Volume 2•2001

WHAT DO I READ NEXT?

A Reader's Guide to Current Genre Fiction

- Fantasy
- Popular Fiction
- Romance
- Horror
- Mystery
- Science Fiction
- Historical
- Inspirational
- Western

ISSN 1052-2212

Volume 2 • 2001

WHAT DO I READ NEXT?

A Reader's Guide
to Current
Genre Fiction

- Fantasy
- Popular Fiction
- Romance
- Horror
- Mystery
- Science Fiction
- Historical
- Inspirational
- Western

NEIL BARRON

TOM BARTON

DANIEL S. BURT

MELISSA HUDAK

D. R. MEREDITH

KRISTIN RAMSDELL

TOM and ENID SCHANTZ

GALE GROUP

THOMSON LEARNING™

Detroit • New York • San Diego • San Francisco
Boston • New Haven, Conn. • Waterville, Maine
London • Munich

Neil Barron, Tom Barton, Daniel S. Burt, Melissa Hudak, D.R. Meredith, Kristin Ramsdell, and Tom & Enid Schantz

Contributors: John Charles, Don D'Ammassa, Stefan Dziemianowicz, and Shelley Mosley

Gale Group Staff:
Coordinating Editor: Beverly Baer
Contributing Editors: Nancy Franklin, Elizabeth Manar, and Heather Price
Managing Editor: Debra M. Kirby

Manager, Composition and Electronic Prepress: MaryBeth Trimper
Assistant Manager, Composition Purchasing and Electronic Prepress: Eveline Abou-el-Seoud
Manufacturing Manager: Dorothy Maki
Buyer: Stacy Melson
Graphic Artist: Michael Logusz

Manager, Data Entry Services: Ronald D. Montgomery
Data Capture Specialists: Civie Green and Beverly Jendrowski
Data Entry Associate: Nancy Sheridan
Manager, Technical Support Services: Theresa Rocklin
Programmer/Analyst: Magdalena Cureton

ISBN 0-7876-3392-5
ISSN 1052-2212

Printed in the United States of America

10 9 8 7 6 5 4 3 2 1

Contents

Introduction

Thousands of books are published each year intended for devoted fans of genre fiction. Dragons, outlaws, lovers, murderers, monsters, and aliens abound on our own world or on other worlds, throughout time--all featured in the pages of fantasy, western, romance, mystery, horror, science fiction, historical, inspirational, and popular fiction. Given the huge variety of titles available each year, added to the numbers from previous years, readers can be forgiven if they're stumped by the question "What do I read next?" And that's where this book comes in.

Designed as a tool to assist in the exploration of genre fiction, *What Do I Read Next?* guides the reader to both current and classic recommendations in nine widely read genres: Mystery, Romance, Western, Fantasy, Horror, Science Fiction, Historical, Inspirational, and Popular Fiction. *What Do I Read Next?* allows readers quick and easy access to specific data on recent titles in these popular genres. Plus, each entry provides alternate reading selections, thus coming to the rescue of librarians and booksellers, who are often unfamiliar with a genre, yet must answer the question frequently posed by their patrons and customers "What do I read next?"

Details on 1,247 Titles

Volume 2 of this year's edition of *What Do I Read Next?* contains 1,247 entries for titles published in late 2000 and 2001. These entries are divided into sections for Mystery, Romance, Western, Fantasy, Horror, Science Fiction, Historical, Inspirational, and Popular Fiction. Experts in each field compile the entries for their respective genres. The experts also discuss topics relevant to their genres in essays that appear at the beginning of each section.

The criteria for inclusion of specific titles vary somewhat from genre to genre. In genres such as Romance and Mystery where large numbers of titles are published each year, the inclusion criteria are more selective, and the experts attempted to select the recently published books they considered the best. In genres such as Horror and Westerns, where the amount of new material is relatively small, a broader range of titles is represented, including many titles published by small or independent houses and some Young Adult books.

The entries are listed alphabetically by main author in each genre section. Most provide the following information:

- **Author or editor's name** and real name if a pseudonym is used. Co-authors, co-editors, and illustrators are also listed where applicable.

- **Book title.**

- **Date and place of publication; name of publisher.**

- **Series name.**

- **Story type:** Specific categories within each genre, identified by the compiling expert. Definitions of these types are listed in the "Key to Genre Terms" section following the Introduction.

- **Subject(s):** Gives the subject matter covered by the title.

- **Major character(s):** Names and brief descriptions of up to three characters featured in the title.

- **Time period(s):** Tells when the story takes place.

- **Locale(s):** Tells where the story takes place.

- **What the book is about:** A brief plot summary.

- **Where it's reviewed:** Citations to reviews of the book, including the source of the review, date of the source, and the page on which the review appears. Reviews are included from genre-specific sources such as *Locus* and *Affaire de Coeur* as well as more general reviewing sources such as *Booklist* and *Publishers Weekly*.

- **Other books by the author:** Titles and publication dates of other books the author has written, useful for those wanting to read more by a particular author.

- **Other books you might like:** Titles by other authors written on a similar theme or in a similar style. These titles further the reader's exploration of the genre.

Indexes Answer Readers' Questions

The nine indexes in *What Do I Read Next?*, used separately or in conjunction with each other, create many pathways to the featured titles, answering general questions or locating specific titles. For example:

"Are there any new Eve Dallas books?"

The SERIES INDEX lists entries by the name of the series of which they are a part.

"I like Regency Romances. Can you recommend any new ones?"

The GENRE INDEX breaks each genre into story types or more specialized areas. In the Romance genre for example, there is a story type heading "Regency." For the definitions of story types, see the "Key to Genre Terms" beginning on page xi.

"I'm looking for a story set in Paris..."

The GEOGRAPHIC INDEX lists titles by their locale. This can help readers pinpoint an area in which they may have a particular interest, such as their hometown, another country, or even Cyberspace.

"Do you know of any science fiction stories set during the 2020s?"

The TIME PERIOD INDEX is a chronological listing of the time settings in which the main entry titles take place.

"What books are available that feature teachers?"

The CHARACTER DESCRIPTION INDEX identifies the major characters by occupation (e.g. Accountant, Editor, Librarian) or persona (e.g. Cyborg, Noblewoman, Stowaway).

"Has anyone written any new books with Sherlock Holmes in them?"

The CHARACTER NAME INDEX lists the major characters named in the entries. This can help readers who remember some information about a book, but not an author or title.

"What has Janette Oke written recently?"

The AUTHOR INDEX contains the names of all authors featured in the entries and those listed under "Other books you might like."

"I want to read a book that's similar to Amy Tan's *The Bonesetter's Daughter*."

The TITLE INDEX includes all main entry titles and all titles recommended under "Other books by the author" and "Other books you might like" in one alphabetical listing. Thus a reader can find a specific title, new or old, then go to that entry to find out what new titles are similar.

"I'm interested in books that depict military life."

The SUBJECT INDEX is an alphabetical listing of all the subjects covered by the main entry titles.

The indexes can also be used together to narrow down or broaden choices. A reader interested in Mysteries set in New York during the 19th century would consult the TIME PERIOD INDEX and GEOGRAPHIC INDEX to see which titles appear in both. Time Travel is a common theme in Science Fiction but occasionally appears in other genres such as Fantasy and Romance. Searching for this theme in other genres would enable a reader to cross over into previously unknown realms of reading experiences. And with the AUTHOR and TITLE indexes, which include all books listed under "Other books by the author" and "Other books you might like," it is easy to compile an extensive list of recommended reading, beginning with a recently published title or a classic from the past.

Suggestions Are Welcome

The editors welcome any comments and suggestions for enhancing and improving *What Do I Read Next?*. Please address correspondence to the Editors, *What Do I Read Next?*, at the following address:

Gale Group
27500 Drake Rd.
Farmington Hills, MI 48331-3535
Phone: 248-699-GALE
Toll-free: 800-347-GALE
Fax: 248-699-8054

About the Genre Experts

Neil Barron, coordinator of the Science Fiction, Fantasy, and Horror Fiction sections, is the editor of the reader guides *Anatomy of Wonder: A Critical Guide to Science Fiction* (Bowker, 4th ed., 1995) and *Fantasy and Horror: A Critical and Historical Guide to Literature, Illustration, Film, TV, Radio, and the Internet* (Scarecrow Press, 1999). He welcomes comments at rneilbarron@hotmail.com.

Tom Barton, (Popular Fiction) is a reference librarian at the Rebecca Crown Library, Dominican University in River Forest, Illinois. A former journalist and community organizer, Barton lives in the West Beverly neighborhood of Chicago.

Daniel S. Burt (Historical Fiction) is a writer and college literature professor who teaches courses on the novel in the nineteenth and twentieth centuries and who for nine years was a dean at Wesleyan University in Middletown, Connecticut. He is the author of *What Historical Novel Do I Read Next?* (Gale, 1997), *The Literary 100: A Ranking of the Most Influential Novelists, Playwrights, and Poets of All Time* (Facts on File, 2001), and *The Biography Book* (Greenwood/Oryx, 2001). He is at work on *The Novel 100* to be published by Facts on File in 2002. Burt lives on Cape Cod, Massachusetts.

Melissa Hudak (Inspirational Fiction) is a medical librarian for Methodist Medical Center in Peoria, Illinois. She was previously employed in public libraries and wrote a column on inspirational literature for *Library Journal.*

D.R. Meredith (Western Fiction) is a full time writer of western historical novels and three mystery series. The award-winning Sheriff series are western mysteries set in rural Texas. *The Sheriff and the Panhandle Murders* and *The Sheriff and the Branding Iron Murders* were actually first published as Westerns (Walker, 1984 and 1985). *Murder by Impulse* (Ballantine, 1988) and *Murder by Deception* (Ballantine, 1989) were both nominated for the Anthony Award. Her latest title in the Megan Clark series is *By Hook or by Book* (Berkley, 2000). In addition to writing, she is book review editor for *Roundup Magazine*, reviews western literature for the *Amarillo Globe-News*, is a speaker at writers' conferences, colleges and universities, libraries, and civic clubs, and is Liaison Chairperson for the American Crime Writers League. She is a member of Western Writers of America, Mystery Writers of America, and Sisters in Crime.

Kristin Ramsdell (Romance Fiction) is a librarian at California State University, Hayward and is a nationally known speaker and consultant on the subject of romance fiction. She writes a romance review column for *Library Journal* and is the author of *Romance Fiction: A Guide to the Genre* (Libraries Unlimited, 1999) and its predecessor, *Happily Ever After: A Guide to Reading Interests in Romance Fiction* (Libraries Unlimited, 1987). She was named Librarian of the Year by Romance Writers of America in 1996.

Tom & Enid Schantz (Mystery Fiction) have been in the mystery business for 30 years. From 1970 to 1980 they ran a rare and out of print mail order business as The Aspen Bookhouse and later as The Rue Morgue Mystery Bookshop. Between 1980 and 2000, they operated a retail mystery bookstore, The Rue Morgue, in Boulder, Colorado. During that same period, they edited a monthly publication, *The Purloined Letter*, which reviews all new mystery titles. They have written a monthly crime fiction column for the *Denver Post* since 1982. In the 1970s, they operated The Aspen Press, which published books of detective stories and items of Sherlockiana. In 1997, they founded The Rue Morgue Press, which continues to publish reprints of classic mysteries from the turn of the century to the 1960s. They continue to operate a mail order book business as The Rue Morgue, which specializes in vintage mystery fiction, and are the recipients of the 2001 Raven from the Mystery Writers of America in honor of their distinguished contribution to mystery bookselling and publishing.

Contributors

John Charles (Romance Fiction), a reference librarian and retrospective fiction selector for the Scottsdale Public Library, also reviews books for both *Library Journal* and *VOYA* (*Voice of Youth Advocates*) and co-authors *VOYA*'s annual "Clueless: Adult Mysteries with Young Adult Appeal" column. John Charles is co-author of the forthcoming *The Mystery Readers' Advisory: The Librarian's Clues to Murder and Mayhem* (ALA, 2001). Along with co-author Shelley Mosley, Charles has twice been the recipient of the Romance Writers of America's Veritas Award.

Don D'Ammassa (Science Fiction and Fantasy) has been reading SF and fantasy for almost 40 years and has been the book reviewer for the *Science Fiction Chronicle* for the past 16 years. He has had fiction published in fantastic magazines and anthologies and has contributed essays to a variety of reference books dealing with fantastic literature.

Stefan Dziemianowicz (Horror Fiction) is a medical editor for a New York-based law book publisher. A co-editor of the quarterly journal, *Necrofile*, he authored the definitive study, *The Annotated Guide to Unknown and Unknown Worlds* (Starmont House, 1991) and is also the author of *Bloody Mary and Other Tales for a Dark Night* (Barnes and Noble, 2000). He has co-edited numerous horror and mystery anthologies--among them the Bram Stoker Award-winning *Horrors! 365 Scary Stories* (Barnes and Noble, 1998).

Shelley Mosley (Romance Fiction), a library manager and romance genre specialist for the Glendale (AZ) Library System, was named 2001 Librarian of the Year by Romance Writers of America. She writes romantic comedies with Deborah Mazoyer under the pen name Deborah Shelley. Their book, *Talk about Love*, was a Holt Medallion finalist for Best First Book. With co-author John Charles, also a *What Do I Read Next?* contributor, she has won two Romance Writers of America's Veritas Awards. In addition to two newspaper columns, she has written articles for *Wilson Library Bulletin*, *Library Journal*, *Romance Writer's Report,* and *VOYA*.

Key to Genre Terms

The following is a list of terms used to classify the story type of each novel included in *What Do I Read Next?* along with brief definitions of the terms. To find books that fall under a particular story type heading, see the Genre Index.

Mystery Story Types

Action/Adventure: Minimal detection; not usually espionage, but can contain rogue police or out of control spies.

Amateur Detective: Detective work is performed by a non-professional rather than by police or a private detective.

Domestic: Fiction relating to household and family matters. Concerned with psychological and emotional needs of family members.

Espionage: Involving the CIA, KGB, or other organizations whose main focus is the collection of information from the other side. Can be either violent or quiet.

Historical: Usually detection set in an earlier time frame than the present.

Humor: A mystery, but the main focus is humorous.

Legal: Main focus is on a lawyer, though it does not always involve courtroom action.

Police Procedural: A story in which the action is centered around a police officer.

Private Detective: Usually detection, involving a professional for hire.

Psychological Suspense: Main focus is on the workings of the mind, usually with some danger involved.

Traditional: Usually means the classic British mystery, but is coming to mean non-private detective fiction.

Romance Story Types

Anthology: A collection of short stories by different authors, usually sharing a common theme.

Contemporary: A romance set in the present.

Contemporary/Exotic: Set in the present but with an especially unusual or exotic setting, e.g. the tent of a desert sheik, or a boat on the Amazon.

Contemporary/Fantasy: A contemporary romance that makes use of fantasy or supernatural elements.

Contemporary/Mainstream: A romance set in the present that would be more properly categorized as fiction rather than romance. Often there is a strong love story line, but the primary emphasis is on other aspects of the plot.

Ethnic: A romance in which the ethnic background of the characters is integral to the story. Usually the focus is on an American ethnic minority group (e.g. African American, Asian American, Native American, Latino) and the two main characters are members of this group. See also Multicultural.

Family Saga: Long narrative, spanning many years, which contains many related characters.

Fantasy: A romance that is not a Gothic or a Romantic Suspense but contains fantasy or supernatural elements.

Futuristic: A romance with a science fiction setting. Often these stories are set on other planets, aboard spaceships or space stations, or on Earth in an imaginary future or, in some cases, past.

Gothic: A romance with a strong mystery suspense plot that emphasizes mood, atmosphere, and/or supernatural or paranormal elements. Unexplained events, ancient family secrets, and a general feeling of impending doom often characterize these tales. These stories are most often set in the past, but several authors (e.g. Phyllis Whitney and Barbara Michaels) write gothics with contemporary settings.

Historical: A romance that takes place in the past that doesn't fall into one of the more specific Historical categories.

Historical/American West: Set in the Western portion of the United States, usually during the second half of the nineteenth century. Stories often involve the hardships of pioneer life (Indian raids, range wars, climatic disasters,

etc.) and the main characters (most often the hero) can be of Native American extraction.

Historical/Americana: A novel set in the past that features uniquely American themes, such as small town life.

Historical Elizabethan: A romance set during the reign of Elizabeth I of England (1558-1603). There is some overlap with the last part of the Historical Renaissance category but the emphasis is British.

Historical/Exotic: Historical romance set in an unusual or exotic place, e.g. a Middle Eastern harem or an archaeological dig in South America.

Historical/Fantasy: Historical romance that makes use of fantasy or supernatural elements.

Historical/Georgian: Set during the reigns of the first three "Georges" of England. Roughly corresponds to the eighteenth century. Stories often focus on the Jacobite Rebellions and the escapades of Bonnie Prince Charlie.

Historical/Medieval: Set during the Middle Ages, approximately the fifth through the fifteenth centuries. Stories feature battles, raids, crusades, and court intrigues; plot-lines associated with the Battle of Hastings (1066) are especially popular.

Historical/Post-American Civil War: Set in the years following the Civil War/War Between the States, generally from 1865 into the 1870s.

Historical/Post-American Revolution: Set mostly in America in the years following the American Revolution. Includes the last part of the eighteenth century.

Historical/Regency: A romance that is set during the Regency period (1811-1820) but is not a "Regency Romance" (see below).

Historical/Renaissance: A romance set in the years of the Renaissance in Europe, generally lasting from the 14th through the 17th centuries.

Historical/Roaring Twenties: Usually has an American setting and takes place in the 1920s.

Historical/Seventeenth Century: A romance set during the seventeenth century. Stories of this type often center around the clashes between the Royalists and the Cromwellians and the Restoration.

Historical/Victorian: Set during the reign of Queen Victoria, 1837-1901. This designation does not include works with a predominately American setting.

Historical/Victorian America: Set in America, usually the Eastern part, during the Victorian Period, 1837-1901.

Holiday Themes: A romance that focuses on or is set during a particular holiday or holiday season (e.g. Christmas, Valentine's Day, Mardi Gras).

Humor: Romance with an amusing story line.

Inspirational: A romance with an uplifting, often Christian, theme, and usually considered "innocent."

Multicultural: A romance in which the ethnic background of the characters is integral to the story. See also Ethnic.

Paranormal: Novel contains supernatural elements. Story may include ghosts, UFOs, aliens, demons, and haunted houses among other unexplained phenomenon.

Regency: A light romance involving the British upper classes, set during the Regency Period, 1811-1820. During this time, the Prince of Wales acted as Prince Regent because of the incapacity of his father, George III. In 1820, "Prinny" became George IV. These stories, in the style of Jane Austen, are essentially comedies of manners and the emphasis is on language, wit, and style. Georgette Heyer set the standard for the modern version of this genre. This designation is also given to stories of similar type that may not fit precisely within the Regency time period.

Reincarnation: A romance in which one of the two main characters has been reincarnated as someone else. Often contains time travel elements.

Romantic Suspense: A romance with a strong mystery suspense plot. This is a broad category including works in the tradition of Mary Stewart as well as the newer women-in-jeopardy tales by writers such as Mary Higgins Clark. These stories usually have contemporary settings but some are also set in the past.

Time Travel: A romance in which characters from one time are transported either literally or in spirit to another time period. The time shifts are usually between the present and another historical period.

Western Story Types

Chase: A traditional Western in which the action of the plot is based on some form of pursuit.

Collection: A book of short stories by a single author.

Historical: A story that emphasizes accuracy of historical settings and characters rather than the characters and themes of the traditional Western. Generally these stories are set in locations or time periods outside the "cowboy" West.

Indian Culture: These historical novels center on the lives, customs, and cultures of characters who are American Indians or who lived among the Indians.

Man Alone: A lone man, alienated from the society that would normally support him, faces overwhelming dangers in this subgenre of the traditional Western.

Modern: Stories set after the closing of the frontier, generally from about 1920 to the present, but retaining the essential characteristics of the Western.

Mystery: A story in which the main plot feature involves the solution to a crime where the perpetrator or motive is not known to characters or readers. The detective is often an amateur, but may be a peace officer.

Quest: Another subgroup, usually of the traditional, the Quest shows its central characters on a journey filled with dangers to reach some worthwhile goal.

Revenge: A character who has suffered an unjust loss returns to take vengeance. This is one of the most common traditional themes.

Saga: A book or series that follows the fortunes of a single family, usually over more than a single generation.

Traditional: The classic Western from Owen Wister to today. Traditional Westerns may deal with virtually any time period or situation, but they are related by shared conventions of setting and characterization.

Young Readers: A Western of any subgenre with characters, plot, and vocabulary primarily aimed at juveniles or young adults.

Fantasy Story Types

Adventure: The character(s) must face a series of obstacles, which may include monsters, conflict with other travelers, war, interference by supernatural elements, interference by nature, and so on.

Alternate History: A story dealing with how society might have evolved if a specific historical event had happened differently, e.g. if the South had won the American Civil War.

Alternate Universe: More accurately, in most cases, alternate history, in which the South won the Civil War, the Nazis triumphed, etc.

Alternate World: The story starts out in the everyday world, but the main character is transported to an alternate/parallel world by supernatural means.

Anthology: A collection of short fiction by different authors usually related in theme or setting.

Collection: A book of short stories by a single author.

Contemporary: The story is set in the everyday world, but elements of the fantastic begin to intrude (e.g., a unicorn appears or the character suddenly has the ability to perform magic).

Historical: This subgenre could also be called Alternate History. Using history as a backdrop, the author adds fantastic elements to build the story.

Humor: Fantasy in which humor, from cerebral to slapstick, is prominent.

Legend: A story based on a legend, myth, or fairy tale that has been rewritten.

Light Fantasy: There is a great deal of humor throughout the story and it is almost guaranteed to have a happy ending.

Literary: Usually refers to novels not published as fantasy and sometimes incorporating unconventional narrative techniques.

Magic Conflict: The main conflict of the story stems from magical interference. Protagonists may be caught in the middle of a conflict between sorcerers or may themselves be engaged in conflict with other sorcerers.

Mystery: Although the story has been classified as Fantasy in this section, there are strong elements of Mystery (e.g., suspense, detectives, etc.).

Political: The novel deals with political issues that are skewed by the use and presence of fantastic elements.

Quest: The character embarks on a journey to achieve a specific goal, such as retrieving a jewel from an evil wizard.

Science Fiction: Although the story has been classified as Fantasy in this section, there are strong elements of Science Fiction.

Space Opera: Intergalactic adventures; westerns in space; a specialized form of Adventure.

Sword and Sorcery: The tried and true formula of this subgenre has a muscle-bound swordsman, who is innocent of thought and common sense, up against evil sorcerers and sorceresses, who naturally lose in the end because they are evil. However, Sword and Sorcery continues to be updated, with heroines instead of heroes and a bit of thought prior to action.

Time Travel: In Science Fiction Time Travel, there is a rational explanation rooted in science for the character's ability to move through time. In Fantasy Time Travel, the rational explanation is rooted in the supernatural.

Young Adult: Commonly indicated by publishers to help librarians categorize fiction likely to be of interest to teenage readers, this subgenre frequently involves a child or teenager maturing by accepting responsibility for self-determined goals and discovering strategies to achieve those goals.

Horror Story Types

Ancient Evil Unleashed: The evils may take familiar forms, like vampires undead for centuries, or malevolent ancient gods released from bondage by careless humans, or ancient prophecies wreaking havoc on today's world. The so-called *Cthulhu Mythos* originated by H.P. Lovecraft, in which *Cthulhu* is prominent among a pantheon of ancient evil gods, is a specific variation of this.

Anthology: A collection of short fiction by different authors, usually related in theme or setting.

Child-in-Peril: The innocence of childhood is often used to heighten the intensity and unpredictability of evil.

Collection: A book of short stories by a single author.

Doppelganger: A double or alter ego, popularized in the works of E.T.A. Hoffmann, Edgar Allan Poe, and Robert Louis Stevenson.

Erotic Horror: Sexuality and horror are often argued to be inextricably linked, as in Bram Stoker's *Dracula* and Sheridan Le Fanu's "Carmilla," although others have argued that they are antithetical. Sexuality became increasingly explicit in the 1980s, sometimes verging on the pornographic, as in Brett Easton Ellis' *American Psycho*.

Evil Children: The presumed innocence of a child is replaced with adult-like malevolence and cunning, contradicting the reader's usual expectations.

Ghost Story: The spirits of the dead, who can be benevolent, as in Charles Dickens, or malevolent, as in the tales of M.R. James.

Mystery: A story in which the identity of evildoers is often concealed and suspense therefore heightened. Psychic detective tales are often mysteries.

Nature in Revolt: Tales in which normally docile plants or animals suddenly turn against humankind, sometimes transformed (giant crabs resulting from radioactivity, predatory rats, plagues, blobs that threaten London or Miami, etc.).

Occult: An adjective suggesting fiction based on a mystical or secret doctrine, but sometimes referring to supernatural fiction generally. Implies that there is a reality beyond the perceived world that only adepts can penetrate. Black Magic may or may not be part of an occult world.

Psychological Suspense: Tales often not supernatural in nature in which the psychological exploration and quirks of characters, rather than outside creations, generate suspense and plot.

Reanimated Dead: These can take many forms, such as mummies and zombies (often the result of Voodoo).

Serial Killer: A multiple murderer, going back to Bluebeard and up to Ed Gein, who inspired Robert Bloch's *Psycho*.

Supernatural Vengeance: Punishment inflicted by God or a godlike creature, whether justly or capriciously: contrast Apocalyptic Horror and Ancient Evil Unleashed.

Vampire Story: Based on mythical bloodsucking creatures possessing supernatural powers and various forms, both animal and human. The concept can be traced far back in history, long before Bram Stoker's famous novel, *Dracula*.

Werewolf Story: *Were* is Old English for man, suggesting the ancient lineage of a creature that once dominated a world in which witches and sorcerers were equally feared. Sometimes used to refer to any shape shifter, whether wolves or other animals.

Wild Talents: The phrase comes from Charles Fort's writings and usually refers to parapsychological powers such as telepathy, psychokinesis, and precognition, collectively called psychic or psi phenomena.

Witchcraft: Characters either profess to be or are stigmatized as witches or warlocks, and practitioners of magic associated with witchcraft. This can include black magic or white magic (e.g. Wicca).

Young Adult: Used by publishers to help categorize fiction likely to be of interest to teenage readers.

Science Fiction Story Types

Alternate Intelligence: Story featuring an entity with a sense of identity and able to self-determine goals and actions. The natural or manufactured entity results from a synergy, generally unpredictable, of individual elements. This subgenre frequently involves a computer-type intelligence.

Alternate Universe: More accurately, in most cases, alternate history, in which the South won the Civil War, the Nazis triumphed, etc. The idea is a venerable one in SF.

Anthology: A collection of short fiction, short stories or novellas or both, written by different authors.

Collection: A book of short stories written by a single author.

Disaster: A tale recounting some event or events seriously disruptive of the social fabric but not as serious as a holocaust; see Post-Holocaust.

Dystopian: The antonym of utopian, sometimes called anti-utopian, in which traditionally positive utopian themes are treated satirically or ironically and the mood is downbeat or satiric.

Espionage Thriller: Analogous to Mystery, in which espionage replaces the narrower world of the private investigator.

First Contact: Any story about the initial meeting or communication of humans with extraterrestrials or aliens. The term may take its name from the eponymous 1945 story by Murray Leinster.

Future Shock: A journalistic term derived from Alvin Toffler's 1970 book and which refers to the alleged disorientation resulting from rapid technological change.

Generation Starship: If pseudoscientific explanations involving faster-than-light drives are rejected, then the time required for interstellar travel will encompass many

human generations.

Genetic Manipulation: Sometimes called genetic engineering, this assumes that the knowledge exists to shape creatures, human or otherwise, using genetic means, as in *Brave New World* (1932).

Hard Science Fiction: Stories in which the author adheres with varying degrees of rigor to scientific principles believed to be true at the time of writing, principles derived from hard (physical, biological) rather than soft (social) sciences.

Humor: SF in which humor, from cerebral to slapstick, is prominent. Early SF was sometimes unintentionally humorous; some modern work is deliberately, and sometimes successfully, so.

Immortality: Usually includes extreme longevity, resulting from fountains of youth, elixirs, or something with a pseudoscientific basis.

Invasion of Earth: An extremely common theme, often paralleling historical events and reflecting fears of the time. Most invasions are depicted as malign, only occasionally benign.

Lost Colony: Stories centering around a colony on another world that loses contact with or is abandoned by its parent civilization and the type of society that evolves under those conditions. Conflict usually arises when contact is re-established between the colony and its home world.

Military: Stories that can range from space wars (compare Space Opera) to more local battles; most such stories tend to glorify military virtues.

Mystery: SF to which traditional mystery/detective structures have been grafted, not always successfully, and in which private eyes go down many mean galaxies; a distant relative of cyberpunk.

Political: Narratives in which themes of power are paramount, whether on a local or galactic scale.

Post-Disaster: Story set in a much degraded environment, frequently involving a reduction in population and the resulting loss of access to processes, resources, technology, etc.

Psychic Powers: Parapsychological or paranormal powers believed by some to be credible, e.g., telepathy, telekinesis, etc.

Religious: Religion of any sort plays a primary role in the plot.

Satire: With an ironic and/or detached point of view, the author is writing on a particular theme (such as religion) using elements of the fantastic to exaggerate and explore the theme.

Space Colony: A permanent space station, usually orbiting Earth but in principal located in deep space or near other planets or stars.

Space Opera: Intergalactic adventures; westerns in space; a specialized form of Adventure.

Techno-Thriller: Stories in which a technological development, such as an invention, is linked to a series of suspenseful ("thrilling") events.

Time Travel: An ancient tradition in SF, whether the traveler goes forward or backward, and replete with paradoxes.

UFO: Unidentified Flying Objects, literally, although sometimes used more generally to refer to any object of mysterious origin or intent. A cliche today in First Contact and Invasion of Earth Stories.

Young Adult: A marketing term for publishers; one or more of the central characters is a teenager often testing his or her skills against adversity to achieve a greater degree of maturity and self-awareness. A category used by librarians to shelve books of likely appeal to teenage readers.

Historical Story Types

Action/Adventure: Plot contains exciting/risky activities or behavior; dangerous experiences.

Arts: Fiction that incorporates some aspect of the arts, whether it be music, painting, drama, etc.

Coming-of-Age: A story in which the primary character is a young person, usually a teenager. The growth of maturity is chronicled.

Family Saga: Long narrative, spanning many years, which contains many related characters.

Ghost Story: The spirits of the dead, who can be benevolent, as in Charles Dickens, or malevolent, as in the tales of M.R. James.

Gothic: Characters or settings contain elements of grotesque, terror, or mystery.

Historical/American Civil War: Set during the American Civil War, 1861-1865.

Historical/American Revolution: Set during the American Revolutionary period.

Historical/American West: Set in the western half of the United States; many stories take place during the second half of the nineteenth century.

Historical/American West Coast: Set in the far western states of America (California, Oregon, Washington, and Alaska).

Historical/Americana: A story dealing with themes unique to the American experience.

Historical/Ancient Egypt: A novel set during the time of the Pharaohs from the fourth century B.C. to the first cen-

tury A.D. and the absorption of Egypt into the Roman Empire.

Historical/Ancient Greece: Set during the flowering of the ancient Greek civilization, particularly during the age of Pericules in the 5th century B.C.

Historical/Ancient Rome: Covering the history of Rome from its founding and the Roman Republic before Augustus through the decline and fall of the Roman Empire in the fifth century.

Historical/Antebellum American South: Set in the South prior to the Civil War.

Historical/Colonial America: Story takes place before the start of the American Revolution in 1775.

Historical/Depression Era: Set mainly in America during the period of economic hardship brought on by the 1929 Stock Market Crash that continued throughout the 1930s.

Historical/Edwardian: Set during the reign of Edward VII of England, 1901-1910.

Historical/Elizabethan: Set during the reign of Elizabeth I of England, 1558-1603.

Historical/Exotic: Setting is an unusual or exotic place.

Historical/Fantasy: Story contains fantasy or supernatural elements.

Historical/French Revolution: Set during the French Revolution, 1789-1795.

Historical/Georgian: Set mostly in the eighteenth century during the reigns of the first three English kings named George.

Historical/Korean War: Set during the conflict (1950-1953) between North Korea and South Korea.

Historical/Medieval: Story is set during the fifth through the fifteenth centuries or what is commonly known as the Middle Ages.

Historical/Napoleonic Wars: Set between 1803-1815 during the wars waged by and against France under Napoleon Bonaparte.

Historical/Post-American Civil War: Set during the years immediately following the Civil War, 1865-1870s.

Historical/Post-French Revolution: Set during the years immediately following the French Revolution; stories usually take place in France or England.

Historical/Pre-history: Set in the years before the Middle Ages.

Historical/Regency: Set mostly during the years known as the Regency period, 1811-1820.

Historical/Renaissance: Story is set during the Renaissance years in Europe, from the fourteenth through the seventeenth centuries.

Historical/Roaring Twenties: Usually has an American setting and takes place in the 1920s.

Historical/Russian Revolution: These stories are set around and during the 1917 Russian Revolution.

Historical/Seventeenth Century: Set during the seventeenth century.

Historical/Victorian: Set during the reign of Queen Victoria, 1837-1901. This story type usually does not take place in America.

Historical/Victorian America: Stories set wholly or in part in America during the reign of Queen Victoria, 1837-1901.

Historical/World War I: Set during the First World War, 1914-1918.

Historical/World War II: Set in the years of the Second World War, 1939-1945.

Indian Culture: These stories are about the lives and culture of the American Indian; the characters are either American Indians or people who lived among them.

Legend: Usually a rewritten version of a legend, myth, or fairy tale.

Lesbian/Historical: Historical fiction with lesbian protagonists.

Literary: Refers to the nature and knowledge of literature.

Military: Stories have a military theme; may deal with life in the armed forces or military battles.

Mountain Man: The characters in these stories live in isolated mountain areas far from civilization and often have to rely on their own resources for survival.

Multicultural: This story type is used when the ethnic background of the characters is essential to the story line.

Mystery: Usually a story where a crime occurs or a puzzle must be solved.

Psychological: Fiction dealing with mental or emotional responses.

Religious: Religion of any sort plays a primary role in the plot.

Romantic Suspense: A romance in which one or both of the characters is in danger or trouble; a strong suspense plot.

Inspirational Story Types

Anthology: A collection of short stories or novellas by different authors; usually linked by a common theme such as Victorian life.

Collection: A book of short stories by a single author.

Contemporary: An inspirational story set in the present day.

Contemporary/Fantasy: A story set in the present that uses elements of fantasy to drive its plot.

Family Saga: Stories focusing on the problems or concerns of a family; estrangement and reunion are common themes.

Fantasy: Inspirational novels using elements of the fantastic or supernatural; themes include such elements as angels.

Historical: Novels set in a time period earlier than the present day.

Historical/American Civil War: Set during the American Civil War, 1861-1865.

Historical/American West: Novels set in the western half of the United States during the era of pioneer expanion (usually from 1870-1900).

Historical/Colonial America: Story takes place before the start of the American Revolution in 1775.

Historical/Post-American Civil War: Novels taking place after the American Civil War, usually from 1865-1870, that emphasize the aftereffects of the war.

Historical/World War II: Set in the years of the Second World War, 1939-1945.

Mystery: An inspirational novel in which crimes occur and some sort of puzzle must be solved; usually the crimes are murders.

Romance: An inspirational novel in which the main plot line revolves around the developing relationship between a couple.

Science Fiction: Stories in which some degree of rational explanation is present. Doesn't usually include supernatural or fantastic elements.

Popular Fiction Story Types

Adult: Fiction dealing with adult characters and mature, developed ideas.

Adventure: Stories that involve risk and chance; exciting in nature and unpredictable.

Americana: Deals with ideas, themes, characters, and objects that are distinctly American.

Collection: A group of short stories or collection of works by the same author; may or may not be linked by themes or characters.

Coming-of-Age: Fiction dealing with a character's formative years; changes in a character's views, ideas, or values.

Contemporary: Story takes place in the present time.

Contemporary/Fantasy: Imaginative, fantastic, creative account of characters, ideas, and themes occurring in the present day; not real--occurs in the character's imagination.

Contemporary/Mainstream: Contemporaneous account of modern life; accurate portrayal of current thoughts and values.

Contemporary Realism: An accurate representation of characters, settings, ideas, themes in the present day. Not idealistic in nature.

Ethnic: Fiction relating to a group of people of identifiable, cultural heritage. Focuses on the ideas and values of this heritage.

Family Saga: Long narrative dealing with family lives in one generation or several generations; continuous portrayal of people and events in one family.

Gay/Lesbian Fiction: Stories portraying homosexual characters or themes.

Gothic: Characters or settings contain elements of grotesque, terror, or mystery.

Historical: Fiction that may use historical events, characters, or settings. Attempts to accurately portray a specific time period through use of details and events.

Historical/American West: Set in the western half of the United States; many stories take place during the second half of the nineteenth century.

Historical/Ancient Rome: Covering the history of Rome from its founding and the Roman Republic before Augustus through the decline and fall of the Roman Empire in the fifth century.

Historical/Seventeenth Century: Fiction set in the seventeenth century.

Historical/World War II: Accurate representation of characters, settings, ideas, and themes during World War II, 1939-1945.

Humor: Amusing account of events and characters; comic in nature, humorous in tone.

Indian Culture: These stories are about the lives and culture of the American Indian; the characters are either American Indians or people who lived among them.

Inspirational: Divine in nature; power that inspires or enlightens. Literature focusing on knowledge or insights

leading to action or changes.

Literary: Relates to the nature and knowledge of literature; can be applied to setting or characters.

Modern: Reflection of the present time period.

Multicultural: Representation of diverse cultures; story does not focus on a "mainstream" culture.

Mystical: Fiction dealing with spiritual elements. Miraculous or supernatural characteristics of events, characters, settings and themes.

Political: Story deals with government issues and affairs.

Psychological: Fiction dealing with mental or emotional responses.

Psychological Suspense: Deals with the character's mental or emotional response to the unknown, unplanned, or a dangerous situation.

Quest: Character's search or pursuit of an understanding or identity.

Romance: A novel detailing the emotional involvement/attachment among its characters. A love affair/love story.

Saga: A long, detailed narrative of events connected through time or from generation to generation.

Satire: Fiction written in a sarcastic and ironic way to ridicule human vices or follies; usually using an exaggeration of characteristics to stress point.

Award Winners

Mystery Awards
by Tom and Enid Schantz

The Agatha

Awarded on May 5, 2001, at Malice Domestic XIII, for works published in 2000. Nominations and final voting by members of the convention.

Best Novel: *Storm Track* by Margaret Maron

Best First Novel: *Death on a Silver Tray* by Rosemary Stevens

Best Non-Fiction: *100 Favorite Mysteries of the Century* edited by Jim Huang

Best Short Story: "The Man in the Civil Suit" by Jan Burke

The Dilys

Awarded by the members of the Independent Mystery Booksellers Association and presented to the book they most enjoyed selling. Presented at Left Coast Crime in March 2001, in Anchorage, Alaska.

The winner: *A Place of Execution* by Val McDermid

The Edgar

Awarded by the Mystery Writers of America at their annual banquet, held in New York City on May 3, 2001. Nominees and final winners are determined by a panel of five different MWA members in each category.

Best Novel: *The Bottoms* by Joe Lansdale

Best First Novel by an American Author: *A Conspiracy of Paper* by David Liss

Best Original Paperback: *The Black Maria* by Mark Graham

Best Short Story: "Missing in Action" by Peter Robinson

Grand Master: Ed Hoch

Special Edgar: Mildred Wirt Benson, a.k.a. Carolyn Keene, author of the original Nancy Drew children's mysteries

Raven Award: For contributions to the field in a non-creative form: Tom & Enid Schantz, Barbara Peters

Ellery Queen Award: Douglas Greene

Robert L. Fish Memorial Award: "The Witch and the Relic Thief" by M.J. Jones

Best Critical or Biographical Work: *Conundrums for the Long Week-End: England, Dorothy Sayers, and Peter Wimsey* by Robert Kuhn McGregor with Ethan Lewis

The Hammett

Given for excellence in the field of crime writing by a U.S. or Canadian author by the North American Branch of the International Association of Crime Writers, the selection process for this award is somewhat different from virtually all other awards. The final decision is made by a constantly changing panel of three outside judges with no connections to the field. The winner receives "The Thin Man."

The winner: *The Blind Assassin* by Margaret Atwood

Los Angeles Times Mystery Book Award

Presented April 28, 2001, at the *Los Angeles Times* Festival of Books

The winner: *A Place of Execution* by Val McDermid

Mary Higgins Clark Award

Award sponsored by Simon and Schuster in recognition of mystery author Mary Higgins Clark.

The winner: *Authorized Personnel Only* by Barbara D'Amato

Anthony Nominees

To be presented at the 2001 World Mystery Convention, also known as Bouchercon, in October 2001 in Washington, D.C. for books published in 2000. The award is named for the late Anthony Boucher, a mystery writer and editor who won three Edgars for mystery criticism. Nominations and final voting by all members of the convention.

Best Novel Nominees: *Deep South* by Nevada Barr; *The Bottoms* by Joe Lansdale; *A Place of Execution* by Val McDermid; *Listen to the Silence* by Marcia

Muller; *He Shall Thunder in the Sky* by Elizabeth Peters; *Legacy of the Dead* by Charles Todd

Best First Mystery Nominees: *Black Dog* by Stephen Booth; *A Conspiracy of Paper* by David Liss; *The Ice Harvest* by Scott Phillips; *Death of a Red Heroine* by Qiu Xiaolong; *Street Level* by Bob Truluck; *Run* by Douglas E. Winter

Best Paperback Original Nominees: *Death Dances to a Reggae Beat* by Kate Grilley; *Bad to the Bone* by Katy Munger; *The Floating Lady Murder* by Daniel Stashower; *Killing Kin* by Chassie West; *A Little Death* by Laura A. Wilson; *The Kidnapping of Rosie Dawn* by Eric Wright

Best Short Story Nominees: "The Seal of the Confessional" by Rhys Bowen; " The Problem of the Potting Shed" by Edward D. Hoch; "Widow's Peak" by Rochelle Krich; "Don't Go Upstairs" by Donald Olson; "Missing in Action" by Peter Robinson

Best Anthology or Short Story Collection Nominees: *Master's Choice II* edited by Lawrence Block; *Malice Domestic 9* edited by Joan Hess; *Magnolias and Mayhem* edited by Jeffrey Marks; *Unholy Orders* edited by Serita Stevens; *Tales out of School* by Carolyn Wheat

Best Non-Fiction or Critical Work Nominees: *The Complete Christie* by Matthew Bunson; *Women of Mystery* by Martha Hailey DuBose; *100 Favorite Mysteries of the Century* edited by Jim Huang; *The American Regional Mystery* by Marvin Lachman; *Hard-Boiled* by Erin A. Smith

Best Fan Publication Nominees: *Deadly Pleasures* edited by George Easter; *The Drood Review of Mystery* edited by Jim Huang; *Murder: Past Tense* edited by Sue Feder; *Mystery News* edited by Chris Aldrich and Lynn Kaczmarek; *The Mystery Readers Journal* edited by Janet Rudolph

Macavity Nominees

The only award we know of that is named for a cat (from T.S. Eliot's *Old Possum's Book of Practical Cats*), this award is for works published in 2000 and presented by members of Mystery Readers International and announced in *The Mystery Readers Journal*.

Best Novel Nominees: *The Bottoms* by Joe Lansdale; *Guns and Roses* by Taffy Cannon; *A Place of Execution* by Val McDermid; *Half Moon Street* by Anne Perry; *The Whole Truth* by Nancy Pickard

Best First Mystery Nominees: *Death Dances to a Reggae Beat* by Kate Grilley; *Three Dirty Women and the Garden of Death* by Julie Wray Herman; *A Conspiracy of Paper* by David Liss; *Crow in Stolen Colors* by Marcia Simpson

Best Biographical/Critical Nominees: *The Doctor and the Detective: A Biography of Sir Arthur Conan Doyle* by Martin Booth, *Women of Mystery* by Martha Hailey Dubose with additional essays by Margaret Caldwell Thomas, *100 Favorite Mysteries of the Century* edited by Jim Huang, *The American Regional Mystery* by Marvin Lachman

Best Mystery Short Story Nominees: "The Man in the Civil Suit" by Jan Burke; "The Chosen" by Joyce Christmas; "A Candle for Christmas" by Reginald Hill

Shamus Nominees

Awarded by the Private Eye Writers of America to those books employing a private detective (defined as a paid investigator who doesn't work for any government agency). The 2001 Shamus winners (for books published in 2000) were to be announced at the Shamus Awards banquet at Bouchercon in Washington, D.C. in October 2001.

Best Hardcover Novel Nominees: *A Smile on the Face of the Tiger* by Loren Estleman; *The Deader the Better* by G.M. Ford; *Havana Heat* by Carolina Garcia-Aguilera; *Ellipsis* by Stephen Greenleaf; *Listen to the Silence* by Marcia Muller

Best First Novel Nominees: *Brigham's Day* by John Gates; *The Heir Hunter* by Chris Larsgaard; *Resurrection Angel* by William Mize; *Lost Girls* by Andrew Pyper; *Street Level* by Bob Truluck

Best Paperback Original Novel Nominees: *The Blazing Tree* by Mary Jo Adamson; *The Sporting Club* by Sinclair Browning; *The Hindenburg Murders* by Max Allan Collins; *Death in the Steel City* by Thomas Lipinski; *Bad to the Bone* by Katy Munger; *Dirty Money* by Steven Womack

Best Short Story Nominees: " The Road's End" by Brendan DuBois; "What's in a Name?" by Jeremiah Healy; "The Sleeping Detective" by Gary Phillips; "The Big Bite" by Bill Pronzini; "The Good Daughter" by Mike Wiecek

Romance Awards
by Kristin Ramsdell

As romance fiction has attained increased recognition as a legitimate literary genre, various publications, organizations, and groups have developed to support the interests of its writers and readers. As part of this mission, a number of these offer awards to recognize the accomplishments of the practitioners. Some awards are juried and are presented for excellence in quality and style of writing; others are based on popularity and are selected by the readers. Usually awards are given for a particular work by a particular writer; however, some awards are presented for a body of work produced over a number of years (a type of career award) and others are given for

various types of contributions to romance fiction in general. The Romance Writers of America, *Romantic Times*, *Affaire de Coeur*, and RRA-L electronic mailing list are the sponsors of most of the awards listed below.

Romance Writers of America Awards

These awards for excellence in romance fiction writing are presented by the Romance Writers of America at the annual RWA conference in July. The awards for 1999 are listed in Volume 2 of *What Do I Read Next? 2000*. The awards for 2000 were presented at the 2001 conference in New Orleans and were not available as of this writing.

Romantic Times Reviewer's Choice Awards

Presented by *Romantic Times* for outstanding romances published in the previous year. Selection is done by the *RT* series romance reviewers. Categories may vary from year to year. The awards for 1999 were announced at the *Romantic Times* Booklovers Convention in Houston, Texas in November 2000 and are listed in Volume 1 of *What Do I Read Next? 2001*. The awards for 2000 were announced at the convention held in Orlando, Florida in November and are not available as of this writing.

Affaire de Coeur Awards

Reader/Writer Poll Awards awarded to romances published in a given year on the basis of a readers' poll conducted by *Affaire de Coeur* magazine and are traditionally published in the August issue of *Affaire de Coeur*. The awards for 1999 are listed in Volume 2 of *What Do I Read Next? 2000*. As of this writing, the awards for 2000 have not yet been determined.

RRA-L Awards

Selected by the members of the RRA-L (Romance Readers Anonymous) electronic mailing list, these awards are usually published on the list in late winter or early spring. The awards for books published in 2000 are included in Volume 1 of *What Do I Read Next? 2001*.

Awards information courtesy of Romance Writers of America, *Affaire de Coeur*, *Romantic Times* Publishing Group, and the RRA-L listserv.

Western Awards
by D.R. Meredith
Western Heritage Awards

The Western Heritage Awards, more commonly called the Wranglers because they are replicas of a Charles Russell bronze of that name, are given by the National Cowboy Hall of Fame to the entries in western literature, music, film, and television which best represent matters relating to the American West or the western experience. Winners for 2000 are:

Outstanding Novel: *Gates of the Alamo* by Stephen Harrigan

Outstanding Juvenile: *Precious Gold, Precious Jade* by Sharon Heisel

Spur Awards

The most widely known and perhaps the most beneficial to both author and publisher for that reason are the Spur awards presented by the Western Writers of America. They are presented at the annual Spur banquet in June of each year for novels published the previous calendar year. To avoid confusion, the Spurs are designated by the year of presentation rather than the year of publication. Thus the Spurs for 2001 are actually awarded to books published in 2000.

The number of Spurs awarded has not always remained constant, as the organization debates whether fiction should be divided into numerous categories, or whether a single Best Western Novel be designated regardless of its length or binding. In other words, should the Best Western Novel stand alone whether it is 100,000 or 65,000 words, historical or traditional, hardbound or paperback original? Or should the novel be categorized by length and binding?

At present, the Western Writers of America recognize three categories of Western novels: Best Western Novel, Best Novel of the West, and Best Paperback Original. The first two categories are divided by length; the Western Novel is defined as a novel of less than 100,000 words, while longer works are considered to be Novels of the West. Best Paperback Original is any book of any length which first appeared in soft cover.

Western Writers of America also awards Spurs to Western nonfiction, juvenile fiction, short stories, short nonfiction, cover art, movie and television scripts, and poetry. The organization also presents the Medicine Pipe Award to the Best First Western Novel, and the Owen Wister Award for Lifetime Achievement in the Western field.

Best Western Novel: *Summer of Pearls* by Mike Blakely, published by Forge

Finalists: *The Witness* by Richard S. Wheeler, published by NAL Signet; *The Spirit Woman* by Margaret Coel, published by Berkley

Best Novel of the West: *The Gates of the Alamo* by Stephen Harrigan, published by Knopf

Finalists: *The Chivalry of Crime* by Desmond Barry, published by Little, Brown; *Monuments* by Clay Reynolds, published by Texas Tech University Press

Best Original Paperback: *Bound for the Promise-Land* by Troy D. Smith, published by iUniverse.com

Finalists: *Apache Ambush* by Austin Olsen, published by Pinnacle; *Requiem at Dawn* by Sheldon Russell, published by Pinnacle; *Blood Red River* by Walter Lucas, published by Pinnacle

Medicine Pipe Bearer Award: *The Chivalry of Crime* by Desmond Barry, published by Little, Brown

Finalists: *Blood Red River* by Walter Lucas, published by Pinnacle; *Bound for the Promise-Land* by Troy D. Smith, published by iUniverse.com

Best Juvenile Fiction: *The Midnight Train Home* by Erika Tamar, published by Random House

Finalists: *Weaver's Daughter* by Kimberley Brubaker Bradley, published by Random House; *Mr. Beans* by Dayton O. Hyde, published by Boyds Mills

Fantastic Fiction Awards
by Neil Barron

Locus provides full listings of dozens of awards given throughout the year and provides a comprehensive historical and current list on its website, www.locusmag.com/SFAwards, often before the monthly issues are published. The second volume of each year's *What Do I Read Next?* lists the awards given earlier in the year, usually the Nebula, Bram Stoker, International Horror, and *Locus* poll awards. Volume 1 lists the remaining major awards, the Hugo and the World Fantasy awards, and sometimes other awards announced too late to make the editorial deadline of the second volume. Because awards are given the year following the year of publication, most of the books listed below are discussed in earlier volumes.

Science Fiction Awards
Nebula Award

Given by the Science Fiction and Fantasy Writers of America, an organization with about 1,300 members, of whom about a quarter vote. The awards, in four fiction categories of varying length, are announced several months before the Hugos and may influence the voting for them. Because of the Nebula rules, some candidates were published more than one year prior to 2001, the year of the award, as noted below. Only the novels are listed here.

Best Novel: *Darwin's Radio* by Greg Bear (1999)

Runners-up: *A Civil Campaign* by Lois McMaster Bujold (1999); *Forests of the Heart* by Charles de Lint (2000); *Crescent City Rhapsody* by Kathleen Ann Goonan (2000); *A Midnight Robber* by Nalo Hopkinson; and *Infinity Beach* by Jack McDevitt (2000)

Grandmaster Award for Lifetime Achievement: Philip Jose Farmer

Horror Awards
Bram Stoker Awards

Active members of the Horror Writers Association vote for this award at an annual summer conference. See also the World Fantasy Awards in *WDIRN? Volume 1, 2001*. 2001 winners for 2000 books.

Best Novel: *The Traveling Vampire Show* by Richard Laymon

Runners-up: *The Indifference of Heaven* by Gary A. Braunbeck; *Silent Children* by Ramsey Campbell; *The Licking Valley Coon Hunters Club* by Brian A. Hopkins (won first novel award); and *The Deceased* by Tom Piccirilli

Best Collection: *Magic Terror* by Peter Straub

Runners-up: *Up out of Cities That Blow Hot and Cold* by Charlee Jacob; *Wind over Heaven and Other Dark Tales* by Bruce Holland Rogers; and *City Fishing* by Steve Rasnic Tem

Best Anthology: *The Year's Best Fantasy & Horror, 13th Annual Collection* edited by Ellen Datlow and Terri Windling

Runners-up: *Brainbox: The Real Horror* edited by Steven Eller; *Extremes: Fantasy & Horror from the Ends of the Earth* edited by Brian A. Hopkins; and *Bad News* edited by Richard Laymon

Life Achievement Award: Nigel Kneale

Grand Master Award: Ray Bradbury

International Horror Guild Awards

Normally presented at the World Horror convention held each spring in different cities, but in 2001 given at the Dragoncon in Atlanta over the Labor Day weekend. A volunteer board of knowledgeable readers selects the candidates and winners of this award, established in 1995. 2001 winners for books published in 2000.

Best Novel: *Declare* by Tim Powers

Runners-up: *The Bottoms* by Joe R. Lansdale; *Silent Children* by Ramsey Campbell; *A Shadow on the Wall* by Jonathan Aycliffe; and *You Come When I Call You* by Douglas Clegg

Best First Novel: *Adams Fall* by Sean Desmond

Runners-up: *House of Leaves* by Mark Z. Danielewski; *Damned If You Do* by Gordon Houghton; *Raveling* by Peter Moore Smith; and *Run* by Douglas E. Winter

Best Collection: *City Fishing* by Steve Rasnic Tem and *Ghost Music and Other Tales* by Thomas Tessier (tie)

Runners-up: *Magic Terror: Seven Tales* by Peter Straub; *The Death Artist* by Dennis Etchison; *Tales of Pain and Wonder* by Caitlin R. Kiernan; and *Toybox* by Al Sarrantonio

Best Anthology: *October Dreams: A Celebration of Halloween* edited Richard Chizmar and Robert Morrish

Runners-up: *Shadows and Silence* edited by Barbara Roden and Christopher Roden; *Dark Terrors 5: The Gollancz Book of Horror* edited by Stephen Jones and David Sutton; *Strange Attraction* edited by

Edward Kramer; and *Embraces: Dark Erotica* edited by Paula Guran

Best Nonfiction: *At the Foot of the Story Tree* by William Sheehan

Runners-up: *Lord of a Visible World: An Autobiography in Letters* by Howard Phillips Lovecraft edited by S.T. Joshi and David E. Schulz; *On Writing: A Memoir of the Craft* by Stephen King; *Horror of the 20th Century: An Illustrated History* by Robert Weinberg; and *The Horror Reader* edited by Ken Gelder

Inspirational Fiction Awards
by Melissa Hudak
Gold Medallion Book Awards

The Evangelical Christian Publishers Association has presented the Gold Medallion Book Awards annually since 1978. Publishers submit entries, which are then judged by a panel of judges composed mainly of Christian retailers. The panel selects a list of finalists and the award winner. The Gold Medallion Book Awards are given to a wide range of book categories, including Bibles, reference works, and theology and doctrine, but there is only one award for fiction.

Best Fiction: *Paul: A Novel* by Walter Wangerin

Finalists: *The Mark* by Tim LaHaye and Jerry B. Jenkins; *Unveiled* by Francine Rivers; *The Great Divide* by T. Davis Bunn; and *Showers in Season* by Terri Blackstock and Beverly LaHaye

Christy Awards

In 1999, a group of Christian publishers decided a new award was needed to bring more attention to the genre of inspirational literature. Under the auspices of the nonprofit group Christian Life Missions, the Christy Awards are to be given annually in six fiction categories. An additional award is given for best new novel. The purpose of the award, according to the awards' website at www.christyawards.com is to "nurture and encourage creativity and quality," "bring a new awareness [and] broaden the readership," and "to provide opportunity to recognize novelists whose work may not have reached bestseller status." The awards are to be announced prior to the Christian Booksellers Association annual international convention. The award itself is named after the popular inspirational fiction book *Christy* by Catherine Marshall.

Best Contemporary/General Novel: *Home to Harmony* by Philip Gulley

Finalists: *The Book of Hours* by T. Davis Bunn; *Bookends* by Liz Curtis Higgs; and *The Trial* by Robert Whitlow

Best Futuristic Novel: *Transgression* by Randall Ingermanson

Finalists: *Eli* by Bill Myers; and *The Mark* by Tim LaHaye and Jerry B. Jenkins

Best Historical Novel (International): *Unashamed* by Francine Rivers

Finalists: *The Black Rood* by Stephen R. Lawhead and *Unveiled* by Francine Rivers

Best Historical Novel (North American): (tie) *Reaping the Whirlwind* by Rosey Dow and *Edge of Honor* by Gilbert Morris

Finalists: *Passing by Samaria* by Sharon Ewell Foster and *Valley of the Shadow* by Stephanie Grace Whitson

Best Romance Novel: *A Touch of Betrayal* by Catherine Palmer

Finalists: *Awakening Mercy* by Angela Benson and *True Devotion* by Dee Henderson

Best Suspense Novel: *The Great Divide* by T. Davis Bunn

Finalists: *Blind Justice* by James Scott Bell; and *Lethal Harvest* by William Cutrer and Sandra Glahn

Best New Novel: *Passing by Samaria* by Sharon Ewell Foster

Finalist: *Refiner's Fire* by Sylvia Bambola

Popular Fiction Awards
by Tom Barton
Book Sense of the Year Award

The American Booksellers Association, a non-profit trade association, gives an annual award for the book their members most enjoyed selling.

Adult Fiction Book of the Year 2001: *The Red Tent* by Anita Diamant

Finalists: *Bee Season* by Myla Goldberg; *The Blind Assassin* by Margaret Atwood; *The Hours* by Michael Cunningham; and *House of Sand and Fog* by Andre Dubus III

National Book Critics Circle Award

The award is given out annually by the National Book Critics Circle which consists of approximately 700 book reviewers.

2000 Winner: *Being Dead* by Jim Crace

Nominees: *A Blind Man Can See How Much I Love You* by Amy Bloom; *The Amazing Adventures of Kavalier & Clay* by Michael Chabon; *Assorted Fire Events: Stories* by David Means; and *White Teeth* by Zadie Smith

Pen/Faulkner Award

The award is given annually to a distinguished work of fiction by a contemporary American author.

2001 Winner: *The Human Stain* by Philip Roth

Nominees: *The Amazing Adventures of Kavalier & Clay* by Michael Chabon; *Harry Gold* by Millicent Dillon; *The Name of the World* by Denis Johnson; and *Off Keck Road* by Mona Simpson

Pultizer Prize for Fiction

The Pulitzer Prize was established in 1917 and is awarded annually to a book of fiction by an American author and preferably about American life.

2001 Winner: *The Amazing Adventures of Kavalier & Clay* by Michael Chabon

Finalists: *Blonde* by Joyce Carol Oates and *The Quick and the Dead* by Joy Williams

Mystery Fiction in Review
by
Tom & Enid Schantz

It may be a little early to call it a trend, but with the new millennium barely under way it appears that publishers are turning more and more from the small mystery book and putting most of their resources into promoting big books and big authors. As a short-term strategy it might pay dividends, but in the long run it's likely to be as effective as a major league team that trades away all of its young minor league prospects in an effort to buy a pennant with pricey but aging veterans. It's all pure speculation, of course, but it seems logical to put the blame for this approach on the mega-corporations that have more or less accidentally found themselves owning publishing companies when putting together mergers. After all, it's been a long time since there was a Simon at Simon & Schuster or a Scribner at Scribners. And though Random House, the biggest publisher in the world, is owned by a single family—the Bertlesmans—it's a far cry from the company Bennett Cerf founded 70 years ago with the intent of "publishing good books at random."

Certainly there was nothing random about Putnam's successful all-out blitz to put Sue Grafton's *P Is for Peril* at Number 1 on the *New York Times* bestseller list in its first week out. Nor did St. Martin's Press—oddly enough owned by another German family, the Holtzbrincks (they dropped the "von" to appear less Teutonic)—pull any punches when three weeks later Janet Evanovich knocked Grafton out of first with *Seven Up*. Only their biggest fans would argue that either author was at her best. Grafton was Grafton and she was there mainly because she'd been there before; Evanovich was still funny, but in terms of plot she seemed, at times, to be writing by the numbers, as well as using them in her titles. Hype and money, not necessarily merit, won the day here, on a field of battle where you're not likely to see any campaign finance reform acts passed in the near future.

There was a time when publishers used bestselling authors to promote their other, smaller authors. The idea was that a sales rep would tell the buyer at a bookstore: "As long as you're buying fifty copies of the new Ross Macdonald,

why not pick up a couple of copies of this new mystery by a young writer we're really keen on?" Today the idea is to push the store into buying yet more copies of the bestselling author's new book. While that new author was being dropped into the publishing waters and told to sink or swim on his or her own, Evanovich was rushing about the country, deigning to appear only at venues where she could be guaranteed crowds in excess of 500, even if it meant the controller at St. Martin's had to open a financial vein or two to finance the publicity campaign needed to guarantee those draws. Gone for good is St. Martin's primary emphasis on publishing lots of mysteries in small editions and making a modest profit on each one. While St. Martin's still publishes more mysteries than anyone else, the list has shrunk dramatically in recent years. For mystery addicts, that's not good news.

Nor is it good news that good writing seems to be less important these days than acquiring books with a "high concept," especially one that's likely to catch the attention of Hollywood. For example, take Francine Mathews' *The Cutout* (published earlier this year and discussed in Volume 1, of the 2001 edition of *WDIRN?*) in which a young CIA analyst finds out after several years that her murdered husband is still alive. There's much that was wonderful about the book, but the ending was spoiled when the author—and her editor—seemingly forgot what they had done with one of the major characters. Keeping track of that character was obviously less important than providing Hollywood with a starring vehicle for a Demi Moore or a Sandra Bullock. Like Mathews' book, Harlan Coben's *Tell No One* was sold to Hollywood for a seven-figure advance months before the book hit the stores. Once again the book's premise—a young doctor suddenly discovers after eight years that his murdered wife may still be alive—will work great as a movie; however, the book's surprise ending is all cheat when you find out that the first-person narrator knew the answer to whodunit all along, a violation of one of the

cardinal rules of mystery writing. It's all right, of course, to write outside the lines, but you have to know they're there and respect them. Yet that didn't stop a reviewer for a Fort Worth newspaper from telling his readers that Coben's book was the second coming of Hammett. We'd prefer the second coming of Maxwell Perkins (Hemingway's and Van Dine's editor at Scribner) who would have told Coben or Mathews to bring their books back when they fixed them.

Hammetts don't come along every day. Indeed, so far as we know there's only been one. What made Hammett great and why he'll be read into the next century, if not the next millennium, is that he took people who hadn't been heroes in fiction before and wrote about them, using words so carefully chosen and put together that it was almost as if he'd reinvented the English language. You won't find Canadian-American writer Rosemary Aubert on the *New York Times* bestseller list any day soon, but we have a feeling that her books will be around long after the fizz has gone out of Evanovich's *Seven Up*. Like Hammett, she writes about people we too often pretend not to see, in her case the battered but not yet defeated homeless who live on the streets, as well as in the parks and abandoned buildings of Toronto. When her first book, *Free Reign*, appeared in 1997, we thought it easily the best first novel of the year, and we thought its 1999 follow-up, *The Feast of Stephen*, was a splendid sequel. Her third book, *The Ferryman Will Be There*, didn't have a fan at *Publishers Weekly*, but believe us: the day will come when that reviewer will be grateful that the magazine's reviews are anonymous. Aubert is staking a spot on the shelf next to the Hammett's.

So is Walter Mosley, who burst onto the mystery scene a few years back with *The Devil in a Blue Dress*, the first book featuring Easy Rawlings, a black veteran who operates as a detective in L.A.'s Watts district post World War II. It was one of those books you knew immediately was destined to be a classic, and it was no surprise when the Independent Mystery Bookseller's Association chose it for inclusion in their 100 Favorite Mysteries of the Century. Like Hammett and Aubert, Mosley gave us a new hero cut from a completely different cloth. As a writer, Mosley's never been afraid to take chances. He's done it again in *Fearless Jones*, whose title character, another black World War II veteran with a lot of attitude, helps track down the bad guys who burn down a gentle black man's modest used bookstore in Watts. Once again Mosley puts faces on the seemingly faceless and gives a voice to those who had none.

The same could be said for Michael Nava, whose *Rag and Bone* is the seventh and last book to feature gay Chicano attorney Henry Rios. Nava says he is shelving Rios and mystery fiction for good, and that's a shame. His beautifully written books may well have been the first significant exposure many straight mystery readers had to the world of gay men that exists outside of television sitcoms like *Will and Grace*. It gives nothing away when we tell you that Nava sends Henry off into a sort of retirement filled with love and grace and honor.

While they weren't deserting the genre or permanently putting their characters out to pasture, a number of other writers gave their series characters the year off and produced non-series mysteries. Publishers can't seem to make up their minds if they like this kind of book, known in the trade as a stand-alone. On one hand, they see it as a way of possibly finding a new audience for a writer whose numbers aren't growing; on the other, they hate to see a series lose any momentum. Some series, however, don't ever seem likely to achieve bestsellerdom. That's probably why Harlan Coben wrote the previously discussed *Tell No One*. His regular series features a Jewish sports agent who, until recently, lived in his parents' New Jersey basement and solves crimes on the side—funny, yes, but probably not the stuff of which bestsellers are made. Doing a stand-alone certainly didn't hurt Dennis Lehane's sales. Lehane, who usually writes about Boston private eyes Patrick Kenzie and Angela Gennaro, tells the story in *Mystic River* of how the sexual molestation of one of a group of three young Boston boys affects their lives after they grow to manhood. Like his series books, this is gritty stuff, written with undeniable power. Marcia Muller turns her back on her popular, though not bestselling, Sharon McCone series with *Point Deception*, the story of a New York writer and the sheriff of a small coastal town who look into an unsolved thirteen-year-old multiple murder. Muller's husband, Bill Pronzini, has been alternating stand-alone suspense novels with his Nameless private eye novels for the past several years, garnering a lot of critical praise if only modest sales.

In an Evil Time is another well-plotted affair in which a loving father decides to kill his wife's stalker, her lawyer ex-husband who uses his legal knowledge to terrorize her without violating the law. Laurie R. King's two series couldn't be much more different. The Mary Russell books feature a young woman who becomes a partner to and then wife of Sherlock Holmes, while the Kate Martinelli series features a San Francisco policewoman who just happens to be a lesbian. Neither is present in *Folly*, the story of a woman who tries to rebuild her life by rebuilding a family home on an isolated island in the Puget Sound only to discover that she's not alone. *The Blue Nowhere* isn't Jeffery Deaver's first stand-alone, though he's probably best known today for his series about paraplegic sleuth Lincoln Rhyme. This thriller paints a fantastic portrait of a computer hacker hired to find another computer hacker, marred only by some uncharacteristically sloppy writing and, for some readers, an excess of computer jargon. Jan Burke's *Flight* is not exactly a stand-alone, but instead of featuring reporter Irene Kelly, the author gives center stage to Irene's cop husband, Frank Hastings.

If publishers aren't always sure about the value of a stand-alone, most agree that writers of cozies aren't going anywhere fast, unless they're named Lilian Jackson Braun

or Diane Mott Davidson. In fact, there was much talk this year on Dorothyl, an Internet mystery discussion group, as to why the cozy had so little respect. This reminded us that years ago we were excited to discover Nancy Atherton's first book, *Aunt Dimity's Death*, a very, very cozy little book about a benevolent English ghost who helps a forlorn young American girl find love and the answers to a family mystery. We still owned a bookstore in those days and personally sold some 550 copies, or about 12 percent of the print run, while managing to talk any number of other stores into heavily stocking the book.

This was in the early days of the so-called hypermodern, a collecting phenomenon that, thankfully, seems to be on its way out. Hypermoderns were usually first novels with small printings that were being touted as great novels, sure to appreciate quickly in the marketplace. Collectors bought them up and dealers put extra copies away, hoping to make a killing at a later date. There was even a newsletter, *Bookline*, which offered tips on potential hypermoderns. Of course, the market required the impossible—that a new great book of the year or decade come along just about every week. A particularly avid hypermodern collector who purchased *Aunt Dimity's Death* from us, based on our glowing review, later chastised us when the book didn't shoot up to some inflated astronomical price. He remarked that we were poor prognosticators in this case and ignored the fact that merit was always our sole criterion for recommending a book. He wouldn't be impressed by the fact the paperback edition is still in print, has gone into double digit printings, and was one of the biggest vote getters in the polling for 100 Favorite Mysteries of the Century. Still, it's true that, for the most part, cozies don't become collectible. We suppose collectors with money need a heavy dose of angst in order to pry open their wallets. Neither do most cozies become bestsellers, Braun and Davidson notwithstanding. In fact, more and more of them are being published as paperback originals rather than starting out life in hardcover.

However, writing a good cozy is as difficult as writing a private eye book or a novel of psychological suspense, if not more so. Ellen Pall's first novel, *Corpse de Ballet*, is a case in point. It's the story of a Regency novelist, Juliet Bodine, who agrees to help a dancer friend develop a ballet based on Dickens' *Great Expectations*. Altogether, it's a substantial and decidedly old-fashioned mystery, with a classic plot and an amateur detective who uses her unusual abilities (including an overdeveloped sense of smell) to solve the crime. But it's even more memorable for the fully realized world in which Juliet moves, the clarity with which the individual characters are drawn, and the sheer fun of being allowed a glimpse of the inner workings of a Manhattan ballet company. And no, it's not just for all those women who dreamed of becoming ballerinas after they saw *The Red Shoes* when they were girls. Even if you've never been to a ballet or cared to do so, you'll be caught up in this book, our pick for best cozy of the year so far.

As a point of information, for years Bantam packaged Jane Haddam's series about retired FBI agent Gregor Demarkian as cozies, which came as quite a surprise to cozy readers. Haddam is now at St. Martin's, and the jackets are a little darker and more appropriate for books that deal sensitively with subjects like suicide and pedophilia within the church, as in *True Believers*. There was never much of a hard edge to Parnell Hall's earlier novels about the henpecked and much put-upon New York private detective Stanley Hastings, so readers familiar with this series won't be surprised that the latest entry is called *Cozy*. Hall shamelessly—and with much good humor—works in many of the traditional trappings of the cozy, including a cat, a quaint New England B&B and, of course, recipes.

You'll find recipes in all kinds of mysteries these days, but when Diane Mott Davidson, the reigning queen of the culinary mystery, proposed putting recipes in her first Goldy Bear (now Schulz) mystery, *Catering to Nobody*, her publisher balked. Davidson persisted, eventually switched publishers, and demurely might have said, "I told you so" while she watched her latest, *Sticks & Scones*, climb onto the *New York Times* bestseller list. The interest in culinary mysteries seems to be growing. Even during the few months we're covering in this edition of *WDIRN*, several other writers have mixed food with mayhem, usually accompanied by recipes, including Peter King (*Eat, Drink and Be Buried*), Phyllis Richman (*Who's Afraid of Virginia Ham?*), Tamar Myers (*The Crepes of Wrath*), and Katherine Hall Page (*The Body in the Moonlight*).

Of course, cozies don't have to have food in them to be popular (though it helps), just as English mysteries don't have to be written by the English. Two of the best practitioners of the English mystery have American accents, which don't slip (so far as we can tell) into their books. Texan Deborah Crombie just keeps getting better and better, and even a little woo-woo doesn't mar *A Finer End*. Elizabeth George's *A Traitor to Memory* was almost as convoluted as P.D. James' *Death in Holy Waters* and should please their many fans, who adore big fat books. We should note that Lee Child, a self-described recovering Englishman, is still happily living in exile in the U.S. and striking back at Crombie and George by setting his books in the U.S. and writing about the very American Jack Reacher, a sort of nomadic Travis McGee. *Echo Burning* is his latest. Other notable English mysteries included Kate Ellis' *An Unhallowed Grave*, Bill James' *Panicking Ralph*, Clare Curzon's *Cold Hands*, Jill McGown's *Scene of Crime*, Frank Smith's *Thread of Evidence*, Denise Mina's gritty *Exile*, and Catherine Aird's disappointing *Little Knell*. M.C. Beaton offered up another delightful Hamish Macbeth tale in *Death of a Dustman* and introduced a charming new couple in the very lightweight *The Skeleton in the Closet*. Peter Lovesey seems to have deserted both the historical mystery, as well as his Bath police inspector Peter Diamond in *The Reaper*, which features a cold-blooded killer who is masquerading as

a very capable and well- liked rector. Told with a nice droll wit, it's up to his usual high standards. A very different clergyman is at the center of Robert Barnard's exceptional *Unholy Dying*, in which both the church and the tabloid press conspire to ruin the life of a kindly parish priest who tries to improve the lot of one of his parishioners, an unwed teenage mother.

One of the best English mysteries of the year was an historical, Gillian Linscott's *Perfect Daughter*. It is the story of a seemingly conventional young English woman who comes to a very bad end one day in 1914, possibly as an indirect result of her association with suffragist and sometimes amateur detective Nell Bray. The popularity of historical mysteries shows no sign of abating. Some of the better recent ones include Alys Clare's *Ashes of the Elements* (12th century England), Max Allan Collins' *Angel in Black* (Nate Heller and the Black Dahlia case), Candace Robb's *A Trust Betrayed* (Scotland, 1297), Laura Joh Rowland's *Black Lotus* (16th century Japan), Jeanne M. Dams' *Green Grow the Victims* (turn of the century Indiana), Ann McMillan's *Civil Blood* (Civil War), Barbara Hambly's *Die upon a Kiss* (early 19th century New Orleans), Charles O'Brien's *Mute Witness* (18th century France), Lynda S. Robinson's *Slayer of Gods* (ancient Egypt), Rosemary Stevens' *The Tainted Snuffbox* (dandy Beau Brummell in 1805 England), and Lindsey Davis' playfully titled *Ode to a Banker* (ancient Rome). P.C. Doherty was around in various guises, as usual, writing about assorted locales and periods. Fans of light, cozy mysteries should enjoy historicals by Carola Dunn (*To Davey Jones Below*), Elizabeth Peters (*Lord of the Silent*), Kate Kingsbury (*A Bicycle Built for Murder*), and Robin Paige (*Death at Epsom Downs*), all set in either the Victorian era or the first half of the 20th century.

If there's one subgenre that seems to be slipping, however, it's the female private eye novel, although Sue Grafton's Kinsey Millhone is still blithely marching through the alphabet with *P Is for Peril* and Dana Stabenow's Kate Shugak continues to catch bad guys in Alaska in *The Singing of the Dead*. There are some relatively new female gumshoes hitting the streets. Julie Smith's new series (her Skip Langdon police procedurals were canceled) combines a cocky young female African American cafe poet with a crusty older Italian white guy in an odd-couple detective agency in New Orleans. Gillian Roberts' P.I. partners Emma and Billie continue to dance around each other in their second outing, *Whatever Doesn't Kill You*, and Katy Munger's Casey Jones continues to talk and act tough in *Better Off Dead*. But some old hands haven't been seen in years, like Karen Kijewski's Cat Colorado or Janet Dawson's Jeri Howard. Lately, women have been turning to jobs even more "unsuitable" (or at least unseemly or unusual) for females, including auto mechanic (Barbara Seranella's *Unfinished Business*), firefighter (Suzanne Chazin's *The Fourth Angel*), forensic anthropologist (Kathy Reich's *Fatal Voyage*), theatrical fight choreographer (Charles Mathes'

The Girl in the Face of the Clock), and stripper (Nancy Bartholomew's *Film Strip*). And you can always throw in one more blue-collar bad girl (Sarah Strohmeyer's *Bubbles Unbound*) to keep Stephanie Plum on her toes.

There are still plenty of guys prowling those mean streets. Not all of them carry private eye licenses, but they've usually got the attitude. The best of these gumshoes can be found in books by John Lantigua (*The Ultimate Havana*), Charles Knief (*Silversword*), Tom Corcoran (*Bone Island Mambo*), and Les Roberts (*The Dutch*). John Shannon's private eye provides an insightful look at life in Orange County in *The Orange Curtain* (as does T. Jefferson Parker in the powerful non-private eye novel *Silent Joe*). Rick Riordan really hit his stride in *The Devil Went Down to Austin*—John Dortmunder is a crook but his adventures appeal to fans of the comic private eye novel—and Donald E. Westlake's *Bad News* is a very funny book about planting dead Indians in old graves. Randy Wayne White's Doc Ford is not exactly a private eye but he's got the attitude (and a hilarious sidekick in his weird genius friend Tomlinson), and *Shark River* is another excellent entry in this always readable series.

There's no question that Robert B. Parker's Spenser is a private eye, but *Potshot* finds our Boston sleuth out west, cleaning up a corrupt small Arizona town. Western settings continue to grow in popularity among mystery writers. James Lee Burke's roots may be in Texas and Louisiana but his heart—and his home—are in Montana, and that helps give *Bitterroot* a special feeling from a very special writer. Other notable books that use the west (rather than just pass through it) are *Desert Noir* by Betty Webb, *Red Mesa* by Aimee and David Thurlo, *Vanishing Point* by Judith Van Gieson, *Crazy Love* by Steve Brewer, *Cruzatte and Maria* by Peter Bowen, *Under the Cover of Law* by Michael McGarrity, *Concrete Desert* by John Talton and *Blue Wolf* by Lise McClendon. If you count Alaska as part of the west, you can throw in Marcia Simpson's *Sound Tracks*, Val Davis' *The Return of the Spanish Lady*, Sue Henry's *Dead North*, and Christopher Lane's *Silent as the Hunter*.

Of the many legal thrillers published during this time period, two stand out: Lisa Scottoline's *The Vendetta Defense*, set in south Philadelphia's Italian community, and John Lescroart's *The Hearing*, in which a heroin addict is unjustly charged with murder. Perri O'Shaughnessy's *Writ of Execution*, about a woman who can't collect her slot machine jackpot without revealing her identity, has movie sale written all over it.

It wasn't easy picking our 25 favorites from this group, although some books really stood out. But you're probably pretty safe, depending on individual taste (after all, some people hate historicals or private eye novels), with the following:

The Ferryman Will Be There by Rosemary Aubert

Unholy Dying by Robert Barnard

Bitterroot by James Lee Burke

Flight by Jan Burke

Echo Burning by Lee Child

Angel in Black by Max Allan Collins

A Finer End by Deborah Crombie

True Believers by Jane Haddam

Cozy by Parnell Hall

Death in Holy Orders by P.D. James

Mystic River by Dennis Lehane

Perfect Daughter by Gillian Linscott

The Reaper by Peter Lovesey

Fearless Jones by Walter Mosley

Rag and Bone by Michael Nava

Corpse de Ballet by Ellen Pall

Silent Joe by T. Jefferson Parker

Right as Rain by George P. Pelecanos

The Devil Went Down to Austin by Rick Riordan

Unfinished Business by Barbara Seranella

The Orange Curtain by John Shannon

Louisiana Hotshot by Julie Smith

Bubbles Unbound by Sarah Strohmeyer

Bad News by Donald E. Westlake

Shark River by Randy Wayne White

In closing, we'd be remiss if we didn't mention several writers whose recent deaths diminish the genre they served so well. Nora DeLoach wrote cozies about a black woman in the Deep South (*Mama Cracks a Mask of Innocence* appeared shortly before she died), something we've not seen anyone else do. Ann George was a poet turned mystery writer who wrote a very funny series about two elderly sisters in Alabama who were from time to time called upon to solve crimes. Fellow Southerner Elizabeth Daniels Squire wrote affectionately about Peaches Dann, a forgetful older sleuth. And there was Hugh Holton, a real-life Chicago cop who graced every room he entered and gave us some fine books featuring black Chicago police commander Larry Cole, the last of which was *The Devil's Shadow*. Finally, there was actor turned bestselling writer Robert Ludlum, whose name for many years was virtually synonymous with the international thriller.

Mystery Titles

CATHERINE AIRD (Pseudonym of Kinn Hamilton McIntosh)

Little Knell

(New York: St. Martin's Press, 2001)

Story type: Traditional; Police Procedural
Series: Inspector Sloan. Book 18
Subject(s): Egyptian Antiquities; Museums; Drugs
Major character(s): C.D. ''Seedy'' Sloan, Police Officer (inspector)
Time period(s): 2000s
Locale(s): Calleshire, England

Summary: When the local museum is bequeathed a collection of valuable ancient Egyptian artifacts, officials are stunned to learn that a 3,000-year-old sarcophagus contains, instead of a mummy, the relatively fresh corpse of a young woman accountant. Sloan's persistent sleuthing eventually connects her with the heroin trade and a money-laundering scheme. Sloan is as likable as ever and the book displays flashes of the author's customary quiet wit, but it's a slight effort compared to some of her earlier works—which is too bad, because she's normally one of the best of the old-fashioned English-village procedural writers.

Where it's reviewed:
Booklist, February 15, 2001, page 1118
Publishers Weekly, February 19, 2001, page 72

Other books by the same author:
Stiff News, 1999
Injury Time, 1997 (short stories)
After Affects, 1996
A Going Concern, 1993
The Body Politic, 1990

Other books you might like:
Caroline Graham, *Barnaby Series Inspector*, 1987-
Ngaio Marsh, *The Roderick Alleyn Series*, 1934-1982
Patricia Moyes, *The Henry Tibbett Series*, 1959-1993
Dorothy Simpson, *The Luke Thanet Series*, 1981-
Susanna Stacey, *The Robert Bone Series*, 1987-

CYNTHIA G. ALWYN

Scent of Murder

(New York: St. Martin's Press, 2001)

Story type: Private Detective
Subject(s): Animals/Dogs; Missing Persons; Serial Killer
Major character(s): Brenna Scott, Animal Trainer; Jett Culpepper, Detective—Private
Time period(s): 2000s
Locale(s): Sacramento, California; Seattle, Washington

Summary: Brenna, founder of a volunteer search-and-rescue team that uses dogs to find missing people, often children, works as an administrative assistant to Jett Culpepper of Culpepper Investigations. While in Seattle for a conference, they are called upon by the police to help track down a little girl reported missing from her home. The child is recovered safely, but Brenna's loyal German Shepherd, Brie, drowns during the search, and Brenna gamely tries to deal with her loss. Back in Sacramento, she and Jett learn that the girl's would-be abductor is targeting other children. The details about the training of search dogs and their amazing abilities are truly fascinating, but the author's gung-ho depiction of police work and her habit of bestowing nicknames on both human and canine characters (''Irish,'' ''String Bean,'' ''Funny Face'') wear a bit thin after a while. Even so, dog lovers should adore this debut novel, if they can get past the harrowing loss of Brenna's canine companion in the opening scenes.

Where it's reviewed:
Publishers Weekly, June 11, 2001, page 64

Other books you might like:
Carole Lea Benjamin, *The Rachel Alexander and Dash Series*, 1996-
Laurien Berenson, *The Melanie Travis Series*, 1995-
Susan Conant, *The Holly Winter Series*, 1989-
Patricia Guiver, *The Delilah Doolittle Series*, 1997-
Virginia Lanier, *The Jo Beth Sidden Series*, 1995-

3

ROSEMARY AUBERT

The Ferryman Will Be There

(Bridgehampton, New York: Bridge Works, 2001)

Story type: Amateur Detective
Series: Ellis Portal. Book 3
Subject(s): Homelessness; Missing Persons; City Life
Major character(s): Ellis Portal, Judge (former), Streetperson (former)
Time period(s): 2000s
Locale(s): Toronto, Ontario, Canada

Summary: Although he has recently come into a sizable sum of money, disgraced former judge Ellis Portal once again finds himself homeless when the rooming house owned by his young friend, Tootie Beet, a former runaway and girl gang member, is condemned so the city can build more upscale housing. He's also called upon by his policeman friend, Matt West, to help him find a missing teenage girl, Carrie Simm, whose famous movie producer father was murdered. With some cautious help from Tootie, whose gang connections lead him to the abandoned buildings throughout the city that have become the precarious refuges of urban homeless youth, Ellis searches for Carrie, ending up at his old haunts in the Don River Valley, where the first book in the series was set. Even though Ellis keeps edging closer and closer to respectability, he still feels most at home in the company of those on the fringes of society, and the series remains as fresh and poignant as it was in the beginning.

Where it's reviewed:
Booklist, May 1, 2001, page 1618
Publishers Weekly, May 21, 2001, page 84
Wall Street Journal, June 5, 2001, page A24

Other books by the same author:
The Feast of Stephen, 1999
Free Reign, 1997

Other books you might like:
G.D. Gearino, *Counting Coup*, 1997
Laurie R. King, *To Play the Fool*, 1995
Barbara Seranella, *No Human Involved*, 1997
John Straley, *The Cecil Younger Series*, 1992-
Mary Willis Walker, *All the Dead Lie Down*, 1998

4

ROBERT BARNARD

Unholy Dying

(New York: Scribner, 2001)

Story type: Traditional; Police Procedural
Series: Charlie Peace and Mike Oddie. Book 5
Subject(s): Clergy; Catholicism; Marriage
Major character(s): Charlie Peace, Police Officer (sergeant); Mike Oddie, Police Officer (inspector); Christopher Pardoe, Religious (Catholic priest)
Time period(s): 2000s
Locale(s): Shipley, England; Leeds, England

Summary: Father Pardoe, a kindly middle-aged priest, has been unjustly accused of having had sexual relations with an unmarried teen mother and is suspended from his parish pending an investigation. It's clear from the outset he is entirely innocent and his only interest in Julie Norris was to help her through a difficult time, offering her emotional support and some modest financial help from a church fund established for that purpose. Enter Cosmo Horrocks, an odious yellow journalist who gets wind of the affair and writes a headline story about it. Pardoe, who's been removed from the presbytery, has taken lodgings with a sensible middle-aged woman, whose heart is as kind as his and is soon offering him the gift of friendship and eventually more. When Horrocks gets himself killed, there's no end of suspects, as all his subjects, colleagues, and family members had ample reason to both fear and detest him. At this point, Peace and Oddie step in to sort matters out. Barnard saves his rancor here for the truly nasty characters in his large cast, such as Horrocks and Julie's smug and unfeeling parents. Mostly, however, it's institutions that he's critical of: loveless marriages that trap families in a self-perpetuating cycle of victims and abusers, and a church that denies its loyal clergy the comfort of loving marriages. Salt-and-pepper cops Peace and Oddie have also appeared as solo investigators in earlier books, and Peace has been teamed with other detectives.

Where it's reviewed:
Publishers Weekly, March 26, 2001, page 66

Other books by the same author:
The Corpse at the Haworth Tandoori, 1999
The Bad Samaritan, 1995
A Hovering of Vultures, 1993
A Fatal Attachment, 1992
A City of Strangers, 1990

Other books you might like:
Colin Dexter, *Service of All the Dead*, 1979
Peter Dickinson, *The Sinful Stones*, 1970
Reginald Hill, *The Dalziel/Pascoe Series*, 1970-
P.D. James, *Death in Holy Orders*, 2001
Peter Lovesey, *The Reaper*, 2001

5

NANCY BARTHOLOMEW

Film Strip

(New York: St. Martin's Press, 2000)

Story type: Amateur Detective
Series: Sierra Lavotoni. Book 3
Subject(s): Entertainment; Humor; Italian Americans
Major character(s): Sierra Lavotoni, Stripper, Detective—Amateur; John Nailor, Detective—Homicide
Time period(s): 2000s
Locale(s): Panama City, Florida

Summary: Somebody is out to kill off the talent at the Tiffany Gentleman's Club. A visiting porn star, Venus Lovemotion, is shot to death during her act and, during the same attack, Sierra takes a hit in her derriere, which is more painful than serious, although it could certainly affect her ability to perform. Then her friend and co-worker, Marla, is suspected of the crime,

and Sierra tries to persuade her cop boyfriend, homicide detective John Nailor, that Marla is innocent. However, she's going to have to mount an investigation of her own to do that. The author manages to keep the humor fresh and emphasizes the camaraderie among the strippers and Sierra's close ties with her volatile and overprotective Italian family.

Where it's reviewed:
Library Journal, October 1, 2000, page 152
New York Times Book Review, December 10, 2000, page 35
Publishers Weekly, October 9, 2000, page 77

Other books by the same author:
Dragstrip, 1999
The Miracle Strip, 1998

Other books you might like:
Sophie Dunbar, *Redneck Riviera*, 1998
Janet Evanovich, *The Stephanie Plum Series*, 1994-
Tony Fennelly, *The Margot Fortier Series*, 1994-
Carl Hiaasen, *Strip Tease*, 1993
Kathleen Taylor, *The Tory Bauer Series*, 1995-

6

M.C. BEATON (Pseudonym of Marion Chesney)

Death of a Dustman
(New York: Mysterious, 2001)

Story type: Traditional; Police Procedural
Series: Hamish Macbeth. Book 17
Subject(s): Small Town Life; Abuse; Blackmail
Major character(s): Hamish Macbeth, Police Officer (village constable)
Time period(s): 2000s
Locale(s): Lochdubh, Scotland

Summary: When a local politician with an environmental conscience establishes a recyling center in the Highlands village of Lochdubh, she appoints garbage collector (or dustman) Fergus Macleod as its head; never mind that he's an alcoholic wife-beater who uses his newfound authority to blackmail the villagers with information gleaned from their garbage. When Fergus, who's become even more officious in his new post, is found dead in a recycling bin, it's up to the canny but laid-back constable Hamish Macbeth to pick out his murderer from a host of suspects. Even this deep into a series by an amazingly prolific author who also writes the Agatha Raisin mysteries, as well as Regency romances under her own name, the formula continues to entertain, sparked by her wry wit and the engaging personality of young Hamish, who isn't nearly as inept a lawman as he'd like people to think.

Where it's reviewed:
Booklist, January 1, 2001, page 923
Library Journal, January 1, 2001, page 162
New York Times Book Review, March 18, 2001, page 18
Publishers Weekly, December 18, 2000, page 57

Other books by the same author:
A Highland Christmas, 1999
Death of an Addict, 1999
Death of a Scriptwriter, 1998
Death of a Dentist, 1997
Death of a Macho Man, 1996

Other books you might like:
Rhys Bowen, *The Evan Evans Series*, 1997-
Gerald Hammond, *The Keith Calder Series*, 1979-
Jonathan Harrington, *The Danny O'Flaherty Series*, 1996-
Frank Parrish, *The Dan Mallett Series*, 1977-
Graham Thomas, *Malice in the Highlands*, 1998

7

M.C. BEATON (Pseudonym of Marion Chesney)

The Skeleton in the Closet
(New York: St. Martin's Minotaur, 2001)

Story type: Traditional; Amateur Detective
Subject(s): Animals/Salamanders; Romance; Small Town Life
Major character(s): Fellworth Dolphin, Waiter/Waitress, Wealthy; Maggie Partlett, Waiter/Waitress
Time period(s): 2000s
Locale(s): Buss, England (Worcestershire)

Summary: When Fell's domineering and penny-pinching mother dies, it takes him awhile to realize what a relief it is to be free of her dour presence and insistent demands. He's even more surprised to learn that he's inherited an astonishing sum of money, especially considering how modestly his parents had always lived. When an interfering aunt makes noises about moving in with him, he claims to be engaged to his co-worker, Maggie, a plain, somewhat lumpish girl who is the closest thing he's ever had to a friend. She's receptive to the ruse, which frees her from similar bondage to her family, and together they quit their menial jobs, move in together, and start spending Fell's newfound money. Both blossom and begin to enjoy life, although they still have obstacles to overcome before Fell can realize Maggie's true worth. There's one nagging problem though: where did all the money come from, and was it somehow connected to a train robbery in the town's past? The two of them set out to investigate and turn up some surprising secrets. *The Skeleton in the Closet* is an engaging fairy tale for grownups that also displays some of the same wry wit that distinguishes the author's long-running series about Agatha Raisin and Hamish Macbeth.

Where it's reviewed:
Library Journal, March 1, 2001, page 133
Publishers Weekly, January 8, 2001, page 50

Other books by the same author:
Death of a Dustman, 2001
Agatha Raisin and the Fairies of Fryfam, 2000
Agatha Raisin and the Witch of Wyckehadden, 2000
A Highland Christmas, 1999
Death of an Addict, 1999

Other books you might like:
Nancy Atherton, *The Aunt Dimity Series*, 1992-
K.K. Beck, *The Jane da Silva Series*, 1992-
April Henry, *Circles of Confusion*, 1999
Charles Mathes, *The Girl at the End of the Line*, 1999
Margot Wadley, *The Gripping Beast*, 2001

8

BARBARA BLOCK

Blowing Smoke

(New York: Kensington, 2001)

Story type: Private Detective
Series: Robin Light. Book 7
Subject(s): Runaways; Animals/Dogs; Psychic Powers
Major character(s): Robin Light, Store Owner (exotic pet store), Detective—Private (part-time unlicensed)
Time period(s): 2000s
Locale(s): Syracuse, New York; Cazenovia, New York

Summary: With her pet store facing possible bankruptcy, Robin is supporting herself through part-time work as a private investigator, but with two cases to deal with right now the work seems more full-time. She's investigating the disappearance of a teenage girl from her affluent Cazenovia home when she's also called upon to check out Pat Humphrey, a woman pet psychic who has been named in the will of wealthy Rose Taylor. Rose's three children are concerned that Pat is a fraud bent on cheating them out of their rightful inheritance. The trouble is that when Robin investigates, she discovers Pat's for real, and she learns Rose Taylor's offspring are far from stellar citizens. When Pat is murdered, Robin has a very different case on her hands. At her side is her faithful cocker spaniel sidekick, Zsa Zsa.

Where it's reviewed:
Booklist, May 1, 2001, page 1622
Publishers Weekly, June 4, 2001, page 61

Other books by the same author:
Endangered Species, 1999
Vanishing Act, 1998
The Scent of Murder, 1997
In Plain Sight, 1996
Twister, 1994

Other books you might like:
Linda Barnes, *The Carlotta Carlyle Series*, 1987-
Carole Lea Benjamin, *The Rachel Alexander and Dash Series*, 1996-
Laurien Berenson, *The Melanie Travis Series*, 1995-
Kathy Hogan Trocheck, *The Callahan Garrity Series*, 1992-
Judith Van Gieson, *The Neil Hamel Series*, 1988-

9

DELLA BORTON (Pseudonym of Lynette Carpenter)

Slow Dissolve

(New York: Fawcett, 2001)

Story type: Amateur Detective
Series: Gilda Liberty. Book 3
Subject(s): Movie Industry; History; Family
Major character(s): Gilda Liberty, Businesswoman (movie theater owner), Detective—Amateur
Time period(s): 2000s
Locale(s): Eden, Ohio

Summary: Gilda is working alone in her movie theater when an elderly man wanders into the lobby and tells her that he

used to be in pictures. He turns out to be Leo Mayer, a former movie director whose mind is fogged by Alzheimer's and who is plagued by disjointed memories of World War II and a mysterious person named Auggie. His current wife, Shirley, has hired a private detective to find out who Auggie is, but then Shirley drowns in their swimming pool and the detective lands in the hospital after being knocked unconscious. Gilda, who comes from a long line of illustrious movie people, puts her family to work on the case. Full of references to Hollywood's glory days (particularly to *Sunset Boulevard*) and featuring a crossword puzzle designed for film buffs, the book should appeal to fans of old-time movies. The author, who as D.B. Borton has written the Cat Caliban mysteries about an aging woman private eye, teaches film on the university level.

Other books by the same author:
Freeze Frame, 2000
Fade to Black, 1999

Other books you might like:
Marian Babson, *The Eve Sinclair/Trixie Dolan Series*, 1986-
Ellen Hart, *The Merchant of Venus*, 2001
Stuart M. Kaminsky, *The Toby Peters Series*, 1977-
Kris Neri, *Revenge of the Gypsy Queen*, 1999
Beth Saulnier, *The Fourth Wall*, 2001

10

GAIL BOWEN

Burying Ariel

(Toronto: McClelland & Stewart, 2001)

Story type: Amateur Detective; Traditional
Series: Joanne Kilbourn. Book 7
Subject(s): Academia; Feminism; Universities and Colleges
Major character(s): Joanne Kilbourn, Professor (political science), Detective—Amateur
Time period(s): 2000s
Locale(s): Regina, Saskatchewan, Canada

Summary: When Ariel Warren, a popular teacher at the small university where Joanne teaches, is murdered, the police take a maintenance worker into custody for the crime. It's widely suspected that they have the wrong person, and one of Ariel's former lovers, a talk-show host known as Charlie D, even seems to suggest, on the air, he may have done it. His father is horrified and asks Joanne to help, but she gets sidetracked when an intended peaceful vigil observing Ariel's death turns into an angry protest against violence toward women.

Where it's reviewed:
Publishers Weekly, April 16, 2001, page 48

Other books by the same author:
Verdict in Blood, 1998
A Killing Spring, 1996
A Colder Kind of Death, 1994
The Wandering Soul Murders, 1993
Love and Murder, 1991

Other books you might like:
J.S. Borthwick, *The Student Body*, 1986
Amanda Cross, *The Kate Fansler Series*, 1964-
Joanne Dobson, *The Karen Pelletier Series*, 1997-
Nora Kelly, *The Gillian Adams Series*, 1984-

Lev Raphael, *The Nick Hoffman Series*, 1996-

PETER BOWEN

Cruzatte and Maria
(New York: St. Martin's Press, 2001)

Story type: Amateur Detective
Series: Gabriel du Pre. Book 8
Subject(s): American West; Native Americans; History
Major character(s): Gabriel du Pre, Inspector (cattle-brand), Musician (fiddler); Charles Van Dusen, FBI Agent
Time period(s): 2000s
Locale(s): Toussaint, Montana

Summary: Gabe has let his daughter Maria talk him into being a consultant to a film company shooting a documentary on the Lewis and Clark expedition. It soon becomes clear that recreating history isn't the filmmakers' only goal; they also want to promote Montana as a desirable place to live and play, which (as it has in past books in the series) infuriates Gabe, who thinks the state is overrun with enough outsiders as it is. Some of his less law-abiding fellow Montanans obviously agree with his sentiments and are picking off river rafters to discourage tourism, and Gabe's old friend, Charles Van Dusen, is assigned to find the killers. In the meantime, Gabe unearths a cache of priceless artifacts, including a journal kept by Meriwether Lewis. Gabe's Metis ancestry (half French, half Indian) continues to dominate the story, particularly as his people, including a long-ago fiddler named Cruzatte, as well as Sacajewea's husband Charbonneau, were for a time members of the expedition.

Where it's reviewed:
Booklist, February 15, 2001, page 1118
Publishers Weekly, February 12, 2001, page 186

Other books by the same author:
Stick Game, 2000
Long Son, 1999
Thunder Horse, 1998
Notches, 1997
Wolf, No Wolf, 1996

Other books you might like:
James Lee Burke, *Black Cherry Blues*, 1989
Margaret Coel, *Spirit Woman*, 2000
Jamie Harrison, *The Jules Clement Series*, 1995-
Jane Langton, *Murder at Monticello*, 2001
Michael McGarrity, *The Kevin Kerney Series*, 1996-

12

JOHN BRADY

A Carra King
(South Royalton, Vermont: Steerforth, 2001)

Story type: Police Procedural
Series: Matt Minogue. Book 6
Subject(s): Archaeology; Celts; Irish Americans
Major character(s): Matt Minogue, Police Officer (inspector)
Time period(s): 2000s
Locale(s): Dublin, Ireland

Summary: When Patrick Shaughnessy, an American tourist from a wealthy family, is found dead in the trunk of a rental car at the Dublin airport, Garda Inspector Matt Minogue is called in to investigate. Shaughnessy turns out not to be your average tourist; in addition to attending exclusive parties for patrons of the arts, he had visited the Stone Age site of the Carra Fields where he had connected with an attractive museum curator who has now gone missing. The site itself is a controversial one, promising as it does to cast a new light on the island's history. Shaughnessy, who was trying to get in touch with his own Irish roots, as well as escape some domestic problems back home, seems to have been drawn to the past and its artifacts, but in death his motives are a puzzle to Minogue.

Where it's reviewed:
Booklist, May 1, 2001, page 1622
Publishers Weekly, May 14, 2001, page 56

Other books by the same author:
The Good Life, 1994
All Souls, 1993
A Kaddish in Dublin, 1990
Unholy Ground, 1989
Stone of the Heart, 1988

Other books you might like:
Vincent Banville, *The John Blaine Series*, 1993-
Ann C. Fallon, *The James Fleming Series*, 1990-
Bartholomew Gill, *The Peter McGarr Series*, 1977-
Jonathan Harrington, *The Danny O'Flaherty Series*, 1996-
Jim Lusby, *The Carl McCadden Series*, 1995-

13

STEVE BREWER

Crazy Love
(Philadelphia: Intrigue, 2001)

Story type: Private Detective; Humor
Series: Bubba Mabry. Book 6
Subject(s): Infidelity; Marriage; Jealousy
Major character(s): Bubba Mabry, Detective—Private; Melvin Howard, Wealthy (millionaire)
Time period(s): 2000s
Locale(s): Albuquerque, New Mexico (USA)

Summary: Even though his wife has been dead for six months, Albuquerque millionaire Melvin Haywood is so obsessed with the infidelity she confessed to on her deathbed that he hires laid-back private eye Bubba Mabry to find out who's been cuckolding him. Although he personally feels it's better to let the past alone, Bubba carries out his assignment, interviewing various residents of The Manor, an upscale closed community full of secrets and lies, as well as all strata of Albuquerque society. No sooner does he identify the wife's lover than the man is murdered—and the police like Bubba as the killer. Along the way, he finds much to reflect upon as to the nature of marriage and loyalty.

Where it's reviewed:
Publishers Weekly, March 12, 2001, page 66

Other books by the same author:
Dirty Pool, 1999
Shaky Ground, 1997
Witchy Woman, 1996
Baby Face, 1995
Lonely Street, 1994

Other books you might like:
Harlan Coben, *The Myron Bolitar Series*, 1995-
Philip Depoy, *The Flap Tucker Series*, 1997-
Parnell Hall, *The Stanley Hastings Series*, 1987-
Rick Riordan, *The Tres Navarre Series*, 1997-
Walter Satterthwait, *The Joshua Croft Series*, 1989-

14

RITA MAE BROWN
SNEAKY PIE BROWN, Co-Author

Claws and Effect

(New York: Bantam, 2001)

Story type: Amateur Detective; Domestic
Series: Mrs. Murphy. Book 9
Subject(s): Animals/Cats; Animals/Dogs; Hospitals
Major character(s): Mrs. Murphy, Animal (cat); Pewter, Animal (cat); Mary Minor ''Harry'' Harristeen, Postal Worker (postmistress), Detective—Amateur
Time period(s): 2000s
Locale(s): Crozet, Virginia

Summary: Harry is getting reports from postal patrons that many of them have received a threatening chain letter demanding money for the local hospital. Then the director of the hospital's physical plant is found dead in the building's basement and a much-loved older doctor is shot to death, with the murder weapon inexplicably turning up at the post office. When Harry's investigation of the events goes south, Mrs. Murphy, Pewter, and their valiant Welsh corgi companion, Tucker, go to work. Two interesting subplots involve the Underground Railroad and the history of fox-hunting, a subject dear to the author's heart.

Where it's reviewed:
Booklist, January 1, 2001, page 923
Publishers Weekly, January 8, 2001, page 50

Other books by the same author:
Pawing through the Past, 2000
Cat on the Scent, 1999
Murder on the Prowl, 1998
Murder, She Meowed, 1996
Pay Dirt, 1995

Other books you might like:
Garrison Allen, *The Big Mike Series*, 1994-
Lilian Jackson Braun, *The Cat Who Series*, 1966-
Mary Daheim, *Suture Self*, 2001
Carole Nelson Douglas, *The Midnight Louie Series*, 1992-
Shirley Rousseau Murphy, *The Joe Grey Series*, 1996-

15

MARSHALL BROWNE

The Wooden Leg of Inspector Anders

(New York: St. Martin's Press, 2001)

Story type: Police Procedural
Subject(s): Organized Crime; Physically Handicapped
Major character(s): D.P. Anders, Police Officer (inspector)
Time period(s): 2000s
Locale(s): Rome, Italy

Summary: Since losing a leg ten years earlier in a confrontation with an anarchist group, Anders has been semi-retired, called out only for special cases. One comes up when the magistrate investigating the murder of a judge in southern Italy is blown up in an explosion. Anders' routine investigation is somewhat altered when he meets the judge's widow and she asks him to prove the Mafia was behind the killings. This book won the Australian Ned Kelly Award for best first crime novel of 1999, the year it came out in the author's native land.

Where it's reviewed:
Booklist, May 1, 2001, page 1624
Publishers Weekly, March 26, 2001, page 65

Other books you might like:
Michael Dibdin, *The Aurelio Zen Series*, 1988-
John Spencer Hill, *The Carlo Arbati Series*, 1995-
Donna Leon, *The Guido Brunetti Series*, 1992-
Magdalen Nabb, *The Salvatore Guarnaccia Series*, 1981-
Edward Sklepowich, *The Urbino Macintyre Series*, 1990-

16

EDNA BUCHANAN

You Only Die Twice

(New York: Morrow, 2001)

Story type: Amateur Detective
Series: Britt Montero. Book 7
Subject(s): Journalism; City Life; Wealth
Major character(s): Britt Montero, Journalist (crime reporter), Detective—Amateur
Time period(s): 2000s
Locale(s): Miami, Florida

Summary: When the nude body of a beautiful woman is found washed up on a Miami beach, the police identify it as that of Kaithlin Jordan, a wealthy socialite who was murdered ten years ago. The problem is that the corpse is only a few hours old. Kaithlin's husband, R.J. Jordan, was found guilty of the crime, although the body was never recovered, and is now on Florida's death row awaiting execution in a matter of weeks. Britt and her usual cadre of helpers go to work trying to piece together what happened and what Kaithlin had been doing for ten years. They get no help from R.J., who is as difficult and unpleasant a person as he was during the original trial. Most of all, though, Britt wants to know how it happened that R.J. was convicted of a crime that never actually took place. In addition to her fiction, the author has written several true-crime books.

Where it's reviewed:
Booklist, January 1, 2001, page 869
Publishers Weekly, March 5, 2001, page 66

Other books by the same author:
Garden of Evil, 1999
Margin of Error, 1997
Act of Betrayal, 1996
Suitable for Framing, 1995
Miami, It's Murder, 1994

Other books you might like:
Robert Crais, *Demolition Angel*, 2000
Carolina Garcia-Aguilera, *The Lupe Solano Series*, 1996-
James W. Hall, *Rough Draft*, 2000
Nancy Pickard, *The Whole Truth*, 2000
Mary Willis Walker, *The Molly Cates Series*, 1994-

17

CAROLE BUGGE

Who Killed Mona Lisa?

(New York: Berkley, 2001)

Story type: Amateur Detective
Series: Claire Rawlings. Book 3
Subject(s): Hotels, Motels; Secrets; Holidays
Major character(s): Claire Rawlings, Editor (publishing house), Detective—Amateur; Meredith Lawrence, Child (12-year-old), Sidekick; Wally Jackson, Police Officer
Time period(s): 2000s
Locale(s): South Sudbury, Massachusetts

Summary: Meredith is the daughter of Claire's college roommate, who died two years earlier and whose husband has since remarried. As Meredith detests her father's new wife, Claire has become something of a mother surrogate to the girl. Claire and Wally are planning a romantic Thanksgiving weekend getaway at the historic Wayside Inn in the Berkshires when Meredith begs to come along, claiming she can't face another holiday with her evil stepmother. Claire acquiesces as she's very fond of the girl, who will also have her own bedroom. They arrive a day ahead of Wally, who is further delayed by work and a surprise snowstorm that effectively cuts the inn off from the outside world. Naturally, there's a murder, and naturally Claire and Meredith—who despite her adolescent love of melodrama is extremely bright—turn detective. The inn has a tradition called the Secret Drawer Society, encouraging guests to write down (anonymously, of course) their deepest secrets for other guests to read. These letters provide clues to the murder. The author has also written two historical mysteries featuring Sherlock Holmes.

Other books by the same author:
Who Killed Dorian Gray?, 2000
Who Killed Blanche Dubois?, 1999

Other books you might like:
Claudia Bishop, *A Taste for Murder*, 1994
Lawrence Block, *The Body in the Library*, 1997
Lee Harris, *The Thanksgiving Day Murder*, 1995
Leslie Meier, *Turkey Day Murder*, 2000
Ann Ripley, *The Garden Tour Affair*, 1999

18

JAMES LEE BURKE

Bitterroot

(New York: Simon & Schuster, 2001)

Story type: Traditional; Legal
Series: Billy Bob Holland. Book 3
Subject(s): Environmental Problems; Ecology; Outdoor Life
Major character(s): Billy Bob Holland, Lawyer
Time period(s): 2000s
Locale(s): Missoula, Montana; Deaf Smith, Texas

Summary: Holland lets himself be pulled away from West Texas for the Bitterroot Valley of Montana by his old friend Doc Voss, who has taken on a ruthless mining company that has next to no regard for the fragile environment their operations are endangering. Their tactics become vengeful when three men rape Doc's teenage daughter Maisey, making a clear message for him to back off. Then one of the rapists is murdered, leaving Doc a chief suspect and in need of a good lawyer—Holland. Waiting for him when he arrives in Montana is another dangerous man, this time from his own past: Wyatt Dixon, paroled from a Texas prison with a score to settle with Holland. There are others, from militia leaders to mobsters, and Holland's job is made more difficult when his son, Lucas, and private detective Temple Carrol arrive on the scene, meaning that the people he loves best are also endangered. The author also writes the Louisiana-based Dave Robicheaux series.

Where it's reviewed:
Booklist, March 15, 2001, page 1331
Library Journal, May 1, 2001, page 125
New York Times Book Review, June 24, 2001, page 22
Publishers Weekly, April 14, 2001, page 1331
Washington Post, June 1, 2001, page C6

Other books by the same author:
Heartwood, 1999
Cimarron Rose, 1997

Other books you might like:
James Crumley, *The Last Good Kiss*, 1978
Jamie Harrison, *The Jules Clement Series*, 1995-
Michael McGarrity, *The Kevin Kerney Series*, 1996-
Jenny Siler, *Iced*, 2001
Judith Van Gieson, *Raptor*, 1990

 19

JAN BURKE

Flight

(New York: Simon & Schuster, 2001)

Story type: Psychological Suspense; Police Procedural
Series: Irene Kelly. Book 8
Subject(s): Airplanes; Missing Persons; Marriage
Major character(s): Frank Harriman, Detective—Homicide; Irene Kelly, Journalist (newspaper reporter)
Time period(s): 2000s
Locale(s): Las Piernas, California

Summary: Reporter Irene Kelly plays a supporting role in this book, the first in the series to star Irene's husband, Frank, a veteran homicide detective for the Las Piernas police department. A cold case is reopened, when the wreckage of a missing small airplane is found along with the remains of Philip Lefebvre, a cop accused of killing the only witness to the brutal murder of a police commissioner and then disappearing with the evidence needed to convict the suspected murderer. As he sifts through the evidence, Frank gradually begins to believe that Lefebvre may not have been guilty after all, nor was the man suspected of the crime. Irene, who knew Lefebvre herself and covered the original story, helps Frank in the investigation, and their amiable teamwork provides a few bright moments in an otherwise dark story, as Frank is increasingly shunned by his fellow officers as he gets closer to the truth.

Where it's reviewed:
Library Journal, March 1, 2001, page 130
Publishers Weekly, January 29, 2001, page 68
Texas Monthly, March 2001, page 32

Other books by the same author:
Bones, 1999
Liar, 1998
Hocus, 1997
Remember Me, Irene, 1996
Dear Irene, 1995

Other books you might like:
Michael Connelly, *The Harry Bosch Series*, 1992-
Robert Crais, *L.A. Requiem*, 1999
Jeffery Deaver, *The Lincoln Rhyme Series*, 1997-
T. Jefferson Parker, *Silent Joe*, 2001
Mary Willis Walker, *The Molly Cates Series*, 1994-

20

ANN CAMPBELL

Wolf in Sheep's Clothing
(New York: Signet, 2001)

Story type: Amateur Detective
Series: Annie O'Hara. Book 2
Subject(s): Antiques; Animals/Dogs; Country Life
Major character(s): Annie O'Hara, Antiques Dealer, Detective—Amateur; Claudius, Animal (wolf-husky hybrid)
Time period(s): 2000s
Locale(s): Lee, New Hampshire

Summary: Halloween is approaching and Annie's antiques shop in a picturesque old tavern is empty of customers, her stove is on the fritz, and her sister-in-law, Lydia, has insisted on parking her gigantic dog, Claudius, with her. If it weren't for her two paying boarders, she would be seriously broke. When one of her tenants, May Upton, is found murdered, Annie realizes she didn't know how bad things could get. Her brother, Tom, had been May's business partner, and he's immediately suspected of killing May for the insurance money she left him. The crisp New England setting and the bond Annie slowly forges with Claudius, who indeed turns out to be her best friend, add to the pleasure of this light mystery.

Other books by the same author:
Wolf at the Door, 2000

Other books you might like:
Carole Lea Benjamin, *The Rachel Alexander & Dash Series*, 1996-
Susan Conant, *The Holly Winter Series*, 1989-
Leslie Meier, *Trick or Treat Murder*, 1996
Tamar Myers, *The Abigail Timberlake Series*, 1996-
Valerie Wolzien, *All Hallows' Eve*, 1992

21

SUZANNE CHAZIN

The Fourth Angel
(New York: Putnam, 2001)

Story type: Police Procedural
Subject(s): Arson; Fires; Single Parent Families
Major character(s): Georgia Skeehan, Fire Fighter (marshal), Single Parent
Time period(s): 2000s
Locale(s): New York, New York

Summary: Georgia, a rookie fire marshal from a family of firefighters, is assigned to a special task force charged with investigating a series of high-accelerant fires, so hot that they're capable of melting the steel framework of a building. Her job is made more difficult by the fact that, as the only female in the department, she is constantly having to prove herself to her fellow firefighters, including her uncooperative partner. She's the first team member to believe the fires are the work of an arsonist, a hunch that's confirmed when she begins getting letters from someone who calls himself ''The Fourth Angel'' and writes in apocalyptic prose. The technical details are riveting and authentic; first-time novelist Chazin is married to a New York deputy fire chief.

Where it's reviewed:
Booklist, December 15, 2000, page 790
People Weekly, March 12, 2001, page 43
Publishers Weekly, January 8, 2001, page 47

Other books you might like:
Christine Andreae, *Smoke Eaters*, 2000
Earl Emerson, *The Mac Fontana Series*, 1988-
Peter Lance, *First Degree Burn*, 1997
Ridley Pearson, *Beyond Recognition*, 1997
Shelley Reuben, *The Wylie Nolan/Max Bramble Series*, 1994-

22

LEE CHILD

Echo Burning
(New York: Putnam, 2001)

Story type: Psychological Suspense; Action/Adventure
Series: Jack Reacher. Book 5
Subject(s): Abuse; Prejudice; American West
Major character(s): Jack Reacher, Drifter, Military Personnel (former military policeman)
Time period(s): 2000s
Locale(s): Echo, Texas

Summary: Perennial drifter and knight-errant Jack Reacher is hitchhiking along a lonely, blistering stretch of West Texas highway when Carmen Greer, a battered wife whose husband is soon to be released from prison, picks him up. It turns out she's looking to hire someone to kill this monster, as there seems to be no other way she can protect herself from him and his family, who despise her because of her Mexican ancestry. Reacher turns down her offer, but does agree to protect her and goes home with her to the family ranch near Pecos. Shortly after that her husband, Sloop, is found dead; Carmen is arrested for the murder; and Reacher, who is convinced her story is genuine, sets out to find the real killer. As always, there's a graceful noir touch to the writing, and it's hard to believe the author was born and raised in England.

Where it's reviewed:
Booklist, May 1, 2001, page 1624
Publishers Weekly, April 23, 2001, page 45

Other books by the same author:
Running Blind, 2000
Tripwire, 1999
Die Trying, 1998
Killing Floor, 1997

Other books you might like:
Michael Connelly, *The Harry Bosch Series*, 1992-
John Connolly, *Every Dead Thing*, 2000
Robert Crais, *L.A. Requiem*, 1999
James W. Hall, *The Thorn Series*, 1987-
Stephen Hunter, *The Bob Swagger Series*, 1993-

23

ALYS CLARE

Ashes of the Elements
(New York: St. Martin's Minotaur, 2001)

Story type: Historical
Series: Helewise of Hawkenlye. Book 2
Subject(s): Middle Ages; Convents; Rural Life
Major character(s): Helewise of Hawkenlye, Religious (abbess); Sir Josse d'Acquin, Knight
Time period(s): 12th century (1191)
Locale(s): Weald of Kent, England

Summary: When a lumberjack is found dead in the Wealden forest near the abbey, the superstitious locals blame it on the Forest People, a band of wild, nomadic men who are said to hide out in the woods. Helewise thinks differently, and once again joins forces with her friend, Sir Josse, to get to the bottom of things. Josse, who has been given a house and land by King Richard, is glad to help her out, but he finds something in the forest even more terrifying than ghosts. On hand to hinder rather than help their investigation is the oafish and corrupt sheriff, Henry Pelham of Tonbridge. There continue to be undertones of unacknowledged sexual tension in the relationship between Helewise and Josse.

Where it's reviewed:
Publishers Weekly, April 2, 2001, page 43

Other books by the same author:
Fortune Like the Moon, 2000

Other books you might like:
Margaret Frazer, *The Sister Frevisse Series*, 1992-
Domini Highsmith, *Master of the Keys*, 1996
Bernard Knight, *The Sir John de Wolfe Series*, 1998-
Sharan Newman, *Death Comes as Epiphany*, 1993
Ellis Peters, *The Brother Cadfael Series*, 1977-1994

24

HARLAN COBEN

Tell No One
(New York: Delacorte, 2001)

Story type: Psychological Suspense
Subject(s): Grief; Love; Internet
Major character(s): David Beck, Doctor (pediatrician)
Time period(s): 2000s
Locale(s): Green River, New Jersey; New York, New York

Summary: Although he's still going through the motions of living, working with children at a low-cost New Jersey clinic, David Beck is a hollow man. He is unable to get on with the real business of living since he lost his beloved wife and childhood sweetheart, Elizabeth, in a dreadful incident one night as they were celebrating the 13th anniversary of their first kiss. Unable to save her from the men who abducted and then murdered her, Beck is paralyzed by guilt, as well as grief over her death. Then one night while he's checking his e-mail, he gets a puzzling message from someone who could only be Elizabeth, referring to events that only they shared. Since he personally did not identify her body, there is the possibility, however remote, that she might still be alive, and soon Beck is off on a desperate search for the truth. The author also writes a series about wise-cracking sports agent Myron Bolitar.

Where it's reviewed:
Booklist, May 1, 2001, page 1624
Library Journal, April 15, 2001, page 130
Publishers Weekly, May 7, 2001, page 220

Other books by the same author:
Darkest Fear, 2000
The Final Detail, 1999
One False Move, 1998
Backspin, 1997
Fade Away, 1996

Other books you might like:
Jeffery Deaver, *The Blue Nowhere*, 2001
Dennis Lehane, *Mystic River*, 2001
T. Jefferson Parker, *Silent Joe*, 2001
Bill Pronzini, *In an Evil Time*, 2001
Stephen White, *The Program*, 2001

25

MAX ALLAN COLLINS

Angel in Black
(New York: New American Library, 2001)

Story type: Historical; Private Detective
Series: Nathan Heller. Book 12
Subject(s): Movie Industry; Organized Crime; History

Major character(s): Nathan Heller, Detective—Private
Time period(s): 1940s (1947)
Locale(s): Los Angeles, California

Summary: Nate is in Los Angeles with his new bride, Peggy, to set up the West Coast branch of his detective agency when he gets a call from an old girlfriend, Beth, announcing that she's pregnant and needs money for an abortion. He can't even remember having been that intimate with her but promises he'll get back to her. The next day he's out with some cop friends when they're called to a horrific crime scene and discover the severed body of a would-be starlet in a vacant lot. Nate is shocked to recognize Beth, aka Elizabeth Short, aka the Black Dahlia, and he doesn't dare tell anyone of his connection with her. The Black Dahlia case is, of course, one of the great unsolved murders in the annals of true crime, and the author comes up with his own ingenious solution to it here. Appended to the novel is an explanation of what is fact and what is fiction in the book and what other solutions have been suggested. The author's research is, as usual, meticulous, and real characters (Orson Welles, Eliot Ness, etc.) rub shoulders with fictional ones as Nate works to discover the killer's identity.

Where it's reviewed:
Booklist, March 1, 2001, page 1230
Publishers Weekly, February 26, 2001, page 62

Other books by the same author:
Majic Man, 1999
Flying Blind, 1998
Damned in Paradise, 1996
Blood and Thunder, 1995
Carnal Hours, 1994

Other books you might like:
Andrew Bergman, *Hollywood and LeVine*, 1975
Raymond Chandler, *The Little Sister*, 1949
James Ellroy, *The Black Dahlia*, 1987
Terence Faherty, *Kill Me Again*, 1996
Stuart M. Kaminsky, *The Toby Peters Series*, 1977-

SARA CONWAY

Murder on Good Friday
(Nashville: Cumberland House, 2001)

Story type: Historical
Subject(s): Anti-Semitism; Religious Conflict; Middle Ages
Major character(s): Lord Godwin, Veteran (ex-Crusader), Lawman (bailiff)
Time period(s): 13th century (1220)
Locale(s): Hexham, England

Summary: When the body of a young boy is found strangled in a field in northern England, the townspeople are eager to find the murderer, especially since the body also bears ritual wounds that suggest he was either crucified or made to appear so. Suspicion immediately falls upon the town's small Jewish population, which consists of nine related people. Lord Godwin must first stop the angry townsfolk from killing the suspects and then conduct his own investigation into the matter. Godwin, who is haunted by his role in the Crusades

and the fact that he survived when many of his comrades perished, no longer has a stomach for religious intolerance and is determined that no innocent man be punished for the sins of another. Author's first novel.

Where it's reviewed:
Publishers Weekly, February 26, 2001, page 63

Other books you might like:
Alys Clare, *The Helewise of Hawkenlye Series*, 1999-
Ian Morson, *The William Falconer Series*, 1994-
Sharan Newman, *The Difficult Saint*, 1999
Sharon Kay Penman, *The Justin de Quincy Series*, 1996-
Candace M. Robb, *A Trust Betrayed*, 2001

TOM CORCORAN

Bone Island Mambo
(New York: St. Martin's Press, 2001)

Story type: Amateur Detective
Series: Alex Rutledge. Book 3
Subject(s): Photography; Islands; Crime and Criminals
Major character(s): Alex Rutledge, Photographer (forensic), Detective—Amateur
Time period(s): 2000s
Locale(s): Key West, Florida

Summary: Once again freelance photographer Alex Rutledge finds himself at the center of a series of murders and other misdeeds. He's innocently bicycling around Key West, photographing buildings for his own pleasure, when a developer accuses him of planning to do an expose of an on-going project. Shortly afterward, the police ask him to photograph a dead body at the same construction site, and then still another body turns up on an outlying island. The police soon suspect he's somehow linked to the crimes, and he's offered a high-paying job by a major real estate broker. Is this a payoff to keep him quiet? The problem is, he doesn't know a thing about what's going on. Eventually he manages to fit the puzzle pieces together, if only to avoid being arrested himself.

Where it's reviewed:
Booklist, May 1, 2001, page 1626

Other books by the same author:
Gumbo Limbo, 1999
The Mango Opera, 1998

Other books you might like:
James W. Hall, *Red Sky at Night*, 1997
Hialeah Jackson, *Farewell, Conch Republic*, 1999
John Leslie, *The Gideon Lowry Series*, 1994-
Laurence Shames, *Florida Straits*, 1992
Jenny Siler, *Easy Money*, 1999

PHILIP R. CRAIG

Vineyard Shadows
(New York: Scribner, 2001)

Story type: Amateur Detective; Domestic

Series: J.W. Jackson. Book 12
Subject(s): Islands; Marriage; Small Town Life
Major character(s): J.W. Jackson, Parent, Beachcomber
Time period(s): 2000s
Locale(s): Martha's Vineyard, Massachusetts

Summary: When two intruders terrorize J.W.'s wife, Zee, and their small daughter, Diana, while he and their young son, Joshua, are out clamming, Zee musters all her resources and ends up killing one man and injuring the other, an act that leaves her badly traumatized. It turns out the intruders were looking for the second husband of J.W.'s ex-wife, Carla, whom he hasn't seen in years. Determined to find who ordered the attack, J.W. works independently of the local police, calling upon some of his own contacts from his past life as a Boston cop. Except for the violence of the opening scene, the book is largely tranquil in tone, focusing as it does upon small-town and family life, the quiet rhythms of the island setting, and the loving relationship between the Jacksons and their small children. Three of J.W.'s recipes are included.

Where it's reviewed:
Booklist, May 1, 2001, page 1626
Library Journal, May 1, 2001, page 130
Publishers Weekly, May 7, 2001, page 228

Other books by the same author:
Vineyard Blues, 2000
A Fatal Vineyard Season, 1999
A Shoot on Martha's Vineyard, 1998
A Deadly Vineyard Holiday, 1997
Death on a Vineyard Beach, 1996

Other books you might like:
Sally Gunning, *The Peter Bartholomew Series*, 1990-
Francine Mathews, *The Merry Folger Series*, 1994-
David Osborn, *Murder on Martha's Vineyard*, 1989
Cynthia Riggs, *Deadly Nightshade*, 2001
Kelly Roos, *Murder on Martha's Vineyard*, 1981

29

DEBORAH CROMBIE

A Finer End

(New York: Scribner, 2001)

Story type: Police Procedural; Traditional
Series: Duncan Kincaid/Gemma James. Book 7
Subject(s): Anglicans; History; Paganism
Major character(s): Duncan Kincaid, Police Officer (superintendent); Gemma James, Police Officer (sergeant); Jack Montford, Architect, Cousin (of Duncan)
Time period(s): 2000s
Locale(s): Glastonbury, England; London, England

Summary: Duncan and Gemma, who are sorting through issues in their relationship, play supporting roles in this unusual story by way of Duncan's kinship with his cousin, Jack Montford, with whom he grew up in Glastonbury. Long a sacred site for many and the home of a great cathedral and the mysterious Glastonbury Tor, the town is now overrun with all manner of New Agers and other pilgrims. Jack has begun unconsciously producing automatic writing in an unfamiliar hand and in Latin as well, and a little research indicates the messages are coming from a long-dead monk with something to say to the town's present inhabitants. In order to help understand what's happening to him, Jack gathers around himself an odd assortment of people, including a pregnant teenager, a woman who believes in the ancient religions, a medieval scholar, another woman who paints mysterious visions, and his own lady love, Winifred, an Anglican priest. When one of the group is murdered, Duncan and Gemma come to help Jack solve this very earthly crime, although they do so largely on the sidelines. The historical background and the pull of the past are handled beautifully, and the mystical aspects of the story are balanced by the complicated and very human relationships that bind the characters together.

Where it's reviewed:
Booklist, March 15, 2001, page 1356
New York Times Book Review, May 20, 2001, page 41
Publishers Weekly, April 16, 2001, page 47

Other books by the same author:
Kissed a Sad Goodbye, 1999
Dreaming of the Bones, 1997
Mourn Not Your Dead, 1996
Leave the Grave Green, 1995
All Shall Be Well, 1994

Other books you might like:
Kate Charles, *Cruel Habitations*, 2001
Jeanne M. Dams, *The Body in the Transept*, 1995
Elizabeth George, *The Thomas Lynley Series*, 1988-
Diane M. Greenwood, *The Theodora Braithwaite Series*, 1991-
Kate Sedley, *The Brothers of Glastonbury*, 2001

30

LAURA CRUM

Breakaway

(New York: St. Martin's Press, 2001)

Story type: Amateur Detective
Series: Gail McCarthy. Book 6
Subject(s): Animals/Horses; Art; Depression
Major character(s): Gail McCarthy, Veterinarian, Detective—Amateur
Time period(s): 2000s
Locale(s): Hawkins Valley, California (Santa Cruz County)

Summary: For days on end Gail has been struggling with a deep depression, barely able to get out of bed in the mornings and feeling none of her usual enthusiasm for life. She's temporarily jolted out of it by an unusual case: a woman artist, Nicolette Devereaux, calls her to her small ranch because her mare has been sexually molested. Gail wants to report this bizarre and unsettling incident to the police, but Nicolette asks her not to speak of it to anyone. While visiting, Gail falls in love with Nicolette's magnificent landscape paintings and makes up her mind to buy one. When more incidents of the same nature take place, Gail becomes concerned, and finally Nicolette herself is killed. Meanwhile, a friend talks Gail into getting help for her condition. The rural California setting and Gail's own cozy homestead are warmly described, along with her love of animals and the outdoors.

Mystery

Other books by the same author:
Slickrock, 1999
Roped, 1998
Roughstock, 1997
Hoofprints, 1996
Cutter, 1994

Other books you might like:
Susan Wittig Albert, *The China Bayles Series*, 1992-
Christine Andreae, *The Lee Squires Series*, 1992-
Nevada Barr, *The Anna Pigeon Series*, 1993-
Earlene Fowler, *The Benni Harper Series*, 1994-
Lia Matera, *Star Witness*, 1997

31

CLARE CURZON (Pseudonym of Eileen-Marie Duell Buchanan)

Cold Hands
(New York: St. Martin's Press, 2001)

Story type: Police Procedural
Series: Mike Yeadings. Book 14
Subject(s): Country Life; Crime and Criminals; Smuggling
Major character(s): Mike Yeadings, Police Officer (superintendent); Rosemary Zyczynski, Police Officer (detective sergeant)
Time period(s): 2000s
Locale(s): Thames Valley, England

Summary: When a customs agent is found murdered, Yeadings discovers the man had been investigating a possible counterfeiting operation, which he traces back to Fraylings Court, a once-stately home whose impoverished owners have turned into a center for theme weekends and classes in various subjects, from the arts to dog-training to poker. He assigns Rosemary, a fair poker player, to go undercover at the estate to see if she can find out who of the many guests and instructors there is involved in the counterfeiting. The investigation itself is straightforward and serious, but many of the scenes at Fraylings Court are light-hearted and even comedic. The author has also written a non-series historical set in the early part of the century.

Where it's reviewed:
Booklist, January 1, 2001, page 923
New York Times Book Review, April 1, 2001, page 17
Publishers Weekly, February 19, 2001, page 72

Other books by the same author:
All Unwary, 1998
Close Quarters, 1997
Past Mischief, 1996
Nice People, 1995
Death Prone, 1994

Other books you might like:
Colin Dexter, *The Inspector Morse Series*, 1975-
Reginald Hill, *The Dalziel/Pascoe Series*, 1970-
Kay Mitchell, *The John Morrisey Series*, 1990-
Peter Robinson, *The Inspector Alan Banks Series*, 1987-
Dorothy Simpson, *The Luke Thanet Series*, 1981-

32

MARY DAHEIM

Suture Self
(New York: Morrow, 2001)

Story type: Amateur Detective; Domestic
Series: Judith McMonigle Flynn. Book 17
Subject(s): Hotels, Motels; Hospitals; Medicine
Major character(s): Judith McMonigle Flynn, Innkeeper, Detective—Amateur; Renie Jones, Cousin (of Judith)
Time period(s): 2000s
Locale(s): Seattle, Washington

Summary: Judith takes an unwelcome break from managing her Hillside Manor bed-and-breakfast to have hip replacement surgery at Good Cheer Hospital, where she shares a room with her volatile cousin, Renie, who's just had surgery to repair her shoulder. Both women are uneasy about being there, as two local celebrities recently died following routine procedures, and while they are convalescing a third patient, a football player, bites the dust. Forced to turn detective from her hospital bed, Judith interviews a number of unwitting suspects in her room, with Renie interjecting her usual caustic commentary. The prolific author also writes a series about Emma Lord, publisher and editor of a small-town Washington newspaper.

Where it's reviewed:
Booklist, January 1, 2001, page 924

Other books by the same author:
A Streetcar Named Expire, 2000
Creeps Suzette, 1999
Legs Benedict, 1999
Snow Place to Die, 1998
Wed and Buried, 1998

Other books you might like:
Claudia Bishop, *The Sarah Quilliam Series*, 1994-
Rita Mae Brown, *Claws and Effect*, 2001
Jo Dereske, *The Miss Zukas Series*, 1994-
Jean Hager, *The Tess Darcy Series*, 1994-
Tamar Myers, *The Magdalena Yoder Series*, 1994-

33

JEANNE M. DAMS

Green Grow the Victims
(New York: Walker, 2001)

Story type: Historical; Amateur Detective
Series: Hilda Johansson. Book 3
Subject(s): Swedish Americans; Miners and Mining; Strikes and Lockouts
Major character(s): Hilda Johansson, Servant, Detective—Amateur
Time period(s): 1900s (1902)
Locale(s): South Bend, Indiana

Summary: Hard-working Hilda is taking a well-deserved break from her job as housekeeper to the wealthy Studebaker family with her beau, Irish fireman Patrick Malloy, at the state fair when a prominent politician is found murdered. The

immediate suspect is Patrick's uncle, Dan Malloy, the victim's chief political opponent, who has mysteriously disappeared. When Patrick's aunt asks Hilda to investigate, she gets leave from the Studebakers, but her efforts are thwarted by the family's reluctance to cooperate and the insistence of the parish priest that he witnessed Dan committing the crime. In the background are the coal strikes of 1902 and the seemingly insurmountable differences between Swedish Protestant Hilda and Irish Catholic Patrick in terms of any possible marriage. The author also writes a contemporary series about Dorothy Martin, an American widow transplanted to an English cathedral town.

Where it's reviewed:
Booklist, May 1, 2001, page 1628
Publishers Weekly, April 16, 2001, page 47

Other books by the same author:
Red, White and Blue Murder, 2000
Death in Lacquer Red, 1999

Other books you might like:
Lauren Belfer, *City of Light*, 1999
Karen Rose Cercone, *Coal Bones*, 1999
Dianne Day, *The Fremont Jones Series*, 1995-
Maureen Jennings, *The William Murdoch Series*, 1997-
Victoria Thompson, *The Sarah Brandt Series*, 1999-

34

DIANE MOTT DAVIDSON

Sticks & Scones

(New York: Bantam, 2001)

Story type: Amateur Detective
Series: Goldy Bear Schulz. Book 10
Subject(s): Castles; Catering Business; Cooks and Cookery
Major character(s): Goldy Bear Schulz, Caterer, Detective—Amateur
Time period(s): 2000s
Locale(s): Aspen Meadow, Colorado

Summary: Goldy has landed a challenging job catering an Elizabethan banquet at Hyde Castle, a real castle imported from England and reassembled stone by stone in Aspen Meadow, where it currently serves as a conference center. On the day of the event, she's awakened before dawn by a shot fired through the window of her home. With her policeman husband Tom out of town and her home now a crime scene, she's forced to report to work six hours early. Then she discovers a body in a nearby creek, and still more shots are fired. Her day becomes frantic as she tries to untangle the crimes and prepare the elaborate food on the menu. As usual, a number of recipes are included and much information on culinary matters.

Where it's reviewed:
Publishers Weekly, March 12, 2001, page 66

Other books by the same author:
Tough Cookie, 2000
Prime Cut, 1998
The Grilling Season, 1997
The Main Corpse, 1996
Killer Pancake, 1995

Other books you might like:
Susan Wittig Albert, *The China Bayles Series*, 1992-
Jerrilyn Farmer, *The Madeline Bean Series*, 1998-
Janet Laurence, *A Deepe Coffyn*, 1989
Katherine Hall Page, *The Faith Sibley Fairchild Series*, 1990-
Virginia Rich, *The Mrs. Eugenia Potter Series*, 1982-1985 continued by Nancy Pickard, 1996-

---

35

LINDSEY DAVIS

Ode to a Banker

(New York: Mysterious, 2001)

Story type: Historical; Private Detective
Series: Marcus Didius Falco. Book 12
Subject(s): Ancient History; Roman Empire; Authors and Writers
Major character(s): Marcus Didius Falco, Detective—Private, Spy
Time period(s): 1st century (74)
Locale(s): Rome, Roman Empire

Summary: Besides performing discreet investigations for public and private clients, Falco likes to scribble a little poetry on the side, and he's delighted when a wealthy Greek banker and patron of the arts, who also runs a publishing house offers to publish his work. His moment of glory never comes, however, as the banker gets himself murdered in a most grisly way. Falco is hired by the court to investigate the circumstances of the man's death, and he quickly discovers just how many enemies the man had from both his occupations. Meanwhile, there are contractors to deal with over the bathhouse he and his wife, Helena, are installing, his parents are having various troubles, and his dog is expecting puppies.

Where it's reviewed:
Booklist, May 1, 2001, page 1628
Mystery News, June/July 2001, page 21

Other books by the same author:
One Virgin Too Many, 2000
Three Hands in the Fountain, 1999
Two for the Lions, 1999
A Dying Light in Corduba, 1998
Time to Depart, 1995

Other books you might like:
Ron Burns, *Roman Nights*, 1991
Albert Noyes, *The Saints' Day Deaths*, 2000
John Maddox Roberts, *The SPQR Series*, 1990-
Steven Saylor, *The Roma Sub Rosa Series*, 1991-
Marilyn Todd, *The Claudia Seferius Series*, 1995-

36

VAL DAVIS (Pseudonym of Angela Irvine and Robert Irvine)

The Return of the Spanish Lady

(New York: St. Martin's Press, 2001)

Story type: Amateur Detective; Traditional
Series: Nicolette Scott. Book 4
Subject(s): Airplanes; Archaeology; Wilderness

Major character(s): Nicolette "Nick" Scott, Archaeologist, Detective—Amateur
Time period(s): 2000s
Locale(s): Alaska; Washington, District of Columbia

Summary: Nick, an historical archaeologist specializing in downed military aircraft, has a dream job working at the Smithsonian's National Air and Space Museum, made even dreamier when she's recruited to join a team of experts who intend to recover a World War II Japanese bomber that went down in the Alaskan wilderness. The expedition is funded by a supposedly philanthropic pharmaceutical company, and it's only after the aircraft has been located that their real agenda comes to light: to recover the bodies of a party of gold miners who died from the deadly Spanish influenza virus in the same area in 1918. Since the virus can survive freezing temperatures, the company intends to extract it, reintroduce it to the modern world after first developing a vaccine, and then reap enormous profits marketing it. First they have to outwit the deadly grizzlies that surround their encampment and of course kill virtually everybody in the search party. There is an absorbing back story about the epidemic itself, the so-called "Spanish Lady," which swept the world and left millions dead and the miners who contracted it, but the present-day plot is downright preposterous and not worthy of the authors' abilities.

Where it's reviewed:
Booklist, January 1, 2001, page 924
Publishers Weekly, January 15, 2001, page 55

Other books by the same author:
Wake of the Hornet, 1999
Flight of the Serpent, 1998
Track of the Scorpion, 1996

Other books you might like:
Christine Andreae, *Grizzly*, 1994
Nevada Barr, *Blood Lure*, 2001
Elizabeth Quinn, *Murder Most Grizzly*, 1993
Marcia Simpson, *Crow in Stolen Colors*, 2000
Dana Stabenow, *Hunter's Moon*, 1999

37

JEFFERY DEAVER

The Blue Nowhere

(New York: Simon & Schuster, 2001)

Story type: Psychological Suspense; Police Procedural
Subject(s): Computers; Serial Killer; Psychological
Major character(s): Wyatt Gillette, Computer Expert (hacker); Frank Bishop, Police Officer; Jon Holloway, Criminal (hacker)
Time period(s): 2000s
Locale(s): Santa Clara County, California (Silicon Valley)

Summary: When serial killer and computer genius Jon Holloway, whose cybername is Phate, starts accessing his victims in a complicated game involving hacking his way into their personal computers and private lives, the police turn to Wyatt Gillette, a man equally gifted at and addicted to computers. Although he is serving prison time for cracking the Defense Department's computer system, Gillette is clearly no psycho-

path. He's the only person alive who is Phate's match, and they play a cat and mouse game that mounts in intensity as the plot proceeds at a breakneck pace. Frank Bishop has been trained in old-fashioned police work, which still plays a role in this case, but increasingly he respects Gillette's abilities and the two work well together. The term "blue nowhere" is a synonym for cyberspace, and Deaver shows its hypnotic influence over the wizards, who can manipulate it in ways not dreamed of by average users. There's a great deal of technical jargon, necessary for readers to understand the twisty, complex plot, but Deaver also shows his characters operating in the Real World (as opposed to the Machine World that some of them are obsessed with). The writing is sometimes clumsy, but the plot is so riveting most readers won't care. The author also writes the Lincoln Rhyme series of police procedurals, as well as numerous other stand-alone thrillers.

Where it's reviewed:
Booklist, March 1, 2001, page 1187
People Weekly, June 18, 2001, page 41
Publishers Weekly, April 30, 2001, page 56

Other books by the same author:
Speaking in Tongues, 2001 (Lincoln Rhyme Series)
The Empty Chair, 2000 (Lincoln Rhyme Series)
The Devil's Teardrop, 1999 (Lincoln Rhyme Series)
The Coffin Dancer, 1998 (Lincoln Rhymes Series)
The Bone Collector, 1997

Other books you might like:
Harlan Coben, *Tell No One*, 2001
Patricia Cornwell, *Post Mortem*, 1990
T. Jefferson Parker, *Red Light*, 2000
Ridley Pearson, *The Lou Boldt Series*, 1991-
John Sandford, *The Lucas Davenport Series*, 1989-

38

JEFFERY DEAVER

Hell's Kitchen

(New York: Pocket, 2001)

Story type: Amateur Detective
Series: Location Scout. Book 3
Subject(s): Arson; City Life; Movies
Major character(s): John Pellam, Filmmaker, Detective—Amateur
Time period(s): 2000s
Locale(s): New York, New York (Hell's Kitchen)

Summary: Pellam, a former Hollywood location scout and stuntman, is now an independent filmmaker living in New York and shooting a low-budget documentary, *West of Eighth*, an oral history of the early days of Hell's Kitchen as told by its oldest residents. When a century-old tenement building is burned to the ground, Ettie Washington, the old woman he's been interviewing, manages to escape her home with severe burns. The police at first suspect her of the crime, but Pellam is convinced the fire was the work of an arsonist and sets out to find him and clear Ettie. This is the final book of a trilogy begun early in the career of this author, who is now best-known for his Lincoln Rhyme police procedurals

featuring a paralyzed criminalist. They were originally published under the name William Jefferies.

Where it's reviewed:
Drood Review, January/February 2001, page 14
Publishers Weekly, January 22, 2001, page 308

Other books by the same author:
Bloody River Blues, 1993 (reprinted 2000)
Shallow Graves, 1992 (reprinted 2000)

Other books you might like:
Thomas Adcock, *The Neil Hockaday Series*, 1989-
Lawrence Block, *Out on the Cutting Edge*, 1989
Wendy Hornsby, *The Maggie MacGowen Series*, 1992-
Mike Lupica, *The Peter Finley Series*, 1986-
Christopher Newman, *The Joe Dante Series*, 1986-

39

NORA DELOACH

Mama Cracks a Mask of Innocence

(New York: Bantam, 2001)

Story type: Amateur Detective
Series: Mama. Book 8
Subject(s): African Americans; Small Town Life; American South
Major character(s): Grace ''Candi'' Covington, Social Worker, Detective—Amateur; Simone Covington, Paralegal
Time period(s): 2000s
Locale(s): Otis, South Carolina

Summary: Simone's back in Otis for another visit with Mama (Grace Covington), helping her distribute clothing to the poor. Instead of busying herself with volunteer work and cooking Simone's favorite dishes, Mama has turned detective again after a young woman, Brenda Long, is found dead in a shallow grave. Mama immediately suspects a parolee whom Brenda had caught stealing. Or maybe it was the teacher who sold drugs on the side, whom Brenda had threatened to report. At any rate, it looks as if it will be a while before Mama gets around to baking any sweet potato pie, and Simone fears that if Mama isn't more careful, she might find herself the killer's next victim.

Where it's reviewed:
Mystery News, June/July 2001, page 32

Other books by the same author:
Mama Pursues Murderous Shadows, 2000
Mama Rocks the Empty Cradle, 1998
Mama Saves a Victim, 1997
Mama Stands Accused, 1997
Mama Stalks the Past, 1997

Other books you might like:
Eleanor Taylor Bland, *The Marti McAlister Series*, 1992-
Teris McMahon Grimes, *The Theresa Galloway Series*, 1996-
Barbara Neely, *The Blanche White Series*, 1992-
Chassie West, *Sunrise*, 1994
James Yaffe, *The Mom Series*, 1988-

40

P.C. DOHERTY

The Anubis Slayings

(New York: St. Martin's Minotaur, 2001)

Story type: Historical
Series: Judge Amerotke. Book 3
Subject(s): Ancient History; Egyptian Religion; Kings, Queens, Rulers, etc.
Major character(s): Amerotke, Judge
Time period(s): 15th century B.C. (1478 B.C.)
Locale(s): Thebes, Egypt

Summary: Even as the defeated Mitanni pay reluctant homage to the triumphant Queen Hatasu, a series of mysterious deaths and palace intrigues threaten her reign. First, a priest is slain in a locked chamber in the Temple of Anubis and the sacred amethyst he was guarding disappears. Then a dancing girl is found dead with no marks of violence upon her, and fish in the palace ponds die mysteriously. Never certain if the incidents are the work of the gods or their human subjects, Amerotke puts himself in great peril to determine what has happened and to protect his pharaoh queen. The author writes many other series set in varying periods of history under a variety of pseudonyms.

Where it's reviewed:
Booklist, May 15, 2001, page 1736
Publishers Weekly, May 14, 2001, page 56

Other books by the same author:
The Horus Killings, 2000
The Mask of Ra, 1999

Other books you might like:
Agatha Christie, *Death Comes as the End*, 1944
Lauren Haney, *The Lieutenant Bak Series*, 1997-
Lee Levin, *King Tut's Private Eye*, 1996
Lynda S. Robinson, *The Lord Meren Series*, 1994-
Carol Thurston, *The Eye of Horus*, 2000

41

P.C. DOHERTY

The Demon Archer

(New York: St. Martin's Minotaur, 2001)

Story type: Historical
Series: Hugh Corbett. Book 11
Subject(s): Middle Ages; Witches and Witchcraft; Kings, Queens, Rulers, etc.
Major character(s): Sir Hugh Corbett, Government Official, Investigator
Time period(s): 14th century (1303)
Locale(s): Ashdown, England

Summary: When a lecherous lord is murdered, Edward I sends Corbett, Clerk of the Secret Seal, to investigate. Lord Henry Fitzalan, who was to act on Edward's behalf in arranging the marriage of his son, Prince William, to Isabella, daughter of King Phillip of France, was reported to have consorted with witches and been a blackmailer, so there is no lack of suspects to choose from. In the company of his manservant, Ranulf,

Corbett travels to Ashdown, where more murders take place. The author writes several other historical mystery series under a variety of pseudonyms.

Where it's reviewed:
Publishers Weekly, January 22, 2001, page 305

Other books by the same author:
The Devil's Hunt, 1998
Satan's Fire, 1995
The Song of a Dark Angel, 1994
The Assassin in the Greenwood, 1993
Murder Wears a Cowl, 1992

Other books you might like:
Susanna Gregory, *The Matthew Bartholomew Series*, 1996-
Paul Harding, *The Brother Athelstan Series*, 1991-
Michael Jecks, *The Sir Baldwin Furnshill Series*, 1995-
Candace M. Robb, *The Owen Archer Series*, 1993-
Caroline Roe, *The Isaac of Girona Series*, 1998-

42
P.C. DOHERTY

The House of Death
(New York: Carroll & Graf, 2001)

Story type: Historical
Series: Alexander the Great. Book 3
Subject(s): Ancient History; War; Espionage
Major character(s): Alexander the Great, Historical Figure, Ruler; Telamon, Doctor
Time period(s): 4th century B.C. (334 B.C.)
Locale(s): Asia Minor; Persia

Summary: On the brink of crossing the Hellespont and invading Persia, Alexander senses all the signs and portents are against him, that his camp is crawling with Persian spies, and that his own generals are plotting against him. To safeguard her son, his formidable mother, Olympias, sends to him his childhood friend, Telamon, whom she charges with his protection. A series of murders (some of them variants of locked-room murders in sealed and guarded tents) and mysterious messages follow, but in the end Alexander triumphs over the Persian King Darius III and Telamon succeeds in overthrowing his friend's secret enemies. The first two books in this series were published under the pseudonym Anna Apostolou. The author has written many other historical mysteries, most of them set in the ancient and medieval worlds.

Where it's reviewed:
Booklist, May 1, 2001, page 1630
Publishers Weekly, May 7, 2001, page 227

Other books you might like:
Ron Burns, *Roman Shadows*, 1992
Lindsey Davis, *The Marcus Didius Falco Series*, 1989-
Margaret Doody, *Aristotle, Detective*, 1980
Mary Reed, *The John the Eunuch Series*, 1999-
   Eric Mayer, co-author
Steven Saylor, *The Roma Sub Rosa Series*, 1991-

43
GAYLORD DOLD

Samedi's Knapsack
(New York: St. Martin's Press, 2001)

Story type: Private Detective
Series: Mitch Roberts. Book 10
Subject(s): Boats and Boating; Hurricanes; Voodoo
Major character(s): Mitch Roberts, Detective—Private
Time period(s): 2000s
Locale(s): Haiti; Miami, Florida

Summary: On his way home to his Colorado ranch after a long London-based love affair has gone sour, Mitch finds himself in Miami, stripped of his credit cards, cash, passport, and rental car, and forced to call Bobby Hilliard, an old friend from his ball-playing days, for help. That's how he gets roped into traveling to Haiti to find Hilliard's missing agent, sent there to buy some paintings and now gone missing. Roberts is appalled at the poverty and squalor of the country and the corruption of its officials, who rule with a combination of cruelty and voodoo and who view his mission with a suspicious eye. With a trusted Haitian guide, Mitch sets out to buy more paintings and locate the missing man, but he finds danger everywhere he turns, including an approaching hurricane. An underrated series whose protagonist moves from place to place, by a writer who makes Haiti come alive for the reader.

Where it's reviewed:
Booklist, April 1, 2001, page 1449
Library Journal, May 1, 2001, page 129
Publishers Weekly, April 16, 2001, page 48

Other books by the same author:
The World Beat, 1993
Rude Boys, 1992
A Penny for the Old Guy, 1991
Disheveled City, 1990
Muscle and Blood, 1989

Other books you might like:
Daniel Easterman, *The Night of the Seventh Darkness*, 1991
James W. Hall, *The Thorn Series*, 1987-
Charles Knief, *The John Caine Series*, 1996-
John Lantigua, *The Willie Cuesta Series*, 2000-
Randy Wayne White, *The Doc Ford Series*, 1990-

44
CAROLE NELSON DOUGLAS

Cat in a Leopard Spot
(New York: Forge, 2001)

Story type: Amateur Detective
Series: Midnight Louie. Book 13
Subject(s): Animals/Cats; Animals/Leopards; Hunting
Major character(s): Midnight Louie, Animal (cat), Detective—Amateur; Temple Barr, Public Relations
Time period(s): 2000s
Locale(s): Las Vegas, Nevada

Summary: When the owner of a nearby ranch is found dead with a leopard missing from a magic act next to him, Louie, Temple, and their cohorts all get together to find out what happened. The victim is not only a hunter himself, but his ranch is the scene of illegal hunts of exotic big game. The leopard, which was kidnapped from his magician owner, is now scheduled to be put down unless Temple and Louie can prove he's innocent of murder. The book is filled with eccentric characters—a woman surgically altered to resemble a cat, animal rights protesters who have staked out the ranch, and a former priest turned radio talk show host—as well as references to earlier cases, mostly by Midnight Louie, who interjects his version of the events intermittently throughout the book.

Where it's reviewed:
Publishers Weekly, March 26, 2001, page 66

Other books by the same author:
Cat in a Kiwi Con, 2000
Cat in a Jeweled Jumpsuit, 1999
Cat in an Indigo Mood, 1999
Cat on a Hyacinth Hunt, 1998
Cat in a Golden Garland, 1997

Other books you might like:
Garrison Allen, *The Big Mike Series*, 1994-
Lilian Jackson Braun, *The Cat Who Series*, 1966-
Rita Mae Brown, *The Mrs. Murphy Series*, 1990-
Pete Hautman, *Short Money*, 1995
Shirley Rousseau Murphy, *The Joe Grey Series*, 1996-

SYBIL DOWNING

The Binding Oath

(Boulder: University Press of Colorado, 2001)

Story type: Historical
Subject(s): German Americans; Prejudice; Journalism
Major character(s): Liz O'Brien, Journalist (newspaper reporter); Phil Van Cise, Lawyer (district attorney)
Time period(s): 1920s (1922)
Locale(s): Denver, Colorado

Summary: Liz, an independent young woman, is one of only two female reporters on the staff of the Denver *Post*. She thinks maybe her big break has come when she is the only journalist to attend a press conference held by the Ku Klux Klan's Grand Dragon, who announces his intent to unseat the city's district attorney, Phil Van Cise. Her editor doesn't think the story is newsworthy, so she digs deeper and uncovers evidence that the KKK is not only involved in a local murder, but is plotting to take over the entire state. Among their targets are all sorts of ethnic minorities, including German-Americans. Van Cise joins with her in an attempt to solve the murder of Emma Volz, a young woman of German descent, and to keep the Klan from forcing a recall election to vote him out of office.

Where it's reviewed:
Publishers Weekly, March 5, 2001, page 62

Other books by the same author:
Ladies of the Goldfield Stock Exchange, 1997

Other books you might like:
K.K. Beck, *Young Mrs. Cavendish and the Kaiser's Men*, 1987
Carola Dunn, *The Daisy Dalrymple Series*, 1994-
Laurie R. King, *A Monstrous Regiment of Women*, 1995
Annette Meyers, *The Olivia Brown Series*, 1999-
Troy Soos, *The Mickey Rawlings Series*, 1994-

46

CAROLA DUNN

To Davy Jones Below

(New York: St. Martin's Press, 2001)

Story type: Historical; Amateur Detective
Series: Daisy Dalrymple. Book 8
Subject(s): Ships; Voyages and Travels; Weddings
Major character(s): Daisy Dalrymple Fletcher, Journalist, Detective—Amateur; Alec Fletcher, Detective—Police (detective chief inspector), Spouse (of Daisy)
Time period(s): 1920s (1926)
Locale(s): *Talavera*, At Sea (crossing the Atlantic Ocean)

Summary: Their long courtship finally over, newlyweds Daisy and Alec are on the second leg of their honeymoon, an ocean voyage to America on board the *Talavera*, a freighter also carrying an all-cabin-class complement of passengers. Their pleasure is dampened by Alec's seasickness and then by two instances of people falling overboard to their deaths—accidents which some witnesses and passengers claim were murders. Daisy, a young aristocrat who horrified her family by first taking up a career in journalism and then falling in love with a policeman, has a naturally inquisitive mind and is, as usual, eager to throw herself into the ensuing investigation after the captain asks Alec to look into the incidents.

Where it's reviewed:
Booklist, March 1, 2001, page 1230
Publishers Weekly, March 5, 2001, page 26

Other books by the same author:
Rattle His Bones, 2000
Dead in the Water, 1998
Damsel in Distress, 1997
Murder on the Flying Scotsman, 1997
Requiem for a Mezzo, 1996

Other books you might like:
K.K. Beck, *Death in a Deck Chair*, 1984
Laurie R. King, *A Letter of Mary*, 1997
Mary Kruger, *No Honeymoon for Death*, 1995
Peter Lovesey, *The False Inspector Dew*, 1982
Walter Satterthwait, *Escapade*, 1995

SELMA EICHLER

Murder Can Upset Your Mother

(New York: Signet, 2000)

Story type: Traditional; Private Detective
Series: Desiree Shapiro. Book 8
Subject(s): Humor; City Life; Food

Major character(s): Desiree Shapiro, Detective—Private
Time period(s): 2000s
Locale(s): New York, New York

Summary: Full-figured, henna-haired Desiree doesn't fit most of her clients' image of a private eye, and the author's chatty style is anything but noir. When she's not fantasizing about food or clothes, Desiree is a crack investigator, this time out to learn who killed Miriam Weisen, a prominent and wealthy philanthropist who had left a message on Desiree's answering machine that there had been two attempts on her life. When she gets around to replying, Desiree gets Miriam's mother instead, who tells her that a third attempt to kill her daughter had been successful and hires her to investigate. Full of guilt for not having replied to Miriam's message sooner, Desiree soon learns that the woman was anything but what she seemed to be and that many people had reason to want her dead. A recipe for eggplant parmigiana is included.

Where it's reviewed:
Publishers Weekly, February 12, 2001, page 189

Other books by the same author:
Murder Can Spoil Your Appetite, 2000
Murder Can Singe Your Old Flame, 1999
Murder Can Spook Your Cat, 1998
Murder Can Wreck Your Reunion, 1997
Murder Can Stunt Your Growth, 1996

Other books you might like:
Carole Lea Benjamin, *The Rachel Alexander and Dash Series*, 1996-
G.A. McKevett, *The Savannah Reed Series*, 1995-
Katy Munger, *The Casey Jones Series*, 1997-
Lynne Murray, *The Josephine Fuller Series*, 1997-
Sharon Zukowski, *The Blaine Stewart Series*, 1991-

KATE ELLIS

An Unhallowed Grave

(New York: St. Martin's Press, 2001)

Story type: Police Procedural
Series: Wesley Peterson. Book 3
Subject(s): Archaeology; History; Marriage
Major character(s): Wesley Peterson, Police Officer (detective sergeant), Archaeologist (amateur)
Time period(s): 2000s
Locale(s): Tradmouth, England

Summary: As usual in this series, there are two mysteries going on here for Trinidad-born black police officer Wesley Peterson. One is the contemporary murder of a local doctor's receptionist, found hanged from a yew tree in the churchyard. As they investigate, the police find that curiously little is known about the woman's past. At a nearby site, archaeologists have unearthed a much older corpse, the skeletal remains of a young woman who supposedly was hanged from the same tree five centuries earlier, a legend borne out by the broken bones in her neck. Research into medieval legal documents offers evidence of a long-ago miscarriage of justice. At the same time, Wesley and his wife, Pamela, are busy caring for their newborn son.

Where it's reviewed:
Publishers Weekly, April 23, 2001, page 52

Other books by the same author:
The Armada Boy, 2000
The Merchant's House, 1999

Other books you might like:
Robert Barnard, *The Charlie Peace/Mike Odhams Series*, 1989-
Kate Charles, *The Lucy Kingsley/David Middleton Brown Series*, 1991-
Deborah Crombie, *A Finer End*, 2001
Aaron Elkins, *The Gideon Oliver Series*, 1982-
Peter Robinson, *The Alan Banks Series*, 1987-

K.J. ERICKSON

Third Person Singular

(New York: St. Martin's Press, 2001)

Story type: Police Procedural
Subject(s): Serial Killer; City Life; Fathers and Sons
Major character(s): Marshall ''Mars'' Bahr, Detective—Police (special detective); Nettie Frisch, Police Officer, Computer Expert
Time period(s): 2000s
Locale(s): Minneapolis, Minnesota

Summary: When a teenager from an affluent suburban family is found stabbed to death in a deserted section of the city's riverfront, with a blood alcohol level that's off the charts although she was never known to drink, Mars and Nettie are assigned the case. The investigation goes nowhere, although they learn a great deal about her family life; her father was abusive and her mother an alcoholic. The point of view then shifts from Mars to the girl's older brother and two other people, and eventually Mars learns that another teenager was murdered in Boston in exactly the same fashion, leading him to believe he is looking for a serial killer. Mars is a very human and sympathetic character, a divorced father who has a warm relationship with his young son, and the author writes with a sure sense of place. Altogether, it's an unusually accomplished debut novel.

Where it's reviewed:
Booklist, December 1, 2000, page 696
Library Journal, January 1, 2001, page 161
Mystery News, February/March 2001, page 24
Publishers Weekly, December 11, 2000, page 67

Other books you might like:
Barbara D'Amato, *The Suze Figueroa/Norm Bennis Series*, 1996-
Tami Hoag, *Dust to Dust*, 2001
David Housewright, *The Holland Taylor Series*, 1995-
John Sandford, *The Lucas Davenport Series*, 1989-
Steve Thayer, *The Weatherman*, 1995

50

JANET EVANOVICH

Seven Up

(New York: St. Martin's Press, 2001)

Story type: Humor; Private Detective
Series: Stephanie Plum. Book 7
Subject(s): City Life; Romance; Crime and Criminals
Major character(s): Stephanie Plum, Bounty Hunter; Joe Morelli, Police Officer; Ricardo Carlos ''Ranger'' Manoso, Bounty Hunter
Time period(s): 2000s
Locale(s): Trenton, New Jersey

Summary: All the series regulars are back in this book, including the semi-deranged Grandma Mazur, Stephanie's annoying sister, Valerie (her perfect marriage now ended), and of course the two men in Stephanie's life, Joe Morelli (with whom she has a long history) and her seductive fellow bounty hunter, Ranger, (with whom she wishes she had at least a short one). At long last Morelli has proposed, which of course leads the contrary Stephanie to back off from making a commitment, especially with Ranger around. There's also her work to attend to, when her bail-bondsman cousin, Vinnie, assigns her to bring in a senior citizen caught smuggling cigarettes into Jersey. It turns out he's also ripped out the heart of his worst enemy, and catching up with him proves to be much more difficult (and dangerous) than Stephanie was expecting. But it's the comedy, rooted in Stephanie's eccentric family, the ethnic working-class Trenton neighborhood where she grew up, and the interminably prolonged failure to resolve her relationships with Joe and Ranger, that dominate the story.

Where it's reviewed:
Booklist, May 1, 2001, page 1598
People Weekly, July 2, 2001, page 38
Publishers Weekly, May 7, 2001, page 227

Other books by the same author:
Hot Six, 2000
High Five, 1999
Four to Score, 1998
Three to Get Deadly, 1997
Two for the Dough, 1996

Other books you might like:
Nancy Bartholomew, *The Sierra Lavatoni Series*, 1998-
Nancy J. Cohen, *The Marla Shore Series*, 1999-
Sparkle Hayter, *The Robin Hudson Series*, 1994-
Sarah Strohmeyer, *Bubbles Unbound*, 2001
Kathleen Taylor, *The Tory Bauer Series*, 1995-

51

NANCY FAIRBANKS (Pseudonym of Nancy Herndon)

Crime Brulee

(New York: Berkley, 2001)

Story type: Amateur Detective
Subject(s): Cooks and Cookery; Travel; Food

Major character(s): Carolyn Blue, Journalist (food writer); Jason Blue, Professor
Time period(s): 2000s
Locale(s): New Orleans, Louisiana

Summary: A humorous article Carolyn writes for her hometown newspaper about dining out abroad lands her an assignment writing a book on the subject, eventually modified to be about her experiences eating out in New Orleans, the location of her professor husband's next academic conference. She's reveling in Creole and Cajun cuisine, when her friend Julienne disappears at a dinner party after a fight with her husband and Carolyn makes up her mind to find her. Interspersed throughout the narrative are excerpts from Carolyn's book, *Eating Out in the Big Easy*, containing recipes (12 in all), as well as comments on the cuisine, culture, and history of this unique city. First book in a projected series. The author has also written several books about Texas police officer Elena Jarvis under her own name.

Other books you might like:
Diane Mott Davidson, *The Goldy Bear Schulz Series*, 1990-
Peter King, *The Gourmet Detective Series*, 1994-
Joanne Pence, *The Angelina Amalfi Series*, 1993-
Phyllis Richman, *The Chas Wheatley Series*, 1997-
Lou Jane Temple, *The Heaven Lee Series*, 1996-

52

JERRILYN FARMER

Dim Sum Dead

(New York: Avon, 2001)

Story type: Amateur Detective; Domestic
Series: Madeline Bean. Book 4
Subject(s): Catering Business; Movie Industry; Food
Major character(s): Madeline Bean, Caterer, Detective— Amateur
Time period(s): 2000s
Locale(s): Los Angeles, California

Summary: It seems as if the ancient game of mah-jongg is suddenly in with the hip Hollywood crowd, and Maddie and her staff are catering a Chinese New Year's party featuring mah-jongg and dim sum, for director Buster Dublin and his girlfriend, Quita McBride. Coincidentally, Maddie's partner, Wesley Westcott, is renovating the mansion that belonged to Quita's first husband, the late film legend Dickey McBride, and has found an antique mah-jongg set along with a diary and a dragon-handled dagger. No sooner has he shown his find to Maddie than it's stolen, and when Quita learns of this, she's so upset Maddie can't help but wonder what secrets the diary contained. When Quita is murdered, Maddie starts snooping around and finds the solution to the crime goes back to the Golden Age of Hollywood.

Other books by the same author:
Killer Wedding, 2000
Immaculate Reception, 1999
Sympathy for the Devil, 1998

Other books you might like:
Della Borton, *The Gilda Liberty Series*, 1999-
Paula Carter, *The Hillary Scarborough Series*, 1999-

Diane Mott Davidson, *The Goldy Bear Schulz Series*, 1990-
Ellen Hart, *The Merchant of Venus*, 2001
Tamar Myers, *The Abigail Timberlake Series*, 1996-

53

JOANNE FLUKE

Strawberry Shortcake Murder

(New York: Kensington, 2001)

Story type: Amateur Detective; Domestic
Series: Hannah Swensen. Book 2
Subject(s): Food; Cooks and Cookery; Small Town Life
Major character(s): Hannah Swensen, Baker, Businesswoman
Time period(s): 2000s
Locale(s): Lake Eden, Minnesota

Summary: Hannah's thrilled when she's selected to be the chief judge of a national flour company's first annual dessert bake-off, figuring it can only help business at her already thriving bakery, The Cookie Jar. What starts out to be a fun event turns deadly, when one of her fellow judges, a high school coach with a reputation for abusing his wife, is found dead, face down in Hannah's strawberry shortcake. Since he'd angered some of the contestants with his sarcastic commentary, Hannah wonders if one of them is just getting even, or if his battered wife had finally snapped. At any rate, she starts investigating with some help from her sister, Andrea, who is married to a policeman. Readers with a sweet tooth will appreciate the recipes, all for desserts and cookies.

Where it's reviewed:
Booklist, February 15, 2001, page 1118
Library Journal, March 1, 2001, page 133
Publishers Weekly, January 29, 2001, page 68

Other books by the same author:
Chocolate Chip Cookie Murder, 2000

Other books you might like:
Susan Wittig Albert, *Chile Death*, 1998
Diane Mott Davidson, *The Goldy Bear Schulz Series*, 1990-
Jerrilyn Farmer, *The Madeline Bean Series*, 1998-
Janet Laurence, *The Darina Lisle Series*, 1989-
Tamar Myers, *The Magdalena Yoder Series*, 1994-

54

LESLIE FORBES

Fish, Blood and Bone

(New York: Farrar, Straus & Giroux, 2001)

Story type: Psychological Suspense
Subject(s): Voyages and Travels; History
Major character(s): Claire Fleetwood, Photographer (forensic)
Time period(s): 1980s (1988); 1880s (1888)
Locale(s): London, England (Whitechapel); Calcutta, India; Tibet

Summary: In this sweeping literary thriller, American-born Claire Fleetwood unexpectedly inherits a decaying London mansion complete with gardens in Whitechapel, the same neighborhood once prowled by Jack the Ripper. When her friend, Sally, is murdered on the property and her biochemist

cousin, Jack, turns up, she learns more about their common ancestor, Maida Ironstone, the mansion's original owner, and her lengthy travels to India and Tibet. Jack persuades Claire to accompany him on a journey retracing Maida's search for a legendary green poppy native to the high Himalayas that reportedly is able to cure or prevent cancer. Part of the novel is told in the form of journal entries written by Maida in 1888. It's a fascinating and intelligent book, marred only slightly by an overabundance of subplots, including one involving Jack the Ripper.

Where it's reviewed:
Booklist, May 1, 2001, page 1630
Entertainment Weekly, June 8, 2001, page 70
Library Journal, May 1, 2001, page 126
New York Times Book Review, June 3, 2001, page 51
Publishers Weekly, April 2, 2001, page 36

Other books by the same author:
Bombay Ice, 1998

Other books you might like:
Cheryl Benard, *Moghul Buffet*, 1998
Lionel Davidson, *The Rose of Tibet*, 1962
Daniel Easterman, *The Ninth Buddha*, 1989
Katherine Neville, *The Eight*, 1988
Eliot Pattison, *The Skull Mantra*, 1999

55

G.M. FORD

Fury

(New York: Morrow, 2001)

Story type: Amateur Detective
Subject(s): Serial Killer; Journalism
Major character(s): Frank Corso, Journalist; Meg Dougherty, Photographer
Time period(s): 2000s
Locale(s): Seattle, Washington

Summary: After a libel suit costs him his job on a New York newspaper, Corso gets hired by the low-rent *Seattle Sun*, where he handles an assignment investigating a series of grisly rapes and murders supposedly committed by death-row inmate Walter Leroy Himes, a.k.a. the Trashman. Corso has a nagging feeling Himes is not guilty, lowlife though he is, and he feels he's vindicated in this when one of the victims confesses she was coerced into identifying Himes, whose execution is imminent. When Corso starts asking questions of the Seattle cops, he gets stonewalled, and he hires Meg, a photographer with a legal background, to help him. The author has also produced a series about Seattle private eye Leo Waterman.

Where it's reviewed:
Booklist, March 15, 2001, page 1357
New York Times Book Review, May 20, 2001, page 41
Publishers Weekly, April 9, 2001, page 53

Other books by the same author:
The Deader the Better, 2000 (Leo Watermam series)
Last Ditch, 1999 (Leo Waterman series)
Slow Burn, 1998 (Leo Waterman series)
The Bum's Rush, 1997 (Leo Waterman series)

Cast in Stone, 1996 (Leo Waterman series)

Other books you might like:
Earl Emerson, *The Thomas Black Series*, 1985-
Dennis Lehane, *Mystic River*, 2001
Ridley Pearson, *The Lou Boldt Series*, 1991-
George P. Pelecanos, *Right as Rain*, 2001
Mary Willis Walker, *The Red Scream*, 1994

 56

EARLENE FOWLER

Arkansas Traveler

(New York: Berkley, 2001)

Story type: Amateur Detective
Series: Benni Harper. Book 8
Subject(s): Race Relations; Prejudice; American South
Major character(s): Benni Harper, Museum Curator
Time period(s): 2000s
Locale(s): Sugartree, Arkansas

Summary: Benni leaves San Celina, California, where she is director of the local folk art museum, for a nostalgic visit to her home town of Sugartree, Arkansas, where she still has many friends and relatives. Accompanied by her best friend, Elvia Aragon, she arrives to find the town in a turmoil. A black woman is running for mayor against a powerful white male incumbent, and two Baptist churches, one predominantly black and the other predominantly white, are planning to merge. A group of home-grown white supremacists, including the mayor's own troubled son, have succeeded in polarizing the town over these events, proving that racism and prejudice are still alive and well. When Benni is joined by her policeman husband, Gabe Ortiz, his ethnic background (Hispanic), which Elvia shares, further angers the group. As events turn ugly, it's just a matter of time before somebody gets killed.

Where it's reviewed:
Publishers Weekly, March 12, 2001, page 66

Other books by the same author:
Seven Sisters, 2000
Mariner's Compass, 1999
Dove in the Window, 1998
Goose in the Pond, 1997
Kansas Troubles, 1996

Other books you might like:
Susan Wittig Albert, *The China Bayles Series*, 1992-
Sinclair Browning, *The Trade Ellis Series*, 1999-
Joan Hess, *The Claire Malloy Series*, 1986-
Janet LaPierre, *The Meg Halloran Series*, 1987-
Marcia Muller, *The Elena Oliverez Series*, 1983-1986

57

ALAN FURST

Kingdom of Shadows

(New York: Random House, 2001)

Story type: Espionage
Subject(s): World War II; Nazis; Espionage

Major character(s): Nicholas Morath, Spy, Nobleman
Time period(s): 1930s (1938)
Locale(s): Paris, France; Budapest, Hungary

Summary: Although not in a series, this is one of a group of atmospheric thrillers the author has written set on the eve of World War II in Europe. Nicholas Morath is a Hungarian aristocrat, who owns a small advertising agency but secretly works as a spy for his uncle, Count Janos Polanyi, who despises the Nazis and will do anything to keep his country from becoming their ally. As the book opens, Hitler is marching into Prague while Morath arrives in Paris to be with his Argentinian mistress and to carry out a mission for Polanyi. His work takes him all over the continent and eventually behind enemy lines, as he fights a dangerous but doomed fight to keep Europe free.

Where it's reviewed:
Booklist, November 15, 2000, page 623
Entertainment Weekly, March 9, 2001, page 76
Library Journal, December 2000, page 187
People Weekly, March 26, 2001, page 48
Publishers Weekly, November 6, 2000, page 67

Other books by the same author:
Red Gold, 1999
The World at Night, 1996
The Polish Officer, 1995
Dark Star, 1991
Night Soldiers, 1988

Other books you might like:
Jack Gerson, *Death Watch '39*, 1991
J. Robert Janes, *The Jean-Louis St. Cyr/Hermann Kohler Series*, 1992-
Philip Kerr, *The Bernie Gunther Series*, 1989-1991
Pavel Kohout, *Widow Killer*, 1998
Paul Watkins, *The Forger*, 2000

58

P.L. GAUS

Clouds Without Rain

(Athens: Ohio University Press, 2001)

Story type: Amateur Detective
Series: Michael Branden. Book 3
Subject(s): Amish; Cultures and Customs; Rural Life
Major character(s): Michael Branden, Professor (history), Detective—Amateur
Time period(s): 2000s
Locale(s): Walnut Creek Township, Ohio (Holmes County)

Summary: The largest concentration of Amish in the country is in Holmes County, Ohio, and its teenagers are not as isolated from the outside world as is perhaps thought. Nor are the Amish communities unaffected by such technology as cell phones and computers or untouched by encroaching development. Michael Branden, an "English," or outsider, who has become a good friend of many of the Old Order Amish, helps the local police (in the person of his childhood friend, Sheriff Bruce Robertson) investigate an incident in which a buggy was overturned when the horse pulling it was shot, resulting in a deadly collision. Series regular Pastor Cal Troyer is also

on hand. An exceptional series, which provides a sympathetic look at this unique subculture.

Where it's reviewed:
Booklist, May 1, 2001, page 1632
Publishers Weekly, May 21, 2001, page 83

Other books by the same author:
Broken English, 2000
Blood of the Prodigal, 1999

Other books you might like:
John Dunning, *Deadline*, 1981
Roma Greth, *Plain Murder*, 1989
Tamar Myers, *The Crepes of Wrath*, 2001
Jodi Picoult, *Plain Truth*, 2000
Deborah Woodworth, *The Sister Rose Callahan Series*, 1997-

59

ROBERTA GELLIS

A Personal Devil
(New York: Forge, 2001)

Story type: Historical
Series: Magdalene la Batarde. Book 2
Subject(s): Middle Ages; Prostitution; Knights and Knighthood
Major character(s): Magdalene la Batarde, Madam; Sir Bellamy of Itchen, Knight
Time period(s): 12th century (1139)
Locale(s): Southwark, England

Summary: Magdalene, owner of the Old Priory Guesthouse, which caters to all the physical desires and comforts of the gentlemen who patronize it, treats the women who work for her fairly and with respect. She is especially close to Sabina, a blind woman, who leaves her employ to become the mistress of Master Mainard, whose physical disfigurements and meager fortune have estranged him from Bertrild, his wife. Bertrild reacts viciously to the arrangement, and when she is murdered, Mainard is the chief suspect. Sabina turns to Magdalene for help, who in turn enlists the aid of her friend Sir Bellamy, the influential knight she met in the first book of the series. The author has also written many mainstream and romantic historical novels.

Where it's reviewed:
Publishers Weekly, February 12, 2001, page 187

Other books by the same author:
A Mortal Bane, 1999

Other books you might like:
Simon Beaufort, *The Sir Geoffrey Mappestone Series*, 1998-
Bernard Knight, *The Sir John de Wolfe Series*, 1998-
Sharan Newman, *The Catherine LeVendeur Series*, 1993-
Ellis Peters, *The Brother Cadfael Series*, 1977-1994
Joan Wolf, *The Hugh Corbaille Series*, 1999-

60

ELIZABETH GEORGE

A Traitor to Memory
(New York: Bantam, 2001)

Story type: Police Procedural; Psychological Suspense
Series: Thomas Lynley/Barbara Havers. Book 11
Subject(s): Sexuality; Music and Musicians; Family Relations
Major character(s): Thomas Lynley, Police Officer (detective inspector); Barbara Havers, Police Officer (detective constable)
Time period(s): 2000s
Locale(s): London, England

Summary: When Eugenie Davies is killed by a car on a nearly deserted London street, the police are quick to realize it was no accident but a deliberate act on the part of the driver, who then disappeared without a trace. But how did it happen that the victim was carrying the name of the man who found her body? Lynley and Havers are assigned the case by their superior officer, Superintendent Malcolm Webberly, whose first murder case when he was a detective inspector two decades ago also concerned Eugenie Davies, who was then involved in a notorious trial. Also, Eugenie's death may be connected to a young violinist, who is suddenly unable to play even a note of music. One of the author's longest books (over 700 pages) and most complex.

Where it's reviewed:
Booklist, May 1, 2001, page 1632

Other books by the same author:
In Pursuit of the Proper Sinner, 1999
Deception on His Mind, 1997
In the Presence of the Enemy, 1996
Playing for the Ashes, 1994
Missing Joseph, 1993

Other books you might like:
Stephen Booth, *The Black Dog*, 2000
Deborah Crombie, *The Duncan Kincaid/Gemma James Series*, 1993-
Martha Grimes, *The Inspector Jury Series*, 1981-
P.D. James, *The Adam Dalgliesh Series*, 1962-
Ruth Rendell, *The Inspector Wexford Series*, 1964-

61

BARTHOLOMEW GILL (Pseudonym of Mark McGarrity)

The Death of an Irish Sinner
(New York: Morrow, 2001)

Story type: Police Procedural
Series: Inspector McGarr. Book 15
Subject(s): Catholicism; Cults; Clergy
Major character(s): Peter McGarr, Police Officer (chief superintendent)
Time period(s): 2000s (2000); 1990s (1990)
Locale(s): Dublin, Ireland

Summary: When best-selling author Mary-Jo Stanton is murdered, the trail to her killer leads McGarr to the militant Catholic sect to which she belonged, Opus Dei, a powerful

secret organization made up of clergy, politicians, and assassins. It's a dangerous investigation he undertakes, one that's blocked at every turn and leads to threats against both McGarr and his beloved family. Opus Dei is willing to go to any lengths to enforce the religious laws its members hold sacred. Once again, this splendid writer has produced a splendid book full of insights into modern Ireland and peopled with intriguing and believable characters, not the least of whom is the determined and compassionate McGarr.

Where it's reviewed:
Booklist, May 15, 2001, page 1736
Publishers Weekly, May 28, 2001, page 52

Other books by the same author:
The Death of an Irish Lover, 2000
The Death of an Irish Tinker, 1997
The Death of an Irish Seawolf, 1996
The Death of an Ardent Bibliophile, 1995
Death on a Cold, Wild River, 1993

Other books you might like:
Vincent Banville, *The John Blaine Series*, 1993-
John Brady, *The Matt Minogue Series*, 1988-
Ann C. Fallon, *The James Fleming Series*, 1990-
Jonathan Harrington, *The Danny O'Flaherty Series*, 1996-
Jim Lusby, *The Carl McCadden Series*, 1995-

62

PHILIP GOODIN

Death of Kings

(New York: Carroll & Graf, 2001)

Story type: Historical
Series: Nick Revill. Book 2
Subject(s): Actors and Actresses; Theater; Kings, Queens, Rulers, etc.
Major character(s): Nick Revill, Actor, Spy
Time period(s): 17th century (1601)
Locale(s): London, England

Summary: With Elizabeth I nearing the end of her reign without a direct heir and refusing even to discuss the matter of a successor, there is great unease in her court and throughout the country. The Earl of Essex, one of Elizabeth's many former lovers and confidantes, is ostensibly planning ways to protect the throne, although there are those who believe he is really plotting to seize it. Enter the queen's own favorite theater company, the Chamberlain's Men, who are approached by an emissary from Essex offering to pay them for performing *Richard II*, a drama about the deposing of a monarch. Nick Revill, one of the players, has been asked to spy on his own company by a representative of the queen herself, and as a result finds himself in danger from people both within and without the Chamberlain's Men.

Other books by the same author:
Sleep of Death, 2000

Other books you might like:
P.F. Chisholm, *A Plague of Angels*, 1998
Judith Cook, *The Slicing Edge of Death*, 1993
Simon Hawke, *A Comedy of Errors*, 2001
Tony Hays, *Murder on the Twelfth Night*, 1993

Faye Kellerman, *The Quality of Mercy*, 1989

63

ED GORMAN

Will You Still Love Me Tomorrow?

(New York: Carroll & Graf, 2001)

Story type: Private Detective; Historical
Series: Sam McCain. Book 3
Subject(s): Communism; Politics; Russians
Major character(s): Sam McCain, Lawyer, Detective—Private
Time period(s): 1950s (1959)
Locale(s): Black River Falls, Iowa

Summary: The author captures the worst of the 1950s, along with the nostalgic best, in this tale of what happens in the small town of Black River Falls when Soviet premier Nikita Khrushchev swings through during a tour of the Midwest. Anti-communist demonstrators are everywhere, and young McCain opens his door one day to find the town's leading liberal, Richard Conners, dead with a hammer and sickle painted in blood on his forehead. There are plenty of suspects among the town's right-wingers, but in very short order they turn up dead as well. The author uses the popular songs and icons of the day to evoke the period, but none is more effective than the rampant McCarthyism that sweeps the town. The prolific author has written many other contemporary mystery series.

Where it's reviewed:
Booklist, November 15, 2000, page 623
Library Journal, January 1, 2001, page 162
Publishers Weekly, October 30, 2000, page 49
Wall Street Journal, February 26, 2001, page A20

Other books by the same author:
Wake Up, Little Susie, 2000
The Day the Music Died, 1999

Other books you might like:
Loren D. Estleman, *Edsel*, 1995
Terence Faherty, *Come Back Dead*, 1997
Joe Gores, *Cases*, 1998
Joseph Kanon, *The Prodigal Spy*, 1998
Richard Parrish, *Defending the Truth*, 1998

64

LAURENCE GOUGH

Funny Money

(Toronto: McClelland & Stewart, 2001)

Story type: Police Procedural
Series: Willows & Parker. Book 12
Subject(s): Runaways; Organized Crime; Prostitution
Major character(s): Jack Willows, Detective—Homicide; Claire Parker, Detective—Homicide
Time period(s): 2000s
Locale(s): Vancouver, British Columbia, Canada

Summary: Claire and Jack are colleagues and lovers, living together with Jack's children and dealing with the usual

problems parents have. Professionally, they're looking for a young prostitute named Chantal, who first hit the streets escaping from an abusive father and is now on the run from the cops, who want to talk to her about the murder of her violent pimp boyfriend. Also looking for Chantal are a couple of inept thugs, Hector and Carlos, who were in the middle of a counterfeiting operation when their boss, Jake Cappalletti, was temporarily disabled by a stroke, and who are now wondering if it was really very smart to pay Chantal off with funny money. All the while Claire's biological clock is ticking; as she watches Jack's children growing up she desperately wants a child of her own. There's a lot of dark humor in this underrated series, as well as solid police procedure.

Other books by the same author:
Shutterbug, 1998
Heartbreaker, 1997
Karaoke Rap, 1997
Memory Lane, 1995
Killers, 1994

Other books you might like:
Earl Emerson, *The Thomas Black Series*, 1985-
Howard Engel, *The Benny Cooperman Series*, 1980-
Medora Sale, *The John Sanders/Harriet Jeffries Series*, 1986-1994
Eric Wright, *The Charlie Salter Series*, 1983-
L.R. Wright, *The Karl Alberg Series*, 1985-

RON GOULART

Groucho Marx and the Broadway Murders
(New York: St. Martin's Minotaur, 2001)

Story type: Historical
Series: Groucho Marx. Book 4
Subject(s): Comedians; Theater; Humor
Major character(s): Groucho Marx, Historical Figure, Entertainer; Frank Denby, Journalist (former crime reporter), Writer (scriptwriter); Jane Denby, Artist (cartoonist)
Time period(s): 1930s (1939)
Locale(s): New York, New York; Los Angeles, California

Summary: When Frank's wife, Jane, is offered a chance to turn her comic strip into a weekly radio show, she insists that it would have to be in collaboration with her husband, which is how the two of them come to be on the Super Chief bound for Manhattan, with Groucho inexplicably along for the ride (in a separate compartment, of course). When they reach the Big Apple, one of the first things they do is see a Broadway show, which unfortunately never makes it past the first act, as one of the actors turns up very dead on the stage. Being experienced sleuths by now, the three of them investigate the murder while trading wisecracks.

Other books by the same author:
Elementary, My Dear Groucho, 1999
Groucho Marx, Private Eye, 1999
Groucho Marx, Master Detective, 1998

Other books you might like:
George Baxt, *The Tallulah Bankhead Murder Case*, 1987
Andrew Bergman, *Tender Is LeVine*, 2001

Terence Faherty, *The Scott Elliott Series*, 1996-
Kinky Friedman, *The Kinky Friedman Series*, 1986-
Stuart M. Kaminsky, *You Bet Your Life*, 1978

SUE GRAFTON

P Is for Peril
(New York: Putnam, 2001)

Story type: Private Detective
Series: Kinsey Millhone. Book 16
Subject(s): Missing Persons; Doctors; Nursing Homes
Major character(s): Kinsey Millhone, Detective—Private, Divorced Person
Time period(s): 1980s (1986)
Locale(s): Santa Teresa, California

Summary: Kinsey is hired by the ex-wife of an elderly physician, who runs a nursing home being investigated for Medicare fraud to find her husband. Missing for over two months, it's not the first time the man has disappeared and the police have been unable to come up with any leads. Both the former and the present Mrs. Purcell are concerned this time, and the current wife thinks he may be dead. The trail is pretty cold by now, but Kinsey promises to do what she can, although there's something about the case she finds disturbing.

Where it's reviewed:
Booklist, March 15, 2001, page 1332
Library Journal, April 15, 2001, page 131
New York Times Book Review, June 10, 2001, page 28
Publishers Weekly, May 21, 2001, page 84

Other books by the same author:
O Is for Outlaw, 2000
N Is for Noose, 1998
M Is for Malice, 1996
L Is for Lawless, 1995
K Is for Killer, 1994

Other books you might like:
Janet Dawson, *The Jeri Howard Series*, 1990-
Susan Dunlap, *The Kiernan O'Shaughnessy Series*, 1989-
Karen Kijewski, *The Kat Colorado Series*, 1988-
Marcia Muller, *The Sharon McCone Series*, 1977-
Sara Paretsky, *The V.I. Warshawski Series*, 1982-

67

SARAH GRAVES (Pseudonym of Mary Kittredge)

Repair to Her Grave
(New York: Bantam, 2001)

Story type: Amateur Detective; Domestic
Series: Jake Tiptree. Book 4
Subject(s): Small Town Life; Single Parent Families; Haunted Houses
Major character(s): Jacobia "Jake" Tiptree, Single Parent, Stock Broker (former)
Time period(s): 2000s
Locale(s): Eastport, Maine

Summary: Jake left Manhattan to escape a stressful lifestyle that included a philandering husband and a teenage son headed down the wrong path. The change has been a healthy one for both Jake and her son, Sam, with the only downside being the hordes of guests that take up their spare bedrooms between Memorial Day and Labor Day. If she's ever going to finish the prolonged job of renovating the house, Jake will have to come up with a way of warding them off—and she does, with dire reports of exploding plumbing and hepatitis. One still shows up at her door, claiming he'd been invited back in January. His name is Jonathan Raines, and although he's posing as a doctoral candidate finishing his dissertation, it soon becomes clear he's really there to investigate the house's history of being haunted. Then when he disappears, Jake has to set her remodeling chores aside once again to investigate.

Other books by the same author:
Wicked Fix, 2000
Triple Witch, 1999
Dead Cat Bounce, 1998

Other books you might like:
Donna Andrews, *The Meg Langslow Series*, 1999-
J.S. Borthwick, *The Sarah Deane Series*, 1982-
Susan Kenney, *One Fell Sloop*, 1990
Francine Mathews, *The Merry Folger Series*, 1994-
Leslie Meier, *The Lucy Stone Series*, 1993-

68

KATE GRILLEY

Death Rides an Ill Wind

(New York: Berkley, 2001)

Story type: Amateur Detective
Series: Kelly Ryan. Book 2
Subject(s): Islands; Hurricanes; Homelessness
Major character(s): Kelly Ryan, Radio Personality
Time period(s): 2000s
Locale(s): St. Chris, Caribbean (island)

Summary: It's the height of the hurricane season on the island paradise of St. Chris, where Kelly works doing a morning show for the local radio station. Islanders are frantically preparing for Hurricane Gilda, a major storm due to hit square on in a matter of hours. When it's over, there's a huge amount of damage, but the only casualty seems to be the dead body of a homeless woman washed up in the bay. However, it turns out the woman died of a fractured skull, a possible murder. The author makes good use of the closed setting (always effective in a mystery) and the small, closely knit island population, giving the reader a good sense of what life is like in her fictionalized version of the Virgin Islands (where she lives).

Other books by the same author:
Death Dances to a Reggae Beat, 2000

Other books you might like:
Donna Andrews, *Murder with Puffins*, 2000
Margaret Maron, *Storm Track*, 2000
Penny Mickelbury, *Paradise Interrupted*, 2001
Marcia Muller, *A Walk through the Fire*, 1999

Laurence Shames, *Tropical Depression*, 1996

69

PATRICIA GUIVER

Delilah Doolittle and the Canine Chorus

(New York: Berkley, 2001)

Story type: Amateur Detective
Series: Delilah Doolittle. Book 5
Subject(s): Animals/Dogs; Pets; Secrets
Major character(s): Delilah Doolittle, Widow(er), Expatriate; Watson, Animal (Doberman pinscher), Sidekick
Time period(s): 2000s
Locale(s): Surf City, California; Las Vegas, Nevada

Summary: When she found herself widowed after a brief marriage and far from her home in England, Delilah realized that despite her solid education she was ill-equipped to earn a living for herself and that her small inheritance wasn't going to be adequate. So she became a pet detective, tracking down stray pets for their anxious owners, an occupation that so far has proved to be anything but humdrum. This time out, it's her own past that she investigates. When someone breaks into her Southern California home and leaves a packet of matches from the same Las Vegas hotel where her shady ex-husband was last seen alive, she begins to wonder again exactly what led to his murder. When she looks through his meager possessions, she finds a deed to a silver mine. Determined to get to the bottom of the matter, she leaves for Las Vegas with Watson, but while she's gone the woman looking after her house is murdered. The book fills in many of the gaps about Delilah's past, her marriage, and how she met many of the secondary characters in the series.

Other books by the same author:
Delilah Doolittle and the Missing Macaw, 2000
Delilah Doolittle and the Careless Coyote, 1998
Delilah Doolittle and the Motley Mutts, 1998
Delilah Doolittle and the Purloined Pooch, 1997

Other books you might like:
Carole Lea Benjamin, *The Rachel Alexander and Dash Series*, 1996-
Laurien Berenson, *The Melanie Travis Series*, 1995-
Simon Brett, *The Mrs. Pargeter Series*, 1986-
Susan Conant, *The Holly Winter Series*, 1989-
Barbara Moore, *The Doberman Wore Black*, 1983

70

JANE HADDAM (Pseudonym of Orania Papazoglou)

True Believers

(New York: St. Martin's Press, 2001)

Story type: Traditional
Series: Gregor Demarkian. Book 17
Subject(s): Catholicism; Clergy; Homosexuality/Lesbianism
Major character(s): Gregor Demarkian, FBI Agent (retired); Bennis Hannaford, Lover (of Gregor)
Time period(s): 2000s
Locale(s): Philadelphia, Pennsylvania

Summary: An apparent murder-suicide in the sacristy of St. Anselm's Catholic Church catches the attention of Sister Mary Scholastica, who suspects that the man didn't actually kill his diabetic wife, as the police claim. She asks Demarkian, retired head of the FBI's Behavioral Sciences Unit, to conduct his own investigation, and it proves to be immensely complicated by various side issues, among them a recent pedophilia scare at the church and parish politics at the neighboring Episcopal church, which ministers to a largely gay male congregation. Meanwhile, Demarkian's lover, Bennis Hannaford, is dealing with major issues of her own. This fine series, originally marketed to a decidedly cozy audience, is in fact much meatier than readers were led to believe, offering a great deal in the way of topical issues, humor, insight into human nature, and intricate and satisfying plotting.

Where it's reviewed:
Booklist, April 1, 2001, page 1449
Library Journal, April 1, 2001, page 137
Publishers Weekly, April 2, 2001, page 42

Other books by the same author:
Skeleton Key, 2000
Deadly Beloved, 1997
And One to Die On, 1996
Baptism in Blood, 1996
Fountain of Death, 1995

Other books you might like:
Joe Gash, *Priestly Murders*, 1984
Sara Paretsky, *Killing Orders*, 1985
James Patterson, *Cradle and All*, 2000
David J. Walker, *A Beer at a Bawdy House*, 2000
Michael C. White, *The Blind Side of the Heart*, 2000

71

PARNELL HALL

Cozy
(New York: Carroll & Graf, 2001)

Story type: Private Detective; Humor
Series: Stanley Hastings. Book 12
Subject(s): Hotels, Motels; Food; Animals/Cats
Major character(s): Stanley Hastings, Detective—Private; Alice Hastings, Sidekick, Spouse (of Stanley)
Time period(s): 2000s
Locale(s): New Hampshire

Summary: With their son Tommie safely off to camp, Stanley's wife Alice—with whom he is incapable of winning an argument—books the two of them into a picturesque country inn from which they can hike through the New Hampshire mountains. Never mind that Stanley despises hiking or that the Blue Frog Ponds Inn turns out to be less than picturesque, boasting paper-thin walls, low ceilings and cartoon frogs on all the doors. Stanley's spirits improve somewhat when guests start being murdered left and right—except for the fact the police consider him to be a prime suspect, along with Alice. With her help, and additional assistance from an enigmatic orange cat, Stanley comes through once again. The author, who also writes the Cora Felton series of crossword puzzle

mysteries, pokes gentle fun at both the private eye and cozy subgenres here.

Where it's reviewed:
Booklist, May 1, 2001, page 1632
Publishers Weekly, May 21, 2001, page 83

Other books by the same author:
Suspense, 1998
Scam, 1997
Trial, 1996
Movie, 1995
Blackmail, 1994

Other books you might like:
Lawrence Block, *The Burglar in the Library*, 1997
Carole Bugge, *Who Killed Mona Lisa?*, 2001
Mary Daheim, *The Judith McMonigle Flynn Series*, 1991-
Jean Hager, *The Tess Darcy Series*, 1994-
Tamar Myers, *The Magdalena Yoder Series*, 1994-

72

PATRICIA HALL (Pseudonym of Maureen O'Connor)

Dead on Arrival
(New York: St. Martin's Press, 2001)

Story type: Police Procedural; Traditional
Series: Laura Ackroyd. Book 6
Subject(s): Poverty; Racism; Emigration and Immigration
Major character(s): Laura Ackroyd, Journalist (newspaper reporter); Michael Thackeray, Police Officer (chief inspector)
Time period(s): 2000s
Locale(s): London, England (Docklands); Bradfield, England (Yorkshire)

Summary: Estranged from her policeman lover, Mike Thackeray, Laura goes to London on an assignment, where she stays with a friend in the newly fashionable Docklands area. While there, she witnesses an attack by some skinheads on two Somali boys, which leaves the younger one dead. Now targeted by the attackers as a witness to the homicide, Laura finds herself in great danger. Back in Bradfield, Thackeray is working on the murder of a Pakistani businessman and the disappearance of a Pakistani woman, events that also may be racially motivated. Both protagonists are trying to work through the issues that led to the rift between them.

Where it's reviewed:
Publishers Weekly, March 5, 2001, page 65

Other books by the same author:
The Italian Girl, 2000
Perils of the Night, 1999
Dead of Winter, 1997
Dying Fall, 1994
Death by Election, 1993

Other books you might like:
Robert Barnard, *The Corpse at the Haworth Tandoori*, 1999
Deborah Crombie, *Kissed a Sad Goodbye*, 1999
Ann Granger, *The Meredith Mitchell/Allan Markby Series*, 1991-
Sarah Lacey, *The Leah Hunter Series*, 1992-

Peter Robinson, *The Inspector Alan Banks Series*, 1987-

BARBARA HAMBLY

Die upon a Kiss
(New York: Bantam, 2001)

Story type: Historical; Amateur Detective
Series: Benjamin January. Book 5
Subject(s): African Americans; American South; Opera
Major character(s): Benjamin January, Slave (freed), Musician (pianist)
Time period(s): 1830s (1835)
Locale(s): New Orleans, Louisiana

Summary: It's Carnival in the country's wickedest city, and January is just leaving the American Theater late one night after rehearsing with the orchestra for a production of *Othello* when he walks into a fight. He ends up rescuing the opera's volatile impresario, Lorenzo Belaggio, from what would have been a fatal assault. January is a big man, a widowed free slave who studied medicine and music in Paris, where he was generally accepted into the city's society, but who in New Orleans is caught between two worlds and at home in neither. The labyrinthine social and racial distinctions of this time and place in American history are thoughtfully explored by the author, resulting in a dense, complicated narrative that both challenges and rewards the attentive reader.

Where it's reviewed:
Booklist, March 15, 2001, page 1333
Publishers Weekly, April 23, 2001, page 52

Other books by the same author:
Sold Down the River, 2000
Graveyard Dust, 1999
Fever Season, 1998
A Free Man of Color, 1997

Other books you might like:
James Lee Burke, *In the Electric Mist with Confederate Dead*, 1993
Ron Burns, *Enslaved*, 1994
Ann McMillan, *Angel Trumpet*, 1999
Miriam Grace Monfredo, *Through a Gold Eagle*, 1996
Robert Skinner, *The Wesley Farrell Series*, 1997-

LYN HAMILTON

The African Quest
(New York: Berkeley, 2001)

Story type: Traditional; Amateur Detective
Series: Lara McClintoch. Book 5
Subject(s): Africa; Archaeology; Treasure
Major character(s): Lara McClintoch, Antiques Dealer, Detective—Amateur
Time period(s): 2000s
Locale(s): Taberda, Tunisia; Toronto, Ontario, Canada

Summary: Lara lets herself be persuaded by her ex-husband and business partner, Clive Swain, that what their shop needs to boost its sales is a posh group tour to an exotic, antiquities-filled country such as Tunisia, and she dutifully assembles some select customers and books them into a charming small hotel in Taberda. It will be the base from which the group takes day tours to various nearby sites in the care of local guides, while Lara scours the countryside for expensive antiquities with which to decorate the home of a high-rolling client back in Toronto. Quite unexpectedly she becomes caught up in the search for a sunken Carthaginian merchant ship laden with treasure, as well as with the murders that strike the people who are looking for it. It turns out that not everybody in Lara's party has come to Tunisia for just the sightseeing and shopping. As usual in this travelogue series, the local color and descriptions of the country are outstanding.

Other books by the same author:
The Celtic Riddle, 2000
The Moche Warrior, 1999
The Maltese Goddess, 1998
The Xibalba Murders, 1997

Other books you might like:
Margot Arnold, *The Penny Spring/Toby Glendower Series*, 1979-
Beverly Connor, *The Lindsay Chamberlain Series*, 1996-
Aaron Elkins, *The Gideon Oliver Series*, 1982-
Elizabeth Peters, *The Amelia Peabody Series*, 1975-
Aaron Marc Stein, *The Tim Mulligan/Elsie Mae Hunt Series*, 1940-1955

STEVE HAMILTON

The Hunting Wind
(New York: St. Martin's Press, 2001)

Story type: Private Detective
Series: Alex McKnight. Book 3
Subject(s): Sports/Baseball; Friendship; Crime and Criminals
Major character(s): Alex McKnight, Detective—Private, Police Officer (former); Randy Wilkins, Sports Figure (former baseball pitcher)
Time period(s): 2000s
Locale(s): Paradise, Michigan (Upper Peninsula); Detroit, Michigan

Summary: McKnight, who was a Detroit cop in a past life and a minor-league catcher before that, finds his past catching up with him one night when Randy Wilkins, a left-handed former pitcher he caught 30 years ago, walks into the Glasgow Inn. That's the pub where Alex spends most of his evenings, nursing Canadian beers and chewing the fat with the locals. After they've filled each other in on how their lives have gone, Randy asks Alex to help him find Maria, the woman he loved back then and walked out on. He hasn't seen or heard from her since. Alex thinks it's a bad idea, but he lets Randy talk him into going down to Detroit with him to make some inquiries. As Alex snoops around, he comes to realize that everything about this case is suspect, including Randy's motives for wanting to find Maria.

Where it's reviewed:
Booklist, May 1, 2001, page 1630

New York Times Book Review, June 24, 2001, page 22
Publishers Weekly, May 21, 2001, page 85

Other books by the same author:
Winter of the Wolf Moon, 2000
A Cold Day in Paradise, 1998

Other books you might like:
Richard Barre, *The Wil Hardesty Series*, 1995-
Loren D. Estleman, *The Amos Walker Series*, 1980-
David Housewright, *The Holland Taylor Series*, 1995-
William Kent Krueger, *The Cork O'Connor Series*, 1998-
Randy Wayne White, *The Doc Ford Series*, 1990-

76

KAREN HARPER

The Twylight Tower

(New York: Delacorte, 2001)

Story type: Historical
Series: Elizabeth I. Book 3
Subject(s): Kings, Queens, Rulers, etc.; Biography; Conspiracies
Major character(s): Elizabeth I, Historical Figure, Ruler (Queen of England); Robert Dudley, Nobleman (Earl of Leicester), Historical Figure
Time period(s): 16th century (1560)
Locale(s): London, England

Summary: Now 26-years-old and queen for nearly two years, Elizabeth is becoming quite accustomed to conspiracies directed against her. Yet another is uncovered, when the wife of Robert Dudley, the horse master of whom she is passionately enamored, dies under suspicious circumstances, followed by the equally suspicious death of a court lutenist. Although the incident is based on an actual event, the portrait the author paints of the young Elizabeth is highly romanticized and at times a trifle anachronistic. Nonetheless, she continues to be a spirited, appealing young woman, who dabbles in detection as a change of pace from her court duties. The author has also produced much contemporary mainstream fiction, as well as historical romances.

Where it's reviewed:
Booklist, February 15, 2001, page 1119
Library Journal, February 1, 2001, page 127
Publishers Weekly, February 25, 2001, page 62

Other books by the same author:
The Tidal Poole, 2000
The Poyson Garden, 1999

Other books you might like:
Fiona Buckley, *The Ursula Blanchard Series*, 1997-
Judith Cook, *The Simon Forman Series*, 1997-
Ann Dukthas, *Time for the Death of a King*, 1994
Kathy Lynn Emerson, *The Susanna, Lady Appleton Series*, 1997-
Edward Marston, *The Nicholas Bracewell Series*, 1988-

77

LEE HARRIS (Pseudonym of Syrell Rogovin Leahy)

The April Fool's Day Murder

(New York: Fawcett, 2001)

Story type: Amateur Detective; Domestic
Series: Christine Bennett. Book 13
Subject(s): Holidays; Small Town Life; Marriage
Major character(s): Christine Bennett Brooks, Housewife, Teacher
Time period(s): 2000s
Locale(s): Oakwood, New Jersey

Summary: Christine, a nun until she left the convent at the age of 30, is now a happily married suburban mother and part-time teacher, who has nothing more pressing on her mind than putting up with her family's April Fool jokes and buying herself a Japanese cut-leaf maple at the local nursery. On her way home she sees one of her neighbors, Willard Platt, lying on his lawn, apparently stabbed to death, with the knife still plunged into his back. After she reports the incident, however, she's embarrassed to learn it was nothing more than an elaborate practical joke. Later, however, Platt really is stabbed to death. As Chris learns more about the dead man's family, she realizes there is much more going on behind their facade of respectability than anyone could have dreamed.

Other books by the same author:
The Mother's Day Murder, 2000
The Father's Day Murder, 1999
The Labor Day Murder, 1998
The New Year's Eve Murder, 1997
The Valentine's Day Murder, 1996

Other books you might like:
Leslie O'Kane, *The Molly Masters Series*, 1996-
Nancy Pickard, *The Jenny Cain Series*, 1984-
Lora Roberts, *The Liz Sullivan Series*, 1994-
Winona Sullivan, *The Sister Cecile Buddenbrooks Series*, 1993-
Valerie Wolzien, *The Susan Henshaw Series*, 1987-

78

CAROLYN HART

Resort to Murder

(New York: Morrow, 2001)

Story type: Amateur Detective; Traditional
Series: Henrie O. Book 6
Subject(s): Islands; Weddings; Hotels, Motels
Major character(s): Henrietta O'Dwyer Collins, Widow(er), Journalist (retired)
Time period(s): 2000s
Locale(s): Bermuda

Summary: Despite the impending wedding of her former son-in-law to an attractive and very wealthy widow, Henrie is struggling with a mild case of depression as she recuperates from pneumonia in an elegant seaside hotel on the tropical island of Bermuda. Meanwhile things aren't going at all right where the wedding is concerned. A granddaughter who

doesn't want to see her father remarry is making trouble, the bride can't stop flirting with every man in sight, the groom can't stand this flirting, and even a few malicious spirits seem to be stirred up over the event. The hotel itself was the scene of a tragedy only a year earlier when a man who was infatuated with the soon-to-be bride jumped to his death. When murder strikes, Henrie soon has more on her mind than her illness. The author also writes the Death on Demand series featuring mystery bookstore owner Annie Laurance Darling.

Where it's reviewed:
Publishers Weekly, March 12, 2001, page 66

Other books by the same author:
Death on the River Walk, 1999
Death in Paradise, 1998
Death in Lovers' Lane, 1997
Scandal in Fair Haven, 1994
Dead Man's Island, 1993

Other books you might like:
Anne George, *The Southern Sisters Series*, 1996-
Patricia Guiver, *The Delilah Doolittle Series*, 1997-
Jean Hager, *The Tess Darcy Series*, 1994-
Charlaine Harris, *The Aurora Teagarden Series*, 1990-
Elizabeth Daniels Squire, *The Peaches Dann Series*, 1994-

79

ELLEN HART (Pseudonym of Patricia Ellen Boenhardt)

The Merchant of Venus
(New York: St. Martin's Press, 2001)

Story type: Amateur Detective; Traditional
Series: Jane Lawless. Book 10
Subject(s): Alcoholism; Homosexuality/Lesbianism; Movie Industry
Major character(s): Jane Lawless, Restaurateur, Detective—Amateur; Cordelia Thorn, Director
Time period(s): 2000s
Locale(s): Minneapolis, Minnesota; New York, New York; Asbury, Connecticut

Summary: In something of a departure from earlier books in this generally light-hearted series, Jane and her friend Cordelia travel to New York and Connecticut to attend the Christmas wedding of Cordelia's younger sister, Octavia, a Broadway actress, to Roland Lester, an 83-year-old reclusive billionaire movie director. When Lester collapses in mid-ceremony and dies shortly after, the affair becomes anything but festive. Jane, who is still recovering from a broken love affair, begins investigating what turns out to be a murder, and she soon realizes it's somehow linked to the unsolved murder 40 years earlier of another Hollywood director, in which Lester, who was the man's lover, was a suspect. Why Lester and Octavia were getting married at all is not the least of the puzzles to be solved. Various subplots and back stories involving McCarthyism, alcoholism, dysfunctional families, and sexual secrets darken the narrative, and even the brazen Cordelia, who can usually be counted on to provide comic relief, is a bit more subdued than usual. The author also writes a series about Minneapolis hotel owner Sophie Greenway.

Where it's reviewed:
Booklist, February 1, 2001, page 1041
Library Journal, February 1, 2001, page 128
Mystery News, February/March 2001, page 28
Publishers Weekly, January 8, 2001, page 50

Other books by the same author:
Hunting the Witch, 1999
Wicked Games, 1998
Robber's Wine, 1996
Faint Praise, 1995
A Small Sacrifice, 1994

Other books you might like:
Marian Babson, *The Eve Sinclair/Trixie Dolan Series*, 1986-
Andrew Bergman, *The Jack LeVine Series*, 1974-
Della Borton, *The Gilda Liberty Series*, 1999-
Kris Neri, *Revenge of the Gypsy Queen*, 1999
Sandra Scoppettone, *The Lauren Laurano Series*, 1991-

80

SUE HENRY

Dead North
(New York: Morrow, 2001)

Story type: Amateur Detective
Series: Jessie Arnold. Book 8
Subject(s): Animals/Dogs; Voyages and Travels; Runaways
Major character(s): Jessie Arnold, Detective—Amateur; Patrick Cutler, Teenager, Runaway
Time period(s): 2000s
Locale(s): British Columbia, Canada; Alaska

Summary: Since losing her home to a fire in *Beneath the Ashes*, Jessie has no fixed abode while waiting for her new one to be built, so she doesn't need much persuasion when it's arranged for her to fly to the lower forty-eight and drive a Winnebago from Idaho to Anchorage via the Alaska Highway. She doesn't mind traveling alone, as long as she has her lead husky, Tank, to keep her company, and she very much enjoys the scenery and the people she meets along the road. One of them is a colorful old man named Max; another is Patrick Cutler, a young runaway whom she befriends but who is being sought by police for his connection with two murders. Gradually Jessie learns the terrible secrets in Patrick's past, but by connecting with him she too has become a target of killers.

Where it's reviewed:
Booklist, May 1, 2001, page 1634

Other books by the same author:
Beneath the Ashes, 2000
Murder on the Yukon Quest, 1999
Deadfall, 1998
Death Takes Passage, 1997
Sleeping Lady, 1996

Other books you might like:
Stan Jones, *White Sky, Black Ice*, 1999
Christopher Lane, *The Ray Attla Series*, 1998-
Megan Mallory Rust, *The Taylor Morgan Series*, 1998-
Marcia Simpson, *Crow in Stolen Colors*, 2000
Dana Stabenow, *The Kate Shugak Series*, 1992-

81

JULIE WRAY HERMAN

Three Dirty Women and the Bitter Brew

(Johnson City, Tennessee: Silver Dagger, 2001)

Story type: Amateur Detective; Domestic
Series: Korine McFaile. Book 2
Subject(s): Gardens and Gardening; Mothers and Sons; Family Problems
Major character(s): Korine McFaile, Landscaper, Detective—Amateur
Time period(s): 2000s
Locale(s): Savannah, Georgia

Summary: Korine, her partner Janey Bascom, and Janey's husband J.J. are attending a landscapers' convention in Savannah, where Korine is stuck with disagreeable Dodie Halloran as a roommate. When Dodie is murdered, Korine becomes a prime suspect, and in order to clear herself of the charge she must unearth the real murderer. At the same time, she's perplexed as to how to deal with her son, Chaz, who has a problem that he can't, or won't, discuss with her. In order to understand what's going on, Korine has to search her own past.

Where it's reviewed:
Publishers Weekly, April 30, 2001, page 60

Other books by the same author:
Three Dirty Women and the Garden of Death, 2000

Other books you might like:
Mary Freeman, *The Rachel O'Connor Series*, 1999-
Janis Harris, *Roots of Murder*, 1999
Ann Ripley, *The Louise Eldridge Series*, 1994-
John Sherwood, *The Celia Grant Series*, 1984-
Nathan Walpow, *The Joe Portugal Series*, 1999-

82

TERI HOLBROOK

Mother Tongue

(New York: Bantam, 2001)

Story type: Amateur Detective; Traditional
Series: Gale Grayson. Book 4
Subject(s): American South; Small Town Life; Vietnamese Americans
Major character(s): Gale Grayson, Historian, Widow(er); Daniel Halford, Detective—Police (Scotland Yard)
Time period(s): 2000s
Locale(s): Statler's Cross, Georgia

Summary: Back home in Georgia after a stint in England (so far, the series has alternated between the two settings), Gale is still mourning her husband's death and hoping to find some measure of peace in her research and writing. However, the normally quiet community is shocked by the murder of three men, one of them a Vietnamese immigrant, and the police investigation is hampered by the unwillingness of certain townspeople to cooperate. Gale's houseguest, Scotland Yard detective Daniel Halford, takes a keen interest in the case, and

together with Gale, her grandmother, and her daughter, sets out to solve it.

Where it's reviewed:
Publishers Weekly, January 15, 2001, page 57

Other books by the same author:
Sad Water, 1999
The Grass Widow, 1996
A Far and Deadly Cry, 1995

Other books you might like:
G.D. Gearino, *What the Deaf Mute Heard*, 1996
Charlaine Harris, *The Lily Bard Series*, 1996-
Virginia Lanier, *The Jo Beth Sidden Series*, 1995-
Margaret Maron, *The Deborah Knott Series*, 1992-
Sharyn McCrumb, *The Ballad Series*, 1990-

83

HUGH HOLTON

The Devil's Shadow

(New York: Forge, 2001)

Story type: Police Procedural
Series: Larry Cole. Book 8
Subject(s): African Americans; Organized Crime; Crime and Criminals
Major character(s): Larry Cole, Police Officer (commander); Julianna Saint, Thief
Time period(s): 2000s (2004-2005)
Locale(s): Chicago, Illinois; Saint Martin, Caribbean

Summary: Julianna Saint—the Devil's Shadow—is a world-class thief, and she's been sent to Chicago on a secret directive from the Vatican. While there she helps the local mob with the daring heist they have planned of the supposedly impenetrable North Michigan Avenue Bank, during which local mystery writer Greg Ennis is accidentally killed. Julianna escapes to an island in the Caribbean with Larry Cole hot on her trail, and when the two connect, Larry finds himself falling for her in a big way. Although the story sets the beautiful and cunning Julianna up for appearances in future books, it's not likely to happen; sadly, the author, the highest-ranking police officer to write mysteries, died in early 2001.

Where it's reviewed:
Booklist, May 1, 2001, page 1634
Publishers Weekly, May 7, 2001, page 222

Other books by the same author:
The Left Hand of God, 2000
Red Lightning, 1998
Violent Crimes, 1997
Chicago Blues, 1996
Windy City, 1995

Other books you might like:
Gary Hardwick, *Cold Medina*, 1996
Stuart M. Kaminsky, *The Abe Lieberman Series*, 1990-
James Patterson, *The Alex Cross Series*, 1995-
Gary Phillips, *The Ivan Monk Series*, 1994-
Michael Raleigh, *The Paul Whelan Series*, 1990-

84

EVAN HUNTER
ED MCBAIN, Co-Author

Candyland

(New York: Simon & Schuster, 2001)

Story type: Psychological Suspense; Police Procedural
Subject(s): Sexual Behavior; Prostitution; Rape
Major character(s): Benjamin Thorpe, Architect; Emma Boyle, Police Officer (Special Victims Unit)
Time period(s): 2000s
Locale(s): New York, New York

Summary: These two authors are, in fact, the same person, but the two separate halves of the book are written in different styles and from different viewpoints. The protagonist of the first section is Benjamin Thorpe, a successful married architect, who makes frequent business trips from his Los Angeles base. Seemingly a normal enough guy, he is in fact a long-term sexual addict, who spends all his free time obsessing about his sexual conquests, seeking out women, indulging in phone sex, and when necessary, visiting prostitutes. On a trip to New York, he attempts to reconnect with various women he's had sexual encounters with on past visits, but he's rebuffed and spends an entire evening feverishly trying to find a new woman, eventually ending up in a massage parlor. In the second half of the book, the action shifts to a precinct house, where police are investigating the brutal murder and rape of a young prostitute—one with whom Thorpe had an encounter the previous night. The officer assigned to the case is Emma Boyle of the Special Victims Unit. The prolific author has written mainstream novels as Hunter and realistic police procedurals as McBain—50 in the 87th Precinct series alone.

Where it's reviewed:
Book, January 1, 2001, page 81
Booklist, November 15, 2000, page 587
Library Journal, December 2000, page 188
New York Times, January 31, 2001, page B9
People Weekly, February 12, 2001, page 41

Other books you might like:
William Caunitz, *One Police Plaza*, 1984
Ed Dee, *The Anthony Ryan/Joe Gregory Series*, 1994-
William Heffernan, *The Paul Devlin Series*, 1988-
Christopher Newman, *The Joe Dante Series*, 1986-
Lawrence Sanders, *The Edward X. Delaney Series*, 1973-

85

JONNIE JACOBS

Witness for the Defense

(New York: Kensington, 2001)

Story type: Legal
Series: Kali O'Brien. Book 4
Subject(s): Adoption; Parenthood
Major character(s): Kali O'Brien, Lawyer; Terri Harper, Parent (hopes to adopt)
Time period(s): 2000s
Locale(s): San Francisco, California

Summary: When Terri Harper comes to Kali asking for legal representation in an adoption procedure, Kali agrees, believing it will be a fairly straightforward assignment. Terri is referred by her half-brother, Steven Cross, a psychologist Kali has worked with in the past. The baby is not yet born, and Terri and her husband, Ted, are caring for the young mother-to-be in their Pacific Heights home. They had tried to adopt previously, but the birth mother had changed her mind, so they are devastated when this adoption, too, goes sour when local radio host Bram Weaver suddenly claims paternity and demands custody of the baby. Kali prepares for a bitter court battle she's certain to lose when Weaver is murdered and Terri becomes the chief suspect. The author has also written a series about suburban single mother Kate Austen.

Where it's reviewed:
Publishers Weekly, March 26, 2001, page 64

Other books by the same author:
Motion to Dismiss, 1999
Evidence of Guilt, 1997
Shadow of Doubt, 1996

Other books you might like:
Perri O'Shaughnessy, *The Nina Reilly Series*, 1995-
Lisa Scottoline, *The Rosato & Associates Series*, 1993-
Marianne Wesson, *The Cinda Hayes Series*, 1998-
Carolyn Wheat, *The Cass Jameson Series*, 1983-
Kate Wilhelm, *The Barbara Holloway Series*, 1991-

86

BILL JAMES

Panicking Ralph

(New York: Norton, 2001)

Story type: Police Procedural
Series: Harpur & Iles. Book 17
Subject(s): Crime and Criminals; Drugs; City Life
Major character(s): Colin Harpur, Police Officer (detective chief superintendent); Desmond Iles, Police Officer (assistant chief constable); Mark Lane, Police Officer (chief constable)
Time period(s): 2000s
Locale(s): England

Summary: Moral ambiguity reigns in this series featuring cynical police officers Colin Harpur and Desmond Iles, who for a long time have been dealing with the criminal element in their unnamed English coastal city. Good people often do bad things and bad people commit good deeds, and sometimes it's hard to keep the players straight without a scorecard. Here Harpur and Iles have been commissioned by their superior, Mark Lane, to totally wipe out the regional narcotics trade, a task as futile as it is ludicrous. The two men give it their best effort, with Harpur forging an uneasy alliance with the local drug lord's chief rivals. Note: American editions of this long-running English series have been coming out in rapid succession, and it's sometimes difficult to tell the order in which they were originally published.

Where it's reviewed:
Booklist, May 1, 2001, page 1634

Library Journal, May 1, 2001, page 130
New York Times Book Review, May 20, 2001, page 34
Publishers Weekly, April 1, 2001, page 43

Other books by the same author:
The Detective Is Dead, 2001
In Good Hands, 2000
Kill Me, 2000
Eton Crop, 1999
Lovely Mover, 1999

Other books you might like:
John Harvey, *The Charlie Resnick Series*, 1989-1998
Quinton Jardine, *The Robert Skinner Series*, 1994-
Val McDermid, *The Tony Hill Series*, 1995-
Ian Rankin, *The John Rebus Series*, 1987-
Peter Robinson, *The Alan Banks Series*, 1987-

DEAN JAMES

Closer than the Bones

(Johnson City, Tennessee: Silver Dagger, 2001)

Story type: Amateur Detective; Traditional
Series: Ernie Carpenter. Book 2
Subject(s): Small Town Life; American South; Authors and Writers
Major character(s): Ernestine ''Ernie'' Carpenter, Teacher (retired), Detective—Amateur
Time period(s): 2000s
Locale(s): Tullahoma, Mississippi

Summary: Local arts patron Mary Tucker McElroy asks Ernie to help her find out who murdered Sukey Lytton, a member of the literary circle that regularly meets at her imposing mansion, Idlewild. To facilitate things, Miss McElroy gathers all the suspects together, including a despised critic, a bestselling woman novelist, and a Pulitzer Prize winner, at Idlewild, and turns Ernie loose on the group. Ernie, a somewhat senior sleuth who retired after 40 years of teaching school, is more than a match for the murderer.

Where it's reviewed:
Publishers Weekly, April 30, 2001, page 60

Other books by the same author:
Cruel as the Grave, 2000

Other books you might like:
Anne George, *The Southern Sisters Series*, 1996-
Carolyn Haines, *Buried Bones*, 2000
Charlaine Harris, *The Aurora Teagarden Series*, 1990-
Carolyn Hart, *The Henrie O Series*, 1993-
Elizabeth Daniels Squire, *The Peaches Dann Series*, 1994-

P.D. JAMES

Death in Holy Orders

(New York: Knopf, 2001)

Story type: Police Procedural; Traditional
Series: Adam Dalgliesh. Book 11

Subject(s): Anglicans; Clergy; Religious Life
Major character(s): Adam Dalgliesh, Police Officer (commander)
Time period(s): 2000s
Locale(s): Suffolk, England (East Anglia)

Summary: Something is very wrong at the small High Church seminary of St. Anselm's. The body of Ronald Treeves, a young ordinand, is found at the foot of the steep cliffs upon which the college is perched, and his father, wealthy industrialist Sir Alfred Treeves, demands a full investigation after getting an anonymous tip that the death wasn't accidental. He takes his request straight to Dalgliesh who, although he expects nothing much to come of it, goes to St. Anselm's to look into the matter. After he arrives, however, a visiting archdeacon who wants to see the college closed down is murdered in the chapel. The murderer clearly seems to be someone within St. Anselm's, and Dalgliesh soon realizes he's up against a formidable adversary as he begins to sort out what turns out to be a very complicated case. The author has also written two mysteries featuring private investigator Cordelia Grey.

Where it's reviewed:
Publishers Weekly, March 19, 2001, page 79

Other books by the same author:
A Certain Justice, 1998
Original Sin, 1994
Devices and Desires, 1989
A Taste for Death, 1986
Death of an Expert Witness, 1977

Other books you might like:
Deborah Crombie, *The Thomas Kincaid/Gemma James Series*, 1993-
Colin Dexter, *The Inspector Morse Series*, 1975-
Elizabeth George, *The Thomas Lynley Series*, 1988-
Val McDermid, *The Tony Hill Series*, 1995-
Sheila Radley, *The Inspector Quantrill Series*, 1978-

J.A. JANCE

Birds of Prey

(New York: Morrow, 2001)

Story type: Amateur Detective; Traditional
Series: J.P. Beaumont. Book 15
Subject(s): Cruise Ships; Remarriage; Old Age
Major character(s): J.P. Beaumont, Police Officer (former)
Time period(s): 2000s
Locale(s): *Starfire Breeze*, At Sea; Alaska

Summary: Beaumont, who has retired from the Seattle police force, is accompanying his octagenarian grandmother and her brand-new husband on their honeymoon cruise to Alaska. Also on board are a group of physicians holding a medical conference and a number of religious extremists, who are targeting them for making medical breakthroughs that thwart God's will. When Margaret Featherman, wife of the conference organizer, falls to her death from the ship's deck, Beaumont finds himself mistaken for an FBI agent and sets out to solve the crime. He's also trying to dodge the many amorous

divorcees, who see him as an ideal candidate for a shipboard romance. By far the coziest in this series of what used to be traditional police procedurals, the book may appeal less to Beaumont's long-time fans than to readers of the author's series about Arizona sheriff Joanna Brady.

Where it's reviewed:
Booklist, February 1, 2001, page 1020
Library Journal, February 1, 2001, page 128

Other books by the same author:
Breach of Duty, 1999
Name Withheld, 1995
Lying in Wait, 1994
Failure to Appear, 1993
Without Due Process, 1992

Other books you might like:
J.S. Borthwick, *My Body Lies over the Ocean*, 1999
Aaron Elkins, *Icy Clutches*, 1990
Sue Henry, *Death Takes Passage*, 1997
Dana Stabenow, *The Liam Campbell Series*, 1998-
John Straley, *The Angels Will Not Care*, 1998

90

RODERIC JEFFRIES

The Ambiguity of Murder

(New York: St. Martin's Press, 2001)

Story type: Police Procedural
Series: Inspector Alvarez. Book 23
Subject(s): Infidelity; Gambling
Major character(s): Alvarez, Police Officer (inspector)
Time period(s): 2000s
Locale(s): Mallorca, Spain

Summary: When the body of a retired Bolivian diplomat is found floating in his swimming pool, Inspector Alvarez immediately suspects he was murdered. As he proceeds with his investigation at his usual leisurely and philosophical pace, he receives threatening phone calls that convince him the drowning was no accident. Although Alvarez is not one to let his official duties interfere with his enjoyment of life, especially when it comes to good brandy and good food, his insight into human nature and long experience as a policeman always get the job done, even when the bureaucracy he must answer to gets in his way.

Where it's reviewed:
Booklist, May 1, 2001, page 1634
Publishers Weekly, March 19, 2001, page 79

Other books by the same author:
An Enigmatic Disappearance, 1998
A Maze of Murders, 1997
An Artistic Way to Go, 1996
An Arcadian Death, 1995
Death Takes Time, 1994

Other books you might like:
Mark Hebden, *The Inspector Pel Series*, 1979-
H.R.F. Keating, *The Ganesh Ghote Series*, 1964-
Donna Leon, *The Guido Brunetti Series*, 1992-
Robert Rosenberg, *The Avram Cohen Series*, 1991-

David Serafin, *The Luis Bernal Series*, 1979-

91

STUART M. KAMINSKY

A Few Minutes Past Midnight

(New York: Carroll & Graf, 2001)

Story type: Historical; Private Detective
Series: Toby Peters. Book 21
Subject(s): Movie Industry; World War II; Communism
Major character(s): Toby Peters, Detective—Private; Charlie Chaplin, Historical Figure, Actor
Time period(s): 1940s (1943)
Locale(s): Los Angeles, California (Hollywood)

Summary: When Charlie Chaplin gets a late night call from a knife-wielding stranger who threatens to kill him unless he stops production on his newest project, a movie about a man who marries and then kills older women for their money, he turns to Hollywood private eye Toby Peters for help. Chaplin, who himself has just married a much younger woman (Oona O'Neill) and has been accused of being a Communist because of his pro-Russian leanings, is the first to admit he has many enemies in Hollywood, but Peters narrows the list by concentrating on the woman Chaplin's would-be attacker warned him off of: Fiona Sinclair, owner of a boardinghouse whose elderly women residents have been dying off left and right. The author lovingly recreates the period atmosphere and, as in all books in this series, offers the reader an affectionate, idealized portrait of the celebrities who figure in the plot. He is also the creator of series featuring Chicago cop Abe Lieberman and Russian police inspector Porfiry Rostnikov.

Where it's reviewed:
Booklist, May 1, 2001, page 1635
Publishers Weekly, June 11, 2001, page 64

Other books by the same author:
A Fatal Glass of Beer, 1997
Dancing in the Dark, 1996
Tomorrow Is Another Day, 1995
The Devil Met a Lady, 1993
The Melting Clock, 1991

Other books you might like:
George Baxt, *The Mae West Murder Case*, 1993
Andrew Bergman, *Hollywood and LeVine*, 1975
Max Allan Collins, *Angel in Black*, 2001
Terence Faherty, *The Scott Elliott Series*, 1996-
Ron Goulart, *The Groucho Marx Series*, 1998-

92

LARRY KARP

The Midnight Special

(Aurora, Colorado: Write Way, 2001)

Story type: Amateur Detective
Series: Thomas Purdue. Book 3
Subject(s): Collectors and Collecting; Antiques; Toys
Major character(s): Thomas Purdue, Doctor (neurologist), Collector (antique music boxes)

Time period(s): 2000s
Locale(s): New York, New York

Summary: Thomas, who collects and restores antique music boxes, gets a call from an old friend of his, Edna Reynolds, who taught him most of the restoration techniques he uses. They met when he was a beginning collector and she a long-time collector of automata, elaborate mechanical toys and dolls that move in complicated and delightful ways. She claims to have just murdered Marcus Wilcox, an interior designer who's been pestering her about selling some of her pieces, but there's no corpse. Thomas has other matters on his agenda, primarily checking out a rare music box one of his pickers has located for him and attending an antique show. The music box never turns up, but actual corpses do, and soon Thomas and his circle of friends, fellow collectors, and scouts have more than one murder to solve.

Where it's reviewed:
Library Journal, March 1, 2001, page 133

Other books by the same author:
Scamming the Birdman, 2000
The Music Box Murders, 1999

Other books you might like:
Michael Delving, *The Dave Cannon Series*, 1967-1979
Jonathan Gash, *The Lovejoy Series*, 1977-
Tamar Myers, *The Abigail Timberlake Series*, 1996-
Anthony Oliver, *The Lizzie Thomas/John Webber Series*, 1980-1987
Neville Steed, *The Peter Marklin Series*, 1986-

93

MICHAEL KILIAN

The Weeping Woman

(New York: Berkley, 2001)

Story type: Historical
Subject(s): Art; Authors and Writers; Literature
Major character(s): Bedford Green, Art Dealer (gallery owner); Sloane Smith, Sidekick
Time period(s): 1920s (1925)
Locale(s): New York, New York (Greenwich Village); Paris, France; Cannes, France

Summary: From the author of the Harrison Raines Civil War mysteries comes this jazz age whodunit featuring art dealer Bedford Green, who walks into his gallery one day to find his assistant, Sloane Smith, dissolved in tears over a postcard she's just received from Paris suggesting that its sender is in serious trouble. As it happens, Bedford is sailing for France within the week, and he impulsively decides to take Sloane with him. With help from such luminaries as Zelda and Scott Fitzgerald, Ernest Hemingway, Pablo Picasso, and others, they search for a missing girl in Paris and Cannes.

Other books by the same author:
A Killing at Ball's Bluff, 2001
Murder at Manassas, 2000

Other books you might like:
George Baxt, *The Dorothy Parker Murder Case*, 1984
K.K. Beck, *The Iris Cooper Series*, 1984-

Howard Engel, *Murder in Montparnasse*, 1999
Annette Meyers, *The Olivia Brown Series*, 1999-
Walter Satterthwait, *Masquerade*, 1998

94

LAURIE R. KING

Folly

(New York: Bantam, 2001)

Story type: Psychological Suspense
Subject(s): Islands; Wilderness; Mental Illness
Major character(s): Rae Newborn, Artisan (woodworker), Mentally Ill Person
Time period(s): 2000s
Locale(s): Folly Island, Washington

Summary: Rae Newborn has had more than her share of suffering, and the tragic loss of her husband and child in an automobile accident has pushed her into a deep depression. Like her great-uncle before her, she decides to heal herself with isolation and hard work, rebuilding his house on a remote island on the Puget Sound. Once ashore with her building materials and supplies, she tosses all her medications into the water, pitches her tent, and begins the laborious process of restoring the house to its former glory. Gradually she senses that she's not alone, that someone or something is watching her. What is not immediately clear is whether she is in actual danger or if her fears are grounded in her own mental illness. Her great-uncle's past also intersects with hers; he had originally built the house to rid himself of the ghosts that haunted him from his experiences during World War I. The plot is complex, perhaps too much so, and there is a murder to solve, but the book's strength is in its atmospheric setting and in Rae's moving attempts to recover her own humanity. The author also writes the Kate Martinelli and Mary Russell/Sherlock Holmes mysteries.

Where it's reviewed:
Booklist, February 15, 2001, page 1116
Mystery News, February/March, 2001, page 22
Publishers Weekly, January 15, 2001, page 55

Other books by the same author:
A Darker Place, 1999 (non-series)
O Jerusalem, 1999 (Mary Russell/Sherlock Holmes series)
The Moor, 1998 (Mary Russell/Sherlock Holmes series)
A Letter of Mary, 1997 (Mary Russell/Sherlock Holmes series)
With Child, 1996 (Kate Martinelli series)

Other books you might like:
Rosemary Aubert, *The Ellis Portal Series*, 1997-
Nevada Barr, *The Anna Pigeon Series*, 1993-
Noreen Gilpatrick, *The Piano Man*, 1991
Abigail Padgett, *Blue*, 1998
Susan Wade, *Walking Rain*, 1996

95

PETER KING

Eat, Drink, and Be Buried

(New York: St. Martin's Press, 2001)

Story type: Amateur Detective; Traditional
Series: Gourmet Detective. Book 6
Subject(s): Food; Cooks and Cookery; Middle Ages
Major character(s): Gourmet Detective, Consultant (food expert), Detective—Amateur
Time period(s): 2000s
Locale(s): London, England

Summary: The Gourmet Detective is called upon by a group of eccentric British aristocrats to create a tasty, but reasonably authentic menu for their annual "Medieval Days" banquet being held at Harlington Castle. No sooner does he arrive than he witnesses what appears to be the murder of a jouster, who actually turns out to have been poisoned rather than beheaded, as it first appeared. While he researches 16th century cuisine, the Gourmet Detective also investigates the crime, finding a surfeit of suspects among his pedigreed clients.

Where it's reviewed:
Library Journal, May 1, 2001, page 132
Publishers Weekly, April 16, 2001, page 47

Other books by the same author:
A Healthy Place to Die, 2000
Death al Dente, 1999
Dying on the Vine, 1998
Spiced to Death, 1997
The Gourmet Detective, 1994

Other books you might like:
Michael Bond, *The Monsieur Pamplemousse Series*, 1983-
Diane Mott Davidson, *Sticks & Scones*, 2001
Kathy Lynn Emerson, *Face Down in the Marrow-Bone Pie*, 1997
Janet Laurence, *A Deep Coffyne*, 1989
Phyllis Richman, *The Chas Wheatley Series*, 1997-

96

KATE KINGSBURY (Pseudonym of Doreen Roberts)

A Bicycle Built for Murder

(New York: Berkley, 2001)

Story type: Historical; Amateur Detective
Subject(s): World War II; Small Town Life; Social Classes
Major character(s): Lady Elizabeth Hartleigh Compton, Widow(er), Noblewoman
Time period(s): 1940s (1942)
Locale(s): Sitting Marsh, England

Summary: Widowed and left impoverished by her gambler husband, Lady Elizabeth still occupies the imposing manor house that is her ancestral home, although there is barely enough money coming in from the rents her tenants pay her to keep the enormous 17th century Jacobean mansion running. Still, she tries to look after her tenants, so when one of them reports that her teenage daughter has gone missing, Lady Elizabeth does her best to find the girl and then, when her

body is discovered on a nearby beach, to apprehend the murderer, since the local constabulary has mostly gone to war. She is also alarmed when the War Office informs her that American soldiers are soon to be quartered at her family home. This is the first in a projected new series by an author, who recently completed a 12-part series set in Edwardian England at a coastal resort known as the Pennyfoot Hotel.

Other books by the same author:
Maid to Murder, 1999
Death with Reservations, 1998
Dying Room Only, 1998
Ring for Tomb Service, 1997
Chivalry Is Dead, 1996

Other books you might like:
Robert Barnard, *Out of the Blackout*, 1984
Joanna Cannan, *Death at the Dog*, 1941 reprinted 2000
Hamilton Crane, *Miss Seeton's Finest Hour*, 1999
Sheila Pim, *Common or Garden Crime*, 1945 reprinted 2001
Elliott Roosevelt, *Murder at the Palace*, 1987

97

CHARLES KNIEF

Silversword

(New York: St. Martin's Press, 2001)

Story type: Private Detective
Series: John Caine. Book 4
Subject(s): Islands; Volcanoes; History
Major character(s): John Caine, Detective—Private
Time period(s): 2000s
Locale(s): Honolulu, Hawaii; San Francisco, California

Summary: After being wounded in a shoot-out in San Francisco, Caine has returned to Hawaii and is recuperating in a luxurious beachfront hotel in Honolulu, where he misses being on his sailboat and finds his enforced inactivity is making the time go by very slowly. So when Donna Wong, a young doctoral candidate in archaeology and anthropology, asks him to help her save some priceless artifacts from a Spanish ship sunk off the coast of one of the islands, he declares himself fit enough to do so. Meanwhile, he's wanted back in San Francisco, when one of the bystanders at the shoot-out dies and the police think he's to blame.

Where it's reviewed:
Booklist, May 1, 2001, page 1635
Publishers Weekly, May 7, 2001, page 228

Other books by the same author:
Emerald Flash, 1999
Sand Dollar, 1997
Diamond Head, 1996

Other books you might like:
Richard Barre, *The Wil Hardesty Series*, 1995-
James W. Hall, *The Thorn Series*, 1987-
John D. MacDonald, *The Travis McGee Series*, 1964-1985
Robert B. Parker, *The Spenser Series*, 1973-
Randy Wayne White, *The Doc Ford Series*, 1990-

98

WILLIAM KENT KRUEGER

Purgatory Ridge

(New York: Pocket, 2001)

Story type: Private Detective
Series: Cork O'Connor. Book 3
Subject(s): Native Americans; Environmental Problems; Small Town Life
Major character(s): Cork O'Connor, Detective—Private, Indian (part Anishinaabe/Ojibway)
Time period(s): 2000s
Locale(s): Aurora, Minnesota

Summary: The lumber mill owned by Karl Lindstrom, who's totally insensitive to its environmental impact, is directly adjacent to a tract of forest that's a sacred site to the local Anishinaabe tribe and which Lindstrom has scheduled for logging operations. An explosion one night at the mill, which kills one of the watchmen, an Ojibway elder, is immediately blamed on the tribe, and Cork is called in to help with the investigation. A definite conflict of interest ensues, since Cork is part Anishinaabe himself and his wife, Jo, is the tribe's lawyer, representing them in their lawsuit against the logging industry. Then a terrorist calling himself the Eco-Warrior claims credit for the bombing and Cork, a former Chicago detective and the ex-sheriff of Aurora, tries to determine the man's identity.

Where it's reviewed:
Booklist, December 15, 2000, page 792
Deadly Pleasures, Winter 2001, pages 31, 47
Publishers Weekly, January 8, 2001, page 45

Other books by the same author:
Boundary Waters, 1999
Iron Lake, 1998

Other books you might like:
Steve Hamilton, *Winter of the Wolf Moon*, 2000
Stan Jones, *White Sky, Black Ice*, 1999
Michael McGarrity, *The Kevin Kerney Series*, 1996-
Kirk Mitchell, *Cry Dance*, 1999
Mark T. Sullivan, *The Purification Ceremony*, 1997

99

MICHAEL KURLAND

The Great Game

(New York: St. Martin's Press, 2001)

Story type: Historical
Series: Professor Moriarty. Book 2
Subject(s): Conspiracies; Victorian Period; Espionage
Major character(s): Professor James Moriarty, Scientist, Criminal; Sherlock Holmes, Detective—Private
Time period(s): 1890s (1891)
Locale(s): London, England; Vienna, Austria

Summary: Known by his nemesis, Sherlock Holmes, as the "Napoleon of Crime," Professor Moriarty conducts an investigation of his own after a stranger, who comes calling at his door, is shot dead with a crossbow bolt and expires before he can explain his urgent mission to the brilliant scientist. Moriarty discovers there is a vast worldwide conspiracy seeking to overthrow the crowned heads of Europe by means of well-chosen assassinations. Enlisting the aid of his network of spies, and even calling upon Holmes to lend a hand, Moriarty sets out to save the world from a conspiracy more sinister than any even he could devise.

Other books by the same author:
The Girls in the High-Heeled Shoes, 1998
Too Soon Dead, 1997
The Infernal Device, 1979 (Professor Moriarty series)
A Plague of Spies, 1969

Other books you might like:
Quinn Fawcett, *The Scottish Ploy*, 2000
John Gardner, *The Professor Moriarty Series*, 1974-
Laurie R. King, *The Mary Russell/Sherlock Holmes Series*, 1994-
Gerard Williams, *Dr. Mortimer and the Barking Man Mystery*, 2001
Wayne Worcester, *The Jewel of Covent Garden*, 2000

100

CHRISTOPHER LANE

Silent as the Hunter

(New York: Avon, 2001)

Story type: Police Procedural
Series: Raymond Attla. Book 4
Subject(s): Eskimos; Animals/Whales; Missing Persons
Major character(s): Raymond Attla, Police Officer
Time period(s): 2000s
Locale(s): Barrow, Alaska

Summary: During the annual whale hunting festival in Barrow, it's the custom for masked revelers to go from door to door throughout the village. When one of the village elders, 97-year-old Aana Clearwater, opens her door to greet her visitors, she's brutally attacked and then disappears without a trace. Ray Attla, an Inupiat Eskimo policeman, is called upon to investigate what appears to be an abduction and perhaps murder, and to find out what happened before the two-day festival draws to a close. The author has also written inspirational and religious fiction.

Other books by the same author:
A Shroud of Midnight Sun, 2000
Season of Death, 1999
Elements of a Kill, 1998

Other books you might like:
Sue Henry, *The Alex Jensen Series*, 1991-
Stan Jones, *White Sky, Black Ice*, 1999
Megan Mallory Rust, *The Taylor Morgan Series*, 1998-
Marcia Simpson, *Crow in Stolen Colors*, 2000
Dana Stabenow, *The Liam Campbell Series*, 1998-

101

JOHN LANTIGUA

The Ultimate Havana
(New York: Signet, 2001)

Story type: Private Detective
Series: Willie Cuesta. Book 2
Subject(s): Cuban Americans; Missing Persons; Crime and Criminals
Major character(s): Willie Cuesta, Detective—Private
Time period(s): 2000s
Locale(s): Miami, Florida (Little Havana); Santiago, Dominican Republic; Havana, Cuba

Summary: Willie is hired to find Carlos Espada, the missing son of a well-known cigar manufacturer, an assignment that takes him to the Dominican Republic, where he gets caught between two rival tobacco companies. He learns that Carlos may be involved with a counterfeit cigar ring that has been manufacturing knockoffs of Ambassadors, very expensive Cuban cigars. As more and more bad guys start gunning for Willie, he realizes he's mixed up in something very dangerous and he'd better find Carlos before both of them get killed.

Other books by the same author:
Player's Vendetta, 1999 (Willie Cuesta series)
Twister, 1992
Burn Season, 1989
Heat Lightning, 1987

Other books you might like:
Carolina Garcia-Aguilera, *Havana Heat*, 2000
Robert Greer, *Limited Time*, 2000
Elmore Leonard, *Cuba Libre*, 1998
Lia Matera, *Havana Twist*, 1998
Randy Wayne White, *North of Havana*, 1997

102

DENNIS LEHANE

Mystic River
(New York: Morrow, 2001)

Story type: Psychological Suspense
Subject(s): Secrets; City Life; Violence
Major character(s): Sean Devine, Police Officer; Jimmy Marcus, Convict (ex-con), Parent (of murdered girl); Dave Boyle, Abuse Victim, Crime Suspect
Time period(s): 1970s (1975); 2000s (2000)
Locale(s): Boston, Massachusetts (East Buckingham)

Summary: When the story opens, three boys—Sean, Jimmy, and Dave—are horsing around on the streets of their working class neighborhood of East Buckingham when a brown Plymouth cruises up and the two plainclothes cops in the car stop and start talking to the boys. One of them, Dave, gets in the car with them when they explain they're taking him to the station house. But the men aren't cops, and when Dave (always the awkward one of the three) is returned four days later, he won't talk about what happened. It's widely (and correctly) assumed that he was molested by sexual predators, and the event changes the lives of all three boys forever. Years later,

they've drifted apart but still live in the old neighborhood. Sean has become a cop, Jimmy (the wild one) has a prison record but has turned his life around, and Dave, who peaked as a high school baseball star, is still struggling with life. When Jimmy's daughter is murdered on the eve of her wedding, Sean is the investigating officer on the case, and Dave, who came home covered with blood on the night of the murder, is the chief suspect. It's a grim, powerful book by a writer whose previous works have all featured Boston private eyes Patrick Kenzie and Angela Gennaro.

Where it's reviewed:
Booklist, November 15, 2000, page 588
Deadly Pleasures, Winter 2001, page 31
Entertainment Weekly, February 16, 2001, page 90
Library Journal, December 2000, page 189
New York Times Book Review, February 18, 2001, page 25

Other books by the same author:
Prayers for Rain, 1999
Gone, Baby, Gone, 1998
Sacred, 1997
Darkness, Take My Hand, 1996
A Drink Before the War, 1994

Other books you might like:
James Lee Burke, *The Dave Robicheaux Series*, 1987-
Michael Connelly, *The Harry Bosch Series*, 1992-
James Crumley, *The Wrong Case*, 1975
Jonathan Lethem, *Motherless Brooklyn*, 2000
George P. Pelecanos, *Right as Rain*, 2001

103

JOHN LESCROART

The Hearing
(New York: Dutton, 2001)

Story type: Legal
Series: Dismas Hardy/Abe Glitsky. Book 9
Subject(s): Trials; Fathers and Daughters; Friendship
Major character(s): Dismas Hardy, Lawyer (defense attorney); Abe Glitsky, Detective—Homicide
Time period(s): 2000s
Locale(s): San Francisco, California

Summary: When a young woman lawyer is murdered in a dark alley one night, the news cuts Abe Glitsky to the quick; he alone knows the victim to be his daughter. He orders his colleagues to come down hard on the obvious suspect, a homeless heroin addict named Cole Burgess who is found near the body, with her jewelry on his person and a gun in his hand. Next, Dis is asked to represent the man, and he finds himself torn between his loyalty to his long-time friend, Abe, and his growing suspicion that Burgess' confession has been coerced by the police. He's also concerned about the trial being used as political currency by an ambitious D.A., who is more interested in furthering her career than in seeking justice. Gradually Glitsky, too, begins to realize the case isn't as simple as it seems and joins Hardy's team, trying to secure a fair hearing for Burgess. At the same time, Hardy and his wife are trying to deal with the fears overwhelming their young daughter, Rebecca.

Where it's reviewed:
Library Journal, January 1, 2001, page 155
Publishers Weekly, March 12, 2001, page 60

Other books by the same author:
Nothing but the Truth, 2000
The Mercy Rule, 1998
Guilt, 1997
A Certain Justice, 1995
The 13th Juror, 1994

Other books you might like:
Stephen Greenleaf, *The John Marshall Tanner Series*, 1979-
Steve Martini, *The Paul Madriani Series*, 1992-
Ed McBain, *The Matthew Hope Series*, 1977-
Grif Stockley, *The Gideon Page Series*, 1992-
William Tapply, *The Brady Coyne Series*, 1984-

104

ROY LEWIS

Dead Secret

(New York: Carroll & Graf, 2001)

Story type: Traditional; Amateur Detective
Series: Arnold Landon. Book 13
Subject(s): Anthropology; Archaeology; Ecology
Major character(s): Arnold Landon, Civil Servant, Detective—Amateur
Time period(s): 2000s
Locale(s): Northumberland, England

Summary: A woodland in rural Northumberland, home of a peat bog where the perfectly preserved body of an ancient man has been found, is being earmarked for a highway bypass, and Arnold Landon of the Department of Museums and Antiquities is called out to the site when a bitter battle develops between developers, politicians, preservationists, the landowner, and archaeologists. Accompanying Landon is his colleague, Portia Tyrrel, but before they can properly determine the archaeological significance of the site, one of the protesters is murdered. The author also writes a series about solicitor Eric Ward.

Other books by the same author:
The Shape Shifter, 1998
Suddenly as a Shadow, 1997
A Short-Lived Ghost, 1995
The Cross Bearer, 1994
Bloodeagle, 1993

Other books you might like:
Rhys Bowen, *Evan Help Us*, 1998
Aaron Elkins, *The Gideon Oliver Series*, 1982-
Kate Ellis, *The Merchant's House*, 1999
Peter Marks, *Skullduggery*, 1987
John Trench, *Dishonoured Bones*, 1955

105

GILLIAN LINSCOTT

The Perfect Daughter

(New York: St. Martin's Press, 2001)

Story type: Historical; Amateur Detective
Series: Nell Bray. Book 9
Subject(s): Politics; Women's Rights; Espionage
Major character(s): Nell Bray, Suffragette, Detective—Amateur
Time period(s): 1910s (1914)
Locale(s): London, England; Teighmouth, England

Summary: The ''perfect daughter'' of the title is Verona North, a 19-year-old whom her parents thought shared their conventional values but who, in private conversations with her older cousin, Nell, was intensely interested in the suffragist movement and other left-wing political beliefs. When she is found hanged to death in her family's boathouse, an apparent suicide, pregnant, and with a heavy dose of morphine in her blood, they blame Nell for their daughter's depraved lifestyle, which they are convinced led to her death. When Nell, plagued with guilt, investigates, she discovers that Verona not only lived with a group of bohemian anarchists, but may truly have been leading a double life and was, in fact, a spy for the secret service.

Where it's reviewed:
Publishers Weekly, March 26, 2001, page 66

Other books by the same author:
Absent Friends, 1999
Dance on Blood, 1998
Dead Man's Sweetheart, 1996
Crown Witness, 1995
Widow's Peak, 1994

Other books you might like:
Clare Curzon, *Guilty Knowledge*, 2000
Michael Gilbert, *Ring of Terror*, 1995
Robert Goddard, *Past Caring*, 1986
Ellen Hawkes, *Shadow of the Moth*, 1983
Laurie R. King, *The Beekeeper's Apprentice*, 1994

106

RANDYE LORDON

East of Niece

(New York: St. Martin's Press, 2001)

Story type: Private Detective
Series: Sydney Sloane. Book 6
Subject(s): Vacations; Automobile Accidents; Homosexuality/Lesbianism
Major character(s): Sydney Sloane, Detective—Private, Lesbian
Time period(s): 2000s
Locale(s): Menton, France (Provence)

Summary: What was meant to be a lazy, relaxing holiday in Provence for Sydney and her lover, Leslie, turns into just another murder investigation for the New York private eye. Her niece, Vickie, the object of the visit, has secretly married

her live-in boyfriend, Gavin, an event followed shortly by the death of Gavin's parents in a car accident. Gavin is quickly moved up to prime suspect status by the local gendarmes, and he disappears. In order to clear him of the crime, Sydney must find him, as well as the real murderer. The sights, sounds and smells of Provence and the Riviera coast are vividly captured during the course of the investigation.

Where it's reviewed:
Booklist, May 1, 2001, page 1635
Publishers Weekly, April 2, 2001, page 42

Other books by the same author:
Mother May I, 1998
Say Uncle, 1998
Father Forgive Me, 1997
Sister's Keeper, 1994
Brotherly Love, 1993

Other books you might like:
Ellen Hart, *The Jane Lawless Series*, 1988-
Elizabeth Pincus, *The Nell Fury Series*, 1992-
J.M. Redmann, *The Micky Knight Series*, 1990-
Sandra Scoppettone, *The Lauren Laurano Series*, 1991-
Mary Wings, *The Emma Victor Series*, 1986-

107

PETER LOVESEY

The Reaper

(New York: Soho, 2001)

Story type: Psychological Suspense
Subject(s): Clergy; Anglicans; Small Town Life
Major character(s): Otis Joy, Religious (clergyman), Imposter
Time period(s): 2000s
Locale(s): Foxford, England (Wiltshire)

Summary: Otis Joy, the handsome young rector of St. Bartholomew's, seems born for the clergy; he's dedicated, conscientious, hard-working (except for his Tuesdays off, invariably spent away from the village), and always able to come up with relevant and thought-provoking sermons and just the right words to comfort or inspire his parishioners. He is, in fact, an imposter and a habitual murderer, who methodically exterminates anyone who threatens to expose or obstruct him and then cleverly arranges to make the deaths appear quite accidental. The book opens as he does away with the bishop who had him removed from his last parish for fiddling the books and has now demanded his resignation from the clergy. Otis truly has a calling as a clergyman and is determined never to give up the life; he passionately loves his work and is popular with his congregation, particularly the ladies, and particularly one lonely housewife, neglected by her oafish husband, who becomes quite infatuated with Otis and is prepared to go to great lengths to make herself available to him. The narrative is at once droll and chilling and the conclusion both surprising and inevitable. Lovesey, the author of the superb Peter Diamond police procedurals and numerous other series and non-series mysteries, continues to demonstrate how truly original and versatile a writer he is.

Where it's reviewed:
Deadly Pleasures, Winter 2001, page 61

New York Times Book Review, April 1, 2001, page 17
Publishers Weekly, March 12, 2001, page 65

Other books by the same author:
The Vault, 2000
Upon a Dark Night, 1998
Bloodhounds, 1996
The Summons, 1995
Diamond Solitaire, 1992

Other books you might like:
Robert Barnard, *Unholy Dying*, 2001
Simon Brett, *Dead Romantic*, 1986
Richard Hull, *The Murder of My Aunt*, 1934
Francis Iles, *Malice Aforethought*, 1931
Anthony Rolls, *Clerical Error*, 1932

108

IRENE MARCUSE

Guilty Mind

(New York: Walker, 2001)

Story type: Amateur Detective; Traditional
Series: Anita Servi. Book 2
Subject(s): Children; Marriage; African Americans
Major character(s): Anita Servi, Social Worker, Detective—
    Amateur
Time period(s): 2000s
Locale(s): New York, New York

Summary: Anita adores her Middle Eastern husband, Benno, and their seven-year-old black almost-adopted daughter, Clea, and they've made a happy home for themselves. Then one night Ellen, an African American graduate student who has been caring for Clea, is murdered after Benno walks her home. The murder weapon is a screwdriver with Benno's fingerprints on it, and the police immediately regard him as a suspect. Determined to clear her husband and certain that he is innocent, Anita still wonders why he was so long coming home that night, and why he is gradually becoming withdrawn and distant. Anita also fears that the investigation will hamper the completion of the adoption process and they might lose Clea, especially when Benno is taken to jail. When she begins asking around, she discovers that there are actually a number of people who might have had reason to kill Ellen, and if she wants to save her family, it's up to her to find the murderer.

Where it's reviewed:
Booklist, May 1, 2001, page 1636
Library Journal, May 15, 2001, page 167
Publishers Weekly, April 30, 2001, page 55

Other books by the same author:
The Death of an Amiable Child, 2000

Other books you might like:
Camilla Crespi, *The Simona Griffo Series*, 1991-
Joanne Pence, *The Angelina Amalfi Series*, 1993-
Marissa Piesman, *The Nina Fischman Series*, 1989-
Carolyn Wheat, *The Cass Jameson Series*, 1983-
Barbara Jaye Williams, *The Brenda Midnight Series*, 1997-

109

MARGARET MARON

Uncommon Clay

(New York: Mysterious, 2001)

Story type: Traditional
Series: Deborah Knott. Book 8
Subject(s): American South; Crafts; Rural Life
Major character(s): Deborah Knott, Judge
Time period(s): 2000s
Locale(s): Colleton County, North Carolina; Randolph County, North Carolina

Summary: When two members of a respected family of potters enter into a bitter divorce after nearly 25 years of marriage, Deborah is called upon to arbitrate the division of their jointly held property, a job that is made no easier when she learns that another family member had committed suicide two years earlier. Then still another is found brutally murdered. One way or another, it looks as if the Nordan family is going to be put out of the pottery business for good, and Deborah intends to find out the truth behind the events. A strong sense of place and of family pervades the story, as is usual in this award-winning series. The author also writes a series about New York police officer Sigrid Harald.

Where it's reviewed:
Booklist, May 1, 2001, page 1605
Library Journal, May 1, 2001, page 132
New York Times Book Review, June 10, 2001, page 26
Publishers Weekly, April 9, 2001, page 54

Other books by the same author:
Storm Track, 2000
Home Fires, 1998
Killer Market, 1997
Up Jumps the Devil, 1996
Shooting at Loons, 1994

Other books you might like:
Anne Underwood Grant, *The Sydney Teague Series*, 1998-
Joan Hess, *The Claire Malloy Series*, 1986-
Sharyn McCrumb, *The Ballad Series*, 1990-
Kathy Hogan Trocheck, *The Callahan Garrity Series*, 1992-
Kate Wilhelm, *The Barbara Holloway Series*, 1991-

110

CHARLES MATHES

The Girl in the Face of the Clock

(New York: St. Martin's Press, 2001)

Story type: Amateur Detective; Traditional
Series: Girl. Book 4
Subject(s): Collectors and Collecting; Fathers and Daughters; Antiques
Major character(s): Jane Sailor, Teacher (theatrical fight choreographer)
Time period(s): 2000s
Locale(s): Cincinnati, Ohio; New York, New York; London, England

Summary: Although not strictly a series, the author's books all share common themes: a plucky heroine, often with an unusual occupation, whose life is altered by secrets from her or her family's past; a quest to uncover them; a cast of oddball supporting characters; and a good deal of travel. This one is no exception, with Jane being called away from her duties instructing actors on how to stage convincing fight scenes by the news that her bedridden father, a painter whose career has taken off since he lapsed into a coma, has suddenly started talking. From his limited speech, she surmises the fall that incapacitated him was no accident and a man named Perry was somehow connected with it. She tracks down Peregrine Mannerback, an eccentric and unpredictable millionaire and clock collector, who promptly offers her a job with his organization, which she takes in order to learn more about the man. There is also a hideous ceramic clock with no hands that is key to the plot, and Jane travels to its manufacturer, now located in London, to find how it ties in. Like its predecessors, it's a curious and often entertaining mix of fairy tale and realism, best enjoyed with a complete suspension of disbelief.

Where it's reviewed:
Booklist, February 15, 2001, page 1119
Library Journal, March 1, 2001, page 134
Publishers Weekly, March 19, 2001, page 79

Other books by the same author:
The Girl at the End of the Line, 1999
The Girl Who Remembered Snow, 1996
The Girl with the Phony Name, 1992

Other books you might like:
Nancy Atherton, *Aunt Dimity's Death*, 1992
M.C. Beaton, *The Skeleton in the Closet*, 2001
April Henry, *Circles of Confusion*, 1999
Larry Karp, *The Music Box Murders*, 1999
Margot Wadley, *The Gripping Beast*, 2001

111

LISE MCCLENDON

Blue Wolf

(New York: Walker, 2001)

Story type: Amateur Detective
Series: Alix Thorssen. Book 4
Subject(s): Animals/Wolves; Ecology; American West
Major character(s): Alix Thorssen, Art Dealer (gallery owner), Detective—Amateur
Time period(s): 2000s
Locale(s): Jackson Hole, Wyoming

Summary: The small resort town of Jackson Hole is divided over the issue of reintroducing wolves into Yellowstone. The ranchers fear for their livestock, while the conservationists feel strongly that this endangered species deserves protection. When a local rancher kills a wolf and claims self-defense, the controversy escalates. Alix is caught in the middle, when a painting of a wolf donated by a local artist, Queen Jones, to an auction benefiting wildlife is questioned by the committee. Then Queen asks Alix to investigate the 25-year-old death of a local boy. The author also has a new series about World War II Kansas City sleuth Dorie Lennox.

Other books by the same author:
Nordic Nights, 1999
Painted Truth, 1995
The Bluejay Shaman, 1994

Other books you might like:
Nevada Barr, *Blood Lure*, 2001
Peter Bowen, *Wolf, No Wolf*, 1996
Barbara Moore, *The Wolf Whispered Death*, 1986
Elizabeth Quinn, *A Wolf in Death's Clothing*, 1995
Judith Van Gieson, *The Wolf Path*, 1992

112

LISE MCCLENDON

One O'Clock Jump
(New York: St. Martin's Press, 2001)

Story type: Historical; Private Detective
Series: Dorie Lennox. Book 1
Subject(s): World War II; Politics; Organized Crime
Major character(s): Dorie Lennox, Detective—Private; Amos
   Haddam, Detective—Private, Veteran (World War I)
Time period(s): 1930s (1939)
Locale(s): Kansas City, Missouri

Summary: There's talk of war in the air as Dorie, a
switchblade-wielding private detective with a bad knee, a
past, and an attitude, takes over the investigation her boss,
Amos Haddam, owner of Sugar Moon Investigations, was
working on when he was hospitalized. Dorie's tough and
stubborn, but not qualified to hold down a real job; that's why
she's working for Amos and waiting outside of a night club
for Iris Jackson, the bargirl a client has hired her to tail, to get
off her shift. When Dorie witnesses Iris jumping off a bridge
into the Missouri River, the case takes another turn. The city
is in the grip of the Prendergast political machine which may
itself be linked with organized crime, and somehow Iris and
her suicide may both be tied in with the mob. There's lots of
World War II nostalgia worked in: swing music, big bands,
dance marathons, FDR's fireside chats, and the like. It's the
first in a projected new series by the author of the contemporary Wyoming-based Alix Thorssen series.

Where it's reviewed:
Booklist, January 1, 2001, page 925
Library Journal, February 1, 2001, page 127
Mystery News, February/March 2001, page 19
New York Times Book Review, March 18, 2001, page 18
Publishers Weekly, February 12, 2001, page 187

Other books by the same author:
Nordic Nights, 1999
Painted Truth, 1995
The Bluejay Shaman, 1994

Other books you might like:
Robert Clark, *Mr. White's Confession*, 1998
Max Allan Collins, *The Million Dollar Wound*, 1986
John Dunning, *Two O'Clock, Eastern Wartime*, 2001
M.T. Jefferson, *In the Mood for Murder*, 2000
Cathie John, *Little Mexico*, 2001

113

SHARYN MCCRUMB

The Songcatcher
(New York: Dutton, 2001)

Story type: Psychological Suspense
Series: Ballad. Book 6
Subject(s): Music and Musicians; History; Appalachia
Major character(s): Lark McCourry, Musician (folksinger)
Time period(s): 2000s; 18th century
Locale(s): Wake County, Tennessee; North Carolina

Summary: Even less of a mystery than earlier books in this
exceptional series, *The Songcatcher* traces the history of a
ballad through seven generations of a Scottish family transplanted to America in the 18th century, eventually ending up
in rural Appalachia. Folksinger Lark McCourry remembers
hearing the song as a child and is trying to recapture it to
record on her next album. She is also trying to make her way
back to her eastern Tennessee home where her estranged
father is dying, but she's trapped when her small plane
crashes in the mountains. Many characters from earlier
books—Sheriff Spencer Arrowood, wisewoman Nora
Bonesteel, etc.—make appearances here, but it's really the
story of a song and a culture making the transition from
Europe to America, using bits of McCrumb's own family
history as inspiration. The author also writes two more conventional mystery series featuring forensic anthropologist
Elizabeth MacPherson and scientist James Owen Mega.

Where it's reviewed:
Booklist, May 15, 2001, page 1733
Publishers Weekly, May 14, 2001, page 51

Other books by the same author:
The Ballad of Frankie Silver, 1998
The Rosewood Casket, 1996
She Walks These Hills, 1994
The Hangman's Beautiful Daughter, 1992
If Ever I Return, Pretty Peggy-O, 1990

Other books you might like:
Deborah Adams, *The Jesus Creek Series*, 1992-
Sallie Bissell, *In the Forest of Harm*, 2001
G.D. Gearino, *Counting Coup*, 1997
Margaret Maron, *The Deborah Knott Series*, 1992-
Michael C. White, *A Dream of Wolves*, 2001

114

MICHAEL MCGARRITY

Under the Color of Law
(New York: Simon & Schuster, 2001)

Story type: Police Procedural; Action/Adventure
Series: Kevin Kerney. Book 6
Subject(s): Terrorism; American West; Drugs
Major character(s): Kevin Kerney, Police Officer (chief)
Time period(s): 2000s
Locale(s): Santa Fe, New Mexico

Summary: Kerney, once again firmly entrenched in police
work, accepts the position of Santa Fe police chief, and no

sooner has he settled in then he has a sensitive case to solve: the murder of the estranged wife of a U.S. ambassador, found stabbed to death with a pair of scissors in her palatial home. The immediate suspect is a Mexican national living in an RV on the property and seen fleeing from the crime scene as the police arrive. Before Kerney can initiate his investigation, the FBI intervenes, shutting him and his officers out of the case. Dissatisfied with the conclusions the FBI reaches, Kerney starts a low-profile investigation of his own and comes up with evidence that links the government with a shady dot.com company. As he probes further, he himself becomes the target of a killer. Meanwhile, Kerney's marriage to strong-willed army officer Sara Brannon takes a new turn when they discover they are soon to become parents.

Other books by the same author:
The Judas Judge, 2000
Hermit's Peak, 1999
Serpent Gate, 1998
Mexican Hat, 1997
Tularosa, 1996

Other books you might like:
Steve Hamilton, *The Alex McKnight Series*, 1998-
Tony Hillerman, *The Fly on the Wall*, 1971
William Kent Krueger, *The Cork O'Connor Series*, 1998-
Walter Satterthwait, *The Joshua Croft Series*, 1989-
Judith Van Gieson, *The Neil Hamel Series*, 1988-

115

JILL MCGOWN

Scene of Crime
(New York: Ballantine, 2001)

Story type: Police Procedural
Series: Inspector Lloyd/Inspector Judy Hill. Book 11
Subject(s): Pregnancy; Christmas; Theater
Major character(s): Lloyd, Police Officer (detective chief inspector); Judy Hill, Police Officer (inspector)
Time period(s): 2000s
Locale(s): Stansfield, England

Summary: Inspectors Lloyd and Hill are partners romantically, as well as professionally, and although they have yet to get married, Judy is pregnant and trying to interest Lloyd, who's some years her senior, in attending childbirth classes. She's also involved in a Christmas production of *Cinderella* being performed by a local theater group. Then Estelle Bignall, wife of the doctor who wrote the play, is gagged and suffocated during what appears to be a break-in burglary of her home. Lloyd and Hill think the murder may not be this simple, but the messy crime scene and the plethora of possible suspects make their investigation difficult.

Where it's reviewed:
Booklist, December 15, 2000, page 792
Publishers Weekly, January 22, 2001, page 305

Other books by the same author:
Plots and Errors, 1999
Picture of Innocence, 1998
Verdict Unsafe, 1996
A Shred of Evidence, 1995

Murder Now and Then, 1993

Other books you might like:
Deborah Crombie, *The Duncan Kincaid/Gemma James Series*, 1993-
Caroline Graham, *Barnaby Series Inspector*, 1987-
Ann Granger, *The Connor O'Neil/Fran Wilson Series*, 1994-
Patricia Hall, *The Laura Ackroyd/Michael Thackeray Series*, 1993-
Janet Neel, *The John McLeish/Francesca Wilson Series*, 1988-

116

RALPH MCINERNY

Triple Pursuit
(New York: St. Martin's Press, 2001)

Story type: Amateur Detective; Traditional
Series: Father Dowling. Book 20
Subject(s): Clergy; Small Town Life; Aging
Major character(s): Roger Dowling, Religious (parish priest), Detective—Amateur; Marie Murkin, Housekeeper; Phil Keegan, Police Officer (captain)
Time period(s): 2000s
Locale(s): Fox River, Illinois (USA)

Summary: The kindly priest and his usual sidekicks—his longtime friend, police captain Phil Keegan; his loyal housekeeper, Marie Murkin; and assorted other townspeople—are all on hand to solve a trio of seemingly unrelated murders, beginning with the apparently accidental death of a young woman, who is only an occasional churchgoer. At the same time, there is unrest at the local senior center, established in the building that formerly housed St. Hilary's, when two elderly widowers clash over a woman who has attracted many admirers. The author also writes two other series, one about lawyer Andrew Broom, the other set at the University of Notre Dame.

Where it's reviewed:
Publishers Weekly, February 26, 2001, page 61

Other books by the same author:
Grave Undertakings, 2000
The Tears of Things, 1996
A Cardinal Offense, 1994
Seed of Doubt, 1993
Desert Sinner, 1992

Other books you might like:
G.K. Chesterton, *The Father Brown Series*, 1911-1935
Margaret Coel, *The Father John O'Malley/Vicky Holden Series*, 1995-
Andrew M. Greeley, *The Blackie Ryan Series*, 1985-
William X. Kienzle, *The Father Koestler Series*, 1979-
Brad Reynolds, *The Father Mark Townsend Series*, 1996-

117

G.A. MCKEVETT (Pseudonym of Sonja Massie)

Sour Grapes

(New York: Kensington, 2001)

Story type: Private Detective; Traditional
Series: Savannah Reid. Book 6
Subject(s): Beauty Contests; Sisters; Eating Disorders
Major character(s): Savannah Reid, Detective—Private, Police Officer (former)
Time period(s): 2000s
Locale(s): California

Summary: Savannah is a woman who likes to eat, and has convinced herself that most of her extra pounds have landed in the right places. Born in Georgia, she favors hearty Southern cooking, but fast food or junk food is good, too. Her newest job is as a security guard at the Miss Gold Coast beauty pageant being held at the Villa Rosa Winery in the heart of California's wine country. By a coincidence, her younger sister, Atlanta, has just flown into town to compete in the contest. Savannah is shocked to see how thin her formerly voluptuous sibling is and suspects that she's suffering from an eating disorder, along with many of the obsessive women who've entered the pageant. When two of the leading contestants are murdered, she also begins to suspect that just about any of the women might have done it.

Where it's reviewed:
Publishers Weekly, December 11, 2000, page 66

Other books by the same author:
Sugar and Spite, 2000
Cooked Goose, 1998
Killer Calories, 1997
Bitter Sweets, 1996
Just Desserts, 1995

Other books you might like:
Diane Mott Davidson, *Killer Pancake*, 1995
Selma Eichler, *The Desiree Shapiro Series*, 1994-
Sharyn McCrumb, *The PMS Outlaws*, 2001
Lynne Murray, *The Josephine Fuller Series*, 1997-
Sarah Shankman, *She Walks in Beauty*, 1991

118

ANN MCMILLAN

Civil Blood

(New York: Viking, 2001)

Story type: Historical; Amateur Detective
Series: Narcissa Powers. Book 3
Subject(s): Civil War; American South; Smallpox
Major character(s): Narcissa Powers, Nurse, Detective—Amateur; Judah Daniel, Healer, Slave (freed); Brit Wallace, Journalist
Time period(s): 1860s (1862)
Locale(s): Richmond, Virginia

Summary: It's May of 1862 and Richmond, capital of the Confederacy, faces threats from both within and without: while Union troops are ready to attack, a silent killer is infiltrating the city in the form of an incipient smallpox epidemic. The disease is being spread by paper money used by war profiteers and killing innocent people, as well as soldiers, and Narcissa and Judah are kept busy nursing the ill and dying. When the disease reaches a Union camp, there are speculations that it could be germ warfare. The utter devastation smallpox caused, given the medical knowledge of the time and the often appalling sanitary conditions that prevailed, is graphically presented, but the focus of the book is still upon the terrible war that forms its background and the unlikely friendship between wealthy white widow Narcissa Powers and the black healer and herbalist Judah Daniel. They're helped in their search to isolate the source of the disease by British journalist Brit Wallace.

Where it's reviewed:
Booklist, May 1, 2001, page 1637
Publishers Weekly, April 23, 2001, page 51

Other books by the same author:
Angel Trumpet, 1999
Dead March, 1998

Other books you might like:
Barbara Hambly, *Fever Season*, 1998
Michael Kilian, *The Harrison Raines Series*, 2000-
Miriam Grace Monfredo, *Sisters of Cain*, 2000
Owen Parry, *The Abel Jones Series*, 1999-
Anne Perry, *Slaves of Obsession*, 2000

119

D.R. MEREDITH

Murder Past Due

(New York: Berkley, 2001)

Story type: Amateur Detective
Series: Megan Clark. Book 3
Subject(s): Libraries; Books and Reading
Major character(s): Megan Clark, Librarian, Anthropologist (paleoanthropologist)
Time period(s): 2000s
Locale(s): Amarillo, Texas

Summary: A paleoanthropologist by training whose professional skills are not exactly in constant demand, Megan Clark lives with her mother and works as a reference librarian in the local library to make ends meet. Her favorite part of the job is the mystery reading group, Murder by the Yard, she conducts at a local bookstore. Her latest project is a tour of famous murder sites in the area, which attracts the attention of Bruce Gorman, a millionaire whose grandson was involved in what appeared to be a murder-suicide with his wife some 20 years ago. Gorman wants the case reopened and asks Meg's group to conduct an investigation for him. Mystery readers will enjoy the frequent references to favorite books and authors in the genre.

Other books by the same author:
By Hook or By Book, 2000
Murder in Volume, 2000

Other books you might like:
Jeff Abbott, *The Jordan Poteet Series*, 1994-
Jo Dereske, *The Miss Zukas Series*, 1994-

Carolyn Hart, *The Death on Demand Series*, 1987-
Neil McGaughey, *The Stokes Moran Series*, 1994-
Barbara Burnett Smith, *The Jolie Wyatt Series*, 1994-

120
PENNY MICKELBURY

Paradise Interrupted
(New York: Simon & Schuster, 2001)

Story type: Private Detective
Series: Carole Ann Gibson. Book 4
Subject(s): Islands; African Americans; Drugs
Major character(s): Carole Ann Gibson, Detective—Private, Lawyer (former)
Time period(s): 2000s
Locale(s): Isle de Paix, Caribbean; Washington, District of Columbia

Summary: With her friend, Jake Graham, a former homicide detective, Carole Ann has opened a high-tech security consulting firm. Their newest client is the Caribbean island nation of Isle de Paix, whose newly elected president has hired GGI to help him reconstruct his country which has been devastated by generations of neglect. Their work is cut out for them, as the island has a history of drug trafficking and corruption, and before Carole Ann even arrives, its entire police force (two constables) is murdered. Despite its troubled past, the island provides a colorful setting for the mystery. A former lawyer, Carole Ann is one of a new breed of highly educated, professional African-American women sleuths.

Where it's reviewed:
Black Issues Book Review, March 2001, page 22
Booklist, December 1, 2000, page 697
Library Journal, February 1, 2001, page 128
Publishers Weekly, December 18, 2000, page 57

Other books by the same author:
The Step Between, 2000
Where to Choose, 1999
One Must Wait, 1998
Night Songs, 1995 (non-series)

Other books you might like:
Evelyn Coleman, *The Patricia Conley Series*, 1998-
Grace F. Edwards, *The Mali Anderson Series*, 1997-
Norman Kelley, *Black Heat*, 2001
Pamela Thomas-Graham, *The Nikki Chase Series*, 1998-
Valerie Wilson Wesley, *The Tamara Hayle Series*, 1994-

121
MARGARET MILES

A Mischief in the Snow
(New York: Bantam, 2001)

Story type: Historical
Series: Charlotte Willett. Book 4
Subject(s): American Colonies; Rural Life; Secrets
Major character(s): Charlotte Willett, Widow(er), Farmer; Richard Longfellow, Farmer
Time period(s): 1760s (1766)

Locale(s): Bracebridge, Massachusetts, American Colonies

Summary: While ice skating alone on a Boar Island pond, Charlotte accidentally falls through the ice and manages to make it to a nearby house occupied by two reclusive women, who allow her to dry herself before their fire. Their only regular visitor from the village is gossipy Alexander Goodwin, who hopes to eventually inherit the huge, magnificently furnished house when its elderly owner dies. He is murdered before that can happen, and Charlotte and Richard wonder if his death is in any way connected with Boar Island and the curse that is said to be upon it. The friendship between Charlotte and her neighbor, Richard, continues to deepen as they investigate the murder. The author does a fine job illuminating the commonplace details of everyday life in colonial America.

Other books by the same author:
No Rest for the Dove, 2000
Too Soon for Flowers, 1999
A Wicked Way to Burn, 1998

Other books you might like:
Robert J. Begiebing, *The Strange Death of Mistress Coffin*, 1991
Margaret Lawrence, *The Hannah Trevor Series*, 1996-
Stephen Lewis, *The Catherine Williams Series*, 1999-
Maan Meyers, *The Kingsbridge Plot*, 1993
S.S. Rafferty, *Cork of the Colonies*, 1975

122
DENISE MINA

Exile
(New York: Carroll & Graf, 2001)

Story type: Amateur Detective; Psychological Suspense
Series: Maureen O'Donnell. Book 2
Subject(s): Abuse; Alcoholism; City Life
Major character(s): Maureen O'Donnell, Social Worker, Detective—Amateur
Time period(s): 2000s
Locale(s): Glasgow, Scotland; London, England

Summary: Maureen, who's somehow survived a history of terrible poverty, abuse, alcoholism, and mental illness, is working at a battered women's shelter in Glasgow when word arrives that Ann Harris, a former shelter client, has disappeared mysteriously. Together with her boss, Maureen heads for London, where Ann was last seen, and the two women investigate, learning eventually that Ann has been murdered. Her boyfriend is the obvious suspect, but out of fairness Maureen looks elsewhere, becoming drawn to Ann's own messy past and thus able to escape her own. The urban landscape that the author portrays is bleak and desperate, but Maureen, who continues to fight her past rather than give into it, is a sympathetic and even admirable character.

Where it's reviewed:
Booklist, January 1, 2001, page 925
Library Journal, February 15, 2001, page 202
New York Times Book Review, March 18, 2001, page 18

Other books by the same author:
Garnethill, 1999

Other books you might like:
Val McDermid, *The Mermaids Singing*, 1995
Abigail Padgett, *The Bo Bradley Series*, 1993-
Ian Rankin, *The Inspector John Rebus Series*, 1987-
Barbara Seranella, *The Munch Mancini Series*, 1997-
Jenny Siler, *Easy Money*, 1999

123

KIRK MITCHELL

Ancient Ones

(New York: Bantam, 2001)

Story type: Police Procedural
Series: Parker & Turnipseed. Book 3
Subject(s): Native Americans; Anthropology; Fossils
Major character(s): Emmett Quanah Parker, Police Officer (Bureau of Indian Affairs), Indian (mixed Comanche); Anna Turnipseed, FBI Agent, Indian (part Modoc)
Time period(s): 2000s
Locale(s): Warm Springs Reservation, Oregon

Summary: When the fossilized remains of a male Caucasian, dating back 14,000 years, are found by a maverick fossil hunter in central Oregon, the event sets off a dramatic chain of events. The discovery would, of course, upset the conventional timeline for human settlement in the area, and the evidence that the human was possibly killed and eaten by a Native American causes further turmoil. The scientific community wants a chance to study the find, and the local Indians want to give the skeleton a proper burial. When a tribal representative disappears amid all the uproar, Parker and Turnipseed are called in to conduct an investigation. Their professional relationship has turned intensely personal, but Anna is unable to achieve the intimacy they both want because of her past history as a sexually abused child, and they are trying to work this out based on advice from a sex therapist.

Where it's reviewed:
Booklist, May 1, 2001, page 1638
Library Journal, April 15, 2001, page 133
Publishers Weekly, March 5, 2001, page 64

Other books by the same author:
Spirit Sickness, 2000
Cry Dance, 1999

Other books you might like:
Margaret Coel, *The Father O'Malley/Vicky Holden Series*, 1995-
James D. Doss, *The Night Visitor*, 2000
Jean Hager, *The Molly Bearpaw Series*, 1992-
Tony Hillerman, *The Joe Leaphorn/Jim Chee Series*, 1970-
Aimee Thurlo, *The Ella Clah Series*, 1995-
    David Thurlo, co-author

124

SKYE KATHLEEN MOODY

K Falls

(New York: St. Martin's Press, 2001)

Story type: Police Procedural
Series: Venus Diamond. Book 5
Subject(s): Ecology; Terrorism; Outdoor Life
Major character(s): Venus Diamond, Government Official (U.S. Fish & Wildlife agent); Louie Song, Government Official (U.S. Fish & Wildlife agent)
Time period(s): 2000s
Locale(s): Astoria, Oregon; Kettle Falls, Washington

Summary: Venus and her fellow agent and good friend Louie Song, who was presumed dead after one of a series of dam bombings along the Columbia River, have gone deep undercover as Juneau and Kay Lynn Jones, living in a trailer park on the outskirts of Kettle Falls. They are intent on hunting down the ecoterrorists who have been blowing up the dams. The key to their identity may lie with Darla Denny, a high school dropout and former bank teller who seems to have hooked up with the group's ringleader when he blew open the safe at the bank where she worked in Astoria. Some incredibly florid prose mars what is an otherwise well-researched and absorbing topical tale taken right out of today's headlines.

Other books by the same author:
Habitat, 1999
Wildcrafters, 1998
Blue Poppy, 1997
Rain Dance, 1996

Other books you might like:
Edward Abbey, *The Monkey Wrench Gang*, 1975
Christine Andreae, *The Lee Squires Series*, 1992-
Nevada Barr, *The Anna Pigeon Series*, 1993-
Richard Hoyt, *The Siskiyou Two-Step*, 1983
Jessica Speart, *The Rachel Porter Series*, 1997-

125

FIDELIS MORGAN

Unnatural Fire

(New York: Morrow, 2001)

Story type: Historical; Humor
Subject(s): Scandal; Journalism; Alchemy
Major character(s): Lady Anastasia Ashby de la Zouche, Noblewoman (Countess of Chapham), Journalist; Alpiew, Servant
Time period(s): 17th century (1699)
Locale(s): London, England

Summary: A playwright and expert on Restoration comedy, the author makes her mystery debut with a sparkling and bawdy tale of two very different women who live by their wits in a man's world. The countess is a 60-year-old faded beauty, once the mistress of Charles II, who now faces life in debtors' prison unless she can find some way to raise money. Alpiew is her former maidservant, a well-endowed and resourceful woman who shares the countess' gift for snooping into other

people's private lives. When Alpiew frees her former employer from jail, they start a profitable enterprise selling juicy bits of gossip to the scandal sheets, but they get more than they bargained for when one of their subjects is murdered and their investigations lead them into the mysterious world of alchemy. Full of broad and often physical humor, as well as pungent descriptions of the seamier side of life in London, it's an original and highly amusing variation of the historical mystery.

Where it's reviewed:
Publishers Weekly, February 26, 2001, page 63

Other books you might like:
Molly Brown, *Invitation to a Funeral*, 1995
Ross King, *Ex-Libris*, 2001
Iain Pears, *An Instance of the Fingerpost*, 1998
Judith Merkle Riley, *The Oracle Glass*, 1994
Patricia Wynn, *The Birth of Blue Satan*, 2001

126

WALTER MOSLEY

Fearless Jones

(Boston: Little, Brown, 2001)

Story type: Amateur Detective; Historical
Subject(s): African Americans; Racism; Crime and Criminals
Major character(s): Paris Minton, Store Owner (used bookstore), Crime Victim; Fearless Jones, Veteran (World War II), Friend (of Paris)
Time period(s): 1950s (1954)
Locale(s): Los Angeles, California (Watts)

Summary: Paris Minton leaves Louisiana for California when he is a teenager because he learns that a black man can get a library card there; not so in New Iberia, where the white librarian refuses him access to the books he longs to read. A bookish, peaceable man, he eventually opens a used bookstore in Watts with the thousands of library discards he manages to acquire, and as long as he makes the rent with a little left to live on, he is in heaven, able to read to his heart's content. Then one day, trouble walks into his store in the form of a beautiful woman in grave peril, and when he tries to help her, his store is burned down and his own life is threatened. Where else to turn but his good friend Fearless Jones, an Army veteran with an attitude who helps him track down the bad guys that did all this? As in his pioneering Easy Rawlins books, the author paints a vivid picture of what it was like to be poor and black in postwar Los Angeles and of the damage racism can do to people's souls.

Where it's reviewed:
Booklist, May 1, 2001, page 1636
Entertainment Weekly, June 22, 2001, page 84
Essence, June 2001, page 80
New York Times Book Review, June 10, 2001, page 24
Publishers Weekly, May 28, 2001, page 53

Other books by the same author:
Gone Fishin', 1997 (Easy Rawlins series)
A Little Yellow Dog, 1996 (Easy Rawlins series)
Black Betty, 1994 (Easy Rawlins series)
White Butterfly, 1992 (Easy Rawlins series)

A Red Death, 1991 (Easy Rawlins series)

Other books you might like:
William Heffernan, *Beulah Hill*, 2000
Chester B. Himes, *The Coffin Ed Johnson/Gravedigger Jones Series*, 1957-1983
Kris Nelscott, *A Dangerous Road*, 2000
James Sallis, *The Lew Griffin Series*, 1992-
Robert Skinner, *The Wesley Farrell Series*, 1997-

127

MARCIA MULLER

Point Deception

(New York: Mysterious, 2001)

Story type: Psychological Suspense
Subject(s): Small Town Life; Missing Persons; Journalism
Major character(s): Rhoda ''Rho'' Swift, Police Officer (sheriff's deputy); Guy Newberry, Journalist (true crime reporter)
Time period(s): 2000s
Locale(s): Signal Port, California (Soledad County)

Summary: In a departure from her long-running Sharon McCone series, the author offers a stand-alone thriller set in a small California coastal town near Mendocino and starring a sheriff's deputy, whose confidence was shaken in a 13-year-old multiple murder in a rugged nearby canyon. When a young woman arrives in Signal Port and is stranded when her car is disabled, nobody has time to stop and help her. When she disappears, Rho again feels that she is somehow to blame. Then New York writer Guy Newberry comes to town to investigate the long-ago murders and starts exposing some of the town's secrets. Eventually Rho joins forces with Guy in reopening the case and gradually they connect it with the present-day events.

Where it's reviewed:
Booklist, May 1, 2001, page 1638
Library Journal, May 15, 2001, page 167

Other books by the same author:
Listen to the Silence, 2000
A Walk through the Fire, 1999
While Other People Sleep, 1998
Both Ends of the Night, 1997
The Broken Promise Land, 1996

Other books you might like:
Mary Kittredge, *Murder in Mendocino*, 1987
Janet LaPierre, *The Port Silva Series*, 1987-
Bill Pronzini, *A Wasteland of Strangers*, 1997
David Rains Wallace, *The Turquoise Dragon*, 1985
Elizabeth C. Ward, *Coast Highway 1*, 1983

128

KATY MUNGER

Better Off Dead

(New York: Avon, 2001)

Story type: Private Detective; Humor
Series: Casey Jones. Book 5

Subject(s): College Life; Rape; Psychology
Major character(s): Casey Jones, Detective—Private (unlicensed)
Time period(s): 2000s
Locale(s): Durham, North Carolina

Summary: Casey Jones is a big woman with a big mouth, fueled by junk food and righteous anger over what happened to her newest client, Helen McInness, who has been traumatized by a violent rape, her attacker's acquittal, and the anonymous threats being made against her. She is a private eye, sort of; because of prison time in her past, Casey's operating without a license, but there's no doubt she knows what she's doing. Leaving Helen in safekeeping with her boyfriend, her partner, and other trusted companions, including a dog named Killer, Casey goes investigating at Duke University, where the the rapist is once again at large. She gets some help from the department of psychopathology (a behavioral science that is the author's own invention). The author has also written as Gallagher Grey.

Other books by the same author:
Bad to the Bone, 2000
Money to Burn, 1999
Out of Time, 1998
Legwork, 1997

Other books you might like:
Nancy Bartholomew, *The Sierra Lavatoni Series*, 1998-
Janet Evanovich, *The Stephanie Plum Series*, 1994-
Sparkle Hayter, *The Robin Hudson Series*, 1994-
Sarah Strohmeyer, *Bubbles Unbound*, 2001
Kathleen Taylor, *The Tory Bauer Series*, 1995-

129

SHIRLEY ROUSSEAU MURPHY

Cat Spitting Mad

(New York: HarperCollins, 2001)

Story type: Traditional; Amateur Detective
Series: Joe Grey. Book 6
Subject(s): Animals/Cats; Fantasy; Small Town Life
Major character(s): Joe Grey, Animal (cat); Dulcie, Animal (cat), Sidekick
Time period(s): 2000s
Locale(s): Molena Point, California

Summary: When two brutal murders and then the kidnapping of a frightened teenage girl, who may have been a witness to them, horrify the sleepy coastal town of Molena Point, the murderer makes them appear to be the work of police chief Max Harper, best friend to Joe's ''owner,'' Clyde Damen. Joe, unique in the annals of crime fiction for not only being able to solve crimes, but having the power of human speech as well, is furious that a man he has come to admire and respect has been made to look guilty in the eyes of the townspeople. He and Dulcie, along with a cute little calico kitten recently introduced to the series, immediately get to work setting things right, a task that involves uncovering a potentially profitable real estate scam.

Where it's reviewed:
Booklist, December 1, 2000, page 697

Library Journal, January 1, 2001, page 162
Publishers Weekly, December 11, 2000, page 67
School Library Journal, May 2001, page 176

Other books by the same author:
Cat to the Dogs, 2000
Cat in the Dark, 1999
Cat Raise the Dead, 1997
Cat under Fire, 1997
Cat on the Edge, 1996

Other books you might like:
Garrison Allen, *The Big Mike Series*, 1994-
Marian Babson, *The Diamond Cat*, 1994
Lilian Jackson Braun, *The Cat Who Series*, 1966-
Rita Mae Brown, *The Mrs. Murphy Series*, 1990-
Carole Nelson Douglas, *The Midnight Louie Series*, 1992-

130

LYNNE MURRAY

At Large

(New York: St. Martin's Press, 2001)

Story type: Amateur Detective
Series: Jo Fuller. Book 3
Subject(s): Infidelity; Women; Charity
Major character(s): Josephine ''Jo'' Fuller, Investigator (philanthropic), Divorced Person
Time period(s): 2000s
Locale(s): Seattle, Washington

Summary: Jo works for a philanthropic foundation checking out charities to see if they qualify for funding, and something about the women's job skills center she's investigating strikes her as fishy. She has to take some time out when her philandering ex-husband's girlfriend, Francesca, is murdered, and Francesca's ex-husband, Teddy Etheridge, shows up asking Jo to find his missing girlfriend. Jo is a large woman, who has long since ceased being defensive about her weight and is supremely confident in her worth and her ability to get tough jobs done. She also is able to laugh at life's little absurdities, of which there are many in this book.

Where it's reviewed:
Publishers Weekly, June 4, 2001, page 61

Other books by the same author:
Large Target, 2000
Larger than Death, 1997

Other books you might like:
Selma Eichler, *The Desiree Shapiro Series*, 1994-
Linda French, *The Teddy Morelli Series*, 1998-
G.A. McKevett, *The Savannah Reed Series*, 1995-
Nancy Pickard, *The Jenny Cain Series*, 1984-
Janet Smith, *The Annie MacPherson Series*, 1990-

TAMAR MYERS

The Crepes of Wrath

(New York: New American Library, 2001)

Story type: Amateur Detective; Domestic
Series: Magdalena Yoder. Book 9
Subject(s): Amish; Hotels, Motels; Cooks and Cookery
Major character(s): Magdalena Yoder, Innkeeper, Detective—Amateur
Time period(s): 2000s
Locale(s): Hernia, Pennsylvania

Summary: When a local Amish woman, reputed to be the worst cook in the county, dies of a drug overdose, bumbling Sheriff Melvin Stoltzfus turns the investigation over to Magdalena. The woman's husband maintains she was murdered because he had shot out the tires of a car belonging to two teenagers who, in the throes of *rumschpringe* (the teenage rebellion that's semi-sanctioned by Amish society) ran over two of his family's pets. Magdalena has no problem leaving her guests on their own, because early in her career running the PennDutch Inn, she made the sensible decision to offer them the true Mennonite lifestyle experience by permitting them to do their own housekeeping (at a slight extra charge). Despite the light tone of the series, the author does offer some insights into Amish society and the interaction between the Amish and the ''English,'' as outsiders are called. A number of Magdalena's recipes are included. The author also writes a series about North Carolina antiques dealer Abigail Timberlake.

Where it's reviewed:
Publishers Weekly, November 27, 2000, page 57

Other books by the same author:
The Hand That Rocks the Ladle, 2000
Play It Again, Spam, 1999
Between a Wok and a Hard Place, 1998
Eat, Drink and Be Wary, 1998
Just Plain Pickled to Death, 1997

Other books you might like:
Claudia Bishop, *The Sarah Quilliam Series*, 1994-
Mary Daheim, *The Judith McMonigle Flynn Series*, 1991-
Roma Greth, *The Hana Shaner Series*, 1988-
Jean Hager, *The Tess Darcy Series*, 1994-
Valerie S. Malmont, *The Tori Miracle Series*, 1994-

132

TIM MYERS

Innkeeping with Murder

(New York: Berkley, 2001)

Story type: Amateur Detective
Subject(s): Hotels, Motels; American South
Major character(s): Alex Winston, Innkeeper
Time period(s): 2000s
Locale(s): Blue Ridge Mountains, North Carolina

Summary: Alex inherits the Hatteras West Inn and Lighthouse from his father and is trying his hand at being an innkeeper, making improvements a little at a time and working hard to make his guests comfortable. The inn is an exact replica of the Cape Hatteras Lighthouse on the Outer Banks, only nestled in the foothills of the Blue Ridge Mountains. When one of his guests is found dead at the top of the lighthouse, it appears at first to have been a heart attack. Then a series of accidents follows, and Alex must get to the bottom of it while all the guests are still at hand. First mystery.

Other books you might like:
Claudia Bishop, *The Sarah & Meg Quilliam Series*, 1994-
Mary Daheim, *The Judith McMonigle Flynn Series*, 1991-
Jean Hager, *The Tess Darcy Series*, 1994-
Parnell Hall, *Cozy*, 2001
Tamar Myers, *The Magdalena Yoder Series*, 1994-

MICHAEL NAVA

Rag and Bone

(New York: Putnam, 2001)

Story type: Private Detective; Legal
Series: Henry Rios. Book 7
Subject(s): Mexican Americans; Homosexuality/Lesbianism; Near-Death Experience
Major character(s): Henry Rios, Lawyer, Homosexual; Elena, Relative (sister of Henry), Lesbian
Time period(s): 2000s
Locale(s): Los Angeles, California

Summary: When he regains consciousness after surviving a severe heart attack, Henry is surprised to see his sister, Elena, at his bedside and to learn that he had been calling out for her during the incident. The two had been estranged as adults and although they had repaired the rift between them, they had never been close. Henry is also surprised to learn that although Elena is a lesbian, she had borne a child whom she put up for adoption shortly after she left the convent after six years as a nun. Now her daughter, Vicky, is grown with a son of her own. Once Henry is discharged from the hospital, Elena returns home to Oakland, where a badly beaten Vicky has shown up with ten-year-old Angelito. Shortly afterward, Vicky's husband is shot, Vicky confesses, and Henry prepares to represent her in what appears to be a clear-cut case of self-defense. Naturally, it turns out to be nothing so simple. Henry, whose life has been severely impacted by the loss of many friends and a long-term lover to AIDS, is going through the mood swings and depression that often accompany a heart attack. Now he is trying to put his life back together and become acquainted with the family he never knew he had. That this will be the last Henry Rios book is a great disappointment to readers who have become hooked on the exquisite writing and emotional depth Nava has brought to both the series and the genre.

Where it's reviewed:
Booklist, February 1, 2001, page 1042
Library Journal, February 1, 2001, page 127
New York Times Book Review, March 18, 2001, page 18
Publishers Weekly, January 22, 2001, page 306

Other books by the same author:
The Burning Plain, 1998
The Death of Friends, 1996
The Hidden Law, 1993
How Town, 1990
Goldenboy, 1988

Other books you might like:
Rosemary Aubert, *The Ellis Portal Series*, 1997-
Joseph Hansen, *The Dave Brandstetter Series*, 1970-
John Straley, *The Cecil Younger Series*, 1992-
John Morgan Wilson, *The Benjamin Justice Series*, 1996-
Mark Richard Zubro, *The Tom Mason Series*, 1988-

134

CHARLES O'BRIEN

Mute Witness

(Scottsdale, Arizona: Poisoned Pen, 2001)

Story type: Historical
Subject(s): Deafness; Theater; Mutism
Major character(s): Anne Cartier, Actress, Teacher
Time period(s): 1780s (1785-1786)
Locale(s): London, England; Paris, France

Summary: Anne Cartier makes plans to leave London for Paris, partly to escape the unwanted attentions of a spurned suitor and partly to learn the truth behind the ostensible suicide of her beloved stepfather, Antoine Dubois, also an actor. In Paris she becomes involved in the theater again and also pursues a second career, teaching the deaf. Under the protection of Colonel Paul de Saint-Martin, she finds time to help investigate a series of jewel thefts. The historical period against which the action is set is so far relatively unused in mystery fiction, and the author employs it effectively. First novel.

Where it's reviewed:
Booklist, May 1, 2001, page 1638
Publishers Weekly, April 30, 2001, page 60

Other books you might like:
Ann Dukthas, *The Prince Lost to Time*, 1995
Katherine Neville, *The Eight*, 1988
Lawrence Norfolk, *Lampriere's Dictionary*, 1991
Anne Perry, *A Dish Taken Cold*, 2001
    novella
Rosemary Stevens, *The Beau Brummell Series*, 2000-

135

LESLIE O'KANE

When the Fax Lady Sings

(New York: Fawcett, 2001)

Story type: Amateur Detective; Domestic
Series: Molly Masters. Book 6
Subject(s): Schools/High Schools; Parenthood; Small Town Life
Major character(s): Molly Masters, Artist (cartoonist), Writer (faxable greeting cards)
Time period(s): 2000s

Locale(s): Carlton, New York (suburb of Albany)

Summary: A dress rehearsal for a PTA fundraiser, in which Molly and six others are performing as identically dressed clowns, is disrupted when one of the clowns opens fire on the director, Corrinne Buldock, who teaches the talented and gifted (TAG) language arts class. There have been rumors that Corrinne, in the wake of splitting up with her boyfriend, had been sexually involved with one of her students. Molly wonders which of the parents or teachers at the school was angry enough with Corrinne to kill her. The author also writes a series about Boulder, Colorado, dog therapist Allida Babcock.

Other books by the same author:
The School Board Murders, 2000
The Fax of Life, 1999
The Cold Hard Fax, 1997
Death and Faxes, 1996
Just the Fax, Ma'am, 1996

Other books you might like:
Jill Churchill, *The Jane Jeffry Series*, 1989-
Jacqueline Girdner, *The Kate Jasper Series*, 1991-
Susan Holtzer, *The Anneke Hagen Series*, 1994-
Dolores Johnson, *The Mandy Dyer Series*, 1997-
Valerie Wolzien, *The Susan Henshaw Series*, 1987-

136

SUSAN OLEKSIW

Friends and Enemies

(Unity, Maine: Five Star, 2001)

Story type: Police Procedural; Traditional
Series: Mellingham. Book 4
Subject(s): Reunions; Small Town Life; Schools/High Schools
Major character(s): Joe Silva, Police Officer (police chief)
Time period(s): 1990s (1996)
Locale(s): Mellingham, Massachusetts

Summary: Joe Silva has never seen the point of high school reunions, and after witnessing the behavior of members of the class of 1969 who are attending their 25th and relaxing in the bar where he likes to hang out, he still doesn't. What's past is past. The past seems very much alive to this particular group of alumni, however, who have long memories of old grudges, bitter rivalries, and unhappy love affairs. When one woman disappears and a man is poisoned and lies near death, Joe's going to have to find out what happened 25 years ago before he can solve the mystery.

Other books by the same author:
Double Take, 2000
Murder in Mellingham, 2000
Family Album, 1995

Other books you might like:
Rita Mae Brown, *Pawing through the Past*, 2000
Sinclair Browning, *The Last Song Dogs*, 1999
Susan Rogers Cooper, *The Milton Kovak Series*, 1988-
April Henry, *Heart-Shaped Box*, 2001
Triss Stein, *Murder at the Class Reunion*, 1993

137

PERRI O'SHAUGHNESSY (Pseudonym of Pamela O'Shaughnessy and Mary O'Shaughnessy)

Writ of Execution

(New York: Delacorte, 2001)

Story type: Legal
Series: Nina Reilly. Book 7
Subject(s): Money; Gambling; Identity
Major character(s): Nina Reilly, Lawyer
Time period(s): 2000s
Locale(s): South Lake Tahoe, California

Summary: Always ready to represent the underdog, Nina meets with a new client who calls herself Jessie Potter and has an unusual problem. Jessie has just won a multimillion dollar jackpot playing the slot,s but can't collect the money until she reveals her actual identity to the casino, something she can't do because she's being stalked and can't risk the publicity. She can't afford not to, either, because she needs the money desperately. So she hatches a scheme to marry a fellow slot player in order to protect her identity. The case turns out to be neither as simple nor as profitable as Nina anticipates, as there are various people after Jessie's money, should she ever collect it, and after Jessie herself, if she doesn't. In addition, there are hints that the jackpot was rigged to begin with.

Where it's reviewed:
Booklist, May 15, 2001, page 1708
Publishers Weekly, June 1, 2001, page 57

Other books by the same author:
Move to Strike, 2000
Acts of Malice, 1999
Breach of Promise, 1998
Obstruction of Justice, 1997
Invasion of Privacy, 1996

Other books you might like:
Jonnie Jacobs, *The Kali O'Brien Series*, 1996-
Lisa Scottoline, *The Rosato & Associates Series*, 1993-
Marianne Wesson, *The Cinda Hayes Series*, 1998-
Carolyn Wheat, *The Cass Jameson Series*, 1983-
Kate Wilhelm, *The Barbara Holloway Series*, 1991-

138

ABIGAIL PADGETT

The Last Blue Plate Special

(New York: Mysterious, 2001)

Story type: Amateur Detective; Traditional
Series: Blue McCarron. Book 2
Subject(s): Homosexuality/Lesbianism; Psychology; Serial Killer
Major character(s): Blue McCarron, Psychologist (social), Lesbian; Roxanne Bouchie, Doctor (prison psychiatrist), Lesbian; BB, Sidekick
Time period(s): 2000s
Locale(s): Borrego Springs, California; San Diego, California

Summary: When two healthy local women politicians die within days of each other of cerebral hemorrhages, Blue crunches a few numbers and confirms her hunch that it's statistically impossible for such a thing to happen. She and her lover and colleague, Roxy, take their findings to the San Diego police and get hired on as consultants. When a third woman, a female evangelist, nearly dies, they find that all three had received threatening mail from someone calling himself "The Sword of Heaven," a serial killer, who has it in for women in positions of authority. His calling card is a picture of a blue willow plate, and when Blue finds one on her own doorstep, she knows she's his next target. Blue, who lives alone in the high desert outside the city in an abandoned motel she bought for a song and is gradually rehabbing, is a worthy successor to the author's previous series character, San Diego child abuse investigator Bo Bradley.

Where it's reviewed:
Booklist, January 1, 2001, page 926
Library Journal, January 1, 2001, page 162
Publishers Weekly, February 19, 2001, page 72

Other books by the same author:
Blue, 1998
The Dollmaker's Daughters, 1997
Moonbird Boy, 1996
Turtle Baby, 1995
Strawgirl, 1994

Other books you might like:
Nevada Barr, *The Anna Pigeon Series*, 1993-
Laurie R. King, *The Kate Martinelli Series*, 1993-
Sarah Lovett, *The Sylvia Strange Series*, 1995-
Anna Salter, *The Michael Stone Series*, 1997-
Mary Willis Walker, *The Molly Cates Series*, 1994-

139

KATHERINE HALL PAGE

The Body in the Moonlight

(New York: Morrow, 2001)

Story type: Amateur Detective; Domestic
Series: Faith Fairchild. Book 11
Subject(s): Small Town Life; Authors and Writers; Cooks and Cookery
Major character(s): Faith Sibley Fairchild, Caterer, Detective—Amateur
Time period(s): 2000s
Locale(s): Aleford, Massachusetts

Summary: When her husband's church decides to host a murder mystery dinner to kick off its restoration campaign, Faith is naturally engaged to cater the affair. The evening, which features four well-known local mystery writers, is a huge success until one of the guests, the attractive Gwen Lord, collapses after polishing off a dessert heavily laced with cyanide. Suddenly Faith's services are no longer in demand by the townspeople, and worse, some even suspect her of the murder, believing her husband, Tom, was overly attentive to this particular parishioner. It's true Tom is despondent over Gwen's death and has become difficult to communicate with. Then her young son's elementary school principal confides he's been receiving threatening phone calls. Faith and the local mystery-writing community go to work trying to sort

matters out. Somewhat darker than earlier entries in this series, it still offers an attractive small-town ambience and a full complement of tempting recipes at the book's end.

Where it's reviewed:
Deadly Pleasures, Winter 2001, page 51
Drood Review, January/February 2001, page 11

Other books by the same author:
The Body in the Big Apple, 1999
The Body in the Bookcase, 1998
The Body in the Fjord, 1997
The Body in the Bog, 1996
The Body in the Basement, 1994

Other books you might like:
Susan Wittig Albert, *The China Bayles Series*, 1992-
Diane Mott Davidson, *The Goldy Bear Schulz Series*, 1990-
Jerrilyn Farmer, *The Madeline Bean Series*, 1998-
Carolyn Hart, *The Christie Caper*, 1991
Joan Hess, *A Conventional Corpse*, 2000

140

ROBIN PAIGE (Pseudonym of Susan Wittig Albert and Bill Albert)

Death at Epsom Downs

(New York: Berkley Prime Crime, 2001)

Story type: Historical; Traditional
Series: Kathryn Ardleigh. Book 7
Subject(s): Victorian Period; Photography; Horse Racing
Major character(s): Lady Kathryn "Kate" Ardleigh Sheridan, Noblewoman, Writer (novelist); Lord Charles Sheridan, Nobleman, Photographer; Lillie Langtry, Actress, Historical Figure
Time period(s): 1890s (1899)
Locale(s): Epsom, England; Newmarket, England

Summary: With Charles recently elevated to the peerage, he and his American-born wife Kate feel compelled to take a more active part in London's social scene, which includes attending such events as Derby Day at Epsom Downs, where the story opens. Charles is photographing the race for the Jockey Club and Kate is gathering information for her newest novel, a horse-racing thriller to be published under her pseudonym, Beryl Bardwell. Kate is sharing a box with Jennie Churchill and the American actress Lillie Langtry, but only later do Kate and Charles learn that not only did a jockey die during the race, but Mrs. Langtry's jewels were stolen from their vault. Charles is commissioned to investigate the theft and what he and Kate learn about Mrs. Langtry's private life puts them both in danger. As usual, the authors blend fact and fiction and illuminate many aspects of Victorian life, such as the agricultural school Kate has opened at their country home of Bishop's Keep for unmarried women in need of a vocation which will both support them and benefit society.

Where it's reviewed:
Library Journal, February 1, 2001, page 127
Publishers Weekly, February 5, 2001, page 72

Other books by the same author:
Death at Whitechapel, 2000
Death at Rottingdean, 1999

Death at Devil's Bridge, 1998
Death at Daisy's Folly, 1997
Death at Gallows Green, 1995

Other books you might like:
Stephanie Barron, *Jane and the Genius of the Place*, 1999
Emily Brightwell, *The Mrs. Jeffries Series*, 1993-
Kate Kingsbury, *The Pennyfoot Hotel Series*, 1993-1999
Anne Perry, *The Thomas and Charlotte Pitt Series*, 1979-
Elizabeth Peters, *The Amelia Peabody Series*, 1975-

141

ELLEN PALL

Corpse de Ballet

(New York: St. Martin's Press, 2001)

Story type: Amateur Detective; Traditional
Subject(s): Ballet; Theater; Dancing
Major character(s): Juliet Bodine, Writer (Regency novelist), Professor (former)
Time period(s): 2000s
Locale(s): New York, New York (Manhattan)

Summary: Juliet, a very successful Regency novelist, is in a work-avoidance mode when she's approached by her old friend, dancer and choreographer Ruth Renswick, for help on the storyline of the new musical production she's staging of *Great Expectations*. Herself a great ballet fan, Juliet jumps at the chance to be backstage during the development and rehearsals. She's fascinated by the exotic creatures who populate the world of dance, but the intense rivalries and competition are more than she bargained for, as are the mysterious accidents that lead to the death of one of the dancers. The police who investigate, including a detective Juliet once knew, label it suicide, but she is certain it was murder and does her best to prove it. The backstage atmosphere and the details about the ballet world are both absorbing and convincing, Juliet is an original and intelligent heroine, the plot is suitably intricate, and the result is a charming, old-fashioned mystery that satisfies on every level. First novel.

Where it's reviewed:
Booklist, May 1, 2001, page 1638
Publishers Weekly, May 7, 2001, page 228

Other books you might like:
Edgar Box, *Death in the Fifth Position*, 1952
Caryl Brahms, *A Bullet in the Ballet*, 1937
    S.J. Simon, co-author
Lucy Cores, *Corpse de Ballet*, 1944
Jane Dentinger, *The Jocelyn O'Roarke Series*, 1983-
Dorian Yeager, *The Victoria Bowering Series*, 1992-

142

ROBERT B. PARKER

Potshot

(New York: Putnam, 2001)

Story type: Private Detective
Series: Spenser. Book 28
Subject(s): Gangs; American West; Robbers and Outlaws

Major character(s): Spenser, Detective—Private; Hawk, Sidekick
Time period(s): 2000s
Locale(s): Potshot, Arizona

Summary: The plot of this newest adventure for the wisecracking, self-assured Boston private eye seems to have been borrowed from the author's forthcoming historical western featuring Wyatt Earp. Spenser is hired to clean up the historic Arizona mining town of Potshot, now a haven for wealthy Los Angelenos, but terrorized by a gang of hard-bitten desert rats and other misfits who resent the lavish lifestyles that have supplanted their old free-wheeling existence and who are determined to redistribute its newfound wealth in their direction by way of extortion and even murder. Spenser brings his taciturn, but lethal sidekick Hawk along, of course, as well as a posse of righteous (if scarcely law-abiding) pals from earlier books: Vinnie Morris, Bobby Horse, Teddy Sapp, and Chollo, who aren't averse to dispensing a little vigilante justice of their own. As usual, the action is swift and the prose smooth, and one hardly minds the timeworn plot. The author also writes two other series, one featuring female Boston private eye Sunny Randall, the other alcoholic Massachusetts police chief Jesse Stone.

Where it's reviewed:
Booklist, February 15, 2001, page 1085
New York Times Book Review, March 25, 2001, page 16
Publishers Weekly, February 26, 2001, page 62

Other books by the same author:
Hugger Mugger, 2000
Hush Money, 1999
Sudden Mischief, 1998
Small Vices, 1997
Chance, 1996

Other books you might like:
Lee Child, *The Jack Reacher Series*, 1997-
Robert Crais, *The Elvis Cole Series*, 1987-
Dennis Lehane, *The Patrick Kenzie Series*, 1994-
Rick Riordan, *The Tres Navarre Series*, 1997-
Walter Satterthwait, *The Joshua Croft Series*, 1989-

T. JEFFERSON PARKER

Silent Joe
(New York: Hyperion, 2001)

Story type: Psychological Suspense
Subject(s): Fathers and Sons; Politics; Gangs
Major character(s): Joe Trona, Police Officer (sheriff's deputy)
Time period(s): 2000s
Locale(s): Orange County, California

Summary: As an infant, Joe Trona is horribly disfigured when his father throws acid in his face, and he is raised in an orphanage until Will Trona, a powerful Orange County supervisor, adopts him into his family. Joe grows up to be his father's right-hand man, accompanying him on his after-hours missions as both chauffeur and bodyguard. During the day, Joe works in the Orange County jail, where he comes to know

many of the criminals and gang members in the area. When his father is murdered one night, Joe is sick with grief and guilt that he was unable to protect him, and he dedicates himself to bringing Will's killer to justice. He must learn some painful secrets about his own past before he's able to do this. Joe is a deeply affecting character, a good man in an evil world, and there is a poignant love story threading its way through the complex plot.

Where it's reviewed:
Booklist, February 25, 2001, page 1085
Library Journal, March 1, 2001, page 132
People Weekly, April 30, 2001, page 43
Publishers Weekly, March 19, 2001, page 78
Wall Street Journal, April 10, 2001, page A20

Other books by the same author:
Red Light, 2000
The Blue Hour, 1999
Where Serpents Lie, 1998
The Triggerman's Dance, 1996
Summer of Fear, 1993

Other books you might like:
Jan Burke, *Flight*, 2001
Michael Connelly, *The Harry Bosch Series*, 1992-
Robert Crais, *Demolition Angel*, 2000
John Shannon, *The Orange Curtain*, 2001
Kate Wilhelm, *Desperate Measures*, 2001

144

ELIOT PATTISON

Water Touching Stone
(New York: St. Martin's Press, 2001)

Story type: Action/Adventure
Series: Shan Tao Yun. Book 2
Subject(s): Buddhism; Resistance Movements; Cultural Conflict
Major character(s): Shan Tao Yun, Dissident, Police Officer (former)
Time period(s): 2000s
Locale(s): Tibet

Summary: Shan, the exiled Beijing police detective who has just been released from four years in the gulag of northern Tibet, is asked by the monks, who have become his mentors and protectors, to find a missing lama and the murderer of a revered teacher. In the company of other outcasts, Shan finds his way across the desert to the dangerous borderland. It's a long, complicated search that he goes on, in which he meets all manner of people, including a young Kazakh woman, and sees many haunting sites, such as sacred shrines and a ruin on the old Silk Road. Always, the long struggle of the Tibetan people against their corrupt Chinese rulers dominates the story, along with much information on Tibetan Buddhism and the spirituality that shapes the country's culture.

Where it's reviewed:
Booklist, May 1, 2001, page 1639
Library Journal, May 1, 2001, page 128
Publishers Weekly, May 14, 2001, page 56

Other books by the same author:
The Skull Mantra, 1999

Other books you might like:
Lionel Davidson, *The Rose of Tibet*, 1962
Daniel Easterman, *The Ninth Buddha*, 1989
Lisa See, *The Flower Net*, 1997
James Ramsey Ullman, *The Sands of Karakorum*, 1953
Christopher West, *The Third Messiah*, 2000

145

CYNTHIA PEALE (Pseudonym of Nancy Zaroulis)

Murder at Bertram's Bower
(New York: Doubleday, 2001)

Story type: Historical; Amateur Detective
Series: Caroline and Addington Ames. Book 2
Subject(s): Social Classes; Emigration and Immigration; Irish Americans
Major character(s): Caroline Ames, Detective—Amateur; Addington Ames, Detective—Amateur; John Alexander MacKenzie, Doctor
Time period(s): 1890s (1892)
Locale(s): Boston, Massachusetts

Summary: Addington and Caroline are siblings living in reduced circumstances in the faded elegance of their inherited Beacon Hill home, where Dr. MacKenzie lives as a boarder. Bertram's Bower is a shelter for fallen women, chiefly prostitutes, some of whom are dying as a Ripper-like killer stalks the back streets of Boston. It may even be Jack the Ripper himself, whom the London police never captured and who is rumored to have escaped to America. At the behest of Caroline's friend Agatha, who runs the shelter with the help of her clergyman brother, Addington agrees to investigate the dreadful murders, aided by Caroline and Dr. MacKenzie. The plight of society's less fortunate and the prejudice of old-time Bostonians against Irish immigrants are two of the social issues explored by the author. Real-life characters, such as William James, are also featured in the book.

Where it's reviewed:
Booklist, February 15, 2001, page 1120
Drood Review, January/February 2001, page 14
Library Journal, March 1, 2001, page 133
Publishers Weekly, January 15, 2001, page 56

Other books by the same author:
The Death of Colonel Mann, 2000

Other books you might like:
Karen Rose Cercone, *The Helen Sorby Series*, 1997-
Dianne Day, *Death Train to Boston*, 1999
Maureen Jennings, *The William Murdoch Series*, 1997-
Robin Paige, *The Kathryn Ardleigh Series*, 1994-
Victoria Thompson, *The Sarah Brandt Series*, 1999-

146

GEORGE P. PELECANOS

Right as Rain
(Boston: Little, Brown, 2001)

Story type: Private Detective
Subject(s): Race Relations; Drugs; African Americans
Major character(s): Derek Strange, Detective—Private, Police Officer (former); Terry Quinn, Police Officer (former)
Time period(s): 2000s
Locale(s): Washington, District of Columbia

Summary: The author introduces a new protagonist, Derek Strange, a black former cop in his mid-fifties who is hired to clear up some loose ends in the fatal shooting of a black off-duty police officer, Chris Wilson, by a white colleague, Terry Quinn. Quinn has been exonerated of the crime, as Wilson failed to identify himself as a police officer, but Wilson's mother is still troubled by Quinn's apparent assumption that her son was a criminal because he was black. Quinn, who himself is haunted by the incident and who resigned from the force because of it, offers to work with Strange in his investigation. Although initially mistrustful of each other, the two men develop a mutual respect and something approaching friendship. Subplots include drug addiction (Strange's sister is a junkie), runaways, and the perils and social evils of urban life in general. The author, who has written a number of other crime novels set in the district, makes good use of the setting, a side of Washington that most tourists and residents never see.

Where it's reviewed:
Deadly Pleasures, Winter 2001, page 47
Library Journal, November 1, 2000, page 36
New York Times Book Review, March 25, 2001, page 27
Publishers Weekly, January 8, 2001, page 51
Washington Post, March 26, 2001, page C4

Other books by the same author:
Shame the Devil, 2000
The Sweet Forever, 1998
King Suckerman, 1997
The Big Blowdown, 1996
Down by the River Where the Dead Men Go, 1995

Other books you might like:
Lawrence Block, *The Matt Scudder Series*, 1976-
James Lee Burke, *The Dave Robicheaux Series*, 1987-
Michael Connelly, *The Harry Bosch Series*, 1992-
Jon A. Jackson, *The Fang Mulheiser Series*, 1977-
Dennis Lehane, *Mystic River*, 2001

147

WILDER PERKINS

Hoare and the Matter of Treason
(New York: St. Martin's Minotaur, 2001)

Story type: Historical
Series: Captain Bartholomew Hoare. Book 3
Subject(s): Ships; Conspiracies; Marriage

Major character(s): Bartholomew Hoare, Military Personnel (naval captain), Handicapped
Time period(s): 1800s (1805)
Locale(s): London, England

Summary: Because his larynx was crushed by a cannonball during a naval battle, Hoare cannot speak above a whisper and is thus judged unfit to command a ship, but he is still entrusted with top secret missions of great importance. As the book opens, he is about to marry the young widow Eleanor Graves, who is being attended by her good friend, Jane Austen. No sooner has the ceremony concluded than he is directed to head for London to find a man who has information about a conspiracy against King George III. Unfortunately, he's unable to find him in time; when he does, the man is dead. Meanwhile, Eleanor and the child they are planning to adopt have moved to London and set up housekeeping there. The final book in the series, it's being published posthumously.

Where it's reviewed:
Publishers Weekly, January 29, 2001, page 68

Other books by the same author:
Hoare and the Headless Captains, 2000
Hoare and the Portsmouth Atrocities, 1998

Other books you might like:
Stephanie Barron, *The Jane Austen Series*, 1996-
John Dickson Carr, *Captain Cutthroat*, 1955
Richard Foxall, *The Dark Forest*, 1972
J.G. Jeffreys, *The Willful Lady*, 1975
Rosemary Stevens, *The Beau Brummell Series*, 2000-

148

ELIZABETH PETERS (Pseudonym of Barbara Mertz)

Lord of the Silent
(New York: Morrow, 2001)

Story type: Historical
Series: Amelia Peabody. Book 13
Subject(s): Archaeology; Egyptian Antiquities; World War I
Major character(s): Amelia Peabody Emerson, Detective—Amateur, Archaeologist; Ramses Emerson, Archaeologist; Nefret Forth, Doctor, Spouse (of Ramses)
Time period(s): 1910s (1915)
Locale(s): Cairo, Egypt; Luxor, Egypt

Summary: Despite the ongoing war with Germany, Amelia and Radcliffe Emerson are back in Egypt for more adventurous excavations when their son, Ramses, now a happily married man, is attacked in the marketplace. Since their archenemy, Sethos, died in the last installment of the series (or did he?), the Emersons must look elsewhere for the culprit. Amelia, terrified the pacifist Ramses might again be recruited for a spy mission by the British Army, whisks him and his bride, Nefret, off to Luxor to investigate some tomb robberies. All in all, a glorious adventure is had by all.

Where it's reviewed:
Booklist, March 1, 2001, page 1188
Library Journal, May 1, 2001, page 132
New York Times Book Review, June 10, 2001, page 28
Publishers Weekly, April 23, 2001, page 52

Other books by the same author:
He Shall Thunder in the Sky, 2000
The Falcon at the Portal, 1999
The Ape Who Guards the Balance, 1998
Seeing a Large Cat, 1997
The Hippopotamus Pool, 1996

Other books you might like:
Dianne Day, *The Fremont Jones Series*, 1995-
Laurie R. King, *O Jerusalem*, 1999
Robin Paige, *The Kathryn Ardleigh Series*, 1994-
Michael Pearce, *The Mamur Zapt Series*, 1988-
Carol Thurston, *The Eye of Horus*, 2000

149

NANCY PICKARD

Ring of Truth
(New York: Pocket, 2001)

Story type: Amateur Detective
Series: Marie Lightfoot. Book 2
Subject(s): Journalism; Crime and Criminals; Clergy
Major character(s): Marie Lightfoot, Journalist (true crime writer), Detective—Amateur
Time period(s): 2000s
Locale(s): Bahia Beach, Florida

Summary: Best-selling crime writer Marie Lightfoot has chosen a sensational murder case set right in her hometown as the subject of her next book. It's the murder of a minister's wife by her husband and his male lover, a case brought swiftly to conviction, with a death sentence imposed on the Reverend Bob Wing. As usual, Marie asks for an interview with the condemned man, but in this case she is refused. As she investigates, she begins to feel that there's more to the case than she originally thought, and she stumbles across a startling piece of evidence not even the police had access to. The author writes two other quite different series, one featuring New England sleuth Jenny Cain and one continuing the Eugenia Potter culinary mysteries originated by Virginia Rich.

Where it's reviewed:
Publishers Weekly, June 4, 2001, page 61

Other books by the same author:
The Whole Truth, 2000

Other books you might like:
Edna Buchanan, *The Britt Montero Series*, 1992-
Jan Burke, *The Irene Kelly Series*, 1993-
Janice Steinberg, *The Margo Simon Series*, 1995-
Mary Willis Walker, *The Molly Cates Series*, 1994-
Jane Waterhouse, *The Garner Quin Series*, 1995-

150

SHEILA PIM

Common or Garden Crime
(Boulder, Colorado: Rue Morgue, 2001)

Story type: Traditional; Amateur Detective

Subject(s): Gardens and Gardening; Small Town Life; World War II
Major character(s): Lucy Bex, Gardener, Detective—Amateur
Time period(s): 1940s (1945)
Locale(s): Clonmeen, Ireland

Summary: Lucy Bex has made a comfortable home for herself and her widowed brother, Linnaeus, in the village of Clonmeen on the outskirts of Dublin, tending to her house and garden, making do with wartime shortages, and wisely observing the ways of her friends and neighbors. When one of them is murdered with monkshood harvested from her own garden, she turns amateur detective and is not content until she solves the crime. When necessary she goes to the police with her discoveries, but she and the authorities conduct separate investigations which eventually lead them to the same conclusions, although Lucy's derive more from her knowledge of botany and her understanding of human nature. First published in England in 1945, it is the author's first mystery and has never before been published in the United States.

Where it's reviewed:
Publishers Weekly, February 19, 2001, page 73

Other books by the same author:
A Hive of Suspects, 1952 (reprinted 2001)
A Brush with Death, 1950
Creeping Venom, 1946

Other books you might like:
Joanna Cannan, Death at the Dog, 1941 reprinted 1999
Eilis Dillon, Sent to His Account, 1954
Bartholomew Gill, The Peter McGarr Series, 1977-
Ann Ripley, The Louise Eldridge Series, 1994-
John Sherwood, The Celia Grant Series, 1984-

151

BILL PRONZINI

In an Evil Time

(New York: Walker, 2001)

Story type: Psychological Suspense
Subject(s): Stalking; Abuse; Cancer
Major character(s): Jack Hollis, Parent
Time period(s): 2000s
Locale(s): San Francisco, California; Los Alegres, California

Summary: Jack Hollis, a loving father with a deep respect for the law, finds his belief in the judicial system tested to the utmost when his daughter Angela starts being stalked and threatened by her viciously abusive ex-husband, David Rakubian, a defense attorney whose knowledge of the law gives him a powerful edge over Angela. The truth is that there is almost nothing that can be done that is both legal and effective to protect Angela and her young son from this monster. Jack decides to take matters into his own hands and hunts Rakubian down, intending to kill him; but when he finds him, the man is already dead. Thinking his son Eric had murdered him, Jack gets rid of the body and cleans up after the killer. When he finds that Eric is innocent, the question of

who killed Rakubian remains unanswered. Then he gets an anonymous note asking him where the body has been hidden. At one point, Jack seeks help from Sharon McCone, protagonist of a popular series created by Pronzini's wife, Marcia Muller. All the while the prostate cancer he has been diagnosed with, but won't take time out to have treated seems to be worsening. The author also writes the long-lived Nameless Detective series about a San Francisco private investigator.

Where it's reviewed:
Booklist, February 15, 2001, page 1120

Other books by the same author:
Nothing but the Night, 1999
A Wasteland of Strangers, 1997
Blue Lonesome, 1995
With an Extreme Burning, 1994
The Lighthouse, 1987 (Marcia Muller, co-author)

Other books you might like:
Brian Garfield, Death Wish, 1972
Reginald Hill, Arms and the Women, 1999
Laurie R. King, Night Work, 2000
Dennis Lehane, Prayers for Rain, 1999
Barbara Seranella, Unfinished Business, 2001

152

PHILIP REED

The Marquis of Fraud

(Long Beach, California: Epic, 2001)

Story type: Action/Adventure; Humor
Subject(s): Animals/Horses; Horse Racing
Major character(s): Cliff Dante, Horse Trainer
Time period(s): 2000s
Locale(s): San Francisco, California; London, England; Glasgow, Scotland

Summary: "Pin hooking" is the art of buying an unbroken colt at auction based on its lineage and the way it moves, breaking and training it for racing, and then selling it six months later for many times its original purchase price. The trainer makes his decision largely on intuition and instinct, and even after training, the horse is sold for its promise, not its performance, since it's never actually been raced. Cliff Dante is a pin hooker, and he's got a fast new colt and two potential clients, but one of them turns out to be a killer and a con artist who steals the colt and ships him off to Europe. Cliff and a friend take off after the horse and the phony client, with a plan for dealing with him when they catch him. The author's previous books deal with used car expert Harold Dodge.

Other books by the same author:
Low Rider, 1998
Bird Dog, 1997

Other books you might like:
Jon Breen, Triple Crown, 1985
Dick Francis, Slayride, 1973
Michael Maguire, Scratchproof, 1977
William Murray, The Shifty Lou Anderson Series, 1984-
Bill Shoemaker, The Coley Killebrew Series, 1994-

153

KATHY REICHS

Fatal Voyage

(New York: Scribner, 2001)

Story type: Police Procedural; Psychological Suspense
Series: Tempe Brennan. Book 4
Subject(s): Airplane Accidents; Disasters
Major character(s): Temperance Brennan, Anthropologist (forensic)
Time period(s): 2000s
Locale(s): Charlotte, North Carolina (USA); Bryson City, North Carolina

Summary: When an airplane crashes in the mountainous North Carolina backwoods, killing 88 passengers (mostly college soccer players) and crew, teams of experts are called in to assess the damage and retrieve the remains. It's a horrifying task, with body parts and airplane debris scattered all over the remote area, and as experienced as she is, it's almost more than Tempe Brennan can bear. It's further complicated by her discovery of a foot that doesn't belong to any of the passengers, and the mystery of whose it is and how it got there ends up getting Tempe, who is determined to get to the bottom of things, into deep trouble with a local politician.

Where it's reviewed:
Booklist, May 15, 2001, page 1737
Publishers Weekly, May 21, 2001, page 79

Other books by the same author:
Deadly Decisions, 2000
Death du Jour, 1999
Deja Dead, 1997

Other books you might like:
Sallie Bissell, *In the Forest of Harm*, 2001
Patricia Cornwell, *The Kay Scarpetta Series*, 1990-
Linda Fairstein, *The Alexandra Cooper Series*, 1996-
Anna Salter, *The Michael Stone Series*, 1997-
Marianne Wesson, *The Cinda Hayes Series*, 1998-

154

PHYLLIS RICHMAN

Who's Afraid of Virginia Ham?

(New York: HarperCollins, 2001)

Story type: Amateur Detective
Series: Chas Wheatley. Book 3
Subject(s): Food; Restaurants; Journalism
Major character(s): Chas Wheatley, Journalist (food critic), Detective—Amateur
Time period(s): 2000s
Locale(s): Washington, District of Columbia

Summary: Her dream job as food critic for the *Washington Examiner* becomes a nightmare when Chas is challenged by a treacherous young reporter, Ringo Laurenge, who tries to co-opt the story she's working on and is obviously gunning for her spot on the newspaper. He's also trying to sabotage her with her friends and colleagues and steal stories from other staff members, so when he's finally done in by a tainted ham,

it's only a question of who of the many people who hated him actually did it. There's lots of yummy detail about food, as one might expect from this recently retired restaurant critic for the *Washington Post*.

Where it's reviewed:
Booklist, April 1, 2001, page 1450
Library Journal, April 1, 2001, page 136
Publishers Weekly, April 2, 2001, page 42

Other books by the same author:
Murder on the Gravy Train, 1999
The Butter Did It, 1997

Other books you might like:
Michael Bond, *The Monsieur Pamplemousse Series*, 1983-
Peter King, *The Gourmet Detective Series*, 1994-
Cecile LaMalle, *The Charly Poisson Series*, 1999-
Joanne Pence, *The Angelina Amalfi Series*, 1993-
Lou Jane Temple, *The Heaven Lee Series*, 1996-

155

CYNTHIA RIGGS

Deadly Nightshade

(New York: St. Martin's Press, 2001)

Story type: Amateur Detective
Subject(s): Small Town Life; Islands; Boats and Boating
Major character(s): Victoria Trumbull, Writer (poet), Aged Person
Time period(s): 2000s
Locale(s): Martha's Vineyard, Massachusetts

Summary: At 92, Victoria Trumbull is independent, sharp as a tack mentally, and still in possession of all her faculties, including excellent hearing, and when she hears screams and scuffling in the harbor one night while she's out walking, she knows that something is very wrong. She discovers a mutilated body floating in the water and immediately calls upon her granddaughter, Elizabeth, who assists the harbormaster in patrolling the shores, to investigate. Elizabeth and her boss, Domingo, a former New York City cop, realize that as a possible witness to the incident Victoria may have put herself in grave danger. The author, a lifetime Vineyard resident, imbues this debut mystery with wonderful local color and offers a realistic and appealing portrait of a very senior sleuth.

Where it's reviewed:
Booklist, April 1, 2001, page 1450
Deadly Pleasures, Spring 2001, page 50
Library Journal, May 1, 2001, page 129
Publishers Weekly, April 23, 2001, page 53

Other books you might like:
Philip R. Craig, *The J.W. Jackson Series*, 1989-
Francine Mathews, *The Merry Folger Series*, 1994-
Stefanie Matteson, *The Charlotte Graham Series*, 1990-
David Osborn, *Murder on Martha's Vineyard*, 1989
Kelly Roos, *Murder on Martha's Vineyard*, 1981

156

RICK RIORDAN

The Devil Went Down to Austin

(New York: Bantam, 2001)

Story type: Private Detective
Series: Tres Navarre. Book 4
Subject(s): Wealth; Computers; Family Relations
Major character(s): Jackson ''Tres'' Navarre, Detective—Private, Professor
Time period(s): 2000s
Locale(s): Austin, Texas; San Antonio, Texas

Summary: Tres leaves San Antonio for a six-week stint teaching English at the University of Texas in Austin, where he also hopes to spend some time with his paraplegic brother, Garrett, and start renovating his grandfather's ranch. It turns into anything but a happy reunion when he discovers that Garrett has mortgaged the ranch to finance a software company he's started up with his friend and partner Jimmy Doebler and Jimmy's wife, Ruby. When Jimmy is murdered, Garrett is accused of the crime, and Tres' old girlfriend, Maia, comes up from San Antonio to defend him.

Where it's reviewed:
Booklist, May 1, 2001, page 1640
Library Journal, May 1, 2001, page 129
Mystery News, June/July 2001, page 16
Publishers Weekly, April 20, 2001, page 59

Other books by the same author:
The Last King of Texas, 2000
Widower's Two-Step, 1999
Big Red Tequila, 1997

Other books you might like:
Jay Brandon, *Local Rules*, 1998
Harlan Coben, *The Myron Bolitar Series*, 1995-
Robert Crais, *The Elvis Cole Series*, 1987-
Bill Crider, *The Truman Smith Series*, 1991-
Robert B. Parker, *The Spenser Series*, 1973-

157

CANDACE M. ROBB

A Trust Betrayed

(New York: Mysterious, 2001)

Story type: Historical
Series: Margaret Kerr. Book 1
Subject(s): Middle Ages; Politics; Rebellions, Revolts, and Uprisings
Major character(s): Dame Margaret Kerr, Detective—Amateur, Spouse
Time period(s): 13th century (1297)
Locale(s): Edinburgh, Scotland; Dunfermline, Scotland; Perth, Scotland

Summary: When Margaret married Roger Sinclair, she looked forward to, if not domestic bliss, a life of entertaining his colleagues, helping him in his shipping business, and most of all bearing and raising his children. Instead she has barely seen him since their wedding two years ago, consigned to keeping his mother Katherine company while he's away fighting the English king. Roger has been missing for several months and his cousin, Jack, goes to Edinburgh to search for him—only to be killed. Determined to find out what has happened, Margaret travels to Edinburgh which is occupied by the English and Roger is nowhere to be found. This is the first in a projected new series about ordinary citizens, whose lives are affected by the political unrest of the times, but even more by the less exalted concerns of everday living, the homely details of which the author knowledgeably describes. She also writes a 14th century series featuring Owen Archer.

Where it's reviewed:
Publishers Weekly, March 5, 2001, page 66

Other books by the same author:
A Gift of Sanctuary, 1998
The King's Bishop, 1996
The Riddle of St. Leonard's, 1996
The Nun's Tale, 1995
The Lady Chapel, 1994

Other books you might like:
P.C. Doherty, *The Hugh Corbett Series*, 1986-
Susanna Gregory, *The Matthew Bartholomew Series*, 1996-
Paul Harding, *The Brother Athelstan Series*, 1991-
Michael Jecks, *The Sir Baldwin Furnshill Series*, 1995-
Ian Morson, *The William Falconer Series*, 1994-

158

GILLIAN ROBERTS (Pseudonym of Judith Greber)

Whatever Doesn't Kill You

(New York: St. Martin's Press, 2001)

Story type: Private Detective
Series: Emma Howe & Billie August. Book 2
Subject(s): Adoption; Mentally Handicapped
Major character(s): Emma Howe, Detective—Private; Billie August, Detective—Private
Time period(s): 2000s
Locale(s): Tiburon, California (Marin County)

Summary: Emma and Billie are an odd-couple pair of private investigators. Emma, who owns the agency, is experienced and cynical, while her rookie assistant, Billie, is young and eager to please her taciturn boss. When a developmentally disabled young man is charged with killing his best friend, Emma is hired to clear him and turns the case over to Billie, who's certain that she'll win a little respect from her employer if she makes good on it. Meanwhile, Emma is busy working on a case in which a young woman is desperate to find her birthmother, against the wishes of the adoptive mother who refuses to help her. Eventually the two cases converge and Billie and Emma find themselves actually working together instead of separately. The author also writes an engaging series about Philadelphia schoolteacher Amanda Pepper.

Where it's reviewed:
Booklist, April 1, 2001, page 1450
Publishers Weekly, April 9, 2001, page 53

Other books by the same author:
Time and Trouble, 1998

Other books you might like:
D.B. Borton, *The Cat Caliban Series*, 1993-
Janet Dawson, *The Jeri Howard Series*, 1990-
Melodie Johnson Howe, *The Claire Conrad & Maggie Hill Series*, 1989-
Marcia Muller, *The Sharon McCone Series*, 1977-
Judith Van Gieson, *Parrot Blues*, 1995

159

LES ROBERTS

The Dutch

(New York: St. Martin's Press, 2001)

Story type: Private Detective
Series: Milan Jacovich. Book 12
Subject(s): Suicide; Internet
Major character(s): Milan Jacovich, Detective—Private
Time period(s): 2000s
Locale(s): Cleveland, Ohio

Summary: Milan is hired by the college professor father of Ellen Carnine, a young dot.com executive who "did the dutch," or killed herself, under a bridge. What seems to be suicide may well turn out to be something quite different as Milan's investigation reaches from corporate boardrooms to the Internet to some of Cleveland's most dangerous neighborhoods.

Other books by the same author:
The Indian Sign, 2000
The Best Kept Secret, 1999
A Shoot in Cleveland, 1998
Cleveland Local, 1997
Collision Bend, 1996

Other books you might like:
Loren D. Estleman, *The Amos Walker Series*, 1980-
Rob Kantner, *The Ben Perkins Series*, 1986-
John Lutz, *The Alo Nudger Series*, 1976-
James Martin, *The Gil Disbro Series*, 1989-
Jonathan Valin, *The Harry Stoner Series*, 1980-

160

LYNDA S. ROBINSON

Slayer of Gods

(New York: Mysterious, 2001)

Story type: Historical
Series: Lord Meren. Book 6
Subject(s): Ancient History; Egyptian Religion; Kings, Queens, Rulers, etc.
Major character(s): Lord Meren, Nobleman, Government Official
Time period(s): 14th century B.C. (circa 1350 B.C.)
Locale(s): Memphis, Egypt

Summary: Twelve years into the reign of the controversial Pharaoh Akhenaten, his queen, the beautiful Nefertiti, vanished, and was later said to have died of the plague. After Akhenaten's death, his son Tutankhamun ascends to the throne. His chief advisor is Lord Meren, who now learns that

Nefertiti was actually poisoned, and he is sent to find her killer by Tutankhamun, to whom the late queen had been a loving second mother. The only person who can help Lord Meren is the Egyptian spy Anath, known as the Eyes of Babylon, a woman who harbors many secrets and is as intelligent as Meren but whose trustworthiness is questionable. As he tries to penetrate the secrets of the past, Lord Meren uncovers a dangerous conspiracy in the present.

Where it's reviewed:
Booklist, May 1, 2001, page 1642
Library Journal, April 1, 2001, page 137
Publishers Weekly, April 9, 2001, page 53

Other books by the same author:
Drinker of Blood, 1998
Eater of Souls, 1997
Murder at the Feast of Rejoicing, 1996
Murder at the God's Gate, 1995
Murder in the Place of Anubis, 1994

Other books you might like:
Agatha Christie, *Death Comes as the End*, 1944
P.C. Doherty, *The Judge Amerotke Series*, 1999-
Lauren Haney, *The Lieutenant Bak Series*, 1997-
Lee Levin, *King Tut's Private Eye*, 1996
Carol Thurston, *The Eye of Horus*, 2000

161

LAURA JOH ROWLAND

Black Lotus

(New York: St. Martin's Minotaur, 2001)

Story type: Historical
Series: Sano Ichiro. Book 6
Subject(s): Samurai; Buddhism; Cults
Major character(s): Sano Ichiro, Investigator; Reiko Ichiro, Spouse
Time period(s): 17th century (1693)
Locale(s): Tokyo, Japan

Summary: As *sosakan-sama* (Most Honorable Investigator of Events, Situations and People) to the shogun, Sano is asked to investigate a case of arson at the Black Lotus Temple which killed three people. Sano suspects that a young girl who was seen fleeing the fire is to blame, but his wife, Reiko, who insists on becoming involved in his investigations, suspects otherwise and goes undercover at the temple. There she uncovers a secret hedonistic cult existing within the sect, which practices prostitution and extortion and may be responsible for the fire. The author makes great use of her exotic setting and quickly puts readers at ease with the unfamiliar surroundings and culture.

Where it's reviewed:
Booklist, January 1, 2001, page 926
Library Journal, March 1, 2001, page 133
Publishers Weekly, January 29, 2001, page 68

Other books by the same author:
The Samurai's Wife, 2000
The Concubine's Tattoo, 1998
The Way of the Traitor, 1997
Bundori, 1996

Shinju, 1994

Other books you might like:
Dale Furutani, *The Matsuyama Kaze Series*, 1998-
Sujata Massey, *The Rei Shimura Series*, 1997-
James Melville, *The Inspector Otani Series*, 1979-
Robert Van Gulik, *The Judge Dee Series*, 1949-1976
Ann Woodward, *The Lady Aoi Series*, 1996-

162

JAY RUSSELL

Greed & Stuff

(New York: St. Martin's Press, 2001)

Story type: Private Detective
Series: Marty Burns. Book 3
Subject(s): Actors and Actresses; Television; Humor
Major character(s): Marty Burns, Detective—Private, Actor
Time period(s): 2000s
Locale(s): Los Angeles, California; Hermosa Beach, California

Summary: A former teen sitcom actor who was out of work for many years, Marty is now playing a private eye on a television series that's tanking with its target audience and doing the occasional investigation for a friend, while he waits to see if the show will be renewed. One of his poker buddies asks Marty to locate some missing footage from an old film noir classic, *The Devil on Sunday*, which his father had a hand in writing and during the filming of which his mother, one of the stars, was murdered. Although his own network once distributed the film, Marty keeps coming up empty-handed, and then his friend turns up dead. Film buffs and general readers alike will enjoy the plentiful cinema trivia and sardonic humor the book is laced with.

Where it's reviewed:
Booklist, December 15, 2000, page 793
Library Journal, January 1, 2001, page 161
Publishers Weekly, January 8, 2001, page 51

Other books by the same author:
Burning Bright, 1997
Celestial Dogs, 1997

Other books you might like:
Robert Campbell, *The Whistler Series*, 1986-
Stan Cutler, *The Rayford Goodman/Mark Bradley Series*, 1991-
Charles Larson, *The Nils-Frederik Blixen Series*, 1973-1985
Les Roberts, *The Saxon Series*, 1988-
Jim Stinson, *The Stony Winston Series*, 1985-

163

JOHN SANDFORD (Pseudonym of John Camp)

Chosen Prey

(New York: Putnam, 2001)

Story type: Police Procedural; Psychological Suspense
Series: Lucas Davenport. Book 12
Subject(s): Sexuality; Serial Killer; Internet

Major character(s): Lucas Davenport, Police Officer (deputy chief)
Time period(s): 2000s
Locale(s): Minneapolis, Minnesota

Summary: Coming to a crossroads in his personal life after his former fiancee, Weather Karkinnen, decides she wants to have his baby, Davenport seeks distraction by immersing himself in a new and complicated case. A number of young women have gone missing in Minnesota and Wisconsin over the past nine years, and there seems to be some kind of connection between an Internet pornography site and a sinister art history professor with a genial manner, a taste for very kinky sex, and a talent for computer graphics.

Where it's reviewed:
Booklist, May 1, 2001, page 1640
Publishers Weekly, April 23, 2001, page 49

Other books by the same author:
Easy Prey, 2000
Certain Prey, 1999
Secret Prey, 1998
Sudden Prey, 1996
Mind Prey, 1995

Other books you might like:
Michael Connelly, *The Harry Bosch Series*, 1992-
Jeffery Deaver, *The Lincoln Rhyme Series*, 1997-
K.J. Erickson, *Third Person Singular*, 2001
T. Jefferson Parker, *The Blue Hour*, 1999
Ridley Pearson, *The Lou Boldt Series*, 1991-

164

BETH SAULNIER

The Fourth Wall

(New York: Warner, 2001)

Story type: Amateur Detective; Humor
Series: Alex Bernier. Book 3
Subject(s): Journalism; Small Town Life; Friendship
Major character(s): Alex Bernier, Journalist (newspaper reporter), Detective—Amateur
Time period(s): 2000s
Locale(s): Gabriel, New York

Summary: While covering a story about SOS, a drive to save the historic Starlight Theater, Alex goes to interview the chairman of the arts council only to find him dead. His heart attack proves to have been caused by an overdose of Viagra and generates a great deal of publicity for SOS, which annoys the developer hoping to convert the old theater into luxury condos. Then a former child star living in Gabriel (home of Benson University and in topography very much like Ithaca, New York) offers to help finance SOS. More bodies follow, including that of an elderly woman, who proves to be a legendary movie star who's long since disappeared from the public eye. The story is told with a good deal of wit, the characters are believable, and the pace lively.

Other books by the same author:
Distemper, 2000
Reliable Sources, 1999

Other books you might like:
Della Borton, *Slow Dissolve*, 2001
P.M. Carlson, *The Maggie Ryan Series*, 1985-1991
Helen Chappell, *The Hollis Ball Series*, 1996-
Jane Rubino, *The Cat Austen Series*, 1996-
Elaine Viets, *The Francesca Vierling Series*, 1997-

165

D.R. SCHANKER

Natural Law

(New York: St. Martin's Press, 2001)

Story type: Legal
Series: Nora Lumsey. Book 2
Subject(s): Rape; Prostitution; Drugs
Major character(s): Nora Lumsey, Lawyer (deputy public defender); Luther Cox, Detective—Police; Sunni Skye, Prostitute, Murderer (accused)
Time period(s): 2000s
Locale(s): Indianapolis, Indiana; Harrison, Indiana

Summary: Now a public defender in Indianapolis, big-boned Nora has a tendency to get emotionally involved with her hard-luck clients. This time she's representing Sunni Skye, a drug-addicted prostitute who is accused of killing Jim Barris, a highly respected professor who was also heartily disliked by most who knew him. Nora also had a connection with Barris, who was for a brief time her lover. She works together with Luther Cox, the police detective who has been assigned the case in rural Indiana, where the body was found. Somehow the matter is connected with a police cover-up of a rape committed by a high-profile university basketball player.

Where it's reviewed:
Booklist, December 15, 2000, page 793
Library Journal, January 1, 2001, page 162
Publishers Weekly, January 22, 2001, page 306

Other books by the same author:
A Criminal Appeal, 1998

Other books you might like:
P.M. Carlson, *The Marty Hopkins Series*, 1992-
Michael A. Kahn, *The Rachel Gold Series*, 1988-
Lisa Scottoline, *Final Appeal*, 1994
Grif Stockley, *The Gideon Page Series*, 1992-
Marianne Wesson, *The Cinda Hayes Series*, 1998-

166

AILEEN SCHUMACHER

Rosewood's Ashes

(Philadelphia: Intrigue, 2001)

Story type: Amateur Detective
Series: Tory Travers. Book 4
Subject(s): Racism; African Americans; History
Major character(s): Tory Travers, Engineer, Single Parent; David Alvarez, Police Officer
Time period(s): 2000s
Locale(s): Rosewood, Florida; Gainesville, Florida; Lake City, Florida

Summary: For years Tory has been estranged from her political kingpin father and only recently has been in communication with him again. Now she has just learned he's in a coma after being involved in a serious accident, and as the only surviving family member, she feels compelled to return to Florida after a long absence to be at his side. Accompanying her is David Alvarez, the El Paso policeman she has a loving relationship with. A major subplot is the horrifying destruction by the Ku Klux Klan in 1923 of the black community of Rosewood, a story that's told in interspersed chapters, primarily from the viewpoint of a young African American woman who lived through it.

Where it's reviewed:
Deadly Pleasures, Spring 2001, page 42
Publishers Weekly, April 30, 2001, page 60

Other books by the same author:
Affirmative Reaction, 1999
Framework for Death, 1998
Engineered for Murder, 1996

Other books you might like:
Sarah Andrews, *The Em Hansen Series*, 1994-
Nevada Barr, *Deep South*, 2000
Earlene Fowler, *Arkansas Traveler*, 2001
William Heffernan, *Beulah Hill*, 2000
Troy Soos, *Hanging Curve*, 1999

167

LISA SCOTTOLINE

The Vendetta Defense

(New York: HarperCollins, 2001)

Story type: Legal
Series: Rosato & Associates. Book 8
Subject(s): Law; Italian Americans; Feuds
Major character(s): Judy Carrier, Lawyer; Anthony "Pigeon Tony" Lucia, Murderer; Frank Lucia, Relative (Pigeon Tony's grandson)
Time period(s): 2000s
Locale(s): Philadelphia, Pennsylvania

Summary: The protagonists in all of the author's legal mysteries are various members of the all-women legal firm of Rosato & Associates; this time it's Judy Carrier who takes center stage. She's been assigned to defend Anthony Lucia, aka "Pigeon Tony," a seventyish Italian man, who is accused of killing Angelo Coluzzi, a long-time rival who killed Tony's wife in Italy nearly 60 years ago. Tony doesn't deny his guilt, but he claims the murder was justified because of the long-standing vendetta between the two men. As intrigued as she is by this simple defense, Judy knows she will have a problem selling it to a jury. Matters are further complicated by her attraction to Tony's grandson and various attempts on her life by members of Coluzzi's gang. The Italian characters and the South Philly neighborhoods they inhabit are wonderfully drawn and the story is told with an engaging wit.

Where it's reviewed:
People Weekly, April 2, 2001, page 45
Publishers Weekly, February 12, 2001, page 185

Other books by the same author:
Moment of Truth, 2000
Mistaken Identity, 1999
Rough Justice, 1997
Legal Tender, 1996
Running from the Law, 1995

Other books you might like:
Jonnie Jacobs, *The Kali O'Brien Series*, 1996-
Lia Matera, *The Laura Di Palma Series*, 1988-
Perri O'Shaughnessy, *The Nina Reilly Series*, 1995-
Barbara Parker, *The Gail Connor Series*, 1994-
Kate Wilhelm, *The Barbara Holloway Series*, 1991-

168

BARBARA SERANELLA

Unfinished Business

(New York: Scribner, 2001)

Story type: Amateur Detective
Series: Munch Mancini. Book 4
Subject(s): Rape; Serial Killer; Single Parent Families
Major character(s): Munch Mancini, Mechanic (auto), Addict
    (recovering); Mace St. John, Detective—Homicide
Time period(s): 2000s
Locale(s): Los Angeles, California (Brentwood)

Summary: Munch, who has put her past as a heroin addict and
outlaw biker behind her, has a respectable job as an auto
mechanic at a Brentwood garage, moonlights as the driver of
her own limousine service, and is raising an adopted seven-
year-old girl, Asia. A socialite client of hers is killed by a
serial rapist, and another, Robin Davies, survives a similar
attack but is horribly traumatized by it. It becomes apparent
the rapist has some connection with the garage where Munch
works and may even have targeted her. She joins forces with
her old friend, Mace St. John, to find the man before he strikes
again. Although she has a boyfriend, Munch finds herself
increasingly attracted to the happily married St. John, but her
ironclad moral code prevents her from ever acting on it.

Where it's reviewed:
Booklist, March 15, 2001, page 1359
Publishers Weekly, April 23, 2001, page 49

Other books by the same author:
Unwanted Company, 2000
No Offense Intended, 1999
No Human Involved, 1997

Other books you might like:
Rosemary Aubert, *The Ellis Portal Series*, 1997-
Wendy Hornsby, *77th Street Requiem*, 1995
Denise Mina, *The Maureen O'Donnell Series*, 1999-
Jenny Siler, *Easy Money*, 1999
John Straley, *The Cecil Younger Series*, 1992-

169

JOHN SHANNON

The Orange Curtain

(New York: Carroll & Graf, 2001)

Story type: Private Detective
Series: Jack Liffey. Book 4
Subject(s): Vietnamese Americans; Gangs; City Life
Major character(s): Jack Liffey, Detective—Private
Time period(s): 2000s
Locale(s): Los Angeles, California; Orange County, California

Summary: When Los Angelenos head south into Orange
County, they call it penetrating the Orange Curtain, and that's
what laconic private eye Jack Liffey does when the disappearance of Minh Phuong, a recent college graduate, takes him to
into the Vietnamese American community in that conservative county. He also searches for her in Los Angeles' own
Little Saigon, where a war is still being fought. Both communities are ruled by street gangs who don't like Liffey poking
around on their turf. Southern California may have changed
since Philip Marlowe walked its mean streets, but the private
eye novel hasn't, and Liffey fits all of Chandler's criteria for
the detective as knight errant. A former aerospace engineer,
who drives a 1979 Concord and specializes in locating missing children, he's a decent guy with a mission, full of perceptive observations about the multicultural city he calls home.
Actually, this is a very much underrated private eye series, in
part because all three previous volumes have been published
only as paperback originals.

Where it's reviewed:
New York Times Book Review, April 1, 2001, page 17
Publishers Weekly, March 16, 2001, page 66

Other books by the same author:
The Poison Sky, 2000
The Cracked Earth, 1999
The Concrete River, 1996

Other books you might like:
Michael Connelly, *The Harry Bosch Series*, 1992-
Robert Crais, *Stalking the Angel*, 1989
T. Jefferson Parker, *Little Saigon*, 1988
T. Jefferson Parker, *Silent Joe*, 2001
Robert Ray, *The Matt Murdock Series*, 1986-

170

BETH SHERMAN

The Devil and the Deep Blue Sea

(New York: Avon, 2001)

Story type: Amateur Detective; Traditional
Series: Anne Hardaway. Book 4
Subject(s): Missing Persons; Small Town Life; Witches and
    Witchcraft
Major character(s): Anne Hardaway, Writer (ghostwriter),
    Detective—Amateur
Time period(s): 2000s
Locale(s): Oceanside Heights, New Jersey

Summary: Anne, who ghostwrites popular how-to and self-help books by celebrity experts, starts learning first-hand about teenage subcultures when her Jersey shore community is invaded by a plague of devil worship which leaves one young wannabe witch dead and another missing. She'd rather not be involved, but the missing girl is the grandniece of an elderly friend of hers, so Anne sets out to find out what's really going on in the name of satanic activities and black magic, but what she finds is anything but otherworldly.

Other books by the same author:
Death's a Beach, 2000
Death at High Tide, 1999
Dead Man's Float, 1998

Other books you might like:
Linda Grant, *Vampyre Bites*, 1998
Rett MacPherson, *The Torie O'Shea Series*, 1997-
Valerie S. Malmont, *The Tori Miracle Series*, 1994-
Abigail Padgett, *The Dollmaker's Daughters*, 1997
Denise Swanson, *The Scumble River Series*, 2000-

171

MARCIA SIMPSON

Sound Tracks

(Scottsdale, Arizona: Poisoned Pen, 2001)

Story type: Amateur Detective
Series: Liza Romero. Book 2
Subject(s): Animals/Whales; Ecology; Boats and Boating
Major character(s): Liza Romero, Pilot (charter boat), Detective—Amateur
Time period(s): 2000s
Locale(s): Wrangell, Alaska

Summary: Liza pilots her boat, *Salmon Eye*, along the Inside Passage of southern Alaska, delivering books and other cargo to the small ports between Ketchikan and Juneau. It's a tricky course, especially in bad weather, but when something crashes into her boat one November day, the last thing Liza expects to find is a humpback whale, since they are instinctively splendid navigators. Soon she realizes both the whales and dolphins in the area have become mysteriously disoriented. Then a state wildlife agent disappears from his boat and is later found drowned, the Vietnam vet husband of a friend goes out of control, and a marine biologist is threatened. The author does a terrific job showing how Alaskans must struggle every day just to survive in their harsh environment, and how they must depend on each other for support.

Where it's reviewed:
Publishers Weekly, April 30, 2001, page 60

Other books by the same author:
Crow in Stolen Colors, 2000

Other books you might like:
Sue Henry, *Beneath the Ashes*, 2000
Stan Jones, *White Sky, Black Ice*, 1999
Megan Mallory Rust, *The Taylor Morgan Series*, 1998-
Dana Stabenow, *The Kate Shugak Series*, 1992-
John Straley, *The Cecil Younger Series*, 1992-

172

FRANK SMITH

Thread of Evidence

(New York: St. Martin's Press, 2001)

Story type: Police Procedural; Traditional
Series: Neil Paget. Book 4
Subject(s): Small Town Life; Prostitution
Major character(s): Neil Paget, Police Officer (detective chief inspector)
Time period(s): 2000s
Locale(s): Shropshire, England

Summary: When a prominent local real estate developer is found stabbed to death in a hotel room, Neil and his fellow officers go searching for the young prostitute who was seen going to his room shortly after midnight on the night the murder took place. However, the girl, Vikki Lane, who woke up next to the bloody corpse with no memory beyond arriving at the room and being knocked unconscious, has gone into hiding, fearing that she might somehow be guilty of the murder. The police find many suspects and as many dead ends in their investigation, and Vikki finds sanctuary with a kind-hearted barmaid who once before befriended her, while the real murderer observes from a distance.

Where it's reviewed:
Booklist, December 15, 2000, page 793
Library Journal, February 1, 2001, page 128

Other books by the same author:
Candles for the Dead, 1999
Stone Dead, 1998
Fatal Flaw, 1996

Other books you might like:
Jo Bannister, *The Frank Shapiro Series*, 1993-
Clare Curzon, *The Mike Yeadings Series*, 1983-
Caroline Graham, *Barnaby Series Inspector*, 1987-
Reginald Hill, *The Dalziel/Pascoe Series*, 1997-
Peter Robinson, *The Inspector Alan Banks Series*, 1987-

173

JULIE SMITH

Louisiana Hotshot

(New York: Forge, 2001)

Story type: Private Detective
Subject(s): American South; African Americans; Internet
Major character(s): Talba Wallace, Detective—Private, Writer (poet); Eddie Valentino, Detective—Private
Time period(s): 2000s
Locale(s): New Orleans, Louisiana

Summary: The author gets this new series off to a flying start, when Talba answers an ad for a private investigator by running a full-scale check on the man placing the ad, Eddie Valentino, and sets the stage for a terrific odd-couple pairing of a cocky young African American woman and a crusty, sixtyish white Italian man. Talba, who moonlights as the cafe poet Baroness de Pontalba, has the computer skills and education Eddie lacks, and he has the experience and perspective

she's too young to have acquired. Her first case is tracking down a man who is luring teenage black girls to their deaths. As in her earlier series about police officer Skip Langdon (who makes a cameo appearance here), the author drenches her narrative in the sights, smells, and sounds of New Orleans.

Where it's reviewed:
Library Journal, May 1, 2001, page 132
Mystery News, June/July 2001, page 13
Publishers Weekly, April 9, 2001, page 54

Other books by the same author:
Mean Rooms, 2000 (short stories)
82 Desire, 1998
Crescent City Kill, 1997
The Kindness of Strangers, 1996
House of Blues, 1995

Other books you might like:
Ace Atkins, *Leavin' Trunk Blues*, 2000
Charlotte Carter, *The Nanette Hayes Series*, 1997-
D.J. Donaldson, *The Andy Broussard Series*, 1988-
Martin Hegwood, *Big Easy Backroad*, 1999
Judith Smith-Levin, *The Starletta Duvall Series*, 1996-

174

MICHELLE SPRING

In the Midnight Hour

(New York: Ballantine, 2001)

Story type: Private Detective; Traditional
Series: Laura Principal
Subject(s): Identity; Missing Persons; Small Town Life
Major character(s): Laura Principal, Detective—Private
Time period(s): 2000s
Locale(s): Cambridge, England; Norfolk, England

Summary: Twelve years ago, John and Olivia Cable's four-year-old son Timmy vanished on a Norfolk beach and was never seen again. Then one day Olivia sees a young Cambridge street musician, who looks the way she thinks Timmy would look as a teenager, and she soon has convinced herself that the boy is her son. John, a well-known Arctic explorer (Olivia is an equally well-known writer), is concerned that his wife needs protection and that the young man she befriends may be simply preying on a bereaved mother's fantasies. He hires Laura both to protect Olivia and to investigate the boy's origins. A smooth blend of the English village cozy and the harder-edged private eye novel.

Where it's reviewed:
Booklist, February 1, 2001, page 1042

Other books by the same author:
Nights in White Satin, 1999
Standing in the Shadows, 1998
Running for Shelter, 1995
Every Breath You Take, 1994

Other books you might like:
Liza Cody, *The Anna Lee Series*, 1980-
Sarah Dunant, *The Hannah Wolfe Series*, 1992-
P.D. James, *An Unsuitable Job for a Woman*, 1972
Nora Kelly, *In the Shadow of Kings*, 1984

Jill Paton Walsh, *The Imogen Quay Series*, 1993-

175

DANA STABENOW

The Singing of the Dead

(New York: St. Martin's Press, 2001)

Story type: Private Detective
Series: Kate Shugak. Book 11
Subject(s): Politics; Eskimos; Prostitution
Major character(s): Kate Shugak, Detective—Private
Time period(s): 2000s; 1910s (1915)
Locale(s): Ahtna, Alaska; Niniltna, Alaska

Summary: Anne Gordaoff, a Native woman running for the Alaskan state senate, hires a reluctant Kate to be her security guard after receiving a number of threatening letters. One evening, while Kate is at Anne's side during a fund-raising event, one of her campaign staffers is murdered in the parking lot. Kate goes to work seeking a connection between the letters and the murder. At the same time, Anne's opponent has hired a researcher to unearth any scandals in her past that might be used against her. What turns up is in some way related to the unsolved murder of a famous good-time girl during the Klondike Gold Rush in 1915, a story that is narrated in flashbacks and somehow has impacted the present day. The author also writes a series about Alaska state trooper Liam Campbell.

Where it's reviewed:
Booklist, May 1, 2001, page 1641
Library Journal, May 1, 2001, page 132
Publishers Weekly, April 2, 2001, page 42

Other books by the same author:
Midnight Come Again, 2000
Hunter's Moon, 1999
Killing Grounds, 1998
Breakup, 1997
Blood Will Tell, 1996

Other books you might like:
Val Davis, *The Return of the Spanish Lady*, 2001
Sue Henry, *The Alex Jensen Series*, 1991-
Stan Jones, *White Sky, Black Ice*, 1999
Megan Mallory Rust, *The Taylor Morgan Series*, 1998-
Marcia Simpson, *Crow in Stolen Colors*, 2000

176

BILL STACKHOUSE

Stream of Death

(Scottsdale, Arizona: Poisoned Pen, 2001)

Story type: Traditional; Police Procedural
Series: Ed McAvoy. Book 1
Subject(s): Fishing; Small Town Life; World War II
Major character(s): Ed McAvoy, Police Officer (police chief)
Time period(s): 2000s; 1940s (1943)
Locale(s): Peekamoose, New York (Catskills); Sicily, Italy

Summary: A fabulous rose-colored diamond that disappeared from Sicily during World War II is fished out of the waters of

Esopus Creek in the Catskills by young Danny Henderson, whose mother is dating Ed McAvoy, the town's police chief. McAvoy, who was invalided out of the Detroit homicide squad after sustaining a gunshot wound, has come to peaceful Peekamoose thinking he's seen an end to violent crime, but fortunately he's still well-equipped to solve one when it happens. The town is filled with eccentric and likable characters, the scenery is attractive, and the fly-fishing details are a pleasant bonus. There's a good measure of quiet humor as well, with the local retirement home that is a haven for retired Mafia (who figure prominently in the plot), an especially clever touch. A promising first novel in a projected new series.

Where it's reviewed:
Booklist, January 1, 2001, page 926
Library Journal, February 1, 2001, page 128
Publishers Weekly, January 29, 2001, page 69

Other books you might like:
Bartholomew Gill, *Death on a Cold, Wild River*, 1993
Macdonald Hastings, *Cork on the Water*, 1951 reprinted 1999
Victoria Houston, *Dead Angler*, 2000
David Leitz, *The Max Addams Series*, 1996-
Archer Mayor, *The Marble Mask*, 2000

177

LES STANDIFORD

Deal with the Dead

(New York: Putnam, 2001)

Story type: Psychological Suspense
Series: John Deal. Book 6
Subject(s): Blackmail; Government; Organized Crime
Major character(s): John Deal, Contractor
Time period(s): 2000s; 1960s (1962)
Locale(s): Miami, Florida

Summary: Building contractor John Deal is delighted when he's offered a lucrative waterfront building project, but his enthusiasm is dimmed when he finds what the cost will be to him. He's visited by members of the Justice Department, who are anything but the good guys; they tell him that his late father (the founder of his building firm) had been a government informer for many years, and now they want John to take his place—or else. He could bear losing the contract, but there are veiled threats against his wife and daughter if he doesn't comply, and he's already filled with guilt over putting his wife in danger in the past. When he reluctantly agrees, there are threats from other quarters. Unless he can find a way to outwit his enemies, he's in a no-win situation, doomed no matter what he does. The author has also written a couple of stand-alone thrillers.

Where it's reviewed:
Booklist, December 1, 2000, page 696

Other books by the same author:
Presidential Deal, 1999
Deal on Ice, 1997
Deal to Die For, 1995
Raw Deal, 1994

Done Deal, 1993

Other books you might like:
Edna Buchanan, *The Britt Montero Series*, 1992-
Carolina Garcia-Aguilera, *The Lupe Solano Series*, 1996-
James W. Hall, *The Thorn Series*, 1987-
Nancy Pickard, *The Whole Truth*, 2000
Randy Wayne White, *The Doc Ford Series*, 1990-

178

ROSEMARY STEVENS

The Tainted Snuff Box

(New York: Berkley Prime Crime, 2001)

Story type: Historical
Series: Beau Brummell. Book 2
Subject(s): Social Classes; Friendship; Animals/Cats
Major character(s): George Bryan ''Beau'' Brummell, Historical Figure, Socialite (dandy)
Time period(s): 1800s (1805)
Locale(s): Brighton, England

Summary: When the Prince of Wales begins getting mysterious letters threatening his life, he takes up holiday residence in Brighton, where he's visited by his good friend, the charming and fashionable Beau Brummell. He also hires as his personal food taster a tiresome baronet, Sir Simon, who is conscientious to the point of sampling a special snuff blend that Beau's friend, Lord Petersham, has offered to the prince. When Simon falls over dead, the prince suspects the poison was intended for himself. In order to clear Petersham, Beau must find the real murderer. At his side always is his pet, Chakkra, the only Siamese cat in England.

Where it's reviewed:
Publishers Weekly, April 16, 2001, page 47

Other books by the same author:
Death on a Silver Tray, 2000

Other books you might like:
Bruce Alexander, *The Sir John Fielding Series*, 1994-
Stephanie Barron, *The Jane Austen Series*, 1996-
Deryn Lake, *The John Rawlings Series*, 1994-
Wilder Perkins, *The Bartholomew Hoare Series*, 1998-
Kate Ross, *The Julian Kestrel Series*, 1993-1997

179

SARAH STROHMEYER

Bubbles Unbound

(New York: Dutton, 2001)

Story type: Amateur Detective; Humor
Subject(s): Mothers and Daughters; Working Mothers; Journalism
Major character(s): Bubbles Yablonsky, Hairdresser, Student—College
Time period(s): 2000s (2001)
Locale(s): Lehigh, Pennsylvania

Summary: Having flunked practically every course the local community college has to offer and struggling to make ends

meet after her rich lawyer ex-husband has cut off her alimony, Bubbles decides it's time to get serious about improving herself. It's not that she doesn't enjoy her work as a hairdresser at Sandy's House of Beauty, it's just that she can't bear having her daughter, a teenager who dyes her own hair with Kool-Aid, always feeling sorry for her. When her guidance counselor suggests journalism, she throws herself into her classes enthusiastically and starts interning at the local newspaper. One day she comes across a crime in progress and finds herself in the middle of a murder investigation, which just might jump-start her career as an investigative journalist—if she lives that long. Bubbles has a warm heart and the requisite complement of wacky relatives, including a pistol-packing mother who has recently escaped from a Polish old folks' home, as well as a sexy sidekick, a photographer nicknamed Stiletto. While she may not have the brain of a rocket scientist, she does have keen powers of observation, particularly when it comes to class distinctions. It doesn't come as much of a surprise to learn that the author of this appealing first novel studied under Janet Evanovich. And it's always nice to add another working-class heroine to the meager ranks of women amateur sleuths who aren't lawyers, entrepreneurs, or other well-heeled professionals.

Where it's reviewed:
Booklist, January 1, 2001, page 927
Deadly Pleasures, Winter 2001, page 51
Library Journal, January 1, 2001, page 161
Mystery News, February/March 2001, page 29

Other books you might like:
Nancy J. Cohen, *The Marla Shore Series*, 1999-
Sophie Dunbar, *The Claire Claiborne Series*, 1993-
Janet Evanovich, *The Stephanie Plum Series*, 1994-
Marlys Millhiser, *The Charlie Greene Series*, 1992-
Kathleen Taylor, *The Tory Bauer Series*, 1995-

180

JAMES SWAIN

Grift Sense

(New York: Pocket, 2001)

Story type: Private Detective
Subject(s): Gambling; Crime and Criminals
Major character(s): Tony Valentine, Consultant, Police Officer (retired)
Time period(s): 2000s
Locale(s): Las Vegas, Nevada

Summary: Tony Valentine makes his living investigating people who cheat at cards in gambling casinos. He's called in by the owner of a second-rate Las Vegas gambling hall, when a card shark named Frank Fontaine proceeds to conspicuously beat the house big time at blackjack, and the surveillance tape suggests the dealer, Nola Briggs, may be in collusion with him. When Frank disappears without a trace, leaving Nola to take the heat, Valentine suggests that the casino free her on bail and he'll see where she goes from there. First novel by a well-known gambling expert.

Where it's reviewed:
Library Journal, May 1, 2001, page 130

Publishers Weekly, May 7, 2001, page 228

Other books you might like:
Jen Banbury, *Like a Hole in the Head*, 1998
Pete Hautman, *Drawing Dead*, 1993
Brian Hodge, *Wild Horses*, 1999
Tom Kakonis, *The Tim Waverly Series*, 1988-
Gary Phillips, *High Hand*, 2001

181

DENISE SWANSON

Murder of a Sweet Old Lady

(New York: Signet, 2001)

Story type: Amateur Detective
Series: Scumble River. Book 2
Subject(s): Small Town Life; Grandmothers; Family
Major character(s): Skye Denison, Psychologist (school)
Time period(s): 2000s
Locale(s): Scumble River, Illinois

Summary: Back in her home town after being fired from a job in Chicago and being dumped by her fiance, Skye is determined to make the best of things until she's saved up enough to leave Scumble River again. Now she works as a psychologist for her old high school and is beginning to get used to the quieter rhythms of small town living. One silver lining to the situation is being able to look in on her grandmother every day and listen to all the family history the old lady still remembers, although her memory of recent events is failing. Then one afternoon she finds her grandmother dead and the housekeeper she'd hired missing. Although it looks as if the old lady died of natural causes, Skye orders an autopsy and is stunned to find her grandma has been murdered.

Other books by the same author:
Murder of a Small-Town Honey, 2000

Other books you might like:
Monica Ferris, *The Betsy Devonshire Series*, 1999-
Rett MacPherson, *The Torie O'Shea Series*, 1997-
Valerie S. Malmont, *The Tori Miracle Series*, 1994-
Leslie Meier, *The Lucy Stone Series*, 1993-
Beth Sherman, *The Anne Hardaway Series*, 1998-

182

JON TALTON

Concrete Desert

(New York: St. Martin's Press, 2001)

Story type: Amateur Detective
Subject(s): Missing Persons; History; Serial Killer
Major character(s): David Mapstone, Professor (of history)
Time period(s): 2000s
Locale(s): Phoenix, Arizona

Summary: When history professor David Mapstone finds himself out of a job when he's denied tenure at San Diego State, he returns to his hometown of Phoenix to teach at the local community college and work as a consultant to the sheriff's office investigating old unsolved cases. He's just settling, in when a former girlfriend, Julie Riding, reappears unexpec-

tedly in his life, asking if he'll help her locate her sister, Phaedra, who's gone missing. The police won't do it, since Phaedra's an adult and there's no evidence of foul play, but Julie is certain there's something terribly wrong about her disappearance. He agrees, and then finds surprising similarities between this case and a 40-year-old one he's investigating involving the disappearance of a woman named Rebecca Stokes in 1959. Worked into the narrative is much interesting information about the city's past. First novel.

Where it's reviewed:
Publishers Weekly, May 14, 2001, page 55

Other books you might like:
Michael McGarrity, *The Kevin Kerney Series*, 1996-
Keith Miles, *Murder in Perspective*, 1997
Richard Parrish, *The Joshua Rabb Series*, 1993-
Bernard Schopen, *The Jack Ross Series*, 1989-
Betty Webb, *Desert Noir*, 2001

183

AIMEE THURLO
DAVID THURLO, Co-Author

Red Mesa

(New York: Forge, 2001)

Story type: Police Procedural; Traditional
Series: Ella Clah. Book 6
Subject(s): Native Americans; Indian Reservations; Parenthood
Major character(s): Ella Clah, Police Officer (tribal special investigator), Indian (Navajo)
Time period(s): 2000s
Locale(s): Navajo Reservation, New Mexico

Summary: Ella is finding it difficult to keep a balance between her personal and her professional lives now that she is the mother of an 18-month-old baby, just as it has always been difficult to balance her identity as a Navajo with her place in the white world. There are always family pressures, as well. In addition to her mother, who disapproves of her working long hours, there is her cousin, Justine, whose new boyfriend looks like bad news to Ella. Then when Justine disappears and what might be her remains are found at Red Mesa, Ella herself becomes a murder suspect and must prove her innocence to her own colleagues. Rich in detail about life on the reservation, as well as forensic crime investigation techniques, this is another strong entry in a series, which also features believable characters and intricate plotting.

Where it's reviewed:
Booklist, December 15, 2000, page 792
Library Journal, March 1, 2001, page 133
Publishers Weekly, January 29, 2001, page 68

Other books by the same author:
Shooting Chant, 2000
Enemy Way, 1998
Bad Medicine, 1997
Death Walker, 1996
Blackening Song, 1995

Other books you might like:
James D. Doss, *The Shaman Series*, 1994-

Jean Hager, *The Molly Bearpaw Series*, 1992-
Tony Hillerman, *The Joe Leaphorn/Jim Chee Series*, 1970-
Kirk Mitchell, *Cry Dance*, 1999
Barbara Moore, *The Wolf Whispered Death*, 1986

184

REBECCA TOPE

Dark Undertakings

(New York: St. Martin's Press, 2001)

Story type: Traditional; Amateur Detective
Subject(s): Death; Drugs; Infidelity
Major character(s): Drew Slocombe, Undertaker, Nurse (former pediatric)
Time period(s): 2000s
Locale(s): Bradbourne, England

Summary: Everyone believes that Jim Lapsford, a robustly healthy man in his middle fifties, died of an unexpected heart attack—everybody, that is, but apprentice undertaker Drew Slocombe. Drew is still haunted by guilt over the death of a child he was caring for in his previous job as a pediatric nurse, even though he was cleared of any wrongdoing. The trouble is that Lapsford's cremation is coming up in just a few days, and there's not much time for Drew to investigate. He quickly learns that Lapsford had been involved in a number of adulterous affairs that ended badly, and that most of his ex-lovers, as well as his wife and son, had good reason to hate him. Lapsford had also been taking black-market Viagra shortly before his untimely demise. Since an autopsy is out of the question, Drew is going to have to find another way to determine the actual cause of death.

Where it's reviewed:
Booklist, May 1, 2001, page 1642
Publishers Weekly, May 7, 2001, page 227

Other books by the same author:
A Dirty Death, 2000

Other books you might like:
Leo Axler, *The Bill Hawley Series*, 1994-
Robert Barnard, *Unholy Dying*, 2001
Tim Cockey, *The Hitchcock Sewell Series*, 2000-
Frank Parrish, *The Dan Mallett Series*, 1977-
Neville Steed, *The Peter Marklin Series*, 1986-

185

MARI ULMER

Carreta de la Muerte (Cart of Death)

(Scottsdale, Arizona: Poisoned Pen, 2001)

Story type: Traditional; Amateur Detective
Series: Taos Festival Mysteries. Book 2
Subject(s): Mexican Americans; Catholicism; Small Town Life
Major character(s): Christina Garcia y Grant, Lawyer (former), Innkeeper (bed and breakfast)
Time period(s): 2000s
Locale(s): Talpa, New Mexico; Taos, New Mexico

Summary: Christy is a young widow who gave up being a lawyer to return to her home town of Talpa, just southwest of Taos, where she inherited a hacienda from her grandmother, which she has turned into a charming bed and breakfast, Casa Vieja. In addition to a large extended family in the town, Christy has many friends, including Iggy Baca, a public defender, and the widower Mac MacLeod, who lives at Casa Vieja and helps her run it (and provides an amiable love interest). There is a murder during the town's fiesta, as well as the theft of some sacred artifacts, followed by the disappearance of Iggy's girlfriend, and Christy and her friends turn detective to solve the crimes. The author does a first-rate job with the local color, being well versed in the Spanish traditions and customs of the area.

Where it's reviewed:
Library Journal, March 1, 2001, page 133
Publishers Weekly, February 26, 2001, page 61

Other books by the same author:
Midnight at the Camposanto, 2000

Other books you might like:
Walter Satterthwait, *The Joshua Croft Series*, 1989-
Richard Martin Stern, *The Johnny Ortiz Series*, 1971-1990
Judith Van Gieson, *The Claire Reynier Series*, 2000-
Robert Westbrook, *The Howard Moon Deer Series*, 1998-
Norman Zollinger, *Lautrec*, 1990

186

JUDITH VAN GIESON

Vanishing Point

(New York: Signet, 2001)

Story type: Traditional; Amateur Detective
Series: Claire Reynier. Book 2
Subject(s): Libraries; American West; Authors and Writers
Major character(s): Claire Reynier, Librarian (archivist), Detective—Amateur
Time period(s): 2000s
Locale(s): Albuquerque, New Mexico; Grand Gulch, Utah

Summary: One of Claire's duties as archivist at the University of New Mexico's Center for Southwestern Research is maintaining the papers of Jonathan Vail, a young novelist and wilderness writer, whose mysterious disappearance over 30 years ago has led to his current status as a cult figure. When a graduate student shows up in her office with a notebook journal he found in the cave in Grand Gulch where Jonathan was last seen alive, on a camping trip with his girlfriend, Claire authenticates it as having been written by Vail, and goes to the site to recover the duffel bag the student had to leave behind. Instead she finds the dead body of the student, either fallen or pushed to the canyon floor, and the duffel bag is nowhere to be found. As Claire investigates the death, she inevitably reopens the search for Vail and meets with his mother, his girlfriend, and a diehard fan who's dedicated himself to keeping Vail's memory alive. Told with the author's usual tight focus and attention to the southwestern landscape, this new series is a worthy successor to the ten books she previously produced featuring Albuquerque private eye Neil Hamel.

Where it's reviewed:
Mystery News, February/March 2001, page 16

Other books by the same author:
The Stolen Blue, 2000
Ditch Rider, 1998
Hotshots, 1996
Parrot Blues, 1995
The Lies That Bind, 1993

Other books you might like:
James D. Doss, *The Shaman Series*, 1994-
Tony Hillerman, *A Thief of Time*, 1988
Walter Satterthwait, *The Joshua Croft Series*, 1989-
Betsy Thornton, *High Lonesome Road*, 2001
Norman Zollinger, *Lautrec*, 1990

187

MARGOT WADLEY

The Gripping Beast

(New York: St. Martin's Press, 2001)

Story type: Traditional; Amateur Detective
Subject(s): Treasure; Islands; Vikings
Major character(s): Isabel Garth, Teacher, Artist
Time period(s): 2000s
Locale(s): Stromness, Scotland (Orkney Islands)

Summary: Isabel, a young American art teacher, has come to Stromness in homage to her late father, an Orkney native whose notebooks she intends to illustrate. On the ferry she meets Johanna, a kindly woman whose young son warns Isabel of the Viking witch, Thora, who lives on the island. No sooner have they landed at the tiny village than Isabel meets Thora and is warned of great danger. It's not long before a series of odd events, from the searching of her room to the disappearance of her drawings to a near-fatal accident in a hired car, convinces Isabel that Thora may have a point. At the heart of the mystery is a lost Viking treasure and eventually Thora's murder. Despite everything, Isabel feels at home on the island and is befriended by several of its inhabitants, some of whom knew her father. Winner of the 2000 St. Martin's/Malice Domestic contest for best first traditional mystery, the book is a respectable specimen of its kind, and the atmospheric setting alone should win over readers who fancy romantic suspense and spunky young heroines in search of their roots.

Where it's reviewed:
Library Journal, February 1, 2001, page 127
Publishers Weekly, March 12, 2001, page 65

Other books you might like:
Jeanne M. Dams, *Holy Terror in the Hebrides*, 1997
Susanna Kearsley, *Shadowy Horses*, 1999
Sharyn McCrumb, *Paying the Piper*, 1991
Elizabeth Peters, *Legend in Green Velvet*, 1976
Josephine Tey, *The Singing Sands*, 1952

188

AYELET WALDMAN

The Big Nap

(New York: Berkley, 2001)

Story type: Amateur Detective; Domestic
Series: Mommy-Track. Book 2
Subject(s): Babysitters; Babies; Judaism
Major character(s): Juliet Applebaum, Parent, Lawyer
Time period(s): 2000s
Locale(s): Los Angeles, California; New York, New York (Brooklyn)

Summary: Feeling grumpy and sleep-deprived since the birth of four-month-old Isaac and neglected by her workaholic screenwriter husband, Juliet reluctantly accepts the offer of a babysitter in the person of a young Hasidic Jewish woman, Fraydl Finkelstein, niece of a neighborhood shopkeeper. Fraydl works wonders with Isaac and for the first time since his birth Juliet gets several hours of uninterrupted sleep. However, the next day Fraydl fails to show up, and when Juliet inquires, she learns the young woman has vanished. Perhaps she fled to avoid an impending arranged marriage, or perhaps it has to do with a young Israeli man Juliet saw her talking to the day before. At any rate, her family refuses to contact the police, so Juliet travels to Brooklyn to see if Fraydl has returned to the Hasidic community there.

Where it's reviewed:
Booklist, May 1, 2001, page 1642
Publishers Weekly, May 21, 2001, page 83

Other books by the same author:
Nursery Crimes, 2000

Other books you might like:
Dorothy Cannell, *Mum's the Word*, 1990
Nancy Goldstone, *Mommy and the Murder*, 1995
Faye Kellerman, *Day of Atonement*, 1992
Lindsay Maracotta, *The Dead Hollywood Moms Society*, 1996
Irene Marcuse, *Guilty Mind*, 2001

189

PENNY WARNER

Blind Side

(Santa Barbara, California: Perseverance Press, 2001)

Story type: Amateur Detective
Series: Connor Westphal. Book 4
Subject(s): Deafness; Animals/Frogs and Toads; Small Town Life
Major character(s): Connor Westphal, Journalist (newspaper owner/editor), Handicapped (deaf); Dan Smith, Detective—Private, Boyfriend (of Connor)
Time period(s): 2000s
Locale(s): Flat Skunk, California (Calaveras County)

Summary: The annual frog jumping contest held just a few miles away is about to get underway, and Connor is running a "Worst Verse" contest in her weekly newspaper in honor of the event. A shadow falls over the festivities when Buford, the defending champion bullfrog from last year, is found dead, and Connor's boyfriend, Dan Smith, is hired to find out who did it. The frog's owner blames the sheriff's son, Jeremiah Mercer, for the murder, as the two were rivals not only in the jumping contest but in matters of the heart. Then a human body turns up in the creek. Connor, who employs Jeremiah at the paper, can't believe he's guilty and she and a new friend join Dan in his investigation to clear Jeremiah and find the real killer.

Other books by the same author:
A Quiet Undertaking, 2000
Right to Remain Silent, 1999
Sign of Foul Play, 1998
Dead Body Language, 1997

Other books you might like:
Carol Cail, *The Maxey Burnell Series*, 1993-
Carol Caverly, *The Thea Barlow Series*, 1994-
Mary Daheim, *The Emma Lord Series*, 1992-
Judy Fitzwater, *The Jennifer Marsh Series*, 1998-
Anne Underwood Grant, *The Sydney Teague Series*, 1998-

190

BETTY WEBB

Desert Noir

(Scottsdale, Arizona: Poisoned Pen, 2001)

Story type: Private Detective
Subject(s): Art; Memory Loss; Identity
Major character(s): Lena Jones, Detective—Private, Police Officer (retired)
Time period(s): 2000s
Locale(s): Scottsdale, Arizona

Summary: Former homicide cop Lena Jones becomes a private detective after an injury forces an early retirement. When her friend, Clarice, an art dealer with a violently abusive husband, is killed, Lena takes it personally and investigates it herself. Although the husband is her first suspect, she discovers Clarice had made a number of enemies, including an Apache artist, a rival gallery owner, and various family members, any of whom might conceivably want to see her dead. A secondary plot is Lena's own mysterious past; shot in the head when she was four, she was raised in a succession of foster homes and still has huge gaps in her memory. As her investigation into Clarice's death continues, it just might lead her to learning more about her own identity. First novel.

Where it's reviewed:
Publishers Weekly, May 21, 2001, page 85

Other books you might like:
Sinclair Browning, *The Trade Ellis Series*, 1999-
Sandra West Prowell, *The Phoebe Siegel Series*, 1993-
C.J. Songer, *The Meg Gillis Series*, 1998-
Jon Talton, *Concrete Desert*, 2001
Betsy Thornton, *The Chloe Newcomb Series*, 1996-

191

CHASSIE WEST

Killer Riches

(New York: Avon, 2001)

Story type: Police Procedural
Series: Leigh Ann Warren. Book 3
Subject(s): African Americans; Family; Vietnam War
Major character(s): Leigh Ann Warren, Police Officer (former), Lawyer; Dillon ''Duck'' Kennedy, Detective—Police
Time period(s): 2000s
Locale(s): Sunrise, North Carolina; Baltimore, Maryland; Ourland, Maryland

Summary: Leigh Ann, a former police officer, was invalided out of the Washington, D.C., force because of a knee injury and has yet to use the law degree she's obtained. She is ready to marry and settle down with Duck, following the example of her foster mother, Nunna, who is currently honeymooning with her new husband. Then a phone call comes, from a man who claims to have kidnapped the honeymooners and threatens to kill them unless Leigh Ann gives him the Silver Star her father was awarded for his service in Vietnam. Leigh Ann has no idea where the medal is, as her parents died when she was small, and she has no known relatives who could help her. Even worse, when she calls in the FBI, they have no records at all of her parents and therefore none of her. So Leigh Ann goes off in search of her birth family and finds them in Ourland, a small African-American community on the Maryland coast, where her parents were born. She also discovers that not all of her newly found family members are glad to see her.

Other books by the same author:
Killing Kin, 2000
Loss of Innocence, 1997 (non-series)
Sunrise, 1994

Other books you might like:
Eleanor Taylor Bland, *The Marti McAlister Series*, 1992-
Nora DeLoach, *The Candi and Simone Covington Series*, 1994-
Barbara Neely, *The Blanche White Series*, 1992-
Judith Smith-Levin, *The Starletta Duvall Series*, 1996-
Valerie Wilson Wesley, *The Tamara Hayle Series*, 1994-

192

DONALD E. WESTLAKE

Bad News

(New York: Mysterious, 2001)

Story type: Humor; Action/Adventure
Series: Dortmunder
Subject(s): Native Americans; Satire; Crime and Criminals
Major character(s): John Dortmunder, Thief; Fitzroy Guilderpost, Con Artist; Little Feather Redcorn, Dancer (chorus girl)
Time period(s): 2000s
Locale(s): New York

Summary: After a five-year hiatus, Dortmunder, ''a man on whom the sun shone only when he needed darkness,'' is back, in one of the most inspired scams in the annals of comic crime fiction. He's just gotten away from the bungled burglary of a discount store when he's invited to take part in an elaborate scheme with a big payoff: part of the take of a highly profitable upstate New York Indian casino. Joe Redcorn, the last survivor of the now-extinct Pottaknobbee tribe, lies buried in a Queens cemetery. Con artist Fitzroy Guilderpost has recruited a Las Vegas showgirl known as Little Feather Redcorn to pose as Joe's great-granddaughter, which would make her the last of the Pottaknobbees. That would entitle her to one-third of the casino profits, which by law were to be divided among the Pottaknobbees and two other tribes. All Dortmunder has to do is switch the coffin containing Little Feather's actual grandfather with Joe Redcorn's coffin so that the DNA results will come out right. Of course Fitzroy intends to get rid of Dortmunder once he's served his purpose, but Dortmunder has already figured this out and has a plan of his own. The author also writes non-series books and other series under various pseudonyms, including Richard Stark and Tucker Coe.

Where it's reviewed:
Booklist, February 15, 2001, page 1086
Library Journal, March 1, 2001, page 132
Publishers Weekly, March 5, 2001, page 65

Other books by the same author:
What's the Worst That Could Happen?, 1996
Don't Ask, 1993
Drowned Hopes, 1990
Good Behavior, 1986
Why Me?, 1983

Other books you might like:
Pete Hautman, *Short Money*, 1995
Carl Hiaasen, *Native Tongue*, 1991
Laurence Shames, *Sunburn*, 1995
Ross Thomas, *Voodoo, Ltd.*, 1992
Randy Wayne White, *The Man Who Invented Florida*, 1994

193

RANDY WAYNE WHITE

Shark River

(New York: Putnam, 2001)

Story type: Action/Adventure; Humor
Series: Doc Ford. Book 8
Subject(s): Islands; Boats and Boating; Treasure
Major character(s): Marion ''Doc'' Ford, Scientist (marine biologist); Tomlinson, Genius, Philosopher (Zen master)
Time period(s): 2000s
Locale(s): Guava Key, Florida; Sanibel Island, Florida

Summary: When Tomlinson is asked to lead a Zen workshop at a luxury resort on Guava Key, he drags Doc away from his marine specimens and lazy evenings at Dinkins Bay Marina to keep him company. He should have stayed home, for the two quickly get mixed up in all sorts of odd and dangerous events, few of which seem to faze the perpetually blissed-out Tomlinson. Among other things, Doc is approached by a

Bahamian woman, who claims to be his sister and who asks for his help in deciphering a map she promises will lead them to a long-lost treasure. The real treasure here is the book itself, like all the others in this wonderfully entertaining series.

Where it's reviewed:
Mystery News, June/July 2001, page 11
New York Times Book Review, June 10, 2001, page 28
Publishers Weekly, May 7, 2001, page 222

Other books by the same author:
Ten Thousand Islands, 2000
Mangrove Coast, 1998
North of Havana, 1997
Captiva, 1996
The Man Who Invented Florida, 1994

Other books you might like:
Tim Dorsey, *Florida Roadkill*, 1999
James W. Hall, *The Thorn Series*, 1987-
Carl Hiaasen, *Sick Puppy*, 2000
Charles Knief, *Silversword*, 2001
John D. MacDonald, *The Travis McGee Series*, 1964-1985

194
KATE WILHELM

Desperate Measures
(New York: St. Martin's Press, 2001)

Story type: Legal
Series: Barbara Holloway. Book 6
Subject(s): Physically Handicapped; Prejudice; Small Town Life
Major character(s): Barbara Holloway, Lawyer (defense attorney)
Time period(s): 2000s
Locale(s): Opal Creek, Oregon; Eugene, Oregon

Summary: As he's about to retire from his Manhattan practice to a small Oregon town, widowed Dr. Graham Minick takes under his wing Alexander Feldman, a young boy with a hideously deformed face whose parents are only too happy to be rid of him. Alex is a gifted artist who grows up in relative isolation, finding release in a comic strip he draws and in the companionship of his guardian, and generally able to handle the reactions of others to his appearance. When a local man is murdered, the townspeople are all too ready to believe Alex did it, unable to see the human being behind the deformity. Barbara agrees to take on his defense, and her young attorney friend, Shelley, an avid fan of Alex's comic strip, is at first shocked at his physical appearance but soon able to see beyond it.

Where it's reviewed:
Booklist, May 1, 2001, page 1643

Other books by the same author:
No Defense, 2000
Defense for the Devil, 1999
Malice Prepense, 1996
The Best Defense, 1994
Death Qualified, 1991

Other books you might like:
Jonnie Jacobs, *The Kali O'Brien Series*, 1996-
Perri O'Shaughnessy, *The Nina Reilly Series*, 1995-
T. Jefferson Parker, *Silent Joe*, 2001
Lisa Scottoline, *The Rosato & Associates Series*, 1993-
Marianne Wesson, *The Cinda Hayes Series*, 1998-

195
GERARD WILLIAMS

Dr. Mortimer and the Barking Man Mystery
(New York: Carroll & Graf, 2001)

Story type: Historical
Subject(s): Victorian Period; Russians; Prostitution
Major character(s): James Mortimer, Doctor, Spouse (of Violet); Violet Branscombe, Doctor, Spouse (of James)
Time period(s): 1890s (1891)
Locale(s): London, England

Summary: With his wife and partner, Violet Branscombe, Dr. Mortimer runs a charitable medical clinic in Whitechapel. He is, of course, the same Dr. James Mortimer who left his walking-stick behind in Sherlock Holmes' chambers at 221B Baker Street, as chronicled in *The Hound of the Baskervilles*. He himself has developed a small reputation as a detective, and with Sherlock Holmes and Dr. Watson engaged in other cases as this narrative opens, he becomes involved in solving the murder of a Russian national in Soho. The case takes the couple deep into London's underworld where they attempt to clear a young revolutionary who has been unjustly accused of the crime.

Other books you might like:
Carole Bugge, *The Haunting of Torre Abbey*, 2000
Arthur Conan Doyle, *The Hound of the Baskervilles*, 1902
Quinn Fawcett, *The Mycroft Holmes Series*, 1994-
Laurie R. King, *The Moor*, 1998
Wayne Worcester, *The Jewel of Covent Garden*, 2000

196
BARBARA JAYE WILSON

Murder and the Mad Hatter
(New York: Avon, 2001)

Story type: Amateur Detective; Traditional
Series: Brenda Midnight. Book 6
Subject(s): Fashion Design; Blackmail; Weddings
Major character(s): Brenda Midnight, Designer (milliner)
Time period(s): 2000s
Locale(s): New York, New York (Greenwich Village)

Summary: As the result of an ill-placed bet, Brenda finds herself about to marry Lemon B. Crenshaw, her boyfriend Johnny's sleazy agent. Bent on revenge, Brenda breaks in Lemmy's apartment to steal his much-prized bra collection, but lands herself right in a murder. She's helped out of this mess by a supporting cast of eccentric friends, who assist her in finding the killer. The Greenwich Village setting is as appealing as ever and, as usual, portrayed as a small town

plopped down in the middle of Manhattan, where everybody knows each other and the only awful things that happen are murders.

Where it's reviewed:
Drood Review, January/February 2001, page 15
Mystery News, February/March 2001, page 29

Other books by the same author:
Hatful of Homicide, 2000
Capped Off, 1999
Accessory to Murder, 1998
Death Flips Its Lid, 1998
Death Brims Over, 1997

Other books you might like:
Jacqueline Girdner, *The Kate Jasper Series*, 1991-
Dolores Johnson, *The Mandy Dyer Series*, 1997-
Christine Jorgensen, *The Stella the Stargazer Series*, 1994-
Tamar Myers, *The Abigail Timberlake Series*, 1996-
Leslie O'Kane, *The Molly Masters Series*, 1996-

197

LAURA WILSON

Dying Voices

(New York: Bantam, 2001)

Story type: Psychological Suspense
Subject(s): Kidnapping; Missing Persons; Mothers and Daughters
Major character(s): Dorothy "Dodie" Blackstock, Editor (magazine)
Time period(s): 1970s (1976); 1990s (1996)
Locale(s): London, England; Camoys, England

Summary: When she was a child of eight, Dodie's beautiful mother, Susan Blackstock, was kidnapped for a ten-million-pound ransom, which her billionaire father, Wolf Blackstock, refused to pay. Dodie never saw her mother again and it was assumed the kidnappers had killed her. Twenty years later, Susan's body is found—but she has only been dead for 48 hours. Determined to find out where she had been for all those years and why she had never tried to contact her, Dodie returns to her childhood home, Camoys Hall, in the English countryside. Layer by layer, the story is revealed to Dodie and to the reader, and it becomes clear that she and the people she loves most are in danger themselves.

Where it's reviewed:
Publishers Weekly, March 12, 2001, page 68

Other books by the same author:
A Little Death, 2000

Other books you might like:
Robert Barnard, *A Murder in Mayfair*, 2000
Patrick Ruell, *Dream of Darkness*, 1991
Michelle Spring, *In a Midnight Hour*, 2001
Barbara Vine, *Grasshopper*, 2000
Minette Walters, *The Breaker*, 1999

198

STUART WOODS

Cold Paradise

(New York: Putnam, 2001)

Story type: Private Detective; Action/Adventure
Series: Stone Barrington. Book 7
Subject(s): Boats and Boating; Wealth; Missing Persons
Major character(s): Stone Barrington, Detective—Private, Lawyer
Time period(s): 2000s
Locale(s): Palm Beach, Florida; New York, New York

Summary: Hired by a software billionaire to find a missing woman in Florida, Stone is only too happy to leave frigid Manhattan for the balmy breezes of Palm Beach, where he is quartered offshore on a luxury yacht. To his surprise, he runs into a woman, now known as Liz, whom he knew as Allison Manning and once defended from a murder charge in an earlier case (*Dead in the Water*). Now she is being threatened by a possible stalker interested in her newfound wealth and by a lawsuit charging her with insurance fraud. Other beautiful women from Stone's past turn up. The ambience, as usual in this glitzy travelogue series, is glamorous, the people wealthy, and the women not only gorgeous but madly attracted to Stone.

Where it's reviewed:
Booklist, March 1, 2001, page 1189
Publishers Weekly, April 16, 2001, page 46

Other books by the same author:
L.A. Dead, 2000
Worst Fears Realized, 1999
Swimming to Catalina, 1998
Dead in the Water, 1997
Dirt, 1996

Other books you might like:
Paul Levine, *The Jake Lassiter Series*, 1990-
A.E. Maxwell, *The Fiddler Series*, 1985-1993
Ed McBain, *The Matthew Hope Series*, 1977-
Barbara Parker, *The Gail Connor Series*, 1994-
Lawrence Sanders, *The Arch McNally Series*, 1992-

199

ERIC WRIGHT

Death of a Hired Man

(New York: St. Martin's Press, 2001)

Story type: Traditional
Series: Mel Pickett. Book 2
Subject(s): Rural Life; Retirement; Marriage
Major character(s): Mel Pickett, Police Officer (retired), Detective—Amateur
Time period(s): 2000s
Locale(s): Larch River, Ontario, Canada; Toronto, Ontario, Canada

Summary: While Pickett and his new wife, Charlotte, are trying to decide which of the four homes they now own between them should be kept and which sold, he rents his

remote cabin north of Toronto to a friend, Norbert Thompson. When the cabin is broken into and Thompson murdered, Pickett can't help but wonder if he himself wasn't actually the intended victim. The police, who are investigating suspects among the victim's family, aren't overly receptive to the idea so Pickett strikes out on his own, finding that his newly retired status vastly complicates his investigation. He is also adjusting to married life and to the existence of a son and granddaughter he didn't know he had. The author of a long-running series about Toronto police inspector Charlie Salter, Wright introduced Pickett several books ago in that series and has also recently begun two other series featuring Lucy Trimble and and Joe Barley.

Where it's reviewed:
Booklist, December 15, 2000, page 18
Library Journal, March 1, 2000, page 134
New York Times Book Review, March 18, 2001, page 18

Other books by the same author:
The Kidnapping of Rosie Dawn, 2000 (Joe Barley series)
Death on the Rocks, 1999 (Lucy Trimble series)
Buried in Stone, 1996 (Mel Pickett series)
Death by Degrees, 1993 (Charlie Salter series)
A Fine Italian Hand, 1992 (Charlie Salter series)

Other books you might like:
Peter Lovesey, *The Peter Diamond Series*, 1991-
Archer Mayor, *The Joe Gunther Series*, 1988-
Medora Sale, *The John Sanders/Harriet Jeffries Series*, 1986-1994
Frank Smith, *The Ian Pepper Series*, 1969-
L.R. Wright, *The Karl Alberg Series*, 1985-

200

PATRICIA WYNN

The Birth of Blue Satan
(Austin, Texas: Pemberley, 2001)

Story type: Historical
Subject(s): Identity, Concealed; Adventure and Adventurers; Romance
Major character(s): Hester Kean, Servant; Gideon Viscount St. Mars, Nobleman, Highwayman
Time period(s): 1710s (1715)
Locale(s): London, England

Summary: Hester Kean, a young single woman who is addressed as ''Mrs.'' out of courtesy (''Miss'' is a term considered to be lacking in respect), is the orphaned daughter of a clergyman, who considers herself fortunate to have been taken in as a servant by her wealthy aunt. Her path crosses that of the dashing Gideon, who is enamored of her beautiful cousin Isabella. When Gideon is falsely accused of murder, he's forced to disguise himself as a highwayman known as Blue Satan in order to protect himself while he searches for the real killer. The book is set during the days shortly following the succession to the throne of the Hanoverian king, George I, and it details the conflict between the Whigs and the Tories, which stands in the way of Gideon's ever winning the hand of Isabella. There's also the fact that it's Hester, not Isabella, who pines for Gideon. There's at least as much romance and derring-do as there is detection in this first mystery by a prolific romance writer.

Where it's reviewed:
Publishers Weekly, February 19, 2001, page 73

Other books you might like:
Bruce Alexander, *The Sir John Fielding Series*, 1994-
Deryn Lake, *The John Rawlings Series*, 1994-
Janet Laurence, *The Canaletto Series*, 1998-
Fidelis Morgan, *Unnatural Fire*, 2001
Rosemary Stevens, *The Beau Brummell Series*, 2000-

Romance Fiction in Review
by
Kristin Ramsdell

"Romance has been elegantly defined as the off-spring of fiction and love."
—Benjamin Disraeli

"A Lady's imagination is very rapid; it jumps from admiration to love, from love to matrimony in a moment."
—Jane Austen (*Pride and Prejudice*)

"...there are lies, damn lies, and statistics."
—Attributed to Mark Twain by Benjamin Disraeli

The romance statistics for 2000 have been tallied; and while they may not be all we would like to have imagined, especially if taken at face value, they clearly show that romance continues to dominate the fiction market with practiced ease. According to the statistical report published annually by the Romance Writers of America (RWA) [Hall, Libby. "ROMstat Report for Year 2000." *Romance Writers Report* 21(September 2001):—forthcoming of this writing], 2289 romance titles were published in 2000 as compared with 2523 in 1999 for an overall decrease of slightly more than 9.2%. Of this total, 2056 romances appeared in print form, 172 came out in e-book format, and 61 were released as audio books, resulting in a decrease in print romances of 7.3% (down from 2218 in 1999) and a whopping 25% drop in e-book releases (down from 272 in 1999). Since this is the first year that audio books have been included in the count, no comparative data exists.

But things are not so bleak as these numbers would indicate. As mentioned in last yeaar's section on statistics, the 1999 figures were skewed because a number of publishers released an extra month's worth of romances in order to bring the publishing dates into line with the actual availability dates of the books, artificially inflating the print releases for the year. In fact, as a quick—and very superficial—calculation will show, if the 13th month is factored out of the 1999 figures, the number of total releases per month for both years is remarkably similar and the number of print releases per month for 2000 is actually up slightly. Obviously, the figures for 1999 were something of an industry-generated aberration, and a look back at previous years will show that this year's numbers have simply brought us back to our normal, steady, upward trend.

Romance continues to dominate the overall popular fiction market and last year accounted for 55.9% of all mass market paperback sales (down from 58.2% in 1999) and 37.2% of total sales of all print formats (down from 38.8% in 1999). Last year the 218,195,000 romances sold generated more than $1.37 billion in sales for the industry. Comparative figures for the other fiction genres show that Mystery/Suspense comprised 28.1% of the market, Science Fiction/Fantasy accounted for 7.2%, General Fiction held 12.9%, and a catch-all group (Religious, Occult, Historical, Western, Male Adventure, Adult, and Movie Tie-ins) was responsible for 14.6% of the total. It is worth noting that the Mystery/Suspense group was up by 2.4% from the previous year, a situation that Hall feels is partly due to the large numbers of romance writers now writing in the suspense/psychological thriller genre. Since the publishing statistics are based on how a book is labeled and marketed (Romance, Mystery, Sci-Fi, etc.) and many romantic suspense novels are often labeled simply Suspense, chances are good that she is right.

A Few Statistical Details

Because the details and trends in romance fiction for 2000 have already been discussed in the essay in the previous volume of *What Do I Read Next?*, I won't duplicate those comments here. Also, because 2001 is only half over as of this writing, I would be presenting an incomplete, and ultimately confusing, picture if I talked about the trends of the year at this point; therefore, these will be discussed in the first volume of next year's *WDIRN?* However, as promised, now that the 2000 romance statistics have been reported, I

will bring you up-to-date on some of those. The source of most of these statistics is Libby Hall's article mentioned above; for more detail and/or additional information, you may wish to consult the original article.

As usual, Contemporary Romance claimed more than half of the romance market, accounting for 58.8% (1208 titles) in 2000, down slightly from 60.5% the year before. Of these, 63% are series romances (primarily Harlequin and Silhouette lines) and 37% were single title releases. These totals also include relevant anthologies, reprints, hardcover releases, Spanish/English language novels, and other novels targeting specific populations.

A distant second to the Contemporary subgenre, Historical Romance accounted for 28.5% (586 titles) of the print market in 2000, down less than 1% of market share from the year before, although the actual number of historical titles published did drop by 67 (10.3%). This number also includes Regency titles, which will be discussed below.

Although included in the overall totals for Historical Romance, Regency Romance is actually its own subgenre and in 2000 accounted for 108 releases. This compares favorably with the 92 releases of the previous year and indicates an increase in titles of almost 17.4%! These 108 titles comprise 18.4% of the Historical market and 5.2% of the total romance market (up from 4% in 1999), making this one of the better years for the Regency in terms of overall market share, something that fans are certain to celebrate.

Alternative Realities Romances (Paranormals) continued their decline in 2000, falling from 80 titles in 1999 to 71 in 2000, but slipping only .1% to 3.5% of the total romance market because of the overall decline in titles. Nevertheless, despite the decline in designated titles, elements of the subgenre continue to flow into other romance subgenres, indicating, perhaps, that the subgenre is not dead, but merely evolving. Stay tuned.

The Romantic Suspense and Gothic subgenres, unfortunately, get short shrift in the statistics tabulations with no specific figures being tallied for either. Still, their influence is felt across all the subgenres, in much the same way as it is with the Alternative Realities subgenre, and it is a rare subgenre that has never been touched by the chilly fingers of mystery, suspense, or horror. As alluded to earlier, for marketing reasons, many books that would normally have fallen within these classifications are now classified simply as Suspense, Mystery, or Horror. While it is admirable to try to expand the market and broaden a particular writer's exposure, it does make it difficult to keep an accurate account of the titles that actually do fall within the romance boundaries.

As with the subgenres listed above, the figures for Multicultural Romances are not listed separately. However, adding the 59 titles from BET Books' Arabesque African American line, the few titles from Genesis, the 24 or so titles from Pinnacle's Encanto series, and the growing number of titles featuring multicultural characters that are published

within a regular series or as single titles, proves the still growing interest in this subgenre. It continues to evolve in interesting ways.

Inspirational Romance continues to hold its own; and although it showed a decrease in actual titles (136 in 1999; 126 in 2000), it continued strong with 6.1% of the overall market.

Anthologies continue to be published, although the numbers released in 2000 plunged 39%, from 87 in 1999 to 53 in 2000. As in the past, almost half of these were Contemporary anthologies, with the combined Historical/Regency group nearly matching them; Inspirationals and Paranormals contributed several each. Although this may simply be a reflection of the ''13th month effect,'' it is interesting that a year after RWA established a Novella category for its Rita Awards, the numbers of anthologies (which consist of novellas, primarily), dropped.

In a direct about-face from 1999, only three of the major publishers released more romance titles in 2000 than in the previous year, with the Bertlesmann group (Ballantine, Bantam, Dell, Delacorte, Doubleday, Fawcett, Ivy, and WaterBrook), Torstar (Harlequin, Mills & Boon, MIRA, Silhouette, and Steeple Hill), and Pocket taking top honors. Interestingly, Bertlesmann and Torstar lagged a bit last year, and this year Torstar's releases jumped a startling 249 to 982, possibly as a result of adding their Mills & Boon line to the tally. One publisher, Avalon, held steady with 36 titles. Torstar is by far the largest publisher, followed at some distance by Kensington (Kensington, Pinnacle, Bouquet, Precious Gems, Zebra) with 274. Pearson (Berkley, NAL, Dutton, Jove, Onyx, Putnam, Signet, Topaz, Viking), Bertlesmann, Dorchester (Leisure and LoveSpell), and Avon/Harper are next in line with 161, 139, 116, and 108, respectively; and BET, Pocket, and St. Martin's produce 30 or more. Warner, and most of the inspirational publishers, produced romance titles in the low double digits, with several houses releasing fewer than ten.

Format continues to be an issue for the industry; and although 2000 saw something of a move away from the e-book and back to the more traditional formats, the e-book and the issues it raises are still very much alive. The fact that more and more libraries are adding e-books to their collections attests to this. However, for the moment, and most likely for the foreseeable future, most romances are, and will probably continue to be, published in print—with the vast majority being released as mass market paperbacks. Hardcovers, although dipping slightly in 2000, should remain on track; and finally, with more and more people spending more and more time in their cars, the demand for audio books (mostly recordings of previously published books) should only increase.

The Future

But what lies ahead for the genre? Obviously, there will be change; it just comes with the territory. Technology is having a tremendous effect on every aspect of life, including publishing, book selling, and libraries; and it will only increase. The fact that only a few major publishers now control most of the romance imprints will also have some influence on the genre, and one can only hope it will be positive. Finally, with the demise of the dot.coms, questions about the viability of Internet commerce by investors and consumers, and the economy's current slump, the future is far less certain—but by no means less interesting—than it was a year ago. As mentioned earlier, I will discuss the various subgenre and industry trends in volume 1 of next year's *WDIRN?*; but at this point, it is safe to say that many of those trends established previously are continuing. With part of the year still to go and with nothing guaranteed in the volatile world of publishing, anything can happen—and often does. 2001 has already proven to be an interesting year—and that is likely to continue.

A Conference Program and an Award

Although the general overview for the year will be included in next year's *What Do I Read Next?*, there are two items of professional interest to librarians I would like to mention. First, at the 2001 Annual Conference of the American Library Association in San Francisco, the Reference and User Services Association/Collection Development and Evaluation Section sponsored a readers advisory program on romance. The Lure of Romance (June 17, 2001) featured two best-selling writers and one librarian and marked one of the first times that romance has been highlighted at a major ALA program. Second, and most importantly, Shelley Mosley, the manager of the Velma Teague Branch of the Glendale (Arizona) Public Library and contributor to the romance section of *What Do I Read Next?*, has been named 2001 Librarian of the Year by the Romance Writers of America.

Recommendations for Romance

Reading tastes vary greatly. What makes a book appeal to one person may make another reject it. By the same token, two people may like the same book for totally different reasons. Obviously, reading is a highly subjective and personal undertaking. For this reason, the recommended readings attached to each entry have tried to cast as broad a net as was reasonably possible. Suggested titles have been chosen on the basis of similarity to the main entry in one or more of the following areas: historical time period, geographic setting, theme, character types, plot pattern or premise, writing style, or overall mood or "feel." All suggestions may not appeal to the same person, but it is to be hoped that at least one would appeal to most.

Because romance reading tastes do vary so widely and readers (and writers) often apply vastly different criteria in

determining what makes a romance good, bad, or exceptional, I cannot claim that the following list of recommendations consists solely of the "best" romance novels of the year. (In fact many of these received no awards or special recognition at all.) It is simply a selection of books that the romance contributors, John Charles and Shelley Mosley, and I found particularly interesting; perhaps some of these will appeal to you, too.

The Secret Swan by Shana Abe

The Temptation of Rory Monahan by Elizabeth Bevarly

The Midnight Bride by Susan Carroll

The Holding by Claudia Dain

The Bad Luck Wedding Night by Geralyn Dawson

The Reluctant Smuggler by Teresa DesJardien

Rules of Attraction by Christina Dodd

You Never Can Tell by Kathleen Eagle

Irish Hope by Donna Fletcher

Some Kind of Wonderful by Barbara Freethy

More than Memory by Dorothy Garlock

Gallant Waif by Ann Gracie

Summer Island by Kristin Hannah

A Belated Bride by Karen Hawkins

To Tame a Rogue by Linda Kay

The Swan Maiden by Susan King

Highland Dream by Tess Mallory

Miss Westlake's Windfall by Barbara Metzger

One Knight in Venice by Tori Phillips

An Offer from a Gentleman by Julia Quinn

Lord Harry's Daughter by Evelyn Richardson

Scandalous by Karen Robards

The Villa by Nora Roberts

The Impossible Texan by Allie Shaw

Just the Way You Aren't by Lynda Simmons

On Bear Mountain by Deborah Smith

Border Lord by Haywood Smith

The Firebrand by Susan Wiggs

Royal Bride by Joan Wolf

For Further Reference

Review Journals

Although *Booklist*, *Publishers Weekly*, and *Library Journal* are continuing their improved coverage of the romance genre, most romance reviews still appear in sources—both print and online—that specialize in romance. Several of the most important sources are listed below.

Library Journal publishes a quarterly romance review column—February 15, May 15, August, and November

15; *Booklist* has a separate romance fiction category, as do the other genres; and *Publishers Weekly* now uses romance reviewers who are generally conversant with the genre.

Affaire de Coeur (www.affairedecoeur.com) includes reviews, articles, and information on the world of romance fiction in general. *Affaire de Coeur* 3976 Oak Hill Road, Oakland, CA 94605-4931; phone, (510) 569-5675; fax, (510) 632-8868. Subscriptions, Monthly, $35 a year (U.S. First Class Rates); $65 for 2 years (U.S. First Class Rates); $30 a year (U.S. Third Class Rates); $55 for 2 years (U.S. Third Class Rates); $65 a year (Canadian Rates); $5 single copy.

All About Romance (www.likesbooks.com) contains selected romance reviews.

Amazon.com (www.amazon.com) includes some published reviews as well as readers' comments.

Barnes&Noble.com (www.bn.com) includes some published reviews as well as readers' comments.

Gothic Journal (GothicJournal.com/romance/). This journal ceased publication with the October/November 1998 issue and is now operating as a website. Back issues are still available. The *Gothic Journal*, P.O. Box 6340, Elko, Nevada 89802-6340; phone, (775)738-3520; fax, (775)738-3524; e-mail, kglass@GothicJournal.com.

Rendezvous: A Monthly Review of Contemporary and Historical Romances, Mysteries, and Women's Fiction (www.geocities.com/Heartland/Estates/9534/rendvous.html) includes reviews of most romances published each month. Published by Love Designers Writers' Club, Inc. 1507 Burnham Avenue, Calumet City, IL 60409; phone, (708) 862-9797. Subscriptions, Monthly, $45 a year; $4 single copy.

The Romance Reader (www.theromancereader.com) has a good selection of ranked, often harsh reviews.

Romantic Times (www.romantictimes.com) includes reviews of most romances published each month, articles, and information about the world of romance fiction. It also includes reviews and other information on other genres and mainstream women's fiction. Published by: Romantic Times Publishing Group, 55 Bergen Street, Brooklyn Heights, NY 11201; phone, (718) 237-1097; fax, (718) 624-4231; Subscriptions, Monthly, $31 for 6 months (U.S. First Class Rates); $62 for 1 year (U.S. First Class Rates); $124 for 2 years; $22 for 6 months (U.S. Fourth Class Rates); $43 for 1 year (U.S. Fourth Class Rates); $85 for 2 years (U.S. Fourth Class Rates); $35 for 6 months (Canadian Rates); $70 for 1 year (Canadian Rates); $139 for 2 years (Canadian Rates); $59 for 6 months (European Rates); $117 for 1 year (European Rates); $234 for 2 years (European Rates).

Websites/Book Clubs/Mail Order Services

In addition to going to the general websites of online book suppliers like Amazon.com, and traditional bookstores such as Borders and Barnes & Noble, readers can now order books directly from some individual publishers' websites. Many of these websites also feature reviews, information on any subscription book clubs the publisher has, and ways for readers to connect with each other. Several of the more popular are listed below.

Publishers

Avon Books, www.avonromance.com

Dorchester Publishing, www.dorchesterpub.com

Harlequin/Silhouette/Mira, www.eharlequin.com

Kensington Books, www.kensingtonbooks.com

Book Suppliers

Amazon.com, www.amazon.com

Barnes & Noble, www.bn.com

Borders, borders.com

1romancestreet.com, www.1romancestreet.com

Reader Service provides books in the Harlequin and Silhouette series on a monthly subscription basis. Write or phone for series descriptions and price information. P.O. Box 1325, Buffalo, NY 14269; phone, (716) 684-1500, or, P.O. Box 603, Fort Erie, Ontario L2A 5X3, Canada; phone, (416) 283-2897.

Conferences

Numerous conferences are held each year for writers and readers of romance fiction. Several of the more important national ones are listed below. For a more complete listing, particularly of regional or local conferences designed primarily for romance writers, consult the *Romance Writers Report*, a monthly publication of the Romance Writers of America.

Rom-Con—Sponsored by *Affaire de Coeur* and East Bay Books. No conference was held in 2000.

Annual Book Lovers Convention—Sponsored by *Romantic Times*. The Romantic Times 17th Annual Book Lovers Convention was held November 9-12, 2000 in Houston, Texas. (This organization also sponsors a number of romance-related tours for readers and writers.) The 18th Annual Book Lovers Convention took place November 14-19, 2001 in Orlando, Florida.

RWA Annual Conference—Sponsored by Romance Writers of America is usually held in July. The 2000 Conference was held July 26-29 in Washington, D.C. The 2001 Conference took place July 18-22 in New Orleans, Louisiana.

Romance Titles

SHANA ABE

Intimate Enemies

(New York: Bantam, 2000)

Story type: Historical/Medieval
Subject(s): Murder; Loyalty; Trust
Major character(s): Lauren MacRae, Warrior, Laird (temporary); Arion du Morgan, Nobleman (earl), Warrior
Time period(s): 12th century (1165; 1177)
Locale(s): Isle of Shot, Scotland

Summary: Lauren MacRae, acting laird, has convinced her clan to form a trial alliance with the British earl Arion du Morgan, in order to fend off Viking invaders. Old rivalries run deep, however, and the alliance is at risk. To top everything off, her clan is forcing her to marry an abusive man. This action-packed story of two brave warriors—one male and one female—is full of lush detail and unforgettable characters.

Where it's reviewed:
Affaire de Coeur, June 2000, page 18
Romantic Times, June 2000, page 36

Other books by the same author:
A Kiss at Midnight, 2000
The Truelove Bride, 1999
A Rose in Winter, 1998
The Promise of Rain, 1998

Other books you might like:
Jill Barnett, *Wicked*, 1999
Jillian Hart, *Malcolm's Honor*, 2000
Connie Mason, *A Touch of Sin*, 2000
Teresa Medeiros, *The Bride and the Beast*, 2000
Haywood Smith, *Highland Princess*, 2000

SHANA ABE

The Secret Swan

(New York: Bantam, 2001)

Story type: Historical/Medieval
Subject(s): Marriage; Plague; Secrets
Major character(s): Tristan Geraint, Nobleman (Earl of Haverlocke); Amiranth St. Clare, Noblewoman
Time period(s): 14th century (1341; 1349)
Locale(s): England

Summary: After marrying Amiranth St. Clare, Tristan Geraint quickly abandons his new wife to go off to war. When he finally returns home eight years later, Tristan finds his wife's cousin, Lily, waiting with news of Amiranth's death from the plague. At first, Tristan is puzzled by how much Lily reminds him of his wife, but as he slowly falls in love with Lily, Tristan begins to suspect he may hunger for the woman he once spurned.

Where it's reviewed:
Romantic Times, April 2001, page 35

Other books by the same author:
A Kiss at Midnight, 2000
Intimate Enemies, 2000
The Truelove Bride, 1999
A Rose in Winter, 1998
The Promise of Rain, 1998

Other books you might like:
Gayle Callen, *My Lady's Guardian*, 2000
Julie Garwood, *The Bride*, 1989
Madeline Hunter, *By Possession*, 2000
Isolde Martyn, *The Maiden and the Unicorn*, 1999
Tina St. John, *Lord of Vengeance*, 1999

203

KYLIE ADAMS (Pseudonym of Jon Salem)

Fly Me to the Moon
(New York: Kensington, 2001)

Story type: Humor; Contemporary
Subject(s): Humor; Singing; Organized Crime
Major character(s): Sofia Cardinella, Young Woman, Businesswoman (nail polish designer); Ben Estes, Singer (lounge act), Stripper
Time period(s): 2000s
Locale(s): New York, New York; Carmel, California

Summary: When Sofia Cardinella leaves her fiance at the altar for the third time, her Mafioso father is not amused. Then Sofia falls for lounge singer Ben Estes, who specializes in Frank Sinatra songs. Her father, a major fan of Old Blue Eyes who can't stand to hear anyone else sing the songs, orders a hit on the object of her affections. Sexy, funny, offbeat, and full of quirky characters, this *Runaway Bride* meets *The Godfather* would be a crime to miss.

Where it's reviewed:
Romantic Times, May 2001, page 96

Other books you might like:
Sue Civil-Brown, *Catching Kelly*, 2000
Millie Criswell, *The Trouble with Mary*, 2001
Janet Evanovich, *Seven Up*, 2001
Olivia Goldsmith, *Bad Boy*, 2001
Tina Wainscott, *The Wrong Mr. Right*, 2000

204

ROCHELLE ALERS
GWYNNE FORSTER, Co-Author
DONNA HILL, Co-Author
FRANCIS RAY, Co-Author

Going to the Chapel
(New York: St. Martin's Press, 2001)

Story type: Contemporary; Multicultural
Subject(s): Weddings; African Americans; Marriage
Time period(s): 2000s

Summary: This exceptionally diverse quartet of novellas by four of the genre's popular African American writers focuses on the topic of weddings and features a wide range of settings that include exotic Barbados, intriguing Nigeria, and the familiar United States. Included are *Stand-In Bride* by Rochelle Alers, *Learning to Love* by Gwynne Forster, *Distant Lover* by Donna Hill, and *Southern Comfort* by Francis Ray.

Where it's reviewed:
Affaire de Coeur, May/June 2001, page 28

Other books by the same author:
Reckless Surrender, 1995

Other books you might like:
Gwynne Forster, *Sealed with a Kiss*, 1995
Donna Hill, *A Scandalous Affair*, 2000
Sandra Kitt, *Serenade*, 1994
    more weddings

Francis Ray, *Forever Yours*, 1994

205

ROCHELLE ALERS

Private Passions
(Washington, D.C.: BET, 2001)

Story type: Contemporary; Multicultural
Series: Hideaway: Second Generation. Book 2
Subject(s): Politics; Multiracial; Scandal
Major character(s): Emily Kirkland, Journalist (television political analyst); Christopher Blackwell Delgado, Political Figure (senator)
Time period(s): 2000s
Locale(s): New Mexico; Jamaica; Mexico

Summary: Jarred into action when a sportscaster announces the engagement of Emily Kirkland, his longtime friend and secret love, to basketball superstar Keith Norris, Senator Chris Delgado heads for Jamaica to convince the vacationing Emily to change her mind. However, Emily's mind doesn't need changing; she has loved Chris all her life. When a subsequent trip to Mexico to visit Chris' dying biological father precipitates their marriage, they know they must keep it secret until New Mexico's gubernatorial election is over. The reason? Chris is a candidate for governor and Emily is a television journalist covering his opponent—a situation that could prove damaging to both their careers. Political intrigue, espionage, and old family secrets bubble over in this sensual romance that features a pair of appealing biracial protagonists (African American/Latino).

Where it's reviewed:
Romantic Times, January 2001, page 82

Other books by the same author:
Just Before Dawn, 2000
Harvest Moon, 1999
Summer Magic, 1999
Heaven Sent, 1998
Hidden Agenda, 1997

Other books you might like:
Brenda Jackson, *Secret Love*, 2000
Sandra Kitt, *Close Encounters*, 2000
Francis Ray, *Incognito*, 1997
Nora Roberts, *Public Secrets*, 1990
Tracey Tillis, *Flashpoint*, 1997

206

VICTORIA ALEXANDER (Pseudonym of Cheryl Griffin)

The Marriage Lesson
(New York: Avon, 2001)

Story type: Historical/Regency
Subject(s): Marriage; Writing; Courtship
Major character(s): Lady Marianne Shelton, Noblewoman, Writer; Thomas Effington, Nobleman (Marquess of Helmsley)
Time period(s): 1810s (1819)
Locale(s): London, England

Summary: Saddled with the duty of chaperoning his brother-in-law's three sisters during their first London Season, Thomas Effington, Marquess of Helmsley, decides the easiest thing to do will be to marry them off as quickly as possible. He doesn't take into consideration Lady Marianne, who is not only determined to have "adventures" and live a little, but who also doesn't intend to marry—ever. She is going to support herself as a writer and never have to depend on a man! Her ideas change, of course, but not before her own adventures, scandalously embroidered, turn into an anonymous weekly column, "The Adventures of a Country Miss in London," that soon has everyone wondering just who the notorious Lord W really is. A humorous, witty, charming story.

Where it's reviewed:
Library Journal, May 15, 2001, page 104
Rendezvous, May 2001, page 17
Romantic Times, May 2001, page 39

Other books by the same author:
The Husband List, 2000
Paradise Bay, 1999
The Wedding Bargain, 1999
Play It Again, Sam, 1998

Other books you might like:
Christina Dodd, *Rules of Engagement*, 2000
Suzanne Enoch, *Meet Me at Midnight*, 2000
Amanda Quick, *Affair*, 1997
Julia Quinn, *How to Marry a Marquis*, 1999
Julia Quinn, *The Viscount Who Loved Me*, 2000

207

SUSAN ANDERSEN

All Shook Up

(New York: Avon, 2001)

Story type: Contemporary; Romantic Suspense
Subject(s): Single Parent Families; Inheritance; Trust
Major character(s): Dru Lawrence, Single Parent, Hotel Owner; J.D. Carver, Construction Worker, Hotel Owner
Time period(s): 2000s
Locale(s): Star Lake, Washington (Star Lake Lodge)

Summary: Dru Lawrence is happy at the Star Lake Lodge. She takes care of her guests and finds time to raise her small son. Then her aunt dies, leaving part of the lodge to Dru and part to her foster son, bad boy J.D. Carver, and Dru's world turns upside down. To make matters worse, unbeknownst to J.D., a former buddy thinks he'll turn him in for murder, so he's out to kill him. The road is filled with lots of suspense in this story of one man's journey from the mean streets of the city to the mountain sanctuary he learns to call home.

Where it's reviewed:
Publishers Weekly, December 18, 2000, page 62
Romantic Times, January 2001, page 77

Other books by the same author:
Baby, Don't Go, 2000
Be My Baby, 1999
Baby, I'm Yours, 1998

Other books you might like:
Claire Cross, *Third Time Lucky*, 2000
Jayne Ann Krentz, *Eclipse Bay*, 2000
Suzann Ledbetter, *East of Peculiar*, 2000
Carla Neggers, *The Waterfall*, 2000
Theresa Weir, *American Dreamer*, 1997

208

CATHERINE ANDERSON

Phantom Waltz

(New York: Onyx, 2001)

Story type: Contemporary
Subject(s): Physically Handicapped; Courage; Love
Major character(s): Bethany Coulter, Handicapped (paraplegic); Ryan Kendrick, Rancher, Wealthy
Time period(s): 2000s
Locale(s): Oregon

Summary: It takes only one look for rancher Ryan Kendrick to fall for Bethany Coulter. Even though she is wheelchair-bound because of a barrel-racing accident years earlier, he thinks she is the most beautiful woman he has ever seen—and he intends to do something serious about it. However, convincing Bethany to trust his love is not going to be easy. Poignant, romantic, and full of snappy, funny dialogue, this heartwarming, sensual romance deals with a issue not often touched by the genre and is another in Anderson's growing list of socially-aware and sensitive romances.

Where it's reviewed:
Rendezvous, May 2001, page 26

Other books by the same author:
Seventh Heaven, 2000
The Work of Hands, 2000
Baby Love, 1999
Cherish, 1998
Simply Love, 1997

Other books you might like:
Mary Balogh, *Dancing with Clara*, 1994
    Regency
Barbara Freethy, *Just the Way You Are*, 2000
Julie Miller, *One Good Man*, 2000
Susan Elizabeth Phillips, *Dream a Little Dream*, 1998
Danielle Steel, *Palomino*, 1981

209

GABRIELLA ANDERSON

A Matter of Pride

(New York: Kensington, 2001)

Story type: Historical/Regency; Paranormal
Series: Destiny Coin Trilogy. Book 2
Subject(s): Scandal; Magic; Singing
Major character(s): Eden Grant, Young Woman, Singer; Trevor St. John, Nobleman (Earl of Ryeburn), Wealthy
Time period(s): 1810s (1819); 1820s (1820)
Locale(s): Boston, Massachusetts; London, England

Summary: Trevor St. John, Earl of Ryeburn, bets his companions a hundred pounds each that he can find a bride within a month. Eden Grant, an American on a tour of Europe before she settles down, is savoring her freedom. The two make a highly unlikely couple, but the Destiny Coin brings them together. A feisty heroine with a sense of humor and an enchanted coin bring magic into the life of a stubborn nobleman in this second book of the Destiny Coin Trilogy.

Where it's reviewed:
Romantic Times, January 2001, page 40

Other books by the same author:
A Matter of Honor, 2001 (Destiny Coin Trilogy. Book 3)
A Matter of Convenience, 2000 (Destiny Coin Trilogy. Book 1)

Other books you might like:
Catherine Coulter, *The Courtship*, 2000
Teresa DesJardien, *Bewitched by Love*, 1996 anthology
Suzanne Enoch, *Meet Me at Midnight*, 2000
Karen Harbaugh, *Cupid's Kiss*, 1999
Joy Reed, *Catherine's Wish*, 2000

210

SHARI ANTON

Knave of Hearts

(Toronto: Harlequin, 2001)

Story type: Historical/Medieval
Subject(s): Marriage; Reunions; Secrets
Major character(s): Marian de Lacy, Noblewoman, Single Parent (of twin girls); Stephen of Wilmont, Nobleman; Lady Carolyn de Grasse, Noblewoman
Time period(s): 12th century (1109)
Locale(s): England

Summary: Expecting to find his intended fiancee, Lady Carolyn, in the London bedchamber he enters, Stephen is startled to find an old lover, Marian de Lacy, and her young daughter, instead. He is even more surprised to learn she and Carolyn are cousins, and when he eventually comes to Branwick Keep to woo Lady Carolyn in earnest, that Marian lives there, too, with her twin daughters. True love eventually wins out, but not until the pair come to terms with the pain of the past and present realities.

Where it's reviewed:
Affaire de Coeur, February 2001, page 24
Romantic Times, February 2001, page 44

Other books by the same author:
By Queen's Grace, 2000
The Conqueror, 2000 (Knights of the Black Rose. Book 3)
By King's Decree, 1998
Lord of the Manor, 1998
Emily's Captain, 1997

Other books you might like:
Rexanne Becnel, *The Mistress of Rosecliffe*, 2000
Jo Beverley, *The Shattered Rose*, 2000
Elizabeth Lowell, *Untamed*, 1993
Patricia Ryan, *Silken Threads*, 1999

Haywood Smith, *Dangerous Gifts*, 1999

211

CATHERINE ARCHER (Pseudonym of Catherine J. Archibald)

Summer's Bride

(Toronto: Harlequin, 2001)

Story type: Historical/Renaissance
Series: Seasons' Brides. Book 3
Subject(s): Feuds; Family Relations; Sea Stories
Major character(s): Genevieve of Harwick, Noblewoman, Stowaway; Marcel Ainsworth, Sea Captain, Nobleman
Time period(s): 15th century
Locale(s): Brackenmoore, England; *Briarwind*, At Sea (en route to Scotland)

Summary: Orphaned Genevieve of Harwick loves Marcel Ainsworth. He's just back after a two year absence, but an aunt needs his services, so he's ready to leave again. Determined not to be left behind this time, Genevieve stows away on Marcel's ship. Marcel can't decide whether to kiss her or kill her in this tale of a stubborn man and a determined woman.

Where it's reviewed:
Romantic Times, January 2001, page 44

Other books by the same author:
Autumn's Bride, 2001 (Seasons' Brides. Book 4)
The Bride of Spring, 2000 (Seasons' Brides. Book 2)
Winter's Bride, 1999 (Seasons' Brides. Book 1)
Fire Song, 1998
Lord Sin, 1997

Other books you might like:
Patricia Cabot, *An Improper Proposal*, 1999
Marsha Canham, *Across a Moonlit Sea*, 1996
Shannon Drake, *Bride of the Wind*, 1992
Miranda Jarrett, *The Captain's Bride*, 1997
Ruth Langan, *The Sea Witch*, 2000

212

JUDITH ARNOLD (Pseudonym of Barbara Keiler)

Looking for Laura

(Don Mills, Ontario: Mira, 2001)

Story type: Contemporary
Subject(s): Widows; Mystery; Humor
Major character(s): Sally Driver, Widow(er), Restaurateur (coffee bar owner); Todd Sloane, Publisher (newspaper), Journalist
Time period(s): 2000s
Locale(s): Winfield, Massachusetts

Summary: In an effort to find out who the ''Laura'' was who wrote love letters to her late husband, Paul, Sally Driver and Paul's bedt friend, Todd Sloane, the town newspaper owner, join forces to solve the mystery—and find love themselves in the process. Humor, wit, and appealing characters, including an adorable five-year-old, recommend this modern romance that also has its share of hometown charm.

Other books by the same author:
Hush, Little Baby, 2001
Her Secret Lover, 1999
The Wrong Bride, 1999
A Stranger's Baby, 1996

Other books you might like:
Jennifer Crusie, *Anyone but You*, 1996
Jennifer Crusie, *The Cinderella Deal*, 1996
Stephanie Mittman, *Head over Heels*, 1999
Deborah Shelley, *Talk about Love*, 1999

213

LAURA BAKER

Raven
(New York: St. Martin's Paperbacks, 2001)

Story type: Romantic Suspense; Paranormal
Subject(s): Native Americans; Treasure, Buried; Legends
Major character(s): Rheada Samuels, Indian (Pueblo), Tour Guide; Kee Blackburn, Indian (Navajo), Investigator
Time period(s): 2000s
Locale(s): Grand Rincons, Utah; Chaco Canyon, Utah; Aztec, Utah

Summary: When her father dies, a youthful Rheada Samuels becomes the infamous artifact thief "Raven" to support her younger sister. Now an adult, Rheada acts as a tour guide and lecturer in the land of the ancient Anasazi, trying to right the wrongs she's perpetrated, and acting as defender of the sacred mask. Agent Kee Blackburn wants revenge, and the object of his hatred is the legendary Raven. A powerful mix of suspense, Native American lore, and mysticism.

Where it's reviewed:
Romantic Times, February 2001, page 87

Other books by the same author:
Broken in Two, 1999
Legend, 1998
Stargazer, 1997

Other books you might like:
Judie Aitken, *A Love Beyond Time*, 1999
Kathleen Eagle, *What the Heart Knows*, 1999
Rachel Lee, *Nighthawk*, 1997
Constance O'Day-Flannery, *Anywhere You Are*, 1999 time travel
Aimee Thurlo, *Black Raven's Pride*, 2000

214

TESSA BARCLAY

A Lovely Illusion
(New York: Severn House, 2001)

Story type: Contemporary
Subject(s): Art
Major character(s): Erica Pencarreth, Museum Curator; Willard Townley, Art Dealer; Alexander "Zan" McNaughton, Vintner
Time period(s): 2000s
Locale(s): Parigos, Greece; London, England; Paris, France

Summary: Erica Pencarreth is stunned by the latest find of her lover, art gallery owner Willard Townley: a slightly damaged painting by artist Claude Monet. When New Zealand vintner Alexander "Zan" McNaughton puts in an early bid on the painting, Erica agrees to help authenticate the work as a favor to Willard. While tracing the provenance of the painting, Erica becomes bothered not only by her growing suspicions something is not right about the painting, but also by her growing attraction to Zan.

Other books you might like:
Liz Fielding, *The Best Man and the Bridesmaid*, 1991
Jayne Ann Krentz, *Silver Linings*, 1991
Rosamunde Pilcher, *Sleeping Tiger*, 1974
Alexandra Raife, *Belonging*, 1999
Sophie Weston, *The Millionaire Affaire*, 2000

215

REXANNE BECNEL

The Matchmaker
(New York: St. Martin's Press, 2001)

Story type: Historical/Regency
Subject(s): Courtship; Secrets
Major character(s): Olivia Byrde, Gentlewoman; Neville Hawke, Nobleman (Baron Hawke of Woodford Court)
Time period(s): 1810s (1818); 1820s (1821)
Locale(s): London, England; Scotland

Summary: Olivia Byrde puts the time she spends observing the eligible bachelors of the *ton* to good use by recording her impressions in a journal which she then uses to match up her friends. While Olivia is quite successful in pairing up other people, she has yet to find the right man for herself. When her journal falls into the hands of Neville Hawke, an emotionally wounded war hero who drinks to forget, Olivia vows to retrieve her embarrassing notes from the one man who just might be the perfect match for her. Witty with some nice echoes of Jane Austen's *Emma*.

Where it's reviewed:
Affaire de Coeur, February 2001, page 26
Romantic Times, February 2001, page 38

Other books by the same author:
The Mistress of Rosecliffe, 2000
The Knight of Rosecliffe, 1999
The Bride of Rosecliffe, 1998
Dangerous to Love, 1997
The Maiden Bride, 1996

Other books you might like:
Victoria Alexander, *The Husband List*, 2000
Jacquie D'Alessandro, *Red Roses Mean Love*, 1999
Suzanne Enoch, *Reforming a Rake*, 2000
Karen Hawkins, *The Abduction of Julia*, 2000
Victoria Malvey, *A Merry Chase*, 2000

Romance

216

JESSICA BENSON

Much Obliged

(New York: Zebra, 2001)

Story type: Regency
Subject(s): Sports/Boxing
Major character(s): John Fitzwilliam, Nobleman (Earl of Claremont); Adelaide "Addie" Winstead, Gentlewoman, Writer
Time period(s): 1810s (1813-1814)
Locale(s): England

Summary: Addie Winstead supports her family by anonymously writing a column on boxing that has all of London talking, including the Earl of Claremont, John Fitzwilliam, whose recent exploits in Gentleman Jackson's establishment are the unflattering subject of Addie's latest column. When John, who at one time was expected to marry Addie, is challenged to a duel in the boxing ring, Addie feels compelled to help him out, especially since John is fighting to protect her honor. Once John realizes who his new "coach" is, he begins to look at Addie in a whole new light. Witty and wonderful.

Where it's reviewed:
Romantic Times, April 2001, page 102

Other books by the same author:
Lord Stanhope's Proposal, 2000

Other books you might like:
Donna Bell, *The Bluestocking's Beau*, 1998
Jo Ann Ferguson, *Rhyme and Reason*, 1998
Kate Huntington, *The Lieutenant's Lady*, 1999
Andrea Pickens, *A Lady of Letters*, 2000
Regina Scott, *The Bluestocking on His Knee*, 1999

217

PATTI BERG

Born to Be Wild

(New York: Avon, 2001)

Story type: Contemporary; Humor
Subject(s): Humor; Social Classes; Burglary
Major character(s): Lauren Remington, Businesswoman (wedding planner), Wealthy; Max Wilde, Caterer, Cook (chef)
Time period(s): 2000s
Locale(s): Palm Beach, Florida

Summary: When the chef who's catering wedding planner Lauren Remington's society event dies, all of the other chefs go to his funeral, leaving her without a caterer. In desperation, she hires Max Wilde's Born to Be Wilde services. Unknown to her, Max has loved her since an encounter that took place years earlier. High society meets the Harley crowd in this fast-paced comedy about worlds colliding.

Where it's reviewed:
Romantic Times, February 2001, page 86

Other books by the same author:
Bride for a Night, 2000

Wife for a Day, 1999
If I Can't Have You, 1998
Looking for a Hero, 1998
Till the End of Time, 1997

Other books you might like:
Millie Criswell, *The Trouble with Mary*, 2001
Jennifer Crusie, *Welcome to Temptation*, 2000
Janet Evanovich, *Hot Six*, 2000
Olivia Goldsmith, *Bad Boy*, 2001
Susan Elizabeth Phillips, *Heaven, Texas*, 1995

218

MARTINE BERNE (Pseudonym of Lisa Bernstein)

The Prize

(New York: Zebra, 2000)

Story type: Historical/Renaissance
Subject(s): Marriage; Revenge; Cultural Conflict
Major character(s): Adrianna, Noblewoman (daughter of an earl); Leith Campbell, Laird
Time period(s): 16th century (1580)
Locale(s): Carlisle, England; Scotland (Inverary Castle)

Summary: Running from her decadent, penniless brother and an unwanted marriage, convent-raised, would-be nun Adrianna is kidnapped by Leith Campbell, a Highland laird seeking to reclaim a stolen Bible and to avenge his brother's death. Unworldly Adrianna is as unprepared for the strange feelings that Leith arouses in her as Leith is unwilling to accept the fact that he is attracted to the daughter of his hated enemy. A jealous woman and Adrianna's persistent, desperate brother cause a few problems, but love does win out in the end.

Where it's reviewed:
Romantic Times, Valentine's Issue 2000, page 41

Other books by the same author:
A Perfect Rogue, 2000

Other books you might like:
Shelley Bradley, *His Stolen Bride*, 2000
Susan King, *The Raven's Moon*, 1997
Janet Lynnford, *Firebrand Bride*, 1999
    more kidnapping
May McGoldrick, *The Enchantress*, 2000
Patricia Potter, *The Abduction*, 1991

219

HEIDI BETTS

Almost a Lady

(New York: Leisure, 2001)

Story type: Historical/Victorian America; Historical/American West
Series: Rose Trilogy. Book 3
Subject(s): Serial Killer; Detection; Romance
Major character(s): Willow Hastings, Detective (Pinkerton agent), Entertainer (undercover saloon singer); Brandt Donovan, Detective (head of security)
Time period(s): 1880s (1886)

Locale(s): New York, New York; Jefferson City, Missouri

Summary: Pinkerton agent Willow Hastings and railroad security chief Brandt Donovan find themselves thrown together in the search for a serial killer and end up falling in love in spite of themselves. Sizzling sexual tension and a complex plot are part of this fast-paced historical that is the final installment in Betts' Rose Trilogy.

Where it's reviewed:
Romantic Times, January 2001, page 43

Other books by the same author:
A Promise of Roses, 2000
Cinnamon and Roses, 2000

Other books you might like:
Emily Carmichael, *Jezebel's Sister*, 2001
Millie Criswell, *Dangerous*, 1998
Maureen McKade, *Mail-Order Bride*, 2000
Maggie Osborne, *The Seduction of Samantha Kincaid*, 2001
Gloria Dale Skinner, *Hellion*, 1998

220

ELIZABETH BEVARLY

First Comes Love

(New York: Silhouette, 2000)

Story type: Humor; Contemporary
Subject(s): Small Town Life; Humor; Teachers
Major character(s): Tess Monahan, Teacher; Will Darrow, Businessman (car repair shop)
Time period(s): 2000s
Locale(s): Marigold, Indiana

Summary: When Tess Monahan, who has never been sick a day in her life, shows up nauseated at an awards banquet, the rumor that she's pregnant spreads like wildfire through the little town of Marigold, Indiana. Will Darrow, her brother's best friend—and the man she's had a crush on since forever—begins to see her in a whole new light when he hears the gossip. Hysterically funny, this book is a can't-put-it-down treat.

Where it's reviewed:
Romantic Times, November 2000, page 112

Other books by the same author:
Dr. Irresistible, 2000
Dr. Mommy, 2000 (From Here to Maternity. Book 2)
A Doctor in Her Stocking, 1999 (From Here to Maternity. Book 1)
Society Bride, 1999 (Fortune's Children: The Brides)
That Boss of Mine, 1999

Other books you might like:
Millie Criswell, *The Trouble with Mary*, 2001
Olivia Goldsmith, *Bad Boy*, 2001
Kasey Michaels, *Too Good to Be True*, 2001
Deborah Shelley, *One Starry Night*, 2000
Tina Wainscott, *The Wrong Mr. Right*, 2000

221

ELIZABETH BEVARLY

The Temptation of Rory Monahan

(New York: Silhouette, 2001)

Story type: Contemporary
Subject(s): Libraries; Seduction
Major character(s): Miriam Thornbury, Librarian; Rory Monahan, Professor (history)
Time period(s): 2000s
Locale(s): Marigold, Indiana

Summary: Practical, sensible librarian Miriam Thornbury is tired of being ignored by cute history professor Rory Monahan; so, with a little help from *Metropolitan* magazine, Miriam unleashes her ''inner temptress'' and goes from invisible to irresistible. Rory definitely notices the new and improved Miriam, but Miriam learns there is big difference between tempting Rory and falling in love with him. Cute with a nice touch of humor.

Where it's reviewed:
Romantic Times, May 2001, page 108

Other books by the same author:
He Could Be the One, 2001
Dr. Irresistible, 2000
How to Trap a Tycoon, 2000
First Comes Love, 2000
Monahan's Gamble, 2000

Other books you might like:
Carrie Alexander, *Black Velvet*, 1998
Kristin Gabriel, *Monday Man*, 1998
Annie Kimberlin, *Romeo and Julia*, 1999
Jayne Ann Krentz, *Perfect Partners*, 1992
Deborah Shelley, *Talk about Love*, 1999

222

JO BEVERLEY

The Devil's Heiress

(New York: Signet, 2001)

Story type: Historical/Regency
Subject(s): Marriage; Money
Major character(s): Clarissa Greystone, Heiress, Noblewoman; George ''Hawk'' Hawkinville, Military Personnel (major), Nobleman
Time period(s): 1810s (1816)
Locale(s): England

Summary: When George Hawkinville returns home from the Napoleonic Wars, he is stunned to learn that he is going to lose his beloved family estate unless he can find a way to either prove a will wrong or marry the woman who has inherited the Duke of Deveril's wealth—and who might very well be responsible for his death. A complex, deception-filled plot, compelling characters, and Beverley's typical brand of sensuality are part of this romance that is part of the trilogy that includes Beverley's short story ''The Demon's Mistress'' in the anthology *In Praise of Younger Men* and then in the novel *The Dragon's Bride*.

Romance

Where it's reviewed:
Rendezvous, June 2001, page 17

Other books by the same author:
The Dragon's Bride, 2001
Devilish, 2000 (Malloren Chronicles. Book 5)
Secrets of the Night, 1999 (Malloren Chronicles. Book 4)
Something Wicked, 1997 (Malloren Chronicles. Book 3)
Tempting Fortune, 1995 (Malloren Chronicles. Book 2)

Other books you might like:
Mary Balogh, *One Night for Love*, 1999
Mary Balogh, *Thief of Dreams*, 1998
Liz Carlyle, *A Woman Scorned*, 2000
Julia London, *The Beautiful Stranger*, 2001
  Rogues of Regent Street series
Anne Stuart, *To Love a Dark Lord*, 1994

223

JO BEVERLEY

The Dragon's Bride
(New York: Signet, 2001)

Story type: Historical/Regency
Subject(s): Dragons; Smuggling; Reunions
Major character(s): Susan Kerslake, Housekeeper, Smuggler; George Connaught "Con" Somerford, Nobleman (Earl of Wyvern)
Time period(s): 1810s (1816)
Locale(s): Devon, England

Summary: Suddenly finding himself the rather reluctant new Earl of Wyvern and master of the forbidding Crag Wyvern, Con Somerford heads for his new estate in Devon and finds himself looking down the barrel of a gun held by none other than the love of his teenage life. Susan, the woman who deeply hurt him 11 years ago, has never forgotten him and now must balance her conflicting feelings for him with her loyalty to her family and her town. Smuggling, a hint of madness, and a fortress filled with bizarre statuary and sadistic toys add to the mix in this darkly sensual story that has links to Beverley's short story "The Demon's Mistress" in the anthology *In Praise of Younger Men* and later in the novel *The Devil's Heiress*.

Where it's reviewed:
Affaire de Coeur, May/June 2001, page 28
Library Journal, May 15, 2001, page 106
Rendezvous, May 2001, page 17

Other books by the same author:
The Devil's Heiress, 2001
Devilish, 2000 (Malloren Chronicles. Book 5)
Secrets of the Night, 1999 (Malloren Chronicles. Book 4)
Something Wicked, 1997 (Malloren Chronicles. Book 3)
Tempting Fortune, 1995 (Malloren Chronicles. Book 2)

Other books you might like:
Mary Balogh, *Thief of Dreams*, 1998
Sabrina Jeffries, *A Dangerous Love*, 2000
Kasey Michaels, *Legacy of the Rose*, 1994
Mary Jo Putney, *Thunder and Roses*, 1993
Anne Stuart, *To Love a Dark Lord*, 1994

224

JO BEVERLEY
CATHY MAXWELL, Co-Author
JACLYN REDING, Co-Author
LAUREN ROYAL, Co-Author

In Praise of Younger Men
(New York: Signet, 2001)

Story type: Anthology
Subject(s): Romance; Difference; Conduct of Life

Summary: Focusing in on one of society's long held conventions—that women marry older men—this captivating quartet of especially well-written short stories challenges the norm and pairs older heroines with younger heroes with rewarding and romantic results. Included are Cathy Maxwell's charming Scottish Regency, "A Man Who Can Dance," Lauren Royal's emotionally involving Restoration romance, "Forevermore," Jaclyn Reding's Regency with a paranormal twist, "Written in the Stars," and Jo Beverley's lively Regency, "The Demon's Mistress." Note: Beverley's story is linked to *The Dragon's Bride* (Signet, 2001) and *The Devil's Heiress* (Signet, 2001).

Where it's reviewed:
Romantic Times, March 2001, page 43

Other books by the same author:
The Devil's Heiress, 2001
The Dragon's Bride, 2001

Other books you might like:
Cathy Maxwell, *The Marriage Contract*, 2001
Pamela Morsi, *Courting Miss Hattie*, 1991
  younger man/older woman
Jaclyn Reding, *White Knight*, 1999
Lauren Royal, *Amber*, 2001

225

CATHERINE BLAIR (Pseudonym of K. Noelle Gracy)

Athena's Conquest
(New York: Zebra, 2001)

Story type: Regency
Subject(s): Books and Reading; Politics; Sisters
Major character(s): Athena Montgomery, Gentlewoman; Dominic Solage, Courier
Time period(s): 1810s
Locale(s): Bath, England; Poole, England

Summary: Athena Montgomery knows she is the serious, clever one in her family, while her sister Cassiopeia is the family beauty so Athena is perfectly content acting as her sister's chaperone while the two sisters stay with their crotchety aunt in Bath. When handsome Dominic Solage, who is rumored to be a French spy, crosses paths with Athena in a bookshop, Athena discounts his compliments as idle flattery only to later realize she does not mind his attentions, but instead is starting to look forward to them.

Where it's reviewed:
Romantic Times, March 2001, page 109

Other books by the same author:
The Hero Returns, 1999
The Scandalous Miss Delaney, 1999

Other books you might like:
Carola Dunn, *Crossed Quills*, 2000
Valerie King, *A Brighton Flirtation*, 2000
Nancy Lawrence, *A Scandalous Season*, 1996
Laura Paquet, *Lord Langdon's Tutor*, 2000
Regina Scott, *The Bluestocking on His Knee*, 1999

226

SHELLEY BRADLEY

His Stolen Bride
(New York: Zebra, 2000)

Story type: Historical/Renaissance
Series: Brothers in Arms. Book 2
Subject(s): Revenge; Kidnapping; Brothers
Major character(s): Lady Averyl Campbell, Noblewoman (daughter of a laird); Drake Thornton McDougall, Laird (dispossessed), Murderer (presumed)
Time period(s): 15th century (1480s)
Locale(s): Scotland

Summary: Accused of murdering his father during a battle, when he knows the deed was done by one of his half-brother's men, Drake McDougall takes revenge in the only way he knows. He kidnaps his half-brother's fiancee, the beautiful, independent, but strangely insecure Averyl Campbell, and takes her off to an isolated island to keep her for ten months, until she turns 18. A classic captor-captive romance with a Scottish twist.

Where it's reviewed:
Romantic Times, December 2000, page 38

Other books by the same author:
His Rebel Bride, 2001
His Lady Bride, 2000
One Wicked Night, 2000
The Lady and the Dragon, 1998

Other books you might like:
Martine Berne, *The Prize*, 2000
Lois Greiman, *Highland Scoundrel*, 1998
Kathleen Harrington, *The MacLean Groom*, 1999
Johanna Lindsey, *A Gentle Feuding*, 2000
Patricia Potter, *The Abduction*, 1991

227

NELL BRIEN (Pseudonym of Shirley Palmer)

Lioness
(Don Mills, Ontario: Mira, 2000)

Story type: Contemporary/Mainstream
Subject(s): Murder; Africa
Major character(s): Cat Stanton, Twin, Architect; Dan Campbell, Guide (bush guide)
Time period(s): 2000s
Locale(s): Africa

Summary: Cat Stanton heads for Africa to learn the truth about her twin brother's brutal death and finds danger and an unexpected love. An uncommon setting for a romance, well-done description, and a back story that is tragic and haunting recommend this romance with definite mainstream appeal.

Where it's reviewed:
Romantic Times, September 2000, page 88

Other books by the same author:
A Veiled Journey, 1999

Other books you might like:
Isak Dinesen, *Out of Africa*, 1937
    early classic/biographical
C.S. Forster, *The African Queen*, 1940
    classic tale of Africa
Iris Johansen, *The Search*, 2000

228

PAMELA BRITTON

Enchanted by Your Kisses
(New York: HarperTorch, 2001)

Story type: Historical/Georgian
Subject(s): Brothers; Espionage; Kidnapping
Major character(s): Ariel D'Archer, Gentlewoman; Nathan Trevain, Gentleman, Spy
Time period(s): 1780s (1781; 1783)
Locale(s): London, England

Summary: Caught in a compromising situation, Ariel D'Archer is ostracized by society and retires in disgrace to the countryside. Two years later, American Nathan Trevain, the future Duke of Davenport, offers his help in restoring Ariel to her place in the *ton*. What Nathan does not tell Ariel is that he needs her help in locating his brother, who disappeared after being impressed by the British Navy. Nathan is determined Ariel will provide him with the information he needs, even if he must kidnap her in the process.

Where it's reviewed:
Affaire de Coeur, March/April 2001, page 17
Romantic Times, March 2001, page 37

Other books by the same author:
My Fallen Angel, 2000

Other books you might like:
Jane Ashford, *Bride to Be*, 1999
Jo Beverley, *My Lady Notorious*, 1993
Jaclyn Reding, *Deception's Bride*, 1993
Patricia Rice, *Love Forever After*, 1990
Barbara Samuel, *The Black Angel*, 1999

229

SUZANNE BROCKMANN

The Defiant Hero
(New York: Ivy, 2001)

Story type: Contemporary; Romantic Suspense
Subject(s): Kidnapping; Terrorism

Major character(s): Meg Moore, Linguist (translator); John Nilsson, Military Personnel (Navy SEAL)
Time period(s): 2000s
Locale(s): Washington, District of Columbia

Summary: When the Kazbekistani Extremists kidnap her 10-year-old daughter and her grandmother, translator Meg Moore responds by taking the Kazbekistani ambassador hostage in the embassy men's room, saying she will negotiate with the only man she trusts under the circumstances, Navy SEAL John Nilsson. A fast-paced, tense, action-filled adventure featuring a multitude of compelling characters. Latest in Brockmann's stories featuring Navy SEALs.

Where it's reviewed:
Romantic Times, March 2001, page 87

Other books by the same author:
Get Lucky, 2000
The Unsung Hero, 2000
Body Guard, 1999
Heartthrob, 1999
Undercover Princess, 1999

Other books you might like:
Shirley Hailstock, *More than Gold*, 2000
    multicultural suspense
Rachel Lee, *After I Dream*, 2000
    SEAL action
Merline Lovelace, *Dark Side of Dawn*, 2001
    military thriller
Merline Lovelace, *Duty and Dishonor*, 1997
Tracey Tillis, *Deadly Masquerade*, 1994

230

SUZANNE BROCKMANN

Over the Edge

(New York: Ivy, 2001)

Story type: Contemporary; Romantic Suspense
Subject(s): Terrorism; Rescue Work; Hostages
Major character(s): Teri Howe, Military Personnel (lieutenant, Navy Reserves), Pilot (helicopter); Stanley Wolchonok, Military Personnel (Navy SEAL)
Time period(s): 2000s
Locale(s): United States; Kazbeckistan, Fictional Country

Summary: When a plane carrying the daughter of an American senator is hijacked and forced to land in Kazbeckistan, helicopter pilot Teri Howe and Senior Chief Petty Officer Stan Wolchonok are part of the SEAL rescue team. They begin the mission as friends; when it is over, they realize they are far more than that. Gritty, fast-paced, and suspenseful with good character development. Latest in Brockmann's series of Navy SEAL adventures.

Other books by the same author:
Get Lucky, 2000
Unsung Hero, 2000
Body Guard, 1999
Heartthrob, 1999
Undercover Princess, 1999

Other books you might like:
Ginna Gray, *The Witness*, 2001
Rachel Lee, *After I Dream*, 2000
    SEALs
Merline Lovelace, *Call of Duty*, 2001
    military theme
Merline Lovelace, *Dark Side of Dawn*, 2001
    military theme

231

DEBRA LEE BROWN

Ice Maiden

(Toronto: Harlequin, 2001)

Story type: Historical/Medieval
Subject(s): Vikings; Marriage
Major character(s): Ulrika "Rika", Warrior (Viking), Abuse Victim; George Grant, Laird
Time period(s): 13th century (1206)
Locale(s): Shetland Islands, Scotland (Fair Isle)

Summary: Rika will do anything to get the money to ransom her brother, Gunnar, and restore him to his rightful role as *jarl*, even marry the strange Scot who is washed up on the shore of her remote island home. George Grant is not about to marry and divorce this strange strapping warrior woman simply so she can claim her dowry; after all, he has a sweet, gentle fiancee waiting for him at home. Of course, getting there is the problem; he will only be released if he marries Rika first. Eventually, the marriage takes place—and the results surprise them both. Interesting characters, good descriptive detail, and political intrigue add to this story that touches on abuse issues.

Where it's reviewed:
Affaire de Coeur, February 2001, page 22
Romantic Times, February 2001, page 43

Other books by the same author:
The Virgin Spring, 2000

Other books you might like:
Suzanne Barclay, *Lion's Legacy*, 1996
J.A. Ferguson, *My Lord Viking*, 2001
Heather Graham, *The Viking's Woman*, 1990
    more Vikings/different treatment
Helen Mittermeyer, *Princess of the Veil*, 2001
    similar setting/wounded heroine
Margaret Moore, *A Warrior's Quest*, 1993

232

PAMELA BURFORD (Pseudonym of Pamela Burford Loeser)

I Do, but Here's the Catch

(Toronto: Harlequin, 2001)

Story type: Contemporary
Series: Wedding Ring. Book 2
Subject(s): Marriage; Communication; Careers
Major character(s): Carlotta "Charli" Rossi, Teacher (high school music), Musician (flutist); Grant Sterling, Lawyer
Time period(s): 2000s

Locale(s): New York, New York (Long Island's South Shore)

Summary: Grant Sterling loves being a bachelor. Unfortunately, his law firm won't consider making him a partner unless he's married. After being introduced to quiet, 30-year-old virgin Charli Rossi, he decides to offer her a marriage of convenience, which to him means separate bedrooms and separate lives. Charli, who misunderstands his proposal, finds herself in a marriage that, has terms she abhors and a husband she loves, but who won't love her back. A tale of a man who's looking for a Stepford Wife but marries an Italian time bomb by mistake.

Where it's reviewed:
Romantic Times, January 2001, page 104

Other books by the same author:
Fiance for Hire, 2001 (Wedding Ring. Book 4)
One Eager Bride to Go, 2001 (Wedding Ring. Book 3)
Love's Funny That Way, 2000 (Wedding Ring. Book 1)
A Class Act, 1999
Summer Heat, 1998

Other books you might like:
Elizabeth Bevarly, *Dr. Mommy*, 2000
Millie Criswell, *The Wedding Planner*, 2000
Leigh Greenwood, *Married by High Noon*, 2000
Myrna Mackenzie, *Simon Says. . .Marry Me!*, 2000
Joan Elliott Pickart, *Man. . .Mercenary. . .Monarch*, 2000

233

PATRICIA CABOT (Pseudonym of Meggin Cabot)

Lady of Skye
(New York: Sonnet, 2001)

Story type: Historical
Subject(s): Healing; Doctors; Small Town Life
Major character(s): Brenna Donnegal, Healer; Reilly Stanton, Nobleman (Eighth Marquis of Stillworth), Doctor; Lord Glendenning, Nobleman
Time period(s): 1840s (1847)
Locale(s): Isle of Skye, Scotland; Lyming, Scotland

Summary: Brenna Donnegal has spent her life helping her father heal the people—and animals—of the Isle of Skye. Now, he's gone, and the lecherous Lord Glendenning has sent for a real doctor who can relieve her of her duties and help persuade her to marry him. Dr. Reilly Stanton is tired of being a member of the worthless upper class, and he's eager to use his new skills as a physician to help the people on the Isle of Skye. He thinks Brenna belongs with him, not the nobleman who wants her. A quirky love triangle of a fiercely independent woman, a man who's out to prove himself, and an oddly lovable, self-centered nobleman fill this book with witty dialogue, unexpected plot twists, and a whole palette of emotions.

Where it's reviewed:
Publishers Weekly, December 11, 2000, page 68
Romantic Times, January 2001, page 38

Other books by the same author:
A Little Scandal, 2000
An Improper Proposal, 1999

Portrait of My Heart, 1998
Where Roses Grow Wild, 1998

Other books you might like:
Debra Lee Brown, *The Virgin Spring*, 2000
Arnette Lamb, *Beguiled*, 1996
Teresa Medeiros, *The Bride and the Beast*, 2000
Jaclyn Reding, *White Heather*, 1997
Amanda Scott, *Border Storm*, 2001

234

LISA CACH

The Mermaid of Penperro
(New York: LoveSpell, 2001)

Story type: Historical/Regency
Subject(s): Mermaids; Smuggling
Major character(s): Konstanze Bugg, Runaway, Singer; Tom Trewella, Banker, Smuggler
Time period(s): 1800s (1804)
Locale(s): Kent, England; Penperro, England

Summary: Running away from her detestable, abusive husband, Konstanze Bugg changes her name to Constance Penrose and begins a new life in an inherited cottage in Cornwall. When Robert Foweather, the leader of the Preventive Water Guard Service, spots Constance swimming in the sea one day and mistakes her for a real mermaid, Tom Trewella convinces Constance to impersonate a mermaid as a way of throwing the King's Men off the trail of the town's smugglers. Much to his surprise, Tom finds out Robert is not the only man susceptible to the new mermaid's seductive song.

Where it's reviewed:
Romantic Times, April 2001, page 42

Other books by the same author:
Bewitching the Baron, 2000
Of Midnight Born, 2000
The Changeling Bride, 1999

Other books you might like:
Jill Barnett, *Dreaming*, 1997
Jillian Hunter, *Fairy Tale*, 1997
Dara Joy, *Tonight or Never*, 1999
Betina Krahn, *The Mermaid*, 1997
Teresa Medeiros, *The Bride and the Beast*, 2000

235

GAYLE CALLEN

His Betrothed
(New York: Avon, 2001)

Story type: Historical/Elizabethan
Subject(s): Conspiracies; Marriage; Spies
Major character(s): Lady Roselyn Harrington Grant, Noblewoman, Widow(er); Sir Spencer Thornton, Nobleman, Spy
Time period(s): 16th century (1588)
Locale(s): London, England; Isle of Wight, England

Summary: When Lady Roselyn Harrington leaves her arrogant fiance, Spencer Thornton, standing in front of the church and runs off with the stable groom, she has no idea that two years later, widowed and living a simple, reclusive life on her family's land on the Isle of Wight, she will save Spencer's life when he is washed up after a battle on her beach. However, Spencer has vowed vengeance for Roselyn's public humiliation of him, and now he has his chance—he will make her fall in love with him and then reject her. True love and politics interfere, and Roselyn and Spencer eventually end up where they were meant to be in the first place—at the altar. Spies, war, and political intrigue are all part of this fast-paced, sensual, occasionally humorous adventure. First in a projected trilogy.

Where it's reviewed:
Library Journal, May 15, 2001, page 104

Other books by the same author:
My Lady's Guardian, 2000 (Medieval Trilogy. Book 3)
A Knight's Vow, 1999 (Medieval Trilogy. Book 2)
The Darkest Knight, 1999 (Medieval Trilogy. Book 1)

Other books you might like:
Julie Beard, *Romance of the Rose*, 1998
Taylor Chase, *Heart of Deception*, 1999
    darker
Denise Domning, *Lady in Waiting*, 1998
    similar period
Ruth Langan, *Conor*, 1999
    Elizabethan adventure

236

STELLA CAMERON

7B

(Don Mills, Ontario: Mira, 2001)

Story type: Historical
Series: Mayfair Square. Book 3
Subject(s): Marriage; Babies; Ghosts
Major character(s): Sibyl Smiles, Gentlewoman; Hunter Lloyd, Lawyer (barrister); Sir Septimus Spivey, Spirit
Time period(s): 1810s
Locale(s): London, England

Summary: Once again the meddling "ghost in a post," Sir Septimus Spivey, sets out to marry off the current tenants of elegant 7 Mayfair Square, simply so he can regain his peace and quiet. Sibyl Smiles is an "independent woman" and while she does want a baby and decides to seduce her barrister neighbor, Hunter Lloyd, in order to get one, she definitely doesn't want a husband. Hunter, on the other hand, is involved in a tricky and dangerous trial situation and can't afford the distraction, even though he is attracted to Sibyl. Light mystery and a dash of ghostly fun add to the appeal of this latest addition to Cameron's series.

Where it's reviewed:
Romantic Times, March 2001, page 40

Other books by the same author:
Finding Ian, 2001
All Smiles, 2000 (Mayfair Square. Book 2)
Key West, 2000

Glass Houses, 2000
More and More, 1998 (Mayfair Square. Book 1)

Other books you might like:
Marion Chesney, *The Miser of Mayfair*, 1996
    another house-based Regency series
Casey Claybourne, *A Ghost of a Chance*, 1996
Christina Dodd, *Rules of Engagement*, 2000
    later period/fast-paced and sensual
Amanda Quick, *Dangerous*, 1993
    lively and sensual

237

STELLA CAMERON

Finding Ian

(New York: Kensington, 2001)

Story type: Contemporary/Mainstream
Subject(s): Adoption; Fathers and Sons; Family Relations
Major character(s): Jade Perron, Businesswoman, Divorced Person; Byron Frazer, Psychologist, Widow(er); Ian Spring, Teenager
Time period(s): 2000s
Locale(s): San Francisco, California; Cornwall, England

Summary: Young and grief-stricken by the tragic death of his wife, Byron Frazer allows his infant son to be adopted, thinking it would be the best for all concerned. Thirteen years later when the boy is suddenly orphaned and sent from Minnesota to live with his adopted mother's sister in Cornwall, Byron, in spite of his good intentions never to become involved in Ian's life, heads for Cornwall to check things out—and finds not only his son, but love, as well. A vulnerable teenager, some meddling secondary characters, and a pair of protagonists badly in need of emotional healing combine in this compelling realistic romance with mainstream appeal.

Where it's reviewed:
Romantic Times, January 2001, page 77

Other books by the same author:
7B, 2001
Glass Houses, 2000
Key West, 2000
The Best Revenge, 1998
The Wish Club, 1998

Other books you might like:
Rexanne Becnel, *The Christmas Wish*, 1993
Barbara Delinsky, *The Passions of Chelsea Kane*, 1992
    reversal of theme
Kathleen Eagle, *What the Heart Knows*, 1999
    father & son issues
Rosamunde Pilcher, *Wild Mountain Thyme*, 1978
    British setting
Belva Plain, *Blessings*, 1988
    reversal of theme

238

CANDACE CAMP

No Other Love

(Don Mills, Ontario: Mira, 2001)

Story type: Historical/Regency
Series: Montford Heirs Trilogy. Book 3
Subject(s): Robbers and Outlaws; Memory Loss; Inheritance
Major character(s): Nicola Falcourt, Healer; Jack Moore, Highwayman, Amnesiac (a.k.a. Gil Martin)
Time period(s): 1780s (1789); 1810s (1815)
Locale(s): England

Summary: After Nicola Falcourt's true love is slain by her evil suitor, she turns to a life of benevolence, helping the unwed mothers of London. During a visit to her sister's, Nicola is abducted by Jack Moore, "The Gentleman," a highwayman known for his Robin Hood ways. A stunning surprise awaits her when she learns the highwayman's true identity in this exciting conclusion to the excellent Montford Heirs trilogy.

Where it's reviewed:
Romantic Times, February 2001, page 41

Other books by the same author:
A Stolen Heart, 2000 (Montford Heirs Trilogy. Book 1)
Promise Me Tomorrow, 2000 (Montford Heirs Trilogy. Book 2)
Swept Away, 1999
Impetuous, 1998
Satan's Angel, 1998

Other books you might like:
Stephanie Laurens, *Captain Jack's Woman*, 1997
Christina Skye, *Come the Night*, 1994
Joan Smith, *A Highwayman Came Riding*, 1998
Shelly Thacker, *Midnight Raider*, 1992
Sylvia Thorpe, *The Highwayman*, 1962

239

LIZ CARLYLE (Pseudonym of S.T. Woodhouse)

A Woman of Virtue

(New York: Sonnet, 2001)

Story type: Historical/Regency
Subject(s): Crime and Criminals; Social Conditions
Major character(s): Cecilia Markham-Sands, Noblewoman (Countess of Walrafen); David Delacourt, Nobleman
Time period(s): 1810s (1818); 1820s (1824)
Locale(s): London, England; Newmarket, England

Summary: After being ruined by the worst rake in England and then refusing his offer of marriage, Cecilia Markham-Sands finds herself reunited with Lord David Delacourt years later when the hedonistic nobleman shows up at the charity mission Cecilia sponsors for reforming prostitutes. Having lost a wager with his brother-in-law, Delacourt must now help out at Cecilia's charity for six months and discovers he is still attracted to the one woman who spurned his advances. When two women from the mission disappear and are later found murdered, Delacourt appoints himself Cecilia's protector and vows to keep the woman he loves safe from danger.

Where it's reviewed:
Romantic Times, March 2001, page 38

Other books by the same author:
A Woman Scorned, 2000
Beauty Like the Night, 2000
My False Heart, 1999

Other books you might like:
Jacquie D'Alessandro, *Red Roses Mean Love*, 1999
Gaelen Foley, *The Duke*, 2000
Sabrina Jeffries, *A Dangerous Love*, 2000
Stephanie Laurens, *All about Love*, 2001
Elizabeth Thornton, *Princess Charming*, 2001

240

EMILY CARMICHAEL (Pseudonym of Emily Krokosz)

Jezebel's Sister

(New York: Jove, 2001)

Story type: Historical/American West; Humor
Subject(s): Conduct of Life; Identity, Concealed; Pioneers
Major character(s): Cassidy "Cass" Rose McAllister, Pioneer; Nathan Stone, Fugitive, Imposter (poses as wagon train leader)
Time period(s): 1860s (1866)
Locale(s): Webster, Kansas; Oregon Trail, West

Summary: Raised in her sister's brothel but not one of the "girls", Cass McAllister endures the town's ostracism, but yearns for respectability—even as she knows it will never happen. When her sister and her women end up in trouble, and a pioneer family needs to sell their complete wagon train "outfit," Cass seizes the opportunity and she and her sister and company set off with the wagon train heading for a new start in the West. The going is not easy for the wagon train is church-related and pious, something that Cass' charges are not at all used to, and the wagon master is drop-dead-gorgeous Preacher Homer Pernell—an imposter with a price on his head and a man on his trail—and someone who has his eyes on Cass. Funny and lively.

Where it's reviewed:
Romantic Times, March 2001, page 39

Other books by the same author:
A Ghost for Maggie, 1999
Finding Mr. Right, 1998
Windfall, 1997
Gold Dust, 1996
Outcast, 1995

Other books you might like:
Heidi Betts, *Almost a Lady*, 2001
Lori Copeland, *Promise Me Forever*, 1994
    humorous
Susan Kay Law, *The Most Wanted Bachelor*, 2000
Pamela Morsi, *Wild Oats*, 1993
    reputations and respectability
Maggie Osborne, *The Brides of Prairie Gold*, 1996
    wagon train romance

241

SUSAN CARROLL

Midnight Bride

(New York: Ballantine, 2001)

Story type: Historical/Fantasy; Paranormal
Series: St. Leger. Book 3
Subject(s): Marriage; Revenge; Supernatural
Major character(s): Kate Fitzleger, Gentlewoman; Valentine St. Leger, Doctor; Rafe Mortmain, Government Official (former customs officer), Villain
Time period(s): 19th century
Locale(s): Cornwall, England

Summary: When Rafe Mortmain returns to Cornwall to take revenge upon the man he holds responsible for his banishment from England, he has no idea that his evil plan will end up changing his life as much as it changes the life of his old enemy, Val St. Leger. An honorable hero with pain-absorbing abilities, a heroine who will risk anything for Val, and a villain who finds a new life join forces in this mesmerizing, magical story that features a dangerous crystal, a meddling ghost, a bit of magic, and nicely continues the St. Leger series.

Other books by the same author:
The Night Drifter, 1999
The Bride Finder, 1998
Parker and the Gypsy, 1997
The Painted Veil, 1995
Christmas Belles, 1992

Other books you might like:
Mary Balogh, *Thief of Dreams*, 1998
 revenge and marriage
Jo Beverley, *The Dragon's Bride*, 2001
Jo Beverley, *Forbidden Magic*, 1998
 darkly magical
Kimberly Cates, *Magic*, 1998
Maggie Shayne, *Destiny*, 2001
 more magic

242

CARLA CASSIDY (Pseudonym of Carla Bracale)

Just One Kiss

(New York: Silhouette, 2001)

Story type: Contemporary
Subject(s): Single Parent Families; Babies; Healing
Major character(s): Marissa Criswell, Single Parent, Health Care Professional (nurse's aide); Jack Coffey, Detective—Private
Time period(s): 2000s
Locale(s): Mason Bridge, Florida

Summary: When single mother Marissa Criswell's toddler deliberately trips private eye Jack Coffey, causing him to break his fingers and leg, she tries her best to make it up to him by typing his paperwork and cleaning his house. Jack isn't interested in Marissa or her son. . .or so he tells himself. A warm, emotion-filled story of love lost and found.

Where it's reviewed:
Romantic Times, January 2001, page 106

Other books by the same author:
An Officer and a Princess, 2001
Lost in His Arms, 2001
Man on a Mission, 2001
Imminent Danger, 2000
Strangers When We Married, 2000

Other books you might like:
Carol Grace, *Fit for a Sheikh*, 2001
 Virgin Brides series
Susan Meier, *Cinderella and the CEO*, 2001
Raye Morgan, *The Boss's Baby Mistake*, 2001
Julianna Morris, *Meeting Megan Again*, 2001
Valerie Parv, *Booties and the Beast*, 2001
 An Older Man series

243

CARLA CASSIDY (Pseudonym of Carla Bracale)

Man on a Mission

(New York: Silhouette, 2001)

Story type: Romantic Suspense; Contemporary
Series: Delaney Heirs. Book 2
Subject(s): Inheritance; Murder; Trust
Major character(s): April Cartwright, Single Parent; Mark Delaney, Rancher
Time period(s): 2000s
Locale(s): Inferno, Arizona

Summary: Someone tried to kill Mark Delaney when they murdered the rancher's social director, and now he doesn't know whom to trust. Even his family is suspect. To gather information, he pretends that the shovel blow to his head has caused brain damage and he settles into the role until the new social director is hired, when suddenly his facade becomes a burden. A suspenseful story where true love sees past the obvious.

Where it's reviewed:
Romantic Times, May 2001, page 109

Other books by the same author:
An Officer and a Princess, 2001
Just One Kiss, 2001
Lost in His Arms, 2001
Imminent Danger, 2000
Waiting for the Wedding, 2000

Other books you might like:
Candace Camp, *Hard-Headed Texan*, 2001
Mary McBride, *Moonglow, Texas*, 2001
Paula Detmer Riggs, *Daddy with a Badge*, 2001
Sharon Sala, *Familiar Stranger*, 2001
Susan Vaughan, *Dangerous Attraction*, 2001

244

RYANNE COREY (Pseudonym of Tonya Wood)

The Heiress and the Bodyguard

(New York: Silhouette, 2001)

Story type: Contemporary
Subject(s): Change; Independence
Major character(s): Billy Lucas, Bodyguard; Julie Roper, Heiress
Time period(s): 2000s
Locale(s): Palm Beach, Florida; Laguna Beach, California

Summary: Pampered, protected, and bored out of her mind, Palm Beach heiress Julie Roper coerces Billy Lucas into giving her an escorted tour of life in the real world. Billy, who has secretly been hired by Julie's brother to protect her, hates deceiving Julie about the real reason he is hanging around. He can't help wondering if by telling Julie the truth about himself, he could lose her forever.

Where it's reviewed:
Romantic Times, April 2001, page 110

Other books by the same author:
Lady with a Past, 2000
When She Was Bad, 1995
The Stranger, 1993
Leather and Lace, 1991
The Valentine Street Hustle, 1990

Other books you might like:
Carrie Alexander, *The Madcap Heiress*, 1996
Kylie Brant, *Guarding Raine*, 1996
Kathy Disanto, *For Love or Money*, 1997
Kristin Gabriel, *Bullets over Boise*, 1998
Lois Greiman, *His Bodyguard*, 1999

245

CATHERINE COULTER

The Scottish Bride

(New York: Jove, 2001)

Story type: Historical/Regency
Series: Bride. Book 4
Subject(s): Marriage; Social Classes; Conduct of Life
Major character(s): Mary Rose Sherbrooke, Bastard Daughter, Bride; Tysen Sherbrooke, Nobleman (Baron Barthwick), Religious (vicar)
Time period(s): 1810s (1815)
Locale(s): Scotland (Kildrummy Castle); Glenclose-on-Rowan, England

Summary: When the dour vicar, Tysen Sherbrooke, suddenly inherits a Scottish castle and becomes Baron Barthwick, he has no idea that his life is about to change totally. His visit to Scotland not only nets him a title but the bride of his dreams as well—a situation that doesn't set too well with his parishioners when he returns. A hero who learns to love, a heroine who teaches him, and a delightful group of children who urge them on add to this lively, fast-paced story that will please fans of Coulter's Bride series.

Where it's reviewed:
Romantic Times, January 2001, page 38

Other books by the same author:
Hemlock Bay, 2001
The Offer, 1997
Rosehaven, 1996
The Cove, 1996
The Heir, 1996

Other books you might like:
Mary Balogh, *One Night for Love*, 1999
Stephanie Laurens, *All about Love*, 2001
Cathy Maxwell, *The Marriage Contract*, 2001
Kate Moore, *Winterburn's Rose*, 2001
Amanda Quick, *Wicked Widow*, 2000

246

CATHERINE COULTER

Warrior's Song

(New York: Signet, 2001)

Story type: Historical/Medieval; Historical
Series: Song. Book 1
Subject(s): Middle Ages; Women Soldiers; Women's Rights
Major character(s): Lady Chandra de Avenell, Warrior, Noblewoman; Jerval de Vernon, Nobleman, Warrior
Time period(s): 13th century (1272)
Locale(s): Chesire, England (Croyland Castle); Cumbria, England (Camberley Castle); Tunis, Africa

Summary: Chandra de Avenell, raised like a boy, has grown up to be a fine warrior. Jerval de Vernon, the man her father forces her to marry, wants a more domestic spouse. This sensual rewrite of Coulter's 1983 book, *1Chandra*, is a twist on *The Taming of the Shrew*, except in this case, the woman is heavily armed.

Other books by the same author:
The Scottish Bride, 2001
The Courtship, 2000
Secret Song, 1991 (Song. Book 4)
Earth Song, 1990 (Song. Book 3)
Fire Song, 1985 (Song. Book 2)

Other books you might like:
Shana Abe, *Intimate Enemies*, 2000
Jill Barnett, *Wicked*, 1999
Donna Fletcher, *Irish Hope*, 2001
Jillian Hart, *Malcolm's Honor*, 2000
Haywood Smith, *Highland Princess*, 2000

247

WILMA COUNTS

The Wagered Wife

(New York: Zebra, 2001)

Story type: Regency
Subject(s): Animals/Horses; Marriage
Major character(s): Caitlyn Maria Woodbridge, Gentlewoman; Trevor Allen Jeffries, Nobleman
Time period(s): 1800s (1808); 1810s (1814)

Locale(s): London, England; Atherton, England; Timberly, England

Summary: Gambling everything and losing to Baron Fiske, Trevor Jeffries finds there is only one way he can repay his debt: marry the baron's unwanted ward, Caitlyn Woodbridge. After a hasty wedding, Trevor abandons his new wife at his recently inherited country estate and enlists in Wellington's army. When Trevor returns home from the war, he finds the shy, unassuming wife he left behind is now a polished beauty who has captivated the *ton*. If Trevor wants his bride back, he must successfully court the woman he discarded.

Where it's reviewed:
Affaire de Coeur, February 2001, page 34
Romantic Times, February 2001, page 111

Other books by the same author:
My Lady Governess, 2000
The Willful Miss Winthrop, 2000
Willed to Wed, 1999

Other books you might like:
Jessica Benson, *Lord Stanhope's Proposal*, 2000
Catherine Blair, *The Hero Returns*, 1999
Kate Huntington, *The Lieutenant's Lady*, 1999
Martha Kirkland, *A Gentleman's Deception*, 1999
Patricia Oliver, *Lady Jane's Nemesis*, 2000

248

MILLIE CRISWELL

The Trouble with Mary

(New York: Ivy, 2001)

Story type: Humor; Contemporary
Subject(s): Humor; Italian Americans; Family Relations
Major character(s): Mary Russo, Restaurateur, Business-woman; Dan Gallagher, Journalist, Critic (food)
Time period(s): 2000s
Locale(s): Baltimore, Maryland (Little Italy)

Summary: When Mary Russo opens her Italian restaurant, food critic Dan Gallagher gives her a scathing review. She's not going to let him get away with it, and neither is her family. This is a warm, wonderful, delightfully funny story of an Italian family that seem so alive you'd swear you knew them. Hilarious!

Where it's reviewed:
Booklist, January 1, 2001, page 927
Publishers Weekly, November 20, 2000, page 52
Romantic Times, January 2001, page 77

Other books by the same author:
The Marrying Man, 2000
The Wedding Planner, 2000
True Love, 1999
Dangerous, 1998
Defiant, 1998

Other books you might like:
Sue Civil-Brown, *Catching Kelly*, 2000
Claire Cross, *Third Time Lucky*, 2000
Janet Evanovich, *Hot Six*, 2000
Jayne Ann Krentz, *Family Man*, 1992

Tina Wainscott, *The Wrong Mr. Right*, 2000

249

HEATHER CULLMAN

Bewitched

(New York: Signet, 2001)

Story type: Historical/Georgian
Subject(s): Marriage; Illness; Love
Major character(s): Emily Merriman, Gentlewoman (American); Michael Vane, Nobleman (Duke of Sherrington), Recluse; Adeline Vane, Noblewoman (Dowager Duchess of Sherrington)
Time period(s): 1820s (1828)
Locale(s): Oxfordshire, England; Dartmoor, England

Summary: Fearing for the succession of the duchy and her own hope for grandchildren, the Dowager Duchess of Sherrington presents her grandson, the current duke and a victim of recurring seizures brought on by a serious brain illness, with an ultimatum—either he marries the American granddaughter of her best friend, or she will declare him insane and commit him to an asylum. Although he reluctantly agrees, the very American Emily is not so docile; after all she has been cursed by a witch, who promised she would bring disaster to any man she loved—and she has three ex-fiances to prove it! The marriage, of course, takes place—understanding, love, and healing eventually follow in this emotionally involving, poignant story.

Where it's reviewed:
Romantic Times, February 2001, page 40

Other books by the same author:
A Perfect Scoundrel, 2000
For All Eternity, 1998
Stronger than Money, 1997
Tomorrow's Dreams, 1996
Yesterday's Roses, 1995

Other books you might like:
Susan Carroll, *The Bride Finder*, 1998
Christina Dodd, *Move Heaven and Earth*, 1995
Hannah Howell, *Beauty and the Beast*, 1992
Laura Kinsale, *Flowers from the Storm*, 1992
Mary Jo Putney, *Thunder and Roses*, 1993

250

CLAUDIA DAIN

The Holding

(New York: Leisure, 2001)

Story type: Historical/Medieval
Subject(s): Middle Ages; Rape; Trust
Major character(s): Lady Cathryn of Greneforde, Noble-woman, Abuse Victim; William le Brouillard, Knight (a.k.a. "The Fog"), Nobleman
Time period(s): 12th century (1155)
Locale(s): Greneforde, England

Summary: As a prize for serving him so long and well, the king gives William le Brouillard, also known as "The Fog,"

the holding of Greneforde, as well as its owner, Lady Cathryn. Cathryn and her people have been victimized by a nefarious nobleman who wants her and her lands for himself. This powerful story is an excellent study on gaining trust, especially when both people have strong reasons for doubts.

Where it's reviewed:
Romantic Times, March 2001, page 40

Other books by the same author:
Tell Me Lies, 2000
Unwrapped, 2000 (anthology)

Other books you might like:
Shana Abe, *Intimate Enemies*, 2000
Rexanne Becnel, *The Mistress of Rosecliffe*, 2000
Donna Fletcher, *The Irish Devil*, 2000
Jillian Hart, *Malcolm's Honor*, 2000
Ana Seymour, *Lady of Lyonsbridge*, 2000

251

DEE DAVIS (Pseudonym of Dee Davis Oberwetter)

After Twilight
(New York: Ivy, 2001)

Story type: Romantic Suspense
Subject(s): Art Restoration; Brothers; Revenge
Major character(s): Kacy Macgrath, Artist; Braedon Roche, Businessman
Time period(s): 2000s
Locale(s): Southhampton, New York; Lindoon, Ireland

Summary: Kacy Macgrath desperately hopes that by changing her name and moving to Ireland she can leave a troubled marriage and her husband's death behind. However, Braedon Roche holds Kacy and her late husband responsible for the forged art that almost ruined his business, and now that Braedon has tracked Kacy to Ireland, he is determined to destroy her. Once Braedon learns Kacy was never connected with the forgeries, he puts aside his thoughts of revenge only to discover someone else is waiting to settle a score with Kacy.

Where it's reviewed:
Romantic Times, January 2001, page 77

Other books by the same author:
Everything in Its Time, 2000

Other books you might like:
Linda Anderson, *When Night Falls*, 2000
Jasmine Cresswell, *The Refuge*, 2000
Kay Hooper, *Haunting Rachel*, 1998
Merline Lovelace, *Dark Side of Dawn*, 2001
Carla Neggers, *Kiss the Moon*, 1999

252

GERALYN DAWSON (Pseudonym of Geralyn Dawson Williams)

The Bad Luck Wedding Night
(New York: Sonnet, 2001)

Story type: Humor; Historical/Victorian

Subject(s): Humor; Cultural Conflict; Weddings
Major character(s): Sarah Simpson, Noblewoman (Lady Weston), Businesswoman (wedding planner); Nicholas Ross, Nobleman (Lord Weston, Earl of Innsbruck), Spy
Time period(s): 1870s; 1880s
Locale(s): Fort Worth, Texas; Scotland; London, England

Summary: Sixteen-year-old Sarah Simpson marries the love of her life, 18-year-old Nicholas Ross, but terrorized by wedding night horror stories, she refuses to let him consummate their marriage. A death in the family forces him to leave the next day, a mysterious pregnant woman in tow. For the next ten years, while Nicholas spies for the British government, and Sarah stays in Texas to run a successful wedding planning service, they correspond, but never get around to annulling their marriage. Then Sarah gets word Nick needs a wedding planner for his sister's upcoming nuptials, and he will only settle for Sarah. An extremely humorous treatment of Victorian mores and a woman who refuses to believe they exist.

Where it's reviewed:
Romantic Times, April 2001, page 38

Other books by the same author:
Sizzle All Day, 2000
Simmer All Night, 1999
The Bad Luck Wedding Cake, 1998
The Wedding Ransom, 1997
The Wedding Raffle, 1996

Other books you might like:
Millie Criswell, *The Marrying Man*, 2000
Suzanne Enoch, *Meet Me at Midnight*, 2000
Jill Marie Landis, *The Orchid Hunter*, 2000
Julia Quinn, *How to Marry a Marquis*, 1999
Judith Stacy, *The Blushing Bride*, 2000

253

CLAIRE DELACROIX

The Beauty
(New York: Dell, 2001)

Story type: Historical/Medieval
Series: Bride Quest. Book 5
Subject(s): Middle Ages; Revenge; Trust
Major character(s): Jacqueline de Crevy, Young Woman; Angus MacGillivray, Knight, Kidnapper
Time period(s): 12th century (1183)
Locale(s): Ceinn-beithe, Scotland

Summary: On her way to join a convent, Jacqueline de Crevy is kidnapped by Angus MacGillivray. Angus has lost his birthright, and seeks vengeance by taking the woman he mistakenly assumes is his enemy's daughter. A wounded hero and a woman terrorized by a previous, vicious attack finally find peace in this richly textured, emotion-filled historical.

Where it's reviewed:
Romantic Times, January 2001, page 40

Other books by the same author:
The Countess, 2000 (Bride Quest. Book 4)
The Damsel, 1999 (Bride Quest. Book 2)
The Heiress, 1999 (Bride Quest. Book 3)

My Lady's Desire, 1998
The Princess, 1998 (Bride Quest. Book 1)

Other books you might like:
Shana Abe, *Intimate Enemies*, 2000
Shari Anton, *The Conqueror*, 2000
Rexanne Becnel, *The Mistress of Rosecliffe*, 2000
Claudia Dain, *The Holding*, 2001
Ana Seymour, *The Rogue*, 2000

254

JAMIE DENTON

Making Mr. Right

(Toronto: Harlequin, 2001)

Story type: Contemporary; Humor
Subject(s): Independence; Responsibility
Major character(s): Jocelyn Camille "Jaycee" Richmond, Businesswoman (family firm), Consultant (image consultant); Simon Hawthorne, Accountant
Time period(s): 2000s
Locale(s): Seattle, Washington

Summary: Tired of being relegated to the role of Better Image's secretary and file clerk, Jaycee Richmond looks for a way to demonstrate to her brothers that she is equally capable of being a partner in the family's firm. When accountant Simon Hawthorne walks through the door seeking someone to give him a new image, Jaycee leaps upon the opportunity. Jaycee promises to help Simon become less nerdy and more "user-friendly" if he will become her first client, but neither one of them knows what to do when their professional relationship turns into something much more personal.

Where it's reviewed:
Romantic Times, January 2001, page 101

Other books by the same author:
Breaking the Rules, 2000
Rules of Engagement, 2000
Valentine Fantasy, 2000
The Seduction of Sydney, 1999
Flirting with Danger, 1998

Other books you might like:
Stephanie Bond, *Seeking Single Male*, 1993
Jennifer Crusie, *Manhunting*, 1993
Kate Hoffmann, *Sweet Revenge*, 1999
Meg Lacey, *Make Me Over*, 1999
Charlotte Maclay, *Courting Cupid*, 1999

255

TERESA DESJARDIEN

The Reluctant Smuggler

(New York: Signet, 2001)

Story type: Regency
Subject(s): Secrets; Smuggling; Sports/Cricket
Major character(s): Charlotte Deems, Gentlewoman, Widow(er); Sebastian Whitbury, Nobleman, Smuggler
Time period(s): 1810s
Locale(s): Severn's Well, England

Summary: After Lord Sebastian Whitbury keeps her young son, Oscar, from tumbling over a cliff one dark night, Charlotte Deems promises she will never tell anyone about Sebastian's own presence on the cliffs. Sebastian is engaged in a bit of smuggling to raise the necessary funds to marry the woman of his dreams and he cheekily insists Charlotte seal their agreement with a kiss. Soon Charlotte finds herself not only becoming a willing accomplice in Sebastian's plans, but also falling in love with the devilishly handsome smuggler.

Where it's reviewed:
Affaire de Coeur, February 2001, page 30
Romantic Times, February 2001, page 111

Other books by the same author:
The Bartered Bridegroom, 2000
The Misfit Marquess, 1999
The Reluctant Lord, 1997
The Skeptical Heart, 1996
Borrowed Kisses, 1995

Other books you might like:
Nancy Butler, *The Prodigal Hero*, 1987
Carola Dunn, *Smuggler's Summer*, 1987
Elisabeth Fairchild, *Miss Dorton's Hero*, 1995
Lynn Kerstan, *Lucy in Disguise*, 1998
Andrea Pickens, *The Hired Hero*, 1999

256

JUDE DEVERAUX

The Summerhouse

(New York: Pocket, 2001)

Story type: Contemporary/Mainstream; Fantasy
Subject(s): Change; Wishes; Conduct of Life
Major character(s): Leslie Headrick, Housewife; Ellie Abbott, Writer; Madison Appleby, Model (former)
Time period(s): 2000s
Locale(s): Maine

Summary: Three 20-year-old women who accidentally meet at the DMV and it turns out they share the same birthday, reunite 20 years later in a charming summerhouse along the Maine coast to share the events of their lives. Nothing, of course, has turned out as expected; but when the mysterious Madam Zoya offers them the option to change any three-week period in their lives, they are forced to seriously take stock of the past and make irrevocable decisions about the future. More women's fiction than romance.

Where it's reviewed:
Romantic Times, May 2001, page 98

Other books by the same author:
Temptation, 2000
High Tide, 1999
An Angel for Emily, 1998
The Blessing, 1998
A Knight in Shining Armor, 1989

Other books you might like:
Victoria Barrett, *Beside a Dreamswept Sea*, 1997
Barbara Delinsky, *Three Wishes*, 2000

Debbie Macomber, *Three Brides, No Groom*, 1997
   more reunions, lighter treatment
Jean Stone, *First Loves*, 1995
   similar premise
Karen Young, *Good Girls*, 1997

257

THEA DEVINE

Seductive

(New York: Kensington, 2001)

Story type: Historical/Victorian
Subject(s): Murder; Inheritance; Stealing
Major character(s): Elizabeth Massey, Noblewoman, Widow(er); Nicholas Massey, Nobleman, Heir
Time period(s): 1890s (1896)
Locale(s): England

Summary: Faced with destitution or taking a lover, recently widowed Elizabeth Massey does the practical thing and takes her late husband's nephew as a lover and tutor in the sexual arts. Russian jewels, a mystery, and a murderer add to the mix in this extremely sexy book that pushes the limits of the romance genre. Part of Kensington's Brava line of erotic romances.

Where it's reviewed:
Library Journal, February 15, 2001, page 153

Other books by the same author:
All I Desire, 1999
Night Moves, 1999
By Desire Bound, 1998
Desire Me Only, 1997
Sinful Secrets, 1996

Other books you might like:
Susan Johnson, *Tempting*, 2001
Nicole Jordan, *The Passion*, 2000
Robin Schone, *The Lover*, 2000
Bertrice Small, *Fascinated*, 2000
   anthology; Susan Johnson, Thea Devine, and Robin Schone, co-authors
Bertrice Small, *Intrigued*, 2001

258

JACQUELINE DIAMOND (Pseudonym of Jackie Hyman)

Excuse Me? Whose Baby?

(Toronto: Harlequin, 2001)

Story type: Humor; Contemporary
Subject(s): Humor; Babies; Child Custody
Major character(s): Alexandra Fenton, Student—Graduate; Jim Bonderoff, Wealthy, Computer Expert
Time period(s): 2000s
Locale(s): Clair De Lune, California (De Lune University)

Summary: Alexandra "Dex" Fenton is a professional student. Jim Bonderoff is a man who's made millions in the software industry. An infertile doctor has "borrowed" an egg from her and sperm from him during medical tests and created a child for herself. Now the doctor is dead, and Jim and Dex are suddenly parents. A wonderful cast of secondary characters surround the befuddled couple, who have to deal with the ultimate secret baby in this very funny romp.

Where it's reviewed:
Romantic Times, January 2001, page 101

Other books by the same author:
Captured by a Sheikh, 2000
Designer Genes, 2000
Kidnapped?, 1999
Mistletoe Daddy, 1999
The Bride Wore Gym Shoes, 1999

Other books you might like:
Jamie Denton, *Making Mr. Right*, 2001
Jennifer Drew, *Mr. Right under Her Nose*, 2001
Holly Jacobs, *I Waxed My Legs for This?*, 2001
Debbi Rawlins, *The Swinging R Ranch*, 2001
Isabel Sharpe, *Follow That Baby!*, 2001

259

CHRISTINA DODD

Rules of Attraction

(New York: Avon, 2001)

Story type: Historical/Victorian
Series: Governess Brides Trilogy. Book 3
Subject(s): Marriage; Reunions; Mystery
Major character(s): Hannah Setterington, Businesswoman (former owner, governess school), Companion; Dougald Pippard, Nobleman (Earl of Raeburn)
Time period(s): 1840s (1843)
Locale(s): Lancashire, England

Summary: Having sold her Distinguished Academy of Governesses, Hannah accepts a position as companion to the new Earl of Raeburn's elderly aunt, only to discover that the earl is none other than the husband she ran away from years before. Appealing secondary characters (a wonderfully dotty aunt is especially memorable) and a hero and heroine who have a past to resolve combine in this fast-paced, sensual romp that nicely concludes Dodd's Governess Brides trilogy.

Where it's reviewed:
Romantic Times, March 2001, page 37

Other books by the same author:
Rules of Engagement, 2000
Rules of Surrender, 2000
Someday My Prince, 1999
The Runaway Princess, 1999
A Knight to Remember, 1997

Other books you might like:
Betina Krahn, *The Perfect Mistress*, 1995
   wonderful secondary characters
Stephanie Laurens, *All about Love*, 2001
Stephanie Laurens, *A Rogue's Proposal*, 1999
Cathy Maxwell, *The Marriage Contract*, 2001
Susan Sizemore, *On a Long Ago Night*, 2000

260

ELIZABETH DOYLE (Pseudonym of Elizabeth Doyle Fowler)

My Lady Pirate
(New York: Kensington, 2001)

Story type: Historical
Subject(s): Pirates; Ships; Kidnapping
Major character(s): Isabella, Orphan; Captain Marques Santana, Pirate
Time period(s): 1720s (1720)
Locale(s): Costa Verde, Portugal; At Sea; Madeira, Portugal

Summary: Isabella, orphaned and raised in a convent, has a fairy tale view of the world. Pirate captain Marques Santana captures this odd, fey female, and finds himself courting her. Interesting secondary characters fill the pages of this sensual but introspective story.

Where it's reviewed:
Romantic Times, March 2001, page 40

Other books by the same author:
Now and Forever, 2000
Precious Passion, 1999

Other books you might like:
Patricia Cabot, *An Improper Proposal*, 1999
Susan Grace, *Forever and Beyond*, 2001
Linda Jones, *On a Wicked Wind*, 1998
   time travel
Sandra Madden, *Take by Storm*, 1999
Patricia Wynn, *Capturing Annie*, 2000

261

ALICE DUNCAN

Cowboy for Hire
(New York: Zebra, 2001)

Story type: Historical/Americana
Subject(s): Movie Industry
Major character(s): Amy Wilkes, Actress; Charlie Fox, Cowboy, Actor
Time period(s): 1900s (1905)
Locale(s): Pasadena, California; El Monte, California

Summary: Amy Wilkes always planned on trading in her secure job working at her uncle's health spa for a safe future as the wife of her reliable, yet boring, banker fiance. However, when a silent film producer offers Amy the chance to star in Peerless Studio's latest feature, Amy does the unexpected and leaps at the chance to do something different. Once Amy finds herself in front of the camera with her ruggedly handsome cowboy-turned-actor costar Charlie Fox, she begins rethinking all her safe plans for her future.

Where it's reviewed:
Romantic Times, March 2001, page 45

Other books by the same author:
Secret Hearts, 1999
Wild Dream, 1997
Texas Lonesome, 1996
One Bright Morning, 1995

Other books you might like:
Eileen Charbonneau, *Waltzing in Ragtime*, 1997
Stef Ann Holm, *Harmony*, 1997
Sharon Ihle, *The Marrying Kind*, 1996
Katie Rose, *Courting Trouble*, 2000
Susan Wiggs, *The Lightkeeper*, 1997

262

CAROLA DUNN
KARLA HOCKER, Co-Author
JUDITH A. LANSDOWNE, Co-Author

Once upon a Waltz
(New York: Zebra, 2001)

Story type: Anthology; Regency
Subject(s): Fairy Tales

Summary: A trio of Regency novellas take their inspiration from some famous fairy tales. In Carola Dunn's *The Firebird*, a young woman who can shape-shift saves a handsome lord who has been turned into a firebird. In *The Dancing Shoes*, Karla Hocker's headmistress heroine must discover where the young ladies she is in charge of disappear to each night. Judith A. Lansdowne's hero is a nobleman with magic powers who tries to break the spell cast over a shrewish young lady in *The Thrushbeard*.

Where it's reviewed:
Romantic Times, March 2001, page 108

Other books by the same author:
Once upon a Time, 2000
Wonderful and Wicked, 2000
Once upon a Kiss, 1999

Other books you might like:
Anne Barbour, *The Grand Hotel*, 2000
Cindy Holbrook, *Valentine Rogues*, 2001

263

KATHLEEN EAGLE

You Never Can Tell
(New York: Morrow, 2001)

Story type: Contemporary; Multicultural
Subject(s): Politics; Murder; Civil Rights Movement
Major character(s): Heather Reardon, Journalist; Kole Kills Crow, Fugitive (former activist), Indian (Sioux)
Time period(s): 2000s
Locale(s): Minnesota (northern border)

Summary: Determined to find the father of her goddaughter and get a story at the same time, journalist Heather Reardon heads for northern Minnesota in search of the legendary activist Kole Kills Crow, a fugitive from prison and a hero from Heather's teenage years. She finds the one thing she never expected—love. A wounded hero who needs to take charge of his past, a heroine who is strong enough to help him, and superb characterization result in a compelling story filled with an emotional intensity that draws readers in and doesn't let them go.

Where it's reviewed:
Library Journal, May 15, 2001, page 106
Rendezvous, June 2001, page 27

Other books by the same author:
The Last Good Man, 2000
What the Heart Knows, 1999
The Last True Cowboy, 1998
The Night Remembers, 1997
Sunrise Song, 1996

Other books you might like:
Rosanne Bittner, *Tame the Wild Wind*, 1996
Dinah McCall, *Tallchief*, 1997
Patricia Simpson, *Just Before Midnight*, 1997
Ruth Wind, *In the Midnight Rain*, 2000
Ruth Wind, *Rainsinger*, 1996

264

JULIE ELLIS

The Hampton Passion

(New York: Severn House, 2001)

Story type: Family Saga; Historical/Roaring Twenties
Subject(s): Family; Labor Conditions
Major character(s): Liz Hampton Adams, Spouse (of Victor);
  Victor Adams, Doctor
Time period(s): 1920s; 1930s (1925-1935)
Locale(s): Atlanta, Georgia; Miami, Florida; Washington, District of Columbia

Summary: Liz Hampton Adams wants more from her marriage, but her husband Victor focuses all of his time and energy on his work as a doctor. While on a business trip in Miami, Liz debates the idea of divorcing Victor, a drastic measure that becomes very attractive after she has an affair with handsome real estate developer Rick Pulaski. However, over the years as the Hampton family experiences both tragedies and triumphs, Liz discards the idea of divorcing Victor when she realizes the one constant thing in her life is her husband's unwavering love.

Other books by the same author:
Kara, 2000
Single Mother, 2000
Villa Fontaine, 1999
When the Summer People Have Gone, 1999
The Italian Affair, 1998

Other books you might like:
Leona Blair, *A World of Difference*, 1984
Catherine Gavin, *The Sunset Dream*, 1984
Iris Gower, *Copper Kingdom*, 1983
Belva Plain, *Random Winds*, 1980
Rosie Thomas, *All Sins Remembered*, 1990

265

JANE FEATHER

The Widow's Kiss

(New York: Bantam, 2001)

Story type: Historical/Renaissance

Subject(s): Marriage; Widows; Witches and Witchcraft
Major character(s): Lady Guinevere Mallory, Noblewoman,
  Widow(er); Hugh of Beaucaire, Nobleman, Military Personnel (soldier)
Time period(s): 16th century (1536-1537)
Locale(s): Derbyshire, England; London, England

Summary: Determined to reclaim family lands for his son, Hugh of Beaucaire sets out to discover the truth about the beautiful, much-widowed Lady Guinevere Mallory, the current owner of the property in question, and the deaths of her four husbands. The intelligent Guinevere is not about to give up her lands and she is definitely a match for Hugh. When he ends up marrying her to save her from charges of murder and witchcraft—and then his life, and that of his son, are threatened—he is forced to deal with his original doubts about the Lady, as well as his love for her. Passionate and lively.

Where it's reviewed:
Romantic Times, January 2001, page 37

Other books by the same author:
The Least Likely Bride, 2000
The Accidental Bride, 1999
Valentine Wedding, 1999
The Emerald Swan, 1998
The Hostage Bride, 1998

Other books you might like:
Katherine Deauville, *Eyes of Love*, 1996
  more mystical/earlier
Lois Greiman, *Highland Scoundrel*, 1998
Jen Holling, *Forever, My Lady*, 2001
Karyn Monk, *The Witch and the Warrior*, 1998
Amanda Quick, *Mystique*, 1995
  lighter

266

CHRISTINE FEEHAN

The Scarletti Curse

(New York: LoveSpell, 2001)

Story type: Gothic; Paranormal
Subject(s): Castles; Murder; Secrets
Major character(s): Don Giovanni Scarletti, Nobleman;
  Nicoletta, Healer, Herbalist
Time period(s): Indeterminate Past
Locale(s): Italy

Summary: Summoned by the Scarletti family to care for a small child, Nicoletta, the village healer and herbalist, attracts the attention of Don Giovanni Scarletti, who invokes his right to the bridal covenant and chooses Nicoletta as his new wife. Nicoletta has no desire to marry Giovanni, especially since not only are all Scarletti men said to be cursed, but both Nicoletta's mother and aunt died under strange circumstances at the Scarletti palazzo. When Giovanni refuses to relinquish his claim on Nicoletta, she finds herself trapped in a new home with a sinister, handsome new husband.

Where it's reviewed:
Romantic Times, March 2001, page 95

Other books by the same author:
Dark Challenge, 2000
Dark Gold, 2000
Dark Magic, 2000
Dark Desire, 1999
Dark Prince, 1999

Other books you might like:
Susan Carroll, *The Night Drifter*, 1999
Michele Jaffe, *The Stargazer*, 1999
Meagan McKinney, *Gentle from the Night*, 1997
Colleen Shannon, *The Wolf of Haskell Hall*, 2001
Susan Wiggs, *Lord of the Night*, 1993

267

MARIE FERRARELLA (Pseudonym of Marie Rydzynski-Ferrarella)

An Uncommon Hero
(New York: Silhouette, 2001)

Story type: Romantic Suspense; Contemporary
Series: Childfinders, Inc.
Subject(s): Child Custody; Runaways; Secrets
Major character(s): Gloria Prescott, Single Parent (a.k.a. Gina Wassel), Fugitive; Ben Underwood, Detective—Private
Time period(s): 2000s
Locale(s): Bedford, California; San Francisco, California; Saratoga, California

Summary: Fleeing an obsessive madman, Gloria Prescott changes her name and goes into hiding with her six-year-old son. Ben Underwood has been hired to find Gloria by a wealthy man who claims she's stolen his son. After locating Gloria, Ben soon finds himself wondering who's lying and who's not. Love goes on the run in this romantic suspense.

Other books by the same author:
A Hero in Her Eyes, 2001 (Childfinders, Inc. series)
Hero for Hire, 2000 (Childfinders, Inc. series)
A Forever Kind of Hero, 1999 (Childfinders, Inc. series)
Baby Talk, 1999
Hero for All Seasons, 1999

Other books you might like:
Beverly Barton, *Her Secret Weapon*, 2000
Merline Lovelace, *The Spy Who Loved Him*, 2001
Sharon Sala, *Mission: Irresistible*, 2000
Pat Warren, *The Way We Wed*, 2001
Margaret Watson, *Someone to Watch Over Her*, 2001

268

AMY J. FETZER

Taming the Beast
(New York: Silhouette, 2001)

Story type: Contemporary
Subject(s): Beauty; Fathers and Daughters
Major character(s): Laura Cambridge, Child-Care Giver; Richard Blackthorne, Businessman, Recluse
Time period(s): 2000s
Locale(s): Moss Island, South Carolina

Summary: Scarred and disfigured in an accident, Richard Blackthorne hides away from the world. When a young daughter he never knew existed turns up on his doorstep, Richard hires Laura Cambridge to be the girl's nanny. Once Laura discovers her new employer is a recluse who refuses to be around anyone, including his young daughter, Laura searches for a way to convince Richard to come out of the shadows and start living again. Powerfully written and emotionally satisfying.

Where it's reviewed:
Romantic Times, April 2001, page 109

Other books by the same author:
The Irish Enchantress, 2001
Renegade Heart, 2000
Wife for Hire, 2000
Going, Going, Wed!, 1999
Irish Princess, 1999

Other books you might like:
Kathleen Eagle, *The Night Remembers*, 1997
Barbara Freethy, *Ask Mariah*, 1997
Kathleen Korbel, *A Rose for Maggie*, 1991
Anne Stuart, *Night of the Phantom*, 1991
Ruth Wind, *The Last Chance Ranch*, 1995

269

DONNA FLETCHER

Irish Hope
(New York: Jove, 2001)

Story type: Historical/Medieval
Series: Irish Eyes
Subject(s): Identity, Concealed; Animals/Dogs; Runaways
Major character(s): Lady Hope, Noblewoman, Imposter (disguised as a boy); Colin of Shanekill, Warrior
Time period(s): 12th century (1170s)
Locale(s): Ireland

Summary: Knowing that an arranged marriage is inevitable, Lady Hope cuts her hair and dresses as a boy, and takes her dog, Lady Gwenyth, on a grand adventure so she can see how the common folk live. Colin of Shanekill takes ''Harold'' under his wing when the boy tries to steal food from his camp. Colin, who's on the road looking for the runaway noblewoman, has no idea she's literally at arm's length, even when he takes her home to Shanekill Keep. A woman running for love and a man running from it collide in this excellent sequel to *The Irish Devil*.

Where it's reviewed:
Affaire de Coeur, March/April 2001, page 35

Other books by the same author:
The Irish Devil, 2000 (Irish Eyes series)
Magical Moments, 1999 (spin-off of *The Wedding Spell*)
Wedding Spell, 1999
Whispers on the Wind, 1997
The Buccaneer, 1995

Other books you might like:
Lynn Bailey, *The Irish Bride*, 2000
    Irish Eyes series

Kate Freiman, *Irish Moonlight*, 2000
Judith E. French, *The Irish Rogue*, 2000
Lisa Hendrix, *To Marry an Irish Rogue*, 2000
    Irish Eyes series
Sonja Massie, *Daughter of Ireland*, 2000
    Irish Eyes series

270

PATRICIA FORSYTHE

The Runaway Princess

(New York: Silhouette, 2001)

Story type: Contemporary
Subject(s): Teachers; Small Town Life; Princes and Princesses
Major character(s): Alexis Chastain, Royalty (princess), Teacher; Jace McTaggart, Rancher, Political Figure (school board president)
Time period(s): 2000s
Locale(s): Sleepy River, Arizona

Summary: A princess who runs away from her castle to teach in a small Arizona town falls in love with a prince of a commoner. Nice blend of humor and pathos.

Where it's reviewed:
Romantic Times, January 2001, page 106

Other books you might like:
Gina Jackson, *Cookies and Kisses*, 2000
Kathryn Jensen, *Mail-Order Cinderella*, 2000
Myrna Mackenzie, *Simon Says. . .Marry Me!*, 2000
Joan Elliott Pickart, *Man. . .Mercenary. . .Monarch*, 2000
Nora Roberts, *Considering Kate*, 2001

271

LORI FOSTER

Annie, Get Your Guy

(Toronto: Harlequin, 2001)

Story type: Humor; Contemporary
Subject(s): Humor; Seduction; Family Relations
Major character(s): Annie Sawyers, Store Owner (bookstore); Guy Donovan, Businessman
Time period(s): 2000s
Locale(s): United States

Summary: Guy Donovan has always treated Annie Sawyers as his friends's kid sister. Annie, however, has loved Guy for as long as she can remember, and nursing him back to health at a secluded mountain cabin becomes part of a master plan for seduction. A very sexy, very funny read.

Where it's reviewed:
Romantic Times, March 2001, page 101

Other books by the same author:
Hot and Bothered, 2001
Messing around with Max, 2001
Sex Appeal, 2001
Married to the Boss, 2000
Scandalized!, 2000

Other books you might like:
Kylie Adams, *Fly Me to the Moon*, 2001
Susan Andersen, *Baby, I'm Yours*, 1998
Rachel Gibson, *Truly Madly Yours*, 1999
Olivia Goldsmith, *Bad Boy*, 2001
Deborah Shelley, *One Starry Night*, 2000

272

LORI FOSTER

Messing around with Max

(Toronto: Harlequin, 2001)

Story type: Humor; Contemporary
Subject(s): Humor; Seduction; Animals/Dogs
Major character(s): Maddie Montgomery, Counselor, Femme Fatale; Max Sawyers, Businessman
Time period(s): 2000s
Locale(s): United States

Summary: Maddie Montgomery treats Max Sawyers like a sex object, but he wants her to see him as a person. After all, he's just rescued a dog with an attitude, and the two of them are ready to settle down. A quirky cast of characters, including advice-giving retired prostitutes, adds to this sensual, steamy, slapstick read.

Where it's reviewed:
Romantic Times, March 2001, page 101

Other books by the same author:
Annie, Get Your Guy, 2001
Hot and Bothered, 2001
Sex Appeal, 2001
Married to the Boss, 2000
Scandalized!, 2000

Other books you might like:
Kylie Adams, *Fly Me to the Moon*, 2001
Susan Andersen, *Baby, I'm Yours*, 1998
Rachel Gibson, *Truly Madly Yours*, 1999
Olivia Goldsmith, *Bad Boy*, 2001
Deborah Shelley, *One Starry Night*, 2000

273

BARBARA FREETHY

Some Kind of Wonderful

(New York: Avon, 2001)

Story type: Contemporary
Subject(s): Babies; Marriage
Major character(s): Caitlyn Devereaux, Store Owner (bridal shop); Matt Winters, Journalist
Time period(s): 2000s
Locale(s): San Francisco, California

Summary: When journalist Matt Winters finds a crying baby at his apartment door late one night, he doesn't have a clue as to what to do, so he goes to his nearest neighbor, Caitlyn Devereaux, for help. Surely, there must be some mistake! However, a search through the diaper bag reveals the baby belongs to Matt's sister, Sarah, and she wants him to take care of the child. Matt and Caitlyn join forces to find the missing

Sarah and end up finding love and healing, as well. Heart-warming, poignant, and nicely written.

Other books by the same author:
Almost Home, 2000
Just the Way You Are, 2000
The Sweetest Thing, 1999
One True Love, 1998
Ask Mariah, 1997

Other books you might like:
Leanne Banks, *Bride of Fortune*, 2000
Debbie Macomber, *Morning Comes Softly*, 1999
Marilyn Pappano, *Father to Be*, 1999
Paula Detmer Riggs, *Daddy by Accident*, 1997
Nora Roberts, *Sea Swept*, 1998
    Quinn Brothers Trilogy. Book 1

274

JUDITH E. FRENCH

The Taming of Shaw MacCade

(New York: Ivy, 2001)

Story type: Historical/Post-American Revolution; Historical/Americana
Subject(s): Feuds; Family Relations; Scandal
Major character(s): Rebecca Raeburn, Pilot (of a river raft); Shaw MacCade, Miner, Mountain Man
Time period(s): 1840s (1849)
Locale(s): Angel Crossing, Missouri

Summary: The Raeburns and the MacCades have been mortal enemies for hundreds of years, their feud even following them from Scotland to their new home in America. Despite the bad blood between their families, Shaw MacCade and Rebecca Raeburn become childhood friends, eventually falling in love. Then Rebecca catches Shaw in a compromising position with her sister, and the feud takes on a whole new meaning. Fast-paced action leads to a most satisfying ending in this twist on the Hatfields and McCoys theme.

Where it's reviewed:
Affaire de Coeur, March/April 2001, page 25
Romantic Times, March 2001, page 42

Other books by the same author:
The Irish Rogue, 2000
Castle Magic, 1999 (anthology)
Morgan's Woman, 1999
McKenna's Bride, 1998
Rachel's Choice, 1998

Other books you might like:
Adele Ashworth, *Stolen Charms*, 1999
Jill Marie Landis, *Blue Moon*, 1999
Holly Newman, *A Lady Follows*, 1999
Judith O'Brien, *The Forever Bride*, 1999
    paranormal
Susan Plunkett, *Untamed Time*, 1999
    time travel

275

KATHERINE GARBERA

Overnight Cinderella

(New York: Silhouette, 2001)

Story type: Contemporary
Subject(s): Family; Self-Confidence; Trust
Major character(s): Cami Jones, Librarian; Duke Merchon, Businessman (vice president of security)
Time period(s): 2000s
Locale(s): Atlanta, Georgia; Hilton Head, South Carolina

Summary: After convincing Pryce Enterprises' president and board to give her a shot at planning the company's big annual gala, research librarian Cami Jones finds herself working closely with Duke Merchon, Vice President of Security. Duke insists on looking over all the details of the event from a security standpoint, but security details are not the only thing Duke notices once he discovers that beneath Cami's plain Jane appearance and drab clothes lurks a strikingly beautiful woman.

Where it's reviewed:
Romantic Times, February 2001, page 105

Other books by the same author:
Her Baby's Father, 2000
Miranda's Outlaw, 1998
The Bachelor Next Door, 1997

Other books you might like:
Pamela Burford, *Fiance for Hire*, 2001
Kathleen Korbel, *A Prince of a Guy*, 1987
Jayne Ann Krentz, *Perfect Partners*, 1992
Barbara McMahon, *Cinderella Twin*, 1998
Alexandra Sellers, *Occupation Casanova*, 2000

276

DOROTHY GARLOCK

More than Memory

(New York: Warner, 2001)

Story type: Contemporary
Subject(s): Reunions; Love; Relationships
Major character(s): Nelda Hanson, Designer (commercial interiors); Lute Hanson, Farmer
Time period(s): 1950s (1958)
Locale(s): Clear Lake, Iowa

Summary: Married to give their child a name, and then divorced and split apart by an autocratic military father, Nelda and Lute reluctantly go their separate ways, not even meeting again at the funeral of their infant daughter. Eight years later, Nelda returns to rural Iowa to sell her grandfather's farm, only to come face to face with a cold and angry Lute at the grave of their little girl—and she realizes that her feelings for him have never really died. Realistic and overflowing with 1950s ambiance.

Where it's reviewed:
Romantic Times, February 2001, page 40

Other books by the same author:
The Edge of Town, 2001
After the Parade, 2000
With Heart, 1999
With Song, 1999
Ribbon in the Sky, 1998

Other books you might like:
Kathleen Eagle, *What the Heart Knows*, 1999
Barbara Freethy, *One True Love*, 1998
Kristin Hannah, *Home Again*, 1996
Dinah McCall, *Legend*, 1998
LaVyrle Spencer, *Bittersweet*, 1990

277

JULIANA GARNETT (Pseudonym of Virginia Brows)

The Knight

(New York: Jove, 2001)

Story type: Historical/Medieval
Subject(s): Knights and Knighthood; Quest; Middle Ages
Major character(s): Aislinn of Amberlea, Noblewoman; Stephen Fitzhugh, Knight
Time period(s): 12th century (1189)
Locale(s): England

Summary: Promised a king's ransom in property by the Earl of Essex if he locates the elusive Holy Grail, landless Sir Stephen Fitzhugh heads for the Abbey of Glastonbury to investigate the clues given him by the earl. He learns that the abbey has burned to the ground and the only person who could possibly help him is Aislinn of Amberlea, the late abbot's charming, beautiful, and independent niece who is not about to betray the abbey's secrets. When the blind miller, a follower of the ''old ways,'' identifies Sir Stephen as the one who will find the Grail, she is forced to reconsider—with romantic and dangerous results. Good historical detail, well-handled sexual tension, and ecclesiastical politics are part of this lively, magical story that makes good use of the Arthurian legends.

Where it's reviewed:
Romantic Times, May 2001, page 38

Other books by the same author:
The Baron, 1999
The Scotsman, 1998
The Vow, 1998
The Magic, 1996
The Quest, 1995

Other books you might like:
Marion Zimmer Bradley, *The Mists of Avalon*, 1982
Helen Holbrook, *Pendragon's Banner*, 1988
    Arthurian legend/mainstream
Elizabeth Lowell, *Enchanted*, 1994
    mystical/medieval setting
Sharon Kay Penman, *Here Be Dragons*, 1985
    medieval setting
Maura Seger, *Tapestry*, 1993
    medieval setting

278

OLIVIA GOLDSMITH

Bad Boy

(New York: Dutton, 2001)

Story type: Contemporary; Humor
Subject(s): Humor; Dating (Social Customs); Friendship
Major character(s): Tracie Higgins, Journalist; Jonathan Delano, Computer Expert
Time period(s): 2000s
Locale(s): Seattle, Washington

Summary: Tracie Higgins' best friend, techno geek Jon Delano, wants to know the secrets of being a man that women can't resist. Taking the challenge, Tracie successfully transforms Good Guy Jon into Bad Boy Johnny. But as soon as other women fall all over him to get his attention, Tracie discovers a terrible secret—she loves him. A very funny tale of a Pygmalion project that backfires.

Where it's reviewed:
Booklist, November 1, 2000, page 492
Library Journal, November 15, 2000, page 96
Publishers Weekly, October 30, 2000, page 43
Romantic Times, January 2001, page 80

Other books by the same author:
Young Wives, 2000
Switcheroo, 1998
Marrying Mom, 1997
The Bestseller, 1996
Simple Isn't Easy, 1995

Other books you might like:
Millie Criswell, *The Trouble with Mary*, 2001
Janet Evanovich, *Hot Six*, 2000
Rachel Gibson, *It Must Be Love*, 2000
Kasey Michaels, *Too Good to Be True*, 2001
Christie Ridgway, *Wish You Were Here*, 2000

279

KATHARINE GORDON

The Long Love

(New York: Severn House, 2001)

Story type: Contemporary/Exotic
Subject(s): Kidnapping; Weddings
Major character(s): Arina Begum, Fiance(e); Sher Ali, Military Personnel, Royalty
Time period(s): 1940s
Locale(s): Glen Laraig, Scotland; India; Pakistan

Summary: Arina Begum leaves her home in Scotland and returns to India to marry Sher Ali, a man Arina was betrothed to when she was three years old. Before Arina even has a chance to get to know her future husband, their nuptial plans fall victim to the unrest and riots caused by the partitioning of British India. While traveling to a more secure site for the wedding, Arina is kidnapped and Sher must find a way to rescue his beloved bride-to-be.

Romance

Where it's reviewed:
Booklist, June 1 & 15, 20001, page 1854

Other books by the same author:
The Palace Garden, 2000
The Peacock Fan, 1996
The Peacock Rider, 1994

Other books you might like:
Emma Drummond, *Beyond All Frontiers*, 1982
Valerie Fitzgerald, *Zemindar*, 1982
Victoria Holt, *The India Fan*, 1988
M.M. Kaye, *The Far Pavilions*, 1978
Rebecca Ryman, *Olivia and Jai*, 1990

280

SUSAN GRACE (Pseudonym of Susan McConnell Koski)

Forever and Beyond

(New York: Kensington, 2001)

Story type: Historical/Regency
Series: Destiny's Lady. Book 2
Subject(s): Pirates; Napoleonic Wars; Adventure and Adventurers
Major character(s): Catherine Grayson, Pirate (a.k.a. "Lady Cat"), Noblewoman; Miles Grayson, Nobleman (viscount), Military Personnel (Navy)
Time period(s): 1800s (1805-1806)
Locale(s): London, England; Paris, France

Summary: Catherine Grayson, formerly known as the dread pirate "Lady Cat," has settled down, married, and given birth to twins. Her husband, Viscount Miles Grayson, has been called away to join the efforts against the French. False reports of his death make Lady Catherine an unwilling pawn in a deadly game of intrigue. There are adventures and surprises galore throughout this very sensual book.

Where it's reviewed:
Romantic Times, January 2001, page 43

Other books by the same author:
Enemies of the Heart, 2001 (Destiny's Lady. Book 3)
Destiny's Lady, 2000 (Destiny's Lady. Book 1)
Golden Fire, 1999

Other books you might like:
Julie Garwood, *Guardian Angel*, 1990
Ruth Langan, *The Sea Witch*, 2000
Kinley MacGregor, *A Pirate of Her Own*, 1999
Lynsay Sands, *Lady Pirate*, 2001
Patricia Wynn, *Capturing Annie*, 2000

281

ANN GRACIE

Gallant Waif

(New York: Harlequin, 2001)

Story type: Historical/Regency
Subject(s): Love; Secrets

Major character(s): Jack Carstairs, Military Personnel (ex-major, Coldstream Guards); Kate Farleigh, Gentlewoman, Impoverished
Time period(s): 1810s (1812-1813)
Locale(s): England

Summary: After returning home wounded from the Peninsular War, disowned by his father, and abandoned by his fiancee, Jack Carstairs turns into a bitter recluse who shuns all human company. Jack's grandmother, Lady Cahill, convinces her newly discovered, and greatly impoverished, goddaughter, Kate Farleigh, to stay with Jack and put his neglected house in order. When Jack discovers his spirited new "housekeeper" is not afraid to stand up to him, he thinks he may have found the one woman who can interest him in love again.

Other books by the same author:
Tallie's Knight, 2001

Other books you might like:
Mary Balogh, *More than a Mistress*, 2000
Loretta Chase, *Lord of Scoundrels*, 1995
Heather Cullman, *Bewitched*, 2001
Merline Lovelace, *The Tiger's Bride*, 1998
Gayle Wilson, *My Lady's Dare*, 2000

282

SUSAN GRANT (Pseudonym of Susan Grant Gunning)

The Star King

(New York: LoveSpell, 2000)

Story type: Futuristic
Subject(s): Space Travel; Space Colonies; Space Exploration
Major character(s): Lt. Jasmine Boswell, Military Personnel (Navy fighter pilot), Space Explorer; Romlijhian B'Kah, Alien, Royalty (crown prince)
Time period(s): Indeterminate Future
Locale(s): Sedona, Arizona; Scottsdale, Arizona; *Quillie*, Spaceship

Summary: Navy fighter pilot Jasmine Boswell crash lands during a battle over the Arabian desert. Crown Prince Romlijhian B'Kah is injured in battle in another desert, yet thanks to a dimensional quirk, the two meet and fall in love. Jasmine awakens from her wounds, her mystery man only a memory. Twenty years later, an alien ship lands on Earth, and when Jasmine, now a divorced mother of two, sees pictures of her true love on it, she'll do anything to get on the space vessel with him. Lots of intergalactic adventures and a love that defies both space and time.

Other books by the same author:
Once a Pirate, 2000

Other books you might like:
Dara Joy, *High Intensity*, 1986
Jayne Ann Krentz, *Sweet Starfire*, 1986
J.D. Robb, *Betrayal in Death*, 2001
Nora Roberts, *Heart of the Sea*, 2000
JoAnn Ross, *Star-Crossed Lovers*, 1993

283

VANESSA GRANT

The Colors of Love

(New York: Zebra, 2000)

Story type: Contemporary
Subject(s): Accidents; Prejudice; Animals/Cats
Major character(s): Jamila "Jamie" Ferguson, Artist (painter); Alexander "Alex" Kent, Doctor; Sara Miller, Child
Time period(s): 2000s
Locale(s): Seattle, Washington

Summary: A rising young artist, who accidentally hits a child chasing after a kitten, and the doctor who cares for her in the emergency room find love despite their many differences. A charming child named Sara, a cat named Squiggles, and good Seattle area detail add interest to this sensual, passionate contemporary by a veteran romance writer.

Where it's reviewed:
Affaire de Coeur, February 2000, page 15
Romantic Times, Valentine's Issue 2000, page 110

Other books by the same author:
Seeing Stars, 2001
Think about Love, 2001
If You Loved Me, 1999
The Chauvinist, 1998
The Moon Lady's Lover, 1994

Other books you might like:
Sandra Brown, *Texas! Sage*, 1991
    conflict
Mary Jane Meier, *Catch a Dream*, 2001
    conflicting characters/child
Nora Roberts, *Born in Fire*, 1997
    artistic heroine
Patricia Simpson, *Just Before Midnight*, 1997

284

VANESSA GRANT

Seeing Stars

(New York: Zebra, 2001)

Story type: Contemporary
Subject(s): Reunions; Adolescence; Astronomy
Major character(s): Claire Welland, Scientist (astronomer); Blake MacKenzie, Businessman (shipbuilder)
Time period(s): 2000s
Locale(s): Arizona; Port Townsend, Washington

Summary: When astronomer and former high school nerd Claire Welland goes back to Port Townsend, Washington for her 15th high school reunion, she connects with Blake MacKenzie, boatbuilder and former "bad boy," and ends up agreeing to help him with a troubled teenager. Despite their differences, Claire and Blake had been aware of each other in high school; and when they meet once again, the feelings they had ignored earlier suddenly flare with a passion that surprises them both. Trust, honesty, and the real meaning of love are issues.

Where it's reviewed:
Romantic Times, January 2001, page 101

Other books by the same author:
Think about Love, 2001
The Colors of Love, 2000
If You Loved Me, 1999
The Chauvinist, 1998
The Moon Lady's Lover, 1994

Other books you might like:
Catherine Anderson, *Seventh Heaven*, 2000
Sandra Brown, *In a Class of Its Own*, 2000
    another reunion
Karen Drogin, *The Right Choice*, 2000
Leigh Michaels, *A Convenient Affair*, 2001
    sweet
Nora Roberts, *Seaswept*, 1998

285

GINNA GRAY

The Witness

(Don Mills, Ontario: Mira, 2001)

Story type: Contemporary; Romantic Suspense
Subject(s): Murder; Wilderness Survival; Native Americans
Major character(s): Lauren Brownley, Musician (pianist); Sam "Grey Wolf" Rawlins, FBI Agent, Indian (half Navajo)
Time period(s): 2000s
Locale(s): Rocky Mountains

Summary: When night club pianist Lauren Brownley witnesses a mob murder, she runs to the police and it quickly becomes clear that the FBI is interested because her evidence could send a major mafioso to prison for a long, long time. Agent Sam Rawlins is given the assignment of keeping her safe; but when their plane goes down in the Rockies, it is only his survival skills and Lauren's determination and grit, that allow them to avoid the killers searching for them. Romance develops along the trail—and marriage soon follows.

Other books by the same author:
The Ties That Bind, 2001
The Prodigal Daughter, 2000
Meant for Each Other, 1999
The Heart's Yearning, 1998

Other books you might like:
Karen Harper, *Heartbreaker*, 1997
Iris Johansen, *The Ugly Duckling*, 1996
Dinah McCall, *Tallchief*, 1997
Fern Michaels, *Charming Lily*, 2001
Karen Robards, *Wait Until Dark*, 2001
    anthology

286

KRISTINE GRAYSON

Thoroughly Kissed

(New York: Zebra, 2001)

Story type: Contemporary; Fantasy

Subject(s): Animals/Cats; Magic
Major character(s): Emma Lost, Professor (University of Wisconsin), Writer (best-selling author); Michael Found, Professor (University of Wisconsin)
Time period(s): 2000s
Locale(s): Madison, Wisconsin; Portland, Oregon

Summary: Ten years after waking up from a thousand year nap and finding her prince has fallen in love with another woman, Emma Lost has finally settled into a new life as a history professor and best-selling author. Just when it seems she has things under control, the magic powers Emma is supposed to inherit arrive earlier than she expects and Emma discovers she has no way of controlling her new talents. Emma needs the help of her magical mentor, but that means a cross-country trip and the only person Emma can find to go with her on this strange journey is her gorgeous, new, and ever-so-normal boss, Michael Found.

Where it's reviewed:
Romantic Times, March 2001, page 87

Other books by the same author:
Utterly Charming, 2000

Other books you might like:
Alice Alfonsi, *Some Enchanted Evening*, 1999
Donna Fletcher, *Wedding Spell*, 1999
Karen Fox, *Prince of Charming*, 2000
Sandra Hill, *Truly, Madly Viking*, 2000
Karen Lee, *Meredith's Wish*, 2000

287

ELENA GREENE
ALICE HOLDEN, Co-Author
REGINA SCOTT, Co-Author

His Blushing Bride

(New York: Zebra, 2001)

Story type: Regency; Anthology
Subject(s): Marriage; Courtship
Time period(s): 1810s
Locale(s): England

Summary: Focusing on the time-honored topics of love, courtship, and marriage, this trio of delightful novellas includes *The Wedding Wager* by Elena Greene, a story of a marriage of convenience that suddenly turns real; *A Picture Perfect Romance* by Alice Holden, a lively tale of a feminist bluestocking who finds a hero worthy of her; and *The June Bride Conspiracy* by Regina Scott, a romance with a dash of well-intentioned deception and unexpected consequences.

Where it's reviewed:
Romantic Times, May 2001, page 93

Other books by the same author:
Lord Langdon's Kiss, 2000

Other books you might like:
Anne Barbour, *The Grand Hotel*, 2000
    Regency anthology
Carola Dunn, *Once upon a Kiss*, 1999
    Regency anthology
Alice Holden, *An Unconventional Miss*, 1997

Regina Scott, *A Dangerous Dalliance*, 2000

288

JENNIFER GREENE

Millionaire M.D.

(New York: Silhouette, 2001)

Story type: Contemporary; Romantic Suspense
Series: Texas Cattleman's Club. Book 1
Subject(s): Babies; Abandonment; Suspense
Major character(s): Winona Raye, Detective—Police; Justin Webb, Doctor (surgeon)
Time period(s): 2000s
Locale(s): Royal, Texas

Summary: Surgeon Justin Webb has asked police detective Winona Raye dozens of times to marry him. She just laughs him off—until someone leaves an abandoned baby on her doorstep. As they become an instant family, events transpire in their quiet little town, set off by the theft of a legendary red diamond. This often humorous romance is complete in this volume, but the mystery of the missing gem continues throughout the Texas Cattleman's Club series.

Where it's reviewed:
Romantic Times, January 2001, page 104

Other books by the same author:
Rock Solid, 2000
You Belong to Me, 2000 (Montana Mavericks series)
Kiss Your Prince Charming, 1999
Prince Charming's Child, 1999
The Honor Bound Groom, 1999

Other books you might like:
Cindy Gerard, *Lone Star Knight*, 2001
    Texas Cattleman's Club series
Kristi Gold, *Her Ardent Sheikh*, 2001
Peggy Moreland, *The Way to a Rancher's Heart*, 2001
Sara Orwig, *World's Most Eligible Texan*, 2001
    Texas Cattleman's Club series
Sheri Whitefeather, *Tycoon Warrior*, 2001
    Texas Cattleman's Club series

289

LOIS GREIMAN

The Fraser Bride

(New York: Avon, 2001)

Story type: Historical/Renaissance
Series: Highland Rogues Trilogy. Book 1
Subject(s): Feuds; Marriage
Major character(s): Anora "Mary" Fraser, Noblewoman; Ramsay MacGowan, Nobleman, Rogue
Time period(s): 16th century (1534)
Locale(s): Scotland

Summary: Fleeing an unwanted marriage and pursued by a mysterious dark warrior, Anora Fraser ends up unconscious and rescued by the notorious MacGowan brothers of Dun Ard. Anora has secrets she will not share; and while her lies convince some, the perceptive Ramsay MacGowan knows

there's more to her story than she will say. Their eventual journey north to Evermyst results in a few surprising truths, and eventually, a satisfactory resolution to almost everyone's problems. Action, mystery, and romance are part of this story of a pair of well-matched protagonists who finally learn to love and trust.

Where it's reviewed:
Library Journal, May 15, 2001, page 104
Romantic Times, April 2001, page 45

Other books by the same author:
Highland Hawk, 2000 (Highland Brides. Book 4)
Highland Enchantment, 1999 (Highland Brides. Book 3)
His Bodyguard, 1999
Highland Scoundrel, 1998 (Highland Brides. Book 2)
The Lady and the Knight, 1997 (Highland Brides. Book 1)

Other books you might like:
Arnette Lamb, *Border Bride*, 1993
Arnette Lamb, *Chieftain*, 1994
Ruth Langan, *Highland Heart*, 1992
Ruth Langan, *The Highlander*, 1994
May McGoldrick, *The Enchantress*, 2000
    Highland Treasure Trilogy. Book 2

290

AMELIA GREY (Pseudonym of Gloria Dale Skinner)

Never a Bride

(New York: Jove, 2001)

Story type: Historical/Regency
Subject(s): Marriage; Mystery; Scandal
Major character(s): Mirabella Whittingham, Noblewoman, Fiance(e); Camden Thurston Brackley, Nobleman (Viscount Stonehurst), Fiance(e)
Time period(s): 1810s
Locale(s): London, England

Summary: Although she knows that her bold behavior may cost her reputation, Mirabella Whittingham sets out to find the man who caused her gentle cousin to take her own life—and she can only do that by kissing her suspects to try to see which one has a telltale scar on his neck. Her plan is complicated when her erstwhile fiance, a man she has never met and who has just returned from America, suddenly shows up and finds her pursuing her "investigations" in another man's arms. Good sexual tension and appealing characters add to this lively Regency-set historical. First by Skinner under this pseudonym.

Where it's reviewed:
Library Journal, May 15, 2001, page 106

Other books you might like:
Jane Ashford, *Bride to Be*, 1999
Jane Feather, *Valentine Wedding*, 1999
Amanda Quick, *Mistress*, 1994
Joan Wolf, *The Gamble*, 1998
Joan Wolf, *The Guardian*, 1997

291

GERI GUILLAUME
ADRIENNE ELLIS REEVES, Co-Author
MILDRED RILEY, Co-Author

Truly

(Washington, D.C.: BET, 2001)

Story type: Anthology; Ethnic
Subject(s): African Americans; Holidays
Time period(s): 2000s

Summary: Valentine's Day is the theme of these three contemporary love stories. Web designer Justin Malloy takes his teenage nephew Valentine's Day shopping at the grand opening of Kallista Hart's new boutique. His nephew is caught shoplifting and Kallista proves to be a pretty tough enforcer in "Stolen Hearts" by Geri Guillaume. "Valentine's Day" by Adrienne Ellis Reeves presents the story of Johnetta Raymond who has given herself until Valentine's Day to prove that she can be a successful writer. When Rafael Thorne comes into her life, her deadline is not the only thing that's bothering her. In Mildred Riley's "Because of You," student nurse Anika Wayne thinks that she'll never see Drew Dawson again. Five years later, her flight crew arrives at the scene of an accident, and the injured man turns out to be none other than Drew.

Other books by the same author:
Be Mine, 2000
What the Heart Knows, 2000

Other books you might like:
Adrienne Ellis Reeves, *Destined*, 1999
Mildred Riley, *No Regrets*, 1999
Mildred Riley, *Trust in Love*, 2000

292

DEBORAH HALE

The Wedding Wager

(Toronto: Harlequin, 2001)

Story type: Historical/Regency
Subject(s): Marriage; Gambling; Social Classes
Major character(s): Leonora Freemantle, Gentlewoman, Teacher; Morse Archer, Military Personnel (sergeant), Imposter (as Captain Maurice Archibald)
Time period(s): 1810s (1812)
Locale(s): England

Summary: Tricked into agreeing to be tutored in the ways of the upper class in order to settle a wager between Miss Leonora Freemantle and her uncle, Sir Hugo Peverill, Sergeant Morse Archer ends up as one of the most eligible bachelors of the season—until fate catches up with him in a most romantic way. A lively, sensual story in the tradition of *My Fair Lady* and *Pygmalion*.

Where it's reviewed:
Library Journal, May 15, 2001, page 106

Other books you might like:
Connie Brockway, *All through the Night*, 1997
    Victorian/more deception
Christina Dodd, *Rules of Surrender*, 2000
    similar theme/humorous
Judith Ivory, *The Proposition*, 1999
Laura Parker, *Risque*, 1996
Amanda Quick, *Mistress*, 1994

293

KRISTIN HANNAH

Summer Island

(New York: Crown, 2001)

Story type: Contemporary/Mainstream
Subject(s): Family Relations; Interpersonal Relations; Reunions
Major character(s): Nora Bridge, Radio Personality (advice talk show host), Journalist (advice columnist); Ruby Bridge, Entertainer (aspiring comedian), Writer; Dean Sloan, Businessman, Wealthy
Time period(s): 2000s
Locale(s): Los Angeles, California; Summer Island, Washington; San Juan Islands, Washington

Summary: When an old lover exposes her to the tabloids, advice columnist and talk-show host Nora Bridge ends up recovering from a car accident and a career loss at the family retreat on Summer Island, accompanied by her estranged would-be comedian daughter, Ruby. Ruby has another, darker agenda, one that she ultimately regrets as she comes to know the mother she had thought she'd lost forever. A rekindled romance adds emotional depth as Ruby learns to face herself, her insecurities, and her past behavior and learns how to let herself love again. A number of secondary plots and characters add to this intense, heart-wrenching story that should appeal to readers of both women's fiction and romance.

Other books by the same author:
Angel Falls, 2000
On Mystic Lake, 1999
Home Again, 1996
When Lightning Strikes, 1994
A Handful of Heaven, 1991

Other books you might like:
Georgia Bockoven, *Things Remembered*, 1998
Barbara Delinsky, *Lake News*, 2000
Barbara Freethy, *Just the Way You Are*, 2000
Kathleen Gilles Seidel, *Summer's End*, 2000
Susan Wiggs, *The You I Never Knew*, 2000

294

DANELLE HARMON (Pseudonym of Danelle F. Colson)

The Wicked One

(New York: Avon, 2001)

Story type: Historical/Georgian
Series: De Montforte. Number 4
Subject(s): Marriage; Love; Sexuality

Major character(s): Eve de la Mouriere, Thief, Patriot (American); Lucien de Montforte, Nobleman (Duke of Blackheath)
Time period(s): 1770s (1771)
Locale(s): England

Summary: After a stellar career of manipulating his siblings into matrimony, the autocratic Duke of Blackheath finally ends up married himself in a lively, sexy story that is sure to please fans of Harmon's earlier books in the series. A fabled aphrodisiac, an intrepid American heroine, and a unique family are elements in this fast-paced, sensual Georgian romance.

Where it's reviewed:
Romantic Times, January 2001, page 39

Other books by the same author:
The Defiant One, 2000
The Beloved One, 1998
The Wild One, 1997
Master of My Dreams, 1993
Captain of My Heart, 1992

Other books you might like:
Jo Beverley, *Devilish*, 2000
Jo Beverley, *My Lady Notorious*, 1993
Christina Dodd, *A Well Pleasured Lady*, 1997
Stephanie Laurens, *All about Love*, 2001
Connie Mason, *A Breath of Scandal*, 2001

295

KAREN HAWKINS

A Belated Bride

(New York: Avon, 2001)

Story type: Historical/Regency
Subject(s): Smuggling; Treasure
Major character(s): Arabella Hadley, Smuggler; Lucien Devereaux, Nobleman (Duke of Wexford)
Time period(s): 1810s (1815)
Locale(s): England (Rosemont)

Summary: The last person Arabella Hadley wants to see lying in the road is Lucien Devereaux, the reckless nobleman who seduced her and abandoned her ten years ago. Unfortunately, Arabella has no choice but to take Lucien home to her estate to recuperate, all the while hoping that the rakish nobleman will not disrupt her carefully laid plans for bringing in the extra money needed to keep her family afloat. Between Arabella's two aunts playing matchmaker with the estranged lovers and Lucien's own carefully orchestrated plans to win back her favor, Arabella starts to think she should have left Lucien in the road where she found him. Witty, humorous, and a joy to read.

Where it's reviewed:
Romantic Times, January 2001, page 43

Other books by the same author:
The Abduction of Julia, 2000

Other books you might like:
Christina Dodd, *That Scandalous Evening*, 2000
Suzanne Enoch, *Reforming a Rake*, 2000
Jane Feather, *Virtue*, 1996

Stephanie Laurens, *Captain Jack's Woman*, 1997
Karen Ranney, *My Wicked Fantasy*, 1998

296

BARBARA HAZARD

The Unsuitable Miss Martingale
(New York: Signet, 2001)

Story type: Regency
Subject(s): Scandal; Marriage; Conduct of Life
Major character(s): Lili Martingale, Orphan, Noblewoman; Graeme Wilder, Nobleman (Viscount Halpern)
Time period(s): 1810s
Locale(s): England

Summary: When Lady Cornelia decides it is time to launch her young orphaned cousin, Lili Martingale, into society, her job is made much more difficult by her former mother-in-law's vicious lies and innuendos about Lili's parentage. Of course, Lili's country upbringing and tendency to say the first thing that comes into her head doesn't always help matters; but when her total lack of artifice attracts an arrogant viscount, much to the dismay of everyone, things become much more interesting, indeed. Class differences and social consequences are definite issues in this gently-paced Regency that contains links to *The Wary Widow*.

Where it's reviewed:
Affaire de Coeur, May/June 2001, page 22
Romantic Times, May 2001, page 93

Other books by the same author:
The Wary Widow, 2000
Midnight Waltz, 1999
Autumn Vows, 1998
Wild Roses, 1998
Lady at Risk, 1997

Other books you might like:
Candice Hern, *An Affair of Honor*, 1996
Georgette Heyer, *Friday's Child*, 1946
    classic Regency tale
Emma Jensen, *His Grace Endures*, 1998
Judith A. Lansdowne, *Mutiny at Almack's*, 1999
Evelyn Richardson, *My Lady Nightingale*, 1999
    social classes/more serious treatment

297

LORRAINE HEATH (Pseudonym of Jan Nowasky)

Never Marry a Cowboy
(New York: Avon, 2001)

Story type: Historical/American West; Historical/Americana
Subject(s): Marriage; Grief; Healing
Major character(s): Ashton Robinson, Invalid; Christian "Kit" Montgomery, Nobleman, Lawman (marshal)
Time period(s): 1870s (1870)
Locale(s): Fortune, Texas

Summary: When a good friend asks him to marry his dying sister, in order for her to realize a childhood dream of having a wedding, Kit Montgomery, U.S. marshal and transplanted Englishman, agrees. Fate has a way of doing the unexpected, however, and although Kit is still trying to come to terms with the five-year-old death of the only woman he had ever loved, Ashton Robinson touches his heart and helps him look beyond the past—and into the future that they both are determined to have. Miracles, healing, and romance.

Where it's reviewed:
Romantic Times, February 2001, page 37

Other books by the same author:
Never Love a Cowboy, 2000
Texas Splendor, 1999
Texas Glory, 1998
Texas Destiny, 1997
Always to Remember, 1996

Other books you might like:
Catherine Anderson, *Annie's Song*, 1996
Catherine Anderson, *Keegan's Lady*, 1996
Robin Lee Hatcher, *Promise Me Spring*, 1991
Jodi Thomas, *The Tender Texan*, 1991
Jodi Thomas, *To Wed in Texas*, 2000

298

SANDRA HEATH (Pseudonym of Sandra Wilson)

Breaking the Rules
(New York: Signet, 2001)

Story type: Regency
Subject(s): Animals/Dogs; Animals/Squirrels; Magic
Major character(s): Ursula Elcester, Gentlewoman; Conan Merrydown, Gentleman
Time period(s): 1810s (1816)
Locale(s): Elcester, England; London, England

Summary: In order to repair her family's fortunes, bookish Ursula Elcester reluctantly agrees to an arranged marriage with Theodore Glendower. When her future husband arrives, along with his charming friend, Conan Merrydown, Ursula is surprised to find Conan is the man who has been haunting her dreams. Ursula's unusual dreams are just one of the strange things going on in Elcester, and soon Ursula and Conan find themselves working together to stop a powerful individual who is determined to rewrite the past.

Where it's reviewed:
Affaire de Coeur, March/April 2001, page 14
Romantic Times, March 2001, page 108

Other books by the same author:
Counterfeit Kisses, 2000
Mistletoe Mischief, 2000
The Wrong Miss Richmond, 2000
Marigold's Marriages, 1999
The Magic Jack-o-Lantern, 1999

Other books you might like:
Anne Barbour, *Lady Hillary's Halloween*, 1998
Rita Boucher, *Lord of Illusion*, 1998
Mary Chase Comstock, *A Midsummer's Magic*, 1994
Teresa DesJardien, *Love's Magic*, 1995
Barbara Metzger, *An Enchanted Affair*, 1996

299
DEE HENDERSON
The Guardian
(Sisters, Oregon: Multnomah, 2001)

Story type: Inspirational; Romantic Suspense
Series: O'Malley. Book Two
Subject(s): Family; Murder; Politics
Major character(s): Marcus O'Malley, Lawman (U.S. Marshal); Shari Hanford, Writer (political speechwriter)
Time period(s): 2000s
Locale(s): Chicago, Illinois; Kentucky; Montana

Summary: Speechwriter Shari Hanford finds her life in immediate jeopardy after she witnesses the murder of a judge about to be appointed to the U.S. Supreme Court. Now the only person who can protect her is U.S. Marshal Marcus O'Malley, who not only struggles with keeping Shari safe but also struggles with the feelings he is developing for her.

Where it's reviewed:
Affaire de Coeur, February 2001, page 21
Library Journal, February 1, 2001, page 77
Publishers Weekly, January 15, 2001, page 52
Romantic Times, February 2001, page 81

Other books by the same author:
The Negotiator, 2000
True Devotion, 2000
Danger in the Shadows, 1999
The Marriage Wish, 1998

Other books you might like:
Karen Ball, *Wilderness*, 1999
Terri Blackstock, *Evidence of Mercy*, 1995
Sally Tyler Hayes, *Magic in a Jelly Jar*, 2001
Tracie Peterson, *Framed*, 1998
Linda Windsor, *Not Exactly Eden*, 2000

300
EMILY HENDRICKSON
The Rake's Revenge
(New York: Signet, 2001)

Story type: Regency
Subject(s): Scandal
Major character(s): Regina Hawthorne, Gentlewoman; Jules St. Aubyn, Nobleman
Time period(s): 1800s
Locale(s): London, England

Summary: After Lord Torrington discards her in favor of marrying another, Regina Hawthorne finds herself labeled "Rejected Regina" by the *ton*. Jules, Lord St. Aubyn, offers to help Regina repair her reputation in return for her assistance with a problem of his own. He initiates a campaign designed to bring Regina back into favor with society only to find that somewhere along the way, he has fallen for the spirited miss himself.

Where it's reviewed:
Romantic Times, March 2001, page 108

Other books by the same author:
Perilous Engagement, 2000
The Dangerous Baron Leigh, 2000
Miss Haycraft's Suitors, 1999
Miss Timothy Perseveres, 1999
Unexpected Wife, 1998

Other books you might like:
Anne Barbour, *A Rake's Reform*, 1999
Catherine Blair, *That Scandalous Miss Delaney*, 1999
Diane Farr, *Fair Game*, 1999
Nancy Lawrence, *A Scandalous Season*, 1996
Barbara Metzger, *Saved by Scandal*, 2000

301
CANDICE HERN
Miss Lacey's Last Fling
(New York: Signet, 2001)

Story type: Regency
Subject(s): Change; Family
Major character(s): Rosalind "Rosie" Lacey, Gentlewoman; Maxwell "Max" Davenant, Rake
Time period(s): 1810s
Locale(s): London, England; Upper Wycombe, England

Summary: Afraid she suffers from the same illness that killed her mother, Rosalind Lacey abandons her dull country existence, caring for her siblings and father to set off for London to enjoy what time she has left. Armed with a list of things to do, Rosalind stays with her outrageous Aunt Fanny who is more than happy to help Rosalind shed her boring past for the delights of the *ton*. After meeting Fanny's handsome young friend, Max Davenant, Rosalind finds flouting the conventions and rules of society is even more fun with a notorious rake like Max.

Where it's reviewed:
Romantic Times, February 2001, page 111

Other books by the same author:
The Best Intentions, 1999
Garden Folly, 1997
An Affair of Honor, 1996
A Change of Heart, 1995

Other books you might like:
Mary Balogh, *The Famous Heroine*, 2000
Elisabeth Fairchild, *Breach of Promise*, 2000
Sandra Heath, *Counterfeit Kisses*, 2000
Emma Jensen, *Best Laid Schemes*, 1998
Barbara Metzger, *Miss Lockharte's Letters*, 1998

302
RITA HERRON
Have Gown, Need Groom
(Toronto: Harlequin, 2001)

Story type: Contemporary; Humor
Series: Hartwell Hope Chests. Book 1
Subject(s): Family Relations; Humor; Dreams and Nightmares

Major character(s): Hannah Howell, Doctor (emergency room physician); Jake Tippins, Detective—Police (undercover)
Time period(s): 2000s
Locale(s): Sugar Hill, Georgia

Summary: Dr. Hannah Howell, following family custom, wears her grandmother's pearl ring to bed the night before her wedding so she can dream of her true love. The problem is the man of her dreams isn't her groom-to-be, but Jake Tippins, who's been shot in the rear stopping a robbery at her father's car dealership. Hannah assumes Jake's a loyal employee, but he's really an undercover cop who thinks her dad's a car thief. Lots of humor and pathos seasoned with a dash of suspense make this a winning recipe for a story.

Where it's reviewed:
Romantic Times, January 2001, page 101

Other books by the same author:
Have Baby, Need Beau, 2001
Saving His Son, 2001
Forgotten Lullaby, 2000
His-and-Hers Twins, 2000
Her Eyewitness, 1999

Other books you might like:
Millie Criswell, *The Pregnant Ms. Potter*, 2001
Muriel Jensen, *Father Formula*, 2001
Mindy Neff, *The Secretary Gets Her Man*, 2001
Debbi Rawlins, *Loving a Lonesome Cowboy*, 2001
Cathy Gillen Thacker, *The Bride Said, "Surprise!"*, 2001

303

BRENDA HIATT (Pseudonym of Brenda Hiatt Barber)

Rogue's Honor
(New York: Avon, 2001)

Story type: Historical/Regency
Subject(s): Marriage; Mystery
Major character(s): Lady Pearl Moreston, Noblewoman, Scholar (bluestocking); Luke St. Clair, Nobleman, Thief
Time period(s): 1810s (1816)
Locale(s): England

Summary: Temporarily posing as a maid in order to avoid marriage to a man she detests and to see how the common folk live, bluestocking Lady Pearl Moreston finds herself waiting tables for members of her own social set. Fearing she will be recognized, she accepts the help of a co-worker, Luke St. Clair, and escapes—but she has nowhere to go, so she stays with Luke. They are instantly attracted to each other, but when she learns of rumors that she has been kidnapped, she leaves without telling him and returns home. Hidden identities, social class conflict, a glimpse of the darker side of the period, and a charming plot add to this lively historical set during the English Regency. Sensual and well-written.

Where it's reviewed:
Rendezvous, June 2001, page 20

Other books by the same author:
Ship of Dreams, 2000
Scandalous Virtue, 1999
Gabriella, 1997

A Christmas Bride, 1993
Daring Deception, 1993

Other books you might like:
Connie Brockway, *All through the Night*, 1997
Cathy Maxwell, *Because of You*, 1999
Mary Jo Putney, *River of Fire*, 1996
Amanda Quick, *Reckless*, 1992
Julia Quinn, *Everything and the Moon*, 1997

304

TERESA HILL

Unbreak My Heart
(New York: Onyx, 2001)

Story type: Contemporary
Subject(s): Mystery; Small Town Life; Family
Major character(s): Allie Bennett, Accountant (former), Volunteer; Stephen Whittaker, Businessman (restores old buildings), Lawyer (non-practicing attorney)
Time period(s): 2000s
Locale(s): Dublin, Kentucky

Summary: When Allie Bennett comes home to Dublin, Kentucky, after her mother's death, she is seeking answers to the past—her sister's death, her father's lack of interest, her mother's secretiveness. She finds them, of course, but she finds a web of mystery, as well—and an unexpected love in the process. Emotionally involving and complex.

Where it's reviewed:
Romantic Times, February 2001, page 88

Other books by the same author:
Twelve Days, 2000

Other books you might like:
Barbara Delinsky, *The Passions of Chelsea Kane*, 1992
  another heroine looking for answers
Kathleen Eagle, *Sunrise Song*, 1996
Barbara Freethy, *Almost Home*, 2000
Stephanie Mittman, *Head over Heels*, 1999
  warm
Ruth Wind, *In the Midnight Rain*, 2000
  poignant/another searching heroine

305

CINDY HOLBROOK

The Missing Grooms
(New York: Zebra, 2001)

Story type: Regency
Subject(s): Animals/Cats; Kidnapping
Major character(s): Julia Wexton, Noblewoman; Garth Tolton, Nobleman
Time period(s): 1810s
Locale(s): London, England

Summary: If Julia Wexton does not find a husband in six months, her father will turn over control of her fortune to his ward, Garth Tolton, who has been a thorn in Julia's side ever since the two were children. Julia immediately begins draw-

ing up a list of prospective husbands only to find that after proposing, each of her suitors suddenly disappears. Now some of the *ton's* most eligible bachelors are missing and everyone is blaming Julia, who in desperation turns to Garth for help in locating her missing grooms.

Where it's reviewed:
Romantic Times, January 2001, page 113

Other books by the same author:
On the First Day of Christmas, 1999
Wedding Ghost, 1999
My Lady's Servant, 1998
Reluctant Bride, 1998
The Country Gentleman, 1997

Other books you might like:
Jenna Jones, *A Delicate Deception*, 1999
Lynn Kerstan, *Lord Dragoner's Wife*, 1999
April Kihlstrom, *Miss Tibbles Investigates*, 2000
Martha Kirkland, *That Scandalous Heiress*, 2000
Lindsay Randall, *A Dangerous Courtship*, 1999

306

CINDY HOLBROOK
DONNA SIMPSON, Co-Author
DEBBIE RALEIGH, Co-Author

Valentine Rogues

(New York: Zebra, 2001)

Story type: Anthology; Regency
Subject(s): Love; Holidays; Courtship
Time period(s): 1810s
Locale(s): England

Summary: Rakish, roguish heroes are featured in this light, lively trio of Valentine's Day novellas by three popular Regency writers. Included are *Valentine Dream* by Cindy Holbrook, *The Merry Cupids* by Debbie Raleigh, and *Wild Honey* by Donna Simpson.

Where it's reviewed:
Romantic Times, February 2001, page 113

Other books you might like:
Kathleen Beck, *My Darling Valentine*, 1992
    anthology
Judy Caille, *A Valentine's Day Fancy*, 1992
Elisabeth Fairchild, *Captain Cupid Calls the Shots*, 2000
Paula Tanner Girard, *A Valentine's Bouquet*, 1992
    anthology
Karen Harbaugh, *Cupid's Mistake*, 1996

307

JEN HOLLING

Forever, My Lady

(New York: HarperTorch, 2001)

Story type: Historical/Elizabethan
Subject(s): Widows; Feuds; Trust

Major character(s): Lady Megan Dixon, Widow(er), Noblewoman; Sir Bryan Hepburn, Nobleman, Government Official (warden)
Time period(s): 16th century (1585)
Locale(s): East March, Scotland (Borderlands)

Summary: When Sir Bryan Hepburn agrees to take a temporary position as warden along the Scottish/English border, his aim is to discover the truth about the murder of the previous warden—not fall in love with a beautiful Scottish widow who is suspected of the crime! Likable characters and a touch of mystery and adventure add to this warm, passionate romance that will appeal to fans of Scottish border tales.

Where it's reviewed:
Romantic Times, January 2001, page 42

Other books by the same author:
A Time for Dreams, 1999

Other books you might like:
Jane Feather, *The Widow's Kiss*, 2001
Lois Greiman, *Highland Enchantment*, 1999
    magical elements
Kathleen Harrington, *The MacLean Groom*, 1999
Patricia Potter, *The Abduction*, 1991
Amanda Scott, *Border Bride*, 1990

308

EMMA HOLLY

Beyond Innocence

(New York: Jove, 2001)

Story type: Historical/Victorian
Subject(s): Scandal; Marriage; Sexuality
Major character(s): Florence Fairleigh, Gentlewoman, Orphan; Edward Burbrooke, Nobleman (Earl of Greystowe); Freddie Burbrooke, Nobleman (Viscount Burbrooke)
Time period(s): 1870s (1873)
Locale(s): London, England

Summary: Edward Burbrooke, Earl of Greystowe, needs to find a suitable wife for his brother, Freddie, in order to save his and the family's reputation. Miss Florence Fairleigh needs to marry well because the small sum her vicar father left her is running out. The solution is obvious, of course; and before long, Florence is being taken in hand by the dowager Duchess of Carlisle and presented to the *ton* as her niece and goddaughter—and cousin to Edward and Freddie. Charmed by Freddie, she agrees to marry him; but why do her thoughts keep turning to his older brother, Edward? This highly sensual story deals with some sensitive issues, including those of sexual identity and society's perceptions and taboos concerning homosexuality.

Other books by the same author:
In the Flesh, 2000
Top of Her Game, 1999
Cooking Up a Storm, 1998

Other books you might like:
Susan Johnson, *Forbidden*, 1991
Susan Johnson, *Seduction in Mind*, 2001
Robin Schone, *Gabriel's Woman*, 2001

Robin Schone, *The Lady's Tutor*, 1999
Bertrice Small, *Captivated*, 1999
    erotic anthology; Susan Johnson, Thea Devine, and Robin Schone, co-authors

309

CHERYL HOLT

My True Love

(New York: Zebra, 2001)

Story type: Historical
Subject(s): Revenge; Romance; Adventure and Adventurers
Major character(s): Penelope Westmoreland, Noblewoman (daughter of a duke), Crime Victim (hostage); Lucas Pendleton, Businessman (shipping company owner)
Time period(s): 19th century
Locale(s): England

Summary: Determined to make the Duke of Roswell acknowledge his late sister's illegitimate son as his own, American Lucas Pendleton breaks into the duke's home, has a fruitless discussion with the duke, and ends up rescuing his daughter from her drunken fiance on his way out. An immediate attraction results and Lucas is quick to realize the potential of the situation—he can use Penelope to blackmail her father into cooperating. Love has a way of complicating even the best of plans, and although everything is eventually worked out, it takes a bit of doing before that happens. Lively action, well-drawn characters.

Where it's reviewed:
Romantic Times, March 2001, page 40

Other books by the same author:
Mountain Dreams, 2000
My Only Love, 2000

Other books you might like:
Gaelen Foley, *The Duke*, 2000
Joan Johnston, *The Bridegroom*, 1999
Jacqueline Navin, *Meet Me at Midnight*, 2001
Patricia Rice, *All a Woman Wants*, 2001

310

MADELINE HUNTER

By Design

(New York: Bantam, 2001)

Story type: Historical/Medieval
Series: Medieval English Trilogy. Book 3
Subject(s): Middle Ages
Major character(s): Joan, Artisan (potter), Servant (indentured); Rhys, Architect (master builder)
Time period(s): 14th century (early)
Locale(s): London, England

Summary: A noblewoman-turned-indentured-servant and a master builder find love amid the political intrigue of the 14th century during the time of Queen Isabella and Roger Mortimer. Realistic, fast-paced, and romantic. Final installment of the trilogy.

Where it's reviewed:
Romantic Times, January 2001, page 39

Other books by the same author:
By Arrangement, 2000
By Possession, 2000

Other books you might like:
Jane Feather, *Brazen Whispers*, 1990
Roberta Gellis, *Roselynde*, 1978
    Roselynde Chronicles. Book 1
Ellen Jones, *The Fatal Crown*, 1991
Susan King, *The Swan Maiden*, 2001
Laura Kinsale, *For My Lady's Heart*, 1991
    politics/realistic detail

311

JUDITH IVORY (Pseudonym of Judy Cuevas)

The Indiscretion

(New York: Avon, 2001)

Story type: Historical/Victorian
Subject(s): Independence
Major character(s): Lydia Jane Bedford-Browne, Noblewoman; Samuel Cody, Businessman, Diplomat
Time period(s): 1890s (1899)
Locale(s): England

Summary: American Samuel Cody, who just missed his own wedding for the second time, and Englishwoman Lydia Bedford-Browne, who is seeking a bit of freedom from her overprotective family, are stranded in the wilds of Dartmoor when the stagecoach on which they are traveling sinks in a bog. Stuck in the middle of nowhere, Lydia and Sam search for a way back to civilization, but once Lydia has a taste of adventure with Sam, her prim and proper life back home suddenly does not seem quite so appealing.

Where it's reviewed:
Publishers Weekly, February 26, 2001, page 64
Romantic Times, April 2001, page 38

Other books by the same author:
The Proposition, 1999
Sleeping Beauty, 1998
Beast, 1997

Other books you might like:
Patricia Gaffney, *To Love and to Cherish*, 2000
Jill Marie Landis, *The Orchid Hunter*, 2000
Constance Laux, *Diamond Rain*, 1999
Linda Francis Lee, *Dove's Way*, 2000
Rebecca Hagan Lee, *Whisper Always*, 1999

312

BRENDA JACKSON

Secret Love

(Washington, D.C.: BET, 2000)

Story type: Contemporary; Multicultural
Series: Madaris Family
Subject(s): African Americans; Secrets; Marriage

Romance

Major character(s): Diamond McSwain, Actress; Jacob "Jake" Madaris, Rancher
Time period(s): 2000s
Locale(s): Texas (Whispering Pines Ranch)

Summary: Wealthy rancher Jake Madaris and Hollywood actress Diamond McSwain marry but keep their marriage a secret, hoping to maintain privacy for Jake. When an intruder enters Diamond's California home, shattering her sense of security, they are forced to rethink their original plan and come to terms with the realities of their love in this installment of Jackson's Madaris Family series.

Where it's reviewed:
Romantic Times, January 2000, page 90

Other books by the same author:
True Love, 2000
Fire and Desire, 1999
One Special Moment, 1998
Whispered Promises, 1996

Other books you might like:
Rochelle Alers, *Hidden Agenda*, 1997
Rochelle Alers, *Private Passions*, 2001
Sandra Kitt, *Sincerely*, 2000
Sandra Kitt, *Suddenly*, 1996
Kayla Perrin, *If You Want Me*, 2001

313

MELANIE JACKSON

Night Visitor

(New York: LoveSpell, 2001)

Story type: Paranormal; Time Travel
Subject(s): Legends; Ghosts; Time Travel
Major character(s): Tafaline "Taffy" Lytton, Photographer (of archaeological sites), Time Traveler; Malcolm MacIntyre, Hero, Spirit (ghost of Duntrune Castle)
Time period(s): 1880s (1888); 17th century (1644)
Locale(s): Scotland

Summary: Archaeological photographer Tafaline "Taffy" Lytton accidentally pricks her finger on the shattered bones of the skeleton of Malcolm MacIntyre, the heroic Piper of Duntrune. Soon, his ghostly apparition appears to Taffy, asking her to join him. She travels 244 years into the past to honor his request—and save his life. Magic and faeries and traveling through time are woven together tighter than a tartan plaid in this ethereal Scottish fantasy.

Where it's reviewed:
Romantic Times, March 2001, page 94

Other books by the same author:
Amarantha, 2001
Manon, 2000
Iona, 1999

Other books you might like:
Diana Gabaldon, *Outlander*, 1991
Jill Jones, *The Scottish Rose*, 1997
Annie Kelleher, *The Ghost and Katie Coyle*, 1999
Tess Mallory, *Highland Dream*, 2001
Christina Skye, *Christmas Knight*, 1998

314

HOLLY JACOBS (Pseudonym of Holly Fuhrmann)

I Waxed My Legs for This?

(Toronto: Harlequin, 2001)

Story type: Contemporary; Humor
Subject(s): Friendship
Major character(s): Carrington Rose "Carrie" Delany, Designer (dress), Saleswoman; Jack Templeton, Lawyer
Time period(s): 2000s
Locale(s): Erie, Pennsylvania; Amore Island, South Carolina

Summary: After Jack Templeton's latest girlfriend dumps him, Carrie Delany casts about for a way to help the best friend she ever had get over his lost love. Planning on teaching Jack how to have fun again, Carrie tricks him into taking a vacation with her at a "couples only" resort. Once they arrive on the island, Carrie finds her plans need modifying when she realizes she is beginning to think of Jack as more than a friend.

Where it's reviewed:
Romantic Times, January 2001, page 101

Other books you might like:
Jennifer Crusie, *Anyone but You*, 1996
Kristin Gabriel, *Send Me No Flowers*, 1999
Jennifer Greene, *Kiss Your Prince Charming*, 1999
Valerie Kirkwood, *Rent-a-Friend*, 1998
Tracy South, *The Fiance Thief*, 1997

315

ELOISA JAMES

Enchanting Pleasures

(New York: Delacorte, 2001)

Story type: Historical/Georgian; Historical/Regency
Subject(s): Courtship; Conduct of Life; Brothers
Major character(s): Gabrielle "Gabby" Jerningham, Gentlewoman, Fiance(e); Erskine "Quill" Dewland, Nobleman, Relative (brother of Peter); Peter Dewland, Nobleman, Relative (brother of Erskine)
Time period(s): 1800s (1806)
Locale(s): London, England

Summary: When an accident renders Quill Dewland unable to either ride a horse or sire a child because the rhythmic motions of those activities result in three-day-long debilitating migraines, his younger brother, Peter, reluctantly agrees to take his place as fiance to Gabrielle Jerningham. Due to arrive from India momentarily, the outspoken, unconventional Gabby is not the elegant Frenchwoman they had all imagined; and how she will ever manage to become the kind of wife that toast of the *ton* Peter needs is the question. Complicating this dilemma is the fact Gabby is far more comfortable with the pragmatic Quill than the cool, correct Peter; and when Quill realizes he wants her for himself, in spite of his disability, things become interesting indeed. Fast-paced, funny, and sexy.

Where it's reviewed:
Affaire de Coeur, May/June 2001, page 28

Other books by the same author:
Midnight Pleasures, 2000
Potent Pleasures, 1999

Other books you might like:
Christina Dodd, *Rules of Engagement*, 2000
Judith McNaught, *Almost Heaven*, 1990
Judith McNaught, *Whitney, My Love*, 1991
Amanda Quick, *Scandal*, 1991
Amanda Quick, *Surrender*, 1990

316

SAMANTHA JAMES (Pseudonym of Sandra Kleinschmidt)

The Truest Heart

(New York: Avon, 2001)

Story type: Historical/Medieval
Subject(s): Politics; Conspiracies
Major character(s): Lady Gillian of Westerbrook, Noble-woman, Fugitive (from the king); Gareth of Summerfield, Nobleman, Criminal (assassin)
Time period(s): 13th century (1215)

Summary: Forced into hiding when King John seeks to kill her and her brother for their father's treachery, Lady Gillian of Westerbrook retreats to the windswept coast of Cornwall and anonymity. When a violent storm deposits a half-drowned, unconscious man on her beach—the very man the king has sent to kill her—her life becomes much less boring, but far more dangerous even though the man has amnesia and can't remember his mission. Politics, intrigue, adventure, and romance.

Other books by the same author:
A Promise Given, 1998
Just One Kiss, 1996
Outlaw Heart, 1993
My Cherished Enemy, 1992

Other books you might like:
Debra Lee Brown, *The Virgin Spring*, 2000
Juliana Garnett, *The Baron*, 1999
Julie Garwood, *Ransom*, 1999
Karyn Monk, *The Witch and the Warrior*, 1998
Ana Seymour, *Lady of Lyonsbridge*, 2000

317

SABRINA JEFFRIES (Pseudonym of Deborah Martin)

A Notorious Love

(New York: Avon, 2001)

Story type: Historical/Regency
Series: Swanlea Spinsters. Book 2
Subject(s): Scandal; Marriage; Travel
Major character(s): Lady Helena Laverick, Gentlewoman, Handicapped (crippled); Daniel Brennan, Businessman (investment advisor)
Time period(s): 1810s (1815)
Locale(s): England

Summary: When her young sister runs off with a ''highly unsuitable'' man, Lady Helena Laverick desperately turns to

her brother-in-law's former man of affairs, Daniel Brennan, for help. She ends up pretending to be his wife as they hare across the country in search of the missing pair. Sensual and adventurous, this fast-paced story follows *A Dangergous Love*.

Other books by the same author:
A Dangerous Love, 2000
The Dangerous Lord, 2000
The Forbidden Lord, 1999
The Pirate Lord, 1998

Other books you might like:
Mary Balogh, *More than a Mistress*, 2000
Jo Beverley, *My Lady Notorious*, 1993
Catherine Coulter, *The Offer*, 1997
Stephanie Laurens, *A Rake's Vow*, 1998
Amanda Quick, *Scandal*, 1991

318

EMMA JENSEN

Fallen

(New York: Ivy, 2001)

Story type: Historical/Regency
Subject(s): Espionage; Legends
Major character(s): Gabriel Loudon, Nobleman (Earl of Rievaulx), Spy (former); Margaret ''Maggie'' MacLeod, Herbalist
Time period(s): 1740s (1746); 1810s (1812)
Locale(s): London, England; Isle of Skye, Scotland

Summary: Driven by guilt, Gabriel Loudon accepts a mission from an old friend to unearth the traitorous spy, L'Ecossais. While searching the Isle of Skye for his dangerous quarry, Gabriel receives an invitation to stay with Maggie MacLeod and her family. Maggie, who has been emotionally bruised by a past love affair, hopes to retreat to a quiet life with her plants, but now Gabriel is evoking passionate feelings Maggie never thought she would experience again.

Where it's reviewed:
Affaire de Coeur, March/April 2001, page 33
Publishers Weekly, March 12, 2001, page 68
Romantic Times, April 2001, page 40

Other books by the same author:
A Grand Design, 2000
The Irish Rogue, 1999
Best Laid Schemes, 1998
His Grace Endures, 1998
Isobel, 1997

Other books you might like:
Connie Brockway, *All through the Night*, 1997
Liz Carlyle, *A Woman Scorned*, 2000
Jean Ross Ewing, *Flowers under Ice*, 1999
Margaret Evans Porter, *Kissing a Stranger*, 1998
Mary Jo Putney, *The China Bride*, 2000

Romance

319

MICHELLE JEROTT (Pseudonym of Michele Albert)

A Great Catch
(New York: Avon, 2000)

Story type: Contemporary
Subject(s): Ships
Major character(s): Tessa Jardine, Sailor (first mate); Lucas Hall, Sea Captain
Time period(s): 2000s
Locale(s): Milwaukee, Wisconsin; Lake Michigan, Great Lakes

Summary: One of the worst drawbacks to Tessa Jardine's new job as first mate on the *S.S. Taliesen*, a renovated steamship offering cruises of the Great Lakes, is her boss, Captain Lucas Hall, who happens to be the same man who romantically dumped Tessa years ago and was also involved in a tanker explosion that killed Tessa's brother, Matt. Working in close quarters is difficult for Tessa and Lucas, especially once they discover they still are attracted to each other; but the only hope Tessa has of both a successful professional and personal relationship with Lucas relies on Tessa letting go of the past and forgiving him.

Where it's reviewed:
Affaire de Coeur, September 2000, page 21

Other books by the same author:
All Night Long, 1999
Absolute Trouble, 1998

Other books you might like:
Patti Berg, *Wife for a Day*, 2000
Barbara Bretton, *At Last*, 2000
Barbara Freethy, *Just the Way You Are*, 2000
Annette Reynolds, *Remember the Time*, 1997
Ruth Wind, *Beautiful Stranger*, 2000

320

SUSAN JOHNSON

Seduction in Mind
(New York: Bantam, 2001)

Story type: Historical/Victorian
Subject(s): Art; Sports/Golf; Seduction
Major character(s): Samuel Lennox, Nobleman (Viscount Ranelagh); Alexandra "Alex" Ionides, Noblewoman (Countess St. Albans), Artist
Time period(s): 1870s (1878)
Locale(s): London, England

Summary: Entranced by the mysterious, beautiful nude in a painting, Samuel Lennox discovers the model is none other than an artist herself: wealthy widow Alexandra Ionides. Samuel is determined he can convince Alexandra to become his next sexual conquest, but surprisingly enough the lady has some ideas of her own.

Other books by the same author:
Tempting, 2001
Legendary Lover, 2000

Temporary Mistress, 2000
A Touch of Sin, 1999
To Please a Lady, 1999

Other books you might like:
Thea Devine, *Seductive*, 2001
Virginia Henley, *Seduced*, 1994
Nicole Jordan, *The Passion*, 2000
Robin Schone, *The Lover*, 2000
Katherine Sutcliffe, *Notorious*, 2000

321

SUSAN JOHNSON

Tempting
(New York: Kensington, 2001)

Story type: Historical/Victorian
Subject(s): Sexuality; Interpersonal Relations; Marriage
Major character(s): Christina, Royalty (princess), Spouse (betrayed); Maxwell Falconer, Nobleman (Marquis of Vale)
Time period(s): 1890s (1892)
Locale(s): England

Summary: Plagued with an adulterous husband and firmly part of a society that condones affairs, Princess Christina refuses to go down that road—until she meets the seductive Maxwell Falconer, Marquis of Vale. Sexy, sensual, and nearly erotic, this story is one of the Brava line of erotic romances by Kensington.

Where it's reviewed:
Library Journal, February 15, 2001, page 153
Romantic Times, March 2001, page 38

Other books by the same author:
Legendary Lover, 2000
Temporary Mistress, 2000
To Please a Lady, 1999
Wicked, 1997
Golden Paradise, 1990

Other books you might like:
Thea Devine, *Seductive*, 2001
Nicole Jordan, *The Passion*, 2000
Robin Schone, *The Lady's Tutor*, 1999
Robin Schone, *The Lover*, 2000
Bertrice Small, *Fascinated*, 2000
anthology; Susan Johnson, Thea Devine, and Robin Schone, co-authors

322

CHRISTINE EATON JONES, Editor

Romancing the Holidays
(Glendale, Arizona: Elan, 2001)

Story type: Anthology; Holiday Themes
Series: Romancing the Holidays. Book 1
Subject(s): Holidays; Holidays, Jewish; Anthology

Summary: This collection contains ten romantic holiday tales written in a wide variety of styles. They include Belmont Delange's "Everybody's Destiny" (Kansas Day), Barbara

White-Rayczek's "Love, Lies, and Cherry Pie" (Washington's Birthday), Deborah Shelley's "Falling for You" (Purim), Pamela Johnson's "Lucky in Love" (St. Patrick's Day), Carrie Weaver's "Sweet April" (April Fool's Day), Su Kopil's "Fragile Beginnings" (Arbor Day), Cathy McDavid's "Better Partners than Adversaries" (Boss's Day), Karen L. Williams' "Devlin's Wicked Wish" (Halloween), Trudy Doolittle's "A Gift of Time" (Christmas), and Christine Eaton Jones' "Coming Home" (New Year's Eve).

Where it's reviewed:
Romantic Times, April 2001, page 96

Other books you might like:
Cathy McDavid, *The Attraction Factor*, 2000
Deborah Shelley, *One Starry Night*, 2000
Carrie Weaver, *Promises, Promises*, 2000

323

JILL JONES

Remember Your Lies
(New York: St. Martin's Paperbacks, 2001)

Story type: Romantic Suspense; Contemporary
Subject(s): Murder; Mystery; Family Relations
Major character(s): Angela Donahue, Police Officer (former), Businesswoman (tour company); Dylan Montana, Detective—Police (undercover cop)
Time period(s): 2000s
Locale(s): Savannah, Georgia

Summary: When J.J. Slade, a reclusive businessman, is murdered, ex-cop Angela Donahue, now a businesswoman with a successful tour company, becomes a suspect. Angela knows that she's never spoken to, met, or even seen the victim, so when witnesses start saying they've seen her eating lunch with him, she knows someone's trying to frame her. To make matters worse, Slade has left his estate to her. Dylan Montana, an undercover cop, believes in her innocence, but his credibility's in question because of his former relationship with her. Danger, threats, blackmail, voodoo, and non-stop suspense make this an edge-of-your-seat thriller.

Where it's reviewed:
Romantic Times, March 2001, page 89

Other books by the same author:
Bloodline, 2000
The Island, 1999
Circle of the Lily, 1998
Essence of My Desire, 1998
The Scottish Rose, 1997 (time travel)

Other books you might like:
Jayne Ann Krentz, *Lost and Found*, 2000
Elizabeth Lowell, *Midnight in Ruby Bayou*, 2000
Meagan McKinney, *The Lawman Meets His Bride*, 2000
Carla Neggers, *The Carriage House*, 2001
Nora Roberts, *Carolina Moon*, 2000

324

LUANNE JONES

Sweethearts of the Twilight Lanes
(New York: Avon, 2001)

Story type: Contemporary
Subject(s): Friendship; Secrets
Major character(s): Theresa Jo "Tess" Redding, Editor (magazine), Writer; Flynn Garvey, Bastard Son
Time period(s): 2000s
Locale(s): Mount Circe, Georgia

Summary: Known as the Suitehearts of Lassiter College, Tess Redding and her three best friends find themselves reunited 14 years later in the small town of Mount Circe after they each receive an anonymous note threatening to reveal a secret. The last thing Tess needs as she prepares to take her *Simply Southern Magazine* national is the slightest hint of a scandal, so Tess reluctantly asks Flynn Garvey, the charming rogue who loved her and left her in college, to help her find out who is behind the blackmail scheme.

Where it's reviewed:
Romantic Times, March 2001, page 93

Other books you might like:
Jennifer Crusie, *Tell Me Lies*, 1998
Curtiss Ann Matlock, *Driving Lessons*, 2000
Emilie Richards, *Whiskey Island*, 2000
Dallas Schulz, *The Way Home*, 1995
Deborah Smith, *A Place to Call Home*, 1997

325

B.D. JOYCE (Pseudonym of Brenda Joyce)

Deadly Love
(New York: St. Martin's Press, 2001)

Story type: Historical; Romantic Suspense
Series: Francesca Cahill. Book 1
Subject(s): Kidnapping; Suspense; Mystery
Major character(s): Francesca Cahill, Activist, Gentlewoman; Rick Bragg, Police Officer (police commissioner)
Time period(s): 1900s (1902)
Locale(s): New York, New York

Summary: Despite her parents' expectations that she marry and settle down, as any young woman in turn-of-the-century New York society should do, Francesca Cahill is a modern woman and she is *involved*. However, when a young neighbor boy is kidnapped—and she finds the ransom note—she ends up becoming more involved than she had expected. Rick Bragg, new police commissioner, has no use for amateur investigators, but Francesca is persistent—so persistent, in fact, that she ends up in more danger than she had ever expected. First in a projected series of early 20th century suspense novels.

Where it's reviewed:
Library Journal, February 15, 2001, page 155

Other books you might like:
Anna Gilbert, *The Long Shadow*, 1984
  historical romantic suspense
Tami Hoag, *Guilty as Sin*, 1996
Linda Howard, *Shades of Twilight*, 1996
  contemporary suspense
Heather Graham Pozzessere, *Slow Burn*, 1994
  contemporary mystery
J.D. Robb, *Naked in Death*, 1996
  another heroine sleuth series/futuristic

326

DONNA KAUFFMAN (Pseudonym of Donna Jean)

Walk on the Wild Side
(New York: Harlequin, 2001)

Story type: Contemporary
Subject(s): Cooks and Cookery; Restaurants
Major character(s): Susan "Sunny" Hadden Chandler, Heiress; Nick D'Angelo, Restaurateur
Time period(s): 2000s
Locale(s): Chicago, Illinois

Summary: Business school graduate Sunny Chandler insists on taking six months off to experience the real world before going to work for her family's corporation. The first job Sunny applies for lands her in the kitchen of an Italian restaurant whose owner, Nick D'Angelo, is certain his new "high society" employee will quit within a month. Determined to prove everyone wrong, Sunny learns that not only does she like working in the small neighborhood restaurant, she is really starting to like her gorgeous new boss.

Where it's reviewed:
Affaire de Coeur, March/April 2001, page 42
Romantic Times, April 2001, page 109

Other books by the same author:
Your Wish Is My Command, 2001
Legend of the Sorcerer, 2000
The Legend MacKinnon, 1999
Dark Night, 1998
Tease Me, 1998

Other books you might like:
Stephanie Bond, *Manhunting in Mississippi*, 2001
Millie Criswell, *The Trouble with Mary*, 2001
Kate Hoffmann, *Mr. Right Now*, 2001
Trish Jensen, *The Harder They Fall*, 1997
Lisa Plumley, *Her Best Man*, 2000

327

DONNA KAUFFMAN

Your Wish Is My Command
(New York: Bantam, 2001)

Story type: Fantasy
Subject(s): Magic; Romance; Genies
Major character(s): Jamie Sullivan, Store Owner (bookstore/cafe), Sports Figure (ex-power boat racing champion);

Sebastien Valentin, Mythical Creature (genii), Matchmaker
Time period(s): 2000s
Locale(s): New Orleans, Louisiana

Summary: When Jamie Sullivan inadvertently summons a "pirate" genii by unsheathing an ancient sword, she is stunned, to say the least. Her surprise only increases when Sebastien announces that his duty is to find the soulmates for three people of Jamie's choice—and one of them ends up being her. A genii, who never thought to fall in love; a highly skeptical heroine; and a lively plot add to the charm of this magical romance that is overlaid with a healthy dose of the fantastic.

Where it's reviewed:
Romantic Times, February 2001, page 90

Other books by the same author:
Walk on the Wild Side, 2001
Legend of the Sorcerer, 2000
The Legend MacKinnon, 1999
Silent Warrior, 1997
Bayou Heat, 1996

Other books you might like:
Donna Fletcher, *Wedding Spell*, 1999
Karen Fox, *Prince of Charming*, 2000
  another enchanted hero
Kathleen Kane, *Simply Magic*, 1999
  historical magic
Johanna Lindsey, *Until Forever*, 1995
Karen Whiddon, *Powerful Magic*, 1995
  sensual and magical

328

LINDA KAY (Pseudonym of Linda Kay West)

To Tame a Rogue
(New York: Kensington, 2001)

Story type: Time Travel; Paranormal
Subject(s): Time Travel; Murder; Inheritance
Major character(s): Arden St. Clare, Time Traveler, Heiress; Captain Royce Warrick, Nobleman, Wealthy
Time period(s): 2000s; 1810s (1816)
Locale(s): New Orleans, Louisiana

Summary: When Arden St. Clare books a very expensive fare with the Any Time, Any Place Travel Agency, she's skeptical about their claim of transporting her to another time. True to their word, she soon finds herself smack dab in Regency England, only a short distance from where kidnappers are attempting to kill an 11-year-old Duke. Helping the boy to escape is nothing compared to dealing with his suspicious uncle. A modern woman has a fine adventure in another land and another time, and the reader is transported right there with her.

Where it's reviewed:
Romantic Times, March 2001, page 94

Other books by the same author:
To Charm a Knight, 2001

Other books you might like:
Casey Claybourne, *Nick of Time*, 2000
Susan Grant, *Once a Pirate*, 2000
Allison Lane, *The Second Lady Emily*, 1998
Cathie Linz, *A Wife in Time*, 1995
Susan Plunkett, *Timepool*, 1999

329

PATRICIA KAY

The Other Woman

(New York: Berkley, 2001)

Story type: Contemporary
Subject(s): Marriage; Love; Reunions
Major character(s): Natalie Ferrenzo, Editor (children's books); Adam Forrester, Lawyer
Time period(s): 2000s; 1970s
Locale(s): New York, New York; New Haven, Connecticut

Summary: Torn apart years earlier when Adam does what is expected of him and marries another, Adam and Natalie accidentally meet again. Both realize they have never stopped loving each other—a realization that plunges them into an affair that is both wonderful and heartbreaking. Adultery, deception, and commitment are issues in this emotionally involving romance. Kay also writes as Trish Alexander.

Where it's reviewed:
Rendezvous, June 2001, page 28

Other books by the same author:
The Millionaire and the Mom, 2001
The Wrong Child, 2000

Other books you might like:
Mary Balogh, *The Secret Pearl*, 1991
   historical
Georgia Bockoven, *Moments*, 1990
Sandra Bregman, *Reach for the Dream*, 1990
   similar theme/family saga
Barbara Delinsky, *More than Friends*, 1993
LaVyrle Spencer, *Bittersweet*, 1990

330

JULIE KENNER

Aphrodite's Kiss

(New York: LoveSpell, 2001)

Story type: Contemporary/Fantasy
Subject(s): Family; Good and Evil; Heroes and Heroines
Major character(s): Zoe Smith, Librarian; George Bailey Taylor, Detective—Private
Time period(s): 2000s
Locale(s): Los Angeles, California; New York, New York

Summary: Halfling Zoe Smith is torn between two worlds: the mortal world and that of the Venerate Counsel of Protectors, a group of immortal superheroes with extraordinary powers. With her 25th birthday coming up, Zoe must either successfully pass a test given by the Counsel or renounce her only chance of being a superhero. While struggling to bring her extrasensory powers under control in time to pass her test,

Zoe finds herself not only fighting her halfling cousin and uncle, who are plotting against the Counsel, but also fighting her attraction to handsome private detective George Taylor.

Where it's reviewed:
Affaire de Coeur, March/April 2001, page 29
Romantic Times, April 2001, page 93

Other books by the same author:
Nobody Does It Better, 2000
Reckless, 2000
The Cat's Fancy, 2000

Other books you might like:
Stephanie Bancroft, *Your Wish Is My Command*, 1998
Tess Farraday, *Sea Spell*, 1998
Dara Joy, *Knight of a Trillion Stars*, 1995
Donna Kauffman, *Legend of the Sorcerer*, 2000
Karen Lee, *Meredith's Wish*, 2000

331

SUSAN KING

The Stone Maiden

(New York: Signet, 2000)

Story type: Historical/Medieval
Subject(s): Feuds; Marriage; Legends
Major character(s): Alainna MacLaren, Laird (of the Clan Laren), Artisan (stone carver); Sebastien le Bret, Knight, Parent
Time period(s): 12th century (1170)
Locale(s): Highlands, Scotland

Summary: For 700 years the Stone Maiden has kept Clan Laren safe. Now, decimated by feuds and battles, the clan will soon lose the Maiden's protection and risks extinction unless Alainna, the new Laird, can find a strong Celtic husband—like the Golden Warrior of her dreams—who will take the MacLaren name and fight for the clan. The king has other ideas and his word is law; so when he sends as Clan Laren's champion, Sebastien le Bret, a Norman knight who has no intention of giving up his name, Alainna and Sebastien have little choice but to make the best of things. Love eventually follows amid the sparks of this lyrical, passionate, well-written romance filled with legend, myth, and a strong sense of Highland history.

Where it's reviewed:
Romantic Times, March 2000, page 37

Other books by the same author:
The Swan Maiden, 2001
The Heather Moon, 1999
Laird of the Wind, 1998

Other books you might like:
Shana Abe, *The Truelove Bride*, 1999
Katherine Deauville, *Eyes of Love*, 1996
Julie Garwood, *Saving Grace*, 1993
Elizabeth Lowell, *Enchanted*, 1994
   lyrical and mystical
Karyn Monk, *The Witch and the Warrior*, 1998

332
SUSAN KING

The Swan Maiden
(New York: Signet, 2001)

Story type: Historical/Medieval
Subject(s): Loyalty; Legends; Identity, Concealed
Major character(s): Juliana Lindsey, Rebel (Highland), Young Woman (''Swan Maiden''); Gawain Avenel, Knight (English), Imposter (''Gabhan MacDuff'')
Time period(s): 13th century (1286); 14th century (1306)
Locale(s): Highlands, Scotland; England

Summary: Juliana Lindsey, Scots rebel and legendary Swan Maiden, has never forgotten the mysterious English knight, her Swan Knight, who saved her from certain capture one night by his fellow soldiers; and Gawain Avenel has never forgotten her—or his native Scotland—either. So when she is eventually captured and publicly humiliated by Gawain's cruel commanding officer, he rescues her once more—this time by marriage—with truly life-changing results. Action-filled adventure and fiery romance combine nicely with mystical legend in this story that depicts the uneasy English-Scottish relationship during the time of Robert the Bruce. Political intrigue, divided loyalties, and blatant deception abound in this complex romance with a bit of a Robin Hood feel.

Where it's reviewed:
Romantic Times, January 2001, page 37

Other books by the same author:
The Stone Maiden, 2000
The Heather Moon, 1999
Laird of the Wind, 1998

Other books you might like:
Shana Abe, *The Truelove Bride*, 1999
Marsha Canham, *The Last Arrow*, 1997
    Robin Hood tale
Arnette Lamb, *Chieftain*, 1994
Karyn Monk, *Once a Warrior*, 1997
Karyn Monk, *The Rose and the Warrior*, 2000

333
KATHERINE KINGSLEY

Lilies on the Lake
(New York: Dell, 2001)

Story type: Historical
Subject(s): Scandal; Marriage
Major character(s): Portia ''Pip'' Merriem, Noblewoman, Scholar (bluestocking); John Henry Lovell, Diplomat, Knight
Time period(s): 1830s (1835-1836)
Locale(s): Egypt; England

Summary: Pip Merriem is determined to honor her promise to her late traveling companion and care for her newborn son. Knowing she can't return to England with a baby and no husband, Pip accepts the proposal of her childhood friend, John Lovell, who just happens to be in Egypt when she needs

help. Naturally, they will divorce once the talk about their unexpected marriage quiets down—or so she thinks. Pip and John discover they still love each other—and now it's a matter of making the marriage work.

Other books by the same author:
The Sound of Snow, 1999
Call Down the Moon, 1998
Once upon a Dream, 1997
In the Wake of the Wind, 1996
No Brighter Dream, 1994

Other books you might like:
Mary Balogh, *Indiscreet*, 1997
Mary Balogh, *Unforgiven*, 1998
Connie Brockway, *As You Desire*, 1997
Laura Kinsale, *The Dream Hunter*, 1994
Cathy Maxwell, *Because of You*, 1999

334
MARTHA KIRKLAND

His Lordship's Swan
(New York: Zebra, 2001)

Story type: Regency
Subject(s): Courtship; Deafness
Major character(s): Evan Trent, Nobleman; Lydia Elizabeth Swann, Gentlewoman
Time period(s): 1810s
Locale(s): England

Summary: Evan Trent uses a coin toss to decide which of the ravishingly beautiful Swann twins he should marry; but when he sends his offer of marriage for the ''eldest'' sister, Evan discovers he is now betrothed to the twins' older, and plainer, sibling, Lydia. Lydia has no interest in marrying a man who does not love her, but she does agree to go along with a mock betrothal if Evan will help her win the attentions of Sebastian Osborne, the man Lydia dreams of marrying. Neither Lydia nor Evan expects their pretend feelings for one another to turn into something very real.

Where it's reviewed:
Romantic Times, April 2001, page 102

Other books by the same author:
An Uncommon Courtship, 2000
Miss Maitland's Letters, 2000
That Scandalous Heiress, 2000
A Gentleman's Deception, 1999
To Catch a Scoundrel, 1999

Other books you might like:
Rebecca Baldwin, *A Tangled Web*, 1993
Jo Beverley, *Deirdre and Don Juan*, 1993
Lynn Collum, *The Valentine Charm*, 2001
Wilma Counts, *The Wagered Wife*, 2001
Dorothy Mack, *The Gold Scent Bottle*, 2000

335

KATHLEEN KIRKWOOD (Pseudonym of Anita Gordon)

His Fair Lady

(New York: Signet, 2001)

Story type: Historical/Medieval
Series: Lords of Danger
Subject(s): Crusades; Quest
Major character(s): Lady Juliana "Ana" Mandeville, Noble-woman, Orphan; Sir Royce de Warrene, Knight (Crusader)
Time period(s): 12th century (1190-1199); 13th century (1200)
Locale(s): England; France

Summary: When Royce de Warrene saves an orphaned waif by placing her in the care of a local village couple in France, he has no idea that his "Ana" is actually the Lady Juliana Mandeville, granddaughter and heiress of an elderly English lord—a dying man who wants her found, and wants Royce to do it. Royce finds that the child, who charmed his heart 10 years ago, is now a lovely young woman, firmly entrenched in the life of her village and wants nothing to do with Royce or his mission. She has no choice, however, and although she fights him all the way, she eventually comes to terms with the situation—and with the fact that she and Royce are destined to be together.

Where it's reviewed:
Romantic Times, February 2001, page 39

Other books by the same author:
Shades of the Past, 1999
A Slip in Time, 1998

Other books you might like:
Julie Garwood, *Saving Grace*, 1993
Deborah Hale, *The Elusive Bride*, 2000
Madeline Hunter, *By Arrangement*, 2000
Lynn Kurland, *If I Had You*, 2000
Anita Mills, *The Fire and the Fury*, 1991

336

SANDRA KITT

She's the One

(New York: Signet, 2001)

Story type: Contemporary; Multicultural
Subject(s): Abortion; Child Custody; African Americans
Major character(s): Deanna Lindsay, Librarian; Patterson Temple, Government Official (fire department)
Time period(s): 2000s
Locale(s): New York, New York

Summary: Deanna Lindsay is stunned when she is named guardian for a six-year-old biracial child of a young woman she knew briefly years ago—and under circumstances she'd like to forget. She knows this is a responsibility she needs to assume in spite of Patterson Temple's reservations about her ability to do the job. A thought-provoking story about friendship, parenting, guilt, and love.

Other books by the same author:
Close Encounters, 2000
Family Affairs, 1999
Between Friends, 1998
Significant Others, 1996
Suddenly, 1996

Other books you might like:
Rochelle Alers, *My Love's Keeper*, 1998
    emotionally involving
Kristin Hannah, *On Mystic Lake*, 1999
    emotionally involving
Margaret Johnson-Hodge, *A New Day*, 1999
Margaret Johnson-Hodge, *The Real Deal*, 1998
Nora Roberts, *Sea Swept*, 1998
    heartwarming

337

JAYNE ANN KRENTZ

Dawn in Eclipse Bay

(New York: Jove, 2001)

Story type: Contemporary; Romantic Suspense
Series: Eclipse Bay. Book 2
Subject(s): Feuds; Dating (Social Customs); Small Town Life
Major character(s): Lillian Harte, Matchmaker (ex-match-making service owner), Artist; Gabe Madison, Business-man (venture capital firm)
Time period(s): 2000s
Locale(s): Portland, Oregon; Eclipse Bay, Oregon

Summary: Finally deciding to follow her true calling as an artist, Lillian Harte closes up her computerized matchmaking business in Portland and heads home to seaside Eclipse Bay to regain her perspective. Unfortunately her last client, who just happens to be her new brother-in-law and a member of the family with whom she has been feuding for years, demands that she supply him with the one remaining date of his contract—and she is left with no other alternative than to go out with him herself. A resentful ex-boyfriend of a former client; a kinky, devious psychologist; and a wonderful collection of other secondary characters add to this fast-paced, funny, sensual romance.

Where it's reviewed:
Library Journal, May 15, 2001, page 107
Romantic Times, May 2001, page 96

Other books by the same author:
Eclipse Bay, 2000 (Eclipse Bay. Book 1)
Eye of the Beholder, 1999
Soft Focus, 1999
Flash, 1998
Sharp Edges, 1998

Other books you might like:
Claire Cross, *Third Time Lucky*, 2000
    suspense and humor
Elizabeth Lowell, *Amber Beach*, 2000
    Pacific Coast setting/suspense
Elizabeth Lowell, *Jade Island*, 1998
    Pacific Coast setting/suspense
JoAnn Ross, *Far Harbor*, 2000

Romance

Theresa Weir, *American Dreamer*, 1997
suspense and humor

338

JAYNE ANN KRENTZ

Lost and Found

(New York: Putnam, 2001)

Story type: Contemporary; Romantic Suspense
Subject(s): Antiques; Suspense; Inheritance
Major character(s): Cady Briggs, Heiress, Businesswoman (antiques and art); Mack Easton, Businessman (finds missing arts/antiques)
Time period(s): 2000s
Locale(s): Santa Barbara, California

Summary: When Cady Briggs' great-aunt, a strong swimmer, drowns, Cady knows it wasn't an accident. As the reluctant heir to her great-aunt's antique business, she hires Mack Easton, whose firm, Lost and Found, is known for its quiet research into lost and stolen arts and antiques. This book has many memorable moments of suspense, including a murder attempt on Cady that encompasses her most dreaded fears. The intrigue is balanced by humorous situations and witty dialogue.

Where it's reviewed:
Library Journal, February 15, 2001, page 202
Romantic Times, January 2001, page 80

Other books by the same author:
Eye of the Beholder, 1999
Soft Focus, 1999
Flash, 1998
Sharp Edges, 1998
Absolutely, Positively, 1996

Other books you might like:
Susan Andersen, *All Shook Up*, 2001
Millie Criswell, *The Trouble with Mary*, 2001
Claire Cross, *Third Time Lucky*, 2000
Carla Neggers, *The Waterfall*, 2000
Nora Roberts, *Genuine Lies*, 1998

339

JAYNE ANN KRENTZ
TESS GERRITSEN, Co-Author
STELLA CAMERON, Co-Author

Stolen Memories

(Toronto: Harlequin, 2001)

Story type: Anthology
Subject(s): Anthology

Summary: Three novels by popular authors are reprinted in this anthology. Katy Randall suspects that her new husband has married her for her money, and not for love in Jayne Ann Krentz's *Test of Time*. A cat burglar steals the heart of a gentleman thief in *Thief of Hearts* by Tess Gerritsen. In Stella Cameron's *Moontide*, a woman returns to England where her husband and baby have died, only to meet up again with the doctor who tried to save them.

Other books by the same author:
Lost and Found, 2001
Eclipse Bay, 2000

Other books you might like:
Stella Cameron, *7B*, 2001
Tess Gerritsen, *Gravity*, 2000
Tess Gerritsen, *Under the Knife*, 2000

340

LYNN KURLAND
PATRICIA POTTER, Co-Author
DEBORAH SIMMONS, Co-Author
GLYNNIS CAMPBELL, Co-Author

A Knight's Vow

(New York: Jove, 2001)

Story type: Historical/Medieval; Anthology
Subject(s): Knights and Knighthood; Middle Ages
Locale(s): England

Summary: This quartet of well-done novellas from some of the genre's more popular writers, focuses on knights, chivalry, and the women who win their hearts. Included are *The Traveller* by Lynn Kurland, *The Minstrel* by Patricia Potter, *The Bachelor Knight* by Deborah Simmons, and *The Siege* by Glynnis Campbell.

Other books by the same author:
If I Had You, 2000

Other books you might like:
Glynnis Campbell, *My Champion*, 2000
Patricia Potter, *The Heart Queen*, 2001
Deborah Simmons, *My Lord De Burgh*, 2000

341

SYLVIE KURTZ

Alyssa Again

(Toronto: Harlequin, 2001)

Story type: Romantic Suspense
Subject(s): Sisters; Sports/Rock Climbing
Major character(s): Brooke Snowden, Teacher; Jack Chessman, Police Officer
Time period(s): 2000s
Locale(s): Boston, Massachusetts; Comfort, New Hampshire; Tilton, New Hampshire

Summary: After being separated for more than 20 years, Brooke Snowden finally locates her sister, Alyssa, only to find Alyssa now lies in a coma caused by a recent climbing accident. Police officer Jack Chessman believes Alyssa's fall was no accident, but rather a murder attempt and he convinces Brooke to assume Alyssa's identity in a bold plan to flush out the potential killer.

Where it's reviewed:
Romantic Times, January 2001, page 102

Other books by the same author:
Blackmailed Bride, 2000
One Texas Night, 1999

Silver Shadows, 1997
Broken Wings, 1996

Other books you might like:
Harper Allen, *Woman Most Wanted*, 2000
Debbi Rawlins, *Her Mysterious Stranger*, 2000
Amanda Stevens, *Lover, Stranger*, 1999
Joanna Wayne, *The Stranger Next Door*, 2000
Gayle Wilson, *Midnight Remembered*, 2000

342

JILL MARIE LANDIS

Summer Moon

(New York: Ballantine, 2001)

Story type: Historical/American West
Subject(s): Mail Order Brides; Ranch Life; Prejudice
Major character(s): Katherine "Kate" Whittington, Teacher, Mail Order Bride; Reed Benton, Lawman (Texas Ranger), Rancher
Time period(s): 1870s (1870)
Locale(s): Texas (Lone Star Ranch)

Summary: When the convent orphanage in Maine where she taught for 11 years closes, educated spinster Kate Whittington answers an ad for a mail order bride, is married by proxy, and heads for Texas and a new life as the wife of rancher Reed Benton. However, the Reed Benton she has been corresponding with is not the same Reed Benton that she has married; and when her "groom" discovers that his late father has arranged the entire thing, the fireworks begin in earnest. A Comanche-raised boy; an angry, badly wounded hero; and a stalwart heroine with issues of her own combine in this compelling, heartwarming story. Abandonment, prejudice, self-esteem, and betrayal are important issues addressed.

Where it's reviewed:
Library Journal, May 15, 2001, page 107

Other books by the same author:
The Orchid Hunter, 2000
Blue Moon, 1999
Glass Beach, 1998
Just Once, 1997
Day Dreamer, 1996

Other books you might like:
Catherine Anderson, *Cherish*, 1998
Dorothy Garlock, *Larkspur*, 1997
Kristin Hannah, *If You Believe*, 1994
LaVyrle Spencer, *The Endearment*, 1982
    another mail-order bride/different treatment
LaVyrle Spencer, *Morning Glory*, 1989

343

CONNIE LANE (Pseudonym of Connie Laux)

Reinventing Romeo

(New York: Dell, 2000)

Story type: Contemporary
Subject(s): Crime and Criminals

Major character(s): Kathleen "Kate" Ellison, FBI Agent; Alex Romero, Businessman, Wealthy
Time period(s): 2000s
Locale(s): New York, New York; Cleveland, Ohio

Summary: When millionaire playboy businessman Alex Romero agrees to testify against the mob, FBI agent Kate Ellison is given the job of keeping him safe until the trial. After a hitman nearly succeeds in killing him, Kate whisks Alex to safety in the suburbs of Cleveland where the two pose as a newlywed couple. Keeping Alex safe is part of Kate's job but acting as his "wife" is putting a whole new spin on their working relationship.

Where it's reviewed:
Affaire de Coeur, Holiday 2000, page 29
Romantic Times, December 2000, page 86

Other books you might like:
Cherry Adair, *Kiss and Tell*, 2000
Susan Andersen, *Baby, Don't Go*, 2000
Patti Berg, *Bride for a Night*, 2000
Suzanne Brockmann, *Body Guard*, 1999
Rachel Gibson, *It Must Be Love*, 2000

344

ELIZABETH LANE

Bride on the Run

(Toronto: Harlequin, 2001)

Story type: Historical/American West
Subject(s): American West; Secrets; Mail Order Brides
Major character(s): Anna DeCarlo, Fugitive, Mail Order Bride; Malachi Stone, Widow(er), Single Parent
Time period(s): 1880s (1889)
Locale(s): Grand Canyon, Arizona; St. Joseph, Missouri

Summary: On the run for a murder she didn't commit, dance hall singer Anna DeCarlo answers an ad for a mail order bride and marries by proxy. Her new husband, Malachi Stone, lives with his two children, isolated from most of the world in a small ferry station at the bottom of the Grand Canyon. The bounty hunters chasing Anna are relentless, and no matter where she is, they've vowed to find her. Suspicion, suspense, and survival are couched in the beauty of the Grand Canyon in this dichotomous tale.

Other books by the same author:
My Lord Savage, 2001
Shawnee Bride, 2000
Apache Fire, 1998
The Tycoon and the Townie, 1997
Lydia, 1996

Other books you might like:
Sandra Chastain, *The Outlaw Bride*, 2000
Kathryn Hockett, *Outrageous*, 2000
Leslie LaFoy, *Maddie's Justice*, 2000
Linda Lael Miller, *Daniel's Bride*, 1992
Maggie Osborne, *A Stranger's Wife*, 1999

345

RUTH LANGAN

The Sea Nymph

(Toronto: Harlequin, 2001)

Story type: Historical/Seventeenth Century
Series: Sirens of the Sea Trilogy. Book 2
Subject(s): Inheritance; Pirates; Identity, Concealed
Major character(s): Bethany Lambert, Privateer; Kane Preston, Nobleman (Earl of Alsmeeth), Highwayman ("Lord of the Night")
Time period(s): 17th century (1665)
Locale(s): *The Undaunted*, At Sea (Atlantic—off the coast of Cornwall); England

Summary: He's really a highwayman. That's okay with her—she's really a privateer. A double dose of disguises and mistaken identity in a world where masks can be both physical and emotional makes this an exciting addition to the Sirens of the Sea Trilogy.

Other books by the same author:
The Sea Sprite, 2001 (Sirens of the Sea Trilogy. Book 3)
The Sea Witch, 2000 (Sirens of the Sea Trilogy. Book 1)
Conor, 1999 (O'Neil Saga. Book 2)
Rory, 1999 (O'Neil Saga. Book 1)
Blackthorne, 1998

Other books you might like:
Stephanie Laurens, *Captain Jack's Woman*, 1997
Teresa Medeiros, *Heather and Velvet*, 1991
Laura Renken, *My Lord Pirate*, 2001
Lynsay Sands, *Lady Pirate*, 2001
Shelly Thacker, *Midnight Raider*, 1992

346

STEPHANIE LAURENS

All about Love

(New York: Avon, 2001)

Story type: Historical/Regency
Series: Bar Cynster. Book 6
Subject(s): Marriage; Murder; Mystery
Major character(s): Phyllida Tallent, Gentlewoman; Alasdair Reginald "Lucifer" Cynster, Gentleman, Collector (silver and jewelry)
Time period(s): 1820s (1820)
Locale(s): Devon, England; London, England

Summary: Despite the fact that he knows his brother and cousins are all happily wed, Lucifer, the last of the current Bar Cynster bachelors, is not about to fall victim to the same fate; so he flees the marriage-minded London social scene and heads for quiet, rural Devon at the invitation of an old friend and fellow collector. When Lucifer arrives to find his friend dead on the floor of his manor house and seconds later is knocked unconscious himself, he begins to realize that Devon will be anything but dull—and when he meets beautiful, independent Phyllida Tallent, the woman who bashed him over the head, he is sure of it. Fast-paced, sensual, and a worthy addition to Laurens' Bar Cynster series.

Where it's reviewed:
Romantic Times, February 2001, page 37

Other books by the same author:
A Season for Scandal, 2001
A Rogue's Reform, 2000
A Secret Love, 2000
A Rogue's Proposal, 1999
Devil's Bride, 1998

Other books you might like:
Jo Beverley, *Devilish*, 2000
Jo Beverley, *Tempting Fortune*, 1995
Christina Dodd, *Rules of Attraction*, 2001
Sabrina Jeffries, *A Dangerous Love*, 2000
Susan Sizemore, *The Price of Passion*, 2001

347

STEPHANIE LAURENS

All about Passion

(New York: Avon, 2001)

Story type: Historical/Regency
Subject(s): Marriage; Surprises
Major character(s): Francesca Rawlings, Gentlewoman, Bride; Gyles Frederick Rawlings, Nobleman (Earl of Chillingworth)
Time period(s): 1820s (1820)
Locale(s): England

Summary: Firmly opposed to the idea of love but knowing he must marry to ensure the line, Gyles Rawlings, Earl of Chillingworth, arranges a marriage of convenience to Francesca, a woman he has seen and talked to, but to whom he has never been formally introduced. A shock awaits him on his wedding day when he realizes that the woman he has wed is not the gentle, sweet girl he walked with by the lake, but her fiery cousin with whom he'd already shared a passionate kiss. Passionate, lively, and laced with fun, this story has links to Laurens' famed Bar Cynster series.

Other books by the same author:
All about Love, 2001
A Secret Love, 2000
A Rogue's Proposal, 1999
Scandal's Bride, 1999
Devil's Bride, 1998

Other books you might like:
Jo Beverley, *Devilish*, 2000
Jo Beverley, *Something Wicked*, 1997
Christina Dodd, *A Well Pleasured Lady*, 1997
Sabrina Jeffries, *A Notorious Love*, 2001

348

SUSAN KAY LAW

The Bad Man's Bride

(New York: Avon, 2001)

Story type: Historical/American West; Historical/Americana
Series: Marrying Miss Bright. Book 1
Subject(s): Prejudice; Small Town Life; Teachers

Major character(s): Anthea Bright, Teacher, Gentlewoman; Gabriel Jackson, Farmer, Guardian
Time period(s): 1880s (1885)
Locale(s): Haven, Kansas

Summary: When limited funds force the three Philadelphia-bred Bright sisters to fend for themselves, Anthea blithely sets off for Kansas to become the new schoolmistress of Haven Township School. There she finds herself confronted with a drafty, delapidated schoolhouse; a group of badly behaved, semi-literate children; some biased, mean spirited- townspeople; and a dangerously attractive ''bad man'' hero determined to make a life for himself and the fragile Lily, a child everyone thinks is his bastard daughter. A spine of steel underlies Anthea's well-mannered finishing school exterior; and no one is going to keep her from educating *all* the children in the town—even if she has to risk her reputation—and her heart—to do it. A tender, sensitive story that also addresses darker issues of social class, scandal, and jealousy, among others.

Where it's reviewed:
Library Journal, May 15, 2001, page 106

Other books by the same author:
The Most Wanted Bachelor, 2000
The Last Man in Town, 1999
Heaven in West Texas, 1997
One Lonely Night, 1997
Home Fires, 1995

Other books you might like:
Stef Ann Holm, *Harmony*, 1997
Jill Marie Landis, *Last Chance*, 1995
Pamela Morsi, *Sealed with a Kiss*, 1998
LaVyrle Spencer, *The Gamble*, 1984
Jodi Thomas, *Forever in Texas*, 1995

349

SUZANN LEDBETTER

South of Sanity

(Don Mills, Ontario: Mira, 2001)

Story type: Humor; Romantic Suspense
Subject(s): Humor; Suspense; Murder
Major character(s): Hannah Garvey, Businesswoman (manages retirement community); David Hendrickson, Police Officer (sheriff)
Time period(s): 2000s
Locale(s): Valhalla Springs, Missouri (retirement community in the Ozarks)

Summary: It's bad enough that the residents of the retirement community she manages get busted for pot, but when her new love, Sheriff David Hendrickson, gets framed for manslaughter, Hannah Garvey wonders why she ever left the big city for the so-called peace and quiet of the Ozarks. Wacky characters in outlandish situations make this sequel to *East of Peculiar* rib-tickling funny.

Where it's reviewed:
Affaire de Coeur, March/April 2001, page 25
Romantic Times, March 2001, page 94

Other books by the same author:
North of Clever, 2001
East of Peculiar, 2000
Colorado Reverie, 1997
Deliverance Drive, 1996
Trinity Strike, 1996

Other books you might like:
Kylie Adams, *Fly Me to the Moon*, 2001
Claire Cross, *Third Time Lucky*, 2000
Janet Evanovich, *Seven Up*, 2001
Sue Grafton, *P Is for Peril*, 2001
Kasey Michaels, *Too Good to Be True*, 2001

350

LINDA FRANCIS LEE

Nightingale's Gate

(New York: Ivy, 2001)

Story type: Historical/Victorian America; Romantic Suspense
Series: Hawthorne Trilogy. Book 3
Subject(s): Suspense; Serial Killer
Major character(s): Alice Kendall, Lawyer, Gentlewoman; Lucas Hawthorne, Businessman (gentleman's club owner), Crime Suspect
Time period(s): 1890s
Locale(s): Boston, Massachusetts

Summary: Accused of murdering a prostitute, Lucas Hawthorne, youngest and most scandal-prone of the Hawthorne brothers and owner of the notorious gentleman's club Nightingale's Gate, hires bright, but untried, attorney Alice Kendall to defend him against the charges. Intrigued by the man, needing the money, and irked at her father's lack of faith in her abilities, Alice accepts, despite her inexperience and the fact that her father is the DA whose protege will be prosecuting the case. As Alice and Lucas work together to prove his innocence, their mutual attraction grows; but it isn't until Lucas can come to terms with his dark and haunted past and forgive himself that they can truly be happy. Courtroom drama, danger, and romantic passion are elements in this final volume in Lee's trilogy about the Hawthorne men of Boston.

Where it's reviewed:
Affaire de Coeur, May/June 2001, page 32

Other books by the same author:
Dove's Way, 2000 (Hawthorne Trilogy. Book 1)
Swan's Grace, 2000 (Hawthorne Trilogy. Book 2)

Other books you might like:
Jane Goodger, *Dancing with Sin*, 1998
    similar setting
B.D. Joyce, *Deadly Love*, 2001
Elizabeth Kary, *Midnight Lace*, 1990
    19th century London, historical suspense
Meagan McKinney, *The Merry Widow*, 1999
Stephanie Mittman, *The Courtship*, 1998
    another attorney heroine/different issues

351

RACHEL LEE (Pseudonym of Sue Civil-Brown)

A January Chill

(Don Mills, Ontario: Mira, 2001)

Story type: Contemporary
Series: Whisper Creek Trilogy. Book 2
Subject(s): Secrets; Family Relations; Healing
Major character(s): Joni Matlock, Pharmacist; Hardy Wingate, Businessman (construction company owner), Architect
Time period(s): 2000s
Locale(s): Whisper Creek, Colorado

Summary: Instilled with her uncle's hatred of Hardy Wingate, the man he blames for his daughter Karen's death 12 years ago, pharmacist Joni Matlock hasn't spoken to Hardy in years. When she sees him one night at the hospital, where his mother is struggling with pneumonia, they connect once more—with results that are both devastating and ultimately healing. Old secrets and resentments bubble to the surface to drive the plot of this dark and emotionally involving story set in a small Colorado mining town in the Rockies.

Where it's reviewed:
Affaire de Coeur, March/April 2001, page 35
Romantic Times, April 2001, page 96

Other books by the same author:
After I Dream, 2000
Snow in September, 2000 (Whisper Creek Trilogy. Book 1)
When I Wake, 2000
Before I Sleep, 1999
Conard County Homecoming, 1999

Other books you might like:
Mary Lynn Baxter, *Tempting Janey*, 2001
Kathleen Eagle, *You Never Can Tell*, 2001
Dinah McCall, *Jackson Rule*, 1996
Dinah McCall, *The Return*, 2000
Sharon Sala, *Reunion*, 2000

352

JOHANNA LINDSEY

Heart of a Warrior

(New York: Morrow, 2001)

Story type: Futuristic
Series: Ly-San-Ter. Book 3
Subject(s): Cultural Conflict; Self-Perception; Science Fiction
Major character(s): Brittany Callaghan, Construction Worker; Dalden Ly-San-Ter, Warrior
Time period(s): Indeterminate Future
Locale(s): California; Spaceship

Summary: On a mission to find the "worldless" King Jorran and stop him from trying to gain control of a world with a mind-altering device, Dalden Ly-San-Ter ends up on Earth being "rescued" from an attack of claustrophobia by Brittany Callaghan. Brittany, a magnificent six-foot tall construction worker, is just the person he needs to help in his quest. Passion, action, and romance soon follow in this sequel to

Lindsey's previous futuristics about the Ly-San-Ters and their adventures.

Where it's reviewed:
Romantic Times, May 2001, page 101

Other books by the same author:
Love Me Forever, 1996
You Belong to Me, 1996 (sequel to *Once a Princess*)
Keeper of the Heart, 1993 (Ly-San-Ter. Book 2)
Once a Princess, 1991
Warrior's Woman, 1990 (Ly-San-Ter. Book 1)

Other books you might like:
Anne Avery, *All's Fair*, 1994
Justine Davis, *The Skypirate*, 1995
Justine Davis, *Storm*, 1994
Dara Joy, *Knight of a Trillion Stars*, 1995
Janelle Taylor, *Moondust and Madness*, 1995

353

JULIA LONDON (Pseudonym of Dinah Dinwiddie)

The Beautiful Stranger

(New York: Dell, 2001)

Story type: Historical/Regency
Subject(s): Friendship; Murder; Responsibility
Major character(s): Arthur Christian, Nobleman; Kerry MacGregor McKinnon, Widow(er)
Time period(s): 1830s (1834; 1837-1838)
Locale(s): London, England; Edinburgh, Scotland; Glenbaden, Scotland

Summary: Upon discovering her late husband left behind a mountain of debts, Kerry McKinnon thinks her life cannot get any worse. Then she accidently shoots a stranger. The stranger turns out to be Englishman Arthur Christian who, unbeknownst to Kerry, has arrived in the Scottish Highlands to oversee the sale of Kerry's village of Glenbaden for a deceased friend. While recuperating in Glenbaden, Arthur is slowly torn between honoring a promise to his friend's family and helping out a woman he has come to love.

Where it's reviewed:
Booklist, June 1 & 15, 2001, page 1854

Other books by the same author:
The Dangerous Gentleman, 2000
The Ruthless Charmer, 2000
Wicked Angel, 1999
The Devil's Love, 1998

Other books you might like:
Catherine Coulter, *The Scottish Bride*, 2001
Debra Dier, *MacLaren's Bride*, 1997
Jillian Hunter, *A Deeper Magic*, 1994
Jaclyn Reding, *White Heather*, 1997
Susan Wiggs, *Miranda*, 1996

354

MERLINE LOVELACE

Dark Side of Dawn

(New York: Signet, 2001)

Story type: Contemporary; Romantic Suspense
Subject(s): Military Life; Suspense; Murder
Major character(s): Joanna West, Pilot (helicopter), Military Personnel (U.S. Air Force captain); Deke Elliot, Pilot, Military Personnel; Alex Taylor, Wealthy, Political Figure (former)
Time period(s): 2000s
Locale(s): Washington, District of Columbia (general area)

Summary: Violating regulations, Captain Joanna West makes a potentially career-ruining decision to land her helicopter in order to save a man's life. She ends up only temporarily grounded, but finds herself the romantic object of her rescuee's affections. Of course, the fact that he's the wealthy grandson of a former president and is handsome and charming to boot, does make him all the more appealing; but the intensity and obsessiveness of his courtship and his controlling nature makes her wary—with good reason. Fast-paced, suspenseful, and well-plotted.

Where it's reviewed:
Romantic Times, January 2001, page 78

Other books by the same author:
The Officer's Bride, 2001
Twice in a Lifetime, 2001
River Rising, 1999
Undercover Groom, 1999
Duty and Dishonor, 1997

Other books you might like:
Suzanne Brockmann, *The Defiant Hero*, 2001
   military mystery
Suzanne Brockmann, *The Unsung Hero*, 2000
Suzanne Forster, *Every Breath She Takes*, 1999
   another stalker/dark and dangerous
Heather Graham, *Tall, Dark, and Deadly*, 1999
   more stalking
Iris Johansen, *Long After Midnight*, 1997

355

MERLINE LOVELACE

The Horse Soldier

(Don Mills, Ontario: Mira, 2001)

Story type: Historical/American West
Subject(s): American West; Reconstruction; Missing Persons
Major character(s): Julia Bonneaux, Southern Belle, Impoverished; Andrew Garrett, Military Personnel (major), Veteran
Time period(s): 1860s (1867)
Locale(s): Fort Laramie, Wyoming (Dakota Territory)

Summary: When Julia Bonneaux, Southern belle, last sees her new husband, Andrew Garrett, Union spy, he's shot and presumed dead. Now, she's on her way West with her small daughter in search of her second husband, who's disappeared.

Julia finds herself stranded at Fort Laramie with none other than her first husband, who has survived both the bullet and the horrors of Andersonville. A woman with one husband too many, who is forced to survive on her own, is only one of the dilemmas in this richly-textured book about life after the Civil War.

Where it's reviewed:
Romantic Times, January 2001, page 37

Other books by the same author:
Dark Side of Dawn, 2001
Mistaken Identity, 2000
Man of His Word, 1999
The Mercenary and the New Mom, 1999
River Rising, 1999

Other books you might like:
Lori Copeland, *Promise Me Forever*, 1994
Lorraine Heath, *Always to Remember*, 1996
Linda Jones, *The Seduction of Roxanne*, 2000
Evelyn Rogers, *Texas Empires: Longhorn*, 2000
Rosalyn West, *The Rebel*, 1998

356

MERLINE LOVELACE
DEBORAH SIMMONS, Co-Author
JULIA JUSTISS, Co-Author

The Officer's Bride

(New York: Harlequin, 2001)

Story type: Anthology; Historical
Subject(s): Love; Marriage

Summary: Three English soldiers find love in this trio of novellas. In Merline Lovelace's *The Major's Wife*, Major Charles Trent returns home from the Crimean War only to find his wife has a new admirer and wants a divorce. Deborah Simmons' *The Companion* features a wounded war hero, who is brought out of his isolation by the love of a dedicated young woman. A young English lieutenant stationed in Portugal risks everything to win the love of his friend's widow in Julia Justiss's *An Honest Bargain*.

Other books you might like:
Jo Beverley, *In Praise of Younger Men*, 2001
Kimberly Cates, *One Night with a Rogue*, 1995
Christina Dodd, *Scottish Brides*, 1999
Mary Jo Putney, *Bride by Arrangement*, 2000
Kathleen E. Woodiwiss, *Three Weddings and a Kiss*, 1995

357

MERLINE LOVELACE

The Spy Who Loved Him

(New York: Silhouette, 2001)

Story type: Romantic Suspense; Contemporary
Series: Year of Loving Dangerously. Book 7
Subject(s): Espionage; Secrets; Women's Rights
Major character(s): Margarita Alfonsa de las Fuentes, Young Woman, Spy (SPEAR agent); Carlos Caballeros, Political Figure (Deputy Minister of Defense), Military Personnel

Time period(s): 2000s
Locale(s): Madrileno, Fictional Country (Central America)

Summary: Secret Agent Margarita Alfonsa de las Fuentes becomes a hostage when a notorious international criminal escapes from prison. Her unflappable fiance, Carlos Caballeros (who has no idea that she's a spy), comes to the rescue. As they run for their lives through the dense, dangerous jungle, he learns her true vocation, and she learns that her Clark Kent is really a Superman. Lots of adventure and suspense as two people, who thought they knew each other find out that they really didn't.

Where it's reviewed:
Romantic Times, January 2001, page 105

Other books by the same author:
Dark Side of Dawn, 2001
The Horse Soldier, 2001
The Officer's Bride, 2001
Twice in a Lifetime, 2001

Other books you might like:
Robyn Amos, *Hero at Large*, 2000
   Year of Loving Dangerously. Book 5
Carla Cassidy, *Strangers When We Married*, 2000
Mary Jo Putney, *Bride by Arrangement*, 2000
Linda Turner, *The Enemy's Daughter*, 2001
   Year of Loving Dangerously. Book 9
Pat Warren, *The Way We Wed*, 2001
   Year of Loving Dangerously. Book 10
Margaret Watson, *Someone to Watch Over Her*, 2001
   Year of Loving Dangerously. Book 8

358

KINLEY MACGREGOR (Pseudonym of Sherrilyn Kenyon)

Master of Desire
(New York: Avon, 2001)

Story type: Historical/Medieval
Subject(s): Politics; Feuds; Middle Ages
Major character(s): Lady Emily, Noblewoman; Draven de Montague, Nobleman (Earl of Ravenswood), Knight
Time period(s): 12th century
Locale(s): England

Summary: In order to maintain peace between two of his feuding noblemen, Henry II forces one of them, Hugh, to send his daughter, Emily, to live in the home of Draven, Earl of Ravenswood, with passionate, and ultimately peace-ensuring, results. Sensual and action-filled.

Where it's reviewed:
Romantic Times, February 2001, page 42

Other books by the same author:
Master of Seduction, 2000
A Pirate of Her Own, 1999

Other books you might like:
Juliana Garnett, *The Baron*, 1999
Julie Garwood, *The Bride*, 1989
Deborah Hale, *The Elusive Bride*, 2000
Teresa Medeiros, *Charming the Prince*, 1999
Ana Seymour, *Lady of Lyonsbridge*, 2000

359

DEBBIE MACOMBER

16 Lighthouse Road
(Don Mills, Ontario: Mira, 2001)

Story type: Contemporary/Mainstream
Series: Cedar Cove Chronicles. Book 1
Subject(s): Small Town Life; Marriage
Major character(s): Olivia Lockhart, Judge; Jack Griffin, Journalist
Time period(s): 2000s
Locale(s): Cedar Cove, Washington

Summary: When the judge denies a couple a divorce on the grounds that they haven't tried hard enough to make it work, the small town of Cedar Cove, Washington, is stunned—and fascinated. The lives of numerous interesting characters intertwine in this gently-paced, heartwarming story that is the first in Macomber's newest "hometown" series, Cedar Cove Chronicles.

Other books by the same author:
Always Dakota, 2001
Thursdays at Eight, 2001
Dakota Born, 2000
Dakota Home, 2000
Return to Promise, 2000

Other books you might like:
Georgia Bockoven, *Things Remembered*, 1998
Colleen Faulkner, *Marrying Owen*, 2000
Barbara Freethy, *Almost Home*, 2000
   small town atmosphere
LaVyrle Spencer, *Morning Glory*, 1989
   1940s farm life
Sherryl Woods, *Angel Mine*, 2000

360

DEBBIE MACOMBER

Thursdays at Eight
(Don Mills, Ontario: Mira, 2001)

Story type: Contemporary/Mainstream
Subject(s): Women; Friendship
Major character(s): Clare Craig, Divorced Person, Single Parent; Liz Kenyon, Widow(er); Julia Murchison, Housewife, Parent
Time period(s): 2000s
Locale(s): California

Summary: Four long-time friends of vastly differing ages (20s to late 50s) meet for breakfast once a week and share the trials and tribulations of their lives in this novel that is more women's fiction than romance and is sure to please Macomber's many fans. A bitter divorcee who learns to forgive, a widow who's not about to waste the rest of her life, a young woman who finds herself, and a 40-year-old faced with a PS baby are the primary players in this heartwarming story of friendship and the part it plays in the lives of most women.

Where it's reviewed:
Rendezvous, May 2001, page 28

Other books by the same author:
Always Dakota, 2001
Dakota Born, 2000
Dakota Home, 2000
Return to Promise, 2000
This Matter of Marriage, 1997

Other books you might like:
Georgia Bockoven, *Things Remembered*, 1998
Barbara Delinsky, *Three Wishes*, 2000
Barbara Delinsky, *The Woman Next Door*, 2001
Mary Alice Monroe, *The Book Club*, 1999
Jean Stone, *Ivy Secrets*, 1996

361

TESS MALLORY

Highland Dream
(New York: LoveSpell, 2001)

Story type: Time Travel; Humor
Subject(s): Time Travel; Humor; Friendship
Major character(s): Jix Ferguson, Writer, Time Traveler; Jamie MacGregor, Detective—Police (Scotland Yard), Time Traveler
Time period(s): 17th century; 2000s
Locale(s): Meadbrooke, Scotland

Summary: Jix Ferguson will do anything to keep her best friend from marrying a slimeball fortune hunter, including getting her drunk and taking her to Scotland. However, an enchanted sword whisks the two of them and a burned-out Scotland Yard detective back to the 17th century, where a barbaric laird mistakes Jix for his son's betrothed. This humorous, highly entertaining time travel shows that often, to find true love, the best-laid plans have to go awry.

Where it's reviewed:
Romantic Times, March 2001, page 94

Other books by the same author:
To Touch the Stars, 1998
Circles in Time, 1997
Midsummer's Night's Magic, 1997 (anthology)
Jewels of Time, 1994

Other books you might like:
Jill Barnett, *Bewitching*, 1999
Lynn Kurland, *The More I See You*, 1999
Teresa Medeiros, *Touch of Enchantment*, 1997
Angie Ray, *A Knight to Cherish*, 1999
Eugenia Riley, *The Bushwhacked Bride*, 1999

362

VICTORIA MALVEY

A Proper Affair
(New York: Sonnet, 2001)

Story type: Historical/Victorian
Subject(s): Marriage; Conduct of Life
Major character(s): Cassandra Abbott Hampsted, Widow(er), Noblewoman (Dowager Duchess of Linley); Bryce Keene, Widow(er), Nobleman (Duke of Amberville)

Time period(s): 1840s (1843)
Locale(s): England

Summary: Married to an elderly duke, widowed, and left penniless, the very proper Cassandra ends up marrying her childhood friend, Bryce Keene, also widowed and the antithesis of everything that Cassandra considers appropriate. They marry for highly pragmatic reasons—she needs a place to go; he needs the help of a "proper wife" in raising his wild 16-year-old niece, Elaina. A typical marriage of convenience that turns into real romance with the added interest of various charming and not so charming secondary characters. Quotes from Cassandra's book *A Lady's Guide to Proper Etiquette* introduce each chapter.

Where it's reviewed:
Affaire de Coeur, May/June 2001, page 19
Romantic Times, May 2001, page 43

Other books by the same author:
A Merry Chase, 2000
Fortune's Bride, 2000
Enchanted, 1999
Temptress, 1999
Portrait of Dreams, 1998

Other books you might like:
Victoria Alexander, *The Marriage Lesson*, 2001
Catherine Archer, *Lady Thorn*, 1997
Patricia Cabot, *A Little Scandal*, 2000
Stella Cameron, *The Wish Club*, 1998
Sabrina Jeffries, *A Dangerous Love*, 2000

363

KAT MARTIN

Perfect Sin
(New York: St. Martin's Paperbacks, 2000)

Story type: Historical/Regency
Subject(s): Treasure, Buried; Adventure and Adventurers; Legends
Major character(s): Cait Harmon, Young Woman, Adventurer; Randall Clayton, Nobleman (7th Duke of Belden)
Time period(s): 1800s (1805)
Locale(s): London, England; Santo Amaro, Fictional Country (remote island)

Summary: When his young cousin commits suicide over a lost fortune, Randall Clayton, seventh Duke of Belden, sets out to find the man who swindled him. Unfortunately, all clues lead to treasure hunter Donovan Harmon, American professor of antiquities, and Randall has fallen in love with his daughter. The search for revenge leads to the accidental discovery of love in this adventure-filled treasure hunt.

Where it's reviewed:
Romantic Times, October 2000, page 38

Other books by the same author:
Silk and Steel, 2000
The Dream, 2000
Night Secrets, 1999
Dangerous Passions, 1998
Wicked Promise, 1998

Other books you might like:
Catherine Coulter, *The Courtship*, 2000
Jill Marie Landis, *The Orchid Hunter*, 2000
Linda Needham, *The Wedding Night*, 1999
    Victorian
Amanda Quick, *Wicked Widow*, 2000
Nan Ryan, *The Seduction of Ellen*, 2001
    Victorian

364

CONNIE MASON

A Breath of Scandal

(New York: Avon, 2001)

Story type: Historical/Georgian
Subject(s): Spies; Gypsies; Identity, Concealed
Major character(s): Lara, Gypsy, Noblewoman; Julian
    "Drago" Thornton, Nobleman (Earl of Mansfield), Spy
    ("Scorpion")
Time period(s): 1750s
Locale(s): Scotland; England

Summary: Shot and left to drown, secret agent and English
nobleman Julian Thornton awakes to find himself rescued,
"married," and renamed Drago, all in an effort by the beautiful gypsy girl Lara to save him from capture. Although their
relationship becomes passionate, Julian eventually leaves
Lara behind for his life in England, little knowing that she is
also the daughter of an English nobleman and will soon be
coming to England for the Season herself. Very sensual.

Where it's reviewed:
Romantic Times, March 2001, page 37

Other books by the same author:
A Taste of Sin, 2000
The Outlaws: Jess, 2000
The Outlaws: Rafe, 2000
To Tame a Renegade, 1998
To Love a Stranger, 1997

Other books you might like:
Jo Beverley, *Something Wicked*, 1997
Christina Dodd, *A Well Pleasured Lady*, 1997
Danelle Harmon, *The Wicked One*, 2001
Stephanie Laurens, *All about Love*, 2001
Margaret Moore, *His Forbidden Kiss*, 2001

365

CATHY MAXWELL

The Marriage Contract

(New York: Avon, 2001)

Story type: Historical/Regency
Subject(s): Marriage; Interpersonal Relations
Major character(s): Anne Burnett, Gentlewoman, Bride
    (proxy bride); Aiden Black, Nobleman (Earl of Tiebauld)
Time period(s): 1810s (1815)
Locale(s): England; Scotland

Summary: Having failed to make an acceptable match, desperate Anne Burnett reluctantly agrees to marry a man she has

never met, and one who doesn't even know he is being
married. Their first meeting is less than auspicious; but as they
come to know each other, respect and love eventually follow.
Well-written, compelling, sensual, and overflowing with
Scottish flavor.

Where it's reviewed:
Romantic Times, February 2001, page 42

Other books by the same author:
A Scandalous Marriage, 2000
Because of You, 1999
Married in Haste, 1999
When Dreams Come True, 1998
Falling in Love Again, 1997

Other books you might like:
Julie Garwood, *Saving Grace*, 1993
    earlier setting/arranged marriage
Susan King, *The Swan Maiden*, 2001
    earlier setting/Scottish flavor
Edith Layton, *The Chance*, 2000
    emotionally involving
Johanna Lindsey, *The Heir*, 2000
Mary Jo Putney, *Bride by Arrangement*, 2000
    anthology

366

AMANDA MCCABE

Scandal in Venice

(New York: Signet, 2001)

Story type: Regency
Subject(s): Art; Scandal
Major character(s): Elizabeth Everdean, Noblewoman, Artist;
    Nicholas "Nick" Hollingsworth, Gentleman, Secretary
Time period(s): 1810s (1814; 1816)
Locale(s): London, England; Venice, Italy

Summary: After accidently killing her lecherous, elderly fiance, Lady Elizabeth Everdean flees her stepbrother's home
in England for Italy, where she becomes artist Elizabeth
Cheswood. Nicholas Hollingsworth agrees to locate Elizabeth
and bring her back home as a favor to her stepbrother, who
saved Nicholas' life in the war. Once Nicholas tracks down
Elizabeth in Venice, he realizes taking the beautiful artist
back to England will destroy her happy new life.

Where it's reviewed:
Affaire de Coeur, March/April 2001, page 39
Romantic Times, April 2001, page 102

Other books you might like:
Nancy Butler, *The Prodigal Hero*, 1997
June Calvin, *Isabella's Rake*, 1997
Elisabeth Fairchild, *A Fresh Perspective*, 1996
Ellen Fitzgerald, *Venetian Masquerade*, 1987
Patricia Oliver, *The Lady in Gray*, 1999

367

DINAH MCCALL (Pseudonym of Sharon Sala)

Storm Warning

(Don Mills, Ontario: Mira, 2001)

Story type: Contemporary; Romantic Suspense
Subject(s): Serial Killer; Psychology Experiments; Fear
Major character(s): Virginia ''Ginny'' Shapiro, Journalist (investigative reporter), Fugitive; Sullivan ''Sully'' Dean, FBI Agent
Time period(s): 2000s
Locale(s): St. Louis, Missouri; Mississippi; Arizona

Summary: Alerted by her childhood friend, Sister Mary Teresa, to the fact that phone calls are somehow triggering the suicides of a select group of their grade school classmates, Ginny calls the convent only to learn that Sister Mary Teresa has become the next victim in the bizarre scenario. Frightened and knowing she is the next—and last—on the killer's list, Ginny runs for her life, not knowing that FBI agent Sully Dean is hot on her trail. They connect in a remote Mississippi fishing camp, interact violently with the locals, and ultimately end up in a safe house near Phoenix. Post-hypnotic suggestion, insanity, and fame are part of this dark, occasionally adventuresome romance.

Where it's reviewed:
Library Journal, May 15, 2001, page 107
Publishers Weekly, April 9, 2001, page 56
Romantic Times, May 2001, page 100

Other books by the same author:
The Return, 2000
Touchstone, 1999
Legend, 1998
Chase the Moon, 1997
Tallchief, 1997

Other books you might like:
Shirley Hailstock, *More than Gold*, 2000
    another heroine on the run
Iris Johansen, *The Ugly Duckling*, 1996
Rachel Lee, *Caught*, 1994
Karen Robards, *Heartbreaker*, 1997
Tracey Tillis, *Deadly Masquerade*, 1994

368

MARY REED MCCALL

Secret Vows

(New York: Avon, 2001)

Story type: Historical/Medieval
Subject(s): Marriage; Middle Ages; Dishonesty
Major character(s): Catherine of Somerset, Noblewoman, Imposter (as the late Elise de Montford); Grayson de Camville, Nobleman (baron), Knight
Time period(s): 13th century (1233)
Locale(s): England

Summary: In order to save the lives of her small children, widowed Catherine of Somerset reluctantly agrees to take her cruel, sadistic brother-in-law's dead sister's place in a mar-

riage to Grayson de Camville. This is not simply a benign arranged marriage; her brother-in-law has destruction on his mind and he plans to use Catherine to accomplish his plans. Good period detail, well-developed characters, and a well-crafted plot are part of this sensual novel of politics, betrayal, greed, and love. First novel.

Other books you might like:
Shana Abe, *The Truelove Bride*, 1999
Juliana Garnett, *The Baron*, 1999
Julie Garwood, *Saving Grace*, 1993
    lighter
Susan King, *The Swan Maiden*, 2001

369

BARBARA MCCAULEY (Pseudonym of Barbara Joel)

Reese's Wild Wager

(New York: Silhouette, 2001)

Story type: Contemporary
Subject(s): Cooks and Cookery; Restaurants
Major character(s): Sydney Taylor, Restaurateur (Le Petit Bistro); Reese Sinclair, Saloon Keeper/Owner (Squire's Tavern and Inn)
Time period(s): 2000s
Locale(s): Pennsylvania

Summary: After Reese Sinclair's dog tears up the flowers in front of Sydney Taylor's new restaurant, Reese suggests they settle their differences with a game of cards. If Sydney wins, Reese will fence his dog in but if Reese wins, Sydney will have to help out in Reese's tavern for two weeks. Determined to teach proper, persnickety Sydney a lesson, Reese hedges the game in his favor, only to later realize he is the one learning a lesson, when Sydney turns out to be nothing like her reputation.

Where it's reviewed:
Romantic Times, April 2001, page 109

Other books by the same author:
Callan's Proposition, 2000
Gabriel's Honor, 2000
Blackhawk's Sweet Revenge, 1999
Killian's Passion, 1999
Secret Baby Santos, 1999

Other books you might like:
Stephanie Bond, *It Takes a Rebel*, 2000
Jennifer Crusie, *Anyone but You*, 1996
Leslie Kelly, *Suite Seduction*, 2000
Charlotte Maclay, *Accidental Roommates*, 1997
Gwen Pemberton, *Wooing Wanda*, 1997

370

SYLVIA MCDANIEL

The Outlaw Takes a Wife

(New York: Zebra, 2001)

Story type: Historical/American West
Series: Burnett Brides. Book 2

Subject(s): American West; Robbers and Outlaws; Family Relations

Major character(s): Elizabeth Anderson, Mail Order Bride, Southern Belle (victim of Reconstructionists); Tanner Burnett, Veteran (Civil War), Outlaw

Time period(s): 1870s (1874)

Locale(s): San Antonio, Texas; Fort Worth, Texas

Summary: When Tanner Burnett rescues Elizabeth Anderson from stagecoach bandits, she never dreams that he's one of them and he never dreams that she's his brother's mail-order bride. A matchmaking mother, a marshal whose brother is an outlaw, and two people scarred by the Civil War add pathos and humor to this prodigal son tale.

Where it's reviewed:
Romantic Times, January 2001, page 41

Other books by the same author:
The Marshal Takes a Wife, 2001 (Burnett Brides. Book 3)
A Scarlet Bride, 2000
The Rancher Takes a Wife, 2000 (Burnett Brides. Book 1)

Other books you might like:
Megan Chance, *Fall from Grace*, 1997
Sandra Chastain, *The Outlaw Bride*, 2000
Lorraine Heath, *Texas Destiny*, 1997
Leslie LaFoy, *Maddie's Justice*, 2000
Penelope Williamson, *The Outsider*, 1997

371

SYLVIA MCDANIEL

A Scarlet Bride

(New York; Zebra, 2000)

Story type: Historical/Victorian America

Subject(s): Trust; Gambling; Marriage

Major character(s): Alexandra Halsted Thurston, Socialite, Divorced Person; Connor Manning, Rake, Landowner

Time period(s): 1890s (1895)

Locale(s): Charleston, South Carolina

Summary: His impulsive bet to seduce the lovely, slightly scandalous divorcee Alexandra Thurston comes back to haunt the charming, debt-ridden Connor Manning when the pair end up falling in love and Alexandra learns of this wager. An unexpected pregnancy, a forced marriage, and issues of trust and betrayal are part of this story that nicely depicts some of the land issues facing Southern landowners and provides an emotionally involving romance at the same time.

Where it's reviewed:
Romantic Times, Valentine's Issue 2000, page 40

Other books by the same author:
The Marshal Takes a Wife, 2001
The Outlaw Takes a Wife, 2001
The Rancher Takes a Wife, 2000
In His Arms Again, 1999
A Hero's Heart, 1998

Other books you might like:
Heidi Betts, *Cinnamon and Roses*, 2000
Heather Graham, *And One Rode West*, 1992
Heather Graham, *And One Wore Gray*, 1992

Margaret Mitchell, *Gone with the Wind*, 1936
classic Civil War story

372

MAY MCGOLDRICK (Pseudonym of Jim McGoldrick and Nikoo McGoldrick)

The Dreamer

(New York: Onyx, 2000)

Story type: Historical/Renaissance

Series: Highland Treasure. Book 1

Subject(s): Marriage; Family Relations; Treasure

Major character(s): Catherine Percy, Fugitive (from Henry VIII); John Stewart, Laird, Nobleman (Earl of Athol)

Time period(s): 16th century (1535)

Locale(s): Yorkshire, England; Scotland (Balvenie Castle)

Summary: When King Henry VIII executes Catherine Percy's father as a traitor, Catherine flees to the Highlands, seeking sanctuary there. When John Stewart, Earl of Athol, comes to Catherine's bedchamber by mistake (his fiancee traded rooms to have an assignation of her own), he insists they marry. As Catherine and John learn to love each other, their potentially idyllic existence is tainted by attempts on Catherine's life. Lots of adventure and secret treasure set the tone for this first book in the Highland Treasure series.

Where it's reviewed:
Romantic Times, May 2000, page 36

Other books by the same author:
The Enchantress, 2000 (Highland Treasure. Book 2)
The Firebrand, 2000
Flame, 1998
The Beauty of the Mist, 1997
Angel of Skye, 1996

Other books you might like:
Shana Abe, *Intimate Enemies*, 2000
Kathleen Givens, *The Wild Rose of Kilgannon*, 1999
Jaclyn Reding, *White Heather*, 1997
Amanda Scott, *Border Storm*, 2001
Haywood Smith, *Border Lord*, 2001

373

MAUREEN MCKADE (Pseudonym of Maureen Webster)

Outlaw's Bride

(New York: Avon, 2001)

Story type: Historical/American West

Subject(s): American West; Revenge; Single Parent Families

Major character(s): Mattie St. Clair, Widow(er), Single Parent; Clint Beaudry, Lawman (former U.S. Marshal), Gunfighter

Time period(s): 1880s (1887)

Locale(s): Green Valley, Colorado

Summary: Since the death of her husband, Mattie St. Clair has been raising her small son alone, making a modest living by taking in boarders. Clint Beaudry lives for revenge, vowing to hunt down and kill the man who raped and murdered his wife. At first, Mattie turns him away, but takes him in when he's

shot in the back. Well-written and packed with emotion, this book has excellent insights into the characters' motivations.

Where it's reviewed:
Romantic Times, February 2001, page 43

Other books by the same author:
Mail-Order Bride, 2000
Untamed Heart, 1999
A Dime Novel Hero, 1998
Winter Hearts, 1997

Other books you might like:
Judith E. French, *Morgan's Woman*, 1999
Jill Gregory, *Cold Night, Warm Stranger*, 1999
Lorraine Heath, *Never Marry a Cowboy*, 2001
Leslie LaFoy, *Maddie's Justice*, 2000
Susan Wiggs, *The Drifter*, 1998

374

MEAGAN MCKINNEY (Pseudonym of Ruth Goodman)

The Lawman Meets His Bride
(New York: Silhouette, 2000)

Story type: Romantic Suspense; Contemporary
Series: Matched in Montana. Book 2
Subject(s): Murder; Mystery; Suspense
Major character(s): Constance Adams, Real Estate Agent; Quinn Loudon, Lawyer (U.S. Attorney), Fugitive
Time period(s): 2000s
Locale(s): Washington, District of Columbia; Mystery, Montana

Summary: Realtor Constance Adams is kidnapped by fugitive Quinn Loudon, an assistant U.S. attorney who's been wounded in a gun battle with federal marshals. Framed by unscrupulous lawmakers, Quinn's only chance of survival is this fearless stranger. Intrigue and danger are around every corner in this exciting romantic suspense.

Where it's reviewed:
Romantic Times, November 2000, page 112

Other books by the same author:
The M.D. Courts His Wife, 2001 (Matched in Montana. Book 3)
The Cowboy Meets His Match, 2000 (Matched in Montana. Book 1)
The Fortune Hunter, 1998
Gentle from the Night, 1997
A Man to Slay Dragons, 1996

Other books you might like:
Susan Andersen, *All Shook Up*, 2001
Jean DeWitt, *The Stranger*, 1998
Leigh Greenwood, *Love on the Run*, 2000
Jayne Ann Krentz, *Lost and Found*, 2001
Carla Neggers, *The Carriage House*, 2001

375

MEAGAN MCKINNEY (Pseudonym of Ruth Goodman)

Still of the Night
(New York: Kensington, 2001)

Story type: Contemporary; Romantic Suspense
Subject(s): Good and Evil; Secrets; Family
Major character(s): Stella St. Vallier, Professor (women's studies); Garrett Shaw, Lawman (undercover U.S. Marshal)
Time period(s): 2000s
Locale(s): Cane Town, Louisiana (Shadow Oaks Plantation)

Summary: Determined to save her family's plantation, Stella St. Vallier takes a sabbatical from her academic career and heads to Shadow Oaks to see what she can do to make the estate profitable again. A local murder, a wounded stranger, and a mystery complicate things as Stella struggles with her common sense and her feelings for her "guest" in this dark, gothically-tinged tale of romantic suspense that is rife with pirate legends, filled with old resentments, and laced with evil.

Where it's reviewed:
Romantic Times, February 2001, page 88

Other books by the same author:
The Lawman Meets His Bride, 2000
One Small Secret, 1999
The Merry Widow, 1999
The Fortune Hunter, 1998
Gentle from the Night, 1997

Other books you might like:
Barbara Erskine, *House of Echoes*, 1996
Kay Hooper, *Amanda*, 1995
Kay Hooper, *Haunting Rachel*, 1998
Karen Robards, *Wait Until Dark*, 2001 anthology; Andrea Kane, Linda Anderson, and Mariah Stewart, co-authors
Anne Stuart, *Shadow Lover*, 1999

376

MARY JANE MEIER

Catch a Dream
(New York: Onyx, 2001)

Story type: Contemporary
Subject(s): Wilderness Survival; Ranch Life; Romance
Major character(s): Meg Delaney, Computer Expert (fantasy game designer); Zack Burkhart, Rancher (llamas), Single Parent
Time period(s): 2000s
Locale(s): Yellowstone Park, Wyoming; Idaho

Summary: Rescued by widowed rancher Zack Burkhart when her self-centered, business-obsessed ex-fiance leaves her stranded in Yellowstone, computer game designer Meg Delaney has every intention of heading back to Salt Lake City. When Zach's five-year-old son, withdrawn and reticent since his mother's death, takes a liking to her and then her ex-fiance tracks her down at Zach's Idaho llama ranch and de-

mands that she return with him, she balks—and ends up with a totally unexpected life and love. Funny, lively, and fast-paced. First novel.

Where it's reviewed:
Romantic Times, March 2001, page 93

Other books you might like:
Susan Andersen, *Baby, I'm Yours*, 1998
Patti Berg, *Bride for a Night*, 2000
Susan Elizabeth Phillips, *Heaven, Texas*, 1995
    fast-paced and funny
Sheila Rabe, *Be My Valentine*, 2001
Christie Ridgway, *This Perfect Kiss*, 2001
    humorous

377

BARBARA METZGER

Miss Westlake's Windfall

(New York: Signet, 2001)

Story type: Regency
Subject(s): Neighbors and Neighborhoods; Orphans; Smuggling
Major character(s): Ada Westlake, Gentlewoman; Charles "Chas" Harrison Ashford, Nobleman (Viscount Ashmead)
Time period(s): 1810s
Locale(s): England

Summary: After turning down yet another offer of marriage from her wealthy neighbor and very good friend, Charles "Chas" Ashford, Ada Westlake discovers a small fortune in coins tucked up a tree in her family's orchard. While the nearly destitute Westlake family could certainly put this windfall to good use, Ada believes the money comes from smugglers and she vows to return the ill-gotten gains to its rightful owner. When Ada turns to Chas for help, Chas is caught between the equally difficult tasks of convincing Ada to keep the money and accept his next offer of marriage. Sparkles with humor.

Where it's reviewed:
Affaire de Coeur, March/April 2001, page 37
Romantic Times, April 2001, page 102

Other books by the same author:
A Worthy Wife, 2000
Saved by Scandal, 2000
Miss Treadwell's Talent, 1999
Lord Heartless, 1998
Miss Lockharte's Letters, 1998

Other books you might like:
Sandra Heath, *The Smuggler's Daughter*, 1996
Emily Hendrickson, *The Debonair Duke*, 1996
Carla Kelly, *Mrs. Drew Plays Her Hand*, 1994
Lynn Kerstan, *Celia's Grand Passion*, 1998
April Kihlstrom, *The Wily Wastrel*, 1999

378

BARBARA METZGER

The Painted Lady

(New York: Signet, 2001)

Story type: Regency; Fantasy
Subject(s): Courtship; Artists and Art; Fantasy
Major character(s): Lilyanne Bannister, Gentlewoman; Kennard Wyndgate "Kasey" Cartland, Nobleman (Duke of Caswell), Artist
Time period(s): 1810s
Locale(s): England (Bannister Home for Healthful Living)

Summary: A bizarre encounter with a talking painting sends the Duke of Caswell in search of help for his obviously dwindling mental state. He ends up in the Bannister Home for Healthful Living, a peaceful estate run by Dr. Osgood Bannister, expert in brain fever, and his niece Lilyanne, who knows there's more to life than she's seen. A charming, funny, romantic tale with a dash of fantasy thrown in for good measure.

Where it's reviewed:
Library Journal, May 15, 2001, page 107

Other books by the same author:
A Worthy Wife, 2000
Miss Treadwell's Talent, 1999
Lord Heartless, 1998
Miss Lockharte's Letters, 1998
The Primrose Path, 1997

Other books you might like:
June Calvin, *Isabella's Rake*, 1997
Casey Claybourne, *A Ghost of a Chance*, 1996
    more "fantastic" meddling
Jo Ann Ferguson, *A Model Marriage*, 1997
    another artist hero
Sandra Heath, *The Halloween Husband*, 1994
    another magical painting
Kasey Michaels, *The Haunted Miss Hampshire*, 1992
    more fantasy

379

FERN MICHAELS

Charming Lily

(New York: Zebra, 2001)

Story type: Contemporary; Romantic Suspense
Subject(s): Parapsychology; Missing Persons
Major character(s): Lily Harper, Mountaineer; Matt Starr, Businessman (CEO of Digitech)
Time period(s): 2000s
Locale(s): Natchez, Tennessee; South

Summary: When Matt Starr suddenly disappears on the eve of their wedding and leaves her waiting at the altar for the second time in ten years, Lily Harper is furious. Then her best friend gives her an antique charm called a "Wish Keeper" and she suddenly begins having strange dreams and visions. After Matt's dog, Gracie, turns up alone, Lily begins to think something really might have happened to him. Experienced

mountaineer and trained survivalist that she is, intrepid Lily decides to go and get her man! Kidnapping, greed, and a dash of the paranormal add to this fast-paced adventure.

Other books by the same author:
Plain Jane, 2001
Listen to Your Heart, 2000
What You Wish For, 2000
Sara's Song, 1998
Yesterday, 1995

Other books you might like:
Jasmine Cresswell, *No Sin Too Great*, 1996
Suzanne Forster, *The Morning After*, 1995
Linda Howard, *Dream Man*, 1995
    paranormal elements
Karen Robards, *Heartbreaker*, 1997
Karen Robards, *Walking After Midnight*, 1995

380

FERN MICHAELS

Plain Jane
(New York: Kensington, 2001)

Story type: Contemporary; Paranormal
Subject(s): Self-Esteem; Rape; Mystery
Major character(s): Jane Lewis, Doctor (psychiatrist), Radio Personality; Michael Sorenson, Doctor (psychiatrist)
Time period(s): 2000s
Locale(s): Rayne, Louisiana

Summary: Still haunted by the memory of the gang rape of a college friend and her subsequent suicide, Jane Lewis, no longer the shy and overweight "Plain Jane" but now a respected psychiatrist with her own radio show, begins to think that one of her patients could have been involved with the rape 12 years ago and she sets out to discover the truth. A pair of quirky crime writers, her high-school heartthrob, and a ghostly dog add interest to this romance that combines a bit of suspense and a dash of humor with some old guilt and self-esteem issues.

Where it's reviewed:
Romantic Times, March 2001, page 90

Other books by the same author:
Charming Lily, 2001
Listen to Your Heart, 2000
What You Wish For, 2000
Sara's Song, 1998
Yesterday, 1995

Other books you might like:
Mary Lynn Baxter, *Hot Texas Nights*, 1996
Jennifer Blake, *Love and Smoke*, 1991
Rebecca Brandewyne, *Dust Devil*, 1996
Sandra Brown, *Breath of Scandal*, 1991
Colleen Faulkner, *Taming Ben*, 2000
    another transformed heroine

381

KASEY MICHAELS (Pseudonym of Kathryn Seidick)

Someone to Love
(New York: Warner, 2001)

Story type: Historical/Regency; Humor
Subject(s): Humor; Family Relations; Relatives
Major character(s): Abigail Backworth Maldon, Widow(er), Matchmaker (for niece); Kipp Rutland, Wealthy, Nobleman (Viscount Willoughby)
Time period(s): 1810s
Locale(s): London, England

Summary: Abigail Backworth Maldon becomes a widow, when her husband dies climbing out of another woman's window. Since he's also gambled away their fortune, she finds herself responsible for an odd assortment of misfit relatives. Faced with poverty, Abigail becomes matchmaker for her lovely but vacuous niece, hoping the girl will snag a wealthy husband. Surprisingly, the rich target, Kipp Rutland, recovering from a broken heart, proposes to Abigail instead, never realizing he's inheriting her weird relatives as well. This is a rollicking good read from cover to cover.

Where it's reviewed:
Affaire de Coeur, March/April 2001, page 41
Booklist, March 1, 2001, page 1232
Publishers Weekly, March 19, 2001, page 82
Romantic Times, April 2001, page 38

Other books by the same author:
Beloved Wolf, 2001 (Coltons series)
His Innocent Temptress, 2001 (Texas Sheikhs series)
Brides of Privilege, 2001 (Coltons series)
Finding Home, 2001 (anthology)
Too Good to Be True, 2001

Other books you might like:
Christina Dodd, *Rules of Surrender*, 2000
Suzanne Enoch, *Reforming a Rake*, 2000
Jill Marie Landis, *The Orchid Hunter*, 2000
Amanda Quick, *Mistress*, 1994
Julia Quinn, *How to Marry a Marquis*, 1999

382

KASEY MICHAELS (Pseudonym of Kathryn Seidick)

Too Good to Be True
(New York: Kensington, 2001)

Story type: Humor; Romantic Suspense
Subject(s): Humor; Suspense; Family Relations
Major character(s): Annie Kendall, Con Artist; Grady Sullivan, Bodyguard, Consultant (security)
Time period(s): 2000s
Locale(s): United States (Peevers Mansion)

Summary: Toilet paper king Archie Peevers may be ancient, but he's still a world class scoundrel. To protect himself from his murderous relatives, Archie hires security expert Grady Sullivan. Archie also hires a fake granddaughter/heir, Annie Kendall, to act as a new target for his greedy family. Annie's as much of a con artist as the old man, but Grady soon falls for

her. A family that redefines dysfunctional, a con artist who's being conned, and a butler who's smarter than everyone else combined make this madcap sequel to *Can't Take My Eyes Off of You* a truly funny one.

Where it's reviewed:
Affaire de Coeur, February 2001, page 33
Publishers Weekly, December 11, 2000, page 68
Romantic Times, February 2001, page 87

Other books by the same author:
Someone to Love, 2001
Can't Take My Eyes Off of You, 2000
Jessie's Expecting, 2000
Marrying Maddie, 2000
Raffling Ryan, 2000

Other books you might like:
Sue Civil-Brown, *Catching Kelly*, 2000
Millie Criswell, *The Trouble with Mary*, 2001
Claire Cross, *Third Time Lucky*, 2000
Janet Evanovich, *Hot Six*, 2000
Jayne Ann Krentz, *Lost and Found*, 2001

383

NADINE MILLER

The Yorkshire Lady

(New York: Signet, 2001)

Story type: Regency
Subject(s): Revenge; Social Conditions
Major character(s): Yves St. Armand, Nobleman (Comte de Rochemont); Rachel Barton, Heiress, Businesswoman (mill owner)
Time period(s): 1810s (1816)
Locale(s): England

Summary: Seeking the name of the nobleman who sold British military secrets to Napoleon and caused the death of the woman he loved, Yves St. Armand finds all clues point to the Earl of Fairborne as the suspected traitor. In order to find evidence, Yves breaks into the nobleman's house only to encounter Rachel Barton, a wealthy mill owner who is being courted by the earl, while he is rifling through the earl's study. Yves convinces Rachel to help him with his investigation, all the while hoping that once he has avenged the woman he loved, he can convince Rachel to share his future.

Where it's reviewed:
Romantic Times, January 2001, page 113

Other books by the same author:
Barbarian Earl, 1999
Touch of Magic, 1999
Madcap Masquerade, 1998
Unlikely Angel, 1998
The Misguided Matchmaker, 1997

Other books you might like:
Elisabeth Fairchild, *Captain Cupid Calls the Shots*, 2000
April Kihlstrom, *The Reluctant Thief*, 1998
Martha Kirkland, *The Seductive Spy*, 1999
Andrea Pickens, *A Lady of Letters*, 2000
Evelyn Richardson, *Lord Harry's Daughter*, 2001

384

MARY ALICE MONROE

The Four Seasons

(Don Mills, Ontario: Mira, 2001)

Story type: Contemporary/Mainstream
Subject(s): Sisters; Family
Major character(s): Rose Season, Relative (sister); Jillian Season, Relative (sister), Model; Beatrice ''Birdie'' Connors, Relative (sister), Doctor
Time period(s): 2000s
Locale(s): Evanston, Illinois

Summary: Drawn together once more by the death of Meredith, their youngest sister, Jilly, Birdie, and Rose must deal with Merry's final request—that they locate Jilly's 26-year-old daughter who had been given up for adoption years ago. Old wounds, healing, and family relationships are key in this powerful novel that is more women's fiction than romance.

Where it's reviewed:
Romantic Times, February 2001, page 90

Other books by the same author:
The Book Club, 1999
The Girl in the Mirror, 1998
The Long Road Home, 1995

Other books you might like:
Elizabeth Berg, *Talk Before Sleep*, 1997
Georgia Bockoven, *Things Remembered*, 1998
Robyn Carr, *The House on Olive Street*, 1999
Patricia Gaffney, *Saving Graces*, 1999
Patricia Potter, *The Perfect Family*, 2001

385

MARGARET MOORE (Pseudonym of Margaret Moore Wilkins)

His Forbidden Kiss

(New York: Avon, 2001)

Story type: Historical/Seventeenth Century
Subject(s): Marriage; Social Classes; Self-Esteem
Major character(s): Vivienne Burroughs, Orphan, Noblewoman; Robert Harding, Lawyer (solicitor)
Time period(s): 17th century (Restoration Era)
Locale(s): London, England

Summary: Attempting to leave London by boat one night rather than be forced into an unwanted marriage by her uncle, Lady Vivienne is ''rescued'' by solicitor Robert Harding, who assumes she is about to drown herself. The attraction between them is strong, but they part with only the memory of a brief, passionate kiss lingering between them. Family issues, love, and money intertwine in this story that makes full use of the colorful Restoration Era.

Where it's reviewed:
Romantic Times, March 2001, page 43

Other books by the same author:
A Scoundrel's Kiss, 1999
The Welshman's Bride, 1999

A Warrior's Bride, 1998
The Dark Duke, 1997
A Warrior's Quest, 1993

Other books you might like:
Jane Feather, *The Accidental Bride*, 1999
Jane Feather, *Reckless Angel*, 1989
Connie Mason, *A Breath of Scandal*, 2001
Haywood Smith, *Secrets in Satin*, 1997

386

MARGARET MOORE (Pseudonym of Margaret Moore Wilkins)

A Rogue's Embrace

(New York: Avon, 2000)

Story type: Historical/Seventeenth Century
Subject(s): Marriage; Inheritance
Major character(s): Elissa Longbourne, Noblewoman, Parent; Sir Richard Blythe, Writer (playwright), Nobleman; Will Longbourne, Child
Time period(s): 17th century (1663)
Locale(s): England

Summary: Forced to wed by the "restored" King Charles II, Sir Richard Blythe and Elissa Longbourne are attracted to each other in spite of themselves. The road to happiness is marred by Elissa's fear for her son's inheritance, a fear that suddenly becomes real when Will's life is threatened. A passionate tale with a colorful English Restoration setting.

Where it's reviewed:
Romantic Times, Valentine's Issue 2000, page 44

Other books by the same author:
His Forbidden Kiss, 2001
The Overlord's Bride, 2001
The Duke's Desire, 2000
A Warrior's Bride, 1998
A Warrior's Way, 1998

Other books you might like:
Jane Feather, *The Least Likely Bride*, 2000
Jane Feather, *Reckless Angel*, 1989
Connie Mason, *A Breath of Scandal*, 2001
Haywood Smith, *Secrets in Satin*, 1997

387

MARY MORGAN

Dangerous Moves

(New York: Zebra, 2000)

Story type: Contemporary
Subject(s): Rodeos; Physically Handicapped
Major character(s): Brooke Stevenson, Health Care Professional (physical therapist); Dillon McRay, Rodeo Rider (bull rider)
Time period(s): 2000s
Locale(s): Oklahoma

Summary: After seeing what her brother went through as a result of a football injury, physical therapist Brooke Steven-

son has little patience for macho men who refuse to take precautions against injuring themselves. Then sexy bull rider Dillon McRay comes into her life intent on riding in the International Championships, back injury or not. Two determined people collide in a battle of wills in this sensual contemporary with the feel of the Old West.

Where it's reviewed:
Romantic Times, February 2000, page 92

Other books you might like:
Patricia Ellis, *Rodeo Hearts*, 2000
    similar setting
Jayne Ann Krentz, *The Cowboy*, 1990
Roxanne Rustand, *Rodeo*, 2001
    similar setting and conflict
Sherryl Woods, *A Love Beyond Words*, 2001

388

DEBRA MULLINS (Pseudonym of Debra Mullins Manning)

The Lawmans Surrender

(New York: Avon, 2001)

Story type: Historical/American West; Historical
Subject(s): American West; Murder; Trust
Major character(s): Susannah Calhoun, Young Woman, Prisoner; Jedidiah Brown, Lawman (U.S. Marshal)
Time period(s): 1880s (1882)
Locale(s): Burr, Wyoming; Silver Flats, Colorado; Denver, Colorado

Summary: When Susannah Calhoun is framed for the murder of a powerful senator's nephew, the only witness to the crime disappears. Even U.S. Marshal Jedidiah Brown, her escort to the Denver jail—and a probable hanging—isn't convinced of her innocence. Their trip made even more treacherous by men determined to kill her, Susannah and Jedidiah find the road to love can be truly dangerous. A very sensual sequel to *Donovan's Bed*.

Where it's reviewed:
Affaire de Coeur, March/April 2001, page 20
Romantic Times, March 2001, page 43

Other books by the same author:
Donovan's Bed, 2000
Once a Mistress, 1999

Other books you might like:
Megan Chance, *Fall from Grace*, 1997
Judith E. French, *Morgan's Woman*, 1999
Leslie LaFoy, *Maddie's Justice*, 2000
Elizabeth Lane, *Bride on the Run*, 2001
Cheryl Anne Porter, *Wild Flower*, 2001

389

HELEN R. MYERS

Dead End

(Don Mills, Ontario: Mira, 2001)

Story type: Romantic Suspense; Contemporary
Subject(s): Mystery; Suspense; Runaways

Major character(s): Brette Barry, Single Parent, Postal Worker (mail carrier); Sam Knight, Teacher (high school shop), Recluse
Time period(s): 1990s (1999)
Locale(s): Wood County, Texas

Summary: Brette Barry sees a bloody handprint on a sign near her home and assumes it's a practical joke, courtesy of her teenaged son and his friend. When she sends her son to clean up the mess, it's gone. . .and so is his friend. As one mystery after another unfolds in their rural community, people begin to wonder about the reclusive high school teacher, Sam Knight, and his role in the latest happenings. Lots of suspense and some hairpin twists will thrill readers of this book.

Where it's reviewed:
Affaire de Coeur, March/April 2001, page 16
Romantic Times, March 2001, page 93

Other books by the same author:
Night Mist, 2001
Lost, 2000
A Fine Arrangement, 1999
More than You Know, 1999
Come Sundown, 1998

Other books you might like:
Sandra Brown, *Standoff*, 2000
Jill Jones, *Remember Your Lies*, 2001
Rachel Lee, *Snow in September*, 2000
Elizabeth Lowell, *Midnight in Ruby Bayou*, 2000
Carla Neggers, *The Carriage House*, 2001

390

CARLA NEGGERS

The Carriage House

(Don Mills, Ontario: Mira, 2001)

Story type: Romantic Suspense; Contemporary
Subject(s): Murder; Single Parent Families; Ghosts
Major character(s): Tess Haviland, Artist (graphic designer), Businesswoman; Andrew Thorne, Architect, Single Parent (widower)
Time period(s): 2000s
Locale(s): Beacon-by-the-Sea, Massachusetts; Boston, Massachusetts

Summary: When graphic artist Tess Haviland accepts an old carriage house in lieu of payment for one of her commissions, she doesn't expect to find a skeleton in the cellar. A neat twist on the classic gothic.

Where it's reviewed:
Affaire de Coeur, February 2001, page 18
Publishers Weekly, November 27, 2000, page 60
Romantic Times, February 2001, page 91

Other books by the same author:
The Cabin, 2001
The Waterfall, 2000
Kiss the Moon, 1999
On Fire, 1999
Claim the Crown, 1997

Other books you might like:
Susan Andersen, *All Shook Up*, 2001
Sandra Brown, *Standoff*, 2000
Jean DeWitt, *The Stranger*, 1998
Jayne Ann Krentz, *Lost and Found*, 2001
Elizabeth Lowell, *Midnight in Ruby Bayou*, 2000

391

CONSTANCE O'DAY-FLANNERY

Time After Time

(New York: Avon, 2001)

Story type: Time Travel
Subject(s): Time Travel; Grief; Healing
Major character(s): Kelly Brennan, Time Traveler, Widow(er); Daniel Gilmore, Widow(er), Gentleman
Time period(s): 1880s (1888); 2000s
Locale(s): Louisiana

Summary: While participating in a wedding in New Orleans, recently widowed Kelly Brennan is drawn back in time to 1888 and into the life of grieving Daniel Gilmore, a man who has also lost his spouse and looks exactly like Kelly's late husband, Michael. A lively child, the typical culture shock time travel issues, and a nice look at post-Civil War Louisiana are part of this romance from one of the veteran authors of this subgenre.

Where it's reviewed:
Affaire de Coeur, March/April 2001, page 27
Romantic Times, March 2001, page 87

Other books by the same author:
Heaven on Earth, 2000
Anywhere You Are, 1999
Sunsets, 1996
Bewitched, 1995
This Time Forever, 1990

Other books you might like:
Jude Deveraux, *Legend*, 1996
Willa Hix, *Then and Now*, 2000
Lynn Kurland, *Veils of Time*, 1999
   anthology
Jenny Lykins, *River of Dreams*, 2000
Ciji Ware, *Midnight on Julia Street*, 1999
   mainstream New Orleans

392

KAYLA PERRIN

If You Want Me

(New York: HarperTorch, 2001)

Story type: Contemporary; Multicultural
Subject(s): African Americans; Reunions; Self-Esteem
Major character(s): Alice Watson, Student, Actress ("Desiree La Croix"); Marcus Quinn, Student, Police Officer
Time period(s): 2000s; 1980s
Locale(s): Chicago, Illinois

Summary: Overweight and the object of high school ridicule, the now successful—and slim—Alice Watson returns to Chi-

cago because of her mother's heart attack and finds herself faced with a chance to settle old problems and renew old dreams—especially those concerning her longtime friend Marcus Quinn. Good reunion story.

Where it's reviewed:
Romantic Times, February 2001, page 89

Other books by the same author:
Midnight Dreams, 1999
Sweet Honesty, 1999
Everlasting Love, 1998
Again, My Love, 1997

Other books you might like:
Barbara Delinsky, *The Passions of Chelsea Kane*, 1992
    not multicultural
Monica Jackson, *The Look of Love*, 1999
Sandra Kitt, *Between Friends*, 1998
Sandra Kitt, *Family Affairs*, 1999
Kathleen Gilles Seidel, *Maybe This Time*, 1990

393

TORI PHILLIPS (Pseudonym of Mary W. Schaller)

One Knight in Venice
(Toronto: Harlequin, 2001)

Story type: Historical/Renaissance; Historical
Series: Cavendish Chronicles. Number 6
Subject(s): Inquisition; Identity, Concealed; Revenge
Major character(s): Jessica Leonardo, Healer; Sir Francis Bardolph, Nobleman, Spy
Time period(s): 16th century (1550)
Locale(s): Venice, Italy

Summary: Sir Francis Bardolph's former mistress is out for revenge now that his attentions are turned to the masked healer, Jessica Leonardo. In the days of the Italian Inquisition, everyone has secrets, and no one trusts anyone. Deadly intrigue lurks in every shadow of this dangerous world where true love is indeed a miracle. This is a spell-binding tale, filled with rich details of life during carnival time in Venice. Characters from other books in the Cavendish Chronicles appear in this book, giving the reader a welcome glimpse of how their lives have gone.

Where it's reviewed:
Affaire de Coeur, March/April 2001, page 37
Romantic Times, April 2001, page 38

Other books by the same author:
Halloween Knight, 2000 (Cavendish Chronicles. Number 5)
Lady of the Knight, 1999 (Cavendish Chronicles. Number 4)
Midsummer's Knight, 1998 (Cavendish Chronicles. Number 2)
Three Dog Knight, 1998 (Cavendish Chronicles. Number 3)
Silent Knight, 1996 (Cavendish Chronicles. Number 1)

Other books you might like:
Shana Abe, *The Truelove Bride*, 1999
Donna Fletcher, *The Irish Devil*, 2000
Judith Merkle Riley, *A Vision of Light*, 1989
Haywood Smith, *Dangerous Gifts*, 1999

Susan Wiggs, *Lord of the Night*, 1993
    RITA Award winner

394

LISA PLUMLEY

Making over Mike
(New York: Zebra, 2001)

Story type: Contemporary; Humor
Subject(s): Business Enterprises; Humor; Change
Major character(s): Amanda Connor, Businesswoman (life coach); Mike Cavaco, Cook (unemployed), Taxi Driver
Time period(s): 2000s
Locale(s): Phoenix, Arizona

Summary: When unemployed short-order cook, Mike Cavaco wins the Life Coach Lotto, a whole life makeover from life coach Amanda Connor, who wants nothing more than for her new business venture to succeed, he suddenly realizes his life will never the the same. Opposites do attract in this lively, funny romp.

Where it's reviewed:
Affaire de Coeur, May/June 2001, page 29

Other books by the same author:
Her Best Man, 2000
Man of the Year, 2000
Lawman, 1999
My Best Friend's Baby, 1999
Outlaw, 1999

Other books you might like:
Jennifer Crusie, *The Cinderella Deal*, 1996
Jayne Ann Krentz, *Perfect Partners*, 1992
Jayne Ann Krentz, *Sweet Fortune*, 1991
Deborah Shelley, *My Favorite Flavor*, 2000
Deborah Shelley, *Talk about Love*, 1999

395

CHERYL ANNE PORTER

Wild Flower
(New York: St. Martin's Paperbacks, 2001)

Story type: Historical/Victorian America; Multicultural
Subject(s): Native Americans; Secrets; Intolerance
Major character(s): Taylor Christie James, Indian (half Cherokee), Bastard Daughter; Grey Talbott, Wealthy
Time period(s): 1870s (1876)
Locale(s): Tahlequah, Oklahoma; St. Louis, Missouri

Summary: Taylor Christie James, half Cherokee and half white, is sprung from the prison on the Indian Nation, where she's scheduled to hang. She escapes to the world of her white father, who abandoned her as a child, but is intercepted by Grey Talbott before she can make contact. Secrets, suspense, and two-way prejudice are woven throughout this story of a woman who finds love in the land of the people she hates.

Where it's reviewed:
Romantic Times, March 2001, page 38

Other books by the same author:
Her Only Chance, 2001
Drive-By Daddy, 2000
Prairie Song, 2000
Captive Angel, 1999
Puppy Love, 1999

Other books you might like:
Megan Chance, *Fall from Grace*, 1997
Sandra Chastain, *The Outlaw Bride*, 2000
Kathryn Hockett, *Outrageous*, 2000
Leslie LaFoy, *Maddie's Justice*, 2000
Maggie Osborne, *The Promise of Jenny Jones*, 1997

396

PATRICIA POTTER

The Heart Queen

(New York: Jove, 2001)

Story type: Historical/Georgian
Series: Scottish Trilogy. Book 2
Subject(s): Marriage; Murder; War
Major character(s): Janet Leslie Campbell, Noblewoman (Countess of Lochaene), Widow(er); Neil Forbes, Nobleman (Marquis of Braemoor)
Time period(s): 1730s (1738); 1740s (1747)
Locale(s): Scotland

Summary: Suspected of murdering her cruel husband and threatened by her greedy in-laws, Janet Campbell appeals to the man she had once loved, but who had betrayed her, Neil Forbes. Janet finds a love and compassion she thought she had lost for good. This romance features well-drawn characters, a compelling plot, and good period detail. Links to *The Black Knave*.

Other books by the same author:
The Perfect Family, 2001
The Black Knave, 2000
Star Keeper, 1999
Starfinder, 1998
Starcatcher, 1997

Other books you might like:
Colleen Faulkner, *Highland Bride*, 2000
Susan King, *The Swan Maiden*, 2001
Arnette Lamb, *Border Bride*, 1993
Amanda Scott, *Border Storm*, 2001
Lyn Stone, *The Highland Wife*, 2001

397

PATRICIA POTTER

The Perfect Family

(New York: Berkley, 2001)

Story type: Contemporary
Subject(s): Reunions; Family Relations; Mystery
Major character(s): Jessica Clayton, Store Owner (bookstore); Ross MacLeod, Foreman (ranch manager)
Time period(s): 2000s
Locale(s): Sedona, Arizona

Summary: When Jessica Clayton accepts a surprise invitation to a family reunion in Sedona, she has no idea why she's been invited or how she fits into the family that is holding it. However, the family is hers; and, as she soon discovers, she holds a key role in its future. Old secrets, family discord, and violence are part of this fast-paced, engrossing story that pits greed against tradition and relative against relative.

Other books by the same author:
The Black Knave, 2000
Star Keeper, 1999
Starfinder, 1998
Starcatcher, 1997
The Marshal and the Heiress, 1996

Other books you might like:
Kay Hooper, *Finding Laura*, 1997
Emilie Richards, *Iron Lace*, 1996
Emilie Richards, *Rising Tides*, 1997
Nora Roberts, *The Villa*, 2001
Anne Stuart, *Shadow Lover*, 1999

398

JULIA QUINN (Pseudonym of Julie Cotler Pottinger)

An Offer from a Gentleman

(New York: Avon, 2001)

Story type: Historical/Regency
Subject(s): Courtship; Fairy Tales; Stepmothers
Major character(s): Sophia Maria "Sophie" Beckett, Bastard Daughter (of the Earl of Penwood), Ward (of the Earl of Penwood); Benedict Bridgerton, Nobleman
Time period(s): 1810s (1815)
Locale(s): London, England

Summary: Treated as a servant by her stepmother and her two stepsisters, Sophie Beckett, illegitimate daughter and ward of the late Earl of Penwood, leads a dismal life. Then one night the servants assume the role of "fairy godparents" and help her attend the Bridgerton Masquerade Ball. Sophie takes the *ton* by storm and attracts the attention of the highly eligible Benedict Bridgerton. When she leaves him at midnight with no idea of who she is, he searches in vain to find her. They are destined to meet again, however; and three years later when they do, the real romance begins. A witty, lively, and warm Cinderella story with a twist.

Where it's reviewed:
Rendezvous, June 2001, page 23

Other books by the same author:
The Duke and I, 2000
The Viscount Who Loved Me, 2000
How to Marry a Marquis, 1999
Brighter than the Sun, 1997
Spendid, 1995

Other books you might like:
Claire Delacroix, *The Damsel*, 1999
    Cinderella elements/earlier time
Jude Deveraux, *Wishes*, 1989
    Cinderella elements
Patricia Grasso, *Violets in the Snow*, 1998

Jill Gregory, *Forever After*, 1993
   Cinderella elements
Barbara Dawson Smith, *A Glimpse of Heaven*, 1995
   Cinderella elements

399

SHEILA RABE

Be My Valentine

(New York: Jove, 2001)

Story type: Holiday Themes; Contemporary
Subject(s): Romance; Courtship
Major character(s): Shelby Barrett, Actress (aspiring), Office Worker (financial consulting office); David Jones, Consultant (financial), Businessman
Time period(s): 2000s
Locale(s): Seattle, Washington

Summary: In a last-ditch effort to get her longtime boyfriend, Matt, to ask her to marry him, Shelby Barrett takes her romance novelist mother's advice and sends herself flowers from the fictional David Jones. When a very real David Jones turns up in her office, furious at being tracked down by the jealous Matt, he is surprised to find himself attracted to her. Enjoyable secondary characters add to this lively, romantic contemporary.

Where it's reviewed:
Romantic Times, January 2001, page 79

Other books by the same author:
All I Want for Christmas, 2000
The Adventuress, 1996
An Innocent Imposter, 1995
Bringing out Betsy, 1994
The Accidental Bride, 1994

Other books you might like:
Suzanne Forster, *Hot Chocolate*, 1999
   anthology/more sensual
Kay Hooper, *Hearts of Gold*, 1994
Mary Jane Meier, *Catch a Dream*, 2001
   humorous and lively
Isabel Sharpe, *Tryst of Fate*, 2000
Anne Stuart, *My Secret Admirer*, 1999
   anthology

400

DEBBIE RALEIGH

A Bride for Lord Challmond

(New York: Zebra, 2001)

Story type: Regency
Subject(s): Social Conditions
Major character(s): Claire Blakewell, Gentlewoman; Simon Townsled, Nobleman
Time period(s): 1810s
Locale(s): England

Summary: One of the first people Simon Townsled encounters after returning home from the war to his Devonshire estate is sharp tongued do-gooder Claire Blakewell, who immediately begins lecturing the weary lord about how he has neglected his estate. Simon discovers there is some measure of truth to her claims and after he begins work on restoring his property, Simon agrees to help Claire with a problem of her own. She hopes to divert her father from his plan of marrying a brazen fortune hunter by pretending Simon is her new suitor, but Simon discovers he wants to be more than a pretend beau for Claire.

Where it's reviewed:
Romantic Times, January 2001, page 113

Other books by the same author:
Lord Carlton's Courtship, 2000
Lord Mumford's Minx, 2000

Other books you might like:
Jessica Benson, *Lord Stanhope's Proposal*, 2000
Dorothea Donley, *A Proper Match*, 1998
Jo Ann Ferguson, *An Unexpected Husband*, 2000
Lynn Kerstan, *Marry in Haste*, 1998
Nancy Lawrence, *A Noble Rogue*, 1998

401

ELLEN RAMSAY

Never Call It Loving

(Sutton, England: Severn House, 2001)

Story type: Contemporary
Subject(s): Infidelity; Family Relations
Major character(s): Fern Graham, Writer; Pietro Petrungero, Singer (opera)
Time period(s): 2000s
Locale(s): Aberdeen, Scotland; Rome, Italy; Vienna, Austria

Summary: Fern Graham is a happily married writer, living with her writer husband in a modest house. She has two great kids who are on the brink of adulthood. Then she's asked by opera star Pietro Petrungero to write his biography, and her well-ordered life pales beside the glitz and glamour of his jet-setting existence. Soon, the two become lovers, even though Pietro is also married. When the press catches wind of it, their affair wreaks havoc on their families. Does Fern throw away her marriage to be with the man she adored as a fan and now worships as a lover? The reader is kept in suspense until the very end of the book.

Other books by the same author:
Harvest of Courage, 1998
Walnut Shell Days, 1997
Butterflies in December, 1996
Dominie's Lassie, 1995
Broken Gate, 1994

Other books you might like:
Nicholas Evans, *The Horse Whisperer*, 1982
Judith Michaels, *Deceptions*, 1982
JoAnn Ross, *Legacy of Lies*, 1995
LaVyrle Spencer, *Home Song*, 1995
Robert James Waller, *The Bridges of Madison County*, 1992

402

DEBBI RAWLINS (Pseudonym of Debbi Quattrone)

Loving a Lonesome Cowboy

(Toronto: Harlequin, 2001)

Story type: Contemporary
Subject(s): Grief; Healing; Child Custody
Major character(s): Sara Conroy, Single Parent, Divorced Person; Ethan Slade, Widow(er), Rancher
Time period(s): 2000s
Locale(s): New Mexico

Summary: Sara Conroy has taken her small daughter and fled from her ex-husband to a small town in New Mexico. Penniless, she becomes the housekeeper for widowed rancher Ethan Slade. She's attracted to Ethan, but he can't seem to stop grieving for his wife, who died six years earlier. A warm book about the healing power of love.

Where it's reviewed:
Romantic Times, January 2001, page 101

Other books by the same author:
The Swinging R Ranch, 2001
His, Hers and Theirs, 1999
Stud for Hire, 1999
Overnight Father, 1999
If Wishes Were. . .Husbands, 1998

Other books you might like:
Leanne Banks, *Bride of Fortune*, 2000
Carla Cassidy, *Code Name: Cowboy*, 1999
Marie Ferrarella, *An Uncommon Hero*, 2001
Neesa Hart, *You Made Me Love You*, 2000
Curtiss Ann Matlock, *Driving Lessons*, 2000

403

LAURA RENKEN

My Lord Pirate

(New York: Jove, 2001)

Story type: Historical/Seventeenth Century
Subject(s): Pirates; Revenge; Kidnapping
Major character(s): Regan Welles, Religious (preparing for life in convent); Talon Drake, Pirate, Nobleman
Time period(s): 17th century
Locale(s): Jamaica; *Dark Fury*, At Sea; Martinique

Summary: Nobleman Talon Drake's family has been slain and his fortune stolen by Harrison Welles. As an act of revenge, Talon, now a pirate, steals Harrison's bride right out from under his nose. Unfortunately, he takes Regan Welles, the wrong woman. Regan, ready to take her vows at a convent, proves to be more than a match for Talon, who has to choose between his need for vengeance and his love for the sister of his enemy. This incredible debut novel has a great plot, lots of action, and an unforgettable hero and heroine.

Where it's reviewed:
Romantic Times, January 2001, page 38

Other books you might like:
Susan Grant, *Once a Pirate*, 2000
    time travel
Miranda Jarrett, *The Captain's Bride*, 1997
Kinley MacGregor, *A Pirate of Her Own*, 1999
Connie Mason, *Pirate*, 1999
Patricia Wynn, *Capturing Annie*, 2000

404

PATRICIA RICE

All a Woman Wants

(New York: Signet, 2001)

Story type: Historical/Victorian
Subject(s): Children; Marriage
Major character(s): Beatrice Cavendish, Heiress; Lachlan MacTavish, Businessman, Kidnapper
Time period(s): 19th century
Locale(s): England

Summary: American businessman Lachlan MacTavish needs a nursemaid for his niece and nephew; gently-bred, totally sheltered Beatrice Cavendish needs a teacher of estate management. So they strike a bargain—he and the children will stay on her estate until they leave for America and he will teach her everything he knows about running an estate. However, Mac has neglected to mention the fact he has kidnapped his late sister's children to save them from their drunken aristocratic father's abuse; and when Bea's pragmatic aunt hears the search is on for Mac and the children, she gives him an ultimatum—marry Bea and help her save the estate or she'll send word to the children's father and grandfather. A wedding soon follows, but it takes a lot of love and understanding before it becomes a marriage.

Where it's reviewed:
Affaire de Coeur, May/June 2001, page 24

Other books by the same author:
Impossible Dreams, 2000
Merely Magic, 2000
Moonlight Mistress, 1999
Volcano, 1999
Blue Clouds, 1998

Other books you might like:
Julie Garwood, *The Gift*, 1991
Julie Garwood, *Prince Charming*, 1994
Susan Kay Law, *The Bad Man's Bride*, 2001
    Marrying Miss Bright. Book 1
Teresa Medeiros, *A Kiss to Remember*, 2001

405

PATRICIA RICE

Nobody's Angel

(New York: Ivy, 2001)

Story type: Contemporary
Subject(s): Art; Revenge
Major character(s): Faith Nicholls, Art Dealer; Adrian Quinn, Convict, Lawyer

Time period(s): 2000s
Locale(s): Knoxville, Tennessee; Charlotte, North Carolina

Summary: After serving four years in prison for a crime he didn't commit, Adrian Quinn has one goal: find the woman who ruined his life and return the favor. Adrian tracks down Faith Nicholls, his ex-business partner's wife and the woman Adrian holds responsible for sending him to jail, intending to convince Faith to tell him where her ex-husband hid all the money he stole. After divorcing her two-timing husband, Faith, however, has blotted out any trace of her past marriage from her present life and she swears she knows nothing about the missing money. Adrian remains convinced that Faith is not only to the key to clearing up his past record, but also just might be the key to a new future.

Where it's reviewed:
Affaire de Coeur, February 2001, page 27
Booklist, January 1, 2001, page 927
Romantic Times, February 2001, page 86

Other books by the same author:
Impossible Dreams, 2000
Merely Magic, 2000
Volcano, 1999
Blue Clouds, 1998
Garden of Dreams, 1998

Other books you might like:
Suzanne Judson, *Harper's Moon*, 1991
Jayne Ann Krentz, *Sweet Fortune*, 1991
Carla Neggers, *Finding You*, 1996
Susan Elizabeth Phillips, *Heaven, Texas*, 1995
Mariah Stewart, *Priceless*, 1999

406

EVELYN RICHARDSON (Pseudonym of Cynthia Johnson)

Lord Harry's Daughter

(New York: Signet, 2001)

Story type: Regency
Subject(s): Napoleonic Wars; Romance; Military Life
Major character(s): Sophia Featherstonaugh, Artist, Noblewoman; Lord Mark Adair, Military Personnel (major), Nobleman (son of the Duke of Cranleigh)
Time period(s): 1810s
Locale(s): Spain; England

Summary: Raised on the campaign trail and used to fending off soldiers' casual flirtations, artist Sophia Featherstonaugh assumes Major Lord Mark Adair is just like all the others—only interested in her as a woman. However, Mark is different; and when he actually looks at her drawings—and truly appreciates them—Sophia begins to look at the major a bit differently, too. Excellent characterizations and descriptions of camp life during the Peninsular War add to this story in which two people must come to terms with their pasts and their inner feelings before they can find happiness together.

Where it's reviewed:
Romantic Times, January 2001, page 113

Other books by the same author:
My Lady Nightingale, 1999

The Gallant Guardian, 1998
My Wayward Lady, 1997
The Reluctant Heiress, 1996
Lady Alex's Gamble, 1995

Other books you might like:
Mary Balogh, *Beyond the Sunrise*, 1999
Marjorie Farrell, *Red, Red Rose*, 1999
Kate Moore, *The Mercenary Major*, 1991
Irene Saunders, *Lady Lucinde's Locket*, 1999
Jeanne Savery, *A Christmas Treasure*, 1994

407

CHRISTIE RIDGWAY

This Perfect Kiss

(New York: Avon, 2001)

Story type: Contemporary
Subject(s): Politics; Acting; Romance
Major character(s): Jilly Skye, Businesswoman (vintage clothing dealer); Rory Kincaid, Businessman (software millionaire), Political Figure (potential senatorial candidate)
Time period(s): 2000s
Locale(s): California

Summary: When Rory Kincaid hires Jilly Skye to help him sort through his late grandfather's collection of costumes and vintage clothing, he has no idea that she has an ulterior motive in taking the job. Jilly is determined to help reunite her friend with her young daughter—the four-year-old child who is Rory's aunt and now his ward and who lives in the mansion where Jilly will be working. Gorgeous, sexy Jilly and Rory get caught by a web cam in a compromising situation and to save his budding political career, they must pretend to be engaged—with funny, sexy, ultimately satisfying results.

Where it's reviewed:
Romantic Times, January 2001, page 80

Other books by the same author:
Beginning with Baby, 2000
Wish You Were Here, 2000
The Millionaire and the Pregnant Pauper, 1999
Big Bad Dad, 1998
Ready, Set. . .Baby, 1998

Other books you might like:
Susan Andersen, *All Shook Up*, 2001
Patti Berg, *Wife for a Day*, 1999
Millie Criswell, *The Trouble with Mary*, 2001
Jennifer Crusie, *Welcome to Temptation*, 2000
Mary Jane Meier, *Catch a Dream*, 2001
    funny

408

KAREN ROBARDS

Scandalous

(New York: Pocket Star, 2001)

Story type: Historical/Regency
Series: Banning Sisters. Book 1

Subject(s): Secrets; Suspense; Murder
Major character(s): Lady Gabriella Banning, Noblewoman, Impoverished; Marcus Banning, Nobleman (Earl of Wickham), Imposter
Time period(s): 1810s (1810)
Locale(s): London, England

Summary: When her abusive father dies, Gabriella Banning is left to care for her two younger sisters. Claire, the middle one, needs a Season in London, and Gabriella has permission from their older half brother, whom she hasn't seen in years, to use his funds. At about the same time, Gabriella receives word that her mysterious sibling has died on his tea plantation in Ceylon. Determined not to let her sisters down, Gabriella decides not to release the news of his death and goes on to London. However, a man claiming to be her brother meets her at the townhouse, and she greets him by shooting him with his own pistol. Danger and intrigue mark the twisting paths of a mysterious hero and the woman who loves him despite herself.

Where it's reviewed:
Affaire de Coeur, March/April 2001, page 24
Romantic Times, March 2001, page 37

Other books by the same author:
Ghost Moon, 2000
The Midnight Hour, 1999
The Senator's Wife, 1998
Heartbreaker, 1997
Walking After Midnight, 1995

Other books you might like:
Shirlee Busbee, *For Love Alone*, 2000
Candace Camp, *A Stolen Heart*, 2000
Suzanne Enoch, *Meet Me at Midnight*, 2000
Lynn Kerstan, *Lord Dragoner's Wife*, 1999
Lisa Kleypas, *Someone to Watch over Me*, 1999

409

KAREN ROBARDS
ANDREA KANE, Co-Author
LINDA ANDERSON, Co-Author
MARIAH STEWART, Co-Author

Wait Until Dark
(New York: Pocket, 2001)

Story type: Anthology; Romantic Suspense
Subject(s): Mystery; Murder; Stalking
Time period(s): 2000s
Locale(s): United States

Summary: This diverse quartet of contemporary romantic suspense novellas features good writing, interesting characters, and plots that, for the most part, work. Included are Karen Robards' sassy, drug-related Tennessee adventure, *Manna from Heaven*, Andrea Kane's gothically-tinged inheritance story, *Stone Cold*, and a pair of very different, but similarly chilling, stalking stories, *Once in a Blue Moon* by Linda Anderson and *'Til Death Do Us Part* by Mariah Stewart.

Other books by the same author:
Walking After Midnight, 1995

Other books you might like:
Linda Anderson, *When Night Falls*, 2000
Andrea Kane, *Run for Your Life*, 2000
Meagan McKinney, *Still of the Night*, 2001
Mariah Stewart, *Brown-Eyed Girl*, 2000

410

J.D. ROBB (Pseudonym of Nora Roberts)

Seduction in Death
(New York: Berkley, 2001)

Story type: Futuristic; Romantic Suspense
Series: Eve Dallas. Book 13
Subject(s): Murder; Serial Killer; Computers
Major character(s): Eve Dallas, Detective—Homicide (lieutenant); Roarke, Businessman, Spouse (Eve's husband)
Time period(s): 2050s (2059)
Locale(s): New York, New York

Summary: A killer, with seduction on his mind, causes Eve Dallas problems before the mystery is solved. Gritty, realistic, and surprisingly romantic, this book nicely continues Robb's popular futuristic crime series.

Other books by the same author:
Judgment in Death, 2000
Conspiracy in Death, 1999
Loyalty in Death, 1999
Holiday in Death, 1998
Vengeance in Death, 1997

Other books you might like:
Tami Hoag, *Guilty as Sin*, 1996
Linda Howard, *Shades of Twilight*, 1996
Iris Johansen, *Long After Midnight*, 1997
B.D. Joyce, *Deadly Love*, 2001

411

NORA ROBERTS

Considering Kate
(New York: Silhouette, 2001)

Story type: Contemporary
Series: Stanislaski. Book 6
Subject(s): Single Parent Families; Family Relations; Dancing
Major character(s): Kate Stanislaski Kimball, Dancer (ballerina), Teacher (dance); Brody O'Connell, Contractor, Single Parent
Time period(s): 2000s
Locale(s): Shepherdstown, West Virginia

Summary: Kate Stanislaski Kimball, world famous ballerina, leaves the glamorous stages of Paris and New York to return to her small hometown in West Virginia to open a school of dance. Brody O'Connell's wife has died of cancer, leaving him with a small son. When he's hired to renovate the historic building which is slated to become Kate's school, the last thing he expects to do is fall in love with her. An interesting addition to the Stanislaski series.

Where it's reviewed:
Romantic Times, February 2001, page 107

Other books by the same author:
Heart of the Sea, 2000 (Irish Trilogy. Book 3)
Night Tales, 2000
The Stanislaski Sisters: Natasha and Rachel, 2000
The Stanislaski Brothers: Mikhail and Alex, 2000
Tears of the Moon, 2000 (Irish Trilogy. Book 2)

Other books you might like:
Kristin Hannah, *Angel Falls*, 2000
Neesa Hart, *You Made Me Love You*, 2000
Christie Ridgway, *Wish You Were Here*, 2000
LaVyrle Spencer, *Small Town Girl*, 1997
Sherryl Woods, *Angel Mine*, 2000

412

NORA ROBERTS

The Villa

(New York: Putnam, 2001)

Story type: Contemporary; Romantic Suspense
Subject(s): Family Relations; Greed; Business Enterprises
Major character(s): Sophia Giambelli, Public Relations (for family winery), Heiress; Tyler MacMillan, Vintner (vineyard manager), Heir
Time period(s): 2000s
Locale(s): Napa Valley, California; Italy

Summary: Once again, Tereza Giambelli, the manipulative, autocratic family matriarch and head of the Giambelli wine empire, revamps her will, this time forcing her granddaughter and step-grandson to agree to work together for a year in order to inherit their parts of the business. Although Sophia and Tyler have no choice but to agree, the sparks are soon flying as the independent pair fight their attraction for each other and deal with a menacing situation that is about to prove deadly. Jealousy, greed, and vengeance drive the plot of this engrossing story that is filled with fascinating characters of all types and that should appeal to fans of family sagas and women's fiction.

Where it's reviewed:
Library Journal, February 15, 2001, page 1555
Romantic Times, March 2001, page 92

Other books by the same author:
Carolina Moon, 2000
Heart of the Sea, 2000 (Irish Trilogy. Book 3)
Night Shield, 2000
Tears of the Moon, 2000 (Irish Trilogy. Book 2)
Jewels of the Sun, 1999 (Irish Trilogy. Book 1)

Other books you might like:
Patricia Potter, *The Perfect Family*, 2001
Mary Jo Putney, *The Burning Point*, 2000
Emilie Richards, *Iron Lace*, 1996
Katherine Stone, *Bed of Roses*, 1998
Anne Stuart, *The Widow*, 1998

413

EVELYN ROGERS

Devil in the Dark

(New York: LoveSpell, 2001)

Story type: Gothic; Historical/Victorian
Subject(s): Brothers; Secrets
Major character(s): Lucinda Fairfax, Heiress; Gideon Blackthorne, Nobleman (Duke of Ravenswood)
Time period(s): 1860s (1860)
Locale(s): Yorkshire, England

Summary: Upon arriving in Yorkshire to claim an estate left to her by her father, American Lucinda Fairfax is nearly run over by a mysterious horseman, Gideon Blackthorne, known to the locals as the "Devil Duke." Despite warnings to stay away from Gideon, who owns the neighboring estate, Lucinda finds her thoughts and dreams constantly haunted by the enigmatic stranger who gradually lures her into a world of danger and deception.

Where it's reviewed:
Romantic Times, January 2001, page 45

Other books by the same author:
Longhorn, 2000
Wicked, 2000
Golden Man, 1999
Second Opinion, 1999
Crown of Glory, 1998

Other books you might like:
Rebecca Brandewyne, *Upon a Moon Dark Moor*, 1996
Patricia Gaffney, *Lily*, 1996
Mandalyn Kaye, *Priceless*, 1998
Constance Laux, *Devil's Diamond*, 1998
Margaret Moore, *The Dark Duke*, 1997

414

ROSEMARY ROGERS

Savage Desire

(Don Mills, Ontario: Mira, 2000)

Story type: Historical/Victorian
Subject(s): Reunions; Marriage; Children
Major character(s): Virginia "Ginny" Brandon Morgan, Adventurer, Spouse; Steve Morgan, Diplomat (ambassador), Wealthy
Time period(s): 1870s (1876)
Locale(s): Mexico; London, England; New Orleans, Louisiana

Summary: Determined to make their marriage work and become a family again, Ginny arrives in London to reconcile with her estranged husband, Steve, and give things a second chance. While the sexual tension still sizzles between them and their will to set things to rights is strong, circumstances send them across the world in an adventure that will prove both exciting and potentially deadly to their lives and their relationship. Although gentler than the earlier Ginny and Steve books, this is a romantic adventure that will appeal to Rogers' many fans. Readers who enjoyed the historicals of the 1970s should take note.

Romance

Where it's reviewed:
Library Journal, February 15, 2001, page 153
Romantic Times, December 2000, page 38

Other books by the same author:
In Your Arms, 1999
All I Desire, 1998
Midnight Lady, 1997
A Dangerous Man, 1996
Sweet Savage Love, 1974

Other books you might like:
Shirlee Busbee, *At Long Last*, 1999
Susan Johnson, *Tempting*, 2001
Nicole Jordan, *The Passion*, 2000
Bertrice Small, *Intrigued*, 2001
Kathleen Woodiwiss, *The Elusive Flame*, 1999

415

KRISTINE ROLOFSON
HEATHER MACALLISTER, Co-Author
JACQUELINE DIAMOND, Co-Author

Tyler Brides
(Toronto: Harlequin, 2001)

Story type: Anthology; Holiday Themes
Series: Tyler
Subject(s): Anthology; Small Town Life; Holidays
Time period(s): 2000s (2001)
Locale(s): Tyler, Wisconsin

Summary: This addition to the Tyler series takes place in a newly opened bed-and-breakfast and readers will enjoy the return of old, favorite characters. In ''Meant for Each Other'' by Kristine Rolofson, a woman's friend and her mother book her into the same room as her former boyfriend. A librarian locked in a dark basement with ''The World's Sexiest Man'' learns he's more than just a pretty face in Heather MacAllister's ''Behind Closed Doors''. Jacqueline Diamond's ''The Bride's Surprise'' presents the story of a bride who must reconsider her relationship with her best friend, a bridesmaid, after finding her in bed with her groom just two hours before the wedding ceremony.

Other books by the same author:
Brides, Boots, and Booties, 2001

Other books you might like:
Jacqueline Diamond, *Designer Genes*, 2000
Jacqueline Diamond, *Excuse Me? Whose Baby?*, 2001
Heather MacAllister, *The Motherhood Campaign*, 2000
Heather MacAllister, *Personal Relations*, 2001
Kristine Rolofson, *Brides, Boots, and Booties*, 2001

416

LAUREN ROYAL

Amber
(New York: Signet, 2001)

Story type: Historical/Seventeenth Century
Series: Chase Family Jewel Trilogy. Book 3
Subject(s): Marriage; Brothers and Sisters

Major character(s): Lady Kendra Chase, Noblewoman; Patrick ''Trick'' Caldwell, Highwayman, Nobleman (Duke of Amberley)
Time period(s): 17th century (1668)

Summary: Lady Kendra Chase is tired of her brother's continuous attempts to introduce her to wealthy noblemen who, in her opinion, are totally unsuitable for marriage. She is stunned when she finds herself in a compromising situation with the handsome highwayman who had held up their coach—and robbed only a Puritan—the day before and her brothers insist that she marry him! Of course, that is before she finds out he is really the Duke of Amberley and only a highwayman part-time. Politics, adventure, and good characterizations are part of this Restoration period romance that follows *Amethyst* and *Emerald*.

Other books by the same author:
Amethyst, 2000 (Chase Family Jewel Trilogy. Book 1)
Emerald, 2000 (Chase Family Jewel Trilogy. Book 2)

Other books you might like:
Jo Beverley, *My Lady Notorious*, 1993
Rosemary Edghill, *Met by Moonlight*, 1998
    similar setting/time-travel
Jane Feather, *The Least Likely Bride*, 2000
    similar setting/lively
Ruth Langan, *Deception*, 1993
    similar period
Laura Parker, *The Gamble*, 1998

417

NAN RYAN

The Seduction of Ellen
(Don Mills, Ontario: Mira, 2001)

Story type: Historical/Victorian America; Paranormal
Subject(s): Legends; Secrets; Native Americans
Major character(s): Ellen Cornelius, Care Giver, Single Parent; Steve Corey, Veteran (Wounded Knee Massacre)
Time period(s): 1890s (1899)
Locale(s): London, England; Lost City of the Anasazi, West

Summary: Ellen Cornelius' Aunt Alexandra, now in her eighties, wants to be young again and stay that way forever. Alexandra hires the mysterious carnival man, Mr. Corey, to take her to the Fountain of Youth. As Alexandra's constant companion, Ellen is forced to go, too, despite her suspicions about their guide. A hidden city, a mysterious stranger, and characters full of secrets make this sensual novel an exciting one.

Where it's reviewed:
Affaire de Coeur, March/April 2001, page 39
Romantic Times, April 2001, page 37

Other books by the same author:
The Countess Misbehaves, 2000
Cloudcastle, 1999
Wanting You, 1999
The Princess Goes West, 1998
Outlaw's Kiss, 1997

Other books you might like:
Jo Ann Ferguson, *Her Only Hero*, 2001
Barbara Freethy, *The Sweetest Thing*, 1999
Jill Marie Landis, *The Orchid Hunter*, 2000
Constance O'Day-Flannery, *Anywhere You Are*, 1999
Christina Skye, *2000 Kisses*, 1999

418

LYNSAY SANDS

Lady Pirate

(New York: Leisure, 2001)

Story type: Humor; Historical/Georgian
Subject(s): Humor; Pirates; Inheritance
Major character(s): Lady Valoree Ainsley, Pirate (captain of pirate ship), Heiress; Daniel Thurborne, Nobleman, Heir
Time period(s): 18th century (late)
Locale(s): London, England; *Valor*, At Sea

Summary: When her brother dies, Valoree Ainsley, who has spent her youth as a "cabin boy," takes command of their pirate ship. Finding out that she needs to be married—and pregnant—to inherit Ainsley Castle, she resigns herself to her fate, vowing to wed a weak man, one who won't hamper her freedom. At the same time, Lord Daniel Thurborne discovers that he, too, has to marry to receive his inheritance. He sets out to convince Valoree that a marriage of convenience would benefit them both, never realizing that the object of his affection would just as soon keelhaul him as kiss him. This tale of a Pygmalion attempt that never quite takes is hysterically funny and a treat to read cover-to-cover.

Where it's reviewed:
Romantic Times, January 2001, page 40

Other books by the same author:
Sweet Revenge, 2000
The Switch, 1999
The Key, 1998
The Deed, 1997

Other books you might like:
Julie Garwood, *Guardian Angel*, 1990
Kinley MacGregor, *A Pirate of Her Own*, 1999
Maggie Osborne, *Lady Reluctant*, 1990
Susan Wiggs, *The Charm School*, 1999
Patricia Wynn, *Capturing Annie*, 2000

419

DEBRA SATINWOOD (Pseudonym of Debra Hamilton)

An English Rose

(New York: Zebra, 2000)

Story type: Historical/Victorian
Subject(s): Blackmail; Courtship; Scandal
Major character(s): Hannah Whitechurch, Gentlewoman, Artist; Beau St. James, Lawyer, Single Parent
Time period(s): 18th century
Locale(s): England (Solitude Cottage)

Summary: Driven by threats of social ruin for his young daughter, attorney Beau St. James seeks to buy artist Hannah

Whitechurch's home and surrounding lands for his blackmailing client. Hannah isn't about to sell, creating an impasse that drives the rest of the conflict in this lively story. An evil villain, charming sisters, and appealing protagonists are an added plus.

Other books by the same author:
Arabesque, 1994
Love's Secret Fire, 1993
The Trysting Moon, 1993
Angel Fire, 1992

Other books you might like:
Jane Goodger, *Dancing with Sin*, 1998
Betina Krahn, *The Last Bachelor*, 1994
Amanda Quick, *Mistress*, 1994
Julia Quinn, *The Viscount Who Loved Me*, 2000

420

VERONICA SATTLER

A True Prince

(New York: Kensington, 2000)

Story type: Historical/Regency; Historical
Subject(s): Women's Rights; Napoleonic Wars; Rebellions, Revolts, and Uprisings
Major character(s): Lady Marisa Lancet, Military Personnel (captain of the Royal Guards), Bodyguard, Royalty (crown prince)
Time period(s): 1810s (1812)
Locale(s): London, England; Baravia, Fictional Country

Summary: Crown Prince Deverell has been playing a shallow fop to gather information. He's fooled everyone, including his father, the king. The king becomes very ill, and, nervous because his son is so ill-prepared to assume the crown, calls him home to be a soldier. The king's worried enough to assign Deverell a bodyguard—Lady Marisa Lancet, Captain of the Royal Guard. A Scarlet Pimpernel kind of guy meets a Joan of Arc kind of woman in this story about two people who are much stronger than the rest of the world gives them credit for being.

Where it's reviewed:
Romantic Times, December 2000, page 35

Other books by the same author:
Once a Princess, 2001
Wild Honey, 1997
Jesse's Lady, 1996 (reissue)
Heaven to Touch, 1994
The Bargain, 1993

Other books you might like:
Shirlee Busbee, *For Love Alone*, 2000
Lynn Kerstan, *Lady Dragoner's Wife*, 1999
Lisa Kleypas, *Someone to Watch over Me*, 1999
Kat Martin, *Perfect Sin*, 2000
Peggy Waide, *Mightier than the Sword*, 2001

421

AMANDA SCOTT (Pseudonym of Lynne Scott-Drennan)

Border Storm

(New York: Zebra, 2001)

Story type: Historical/Elizabethan
Series: Border. Book 2
Subject(s): Hostages; Massacres; Murder
Major character(s): Laurie Halliot, Prisoner; Sir Hugh Graham, Wealthy, Nobleman
Time period(s): 16th century (1590s)
Locale(s): Scotland (English/Scottish border)

Summary: When Laura Halliot's sister disappears after being accused of murdering an English official, Laurie agrees to take her place as prisoner of Sir Hugh Graham of Brackengill. Concerned for Laurie's reputation, her father insists that she and Hugh be hand-fasted before she's placed into his custody. Soon, feelings develop between Hugh and Laurie that have nothing to do with jailers and their prisoners. Action and intrigue fill the pages of this tumultuous romance between two enemies torn between loyalty to each other and loyalty to their warring countries.

Where it's reviewed:
Romantic Times, January 2001, page 37

Other books by the same author:
Border Fire, 2000
Dangerous Lady, 1999
Highland Spirits, 1999
Highland Secrets, 1998
Highland Treasure, 1998

Other books you might like:
Debra Lee Brown, *The Virgin Spring*, 2000
Colleen Faulkner, *Highland Bride*, 2000
Julie Garwood, *Ransom*, 1999
Kathleen Givens, *The Wild Rose of Kilgannon*, 1999
Teresa Medeiros, *The Bride and the Beast*, 2000

422

COLLEEN SHANNON (Pseudonym of Colleen Jeske)

The Wolf of Haskell Hall

(New York: LoveSpell, 2001)

Story type: Gothic; Historical/Victorian
Subject(s): Animals/Wolves; Werewolves
Major character(s): Delilah Haskell Trent, Heiress; Ian Griffith, Steward (estate manager), Werewolf
Time period(s): 1870s (1878)
Locale(s): Haskell, England

Summary: Haskell women and Griffith men have been romantically linked for centuries, but a curse placed upon the Haskell family by a gypsy a century ago has led to the last five Haskell heiresses being brutally killed by wolves. When American Delilah Haskell Trent arrives to take control of Haskell Hall, she is captivated by the wild beauty of the moors and fascinated with her mysterious estate manager, Ian Griffith. Despite rumors of werewolves that stalk the moors at night, Delilah and Ian continue to find ways to meet until

Delilah realizes the man she now desires may be the same man fated to kill her.

Where it's reviewed:
Romantic Times, January 2001, page 45

Other books by the same author:
Heaven's Hero, 2000
Heaven's Rogue, 1999
Steadfast, 1998
The Gentle Beast, 1996
Golden Fires, 1993

Other books you might like:
Catherine Coulter, *The Countess*, 1999
Susan Krinard, *Touch of the Wolf*, 1999
Meagan McKinney, *Gentle from the Night*, 1997
Margaret Moore, *The Rogue's Return*, 1997
Patricia Rice, *Merely Magic*, 2000

423

ISABEL SHARPE (Pseudonym of Muna Shehadi Sill)

Follow That Baby!

(Toronto: Harlequin, 2001)

Story type: Humor; Contemporary
Subject(s): Babies; Humor; Child Custody
Major character(s): Melanie Brooks, Teacher; Joe Jantzen, Detective—Private
Time period(s): 2000s
Locale(s): Birchfield, Wisconsin

Summary: After Melanie Brooks' best friend tells her that her husband is abusive, she hides their toddler in Melanie's house. Private detective Joe Jantzen is soon on the tot's trail, so Melanie tries to trick him by dressing the baby boy as a girl. Sparks fly between Melanie and Joe as she's forced to deceive him in this romantic comedy.

Where it's reviewed:
Romantic Times, January 2001, page 101

Other books by the same author:
Beauty and the Bet, 2000
The Way We Weren't, 2000
Tryst of Fate, 2000

Other books you might like:
Elizabeth Bevarly, *First Comes Love*, 2000
Jacqueline Diamond, *Excuse Me? Whose Baby?*, 2001
Liz Ireland, *The Sheriff and the E-Mail Bride*, 2000
Kasey Michaels, *Raffling Ryan*, 2000
Tina Wainscott, *The Wrong Mr. Right*, 2000

424

ALLIE SHAW (Pseudonym of Alyse Pleiter)

The Impossible Texan

(New York: Ivy, 2001)

Story type: Historical/Victorian America; Historical/American West
Subject(s): Campaigns, Political; Intolerance; Journalism

Major character(s): Marlena Maxwell, Young Woman; Tyler Hamilton III, Public Relations (campaign manager)
Time period(s): 1880s (1888)
Locale(s): Austin, Texas

Summary: When Marlena Maxwell's Texas senator father loses his campaign manager, she thinks she's done a pretty good job taking over for him. Much to everyone's surprise, he imports Bostonian Tyler Hamilton III to run the campaign. Wounds from the Civil War are still raw though, and this northerner finds little welcome in Texas. Sizzling tension and a terrific plot are only two of the things that make this an incredible debut novel.

Where it's reviewed:
Romantic Times, May 2001, page 38

Other books you might like:
Geralyn Dawson, *The Bad Luck Wedding Night*, 2001
Lorraine Heath, *Always to Remember*, 1996
Betina Krahn, *Sweet Talking Man*, 2000
Sylvia McDaniel, *The Outlaw Takes a Wife*, 2001
Maggie Osborne, *A Stranger's Wife*, 1999

425

MAGGIE SHAYNE (Pseudonym of Margaret Benson)

Destiny
(New York: Jove, 2001)

Story type: Reincarnation; Fantasy
Series: Witch Trilogy. Book 3
Subject(s): Witches and Witchcraft; Good and Evil; Immortality
Major character(s): Nidaba, Witch, Immortal; Nathan "Eannatum" King, Witch, Immortal
Time period(s): 2000s
Locale(s): Sumer, Ancient Civilization (in the Middle East); New York, New York

Summary: Antiquities expert Nathan King (Eannatum) recognizes the newspaper picture of an unidentified accident victim as Nidaba, the woman he loved 4000 years ago in the Kingdom of Sumer, long before either of them realized that they were immortal. Nathan realizes the Dark Ones, who seek to kill them, are close by—and so he kidnaps Nidaba in order to keep her safe and help her heal. Flashbacks to their earlier life explain the complexities of the current situation. Third in Shayne's trilogy of the struggle between the Light and Dark Immortal High Witches.

Where it's reviewed:
Library Journal, February 15, 2001, page 155
Romantic Times, February 2001, page 86

Other books by the same author:
The Brands Who Came for Christmas, 2000
Infinity, 1999 (Witch Trilogy. Book 2)
Eternity, 1998 (Witch Trilogy. Book 1)
Forever Enchanted, 1997
Fairytale, 1996

Other books you might like:
Marion Zimmer Bradley, *Witchlight*, 1996
Susan Carroll, *The Bride Finder*, 1998

Susan Carroll, *Midnight Bride*, 2001
Sandra Heath, *Halloween Magic*, 1996
  Regency good and evil
Jill Jones, *Circle of the Lily*, 1998
  good and evil issues

426

LYNDA SIMMONS

Just the Way You Aren't
(New York: Zebra, 2001)

Story type: Contemporary
Subject(s): Artists and Art; Family
Major character(s): Sunny Anderson, Artist; Michael Wolfe, Businessman (project manager for hotel)
Time period(s): 2000s
Locale(s): New York, New York

Summary: After crashing the Concord Hotel's grand masquerade gala in order to catch the unveiling of the mural she painted, artist Sunny Anderson unexpectedly bumps into the hotel's project manager, Michael Wolfe. Since Sunny is in costume and does not want anyone to know she is at the gala uninvited, she pretends to be another woman. Michael is intrigued by the enigmatic beauty flirting with him and he pursues her for a romantic, no-strings attached fling; but he gradually loses interest in his mystery woman once he discovers how much fun being around Sunny can be.

Other books by the same author:
Charmed and Dangerous, 2000
This Magic Moment, 2000
Perfect Fit, 1999

Other books you might like:
Stephanie Bond, *It Takes a Rebel*, 2000
Kristin Gabriel, *Send Me No Flowers*, 1999
Maddie James, *Crazy for You*, 1999
Leslie Kelly, *Suite Seduction*, 2000
Lisa Plumley, *Her Best Man*, 2000

427

SUZANNE SIMMONS (Pseudonym of Suzanne Simmons Guntrum)

Lip Service
(New York: St. Martin's Press, 2001)

Story type: Romantic Suspense; Contemporary
Subject(s): Inheritance; Suspense; Secrets
Major character(s): Schuyler Grant, Heiress; Trace Ballinger, Lawyer
Time period(s): 2000s
Locale(s): Rhinebeck, New York

Summary: Trace Ballinger has been "Crazy" Cora Grant's attorney for years, and now he's the executor of her estate. Cora's niece Schuyler, heiress to the fortune, finds herself a target for the people who covet her inheritance. This romantic suspense has gothic elements, as well as a sensual romance.

Where it's reviewed:
Publishers Weekly, February 19, 2001, page 308

Romantic Times, February 2001, page 89

Other books by the same author:
Lady's Man, 1999
No Ordinary Man, 1998
You and No Other, 1998
Paradise Man, 1997
Bed of Roses, 1995

Other books you might like:
Susan Andersen, *All Shook Up*, 2000
Linda Anderson, *The Secrets of Sadie Maynard*, 1999
Jill Jones, *Remember Your Lies*, 2001
Jayne Ann Krentz, *Lost and Found*, 2001
Carla Neggers, *The Carriage House*, 2001

428

SUSAN SIZEMORE

The Price of Passion

(New York: Avon, 2001)

Story type: Historical/Victorian; Historical/Exotic
Subject(s): Adventure and Adventurers; Egyptian Antiquities; Revenge
Major character(s): Cleopatra "Cleo" Fraser, Archaeologist (Egyptologist); Azrael "Angel" David Evans, Archaeologist (Egyptologist)
Time period(s): 1860s (1868); 1870s (1878)
Locale(s): Nile Delta, Egypt; Muirford, Scotland

Summary: Cleo Fraser is back in Scotland to help with the establishment of a museum that will display some of her archaeologist father's latest finds. Raised in the Middle East, Cleo is an Egyptologist in her own right, and she must deal not only with Victorian society's rigid expectations about the role of women, but her attraction to the archaeologist, who stole her virginity when she was a teenager, and is now in Scotland on a mission of his own. Danger, passion, and intrigue are part of this sensual, fast-paced adventure.

Where it's reviewed:
Library Journal, February 15, 2001, page 154
Romantic Times, January 2001, page 41

Other books by the same author:
On a Long Ago Night, 2000
His Last Best Hope, 1999
The Price of Innocence, 1999
One of These Nights, 1997
My First Duchess, 1993

Other books you might like:
Connie Brockway, *As You Desire*, 1997
Danelle Harmon, *The Wicked One*, 2001
  earlier time period
Laura Kinsale, *The Dream Hunter*, 1994
Stephanie Laurens, *All about Love*, 2001
Amanda Quick, *With This Ring*, 1998

429

BERTRICE SMALL

Intrigued

(New York: Kensington, 2001)

Story type: Historical/Seventeenth Century
Subject(s): Marriage; Politics
Major character(s): Autumn Leslie, Noblewoman; Gabriel Bainbridge, Nobleman (Duke of Garwood)
Time period(s): 17th century (1650-1663)
Locale(s): France; England

Summary: In a fashion that her great-grandmother, Skye O'Malley, would have admired, Autumn Leslie lives life on her own terms as she works her way through one husband and two kings, ultimately ending up in the arms of the man she is destined to marry—a man she first meets at gun point. Fast-paced, sensual, and occasionally outrageous.

Where it's reviewed:
Library Journal, February 15, 2001, page 154
Romantic Times, February 2001, page 37

Other books by the same author:
A Memory of Love, 2000
Bedazzled, 2000
Fascinated, 2000 (anthology; Susan Johnson, Thea Devine, and Robin Schone, co-authors)
Besieged, 2000
Skye O'Malley, 1980

Other books you might like:
Jane Feather, *The Diamond Slipper*, 1997
Virginia Henley, *The Pirate and the Pagan*, 1990
Susan Johnson, *Forbidden*, 1991
Susan Johnson, *Tempting*, 2001
Nicole Jordan, *The Passion*, 2000

430

DEBORAH SMITH

On Bear Mountain

(New York: Little, Brown, 2001)

Story type: Contemporary
Subject(s): Animals/Bears; Family; Sculptors and Sculpting
Major character(s): Ursula Powell, Store Owner (bookstore); Quentin Riconni, Businessman (architectural salvage company)
Time period(s): 1960s; 2000s
Locale(s): Tiberville, Georgia; Atlanta, Georgia; New York, New York

Summary: After discovering a long lost abstract sculpture by his father was not destroyed but instead actually sits on a farm owned by Ursula Powell, Quentin Riconni travels to Bear Creek hoping he can convince Ursula to sell the piece back to him. Quentin discovers Ursula will not part with the artwork for love or money since it has played such a powerful role in the history of her family. Interestingly enough, the same piece of sculpture that threatens to keep Ursula and Quentin apart may be the one thing that finally brings them together. Beautifully written.

Where it's reviewed:
Booklist, September 1, 2000, page 8
Library Journal, November 1, 2000, page 138
Publishers Weekly, November 27, 2000, page 50
Romantic Times, February 2001, page 90

Other books by the same author:
When Venus Fell, 1998
A Place to Call Home, 1997
Silk and Stone, 1994
Blue Willow, 1993
Miracle, 1991

Other books you might like:
Kristin Hannah, *Summer Island*, 2001
Neesa Hart, *You Made Me Love You*, 2000
Curtiss Ann Matlock, *Lost Highways*, 1999
Patricia Rice, *Impossible Dreams*, 2000
Mariah Stewart, *Devlin's Light*, 1997

431

HAYWOOD SMITH

Border Lord

(New York: St. Martin's Paperbacks, 2001)

Story type: Historical/Elizabethan
Subject(s): Hostages; Fathers; Healing
Major character(s): Catherine Armstrong, Crime Victim (hostage); Duncan ''Black Bastard'' Maxwell, Outlaw
Time period(s): 16th century (1590-1591)
Locale(s): Solway Firth, Scotland; Annanlea, Scotland

Summary: The last thing Catherine Armstrong remembers before her ship sinks is the feel of someone's hands around her neck, trying to strangle her. She washes ashore, ending up the hostage of the infamous outlaw the Black Bastard. Before long, Catherine learns this ruthless man is actually Duncan Maxwell, a devoted father trying to raise seven motherless children. As Catherine begins to develop feelings for Duncan, he distances himself—after all, everyone he marries dies. A hostage claims the heart of her captor in this extraordinary book that captures the heart of its reader.

Where it's reviewed:
Affaire de Coeur, March/April 2001, page 30
Romantic Times, April 2001, page 43

Other books by the same author:
Highland Princess, 2000
Dangerous Gifts, 1999
Damask Rose, 1998
Secrets in Satin, 1997
Shadows in Velvet, 1996

Other books you might like:
Shana Abe, *Intimate Enemies*, 2000
Judith E. French, *The Irish Rogue*, 2000
Kathleen Givens, *The Wild Rose of Kilgannon*, 1999
Connie Mason, *A Taste of Sin*, 2000
Amanda Scott, *Border Storm*, 2001

432

SHERIDON SMYTHE (Pseudonym of Sherrie Eddington and Donna Smith)

Hero for Hire

(New York: Jove, 2001)

Story type: Historical/Victorian America
Subject(s): Friendship; Seduction
Major character(s): Mackenzy ''Mac'' Cord, Bounty Hunter; Savannah Carrington, Heiress
Time period(s): 1890s (1892)
Locale(s): Angel Creek, South Carolina; Jamestown, New York; Paradise, Virginia

Summary: When bounty hunter Mackenzy Cord finally locates Savannah Carrington, Mackenzy's childhood friend and the missing daughter of a wealthy banker, she is being held in jail on charges of bank robbery. By pretending to be her husband, Mackenzy manages to get Savannah released, but Savannah informs him she is not going home until she recovers the money stolen from her by the real bank robber. Now all Mackenzy has to do is help Savannah find her money and convince her to stop considering him as her friend and start thinking of him as a potential husband.

Where it's reviewed:
Affaire de Coeur, May/June 2001, page 16
Romantic Times, May 2001, page 42

Other books by the same author:
A Perfect Fit, 2000
Mr. Hyde's Assets, 2000
Cupid's Workshop, 1999
Love Lesson, 1999
Where the Heart Is, 1999

Other books you might like:
Judith E. French, *Morgan's Woman*, 1997
Stef Ann Holm, *Harmony*, 1997
Maureen McKade, *A Dime Novel Hero*, 1998
Teresa Medeiros, *Nobody's Darling*, 1998
Debra Mullins, *Donovan's Bed*, 2000

433

CHERYL ST. JOHN (Pseudonym of Cheryl Ludwigs)

Sweet Annie

(Toronto: Harlequin, 2001)

Story type: Historical/American West
Subject(s): American West; Family Relations; Healing
Major character(s): Annie Sweetwater, Handicapped (wheelchair bound); Luke Carpenter, Businessman (livery owner)
Time period(s): 1870s (1878); 1880s (1888)
Locale(s): Copper Creek, Colorado

Summary: Annie Sweetwater, who has a leg and hip deformity, is imprisoned in her wheelchair by loving, overprotective parents. Luke Carpenter, who took a beating from her brother when he let Annie ride his horse ten years earlier, is still in love with her and determined to help her live a normal life. Now she has to make a dreadful choice—her family or

Romance

the man she loves. An emotion-filled story of both the healing and the crippling power of love.

Where it's reviewed:
Romantic Times, February 2001, page 46

Other books by the same author:
For This Week I Thee Wed, 1999
The Doctors Wife, 1999
Joe's Wife, 1999
The Mistaken Widow, 1998
A Husband by Any Other Name, 1996

Other books you might like:
Lorraine Heath, *Never Love a Hero*, 2000
Linda Jones, *The Seduction of Roxanne*, 2000
Mary McBride, *The Marriage Knot*, 1999
Stephanie Mittman, *The Courtship*, 1998
Laura Renken, *My Lord Pirate*, 2001

434

CYNTHIA STERLING (Pseudonym of Cynthia Myers)

A Husband by Law
(New York: Jove, 2001)

Story type: Historical/American West
Subject(s): Military Life; Marriage
Major character(s): Michael Trent, Military Personnel (U.S. Army First Dragons); Ellen Winthrop, Bride
Time period(s): 1840s (1846)
Locale(s): Texas; New Mexico; California

Summary: In order to travel from Texas to California with the United States Army, Englishwoman Ellen Winthrop must find a soldier to marry her. To avoid court martial proceedings, Lieutenant Michael Trent is encouraged by his commanding officer to accept Ellen's proposal. Both Michael and Ellen agree to a marriage in name only, but by the time their trip is over, they realize their feelings for one another are very real.

Where it's reviewed:
Affaire de Coeur, March/April 2001, page 19
Romantic Times, March 2001, page 44

Other books by the same author:
Runaway Ranch, 2001
Great Caesar's Ghost, 2000
Nobility Ranch, 2000
Last Chance Ranch, 2000
Willing Spirit, 1999

Other books you might like:
Emily Carmichael, *Jezebel's Sister*, 2001
Lorraine Heath, *Never Marry a Cowboy*, 2001
Debra Mullins, *The Lawman's Surrender*, 2001
Maggie Osborne, *The Promise of Jenny Jones*, 1997
Cheryl Anne Porter, *Captive Angel*, 1999

435

AMANDA STEVENS (Pseudonym of Marilyn Medlock Amann)

Nighttime Guardian
(New York: Harlequin, 2001)

Story type: Romantic Suspense
Subject(s): Pearls; Rivers
Major character(s): Nathan Dallas, Journalist; Shelby August, Accountant
Time period(s): 2000s
Locale(s): Arcadia, Arkansas

Summary: When she is a young girl Shelby August swears that she saw the Pearl River Monster, but her claim is dismissed as a hoax by everyone in Arcadia except for her friend, Nathan Dallas. Twenty years later, Shelby returns to Arcadia to take care of her grandmother's pearl shop and strange things start happening. Mysterious noises in the night, wet footprints, and strange ripples in the river seem to indicate Shelby's monster is back and Shelby turns to Nathan, the only person who ever believed her, for help.

Where it's reviewed:
Romantic Times, March 2001, page 102

Other books by the same author:
Forbidden Lover, 2000
The Bodyguard's Assignment, 2000
Secret Admirer, 2000
The Littlest Witness, 2000
Lover, Stranger, 1999

Other books you might like:
Lisa Bingham, *When Night Draws Near*, 1993
Carla Cassidy, *Swamp Secrets*, 1993
Helen R. Myers, *Waiting for Willa*, 1995
Patricia Simpson, *The Haunting of Brier Rose*, 1993
Anne Stuart, *A Dark and Stormy Night*, 1997

436

SALLY STEWARD

Private Vows
(Toronto: Harlequin, 2001)

Story type: Romantic Suspense
Subject(s): Memory Loss
Major character(s): Mary Jackson, Teacher; Cole Grayson, Detective—Private
Time period(s): 2000s
Locale(s): Dallas, Texas

Summary: On the way home from a job, private investigator Cole Grayson nearly runs down a woman wearing a white wedding gown stained with blood. When Cole stops to help, he discovers the woman has no idea who she is or how she got blood on her dress; and when asked her name, she comes up with Mary Jackson. For some reason, Mary seems afraid of both the police and a man from her past, so she turns to the only person she knows and trusts for help: Cole.

Where it's reviewed:
Romantic Times, February 2001, page 103

Other books by the same author:
Ghost of Summer, 1999
Secrets Rising, 1998
Lovers and Liars, 1997
Undercover Lover, 1996

Other books you might like:
B.J. Daniels, *Mystery Bride*, 1988
Linda Howard, *White Lies*, 1988
Margaret Watson, *The Fugitive Bride*, 1999
Joanna Wayne, *The Outsider's Redemption*, 2000
Gayle Wilson, *The Bride's Protector*, 1999

437

LYN STONE

The Highland Wife
(Toronto: Harlequin, 2001)

Story type: Historical/Medieval
Subject(s): Marriage; Interpersonal Relations; Deafness
Major character(s): Mairi MacInness, Noblewoman (Highlander); Robert ''Rob'' MacBain, Nobleman (baron from the lowlands), Handicapped (deaf)
Time period(s): 14th century (1335)
Locale(s): Scotland

Summary: Rejected by his betrothed, deaf lowland nobleman Baron Rob MacBain heads for the Highlands and a hastily arranged marriage with Mairi MacInness, a woman he has never met, only to find himself caught up in a deadly attack on Mairi's home, Craigmuir. At her dying father's command, Mairi and Rob are quickly wed and, although Mairi strenuously objects to leaving her home and her people to her greedy cousin, Ranald, they head for Rob's home. Rob's sensitivity about his deafness and the fact that Mairi did not know about it make for a rocky beginning to their relationship. That Ranald wants Mairi for himself and Rob's original fiancee reappears on the scene just add to the problems. Lots of action and well-developed characters.

Where it's reviewed:
Affaire de Coeur, March/April 2001, page 18
Romantic Times, March 2001, page 45

Other books by the same author:
Live-In Lover, 2001
My Lady's Choice, 2000
Beauty and the Badge, 1999
Bride of Trouville, 1999
The Arrangement, 1997

Other books you might like:
Shana Abe, *The Truelove Bride*, 1999
  supernatural elements
Julie Garwood, *The Bride*, 1989
Julie Garwood, *Saving Grace*, 1993
Samantha James, *A Promise Given*, 1998
Susan King, *The Swan Maiden*, 2001

438

KATHERINE SUTCLIFFE

Fever
(New York: Sonnet, 2001)

Story type: Historical/Victorian; Historical/Victorian America
Subject(s): Inheritance; Social Classes; American South
Major character(s): Juliette Broussard, Orphan, Heiress; Chantz Boudreaux, Bastard Son, Overseer
Time period(s): 1850s (1853)
Locale(s): France; Louisiana

Summary: Juliette Broussard has lived at a French convent since her courtesan mother died and her disillusioned father left her there years earlier. When Max Hollinsworth comes to visit, she is overjoyed to learn that he is her godfather and is going to take her to Louisiana to reclaim her mother's family's rundown sugar plantation, Belle Jarod. Max, however, has other things in mind, like marrying her off to his good-for-nothing son so he can gain control of her property. Of course, willful, fiery Juliette has no intention of marrying Tylor, especially when she falls in love with Max's bastard son, Chantz Boudreaux, the one man who can help put her plantation back on its feet. Filled with adventure, earthy passion, assorted problems from difficult people to alligators and yellow fever, and a depiction of slavery that will not set well with many of today's readers.

Where it's reviewed:
Publishers Weekly, May 28, 2001, page 57
Rendezvous, May 2001, page 25

Other books by the same author:
Darkling I Listen, 2001 (contemporary)
Notorious, 2000
Hope and Glory, 1999
Whitehorse, 1999
Love's Illusion, 1998

Other books you might like:
Jennifer Blake, *Arrow to the Heart*, 1993
  Southern setting
Sandra Chastain, *Jasmine and Silk*, 1993
  Southern setting
Thea Devine, *Southern Seduction*, 1991
  passionate/similar time period
Karen Ranney, *After the Kiss*, 2000
Nan Ryan, *You Belong to My Heart*, 2000
  Southern/Civil War period

439

JODI THOMAS (Pseudonym of Jodi Koumalats)

To Wed in Texas
(New York: Jove, 2000)

Story type: Historical/American West; Historical/Post-American Civil War
Subject(s): Small Town Life; Family
Major character(s): Karlee Whitworth, Spinster, Relative; Daniel McLain, Religious (pastor), Widow(er)
Time period(s): 1860s

Locale(s): Jefferson, Texas

Summary: When a woman pops out of a trunk and announces herself as his late wife's first cousin here to help care for his young daughters, the recently widowed Pastor Daniel McLain is startled, to say the least. He'd been expecting his elderly Aunt Rosy, not this outspoken, slightly hoydenish spinster. However, Karlee is just what he needs; and as Daniel works to bring peace and civility to his rough and wild Texas town, Karlee makes a home for him and his children—and she ends up with a home and a love for herself, as well. Warm, funny, and tender.

Where it's reviewed:
Romantic Times, February 2000, page 42

Other books by the same author:
Twilight in Texas, 2001
The Texan's Touch, 1998
Forever in Texas, 1995
The Texan and the Lady, 1994
The Tender Texan, 1991

Other books you might like:
Deborah Camp, *Black-Eyed Susan*, 1990
Lori Copeland, *The Courtship of Cade Kolby*, 1997
Robin Lee Hatcher, *Promise Me Spring*, 1991
Lorraine Heath, *Never Marry a Cowboy*, 2001
Jill Marie Landis, *Come Spring*, 1995

440

JODI THOMAS (Pseudonym of Jodi Koumalats)

Twilight in Texas

(New York: Jove, 2001)

Story type: Historical/American West; Historical/Post-American Civil War
Subject(s): Reunions; Spies; Romance
Major character(s): Molly Donivan, Doctor; Wolf "Benjamin" Hayward, Lawman (Texas Ranger), Spy (former Confederate spy)
Time period(s): 1870s (Reconstruction era)
Locale(s): Austin, Texas

Summary: Eight years ago Wolf and Molly briefly met during the Civil War and fell in love at first sight. Now, they meet once again in Texas; and while Wolf recognizes Dr. Molly Donivan as the angel who stole his heart, she doesn't associate Texas Ranger Wolf Hayward with the young Union soldier named Benjamin she still dreams of. The reason? Wolf was a Southern spy in the Union Army and Molly was the daughter of a Union doctor—a situation that could threaten their growing relationship, if Molly ever learns the truth. Poignant, emotionally compelling, and tender.

Other books by the same author:
To Wed in Texas, 2000
The Texan's Touch, 1998
Forever in Texas, 1995
The Texan and the Lady, 1994
The Tender Texan, 1991

Other books you might like:
Catherine Anderson, *Forever After*, 1998

Lorraine Heath, *Always to Remember*, 1996
Lorraine Heath, *Texas Destiny*, 1997
Jill Marie Landis, *Last Chance*, 1995
Jill Marie Landis, *Sunflower*, 1989

441

PATRICIA VERYAN

The Riddle of the Shipwrecked Spinster

(New York: St. Martin's Press, 2001)

Story type: Historical/Georgian
Subject(s): Identity, Concealed; Conspiracies; Marriage
Major character(s): Cordelia "Mary Westerman" Stansbury, Runaway, Imposter; Piers Cranford, Nobleman, Twin (brother of Peregrine); Peregrine Cranford, Gentleman, Twin (brother of Piers)
Time period(s): 1740s (1747; 1749)
Locale(s): England

Summary: Humiliated when her scheming mother engineers a compromising situation in an effort to secure her an offer of marriage from Gervaise Valerian, one of the *ton's* most eligible bachelors, plain, dowdy Cordelia Stansbury does the only thing her pride will allow—she runs away to sea. A year later, she returns a much-changed woman with a tale of shipwreck and life on an island with a band of savages, and is forced to deal with the fact that her reputation is in shreds and her erstwhile fiance refuses to marry her. Meanwhile, Gervaise's cousin, Piers Cranford, has been coerced by their mutual uncle into offering to take Gervaise's place—despite the fact that Piers is becoming attracted to a charming young newcomer to his neighborhood. Politics, hidden identities, subterfuge, and real danger work their magic in this story with a *Twelfth Night* plot and beautifully rendered language. Links to Veryan's earlier Tales of the Jeweled Men and Golden Chronicles series.

Where it's reviewed:
Affaire de Coeur, March/April 2001, page 39

Other books by the same author:
The Riddle of the Reluctant Rake, 1999
The Riddle of the Lost Lover, 1998
The Riddle of Alabaster Royal, 1997
Lanterns, 1996
Never Doubt I Love, 1995

Other books you might like:
Rosemary Edghill, *The Ill-Bred Bride*, 1990
Jean Ross Ewing, *Rogue's Reward*, 1995
    Regency setting
Candice Hern, *An Affair of Honor*, 1996
Georgette Heyer, *The Convenient Marriage*, 1934
Georgette Heyer, *The Masqueraders*, 1934

442

PEGGY WAIDE

Mightier than the Sword

(New York: Leisure, 2001)

Story type: Historical/Regency

Subject(s): Identity, Concealed; Napoleonic Wars; Espionage
Major character(s): Rebecca Marche, Wealthy; Adam Hawksmore, Nobleman (Earl of Kerrick), Fugitive
Time period(s): 1810s (1816)
Locale(s): England

Summary: Adam Hawksmore has been framed as a traitor and wounded, has escaped. In order to smoke out the real traitor, Rebecca Marche, who's loved Adam since childhood, disguises him as a poet. Intrigue is interspersed with many light moments as the alpha male Adam, dressed up in outlandish, foppish garb, tries his darndest to come up with poetry on the spot. A fun read.

Where it's reviewed:
Romantic Times, March 2001, page 45

Other books by the same author:
Potent Charms, 2000
Duchess for a Day, 1999

Other books you might like:
Shirlee Busbee, *For Love Alone*, 2000
Candace Camp, *A Stolen Heart*, 2000
Susan Grace, *Forever and Beyond*, 2001
Lynn Kerstan, *Lady Dragoner's Wife*, 1999
Gayle Wilson, *My Lady's Dare*, 2000

443

TINA WAINSCOTT

Back in Baby's Arms

(New York: St. Martin's Paperbacks, 2001)

Story type: Contemporary; Romantic Suspense
Subject(s): Memory Loss; Boatbuilding; Boats and Boating
Major character(s): Maddie Schaeffer, Widow(er), Businesswoman; Chase, Amnesiac
Time period(s): 2000s
Locale(s): Sugar Bay, Florida

Summary: Pampered Maddie Schaeffer's husband dies in a foolish, daredevil boating accident. Paralyzed by grief, she remains cushioned and isolated by her family until a stranger comes to their little town. This man, who forces her to face her past, is, ironically, one who can't remember his own. A mysterious man, the hint of danger, and a woman who finally finds herself are the elements of this book with a surprise ending.

Where it's reviewed:
Romantic Times, January 2001, page 78

Other books by the same author:
A Trick of the Light, 2000
The Wrong Mr. Right, 2000
In a Heartbeat, 1999
Second Time Around, 1997
Dreams of You, 1996

Other books you might like:
Margot Dalton, *Tangled Lives*, 1998
Jean DeWitt, *The Stranger*, 1998
Lindsay McKenna, *Morgan's Marriage*, 1996
Sharon Sala, *Remember Me*, 1999
Rebecca York, *Midnight Caller*, 1999

444

SHEILA WALSH

The Lady from Lisbon

(New York: Signet, 2001)

Story type: Regency
Subject(s): Love
Major character(s): Cressida Merriton, Gentlewoman; Alastair Langley, Nobleman (Earl of Langley)
Time period(s): 1810s
Locale(s): London, England

Summary: Lady Beatrice Kilbride convinces her nephew Lord Alastair Langley to escort her goddaughter, Cressida Merriton, from Portsmouth to London where Cressida is to enjoy a season of her own under Lady Kilbride's auspices. Cressida, who has not seen her godmother for years, is quite surprised to find waiting for her a depressed Lady Kilbride who has isolated herself from the world. Against Alastair's wishes, Cressida takes it upon herself to reintroduce her godmother to society and her old friends, and along the way Cressida wins the love of both Lady Kilbride and Alastair.

Where it's reviewed:
Affaire de Coeur, February 2001, page 24
Romantic Times, February 2001, page 111

Other books by the same author:
Kate and the Marquess, 1997
The Perfect Bride, 1994
Lord Gilmore's Bride, 1990
Arrogant Lord Alistair, 1989
The Notorious Nabob, 1989

Other books you might like:
Shannon Donnelly, *A Compromising Situation*, 2000
Barbara Hazard, *The Wary Widow*, 2000
Martha Kirkland, *An Uncommon Courtship*, 2000
Allison Lane, *The Prodigal Daughter*, 1996
Evelyn Richardson, *Lord Harry's Daughter*, 2001

445

PAT WARREN

The Way We Wed

(New York: Silhouette, 2001)

Story type: Romantic Suspense; Contemporary
Series: Year of Loving Dangerously. Book 10
Subject(s): Espionage; Suspense; Healing
Major character(s): Tish Buckner, Young Woman, Spy (SPEAR agent); Jeff Kirby, Doctor, Spy (SPEAR agent)
Time period(s): 2000s
Locale(s): Condor Mountain, California; New York, New York (Manhattan); Arizona

Summary: Tish Buckner and Jeff Kirby meet while they're both secret agents for SPEAR. After a passionate affair, they elope. A sudden tragedy drives them apart, and just as their relationship is on the mend, Jeff receives word Tish is in a coma as a result of a bomb blast. This emotional story is deftly told in flashbacks.

Where it's reviewed:
Romantic Times, April 2001, page 110

Other books by the same author:
Daddy by Surprise, 2000
The Baby Quest, 2000
The Lawman and the Lady, 2000
Stand-In Father, 1998
Stranded on the Ranch, 1998

Other books you might like:
Robyn Amos, *Hero at Large*, 2000
    Year of Loving Dangerously. Book 5
Carla Cassidy, *Strangers When We Married*, 2000
Merline Lovelace, *The Spy Who Loved Him*, 2001
    Year of Loving Dangerously. Book 7
Linda Turner, *The Enemy's Daughter*, 2001
    Year of Loving Dangerously. Book 9
Margaret Watson, *Someone to Watch Over Her*, 2001
    Year of Loving Dangerously. Book 8

446

MARGARET WATSON

Someone to Watch over Her

(New York: Silhouette, 2001)

Story type: Romantic Suspense
Series: Year of Loving Dangerously. Book 8
Subject(s): Espionage; Kidnapping
Major character(s): Jessica Burke, Scientist, Student; Marcus Waters, Spy (SPEAR)
Time period(s): 2000s
Locale(s): Cascadilla, Caribbean

Summary: SPEAR agent Marcus Waters' first instinct upon discovering an unconscious young woman on the beach of the Caribbean island where he is ''vacationing'' is to hide her. Marcus' instincts prove to be right on target for it turns out the woman is scientist Jessica Burke who has just escaped from her kidnappers. Marcus later learns that the man behind Jessica's kidnapping is the mysterious Simon, the same traitor he is looking for. Marcus vows to protect Jessica from Simon, but can he protect himself from falling in love with her?

Where it's reviewed:
Romantic Times, February 2001, page 106

Other books by the same author:
A Thanksgiving to Remember, 2000
Family on the Run, 2000
The Fugitive Bride, 1999
The Marriage Protection Program, 1999
Cowboy with a Badge, 1998

Other books you might like:
Robyn Amos, *Hero at Large*, 2000
Beverly Barton, *Her Secret Weapon*, 2000
Carla Cassidy, *Strangers When We Married*, 2000
Merline Lovelace, *The Spy Who Loved Him*, 2001
Eileen Wilks, *Night of No Return*, 2000

447

SUSAN WIGGS

The Firebrand

(Don Mills, Ontario: Mira, 2001)

Story type: Historical/Victorian America
Series: Chicago Fire Trilogy. Book 3
Subject(s): Women's Rights; Fires; Intolerance
Major character(s): Lucy Hathaway, Store Owner (bookstore), Suffragette; Randolph Higgins, Wealthy, Banker
Time period(s): 1870s (1871-1876)
Locale(s): Chicago, Illinois

Summary: Caught up in the horrors of the Great Chicago Fire, suffragette Lucy Hathaway barely escapes with her life. . .and a baby someone has thrown to her from a fiery hotel. Unable to locate the parents of the child, Lucy raises her as her own. Randolph Higgins, prominent Chicago banker, has grieved the loss of his daughter for years. Then one day, while being turned down for a loan, Lucy sees the picture of Randolph's baby daughter in his office, and she knows she'll have to tell him the truth, even if it means giving up her beloved Maggie. A hero, with as many scars inside as out, and a heroine, who does the right thing at great cost, find healing in this powerful story that sweeps the reader along as it rises like a phoenix from the ashes of the fire. A most satisfying ending to an incredible trilogy.

Where it's reviewed:
Booklist, April 15, 2001, page 75
Romantic Times, April 2001, page 35

Other books by the same author:
The Hostage, 2000 (Chicago Fire Trilogy. Book 1)
The Mistress, 2000 (Chicago Fire Trilogy. Book 2)
The Charm School, 1999
The Horsemaster's Daughter, 1999
The Drifter, 1998

Other books you might like:
Betina Krahn, *Sweet Talking Man*, 2000
Jill Marie Landis, *The Orchid Hunter*, 2000
Maggie Osborne, *A Stranger's Wife*, 1999
Nan Ryan, *A Lifetime of Heaven*, 1999
LaVyrle Spencer, *The Gamble*, 1984

448

BRONWYN WILLIAMS (Pseudonym of Dixie Browning and Mary Williams)

Longshadow's Woman

(Toronto: Harlequin, 2001)

Story type: Historical/Americana
Subject(s): Abuse; Animals/Horses; Farm Life
Major character(s): Carrie Adams, Spouse; Jonah Longshadow, Convict, Horse Trainer
Time period(s): 19th century
Locale(s): Shingle Landing, North Carolina

Summary: Desperately needing help around her small farm, Carrie Adams reluctantly purchases the services of convict Jonah Longshadow. Jonah plans on leaving as soon as he

completes his work but once he meets Carrie's abusive gambler of a husband, he finds himself looking for reasons to hang around. When Jonah is once again falsely imprisoned, Carrie finds the courage within herself to fight for the man she now loves.

Where it's reviewed:
Romantic Times, March 2001, page 42

Other books by the same author:
The Paper Marriage, 2000
The Mariner's Bride, 1999
Beholden, 1998
Entwined, 1998
Stormwalker, 1998

Other books you might like:
Catherine Anderson, *Coming Up Roses*, 1999
Megan Chance, *A Season in Eden*, 1999
Alexis Harrington, *Allie's Moon*, 2000
Julianne MacLean, *Prairie Bride*, 2000
Maggie Osborne, *The Brides of Bowie Stone*, 1994

449

GAYLE WILSON (Pseudonym of Mona Gay Thomas)

Anne's Perfect Husband
(Toronto: Harlequin, 2001)

Story type: Historical/Regency
Subject(s): Love; Responsibility
Major character(s): Ian Sinclair, Military Personnel (former), Guardian; Anne Darlington, Gentlewoman, Ward
Time period(s): 1810s (1813-1814)
Locale(s): England

Summary: Upon being informed he has been named guardian of Anne Darlington, Ian Sinclair waits for a little girl to arrive at his home. Ian is quite surprised to discover the girl is actually a young woman and despite the fact that Anne's father was responsible for ending Ian's military career, he is determined to find a suitable husband for his new ward. Anne, however, is positive the perfect candidate for her future husband is Ian himself.

Where it's reviewed:
Romantic Times, March 2001, page 44

Other books by the same author:
Her Private Bodyguard, 2000
Midnight Remembered, 2000
Renegade Heart, 2000
My Lady's Dare, 2000
Each Precious Hour, 1999

Other books you might like:
Mary Balogh, *The Red Rose*, 2000
Nicole Byrd, *Robert's Lady*, 2000
Deborah Hale, *A Gentleman of Substance*, 1999
Deborah Simmons, *The Gentleman Thief*, 2000
Patricia Veryan, *Give All to Love*, 1987

450

JOAN WOLF

Royal Bride
(New York: Warner, 2001)

Story type: Historical/Regency
Subject(s): Marriage; Politics; Kings, Queens, Rulers, etc.
Major character(s): Charity Beaufort, Royalty (Princess of Jura), Bride (marriage of convenience); Augustus Adamov, Ruler (Prince of Jura)
Time period(s): 1810s (1815)
Locale(s): England; Jura, Fictional Country; Europe

Summary: When her older sister, Lydia, who is engaged to marry the Prince of Jura for political reasons, elopes with her fiance's clever cousin, Lady Charity Beaufort steps into the breach and marries Prince Augustus herself—with highly successful results. Political intrigue, greed, and a quest for power structure the plot of this readable, romantic, arranged-marriage tale that features a number of well-depicted secondary characters and a pair of brave, loyal, well-matched protagonists. A charming, fast-paced adventure.

Where it's reviewed:
Library Journal, February 15, 2001, page 155
Romantic Times, March 2001, page 40

Other books by the same author:
The Gamble, 1998
The Arrangement, 1997
The Guardian, 1997
The Deception, 1996
The Reindeer Hunters, 1994

Other books you might like:
Mary Balogh, *Promise of Spring*, 1990
    another arranged marriage
Marion Chesney, *The Desirable Duchess*, 1993
    another marriage of convenience
Georgette Heyer, *The Convenient Marriage*, 1934
    classic arranged marriage
Johanna Lindsey, *Once a Princess*, 1991
Mary Jo Putney, *Bride by Arrangement*, 2000
    anthology

451

SHERRYL WOODS

Do You Take This Rebel?
(New York: Silhouette, 2001)

Story type: Contemporary
Series: Calamity Janes. Book 1
Subject(s): Family Relations; Friendship; Child Custody
Major character(s): Cassie Collins, Single Parent; Cole Davis, Rancher
Time period(s): 2000s (2001)
Locale(s): Winding River, Wyoming

Summary: When Cole Davis finds out the reason Cassie Collins left town ten years earlier was that she carried his baby, he insists they marry. Cassie doesn't want to marry him, but the other alternative is risking custody of her son. On the other

Romance

hand, with a nine-year-old smart enough to run an Internet scam, two parents don't seem like such a bad idea. . . . This is the first book in a series featuring five friends from the class of '91—The Calamity Janes.

Where it's reviewed:
Romantic Times, May 2001, page 110

Other books by the same author:
About That Man, 2001
Courting the Enemy, 2001 (Calamity Janes. Book 2)

The Calamity Janes, 2001 (Calamity Janes. Book 4)
To Catch a Thief, 2001 (Calamity Janes. Book 3)
Wrangling the Redhead, 2001 (Calamity Janes. Book 5)

Other books you might like:
Pamela Burford, *I Do, but Here's the Catch*, 2001
Millie Criswell, *The Wedding Planner*, 2000
Ruth Jean Dale, *Fiance Wanted*, 2000
Jennifer Greene, *Millionaire M.D.*, 2001
Leigh Greenwood, *Married by High Noon*, 2000

Western Books in Review
by
D.R. Meredith

The trends indicated in the last volume of *What Do I Read Next?* continue: books by and about women and minorities, and solid historical Westerns rather than traditional shoot'em-ups, are gaining ground. Even the growth industry books about famous outlaws are as lacking as they were in the first half of this year, although we do have one about Billy the Kid: *The Stone Garden: The Epic Life of Billy the Kid* by Bill Brooks. And there is only one book about George Armstrong Custer, *American Woman* by R. Garcia y Robertson. That is remarkable.

The number of books in which African Americans in the West are the protagonists are increasing even more than in the first part of the year. *Broken Ranks* by Hiram King, about a black gunfighter, and *Johnny Blue and the Hanging Judge* by Joseph A. West are two examples. The books about minorities now include minorities other than African American, Mexican American, and Indian. One such book, that also demonstrates a noticeable trend of basing a novel on an actual historical incident, is *Last Daughter of Happiness* by Yan Geling.

I am encouraged by the number of novels based on actual historical incidents, as it demonstrates the overall comeback of historical novels in general, and the strength of Western historical novels in particular. As there are numerous exciting events that occurred in the West, writers have a plethora of subjects. These books range from Elmer Kelton's classic, *The Time It Never Rained*, based on the six year drought in West Texas, to *Gunman's Rhapsody* by Robert B. Parker about Wyatt Earp and the gunfight at that famous corral, to *Grand Ambition* by Lisa Michaels about a pair of newlyweds who disappear while rafting down the Colorado rapids. I expect to see many more such historical novels with Western settings and history, and I predict at least one or two will make the bestseller lists. There are too many good writers choosing the West as a subject for sales not to increase. One example is Robert B. Parker, mentioned above. The creator of the famous fictional detective,

Spencer, Parker now weighs in with a book about the West, and a fine one at that.

Another noticeable trend in the Western titles in this volume is the number of series. Not that it is a new trend, as such stalwarts as Louis L'Amour with his Sackett stories and Max Brand's various series characters prove, but other than the adult Westerns, most others have been stand-alone novels. There are always examples, of course, but, for the first time in a long while, the trend is noticeable. The Western writer may have noticed the popularity of modern mystery series, or been encouraged by editors who recognize the popularity of serial characters from also editing mysteries, but whatever the reason, I believe serial characters will attract readers.

There are the usual cross-genre romance writers such as Rosanne Bittner and her Sioux Indian series, but also we have Peter Bowen with his comic Yellowstone Kelly novels, represented here by *Kelly and the Three-Toed Horse*. Don Coldsmith, of course, has long written serial Westerns with his Spanish Bit series, the latest of which is *Raven Mocker*. Ray Hogan's *Doomsday Marshal* is an example of a traditional Western with a serial character, as is Dusty Richards' Arizona ranger series. James A. Vesely is writing a trilogy about the Corrales Valley in New Mexico which features generations of the same family, a variation on the serial character. With strong historical themes and serial characters, writers are creating books that appeal to a wider audience than merely the Western genre reader. For the first time in two decades I see the Western novel as more novel than shoot'em-up.

Another continuing trend is the short story anthology. Where once a writer couldn't pay a publisher to put out an anthology of Western short stories, now we have a selection of anthologies featuring different themes and time periods. Some are reprints of short stories which first appeared in the pulp magazines, such as Max Brand's *Men Beyond the Law*, while others are stories with modern settings such as *Laming*

out and Other Stories by Mary Clearman Blew, and Jose Skinner's *Flight and Other Stories*. Glendon Swarthout's *Easterns and Westerns* includes stories also set in urban areas, but all the selections deal with generational conflict.

In addition to the continued publication of short story anthologies, I also see a trend of reprinting the classic Western novels, so that our current generation of readers and writers can enjoy them. In this volume of *WDIRN?* alone are Owen Wister's *The Virginian*, Elmer Kelton's *The Time It Never Rained*, considered by some critics to be one of the ten best American novels, and Max Brand's *Beyond the Outposts*. I cannot emphasize enough how important it is that contemporary writers read these classic Western novels. They combine character, sense of place, and theme. *The Virginian* is considered to be the first genuine Western, and introduces to the genre several plot elements that are still used today. ''Smile when you say that'' may be a cliche, but it was first used by Wister. The schoolmarm and the afternoon buggy ride are plot elements also first introduced by him.

The Time It Never Rained is based on an actual historical event that is not a gunfight nor a battle with Indians, but a drought in West Texas which destroyed many small rural towns and sent many farmers and ranchers into bankruptcy. In the character of Charlie Flagg, Kelton created the rugged Western hero who never participated in a gunfight, who had difficulty relating to women, and who never really understood his own paternalistic attitude toward Mexican Americans. Charlie Flagg never asked for help or charity, but never turned down a man who asked him. He was a man of his time who fought to survive against a bleak and unforgiving Nature. Charlie Flagg is the real hero of the West, a man who tries whatever might work to save his ranch, not against land grabbers, but against the environment. *Beyond the Outposts* is the story of a boy's search for his father, who is guilty of killing three men in what everyone but the jury saw as self-defense. During the search he discovers his own manhood.

Another trend, and this I find very encouraging, is the increase in Westerns for young readers. The Republic of Texas Press leads the way with two series, one directed at young girls and the other at young boys. Patrick Dearen creates a series called Lone Star Heroes in which a young boy and his cousin share adventures in early Texas. Melinda Rice creates Lone Star Heroines which features different time periods and ethnic groups, from a young Mexican American girl at the Battle of Gonzales to an Anglo girl during WWII. *Get Along, Little Dogies: The Chisholm Trail Diary of Hallie Lou Wells* by Lisa Waller Rogers is based on actual diaries and journals of cattle drives, so Rogers represents two trends: novels based on actual historical events, and books for young readers.

As has always been the case with Westerns, sense of place is one of the most important elements, and there are several books that illustrate this, beginning with *The Time It Never Rained*. One can taste the dust in one's mouth as a dry norther blows in. *Moon Medicine* by Mike Blakely evokes the sage brush and isolation of the Texas Panhandle, while *The Master Executioner* tells us almost more than we want to know about hangings. *Lambing out and Other Stories* is a collection set in contemporary times which features hardship in Montana. One sweats along with the characters. Sybil Downing's *The Binding Oath* takes us into the middle of 1920s Denver and the gathering of the Ku Klux Klan. These and several other novels illustrate the realism of the contemporary Western.

Another noticeable trend is the number of mysteries set in the West which use sense of place as a plot element. Some of the best of these are Elizabeth Dearl's Taylor Madison mysteries such as *Twice Dead*, and Sue Henry's *Dead North*. One mystery which blends Western past and Western present is Carol Cail's *The Seeds of Time* in which a contemporary archaeologist comes into contact with a nineteenth century prostitute.

From mystery to realism to the presence of women, minorities, and ordinary men in heroic situations, today's Western is a novel in the truest sense of the word.

Recommended Titles

Now comes that part of my review of Westerns that I dread the most: the selecting of the twenty-five best titles in this volume. I want to emphasize again that these are my choices and are a result of my subjective taste. Another reader might very well choose entirely different titles for entirely different reasons.

1. *The Time It Never Rained* by Elmer Kelton. Simply one of the best Westerns ever written, it has everything: plot, characterization, and sense of place.

2. *The Master Executioner* by Loren D. Estleman. One of Estleman's quirky stories, this is about a hangman. The realism is superb and the sense of place such as the execution chamber at Leavenworth sends chills up one's spine.

3. *Moon Medicine* by Mike Blakely. A wonderful story set at Adobe Walls.

4. *Blue Horizons* by Irene Bennett Brown. Book II of Women of Paragon Springs, this is a story of courage and reflection.

5. *Once They Wore the Gray* by Johnny D. Boggs. Enlisting in the Union Army in order to escape the horrors of a prison camp, these Confederates become ''Galvanized Yankees.''

6. *The Virginian* by Owen Wister. The classic first Western. Required reading for fans of the genre.

7. *Johnny Blue and the Hanging Judge* by Joseph A. West. Another of West's humorous tales about an African American and a white man who are inseparable friends.

8. *Ghost Town* by Ed Gorman. One of Gorman's delightful traditional Westerns with his customary touch of humor and pathos.

9. *An Ordinary Woman* by Cecelia Holland. Another novel based on historical fact about the first American woman to reach California.

10. *Snow Mountain Passage* by James D. Houston. A retelling of the tragedy of the Donner party from the point of view of James Reed. Wonderful sense of place.

11. *Spirit Sickness* by Kirk Mitchell. A Western mystery with lots of Indian culture.

12. *American Woman* by R. Garcia y Robertson. A view of the Custer massacre through the eyes of a Quaker woman married to a Sioux.

13. *Get Along, Little Dogies: The Chisholm Trail Diary of Hallie Lou Wells* by Lisa Waller Rogers. One of the best books for young readers, it is the story of a young girl on a cattle drive.

14. *Rise to Rebellion* by Jeff Shaara. An historical novel about America's first frontier: the colonies in revolt.

15. *Flight and Other Stories* by Jose Skinner. Contemporary collection that explores the Hispanic American experience in the West.

16. *Easterns and Westerns* by Glendon Swarthout. Stories set in both the east and the west.

17. *Grace* by Jane Roberts Wood. Life in a rural Texas town during WWII. Excellent sense of place.

18. *The Lost Daughter of Happiness* by Yan Geling. A young Chinese girl is forced into prostitution.

19. *Seasons of Harvest* by James A. Vesely. The first in a trilogy about the settlement of the Corrales Valley in New Mexico. This volume starts with prehistoric Indians and continues through the Spanish Conquest.

20. *The Power of the Dog* by Thomas Savage. A powerful novel about two brothers and the woman who separates them.

21. *Comanche Peace Pipe* by Patrick Dearen. Wonderful characterization in this book for young readers.

22. *MacGregor's Lantern* by Corinne Joy Brown. A novel about a woman in business.

23. *Beyond the Outposts* by Max Brand. A classic boy's coming-of-age story.

24. *Bodie Gone* by Bill Hyde. A time travel Western mystery that alternates between the present and the California Gold Rush.

25. *Gunman's Rhapsody* by Robert B. Parker. A fine Western written by a superb mystery writer.

For More Information about Western Fiction

The Western Writers of America maintain a database of bookstores willing to stock and/or order Western titles. For information on the database, or to add your favorite bookstore to it, write to Candy Moulton, Editor, *Roundup* Magazine, Box 29 Star Route, Encampment, WY 82325.

For general information on what's happening in Western writing, subscribe to *Roundup* magazine at the above address. *Roundup* is the official publication of the Western Writers of America and includes reviews of Western fiction and nonfiction done by yours truly. In addition, there is a series of features on writers of the 20th century, a section on what's doing in Hollywood by Miles Hood Swarthout, and articles on new directions in Western writing.

For the computer literate, there is no source like Amazon.com for finding out-of-print Westerns, or just titles by a favorite that you are missing. Remember also to periodically check for titles in your local used bookstores, estate sales, flea markets, garage sales, and your local Friends of the Library book sale. And speaking of libraries, if the title you want is in hardback, ask your local library to get it for you on interlibrary loan. Some libraries will order original paperbacks on interlibrary loan, but you will need to ask. As a last resort, contact a rare book dealer for some desired title you want, but be prepared to pay dearly. I found one of my first printing, original paperbacks, used, for $108. I didn't make a whole lot more than that when I wrote it.

Western Titles

452

ROSANNE BITTNER

Mystic Warriors
(New York: Forge, 2001)

Story type: Historical; Saga
Series: Mystic Indian
Subject(s): Indians of North America
Major character(s): Buffalo Dreamer, Indian (Lakota Sioux), Spouse (of Rising Eagle); Rising Eagle, Spouse (of Buffalo Dreamer), Indian (Lakota Sioux); Brave Horse, Relative (son of Rising Eagle), Indian (Lakota Sioux)
Time period(s): 19th century (post-Civil War)
Locale(s): Fort Laramie, Wyoming

Summary: Those who have seen the sacred white buffalo are said to be blessed. Buffalo Dreamer and her husband, Rising Eagle, have not only seen the white buffalo, but have eaten its heart. They have been told that as long as the Lakota have the skin of the white buffalo, the tribe will also be blessed. Then the sacred skin is stolen, settlers invade the land of the Lakota, and a brutal cavalry force begins killing the tribe's women and children. To restore order in the Lakota nation, Rising Eagle and his son, Brave Horse, join forces with Sitting Bull and Crazy Horse to lead allied tribes against the white man.

Other books by the same author:
Mystic Dreamers, 2000
Mystic Visions, 2000
Tame the Wild Wind, 1996
Chase the Sun, 1995
Wildest Dreams, 1994

Other books you might like:
Michael Blake, *Dances with Wolves*, 1990
Joseph Bruchac, *The Arrow over the Door*, 1998
Amanda Cockrell, *The Long Walk*, 1996
Terry C. Johnston, *Dream Catcher*, 1994
Alan LeMay, *The Searchers*, 1954

453

MIKE BLAKELY

Moon Medicine
(New York: Forge, 2001)

Story type: Historical
Subject(s): American West; Indians of North America
Major character(s): Honore Greenwood, Scout (also known as ''Plenty Man''); Jibber, Sidekick; Charles Bent, Trader, Historical Figure
Time period(s): 19th century; 20th century (1828-1927)
Locale(s): Bent's Fort, Colorado; Taos, New Mexico; Adobe Walls, Texas

Summary: After murdering his fencing master for raping his sweetheart, Honore Greenwood stows away on a ship bound for America with nothing but the clothes on his back and a stolen violin. On the ship he acquires a friend, a sailor named Jibber, who accompanies him West. In Taos, his heart is broken when he falls in love with a woman already betrothed, and he flees into the wilderness, where he builds what is later called Adobe Walls. At the age of 98, he shares his life.

Where it's reviewed:
Roundup, August 2001, page 26

Other books by the same author:
Summer of Pearls, 2000
Comanche Dawn, 1998
Dead Reckoning, 1996
Spanish Blood, 1996
Too Long at the Dance, 1996

Other books you might like:
Frederic Bean, *Renegade*, 1993
Giff Cheshire, *Renegade River*, 1998
Tracy Dunham, *The Ghost Trail*, 1998
Paul A. Hawkins, *The Seekers*, 1994
Richard S. Wheeler, *Cheyenne Winter*, 1992

454

MARY CLEARMAN BLEW

Lambing Out & Other Stories

(Norman: University of Oklahoma Press, 2001)

Story type: Modern; Collection
Subject(s): Animals/Sheep; American West
Time period(s): 2000s
Locale(s): Montana

Summary: Seven short stories reflect the harsh weather and personal hardships of persons living in rural Montana.

Other books by the same author:
All but the Waltz, 2001
Balsamroot, 2001
Sister Coyote, 2000
Bone Deep in Landscape, 1999
Runaway, 1990

Other books you might like:
Rick Bass, *The Sky, the Stars, the Wilderness*, 1997
Max Brand, *The Ghost Wagon and Other Great Western Adventures*, 1996
H.A. DeRosso, *Riders of the Shadowlands*, 1999
T.T. Flynn, *Death Marks Time in Trampas: A Western Quintet*, 1998
Robert Franklin Gish, *First Horses*, 1993

455

JOHNNY D. BOGGS

Once They Wore the Gray

(Thorndike, Maine: Thorndike, 2001)

Story type: Historical; Saga
Subject(s): War; Indians of North America
Major character(s): Gil Metaire, Military Personnel (Confederate Army sergeant); John J. Rankin, Military Personnel (Union Army major); Rebecca Rankin, Relative (Major Rankin's daughter)
Time period(s): 1860s (1865)
Locale(s): Santa Fe Trail, Kansas; Rock Island, Illinois

Summary: Sergeant Gil Metaire and several Confederate prisoners of war are determined to survive, and it appears the best way to do that, however reluctant they might be, is to enlist in the Union army and be sent to the frontier to fight the Indians and keep the Santa Fe Trail open. Gil doesn't want to become a Galvanized Yankee as these Confederates are called, but he doesn't want to die in the prison camp either. Fortunately, the commanding officer at Fort Zarah on the Santa Fe Trail is an understanding man. His daughter, Rebecca, with whom Gil falls in love, is sympathetic with the Confederates' condition. However, an understanding commanding officer doesn't keep away the Indians set to kill all white men, and it doesn't solve the problem of the Blackwater River Guards, a Confederate troop better known for looting and murder than patriotism.

Where it's reviewed:
Roundup Magazine, October 2001, page 24

Other books by the same author:
The Lonesome Chisholm Trail, 2000
Ten and Me, 1999
Riding with Hannah and the Horseman, 1998
Hannah and the Horseman, 1997
This Man Colter, 1997

Other books you might like:
Tom Austin, *The Blood Oath*, 1997
   O'Malley Saga. Book 1
Frederic Bean, *Santa Fe Showdown*, 1993
Robert W. Broomall, *Conroy's First Command*, 1994
Frank Cannon, *Feud at Sweetwater Creek*, 1988
Hank Edwards, *Gray Warrior*, 1995

456

PETER BOWEN

Kelly and the Three-Toed Horse

(New York: St. Martin's Press, 2001)

Story type: Historical; Saga
Subject(s): American West; Indians of North America; Humor
Major character(s): Luther "Yellowstone" Kelly, Scout, Gunfighter; Alys, Archaeologist; Blue Fox, Indian (Cheyenne), Mentally Ill Person (psychopath)
Time period(s): 19th century (post-Civil War)
Locale(s): Wyoming

Summary: After the fossil of a three-toed horse is found, Yellowstone Kelly is hired to guide an archaeological expedition through Wyoming Territory. Alys, a member of the expedition whose job it is to record the finds, is smitten by Kelly. Blue Fox, a psychopathic Cheyenne educated at Dartmouth, keeps trying to kill Kelly and anyone else on the expedition who crosses his sights. Kelly keeps believing that he has killed Blue Fox, but Blue Fox continues to reappear in a comic chase. Wonderful humor.

Where it's reviewed:
Publishers Weekly, February 26, 2001, page 62

Other books by the same author:
Stick Game, 2000
Long Son, 1999
Thunder Horse, 1998
Notches, 1997
Wolf, No Wolf, 1996

Other books you might like:
Frederic Bean, *Murder at the Spirit Cave*, 1999
Mike Blakely, *Spanish Blood*, 1996
Tim Champlin, *Deadly Season*, 1997
Jack Curtis, *The Mark of Cain*, 1994
Ed Gorman, *Trouble Man*, 1999

457

G.G. BOYER

Morgette in the Yukon

(New York: Leisure, 2001)

Story type: Traditional; Quest
Series: Morgette

Subject(s): American West; Gold Discoveries
Major character(s): Dolf Morgette, Miner; Jack Quillen, Miner; Rudy Dwan, Outlaw, Outcast
Time period(s): 19th century (post-Civil War)
Locale(s): Sky Pilot Fork, Alaska

Summary: Dolf Morgette heads west and north as far as a man can go—to Alaska to join the gold rush. With him is his pregnant wife, Margaret, and Jack Quillen, the only man who knows the location of Sky Pilot Fork. Morgette is responsible for protecting Quillen from thieves and claim jumpers, including Morgette's old enemy, Rudy Dwan.

Other books by the same author:
Guns of Morgette, 2000
Winchester Affidavit, 1997

Other books you might like:
Frederic Bean, *Renegade*, 1993
Giff Cheshire, *Renegade River*, 1998
Tracy Dunham, *The Ghost Trail*, 1998
Paul A. Hawkins, *The Seekers*, 1994
Richard S. Wheeler, *Cheyenne Winter*, 1992

458

MAX BRAND

Beyond the Outposts

(New York: Leisure, 2001)

Story type: Traditional; Revenge
Subject(s): Crime and Criminals; American West; Outcasts
Major character(s): Lew Dorset, Frontiersman; Will Dorset, Parent (of Lew Dorset); Chris Hudson, Sidekick
Time period(s): 19th century (pre-Civil War)
Locale(s): West

Summary: When Will Dorset kills three of the Connell brothers for burning down his house, everybody in Virginia figures it was self-defense since it was six against one. Somebody has to go to jail, but Will Dorset doesn't stay there long before he escapes to the frontier. When young Lew Dorset grows up he sets out to find his father with not much more than the clothes on his back and a shiny new rifle given to him by Chris Hudson. After many adventures on the prairies, including surviving an attack by the Cheyenne, he finds shelter with the Sioux, as well as a surprise ending to his search.

Other books by the same author:
The Stone That Shines, 2001
Tales of the Wild West, 2000
The Bright Face of Danger, 2000
The Overland Kid: A Western Trio, 1999
The Quest of Lee Garrison, 1999

Other books you might like:
Patrick E. Andrews, *Texican Blood Fight*, 1992
Michael Blake, *Dances with Wolves*, 1990
Robert J. Conley, *Back to Malachi*, 1997
Max Evans, *Bluefeather Fellini*, 1993
Page Lambert, *Shifting Stars: A Novel of the West*, 1997

459

MAX BRAND

Men Beyond the Law

(New York: Leisure, 2001)

Story type: Historical; Collection
Subject(s): American West; Crime and Criminals
Time period(s): 19th century (post-Civil War)

Summary: Three short novels feature men who are beyond the law through no fault of their own. The titles included are *Werewolf*, *The Finding of Jeremy*, and *The Trail Up Old Arrowhead*.

Other books by the same author:
The Stone That Shines, 2001
Tales of the Wild West, 2000
The Peril Trek: A Western Trio, 2000
The Masterman: A North-Western Story, 2000
The Bright Face of Danger, 2000

Other books you might like:
Walt Coburn, *The Secret of Crutcher's Cabin: A Western Trio*, 1999
T.T. Flynn, *Long Journey to Deep Canon*, 1998
Ray Hogan, *Legend of a Badman*, 1997
Elmore Leonard, *The Tonto Woman and Other Western Stories*, 1998
Finley Stewart, *Best Stories from the Texas Storytelling Festival*, 1995

460

MAX BRAND

The Tyrant

(Thorndike, Maine: Thorndike, 2001)

Story type: Traditional; Quest
Subject(s): American West
Major character(s): Jean Limousin, Gambler, Frontiersman; Francois Limousin, Parent (Jean's father); Pierre Reynal, Gambler
Time period(s): 19th century (post-Civil War)
Locale(s): Quebec, Canada; West

Summary: Jean Limousin grows up on his father, Francois Limousin's, estate outside Quebec. Francois forbids gambling of any sort on his land, so when Jean is tempted into playing cards with Pierre Reynal, he knows he is risking trouble. When he falls deeply in debt, his mother gives him her jewels to pawn. After his father discovers the plot and forces Jean to leave the estate, his mother, worn from years of living with her tyrant husband, dies. Jean flees west with Pierre, who regrets his part in the tragedy. They settle in a cabin, shooting game for food and trapping furs for cash. Francois finds them, but he is only interested in revealing his new plan of marrying for money. A tragic story by a master storyteller.

Other books by the same author:
Don Diablo: A Western Trio, 2001
The Welding Quirt: A Western Trio, 2001
The Bright Face of Danger, 2000
The Outlaw Redeemer, 2000

Western

The Peril Trek: A Western Trio, 2000

Other books you might like:
Rick Bass, *The Sky, the Stars, the Wilderness*, 1997
Frank Bonham, *One Ride Too Many*, 1997
H.A. DeRosso, *Riders of the Shadowlands*, 1999
T.T. Flynn, *Death Marks Time in Trampas: A Western Quintet*, 1998
Robert Franklin Gish, *First Horses*, 1993

461

BILL BROOKS

The Stone Garden

(New York: Forge, 2001)

Story type: Historical; Saga
Subject(s): American West; Crime and Criminals; Outcasts
Major character(s): Billy Bonney, Outlaw, Historical Figure; Pat Garrett, Lawman (sheriff), Historical Figure; Celsa, Girlfriend (of Billy the Kid)
Time period(s): 1880s (1881); 1900s (1908)
Locale(s): Lincoln County, New Mexico; Fort Sumner, New Mexico

Summary: At midnight, July 14, 1881, Sheriff Pat Garrett shoots Billy the Kid in Pete Maxwell's bedroom in Fort Sumner, New Mexico Territory. Or does he? The following morning Billy is buried between two of his friends. The young Mexican girl, Celsa, puts flowers on what she believes is his grave. But is it? According to Brooks' account, Pat Garrett will claim he shot Billy, if Billy will swear to leave New Mexico and never return. Garrett believes people will eventually forget about Billy. However, Billy becomes the stuff of myth and legend, and Garrett becomes the most hated man in New Mexico for killing him. And who kills Pat Garrett 27 years later? Is it Billy or someone else?

Where it's reviewed:
Roundup Magazine, October 2001, page 26

Other books by the same author:
Dust on the Wind, 1997
The Last Law There Was, 1995
Buscadero, 1993

Other books you might like:
Frederic Bean, *The Outlaw*, 1993
Loren D. Estleman, *Journey of the Dead*, 1998
Elizabeth Fackler, *Billy the Kid*, 1995
Fred N. Kimmel, *The Lincoln County Trilogy*, 1998
Preston Lewis, *The Demise of Billy the Kid*, 1995

462

SIGMUND BROUWER

Thunder Voice

(Minneapolis: Bethany House, 2001)

Story type: Historical; Mystery
Series: Sam Keaton: Legends of Laramie
Subject(s): American West; Crime and Criminals

Major character(s): Sam Keaton, Lawman (marshal); Leigh Tafton, Widow(er); Jake Wilson, Lawman (Sam Keaton's deputy)
Time period(s): 1870s (1876)
Locale(s): Laramie, Wyoming

Summary: Marshal Sam Keaton isn't surprised at the death of the town drunk; he had lived a risky life. He is surprised though when two Texas Rangers show up in town asking questions about the drunk's death. Then the widow Leigh Tafton arrives on the train from back east claiming that her sister's death and the drunk's murder are related. Sam is curious and agrees to help her until it becomes apparent that there is a root at the bottom of the problem, and Sam is offered a most interesting and most tempting marriage proposal. This book was originally published in 1995.

Other books by the same author:
Cyber Quest, 2000
Evening Star, 2000
Silver Moon, 2000
Pony Express Christmas, 2000
Into His Arms, 1999

Other books you might like:
Frederic Bean, *Murder at the Spirit Cave*, 1999
Mike Blakely, *Spanish Blood*, 1996
Tim Champlin, *Deadly Season*, 1997
Jack Curtis, *The Mark of Cain*, 1994
Ed Gorman, *Trouble Man*, 1999

463

CORINNE JOY BROWN

MacGregor's Lantern

(Thorndike, Maine: Thorndike, 2001)

Story type: Historical; Man Alone
Subject(s): Cattle Wars; American West
Major character(s): Sir Kerr McKennon, Rancher (Scotsman); Margaret Dowling, Spouse (of Kerr McKennon); Hugh Redmond MacGregor, Rancher (Scotsman)
Time period(s): 19th century (post-Civil War)
Locale(s): Colorado; Philadelphia, Pennsylvania

Summary: Near the close of the 19th century, wealthy Scottish and English businessmen competed for control of large American cattle ranches. Two Scots, Sir Kerr McKennon and Hugh Redmond MacGregor, are partners in enterprises in Colorado and Wyoming, but the partnership breaks up. McKennon, determined to prove his superiority over his erstwhile partner, takes out a loan from a Philadelphia bank and marries the banker's daughter, Margaret Dowling. The marriage is not a success, but Margaret loves the wild country of the West. When Kerr McKennon is killed, Margaret is determined to run the ranching operations herself, despite the competition with MacGregor. A fine novel about a strong woman.

Other books you might like:
Patrick E. Andrews, *Texican Blood Fight*, 1992
Michael Blake, *Marching to Valhalla*, 1996
Robert J. Conley, *Back to Malachi*, 1997
Ed Gorman, *Dark Trail*, 1998
Page Lambert, *Shifting Stars: A Novel of the West*, 1997

464

IRENE BENNETT BROWN

Blue Horizons

(Thorndike, Maine: Thorndike, 2001)

Story type: Historical; Saga
Series: Women of Paragon Springs. Book 2
Subject(s): American West; Crime and Criminals
Major character(s): Meg Brennon, Pioneer, Abuse Victim; Ted Malloy, Spouse (of Meg Brennon); Jack Ambler, Pioneer, Farmer
Time period(s): 19th century (post-Civil War)
Locale(s): Paragon Springs, Kansas; St. Louis, Missouri

Summary: Fearful but determined, Meg Brennon leaves her beloved homestead at Paragon Springs to return to St. Louis to find and divorce her abusive husband, Ted Malloy. She fled the marriage years before and she hopes he no longer wants to control her. She is wrong. Ted first begs, then threatens, then assaults her. Her lawyer tells her to return home until her case comes up in court, but under no circumstances let Ted know where she lives. She returns home to find that her neighbor, Jack Ambler, resents her even more and he continues his attacks against her property. Meg must hold on to her land, get a divorce, and deal with her feelings toward her St. Louis lawyer.

Where it's reviewed:
Roundup Magazine, October 2001, page 24

Other books by the same author:
Long Road Turning, 2000
The Plainswoman, 1994

Other books you might like:
Jane Candia Coleman, *The O'Keefe Empire*, 2001
Karen Joy Fowler, *Sister Noon*, 2001
Cecelia Holland, *An Ordinary Woman*, 2001
Jane Kirkpatrick, *All Together in One Place*, 2000
Jane Kirkpatrick, *No Eye Can See*, 2001

465

JAMES LEE BURKE

Bitterroot

(New York: Simon & Schuster, 2001)

Story type: Modern; Mystery
Series: Billy Bob Holland
Subject(s): American West; Crime and Criminals
Major character(s): Billy Bob Holland, Lawyer; Wyatt Dixon, Criminal; Tobin Voss, Doctor
Time period(s): 2000s (2001)
Locale(s): Bitterroot Mountains, Montana

Summary: Former Texas Ranger and now lawyer Billy Bob Holland goes to the Bitterroot Mountains of Montana to offer aid to his old friend, Tobin Voss, better known as Doc Voss. A hero of the Vietnam War, Voss never talks about what bothers him most, such as the death of his wife, but he has within himself some of the violence that erupted during the war. Billy Bob has problems of his own, including being stalked by Wyatt Dixon, recently paroled from prison. Dixon

blames Billy Bob for both his imprisonment and his sister's death and swears to kill him. The body count mounts and Billy Bob's tortured mind tries to cope with the mysteries.

Other books by the same author:
Purple Cane Road, 2000
Heartwood, 1999
Sunset Limited, 1999
Heaven's Prisoners, 1997
The Pinball Effect, 1997

Other books you might like:
Frederic Bean, *Murder at the Spirit Cave*, 1999
Peter Bowen, *Thunder Horse*, 1998
Sinclair Browning, *Rode Hard, Put Away Dead*, 2001
Elizabeth Dearl, *Twice Dead*, 2001
Sue Henry, *Dead North*, 2001

466

CAROL CAIL

The Seeds of Time

(Vancouver, Washington: Deadly Alibi, 2001)

Story type: Modern; Mystery
Subject(s): American West; Time Travel; Crime and Criminals
Major character(s): Delia Pitman, Prostitute, Dancer (barroom); Annie Darrow, Archaeologist; Jake, Archaeologist
Time period(s): 19th century (post-Civil War); 2000s
Locale(s): Melissandra, Colorado

Summary: An archaeological dig in Melissandra, Colorado, uncovers a string of unsolved 19th century serial murders. Delia Pitman, a barroom dancer and part-time prostitute from the 19th century makes contact through time with archaeologist Annie Darrow and her assistant, Jake. Delia begs for help from Annie and Jake, and as it turns out, Delia may be able to save Annie's life. A good time travel mystery set in the West.

Where it's reviewed:
Publishers Weekly, June 11, 2001, page 65

Other books by the same author:
Who Was Sylvia, 1999

Other books you might like:
Judy Alter, *Libbie*, 1994
Frederic Bean, *Murder at the Spirit Cave*, 1999
Sinclair Browning, *Rode Hard, Put Away Dead*, 2001
Elizabeth Dearl, *Diamondback*, 2000
    Tracy Madison series
Ed Gorman, *The Fatal Frontier*, 1997
    Martin Greenberg, co-editor

467

DON COLDSMITH

Raven Mocker

(Norman: University of Oklahoma Press, 2001)

Story type: Traditional; Indian Culture

Western

Series: Spanish Bit Saga. Number 30
Subject(s): American West; Indians of North America
Major character(s): Snakewater, Shaman; Corn Flower, Indian (Cherokee), Shaman; Three Fingers, Chieftain (Cherokee)
Time period(s): 19th century

Summary: When the wise woman and healer Snakewater dies, her position is taken over by Corn Flower who also takes Snakewater's name. As a very old woman, Snakewater tells of accusations of being a raven mocker, a spirit that kills young people and steals their years to add to her own life. Innocent of such charges, Snakewater flees the village after assuring the peace chief, Three Fingers, that she is innocent. She joins a traveling band and discovers she is a storyteller. Eventually she joins the Elk-Dog people to whom she teaches the Sun Dance.

Where it's reviewed:
Publishers Weekly, February 19, 2001, page 71
Roundup Magazine, August 2001, page 25

Other books by the same author:
The Long Journey Home, 2001
The Lost Band, 2000
South Wind, 1998
Medicine Hat, 1997
Tallgrass: A Novel of the Great Plains, 1997

Other books you might like:
Margaret Allen, *Keeper of the Stone*, 1995
Irwin R. Blacker, *Taos*, 1959
William Bright, *A Coyote Reader*, 1993
Robert Franklin Gish, *When Coyote Howls*, 1994
Janette Oke, *Drums of Change*, 1996

468

JANE CANDIA COLEMAN

The O'Keefe Empire

(New York: Leisure, 2001)

Story type: Traditional; Man Alone
Subject(s): American West; Cattle Drives
Major character(s): Alex O'Keefe, Rancher; Joanna O'Keefe, Spouse (of Alex), Rancher; Angus McLeod, Sidekick, Cowboy
Time period(s): 19th century (post-Civil War)
Locale(s): New Mexico

Summary: Alex O'Keefe dreams of free acres for the taking in New Mexico Territory. His wife, Joanna, becomes just as enthusiastic, sells the family holdings, and follows Alex by train. When she arrives, Alex is dead and the ranch he dreamed of is being held hostage by the railroad's high shipping fees. Determined to save their dream, she plans to drive her cattle overland to San Diego with the help of Angus McLeod despite those who tell her it can't be done.

Other books by the same author:
Doc Holliday's Gone: A Western Duo, 2000
I, Pearl Hart, 1998
Moving On, 1997
Doc Holliday's Woman, 1995
Stories from Mesa Country, 1991

Other books you might like:
Jack Ballas, *Powder River*, 1995
Ralph Compton, *The Border Empire*, 1997
Wynema McGowan, *While the Rivers Run*, 1996
Geo. W. Proctor, *Comes the Hunter*, 1992
Ellen Recknor, *Leaving Missouri*, 1997

469

BARRY CORD

The Masked Gun

(Bath, England: Chivers, 2001)

Story type: Traditional; Man Alone
Subject(s): American West; Crime and Criminals; Outcasts
Major character(s): Mido Peters, Lawman (sheriff); Jake Grady, Rancher; Ben Codine, Outlaw
Time period(s): 19th century (post-ivil War)
Locale(s): Labelle, Texas

Summary: Sheriff Mido Peters prepares himself for a lawless New Year's Eve after word gets around that rich Jake Grady has promised drinks on the house to any man. That means trouble, and Peters knows it. What he doesn't expect is for Ben Codine to gun down Ira Flint. One is a phony lawman and the other is an outlaw. There is trouble brewing in Labelle and Sheriff Peters is right in the middle of it.

Other books by the same author:
Gallows Ghost, 2000
Hell in Paradise Valley, 1999
Last Chance at Devil's Canyon, 1999
Trail Boss from Texas, 1989
The Guns of Hammer, 1956 (1999)

Other books you might like:
Frederic Bean, *The Outlaw*, 1993
Loren D. Estleman, *Journey of the Dead*, 1998
Elizabeth Fackler, *Road from Betrayal*, 1994
Elmer Kelton, *Honor at Daybreak*, 1991
Steven Krauzer, *God's Country*, 1993

470

RALPH COTTON

Blood Rock

(New York: Signet, 2001)

Story type: Traditional; Quest
Subject(s): American West; History; Adventure and Adventurers
Major character(s): Samuel Burrack, Lawman (Arizona ranger), Adventurer; Clyde Sazes, Lawman (ranger); Junior Lake, Outlaw, Murderer
Time period(s): 19th century (post-Civil War)
Locale(s): Blood Rock, Mexico

Summary: Before he becomes a famous Arizona ranger, Sam Burrack is just another young man roaming the West in search of adventure. When his best friend is killed, he joins up with the famous Ranger Clyde Sazes, who teaches him to track, hunt, and shoot. When Sazes is killed by Junior Lake, Sam,

now a deputy, vows to avenge his friend in the town of Blood Rock, Mexico.

Other books by the same author:
Riders of Judgment, 2001
Hangman's Choice, 2000
Border Dogs, 1999
Hard Justice, 1999
Badlands, 1998

Other books you might like:
Patrick E. Andrews, *Texican Blood Fight*, 1992
Jack Ballas, *Powder River*, 1995
Ralph Hayes, *Revenge of the Buffalo Hunter*, 1992
T.V. Olsen, *The Golden Chance*, 1992
James A. Ritchie, *The Payback*, 1992

471

ANN HOWARD CREEL

The Magic of Ordinary Days
(New York: Viking, 2001)

Story type: Modern
Subject(s): American West; World War II
Major character(s): Livvy Dunne, Spouse (of Ray Singleton); Ray Singleton, Farmer; Rose, Prisoner (Japanese internment camp)
Time period(s): 1940s (1941-1945)
Locale(s): Colorado

Summary: Livvy Dunne becomes pregnant by an army officer in WWII Colorado, and is forced into marriage by her stern minister father. She lives with Ray Singleton on his lonely Colorado farm, two people who know very little about each other and are inexperienced around the opposite sex. Ray is devoted to Livvy and she is happy to a degree, but she wishes he would talk to her more. Livvy becomes entangled with Rose and Lorelei, two Japanese American women in a local internment camp, and is guilty of deceit and manipulation of Ray. A honest picture of the homefront in the West during WWII.

Where it's reviewed:
Publishers Weekly, June 11, 2001, page 57

Other books you might like:
Randy Lee Eickhoff, *Return to Ithaca*, 2001
Lee Martin, *Quakertown*, 2001
Jane Roberts Wood, *Grace*, 2001

472

PATRICK DEAREN

Comanche Peace Pipe
(Plano, Texas: Republic of Texas, 2001)

Story type: Young Readers; Indian Culture
Series: Lone Star Heroes. Book 1
Subject(s): American West; Indians of North America
Major character(s): Fish Rawlings, Child; Hunting Bear, Indian (Comanche), Child; Gid Rawlings, Cousin (of Fish)
Time period(s): 1860s (1867)
Locale(s): Texas

Summary: Eleven-year-old Fish Rawlings and his cousin, Gid, are riding across Texas in a wagon train. When Fish helps a Comanche youth his own age, he knows he can't tell anyone about Hunting Bear because all the adults on the wagon train hate Comanches. Hunting Bear also knows he can't tell the men of his village about Fish, or the tribe will attack the wagon train. The Comanches decide to attack anyway, and it is up to Fish and Hunting Bear to make peace among the adults.

Other books by the same author:
On the Pecos Trail, 2001 (Lone Star Heroes series)
The Hidden Treasure of the Chisos, 2001 (Lone Star Heroes series)

Other books you might like:
Phyllis de la Garza, *Camels West*, 1998
James Rice, *Victor Lopez at the Alamo*, 2001
Melinda Rice, *Fire on the Hillside*, 2001
    Lone Star Heroines series
Melinda Rice, *Messenger on the Battlefield*, 2001
    Lone Star Heroines series
Melinda Rice, *Secrets in the Sky*, 2001
    Lone Star Heroines series

473

PATRICK DEAREN

The Hidden Treasure of the Chisos
(Plano, Texas: Republic of Texas, 2001)

Story type: Traditional; Young Readers
Series: Lone Star Heroes. Book 3
Subject(s): American West; History; Adventure and Adventurers
Major character(s): Fish Rawlings, Child; Gid Rawlings, Cousin (of Fish); Child-of-the-Waters, Indian (Apache)
Time period(s): 1860s (1869)
Locale(s): Big Bend, Texas

Summary: According to legend, there's a lost gold mine in the Chisos Mountains in the Big Bend region of Texas. When Fish Rawlings and his cousin, Gid, find a dying Indian in the desert, they have reason to believe that the gold mine really exists and now they know where it is. But do they dare try to find it? The boys would have to cross a desert prowled by Apaches, and ride down a trail infested with devil animals. Even with the Apache boy Child-of-the-Waters as a guide, do they dare take the chance?

Other books by the same author:
Comanche Peace Pipe, 2001 (Lone Star Heroes. Book 1)
On the Pecos Trail, 2001 (Lone Star Heroes. Book 2)

Other books you might like:
Phyllis de la Garza, *Camels West*, 1998
James Rice, *Victor Lopez at the Alamo*, 2001
Melinda Rice, *Fire on the Hillside*, 2001
    Lone Star Heroines series
Melinda Rice, *Messenger on the Battlefield*, 2001
    Lone Star Heroines series
Melinda Rice, *Secrets in the Sky*, 2001
    Lone Star Heroines series

Western

474

PATRICK DEAREN

On the Pecos Trail

(Plano, Texas: Republic of Texas, 2001)

Story type: Traditional; Young Readers
Series: Lone Star Heroes. Book 2
Subject(s): American West; Cattle Drives
Major character(s): Fish Rawlings, Child; Gid Rawlings, Cousin (of Fish); Guy Rawlings, Relative (Fish's uncle), Rancher
Time period(s): 1860s (1868)
Locale(s): Seep Springs, Texas

Summary: All his life Fish Rawlings has wanted to be a cowboy, but when his father dies on a cattle drive, all the joy of life leaves him. Then his uncle, Guy, convinces his ma that Fish needs to go on a cattle drive to Horsehead Crossings on the Pecos to help him get over his pa's death. At first Fish isn't sure about this, but then he saves his cousin, Gid, from a runaway horse, and the excitement never seems to stop. Amid sandstorms, stampedes, lightning and twisters, the action goes on and on and Fish regains his joy in living.

Other books by the same author:
Comanche Peace Pipe, 2001 (Lone Star Heroes. Book 1)
The Hidden Treasure of the Chisos, 2001 (Lone Star Heroes. Book 3)

Other books you might like:
Phyllis de la Garza, *Camels West*, 1998
James Rice, *Victor Lopez at the Alamo*, 2001
Melinda Rice, *Fire on the Hillside*, 2001
    Lone Star Heroines series
Melinda Rice, *Messenger on the Battlefield*, 2001
    Lone Star Heroines series
Melinda Rice, *Secrets in the Sky*, 2001
    Lone Star Heroines series

475

ELIZABETH DEARL

Twice Dead

(Brighton, Michigan: Avid, 2001)

Story type: Modern; Mystery
Series: Taylor Madison
Subject(s): American West; Mystery and Detective Stories
Major character(s): Taylor Madison, Detective—Amateur, Writer; Cal Arnette, Lawman; Dorothy Stenson, Neighbor
Time period(s): 2000s (2001)
Locale(s): Perdue, Texas

Summary: Taylor Madison just got a new contract for a novel and her boy friend, Cal Arnette, is running for sheriff. It looks like he might win if Taylor's neighbor, Dorothy Stenson, doesn't tell everyone that she saw Cal leaving Taylor's house early one morning. Sex outside of wedlock isn't approved of in Perdue, Texas, and Taylor is afraid she might lose Cal votes. Then murder happens and Taylor doesn't have time to worry about what the neighbors think.

Other books by the same author:
Diamondback, 2000 (Taylor Madison series)

Other books you might like:
Frederic Bean, *Murder at the Spirit Cave*, 1999
Peter Bowen, *Thunder Horse*, 1998
    Gabriel Du Pree series
Sinclair Browning, *Rode Hard, Put Away Dead*, 2001
John Paxson, *A Golden Trail of Murder*, 2001
M.K. Preston, *Perhaps She'll Die*, 2001

476

H.A. DEROSSO

.44

(Bath, England: Chivers, 2001)

Story type: Traditional; Chase
Subject(s): American West; Crime and Criminals
Major character(s): Dan Harland, Gunfighter; Jim Lancaster, Rancher; Buckskin Tom Elliott, Rancher
Time period(s): 1880s (1881)
Locale(s): West

Summary: Dan Harland has a reputation with his .44. Tired of the hypocrisy, Harland decides if he is going to be treated like a gunman, he may as well live like one. He hires out his gun to Buckskin Tom Elliott to kill Jim Lancaster. When Lancaster draws first, then doesn't fire, Harland is sick at heart. The man had deliberately let Harland kill him, and Harland can't stand it. He has to know why Elliott wanted Lancaster killed and who ordered it.

Other books by the same author:
Riders of the Shadowlands, 1999
Under the Burning Sun, 1997

Other books you might like:
Max Brand, *The Bright Face of Danger*, 2000
Peter Dawson, *Rattlesnake Mesa*, 1997
Ed Gorman, *Trouble Man*, 1999
Douglas Hirt, *The Silent Gun*, 1993
Arthur Moore, *Rebel*, 1992

477

SYBIL DOWNING

The Binding Oath

(Boulder: University Press of Colorado, 2001)

Story type: Historical; Saga
Subject(s): American West; Historical; Racism
Major character(s): Liz O'Brien, Journalist (reporter); Phil Van Cise, Lawyer (district attorney); Frank Capillupo, Pilot
Time period(s): 1920s (1922)
Locale(s): Denver, Colorado

Summary: When the Ku Klux Klan gathers strength during the disillusionment following WWI, Colorado has one of the largest memberships outside the South. In June of 1922, the Grand Dragon of Colorado's Ku Klux Klan calls a press conference to announce their plans to recall district attorney Phil Van Cise and replace him with a Klan member. Only a

brash young reporter from Denver's newspaper attends. Liz O'Brien's editor dismisses the story, but when Liz stumbles across a body in Denver's slums, she is convinced that the Klan's reign of terror has already begun. With the help of Van Cise and an airmail pilot named Frank Capillupo, Liz races to solve the murder.

Where it's reviewed:
Roundup Magazine, October 2001, page 25

Other books by the same author:
The Ladies of the Goldfield Stock Exchange, 1997
Fire in the Hole, 1996

Other books you might like:
Frederic Bean, *Murder at the Spirit Cave*, 1999
Peter Bowen, *Thunder Horse*, 1998
Sinclair Browning, *Rode Hard, Put Away Dead*, 2001
Jack Curtis, *The Mark of Cain*, 1994
J.A. Jance, *Outlaw Mountain*, 1999

478

RANDY LEE EICKHOFF

Return to Ithaca

(New York: Forge, 2001)

Story type: Modern; Man Alone
Subject(s): Military Life; Indians of North America; American West
Major character(s): Henry Morgan, Military Personnel (retired); Billy Morgan, Relative (Henry's brother); Dog Tiresias, Indian (Sioux), Cowboy
Time period(s): 20th century (1960s-1990s)
Locale(s): Kentucky; Ithaca, West

Summary: Eickhoff blends a Western and a Vietnam war story to create a literary novel about Henry Morgan, one of the very few survivors of an elite team working with the Montagnard tribesmen. Telling the story of his attempts to come home to the fictional high plains town of Ithaca and his ranch there, he is near the end of his life and living in a monastery in Kentucky. He recounts the death of his brother, Billy, and his guilt in not being able to save him. Interspersed with Morgan's account is narrative by Dog, a Sioux Indian hand who works on the ranch. Eickhoff attempts to point to the similarities between the fate of Vietnam veterans and a disjoined and rejected life.

Where it's reviewed:
Publishers Weekly, June 11, 2001, page 59

Other books by the same author:
Bowie, 1998 (Leonard C. Eickhoff, co-author)
The Fourth Horseman, 1997

Other books you might like:
Judy Alter, *Libbie*, 1994
Win Blevins, *Stone Song*, 1995
Frederick J. Chiaventone, *A Road We Do Not Know*, 1996
Harry Combs, *Brules*, 1994
Will Henry, *No Survivors*, 1950

479

LOREN D. ESTLEMAN

The Master Executioner

(New York: Forge, 2001)

Story type: Historical; Saga
Subject(s): American West; Crime and Criminals
Major character(s): Oscar Stone, Executioner; Fabian Rudd, Executioner; Gretchen Stone, Spouse (of Oscar Stone)
Time period(s): 19th century (1866-1898)
Locale(s): Fort Leavenworth, Kansas

Summary: Oscar Stone witnesses the hanging of four Confederates during the Civil War, and vows to never watch another execution. Released from the Union army, he becomes a carpenter, marries Gretchen, and the two travel to Kansas to start a new life. The only work Oscar can find is building a gallows. When the hangman, Fabian Rudd, gives him an invitation to a hanging to see how a proper one is done, Oscar knows he has found his true work. For over 30 years, he is the master executioner in the West even though it costs him his marriage after Gretchen discovers his new livelihood. A most unusual story by a talented writer.

Where it's reviewed:
Roundup Magazine, August 2001, page 26

Other books by the same author:
The Rocky Mountain Moving Picture Association, 1999
Journey of the Dead, 1998
Billy Gashade, 1997
City of Widows, 1994
Sudden Country, 1991

Other books you might like:
Jack Ballas, *Gun Boss*, 1999
L.D. Clark, *A Bright Tragic Thing*, 1992
W. Michael Gear, *Big Horn Legacy*, 1988
Preston Lewis, *Mix-Up at the O.K. Corral*, 1996
Ellen Recknor, *Me and the Boys*, 1995

480

ANDREW J. FENADY

There Came a Stranger

(New York: Forge, 2001)

Story type: Traditional; Man Alone
Subject(s): American West
Major character(s): Chad Walker, Rancher; Adam Dawson, Military Personnel (ex-soldier), Drifter; Lorena Walker, Spouse (of Chad)
Time period(s): 19th century (post-Civil War)
Locale(s): Pinto, Texas

Summary: Chad Walker is one of those individuals who doesn't care about anyone else, including his wife, Lorena, and his horse, so the town of Pinto, Texas, is shocked when he takes up with Adam Dawson. After leaving the army and his friend and commanding officer, Autie, better known as George Custer, Adam has become a drifter and swears he will never kill another man no matter what. However, he doesn't

Western

count on falling in love with another man's wife and ending up in both a land war and a love war.

Where it's reviewed:
Publishers Weekly, June 11, 2001, page 60
Roundup Magazine, August 2001, page 26

Other books by the same author:
The Rebel: Johnny Yuma, 1999
The Summer of Jack London, 1998
Runaways, 1994

Other books you might like:
Don Coldsmith, *The Long Journey Home*, 2001
Cynthia Haseloff, *Changing Trains*, 2001
Ken Hodgson, *Lone Survivor*, 2001
Jory Sherman, *The Ballad of Pinewood Lake*, 2001
Richard S. Wheeler, *Restitution*, 2001

481

BARBARA SPENCER FOSTER

Girl of the Manzanos

(Santa Fe, New Mexico: Sunstone, 2001)

Story type: Historical
Subject(s): American West; Pioneers
Major character(s): Mardee Spenser, Heroine; Jeff Corbin, Lawyer; Frankie Moseby, Young Man (Mexican American)
Time period(s): 1910s (1912)
Locale(s): Santa Fe, New Mexico; Eastview, New Mexico

Summary: New Mexico has just achieved statehood and Mardee Spenser is looking past the small town of Eastview toward Santa Fe. She interprets for her father during the statehood meetings where she meets Jeff Corbin, an ambitious young lawyer who declares his love for her and promises to get her a job in the new governor's office. Mardee leaves her family for Santa Fe, but her fate among the politically ambitious is uncertain. Will Jeff Corbin keep his word to get her a job, and what of Frankie Moseby, the half-Mexican boy who has always loved her?

Other books you might like:
K. Follis Cheatham, *The Adventures of Elizabeth Fortune*, 2000
Jane Candia Coleman, *Moving On*, 1997
Bill Dugan, *Brady's Law*, 1993
Jason Manning, *The Black Jacks*, 1997
P.G. Nagle, *Glorieta*, 1998

482

BENNETT FOSTER

Cow Thief Trail

(Bath, England: Chivers, 2001)

Story type: Traditional; Revenge
Subject(s): American West; Historical; Crime and Criminals
Major character(s): Miles Trask, Cowboy, Outcast; Asa Ryland, Rancher; Whitey Arburg, Lawman (sheriff)
Time period(s): 19th century (post-Civil War)
Locale(s): Tramparas, Texas

Summary: Five years ago Miles Trask was a wild, grieving young man, forced off his own land by a crooked uncle when his father died. He was also betrayed by Asa Ryland, the richest rancher around, and Whitey Arburg the sheriff—when he chose to wear the badge. Now Miles is back and he is ready for revenge against those who wronged him. There will be killing before it is all over.

Other books by the same author:
Lone Wolf, 1999
Mexican Saddle, 1999
Dust of the Trail, 1998
Rawhide Road, 1997
Badlands, 1938

Other books you might like:
Patrick E. Andrews, *Texican Blood Fight*, 1992
Erie Atkins, *Killing Revenge*, 1994
Ed Gorman, *Wolf Moon*, 1993
Robert Lake, *Texas Iron*, 1991
T.V. Olsen, *The Burning Sky*, 1991

483

KAREN JOY FOWLER

Sister Noon

(New York: Putnam, 2001)

Story type: Historical; Saga
Subject(s): American West; Mystery
Major character(s): Lizzie Hayes, Spinster, Volunteer; Mary Ellen Pleasant, Wealthy; Jenny Ijub, Orphan, Child
Time period(s): 19th century (post-Civil War)
Locale(s): San Francisco, California

Summary: Aging spinster and socialite Lizzie Hayes is the volunteer treasurer of the Ladies' Relief and Protection Society Home, when the reputed madam, Mrs. Mary Ellen Pleasant, arrives with a four-year-old girl in tow. Supposedly the girl, Jenny Ijub, is an orphan, but Lizzie believes that she is the illegitimate daughter of a wealthy man, a man who might be persuaded to donate to the upkeep of the Society.

Where it's reviewed:
Publishers Weekly, April 9, 2001, page 48

Other books by the same author:
Black Glass, 1998
The Sweetheart Season, 1996
Sarah Canary, 1991

Other books you might like:
David Ballantine, *Chalk's Woman*, 2000
Sinclair Browning, *Rode Hard, Put Away Dead*, 2001
Jane Candia Coleman, *Borderlands: Western Stories*, 2000
Cynthia Haseloff, *Changing Trains*, 2001
Ellen Gray Massey, *Borderland Homecoming*, 2000

484

CHARLES E. FRIEND

Shannon: US Marshal

(New York: Avalon, 2001)

Story type: Traditional; Man Alone
Subject(s): American West; Crime and Criminals
Major character(s): Clay Shannon, Lawman; Charlotte Alvarez, Rancher; King Kruger, Villain
Time period(s): 19th century (post-Civil War)
Locale(s): Los Santos, New Mexico

Summary: After the deaths of his wife and son and the closing of the mines in Whiskey Creek, Sheriff Clay Shannon is ready to retire and search for a new life. A former deputy asks Shannon to come to Los Santos, New Mexico, to protect the family and ranch of Charlotte Alvarez against a land grabbing villain named King Kruger. Shannon isn't interested until Charlotte gets him an appointment as a US Marshal, then he begins to investigate the corrupt Kruger. It's not the easiest job though, and Shannon wonders if he made a mistake becoming a lawman again.

Other books by the same author:
Shannon's Law, 2000
Shannon's Way, 1999

Other books you might like:
A.J. Arnold, *Dead Man's Cache*, 1988
Jack Curtis, *No Mercy*, 1995
Ernest Haycox, *Rim of the Desert*, 1940
Elmer Kelton, *Cloudy in the West*, 1997
T.V. Olsen, *The Golden Chance*, 1992
    Spur winner

485

R. GARCIA Y ROBERTSON

American Woman

(New York: Forge, 2001)

Story type: Historical; Indian Culture
Subject(s): American West; Indians of North America
Major character(s): Sarah Kilory, Spouse (of Yellow Legs); Yellow Legs, Spouse (of Sarah Kilory), Indian (Sioux); George Armstrong Custer, Military Personnel, Historical Figure
Time period(s): 1860s; 1870s (1860-1876)
Locale(s): Little Big Horn, Montana

Summary: Sarah Kilory, a young Quaker woman, goes West to teach school in Indian Territory. After falling in love, she becomes the second wife of a Sioux warrior named Yellow Legs. Sarah then takes the name American Woman, and it is through her eyes that we see events leading up to the massacre of General Custer's troops at the Battle of the Little Big Horn.

Where it's reviewed:
Roundup Magazine, October 2001, page 26

Other books by the same author:
The Virgin and the Dinosaur, 1996
The Spiral Dance, 1991

Other books you might like:
Sanora Babb, *Cry of the Tinamou*, 1997
Rick Bass, *The Sky, the Stars, the Wilderness*, 1997
Win Blevins, *Stone Song*, 1995
Frederick J. Chiaventone, *A Road We Do Not Know*, 1996
E. Donald Two-Rivers, *Survivor's Medicine*, 1998

486

RACHEL GIBSON

True Confessions

(New York: Avon, 2001)

Story type: Modern
Subject(s): American West; Romance
Major character(s): Hope Spencer, Journalist (tabloid reporter); Dylan Taber, Lawman (sheriff)
Time period(s): 2000s (2001)
Locale(s): Gospel, Idaho

Summary: When Hope Spencer roars into Gospel, Idaho, in her turquoise Tony Lamas and tight jeans, Sheriff Dylan Taber knows she's trouble with a capital T. He doesn't expect to fall in love with her, not when he is a single father with a youthful bad reputation to live down. Hope, on the other hand, is hoping to recover from a bad marriage and write a few captured-seduced-abducted by alien stories for the tabloid she works for. She certainly doesn't expect to fall in love with a small town western sheriff.

Where it's reviewed:
Publishers Weekly, June 11, 2001, page 67

Other books by the same author:
It Must Be Love, 2000
Truly Madly Yours, 1999
Simply Irresistible, 1998

Other books you might like:
Frederic Bean, *Murder at the Spirit Cave*, 1999
Sinclair Browning, *Rode Hard, Put Away Dead*, 2001
Carol Cail, *The Seeds of Time*, 2001
Randall Beth Platt, *The Royalscope Fe-As-Ko*, 1997
Ellen Recknor, *Me and the Boys*, 1995

487

ED GORMAN

Ghost Town

(New York: Berkley, 2001)

Story type: Traditional; Man Alone
Subject(s): American West; Crime and Criminals
Major character(s): Bryce Lamont, Thief (paroled); Jed Wylie, Outlaw, Thief; Frank Stodla, Outlaw, Thief
Time period(s): 19th century (post-Civil War)
Locale(s): Wyatt, Wisconsin

Summary: Bryce Lamont tracks down Jed Wylie and Frank Stodla, his two cohorts who took the diamonds Bryce helped steal and watched him go to jail. He finds them in Wyatt, Wisconsin, walking the straight and narrow like honest men, and plans how he will steal back the fifty thousand dollars worth of diamonds. Then a gang of thieves clean out the bank,

Western

robbing Bryce of what he can't replace, and he plans to track them down and take revenge. In the meantime, malaria is killing the townspeople one by one.

Other books by the same author:
Trouble Man, 1999
Dark Trail, 1998
Gunslinger, 1995
The Sharpshooter, 1993
Wolf Moon, 1993

Other books you might like:
Frederic Bean, *Border Justice*, 1994
Clifford Blair, *Bushwhacker's Gun*, 1996
Hascal Giles, *Texas Tough*, 1992
James A. Janke, *A Tin Star for Braddock*, 1992
Richard S. Wheeler, *Dark Passage*, 1998

488

ZANE GREY

To the Last Man

(New York: Forge, 2001)

Story type: Traditional; Revenge
Subject(s): American West; Cattle Wars; Ranch Life
Major character(s): Jean Isbel, Rancher; Ellen Jorth, Young Woman (daughter of a sheep rancher); Gass Isbel, Parent (Jean Isbel's father)
Time period(s): 19th century (post-Civil War)
Locale(s): Pleasant Valley, Arizona

Summary: Set against the real background of the Pleasant Valley war, a feud between cattlemen and sheep ranchers, *To the Last Man* is the story of the romance between Jean Isbel, son of a cattleman, and Ellen Jorth, daughter of a sheep rancher. This is a tragic range war both in reality and in fiction.

Other books by the same author:
The Westerners: Stories of the West, 2000
Woman of the Frontier, 2000
Rangers of the Lone Star, 1999
Last of the Duanes, 1996
Riders of the Purple Sage, 1912

Other books you might like:
Jack Ballas, *Gun Boss*, 1999
L.D. Clark, *A Bright Tragic Thing*, 1992
Charles Hackenberry, *Friends*, 1993
Paul A. Hawkins, *White Moon Tree*, 1994
Suzann Ledbetter, *Pure Justice*, 1997

489

FRED GROVE

Red River Stage

(Thorndike, Maine: Thorndike 2001)

Story type: Traditional; Collection
Subject(s): American West; Short Stories

Summary: This is a collection of 12 short stories, including two Spur Award winners.

Other books by the same author:
A Distance of Ground, 2000
Destiny Valley, 2000
Into the Far Mountains, 1999
Man on a Red Horse, 1998
Bitter Trumpet, 1989

Other books you might like:
Sanora Babb, *Cry of the Tinamou*, 1997
Max Brand, *Men Beyond the Law*, 2001
Will Henry, *Tumbleweeds*, 2001
Billy Bob Hill, *Texas Short Stories 2*, 2000
Frances Fuller Victor, *Women of the Gold Rush*, 1998

490

SUE HENRY

Dead North

(New York: Morrow, 2001)

Story type: Modern; Mystery
Series: Jessie Arnold
Subject(s): American West; Mystery and Detective Stories
Major character(s): Jessie Arnold, Detective—Amateur; Patrick Cutler, Teenager, Runaway; Maxie McNabb, Widow(er)
Time period(s): 2000s
Locale(s): Cody, Wyoming; Fairbanks, Alaska

Summary: A beautifully written novel in the Jessie Arnold series, this one finds Jessie and Tank, her lead dog, in Idaho where she has agreed to pick up an RV and drive it back to Fairbanks. On the way, she picks up a runaway teenager, Patrick Cutler from Cody, Wyoming, and befriends a feisty widow named Maxie McNabb. Neither Jessie nor Maxie entirely believe Patrick's story about why he's on his way to Fairbanks, but they don't confront the teenager because he seems frightened. Along with some marvelous characters that range from an aging truck driver to an elderly friend of Patrick's, the trio engage in a series of chase scenes trying to escape Patrick's stepfather, who killed Patrick's mother and is now searching for him.

Where it's reviewed:
Publishers Weekly, June 11, 2001, page 64

Other books by the same author:
Beneath the Ashes, 2000
Murder on the Iditarod Trail, 1998

Other books you might like:
Judy Alter, *Libbie*, 1994
Mike Blakely, *Summer of Pearls*, 2000
Sinclair Browning, *Rode Hard, Put Away Dead*, 2001
Elizabeth Dearl, *Diamondback*, 2000
Will Henry, *No Survivors*, 1950

491

JOHN HOCKENBERRY

A River out of Eden

(New York: Doubleday, 2001)

Story type: Modern; Man Alone

Subject(s): Environmental Problems
Major character(s): Francine Smohalla, Scientist (marine biologist); Charley Shen-oh-way, Parent (Francine's father), Murderer; Jack Charnock, Scientist, Terrorist
Time period(s): 2000s (2001)
Locale(s): Washington

Summary: Francine Smohalla is a half-white, half-Chinook marine biologist in charge of the salmon hatchery at the Bonneville Dam. She is torn between her desire to serve her profession and her native heritage, which says let the river be free. Her father, Charley Shen-oh-way, demands that the dams on the Columbia be destroyed and runs around murdering people in pursuit of his goal. Jack Charnock, a weapons designer at the nearby nuclear facility, Hansford Nuclear Reservation, also believes in the river being free and has the knowledge to design weapons to destroy the dams. Francine knows she must stop her father's killing spree and prevent Charnock from blowing up the dams, but she is in a race against time.

Where it's reviewed:
Library Journal, June 1, 2001, page 216

Other books you might like:
Frederic Bean, *Murder at the Spirit Cave*, 1999
Peter Bowen, *Thunder Horse*, 1998
Carol Cail, *The Seeds of Time*, 2001
Elizabeth Dearl, *Diamondback*, 2000
    Taylor Madison series
Elizabeth Dearl, *Twice Dead*, 2001

492

RAY HOGAN

The Doomsday Marshal and the Mountain Man

(New York: Leisure, 2001)

Story type: Traditional; Man Alone
Series: Doomsday Marshal
Subject(s): American West; Crime and Criminals
Major character(s): John Rye, Lawman (marshal); Hode Wilkinson, Outlaw, Mountain Man; Morning Sky, Indian (Kiowa), Captive (of Hode Wilkinson)
Time period(s): 19th century (post-Civil War)
Locale(s): Springtown, New Mexico; Cimarron, New Mexico

Summary: Hode Wilkinson is 300 pounds of the meanest mountain man in the West. Guilty of murdering at least nine people and kidnapping a Kiowa girl named Morning Sky, Hode is on the run. Tracking him is the legendary John Rye, known as the Doomsday Marshal. John is determined to capture Wilkinson and return him to justice—if the Kiowas don't get him first.

Other books by the same author:
Stonebreaker's Ridge, 2000
The Doomsday Marshal and the Comancheros, 2000
Guns of Freedom, 1999
Legend of a Badman, 1997
Soldier in Buckskin, 1996

Other books you might like:
Rick Bass, *The Sky, the Stars, the Wilderness*, 1997
Frank Bonham, *One Ride Too Many*, 1997
T.T. Flynn, *Rawhide*, 1996
Clarence E. Mulford, *Bar-20 Days*, 1993
Ken Wilkerson, *Blue Ride: Stories from Old Desert Towns*, 1998

493

CECELIA HOLLAND

An Ordinary Woman

(New York: Forge, 2001)

Story type: Historical; Saga
Subject(s): American West; Emigration and Immigration
Major character(s): Nancy Kelsey, Settler, Historical Figure; Ben Kelsey, Historical Figure, Settler; Andrew Kelsey, Historical Figure, Settler
Time period(s): 1840s (1841)
Locale(s): West

Summary: This account is based on journals written at the time by Nancy Kelsey, 18, about the journey west with her husband, Ben, and his brother, Andrew. Nancy was the first American woman to reach California, and Holland describes her journey in meticulously accurate detail.

Other books by the same author:
The Pillar of the Sky, 2000
Lily Nevada, 1999
Railroad Schemes, 1997
Jerusalem, 1987
The Kings in Winter, 1968

Other books you might like:
Don Coldsmith, *The Long Journey Home*, 2001
Jane Candia Coleman, *Moving On*, 1997
Jane Kirkpatrick, *All Together in One Place*, 2000
Kay L. McDonald, *Beyond the Vision*, 2000
Vella Munn, *Soul of the Sacred Earth*, 2000

494

JAMES D. HOUSTON

Snow Mountain Passage

(New York: Knopf, 2001)

Story type: Historical; Saga
Subject(s): American West; Migration
Major character(s): James Frazier Reed, Pioneer, Historical Figure; Patty Reed, Relative (daughter of James Reed), Historical Figure; George Donner, Pioneer, Historical Figure
Time period(s): 1840s (1846)
Locale(s): Donner Pass, California; Sacramento, California

Summary: This account of the Donner party and the tragedy that resulted is told by James Frazier Reed. Interspersed with Reed's account are trail notes written from memory 75 years later by his daughter, Patty. A powerful and historically accurate portrayal of the Donner party.

Where it's reviewed:
Publishers Weekly, March 19, 2001, page 77

Other books by the same author:
The Last Paradise, 1998
Continental Drift, 1978

Other books you might like:
John Edward Ames, *The Unwritten Order*, 1996
Don Coldsmith, *The Lost Band*, 2000
Kathleen O'Neal Gear, *The Summoning God*, 2000
    W. Michael Gear, co-author
Jane Kirkpatrick, *All Together in One Place*, 2000
JoAnn Levy, *For California's Gold*, 2000

495

BILL HYDE

Bodie Gone

(Santa Fe, New Mexico: Sunstone, 2001)

Story type: Modern; Mystery
Subject(s): American West; Time Travel
Major character(s): Frances DeQuill, Socialite, Journalist; Peter Quinn, Miner (Irish American); Pierre Lovell, Trapper (French Canadian)
Time period(s): 1840s (1849); 2000s (2001)
Locale(s): San Francisco, California; Bridgeport, California; Bodie, California

Summary: Frances DeQuill is an affluent housewife and part-time journalist whose investigation of strange happenings in her hometown of Bridgeport and the nearby ghost town of Bodie leads to her being thrown in jail. Her quest for an explanation sends her back to 1849 and the Gold Rush, where she meets miners Peter Quinn and Pierre Lovell. A time travel book with a twist ending.

Other books you might like:
David Ballantine, *Chalk's Woman*, 2000
Sinclair Browning, *Rode Hard, Put Away Dead*, 2001
Jane Kirkpatrick, *All Together in One Place*, 2000
JoAnn Levy, *For California's Gold*, 2000
Ellen Gray Massey, *Borderland Homecoming*, 2000

496

ELMER KELTON

The Time It Never Rained

(New York: Forge, 1999)

Story type: Modern; Man Alone
Subject(s): American West; Ranch Life; Drought
Major character(s): Charlie Flagg, Rancher; March Nicholson, Government Official (Agriculture Department); Rounder Pike, Rancher
Time period(s): 1950s
Locale(s): Rio Seco, Texas

Summary: The drought is years old, the cattle and sheep fed by hauling in grain, for all the grass has withered and died. The government in the person of March Nicholson hands out checks to try to keep the farmers and ranchers afloat, but Charlie Flagg is old-fashioned. He refuses help even though Rounder Pike tells him it's the only way to survive. Government help comes with government orders and Charlie Flagg is not going to take orders from anyone about what to do with his own land. He'll go his own way and survive the drought, or not, on his own. This is one of the finest Westerns ever written, winner of the Spur and the Western Heritage Awards.

Other books by the same author:
Badger Boy, 2001
The Buckskin Line, 1999
The Smiling Country, 1998
Cloudy in the West, 1997
The Pumpkin Rollers, 1996

Other books you might like:
Jane Valentine Barker, *Mari*, 1997
Matt Braun, *Texas Empire*, 1997
Wayne Davis, *John Stone and the Choctaw Kid*, 1993
Laura Kalpakian, *Caveat*, 1998
Randall Beth Platt, *The Royalscope Fe-As-Ko*, 1997

497

HIRAM KING

Broken Ranks

(New York: Leisure, 2001)

Story type: Traditional; Man Alone
Subject(s): American West; African Americans
Major character(s): Ples Butler, Gunfighter (African American); Kalem Jones, Military Personnel (buffalo soldier); Jerico, Military Personnel (buffalo soldier)
Time period(s): 1860s (1865)
Locale(s): Fort Leavenworth, Kansas

Summary: For many ex-slaves who want to make a new life for themselves joining the army sounds like the way to do it. The Tenth Cavalry Regiment will be entirely African American and the soldiers will receive an education and have a career. Trouble starts for the recruits like Jerico and Kalem Jones before they have a chance to fight the Indians. They must travel from St. Louis to Fort Leavenworth, a lot of the way through hostile ex-Confederate territory. To counterbalance the hostile Southerners, the army hires Ples Butler, a black gunfighter who swears to get the train of recruits to Leavenworth come hell or high water.

Other books by the same author:
Dark Trail, 1998
High Prairie, 1997

Other books you might like:
Charles Brashear, *Killing Cynthia Ann*, 1999
David Anthony Durham, *Gabriel's Story*, 2001
Don Johnson, *Brasada*, 1999
Lauran Paine, *The White Bird*, 1999
Michael Zimmer, *Where the Buffalo Roam*, 1999

498

TRACY KNIGHT

Beneath a Whiskey Sky

(New York: Leisure, 2001)

Story type: Traditional; Man Alone
Subject(s): American West
Major character(s): Sim McCracken, Gunfighter, Drifter; Charles McCracken, Relative (Sim's brother), Handicapped; Amos Pell, Rancher
Time period(s): 19th century (post-Civil War)
Locale(s): Missouri

Summary: Amos Pell hires Sim McCracken to kill a young preacher, but when the minister asks Sim to assess his own life, Sim lets him go and decides to leave his past behind. Pell is not happy with Sim and sends men after him to balance his account with a bullet. Then there's the problem of Charlie, Sim's handicapped brother, whom Sim must take to a hospital, not an easy chore with a gunman breathing down your neck.

Other books you might like:
Don Coldsmith, *The Long Journey Home*, 2001
Jane Candia Coleman, *Moving On*, 1997
Jane Kirkpatrick, *All Together in One Place*, 2000
Aaron Latham, *Code of the West*, 2001
Preston Lewis, *Hard Texas Winter*, 1981

499

JOE R. LANSDALE

The Magic Wagon

(Burton, Michigan: Subterranean, 2001)

Story type: Traditional
Subject(s): American West; Humor
Major character(s): Buster Fogg, Drifter; Billy Bob Daniels, Sidekick; Albert, Slave (freed)
Time period(s): 19th century (post-Civil War)
Locale(s): Mud Creek, Texas

Summary: Buster Fogg joins Billy Bob Daniels' patent medicine show after his family is killed in a tornado. Also with the show are Albert, an ex-slave, and Rot Toe, the wrestling ape. As the show rolls into Mud Creek, Texas, Billy Bob is challenged to a gunfight by Texas Jack, who, it is said, even frightened Wild Bill Hickok whom Billy Bob claims is his father. Buster and Albert have to figure out a way to rescue Billy Bob from his situation.

Where it's reviewed:
Publishers Weekly, May 14, 2001, page 55

Other books by the same author:
Blood Dance, 2000
The Bottoms, 2000
Freezer Burn, 1999
Rumble Tumble, 1999
The Long Ones, 1999

Other books you might like:
Jane Candia Coleman, *Doc Holliday's Gone: A Western Duo*, 2000
Cynthia Haseloff, *Changing Trains*, 2001
Cecelia Holland, *Lily Nevada*, 1999
Jane Kirkpatrick, *All Together in One Place*, 2000
Suzanne Lyon, *Lady Buckaroo*, 2000

500

AARON LATHAM

Code of the West

(New York: Simon & Schuster, 2001)

Story type: Historical; Saga
Subject(s): American West
Major character(s): Jimmy Goodnight, Captive, Cowboy; Revelie Goodnight, Spouse (of Jimmy); Jack Loving, Cowboy
Time period(s): 19th century (post-Civil War)
Locale(s): Palo Duro Canyon, Texas

Summary: This take on the King Arthur legend is built on the historical bones of Charlie Goodnight and Oliver Loving, with the facts changed to fit the myth. Charlie Goodnight becomes Jimmy, while Oliver Loving is known as Jack Loving. Goodnight's wife, Revelie in the book, plays Guinevere. The story is symbolic, but may put off many western readers who know the real story of Goodnight and Loving.

Where it's reviewed:
Library Journal, March 15, 2001, page 105
Publishers Weekly, February 19, 2001, page 69

Other books you might like:
Matt Braun, *Texas Empire*, 1997
Jerry Craven, *Snake Mountain*, 2000
Zane Grey, *Woman of the Frontier*, 2000
Elmer Kelton, *The Smiling Country*, 1998

501

MICHAEL LITTLE

Queen of the Rodeo

(Eugene, Oregon: Triple Tree, 2001)

Story type: Modern
Subject(s): Rodeos; American West; Humor
Major character(s): Donna Cooper, Rodeo Rider, Heroine; Tyler Griffin, Rancher, Rodeo Rider; Darryl King, Villain
Time period(s): 2000s
Locale(s): Reno, Nevada

Summary: : About the time that Donna Cooper's term as Miss Reno Rodeo is set to expire, she meets Tyler Griffin, the cutest hunk of Texas cowboy that Donna has ever seen. She already has doubts about marrying Darryl King, a beer drinking hardware store heir, and after meeting Tyler, she knows that Darryl is history. Tyler and Donna set the wedding day, but they don't take into account Darryl's new fondness for a chainsaw. Regardless of what Darryl and Tyler's ex-girlfriend in Texas think up, Donna intends to keep her man.

Other books you might like:
Judy Alter, *A Ballad for Sallie*, 1992
Judy Alter, *Cherokee Rose*, 1996
Frederic Bean, *Lorena*, 1996
Jane Candia Coleman, *I, Pearl Hart*, 1998
Loren D. Estleman, *White Desert*, 2000

502
WOLF MACKENNA

Gunning for Regret
(New York: Berkley, 2001)

Story type: Traditional; Man Alone
Subject(s): American West; Indians of North America
Major character(s): Dix Granger, Lawman (sheriff); Yancy Wade, Sidekick, Lawman (Dix's deputy); Cash Malone, Thief (bank robber)
Time period(s): 19th century (post-Civil War)
Locale(s): Regret, Arizona

Summary: Sheriff Dix Granger and his deputy, Yancy, have captured Cash Malone, a first time bank robber who probably ought to take up another line of work. Before Dix and Yancy can get Malone home and in jail, a sandstorm comes up and they are forced to take shelter in a worn-out little town called Regret: population 6. Just as the sandstorm is about over one of Regret's residents shoots a young Apache boy. Now it's up to Dix, Yancy, and Cash Malone to defend Regret against an Indian attack.

Other books by the same author:
Dust Riders, 2000

Other books you might like:
Robert J. Conley, *Broke Loose*, 2000
Robert J. Conley, *Fugitive's Trail*, 2000
Preston Lewis, *The Demise of Billy the Kid*, 1995
Ellen Recknor, *Leaving Missouri*, 1997
Ellen Recknor, *Prophet Annie*, 1999

503
LEE MARTIN

Quakertown
(New York: Dutton, 2001)

Story type: Modern
Subject(s): American West; African Americans; Racism
Major character(s): Little Washington Jones, Gardener; Camellia Jones, Relative (Washington's daughter); Andrew Bell, Banker
Time period(s): 1920s
Locale(s): Denton, Texas

Summary: Little Washington Jones is an exceptional gardener in the Quakertown neighborhood of the 1920s North Texas town of Denton. He is respected by both white and black residents, and his principle worry is the fact that his daughter, Camellia, is in love with a white banker's son. Little knows that the father, gentlemanly as he is, would never countenance a relationship between his son and Little's daughter. When the father, Andrew Bell, asks Little to help divide the neighbor-

hood of Quakertown into white and black divisions, he accepts even though he senses trouble ahead. A wonderful sense of place and well-drawn characters make this an exceptional literary novel of the West.

Where it's reviewed:
Publishers Weekly, June 11, 2001, page 60

Other books by the same author:
Trail of the Reckless Gun, 2000
Trail of the Fast Gun, 1999
Trail of the Long Riders, 1999
Trail of the Circle Star, 1998
The Least You Need to Know, 1996

Other books you might like:
Judy Alter, *Libbie*, 1994
Judy Alter, *Mattie*, 1988
K. Follis Cheatham, *The Adventures of Elizabeth Fortune*, 2000
Max Evans, *Faraway Blue*, 1999
Michael Zimmer, *Where the Buffalo Roam*, 1999

504
GARY MCCARTHY

The Buffalo Hunters
(New York: Leisure, 2001)

Story type: Traditional; Quest
Subject(s): American West; Animals/Buffalo
Major character(s): Thomas Atherton, Cowboy; Buffalo Bill Cody, Historical Figure; Sally, Outcast, Thief (pickpocket)
Time period(s): 19th century (post-Civil War)
Locale(s): Cheyenne, Wyoming

Summary: Thomas Atherton is a young stable master from Massachusetts who dreams of going west and earning enough money to come back and marry Miss Alice Rutherford, his employer's daughter. Then he meets Buffalo Bill Cody and hears about a $5,000 reward to the man who finds a surviving herd of buffalo. He is certain that he can win the prize, but he doesn't count on Sally, the girl pickpocket, who cleans him out and leaves him working at a saloon in Cheyenne, Wyoming.

Other books by the same author:
Wind River, 1998
Yellowstone, 1998
Mesa Verde, 1997
Grand Canyon, 1996
The Humboldt River, 1996

Other books you might like:
Doug Bowman, *West to Comanche County*, 2000
Tim Champlin, *Treasure of the Templars*, 2000
Douglas Hirt, *Shadow Road*, 2000
Kevin McCalley, *The Other Side*, 2000
Richard S. Wheeler, *Flint's Gift*, 1999

505

MICHAEL MCGARRITY

Under the Color of Law
(New York: Dutton, 2001)

Story type: Modern; Mystery
Series: Kevin Kerney
Subject(s): American West; American History; Crime and Criminals
Major character(s): Kevin Kerney, Police Officer (chief); Phyllis Terrell, Spouse (of an ambassador); Joseph Mitchell, Religious (Catholic priest)
Time period(s): 2000s (2001)
Locale(s): Santa Fe, New Mexico

Summary: Another mystery with a strong western flavor, this adventure finds Kevin Kerney as the new police chief of Santa Fe. He hardly has time to pour his first cup of coffee before Phyllis Terrell, the wife of an ambassador is found dead. Then Father Joseph Mitchell is discovered murdered in the Christian Brothers Residence of the College of Santa Fe. The FBI move in and freeze out the police, but Kerney keeps digging for clues. Santa Fe is his town and he'll catch his own murderers.

Where it's reviewed:
Publishers Weekly, June 18, 2001, page 62

Other books by the same author:
Serpent Gate, 1999
Mexican Hat, 1997
Tularosa, 1996

Other books you might like:
Frederic Bean, *Murder at the Spirit Cave*, 1999
Peter Bowen, *Thunder Horse*, 1998
Sinclair Browning, *Rode Hard, Put Away Dead*, 2001
Elizabeth Dearl, *Diamondback*, 2000
  Taylor Madison series
Ed Gorman, *The Fatal Frontier*, 1997
  Martin Greenberg, co-editor

506

LISA MICHAELS

Grand Ambition
(New York: Norton, 2001)

Story type: Man Alone; Quest
Subject(s): American West; Rafting
Major character(s): Glen Hyde, Spouse (of Bessie), Adventurer; Bessie Hyde, Spouse (of Glen), Adventurer; Reith Hyde, Parent (Glen's father)
Time period(s): 1920s (1928)
Locale(s): Colorado River, Colorado

Summary: Michaels recounts the honeymoon adventure of Glen and Bessie Hyde as they raft down the dangerous Colorado River. They disappear before reaching the end of their journey and their bodies are never found, despite a search by Reith Hyde, Glen's father. A blend of love story and western adventure, based on an actual historical event, this is a four hankie book.

Where it's reviewed:
Publishers Weekly, June 11, 2001, page 58

Other books by the same author:
Spilt, 1999

Other books you might like:
Frederic Bean, *Murder at the Spirit Cave*, 1999
Peter Bowen, *Kelly and the Three-Toed Horse*, 2001
Sinclair Browning, *Rode Hard, Put Away Dead*, 2001
Elizabeth Dearl, *Diamondback*, 2000
  Tracy Madison series
Ken Hodgson, *Lone Survivor*, 2001

507

KIRK MITCHELL

Ancient Ones
(New York: Bantam, 2001)

Story type: Modern; Mystery
Subject(s): American West; Indians of North America
Major character(s): Emmett Quanah Parker, Police Officer (Bureau of Indian Affairs), Indian (Comanche); Anna Turnipseed, FBI Agent, Indian (Modoc); Thaddeus Rankin, Anthropologist
Time period(s): 2000s
Locale(s): Oregon

Summary: Comanche Emmett Quanah Parker, Criminal Investigator for the Bureau of Indian Affairs, and his girl friend, Anna Turnipseed, Special FBI Agent, are entering counseling to help Anna deal with her abusive past, when a 14,000-year-old skeleton is discovered in Oregon. Both are sent to investigate, but the problem is that the skeleton is clearly Caucasian, not Indian, and no one—police, tribal representatives, or an eccentric anthropologist named Thaddeus Rankin—seems to be in charge. As the number of murder victims climbs, so does the number of suspects, and Emmett and Anna have to postpone counseling to hunt down a murderer.

Where it's reviewed:
Library Journal, April 15, 2001, page 133

Other books by the same author:
Spirit Sickness, 2000
Cry Dance, 1999
Deep Valley Malice, 1996
High Desert Malice, 1995

Other books you might like:
Frederic Bean, *Murder at the Spirit Cave*, 1999
Peter Bowen, *Thunder Horse*, 1998
Sinclair Browning, *Road Hard, Put Away Dead*, 2001
Robert J. Conley, *Back to Malachi*, 1997
Dan Cushman, *Valley of the Thousand Smokes*, 1996

508

KIRK MITCHELL

Spirit Sickness
(New York: Bantam, 2000)

Story type: Modern; Mystery

Western

Subject(s): American West; Indians of North America; Mystery and Detective Stories

Major character(s): Emmett Quanah Parker, Police Officer (Bureau of Indian Affairs), Indian (Comanche); Anna Turnipseed, FBI Agent, Indian (Modoc)

Time period(s): 2000s

Locale(s): Navajo Reservation, New Mexico

Summary: When a Navajo tribal patrolman and his wife are found in a burned out patrol car with the windows broken out to release the spirits of the dead, Bureau of Indian Affairs Criminal Investigator Emmett Quanah Parker knows that there is evil loose on the Navajo Reservation. He is joined by FBI Special Agent Anna Turnipseed, a member of the Modoc tribe, in tracking down the murderer, who mixes personal madness with Navajo mythology.

Other books by the same author:
Ancient Ones, 2001
Cry Dance, 1999
Deep Valley Malice, 1996
High Desert Malice, 1995

Other books you might like:
Wayne Barton, *Wildcat*, 1995
    Stan Williams, co-author
Frederic Bean, *Murder at the Spirit Cave*, 1999
Andrew Huebner, *American by Blood*, 2000
Giles Tippette, *Southwest of Heaven*, 1999
Charles G. West, *Wings of the Hawk*, 2000

509

SKYE KATHLEEN MOODY

K Falls

(New York: St. Martin's Press, 2001)

Story type: Modern; Mystery

Series: Venus Diamond. Number 5

Subject(s): American West; Crime and Criminals

Major character(s): Venus Diamond, Government Official (U.S. Fish and Wildlife agent); Darla Denny, Sidekick (of Gerald); Gerald, Terrorist

Time period(s): 2000s (2001)

Locale(s): Kettle Falls, Washington

Summary: U.S. Fish and Wildlife agent Venus Diamond is tracking down an eco-terrorist, who is bombing dams along the Columbia River. Known only as Gerald, the terrorist is seemingly the invisible man. Finally Venus and another agent set up housekeeping in Kettle Falls, Washington, and make the acquaintance of Darla Denny, Gerald's companion. Venus has very little time to uncover Gerald's identity before he blows up the Grand Coulee Dam and two presidential contenders at the same time. A book with a wonderful sense of place.

Where it's reviewed:
Publishers Weekly, June 18, 2001, page 63

Other books by the same author:
Habitat, 1999
Wildcrafters, 1998
Blue Poppy, 1997
Rain Dance, 1996

Other books you might like:
Frederic Bean, *Murder at the Spirit Cave*, 1999
Sinclair Browning, *Rode Hard, Put Away Dead*, 2001
Elizabeth Dearl, *Diamondback*, 2000
    Taylor Madison series
J.A. Jance, *Outlaw Mountain*, 1999
    Joanna Brady series
J.A. Jance, *Rattlesnake Crossing*, 1998
    Joanna Brady series

510

VELLA MUNN

Cheyenne Summer

(New York: Forge, 2001)

Story type: Historical; Indian Culture

Subject(s): American West; Indians of North America

Major character(s): Grey Bear, Indian (Cheyenne), Warrior; Lone Hawk, Indian (Cheyenne), Warrior; Touches the Wind, Indian (Cheyenne)

Time period(s): 19th century (pre-Civil War)

Locale(s): West

Summary: Lightning sets off a fire that destroys half a Cheyenne village. Grey Bear and Lone Hawk search for missing children and horses feared lost in the fire. However, Grey Bear can only think of fighting the Pawnee, while Lone Hawk worries about saving the remaining Cheyenne. Two Indian women, Touches the Wind and Seeks Fire, must struggle to survive the consequences of Grey Bear's temper, which lead to death and exile.

Other books by the same author:
Soul of the Sacred Earth, 2000
Blackfeet Season, 1999
Seminole Song, 1998
Daughter of the Forest, 1995
Midnight Sun, 1993

Other books you might like:
Sanora Babb, *Cry of the Tinamou*, 1997
Rosanne Bittner, *Chase the Sun*, 1995
Rosanne Bittner, *Tame the Wild Wind*, 1996
Tracy Dunham, *The Changing Trail*, 1999
Tracy Dunham, *The Ghost Trail*, 1998

511

JOHN D. NESBITT

Man from Wolf River

(New York: Leisure, 2001)

Story type: Traditional; Man Alone

Subject(s): American West

Major character(s): Owen Felver, Cowboy, Drifter; Jenny Quoin, Heroine, Pioneer; Henry Coper, Villain

Time period(s): 19th century (post-Civil War)

Locale(s): Cameron, Wyoming

Summary: Owen Felver, the man from Wolf River, is on his way to the Laramie Mountains in search of work. When he stops over in Cameron, Wyoming, for a beer, he interrupts

Henry Coper who is trying to harass young Jenny Quoin. Interfering in Coper's business will land Owen in more trouble than he can handle.

Other books by the same author:
Coyote Trail, 1999
Wild Rose of Ruby Canyon, 1997
One Foot in the Stirrup, 1996
Twin Rivers, 1995
One-Eyed Cowboy Wild, 1994

Other books you might like:
Tim Champlin, *Treasure of the Templars*, 2000
David Claire, *Winter Range*, 2000
Ed Gorman, *Lawless*, 2000
Preston Lewis, *Hard Texas Winter*, 1981
E. Donald Two-Rivers, *Survivor's Medicine*, 1998

512

KERRY NEWCOMB

Texas Born

(New York: St. Martin's Paperbacks, 2001)

Story type: Historical; Saga
Series: Anthem Saga. Book 2
Subject(s): American West
Major character(s): John Anthem, Rancher; Cole Anthem, Relative (John Anthem's son); Billy Anthem, Relative (John Anthem's son)
Time period(s): 19th century (1863-)
Locale(s): Bonnet Ranch, Texas

Summary: The second of a five book series, this volume begins with John Anthem, a successful rancher whose sons are mavericks. The older son, Cole, goes off to fight in the Civil War, while the younger, Billy, follows his own ways. When a Mexican outlaw comes after John Anthem, father and sons pull together to defend the family.

Other books by the same author:
Texas Anthem, 2000
Scorpion, 1994
Ride the Panther, 1992
Sword of Vengeance, 1991
Warriors of the Night, 1991

Other books you might like:
Matt Braun, *Texas Empire*, 1997
Jerry Craven, *Snake Mountain*, 2000
Zane Grey, *Woman of the Frontier*, 2000
Elmer Kelton, *The Smiling Country*, 1998
Jory Sherman, *The Baron Range*, 1998

513

JOHN NICHOLS

The Voice of the Butterfly

(San Francisco: Chronicle, 2001)

Story type: Modern
Subject(s): American West; Ecology

Major character(s): Charlie McFarland, Hippie, Environmentalist; Susan Delgado, Journalist; Lydia Arlington Babcock, Environmentalist
Time period(s): 2000s (2001)
Locale(s): West

Summary: : Aging hippie Charlie McFarland leads a coalition of butterfly lovers against the local town's hierarchy, who want to bulldoze a road through the last habitat of the Rocky Mountain Phistic Copper butterfly. Among the coalition members is 90-year-old Lydia Arlington Babcock, Charlie's son who works at the local Burger Boy, and his ex-wife when she's not in jail. Stalking Charlie and the coalition is Susan Delgado who lusts for Charlie and a good story.

Where it's reviewed:
Publishers Weekly, June 4, 2001, page 55

Other books by the same author:
Nirvana Blues, 2000
The Magic Journey, 2000
The Milagro Bean Field War, 2000

Other books you might like:
Mike Blakely, *Summer of Pearls*, 2000
Sinclair Browning, *Rode Hard, Put Away Dead*, 2001
Wayne Davis, *John Stone and the Choctaw Kid*, 1993
Elizabeth Dearl, *Diamondback*, 2000
 Taylor Madison series
Will Henry, *No Survivors*, 1950

514

T.V. OLSEN

Lone Hand

(New York: Leisure, 2001)

Story type: Traditional; Collection
Subject(s): American West
Time period(s): 19th century (post-Civil War)

Summary: A short novel, *Lone Hand*, and ten short stories showcase Olsen's skill at characterization. Included are two stories that have never been published before: "Center-Five" and "Five Minutes."

Other books by the same author:
There Was a Season, 1997
Red Is the River, 1993
The Golden Chance, 1992
The Burning Sky, 1991
Under the Gun, 1989

Other books you might like:
Max Brand, *The Bright Face of Danger*, 2000
Charles Brashear, *Comeuppance at Kicking Horse Casino and Other Stories*, 2000
Peter Dawson, *Claiming of the Deerfeet: A Western Duo*, 2000
Earl P. Murray, *Midnight Sun and Other Stories of the Unexplained*, 2000
Les Savage Jr., *The Shadow in Renegade Basin*, 2000

515

GLEN ONLEY

Beyond Contentment

(Santa Fe, New Mexico: Sunstone, 2001)

Story type: Modern; Man Alone
Subject(s): American West; Crime and Criminals
Major character(s): Blaine Wells, Heir—Lost, Hero; Becky Adkins, Child, Survivor; Walter Dutton, Pilot
Time period(s): 2000s
Locale(s): Albuquerque, New Mexico; Pecos Wilderness, New Mexico

Summary: After the brutal murders of his wife and daughter, Blaine Wells drops out of society and lives a hermit-like existence in the Pecos Wilderness of New Mexico. He asks only to be left alone. But when a private plane crashes near his cabin, he knows he must rescue any survivors. Among them are a little girl, Becky Adkins, whose father was killed, and the co-pilot, Walter Dutton. The others have deserted them in favor of hunting for a settlement and a source of water. After the survivors are rescued, Blaine often thinks of little Becky. Finally, he contacts his sister-in-law and learns that he has inherited half of a large ranch from his late wife's family. Now Blaine must decide whether to accept his inheritance or return to his wilderness sanctuary.

Other books you might like:
Wayne Barton, *Wildcat*, 1995
    Stan Williams, co-author
Wayne Davis, *John Stone and the Choctaw Kid*, 1993
Loren D. Estleman, *The Rocky Mountain Moving Picture Association*, 1999
A.B. Guthrie Jr., *Arfive*, 1970
Laura Kalpakian, *Caveat*, 1998

516

JACKSON O'REILLY (Pseudonym of Robert Jordan)

Cheyenne Raiders

(New York: Forge, 2001)

Story type: Historical; Indian Culture
Subject(s): American West; Indians of North America
Major character(s): Thomas McCabe, Government Official (Bureau of Indian Affairs); Night Bird Woman, Indian (Cheyenne); Spotted Fox, Indian (Cheyenne)
Time period(s): 1830s (1837)
Locale(s): Wyoming

Summary: Yale graduate Thomas McCabe joins the Bureau of Indian Affairs and is sent as an Indian agent to a nomadic tribe called the Cheyenne. McCabe is totally unprepared for the rigors of living with a nomadic tribe, but thanks to the help of his mentor, Spotted Fox, he gradually adapts. When he falls in love with Night Bird Woman, he must find a way for the tribe to totally accept him because she is betrothed to another man. McCabe must first challenge her suitor, then survive the Test of Fire. It is during this test that he receives a Spirit Vision, one that prepares him to remake the lives of the imperiled Cheyenne.

Other books you might like:
Paula Gunn Allen, *Spider Woman's Granddaughters*, 1990
Rosanne Bittner, *Song of the Wolf*, 1992
Diane Glancy, *Flutie*, 1998
Cynthia Haseloff, *Man with Medicine*, 1996
Page Lambert, *Shifting Stars: A Novel of the West*, 1997

517

WAYNE D. OVERHOLSER

Hearn's Valley

(Bath, England: Chivers, 2001)

Story type: Man Alone; Quest
Subject(s): American West
Major character(s): Big Vic Hearn, Rancher; Hugh Moberly, Rancher
Time period(s): 19th century (post-Civil War)
Locale(s): West

Summary: They call it Hearn's Valley because Big Vic Hearn owns every square inch of it and controls everyone on it with hired guns. Then one day Hugh Moberly appears: the same Hugh Moberly whose father used to own part of the valley and who is faster than any of Big Vic's hired gunslingers. There is no question that one of them will die before the fight is over.

Other books by the same author:
Nugget City, 1997

Other books you might like:
Frederic Bean, *Blood Trail*, 1993
Richard Clark, *The Arizona Panhandle*, 1989
Al Dempsey, *What Law There Was*, 1990
Richard S. Wheeler, *Restitution*, 2001
G. Clifton Wisler, *Baron of the Brazos*, 1991

518

LAURAN PAINE

The Dark Trail

(Thorndike, Maine: Thorndike, 2001)

Story type: Traditional; Man Alone
Subject(s): American West
Time period(s): 19th century (post-Civil War)

Summary: Two short novels concerning personal conflict.

Other books by the same author:
The Killer Gun, 2001
The Running Iron, 2000
The Mustangers, 1999
The White Bird, 1999
The Grand Ones of San Ildefonso, 1997

Other books you might like:
Mary Clearman Blew, *Lambing Out & Other Stories*, 2001
Will Henry, *Tumbleweeds*, 2001
Jose Skinner, *Flight and Other Stories*, 2001
Glendon Swarthout, *Easterns and Westerns*, 2001
E. Donald Two-Rivers, *Survivor's Medicine*, 1998

519

LAURAN PAINE

The Killer Gun

(New York: Leisure, 2001)

Story type: Traditional; Man Alone
Subject(s): American West; Crime and Criminals
Major character(s): George Washington Mars, Businessman (gunsmith), Veteran (wounded in War of 1812); Hernando Espanol, Relative (brother is murdered); Manuel Ortiz, Fugitive, Murderer (killed Hernando's brother)
Time period(s): 19th century (post-Civil War)
Locale(s): Pueblo Juarez, New Mexico

Summary: George Washington Mars is an old man with a limp and aching bones. He owns a gun shop and an idea: make a Colt .45 which will fire when half cocked, so the shooter will win in a duel. When Hernando Espanol's brother, Jorge, is shot by Manuel Ortiz, Mars wonders how events would have turned out if Jorge had been using George's new gun. Mars soon learns the results of a duel with his gun when it is stolen one night and passed from hand to hand, each passage marked by a dead body until it becomes known as the killer gun.

Other books by the same author:
The Grand Ones of San Ildefonso, 1997
Lockwood, 1996
The Devil on Horseback, 1995
The Prairieton Raid, 1994
The Squaw Men, 1992

Other books you might like:
Dan Parkinson, *Dust on the Wind*, 1992
Dan Parkinson, *The Guns of No Man's Land*, 1992
Lewis B. Patten, *Tincup in the Storm Country*, 1996
Frank Roderus, *Hayseed*, 1998
Jack Schaefer, *Monte Walsh*, 1963

520

ROBERT B. PARKER

Gunman's Rhapsody

(New York: Putnam, 2001)

Story type: Historical; Man Alone
Subject(s): American West; Crime and Criminals
Major character(s): Wyatt Earp, Historical Figure, Lawman; Josie Marcus, Historical Figure, Actress; John Henry ''Doc'' Holliday, Gambler, Historical Figure
Time period(s): 1880s (1881)
Locale(s): Tombstone, Arizona

Summary: This is an account of Wyatt Earp and the gunfight at the O.K. Corral with all the players in its vast cast: the other Earp brothers, Doc Holliday, Johnny Behan, and Josie Marcus. According to this account, it is Earp's love for Josie Marcus that leads to Behan's acts of cowardice and the conspiracy that eventually ended in the West's most famous gunfight. This is a fast-paced and exciting retelling of the Earp legend.

Where it's reviewed:
Publishers Weekly, May 14, 2001, page 51

Other books by the same author:
Hugger Mugger, 2000
Troubles in Paradise, 2000
Perish Twice, 2000
Family Honor, 1999
Hush Money, 1999

Other books you might like:
Matt Braun, *Doc Holliday*, 1997
Matt Braun, *Wyatt Earp*, 1994
Jane Candia Coleman, *Doc Holliday's Woman*, 1995
Randy Lee Eickhoff, *The Fourth Horseman*, 1997
Loren D. Estleman, *Bloody Season*, 1988

521

RICHARD PARRY

The Wolf's Pack

(New York: Forge, 2001)

Story type: Historical; Quest
Series: Nathan Blaylock
Subject(s): American West; Gold Discoveries
Major character(s): Nathan Blaylock, Gunfighter, Gambler; Jim Riley, Sidekick, Gunfighter; E.T. Barnette, Banker, Landowner
Time period(s): 1900s (1902)
Locale(s): Fairbanks, Alaska

Summary: Nathan Blaylock is the illegitimate son of Wyatt Earp and Mattie Blaylock. He is taught his skills with a gun by his mentor, Jim Riley. Nathan and Riley work briefly for E.T. Barnette, who is determined to establish a trading post at Tanana Crossing. When gold is discovered, the trading post becomes Fairbanks, and Barnette builds a huge bank to hold all the gold he exacts from the miners as tribute. When Nathan and Riley oppose the Fairbanks kingpin, they call in Wyatt Earp and his gang of retired gunfighters to help.

Other books by the same author:
The Wolf's Cub, 1997
The Winter Wolf, 1995

Other books you might like:
Doug Bowman, *West to Comanche County*, 2000
Tim Champlin, *Treasure of the Templars*, 2000
Douglas Hirt, *Shadow Road*, 2000
Preston Lewis, *Mix-Up at the O.K. Corral*, 1996
Richard S. Wheeler, *Flint's Gift*, 1999

522

LEWIS B. PATTEN

Death Rides the Denver Stage

(New York: Leisure, 2001)

Story type: Traditional; Man Alone
Subject(s): American West; Civil War
Major character(s): Clee Fahr, Cowboy, Drifter; Eames Jeffords, Trader; Sam Massey, Mine Owner
Time period(s): 1860s (1861)
Locale(s): Denver, Colorado

Summary: Clee Fahr arrives in Denver just as the town is about to tear itself apart over the Civil War. An old enemy of Clee's, Eames Jeffords, is buying rifles for the Confederates, while mine owner Sam Massey is gathering a volunteer troop to join the Union cause. Clee is torn between the two, but soon finds himself a target of both sides.

Other books by the same author:
The Woman at Ox-Yoke: A Western Duo, 2000
Tincup in the Storm Country, 1996
Best Western Stories of Lewis B. Patten, 1989
Trail of the Apache Kid, 1979
Hunt the Man Down, 1977

Other books you might like:
Wayne Barton, *Wildcat*, 1995
    Stan Williams, co-author
Frederic Bean, *The Outlaw*, 1993
Johnny D. Boggs, *Riding with Hannah and the Horseman*, 1998
Harold Coyle, *Look Away*, 1996
Harold Coyle, *Until the End*, 1996

523

JOHN PAXSON

A Golden Trail of Murder

(New York: Avalon, 2001)

Story type: Modern; Mystery
Subject(s): American West; Crime and Criminals
Major character(s): Rancher, Journalist, Carpenter; Ben Tripp, Detective—Private
Time period(s): 2000s
Locale(s): Montana

Summary: With the discovery during the spring thaw of a body buried in a snow bank, Rancher and PI Ben Tripp are busy tracking down the killer. Tripp discovers a scheme to steal valuable land is behind the killing. A modern day range war Western.

Where it's reviewed:
Publishers Weekly, June 11, 2001, page 65

Other books you might like:
Frederic Bean, *Murder at the Spirit Cave*, 1999
Sinclair Browning, *Rode Hard, Put Away Dead*, 2001
Carol Cail, *The Seeds of Time*, 2001
Randall Beth Platt, *The Royalscope Fe-As-Ko*, 1997
Ellen Recknor, *Me and the Boys*, 1995

524

MARTHAYN PELEGRIMAS

On the Strength of Wings

(Thorndike, Maine: Thorndike, 2001)

Story type: Historical; Saga
Subject(s): American West; Emigration and Immigration
Major character(s): Abigail Gray, Spouse (of Samuel Gray), Pioneer; Julia Markham, Abuse Victim; Samuel Gray, Pioneer, Spouse (of Abigail)
Time period(s): 1820s (1828)

Locale(s): Oregon Trail, West

Summary: Abigail Gray is furious her husband, Samuel Gray, has decided to travel west to Oregon by wagon train and set up a ship building operation. She is comfortable in Baltimore and doesn't want to go, but doesn't have a choice. When she discovers that she is pregnant, Abigail ignores her condition since the baby will be born after they reach Oregon. Then Samuel is bitten by a snake and dies of a heart attack, leaving her alone with only two friends, Sarah and Coral, for company. At Fort Bridger, Abigail rescues Julia Markham from an abusive husband and smuggles her onto the wagon train. Together the woman decide the course of their lives and go to California instead of Oregon.

Other books you might like:
Judy Alter, *Jessie*, 1995
Judy Alter, *Mattie*, 1988
Irene Bennett Brown, *Long Road Turning*, 2000
Jane Kirkpatrick, *All Together in One Place*, 2000
Jane Roberts Wood, *The Train to Estelline*, 1987

525

GEORGE POST

Life of a Lakota Warrior and Another Short Story

(Kearney, Nebraska: Morris, 2001)

Story type: Traditional; Indian Culture
Subject(s): American West; Indians of North America
Time period(s): 19th century

Summary: Two long short stories about relationships between the white man and the Sioux.

Other books you might like:
Sanora Babb, *Cry of the Tinamou*, 1997
Rosanne Bittner, *Chase the Sun*, 1995
Rosanne Bittner, *Tame the Wild Wind*, 1996
Tracy Dunham, *The Changing Trail*, 1999
Tracy Dunham, *The Ghost Trail*, 1998

526

M.K. PRESTON

Perhaps She'll Die

(Philadelphia: Intrigue, 2001)

Story type: Modern; Mystery
Subject(s): American West; Crime and Criminals; Racism
Major character(s): Chantalene Morrell, Detective— Amateur, Gypsy
Time period(s): 2000s
Locale(s): Tetumka, Oklahoma

Summary: Chantalene Morrell, a Gypsy, returns to her home town of Tetumka, Oklahoma, on a mission: discover who killed her father and caused the disappearance of her mother. Her questions cause more murders, and Chantalene examines her own memories and faces the hostile town. Good mystery and strong sense of place.

Where it's reviewed:
Publishers Weekly, June 11, 2001, page 66

Other books you might like:
Frederic Bean, *Murder at the Spirit Cave*, 1999
Sinclair Browning, *Rode Hard, Put Away Dead*, 2001
Elizabeth Dearl, *Diamondback*, 2000
　　Tracy Madison series
J.A. Jance, *Outlaw Mountain*, 1999
　　Joanna Brady series
J.A. Jance, *Rattlesnake Crossing*, 1998
　　Joanna Brady series

527

BILL PRONZINI

The Gallows Land

(New York: Berkley, 2001)

Story type: Traditional; Man Alone
Subject(s): American West
Major character(s): Roy Boone, Drifter; Jennifer Todd, Abuse
　　Victim, Pioneer; Mase Todd, Villain
Time period(s): 1870s (1878)
Locale(s): Arizona

Summary: After the death of his wife, Roy Boone drifts
throughout Arizona hoping to find meaning to his life. He
meets a beautiful young woman, Jennifer Todd, who has been
brutally beaten by her husband, Mase Todd. Jennifer gives
Roy food and water and he rides on, but decides to return
because he is worried Mase might kill his wife. He finds that
Jennifer has disappeared and Roy barely escapes two bullets.
Figuring Jennifer knows the reason someone is tracking him,
he begins a desperate search for her before the next bullet
catches up with him.

Other books by the same author:
Firewind, 1990
More Wild Westerns, 1989
The Hangings, 1989
The Last Days of Horse-Shy Halloran, 1987

Other books you might like:
Tim Champlin, *Treasure of the Templars*, 2000
David Claire, *Winter Range*, 2000
Ed Gorman, *Lawless*, 2000
Preston Lewis, *Hard Texas Winter*, 1981
Johnny Quarles, *Shadow of the Gun*, 1995

528

ROBERT H. REDDING

Steele

(New York: Avalon, 2001)

Story type: Traditional; Chase
Subject(s): American West; Indians of North America
Major character(s): Steele, Miner, Rancher; Elizabeth White,
　　Heroine; Two Dogs, Indian (Cheyenne), Chieftain
Time period(s): 1870s (1876)
Locale(s): Little Big Horn, Montana

Summary: Steele has his wages from mining in Idaho and is
drifting through Montana Territory, when he meets a group of
greenhorns on their way to the Black Hills to prospect for
gold. Among this group is Elizabeth White with whom Steele
falls in love. A group of crooked promoters influence Elizabeth and her father to sign on with them and go to the Black
Hills. To the promoters' disgust Steele signs on, too, as a
wagon master. Among the promoters is the Cheyenne war
chief Two Dogs, who speaks of a huge battle coming between
the Indians and the whites. Steele turns the tables on the
promoters and chases them across Montana, arriving at the
Little Big Horn in time to witness Custer's Last Stand.

Other books by the same author:
McCall, 2000

Other books you might like:
Judy Alter, *Libbie*, 1994
Don Bendell, *Chief of Scouts*, 1993
　　Chief of Scouts. Book 1
Michael Blake, *Dances with Wolves*, 1990
Will Henry, *No Survivors*, 1950
Terry C. Johnston, *Seize the Sky*, 1991
　　editor

529

JAMES RICE

Victor Lopez at the Alamo

(Gretna, Louisiana: Pelican, 2001)

Story type: Traditional; Chase
Subject(s): American West; War
Major character(s): Victor Lopez, Child (Mexican); Jose, Mil-
　　itary Personnel (Mexican); Pedro, Military Personnel
　　(Mexican)
Time period(s): 1830s (1836)
Locale(s): San Antonio, Texas

Summary: This book for young readers recounts the story of
Victor Lopez, a Mexican boy who is coerced into Santa
Anna's army as it marches toward San Antonio and the
Alamo. He has trouble almost immediately with an older boy,
Jose, who cruelly beats him up for his blanket. Victor is
nursed back to health by an old man named Pedro, who
doesn't much want to be in the army either. The story ends at
the Alamo where Victor learns the true cost of war.

Other books you might like:
Katherine Ayres, *North by Night*, 1998
Joseph Bruchac, *The Arrow over the Door*, 1998
Joseph Bruchac, *The Heart of a Chief*, 1998
Phyllis de la Garza, *Camels West*, 1998
Suzanne Pierson Ellison, *Best of Enemies*, 1998

530

MELINDA RICE

Fire on the Hillside

(Plano, Texas: Republic of Texas, 2001)

Story type: Traditional; Young Readers
Series: Lone Star Heroines

Subject(s): American West
Major character(s): Katherine Haufmann, Teenager; Opa Haufmann, Grandparent (of Katherine); Hannah Haufmann, Child (Katherine's sister)
Time period(s): 1840s (1847)
Locale(s): Fredericksburg, Texas

Summary: Thirteen-year-old Katherine Haufmann is not certain she is going to like Texas. She misses Germany and her friends there. Everyone else in her family loves Fredericksburg and this wide open Texas land, even her little sister, Hannah. Then one night Katherine notices fires in the distant countryside and night after night the fires appear in the same place. With her Opa's help, Katherine sets out to discover the mystery of the fires. Katherine's story is based on real events, and the book includes a chapter on and picture of the real Katherine.

Other books by the same author:
Messenger to the Battlefield, 2001 (Lone Star Heroines series)
Secrets in the Sky, 2001 (Lone Star Heroines series)

Other books you might like:
Phyllis de la Garza, *Camels West*, 1998
Patrick Dearen, *Comanche Peace Pipe*, 2001
    Lone Star Heroes. Book 1
Patrick Dearen, *The Hidden Treasure of the Chisos*, 2001
    Lone Star Heroes. Book 3
Patrick Dearen, *On the Pecos Trail*, 2001
    Lone Star Heroes. Book 2
Laurie Lawlor, *West Along the Wagon Road, 1852*, 1998

531

MELINDA RICE

Messenger on the Battlefield

(Plano, Texas: Republic of Texas, 2001)

Story type: Traditional; Young Readers
Series: Lone Star Heroines
Subject(s): American West; Frontier and Pioneer Life
Major character(s): Isabelina Montoya, Child (Mexican); Feliciana Montoya, Relative (older sister of Isabelina); Rodrigo Cantares, Military Personnel (Mexican army)
Time period(s): 1830s (1835)
Locale(s): San Antonio, Texas

Summary: Eleven-year-old Isabelina Montoya is excited about her sister Feliciana's wedding to Rodrigo Cantares, a handsome young officer in the Mexican army. Then comes word that Texas is declaring its independence from Mexico and the Montoya family is torn between the two sides. Should they remain loyal to Mexico, or declare allegiance to their real home, Texas?

Other books by the same author:
Fire on the Hillside, 2001
Secrets in the Sky, 2001

Other books you might like:
Phyllis de la Garza, *Camels West*, 1998
Patrick Dearen, *Comanche Peace Pipe*, 2001
    Lone Star Heroes. Book 1
Patrick Dearen, *The Hidden Treasure of the Chisos*, 2001
    Lone Star Heroes. Book 3

Patrick Dearen, *On the Pecos Trail*, 2001
    Lone Star Heroes. Book 2
James Rice, *Victor Lopez at the Alamo*, 2001

532

MELINDA RICE

Secrets in the Sky

(Plano, Texas: Republic of Texas, 2001)

Story type: Modern; Young Readers
Series: Lone Star Heroines
Subject(s): American West
Major character(s): Bethany Parker, Child; Josephine Nicholson, Military Personnel, Pilot; Lynn Strickland, Military Personnel, Pilot
Time period(s): 1940s (1943)
Locale(s): Sweetwater, Texas

Summary: Twelve-year-old Bethany Parker is stuck at home while her brother is fighting in WWII. When Bethany meets Josephine Nicholson and Lynn Strickland, members of the Women Air Force Service Pilots who have come to Sweetwater to train, she also wants to be a woman pilot. She would call herself the Purple Baroness. When Josephine is killed in a training flight crash, Bethany is sure that it was sabotage by a German spy and she sets out to prove it.

Other books by the same author:
Fire on the Hillside, 2001 (Lone Star Heroines series)
Messenger on the Battlefield, 2001 (Lone Star Heroines series)

Other books you might like:
Phyllis de la Garza, *Camels West*, 1998
Patrick Dearen, *Comanche Peace Pipe*, 2001
    Lone Star Heroes. Book 1
Patrick Dearen, *The Hidden Treasure of the Chisos*, 2001
    Lone Star Heroes. Book 3
Patrick Dearen, *On the Pecos Trail*, 2001
    Lone Star Heroes. Book 2
James Rice, *Victor Lopez at the Alamo*, 2001

533

LISA WALLER ROGERS

Get Along, Little Dogies

(Lubbock: Texas Tech University Press, 2001)

Story type: Traditional; Young Readers
Subject(s): American West; Frontier and Pioneer Life; Cattle Drives
Major character(s): Hallie Lou Wells, Teenager; Dovey, Servant (Hallie Lou's maid); Ab Blocker, Cowboy
Time period(s): 1870s (1878)
Locale(s): Chisholm Trail, Texas

Summary: When her father decides to stay home with her pregnant mother, 14-year-old Hallie Lou is allowed to accompany the cattle drive up the Chisholm Trail with her maid, Dovey, and her brother. The man in charge of the drive is legendary Ab Blocker, and Hallie Lou has more excitement

than she can handle. The novel is written in the form of a trail journal, which adds to the realism.

Where it's reviewed:
Amarillo Globe News, April 8, 2001, page 18D

Other books you might like:
Phyllis de la Garza, *Camels West*, 1998
Patrick Dearen, *Comanche Peace Pipe*, 2001
    Lone Star Heroes. Book 1
Melinda Rice, *Fire on the Hillside*, 2001
    Lone Star Heroines series
Melinda Rice, *Messenger on the Battlefield*, 2001
    Lone Star Heroines series
Melinda Rice, *Secrets in the Sky*, 2001
    Lone Star Heroines series

534

HAROLD G. ROSS

Brannick: And the Untamed West

(Manhattan, Kansas: Sunflower University Press, 2001)

Story type: Historical; Man Alone
Subject(s): American West; Pioneers
Major character(s): Jim Brannick, Farmer, Lawman; Brad Collins, Cowboy
Time period(s): 19th century; 20th century (1882-1920s)
Locale(s): Flint Hills, Kansas

Summary: This novel is based on the life of the author's grandfather, a pioneer farmer and lawman of early Kansas.

Other books by the same author:
Homage to the Gods, 1998
Along Golden Hills, 1996
Where Eagles Fly, 1995
Passing Day, 1993

Other books you might like:
K. Follis Cheatham, *The Adventures of Elizabeth Fortune*, 2000
Max Evans, *Faraway Blue*, 1999
Elmer Kelton, *The Wolf and the Buffalo*, 1980
Hiram King, *Dark Trail*, 1998
Michael Zimmer, *Where the Buffalo Roam*, 1999

535

AL SARRANTONIO

West Texas

(Lancaster, Pennsylvania: Stealth, 2001)

Story type: Traditional; Chase
Subject(s): American West; African Americans; Crime and Criminals
Major character(s): Thomas Mullins, Military Personnel (African American); Captain Seavers, Military Personnel (captain of black troops); Lincoln Reeves, Military Personnel (African American trooper)
Time period(s): 19th century (post-Civil War)
Locale(s): Fort Davis, Texas

Summary: There is a serial killer loose in West Texas, and Thomas Mullins is the man who knows most about the region. Thomas is no longer a buffalo soldier, thanks to Captain Seavers, and no one can force him to search the dry, desolate land for a missing senator's son. However, to be reinstated as a buffalo soldier at his former rank and pay, Mullins will search for the son and the other people reported missing in the area. With the aid of Trooper Reeves, Mullins tracks the most dangerous man he has ever hunted.

Other books by the same author:
Kitt Peake, 1993

Other books you might like:
Tim Champlin, *Wayfaring Strangers*, 2000
K. Follis Cheatham, *The Adventures of Elizabeth Fortune*, 2000
Max Evans, *Faraway Blue*, 1999
Bruce A. Glasrud, *The African American West: A Century of Short Stories*, 2000
    editor
Elmer Kelton, *The Wolf and the Buffalo*, 1980

536

LES SAVAGE JR.

The Bloody Quarter

(New York: Leisure, 2001)

Story type: Traditional; Man Alone
Subject(s): American West; Revenge
Major character(s): Paul Hagar, Rancher; Ed Garland, Rancher; Napoleon Nicholet, Lawyer
Time period(s): 19th century (post-Civil War)
Locale(s): Converse County, Wyoming

Summary: Paul Hager is a drifter, working for different people and at different jobs. Finally, it appears his luck has changed. He files homestead papers on a quarter section of land in Converse County, Wyoming. The fact that it is called the Bloody Quarter doesn't frighten him off, not even when he ends up in a range war with Ed Garland, and his only ally is a lawyer named Napoleon Nicholet.

Other books by the same author:
In the Land of Little Sticks, 2000
The Shadow in Renegade Basin, 2000
Phantoms in the Night, 1998
Coffin Gap, 1997
Medicine Wheel, 1996

Other books you might like:
Frank Bonham, *One Ride Too Many*, 1997
Walt Coburn, *The Secret of Crutcher's Cabin: A Western Trio*, 1999
T.T. Flynn, *Rawhide*, 1996
Louis L'Amour, *Monument Rock*, 1998
Frank Norris, *The Best Short Stories of Frank Norris*, 1998

Western

537

LES SAVAGE JR.

The Cavan Breed

(Thorndike, Maine: Thorndike, 2001)

Story type: Traditional; Quest
Subject(s): American West; Mexican Americans
Major character(s): Teresa Cavan, Servant, Heroine; Don Biscara, Landowner; Kelly Morgan, Mountain Man
Time period(s): 1830s (1837)
Locale(s): Santa Fe, New Mexico

Summary: Pregnant and deserted by a Mexican soldier, Teresa marries a much older man who abuses her. After her husband and baby are killed by Apache raiders and she is kidnapped, Teresa manages to escape and flee to the hacienda of Don Biscara where her mother works. Don Biscara orders her whipped after she refuses to become his mistress. It is mountain man Kelly Morgan who rescues her, and she allies herself with a coalition of Pueblo Indians who seize power in Santa Fe. Teresa becomes wealthy and powerful, but war is coming with the United States, and Kelly Morgan, a man of no money or possessions, offers her what she desires most: freedom.

Other books by the same author:
In the Land of Little Sticks, 2000
The Sting of Senorita Scorpion, 2000
The Shadow in Renegade Basin, 2000
Phantoms in the Night, 1998
Coffin Gap, 1997

Other books you might like:
Wayne Barton, *Warhorse*, 1988
  Stan Williams, co-author
Patrick Dearen, *The Illegal Man*, 1998
Loren D. Estleman, *Journey of the Dead*, 1998
Laura Kalpakian, *Caveat*, 1998
Wendi Lee, *The Overland Trail*, 1996

538

THOMAS SAVAGE

The Power of the Dog

(Boston: Little, Brown, 2001)

Story type: Modern; Saga
Subject(s): American West; Ranch Life
Major character(s): Phil Burbank, Rancher, Relative (brother to George); George Burbank, Rancher; Rose Gordon, Widow(er)
Time period(s): 1920s (1925)
Locale(s): Montana

Summary: George and Phil Burbank are two of the richest ranchers in the valley and two of the closest brothers, never having a disagreement. When George marries Rose and brings her back to the ranch, Phil wages a brutal war against her. Then her brilliant young son, Peter, comes to visit, sees Phil's cruelty and plots a devilish revenge. A literary Western that is a piece of gritty realism.

Other books by the same author:
The Corner of Rife and Pacific, 1988

The Sheep Queen, 1977

Other books you might like:
Dan Parkinson, *Dust on the Wind*, 1992
Dan Parkinson, *The Guns of No Man's Land*, 1992
Lewis B. Patten, *Tincup in the Storm Country*, 1996
Frank Roderus, *Potter's Fields*, 1996
Jack Schaefer, *Monte Walsh*, 1963

539

JEFF SHAARA

Rise to Rebellion

(New York: Ballantine, 2001)

Story type: Historical; Saga
Subject(s): Revolutionary War; Adventure and Adventurers
Major character(s): John Adams, Historical Figure, Political Figure; Abigail Adams, Historical Figure; George Washington, Historical Figure, Military Personnel
Time period(s): 1770s (1770-1776)
Locale(s): Philadelphia, Pennsylvania; Boston, Massachusetts

Summary: Set during the Revolutionary War, when the eastern seaboard was the frontier, this novel provides Shaara another opportunity to create living characters out of historical figures, as he draws meticulous portraits of John Adams; his wife, Abigail; and gentlemanly, but tough George Washington. Western readers should enjoy this book.

Where it's reviewed:
Publishers Weekly, March 15, 2001, page 106

Other books by the same author:
Gone for Soldiers, 2000
The Last Full Measure, 1998
Gods and Generals, 1996 (Michael Shaara, co-author)

Other books you might like:
Rick Bass, *The Sky, the Stars, the Wilderness*, 1997
Mike Blakely, *Comanche Dawn*, 1998
Bruce A. Glasrud, *The African American West: A Century of Short Stories*, 2000
  editor
Jim R. Woolard, *Cold Moon*, 1998
Jim R. Woolard, *The Winds of Autumn*, 1996

540

JOSE SKINNER

Flight and Other Stories

(Reno: University of Nevada Press, 2001)

Story type: Modern; Collection
Subject(s): American West; Mexican Americans; Short Stories
Time period(s): 2000s
Locale(s): West

Summary: A debut collection of short stories exploring the Hispanic-American experience in the West. Skinner presents a wide range of themes, among them: racial misunderstanding, romance, gay encounters, and coming-of-age.

Other books you might like:

Max Brand, *The Bright Face of Danger*, 2000
Jane Candia Coleman, *Borderlands: Western Stories*, 2000
Will Henry, *Ghost Wolf of Thunder Mountain*, 2000
Les Savage Jr., *The Shadow in Renegade Basin*, 2000
Richard S. Wheeler, *Tales of the American West*, 2000

541

GLENDON SWARTHOUT

Easterns and Westerns

(East Lansing: Michigan State University Press, 2001)

Story type: Collection
Subject(s): American West; Short Stories
Time period(s): 19th century (post-Civil War)

Summary: The only collection of short fiction that Swarthout ever wrote, these 13 short stories and one novella illustrate his gift for delineating the themes of generational conflict, hypocrisy, loss, sacrifice, love, and war.

Where it's reviewed:
Roundup Magazine, October 2001, page 27

Other books by the same author:
The Shootist, 1998
The Homesman, 1988
The Old Colts, 1985
The Eagle and the Iron Cross, 1966

Other books you might like:
Max Brand, *The Black Rider and Other Stories*, 1996
Jane Candia Coleman, *Moving On*, 1997
Will Henry, *Ghost Wolf of Thunder Mountain*, 2000
Les Savage Jr., *In the Land of Little Sticks*, 2000
Richard S. Wheeler, *Aftershocks*, 1999

542

JON TALTON

Concrete Desert

(New York: St. Martin's Press, 2001)

Story type: Modern; Mystery
Series: David Mapstone
Subject(s): American West; Crime and Criminals; Mystery and Detective Stories
Major character(s): David Mapstone, Professor (of history); Creeper, Murderer
Time period(s): 2000s (2001)
Locale(s): Phoenix, Arizona

Summary: A strong sense of place permeates this story of former cop and teacher David Mapstone. After being fired, he goes back to work for the police investigating old cases. This case, forty years old, may tie into the disappearance of his former girlfriend's sister. The question is if the killer is the mysterious Creeper who appeared briefly, then disappeared. The historical anecdotes about Phoenix add interest to the plot.

Where it's reviewed:
Publishers Weekly, May 14, 2001, page 55

Other books you might like:

Frederic Bean, *Murder at the Spirit Cave*, 1999
Sinclair Browning, *Rode Hard, Put Away Dead*, 2001
Elizabeth Dearl, *Diamondback*, 2000
    Taylor Madison series
Elizabeth Dearl, *Twice Dead*, 2001
Loren D. Estleman, *White Desert*, 2000

543

AIMEE THURLO
DAVID THURLO, Co-Author

Shooting Chant

(New York: Forge, 2000)

Story type: Modern; Mystery
Series: Ella Clah
Subject(s): Indians of North America; Crime and Criminals; Mystery and Detective Stories
Major character(s): Ella Clah, Police Officer (tribal special investigator), Indian (Navajo); Clifford Clah, Indian (Navajo), Shaman (Ella's brother); James Yellowhair, Indian, Political Figure (kidnapped)
Time period(s): 2000s (2001)
Locale(s): Shiprock, New Mexico

Summary: Once an FBI agent, Ella Clah is now a Special Investigator with the Navajo Police and has not been accepted completely by either the Navajo or the white worlds. Her brother, Clifford, a shaman of the tribe, asserts that Ella's gift as an investigator is from the spirits who guard the Dineh, as the Navajo call themselves. Ella disagrees, believing it is her FBI training. Wherever her gift comes from, Ella has a full case load. She is pregnant, but refuses to marry the father. Still, she worries about doing such a dangerous job while trying to raise a child. Then there is the kidnapping of State Senator James Yellowhair; the tension between the traditionalist and modernist elements in the Navajo world; and worse yet, the theft of records of pregnant women, including Ella, from a health care clinic and the murder of one of the women.

Other books by the same author:
Bad Medicine, 1998 (Ella Clah series)
Enemy Way, 1998 (Ella Clah series)
Death Walker, 1996 (Ella Clah series)
Timewalker, 1996
Blackening Song, 1995

Other books you might like:
Rick Bass, *The Sky, the Stars, the Wilderness*, 1997
Frederic Bean, *Murder at the Spirit Cave*, 1999
Sinclair Browning, *Rode Hard, Put Away Dead*, 2001
Elizabeth Dearl, *Diamondback*, 2000
    Taylor Madison series
Tony Hillerman, *The Mysterious West*, 1994

Western

544

MARI ULMER

Carreta de la Muerte (Cart of Death)

(Scottsdale, Arizona: Poisoned Pen, 2001)

Story type: Modern; Mystery
Subject(s): American West; Indians of North America; Mystery and Detective Stories
Major character(s): Christina Garcia y Grant, Lawyer (Mexican/Anglo), Innkeeper (bed and breakfast owner); Doris Jordon, Sidekick, Lawyer; Iggy Baca, Lawyer (Mexican American)
Time period(s): 2000s
Locale(s): Taos, New Mexico; Talpa, New Mexico

Summary: A wonderful western mystery rampant with the culture and sense of place of Taos, New Mexico, this tale features a group of amateur sleuths led by Christina Garcia y Grant. Christina has given up her legal practice to run a bed and breakfast in a tiny town south of Taos. Her fellow sleuths (and lawyers) are Iggy Baca and Doris Jordon. The plot revolves around Iggy's missing girlfriend, and while Christina remains tied up with plans for the coming fiesta, Iggy and widower Mac McCloud search for the missing girl.

Where it's reviewed:
Publishers Weekly, February 26, 2001, page 61

Other books you might like:
Frederic Bean, *Murder at the Spirit Cave*, 1999
Peter Bowen, *Thunder Horse*, 1998
Sinclair Browning, *Rode Hard, Put Away Dead*, 2001
Elizabeth Dearl, *Diamondback*, 2000
    Tracy Madison series
Richard S. Wheeler, *Dark Passage*, 1998

545

JAMES M. VESELY

The Awakening Land

(Lincoln, Nebraska: Writers Club, 2001)

Story type: Historical; Saga
Series: Corrales Valley Trilogy. Book II
Subject(s): American West; Frontier and Pioneer Life
Major character(s): Louis Bonneau, Immigrant (French); Gaetano Perna, Immigrant (Sicilian); Owen Forbes Parrish, Rancher
Time period(s): Multiple Time Periods (17th-19th centuries)
Locale(s): Corrales Valley, New Mexico

Summary: The second volume in the Corrales Valley Trilogy follows the Apodaca family from the time of the Pueblo Revolt until the 19th century. During that time, more immigrants move to the Corrales Valley. First are Louis and Julian Bonneau, who are fleeing the guillotine in France. Next is Gaetano Perna, a Sicilian who flees a Mafia vendetta. The last is Owen Forbes Parrish, a veteran of the Civil War and a Colorado rancher, who wants to buy part of the valley for his son.

Other books by the same author:
Seasons of Harvest, 2001 (Corrales Valley Trilogy. Book I)

Shadows on the Land, 2001 (Corrales Valley Trilogy. Book III)

Other books you might like:
Irwin R. Blacker, *Taos*, 1959
Mike Blakely, *The Glory Trail*, 1990
Dorothy Cave, *Mountains of the Blue Stones*, 1998
Jane Candia Coleman, *Moving On*, 1997
Genevieve Gray, *Fair Laughs the Morn*, 1994

546

JAMES M. VESELY

Seasons of Harvest

(Lincoln, Nebraska: Writers Club, 2001)

Story type: Historical; Saga
Series: Corrales Valley Trilogy. Book I
Subject(s): American West; Mexican Americans; Conquest
Major character(s): Neska, Indian (Anasazi); Miguel Apodaca, Military Personnel (Spanish conquistador); Primitivo Apodaca, Military Personnel (Spanish conquistador)
Time period(s): Multiple Time Periods (13th-17th centuries)
Locale(s): Corrales Valley, New Mexico

Summary: The first volume in a trilogy about the founding and history of Corrales, New Mexico, begins with the migration of the Anasazi led by Neska, and continues through the arrival of Primitivo Apodaca with the first Spanish conquistador. Young Miguel Apodaca, Primitivo's grandson, is also a conquistador, but one who is so appalled by the cruelties of the Spanish Conquest that he deserts his post and flees into the New Mexico wilderness to begin a new life.

Where it's reviewed:
Roundup Magazine, October 2001, page 27

Other books by the same author:
Shadows on the Land, 2001 (Corrales Valley Trilogy. Book III)
The Awakening Land, 2001 (Corrales Valley Trilogy. Book II)

Other books you might like:
Margaret Allen, *The Last Mammoth*, 1995
Mike Blakely, *Comanche Dawn*, 1998
Joseph Bruchac, *The Waters Between*, 1998
Don Coldsmith, *Tallgrass: A Novel of the Great Plains*, 1997
Karen Osborn, *Between Earth and Sky*, 1996

547

JAMES M. VESELY

Shadows on the Land

(Lincoln, Nebraska: Writers Club, 2001)

Story type: Modern
Series: Corrales Valley Trilogy. Book III
Subject(s): American West; Ranch Life; World War II
Major character(s): James Parrish, Veteran (WWI), Rancher; Rueben Apodaca, Handicapped (clubfoot); Joe Apodaca, Military Personnel (WWII)
Time period(s): 19th century; 20th century

Locale(s): Corrales Valley, New Mexico

Summary: The final volume of the Corrales Valley Trilogy follows the fortunes of James Parrish, a veteran of WWI, and Rueben and Joe Apodaca during WWII. James marries Emily MacKenzie, who becomes a heroine during the Spanish flu epidemic of 1918. After Pearl Harbor, Joe Apodaca and Holt Parrish enlist and find themselves part of the Bataan Death March. Rueben, unable to join the military because of his clubfoot, graduates from the University of Chicago and becomes part of the team that builds the first atomic bomb.

Other books by the same author:
Seasons of Harvest, 2001 (Corrales Valley Trilogy. Book I)
The Awakening Land, 2001 (Corrales Valley Trilogy. Book II)

Other books you might like:
Frederic Bean, *The Pecos River*, 1995
    Rivers West. Book 13
Irwin R. Blacker, *Taos*, 1959
Mike Blakely, *Baron of the Sacramentos*, 1991
Andrew Glass, *The Sweetwater Run*, 1996
Jory Sherman, *Rio Grande*, 1994

548

JOSEPH A. WEST

Johnny Blue and the Hanging Judge

(New York: Signet, 2001)

Story type: Traditional; Chase
Series: Johnny Blue
Subject(s): American West; Crime and Criminals; Humor
Major character(s): Johnny Blue Dupree, Cowboy, Sidekick; Shade Hannah, Villain; Unnamed Character, Narrator (me)
Time period(s): 19th century (post-Civil War)
Locale(s): Fort Smith, Arkansas

Summary: The unnamed narrator of this first person account of me and Johnny Blue Dupree on the run from the law, due to a mistake involving a bank and a wagon load of gold, is a humorous good old boy. There is no way the two men can hide since Johnny Blue is black and the unnamed me is white. Johnny Blue hears his sister, sold down the river during the days of slavery, is in South Texas. Since me also considers the girl his sister, the two head for Texas. Somehow they end up working as marshals for hanging Judge Parker out of Fort Smith, Arkansas. The exact details are a little obscure, but me explains it as best he can. It's just that odd things are always happening to me and Johnny Blue, two of the most original characters in Westerns today.

Other books by the same author:
Me and Johnny Blue, 2000

Other books you might like:
Robert J. Conley, *Barjack*, 2000
Robert J. Conley, *Broke Loose*, 2000
Preston Lewis, *The Demise of Billy the Kid*, 1995
Ellen Recknor, *Leaving Missouri*, 1997
Ellen Recknor, *Me and the Boys*, 1995

549

OWEN WISTER

The Virginian

(New York: Penguin, 2001)

Story type: Historical; Man Alone
Subject(s): American West; Crime and Criminals
Major character(s): The Virginian, Cowboy; Trampas, Outlaw, Outcast; Molly Wood, Teacher, Girlfriend
Time period(s): 19th century (post-Civil War)
Locale(s): Medicine Bow, Wyoming

Summary: In this reprint of the classic first Western, the reader meets again the nameless hero called The Virginian; the rustler, Trampas; and the schoolmarm, Molly Wood. It is this novel that introduces many devices which later become stereotypes in Westerns such as the gunfight and the afternoon ride with the hero, only in this classic one sees the literary use of the later stereotypes.

Other books by the same author:
Lin McLean, 1998

Other books you might like:
Max Brand, *The Masterman: A North-Western Story*, 2000
Robert J. Conley, *Fugitive's Trail*, 2000
Loren D. Estleman, *White Desert*, 2000
Douglas Hirt, *Shadow Road*, 2000
Cameron Judd, *Brazos*, 2000

550

JANE ROBERTS WOOD

Grace

(New York: Dutton, 2001)

Story type: Modern
Subject(s): American West; World War II
Major character(s): Grace Gillian, Teacher (high school English); Bucy Gillian, Spouse (of Grace); Bobby Moore, Teenager
Time period(s): 1940s (1944)
Locale(s): Cold Springs, Texas

Summary: This is a modern Western in that it is set in East Texas in 1944. Deserted by her husband, Bucy, high school English teacher Grace Gillian must decide whether she will accept the attentions of her recently bereaved neighbor, a sergeant she meets, or her own husband. A subplot concerns young Bobby Moore, who is desperate to help the war effort even though his vision is too poor for him to enlist. While the plot doesn't read like a Western, the sense of place clearly is more ''Western'' than otherwise.

Where it's reviewed:
Publishers Weekly, March 19, 2001, page 75
Roundup Magazine, October 2001, page 28

Other books by the same author:
Dance a Little Longer, 1993 (Lucinda ''Lucy'' Richards Trilogy. Book 3)
A Place Called Sweet Shrub, 1990 (Lucinda ''Lucy'' Richards Trilogy. Book 2)

Western

The Train to Estelline, 1987 (Lucinda ''Lucy'' Richards Trilogy. Book 1)

Other books you might like:

Jane Candia Coleman, *Doc Holliday's Gone: A Western Duo*, 2000

Cynthia Haseloff, *Changing Trains*, 2001

Cecelia Holland, *Lily Nevada*, 1999

Jane Kirkpatrick, *All Together in One Place*, 2000

Suzanne Lyon, *Lady Buckaroo*, 2000

551

GELING YAN

The Lost Daughter of Happiness

(New York: Hyperion, 2001)

Story type: Historical; Quest

Subject(s): American West; Prostitution; Racism

Major character(s): Fusang, Prostitute (Chinese); Chris, Businessman (Anglo); Da Yong, Criminal (Chinese)

Time period(s): 19th century (post-Civil War)

Locale(s): San Francisco, California

Summary: Fusang, a young Chinese girl, is kidnapped and forced into prostitution in San Francisco during the Gold Rush. She is loved by two very different men: Chris, a prominent white businessman, and Da Yong, a Chinese criminal. She must choose between her two lovers, and her choice will alter her life. Based on an historical event, this tale is intriguing with a strong sense of place. Translated by Cathy Silber.

Where it's reviewed:

Library Journal, February 15, 2001, page 203

Publishers Weekly, March 5, 2001, page 62

Other books you might like:

Frederic Bean, *Lorena*, 1996

Sarah Bird, *Virgin of the Rodeo*, 1993

Jane Candia Coleman, *Doc Holliday's Woman*, 1995

Jane Kirkpatrick, *All Together in One Place*, 2000

JoAnn Levy, *For California's Gold*, 2000

Magic in Detective Stories and Murder Mysteries
by
Don D'Ammassa

Blends of science fiction and traditional detective stories or murder mysteries are a long-standing tradition and have resulted in a large number of very fine novels. A few authors have tried to consummate a similar marriage of forms within the fantasy field, but unfortunately there is a major obstacle inherent in the nature of fantasy. The one movie which tried to combine the two, *Cast a Deadly Spell*, succeeded only because of its humorous tone. It is difficult to write a convincing locked room murder mystery that doesn't cheat the reader, or at least hold the possibility of cheating, in a setting where magic is possible. How does a detective go about finding physical evidence when the murder weapon was a sorcerous curse? Can you write a suspense murder mystery set in a world where the recently dead can be brought back to life to identify their killers? Is it possible to avoid frustrating the reader when the rules aren't clear from the outset and are subject to change at any time?

Some authors have approached these blends by using contemporary or historical settings and keeping the fantastic element limited to one item not critical to the central mystery. John Dickson Carr, author of scores of traditional murder mysteries, set three of them in historical England, but in each case used a protagonist from the present, who was magically transported back through time into a period when sophisticated police procedures didn't exist. The three were *Fire, Burn* (1957), *Fear Is the Same* (1956), and *The Devil in Velvet* (1951). A modern day detective finds himself in the early days of Scotland Yard in the first; two involuntary time travelers visit Regency England to solve a murder in the second; and a scholar is magically transported to the 17th century just in time to play detective in the third.

Similarly, Andrew Greeley has written six adventures of Nuala Ann MacGrail, an amateur detective aided by a series of psychic visions she can't control. Due to the sporadic nature of the visions, most of the evidence she gathers has to be acquired by conventional means. *Irish Gold* (1995) and *Irish Lace* (1996) are quite traditional

mysteries other than the psychic element. MacGrail solves the mystery of the death of one of Al Capone's rivals in *Irish Whiskey* (1998) and a political assassination in *Irish Mist* (1999), and locates buried treasure while solving a murder mystery in *Irish Eyes* (2000). The most recent in the series, *Irish Love* (2001), has a much more active fantastic element and much less mystery.

Dorothy Gilman's charming protagonist in *The Clairvoyant Countess* (1975) also has brief glimpses of magical enlightenment, but, like MacGrail, must solve the case with more mundane methods. Silver Ravenwolf's *Murder at Witches' Bluff* (2000) makes use of authentic Wiccan ceremonies and beliefs in its portrayal of murder at a convocation of contemporary witches in Appalachia.

An alternative approach is to embrace the fantastic elements in a contemporary setting, but specifically define and delimit them so that the reader understands the rules and can factor them into solving the puzzle. Charles De Lint does this in *Mulengro* (1985), a serial killer story in which the villain is actually a supernatural entity drawn from gypsy folklore. An interesting variation on this is Barbara Hambly's *Those Who Hunt the Night* (1988), wherein someone is hunting down and murdering the relatively innocuous vampires living secretly within London society. Their physical limitations make it difficult for them to investigate, so they hire a living detective to protect themselves. Similar situations arise with some regularity in Laurell Hamilton's Anita Blake, Vampire Hunter series, which started with *Guilty Pleasures* (1993) and reached its tenth volume with *Narcissus in Chains* (2001). Of course, Hamilton occasionally introduces new creatures or powers in mid-volume, frustrating any attempt by the reader to outguess the plot. An even more unusual premise is the basis of Shirley Rousseau Murphy's Cat series, which describes a secret group of intelligent cats living within human society who intercede in our affairs and solve crimes. The cats track down a murderer in *Cat on the Edge* (1996) and a brilliant burglar in *Cat Raise*

the Dead (1997), and clear a falsely accused person in *Cat in the Dark* (1999).

The tough private eye story adapts more readily to fantasy because it is less dependent upon presenting a puzzle and challenging the reader to solve it. Glen Cook's Garrett series is the most successful, and certainly the longest, such series, beginning with *Sweet Silver Blues* (1987) and currently extending to his latest adventure, *Faded Steel Heat* (1999). Garrett mixes his detection with more covert adventure, rescuing kidnap victims from ogres, saving victims slated to be sacrificed to mysterious gods, tracing missing persons, finding himself the target of a sorcerer intent on stopping an investigation, serving as a bodyguard, and tracking down a serial killer. Cook largely ignores the implications of magic on the crimes, focusing the reader's attention on the action elements rather than the puzzles. Similarly, *Darkworld Detective* (1982) by J. Michael Reaves subordinates the mystery to the action in a series of episodic private eye stories. Mike Resnick uses humor to gloss over the problem in *Stalking the Unicorn* (1987), his Chandleresque detective story set in an alternate New York City where magic works and everyone knows that it does. James Gunn also uses a conventional private detective in *The Magicians* (1976), in this instance hired to identify a mysterious character who turns out to have genuine magical powers. The private detective in *Once upon a Murder* (1987) by Robert L. Randisi and Kevin D. Randle must solve a puzzle simultaneously in our own universe and a parallel one where magic works.

Various historical settings have also been used as the backdrop for fantastic mysteries. Perhaps the most exotic of these are the Asian variants found in the novels of Barry T. Hughart. In *Bridge of Birds* (1984), Number Ten Ox and his companion search for the cure for a disease in a magical alternate China, and must solve an ancient mystery to accomplish their task. They return for two more adventures. In *The Story of the Stone* (1988), a monk has been murdered, apparently to gain possession of a manuscript believed to be worthless. The protagonists discover that it is actually a key to a powerful magic, but it is clear from the outset that the murder was achieved by conventional means, and the mystery plot is quite effective. Hughart confronts the issue of magic and murder directly in *Eight Skilled Gentlemen* (1991). Someone is systematically murdering mandarins, and everyone believes that a demonic force is responsible. It is up to the protagonists to prove that they were killed by the quite ordinary methods used by a human killer.

Other historical settings include various time periods and locations. Esther Friesner sets *Druid's Blood* (1988) in an alternate Victorian England where magic works. *The Anubis Murders* (1992) by Gary Gygax takes place in an ancient Egypt where gods are real, and in which a murder is falsely blamed on the intervention of one of the gods. William Kotzwinkle's *Fata Morgana* (1977) uses Paris in 1860 as its location. The more recent *Point of Dreams* (2001) by

Melissa Scott and Lisa A. Barnett takes place in an alternate version of Renaissance Europe.

The most fully realized traditional fantasy world in which detection is the focus of the plot is that of Randall Garrett's novel *Too Many Magicians* (1966), and two collections of shorter tales, *Lord Darcy Investigates* (1981) and *Murder and Magic* (1979). Garrett very skillfully delineates what magic is and how it works so that it can be factored into solving the mystery. Michael Kurland continues this series with some success in *A Study in Sorcery* (1989) and *Ten Little Wizards* (1988). Most titles in Daniel Hood's Liam Rhenford series are variations of standard mystery plots with fantastic elements, such as the theft of a magic jewel, the murder of a wizard, and other crimes. The titles include *Fanuilh* (1994), *Wizard's Heir* (1995), *Beggar's Banquet* (1997), and *Scales of Justice* (1998). Several others meet the same criteria. In J. Robert King's *Carnival of Fear* (1993), a carnival is plagued by a series of murders as it travels through a fictional country where there are overtones of magic. A young woman is unjustly accused of assassination and must track down the real culprit in Mindy L. Klasky's promising first novel *The Glasswright's Apprentice* (2000). A murderer possesses the body of others in order to commit his crimes in *Four and Twenty Blackbirds* (1997) by Mercedes Lackey.

The amateur detective is also a common device in fantasy, as well as traditional mysteries. Phyllis Ann Karr uses the falsely accused suspect, or friends thereof, to solve crimes in a trio of medieval mysteries that are otherwise unrelated. In *At Amberleaf Fair* (1986), it's the prime suspect who untangles the mystery. Friends help to clear the name of a sorceress in *Frostflower and Windbourne* (1982) and it is Queen Guinevere who is accused of causing the death of a knight in Camelot itself in *The Idylls of the Queen* (1982). Two royal bodyguards find themselves playing detective in *The Crooked House* (2000) by Dave Duncan. The authorities appoint some inept sleuths, hoping that they will fail to uncover the probable aristocratic connections to a murder, in John Maddox Roberts' *Murder in Tarsis* (1996). The protagonist of *Hour of the Octopus* (1994) by Joel Rosenberg invents the idea of being a private detective to solve a crime in his magical universe. Melisa Michaels tells the story of a rock artist's bodyguard who must defeat a villain able to use faerie magic in *Cold Iron* (1997). The protagonist actually crosses over into Faerie to solve a second crime in the sequel, *Sister to the Rain* (1998).

A few writers have used blends of magic and mystery entirely for humorous effect, in which cases the practical problems are largely irrelevant. The best of these are *The Castle Murders* (1991) by John DeChancie, and *Dragons on the Town* (1992) by Thorarinn Gunnarsson, in which Sherlock Holmes and friends have to solve a mystery in a contemporary but magical alternative New York City. The decline in popularity of humorous fantasy in the United States

in recent years may explain why more authors have not taken this path.

The first half of 2001 saw the publication of a number of good novels, though none of them even remotely what we might consider a mystery story such as those discussed above. Very few fantasy novels during this period were actually outstanding, and even fewer explored new territory. At the same time, several very good single author short story collections appeared, mostly from newer writers in the field. These included three first books, *Redgunk Tales* by William Eakin, *Meet Me in the Moon Room* by Ray Vukcevich, and *Stranger Things Happen* by Kelly Link, all from smaller publishing houses.

Recommended Books

The best books of this period are:

Issola by Steven Brust

The Curse of Chalion by Lois McMaster Bujold

The Wooden Sea by Jonathan Carroll

Redgunk Tales by William Eakin

The Beyond by Jeffrey Ford

Tales from Earthsea by Ursula K. Le Guin

Stranger Things Happen by Kelly Link

Perdido Street Station by China Mieville

Thief of Time by Terry Pratchett

Not Quite Scaramouche by Joel Rosenberg

Point of Dreams by Melissa Scott and Lisa A. Barnett

Summers at Castle Auburn by Sharon Shinn

The Blade of Tyshalle by Matthew Stover

Meet Me in the Moon Room by Ray Vukcevich

Fantasy Titles

552

MARK ANTHONY

The Dark Remains

(New York: Bantam, 2001)

Story type: Contemporary
Series: Last Rune. Book 3
Subject(s): Magic
Major character(s): Travis Wilder, Saloon Keeper/Owner; Grace Beckett, Doctor; Beltran, Knight
Time period(s): 2000s (2001)
Locale(s): Denver, Colorado; Eldh, Fictional Country

Summary: Grace Beckett and Travis Wilder return from the magical realm of Eldh with one of its knights, who is seriously wounded. Shortly after getting him to a hospital, they discover that they have been followed by an evil force and must return to Eldh, where a demon has become so powerful that he endangers the gods of that reality.

Where it's reviewed:
Publishers Weekly, February 26, 2001, page 63
Science Fiction Chronicle, April 2001, page 36

Other books by the same author:
The Keep of Fire, 1999
Beyond the Pale, 1998
Escape from Undermountain, 1996
Curse of the Shadowmage, 1995
Crypt of the Shadowking, 1993

Other books you might like:
Tom Deitz, *Darkthunder's Way*, 1989
Esther Friesner, *New York by Knight*, 1986
Laurell K. Hamilton, *A Kiss of Shadows*, 2000
Will Shetterly, *Nevernever*, 1993
Roger Zelazny, *Nine Princes in Amber*, 1970

553

PIERS ANTHONY

DoOon Mode

(New York: Tor, 2001)

Story type: Quest
Series: Mode. Book 4
Subject(s): Magic
Major character(s): Colleen, Young Woman; Darius, Ruler (king); Burgess, Alien
Time period(s): Indeterminate
Locale(s): Alternate Universe

Summary: Colleen travels through alternate realities accompanied by an alien, talking cats, a king, and a telepathic horse. Her adventures come to a climax when she and her companions confront an evil warlord who has recognized that she is a pivot point in the future of the alternate realities and who seeks to use her to extend his own power.

Where it's reviewed:
Publishers Weekly, March 5, 2001, page 66

Other books by the same author:
The Dastard, 2000
Reality Check, 1999
Xone of Contention, 1999
The Muse of Art, 1999
Faun and Games, 1997

Other books you might like:
John DeChancie, *MagicNet*, 1993
Philip Jose Farmer, *The Gates of Creation*, 1966
Esther Friesner, *Majyk by Accident*, 1993
Craig Shaw Gardner, *Slaves of the Volcano God*, 1989
Lawrence Watt-Evans, *Out of This World*, 1994

554

ROBERT ASPRIN

JODY LYNN NYE, Co-Author

License Invoked

(New York: Baen, 2001)

Story type: Mystery
Subject(s): Magic
Major character(s): Fionna Kenmare, Singer; Elizabeth Mayfield, Government Official; Don Winslow, Secretary
Time period(s): 2000s (2001)
Locale(s): New Orleans, Louisiana

Summary: Popular singer Fionna Kenmare is touring an alternate U.S. where magic is an accepted part of life. Someone is making supernatural attacks against her, and both the American and British governments assign agents to safeguard her person in this light mystery laced with mild humor.

Where it's reviewed:
Locus, March 2001, page 33
Science Fiction Chronicle, April 2001, page 38

Other books by the same author:
Sweet Myth-Tery of Life, 1994
Phule's Paradise, 1992
Phule's Company, 1990
Mythnomers and Im-Pervections, 1987
M.Y.T.H. Inc. Link, 1986

Other books you might like:
Laurell K. Hamilton, *A Kiss of Shadows*, 2000
David Lee Jones, *Zeus and Co.*, 1993
Jody Lynn Nye, *Mythology 101*, 1990
Rachel Pollack, *Temporary Agency*, 1994
Mike Resnick, *Stalking the Unicorn*, 1987

555

CHERITH BALDRY

Exiled from Camelot

(Oakland, California: Green Knight, 2001)

Story type: Quest
Subject(s): Arthurian Legend
Major character(s): Sir Kay, Knight; Loholt, Young Man; Brisane, Sorceress
Time period(s): Indeterminate Past
Locale(s): England

Summary: When King Arthur's illegitimate son, Loholt, appears, Arthur overlooks his faults because he is desperate for an heir. Among the strongest enemies of Loholt is Sir Kay, who becomes the prime suspect when Loholt is murdered. Cast out from the Round Table, Kay becomes involved with a sorceress in an attempt to clear his name and solve the murder. This is a first novel.

Where it's reviewed:
Science Fiction Chronicle, July 2001, page 43

Other books you might like:
Daffyd ab Hugh, *Far Beyond the Wave*, 1994
Gillian Bradshaw, *In Winter's Shadow*, 1983

Vera Chapman, *The King's Damosel*, 1976
Phyllis Ann Karr, *The Idylls of the Queen*, 1982
Diana L. Paxson, *The Hallowed Isle*, 1999

556

NANCY VARIAN BERBERICK

The Inheritance

(Renton, Washington: Wizards of the Coast, 2001)

Story type: Sword and Sorcery
Series: Dragonlance
Subject(s): Magic
Major character(s): Elansa Sungold, Mythical Creature (elf); Char, Mythical Creature (dwarf); Prince Kethrenan, Royalty
Time period(s): Indeterminate
Locale(s): Qualinesti, Fictional Country

Summary: When Elansa Sungold is kidnapped by a band of outlaws, she expects her people to rescue her in short order. When that doesn't happen, she looks at her captors in a new way and discovers a bond forming, but she isn't certain whom she can trust any longer.

Other books by the same author:
Dalamar the Dark, 2000
Tears of the Night Sky, 1998 (Linda Baker, co-author)
The Panther's Hoard, 1994
A Child of Elvish, 1992
The Jewels of Elvish, 1989

Other books you might like:
Lynn Abbey, *Simbul's Gift*, 1997
Philip Brugalette, *The Nine Gates*, 1992
Monte Cook, *The Glass Prison*, 1999
Simon Hawke, *The Seeker*, 1994
Mary Herbert, *Lightning's Daughter*, 1991

557

MARION ZIMMER BRADLEY, Editor

Sword and Sorceress XVIII

(New York: DAW, 2001)

Story type: Anthology; Sword and Sorcery
Subject(s): Short Stories

Summary: The themes presented in these 20 original fantasy stories involve impossible tasks, invading armies, learning how to use magic, and discovering one's true self. The contributors include Lawrence Watt-Evans, Diana Paxson, Rosemary Edghill, Denise Lopes Heald, Dave Smeds, Dorothy Heydt, and others.

Other books by the same author:
Lady of Avalon, 1997
Exile's Song, 1996
Witchlight, 1996
Lady of Trillium, 1995
The Forest House, 1993

Other books you might like:
Rosemary Edghill, *The Cloak of Night and Daggers*, 1997

Denise Lopes Heald, *Mistwalker*, 1994
Diana L. Paxson, *The Book of Stone*, 2000
Dave Smeds, *The Sorcery Within*, 1985
Lawrence Watt-Evans, *Night of Madness*, 2000

558

STEVEN BRUST

Issola

(New York: Tor, 2001)

Story type: Quest
Series: Vlad Taltos. Book 9
Subject(s): Magic
Major character(s): Vlad Taltos, Criminal (assassin); Lady Teldra, Noblewoman; Morrolan e'Drien, Prisoner
Time period(s): Indeterminate
Locale(s): Dragaera, Fictional Country

Summary: An assassin, Vlad Taltos, is seeking a place where he can live in peace and quiet for a while. When his friend, Lady Teldra, tracks him down and tells him that two of his friends have disappeared, he is forced to come out of retirement and venture into the realm of the creatures, who may have created his entire world.

Other books by the same author:
Dragon, 1998
Orca, 1996
Agyar, 1993
The Phoenix Guards, 1991
Phoenix, 1990

Other books you might like:
Raymond E. Feist, *Krondor: The Assassins*, 1999
Eric Flint, *The Philosophical Strangler*, 2001
Maggie Furey, *The Heart of Myrial*, 1999
Robin Hobb, *Assassin's Quest*, 1997
Tad Williams, *The River of Blue Fire*, 1998

559

LOIS MCMASTER BUJOLD

The Curse of Chalion

(New York: Avon Eos, 2001)

Story type: Political
Subject(s): Magic
Major character(s): Lupe dy Cazaril, Secretary; Iselle dy Chalion, Noblewoman; Dondo dy Jirondal, Nobleman
Time period(s): Indeterminate
Locale(s): Chalion, Fictional Country

Summary: A nobleman from Chalion escapes slavery and returns to his homeland, seeking a quiet position to support himself. He becomes secretary to the sister of the heir apparent to the throne, which exposes him to his old enemies and requires him to offer up his life to protect his charge. To ensure her safety, he must lift a curse that hovers over the royal family.

Other books by the same author:
A Civil Campaign, 1999
Komarr, 1998

Cetaganda, 1996
Mirror Dance, 1994
The Spirit Ring, 1992

Other books you might like:
Stephen R. Donaldson, *A Man Rides Through*, 1987
Dave Duncan, *Sky of Swords*, 2000
Simon R. Green, *Beyond the Blue Moon*, 2000
Katherine Kurtz, *King Kelson's Bride*, 2000
George R.R. Martin, *A Game of Thrones*, 1996

560

CHRIS BUNCH

Corsair

(New York: Warner Aspect, 2001)

Story type: Adventure
Subject(s): Pirates
Major character(s): Gareth Radnor, Sea Captain; Thom Tehidy, Sailor; Labala, Sorcerer
Time period(s): Indeterminate
Locale(s): Saros, Fictional Country; *Steadfast*, At Sea

Summary: Gareth Radnor seeks vengeance against the pirates who murdered his family, so he assembles a crew and goes to sea himself. He attacks the pirates whenever he sees them, continuing even after his own kingdom has negotiated a peace with the sea raiders. Then he discovers that the pirates are more than they seem; in addition to their crimes, they are also inhuman.

Other books by the same author:
Firemask, 2000
Storm Force, 2000
The Last Legion, 1999
Warrior King, 1999
Seer King, 1998

Other books you might like:
Poul Anderson, *Conan the Rebel*, 1980
John Gregory Betancourt, *Rogue Pirate*, 1987
Hugh Cook, *The Questing Hero*, 1987
L. Sprague de Camp, *The Clocks of Iraz*, 1971
Tim Powers, *On Stranger Tides*, 1987

561

JACQUELINE CAREY

Kushiel's Dart

(New York: Tor, 2001)

Story type: Magic Conflict
Subject(s): Political Thriller
Major character(s): Phedre no Delaunay, Slave; Joscelin Verreuil, Nobleman; Childric d'Essoms, Nobleman
Time period(s): Indeterminate
Locale(s): Terre d'Ange, Fictional Country

Summary: Terre d'Ange is threatened by factionalism within and more obvious enemies from without. A large cast of characters indulge in court intrigues and open confrontations in an effort to shape the future of their people, but a young girl

sold into involuntary servitude may ultimately have more to say in the matter than any of them. This is a first novel.

Where it's reviewed:
Publishers Weekly, May 14, 2001, page 58

Other books you might like:
Lois McMaster Bujold, *The Curse of Chalion*, 2001
Simon R. Green, *Beyond the Blue Moon*, 2000
Robert Jordan, *Winter's Heart*, 2000
Katherine Kurtz, *King Kelson's Bride*, 2000
George R.R. Martin, *A Storm of Swords*, 2000

562

JONATHAN CARROLL

The Wooden Sea

(New York: Tor, 2001)

Story type: Contemporary
Subject(s): Time Travel
Major character(s): Francis ''Frannie'' McCabe, Police Officer; George Dalemwood, Writer; Caz de Floon, Businessman
Time period(s): 21st century (2001-2028); 1970s (1970)
Locale(s): Crane's View, New York

Summary: Frannie McCabe enjoys his life and his job as chief of police in a small town. When a three legged dog dies in his office and refuses to remain in its grave, it is just the first of a series of bizarre events which will lead to his meeting older and younger versions of himself, and discovering the true purpose of the universe.

Where it's reviewed:
Booklist, December 15, 2000, page 785
Locus, February 2001, page 20
Publishers Weekly, January 8, 2001, page 47
Realms of Fantasy, April 2001, page 29
Science Fiction Chronicle, April 2001, page 35

Other books by the same author:
The Marriage of Sticks, 1999
Kissing the Beehive, 1998
From the Teeth of Angels, 1994
Outside the Dog Museum, 1992
Sleeping in Flame, 1989

Other books you might like:
James P. Blaylock, *The Paper Grail*, 1991
John Crowley, *Daemonomania*, 2001
Paul Di Filippo, *The Steampunk Trilogy*, 1994
Richard Grant, *Kaspian Lost*, 1999
Tim Powers, *Earthquake Weather*, 1997

563

ANN CHAMBERLIN

The Merlin of the Oak Wood

(New York: Tor, 2001)

Story type: Historical
Series: Joan of Arc Tapestries. Book 2
Subject(s): Legends

Major character(s): Joan of Arc, Historical Figure, Warrior; Gilles de Rais, Nobleman, Historical Figure
Time period(s): 15th century (1425-1428)
Locale(s): France

Summary: Fifteenth century France is in shambles, devastated by battles for the throne and with external enemies. Young Jehannette D'Arc hears voices in her head that tell her to take up arms and unite the country, and to ensure her victory they lend her certain magical powers.

Where it's reviewed:
Publishers Weekly, April 30, 2001, page 61

Other books by the same author:
The Merlin of St. Gilles' Well, 1999

Other books you might like:
Lynn Abbey, *Unicorn and Dragon*, 1987
Gael Baudino, *Strands of Sunlight*, 1994
James Branch Cabell, *The Silver Stallion*, 1926
Thomas Harlan, *The Shadow of Ararat*, 1999
R.A. MacAvoy, *Damiano*, 1984

564

STEPAN CHAPMAN

Dossier

(Berkeley, California: Creative Arts, 2001)

Story type: Collection
Subject(s): Short Stories

Summary: This collection contains 17 stories, most of them quite short. Although they sometimes make use of the trappings of science fiction, for the most part the stories use magical devices. Mostly concerned with imagery, the tales rarely have strong narrative qualities. The majority of the collection is original to this book.

Other books by the same author:
Troika, 1997
Danger Music, 1996

Other books you might like:
Donald Barthelme, *City Life*, 1970
Avram Davidson, *Everybody Has Somebody in Heaven*, 2000
Harlan Ellison, *Angry Candy*, 1988
R.A. Lafferty, *Tales of Midnight*, 1992
Gene Wolfe, *Strange Travelers*, 2000

565

DEBORAH CHESTER

The Chalice

(New York: Ace, 2001)

Story type: Sword and Sorcery
Series: Sword, Ring, and Chalice. Book 3
Subject(s): Quest
Major character(s): Dain, Mythical Creature (half-elf), Nobleman; Phenesa, Royalty (princess); Gavril, Royalty (prince)
Time period(s): Indeterminate
Locale(s): Nether, Fictional Country

Summary: A half-elf nobleman continues his rivalry with the heir to the throne, both of whom are in love with the same woman. An assassination attempt, using poison, goes awry and she falls into a coma, and the two men who love her set out on a quest to find the cure before they both lose her. At the same time, a sinister force is plotting to usurp the throne.

Other books by the same author:
The Ring, 2000
The Sword, 2000
The Crystal Eye, 1999
The Crimson Claw, 1998
The Golden One, 1998

Other books you might like:
Troy Denning, *The Oath of Stonekeep*, 1999
Doranna Durgin, *Seer's Blood*, 2000
Holly Lisle, *The Courage of Falcons*, 2000
R.A. Salvatore, *Bastion of Darkness*, 2000
Paula Volsky, *The Sorcerer's Curse*, 1989

566

EOIN COLFER

Artemis Fowl

(New York: Hyperion, 2001)

Story type: Young Adult; Humor
Subject(s): Fairies
Major character(s): Artemis Fowl, Thief, Child (12-year-old); Butler, Servant; Holly Short, Mythical Creature (fairy)
Time period(s): 2000s (2001)
Locale(s): United States

Summary: Artemis Fowl is a 12-year-old master thief, international entrepreneur, and scientific genius. Even he may have bitten off more than he can chew when he steals a copy of the secret book of magic used by fairies. A series of wild adventures follow, including time travel, well armed leprechauns, and a host of other strange characters. This is a first fantasy novel.

Where it's reviewed:
Booklist, April 15, 2001, page 1554
Locus, May 2001, page 29
Publishers Weekly, April 9, 2001, page 75

Other books you might like:
Emma Bull, *War for the Oaks*, 1987
Rick Cook, *Mall Purchase Night*, 1993
Esther Friesner, *Hooray for Hellywood*, 1990
Craig Shaw Gardner, *A Multitude of Monsters*, 1986
Norton Juster, *The Phantom Tollbooth*, 1961

567

ELAINE CUNNINGHAM

The Floodgate

(Renton, Washington: Wizards of the Coast, 2001)

Story type: Magic Conflict
Series: Forgotten Realms
Subject(s): Magic

Major character(s): Matteo, Wizard; Andris, Warrior; Akhlaur, Wizard
Time period(s): Indeterminate
Locale(s): Halruaa, Fictional Country

Summary: Matteo is finally beginning to master the magical powers which were awakened within him. Unfortunately, the evil sorcerer Akhlaur has been thwarted but not defeated, and now he launches a fresh attack on the land of Halruaa.

Other books by the same author:
The Magehound, 2000
The Dream Spheres, 1999
Evermeet, 1998
Thornhold, 1998
Silver Shadows, 1996

Other books you might like:
Mark Anthony, *Escape from Undermountain*, 1996
Troy Denning, *The Veiled Dragon*, 1996
Simon Hawke, *Nomad*, 1994
Paul Kidd, *Mus of Kerbridge*, 1995
Chris Pierson, *Dezra's Quest*, 1999

568

CECILIA DART-THORNTON

The Ill-Made Mute

(New York: Warner, 2001)

Story type: Quest
Series: Bitterbynde. Book 1
Subject(s): Magic
Major character(s): Imrhien, Young Woman, Handicapped (mute and disfigured); Thorn, Ranger
Time period(s): Indeterminate
Locale(s): Erith, Fictional Country

Summary: A young woman sets out on a perilous journey to a distant land in search of a wise woman. Unfortunately, the legends of monsters along the way prove to be true, but she is saved in the nick of time by a heroic ranger named Thorn, who becomes her protector and agrees to accompany her on her quest. Opening volume of a series and a first novel.

Where it's reviewed:
Science Fiction Chronicle, April 2001, page 35

Other books you might like:
James Barclay, *Noonshade*, 2000
Terry Brooks, *The Elfqueen of Shannara*, 1992
Stephen R. Donaldson, *Lord Foul's Bane*, 1977
Terry Goodkind, *Wizard's First Rule*, 1994
Andre Norton, *The Warding of Witch World*, 1996

569

PETER DAVID

Sir Apropos of Nothing

(New York: Pocket, 2001)

Story type: Alternate World
Subject(s): Magic

Major character(s): Apropos, Thief, Abuse Victim; Princess Entipy, Royalty; Tacit, Thief
Time period(s): Indeterminate
Locale(s): Istaria, Fictional Country

Summary: Apropos is raised as an abused child in a poor village of Istaria, and eventually he adopts a career as a thief. Then the inadvertent death of a young woman affects him deeply and he teams up with a heroic warrior to help protect a princess. His endeavors alter his personality and his destiny after a series of fast paced adventures.

Other books by the same author:
Excalibur: Renaissance, 2000
Excalibur: Requiem, 2000
Excalibur: Restoration, 2000
Dark Allies, 1999
Double or Nothing, 1999

Other books you might like:
Clayton Emery, *The Star of Gursrah*, 1999
Fritz Leiber, *Ill Met in Lankhmar*, 1995
Juliet McKenna, *The Thief's Gamble*, 1999
Mickey Zucker Reichert, *Shadow Climber*, 1988
Michael Shea, *The Mines of Behemoth*, 1997

570

TOM DEITZ

Summerblood

(New York: Bantam, 2001)

Story type: Magic Conflict
Series: Avall. Book 3
Subject(s): Magic
Major character(s): Avall, Ruler (king); Merryn, Noblewoman; Rann, Warrior
Time period(s): Indeterminate
Locale(s): Eron, Fictional Country

Summary: Avall has assumed the throne of Eron despite his lack of experience and he hopes to help his people heal in the aftermath of a devastating war and a terrible plague. His efforts are hindered by the rising power of a secretive cult's priesthood who want to deprive him of his authority and rule the land themselves.

Other books by the same author:
Warstalker's Track, 1999
Demons in the Green, 1997
Landslayer's Law, 1997
Ghostcountry's Wrath, 1995
Above the Lower Sky, 1994

Other books you might like:
David Feintuch, *The Still*, 1997
Raymond E. Feist, *Krondor the Betrayal*, 1998
Simon R. Green, *Beyond the Blue Moon*, 2000
Ricardo Pinto, *The Chosen*, 1999
Jennifer Roberson, *Sword Born*, 1998

571

TROY DENNING

The Summoning

(Renton, Washington: Wizards of the Coast, 2001)

Story type: Magic Conflict; Sword and Sorcery
Series: Return of the Archwizards. Book 1
Subject(s): Magic
Major character(s): Galaeron Nihmedu, Mythical Creature (elf); Vala, Warrior; Melegaunt Tanthul, Wizard
Time period(s): Indeterminate
Locale(s): Anauroch, Fictional Country

Summary: A squad of elven warriors discovers a group of tomb robbers, but the thieves don't appear to be after conventional riches. Then both parties are attacked, and they must join forces against an evil which is gathering strength preparatory to launching an all-out war for control of the world. Opening volume in a new subseries of the Forgotten Realms world.

Where it's reviewed:
Science Fiction Chronicle, April 2001, page 38

Other books by the same author:
The Oath of Stonekeep, 1999
Faces of Deception, 1998
Pages of Pain, 1996
The Veiled Dragon, 1996
The Crimson Legion, 1992

Other books you might like:
Richard Awlinson, *Shadowdale*, 1989
David Cook, *Soldiers of Ice*, 1993
Elaine Cunningham, *Tangled Webs*, 1996
Mary Kirchoff, *The Medusa Plague*, 1994
R.A. Salvatore, *Bastion of Darkness*, 2000

572

L. WARREN DOUGLAS

The Veil of Years

(New York: Baen, 2001)

Story type: Quest
Subject(s): Magic
Major character(s): Pierette, Witch; Episkopos Theodosius, Religious
Time period(s): 2nd century B.C. (124 B.C.)
Locale(s): Mediterranean

Summary: Pierette is a young witch, who has lived near a sacred magical pool all her life. Now she sets out on a journey across the ancient world, encountering myriad characters and avoiding dangerous situations, as she discovers the effects of Roman culture on the surrounding peoples. This novel is related to *The Silent Pool*, but is not a sequel.

Other books by the same author:
The Silent Pool, 2001
Simply Human, 2000
Glaice, 1996
The Wells of Phyre, 1996

Cannon's Orb, 1994

Other books you might like:
Marion Zimmer Bradley, *The Forest House*, 1993
Jessica Bryan, *Across a Wine Dark Sea*, 1991
Sarah Isidore, *The Hidden Land*, 1999
Talbot Mundy, *Tros of Samothrace*, 1925
Thomas Burnett Swann, *How Are the Mighty Fallen*, 1974

573

SARA DOUGLASS

Battleaxe

(New York: Tor, 2001)

Story type: Magic Conflict
Series: Wayfarer Redemption. Book 1
Subject(s): Magic
Major character(s): Faraday, Noblewoman; Axis, Nobleman; Gorgrael, Sorcerer
Time period(s): Indeterminate
Locale(s): Achar, Fictional Country

Summary: Faraday is betrothed to a man whom she doesn't love, and when she discovers that all she believes about the history of her people is untrue, she rebels against marrying him. She eventually escapes accompanied by her fiance's half-brother, with whom she promptly falls in love, but their fate is entangled with the latest efforts by an evil sorcerer and his frozen army to subdue the world. This is the author's first novel to be published outside Australia.

Where it's reviewed:
Locus, March 2001, page 33

Other books you might like:
David Farland, *Wizardborn*, 2001
Dennis Jones, *The Mask and the Sorceress*, 2001
Katharine Kerr, *The Fire Dragon*, 2001
John Marco, *The Saints of the Sword*, 2001
Karen Michalson, *Enemy Glory*, 2001

574

DIANE DUANE

The Wizard's Dilemma

(New York: Harcourt, 2001)

Story type: Young Adult
Series: Young Wizards. Book 5
Subject(s): Magic
Major character(s): Kit Rodriguez, Teenager, Wizard; Nita Callahan, Teenager, Wizard; S'ree, Animal (whale), Wizard
Time period(s): 2000s (2001)
Locale(s): New York

Summary: Two teenaged wizards remain friends, although they are no longer as close as they once were. Then one of them discovers that her mother has cancer and decides to make a bargain with a particularly dangerous entity in an effort to save her life. The consequences of this action bring the twosome close together again.

Other books by the same author:
Honor Blade, 2000
Intellivore, 1997
The Venom Factor, 1994
The Door into Sunset, 1993
Deep Wizardry, 1985

Other books you might like:
Diana Wynne Jones, *The Magicians of Caprona*, 1980
J.K. Rowling, *Harry Potter and the Chamber of Secrets*, 1999
Vivian Vande Velde, *Curses Inc.*, 1997
Jane Yolen, *The Wizard's Map*, 1999
Mary Frances Zambreno, *Journeyman Wizard*, 1994

575

WILLIAM R. EAKIN

Redgunk Tales

(Montpelier, Vermont: Invisible Cities, 2001)

Story type: Collection
Subject(s): Short Stories
Locale(s): Redgunk, Arkansas

Summary: These 13 short stories, published between 1996 and 2000, are all set in the fictional town of Redgunk, Arkansas. Although aliens appear in two of the stories, and clones in one, they are predominantly fantasy and not science fiction. They involve mummies who fall in love with the local cleaning lady, a ghost obsessed with mowing his lawn, unicorns, doppelgangers, and serial killers. Although there are elements of horror, the overall tone is whimsical. This is the author's first book.

Other books you might like:
Michael Bishop, *Blue Kansas Sky*, 2000
Avram Davidson, *The Adventures of Dr. Esterhazy*, 1990
Paul Di Filippo, *The Steampunk Trilogy*, 1994
R.A. Lafferty, *Not to Mention Camels*, 1976
Gene Wolfe, *Endangered Species*, 1989

576

TERESA EDGERTON

The Queen's Necklace

(New York: Avon Eos, 2001)

Story type: Magic Conflict
Subject(s): Magic
Major character(s): Wilrowan Krogan-Blackheart, Military Personnel; Lilliana Brakeburn-Blackheart, Noblewoman; Raith, Bodyguard
Time period(s): Indeterminate
Locale(s): Mountfalcon, Mythical Place; Winterscar, Mythical Place

Summary: The human race has been free of its evil goblin rulers for many generations and the monsters are believed extinct. They secretly survive, gathering magical implements in anticipation of their return, and a dashing soldier finds it difficult to convince people to take his belief in their existence seriously. A novel of court intrigue and hidden menace.

Other books by the same author:
The Grail and the Ring, 1994
The Castle of the Silver Wheel, 1993
Goblin Moon, 1991
The Gnomes' Engine, 1991
Child of Saturn, 1989

Other books you might like:
C.J. Cherryh, *The Goblin Mirror*, 1993
L. Sprague de Camp, *The Goblin Tower*, 1968
Oliver Johnson, *The Forging of the Shadows*, 1996
Carl Miller, *The Goblin Plain War*, 1991
Stan Nicholls, *Legion of Thunder*, 1996

577
CLAYTON EMERY

Johan
(Renton, Washington: Wizards of the Coast, 2001)

Story type: Magic Conflict
Series: Magic: The Gathering
Subject(s): Magic
Major character(s): Johan, Ruler; Hazezon Tamar, Wizard; Jaeger, Mythical Creature (tigerman)
Time period(s): Indeterminate
Locale(s): Jamuraa, Fictional Country

Summary: The cruel ruler Johan is determined to conquer the neighboring land of Bryce. It appears that he is likely to succeed, until his plans are disrupted by a moderately talented wizard and a tigerman with superhuman strength. Swordplay and magical combat ensue before the issue is decided.

Other books by the same author:
The Star of Gursrah, 1999
Mortal Consequences, 1998
The Cardmaster, 1997
Dangerous Games, 1996
Sword Play, 1996

Other books you might like:
Lynn Abbey, *Planeswalker*, 1998
William R. Forstchen, *Arena*, 1994
Jeff Grubb, *The Gathering Dark*, 1999
J. Robert King, *The Thran*, 1999
Robert E. Vardeman, *Dark Legacy*, 1996

578
DAVID FARLAND

Wizardborn
(New York: Tor, 2001)

Story type: Magic Conflict
Series: Runelords. Book 3
Subject(s): Magic
Major character(s): Gaborn Val Orden, Nobleman; Raj Ahten, Warrior; Averan, Young Woman
Time period(s): Indeterminate
Locale(s): Rofehaven, Fictional Country

Summary: Gaborn's enemy, Raj Ahten, has been defeated and is barely capable of controlling his own people. That bodes

well, since Gaborn has now lost his magical powers, and must rely on sword and muscle to defeat the evil Reavers, monsters who plague both kingdoms. The key to survival is a young girl, who has absorbed some of the Reaver memories and may know the secret of their lair.

Other books by the same author:
Brotherhood of the Wolf, 1999
The Runelords, 1998

Other books you might like:
Stephen R. Donaldson, *Lord Foul's Bane*, 1977
Terry Goodkind, *Soul of the Fire*, 1999
Oliver Johnson, *The Forging of the Shadows*, 1996
George R.R. Martin, *A Storm of Swords*, 2000
Jane Routley, *Fire Angels*, 1998

579
RAYMOND E. FEIST

Krondor: Tear of the Gods
(New York: Avon, 2001)

Story type: Magic Conflict
Series: Riftwar Legacy. Book 3
Subject(s): Magic
Major character(s): Arutha, Ruler (prince); Squire James, Spy; Jazhara, Magician
Time period(s): Indeterminate
Locale(s): Krondor, Fictional Country

Summary: An agent of the throne of Krondor investigates a wave of criminal activity and discovers a horde of monsters under the city. He teams up with the court magician to track down a magical artifact which has fallen into evil hands, knowing that unless he recovers it, the future of his people could be relentlessly awful.

Where it's reviewed:
Library Journal, November 15, 2000, page 48
Publishers Weekly, February 12, 2001, page 188

Other books by the same author:
Krondor: The Assassins, 1999
Krondor: The Betrayal, 1998
Shards of a Broken Crown, 1998
Rage of a Demon King, 1997
Rise of a Merchant Prince, 1995

Other books you might like:
Simon R. Green, *The Bones of Haven*, 1992
Fritz Leiber, *The Knight and Knave of Swords*, 1988
Michael Moorcock, *The Runestaff*, 1969
Andrew J. Offutt, *My Lord Barbarian*, 1977
Lawrence Watt-Evans, *The Misenchanted Sword*, 1985

580
ERIC FLINT

The Philosophical Strangler
(New York: Baen, 2001)

Story type: Humor
Subject(s): Magic

Major character(s): Ignace, Criminal; Greyboar, Criminal (strangler); Leuwen, Saloon Keeper/Owner
Time period(s): Indeterminate
Locale(s): Grotum, Fictional Country

Summary: The stories of Greyboar, a professional strangler for hire, and his companion, Ignace, are told in a series of episodic adventures. The twosome make a living by assassinating people, but things get more complicated when Greyboar becomes fascinated with philosophy. Despite the violent theme, the novel is humorous.

Where it's reviewed:
Booklist, April 15, 2001, page 1539
Publishers Weekly, April 23, 2001, page 54

Other books by the same author:
1632, 2000
Fortune's Stroke, 2000 (David Drake, co-author)
Rats Bats and Vats, 2000 (Dave Freer, co-author)
Destiny's Shield, 1999 (David Drake, co-author)
Mother of Demons, 1997

Other books you might like:
Robert Asprin, *Hit or Myth*, 1983
Esther Friesner, *Sphynxes Wild*, 1989
Craig Shaw Gardner, *The Last Arabian Night*, 1993
Fritz Leiber, *Heroes and Horrors*, 1978
Terry Pratchett, *The Last Continent*, 1998

581

JEFFREY FORD

The Beyond
(New York: Avon Eos, 2001)

Story type: Literary
Series: Cley. Book 3
Subject(s): Fantasy
Major character(s): Cley, Religious (physiognomist); Misrix, Demon
Time period(s): Indeterminate
Locale(s): The Beyond, Mythical Place

Summary: Cley, the physiognomist, has witnessed the fall of the old order in his world, and now he's on a perilous new journey, wandering solitarily through the unknown lands known as The Beyond. Unbeknownst to him, his efforts are being watched by Misrix, the demonic offspring of his old nemesis.

Where it's reviewed:
Locus, January 2001, page 22

Other books by the same author:
Memoranda, 1999
The Physiognomist, 1997
Vanitas, 1988

Other books you might like:
Kobo Abe, *The Woman in the Dunes*, 1964
Iain Banks, *The Bridge*, 1986
H.P. Lovecraft, *The Dreamquest of Unknown Kadath*, 1955
Michael Moorcock, *Fabulous Harbors*, 1995
Herbert Read, *The Green Child*, 1935

582

ALAN DEAN FOSTER

Kingdoms of Light
(New York: Warner, 2001)

Story type: Quest
Subject(s): Magic
Major character(s): Cezer, Animal (cat); Taj, Animal (bird); Oskar, Animal (dog)
Time period(s): Indeterminate
Locale(s): Gowdlands, Fictional Country

Summary: Six animals are transformed into human form by a wizard's dying spell. Their quest is to save the world from dark necromancy, and to do so they will have to travel to another plane of existence to claim a magical power that can save their world, or destroy it.

Where it's reviewed:
Library Journal, January 1, 2001, page 163
Publishers Weekly, January 22, 2001, page 307

Other books by the same author:
Dirge, 2000
Phylogenesis, 1999
Carnivores of Light and Darkness, 1998
Parallelities, 1998
Jed the Dead, 1997

Other books you might like:
Elizabeth Boyer, *The Keeper of the Cats*, 1995
Diane Duane, *The Book of Night with Moon*, 1997
Esther Friesner, *Majyk by Design*, 1974
Gabriel King, *The Wild Road*, 1998
Christopher Rowley, *The Ancient Enemy*, 2000

583

NEIL GAIMAN

American Gods
(New York: Morrow, 2001)

Story type: Contemporary
Subject(s): Legends
Major character(s): Shadow, Convict; Mr. Wednesday, Mythical Creature
Time period(s): 2000s (2001)
Locale(s): United States

Summary: Shadow is given an early release from prison when his wife dies in an accident. He is soon employed by Mr. Wednesday, an enigmatic man, and visited by the ghost of his wife. His adventures grow more bizarre when he discovers that each wave of immigrants brought some of the supernatural entities of their homeland with them when they came to America.

Other books by the same author:
Smoke and Mirrors, 1998
Stardust, 1998
Neverwhere, 1997
Good Omens, 1990 (Terry Pratchett, co-author)

Fantasy

Other books you might like:
Emma Bull, *War for the Oaks*, 1987
Brett Davis, *The Faery Convention*, 1995
Charles De Lint, *Mulengro*, 1985
Esther Friesner, *New York by Knight*, 1986
Laurell K. Hamilton, *A Kiss of Shadows*, 2000

584

DAVID GEMMELL

Ravenheart

(New York: Ballantine Del Rey, 2001)

Story type: Magic Conflict
Series: Rigante. Book 3
Subject(s): Magic
Major character(s): Alterith Shaddler, Teacher; Kaelin Ring, Teenager; Jaim Grymaugh, Warrior
Time period(s): Indeterminate
Locale(s): Eldacre, Fictional Country

Summary: The inhabitants of Eldacre have been conquered by the Varlish, who treat them as second class citizens. Kaelin Ring is a young man influenced by his warrior friend, Jaim Grymaugh, who is determined to demonstrate his ability to stand with any man, regardless of the consequences. Grymaugh's eventual fate seems certain, but what is the future for a boy in a country his people no longer control?

Other books by the same author:
Hero in the Shadows, 2000
Ironhand's Daughter, 1995
Druss the Legend, 1994
In the Realm of the Wolf, 1992
The Lion of Macedon, 1992

Other books you might like:
Maggie Furey, *Harp of Winds*, 1994
Simon R. Green, *Blue Moon Rising*, 1991
Dennis L. McKiernan, *The Eye of the Hunter*, 1992
Jennifer Roberson, *Sword Born*, 1998
Lawrence Watt-Evans, *Dragon Weather*, 1999

585

DAVID GEMMELL

The Sword in the Storm

(New York: Ballantine Del Rey, 2001)

Story type: Magic Conflict
Series: Rigante. Book 1
Subject(s): Magic
Major character(s): Connavar, Warrior; Meria, Housewife; Banouin, Trader
Time period(s): Indeterminate
Locale(s): Rigante, Fictional Country

Summary: When his land is invaded, a young man becomes a powerful warrior, aided by the magic sword he was given by a mysterious, inhuman race which has been watching over him. Although he is unable to defeat the enemy, he acquits himself well and rescues many of his kind.

Other books by the same author:
Ravenheart, 2001
Hero in the Shadows, 2000
Ironhand's Daughter, 1995
Druss the Legend, 1994
The Lion of Macedon, 1992

Other books you might like:
Steven Frankos, *Beyond the Lich Gate*, 1994
Maggie Furey, *The Heart of Myrial*, 1999
Barbara Hambly, *The Dark Hand of Magic*, 1990
Ardath Mayhar, *Lords of the Triple Moons*, 1983
Dan Parkinson, *The Covenant of the Forge*, 1993

586

ED GREENWOOD

The Vacant Throne

(New York: Tor, 2001)

Story type: Magic Conflict
Subject(s): Magic
Major character(s): Hawkril, Warrior; Craer, Thief; Sarasper, Healer
Time period(s): Indeterminate
Locale(s): Aglirta, Fictional Country

Summary: An unlikely band of four warriors raised the curse that prevented the rightful king of Aglirta from assuming his throne. Now that the magical impediment has been removed, new problems rise in its place, including ambitious rivals and subversive supernatural forces. The foursome discover that their job is not yet done and go to the aid of their ruler once more. Sequel to *The Kingless Land*.

Other books by the same author:
The Kingless Land, 2000
Silverfall, 1999
Elminster in Myth Drannor, 1997
Stormlight, 1996
All Shadows Fled, 1995

Other books you might like:
Storm Constantine, *Sea Dragon Heir*, 2000
Karen Michalson, *Enemy Glory*, 2001
Jennifer Roberson, *Sword Born*, 1998
Jo Walton, *The King's Peace*, 2000
Lawrence Watt-Evans, *Touched by the Gods*, 1997

587

THOMAS HARLAN

The Storm of Heaven

(New York: Tor, 2001)

Story type: Magic Conflict; Alternate History
Series: Oath of Empire. Book 3
Subject(s): Magic
Major character(s): Dahak, Sorcerer; Prince Maxian, Royalty; Dwyrn, Sorcerer
Time period(s): Indeterminate
Locale(s): Alternate Earth

Summary: A three sided war rages in an ancient world that somewhat resembles our own. The Roman Empire is at war with Persia, as well as an Arab empire, and there are other powers rising as well. Since all of the various armies are aided by the presence of sorcerers, the outcome of every battle is unpredictable, and Prince Maxian despairs that he can steer his people on a safe course.

Other books by the same author:
The Gate of Fire, 2000
The Shadow of Ararat, 1999

Other books you might like:
Jo Clayton, *A Bait of Dreams*, 1985
John Ford, *The Dragon Waiting*, 1983
Esther Friesner, *Child of the Eagle*, 1996
J. Gregory Keyes, *Newton's Cannon*, 1998
Andre Norton, *Leopard in Exile*, 2001
      Rosemary Edghill, co-author

588

NINA KIRIKI HOFFMAN

Past the Size of Dreaming
(New York: Ace, 2001)

Story type: Contemporary
Series: Matilda Black. Book 2
Subject(s): Ghosts
Major character(s): Matilda Black, Witch; Edmund Reynolds, Witch; Deirdre Eberhard, Veterinarian
Time period(s): 2000s (2001)
Locale(s): Oregon

Summary: Two benevolent witches move into a house, which is full of memories for one of them. It also has a personality of its own, and it insists that they search out the scattered friends who once lived there, in order to bring them back together to combat an evil force.

Where it's reviewed:
Booklist, March 15, 2001, page 1360
Library Journal, February 15, 2001, page 110
Locus, April 2001, page 23
Publishers Weekly, January 29, 2001, page 70
Science Fiction Chronicle, June 2001, page 37

Other books by the same author:
The Red Heart of Memories, 1999
I Was a Sixth Grade Zombie, 1998
The Silent Strength of Stones, 1995
The Thread That Binds the Bones, 1993
Unmasking, 1992

Other books you might like:
James P. Blaylock, *The Rainy Season*, 1999
Terry Brooks, *Running with the Demon*, 1997
Christopher Golden, *Ghost Roads*, 1999
      Nancy Holder, co-author
Richard Grant, *In the Land of Winter*, 1997
James Stoddard, *The High House*, 1999

589

TOM HOLT

Nothing but Blue Skies
(London: Orbit, 2001)

Story type: Humor; Contemporary
Subject(s): Environmental Problems
Major character(s): Karen, Mythical Creature (dragon), Real Estate Agent; Gordon Smelt, Entertainer; Steven Harrison, Government Official
Time period(s): 2000s (2001)
Locale(s): England

Summary: Karen works as a realtor, but she is actually a Chinese water dragon in disguise, one of a number of such creatures living in England. The dragons are in fact responsible for the perpetually bad weather there, and a secret society of angry weatherman has kidnapped Karen's father as part of their efforts to expose the truth and prove that they're not responsible.

Where it's reviewed:
Science Fiction Chronicle, July 2001, page 42

Other books by the same author:
Snow White and the Seven Samurai, 2000
Valhalla, 2000
Paint Your Dragon, 1996
Djinn Rummy, 1995
Faust Among Equals, 1994

Other books you might like:
Rick Cook, *Mall Purchase Night*, 1993
John DeChancie, *Bride of the Castle*, 1994
Esther Friesner, *Gnome Man's Land*, 1991
Craig Shaw Gardner, *Revenge of the Fluffy Bunnies*, 1990
Terry Pratchett, *The Truth*, 2000

590

TANYA HUFF

The Second Summoning
(New York: Tor, 2001)

Story type: Contemporary
Series: Keeper's Chronicles. Book 2
Subject(s): Angels
Major character(s): Claire Hansen, Magician (keeper); Austin, Animal (cat); Diana Hansen, Young Woman
Time period(s): 2000s (2001)
Locale(s): New York

Summary: Claire Hansen's job is to prevent rifts in the natural world from spreading or being noticed by the local inhabitants. Her job gets particularly difficult when an angel and a demon both manifest themselves in human bodies, as hormone driven teenagers. With her talking cat and other companions, she sets out to neutralize this new threat.

Where it's reviewed:
Locus, February 2001, page 27
Science Fiction Chronicle, April 2001, page 37

Fantasy

Other books by the same author:
Stealing Magic, 1999
The Quartered Sea, 1999
The Wizard of the Grove, 1999
Summon the Keeper, 1998
No Quarter, 1996

Other books you might like:
Storm Constantine, *Stalking Tender Prey*, 1995
Neil Gaiman, *Good Omens*, 1990
    Terry Pratchett, co-author
Christopher Golden, *Out of the Madhouse*, 1999
    Nancy Holder, co-author
Sherrilyn Kenyon, *Daemon's Angel*, 1995
James Stoddard, *The High House*, 1999

591

KIM HUNTER

Knight's Dawn
(London: Orbit, 2001)

Story type: Magic Conflict
Series: Red Pavilions. Book 1
Subject(s): Magic
Major character(s): Soldier, Knight, Amnesiac; Spagg, Businessman; Pugorchoff, Magician
Time period(s): Indeterminate
Locale(s): Guthrum, Fictional Country

Summary: A knight wakes up with no memory of his past, apparently having just survived a battle, even though none has taken place in living memory. He tries to make a life for himself in a nearby city, but is unable to adjust, so he finally joins a mercenary group in an effort to discover his past, and his purpose. This is a first novel.

Where it's reviewed:
Science Fiction Chronicle, April 2001, page 37

Other books you might like:
Robert Don Hughes, *The Power and the Prophet*, 1985
Oliver Johnson, *The Last Star at Dawn*, 1999
Richard A. Knaak, *Ruby Flames*, 1999
Mercedes Lackey, *Owlknight*, 1999
Michael Moorcock, *Hawkmoon*, 1995

592

IAN IRVINE

A Shadow on the Glass
(New York: Warner Aspect, 2001)

Story type: Magic Conflict
Series: View from the Mirror. Book 1
Subject(s): Magic
Major character(s): Llian, Historian; Karan, Psychic; Mendark, Sorcerer
Time period(s): Indeterminate
Locale(s): Aachim, Alternate Universe; Faellem, Alternate Universe

Summary: Humankind exists on a series of alternate worlds, although the means of traveling among them has somehow been lost. A historian and a young woman with psychic powers become fugitives in their own world, when they inadvertently run afoul of a plot to alter the balance of power. This is a first novel.

Other books you might like:
Raymond E. Feist, *A Darkness at Sethanon*, 1986
R.A. Salvatore, *The Demon Apostle*, 1999
Freda Warrington, *The Sapphire Throne*, 2000
Tad Williams, *The Mountain of Black Glass*, 1999
Janny Wurts, *The Warhost of Vastmark*, 1995

593

DENNIS JONES

The Mask and the Sorceress
(New York: Avon Eos, 2001)

Story type: Magic Conflict
Series: House of Pandragore. Book 2
Subject(s): Magic
Major character(s): Theatana, Royalty (princess), Mentally Ill Person; Elyssa, Noblewoman; Lashgar, Nobleman
Time period(s): Indeterminate
Locale(s): The Ascendancy, Fictional Country

Summary: Theatana is a member of the ruling family of The Ascendancy, but she is mentally unstable and has been confined for her own protection as well as the security of the empire. She escapes and flees to unknown lands, where she recruits allies, some magical, in her campaign to wrest the throne from her family and rule in their place.

Where it's reviewed:
Publishers Weekly, February 19, 2001, page 73

Other books by the same author:
The Stone and the Maiden, 1999
The Winter Palace, 1988
The Russian Spring, 1984
Rubicon One, 1983

Other books you might like:
Anne Bishop, *Queen of Darkness*, 2000
James Clemens, *Wit'ch War*, 2000
Storm Constantine, *Sea Dragon Heir*, 2000
Simon R. Green, *Beyond the Blue Moon*, 2000
Barbara Hambly, *Knight of the Demon Queen*, 2000

594

KATHARINE KERR

The Fire Dragon
(New York: Bantam, 2001)

Story type: Magic Conflict
Series: Dragon Mage. Book 3
Subject(s): Magic
Major character(s): Maryn, Royalty (prince); Lilli, Magician, Apprentice; Rhodry Maelwaedd, Nobleman
Time period(s): Indeterminate
Locale(s): Deverry, Fictional Country

Summary: In the concluding volume of the trilogy, a new king is ready to declare himself in Deverry, but there is still one clan in open rebellion, a sorceress is plotting against the throne, and hordes of barbarians are invading from the north. The king's reputation plummets when he pursues his infatuation with a young apprentice and it appears that the kingdom will fall into chaos.

Where it's reviewed:
Booklist, November 15, 2000, page 625
Library Journal, January 1, 2001, page 163

Other books by the same author:
The Black Raven, 1998
The Red Wyvern, 1997
Days of Air and Darkness, 1994
Freezeframes, 1994
Days of Blood and Fire, 1993

Other books you might like:
Joanne Bertin, *The Last Dragonlord*, 1998
B.W. Clough, *The Dragon of Mishbil*, 1985
Esther Friesner, *The Silver Mountain*, 1986
Robert Don Hughes, *The Faithful Traitor*, 1992
Craig Mills, *The Bane of Lord Caladon*, 1982

595

J. GREGORY KEYES

The Shadows of God

(New York: Ballantine Del Rey, 2001)

Story type: Alternate Universe
Series: Age of Unreason. Book 4
Subject(s): Alternate History
Major character(s): Benjamin Franklin, Historical Figure, Political Figure; Red Shoes, Shaman; Adrienne de Montchevreuil, Scientist
Time period(s): Indeterminate
Locale(s): Alternate Earth

Summary: In what appears to be the concluding volume of this alternate history fantasy, Ben Franklin teams up with a shaman named Red Shoes for the final confrontation. Napoleon has conquered much of Europe using magic to aid his armies, and Russia and England are gobbling up the new world. To win the day, they must defeat a female scientist, who has wedded magic to technology and forged them into an apparently irresistible weapon.

Where it's reviewed:
Booklist, April 15, 2001, page 1540
Publishers Weekly, May 14, 2001, page 57
Science Fiction Chronicle, July 2001, page 43

Other books by the same author:
Empire of Unreason, 2000
A Calculus of Angels, 1999
Newton's Cannon, 1998
The Blackgod, 1997
Waterborn, 1996

Other books you might like:
Poul Anderson, *Operation Luna*, 1999
Jo Clayton, *A Bait of Dreams*, 1985

Esther Friesner, *Druid's Blood*, 1988
Thomas Harlan, *The Gate of Fire*, 2000
Stephen Leigh, *The Abraxas Marvel Circus*, 1990

596

J. ROBERT KING

Planeshift

(Renton, Washington: Wizards of the Coast, 2001)

Story type: Sword and Sorcery
Series: Magic: The Gathering
Subject(s): Quest
Major character(s): Gerrard, Warrior; Captain Sisay, Warrior; Tsabo Tavoc, Warrior
Time period(s): Indeterminate
Locale(s): Dominaria, Fictional Country

Summary: The armies of Phyrexia have crossed between worlds and invaded the land of Dominaria. The local residents use magic instead of technology, and the two rival realities collide in a series of battles as the defenders seek to end the war by attacking the heart of the Phyrexian Empire.

Other books by the same author:
Invasion, 2000
Mad Merlin, 2000
Planar Powers, 1997
Rogues to Riches, 1995
The Summerhill Hounds, 1995

Other books you might like:
Piers Anthony, *Phaze Doubt*, 1990
Loren Coleman, *Bloodlines*, 1998
Jeff Grubb, *The Shattered Alliance*, 2000
Frances Lebaron, *Mercadian Masques*, 1999
Lawrence Watt-Evans, *Out of This World*, 1994

597

RICHARD A. KNAAK

Day of the Dragon

(New York: Pocket, 2001)

Story type: Sword and Sorcery
Subject(s): Magic
Major character(s): Rhonin, Wizard; Nekros Skullcrusher, Mythical Creature (orc); Lord Prestor, Nobleman
Time period(s): Indeterminate
Locale(s): Azeroth, Alternate Universe

Summary: An unconventional but respected wizard travels to a remote land to investigate rumors of strange events. Elsewhere, a scheming nobleman uses his powers to subjugate the will of his rivals in a bid to become ruler of them all. The wizard must form an alliance with the reclusive dragons in order to save the world. This is supposedly based on the *Warcraft* computer game.

Where it's reviewed:
Science Fiction Chronicle, April 2001, page 40

Other books by the same author:
Reavers of the Blood Sea, 1999

Fantasy

The Ruby Flames, 1999
The Horse King, 1997
Land of the Minotaurs, 1996
Frostwing, 1995

Other books you might like:
Joanne Bertin, *The Last Dragonlord*, 1998
Robert Charrette, *Never Deal with a Dragon*, 1981
Susan Dexter, *The Ring of Allaire*, 1981
Elizabeth Kerner, *The Lesser Kindred*, 2000
Jean Rabe, *The Dawn of a New Age*, 1996

598

RICHARD A. KNAAK

Legacy of Blood

(New York: Pocket, 2001)

Story type: Sword and Sorcery
Series: Diablo. Book 1
Subject(s): Magic
Major character(s): Norrec Vizharan, Warrior; Augustus Malevolyn, Military Personnel; Sadun Tryst, Warrior
Time period(s): Indeterminate
Locale(s): Aranoch, Fictional Country

Summary: Three companions enter an ancient tomb in search of magical artifacts. They find some enchanted armor, but they also discover a small army of the living dead. Norrec Vizharan escapes with the armor, but when he puts it on, he discovers that his body is possessed by the spirit of a long dead and very evil man.

Other books by the same author:
Day of the Dragon, 2001
Reavers of the Blood Sea, 1999
Ruby Flames, 1999
The Horse King, 1997
Frostwing, 1995

Other books you might like:
Stephen R. Donaldson, *Lord Foul's Bane*, 1977
Robert E. Howard, *Skulls in the Stars*, 1978
David Mason, *The Deep Gods*, 1973
Andre Norton, *The Horn Crown*, 1981
Karl Edward Wagner, *Death Angel's Shadow*, 1973

599

KATHERINE KURTZ

St. Patrick's Gargoyle

(New York: Ace, 2001)

Story type: Contemporary; Magic Conflict
Subject(s): Legends
Major character(s): Paddy, Mythical Creature (gargoyle); Francis Templeton, Aged Person, Knight
Time period(s): 2000s (2001)
Locale(s): Dublin, Ireland

Summary: Gargoyles are actually angels in disguise, and one of them enlists the aid of a human in tracking down some property stolen from a church. In the process, the gargoyle inadvertently reveals his true form, dooming the human, but

gains an extension of his life by recruiting the man to help defeat an evil force.

Where it's reviewed:
Booklist, February 1, 2001, page 1042
Library Journal, February 15, 2001, page 205
Locus, February 2001, page 23
Science Fiction Chronicle, April 2001, page 35

Other books by the same author:
King Kelson's Bride, 2000
Two Crowns for America, 1996
The Bastard Prince, 1994
King Javan's Year, 1992
Deryni Magic, 1991

Other books you might like:
Piers Anthony, *Geis of the Gargoyle*, 1995
Margot Benary-Isbert, *The Wicked Enchantment*, 1955
Anthony Burgess, *The Eve of St. Venus*, 1964
Neil Gaiman, *Good Omens*, 1990
    Terry Pratchett, co-author
Thorne Smith, *Turnabout*, 1931

600

KATHERINE KURTZ
DEBORAH TURNER HARRIS, Co-Author

The Temple and the Crown

(New York: Warner Aspect, 2001)

Story type: Historical
Series: Temple. Book 2
Subject(s): Magic
Major character(s): Arnault de St. Clair, Knight, Religious; Brother Torquil, Religious; Robert Bruce, Leader
Time period(s): 14th century (1306)
Locale(s): England; Scotland

Summary: King Edward of England has violently suppressed the rebels in Scotland, and in France the new king challenges the power of the Pope. Both acts are actually caused by a secret order of alchemists, who are manipulating the rulers of Europe in their efforts to steal a trove of magical artifacts that have been hidden by the Knights Templar.

Where it's reviewed:
Booklist, April 15, 2001, page 1540

Other books by the same author:
St. Patrick's Gargoyle, 2001
King Kelson's Bride, 2000
The Temple and the Stone, 1998 (Temple. Book 1; Deborah Turner Harris, co-author)
The Bastard Prince, 1994
King Javan's Year, 1992

Other books you might like:
Terry Brooks, *Angel Fire East*, 1999
Kenneth Flint, *A Storm upon Ulster*, 1981
R. Garcia y Robertson, *The Spiral Dance*, 1991
Morgan Llywelyn, *Bard*, 1984
Jennifer Roberson, *Scotland the Brave*, 1996

601

MERCEDES LACKEY
ROSEMARY EDGHILL, Co-Author

Beyond World's End

(New York: Baen, 2001)

Story type: Magic Conflict
Series: Serrated Edge. Book 5
Subject(s): Fairies
Major character(s): Eric Banyon, Student; Lydia Ashborn, Student; Beth Kentraine, Student
Time period(s): 2000s (2001)
Locale(s): New York, New York; California

Summary: A rift has opened between the world of the fairies and the one with which we are familiar. Eric Banyon knows this because a fairy knight appeared to him, but he is trying to forget it. Unfortunately, political maneuverings in the land of the fairies are about to spill over into our world, and those aware of the gateway are going to be caught up in what follows.

Where it's reviewed:
Booklist, January 1, 2001, page 928
Library Journal, January 1, 2001, page 163
Publishers Weekly, December 18, 2000, page 59

Other books by the same author:
Brightly Burning, 2000
The Black Swan, 1999
Werehunter, 1999
Fiddler's Fair, 1998
Storm Breaking, 1996

Other books you might like:
Emma Bull, *War for the Oaks*, 1987
Rick Cook, *Mall Purchase Night*, 1993
Esther Friesner, *Elf Defense*, 1988
Laurell K. Hamilton, *A Kiss of Shadows*, 2000
Will Shetterly, *Elsewhere*, 1991

602

MERCEDES LACKEY

The Serpent's Shadow

(New York: DAW, 2001)

Story type: Historical
Subject(s): Magic
Major character(s): Maya Witherspoon, Doctor, Healer; Gupta, Servant; Peter Scott, Nobleman
Time period(s): 1900s (1909)
Locale(s): London, England

Summary: Returning to England following the mysterious death of her parents, Maya Witherspoon works as a physician and conceals the fact that she has a magical ability to heal people. She is followed by a handful of Indian magicians who want to control her powers for their own purposes.

Where it's reviewed:
Booklist, February 15, 2001, page 1122
Library Journal, February 15, 2001, page 205

Locus, February 2001, page 27
Science Fiction Chronicle, February 2001, page 42

Other books by the same author:
Brightly Burning, 2000
Owlknight, 1999
The Black Swan, 1999
Werehunter, 1999
Fiddler's Fair, 1998

Other books you might like:
James P. Blaylock, *Homunculus*, 1986
Terry Brooks, *Running with the Demon*, 1997
Paul Di Filippo, *The Steampunk Trilogy*, 1994
Mark Frost, *The List of Seven*, 1993
Barbara Hambly, *Bride of the Rat God*, 1994

603

MILLER LAU

Talisker

(London: Earthlight, 2001)

Story type: Contemporary; Mystery
Series: Last Clansman. Book 1
Subject(s): Magic
Major character(s): Duncan Talisker, Businessman; Alessandro Chaplin, Detective—Police; Malky MacLeod, Warrior
Time period(s): 2000s (2001)
Locale(s): Scotland; Sutra, Alternate Universe

Summary: A man falsely convicted of murder is freed, and immediately falls under suspicion when a new crime is committed. He and the police officer who investigated him then travel to an alternate universe where an ancient evil force is threatening to rise and affect the lives of people in both realities. This is the first title to appear under this author name, which is a pseudonym for an unidentified writer.

Other books you might like:
Terry Brooks, *Angel Fire East*, 1999
Emma Bull, *War for the Oaks*, 1987
Esther Friesner, *New York by Knight*, 1986
Garfield Reeves-Stevens, *Shifter*, 1990
    Judith Reeves-Stevens, co-author
James Stoddard, *The High House*, 1999

604

URSULA K. LE GUIN

Tales from Earthsea

(New York: Harcourt, 2001)

Story type: Collection
Series: Earthsea
Subject(s): Short Stories
Locale(s): Earthsea, Fictional Country

Summary: This is a collection of five original stories, all set in Earthsea, the locale used in four previous fantasy novels. The stories involve the quest for freedom, the efforts by a magician to use his powers to avert an earthquake, and other matters. One story is set in the years before any of the novels

Fantasy

take place and one is a bridge to a new novel that is forthcoming.

Where it's reviewed:
Publishers Weekly, March 5, 2001, page 66

Other books by the same author:
The Telling, 2000
Four Ways to Forgiveness, 1995
Tehanu, 1990
Three Hainish Novels, 1987
Always Coming Home, 1985

Other books you might like:
James Branch Cabell, *The Silver Stallion*, 1926
Avram Davidson, *The Island under the Earth*, 1969
Terry Goodkind, *Wizard's First Rule*, 1994
Carol Severance, *Storm Caller*, 1993
Lawrence Watt-Evans, *Dragon Weather*, 1999

J. ARDIAN LEE

Son of the Sword
(New York: Ace, 2001)

Story type: Time Travel; Historical
Subject(s): Magic
Major character(s): Dylan Matheson, Time Traveler, Martial Arts Expert (instructor); Cait Matheson, Young Woman; Sinann, Mythical Creature (fairy)
Time period(s): 2000s (2001); 1710s (1713)
Locale(s): Scotland

Summary: A martial arts instructor in contemporary Scotland finds a magical sword which transports him back through time to the 18th century. There he is greeted by a fairy, becomes involved with warfare and magic, and discovers his true love. This is a first novel.

Other books you might like:
T.A. Barron, *The Ancient One*, 1992
John Dickson Carr, *Fire, Burn*, 1957
Diana Gabaldon, *Voyager*, 1994
Edmond Hamilton, *A Yank at Valhalla*, 1973
Zoe Sherburne, *Why Have the Birds Stopped Singing?*, 1964

KELLY LINK

Stranger Things Happen
(Brooklyn, New York: Small Beer Press, 2001)

Story type: Collection
Subject(s): Short Stories

Summary: This collection contains 11 stories, all originally published between 1995 and 2000, most of which are fantasy. The themes include a girl so alienated that she literally vanishes, a party for disasters, an unusual fairy tale, a very strange story of possible alien invasion, and a mildly supernatural story about a peculiar family. This is the author's first book.

Other books you might like:
Charles Beaumont, *The Howling Man*, 1992

Avram Davidson, *The Avram Davidson Treasury*, 1998
Nancy Kress, *Beaker's Dozen*, 1998
David Morrell, *Black Evening*, 2000
Ray Vukcevich, *Meet Me in the Moon Room*, 2001

JOHN MARCO

The Saints of the Sword
(New York: Bantam, 2001)

Story type: Magic Conflict
Series: Tyrants and Kings. Book 3
Subject(s): Magic
Major character(s): Alazrian Leth, Teenager, Nobleman; Jahl Rob, Religious; Tassis Gayle, Ruler
Time period(s): Indeterminate
Locale(s): Nar, Fictional Country

Summary: The emperor of Nar has finally decided to bring an end to war and turmoil, but cannot convince his enemies that he truly wants peace. When two powerful leaders begin uniting their forces against him, the emperor uses the son of one of his enemies as a pawn in a plan to hold onto his throne. The boy has magical powers, however, and eventually sets his own agenda.

Where it's reviewed:
Booklist, February 1, 2001, page 1042
Library Journal, February 15, 2001, page 265

Other books by the same author:
The Grand Design, 2000
The Jackal of Nar, 1999

Other books you might like:
Joanne Bertin, *The Dragon and the Phoenix*, 1999
Sara Douglass, *Battleaxe*, 2001
George R.R. Martin, *A Storm of Swords*, 2000
Douglas Niles, *The War of Three Waters*, 1997
R.A. Salvatore, *The Sword of Bedwyr*, 1996

JULIET MARILLIER

Son of the Shadows
(New York: Forge, 2001)

Story type: Historical
Series: Sevenwaters. Book 2
Subject(s): Women
Major character(s): Liadan, Noblewoman; Conor, Religious (druid); Bran, Warrior
Time period(s): Indeterminate Past
Locale(s): Ireland

Summary: The daughter of a noble house in Celtic Ireland defies the family when she falls in love with the enigmatic leader of a band of outlaws. In order to get her way, she must abandon her family, or convince them to change their attitude. She also must contend with an ancient prophecy that predicts doom if she leaves her home.

Other books by the same author:
Daughter of the Forest, 2000

Other books you might like:
Risa Aratyr, *Hunter of Light*, 1995
Kenneth Flint, *Cromm*, 1990
Casey Flynn, *The Enchanted Isles*, 1991
Gregory Frost, *Tain*, 1986
Morgan Llywelyn, *Druids*, 1991

609

TERRY MCGARRY

Illumination

(New York: Tor, 2001)

Story type: Quest
Subject(s): Magic
Major character(s): Liath n'Geara l'Danor, Magician; Karanthe Illuminator, Magician; Torrin n'Maeryn l'Eilody, Nobleman
Time period(s): Indeterminate
Locale(s): Alternate Universe

Summary: Liath has finally mastered the powers of magic, but just as she acquires the badge of office, she mysteriously loses her powers. The council of magicians is willing to help her, but only if she performs a service for them first. She must track down and capture a rogue magician, but as her quest continues, she begins to wonder which party is actually serving the cause of evil. This is a first novel.

Other books you might like:
Terry Goodkind, *Faith of the Fallen*, 2000
Valery Leith, *The Riddled Night*, 2000
Patricia McKillip, *The Tower at Stony Wood*, 2000
Ricardo Pinto, *The Chosen*, 1999
Angus Wells, *Wild Magic*, 1993

610

KAREN MICHALSON

Enemy Glory

(New York: Tor, 2001)

Story type: Magic Conflict
Subject(s): Magic
Major character(s): Llewelyn, Religious, Magician; Walworth, Nobleman (duke); Brother Cristo, Religious
Time period(s): Indeterminate
Locale(s): Threla, Fictional Country

Summary: In a world divided between the realm of the supernatural and another where rival cults of good and evil contend for the souls of the inhabitants, a young man becomes a magician in a religious order. He becomes involved in a revolution, becomes embittered with the world, and eventually begins to use his magical talents more aggressively. First in a projected series and a first novel.

Where it's reviewed:
Library Journal, January 1, 2001, page 163
Locus, February 2001, page 27
Publishers Weekly, January 8, 2001, page 53

Other books you might like:
Dennis Jones, *The Mask and the Sorceress*, 2001
Robert Jordan, *Winter's Heart*, 2000
John Marco, *The Saints of the Sword*, 2001
George R.R. Martin, *A Storm of Swords*, 2000
Ricardo Pinto, *The Chosen*, 1999

611

CHINA MIEVILLE

Perdido Street Station

(New York: Ballantine Del Rey, 2001)

Story type: Alternate World
Subject(s): Magic
Major character(s): Isaac Dan Der Grimnebulin, Scientist; Lin, Artist, Alien (Khepri); Motley, Criminal
Time period(s): Indeterminate
Locale(s): New Crobuzon, Fictional Country

Summary: A scientist in a magical city, where humans live with a number of alien species, accepts a commission to restore wings to a creature, which has lost the power of flight. His wife simultaneously agrees to create a sculpture of a criminal mastermind, whose body has been distorted in very strange ways. The two plots become intertwined as dark forces move within the couple's city.

Where it's reviewed:
Booklist, February 15, 2001, page 1122
Library Journal, February 15, 2001, page 204
Publishers Weekly, January 8, 2001, page 52

Other books by the same author:
King Rat, 1998

Other books you might like:
Neal Barrett Jr., *The Prophecy Machine*, 2000
Avram Davidson, *The Island under the Earth*, 1969
Peter Garrison, *The Magic Dead*, 2000
Mary Gentle, *Rats and Gargoyles*, 1990
Lawrence Watt-Evans, *Night of Madness*, 2000

612

L.E. MODESITT JR.

The Shadow Sorceress

(New York: Tor, 2001)

Story type: Magic Conflict
Series: Spellsong. Book 4
Subject(s): Magic
Major character(s): Secca, Sorceress, Noblewoman; Lord Robero, Ruler; Richina, Sorceress
Time period(s): Indeterminate
Locale(s): Nordwei, Fictional Country

Summary: When the most prominent sorceress in the land dies, she leaves her people virtually undefended. Now her apprentice must complete her training on her own and master the art of magical music to put down a rebellion and prevent the immature ruler from being driven from his throne before he is old enough to defend himself.

Other books by the same author:
The Octagonal Raven, 2001
Scion of Cyador, 2000
Timegods' World, 2000
Darksong Rising, 1999
Gravity Dreams, 1999

Other books you might like:
Sarah Ash, *Songspinners*, 1996
Greg Bear, *The Infinity Concerto*, 1984
Ellen Kushner, *Thomas the Rhymer*, 1990
Ardath Mayhar, *Soul-Singer of Tyrnos*, 1981
Andrea Shettle, *Flute Song Magic*, 1990

613

REBECCA NEASON

The Thirteenth Scroll

(New York: Warner Aspect, 2001)

Story type: Magic Conflict
Subject(s): Magic
Major character(s): Lysandra, Healer; Aurya, Sorceress; Giraldus, Nobleman
Time period(s): Indeterminate
Locale(s): Aghamore, Fictional Country

Summary: A sorceress believes that she can help her lover to become the next king of Aghamore, but only if she acts preemptively to destroy a child who is a magical stumbling block. Elsewhere, a village healer has a vision in which she learns of the sorceress' plot, and decides to forestall her.

Where it's reviewed:
Science Fiction Chronicle, June 2001, page 40

Other books by the same author:
Shadow of Obsession, 1998
The Path, 1997
Guises of the Mind, 1993

Other books you might like:
Storm Constantine, *Sea Dragon Heir*, 2000
Nancy Kress, *The Golden Grove*, 1984
Jennifer Roberson, *Shapechanger's Song*, 2001
Joan D. Vinge, *Willow*, 1988
Lawrence Watt-Evans, *Dragon Weather*, 1999

614

ADAM NICHOLS

The Curer

(London: Millennium, 2001)

Story type: Magic Conflict
Series: Whiteblade. Book 3
Subject(s): Magic
Major character(s): Pawli, Teenager; Brynmaur, Healer; Khurdis Blackeye, Sorcerer
Time period(s): Indeterminate
Locale(s): Three Valleys, Fictional Country

Summary: Pawli is a teenager, who believes he has a magical gift, but his uncle refuses to believe it even though he himself

has healing powers. Then an evil sorcerer tries to extend his rule to include their homeland and the boy and his uncle discover that it lies in their hands alone to thwart his plans.

Other books by the same author:
The Songster, 1999
The Paladin, 1997
The Pathless Way, 1996
The War of the Lord's Veil, 1994

Other books you might like:
L. Sprague de Camp, *The Pixilated Peeress*, 1991
David Farland, *The Runelords*, 1998
Oliver Johnson, *The Forging of the Shadows*, 1996
Mindy L. Klasky, *The Glasswright's Apprentice*, 2000
John Marco, *The Jackal of Nar*, 1999

615

PATRICK NIELSEN-HAYDEN, Editor

Starlight 3

(New York: Tor, 2001)

Story type: Anthology
Subject(s): Short Stories

Summary: This is an original collection of 16 stories, almost all of which are fantasy. The themes include the arrival of angels on Earth, a werewolf story, a woman whose physical orientation is strangely altered, a spoof of J.R.R. Tolkien, and a world in which dancing is mandatory. Contributors include D.G. Compton, Maureen McHugh, Madeleine Robins, Geoffrey Landis, and Susan Palwick.

Other books by the same author:
Starlight 2, 1999
Starlight, 1996

Other books you might like:
D.G. Compton, *The Steel Crocodile*, 1970
Geoffrey A. Landis, *Mars Crossing*, 2000
Maureen McHugh, *Mission Child*, 1998
Susan Palwick, *Flying in Place*, 1992
Madeleine Robins, *The Stone War*, 1999

616

DOUGLAS NILES

The Messenger

(Renton, Washington: Wizards of the Coast, 2001)

Story type: Sword and Sorcery
Series: Icewall. Book 1
Subject(s): Magic
Major character(s): Kerrick Fallabaine, Mythical Creature (elf); Grimwar Bane, Mythical Creature (ogre); Moreen Bayguard, Warrior, Hunter
Time period(s): Indeterminate
Locale(s): Icewall, Fictional Country

Summary: A disgraced elf is exiled and sent on a perilous ocean voyage. Elsewhere, fierce ogres have been raiding peaceful villages and slaughtering the leaders of a primitive

people. They are now led by a determined woman whose life is about to cross that of the elf.

Other books by the same author:
The Puppet King, 1999
The Last Thane, 1998
The War of Three Waters, 1997
Darkenheight, 1996
Pawns Prevail, 1995

Other books you might like:
Nancy Varian Berberick, *Stormblade*, 1988
David Cook, *King Pinch*, 1995
Troy Denning, *The Ogre's Pact*, 1994
Ed Greenwood, *Silverfall*, 1999
Dan Parkinson, *The Gully Dwarves*, 1996

617

GARTH NIX

Lirael

(New York: HarperCollins, 2001)

Story type: Young Adult
Subject(s): Magic
Major character(s): Lirael, Teenager, Orphan; Dog, Animal (dog); Sameth, Royalty (prince)
Time period(s): Indeterminate
Locale(s): Old Kingdom, Fictional Country

Summary: Lirael is an orphan, valued little because she apparently has no magical abilities. Then magic reveals that she holds the key to the salvation of her people, but only if she and a magically conjured dog can complete a hazardous quest. This is the sequel to *Sabriel*.

Where it's reviewed:
Publishers Weekly, March 19, 2001, page 101

Other books by the same author:
Castle, 2000
The Fall, 2000
Shade's Children, 1997
The Calusari, 1997
Sabriel, 1995

Other books you might like:
Bruce Coville, *The Dragonslayers*, 1974
Pamela Dean, *The Whim of the Dragon*, 1989
Gayle Greeno, *Sunderlies Seeking*, 1998
Diana Wynne Jones, *The Crown of Dalemark*, 1993
Jane Yolen, *Child of Faerie, Child of Earth*, 2000

618

ANDRE NORTON
SASHA MILLER, Co-Author

Knight or Knave

(New York: Tor, 2001)

Story type: Magic Conflict
Series: Book of Oak. Book 2
Subject(s): Magic

Major character(s): Ysa, Ruler (queen); Florian, Ruler (prince); Ashen Deathdaughter, Rebel
Time period(s): Indeterminate
Locale(s): Rendel, Fictional Country

Summary: Prince Florian has assumed the throne, but he is a weak minded, fickle young man who is dominated by his more thoughtful mother, Queen Ysa. Unfortunately, Ashen Deathdaughter, his illegitimate half sister, has not abandoned her efforts to seize the throne, and there is another magical evil force gathering outside the country's borders.

Other books by the same author:
Leopard in Exile, 2001 (Rosemary Edghill, co-author)
Time Traders II, 2001
To the King a Daughter, 2000 (Sasha Miller, co-author)
The Warding of Witch World, 1996
The Mirror of Destiny, 1995

Other books you might like:
Dave Duncan, *Sky of Swords*, 2000
Kate Elliott, *The Burning Stone*, 1999
Katharine Kerr, *The Bristling Wood*, 1989
George R.R. Martin, *A Storm of Swords*, 2000
Melanie Rawn, *The Mageborn Traitor*, 1997

619

ANDRE NORTON
ROSEMARY EDGHILL, Co-Author

Leopard in Exile

(New York: Tor, 2001)

Story type: Alternate Universe
Series: Carolus Rex. Book 2
Subject(s): Magic
Major character(s): Rupert Dyer, Nobleman, Spy; Sarah Roxbury, Witch, Noblewoman; Marquis de Sade, Nobleman, Sorcerer
Time period(s): 1800s (1807)
Locale(s): Paris, Alternate Earth; New Orleans, Alternate Earth

Summary: In an alternate 19th century where the British colonies never won their independence, Napoleon is waging a successful war in Europe thanks to the sorcery of the Marquis de Sade. A husband and wife spy team for the British Empire, who are also practicing witches, oppose his maneuverings in North America.

Where it's reviewed:
Science Fiction Chronicle, June 2001, page 38

Other books by the same author:
Time Traders II, 2001
To the King a Daughter, 2000 (Sasha Miller, co-author)
The Shadow of Albion, 1999 (Rosemary Edghill, co-author)
The Warding of Witch World, 1996
The Mirror of Destiny, 1995

Other books you might like:
Poul Anderson, *Operation Luna*, 1999
Esther Friesner, *Child of the Eagle*, 1996
Thomas Harlan, *The Storm of Heaven*, 2001
J. Gregory Keyes, *Empire of Unreason*, 2000

Fantasy

Melissa Scott, *The Armor of Light*, 1988
Lisa A. Barnett, co-author

620

TERRY PRATCHETT

Thief of Time

(New York: HarperCollins, 2001)

Story type: Humor
Series: Discworld. Book 26
Subject(s): Inventions
Major character(s): Lu-Tze, Religious (monk); Ronnie Soak, Businessman; Lobsang, Religious (monk)
Time period(s): Indeterminate
Locale(s): Discworld, Alternate Universe

Summary: In Discworld, time can be handled like any other commodity. An order of monks has the job of taking time from where it's not needed and moving it to places where it is. Then someone invents the first perfectly accurate clock, and by its very existence it endangers the fabric of time itself. Only the loyal monks can act to save the day, but can they do so in time?

Other books by the same author:
The Truth, 2000
The Fifth Elephant, 1999
Carpe Jugulum, 1998
Hogfather, 1998
The Last Continent, 1998

Other books you might like:
David Bear, *Keeping Time*, 1979
James Branch Cabell, *Jurgen*, 1919
Rick Cook, *Mall Purchase Night*, 1993
L. Sprague de Camp, *The Pixilated Peeress*, 1991
John DeChancie, *Castle Spellbound*, 1992

621

IRENE RADFORD

Guardian of the Vision

(New York: DAW, 2001)

Story type: Historical
Series: Merlin's Descendants. Book 3
Subject(s): Magic
Major character(s): Griffin Kirkwood, Magician, Religious; Donovan Kirkwood, Magician; Roanna Douglas, Witch
Time period(s): 16th century (1553-1563)
Locale(s): England; France

Summary: In Elizabethan England, two descendants of Merlin face their duty in different ways. One brother abandons his position and travels to France to become a priest. The other prepares to assume his duties to protect the crown, but has been unable to awaken the magical powers he is heir to. Elsewhere a witch has attempted to bind a demon to serve her, but instead has become its agent in a war against the forces of good.

Where it's reviewed:
Science Fiction Chronicle, April 2001, page 36

Other books by the same author:
Guardian of the Trust, 2000
The Wizard's Treasure, 2000
Guardian of the Balance, 1999
The Renegade Dragon, 1999
The Dragon's Touchstone, 1997

Other books you might like:
Allen Andrews, *The Pig Plantagenet*, 1980
James P. Blaylock, *Homunculus*, 1986
Michael G. Coney, *King of the Scepter'd Isle*, 1990
Barbara Hambly, *Bride of the Rat God*, 1994
Tim Powers, *The Stress of Her Regard*, 1989

622

MICHAEL REAVES

Hell on Earth

(New York: Ballantine Del Rey, 2001)

Story type: Contemporary
Subject(s): Angels
Major character(s): Colin, Orphan; Zoel, Angel; Asdeon, Demon
Time period(s): 2000s (2001)
Locale(s): Oregon; Alabama; New York, New York (Greenwich Village)

Summary: The devil has stolen a magical talisman that is the key to ending the world and causing final judgment to take place. Colin is an orphan whose destiny is to prevent the devil from doing so, but only if he is assisted by an angel and a demon. His two allies have mixed emotions about the outcome, however, and their loyalties are fluid and unpredictable.

Where it's reviewed:
Booklist, April 1, 2001, page 1450
Publishers Weekly, March 12, 2001, page 67

Other books by the same author:
Street Magic, 1991
The Burning Realm, 1988
The Shattered World, 1984
Darkworld Detective, 1982
I, Alien, 1978

Other books you might like:
Steven Brust, *To Reign in Hell*, 1984
Esther Friesner, *New York by Knight*, 1986
Neil Gaiman, *Good Omens*, 1990
    Terry Pratchett, co-author
Garfield Reeves-Stevens, *Shifter*, 1990
    Judith Reeves-Stevens, co-author
Jan Siegel, *The Dragon Charmer*, 2001

623

THOMAS M. REID

The Temple of Elemental Evil

(Renton, Washington: Wizards of the Coast, 2001)

Story type: Sword and Sorcery
Series: Greyhawk

Subject(s): Magic
Major character(s): Shanhaevel, Mythical Creature (elf); Hedrack, Religious; Burne, Warrior
Time period(s): Indeterminate
Locale(s): Hommlet, Fictional Country

Summary: An apprentice elf watches his master die in an ambush. He then discovers his master was part of a band of companions dedicated to ensuring that the evil force from a ruined temple never again menaces the world. Unfortunately, a demonic creature is being assisted by an ambitious priest who wants to restore the power of his lost order. This is a first novel.

Other books you might like:
Catherine Cooke, *The Hidden Temple*, 1988
L. Sprague de Camp, *The Pixilated Peeress*, 1991
Robert E. Howard, *Red Nails*, 1977
Fritz Leiber, *Swords Against Death*, 1970
Andre Norton, *Sorceress of the Witch World*, 1968

624

JENNIFER ROBERSON, Editor

Out of Avalon
(New York: DAW, 2001)

Story type: Anthology
Subject(s): Short Stories; Arthurian Legend

Summary: King Arthur and the land he ruled are the subjects of the 15 original stories in this collection. They deal with the Knights of the Round Table, the Holy Grail, the Lady of the Lake, and other elements from the legend. The contributors include Marion Zimmer Bradley, Michelle West, Katharine Kerr, David Farland, and Rosemary Edghill.

Other books by the same author:
Shapechanger's Song, 2001
Sword Born, 1998
Scotland the Brave, 1996
A Tapestry of Lions, 1992
Sword Breaker, 1991

Other books you might like:
Monica Barrie, *Queen of Knights*, 1985
Marion Zimmer Bradley, *The Mists of Avalon*, 1982
Gillian Bradshaw, *Hawk of May*, 1980
Parke Godwin, *Firelord*, 1980
Robert Nathan, *The Fair*, 1964

625

JENNIFER ROBERSON

Shapechanger's Song
(New York: DAW, 2001)

Story type: Magic Conflict
Series: Cheysuli
Subject(s): Magic
Major character(s): Alix, Mythical Creature (shapechanger); Carillon, Ruler (prince)
Time period(s): Indeterminate
Locale(s): Homana, Fictional Country

Summary: This is an omnibus of the first two books in the Cheysuli series. In the first, the uneasy peace between humans and shapechanging Cheysuli ends with a forbidden elopement. In the second, the rightful ruler of Homana attempts to protect the surviving shapechangers and restore full rights to them.

Where it's reviewed:
Science Fiction Chronicle, April 2001, page 37

Other books by the same author:
Sword Born, 1998
Scotland the Brave, 1996
A Tapestry of Lions, 1992
Sword Breaker, 1991
Daughter of the Lion, 1989

Other books you might like:
Eleanor Arnason, *Daughter of the Bear King*, 1987
Clare Bell, *The Jaguar Princess*, 1993
Jo Clayton, *Blue Magic*, 1988
Louise Cooper, *The Sleep of Stone*, 1991
Quinn Taylor Evans, *Daughter of the Mist*, 1996

626

JOEL ROSENBERG

Not Quite Scaramouche
(New York: Tor, 2001)

Story type: Humor; Quest
Series: Guardians of the Flame. Book 9
Subject(s): Princes and Princesses
Major character(s): Jason Cullinane, Nobleman; Kethol, Warrior; Erenor, Wizard
Time period(s): Indeterminate
Locale(s): Cullinane, Fictional Country

Summary: The heir to the throne has renounced it for his family and the result is an empire rife with political intrigues, ambitious plotters, and seductive women. His friends and protectors, a disparate band of warriors and magicians, try to keep things from falling completely apart. Light adventure laced with humorous anecdotes.

Other books by the same author:
Not Exactly the Three Musketeers, 1999
The Crimson Sky, 1998
The Silver Stone, 1996
The Fire Duke, 1995
The Road Home, 1995

Other books you might like:
Steven Brust, *The Phoenix Guards*, 1991
Jack L. Chalker, *The Run to Chaos Keep*, 1991
Robert A. Heinlein, *Glory Road*, 1992
Diana Wynne Jones, *The Magicians of Caprona*, 1980
Lawrence Watt-Evans, *Split Heirs*, 1993
  Esther Friesner, co-author

Fantasy

627

CHRISTOPHER ROWLEY

The Shasht War

(New York: Roc, 2001)

Story type: Magic Conflict
Series: Arna. Book 2
Subject(s): Magic
Major character(s): Thru Gillo, Military Personnel; Filek, Doctor; Simona, Young Woman
Time period(s): Indeterminate
Locale(s): Arna, Fictional Country

Summary: The armies of humankind are once again on the march, attacking the peaceful inhabitants of Arna, who were at one time lowly apes but are now intelligent. Thru Gillo is an officer in the defending army, but he is captured and taken behind enemy lines, where he will escape only through the friendship of a human woman.

Other books by the same author:
The Ancient Enemy, 2000
The Dragon Ultimate, 1999
The Dragons of Argonath, 1998
The Dragon at World's End, 1997
The Wizard and the Floating City, 1996

Other books you might like:
Neal Barrett Jr., *Aldair in Albion*, 1976
Pierre Boulle, *Planet of the Apes*, 1963
John Crowley, *Beasts*, 1976
Raymond E. Feist, *Silverthorn*, 1985
Mary Gentle, *Rats and Gargoyles*, 1990

628

KRISTINE KATHRYN RUSCH

Stories for an Enchanted Afternoon

(Urbana, Illinois: Golden Gryphon, 2001)

Story type: Collection
Subject(s): Short Stories

Summary: This collection gathers ten short stories and a novelette, all previously published between 1988 and 2000. The novelette features Civil War photographer Matthew Brady, who is transported to the future to get glimpses of wars to come. The story themes include humor, teleportation, and magic realism.

Other books by the same author:
The Rival, 1997
The Changeling, 1996
The Devil's Churn, 1996
The New Rebellion, 1996
Alien Influences, 1994

Other books you might like:
Avram Davidson, *Strange Seas and Shores*, 1971
Charles De Lint, *Spiritwalk*, 1992
Nancy Kress, *Beaker's Dozen*, 1998
Theodore Sturgeon, *The Perfect Host*, 1998
Jane Yolen, *Sister Emily's Lightship*, 2000

629

SEAN RUSSELL

The One Kingdom

(New York: Avon, 2001)

Story type: Magic Conflict
Series: Swans' War. Book 1
Subject(s): Magic
Major character(s): Toren Renne, Nobleman; Elise Wills, Noblewoman; Valeman Tan, Adventurer
Time period(s): Indeterminate
Locale(s): Ayr, Fictional Country

Summary: The King of Ayr fails to name a successor before his death, and now the kingdom is torn between two powerful families, aided and abetted by other nobles and sorcerers, many of whom believe they would be better off in a splintered, chaotic land.

Where it's reviewed:
Locus, January 2001, page 21
Science Fiction Chronicle, April 2001, page 34

Other books by the same author:
The Compass of the Soul, 1998
Beneath the Vaulted Hills, 1997
Sea Without a Shore, 1996
Gatherer of Clouds, 1992
The Initiate Brother, 1991

Other books you might like:
Anne Bishop, *The Invisible Ring*, 2000
James Clemens, *Wit'ch Storm*, 1999
Simon R. Green, *Beyond the Blue Moon*, 2000
Barbara Hambly, *Mother of Winter*, 1996
Dennis Jones, *The Stone and the Maiden*, 1999

630

FRED SABERHAGEN

God of the Golden Fleece

(New York: Tor, 2001)

Story type: Legend
Series: Book of Gods. Book 4
Subject(s): Mythology
Major character(s): Jason, Adventurer; Proteus, Adventurer; Medea, Ruler (princess)
Time period(s): Indeterminate Past
Locale(s): Mediterranean

Summary: This is an inventive retelling of the story of Jason and the Argonauts and their quest to retrieve the golden fleece. Princess Medea is smitten with Jason, but neither of them is aware of the role to be played by Proteus, a member of the crew who has lost most of his memory after a mysterious battle with a creature from out of the sea.

Where it's reviewed:
Science Fiction Chronicle, June 2001, page 38

Other books by the same author:
The Arms of Hercules, 2000
Vlad Tepes, 2000

Ariadne's Web, 1999
Shiva in Steel, 1998
The Face of Apollo, 1998

Other books you might like:
Patrick Adkins, *Sons of the Titans*, 1990
Alan Dean Foster, *Clash of the Titans*, 1981
David Gemmell, *The Lion of Macedon*, 1992
Jane Lindskold, *The Pipes of Orpheus*, 1995
Richard Purtill, *The Mirror of Helen*, 1983

631

R.A. SALVATORE

Ascendance

(New York: Ballantine Del Rey, 2001)

Story type: Magic Conflict
Subject(s): Magic
Major character(s): Jilseponie Wyndom, Noblewoman; Aydrian, Sorcerer; De'Unnero, Mythical Creature (weretiger)
Time period(s): Indeterminate
Locale(s): Corona, Fictional Country

Summary: The King of Corona causes considerable turmoil with his choice of a new queen. She in turn is reluctant to marry, and still mourns her child, who was carried off and is presumed dead. The boy survives, however, and is raised by enemies of the throne who teach him powerful magic. Allied with a shapechanging villain, he decides to move against the royal family.

Other books by the same author:
Bastion of Darkness, 2000
The Icewind Trilogy, 2000
Servant of the Shard, 2000
The Demon Apostle, 1999
Vector Prime, 1999

Other books you might like:
Dave Duncan, *The Reluctant Swordsman*, 1988
Ken Hood, *Demon Knight*, 1998
Richard A. Knaak, *The Shrouded Realm*, 1991
Lawrence Watt-Evans, *Blood of a Dragon*, 1991
Janny Wurts, *The Warhost of Vastmark*, 1995

632

MELISSA SCOTT
LISA A. BARNETT, Co-Author

Point of Dreams

(New York: Tor, 2001)

Story type: Mystery; Alternate World
Series: Pointsman Rath. Book 2
Subject(s): Theater
Major character(s): Nicolas Rathe, Detective—Police; Philip Eslingen, Military Personnel; Trijn, Police Officer
Time period(s): Indeterminate
Locale(s): Astreiant, Fictional City

Summary: In an alternate version of Renaissance Europe, the city of Astreiant is enchanted with a new play. They are less pleased when a murder takes place, and the body turns up on the stage. At a time of the year when ghosts are literally all around, a detective must solve the crime despite no cooperation from many of those involved.

Where it's reviewed:
Booklist, February 15, 2001, page 1122
Library Journal, February 15, 2001, page 204
Publishers Weekly, January 8, 2001, page 52

Other books by the same author:
Point of Hopes, 2000 (Lisa A. Barnett, co-author)
The Jazz, 2000
The Shape of Their Hearts, 1998
The Garden, 1997
Burning Bright, 1993

Other books you might like:
John Dickson Carr, *The Devil in Velvet*, 1951
Randall Garrett, *Lord Darcy Investigates*, 1981
J. Robert King, *Carnival of Fear*, 1993
Michael Reaves, *Darkworld Detective*, 1982
Mike Resnick, *Stalking the Unicorn*, 1987

633

SHARON SHINN

Summers at Castle Auburn

(New York: Ace, 2001)

Story type: Light Fantasy
Subject(s): Magic
Major character(s): Coriel Halsing, Witch; Jaxon Halsing, Nobleman; Prince Bryan, Royalty
Time period(s): Indeterminate
Locale(s): Alora, Fictional Country; Castle Auburn, Mythical Place

Summary: Coriel, the illegitimate daughter of a nobleman, is treated to summers at a remote castle, where she learns the rudiments of witchcraft from her grandmother. She also meets many members of the nobility, including the heir apparent to the throne, and eventually gets involved with romance and court politics.

Where it's reviewed:
Booklist, April 15, 2001, page 1544
Publishers Weekly, April 2, 2001, page 44
Science Fiction Chronicle, July 2001, page 43

Other books by the same author:
Heart of Gold, 2000
Wrapt in Crystal, 1999
The Alleluia Files, 1998
Jovah's Angel, 1997
Archangel, 1996

Other books you might like:
Marion Zimmer Bradley, *Lady of Avalon*, 1997
Lois McMaster Bujold, *The Curse of Chalion*, 2001
Stephen R. Donaldson, *The Mirror of Her Dreams*, 1986
Tad Williams, *Caliban's Hour*, 1994
Jane Yolen, *Child of Faerie, Child of Earth*, 2000

Fantasy

634

JAN SIEGEL

The Dragon Charmer

(New York: Ballantine Del Rey, 2001)

Story type: Contemporary
Subject(s): Witches and Witchcraft
Major character(s): Fern Capel, Witch; Gaynor Moberley, Businessman; Allison Redmund, Young Woman
Time period(s): 2000s (2001)
Locale(s): London, England

Summary: Fern Capel has decided to set her witchcraft aside long enough to get married, but events are going to make it difficult for her to keep to her resolve. Before long, there are problems with wizardry, a werewolf, demonic possession, and kidnapping. This is a sequel to *Prospero's Children*.

Other books by the same author:
Prospero's Children, 2000

Other books you might like:
Pamela Dean, *Juniper, Gentian, and Rosemary*, 1998
Richard Grant, *In the Land of Winter*, 1997
Brenda Jordan, *The Brentwood Witches*, 1987
James Long, *Ferney*, 1998
James Stoddard, *The High House*, 1999

635

ROBERT SILVERBERG

The King of Dreams

(New York: Avon Eos, 2001)

Story type: Alternate Universe
Series: Majipoor. Book 7
Subject(s): Plague
Major character(s): Lord Prestimion, Ruler; Prince Dekkeret, Royalty; Fiorinda, Servant
Time period(s): Indeterminate
Locale(s): Majipoor, Alternate Universe

Summary: After many years of strife, it appears that the land of Majipoor is finally going to enjoy a period of peace. Then ancient forces unleash a new weapon, a plague of insanity and horror that sweeps across the countryside. Two members of the aristocracy must risk their own lives to save their people.

Where it's reviewed:
Publishers Weekly, April 30, 2001, page 61

Other books by the same author:
Lord Prestimion, 1999
The Alien Years, 1998
The Sorcerers of Majipoor, 1997
Hot Sky at Midnight, 1994
Letters from Atlantis, 1990

Other books you might like:
Neal Barrett Jr., *The Prophecy Machine*, 2000
Deborah Grabien, *Plainsong*, 1991
Mary Herbert, *City of the Sorcerers*, 1994
Anne Logston, *Shadow Dance*, 1992
Elizabeth Scarborough, *Last Refuge*, 1992

636

JOHN SKIPP
MARC LEVINTHAL, Co-Author

The Emerald Burrito of Oz

(Northridge, California: Babbage, 2001)

Story type: Alternate Universe
Subject(s): Magic
Major character(s): Aurora Q. Jones, Businesswoman; Gene Speilman, Immigrant; Ozma, Royalty (princess)
Time period(s): 2000s (2007)
Locale(s): Oz, Mythical Place

Summary: A young man takes advantage of a portal that allows emigration to Oz, taking along only his laptop computer. He arrives in time to get caught in a war between Princess Ozma and the Hollow Man, who is raising an army to seize control of the government. His laptop computer suddenly becomes sentient, and his presence is instrumental in resolving the conflict.

Where it's reviewed:
Science Fiction Chronicle, April 2001, page 37

Other books by the same author:
Animals, 1993 (Craig Spector, co-author)
The Bridge, 1991 (Craig Spector, co-author)
Dead Lines, 1989 (Craig Spector, co-author)
The Cleanup, 1987 (Craig Spector, co-author)
The Light at the End, 1986 (Craig Spector, co-author)

Other books you might like:
Donald Abbott, *How the Wizard Saved Oz*, 1997
L. Frank Baum, *Ozma of Oz*, 1907
Philip Jose Farmer, *A Barnstormer in Oz*, 1982
Jeff Freedman, *The Magic Dishpan of Oz*, 1994
John R. Neill, *Lucky Bucky in Oz*, 1942

637

LISA SMEDMAN

Tails You Lose

(New York: Roc, 2001)

Story type: Alternate World
Series: Shadowrun. Number 39
Subject(s): Magic
Major character(s): Gray Squirrel, Businessman; Alma Johnson, Security Officer; Eldest Brother, Mythical Creature (troll)
Time period(s): 21st century
Locale(s): North America

Summary: The protagonist is a security officer working for a large corporation in a future alternative Earth where magic works. Someone has created her own doppelganger and used that figure to arrange for the kidnapping of an executive, leaving her to take the blame. She has to avoid the authorities and battle Chinese magic to get him back and clear her name.

Where it's reviewed:
Science Fiction Chronicle, July 2001, page 44

Other books by the same author:
The Forever Drug, 1999
Blood Sport, 1998
Psychotrope, 1998
The Lucifer Deck, 1997

Other books you might like:
Stephen Kenson, *Crossroads*, 1999
Jack Koke, *Beyond the Pale*, 1998
Mel Odom, *Headhunters*, 1997
Nyx Smith, *Steel Rain*, 1997
Michael A. Stackpole, *Wolf and Raven*, 1998

638

CHRISTOPHER STASHEFF

A Wizard in a Feud

(New York: Tor, 2001)

Story type: Science Fiction
Series: Rogue Wizard. Book 9
Subject(s): Space Colonies
Major character(s): Gar Pike, Spaceman; Alea, Spacewoman;
   Moira, Young Woman
Time period(s): Indeterminate Future
Locale(s): Outer Space

Summary: A wizard and his companions visit a lost colony
world that was settled by a contingent from Scotland. They
discover that the colonists share the world with the equivalent
of fairies and get involved in the local political problems,
while resolving their own internal difficulties.

Other books by the same author:
A Wizard in Peace, 1996
The Sage, 1996
A Wizard in War, 1995
Quicksilver's Knight, 1995
We Open on Venus, 1994

Other books you might like:
C.S. Friedman, *Black Sun Rising*, 1991
Roland Green, *Tale of the Comet*, 1997
D.J. Heinrich, *The Fall of Magic*, 1993
Nalo Hopkinson, *The Midnight Robber*, 2000
Lawrence Watt-Evans, *Out of This World*, 1994

639

MATTHEW STOVER

Blade of Tyshalle

(New York: Ballantine Del Rey, 2001)

Story type: Alternate World
Subject(s): Virtual Reality
Major character(s): Hari Michaelson, Actor; Pallas Raithe,
   Diplomat (ambassador); Tan'Elkoth, Nobleman
Time period(s): Indeterminate Future
Locale(s): California; Overworld, Alternate Universe

Summary: Hari Michaelson is an actor in our universe, and a
ruthless assassin in the alternate reality known as Overworld.
Over the years, he has made numerous enemies and now it
appears that one of them is plotting vengeance. At the same

time, he finds himself the unlikely protector of the magical
realm when it is menaced by corporate ambitions.

Where it's reviewed:
Publishers Weekly, March 5, 2001, page 67

Other books by the same author:
Heroes Die, 1998
Jericho Moon, 1998
Iron Dawn, 1997

Other books you might like:
Piers Anthony, *Phaze Doubt*, 1990
Michael Cassutt, *Dragon Season*, 1991
Jo Clayton, *A Bait of Dreams*, 1985
Gregory Frost, *Lyrec*, 1984
Melissa Scott, *The Armor of Light*, 1988
   Lisa A. Barnett, co-author

640

STEPHEN D. SULLIVAN

The Phoenix

(Renton, Washington: Wizards of the Coast, 2001)

Story type: Sword and Sorcery
Series: Legend of Five Rings. Book 4
Subject(s): Magic
Major character(s): Isawa Tadaka, Warrior; Isawa Kaede,
   Housewife; Junzo, Wizard
Time period(s): Indeterminate
Locale(s): Rokugan, Fictional Country

Summary: The various clans of Rokugan, a world similar to
feudal Japan, are battling amongst themselves again and not
paying attention to the evil wizard whom they defeated but
did not destroy in battles past. Now he has raised an army of
inhuman creatures superior to those he used before, and there
is no united resistance to his efforts to conquer all of the clans.

Where it's reviewed:
Science Fiction Chronicle, April 2001, page 38

Other books by the same author:
The Scorpion, 2000

Other books you might like:
Kara Dalkey, *Genpei*, 2000
A.L. Lassieur, *The Unicorn*, 2000
Tim Lukeman, *Koren*, 1981
E. Hoffman Price, *The Jade Enchantress*, 1982
Ree Soesbee, *The Crane*, 2000

641

PATRICK THOMAS

Murphy's Lore: Fools' Day

(Farmingdale, New York: Padwolf, 2001)

Story type: Light Fantasy
Series: Murphy's Lore
Subject(s): Fairies
Major character(s): John Murphy, Saloon Keeper/Owner; Pan,
   Deity; Donald Washington, Businessman
Time period(s): 2000s (2001)

Locale(s): Bulfinche's Pub, Mythical Place

Summary: A fairy steals a nuclear weapon, causing the U.S. military to launch a pre-emptive strike on the land of Faerie. Refugees cross into our world, bringing magic and monsters, and the situation continues to worsen. Then a time traveler recruits the patrons of a mystical tavern to help avert the crisis and change the future.

Other books by the same author:
Murphy's Lore, 1997

Other books you might like:
Poul Anderson, *A Midsummer Tempest*, 1975
Steven Brust, *Cowboy Feng's Space Bar and Grill*, 1990
L. Sprague de Camp, *Tales from Gavagan's Bar*, 1953
    Fletcher Pratt, co-author
Esther Friesner, *Elf Defense*, 1988
Spider Robinson, *Callahan's Legacy*, 1996

642

BRIAN M. THOMSEN, Editor
MARTIN H. GREENBERG, Co-Editor

Oceans of Magic

(New York: DAW, 2001)

Story type: Anthology
Subject(s): Short Stories; Sea Stories

Summary: These 13 original fantasy stories involve the ocean or travel thereon. The stories are grouped by historical tales, sea adventures, and stories of the gods and other creatures who live in the ocean. The contributors include Tanya Huff, Kristine Kathryn Rusch, Mel Odom, Mickey Zucker Reichert, and Jeff Grubb.

Other books by the same author:
The Mage in the Iron Mask, 1996
Once around the Realms, 1995

Other books you might like:
Jeff Grubb, *The Eternal Ice*, 2000
Tanya Huff, *The Quartered Sea*, 1999
Mel Odom, *The Sea Devil's Eye*, 2000
Mickey Zucker Reichert, *Beyond Ragnarok*, 1995
Kristine Kathryn Rusch, *The Rival*, 1997

643

GAV THORPE

The Thirteenth Legion

(Nottingham, England: Black Library, 2001)

Story type: Magic Conflict; Space Opera
Series: Warhammer
Subject(s): Space Exploration
Major character(s): Kage, Military Personnel, Convict; Franx, Military Personnel, Convict; Poal, Military Personnel, Convict
Time period(s): Indeterminate Future
Locale(s): Outer Space; Ichar IV, Planet—Imaginary

Summary: A group of convicts are given the choice of continuing as prisoners or forming a military unit in an interstellar war. The unique twist to this series is that magic works in this universe, and rather than fighting aliens, they're going to be battling orcs and trolls. This is a first novel.

Other books you might like:
Dan Abnett, *First and Only*, 2000
Barrington J. Bayley, *Eye of Terror*, 2000
Brian Craig, *The Ghost Dancers*, 1991
William King, *Space Wolf*, 2000
Lawrence Watt-Evans, *Out of This World*, 1994

644

HARRY TURTLEDOVE

Through the Darkness

(New York: Tor, 2001)

Story type: Magic Conflict
Series: Darkness. Book 3
Subject(s): Magic
Major character(s): Swemmel, Ruler (king); Sabrino, Military Personnel; Panfilo, Military Personnel
Time period(s): Indeterminate
Locale(s): Unkerlant, Fictional Country; Algarvia, Fictional Country; Kuusamo, Fictional Country

Summary: A magical war has embroiled the entire world, with three minor powers allied against the more aggressive Algarvian Empire. Sorcerers sacrifice thousands of human lives in order to fuel their magic, and one group seeks a more benevolent, but powerful form of sorcery that may save them from conquest and death.

Where it's reviewed:
Booklist, February 15, 2001, page 1086
Publishers Weekly, February 19, 2001, page 74

Other books by the same author:
Colonization: Down to Earth, 2000
Into the Darkness, 1999
Second Contact, 1999
Between the Rivers, 1998
Videssos Besieged, 1998

Other books you might like:
Robin W. Bailey, *Brothers of the Dragon*, 1993
Michael Cassutt, *Dragon Season*, 1991
David B. Coe, *The Children of Amarid*, 1997
Alan Cole, *The Warrior Returns*, 1996
David Feintuch, *The Still*, 1997

645

ERIC VAN LUSTBADER

The Ring of Five Dragons

(New York: Tor, 2001)

Story type: Magic Conflict
Series: Pearl. Book 1
Subject(s): Magic
Major character(s): Nith Sahor, Religious; Eleusis Ashera, Government Official; Kurgan, Nobleman
Time period(s): Indeterminate
Locale(s): Kundala, Fictional Country

Summary: The land of Kundala has been conquered by a technologically oriented society that has suppressed the sorcery of its people. Individuals on both sides seek to uncover the secrets of sorcery and are determined to control the source of that power.

Where it's reviewed:
Booklist, April 15, 2001, page 1510
Publishers Weekly, April 23, 2001, page 54
Science Fiction Chronicle, June 2001, page 36

Other books by the same author:
Beneath an Opal Moon, 1980
Dai-San, 1978
The Shallows of Night, 1978
The Sunset Warrior, 1977

Other books you might like:
Terry Goodkind, *Faith of the Fallen*, 2000
Robert Jordan, *Winter's Heart*, 2000
George R.R. Martin, *A Storm of Swords*, 2000
L.E. Modesitt Jr., *The Colors of Chaos*, 1999
Andre Norton, *Witch World*, 1963

646

RAY VUKCEVICH

Meet Me in the Moon Room

(Brooklyn, New York: Small Beer Press, 2001)

Story type: Collection
Subject(s): Short Stories

Summary: Thirty-three short stories, all originally published between 1990 and 2000 are collected here. The stories are each based on a strange image: fish growing hats, playing catch with cats, a dead Santa Claus in a department store, creatures living in a character's nose, and averting disasters by not believing in them. This is the author's first book.

Other books you might like:
Charles Beaumont, *The Magic Man*, 1965
Avram Davidson, *Strange Seas and Shores*, 1971
Kelly Link, *Stranger Things Happen*, 2001
Richard Matheson, *Shock Waves*, 1970
Thomas Tessier, *Fog Heart*, 1997

647

MARGARET WEIS
TRACY HICKMAN, Co-Author

Dragons of a Lost Star

(Renton, Washington: Wizards of the Coast, 2001)

Story type: Magic Conflict
Series: War of Souls. Book 2
Subject(s): Magic
Major character(s): Palin Majere, Warrior; Beryl, Mythical Creature (dragon), Ruler; Mina, Warrior
Time period(s): Indeterminate
Locale(s): Krynn, Fictional Country

Summary: The land of Krynn is beset by two dangers this time. A mysterious warrior with charismatic skills is leading an army of conquest, and Beryl, the dragon ruler of part of the world, moves against her own subjects in order to enhance her power. A handful of conspirators plot to fool Beryl into overextending herself.

Where it's reviewed:
Science Fiction Chronicle, April 2001, page 34

Other books by the same author:
Dragons of a Fallen Sun, 2000 (Tracy Hickman, co-author)
Knights of the Black Earth, 1995 (Don Perrin, co-author)
The King's Test, 1991
The Elven Star, 1990
The Lost King, 1990

Other books you might like:
Timothy Brown, *The Dark Knight of Karameikos*, 1995
Tina Daniell, *Dark Heart*, 1992
Troy Denning, *Dragonwall*, 1990
Douglas Niles, *The Kinslayer Wars*, 1991
Jean Rabe, *Red Magic*, 1991

648

ANGUS WELLS

Yesterday's Kings

(New York: Bantam, 2001)

Story type: Magic Conflict
Subject(s): Magic
Major character(s): Cullyn, Woodsman; Eben, Sorcerer; Lord Bartram, Nobleman
Time period(s): Indeterminate
Locale(s): Kandara, Fictional Country

Summary: The Kandarans successfully seize some of the land belonging to the Durrym, and the latter retreat behind a wall of impenetrable magic. They haven't abandoned their territory, however, and their spies clash with the occupying forces. Cullyn, a young woodsman with no political leanings, is caught in the middle and becomes a pivotal figure in resolving their conflict.

Where it's reviewed:
Science Fiction Chronicle, June 2001, page 37

Other books by the same author:
Exile's Challenge, 1996
Exile's Children, 1995
Lords of the Sky, 1995
Wild Magic, 1993
Dark Magic, 1992

Other books you might like:
Raymond E. Feist, *Shadow of a Dark Queen*, 1994
Simon R. Green, *Beyond the Blue Moon*, 2000
L.E. Modesitt Jr., *The Fall of Angels*, 1996
Andre Norton, *Spell of the Witch World*, 1976
Eric Van Lustbader, *The Ring of Five Dragons*, 2001

Fantasy

649

MICHELLE WEST

Sea of Sorrows

(New York: DAW, 2001)

Story type: Quest; Magic Conflict
Series: Sun Sword. Book 4
Subject(s): Magic
Major character(s): Valedan Di'Leonne, Nobleman; Jewel, Sorceress; Avantar, Guard
Time period(s): Indeterminate
Locale(s): Essalieyan Empire, Fictional Country

Summary: Valedan is finally beginning to acquire the authority that is rightfully his, but control of the empire still eludes his grasp and a new war is threatening to break out. His efforts are reinforced by a quest undertaken by a sorceress, her loyal guard, and a band of varied companions who set out for a fabled distant city, although they are menaced by a spell, which makes their presence known to their enemies.

Other books by the same author:
The Shining Court, 1999
The Uncrowned King, 1998
The Broken Crown, 1997
Hunter's Death, 1996
Hunter's Oath, 1995

Other books you might like:
Kate Elliott, *The Burning Stone*, 1999
Maggie Furey, *Dhammara*, 1997
Gayle Greeno, *Sunderlies Seeking*, 1998
Melanie Rawn, *The Skybowl*, 1994
Jennifer Roberson, *Sword Born*, 1998

650

JACK WHYTE

Uther

(New York: Forge, 2001)

Story type: Legend
Series: Camulod Chronicles. Book 7
Subject(s): Arthurian Legend
Major character(s): Uther Pendragon, Ruler (King of Cambria); Caius Merlyn Britannicus, Sorcerer, Warrior; Ygraine, Bride (arranged marriage)
Time period(s): 5th century
Locale(s): England

Summary: This series retells the Arthurian legend as an historical novel. The present volume centers on Uther Pendragon, cousin to Merlyn, who has forsworn his Roman blood in preference to that of his Celtic forebears. As he grows older

and more influential, his opinions affect the future of Camulod.

Other books by the same author:
The Fort at River's Bend, 1999 (Camulod Chronicles. Book 5)
The Sorcerer: Metamorphosis, 1999 (Camulod Chronicles. Book 6)
The Singing Sword, 1996 (Camulod Chronicles. Book 2)
The Skystone, 1996 (Camulod Chronicles. Book 1)
The Eagles' Brood, 1994 (Camulod Chronicles. Book 3)

Other books you might like:
Cherith Baldry, *Exiled from Camelot*, 2001
Cary James, *King and Raven*, 1995
Stephen R. Lawhead, *Pendragon*, 1994
Ian McDowell, *Mordred's Curse*, 1996
Richard Monaco, *The Grail War*, 1979

651

TAD WILLIAMS

Sea of Silver Light

(London: Orbit, 2001)

Story type: Alternate Universe
Series: Otherland. Book 4
Subject(s): Magic
Major character(s): Irene Sulaweyo, Teacher; Stephen Sulaweyo, Teenager; Paul Jonas, Military Personnel
Time period(s): Indeterminate
Locale(s): Otherland, Alternate Universe

Summary: After a series of adventures in a string of alternate worlds, a team of disparate adventurers approaches the sea of silver light, which appears to be a haven. Their dangers aren't over yet though, because some of the fundamental laws that operate these alternate realities appear to be changing, and chaos is spreading throughout the various worlds.

Where it's reviewed:
Booklist, March 15, 2001, page 1333
Locus, May 2001, page 29
Publishers Weekly, April 9, 2001, page 56

Other books by the same author:
The Mountain of Black Glass, 1999
The River of Blue Fire, 1998
The City of Golden Shadow, 1996
Caliban's Hour, 1994
To Green Angel Tower, 1993

Other books you might like:
K.A. Applegate, *Realm of the Reaper*, 1999
Jack L. Chalker, *The Labyrinth of Dreams*, 1987
Philip Jose Farmer, *The Maker of Universes*, 1965
Mick Farren, *The Synaptic Manhunt*, 1976
Michael Moorcock, *Fabulous Harbors*, 1995

Lovecraftian Fiction and the Cthulhu Mythos
by
Stefan Dziemianowicz

No one who is familiar with modern horror fiction can be unfamiliar with the literary legacy of H.P. Lovecraft. Lovecraft's brief career as a professionally published writer spanned the years 1923 to 1937 and comprised only a few dozen stories, the majority published in the pulp fiction magazine *Weird Tales*. Yet several of those stories are among the best known and most frequently reprinted horror tales of the twentieth century, and some critics cite them as a convenient starting point for discussions of modern horror, much the same way that they consider the fiction of M.R. James the starting point for the modern ghost story.

Contemporary horror fiction abounds with references to Lovecraft and his creations. His influence has been so pervasive and enduring that his name has become an adjective for a specific type of horror story. But though the meaning of the term ''Lovecraftian horror'' should be self-evident to anyone who has read Lovecraft's fiction, the description is applied in a variety of ways that sometimes seem contradictory. To some, Lovecraftian refers to stories in the spirit and style of Lovecraft's fiction. To others, it refers primarily to the Cthulhu Mythos, a myth pattern derived from elements in Lovecraft's fiction and elaborated mostly by writers other than Lovecraft, both in his lifetime and after his death.

To understand the source of this confusion, it is helpful to go back to Lovecraft himself, who was not only a writer of fiction but an articulate theorist on the aesthetic of the horror story. In a letter written to *Weird Tales* editor Farnsworth Wright in 1927, Lovecraft summarized the intent of his stories by revealing that he did not superimpose human form, laws, emotions, interests or any other human qualities on the other worlds or universes described in his tales. While writing, he had to forget about all things human and forget that any such attributes existed.

At the time Lovecraft wrote, and especially in the popular fiction market where his work sold, conventions from the Gothic era still held sway. Stories tended to be filled with cliches that had shaped expectations for the weird tale a century before: evil villains menacing virtuous heroes and heroines; familiar supernatural monsters such as the ghost, vampire, or werewolf enjoying a brief, threatening romp in our world before being exorcised and order restored. Though stories of this kind abounded, and were among some of the writings that shaped his own tastes for weird fiction, Lovecraft found them too old-fashioned and limited to be effective. They did not speak to a modern age that had seen horror on the awesome scale of World War I, and whose advances in science and the social sciences were fast exposing the limits of human understanding.

For the most part, Lovecraft studiously avoided putting traditional monsters to work in his horror fiction. He evoked a mood of horror through careful crafting of atmosphere, as well as a florid prose style, clogged with archaisms and evocative terms like ''eldritch'' and ''noisome,'' that his parodists would later use to ridicule him. The search for an ideal incarnation of the otherworldliness that he strove to articulate through his fiction led Lovecraft to imagine species of creatures impervious to human concepts of time and space. They appeared as vast physical abominations of known biology, and bore such unwieldy and unpronounceable names as Cthulhu, Yog-Sothoth and Shub Niggurath. Part of Lovecraft's conceit about these entities is that human beings, who have only a primitive understanding of their existence, would look upon them as gods to be placated and worshiped. He conceived of ancient books of lore about these creatures written by mystics driven mad by their knowledge of them, of which the most famous was the Necronomicon, penned circa 730 A.D. by the mad Arab Abdul Alhazred. And he imagined entire locales—Arkham, Dunwich, Innsmouth—based in his native New England, where belief in the godhood of these beings fostered a subclass of creepy degenerates misguided in their belief that they could summon and be favored by these beings.

Lovecraft wrote slightly more than a dozen stories that specifically developed this myth pattern, the titles of which

will be familiar to any reader of twentieth century horror fiction: ''The Call of Cthulhu,'' ''The Dunwich Horror,'' ''The Shadow over Innsmouth,'' ''At the Mountains of Madness,'' ''Dreams in the Witch House,'' ''The Shadow out of Time,'' ''The Thing on the Doorstep,'' and so on. These original fusions of cutting- edge science fiction and Gothic horror began seeing print in 1924 and constituted most of his output for the last few years of his life.

They were appreciated not only by readers, who commented on their uniqueness in magazine letter columns, but by Lovecraft's fellow writers. Lovecraft was a friend and correspondent with many other writers for *Weird Tales*, and in a spirit of camaraderie some of them began making reference to specific Lovecraftian names and themes in their own fiction. In his 1925 story, ''The Dog-Eared God,'' Frank Belknap Long was the first author besides Lovecraft to mention his imaginary *Necronomicon*, which has often been requested from used book dealers. In the next twelve years, Long was joined by well-known writers, such as Clark Ashton Smith and Robert E. Howard, and several Lovecraft disciples, including Robert Bloch and Henry Kuttner, in expanding Lovecraft's myth pattern. Lovecraft encouraged them to imagine their own otherworldly entities and books of forbidden lore and just as they borrowed from Lovecraft, so did he mention their creations in his own writings. Understandably, no other writer wrote stories quite like Lovecraft's because no other writer so wholeheartedly subscribed to Lovecraft's vision. But by the time of Lovecraft's death in 1937, the myth pattern he had initiated numbered several dozen stories by a variety of contributors, making it the first shared-world in horror fiction.

Lovecraft never referred to his Cthulhu stories as the Cthulhu Mythos. That task fell to August Derleth, a Lovecraft protege who was one of the more prolific contributors to the story pattern while Lovecraft was alive and who became Lovecraft's publisher after his death. Promoting Lovecraft in the 1940s, Derleth wrote introductions to collections of his stories in which he somewhat revised Lovecraft's 1927 comments. Derleth indicated that Lovecraft wrote his stories with the idea that the world had at some point been inhabited by a race—not human—who despite practicing black magic was defeated, but still somehow are present and eager to regain power and take control of earth.

The mention of black magic forced a new perspective on Lovecraft's fiction, reverting his extra-dimensional entities to participants in the conventional battle between good and evil that Lovecraft had sought to transcend through his fiction. In subsequent writings on Lovecraft, Derleth noted parallels between the ''gods'' in Lovecraft's fiction—the malign Great Old Ones, led by Cthulhu, and the benign Elder Gods, who represented their counterparts—and the Christian Mythos, ''specifically in regard to the expulsion of Satan from Eden and the power of evil.'' Derleth also began codifying what he dubbed the Cthulhu Mythos, organizing the deities into strategic alliances and affiliations based on

their apparent elemental domain (earth, fire, water, wind) and familial relationships, cataloguing the books of lore Lovecraft and others had invented, and mapping the terrain of Lovecraft's shunned New England towns. The Mythos, as promulgated by Derleth, was largely in these details. What's more, these details fit together to form an all-encompassing pattern, parts of which Lovecraft and his colleagues had only hinted and which were still begging to be written.

Thus, in 1945, Derleth published *The Lurker at the Threshold* under his Arkham House imprint. The novel, supposedly completed by Derleth from a fragment Lovecraft left at his death, was billed as a collaboration between the two authors. It proved the first of a series of such ''posthumous collaborations'' produced over the next three decades, most of them spun from a sentence or two of a story idea Lovecraft had jotted down in his commonplace book. The stories, all of which were eventually collected in the omnibus *The Watchers out of Time and Others* (1974), were solid advertisements for the Cthulhu Mythos as Derleth described it. Most were tales of human beings struggling to save the earth from evil Lovecraftian gods, in narratives densely laden with the data of the Mythos. Superficially, they sounded like Lovecraft's stories, but frequently they presented as gospel the quasi-religious interpretations that the narrow-minded humans in Lovecraft's tales resorted to in their efforts to comprehend mind-boggling philosophical and scientific concepts.

In 1969, Derleth compiled the important anthology *Tales of the Cthulhu Mythos*. This omnibus volume brought together a sampling of the best contributions to Lovecraft's shared universe written by many of his contemporaries in the pulp magazines. In addition, it introduced new mythos fiction by four new writers: Ramsey Campbell, Brian Lumley, Colin Wilson, and James Wade. They were by no means the only writers since Lovecraft's death other than Derleth to work in the Lovecraftian milieu, but they were the first new writers officially sanctioned by Lovecraft's publisher. Though they broke no real new ground, the stories called attention to a new generation of writers, working under Lovecraft's influence, who followed the precepts of the Mythos as outlined by Derleth.

Derleth's anthology virtually opened the floodgates to a torrent of Mythos fiction written by a new generation who had fallen under Lovecraft's spell. In the years since its publication, more than a score of similar anthologies have followed its lead, publishing mythos tales by writers new and old. The Cthulhu Mythos has particularly gained firm footing in the specialty press, where an entire subculture dedicated to Lovecraft and the Cthulhu Mythos has taken root. Small press magazines such as *Nyctalops, Beyond the Dark Gateway* and *Crypt of Cthulhu* rose and fell primarily on the strength of their mythos affiliations. Others with less renown and minuscule print runs are still published today. Specialty press publishers such as Mythos Books specialize in collections of Lovecraft pastiches and mythos tales.

Chaosium, a publisher of fantasy role-playing materials, has tied in to its popular Call of Cthulhu game, set in the world of Lovecraft's fiction, an ambitious series of anthologies edited by Robert M. Price (*The Innsmouth Cycle, The Dunwich Cycle, The Hastur Cycle,* etc.) which combine thematically specific fiction by Lovecraft, the writers who influenced him, and the writers whom he himself has influenced.

In the past half-century, Lovecraft and the mythos have percolated into numerous literary realms where their appearance might never have been suspected. Fred Chappell worked them into the southern gothic tradition in his novel *Dagon.* Writers have worked mythos elements into tales of erotic horror fiction. There is even a subgenre of comic mythos fiction that ranges from the outright parody of Peter Cannon's (writing as H.P.G. Wodehouse) *Scream for Jeeves,* a splicing of the styles of Lovecraft and P.G. Wodehouse, and William Browning Spencer's *Resume with Monsters,* a black comedy with Lovecraftian overtones. Nancy Collins, Poppy Z. Brite, Caitlin Kiernan, Harlan Ellison, Kim Newman and countless other contemporary writers whose horror fiction is far from Lovecraftian have evoked Lovecraft and the concepts in his fiction.

The quantity of Cthulhu Mythos fiction now tallies in the thousands, dwarfing in total words Lovecraft's entire literary output. There are now hundreds of unspeakable entities and books of dark lore about them, contributed mostly by writers who believe that these elements are the essence of a mythos tale. Concern over the resulting attenuation and twisting of Lovecraft's aesthetic for the weird tale has prompted a response on some fronts. Editors like Ramsey Campbell, in his anthology *New Tales of the Cthulhu Mythos* (1980) seek stories largely devoid of the usual mythos accretions and instead devoted to the Lovecraftian principle of suggesting "something larger and more terrible than was ever stated." However one views Lovecraft and his fiction, the Cthulhu Mythos has become a cottage industry in horror publishing, and there are enough books full of fiction and commentary for readers to form their own opinions about it.

The bibliography below, far from exhaustive, is offered as a core library for those who wish to know more about Lovecraft's fiction and the Cthulhu Mythos.

Collections:

Bloch, Robert. *Mysteries of the Worm* (Chaosium, 1993)

Campbell, Ramsey. *Cold Print* (Headline, 1993)

Derleth, August. *In Lovecraft's Shadow* (Mycroft and Moran, 1998)

Kuttner, Henry. *The Book of Iod* (Chaosium, 1995)

Lovecraft, H.P. *The Dunwich Horror and Others* (Arkham House, 1963)

Lovecraft, H.P. *At the Mountains of Madness and Other Novels* (Arkham House, 1964)

Lovecraft, H.P. *Dagon and Other Macabre Tales* (Arkham House,1965)

Lovecraft, H.P. and August Derleth. *The Watchers out of Time and Others* (Arkham House, 1974)

Wodehouse, H.P.G. *Scream for Jeeves: A Parody* (Wodecraft Press, 1994)

Novels:

Bloch, Robert. *Strange Eons* (Whispers Press, 1978)

Chappell, Fred. *Dagon* (Harcourt Brace & World, 1968)

Lumley, Brian. *The Burrowers Beneath* (DAW, 1974)

Spencer, William Browning. *Resume with Monsters* (Permanent Press, 1995)

Wilson, Colin. *The Mind Parasites* (Arkham House, 1967)

Anthologies:

Berglund, E.P. (ed.). *Disciples of Cthulhu* (DAW, 1976)

Campbell, Ramsey (ed.). *New Tales of the Cthulhu Mythos* (Arkham House, 1980)

Derleth, August (ed.). *Tales of the Cthulhu Mythos* (Arkham House, 1969)

Price, Robert M. (ed.). *Tales of the Lovecraft Mythos* (Fedogan & Bremer, 1992)

Turner, James (ed.). *Cthulhu 2000: A Lovecraftian Anthology* (Arkham House, 1995)

Turner, James (ed.). *Eternal Lovecraft: The Persistence of HPL in Popular Culture* (Golden Gryphon, 1998)

Non-Fiction:

Carter, Lin. *Lovecraft: A Look Behind the Cthulhu Mythos* (Ballantine, 1972)

Jarocha-Ernst, Chris. *A Cthulhu Mythos Bibliography and Concordance* (Armitage House, 1999)

Price, Robert M. *H.P. Lovecraft and the Cthulhu Mythos* (Starmont House, 1990)

The second volume of each year's *What Do I Read Next?* will contain an interim list of best books published roughly the first half of the calendar years and following the topical essay. A more definitive list, covering the entire preceding calendar year, will follow the year-in-review essay, included in Volume 1. Most of the titles in the interim list will be retained, but a few might be dropped, replaced by better books published in the year.

BestNovels:

Bitten by Kelley Armstrong

The Living Blood by Tananarive Due

Threshold by Caitlin Kiernan

Declare by Tim Powers

Best Collections:

Talking in the Dark by Dennis Etchison

231

The Black Gondolier and Other Stories by Fritz Leiber

Eye by David J. Schow

Best Anthologies:

Meddling with Ghosts edited by Ramsey Campbell

The Year's Best Fantasy and Horror: Fourteenth Annual Collection edited by Ellen Datlow and Terri Windling

Horror Titles

652

FEDERICO ANDAHAZI

The Merciful Women
(New York: Grove, 2000)

Story type: Serial Killer
Subject(s): Creative Writing; Sexuality; Vampires
Major character(s): John Polidori, Doctor; Annette Legrand, Aged Person; George Gordon Byron, Writer (poet), Historical Figure (Lord Byron)
Time period(s): 1810s (1816)
Locale(s): Geneva, Switzerland

Summary: This ''true'' story tells how John Polidori, a companion of Lord Byron and Percy Shelley, comes to write the first popular vampire tale, ''The Vampyre,'' as part of the ghost-story writing contest at the Villa Diodati in 1816 that also produced Mary Shelley's *Frankenstein*. While staying at the villa and being humiliated by his friends, Polidori is taken into confidence by Annette Legrand, an grotesque unformed twin surgically removed from her more beautiful sister, and who miraculously has managed to survive through her sister's steady supply of sexual fluids from men. Annette inspires Polidori to write his story in exchange for sexual favors, and may have similarly inspired other imaginative writers over the decades. First published in Spain in 1998 as *Las Piadosas*, and translated into English by Alberto Manguel.

Other books by the same author:
The Anatomist, 1998

Other books you might like:
Brian W. Aldiss, *Frankenstein Unbound*, 1973
Emmanuel Carrere, *Bravoure*, 1984
Tom Holland, *Lord of the Dead*, 1995
Tim Powers, *The Stress of Her Regard*, 1989
Kathryn Ptacek, *In Silence Sealed*, 1988

653

KELLEY ARMSTRONG

Bitten
(New York: Viking, 2001)

Story type: Werewolf Story
Subject(s): Family Life; Horror; Werewolves
Major character(s): Elena Michaels, Journalist, Werewolf; Clay Danvers, Werewolf; Jeremy, Artist, Werewolf
Time period(s): 2000s
Locale(s): Bear Valley, New York; Toronto, Ontario, Canada

Summary: Elena Michaels is the only known female werewolf in the world, and one of only three werewolves converted by a bite. A self-described ''mutt,'' who has left her Pack to seek an independent life as a journalist, she is summoned back to the Pack estate at Stonehaven to help track down renegade werewolves whose conversion of ordinary criminals is creating bloody havoc and calling attention to the Pack's existence. Once back at Stonehaven, Elena finds herself wrestling with choices between living among humans or returning to the Pack, and whether to keep her human lover, Philip, or return to loving Clay, the werewolf who converted her. A first novel.

Other books you might like:
P.D. Cacek, *Canyons*, 2000
Michael Cadnum, *St. Peter's Wolf*, 1991
Dennis Danvers, *Wilderness*, 1991
Anne Rice, *The Witching Hour*, 1990
Whitley Strieber, *The Wild*, 1990

654

JEFFREY BARLOUGH

The House in the High Wood
(New York: Ace, 2001)

Story type: Supernatural Vengeance
Series: Western Lights. Number 2
Subject(s): Revenge; Rural Life; Supernatural

Major character(s): Mark Trench, Businessman; Oliver Langley, Writer; Thomas Dogger, Lawyer
Time period(s): 19th century
Locale(s): Shilston Upcot, England

Summary: Strange disruptions of nature and spectral appearances begin occurring in and around Shilston Upcot after secretive Bede Wintermarch moves into the long-abandoned Skylingden House. Squire Mark Trench and his houseguest, Oliver Langley, investigate and uncover a trail of clues that involves the former inhabitants of Skylingden House, the shaming and death of a woman in decades past, the unresolved mysterious disappearance of the squire's father years before, and the signs pointing to the gestation of a terrible supernatural vengeance against the town and its inhabitants. This is the second book in a series set in an alternative world where a comet strike has decimated most of known civilization centuries before and remnants of the prehistoric era coexist with people of the modern day.

Other books by the same author:
Dark Sleeper, 1998

Other books you might like:
Jonathan Aycliffe, *A Shadow on the Wall*, 2000
Charles Dickens, *Bleak House*, 1853
Susan Hill, *The Woman in Black*, 1983
J. Sheridan Le Fanu, *Uncle Silas*, 1864
Charles Palliser, *The Unburied*, 1999

655

BERTICE BARRY

The Haunting of Hip Hop

(New York: Doubleday, 2001)

Story type: Ghost Story
Subject(s): African Americans; Ghosts; Music and Musicians
Major character(s): Harry Hudson, Musician; Ava Vercher, Lawyer; Charles Campbell, Real Estate Agent
Time period(s): 2000s
Locale(s): New York, New York

Summary: Rap producer Harry ''Freedom'' Hudson finds himself drawn irresistibly to an abandoned house in Harlem. Though Harry hopes to buy the house for his own, he is unaware that it harbors ghosts of African Americans from the past, who feel that his music betrays the black heritage and who hope to persuade him to change his tune.

Other books by the same author:
Redemption Song, 2000

Other books you might like:
Tananarive Due, *The Living Blood*, 2001
Marvin Kaye, *Fantastique*, 1992
Adrian Savage, *Symphony*, 1992
Fred Mustard Stewart, *The Mephisto Waltz*, 1969

656

EDWARD P. BERGLUND

Shards of Darkness

(Poplar Bluff, Missouri: Mythos, 2000)

Story type: Collection
Subject(s): Horror; Short Stories; Supernatural

Summary: Many of these 11 stories, all previously published, contain a Lovecraftian slant and are set in the imaginary Lovecraftian milieu of O'Khymer, Oregon. Selections include ''The Feaster from the Stars,'' in which a man discovers the house he inherits from his parents was, and continues to be, a site of unspeakable supernatural evil; ''Dream Sendings,'' a dream fantasy that oscillates between an undersea city and the land; and ''The Towers,'' in which a traveler is dangerously coerced into the strange worship of a man he meets on the road. With an introduction by Robert M. Price.

Other books you might like:
James Ambuehl, *Correlated Contents*, 1998
Lin Carter, *The Xothic Cycle*, 1997
Wilum H. Pugmire, *Dreams of Lovecraftian Horror*, 1999
Stanley Sargent, *Ancient Exhumations*, 1999
Jeffery Thomas, *Bones of the Old Ones and Other Lovecraftian Tales*, 1995

657

DEBORAH BOEHM

Ghost of a Smile

(New York: Kodansha, 2001)

Story type: Collection
Subject(s): Folk Tales; Short Stories; Supernatural
Locale(s): Japan

Summary: Boehm, a renowned translator, provides eight contemporary retellings of classic Japanese folk tales. Contents include the allegorical ''Naked in the Moonlight,'' about a merchant's frustrated efforts to gain admission to the exclusive nightclub Hell; ''The Beast in the Mirror,'' about a werewolf sumo wrestler; and ''The Snake Spell,'' about a reserved librarian, who is transformed by a spell into an irresistable love interest.

Where it's reviewed:
Publishers Weekly, January 8, 2001, page 44

Other books you might like:
Lafcadio Hearn, *Kwaidan*, 1904
Lafcadio Hearn, *Some Chinese Ghosts*, 1887
Yumiko Kurahashi, *The Woman with the Flying Head and Other Stories*, 1998
Tom Te-Wu Ma, *Chinese Ghost Stories for Adults*, 2000
Murasaki Shikibu, *Genjii Monogatari*, 1974

658

GARY A. BRAUNBECK
ALAN M. CLARK, Co-Author
ALAN M. CLARK, Illustrator

Escaping Purgatory

(Eugene, Oregon: IFD, 2001)

Story type: Collection
Subject(s): Fantasy; Horror; Short Stories

Summary: Five stories and a wraparound prologue/epilogue each present a variation on the theme of people trying to escape Purgatory. In ''Mr. Hands,'' Purgatory takes the shape of a hideous monster created from a mother's rage and deployed to stalk and kill child molesters and murderers. In ''The Big Hollow,'' the dead in a local cemetery, unable to resolve problems in their past, live an afterlife dogged by the same doubts, fears, and unresolved issues as they did in life. ''A Host of Shadows'' imagines a life of infirmity and old age for Jack the Ripper that is its own Purgatory. All of the stories are illustrated by Clark, who also collaborated on the fiction and whose paintings inspired some of the stories.

Other books by the same author:
Things Left Behind, 1997

Other books you might like:
Peter Crowther, *Dante's Disciples*, 1996
    Edward Kramer, co-editor
Elizabeth Engstrom, *The Alchemy of Love*, 1998
Elizabeth Engstrom, *Imagination Fully Dilated*, 1998
    Alan Clark, co-editor
Edward Kramer, *The Crow: Shattered Lives, Broken Dreams*, 1998
    James O'Barr, co-editor

659

GARY A. BRAUNBECK

This Flesh Unknown

(Scarborough, Maine: Foggy Windows, 2001)

Story type: Erotic Horror; Doppelganger
Subject(s): Fantasy; Marriage; Sexuality
Major character(s): Paul Howe, Restaurateur; Vanessa Howe, Museum Curator; Rowan Byrne, Artist
Time period(s): 2000s
Locale(s): Ohio

Summary: Their sex lives in decline following the death of their young daughter, for which they blame themselves, Paul and Vanessa each are seduced by a mysterious lover who satisfies them totally. Their daughter returns from the grave to warn them that their paramours are actually private fantasies made flesh by their unfulfilled desires, and that Paul and Vanessa are in danger of being supplanted by them if they don't re-establish intimacy between themselves.

Other books by the same author:
The Indifference of Heaven, 2000
Things Left Behind, 1997

Other books you might like:
Ron Dee, *Succumb*, 1984
Ed Kelleher, *Animus*, 1993
    Harriette Vidal, co-author
Richard Matheson, *Earthbound*, 1994
T.L. Parkinson, *The Man Upstairs*, 1991
Ray Russell, *Incubus*, 1976

660

EDWARD BRYANT

The Baku

(Burton, Michigan: Subterranean, 2001)

Story type: Collection
Series: Rook
Subject(s): Horror; Supernatural; Nuclear Weapons

Summary: *The Baku* contains three stories, all dealing with aspects of nuclear holocaust. The title tale concerns a representative for a nuclear energy provider haunted by the ghosts of atom bomb victims. ''The Hibakusha Gallery'' tells of a futuristic photo arcade where people with strange desires come to have their pictures taken as nuclear holocaust victims. ''Jody After the War'' is a tale of love in the ruins of a nuclear war. Also included is an unfilmed script the author adapted from the title story. Published as a signed limited edition.

Where it's reviewed:
Publishers Weekly, March 26, 2001, page 69

Other books by the same author:
Darker Passions, 1992
Thermals of August, 1992
Fetish, 1991
The Cutter, 1991
Man of the Future, 1990

Other books you might like:
Harlan Ellison, *Slippage*, 1997
George R.R. Martin, *Portraits of His Children*, 1987
Robert R. McCammon, *Blue World*, 1989
Dan Simmons, *Prayers to Broken Stones*, 1990
F. Paul Wilson, *Soft and Others*, 1989

661

THOMAS BURKE

The Golden Gong

(Ashcroft, British Columbia: Ash-Tree Press, 2001)

Story type: Collection
Subject(s): Horror; Short Stories; Suspense

Summary: This collection of 20 macabre stories is by a British writer from the first half of the 20th century who specialized in contes cruels and tales of psychological suspense. Many are set in the Limehouse district and slums of England, including ''The Hands of Mr. Ottermole,'' about a Jack the Ripper-type killer and the bizarre motive for his murders; the zombie tale ''The Hollow Man;'' and ''The Man Who Lost His Head,'' a tale of personality exchange. Edited and with an introduction by Jessica Amanda Salmonson.

Horror

Other books by the same author:
Dark Nights, 1944
Night Pieces, 1935
Whispering Windows, 1921
Limehouse Nights, 1916

Other books you might like:
Villiers de l'Isle-Adam, *Contes Cruels*, 1893
William Fryer Harvey, *The Beast with Five Fingers*, 1947
Maurice Level, *Tales of Mystery and Horror*, 1920
Gouverneur Morris, *It and Other Stories*, 1912
W.C. Morrow, *The Monster Maker and Other Stories*, 2000

662

JACK CADY

The Haunting of Hood Canal

(New York: St. Martin's Press, 2001)

Story type: Ancient Evil Unleashed; Supernatural Vengeance
Subject(s): Horror; Small Town Life; Supernatural
Major character(s): Sugar Bear Smith, Blacksmith; Greek Annie, Witch; Petey Mulholland, Gambler
Time period(s): 2000s
Locale(s): Hood Canal, Washington

Summary: When Sugar Bear Smith kills a suspected child molester and dumps his car and corpse in nearby Hood Canal, it awakens a water fury that begins pulling pulling cars off the road surrounding the canal and into its waters. The water fury and its ravenous appetite are just a metaphor for a type of evil that is slowly infiltrating hitherto placid Hood Canal, manifesting in the form of business interests and destructive commercialism.

Other books by the same author:
The Off Season, 1995
Inagehi, 1994
Street, 1994
The Jonah Watch, 1981
The Well, 1980

Other books you might like:
Scott Bradfield, *What's Wrong with America*, 1994
Thomas M. Disch, *The Sub*, 1998
Kim Newman, *The Quorum*, 1994
Joan Samson, *The Auctioneer*, 1975
Gus Weill, *Flesh*, 1990

663

RAMSEY CAMPBELL, Editor

Meddling with Ghosts

(London: British Library, 2001)

Story type: Anthology; Ghost Story
Subject(s): Ghosts; Short Stories; Supernatural

Summary: These 16 previously published stories are assembled as a tribute to the influence of M.R. James, the dean of modern ghost fiction, who emphasized the importance of malevolent ghosts and reticence in their description as the key to writing an effective ghost story. Selections are divided into stories by predecessors, contemporaries, and successors of James and include F. Marion Crawford's ''The Upper Berth,'' about a man who discovers too late his room on a ship is haunted by the ghost of someone who died in it; Percival Landon's ''Thurnley Abbey,'' about a man who sleeps in a room haunted by the specter of a nun walled up in it centuries before; and Fritz Leiber's ''Smoke Ghost,'' a modern tale of a ghost conjured from the angst and tensions of the modern city and which manifests in the smoke and soot of the cityscape. With an annotated bibliography by Rosemary Pardoe of other Jamesian writers and fiction.

Other books by the same author:
Uncanny Banquet, 1992
Fine Frights, 1988
New Terrors, 1984
New Tales of the Cthulhu Mythos, 1980
Superhorror, 1976

Other books you might like:
V.H. Collins, *Ghosts and Marvels*, 1924
    editor
Richard Dalby, *Ghosts and Scholars*, 1987
    Rosemary Pardoe, co-editor
Inge Dupont, *Morgan Library Ghost Stories*, 1990
    Hope Mayo, co-editor
Barbara Roden, *Shadows and Silence*, 2000
    Christopher Roden, co-editor
Wendy Webb, *Gothic Ghosts*, 1997
    Charles L. Grant, co-editor

664

HUGH B. CAVE

The Evil Returns

(New York: Leisure, 2001)

Story type: Occult; Child-in-Peril
Subject(s): Horror; Mothers; Voodoo
Major character(s): Margal, Sorcerer; Ken Forrest, Government Official; Sandra Dawson, Housewife
Time period(s): 2000s
Locale(s): Port-au-Prince, Haiti; Miami, Florida

Summary: Having survived the fire his enemies thought had killed him, the crippled voodoo houngan Margal seeks to increase his power. Abducting the child of an American diplomat, he flees to the United States, hoping to use his black magic to gain access to, and ultimately control, the president of the United States. A sequel to *The Evil*.

Other books by the same author:
Lucifer's Eye, 1991
The Lower Deep, 1990
Disciples of Dread, 1988
Shades of Evil, 1982
The Evil, 1981

Other books you might like:
Ramsey Campbell, *The Nameless*, 1981
Nicholas Conde, *The Religion*, 1982
Owl Goingback, *Evil Whispers*, 2001
Michael Reaves, *Voodoo Child*, 1998
John Saul, *Darkness*, 1991

665

RICHARD CHIZMAR, Editor

Night Visions 10

(Burton, Michigan: Subterranean, 2001)

Story type: Anthology
Subject(s): Horror; Short Stories; Supernatural

Summary: This volume revives an anthology series that ran initially from 1984 to 1991, each volume featuring three authors contributing 40,000 words of previously unpublished fiction. Selections include Jack Ketchum's ''The Passenger,'' about a woman forced to endure a night of horror at the hands of murderers on the run who kidnap her after her car breaks down; John Shirley's ''Her Hunger,'' about a supernatural predator who uses sex to prey on teenagers in the southern California night scene; and five stories by David B. Silva, including the paranoid dark fantasy ''Signing Off,'' and ''Memory's Weave,'' about a brother and sister who reunite to slay a supernatural menace they thought they laid to rest in childhood.

Where it's reviewed:
Locus, June 2001, page 27
Publishers Weekly, March 26, 2001, page 68

Other books by the same author:
The Earth Strikes Back, 1994
Chillers, 1992
Cold Blood, 1991

Other books you might like:
Dana M. Anderson, *Cafe Purgatorium*, 1991
John Farris, *Night Visions 8*, 1991
    editor
Thomas Tessier, *Night Visions 9*, 1991
    editor
Stanley Wiater, *Night Visions 7*, 1990
    editor
F. Paul Wilson, *Night Visions 6*, 1989
    editor

666

SIMON CLARK

Blood Crazy

(New York: Leisure, 2001)

Story type: Child-in-Peril
Subject(s): Horror; Murder; Massacres
Major character(s): Nick Aten, Teenager; Tug Slatter, Teenager; Sarah Hayes, Teenager
Time period(s): 1990s
Locale(s): Doncaster, England

Summary: One morning, for reasons no one can explain, the adults of Doncaster fall under a strange influence that compels them to slaughter all children younger than the age of 19. Nick and his friends try gamely to dodge their murderous loved ones, but find it difficult to cope with the omnipresent threat of their killing, as well as the many personal conflicts they grappled with when the world was normal. First published in England in 1995.

Other books by the same author:
Darkness Demands, 2001
The Judas Tree, 2000
The Fall, 1998
Vampyrrhic, 1998
King Blood, 1997

Other books you might like:
Jack Ketchum, *Ladies Night*, 1998
Stephen Laws, *Chasm*, 1998
Alan Rodgers, *Blood of the Children*, 1989
John Russo, *Night of the Living Dead*, 1974

667

SIMON CLARK

Darkness Demands

(Abingdon, Maryland: CD Publications, 2001)

Story type: Ancient Evil Unleashed; Child-in-Peril
Subject(s): Children; Supernatural; Writing
Major character(s): John Newton, Writer (true crime); Paul Newton, Teenager; Elizabeth Newton, Housewife
Time period(s): 2000s
Locale(s): Skelbrooke, England

Summary: Newly moved with his family to rural Skelbrooke, bestselling true-crime writer John Newton begins receiving anonymously posted notes demanding that he leave a variety of unusual items on a grave in the nearby cemetery, or suffer extreme consequences. From fearful townspeople who are also receiving the notes, John pieces together a story concerning an evil entity who lives under the ground of the countryside, and whose demands, made for centuries of the luckless dwellers in the region, invariably end with a request for young children.

Other books by the same author:
The Judas Tree, 2000
The Fall, 1998
Vampyrrhic, 1998
King Blood, 1997
Nailed by the Heart, 1995

Other books you might like:
Jonathan Aycliffe, *Whispers in the Dark*, 1993
Ramsey Campbell, *Midnight Sun*, 1991
Vincent Courtney, *Goblins*, 1994
Chris Curry, *Panic*, 1994
Sidney Williams, *Gnelfs*, 1991

668

MAX ALLAN COLLINS

The Mummy Returns

(New York: Berkley/Boulevard, 2001)

Story type: Reanimated Dead; Occult
Subject(s): Egyptian Antiquities; Mummies; Supernatural
Major character(s): Richard O'Connell, Mercenary; Evelyn O'Connell, Archaeologist; Alex O'Connell, Child
Time period(s): 1930s
Locale(s): London, England; Thebes, Egypt

Horror

Summary: While playing with artifacts brought back by his parents from Egypt, Alex O'Connell finds himself unable to remove the bracelet of the Scorpion King from his wrist. Alex soon becomes a pawn between sinister Egyptian agents, who hope to revive the Scorpion King and return the world to the dark gods he worshipped, and Imhotep, a reanimated mummy and his sworn enemy. Novelization of the screenplay by Stephen Sommers, and a sequel to the 1999 novel and movie *The Mummy.*

Where it's reviewed:
Locus, April 2001, page 31
Publishers Weekly, February 19, 2001, page 92

Other books you might like:
David Case, *The Third Grave*, 1981
Carl Dreadstone, *The Mummy*, 1977
Charles L. Grant, *The Long Night of the Grave*, 1986
Kathryn Meyer Griffith, *The Calling*, 1994
Michael Paine, *Cities of the Dead*, 1988

669

NANCY COLLINS

Avenue X and Other Dark Streets
(Philadelphia: Xlibris, 2000)

Story type: Collection
Subject(s): Horror; Short Stories; Supernatural

Summary: This volume collects 13 edgy and often raunchy tales of horror and fantasy. Selections include "Cavalerada," about the horrors a band of outlaws encounter shooting up a Mexican town on *Dia de Los Muertos*; "The Thing from Lovers Lane," about a Lovecraftian monster that stalks the woods outside a town, seeking to spawn offspring with its unsuspecting women; and "Vampire King of the Goth Chicks," a story in the author's celebrated Sonja Blue vampire series, in which a tough-as-nails female vampire viciously shows up a fake vampire preying on the Goth subculture of a town.

Other books by the same author:
Angels on Fire, 1998
Midnight Blue, 1995
Walking Wolf, 1995
Nameless Sins, 1994
Wild Blood, 1994

Other books you might like:
Poppy Z. Brite, *Are You Loathsome Tonight?*, 1998
Joe R. Lansdale, *High Cotton*, 2000
John Shirley, *Darkness Divided*, 2001
Lucy Taylor, *Painted in Blood*, 1997
Karl Edward Wagner, *Exorcisms and Ecstasies*, 1997

670

ELLEN DATLOW, Editor
TERRI WINDLING, Co-Editor

The Year's Best Fantasy and Horror: Fourteenth Annual Collection
(New York: St. Martin's Griffin, 2001)

Story type: Anthology
Series: Year's Best Fantasy and Horror. Number 14
Subject(s): Fantasy; Horror; Short Stories

Summary: Forty-four stories and eight poems, all published for the first time in the year 2000, represent, in the editors' estimation, the best fantasy and horror fiction of the year. Highlights among the horror selections include Tia Travis' "Down Here in the Garden," a tale of guilt and terrible revenge based on the history of the Donner Party; Stewart O'Nan's "Endless Summer," the first-person narrative of a psychopath; Jack Ketchum's "Gone," a tale of nonsupernatural Halloween horrors; and Dennis Etchison's "My Present Wife," a subtly disarming tale of psychological suspense and festering evil. The book also contains overviews of the year in fantasy and horror fiction by the editors, fantasy and horror in the media by Ed Bryant, the year in comics by Seth Johnson, and obituaries by James Frenkel.

Where it's reviewed:
Kirkus Reviews, June 1, 2001, page 779

Other books by the same author:
Silver Birch, Blood Moon, 1999
Sirens and Other Daemon Lovers, 1998
Ruby Slippers, Golden Tears, 1995
Black Thorn, White Rose, 1994
Snow White, Blood Red, 1993

Other books you might like:
Richard Chizmar, *Subterranean Gallery*, 1999
    William Schafer, co-editor
Elizabeth Engstrom, *Imagination Fully Dilated II*, 2000
    Alan Clark, co-editor
Stephen Jones, *Dark Terrors 5*, 2000
    David Sutton, co-editor
Stephen Jones, *The Mammoth Book of Best New Horror 12*, 2001
    editor
Richard Laymon, *Bad News*, 2000
    editor

671

SEAN DESMOND

Adams Fall
(New York: St. Martin's Press, 2000)

Story type: Serial Killer; Ghost Story
Subject(s): Academia; School Life; Serial Killer
Major character(s): Unnamed Character, Narrator, Student—College; Maeve O'Hara, Student—College; Daniel Edmonds, Spirit
Time period(s): 2000s
Locale(s): Cambridge, Massachusetts

Summary: The nameless narrator of this novel, a senior at Harvard University, relates the tragedy of his roommate's suicide, and the apparent arousal this causes of the ghost of a student suicide from decades before. A series of gruesome deaths follow, all of them pinned on the narrator who begins to crumble psychologically under their burden. Is he as innocent as he seems? First novel.

Other books you might like:
Douglas Clegg, *Mischief*, 2000
Charles L. Grant, *The Pet*, 1986
Barry Hoffman, *Born Bad*, 2000
Tom Piccirilli, *The Night Class*, 2001
Patrick Redmond, *Something Dangerous*, 1999

672

TANANARIVE DUE

The Living Blood
(New York: Pocket, 2001)

Story type: Occult
Subject(s): Africa; African Americans; Medicine
Major character(s): Jessica Jacob-Wolde, Journalist; Fana Jacob-Wolde, Child; Lucas Shepard, Scientist
Time period(s): 2000s
Locale(s): Miami, Florida; Lalibella, Ethiopia

Summary: Jessica Jacob-Wolde pursues her immortal husband, Dawit, to Ethiopia to show him Fana, the daughter conceived after Jessica was resurrected with Dawit's immortal blood, and who is beginning to show awesome and undisciplined supernatural powers. En route to her destination, Jessica dispenses Dawit's lifesaving blood to the sick and dying—an act that draws the attention of a microbiologist whose son is dying of leukemia, as well as an evil businessman out to exploit the blood's magical properties for personal gain. Sequel to *My Soul to Keep*.

Where it's reviewed:
Kirkus Reviews, January 15, 2001, page 70
Publishers Weekly, March 19, 2001, page 81

Other books by the same author:
My Soul to Keep, 1997
The Between, 1995

Other books you might like:
Thomas F. Monteleone, *The Resurrectionist*, 1995
Seth Pfefferle, *Stickman*, 1987
Anne Rice, *Merrick*, 2000
Chelsea Quinn Yarbro, *Out of the House of Life*, 1990

673

DENNIS ETCHISON

Talking in the Dark
(Lancaster, Pennsylvania: Stealth, 2001)

Story type: Collection
Subject(s): Horror; Short Stories; Suspense

Summary: This is a retrospective collection of 24 atmospheric stories of dread, terror, and alienation, one original to the volume. Most are set in southern California and feature ordinary characters whose lives take suddenly menacing turns. Selections include ''It Only Comes out at Night,'' about a highway rest stop stalked by a serial killer; ''The Dark Country'' and ''The Scar,'' both nonsupernatural tales of troubled relationships erupting into grim violence; and a trio of stories—''The Late Shift,'' ''The Machine Demands a Sacrifice,'' and ''The Dead Line''—about the exploitative uses for zombies created by modern medical science.

Where it's reviewed:
Locus, July 2001, page 35

Other books by the same author:
The Death Artist, 2000
The Blood Kiss, 1988
Red Dreams, 1984
The Dark Country, 1982

Other books you might like:
Harlan Ellison, *Slippage*, 1997
Richard Christian Matheson, *Dystopia*, 2000
David J. Schow, *Seeing Red*, 1989
Peter Straub, *Magic Terror*, 2000
Thomas Tessier, *Ghost Music*, 2000

674

J. MEADE FALKNER

The Lost Stradivarius
(East Sussex, England: Tartarus, 2000)

Story type: Collection
Subject(s): Horror; Short Stories; Supernatural

Summary: This collection contains three weird tales, one never before reprinted. The centerpiece of the volume is the title tale, a novel originally published in 1895 about a violin possessed by the soul of a former owner and occultist, which has a devilish and debauching effect on subsequent owners.

Other books by the same author:
The Nebuly Coat, 1903
Moonfleet, 1898

Other books you might like:
Algernon Blackwood, *Best Ghost Stories of Algernon Blackwood*, 1973
M.R. James, *Ghost Stories of an Antiquary*, 1904
J. Sheridan Le Fanu, *Best Ghost Stories of J. Sheridan Le Fanu*, 1964
Vernon Lee, *The Snake Lady and Other Stories*, 1954
Fitz-James O'Brien, *Supernatural Tales of Fitz-James O'Brien*, 1988

675

MICK FARREN

More than Mortal
(New York: Tor, 2001)

Story type: Vampire Story
Subject(s): Arthurian Legend; Horror; Vampires

Horror

Major character(s): Victor Renquist, Vampire; Fenrior, Vampire; Columbine Dashwood, Vampire
Time period(s): 2000s
Locale(s): Morton Downs, England

Summary: When an archaeological dig at Morton Downs coincides with strange dreams experienced by female vampires in his entourage, vampire lord Victor Renquist investigates. Signs indicate the excavation has uncovered the resting place of Taliesin, better known as Merlin, who like the vampires was one of a species created by the extraterrestrial Nephilim as part of their biogenetic experiments on Earth eons before. While trying to determine whether Taliesin's resurrection will shift the balance of power from vampires to humans, Renquist must contend with the willfulness of his vampire women and the aggression of a rival vampire lord whose territory he visits. A sequel to *Darklost*.

Where it's reviewed:
Kirkus Reviews, June 1, 2001, page 772
Publishers Weekly, July 9, 2001, page 51

Other books by the same author:
Darklost, 2000
Jim Morrison's Adventures in the Afterlife, 1999
The Time of Feasting, 1996
Necrom, 1991

Other books you might like:
Anne Rice, *Queen of the Damned*, 1988
Michael Romkey, *The Vampire Papers*, 1994
Fred Saberhagen, *Dominion*, 1982
Michael Talbot, *The Delicate Dependency*, 1982
Chelsea Quinn Yarbro, *Better in the Dark*, 1993

676

JOHN FARRIS

The Fury and the Terror

(New York: Tor, 2001)

Story type: Wild Talents
Subject(s): Espionage; Government; Psychic Powers
Major character(s): Eden Waring, Student—College (valedictorian), Psychic; Tom Sherard, Spy; Rona Harvester, Political Figure
Time period(s): 2000s
Locale(s): Shasta, California; Plenty Coups, Montana; Washington, District of Columbia

Summary: Eden Waring, the unwitting daughter of two extraordinarily endowed psychic adepts, becomes a pawn between the FBI, the First Lady of the United States, and MORG—the Multiphasic Operations Research Group, which is dedicated to developing persons with psychic talents as part of the national weapons arsenal—when a struggle for power to lead America follows a debilitating stroke that incapacitates the President of the United States. A sequel to the author's landmark novel *The Fury*.

Where it's reviewed:
Publishers Weekly, February 26, 2001, page 56

Other books by the same author:
Sacrifice, 1994

Fiends, 1989
The Axman Cometh, 1989
All Heads Turn When the Hunt Goes By, 1977
The Fury, 1976

Other books you might like:
Mark Burnell, *Freak*, 1994
Douglas Clegg, *Dark of the Eye*, 1994
Tananarive Due, *The Living Blood*, 2001
Stephen King, *Firestarter*, 1980
Thomas F. Monteleone, *The Resurrectionist*, 1995

677

PAUL FINCH

After Shocks

(Ashcroft, British Columbia: Ash-Tree Press, 2001)

Story type: Collection
Subject(s): Horror; Short Stories; Supernatural

Summary: The 18 stories of horror and the supernatural in this collection are mostly modern extensions of the classic ghostly tradition and its principles of subtlety and atmosphere. Selections include the title story, about a remote railway station haunted by the ghosts of soldiers from the great war; "The Altar," in which a priest discovers that his congregation in a slum is slowly being seduced by a powerful religion that speaks more directly to their misery and needs; and "September," in which two boys are menaced by farm equipment animated by the spirit of the comatose farmer whose land they have strayed onto.

Other books by the same author:
The Dark Satanic, 1999

Other books you might like:
Steve Duffy, *The Night Comes On*, 1998
Derek M. Fox, *Treading on the Past*, 2000
Terry Lamsley, *Conference with the Dead*, 1996
L.H. Maynard, *Echoes of Darkness*, 2000
    M.P.N. Sims, co-author
Mark Morris, *Close to the Bone*, 1994

678

SHAMUS FRAZER

Where Human Pathways End

(Ashcroft, British Columbia: Ash-Tree Press, 2001)

Story type: Collection
Subject(s): Horror; Short Stories; Supernatural

Summary: This is the sole collection of supernatural fiction by a writer better known in his lifetime as a social satirist. Selections include "The Tune in Dan's Cafe," about a pub with a haunted jukebox that plays only the favorite song of a criminal shot to death on its premises, and "The Yew Tree," about a malevolent tree endowed with horrible life drawn from the dead in the graveyard where it grew. Five of the book's ten selections (one a poem) are published for the first time, including the sardonic deal-with-the-devil story "Mr. Nicholas Loses Grip," and "Obituary," in which a nosy journalist discovers firsthand the peculiar tastes of a former

celebrity who shuns the limelight. Edited and introduced by Richard Dalby, and featuring a memoir by the author's wife.

Where it's reviewed:
Hellnotes, April 6, 2001, page 2

Other books by the same author:
Blow Blow Your Trumpets, 1945
Goodnight Sweet Ladies, 1940
A Shroud as Well as a Shirt, 1935
Porcelain People, 1934
Acorned Hog, 1933

Other books you might like:
Charles Birkin, *A Haunting Beauty*, 2000
R. Chetwynd-Hayes, *The Unbidden*, 1971
Frederick Cowles, *The Night Wind Howls*, 1996
Nigel Kneale, *Tomato Cain and Other Stories*, 1949
H. Russell Wakefield, *Reunion at Dawn*, 2000

679

CHRISTOPHER GOLDEN

Prowlers

(New York: Pocket/Pulse, 2001)

Story type: Werewolf Story; Young Adult
Series: Prowlers. Number 1
Subject(s): Horror; Teen Relationships; Supernatural
Major character(s): Jack Dwyer, Teenager; Molly Hatcher, Teenager; Owen Tanzer, Teenager
Time period(s): 2000s
Locale(s): Boston, Massachusetts

Summary: Jack Dwyer's murdered friend, Artie, returns from the Ghostlands to tell him about the Prowlers, a feral race who masquerade as humans and who kill with impunity. The information offers little consolation to Jack, who now finds his life and the lives of his friends and family endangered, and the all-too-knowledgeable authorities only marginally helpful. First novel in a series for young adult readers.

Other books by the same author:
Buffy the Vampire Slayer: Spike and Dru: Pretty Maids All in a Row, 2000
Head Games, 2000
Buffy the Vampire Slayer: Sins of the Father, 1999
Strangewood, 1999

Other books you might like:
P.D. Cacek, *Canyons*, 2000
Henry Garfield, *Moondog*, 1995
Annette Klause, *Blood and Chocolate*, 1997
Whitley Strieber, *Wolfen*, 1978
Melanie Tem, *Wilding*, 1992

680

EDWARD GOREY, Editor
EDWARD GOREY, Illustrator

The Haunted Looking Glass

(New York: New York Review of Books, 2001)

Story type: Anthology

Subject(s): Horror; Suspense; Supernatural

Summary: This is a reprint of a collection of 12 classic ghost tales, first published in 1959 and illustrated by the editor. Selections include E. Nesbit's ''Man-Size in Marble,'' about a couple whose misfortune is to visit a rural town on the night when the stone effigies decorating coffins in the church are afoot; Robert Louis Stevenson's ''The Body Snatcher,'' about the gruesome fate that befalls a team of men who supply physicians in Victorian England with corpses to study; and Bram Stoker's ''The Judge's House,'' in which a young student falls under the evil influence of the ghost of a judge who once lived in the rooms he lets.

Where it's reviewed:
Publishers Weekly, February 26, 2001, page 64

Other books you might like:
Michael Cox, *Twelve Tales of the Supernatural*, 1997
Michael Cox, *Twelve Victorian Ghost Stories*, 1997
Roald Dahl, *Roald Dahl's Book of Ghost Stories*, 1983
   editor
Richard Dalby, *Twelve Gothic Tales*, 1998
   editor
Barbara Roden, *Forgotten Ghosts*, 1996
   Christopher Roden, co-editor

681

ED GORMAN

The Dark Fantastic

(New York: Leisure, 2001)

Story type: Collection
Subject(s): Horror; Suspense; Supernatural

Summary: This collection of 17 stories of horror, fantasy, and suspense are all inflected with the mood and atmosphere of noir fiction. Selections include ''Different Kinds of Dead,'' about a traveling salesman's life-changing encounter with a ghost on the road; ''Lover Boy,'' a futuristic tale of virtual reality and sexuality; and ''The Broker,'' which reveals the supernatural truth behind a woman whose pimp passes her off as the ultimate in sexual thrills.

Other books by the same author:
Cages, 1996
Out There in the Darkness, 1995
Prisoners and Other Stories, 1992

Other books you might like:
Rick Hautala, *Bedbugs*, 2000
Dean R. Koontz, *Strange Highways*, 1995
Richard Laymon, *Dreadful Tales*, 2000
William F. Nolan, *Things Beyond Midnight*, 1984
F. Paul Wilson, *Soft and Others*, 1989

682

CHARLES L. GRANT

When the Cold Wind Blows

(New York: Roc, 2001)

Story type: Werewolf Story

Series: Black Oak. Number 4
Subject(s): Werewolves; Witches and Witchcraft
Major character(s): Ethan Proctor, Investigator; Paul Tazaretti, Investigator; Vivian Chambers, Bodyguard
Time period(s): 2000s
Locale(s): Alton, Georgia

Summary: The Black Oak investigative team's latest lead on the trail to find Taylor Blaine's missing daughter, Celeste, takes them to a small town on the outskirts of Atlanta, where a series of violent killings point to a werewolf. Worse, the killer may be all the more difficult to identify, owing to a close affiliation with the local authorities. Fourth in a series about a team of private investigators whose work often brings them into contact with the supernatural.

Other books by the same author:
Hunting Ground, 2000
Winter Knight, 1999
Genesis, 1998
The Hush of Dark Wings, 1998
Stunts, 1990

Other books you might like:
Crosland Brown, *Tombley's Walk*, 1991
Geoffrey Caine, *Wake of the Werewolf*, 1991
D.J. Donaldson, *Blood on the Bayou*, 1991
Ronald Kelly, *Moon of the Werewolf*, 1991
Les Whitten, *Moon of the Wolf*, 1967

683

STEPHEN GRESHAM

In the Blood

(New York: Pinnacle, 2001)

Story type: Vampire Story
Subject(s): Vampires
Major character(s): Jacob Tracker, Clerk; Orpheus Beauregard "Bo" Smith, Restaurateur; Brianna McVicar, Young Woman
Time period(s): 2000s
Locale(s): Soldier's Crossing, Alabama

Summary: Demolition of Sweet Gum, the Tracker family house built at the time of the American Civil War, discloses numerous skeletons buried in its walls. Soon, members of the Tracker family, who comprise most of the small town of Soldier's Crossing, are turning into vampires, as a result of the bite of family members infected by the house's taint. As blood calls to blood, only those who are not pure blood Trackers can hope to resist the vampire scourge and prevent its inexorable spread.

Other books by the same author:
The Living Dark, 1991
Blood Wings, 1990
Demon's Eye, 1989
Abracadabra, 1988
Runaway, 1988

Other books you might like:
Scott Baker, *Ancestral Hungers*, 1995
Ron Dee, *Dusk*, 1991
Pat Graversen, *Sweet Blood*, 1992

Wendy Haley, *This Dark Paradise*, 1994
Tanith Lee, *Darkness, I*, 1995

684

NICOLA GRIFFITH, Editor
STEPHEN PAGEL, Co-Editor

Bending the Landscape: Horror

(New York: Overlook, 2001)

Story type: Anthology
Subject(s): Homosexuality/Lesbianism; Horror; Sexuality

Summary: Eighteen new stories refract gay themes and issues through the lens of horror fiction. Selections include Leslie What's "The Were-Slut of Avenue A," in which a woman's desire to bond with her lover by sharing her gift of lycanthropy has unexpectedly alienating results; Gary Bowen's "Blood Requiem," a tale of vampirism and the persecution of gays during World War II; and Mark W. Tiedeman's dystopic "Passing," about a viciously antigay future.

Where it's reviewed:
Kirkus Reviews, March 1, 2001, page 279
Publishers Weekly, March 5, 2001, page 67

Other books by the same author:
Bending the Landscape: Science Fiction, 1998
Bending the Landscape: Fantasy, 1997

Other books you might like:
Eric Garber, *Embracing the Dark*, 1991
  editor
Pam Keesey, *Darker Angels: Lesbian Vampire Stories*, 1995
  editor
William J. Mann, *Grave Passions*, 1997
  editor
Michael Rowe, *Queer Fear*, 2000
  editor
Julie K. Trevelyan, *The Ghost of Carmen Miranda and Other Spooky Gay and Lesbian Tales*, 1999
  Scott Brassart, co-editor

685

CHARLAINE HARRIS

Dead Until Dark

(New York: Ace, 2001)

Story type: Vampire Story; Mystery
Subject(s): Psychic Powers; Small Town Life; Vampires
Major character(s): Sookie Stackhouse, Waiter/Waitress; Bill Compton, Vampire; Jason Stackhouse, Foreman
Time period(s): 2000s
Locale(s): Bon Temps, Louisiana

Summary: In a world where humans uneasily accept the co-existence of vampires in their midst, Sookie Stackhouse, whose secret telepathic skills set her apart as an oddity in her small Louisiana town, develops an alliance with Bill Compton, vampire scion of a local family whom the towns-folk would just as soon be rid of. When those members of Sookie's social circle associating with vampires begin turning

up murdered, Sookie must turn sleuth to exonerate Bill and find the culprit she thinks is framing him.

Where it's reviewed:
Locus, July 2001, page 23
Locus, June 2001, page 35

Other books by the same author:
Shakespeare's Trollop, 2000
A Fool and His Honey, 1999
Dead over Heels, 1996
A Bone to Pick, 1992
Real Murders, 1990

Other books you might like:
Vincent Courtney, *Vampire Beat*, 1990
P.N. Elrod, *Bloodlist*, 1990
Sherry Gottlieb, *Love Bite*, 1994
Laurell K. Hamilton, *Guilty Pleasures*, 1993
Tanya Huff, *Blood Price*, 1991

686

RICK HAUTALA

The Mountain King

(New York: Leisure, 2001)

Story type: Collection
Subject(s): Horror; Rural Life; Short Stories
Locale(s): Maine

Summary: Rural Maine provides the setting for these four stories. The title tale concerns a man suspected of murdering his friend, who is determined to prove the friend was abducted by a monster in the mountains. The other three stories are part of the author's Little Brothers series, about creatures of Native American mythology with a ravenous appetite for human flesh.

Other books by the same author:
Bedbugs, 2000
Impulse, 1996
Shades of Night, 1995
Twilight Time, 1994
Little Brothers, 1988

Other books you might like:
David Case, *The Cell and Other Tales of Horror*, 1971
John Farris, *Scare Tactics*, 1989
Brian Lumley, *Dagon's Bell and Other Discords*, 1994
Graham Masterton, *Flights of Fear*, 1996
Robert R. McCammon, *Blue World*, 1989

687

H.F. HEARD

Dromenon

(East Sussex, England: Tartarus, 2001)

Story type: Collection
Subject(s): Horror; Short Stories; Supernatural

Summary: *Dromenon* consists of ten stories representing the collected weird fiction of a mid-20th century British writer. The title story tells of a man who discovers a mystical channel

to religious experience embodied in the architecture of a Gothic cathedral. ''The Cup'' is the story of a thief whose mystic vision while attempting to steal a religious artifact results in his conversion. ''The Rousing of Mr. Bradegar'' concerns a man transported by a stroke back to the days of his youth. In ''The Weird Fog,'' plants alter the landscape of human civilization by emitting a fog that destroys visibility.

Other books by the same author:
The Black Fox, 1950
The Lost Cavern and Other Tales of the Fantastic, 1948
Doppelgangers, 1947
The Great Fog and Other Weird Tales, 1944
A Taste for Honey, 1941

Other books you might like:
John Burke, *We've Been Waiting for You*, 2000
Shamus Frazer, *Where the Human Pathways End*, 2001
Alexander Hamilton, *Beam of Malice*, 1966
Gerald Kersh, *On an Odd Note*, 1958
H. Russell Wakefield, *Imagine a Man in a Box*, 1931

688

BARRY HOFFMAN

Judas Eyes

(Springfield, Pennsylvania: Gauntlet/Edge, 2001)

Story type: Werewolf Story
Subject(s): Psychic Powers; Rape; Werewolves
Major character(s): Lamar Briggs, Detective—Police; Shara Farris, Detective—Private; Mica Swann, Fugitive
Time period(s): 2000s
Locale(s): Philadelphia, Pennsylvania; Atlanta, Georgia

Summary: Shara, a private detective, teams up with Lamar Briggs to track down a predator, who is cutting a wide swath across the eastern United States, killing men in the act of rape. The murderer proves no ordinary killer, as Shara pieces together clues gleaned from her psychic rapport. The criminal, former dominatrix Mica Swann, is a woman whose family has been so devastated by rape that her internalized rage emerges as a wolf-like monster that slaughters her male victims. A sequel to *Eyes of Prey*.

Where it's reviewed:
Publishers Weekly, June 4, 2001, page 63

Other books by the same author:
Guardian of Lost Souls, 2001
Born Bad, 2000
Eyes of Prey, 1998
Hungry Eyes, 1997
Firefly. . .Burning Bright, 1996

Other books you might like:
Kelley Armstrong, *Bitten*, 2001
Nancy Collins, *Wild Blood*, 1994
Pam Keesey, *Women Who Run with the Werewolves*, 1996
    editor
Lucy Taylor, *Dancing with Demons*, 1998
Edo van Belkom, *Teeth*, 2001

689

JEMIAH JEFFERSON

Voice of the Blood
(New York: Leisure, 2001)

Story type: Vampire Story
Subject(s): Vampires
Major character(s): Ariane Dempsey, Scientist; Orfeo Ricari, Vampire; Daniel, Vampire
Time period(s): 2000s
Locale(s): San Francisco, California; Hollywood, California

Summary: Ariane agrees to honor the request of Orfeo, a 200-year-old vampire, that she kill him, in exchange for time to study his life. However, in the course of working closely with Orfeo, Ariane loses her scientific objectivity, becoming increasingly enamored of the vampire life until she forces him to convert her. First novel.

Other books you might like:

Poppy Z. Brite, *Lost Souls*, 1992
Nancy Collins, *Sunglasses After Dark*, 1989
Sephera Giron, *Eternal Sunset*, 2000
Kyle Marfinn, *Gothique*, 2000
Gail Petersen, *The Making of a Monster*, 1993

690

ROY JOHANSEN

Beyond Belief
(New York: Bantam, 2001)

Story type: Child-in-Peril; Wild Talents
Subject(s): Magicians; Psychic Powers; Religion
Major character(s): Joe Bailey, Detective—Police, Magician (former); Jesse Randall, Child; Garrett Lyles, Murderer
Time period(s): 2000s
Locale(s): Atlanta, Georgia

Summary: Joe Bailey, a magician turned detective, investigates suspicions that young Jesse Randall, a boy with presumed psychic powers, unintentionally killed a parapsychology professor with a shadow storm of awesome energy liberated during his dreams. Though Bailey believes the boy is a fake, Garrett Lyles, an excommunicated member of a fringe millennial cult, believes that Jesse is the long-prophesied ''Child of Light,'' and he will stop at nothing—even murder—to guarantee the boy's safety.

Where it's reviewed:

Kirkus Reviews, January 15, 2001, page 217
Publishers Weekly, March 26, 2001, page 65

Other books by the same author:

The Answer Man, 1999

Other books you might like:

Nicholas Conde, *The Religion*, 1982
John Coyne, *Child of Shadows*, 1990
John Farris, *The Fury*, 1976
Dean R. Koontz, *Servants of Twilight*, 1984

691

STEPHEN JONES, Editor
DAVID SUTTON, Co-Editor

Dark Terrors 5
(London: Orion, 2001)

Story type: Anthology
Series: Dark Terrors. Number 5
Subject(s): Horror; Short Stories; Supernatural

Summary: Most of these 31 stories of horror, fantasy, and the supernatural are published here for the first time. Selections include Christopher Fowler's ''At Home in the Old Pubs of London,'' an urban horror story about a psychopath who obsessively haunts the taverns of London; Caitlin Kiernan's ''Valentia,'' a blend of horror and mythic fantasy about a paleontologist's discovery of a strange archaeological artifact; David J. Schow's ''Why Rudy Can't Read,'' a tale of sexual politics, wild talents and grim retribution; and Ramsey Campbell's ''No Story in It,'' a nightmarish tale of a writer forced to a horrific act of desperation by his failure in the marketplace. The book includes additional works by Peter Straub, Dennis Etchison, Brian Hodge, Kim Newman, Lisa Tuttle, and others. This is the most recent of the anthologies in the long running Pan Book of Horror series. Published in hardcover in 2000.

Other books by the same author:

Dark Terrors 4, 1999 (editor)
Dark Terrors 3, 1997 (editor)
Dark Terrors, 1996 (editor)
Dark Terrors 2, 1996 (editor)
The Best Horror from Fantasy Tales, 1990 (editor)

Other books you might like:

Richard Chizmar, *Subterranean Gallery*, 1999
    William Schafer, co-editor
Dennis Etchison, *Cutting Edge*, 1986
    editor
Kirby McCauley, *Dark Forces*, 1980
    editor
Al Sarrantonio, *999*, 1999
    editor
Herbert van Thal, *The 21st Pan Book of Horror Stories*, 1980
    editor

692

JACK KETCHUM (Pseudonym of Dallas Mayr)

The Lost
(New York: Leisure, 2001)

Story type: Psychological Suspense
Subject(s): Murder; Suspense; Teen Relationships
Major character(s): Ray Pye, Hotel Worker; Charlie Schilling, Police Officer; Kathy Wallace, Teenager
Time period(s): 1960s
Locale(s): Sparta, New Jersey

Summary: In 1965, Ray Pye wantonly kills two girls in a secluded camping area for what he construes as their sexually illicit relationship. Years later, the local police are still trying

to pin the murders on him, and Ray, whose sociopathic tendencies are keyed to his macho self-image, has become a powder keg of confused emotions, waiting for the right spark to touch him off for a violent explosion. Also published as a signed limited edition from CD Publications.

Where it's reviewed:
Hellnotes, June 1, 2001, page 2
Hellnotes, June 1, 2001, page 3
Publishers Weekly, April 23, 2001, page 54

Other books by the same author:
Ladies Night, 1998
She Wakes, 1989
The Girl Next Door, 1989
Hide and Seek, 1984
Off Season, 1980

Other books you might like:
Douglas Borton, *Kane*, 1990
John Farris, *The Aman Cometh*, 1989
Stephen King, *Rose Madder*, 1995
Dean R. Koontz, *Intensity*, 1996
Joe R. Lansdale, *The Savage Season*, 1990

693

CAITLIN R. KIERNAN

Threshold
(New York: Roc, 2001)

Story type: Wild Talents; Ancient Evil Unleashed
Subject(s): Horror; Paleontology; Psychic Powers
Major character(s): Chance Matthews, Scientist (paleontologist), Psychic; Deacon Silvey, Worker, Psychic; Dancy Flammarion, Teenager, Psychic
Time period(s): 2000s
Locale(s): Birmingham, Alabama

Summary: Chance, Deacon, and Dancy are all possessed of psychic skills and arcane knowledge. Though they barely understand its import, Darcy senses it encompasses all the tragedy in their lives and is tied to a primordial locus of supernatural power they must strive to understand and overcome.

Other books by the same author:
Tales of Pain and Wonder, 2000
Candles for Elizabeth, 1998
Silk, 1998

Other books you might like:
Ramsey Campbell, *Incarnate*, 1983
Douglas Clegg, *You Come When I Call You*, 2000
Stephen King, *It*, 1986
Nicholas Royle, *Counterparts*, 1993
Conrad Williams, *Head Injuries*, 1998

694

JEREMY LASSEN, Editor

After Shocks
(San Diego: Freak Press, 2001)

Story type: Anthology
Series: After Shocks
Subject(s): Horror; Short Stories; Supernatural
Locale(s): California

Summary: These 12 previously unpublished stories of horror, fantasy, and magic realism all have southern California settings. Selections include Stephen Woodworth's ''Street Runes'' and Lisa Morton's ''El Cazador,'' both concerned with supernatural horrors encrypted in the work of urban graffiti artists; James Van Pelt's ''Parallel Highways,'' about a latter-day Flying Dutchman unable to exit the Los Angeles freeway; Christa Faust's ''Bodywork,'' in which a woman finds a bizarre makeover artist in the garage and car culture of southern L.A.; and Brian Hodge's ''Driving the Last Spike,'' in which two people sucked dry of their dreams by life on the west coast perpetrate a poetic justice on the person most responsible for their disillusionment.

Where it's reviewed:
Publishers Weekly, March 26, 2001, page 68

Other books you might like:
Dennis Etchison, *The Death Artist*, 2000
Richard Christian Matheson, *Dystopia*, 2000
Frank D. McSherry Jr., *Hollywood Ghosts*, 1991
    Charles G. Waugh, Martin H. Greenberg, co-editors
William F. Nolan, *California Sorcery*, 1999
    William K. Schafer, co-editor
David J. Schow, *Lost Angels*, 1990

695

J. SHERIDAN LE FANU

Spalatro: Two Italian Tales
(Mountain Ash, Wales: Sarob, 2001)

Story type: Collection
Subject(s): Fantasy; Short Stories; Supernatural

Summary: The two stories reprinted here for the first time since their initial periodical appearance in the mid-19th century have only recently been discovered to be the work of Le Fanu, one of the most influential writers of horror fiction in the past two centuries. The title story is presented as the confession of a sentenced criminal who relates the story of his life, one filled with supernatural experiences and bloody murders that have shaped his character. ''Borrhomeo the Astrologer'' is the tale of an alchemist's pursuit of the fabled elixir vitae, and the horrible doom that awaits him after he drinks it. Edited and introduced by Miles Stribling.

Other books by the same author:
The Watcher and Other Weird Stories, 1894
The Purcell Papers, 1880
In a Glass Darkly, 1872
The Chronicles of the Golden Friars, 1871
Ghost Stories and Tales of Mystery, 1851

Horror

Other books you might like:

Marjorie Bowen, *Kecksies and Other Twilight Tales*, 1976
Mary Elizabeth Braddon, *The Cold Embrace*, 2000
Julian Hawthorne, *The Rose of Death and Other Mysterious Delusions*, 1997
M.R. James, *A Warning to the Curious*, 1925
Vernon Lee, *Hauntings: Fantastic Stories*, 1890

696

TIM LEBBON

As the Sun Goes Down

(San Francisco: Night Shade, 2000)

Story type: Collection
Subject(s): Horror; Short Stories; Supernatural

Summary: These 16 stories, half original to the collection, are by a British writer who melds horror, fantasy, and science fiction themes. Most of the stories focus on the cruelty of humans to one another, especially when in life-threatening or apocalyptic situations, as in "The Beach," "Recipe for Disaster," and "Dust," the latter concerned with the horrific fates of a spaceship crew that crash-lands on a planet where their rocket is slowly being buried beneath the sand. In "The Empty Room," a young boy recalls how he let a friend who became trapped in a subterranean room with a supernatural menace languish with no help. "Life Within" tells of a young boy who becomes emotionally obsessed with the birth of his pet dog's litter, to the point where he dangerously identifies with their fate. With an introduction by Ramsey Campbell.

Where it's reviewed:

Hellnotes, February 2, 2001, page 2
Locus, July 2001, page 27
Publishers Weekly, April 2, 2001, page 44

Other books by the same author:

Naming of Parts, 2000
White, 1999
Faith in the Flesh, 1998
Mesmer, 1997

Other books you might like:

Chaz Brenchley, *Blood Waters*, 1996
Simon Clark, *Salt Snake and Other Bloody Cuts*, 1999
Christopher Fowler, *Personal Demons*, 1998
Stephen Laws, *The Midnight Man*, 2000
Mark Morris, *Close to the Bone*, 1994

697

TIM LEBBON
GAVIN WILLIAMS, Co-Author

Hush

(Cardiff, Wales: Razorblade, 2000)

Story type: Ancient Evil Unleashed
Subject(s): Occult; Supernatural
Major character(s): Jacob Alistair Naylor, Activist; Lila, Young Woman; Fade, Magician
Time period(s): 2000s
Locale(s): Beckington, England

Summary: When Jacob botches an antivivisectionist attack on a laboratory, he falls into company with Lila, a young woman whom he found imprisoned inside. With Lila's help, Jacob is reminded of the Order, an occult army whose mission is "to guard against aggressive incursions from transcorporeal realms," and his identity as Hush, a former adept of the Order whose grievous injury in a past supernatural encounter resulted in his memory being wiped clean. Having spent the past 15 years fitting imperfectly into human society, Jacob/Hush is now called on to help the Order fight a steamrolling supernatural onslaught.

Where it's reviewed:

Hellnotes, March 30, 2001, page 4

Other books you might like:

Ramsey Campbell, *Ancient Images*, 1989
Christopher Fowler, *Rune*, 1990
Brian Lumley, *The Burrowers Beneath*, 1974
Mark Morris, *Genesis*, 1999

698

FRITZ LEIBER

The Black Gondolier and Other Stories

(Seattle: Midnight House, 2001)

Story type: Collection
Subject(s): Horror; Fantasy; Short Stories

Summary: This is a retrospective collection of 18 stories of horror and dark fantasy by a writer renowned for both his literary sensibility and his ingenious updating of classic horror themes for modern times. Selections include the title story and "The Black Gondolier," both of which tackle the theme of energy sources that are sentient entities malevolently protecting their anonymity; "The Dead Man," about a physician's experiments with post-hypnotic suggestion and the afterlife; and the mock Gothic "Spider Mansion." With an introduction by John Pelan and an afterword by Steve Savile.

Where it's reviewed:

Hellnotes, April 6, 2001, page 4

Other books by the same author:

The Ghost Light, 1984
Heroes and Horrors, 1978
Night Monsters, 1969
Shadows with Eyes, 1962
Nights Black Agents, 1947

Other books you might like:

Ray Bradbury, *The October Country*, 1955
Joseph Payne Brennan, *Nine Horrors and a Dream*, 1958
Robert A. Heinlein, *The Unpleasant Profession of Jonathan Hoag*, 1959
Henry Kuttner, *A Gnome There Was*, 1950
Richard Matheson, *Shock*, 1961

699

THOMAS LORD

Bound in Blood

(New York: Kensington, 2001)

Story type: Vampire Story
Subject(s): Homosexuality/Lesbianism; Mothers and Sons; Vampires
Major character(s): Jean Luc ''Jack'' Courbet, Writer, Vampire; Claude Halloran, Actor, Model; Noel Courbet, Actress, Vampire
Time period(s): 2000s
Locale(s): New York, New York

Summary: Vampire Jack Courbet preys on Manhattan's gay community even as he cultivates his affections for the mortal Claude. Jack's biggest nemesis is not the police detectives who are investigating his murders, but his mother Noel, who like Jack was converted by his stepfather, and who has never forgiven her son for killing her husband two centuries before. A first novel.

Other books you might like:

Gary Bowen, *Diary of a Vampire*, 1995
Poppy Z. Brite, *Lost Souls*, 1992
John Peyton Cooke, *Out for Blood*, 1991
Mary Ann Mitchell, *Sips*, 2000
Anne Rice, *Interview with the Vampire*, 1976

700

ALVIN LU

The Hell Screens

(New York: Four Walls Eight Windows, 2000)

Story type: Occult; Ghost Story
Subject(s): Asian Americans; Ghosts; Serial Killer
Major character(s): Cheng-Ming, Student; Sylvia, Student; Fatty, Filmmaker
Time period(s): 2000s
Locale(s): Taipei, Taiwan

Summary: Cheng-Ming's academic interest in a serial killer whom some claim committed suicide acquaints him with the killer's former associates and an assortment of people obsessed with the afterlife. Increasingly sensitized to the spirit world, Cheng-Ming soon has visions of ghosts and is threatened by the gradual erosion of boundaries separating the real world he knows from the world of the supernatural. This first novel subtly employs the supernatural as a device for probing questions of personal and cultural identity.

Other books you might like:

Ryunosuke Akutagawa, *The Essential Akutagawa*, 1999
Deborah Boehm, *Ghost of a Smile*, 2001
Philip K. Dick, *The Man in the High Castle*, 1962
Yumiko Kurahashi, *The Woman with the Flying Head and Other Stories*, 1998
Dan Simmons, *Song of Kali*, 1985

701

LEOPOLDO LUGONES

Strange Forces

(Pittsburgh: Latin American Literary Review, 2001)

Story type: Collection
Subject(s): Fantasy; Short Stories; Supernatural

Summary: These 12 tales of horror and fantasy with a metaphysical twist were first published in 1906 by an Argentinian writer. Selections include ''The Bloat Toad,'' a tale of physical horror in which a boy is menaced by an amphibious anomaly; ''An Inexplicable Phenomenon,'' about a scientist haunted by the image of an ape that only he can see; ''Psychon,'' about a man driven mad when he learns to liberate liquid thought; and the spirit narrative ''Origins of the Flood.'' Translated by Gilbert Alter-Gilbert.

Other books you might like:

Jorge Luis Borges, *Labyrinths*, 1962
Dino Buzzati, *Catastrophe*, 1985
Thomas Colchie, *A Hammock Beneath the Mangoes*, 1991
Julio Cortazar, *The End of the Game and Other Stories*, 1967
Horacio Quiroga, *The Decapitated Chicken and Other Stories*, 1976

702

BRIAN LUMLEY

Avengers

(New York: Tor, 2001)

Story type: Vampire Story
Series: Necroscope. Number 13
Subject(s): Espionage; Psychic Powers; Vampires
Major character(s): Jake Cutter, Spy; Nephran Malinari, Vampire; Ben Trask, Spy
Time period(s): 2000s
Locale(s): London, England; Sirpsindigi, Turkey

Summary: Nephran Malinari and the Lady Vavara, vampires from the otherworldy vampire universe Sunside/Starside, have escaped near-death in Greece, and continue their mission to seed the world with the spores of virulent fungi that could convert the entire world to vampirism. Meanwhile, Jake Cutter, a Necroscope and the sole human with the power to fight the vampire onslaught, wrestles with a vampire consciousness he was tricked into admitting into his own mind. Jake also banters with Harry Keogh, the original Necroscope, who instructs him in the proper use of his powers, but whom he holds at arm's length, owing to Harry's own vampire taint.

Other books by the same author:

Defilers, 2000
Invaders, 1999
Resurgence, 1996
The Lost Years, 1995
The Last Aerie, 1993

Other books you might like:

Ron Dee, *Blood Lust*, 1990
Robert R. McCammon, *They Thirst*, 1981
Yvonne Navarro, *Afterage*, 1993

Dan Simmons, *Children of the Night*, 1992
John Steakley, *Vampire*, 1990

703

BRIAN LUMLEY

The Whisperer and Other Voices
(New York: Tor, 2001)

Story type: Collection
Subject(s): Horror; Short Stories; Supernatural

Summary: These nine selections of supernatural and non-supernatural horror range in their approach from the gruesomely comic ''The Disapproval of Jeremy Cleave,'' in which a glass eye and prosthetic leg salvaged from a dead man stalk his amorous widow, to the suspenseful ''No Sharks in the Med,'' about a newlywed couple desperately trying to escape pursuing murderers on a private island. The short novel *The Return of the Deep Ones*, a homage to the Cthulhu Mythos of H.P. Lovecraft, is about a man who discovers that he is related to a race of aquatic creatures descended from a monstrous supernatural entity.

Where it's reviewed:
Hellnotes, March 2, 2001, page 4
Kirkus Reviews, November 1, 2000, page 1509

Other books by the same author:
A Coven of Vampires, 1998
Dagon's Bell and Other Discords, 1994
Return of the Deep Ones and Other Mythos Tales, 1994
Fruiting Bodies and Other Fungi, 1993
The Last Rite, 1993

Other books you might like:
Stephen King, *Night Shift*, 1978
Richard Laymon, *A Good Secret Place*, 1993
Brian McNaughton, *Worse Things Waiting*, 2000
Stanley Sargent, *Ancient Exhumations*, 1999
F. Paul Wilson, *The Barrens and Others*, 1998

704

ARTHUR MACHEN

A Fragment of Life
(East Sussex, England: Tartarus, 2000)

Story type: Occult
Subject(s): Fantasy; Marriage; Supernatural
Major character(s): Edward Darnell, Clerk; Mary Darnell, Housewife; Alice, Servant
Time period(s): 1900s
Locale(s): Shepherd's Bush, England

Summary: Bogged down in the mundane routines of their newly married life, Edward and Mary find a way to recapture the wonder of life as they perceived it when children. The ecstasy Edward experiences in his flight from the ordinary transports him to a world of supernatural potential and a forgotten mystical legacy. The story is published as it first appeared in a magazine in 1904, and with the revised ending written for its publication in 1906 for Machen's collection *The House of Souls*.

Other books by the same author:
The Terror, 1917
The Great Return, 1915
The Hill of Dreams, 1907
The House of Souls, 1906
The Three Impostors, 1895

Other books you might like:
Algernon Blackwood, *Julius LeVallon, an Episode*, 1916
Robert Hichens, *Flames*, 1897
Edgar Jepson, *Number 19*, 1910
H.P. Lovecraft, *The Dream Quest of Unknown Kadath*, 1955
Sarban, *The Doll Maker and Other Tales of the Uncanny*, 1953

705

ELIZABETH MASSIE

Wire Mesh Mothers
(New York: Leisure, 2001)

Story type: Psychological Suspense; Evil Children
Subject(s): Murder; Serial Killer; Detection
Major character(s): Kate McDolen, Teacher; Angela ''Tony'' Petinske, Teenager; Mistie Dawn Henderson, Child, Abuse Victim
Time period(s): 2000s
Locale(s): Pippins, Virginia

Summary: Hoping to save an abused child from further torment and neglect, Kate McDolen abducts young Mistie Dawn, intending to flee over the Canadian border. Before she can even leave her small Virginia town, though, she is carjacked by Tony, a delinquent teenage girl on the lam for a murder, who takes both Kate and Mistie Dawn as hostages on a terrifying cross-country trip to Texas to see her estranged father.

Other books by the same author:
Welcome Back to the Night, 1999
Shadow Dreams, 1996
Sineater, 1994
Southern Discomfort, 1993

Other books you might like:
Lynda Barry, *Cruddy*, 1999
Ramsey Campbell, *The One Safe Place*, 1995
Richard Laymon, *Come out Tonight*, 1999
Billie Sue Mosiman, *Night Cruise*, 1992
Whitley Strieber, *Billy*, 1990

706

GRAHAM MASTERTON

The Doorkeepers
(New York: Severn House, 2001)

Story type: Occult
Subject(s): Alternate History; Business; Occult
Major character(s): Josh Winward, Animal Lover; Frank Mordant, Businessman; Ellen Tibibnia, Psychic
Time period(s): 2000s
Locale(s): London, England

Summary: Josh Winward travels to London to reclaim the body of his murdered sister, Julia, and is surprised to hear that no one knew of her whereabouts for a year. Private investigation and the lucky decoding of a magic ritual in the words of an old nursery rhyme transport Josh to an alternate London. This is a second-rate world where the teachings of Oliver Cromwell are still revered, and where Julia's murderer, an exploitative businessman who makes snuff films on the side, is determined to dispose of anyone who probes too deeply into his work.

Other books by the same author:
The Chosen Child, 1997
The House That Jack Built, 1996
Spirit, 1995
The Sleepless, 1993
Prey, 1992

Other books you might like:
Jack Finney, *Time and Again*, 1970
Christopher Fowler, *Roofworld*, 1988
Stephen Laws, *Macabre*, 1994
Steve Lockley, *The Ragchild*, 2000
    Paul Lewis, co-author
China Mieville, *King Rat*, 1998

707

L.H. MAYNARD, Editor
M.P.N. SIMS, Co-Editor

Darkness Rising: Night's Soft Pains

(Gillette, New Jersey: Wildside/Cosmos, 2001)

Story type: Anthology
Series: Darkness Rising
Subject(s): Horror; Supernatural; Short Stories

Summary: Eighteen stories of atmospheric, understated horror are presented here. The sole reprint, Howard Jones' ''Marriott's Monkey,'' is a tale of obsession and psychological horror, concerning a man haunted by the memory of a demonic simian, whose bite may or may not have infected him with its beastliness. Other selections include Kurt Newton's ''The Old Mill,'' about a monstrous creature in an abandoned mill that steals the child of a human couple, and Walt Jarvis' ''Beggar and Child,'' in which a man is haunted—possibly psychologically, possibly supernaturally—by the vision of a beggar woman whose death he accidentally caused.

Other books by the same author:
Echoes of Darkness, 2000

Other books you might like:
Claudia O'Keefe, *Ghosttide*, 1993
    editor
Paul F. Olson, *Post Mortem*, 1989
    David B. Silva, co-editor
Gerald Page, *Nameless Places*, 1975
    editor
Barbara Roden, *Shadows and Silence*, 2000
    Christopher Roden, co-editor
Wendy Webb, *Gothic Ghosts*, 1997
    Charles L. Grant, co-editor

708

BRIAN MCNAUGHTON

Downward to Darkness

(Gillette, New Jersey: Wildside, 2000)

Story type: Occult; Witchcraft
Subject(s): Horror; Supernatural; Witches and Witchcraft
Major character(s): Patrick Laughlin, Teenager; Frank Laughlin, Artist; Jane Miniter, Teenager
Time period(s): 2000s
Locale(s): Mount Tabor, Connecticut

Summary: Shortly after the Laughlins move into the old mill house that belonged to a relative of his Rose Laughlin's, Rose's son Patrick and husband Frank are each haunted by the vision of a supernaturally seductive woman. On Halloween night, during a party the Laughlins throw, the ancient legacy of witchcraft associated with Mordred Glendower, one of Rose's ancestors, is resurrected through the agency of the woman to take root in the modern day. A revision of *Satan's Mistress*, first published by the author in 1978.

Other books by the same author:
Gemini Rising, 2000
More Nasty Stories, 2000
Nasty Stories, 2000
Worse Things Waiting, 2000
The Throne of Bones, 1997

Other books you might like:
Lisa Cantrell, *Torments*, 1990
Simon Clark, *Darkness Demands*, 2001
Dennis Higman, *Pranks*, 1983
Richard Laymon, *Once upon a Halloween*, 2000
Jeffrey Sackett, *Candlemas Eve*, 1988

709

BRIAN MCNAUGHTON

Gemini Rising

(Gillette, New Jersey: Wildside, 2000)

Story type: Occult; Ancient Evil Unleashed
Subject(s): Cults; Mothers and Daughters; Supernatural
Major character(s): Marcia Creighton, Journalist; Ken Creighton, Architect; Melody Creighton, Teenager
Time period(s): 2000s
Locale(s): Riveredge, New Jersey

Summary: Violent deaths, unexplained supernatural phenomena and the presence of hippies and cultists are on the increase in Riveredge. Suspicions inevitably tie them to Marcia Creighton, whose daughter Melody was born out of wedlock during her mostly forgotten life in a hippie commune decades before, and who seems to know secrets about the occult forces behind them that are a mystery to her mother and stepfather. Loosely based on H.P. Lovecraft's story ''The Dunwich Horror,'' this is a revision of the novel *Satan's Love Child*, first published in 1977.

Other books by the same author:
Downward to Darkness, 2000
Worse Things Waiting, 2000

Even More Nasty Stories, 2000
Nasty Stories, 2000
The Throne of Bones, 1997

Other books you might like:
D.A. Fowler, *The Devil's End*, 1992
Ira Levin, *Son of Rosemary*, 1967
David Selzer, *The Omen*, 1976
Peter Straub, *Mr. X*, 1999

710

BRIAN MCNAUGHTON

Nasty Stories

(Gillette, New Jersey: Wildside, 2000)

Story type: Collection
Subject(s): Horror; Fantasy; Short Stories

Summary: Most of these 25 stories, eight original to the volume, are leavened with morbid humor and end with sardonic twists. ''The Conversion of Saint Monocarp'' concerns the comeuppance a young woman gets when she performs one too many soul transfers trying to obtain the perfect body for her lover. ''Nothing but the Best'' is an amusing tale of the dangers of shapeshifing by occult means. A subset of stories including ''The Dunwich Lodger'' and ''Herbert West—Reincarnated'' are wry variations on Lovecraftian themes.

Other books by the same author:
More Nasty Stories, 2000
The Throne of Bones, 1997

Other books you might like:
P.H. Cannon, *Scream for Jeeves*, 1994
Lord Dunsany, *A Dreamer's Tales*, 1910
William I.I. Read, *Degrees of Fear*, 2000
Don Webb, *A Spell for the Fulfillment of Desire*, 1996
John Whitbourn, *Binscombe Tales*, 1998

711

BRIAN MCNAUGHTON

Worse Things Waiting

(Gillette, New Jersey: Wildside, 2000)

Story type: Occult; Witchcraft
Subject(s): Horror; Supernatural; Witches and Witchcraft
Major character(s): Amy Miniter, Real Estate Agent; Martin Paige, Writer; Howard Ashcroft, Occultist
Time period(s): 2000s
Locale(s): Mount Tabor, Connecticut

Summary: Real estate agent Amy Miniter attempts to sell a Mount Tabor home with an unsavory past that has adversely affected her own life, unaware her efforts have resurrected centuries old forces of witchcraft trying to gain a foothold in the modern world. An informal sequel to *Downward to Darkness*, this is a revision of the author's 1979 novel *Satan's Seductress*.

Other books by the same author:
Downward to Darkness, 2000
More Nasty Stories, 2000

Nasty Stories, 2000
Worse Things Waiting, 2000
The Throne of Bones, 1997

Other books you might like:
Marion Zimmer Bradley, *Witch Hill*, 1990
Ramsey Campbell, *Nazareth Hill*, 1996
Ruby Jean Jensen, *Night Thunder*, 1995
Graham Masterton, *The House That Jack Built*, 1996
Tamara Thorne, *Haunted*, 1995

712

BILLIE SUE MOSIMAN

Red Moon Rising

(New York: DAW, 2001)

Story type: Vampire Story
Subject(s): Illness; Teen Relationships; Vampires
Major character(s): Della Joan Cambian, Teenager, Vampire; Mentor, Vampire; Charles Upton, Businessman, Wealthy
Time period(s): 2000s
Locale(s): Houston, Texas

Summary: With the guidance of Mentor, a vampire elder, Della Cambian has learned how to live with her mutated form of porphyria and avoided becoming either a vampiric predator or craven. Billionaire Charles Upton, afflicted with the deadly form of regular porphyria, has begun looking into vampire legends to find a cure, and his manipulations threaten the delicate balance of life not only for Della, but for all other vampires with her condition who have learned how to fit unobtrusively into normal mortal company.

Other books by the same author:
Stiletto, 1996
Night Cruise, 1992
Deadly Affections, 1990

Other books you might like:
Scott Ciencin, *Parliament of Blood*, 1992
John Peyton Cooke, *Out for Blood*, 1991
Pat Graversen, *Precious Blood*, 1993
Stephen Spruill, *Rulers of Darkness*, 1995
Karen Taylor, *Blood of My Blood*, 2000

713

NATASHA MOSTERT

The Midnight Side

(New York: Morrow, 2001)

Story type: Wild Talents
Subject(s): Afterlife; Dreams and Nightmares
Major character(s): Isabelle Dewitt, Architect; Justin Temple, Businessman; Michael Chapman, Photographer
Time period(s): 2000s
Locale(s): London, England

Summary: Isa Dewitt is made sole beneficiary of her friend, Alette Temple, who hopes that Isa will follow instructions Alette had written before her suspicious death to ruin the pharmaceutical company of her despised husband, Justin. Alette makes contact with Isa after her death through the lucid

dreaming the two women shared as girls, and as Isa begins to fall in love with Justin, she suspects that Alette is so obsessive in her determination to destroy Justin that she might very well reach from beyond the grave to overwhelm Isa's personality. First novel.

Where it's reviewed:
Kirkus Reviews, December 1, 2000, page 1637

Other books you might like:
Ramsey Campbell, *To Wake the Dead*, 1980
Tananarive Due, *The Between*, 1995
Stephen King, *Insomnia*, 1994
Daniel Quinn, *Dreamer*, 1988
Kelley Wilde, *Makoto*, 1990

714

J. NEWMAN

Holy Rollers

(Grandview, Missouri: DarkTales, 2001)

Story type: Psychological Suspense
Subject(s): Fundamentalism; Religion
Major character(s): Jack Morris, Spouse; Mary Morris, Housewife; Joseph Franks, Detective—Police
Time period(s): 2000s
Locale(s): South

Summary: Under the pretense of being devout members of the Sons of the Ever-Glowing Light fundamentalist sect, two psychopathic brothers invade the house of Jack Morris and his wife Mary, subjecting them to physical and psychological tortures to get them to repent their "sinful" ways. First book.

Other books you might like:
Simon Maginn, *Virgins and Martyrs*, 1995
Robert R. McCammon, *Mystery Walk*, 1984
Michael Paine, *The Colors of Hell*, 1990
Tamara Thorne, *Moonfall*, 1996
Elleston Trevor, *The Sister*, 1994

715

WILLIAM F. NOLAN

Things Beyond Midnight

(Northridge, California: Babbage, 2001)

Story type: Collection
Subject(s): Horror; Short Stories; Supernatural

Summary: The twenty stories and a screenplay in *Things Beyond Midnight* represent the author's best dark fantasy fiction written before 1984. The stories are simple weird tales, mixing elements of fantasy, suspense, and science fiction and ending with carefully crafted horrific twists. Contents include "He Kilt It with a Stick," in which a man's lifelong disdain of cats is equal only to their malevolent attitude towards him; "Something Nasty," in which an adult's effort to scare a child with the threat of something nasty inside her rebounds horribly; and "Dark Winner," in which a man's efforts to revisit his childhood home lead to his absorption by his childhood self. With an introduction by Richard Christian Matheson. First published in 1984.

Other books by the same author:
Night Shapes: Excursions into Terror, 1995
Blood Sky, 1991
Alien Horizons, 1974
Impact 20, 1963

Other books you might like:
Charles Beaumont, *Selected Stories*, 1988
Jerome Bixby, *Space by the Tail*, 1964
Ed Gorman, *The Dark Fantastic*, 2001
George Clayton Johnson, *All of Us Are Dying*, 1999
Richard Matheson, *Collected Stories*, 1989

716

OLIVER ONIONS

Ghost Stories

(East Sussex, England: Tartarus, 2001)

Story type: Collection
Subject(s): Horror; Short Stories; Supernatural

Summary: Twenty-two stories represent the complete ghostly fiction of an artist turned writer whose fiction appeared in the late Victorian and Edwardian eras. Included is the landmark story "The Beckoning Fair One," about an artist overwhelmed by the obsessively amorous ghost of a woman who haunts the house in which he lets a room. Other selections include "The Painted Face," a tale of precognition and possible reincarnation, and "The Rosewood Door," in which a doorway salvaged from a house under demolition gives access to a supernatural dimension. Reprint of a volume first published in 1935.

Other books by the same author:
Bells Rung Backwards, 1953
The Painted Face, 1929
Ghosts in Daylight, 1924
Tower of Oblivion, 1921
Widdershins, 1911

Other books you might like:
Robert W. Chambers, *The King in Yellow*, 1895
Walter de la Mare, *The Riddle and Other Stories*, 1923
Arthur Hichens, *Tongues of Conscience*, 1900
Henry James, *The Ghostly Tales of Henry James*, 1948
Arthur Quiller-Couch, *Old Fires and Profitable Ghosts*, 1900

717

TIM PARKS

Mimi's Ghost

(New York: Arcade, 2001)

Story type: Serial Killer
Subject(s): Family; Ghosts; Murder
Major character(s): Morris Duckworth, Con Artist, Serial Killer; Paola Trevisan, Spouse (of Morris), Relative (Mimi's sister); Bobo Posenato, Businessman
Time period(s): 1990s
Locale(s): Verona, Italy

Summary: Acting in the belief that he is being guided by the loving ghost of Massimina "Mimi" Trevisan—the girlfriend

Horror

whom he murdered in a botched extortion caper and whose spirit he suddenly begins seeing manifesting in works of classical art—Morris Duckworth embarks on a partly inadvertent murder spree, killing his brother-in-law business associate, his wife and those who would stand in the way of his efforts to assume control of the Trevisan family wine business, which he has been led to believe he rightfully should run. A black comedy sequel to the pseudonymously published *Cara Massimina* (a.k.a. *Juggling the Stars*).

Where it's reviewed:
Kirkus Reviews, December 1, 2000, page 1639

Other books by the same author:
Destiny, 1999
Europa, 1997
Shear, 1993
Goodness, 1991
Cara Massimina, 1990

Other books you might like:
Ramsey Campbell, *The Count of Eleven*, 1991
Brett Easton Ellis, *American Psycho*, 1991
Patricia Highsmith, *The Talented Mr. Ripley*, 1955
Henry Kressing, *The Cook*, 1965

718

NORMAN PARTRIDGE

The Man with the Barbed Wire Fists

(San Francisco: Night Shade, 2001)

Story type: Collection
Subject(s): Horror; Short Stories; Supernatural

Summary: This volume collects 24 stories, including two originals, many laced with dark humor and explorations of the dark side of life in ordinary America. Included are the title story, a variant on the Frankenstein theme; ''The Hollow Man,'' told from the viewpoint of a terrifying creature that commandeers the bodies of its victims; ''Where the Woodbine Twineth,'' a rural horror story; and ''The Last Kiss,'' a morbidly amusing tale of a young man whose obsessive love for a fellow student leads to his becoming a serial killer. The novellas *Spyder*, *The Red Right Hand*, and *The Bars on Satan's Jailhouse* all published originally as chapbooks, are included, as well as an introduction and bibliography by the author.

Other books by the same author:
The Crow: Wicked Prayer, 2000
Wildest Dreams, 1998
Bad Intentions, 1996
Slippin into Darkness, 1996
Mr. Fox and Other Feral Tales, 1992

Other books you might like:
Nancy Collins, *Nameless Sins*, 1994
Dennis Etchison, *Red Dreams*, 1984
Ed Gorman, *Prisoners and Other Stories*, 1992
Joe R. Lansdale, *Bestsellers Guaranteed*, 1993
Elizabeth Massie, *Shadow Dreams*, 1996

719

ROGER PATER

Mystic Voices

(Ashcroft, British Columbia: Ash-Tree Press, 2001)

Story type: Occult; Collection
Subject(s): Clergy; Religion; Supernatural

Summary: This collection of 14 connected stories is related as the experiences of a 19th century cleric to his nephew, all involving premonitions and ''direct speech,'' in which a state of religious grace renders the narrator sensitive to supernatural communications. ''The Warnings'' concerns the narrator's premonition of his brother's death while attending a Shakespeare play. In ''The Persecution Chalice,'' an Easter visit to another parish immures the narrator in a pageant of menace and awe transpiring centuries before. In ''The Priest's Hiding Place,'' the cleric discovers a secret hiding place for priests last used ages ago still resonates with the cadences of the services they gave there. Originally published in 1923, this volume is edited by David G. Rowlands, who has also synopsized the author's book *My Cousin Philip*, which describes factual events in the author's life that led to the writing of the stories.

Other books by the same author:
My Cousin Philip, 1924

Other books you might like:
A.C. Benson, *The Hill of Trouble and Other Stories*, 1903
Robert Hugh Benson, *The Light Invisible*, 1903
M.R. James, *Ghost Stories of an Antiquary*, 1904
Basil Smith, *The Scallion Stone*, 1980
E.G. Swain, *Stoneground Ghost Tales*, 1912

720

CLIVE PEMBERTON

The Weird O' It

(Seattle: Midnight House, 2000)

Story type: Collection
Subject(s): Horror; Short Stories; Supernatural

Summary: This reprint of a horror fiction collection published in the early 20th century includes an additional previously uncollected story. The stories are basic weird tales with an often gruesome element, including ''The Spider,'' in which a house is menaced by a giant blood drinking spider; ''The Pool,'' about a pool haunted by the ghost of a drowning victim; and ''The Will of Luke Carlowe,'' the tale of a strange bequest and a return from the grave. The previously uncollected ''The Mark of the Beast'' tells of the transmigration of a beast's soul into a man's body. Introduction by John Pelan.

Other books by the same author:
The Way of the World, 1921
A Member of Tattersals, 1920
The Harvest of Deceit, 1908

Other books you might like:
Eugene Ascher, *Uncanny Adventures*, 1946
Hugh B. Cave, *Murgunstrumm and Others*, 1977

Frederick Cowles, *Fear Walks the Night*, 1993
Dick Donovan, *The Corpse Light and Other Tales of Terror*, 1999
R. Thurston Hopkins, *Horror Parade*, 1945

721

ALICE PERRIN

The Sistrum and Other Ghost Stories
(Mountain Ash, Wales: Sarob, 2001)

Story type: Collection
Subject(s): Horror; Short Stories; Supernatural

Summary: These 15 stories of the weird and supernatural are by a British writer from the turn of the 20th century. Many of the selections are set in colonial India, the author's temporary home, including "Caulfield's Crime," about a man hounded by a beast that has absorbed the soul of a native he killed; "In the Next Room," about a haunted dwelling in which a crime from the past is re-enacted; and the title story, which concerns an antiquarian artifact once the center of a savage primitive ritual and now continuing to exert its malignant influence on its modern owners. Edited and introduced by Richard Dalby.

Other books by the same author:
Rough Passages, 1926
Tales That Are Told, 1917
Red Records, 1906
East of Suez, 1901

Other books you might like:
B.M. Croker, *Number 90 and Other Ghost Stories*, 2000
Vernon Lee, *The Snake Lady and Other Stories*, 1954
Mary E. Penn, *In the Dark and Other Ghost Stories*, 2000
Edith Wharton, *The Ghost Feeler*, 1996

722

TOM PICCIRILLI

The Night Class
(Centreville, Virginia: Shadowlands, 2001)

Story type: Wild Talents; Psychological Suspense
Subject(s): Murder; College Life; Suspense
Major character(s): Caleb Prentiss, Student—College
Time period(s): 2000s
Locale(s): United States

Summary: Struggling with scholastics and with alcoholic proclivities, Caleb Prentiss returns to college after winter break and discovers that Sylvia Campbell, a young woman who temporarily stayed in his dorm room during the interval, was murdered there. The sudden eruption of bleeding stigmata on his hands exacerbates Cal's obsession with discovering the reason why his school wants to hush the killing up, and eventually leads him to clues that implicate the school and members of the faculty in the murder.

Other books by the same author:
The Deceased, 2000
Hexes, 1999
Deep into That Darkness Peering, 1998
Pentacle, 1995

Dark Father, 1990
Other books you might like:
Douglas Clegg, *Goat Dance*, 1989
Sean Desmond, *Adams Fall*, 2000
Bentley Little, *The University*, 1995
Mark Morris, *Toady*, 1990
Donna Tartt, *The Secret History*, 1992

723

TIM POWERS

Declare
(New York: Morrow, 2001)

Story type: Occult; Ancient Evil Unleashed
Subject(s): Demons; Espionage; Mythology
Major character(s): Andrew Hale, Professor, Spy; Kim Philby, Spy, Historical Figure; Elena Teresa Ceniza-Bendiga, Spy
Time period(s): 1940s; 1960s
Locale(s): London, England; Mount Ararat, Turkey

Summary: As an agent in a secret branch of British Intelligence, Andrew Hale participates in Operation Declare, a covert espionage maneuver through which he learns that the djinn on Mount Ararat—fallen angels of biblical renown—are being used as protective occult weapons by the Soviet Union. Hale's failure to destroy the djinn during a horrific mission in World War II sets the stage for a return to Mount Ararat at the height of the Cold War, where he discovers an occult destiny predetermined before his birth which ties him to the legendary British double agent Kim Philby.

Other books by the same author:
Earthquake Weather, 1997
Expiration Date, 1995
Last Call, 1992
The Stress of Her Regard, 1989
On Stranger Tides, 1987

Other books you might like:
Robert R. McCammon, *The Wolf's Hour*, 1989
Kim Newman, *The Bloody Red Baron*, 1995
Dennis Wheatley, *They Used Dark Forces*, 1964
F. Paul Wilson, *Black Wind*, 1989
F. Paul Wilson, *The Keep*, 1981

724

TIM POWERS

Night Moves and Other Stories
(Burton, Michigan: Subterranean, 2001)

Story type: Collection
Subject(s): Fantasy; Horror; Short Stories

Summary: Six stories, two written in collaboration with James Blaylock, represent the complete short fiction of a writer known for his indefinable blends of fantasy, horror, and science fiction themes. The title story concerns a man pursued all his life by a strange woman, who turns out to be the person his aborted older sister would have been. "The Way Down the Hill" tells of a species that ensures its immortality by periodically displacing the souls of newborn children and

Horror

using their bodies to grow to maturity. In "Where They Are Hid," a man is haunted by the twin brother he never knew, who has found a way to jump back in time into an alternate reality. Introduction by Blaylock and story notes by the author. Published as a signed limited edition.

Other books by the same author:
Delcare, 2001
Earthquake Weather, 1997
Expiration Date, 1995
Last Call, 1992
The Stress of Her Regard, 1989

Other books you might like:
James P. Blaylock, *Thirteen Phantasms*, 2000
Ray Bradbury, *The Stories of Ray Bradbury*, 1981
Jack Cady, *The Night We Buried Road Dog*, 1998
Charles De Lint, *Dreams Underfoot*, 1993
Harlan Ellison, *Deathbird Stories*, 1975

725

ROBERT M. PRICE, Editor

Acolytes of Cthulhu
(Minneapolis: Fedogan & Bremer, 2001)

Story type: Anthology
Subject(s): Horror; Short Stories; Supernatural

Summary: Twenty-five stories show the influence of horror master H.P. Lovecraft and the mythology of otherworldy beings he created to embody the awesome and alienating indifference of the universe toward mankind. Selections are more Gothic than genuinely Lovecraftian and include Earl Pierce's tale of a family's vampire curse, "Doom of the House of Duryea;" Manly Wade Wellman's "The Letters of Cold Fire," about the dangers of studying a book of forbidden lore; Peter Cannon's tale of a magically cursed talisman, "The Pewter Ring;" and Arthur Pendragon's "The Crib of Hell," the story of a witch's curse and a family's tainted blood line. Also included are stories by David H. Keller, John Glasby, Jorge Luis Borges, and Joseph Payne Brennan.

Other books by the same author:
The Innsmouth Cycle, 1998
The Hastur Cycle, 1997
The Nyarlathotep Cycle, 1997
The New Lovecraft Circle, 1996
Tales of the Lovecraft Mythos, 1992

Other books you might like:
Edward P. Berglund, *Disciples of Cthulhu*, 1973
    editor
August Derleth, *Tales of the Cthulhu Mythos*, 1969
Steve Jones, *Shadows over Innsmouth*, 1994
    editor
Thomas K. Stratman, *Cthulhu's Heirs*, 1994
    editor
Robert Weinberg, *Lovecraft's Legacy*, 1990
    Martin H. Greenberg, co-editor

726

JEAN RABE, Editor
MARTIN H. GREENBERG, Co-Editor

Historical Hauntings
(New York: DAW, 2001)

Story type: Ghost Story
Subject(s): Ghosts; Historical

Summary: The ghosts in these 18 tales of hauntings embody aspects of the historical past. Selections are all original to the book and include Brian M. Thomsen's "In the Charnel House," in which an unemployed lawyer finds himself haunted by specters of the Nazi holocaust that have a peculiar resonance with his life, and Brian Hopkins' "Diving the Coolidge," about a man whose undersea salvage operation becomes an odyssey that forces him to confront his personal past. Stories by Andre Norton, John Helfers, Bruce Holland Rogers, and others are also included.

Other books you might like:
Claudia O'Keefe, *Ghosttide*, 1993
Paul F. Olson, *Post-Mortem*, 1989
    David B. Silva, co-editor
Peter Straub, *Peter Straub's Ghosts*, 1995
Gahan Wilson, *Gahan Wilson's Ultimate Haunted House*, 1996

727

STEPHEN MARK RAINEY

Balak
(Gillette, New Jersey: Wildside, 2000)

Story type: Occult
Subject(s): Cults; Horror; Supernatural
Major character(s): Claire Challis, Artist; Mike Selby, Paralegal; Ingram Potter, Detective—Police
Time period(s): 2000s
Locale(s): Chicago, Illinois

Summary: Claire Challis learns of the Church of the Seven Stars and its strange adherents while helping to track down a missing child. It turns out that leaders of the church abducted Claire's own child several years before, as a sacrifice to Balak, the demonic being of biblical renown whom they worship, and they are now grooming her as the last sacrifice necessary for their takeover of the world.

Other books by the same author:
The Last Trumpet, 2000
Fugue Devil and Other Weird Horrors, 1993

Other books you might like:
Ray Garton, *Dark Channel*, 1992
Ira Levin, *Son of Rosemary*, 1997
John Shirley, *Cellars*, 1982
Whitley Strieber, *The Night Church*, 1983
Robert Weinberg, *The Black Lodge*, 1991

728

STEPHEN MARK RAINEY

The Last Trumpet
(Gillette, New Jersey: Wildside, 2000)

Story type: Collection
Subject(s): Horror; Short Stories; Supernatural

Summary: Several of these 13 previously published stories contain Lovecraftian themes. They include ''Sabbath of the Black Goat,'' about a household terrorized by extradimensional beings, and ''Threnody'' and ''The Spheres of Sound,'' both concerned with music as a passport to otherworldly realms of horror. ''The Spiritual Radio'' is a dream fantasy and ''The Grey House'' an old-fashioned tale of an abandoned house haunted by an unspeakable evil.

Other books by the same author:
Balak, 2000
Fugue Devil and Other Weird Horrors, 1993

Other books you might like:
Edward P. Berglund, *Shards of Darkness*, 2000
Stanley Sargent, *Ancient Exhumations*, 1999
William R. Stotler, *The Final Diary Entry of Kees Hujgens*, 1995
Steve Rasnic Tem, *Decoded Mirrors*, 1992
Jeffrey Thomas, *Bones of the Old Ones and Other Lovecraftian Tales*, 1995

729

OCTAVIO RAMOS JR.

Smoke Signals
(North Webster, Indiana: Delirium, 2001)

Story type: Collection
Subject(s): Horror; Short Stories; Supernatural

Summary: Eight stories of horror and dark fantasy, several with southwestern themes and settings, are collected here. Contents include ''Chico's Hand,'' in which a magically endowed spider substitutes for an outlaw's amputated hand; ''The Call,'' about a man with a preternatural sympathy for spirits of the woods; and ''Punk Bitch,'' in which a punk rocker turns gruesome self-mutilation into a type of performance art. First collection.

Other books you might like:
Casey Czichas, *The Candlelight Readers*, 1999
Greg G. Gifune, *Down to Sleep*, 1999
Michael Laimo, *Demons, Freaks and Other Abnormalities*, 1999
Newton E. Streeter, *Noise and Other Night Terrors*, 1998
Stacy Layne Wilson, *Horrors of the Holy*, 2000

730

WILLIAM I.I. READ

Degrees of Fear
(Mountain Ash, Wales: Sarob, 2000)

Story type: Collection
Subject(s): Horror; Humor; Short Stories
Major character(s): Dennistoun, Professor (don)
Time period(s): 20th century
Locale(s): England

Summary: In these eight stories of supernatural humor, all hell breaks loose when Dennistoun and and his fellow dons of Usher College bumble into things that mankind was not meant to know. Selections include ''Call of the Tentacle,'' in which Dennistoun is fooled into thinking that a convention on the paranormal at Lovecraft's Miskatonic University is actually a conference on domestic science and cooking, and ''The Dentures of Count Usher,'' a comic riff on the vampire theme. Other selections include spoofs of the Jamesian ghost story.

Other books by the same author:
Call of the Tentacle, 1997

Other books you might like:
P.H. Cannon, *Scream for Jeeves*, 1994
James Hynes, *Publish and Perish*, 1997
William Browning Spencer, *The Return of Count Electric and Other Stories*, 1993
John Whitbourn, *Binscombe Tales*, 1998
Gahan Wilson, *The Cleft and Other Odd Tales*, 1998

731

SARBAN (Pseudonym of John W. Wall)

Ringstones and Other Curious Tales
(East Sussex, England: Tartarus, 2000)

Story type: Collection
Subject(s): Horror; Short Stories; Supernatural

Summary: Five of these six stories of the macabre were originally publshed under this same title in 1951. The title story, a high-water mark of horror fiction written after World War II, features a governess who discovers that the three mysterious and precocious children she is hired to look after may be remnants of the ancient race who gave rise to legends of the fairies. Also included is ''Number Fourteen,'' about a crippled girl whose strange religion empowers her to control the beautiful ballerina she idolizes. This story was found among the author's papers after his death.

Other books by the same author:
The Doll Maker and Other Tales of the Uncanny, 1953
The Sound of His Horn, 1952

Other books you might like:
Robert Aickman, *The Unsettled Dust*, 1990
Algernon Blackwood, *The Doll and One Other*, 1946
John Buchan, *The Watcher by the Threshold and Other Tales*, 1902
Arthur Machen, *The Three Impostors*, 1895
Francis Brett Young, *Cold Harbour*, 1924

Horror

732

DAVID J. SCHOW

Eye

(Burton, Michigan: Subterranean, 2001)

Story type: Collection
Subject(s): Short Stories; Horror

Summary: This baker's dozen of edgy tales of horror and suspense is written by an author known for his hardboiled approach and caustic wit. Selections include tales of pure paranoia, such as "2¢ Worth," a variation on Ray Bradbury's "Pedestrian," in which a man's choice to purchase a book does not go over well in a world given over to alternative forms of entertainment, and "Entr'acte," in which a man cannot prove to himself that his wife is not an alen after receiving an anhonymous phone call warning him that she is. "Bagged" is a modern vampire tale with a black comedy twist, and "Holiday" a creepy yarn about a tattoo slowly absorbing its owner. Extensive story notes by the author are included.

Other books by the same author:
Crypt Orchids, 1998
Black Leather Required, 1994
Lost Angels, 1990
The Shaft, 1990
Seeing Red, 1989

Other books you might like:
Dennis Etchison, *Talking in the Dark*, 2001
Caitlin R. Kiernan, *Tales of Pain and Wonder*, 2000
Richard Christian Matheson, *Dystopia*, 2000
John Shirley, *Darkness Divided*, 2001
Michael Marshall Smith, *What You Make It*, 1999

733

DAVID SEARCY

Ordinary Horror

(New York: Viking, 2001)

Story type: Nature in Revolt
Subject(s): Gardens and Gardening
Major character(s): Frank Delabano, Aged Person; Mike Getz, Salesman; Julie Getz, Child
Time period(s): 2000s (2001)
Locale(s): Texas

Summary: A gopher problem in his garden spurs Frank Delabano to order an exotic plant, guaranteed in a strange advertisement to control pests. After planting it, Frank notices a curious absence of pets around the neighborhood, general feelings of malaise, and a strange warping of reality that suggest the plant, and its effects, have unnatural—and possibly uncanny—properties. First novel.

Where it's reviewed:
Booklist, November 15, 2000, page 619
Kirkus Reviews, November 1, 2000, page 1513
Library Journal, January 1, 2001, page 157
Publishers Weekly, December 18, 2000, page 59

Other books you might like:
Robert Charles, *Flowers of Evil*, 1982
Alison Drake, *Lagoon*, 1990
Harry Adam Knight, *The Fungus*, 1989
J.N. Williamson, *The Night Seasons*, 1991
John Wyndham, *The Day of the Triffids*, 1991

734

DARREN SHAN

Cirque Du Freak

(New York: Little Brown, 2001)

Story type: Vampire Story; Child-in-Peril
Subject(s): Carnivals; Teen Relationships; Vampires
Major character(s): Darren Shan, Child; Steve Leonard, Child; Larten Crepsley, Vampire
Time period(s): 2000s
Locale(s): England

Summary: After attending the forbidden Cirque du Freak, a traveling sideshow not for the faint of heart, young Darren steals Madam Octa, the trained tarantula of the sinister Larten Crepsley. Larten is actually the vampire Vur Horston, and when Madam Octa poisons Darren's friend, Steve, Crepsley agrees to help cure him only if Darren will accept conversion to vampirism and become his traveling partner. A first novel for young adult readers, and the first of a projected series of books. Originally published in the UK in 2000.

Other books you might like:
Ray Bradbury, *Something Wicked This Way Comes*, 1962
Richie Tankersley Cusick, *Vampire*, 1991
Christopher Pike, *The Last Vampire*, 1994
R.J. Smith, *The Vampire Diaries*, 1992
S.P. Somtow, *The Vampire's Beautiful Daughter*, 1997

735

JOHN SHIRLEY

Darkness Divided

(Lancaster, Pennsylvania: Stealth, 2001)

Story type: Collection
Subject(s): Horror; Short Stories; Supernatural

Summary: Many of these 22 macabre stories—four original to the book, two written in collaboration—have a quirky streak of social consciousness. "My Victim" and "Tighter" suggest that assassination and violent murder are vital skills for being successful in contemporary business. "Jody and Annie on TV," about a thrill killing pair of teens who get their kicks watching their crimes reported on television, and "In the Road" both map the impact of parental and social neglect on the growing child. "Sweetbite Point" revisits the characters of the author's otherworldly vampire novel *Wetbones* (1991). Introduction by Poppy Z. Brite.

Other books by the same author:
Really, Really, Really, Really Weird Stories, 1999
Black Butterflies, 1998
New Noir, 1993
Heatseeker, 1989

The Exploded Heart (1996)
Other books you might like:
Nancy Collins, *Nameless Sins*, 1994
Brian Hodge, *The Convulsion Factory*, 1996
Richard Christian Matheson, *Dystopia*, 2000
David J. Schow, *Eye*, 2001
Lucius Shepard, *Barnacle Bill the Spacer and Other Stories*, 1997

736

JOHN SHIRLEY

The View from Hell

(Burton, Michigan: Subterranean, 2001)

Story type: Occult
Subject(s): Horror; Occult; Violence
Major character(s): Jack Younger, Producer; Hank Eckman, Businessman; Felix Banqueros, Teacher
Time period(s): 2000s
Locale(s): San Francisco, California; Santa Monica, California; Los Angeles, California

Summary: Three disembodied interdimensional beings—H, V, and Z—study the short, miserable lives of human beings by manipulating their consciousness and perceptions, and steering them to violent actions on the assumption that it may be possible to prevent them. A signed limited edition hardcover.

Other books by the same author:
Demons, 2000
Wetbones, 1992
In Darkness Waiting, 1988
Cellars, 1982

Other books you might like:
Stephen Lee Climer, *Soul Temple*, 2000
Tom Elliott, *The Dwelling*, 1988
Bentley Little, *The House*, 1999
Anne Rice, *Memnoch the Devil*, 1995
Dan Simmons, *Carrion Comfort*, 1988

737

DAVID B. SILVA

Through Shattered Glass

(Springfield, Pennsylvania: Gauntlet, 2001)

Story type: Occult; Collection
Subject(s): Horror; Short Stories; Supernatural

Summary: Many of these 17 stories of understated horror draw on emotional pain and the private dynamics of families for their themes. "The Calling" and "Metastasis" both offer supernatural horrors as metaphors for the ravages of cancer. "Dwindling" concerns a young boy who finds that he and his siblings are little more than figments of their parents' imagination. In "Ice Sculptures," gruesome fates await artists who find not only their souls but their physical integrity have been carved into a colleague's melting ice sculptures. With an introduction by Dean R. Koontz. Published in a signed limited edition.

Where it's reviewed:
Publishers Weekly, March 19, 2001, page 82
Other books by the same author:
The Night in Fog, 1998
The Disappeared, 1995
The Presence, 1994
Come Thirteen, 1988
Child of Darkness, 1986
Other books you might like:
Michael Blumlein, *The Brains of Rats*, 1989
Ray Bradbury, *The October Country*, 1955
Dean R. Koontz, *Strange Highways*, 1995
Robert R. McCammon, *Blue World*, 1989
Mark Morris, *Close to the Bone*, 1994

738

MICHAEL SLADE (Pseudonym of Jay Clarke and Rebecca Clarke)

Hangman

(New York: Signet, 2001)

Story type: Serial Killer
Subject(s): Crime and Criminals; Serial Killer
Major character(s): Zinc Chandler, Detective—Police (inspector); Maddy Thorne, Detective—Police (inspector); Justin Whitfield, Journalist
Time period(s): 2000s
Locale(s): Seattle, Washington; Vancouver, British Columbia, Canada

Summary: A serial killer is terrorizing the Pacific Northwest, viciously killing and dismembering his victims in a crude approximation of the puzzle game, Hangman. Canadian police inspectors Zinc Chandler and Maddy Thorne are challenged by the killer to find the link that connects all of the victims, and how they relate to the fate of Peter Bryce Haddon, a convicted child killer who was hanged in 1993 and who claimed up to his death that he was innocent of the crime.

Other books by the same author:
Burnt Bones, 2000
Primal Scream, 1999
Evil Eye, 1996
Zombie, 1996
Ripper, 1994
Other books you might like:
Randall Boyll, *Shocker*, 1990
Ed Gorman, *The Poker Club*, 2000
Thomas Harris, *Red Dragon*, 1981
Edward Lee, *Dahmer's Not Dead*, 1999
    Elizabeth Steffen, co-author
John Saul, *Black Lightning*, 1995

739

SHANE RYAN STALEY, Editor

The Dead Inn

(North Webster, Indiana: Delirium, 2001)

Story type: Anthology

Horror

Subject(s): Horror; Short Stories; Supernatural

Summary: These 25 stories of mostly hardcore horror and the supernatural, all but two original to the book, are presented as the bill of fare at an imaginary wayside inn. Stories are grouped into three categories: Gross Oddities is represented by Don D'Ammassa's "Something in Common," in which a couple find that brutal violence towards one another invigorates their loveless marriage; Erotic Perversities features Dominick Cancilla's "A Little Seduction," in which a sweet-talking homunculus seduces a woman into a gruesome form of procreation; and Supernatural Entities includes Kurt Newton's "Dancing upon the Dirt of Falling Angels," which follows the thoughts and agonies of a pair of headbangers, who discover the mosh pit is a sacrificial altar to a demon god invoked by a popular rock band. Also included are stories by Charlee Jacob, John B. Rosenman, Mark McLaughlin, Trey R. Barker, and others.

Where it's reviewed:
Hellnotes, March 16, 2001, page 2

Other books you might like:
Victor Heck, *Psycho Ward: The Asylum. Volume 1*, 1999
  editor
Michael Laimo, *Bloodtype*, 2001
  editor
John Pelan, *Darkside: Horror for the Next Millennium*, 1996
  editor
John Skipp, *Book of the Dead*, 1989
  Craig Spector, co-editor
David Whitman, *Scary Rednecks and Other Inbred Horrors*, 2000
  Weston Ochse, co-author

740

JOHN RICHARD STEPHENS, Editor

Into the Mummy's Tomb
(New York: Berkley, 2001)

Story type: Anthology
Subject(s): Horror; Short Stories; Supernatural

Summary: Eighteen stories and excerpts feature mummies and other marvels of ancient Egypt. Selections range from whimsical stories such as Edgar Allan Poe's "Some Words with a Mummy" and Mark Twain's "The Majestic Sphinx," to H.P. Lovecraft's horror opus "Under the Pyramids," in which a man trapped inside a pyramid discovers the truth about the inspiration for Egyptian statuary; Tennessee William's "The Vengeance of Nitocris," in which the sister of a murdered pharaoh seeks revenge on the mummy who killed him; and Sir Arthur Conan Doyle's "Lot 249," the tale of a reanimated mummy.

Other books by the same author:
Vampires, Wine and Roses, 1997
The King of the Cats and Other Feline Fairy Tales, 1993
The Enchanted Cat, 1990

Other books you might like:
Vic Ghidalia, *The Mummy Walks Among Us*, 1971
  editor

Martin H. Greenberg, *Mummy Stories*, 1990
  editor
Peter Haining, *The Mummy*, 1988
Bill Pronzini, *Mummy!*, 1980

741

STEVE RASNIC TEM

City Fishing
(Woodinville, Washington: Silver Salamander, 2000)

Story type: Collection
Subject(s): Horror; Short Stories; Supernatural

Summary: This retrospective collection contains 38 short stories, four original to the book, most of which feature characters in the grip of emotions that shift their sense of reality and darken perspectives on their world and experiences. Many feature parent-child relationships, including "The Battering," about a young daughter whose paranormal powers draw the abusive tendencies of adults, and the title story, a grim coming-of-age tale set in a surreal urban environment. "Derangement" is a creepy meditation on the ambiguity of insanity, and "Bite" about a father whose psychological disturbance manifests itself in a dangerously physical fashion.

Where it's reviewed:
Locus, March 2001, page 31

Other books by the same author:
The Far Side of the Lake, 2001
Decoded Mirrors, 1992
Fairytales, 1990

Other books you might like:
Angela Carter, *The Bloody Chamber*, 1979
Fred Chappell, *More Shapes than One*, 1991
Thomas Ligotti, *Songs of a Dead Dreamer*, 1989
Joyce Carol Oates, *Demon and Other Tales*, 1996
Darrell Schweitzer, *Transients and Other Disquieting Tales*, 1993

742

THOMAS TESSIER

Father Panic's Opera Macabre
(Burton, Michigan: Subterranean, 2001)

Story type: Occult
Subject(s): Mystery; Sexuality; Travel
Major character(s): Neil O'Netti, Writer; Marisa Panic, Young Woman; Anton Panic, Religious
Time period(s): 2000s (2001)
Locale(s): The Marches, Italy

Summary: Stranded at the remote family house of the Panic family in the Italian countryside, Neil falls in love with Marisa Panic, who apprises him of the family's gypsy origins and past trade running a roving carnival. The knowledge works a transformation on Neil, plunging him into a surreal world of horror and slaughter where the Panic family presides over the execution of helpless victims, including Neil. Published as a signed limited edition.

Where it's reviewed:
Publishers Weekly, January 1, 2001, page 60

Other books by the same author:
Fog Heart, 1997
Secret Strangers, 1990
Rapture, 1987
Finishing Touches, 1986
Phantom, 1982

Other books you might like:
Ramsey Campbell, *The Long Lost*, 1993
Robert Girardi, *Vaporetto 13*, 1997
Graham Joyce, *Indigo*, 1999
Daniel Rhodes, *Next After Lucifer*, 1988

743

TAMARA THORNE (Pseudonym of Chris Curry)

Eternity

(New York: Pinnacle, 2001)

Story type: Occult; Serial Killer
Subject(s): Occult; Serial Killer
Major character(s): Zach Tully, Police Officer; Kate McPherson, Tour Guide; Phil Katz, Doctor
Time period(s): 2000s
Locale(s): Eternity, California

Summary: Eternity, in the mountains of northern California, is a haven for New Age wackos and crackpots of all sorts, owing to the strange events and people within its borders, and a Stonehenge-like circle of rocks on its outskirts. When Zach Tully takes the local sheriff's job, in the wake of the murder of the previous sheriff, his hunt for a serial killer who has long terrorized the town leads to clues that the stones are a doorway between dimensions that permit travel through time and space for disappeared people.

Other books by the same author:
Moonfall, 1996
Haunted, 1995

Other books you might like:
Jack Cady, *The Off Season*, 1995
Leigh Clark, *Evil Reincarnate*, 1994
Dennis Etchison, *Shadowman*, 1993
Graham Masterton, *The Doorkeepers*, 2001
Michael Slade, *Cutthroat*, 1992

744

EDO VAN BELKOM

Death Drives a Semi

(Kingston, Ontario: Quarry, 2001)

Story type: Collection
Subject(s): Supernatural

Summary: Edo van Belkom's twenty stories of horror, fantasy, and the supernatural mostly feature ordinary people subjected to bizarrely extraordinary experiences. Selections include the title story, in which Death, incarnated as the reckless driver of a tractor trailer, menaces the driver of an automobile in a life

and death showdown; "But Somebody's Got to Do It," narrated by a man who works in a crematorium burning the infectious bodies of zombies in the midst of a zombie plague; and "The Basement," a sentimental afterlife fantasy. Introduced by Robert Sawyer. Originally published in 1998.

Other books by the same author:
Six Inch Spikes, 2001
Teeth, 2001
Lord Soth, 1996
Wyrm Wolf, 1995

Other books you might like:
Mel D. Ames, *Tales of Titillation and Terror*, 1996
Adam-Troy Castro, *Lost in Booth Nine*, 1993
Brian Hopkins, *Something Haunts Us All*, 1995
Robert Steven Rhine, *My Brain Escapes Me*, 1999
David Niall Wilson, *The Fall of the House of Escher and Other Illusions*, 1995

745

EDO VAN BELKOM

Six Inch Spikes

(Grandview, Missouri: DarkTales, 2001)

Story type: Collection; Erotic Horror
Subject(s): Erotica; Horror; Short Stories

Summary: Sixteen stories deal with sexual themes, often graphically, and in approaches ranging from the darkly comic to the physically repellant. Selections include "Letting Go," a poignant tale of love and loss in which a man watches his AIDS-infected companion taken by death as though by a lover; "Bust," where a victim of breast augmentation at the hands of an irresponsible plastic surgeon exacts a gruesome physical revenge; and "Teeth," which takes the theme of the vagina dentata to horrific extremes.

Where it's reviewed:
Publishers Weekly, June 25, 2001, page 55

Other books by the same author:
Teeth, 2001
Death Drives a Semi, 1998
Yours Truly, Jackie the Stripper, 1998
Lord Soth, 1996
Wyrm Wolf, 1995

Other books you might like:
Ramsey Campbell, *Scared Stiff*, 1987
Ron Dee, *Sex and Blood*, 1994
Nancy Kilpatrick, *Cold Comfort*, 2001
Amarantha Knight, *The Darker Passions Reader*, 1996
Richard Sutphen, *Sexpunks and Savage Sagas*, 1991

746

ROGER WEINGARTEN, Editor

Ghost Writing

(Montpelier, Vermont: Invisible Cities, 2000)

Story type: Anthology
Subject(s): Horror; Short Stories; Supernatural

Horror

Summary: Subtle horrors are featured in these 21 literary stories of fantasy and the supernatural, 15 of which are original to the volume. Selections include John Updike's "The Indian," in which a ghostly Native American provides a focus for a brief study of the decline of New England culture; T. Coraghessan Boyle's amusing "The Miracle at Ballinspittle," about an unlikely emissary for a miraculous manifestation on Earth; Louise Erdrich's "Le Mooz," a humorous adventure drawn from Native American folklore; and Jennifer Rachel Baumer's "The Party over There," in which a woman uses mirror magic to trap her abusive lover.

Other books you might like:

Michael Cox, *The Oxford Book of Twentieth Century Ghost Stories*, 1996
   editor
Larry Dark, *The Literary Ghost*, 1991
   editor
Bradford Morrow, *The New Gothic*, 1992
   Patrick McGrath, co-editor
Joyce Carol Oates, *American Gothic Tales*, 1996
   editor
Robert Weinberg, *The Mists from Beyond*, 1993
   Stefan Dziemianowicz, Martin H. Greenberg, co-editors

747

EDWARD LUCAS WHITE

Sesta and Other Strange Stories

(Seattle: Midnight House, 2001)

Story type: Collection
Subject(s): Horror; Short Stories; Supernatural

Summary: Collected here are fifteen stories and two poems, nine original to the volume, by a writer whose work in the first half of the 20th century was based largely on vivid personal nightmares. Included are "Canean," about a woman whose soul is almost lost when it mischievously migrates into the body of a rat; "The Tooth," in which a dentist's obsession with an historical artifact precipitates a curse, leading to the doom of him and his fiancee; and "The Startling Blonde," a tale of madness. Edited and introduced by Lee Weinstein.

Other books by the same author:

House of the Nightmare, 2000
Lukundoo and Other Stories, 1927
The Song of the Sirens, 1919

Other books you might like:

Robert W. Chambers, *The King in Yellow*, 1895
F. Marion Crawford, *For the Blood Is the Life and Other Stories*, 1996
August Derleth, *Not Long for This World*, 1948
Clive Pemberton, *The Weird O' It*, 2000
Jack Snow, *Dark Music and Other Spectral Tales*, 1947

748

DAVID WHITMAN

Deadfellas

(Grandview, Missouri: DarkTales, 2001)

Story type: Reanimated Dead; Doppelganger
Subject(s): Death; Organized Crime
Major character(s): Tim Machen, Criminal; Francis O'Connor, Criminal; Benny, Criminal
Time period(s): 2000s (2001)
Locale(s): United States

Summary: This black comedy about organized crime chronicles the problems two different groups of mob assassins have carrying out their hits on zombie victims who won't stay dead. *Deadfellas* is the first solo publication of an author who collaborated with Weston Ochse on the collection *Scary Rednecks and Other Inbred Horrors* (2000).

Other books you might like:

Joe R. Lansdale, *Dead in the West*, 1986
Philip Nutman, *Wet Work*, 1993
George A. Romero, *Dawn of the Dead*, 1978
John A. Russo, *Night of the Living Dead*, 1974
Del Stone, *Dead Heat*, 1996

749

F. PAUL WILSON
ALAN CLARK, Illustrator

The Christmas Thingy

(Abingdon, Maryland: CD Publications, 2000)

Story type: Child-in-Peril
Subject(s): Children; Christmas; Supernatural
Major character(s): Mrs. Murgatroyd, Housekeeper; Jessica Atkins, Child, Handicapped
Time period(s): 2000s
Locale(s): London, England

Summary: Lonely at holiday time in her new temporary home in London, crippled American child Jessica wishes for a playmate. Her prayers are answered by the arrival of the Christmas Thingy, a monster who becomes her secret friend, but whom the family housekeeper warns stole all the Christmas presents of the last child who summoned it to the house. A picture book for young children profusely illustrated by Alan Clark.

Other books by the same author:

Hosts, 2001
All the Rage, 2000
Conspiracies, 1999
Legacies, 1998
Pelts, 1990

Other books you might like:

Charles Dickens, *A Christmas Carol*, 1843
Edward Gorey, *The Haunted Tea Cosy*, 1997
David G. Hartwell, *Christmas Forever*, 1993
   editor
Dean R. Koontz, *Santa's Twin*, 1996
Gahan Wilson, *Eddy Deco's Last Caper*, 1987

750

T. WINTER-DAMON
RANDY CHANDLER, Co-Author

Duet for the Devil

(Orlando, Florida: Necro Publications, 2000)

Story type: Serial Killer
Subject(s): Drugs; Murder; Serial Killer
Major character(s): Frank Hawkes, Detective—Private; Truman Gilmore, Salesman; Maldoror, Serial Killer
Time period(s): 2000s
Locale(s): Ocala, Florida

Summary: A contemporary Zodiac Killer is racking up kills across Florida. While private detective Frank Hawkes investigates the possibility of occult motives for the killer's activities, other manhunters recognize the handiwork of the creators of Blue Devil, a drug that forges a psychic link between the administrator and the killer, and is being studied as a possible weapon with top secret military uses.

Other books you might like:

Thomas Harris, *Red Dragon*, 1981
Dean R. Koontz, *False Memory*, 1999
Edward Lee, *Dahmer's Not Dead*, 1999
    Elizabeth Steffen, co-author
John Maxim, *Mosaic*, 1999
Rex Miller, *Slob*, 1987

751

T.M. WRIGHT

Sleepeasy

(New York: Leisure, 2001)

Story type: Occult
Subject(s): Afterlife; Detection; Supernatural
Major character(s): Harry Briggs, Detective—Private, Teacher; Sam Goodlow, Detective—Private; Sidney Greenstreet, Criminal
Time period(s): 1990s
Locale(s): Silver Lake, Fictional Country; New York, New York

Summary: When philosophy professor Harry Briggs dies, he finds himself transported to Silver Lake, a strange realm in the afterlife where he is incarnated as a hardboiled detective of his imagination. Worse, his subconscious, manifesting as a murdering criminal in the guise of Sidney Greenstreet, has escaped to the world of the living, forcing Harry to return and track him down to prevent him acting on his every wild impulse. First published in 1993.

Other books by the same author:

The Ascending, 1994
Goodlow's Ghosts, 1993
Little Boy Lost, 1992
Boundaries, 1990
The School, 1990

Other books you might like:

Ray Bradbury, *Death Is a Lonely Business*, 1992
Rick Hautala, *Beyond the Shroud*, 1996
William Hjortsberg, *Falling Angel*, 1978
Mark Morris, *The Immaculate*, 1996
J.J. Thrasher, *Charlie's Bones*, 1998

Horror

Alternate Histories in Science Fiction
by
Don D'Ammassa

Alternate histories, also known as Uchronia or Euchronias, have a long and honored position in science fiction, and some overlap into mainstream fiction as well. The question "What if. . .?" has fascinated readers and writers for centuries and is certainly not exclusively an interest of science fiction fans, although it has become a long standing and increasingly popular theme within the genre. The *Back to the Future* movies and the television program *Sliders* both enjoyed popularity because of our curiosity about the consequences of decisions in the past and their effects on our present, and there have been innumerable war games designed to explore situations and conflicts that never actually took place.

The change in history can be subtle, as in Robert Sobel's *For Want of a Nail* (1973), in which a thrown horseshoe changes the world. Or, the effects can be massive, as is the case with Harry Harrison's Eden series—*West of Eden* (1984), *Winter in Eden* (1986) and *Return to Eden* (1988)—in which dinosaurs evolve into the dominant intelligent species on Earth and humans never become more than barbaric nomads. The Ptolemaic view of the universe proved to be correct in Richard Garfinkle's *Celestial Matters* (1996) and the Mediterranean is dry land in Harry Turtledove's *Down in the Bottomlands* (1999). The relationship of the alternate history to our own is handled in various ways. Some authors use the device of branching history, with different choices resulting in divergent worlds existing in parallel, occasionally with travel possible between the two, as in *The Woodrow Wilson Dime* (1968). In other cases, time travel changes history from its "correct" course, and there is only one reality, but it's not the one with which we're familiar. This is a common motif in "Change War" stories, which are discussed later. The majority of alternate histories avoid the question altogether, simply presenting the variant world and telling a story set within its boundaries.

There are innumerable events in history which lend themselves to such speculation. What might have happened to Europe had the Turkish fleet not been defeated at Lepanto? What if Julius Caesar had been warned of the conspiracy to assassinate him? How might history have changed if the Spanish Armada had successfully invaded England? While there have indeed been several novels exploring less famous moments in history, most alternate histories cluster around the outcomes of wars, and since Americans write the majority of English language science fiction, it is not surprising that the Revolution, the Civil War, and World War II are the most popular choices.

Those that deal with the Revolutionary War usually assume that Washington is defeated militarily, although in some cases the colonies and England reconcile without hostilities. Joan Aiken's *The Wolves of Willoughby Chase* (1962) and its sequels are set in such a world, as are *A Transatlantic Tunnel, Hurrah!* (1972) by Harry Harrison, *The Whenabouts of Burr* (1975) by Michael Kurland, and *The Two Georges* (1996) by Richard Dreyfuss and Harry Turtledove. The most impressive efforts using this setting are Michael Moorcock's *Gloriana* (1978) and Keith Roberts' excellent series of linked stories collected as *Pavane* (1968). In most of these cases, the exotic setting is presented with very little detail about the individual steps by which history changed from the crisis point, and the plots are usually melodramatic adventures or mysteries.

The American Civil War is a very popular point of divergence. How would the 20th century be changed if the Confederacy had successfully seceded? The classic science fiction treatment is *Bring the Jubilee* (1952) by Ward Moore, but speculation has not been confined to genre writers. MacKinlay Kantor's *If the South Had Won the Civil War* (1960) examines the mechanics of the Confederacy's victory, and Oscar Lewis' *The Lost Years* (1951) portrays an ex-President Abraham Lincoln disgraced and impoverished following his failure to reunite the nation. In *A More Perfect Union* (1971) the Civil War never takes place because the South secedes peacefully. More recently, two writers have

produced series of novels which trace the course of history from the Civil War into the decades that followed, concentrating very heavily on the details of the historical process, sometimes spending more time on them than on the actual story. Harry Harrison's *The Stars and Stripes Forever* (1998) and its sequel concentrate on a relatively small cast of characters, but Harry Turtledove uses a very large number of historical and fictional characters in his novels such as *Guns of the South* (1992), *How Few Remain* (1997), *American Front* (1998), and *Walk in Hell* (1999).

Oddly enough, World War I has attracted very little attention from alternate history writers, although one recent novel, *Pashazade* (2001) by Jon Courtenay Grimwood, is set in a 20th century in which the Central Powers won, possibly because the United States failed to intercede. Jack Finney's *The Woodrow Wilson Dime* (1968) has a similar setting.

World War II, on the other hand, is the single most popular divergence point, and there have been at least a score of novels in which the Nazis successfully conquer Europe, and in some cases America as well. Several mainstream thriller writers have chosen a Nazi occupied England or America as their setting, most notably Len Deighton in *SS-GB* (1978) and Robert Harris in *Fatherland* (1992). Newt Gingrich and William R. Forstchen collaborated on *1945* (1995), which was supposed to be the first in a series, although the proposed sequel never appeared. Philip K. Dick's *The Man in the High Castle* (1962), set many years after the U.S. was divided in two by Japanese and German occupation forces, won a Hugo Award as the best science fiction novel of the year. *The Sound of His Horn* (1960) by Sarban is a highly atmospheric, almost surrealistic story in which "lesser" humans are hunted for sport in a Nazi dominated future. Brad Linaweaver explores the consequences if the Nazis had developed atomic weapons in *Moon of Ice* (1988).

Although most World War II alternate histories concentrate on Germany, Alfred Coppel describes in great detail the Allied invasion of Japan in *The Burning Mountain* (1983). Another unusual variant is *The Trial of Adolf Hitler* (1978) by Philippe Van Rjndt, set in a history where the Allies did win, but Hitler did not commit suicide and was captured. Perhaps the strangest World War II related alternate history is Harry Turtledove's recent Colonization series. In the midst of World War II, aliens invade the Earth, forcing the Allies to make an uneasy peace with Hitler and Tojo in order to defeat the common enemy.

Although these three wars are the most popular choices for critical points in history, other writers have explored a variety of scenarios. Kingsley Amis considers a world in which Christianity never gained its current preeminence in *The Alteration* (1976). Pierre Barbet chooses the life and untimely death of the Maid of Orleans for *The Joan of Arc Replay* (1978), although technically this is not an alternate history, since human society is reconstructed on another planet by curious aliens. A very different Australia emerges

in *Kelly Country* (1983) by A. Bertram Chandler, one in which the anti-government rogue Ned Kelly was not trapped and killed but instead led a successful revolutionary movement. Would the British Empire have fallen if its scientists had developed an atomic bomb? We discover the answer in *Queen Victoria's Bomb* (1967) by Ronald Clark.

The role of technology is also explored in L. Sprague de Camp's classic *Lest Darkness Fall* (1941), in which an archaeologist is transported to the late Roman Empire. Kirk Mitchell wrote three novels set in an alternate history where the Roman Empire survives into the 20th century, including *Procurator* (1984), *The New Barbarians* (1986), and *Cry Republic!* (1989). Mitchell also wrote an interesting novel in which a descendant of Bret Harte attempts to derail the career of Mark Twain to enhance his ancestor's reputation, *Never the Twain* (1987). The possibility of a North America in which Native Americans maintain control of part of the continent is explored in *The Indians Won* (1980) by Martin Cruz Smith, *Apacheria* (1998) by Jake Page, and most notably in *Climb the Wind* (1999) by Pamela Sargent. A dubious American hero survives his last disgrace in *The Court Martial of George Armstrong Custer* (1976) by Douglas Jones. Comparatively recent events have also been the basis for alternate histories, including *President Kissinger* by Donald Munson and Monroe Rosenthal (1974); *If Israel Lost the War* (1969) by Richard Chesnoff, Edward Klein, and Robert Littell; and John Batchelor's *Peter Nevsky and the True Story of the Russian Moon Landing* (1993).

A special case of the alternate history is the "Change War" story, made popular in particular by Fritz Leiber and Poul Anderson, each of whom wrote a series of novels and shorter works in which organizations exist to prevent time travelers from altering the past and changing the course of history. Most stories of this type either involve efforts to prevent interference either before or after the fact, less frequently manipulating events after the change to restore the original timeline. Leiber's award-winning *The Big Time* (1961) does not in fact specifically deal with any historical period but rather with a kind of limbo existence outside normal time where agents go to rest and recuperate between assignments. The best of this series was collected as *Changewar* (1983). Anderson's Time Patrol stories include *The Guardians of Time* (1960), *Time Patrolman* (1983), *The Year of the Ransom* (1983), *Annals of the Time Patrol* (1984), *The Shield of Time* (1990), and *Time Patrol* (1991).

Another short but notable Changewar series, by H. Beam Piper, was collected as *Lord Kalvan of Otherwhen* (1965) and *Paratime* (1981). These have been collected more recently in the 2001 omnibus, *The Complete Paratime*. John Jakes pits two time travelers against each other, one a black militant, the other a white supremacist in *Black in Time* (1970). The invasion of England by the Spanish Armada gets some extra-temporal assistance in *Times Without Number* (1962) by John Brunner. Isaac Asimov's *The End of*

Eternity (1955) involves a rogue time agent, who falls in love with a woman from another time and nearly destroys the universe by manipulating history. Also notable is *Crossroads of Time* (1956) by Andre Norton. The battle to change time is given an amusing twist in the kitchen sink novel *The Eyre Affair* (2001) by Jasper Fforde.

There is no question that alternate histories have an enduring popularity, and in fact the number of such stories has increaased dramatically in recent years, with Harry Turtledove and Jake Page being just two who have adopted it almost entirely for their work. One publisher even briefly began using the term ''alternate history'' on the spines of its books in an attempt to define it as a separate genre. The best of these blend traditional storytelling techniques, strong characterization, and skilled prose with the speculation. Others, which rely chiefly on creating amusing juxtapositions of characters and playing with historical trends will more likely enjoy a brief popularity but rapidly fade away.

Readers wishing to learn more about this popular subgenre should see the entries ''Alternate Worlds,'' ''Parallel Worlds,'' and ''History in SF'' in *The Encyclopedia of Science Fiction* (1993), edited by John Clute and Peter Nicholls; the detailed bibliography in *Alternative Histories* (1986), edited by Martin H. Greenberg and Charles G. Waugh; and Karen Hellekson's new study, *The Alternate History: Refiguring Historical Time* (Kent State, 2001).

The closest thing to an outstanding alternate history in early 2001 was Robert Charles Wilson's *The Chronoliths*, which is essentially a changewar story with the battle between our own near future and one twenty years further on. Otherwise, for science fiction readers, the first half of the year 2001 was considerably diverse in theme and style, with a good blend of hard science fiction, military adventure, serious cultural speculation, mystery, satire, and other worlds adventures. There were also three very fine retrospective collections of short stories by Arthur C. Clarke, Fredric Brown, and William Tenn.

Recommended Titles

The outstanding books for this period were:

Manifold: Space by Stephen Baxter

The Pickup Artist by Terry Bisson

Jupiter by Ben Bova

From These Ashes by Fredric Brown

Hammerfall by C.J. Cherryh

The Collected Stories of Arthur C. Clarke by Arthur C. Clarke

Children of Hope by David Feintuch

Reunion by Alan Dean Foster

Water of Death by Paul Johnston

Probability Sun by Nancy Kress

Deepsix by Jack McDevitt

Ship of Fools by Richard Paul Russo

Child of Venus by Pamela Sargent

Immodest Proposals by William Tenn

The Chronoliths by Robert Charles Wilson

Return to the Whorl by Gene Wolfe

For More Information about Fantastic Fiction by Neil Barron

The February issue of *Locus* provides a detailed statistical overview of the preceding year, with a recommended reading list assembled from choices by contributors, who each provide their own comments. The overall figures were down slightly for 2000. Original U.S. works totaled 1027 books, hardcover and paperback, with reprints adding 900 titles. *Locus* admits that it doesn't count everything, missing many small press books and ''mainstream'' novels with SF or fantasy elements. In 2000 the increasingly large number of print on demand (POD) reprints, mostly trade paperbacks, affected the totals, and *Locus* admits that the 87 titles they logged omitted many others. For the original books, SF novels totaled 230, fantasy 258, and horror 80, plus others in the anthologies (67) and collections (77) categories. A large separate category is ''media-related,'' the hundreds of film, TV and gaming spin- offs, which totaled 183 mostly forgettable books from a literary standpoint, but of great importance to publisher profits. The paid circulations of the dwindling number of fantastic fiction magazines continued their decline, with the revived *Amazing Stories* ceasing publication in mid-2000, ending the life of the first all-SF magazine, which began in 1926.

Reviews of Stanley Kubrick's 1968 film, *2001*, were generally not favorable, but in succeeding years the film established itself as a cult classic, and not simply as a SF film. It's been the subject of a handful of books and many essays, such as Carolyn Geduld, *The Lost Worlds of 2001* (1979), Piers Bizony, *2001: Filming the Future* (1994), and David G. Stork who edited *Hal's Legacy: 2001's Computer as Dream and Legacy* (1997). The latest study, and the first in a new Modern Library film series, is *The Making of ''2001: A Space Odyssey''*, edited by Stephanie Schwann. While unavoidably repeating some material from earlier studies, it also adds much new material and is strongly recommended to all types of libraries.

Illustration has always been an essential component of written SF, especially on the garish covers of the pulps, whose icons have been made familiar by decades of repetition—spaceships, robots, space captains with ray guns at the ready, bimbos in abbreviated clothing and plastic bubbles over their heads, and of course bug-eyed monsters (BEMs). These icons, and those from several other genres, such as detective, fantasy, and ''hot'' and ''spicy'' pulps, plus less commonly seen British pulps, are the focus of British writer Peter Haining in his *The Classic Era of American Pulp*

Magazines (Chicago Review). This colorful survey is casually written but adds little to its subject. Better choices include *Pulp Culture: The Art of the Fiction Magazines* (Collectors Press, 1998) by Frank M. Robinson and Lawrence Davidson, and Robert Lesser's *Pulp Art* (Gramercy Books, 1997), which reproduces the work from the original paintings or drawings.

Frank Kelley Freas (1922-) is unquestionably the best known contemporary SF illustrator and has been nominated 20 times for the Hugo award and won ten times. He's been a full-time illustrator since 1952. His latest book, *As He Sees It* (Paper Tiger, distr. by Sterling), is his fifth and the first in almost two decades. The emphasis here is on his work, mostly in color, created since 1984. Paper Tiger has published several dozen oversize books profiling the work of British and American illustrators of the fantastic, many of them distributed by Sterling in the U.S., and libraries should consider acquiring a few (see www.papertiger.co.uk for details).

As space travel shifted from fiction to fact in the 1960s, illustration accompanied it. A lot of the latter was hardware oriented and appealed more to the technically inclined. Preceding this was the more speculative astronomical art, the dean of which was Chesley Bonestell (1888-1986). A thorough retrospective of his work is by Ron Miller and Frederick C. Curant III, *The Art of Chesley Bonestell* (Paper Tiger/Sterling). This oversize book reproduces his illustrations from the pioneering 1949 book, *The Conquest of Space*, plus his many other illustrations from *Life*, *Collier's* and other magazines and books. It includes biographical information and reproductions of his architectural renderings and other work, including Bonestell's favorite among all his paintings, a pastoral oil on board titled *The Engulfed Cathedral*, inspired by the Debussy composition. This is the second book on Bonestell by these authors, who wrote a similar but less comprehensive work, *Worlds Beyond: The Art of Chesley Bonestell*, published by a small specialty press in 1983. As landscape and religious paintings are recognized genres, so space art in a secular age has its place, and public libraries especially should consider this book.

When major publishers like Doubleday and Simon & Schuster began their SF lines in the early 1950s, they sought cover art more "respectable" than the typical pulp art on paperbacks or on the books of the specialty SF presses. So did Ian Ballantine when he began his line of original paperbacks for a more serious audience in 1952. They often chose Richard Powers (1921-1996), whose work is now explored in detail in Jane Frank's *The Art of Richard Powers* (Paper Tiger, distr. by Sterling). Powers' abstract surrealism was totally unlike the pulp-inspired illustrations that adorned most SF of the period and drew from the European fine art tradition, especially surrealists like Matta, Miro and, especially Yves Tanguy. He was a prolific and gifted illustrator, as well as a respected fine artist. All the illustrations are reproduced from the original art, and the text is intelligent and informative. Strongly recommended to any library with an interest in book illustration or science fiction.

Many histories of comic books are written for fans and are often heavily illustrated. Bradford W. Wright's *Comic Book Nation: The Transformation of Youth Culture in America* (Johns Hopkins) is a clearly written cultural history of American comic books, including some of the SF comics. A useful survey for the non-fan (which includes most librarians I suspect), as well as for the scholar.

The fourth of H.G. Wells' scientific romances, *The War of the Worlds*, may be his best known because of the 1938 Halloween radio dramatization by Orson Welles and his Mercury Theatre of the Air. The program was estimated to have been heard by about six million people, of whom about a million were alarmed or terrified. *The Complete War of the Worlds: Mars' Invasion of Earth from H.G. Wells to Orson Welles* edited by Brian Holmsten and Alex Lubertozzi (Sourcebooks, 2001) reprints the novel, with illustrations from the British serial version, plus the radio script, and includes valuable background information about the program and later dramatizations elsewhere. Also included is an audio CD, which includes the complete hour-long radio play plus four short recordings that deal with the famous broadcast. The bibliography lists many of the contemporary and later accounts of the broadcast, including 25 websites. Strongly recommended to high school and public libraries, and university libraries supporting media studies, all of which will have to keep an eye on the CD.

A few collections of H.P. Lovecraft have been annotated in *WDIRN?* Much of the philosophy underlying many of his distinctive horror stories is explained in his long essay, "Supernatural Horror in Literature," originally published in 1927 and revised several times until his death in 1937. The latest edition is annotated in detail by the foremost Lovecraft scholar, S.T. Joshi (Hippocamus Press, 2000). This essay was important and influential, and libraries desiring strength in critical works about fantastic literature should have either this edition, the less expensive Dover trade paperback (1973), or the standard Arkham edition of HPL's *Dagon and Other Macabre Tales* which was first published in 1965 and has been reprinted. See also the essay on horror fiction in this volume.

Robert Louis Stevenson's most popular book may be *Treasure Island*, but not far behind is his 1886 novel, *The Strange Case of Dr. Jekyll and Mr. Hyde*, whose plot he learned from his nurse. Stevenson gradually came to live a double life himself, and the theme of doubles occurs regularly in his other fiction. A readable and useful study in literary genealogy is *In Search of Dr. Jekyll & Mr. Hyde* (Renaissance Books) by Raymond T. McNally and Radu R. Florescu, whose earlier similar studies were devoted to *Dracula* and *Frankenstein*. It is also a useful supplement to the annotated editions of the novel, such as *The Definitive Dr. Jekyll and Mr. Hyde Companion* (1983), edited by Harry M. Geduld.

SF and fantasy have been taught at various levels in the U.S. (rarely abroad) for many years. The latest textbook for high school/college classroom use is edited by Garyn G. Roberts, *The Prentice Hall Anthology of Science Fiction and Fantasy* (2001), a hefty trade paperback with 85 tales, each with a headnote, and a variety of lists among its almost 1,200 pages. The historical and nationality scope is wide, in sharp contrast to the competing anthology edited by Ursula K. Le Guin and Brian Attebery, *The Norton Book of Science Fiction* (1993), with 67 stories in 864 pages, plus a separate 129 page teacher's guide. A comprehensive anthology, quite apart from its value as a teaching aid.

Necrology

This section highlights selected figures associated with fantastic literature or film who have died since the previous fall. The most detailed obituaries, often accompanied by appreciations, are found in the monthly news magazine, *Locus*, and the date of the issue is cited here. Standard reference works such as *The Encyclopedia of Science Fiction* (1993) or *The Encyclopedia of Fantasy* (1997) or the St. James guide to genre fiction writers provide additional details.

Douglas Adams (1952-May 11, 2001) was best known for his *Hitch Hiker's Guide to the Galaxy* and its several sequels. He wrote the script for the film based on the first book, to be released by Disney in 2002. The book was derived from a BBC radio, later a TV series. In it he revealed the answer to The Ultimate Question of Life, the Universe, and Everything (in case you've forgotten, it was the number 42). The appeal of his books transcended SF fandom, and their satirical humor is a delight. (June 2001)

Marion Zimmer Bradley (1930-September 25, 1999) was a prolific author of SF and fantasy works. Her best known work was the bestselling 1983 novel, *The Mists of Avalon*, a feminist-mystical retelling of the Arthurian legends from the viewpoint of Morgan Le Fay. She was also well known for her long-running Darkover adventure novels and shorter fiction, which began in 1962. As her health declined, she founded and edited *Marion Zimmer Bradley's Fantasy Magazine*, which ceased publication with issue 50 in late fall 2000. (November 1999)

L. Sprague de Camp (1907-November 6, 2000) was one of the last of the so-called "Golden Age" (1938-1946) writers for *Astounding Science Fiction*. His long interest in earlier civilizations was evident in much of his fiction, most notably in his 1941 masterpiece, *Lest Darkness Fall*, in which a man is transported to the late Roman Empire and, armed with a good knowledge of practical matters and a sense of humor, changes history. His many collaborations with Fletcher Pratt, such as *The Incomplete Enchanter* (1941) and *The Castle of Iron* (1950) all featured Harold Shea and display the considerable humor and wit found in most of his works. (December 2000)

Gordon R. Dickson (Canada, 1923-January 3, 2001) wrote more than 100 short stories, collected into 24 collections, plus 55 novels. He lived in Minneapolis since 1937 and became a full-time writer in 1950. His humorous "Hoka" stories, co-authored with fellow Twin Cities writer Poul Anderson, were assembled in several collections, most recently *Hokas Pokas!* (2000). He is also well known for his "Childe" or "Dorsai" series of stories, beginning with *Dorsai!* in 1959. (March 2001)

Richard Laymon (1947-February 14, 2001) was the president of the Horror Writers Association when he died in Los Angeles. His first novel, *The Cellar*, was issued in 1980, with sequels in 1986 and two posthumous novellas published in 2001, *Friday Night in Beast House* and *Night in the Lonesome October*. His explicit horror novels were published more in the UK than the US. His 2000 novel, *The Traveling Vampire Show*, was widely praised. (March 2001)

Keith Roberts (UK, 1935-October 5, 2000) achieved prominence with his second book, 1968's *Pavane*, an episodic cyclic series set in an alternative world, a Catholic-dominated Britain passed over by the industrial revolution. Other works include *The Chalk Giants* (1974), *The Grain Kings* (1976) and a 1987 novel, *Graine*, which won the British SF Award and was nominated for the Arthur G. Clarke Award. (November 2000)

Curt Siodmak (1902-September 2, 2000) was perhaps best known for one of his many films, *The Wolf Man* (1942), and his 1943 novel, *Donovan's Brain*, which had three film adaptations. He had 18 novels published in Germany before he emigrated to the U.S. in 1933, barely escaping the Nazis. In February 2001, his *Wolf Man's Maker: Memoir of a Hollywood Writer* (Scarecrow Press) was published. (October 2000)

Science Fiction Titles

752

BRIAN W. ALDISS

Supertoys Last All Summer Long

(London: Orbit, 2001)

Story type: Collection
Subject(s): Short Stories

Summary: These 19 stories were originally published between 1969 and 1999, although the majority first appeared during the 1990s. The stories deal with familiar SF themes—population control, self-aware robots, aliens, time travel, and others, but predominantly in non-traditional ways. Most of the stories have an element of humor, generally satirical.

Where it's reviewed:
Locus, May 2001, page 15
Science Fiction Chronicle, June 2001, page 39

Other books by the same author:
Common Clay, 1996
A Tupolev Too Far, 1994
Dracula Unbound, 1991
Man in His Time, 1988
Helliconia Winter, 1985

Other books you might like:
Michael Bishop, *Close Encounters with the Deity*, 1986
Philip K. Dick, *The Second Variety*, 1991
R.A. Lafferty, *Strange Doings*, 1972
Robert Sheckley, *The Robot Who Looked Like Me*, 1982
Gene Wolfe, *The Book of Days*, 1981

753

ROBERT ASPRIN
LINDA EVANS, Co-Author

The House That Jack Built

(New York: Baen, 2001)

Story type: Time Travel
Series: Time Scout. Book 4

Subject(s): Time Travel
Major character(s): Kit Carson, Time Traveler; John Caddrick, Political Figure (senator); Skeeter Jackson, Con Artist
Time period(s): Indeterminate Future
Locale(s): England; Time Terminal 86, Mythical Place

Summary: Life becomes extremely complicated for time agent Kit Carson when a government official hires an assassin and attempts to bring an end to all time travel. As if that wasn't bad enough, someone has allowed Jack the Ripper to leave England and enter the immaterial world of time travel, and he has brought his knife with him.

Where it's reviewed:
Science Fiction Chronicle, April 2001, page 39

Other books by the same author:
Wagers of Sin, 1996 (Linda Evans, co-author)
Time Scout, 1995 (Linda Evans, co-author)
The Bug Wars, 1979
The Cold Cash War, 1977

Other books you might like:
Karl Alexander, *Time After Time*, 1979
Poul Anderson, *The Corridors of Time*, 1965
Matthew J. Costello, *Time of the Fox*, 1990
Gordon Eklund, *Serving in Time*, 1975
Fritz Leiber, *Changewar*, 1983

754

J.D. AUSTIN

Bobby's Girl

(New York: Ace, 2001)

Story type: Invasion of Earth
Subject(s): Aliens
Major character(s): Ket Mhulhar, Alien, Fugitive; Bobby Albertson, Director; Celin Kwa, Alien
Time period(s): 2000s (2001)
Locale(s): Los Angeles, California; Thradon, Planet—Imaginary

Summary: When the war begins to go badly on the planet Thradon, Ket Mhulhar goes into hiding on Earth, taking a job as a script girl for a movie project. Circumstances reveal she is a highly trained warrior with super strength, and director Bobby Albertson falls in love with her. Unfortunately, her old enemies figure out where she's gone, and they come to Earth looking for her.

Where it's reviewed:
Science Fiction Chronicle, June 2001, page 40

Other books you might like:
John Boyd, *The Andromeda Gun*, 1974
John DeChancie, *Living with Aliens*, 1995
Herbert Kastle, *The Reassembled Man*, 1964
Paul Preuss, *Human Error*, 1985
Oscar Rossiter, *Tetrasomy Two*, 1974

755

KAGE BAKER

The Graveyard Game

(New York: Harcourt, 2001)

Story type: Time Travel
Series: Company. Book 4
Subject(s): Time Travel
Major character(s): Joseph, Time Traveler; Lewis, Time Traveler
Time period(s): Multiple Time Periods
Locale(s): San Francisco, California

Summary: Agents of a time travel organization founded in the 24th century, but recruited from various times, begin to suspect that their superiors are lying to them. There is no news of the future beyond the year 2355, and those agents who become troublesome are confined in past epochs with no way to escape.

Where it's reviewed:
Booklist, December 15, 2000, page 793
Library Journal, October 15, 2000, page 108
Locus, March 2001, page 33
New York Times Book Review, January 21, 2001, page 16

Other books by the same author:
Mendoza in Hollywood, 2000
Sky Coyote, 1999
In the Garden of Iden, 1997

Other books you might like:
Poul Anderson, *There Will Be Time*, 1973
Isaac Asimov, *The End of Eternity*, 1955
Ray Cummings, *The Man Who Mastered Time*, 1929
Joseph Delaney, *The Lords Temporal*, 1987
Fritz Leiber, *The Big Time*, 1961

756

STEPHEN BAXTER

Manifold: Space

(New York: Ballantine Del Rey, 2001)

Story type: First Contact

Subject(s): Space Exploration
Major character(s): Reid Malenfant, Space Explorer; Nemoto, Scientist; Xenia Makarova, Scientist
Time period(s): 21st century (2020-2042); 24th century (2340)
Locale(s): Outer Space; Kazakhstan; United States

Summary: An enterprising space pilot finds an alien artifact that allows him to teleport his ship around the universe. While he is attempting to communicate with the aliens he encounters, scientists back on Earth discover that the solar system has been visited before, and that on each occasion there was a massive eradication of life.

Where it's reviewed:
Booklist, December 15, 2000, page 763
Library Journal, January 1, 2001, page 162
Locus, January 2001, page 19
Publishers Weekly, January 8, 2001, page 52
Science Fiction Chronicle, April 2001, page 36

Other books by the same author:
Manifold: Time, 2000
Mammoth, 1999
Moonseed, 1998
Titan, 1997
Voyage, 1997

Other books you might like:
Roger MacBride Allen, *The Ring of Charon*, 1990
Greg Bear, *Eternity*, 1990
Jeffrey A. Carver, *The Infinity Link*, 1984
Alexander Jablokov, *Deepdrive*, 1998
Frederik Pohl, *Gateway*, 1978

757

HILARI BELL

A Matter of Profit

(New York: Harper, 2001)

Story type: Espionage Thriller
Subject(s): Aliens
Major character(s): Ahvren, Military Personnel; Sabri, Rebel; Redahd, Government Official
Time period(s): Indeterminate Future
Locale(s): T'Chin, Planet—Imaginary

Summary: Ahvren has returned to his home world after a successful military campaign. There he discovers his sister has rebelled against the pressure for her to conform to an arranged marriage. His personal problems become interlinked with his assignment to discover whether or not there is a conspiracy to assassinate the planetary emperor.

Other books by the same author:
Navohar, 2000

Other books you might like:
Lois McMaster Bujold, *Cetaganda*, 1996
C.J. Cherryh, *Precursor*, 1999
Julie E. Czerneda, *A Thousand Words for Stranger*, 1997
Colin Kapp, *The Wizard of Anharitte*, 1973
Janet Morris, *The Carnelian Throne*, 1979

758

DAVID BISCHOFF

The Diplomatic Touch
(Scarborough, Maine: Foggy Windows, 2001)

Story type: Humor
Subject(s): Space Exploration
Major character(s): Thomas Diadem, Diplomat; Sarah Diadem, Diplomat; Persimmons, Government Official (minister)
Time period(s): Indeterminate Future
Locale(s): Nocturne III, Planet—Imaginary; Outer Space

Summary: Thomas and Sarah Diadem are interstellar diplomats, who have been given the assignment of convincing the government of Nocturne III to join a consortium of worlds. The alien inhabitants of that world have a peculiar society involving some unusual sexual encounters and a great deal of slapstick comedy.

Other books by the same author:
Alien Island, 1996
Genocide, 1994
Night of the Living Shark, 1991
Abduction, 1990
The Unicorn Gambit, 1986

Other books you might like:
Poul Anderson, *The Makeshift Rocket*, 1962
John DeChancie, *Living with Aliens*, 1995
Andrew Harman, *A Midsummer Night's Gene*, 1997
Keith Laumer, *Retief and the Rascals*, 1993
Robert Sheckley, *Mindswap*, 1966

759

TERRY BISSON

The Pickup Artist
(New York: Tor, 2001)

Story type: Satire
Subject(s): Futuristic Fiction
Major character(s): Hank Shapiro, Government Official; Henry, Young Woman; Lou, Saloon Keeper/Owner
Time period(s): 21st century
Locale(s): United States

Summary: In order to make room for new art, older movies, books, and music are systematically declared obsolete, outlawed, and destroyed. The protagonist is one of those who confiscates the proscribed materials, but when he succumbs to temptation and samples some himself, he finds himself drawn into a revolutionary underworld.

Where it's reviewed:
Publishers Weekly, February 19, 2001, page 74
Science Fiction Chronicle, April 2001, page 35

Other books by the same author:
In the Upper Room and Other Stories, 2000
Pirates of the Universe, 1996
Virtuosity, 1995
Bears Discover Fire, 1993

Fire on the Mountain, 1988

Other books you might like:
Benjamin Appel, *The Funhouse*, 1959
Ray Bradbury, *Fahrenheit 451*, 1953
Philip Jose Farmer, *Dayworld*, 1985
Vincent King, *Light a Last Candle*, 1969
Fritz Leiber, *The Silver Eggheads*, 1962

760

BEN BOVA

Jupiter
(New York: Tor, 2001)

Story type: Hard Science Fiction
Subject(s): Space Exploration; Aliens
Major character(s): Grant Archer, Scientist; Egon Karlstad, Scientist; Elaine O'Hara, Scientist
Time period(s): Indeterminate Future
Locale(s): Jupiter

Summary: Scientists based on Jupiter's moons are investigating the possibility that the enormous life forms found in the atmosphere of the giant planet may actually be intelligent. Religious fanatics dominate the government and want to suppress anything that might call into question the literal truth of the Bible, and they send a young graduate student to spy on the project.

Where it's reviewed:
Booklist, January 1, 2001, page 928
Library Journal, January 1, 2001, page 163
Publishers Weekly, November 27, 2000, page 58
Science Fiction Chronicle, April 2001, page 34

Other books by the same author:
Venus, 2000
Return to Mars, 1999
Moonwar, 1998
Twice Seven, 1998
Brothers, 1996

Other books you might like:
Poul Anderson, *Three Worlds to Conquer*, 1964
John Glasby, *Project Jove*, 1971
James P. Hogan, *The Gentle Giants of Ganymede*, 1978
Donald Moffitt, *The Jupiter Theft*, 1977
Paul Preuss, *The Diamond Moon*, 1990

761

BEN BOVA

The Precipice
(New York: Tor, 2001)

Story type: Hard Science Fiction
Series: Asteroid Wars. Book 1
Subject(s): Space Exploration
Major character(s): Dan Randolph, Businessman; Pancho Lane, Astronaut; Martin Humphries, Businessman
Time period(s): Indeterminate Future
Locale(s): Earth; Asteroid

Science Fiction

Summary: Dan Randolph and Martin Humphries both want to exploit the asteroids. Randolph believes the resources are essential to preserving civilization in the face of massive ecological disaster; Humphries sees it as a means to gaining dictatorial powers. Humphries manipulates his rival into a treacherous alliance, and then attempts to strand him in space.

Other books by the same author:
Jupiter, 2001
Venus, 2000
Return to Mars, 1999
Moonwar, 1998
Twice Seven, 1998

Other books you might like:
Poul Anderson, *Tales of the Flying Mountains*, 1971
C.J. Cherryh, *Hellburner*, 1992
Michael Flynn, *Falling Stars*, 2001
Scott Mackay, *The Meek*, 2001
Alan E. Nourse, *Scavengers in Space*, 1959

762

FREDRIC BROWN

From These Ashes

(Framingham, Massachusetts: NESFA, 2001)

Story type: Collection
Subject(s): Short Stories

Summary: This volume brings together the complete science fiction and fantasy of Fredric Brown, well over 100 stories, including many short shorts. The stories originally appeared during the 1940s through 1960s. Their themes include humor, magic, aliens, other planets, and make extensive use of surprise endings.

Where it's reviewed:
Booklist, April 15, 2001, page 1539

Other books by the same author:
The Best of Fredric Brown, 1977
Paradox Lost, 1974
Daymares, 1968
Nightmares and Geezenstacks, 1961
The Mind Thing, 1961

Other books you might like:
Harry Harrison, *50 in 50*, 2001
Murray Leinster, *First Contacts*, 1998
Richard Matheson, *The Shores of Space*, 1957
Eric Frank Russell, *Major Ingredients*, 2000
Clifford D. Simak, *Over the River and through the Woods*, 1996

763

ORSON SCOTT CARD

Shadow of the Hegemon

(New York: Tor, 2001)

Story type: Espionage Thriller
Series: Ender's Shadow. Book 2
Subject(s): Political Thriller

Major character(s): Bean, Military Personnel; Peter Wiggin, Government Official; Petra Arkanian, Military Personnel
Time period(s): 21st century
Locale(s): Earth

Summary: With an alien threat at least temporarily averted, the young people who masterminded the victory return to Earth. Unfortunately, old political and international animosities have sprung to life in the absence of a common enemy, and some of the more unscrupulous plan to make use of those who returned to pursue their own goals. Eventually, new leaders emerge who plan to reshape human society into a more unified force.

Where it's reviewed:
Booklist, November 1, 2000, page 490
Library Journal, December 2000, page 196
Locus, December 2000, page 29
Publishers Weekly, November 20, 2000, page 50
Science Fiction Chronicle, February 2001, page 42

Other books by the same author:
Enchantment, 1999
Ender's Shadow, 1999
Heartfire, 1998
Pastwatch, 1996
Alvin Journeyman, 1995

Other books you might like:
Poul Anderson, *Harvest of Stars*, 1993
Gordon R. Dickson, *Wolf and Iron*, 1990
Joe Haldeman, *The Coming*, 2000
Robert A. Heinlein, *Friday*, 1982
Mack Reynolds, *Border, Breed, nor Birth*, 1972

764

JACK L. CHALKER

Melchior's Fire

(New York: Baen, 2001)

Story type: Space Opera
Subject(s): Space Colonies
Major character(s): Randi Queson, Scientist; Jerry Nagel, Spaceman; An Li, Spacewoman
Time period(s): Indeterminate Future
Locale(s): Sepuchus, Planet—Imaginary; *Henry Morton Stanley*, Spaceship; Outer Space

Summary: This two-part adventure story involves a star traveling salvage crew. First, they visit an abandoned colony world and narrowly escape being captured and absorbed by a giant, intelligent shape changing creature. Then financially distressed, they become involved in an interstellar treasure hunt. This book is a sequel to *Balshazzar's Serpent*.

Other books by the same author:
Balshazzar's Serpent, 2000
The Moreau Factor, 2000
Priam's Lens, 1999
The Sea Is Full of Stars, 1999
The Wonderland Gambit, 1996

Other books you might like:
Poul Anderson, *Satan's World*, 1968

Gordon R. Dickson, *Mission to Universe*, 1965
Murray Leinster, *Get Off My World!*, 1966
Richard Paul Russo, *Ship of Fools*, 2001
Timothy Zahn, *The Icarus Hunt*, 1999

765

C.J. CHERRYH

Hammerfall
(New York: Avon Eos, 2001)

Story type: Lost Colony
Series: Gene Wars. Book 1
Subject(s): Disasters; Technology
Major character(s): Marak Trin, Warrior; Ila, Ruler; Hati Makri, Warrior
Time period(s): Indeterminate Future
Locale(s): Lakht, Planet—Imaginary

Summary: On a barbaric colony world, the local dictator demands that all of the insane be brought to her city. She has discovered that they share a common dream of a mysterious tower, and believes this indicates she has been found by someone who followed her when she fled to this system in the midst of an interstellar war.

Other books by the same author:
Precursor, 1999
Finity's End, 1997
Cloud's Rider, 1996
Inheritor, 1996
Invader, 1995

Other books you might like:
Tony Daniel, *Metaplanetary*, 2001
Michael Flynn, *The Nanotech Chronicles*, 1991
Peter Hamilton, *The Reality Dysfunction*, 1996
Linda Nagata, *The Bohr Maker*, 1995
Andre Norton, *Voorloper*, 1980

766

ARTHUR C. CLARKE

The Collected Stories of Arthur C. Clarke
(New York: Tor, 2001)

Story type: Collection
Subject(s): Short Stories

Summary: This collection contains all of the author's short science fiction stories, over 100 total, including many of the acknowledged classics in the field. Originally published between 1937 and 2000, the stories cover a wide range of themes and subjects, including humor, hard SF, first contact, aliens, other worlds, tall tales, scientific puzzles, and wild adventures.

Where it's reviewed:
Booklist, January 1, 2001, page 928
Locus, December 2000, page 27

Other books by the same author:
3001: The Final Odyssey, 1997
The Fountains of Paradise, 1979

Imperial Earth, 1976
Rendezvous with Rama, 1973
A Fall of Moondust, 1961

Other books you might like:
Isaac Asimov, *The Edge of Tomorrow*, 1985
Robert A. Heinlein, *The Past through Tomorrow*, 1967
Henry Kuttner, *The Best of Henry Kuttner*, 1975
Robert Sheckley, *The Collected Stories of Robert Sheckley*, 1992
Clifford D. Simak, *Over the River and through the Woods*, 1996

767

TONY DANIEL

Metaplanetary
(New York: Avon Eos, 2001)

Story type: Alternate Intelligence; Dystopian
Subject(s): Artificial Intelligence
Major character(s): Roger Sherman, Military Personnel (retired); Ames, Ruler; Alethea, Artist
Time period(s): Indeterminate Future
Locale(s): Earth; Outer Space

Summary: The inner planets of the solar system have become a closely interlocked dictatorship, using artificial intelligence and nanotechnology to hold things together. The outer worlds are less structured, and some artificial intelligences escape to freedom from the virtual slavery of the inner system. Eventually the loss of resources results in a war that will determine the future of what it is to be a human being.

Where it's reviewed:
Publishers Weekly, February 26, 2001, page 63
Science Fiction Chronicle, March 2001, page 43

Other books by the same author:
The Robot's Twilight Companion, 1999
Earthling, 1997
Warpath, 1993

Other books you might like:
Colin Greenland, *Take Back Plenty*, 1990
Cecelia Holland, *Floating Worlds*, 1975
Alexander Jablokov, *Deepdrive*, 1998
Alastair Reynolds, *Revelation Space*, 2000
Vernor Vinge, *A Fire upon the Deep*, 1992

768

JACK DANN, Editor
GARDNER DOZOIS, Co-Editor

Genometry
(New York: Ace, 2001)

Story type: Anthology; Genetic Manipulation
Subject(s): Short Stories; Genetic Engineering

Summary: *Genometry* consists of 11 stories dealing with the concept of genetic engineering. All but one were originally published between 1984 and 1997, with the other from the early 1960s. The authors include Cordwainer Smith, John

Brunner, Bruce Sterling, Frederik Pohl, and others, and they explore a wide variety of consequences, both good and bad, of this field of study.

Where it's reviewed:
Science Fiction Chronicle, March 2001, page 45

Other books by the same author:
The Memory Cathedral, 1996
Echoes of Thunder, 1991
The Man Who Melted, 1984
Junction, 1981
Starhiker, 1967

Other books you might like:
Brian W. Aldiss, *An Island Called Moreau*, 1981
Lois McMaster Bujold, *Falling Free*, 1988
Anne Harris, *Accidental Creatures*, 1998
Hayford Peirce, *The Phylum Monsters*, 1989
Robert Reed, *Black Milk*, 1989

769

JACK DANN, Editor
GARDNER DOZOIS, Co-Editor

Space Soldiers

(New York: Ace, 2001)

Story type: Anthology; Military
Subject(s): Short Stories

Summary: Nine stories, all previously published, each deal with some aspect of military service in outer space. The stories are set elsewhere in our solar system and in other parts of the galaxy. The contributors include Mack Reynolds, Tom Purdom, William Barton, Fritz Leiber, Stephen Baxter, Fred Saberhagen, and Alastair Reynolds.

Where it's reviewed:
Science Fiction Chronicle, June 2001, page 40

Other books by the same author:
The Memory Cathedral, 1996
Echoes of Thunder, 1991
The Man Who Melted, 1984
Junction, 1981
Timetipping, 1980

Other books you might like:
William Barton, *When Heaven Fell*, 1995
Joe Haldeman, *The Forever War*, 1974
Alastair Reynolds, *Revelation Space*, 2000
Mack Reynolds, *The Galactic Medal of Honor*, 1976
Fred Saberhagen, *Berserker Fury*, 1997

770

ROXANN DAWSON
DANIEL GRAHAM, Co-Author

Entering Tenebrea

(New York: Pocket, 2001)

Story type: Space Opera
Series: Tenebrea. Book 1
Subject(s): Cloning

Major character(s): Hal K'Rin, Alien, Government Official; Andrea Flores, Vigilante; Eric, Clone
Time period(s): Indeterminate Future
Locale(s): Jod, Planet—Imaginary; Clemnos, Planet—Imaginary

Summary: When a woman sees her family slaughtered by alien terrorists, she leaves Earth on a mission of vengeance. On an alien world, she seeks to join an elite organization, and discovers the injustices of how clones are treated on other planets. This is a first novel by this collaborative team.

Where it's reviewed:
Science Fiction Chronicle, July 2001, page 44

Other books you might like:
Poul Anderson, *Mayday Orbit*, 1961
C.J. Cherryh, *The Pride of Chanur*, 1982
Nancy Kress, *Probability Sun*, 2001
Jack Vance, *The Star King*, 1964
Sean Williams, *A Dark Imbalance*, 2001
   Shane Dix, co-author

771

ARWEN ELYS DAYTON

Resurrection

(New York: Roc, 2001)

Story type: Space Opera
Subject(s): Aliens
Major character(s): Pruit, Military Personnel, Alien; Adaiz, Alien, Spy
Time period(s): 2000s (2001)
Locale(s): Egypt

Summary: The inhabitants of the planet Herrod are about to be wiped out by their enemies from Lucien. Their only hope is to find an ancient technology they lost long ago, remnants of which may be found in the ruins of an age-old expedition to the primitive planet Earth. This is a first novel.

Other books you might like:
J.D. Austin, *Bobby's Girl*, 2001
Jeffrey Lloyd Castle, *Vanguard to Venus*, 1957
Dean R. Koontz, *Strangers*, 1986
Ashley McConnell, *The Morpheus Factor*, 2001
Kate Orman, *Set Piece*, 1995

772

DENNY DEMARTINO

Heart of Stone

(New York: Ace, 2001)

Story type: Mystery
Series: Astrologer. Book 1
Subject(s): Astrology
Major character(s): Philipa Cyrion, Astrologer; Artemis Hadrien, Police Officer
Time period(s): 22nd century (2130)
Locale(s): Earth

Summary: In the 22nd century, scientists have discovered the secret of travel to the stars, and have also learned that astrology has a scientific basis, since our universe is connected to a series of other realities, including one that functions as the afterlife. When an astrologer's husband is murdered without the stars warning her, she comes to doubt her specialty, but decides to find out who's responsible by more conventional means. This is a first novel.

Other books you might like:
David Bear, *Keeping Time*, 1979
Moyra Caldecott, *Child of a Dark Star*, 1984
Katherine Kurtz, *The Legacy of Lehr*, 1986
Atanielle Annyn Noel, *Murder on Usher's Planet*, 1987
Mary Rosenblum, *The Stone Garden*, 1995

773

ROBERT DOHERTY

Area 51: The Grail

(New York: Dell, 2001)

Story type: Invasion of Earth; UFO
Series: Area 51. Book 5
Subject(s): Aliens
Major character(s): Mike Turcotte, Military Personnel; Lisa Duncan, Scientist, Captive; Che Lu, Military Personnel
Time period(s): 2000s (2001)
Locale(s): China; United States; Israel

Summary: Aliens once occupied the Earth, and now they have secretly returned. Area 51 is a covert government agency working to defeat them, and their current mission is to find the Holy Grail, which is actually an alien artifact with enormous power. The leader of the recovery group is hampered by the knowledge that the woman he loves is a prisoner of the aliens.

Other books by the same author:
Area 51: The Sphinx, 2000
Area 51: The Reply, 1998
Area 51, 1997
The Rock, 1996

Other books you might like:
Paul Adler, *Saucer Hill*, 1979
David Bischoff, *Revelation*, 1991
Martin Caidin, *The Mendelov Conspiracy*, 1969
John Dalton, *The Cattle Mutilations*, 1980
Louis Goth, *Red 12*, 1979

774

GREG DONEGAN

Devil's Sea

(New York: Berkley, 2001)

Story type: Invasion of Earth
Series: Atlantis. Book 3
Subject(s): Aliens
Major character(s): Eric Dane, Military Personnel; Ariana Michelet, Scientist; Kaia, Nobleman
Time period(s): 1st century (79); 21st century
Locale(s): Cambodia; Undersea Environment/Habitat; Italy

Summary: An alien force attacking from another dimension menaced Earth in the far past, and destroyed Atlantis before being repulsed. Now an elite military force responds to their latest attempts to invade the world by preparing a counterattack that will eliminate the threat forever.

Where it's reviewed:
Science Fiction Chronicle, April 2001, page 39

Other books by the same author:
Bermuda Triangle, 2000
Atlantis, 1999

Other books you might like:
John Brunner, *The Atlantic Abomination*, 1960
Robert Doherty, *The Grail*, 2000
Murray Leinster, *Creatures of the Abyss*, 1961
Joseph Rosenberger, *The Bermuda Triangle Action*, 1980
John Wyndham, *Out of the Deeps*, 1953

775

GARDNER DOZOIS, Editor
SHEILA WILLIAMS, Co-Editor

Isaac Asimov's Father's Day

(New York: Ace, 2001)

Story type: Collection
Subject(s): Short Stories; Fathers and Daughters; Fathers and Sons

Summary: These nine stories are all reprinted from *Isaac Asimov's Science Fiction*, where they appeared between 1990 and 1998. Each of the stories deals with the relationship between a father and his child or children, in future settings, and on other worlds. Contributors include Pamela Sargent, Harry Turtledove, Robert Reed, Jonathan Lethem, and James Patrick Kelly.

Other books by the same author:
Geodesic Dreams, 1992
The Peacemaker, 1983
Strangers, 1978
The Visible Man, 1977
Nightmare Blue, 1975 (George Alec Effinger, co-author)

Other books you might like:
James Patrick Kelly, *Think Like a Dinosaur*, 1997
Jonathan Lethem, *Amnesia Moon*, 1995
Robert Reed, *Marrow*, 2000
Pamela Sargent, *Climb the Wind*, 1999
Harry Turtledove, *Sentry Peak*, 2000

776

GARDNER DOZOIS, Editor

The Year's Best Science Fiction: Eighteenth Annual Collection

(New York: St Martin's Press, 2001)

Story type: Anthology
Subject(s): Short Stories

Summary: This comprehensive and representative sampling of short science fiction published during the year 2000 includes a

complete short novel by Ian McDonald. Other contributors are Ursula K. Le Guin, Alastair Reynolds, Lucius Shepard, Peter Hamilton, Brian Stableford, Tananarive Due, Stephen Baxter, and Nancy Kress.

Other books by the same author:
Geodesic Dreams, 1992
The Peacemaker, 1983
Strangers, 1978
The Visible Man, 1977
Nightmare Blue, 1975 (George Alec Effinger, co-author)

Other books you might like:
Tananarive Due, *The Living Blood*, 2001
Nancy Kress, *Probability Sun*, 2001
Alastair Reynolds, *Revelation Space*, 2000
Lucius Shepard, *Barnacle Bill the Spacer and Other Stories*, 1997
Brian Stableford, *The Cassandra Complex*, 2001

DAVID DRAKE, Editor

Foreign Legions

(New York: Baen, 2001)

Story type: Anthology
Subject(s): Short Stories

Summary: The stories in this anthology are set in the same universe as the editor's short story, "Ranks of Bronze," which is also included. In this story, aliens capture a group of Roman soldiers to use as mercenaries, making them nearly immortal in the process. The Romans bide their time, eventually gaining the upper hand. Other stories are contributed by David Weber, S.M. Stirling, and Eric Flint.

Other books by the same author:
Lieutenant Leary Commanding, 2000
Servants of the Dragon, 1999
With the Lightnings, 1998
The Tank Lords, 1997
Ranks of Bronze, 1986

Other books you might like:
Poul Anderson, *The High Crusade*, 1960
Eric Flint, *1632*, 2000
William R. Forstchen, *Rally Cry*, 1990
Jerry Pournelle, *Storms of Victory*, 1987
    Roland Green, co-author
David Weber, *In Enemy Hands*, 1997

BILL FAWCETT, Editor

Bolos: Old Guard

(New York: Baen, 2001)

Story type: Anthology
Series: Bolos. Book 5
Subject(s): Short Stories

Summary: This is a collection of four long stories set in the universe of the Bolos, created by the late Keith Laumer. Bolos

are supertanks of the future, deployed on distant worlds, each with the organic mind of a human being to guide its actions. The contributors are Mark Thies, Dean Wesley Smith, J. Steven York, William H. Keith, and John Mina.

Other books by the same author:
Honor of the Regiment, 1993
Cats in Space and Other Places, 1992

Other books you might like:
David Drake, *The Tank Lords*, 1997
Leo Frankowski, *A Boy and His Tank*, 1999
William H. Keith Jr., *Bolo Rising*, 1999
Keith Laumer, *Rogue Bolo*, 1986
S.M. Stirling, *The Ship Avenged*, 1997

DAVID FEINTUCH

Children of Hope

(New York: Ace, 2001)

Story type: Space Colony; Religious
Series: Nicholas Seafort. Book 7
Subject(s): Aliens; Political Thriller
Major character(s): Nicholas Seafort, Spaceship Captain; Randall Carr, Teenager; Anthony Carr, Government Official
Time period(s): 23rd century (2246-2247)
Locale(s): Hope, Planet—Imaginary; *Olympiad*, Spaceship

Summary: Young Randall Carr blames Nicholas Seafort for the death of his father, so he assaults him when he arrives at the planet Hope, commanding a new starship. Seafort survives and adopts the repentant Carr, just as the political situation between Earth and Hope reaches a critical point, with the theocracy stirring up trouble on every side. Then an armada of aliens enters the system and the situation becomes a crisis.

Where it's reviewed:
Science Fiction Chronicle, June 2001, page 37

Other books by the same author:
Patriarch's Hope, 1999
Fisherman's Hope, 1996
Voices of Hope, 1996
Challenger's Hope, 1995
Prisoner's Hope, 1995

Other books you might like:
C.J. Cherryh, *Downbelow Station*, 1984
Joe Haldeman, *The Forever War*, 1974
Alastair Reynolds, *Revelation Space*, 2000
Dan Simmons, *Endymion*, 1995
Vernor Vinge, *A Deepness in the Sky*, 1999

780

JASPER FFORDE

The Eyre Affair

(London: New English Library, 2001)

Story type: Time Travel

Subject(s): Alternate History
Major character(s): Thursday Next, Police Officer; Acheron Hades, Criminal; Tamworth, Government Official
Time period(s): 2000s (2001)
Locale(s): Alternate Earth

Summary: In an alternate version of Earth, a police agent chases an arch criminal, who has stolen the original manuscript of a classic novel. She believes she's living in the original timeline, but her father remembers an entirely different history. This is a first novel.

Other books you might like:
Bradley Denton, *Wrack and Roll*, 1986
Phyllis Eisenstein, *Shadow of Earth*, 1979
Jon Courtenay Grimwood, *Pashazade: The First Arabesk*, 2001
Michael Moorcock, *Gloriana*, 1978
Keith Roberts, *Pavane*, 1968

781

ERIC FLINT
DAVID DRAKE, Co-Author

The Tide of Victory
(New York: Baen, 2001)

Story type: Invasion of Earth
Series: Belisarius. Book 5
Subject(s): Aliens
Major character(s): Belisarius, Military Personnel (general); Malwa, Alien; Antonina, Noblewoman
Time period(s): 6th century (533)
Locale(s): India

Summary: The alien Malwa has still not been driven from the Earth. General Belisarius and his companions must battle a fresh assault, while dealing with various factions from the Indian subcontinent, Ethiopia, and surrounding nations. Much of the story deals with the military campaigns against the alien-controlled enemy.

Other books by the same author:
The Philosophical Strangler, 2001
1632, 2000
Fortune's Stroke, 2000 (David Drake, co-author)
Destiny's Shield, 1999 (David Drake, co-author)
Mother of Demons, 1997

Other books you might like:
John Barnes, *Caesar's Bicycle*, 1997
L. Sprague de Camp, *Lest Darkness Fall*, 1941
David Drake, *Ranks of Bronze*, 1986
Crawford Kilian, *Rogue Emperor*, 1988
James White, *The First Protector*, 2000

782

MICHAEL FLYNN

Falling Stars
(New York: Tor, 2001)

Story type: Disaster
Series: Star. Book 4

Subject(s): Disasters
Major character(s): Jimmy Poole, Computer Expert; Mariesa Van Huyten, Businesswoman; Roberta Carson, Writer (poet)
Time period(s): 21st century
Locale(s): Outer Space; United States

Summary: Several asteroids have been diverted from their usual course, and some of them nearly strike the Earth. An exploratory mission discovers an alien installation within the asteroid belt. Now a new voyage must be launched to discover the purpose of this hidden control room, and avert a worldwide disaster that could threaten the future of the human race.

Where it's reviewed:
Locus, March 2001, page 64

Other books by the same author:
Lodestar, 2000
Rogue Star, 1998
The Forest of Time and Other Stories, 1997
Firestar, 1996
In the Country of the Blind, 1990

Other books you might like:
Poul Anderson, *Tales of the Flying Mountains*, 1971
Ben Bova, *Privateers*, 1985
C.J. Cherryh, *Hellburner*, 1992
Elizabeth Hand, *Icarus Descending*, 1993
Alan E. Nourse, *Scavengers in Space*, 1959

783

ALAN DEAN FOSTER

Interlopers
(New York: Ace, 2001)

Story type: Invasion of Earth
Subject(s): Aliens
Major character(s): Cody Westcott, Archaeologist; Kelli Alwydd Westcott, Archaeologist; Karl Oelefse von Eichstatt, Scientist
Time period(s): 2000s (2001)
Locale(s): Arizona; Peru

Summary: An archaeologist experiments with a drug described in an ancient Incan text and suddenly has the ability to see invisible parasites, which inhabit the world and prey on humans. They are intelligent and aware of his knowledge, and attempt to prevent him from interfering with their secret activities by menacing him and his friends.

Where it's reviewed:
Science Fiction Chronicle, July 2001, page 44

Other books by the same author:
Dirge, 2000
Phylogenesis, 1999
Parallelities, 1998
Jed the Dead, 1997
Mad Amos, 1996

Other books you might like:
John Brunner, *Echo in the Skull*, 1959
John Christopher, *The Possessors*, 1964
Matthew J. Costello, *Wurm*, 1991

Dean Ing, *Anasazi*, 1980
Richard Laymon, *Flesh*, 1987

784
ALAN DEAN FOSTER

Reunion
(New York: Ballantine Del Rey, 2001)

Story type: Space Opera
Series: Flinx. Book 8
Subject(s): Aliens; Genetic Engineering
Major character(s): Philip Lynx, Space Explorer; Mahmahmi Lynx, Businesswoman; Voocim, Military Personnel, Alien (Aann)
Time period(s): 30th century
Locale(s): Pyrassis, Planet—Imaginary; Outer Space

Summary: Philip Lynx travels to a desert world controlled by the alien Aann in search of data concerning his childhood as a genetically engineered experiment. Stranded, he battles a variety of local predators before being captured by the Aann, then escapes and discovers a gigantic alien artifact that has been dormant for a half billion years.

Where it's reviewed:
Locus, May 2001, page 29
Science Fiction Chronicle, June 2001, page 37

Other books by the same author:
Dirge, 2000
Phylogenesis, 1999
Parallelities, 1998
Jed the Dead, 1997
The Howling Stones, 1997

Other books you might like:
James P. Hogan, *Code of the Lifemaker*, 1983
Jack McDevitt, *Deepsix*, 2001
David F. Nighbert, *Timelapse*, 1988
Alastair Reynolds, *Revelation Space*, 2000
Jack Vance, *Araminta Station*, 1988

785
GEORGE FOY

The Last Harbor
(New York: Bantam, 2001)

Story type: Future Shock
Subject(s): Futuristic Fiction
Major character(s): Slocum, Businessman, Unemployed; Melisande Sloan, Young Woman; MacTavish, Guard
Time period(s): Indeterminate Future
Locale(s): North America

Summary: Slocum is an out of work businessman trying to scrape together a life along the seacoast. Then a mysterious woman appears on a colossal sea vessel, and his interaction with her is complicated by politics and a new disease which threatens to be more devastating than AIDS.

Where it's reviewed:
Locus, May 2001, page 27

Science Fiction Chronicle, July 2001, page 43

Other books by the same author:
The Memory of Fire, 2000
Contraband, 1997
The Shift, 1996

Other books you might like:
J.G. Ballard, *Vermilion Sands*, 1971
Paul Di Filippo, *Lost Pages*, 1998
William Gibson, *Mona Lisa Overdrive*, 1988
Michael Moorcock, *Fabulous Harbors*, 1995
Jamil Nasir, *Distance Haze*, 2000

786
DAVID GARNETT

Space Wasters
(London: Orbit, 2001)

Story type: Humor
Subject(s): Space Travel
Major character(s): Wayne Norton, Tourist; Kiru Norton, Tourist; Dulsedech, Alien
Time period(s): Indeterminate Future
Locale(s): Cafe World, Planet—Imaginary; Outer Space; Algol, Planet—Imaginary

Summary: Wayne Norton and his wife are vacationing on a resort world when she disappears, apparently having been kidnapped. Wayne is maneuvered into acting as the agent of an interstellar bureau of taxation in order to get her back, and has a series of comic adventures as he travels to another planet.

Where it's reviewed:
Science Fiction Chronicle, July 2001, page 44

Other books by the same author:
Cosmic Carousel, 1976
The Forgotten Dimension, 1975
Time in Eclipse, 1974
The Starseekers, 1971
Mirror in the Sky, 1969

Other books you might like:
Douglas Adams, *Dirk Gently's Holistic Detective Agency*, 1987
Neal Barrett Jr., *Stress Pattern*, 1974
John DeChancie, *The Kruton Interface*, 1993
Esther Friesner, *The Sherwood Game*, 1995
Harry Harrison, *Bill, the Galactic Hero*, 1965

787
DAVID GERROLD

Bouncing Off the Moon
(New York: Tor, 2001)

Story type: Young Adult
Series: Dingillian. Book 2
Subject(s): Artificial Intelligence
Major character(s): Chigger Dingillian, Teenager; Alexei Krislov, Spaceman; Douglas Dingillian, Teenager

Time period(s): 21st century
Locale(s): Moon (Earth's)

Summary: The three Dingillian brothers have successfully escaped the control of their feuding parents. Now they need to get off a geosynchronous space station and find a new home because a handful of corporations and government agencies are chasing them, trying to gain control of a secret technology their father concealed within their baggage. A friend takes them to the moon, and the chase is on again.

Where it's reviewed:
Publishers Weekly, February 19, 2001, page 73
Science Fiction Chronicle, April 2001, page 35

Other books by the same author:
Jumping Off the Planet, 2000
The Middle of Nowhere, 1995
Under the Eye of God, 1993
A Season for Slaughter, 1992
Voyage of the Star Wolf, 1990

Other books you might like:
Ben Bova, *Colony*, 1978
John Christopher, *The Lotus Caves*, 1969
Arthur C. Clarke, *Earthlight*, 1955
Lester Del Rey, *Moon of Mutiny*, 1961
Monica Hughes, *Earthdark*, 1977

788

KURT R.A. GIAMBASTINI

The Year the Cloud Fell

(New York: Roc, 2001)

Story type: Alternate Universe
Subject(s): Alternate History
Major character(s): George Armstrong Custer Jr., Military Personnel; Storm Arriving, Warrior; Speaks While Leaving, Young Woman
Time period(s): 1880s (1886)
Locale(s): North America

Summary: In an alternate America where the Cheyenne nation remains independent, George Custer's son sets out in a dirigible to survey the contested land. He crashes and is taken in by the Cheyenne, who believe he is fated to intercede on their behalf and force the United States to recognize them as a separate people. This is a first novel.

Where it's reviewed:
Science Fiction Chronicle, April 2001, page 39

Other books you might like:
Harry Harrison, *Stars & Stripes Forever*, 1998
Michael Kurland, *The Whenabouts of Burr*, 1975
Jake Page, *Apacheria*, 1998
William Sanders, *The Wild Blue and the Gray*, 1991
Pamela Sargent, *Climb the Wind*, 1999

789

JAMES C. GLASS

Empress of Light

(New York: Baen, 2001)

Story type: Lost Colony
Series: Shanji. Book 2
Subject(s): Space Colonies
Major character(s): Kati, Ruler (empress); Yesugen, Military Personnel; Huomeng, Government Official
Time period(s): Indeterminate Future
Locale(s): Shanji, Planet—Imaginary

Summary: Two planets circling neighboring stars have been at war for some time, but now Shanji has overwhelmed its enemies thanks to the awe inspiring power of its new empress. Just when it appears that she can finally rest and return to her family, factions on both sides begin to provoke new violence and it seems the war will break out again.

Other books by the same author:
Shanji, 1999

Other books you might like:
Roger MacBride Allen, *Rogue Powers*, 1986
Poul Anderson, *Mirkheim*, 1977
Alfred Coppel, *Glory's War*, 1995
Bob Shaw, *The Ragged Astronauts*, 1986
Dan Simmons, *Endymion*, 1995

790

KEN GODDARD

Outer Perimeter

(New York: Bantam, 2001)

Story type: Mystery
Subject(s): Aliens
Major character(s): Colin Cellars, Detective—Police; Ed Dombrowski, Military Personnel; Melissa Washington, Scientist
Time period(s): 2000s (2001)
Locale(s): Oregon

Summary: Colin Cellars is a police investigator whose reputation is endangered by his personal involvement in a recent murder. He pursues that investigation, as well as another featuring the disappearance of dozens of people, and his efforts run afoul of a government effort to suppress the fact that aliens are secretly visiting the Earth.

Where it's reviewed:
Booklist, December 1, 2000, page 696
Publishers Weekly, January 8, 2001, page 48
Science Fiction Chronicle, February 2001, page 42

Other books by the same author:
First Evidence, 1999

Other books you might like:
Kevin J. Anderson, *Antibodies*, 1997
Gary A. Braunbeck, *In Hollow Houses*, 2000
Charles L. Grant, *Whirlwind*, 1995
Clifford D. Simak, *All Flesh Is Grass*, 1965

Mark Sumner, *Insanity, Illinois*, 1998

Brad Ferguson, *The World Next Door*, 1990
James P. Hogan, *Paths to Otherwhere*, 1996
Kirk Mitchell, *Never the Twain*, 1987
Hayford Peirce, *Napoleon Disentimed*, 1987

791

THOMAS S. GRESSMAN

Operation Sierra-75

(New York: Warner Aspect, 2001)

Story type: Space Opera
Series: Vor. Book 5
Subject(s): Space Exploration
Major character(s): Maxwell Taggart, Military Personnel (captain); Rebecca Cortez, Military Personnel (lieutenant), Doctor; Gunny Frost, Military Personnel
Time period(s): Indeterminate Future
Locale(s): Sierra 75, Planet—Imaginary

Summary: Earth has been pulled into a pocket universe with myriad other planets. A spaceship disappears while investigating one of the worlds closest to the Earth, and a military expedition follows to find out what happened to it. The expedition members find themselves on a bizarre world where reality seems to change, and where some malevolent force is hunting them.

Other books by the same author:
Shadows of War, 1998
Sword and Fire, 1998
The Hunters, 1997

Other books you might like:
Roger MacBride Allen, *The Ring of Charon*, 1990
Stephen Baxter, *The Raft*, 1992
Gordon R. Dickson, *Mission to Universe*, 1965
Philip Jose Farmer, *The Maker of Universes*, 1965
Harry Harrison, *Deathworld*, 1976

792

JON COURTENAY GRIMWOOD

Pashazade: The First Arabesk

(London: Earthlight, 2001)

Story type: Mystery
Subject(s): Alternate History
Major character(s): Ashraf al-Mansur, Nobleman, Fugitive; Hani, Child; Zara Effendi, Young Woman
Time period(s): 2000s (2001)
Locale(s): Africa, Alternate Earth

Summary: Ashraf al-Mansur escapes imprisonment in North America and returns to his native North Africa in a world where Germany won the First World War. There he meets the woman he is pledged to marry, although she doesn't like him very much, and becomes responsible for his young cousin after her guardian is murdered. Unfortunately, he quickly becomes the prime suspect in the crime.

Other books by the same author:
Lucifer's Dragon, 1998
Neoaddix, 1997

Other books you might like:
George Alec Effinger, *Relatives*, 1973

793

HARRY HARRISON

50 in 50

(New York: Tor, 2001)

Story type: Collection
Subject(s): Short Stories

Summary: To celebrate his 50 years as a writer, Harrison has selected what he considers his 50 best short stories. They are grouped thematically, including aliens, marvelous inventions, humor, psychological twists, and others. Adventure predominates but there is some satire as well.

Other books by the same author:
Stars and Stripes in Peril, 2000
The Stainless Steel Rat Joins the Circus, 1999
Stars & Stripes Forever, 1998
King and Emperor, 1996
Galactic Dreams, 1994

Other books you might like:
Gordon R. Dickson, *The Man the Worlds Rejected*, 1986
Keith Laumer, *The Best of Keith Laumer*, 1976
Murray Leinster, *First Contacts*, 1998
Alan E. Nourse, *Psi High and Others*, 1967
Robert Sheckley, *Citizen in Space*, 1955

794

JOHN G. HEMRY

Stark's Command

(New York: Ace, 2001)

Story type: Military
Series: Stark. Book 2
Subject(s): Space Colonies
Major character(s): Ethan Stark, Military Personnel (sergeant); Vic Reynolds, Military Personnel; James Campbell, Government Official
Time period(s): Indeterminate Future
Locale(s): Moon (Earth's)

Summary: A military contingent at the moon colony has successfully mutinied. The civilian population is willing to cooperate with them against fresh forces sent up from Earth, but only if the mutineers support their bid to become an independent state. Ethan Stark, acting military commander, must find a way to integrate the two groups if the rebellion is to remain viable.

Other books by the same author:
Stark's War, 2000

Other books you might like:
Ben Bova, *Moonwar*, 1998
Lester Del Rey, *Moon of Mutiny*, 1961
Philip Jose Farmer, *Tongues of the Moon*, 1961

Robert A. Heinlein, *The Moon Is a Harsh Mistress*, 1966
Jeff Sutton, *First on the Moon*, 1958

795

MATTHEW HUGHES

Fool Me Twice

(New York: Warner Aspect, 2001)

Story type: Humor
Subject(s): Futuristic Fiction
Major character(s): Filidor Vesh, Apprentice; Emmlyn Podarke, Thief; Faubon Basspriot, Police Officer
Time period(s): Indeterminate Future
Locale(s): Earth

Summary: This sequel to *Fool's Errant* follows the adventures of Filidor Vesh, an innocuous young man, whose credentials are stolen by a lively young woman. He chases her to a remote part of a far future Earth to regain his property, encountering aliens, pirates, and other characters along the way, each confrontation developed to humorous effect.

Other books by the same author:
Fool's Errant, 2000

Other books you might like:
Robert Asprin, *Phule Me Twice*, 2000
   Peter J. Heck, co-author
Edmund Cooper, *Kronk*, 1971
Gordon R. Dickson, *The Magnificent Wilf*, 1995
Robert Sheckley, *Journey Beyond Tomorrow*, 1962
Jack Vance, *The Night Lamp*, 1996

796

CHARLES INGRID

The Sand Wars. Volume Two

(New York: DAW, 2001)

Story type: Space Opera
Series: Sand Wars. Volume 2
Subject(s): Space Travel
Major character(s): Jack Storm, Military Personnel, Spaceman
Time period(s): Indeterminate Future
Locale(s): Outer Space

Summary: This is an omnibus of the second three novels in the Sand Wars series, *Alien Salute*, *Return Fire*, and *Challenge Met*. Jack Storm is heavily involved in the battle against the alien Thraks when a third force appears, another race with territorial ambitions. Humans and Thraks become temporary allies, but Storm suspects that the alliance is flawed by treachery, and eventually must disprove charges that he is a traitor.

Where it's reviewed:
Science Fiction Chronicle, April 2001, page 38

Other books by the same author:
Soulfire, 1995
The Downfall Matrix, 1994
The Path of Fire, 1992
The Last Recall, 1991
The Marked Man, 1989

Other books you might like:
Roger MacBride Allen, *Allies and Aliens*, 1995
Poul Anderson, *The Star Fox*, 1966
Alan Dean Foster, *Dirge*, 2000
Keith Laumer, *The Glory Game*, 1973
Barry Longyear, *Manifest Destiny*, 1980

797

PAUL JOHNSTON

Water of Death

(New York: St Martin's Press, 2001)

Story type: Mystery
Series: Edinburgh. Book 3
Subject(s): Environmental Problems
Major character(s): Quintillian Dalrymple, Detective—Police; Lewis Hamilton, Government Official; Agnes Kennedy, Criminal
Time period(s): 2020s (2025)
Locale(s): Edinburgh, Scotland

Summary: After the collapse of the United Kingdom, Edinburgh becomes an independent nation with a repressive government. Quint is a detective employed by that government to discover who has been putting poison into bottles of black market whiskey, but his investigation uncovers an even more dangerous threat to the city.

Where it's reviewed:
Booklist, March 1, 2001, page 1231
Publishers Weekly, February 12, 2001, page 187

Other books by the same author:
The House of Dust, 2001
The Bone Yard, 1998
Body Politic, 1997

Other books you might like:
Wilhelmina Baird, *Clipjoint*, 1994
Eric James Fullilove, *Circle of One*, 1996
Donald James, *Monstrum*, 1997
Mel Odom, *Lethal Interface*, 1992
Richard Paul Russo, *Carlucci's Edge*, 1995

798

ROBERT L. KATZ

Edward Maret

(Holliston, Massachusetts: Willowgate, 2001)

Story type: Political
Subject(s): Cyborgs
Major character(s): Edward Maret, Cyborg; Jason Deseret, Police Officer; Vincent Fitzmichael, Businessman
Time period(s): Indeterminate Future
Locale(s): Earth; Outer Space

Summary: Edward Maret is heir to a family fortune, but he has two enemies, one who covets his money, the other the woman he is engaged to marry. They erase Maret's memories and convert his body into that of a cyborg, in which form he is compelled to serve in humanity's battle against an alien race encountered in space. Eventually his memories return and he

seeks revenge on those who wronged him. This is a first novel.

Where it's reviewed:
Publishers Weekly, February 26, 2001, page 64
Science Fiction Chronicle, March 2001, page 44

Other books you might like:
John Gregory Betancourt, *Rememory*, 1990
Algis Budrys, *Who?*, 1958
Karl Hansen, *War Games*, 1981
Keith Laumer, *A Plague of Demons*, 1965
Frederik Pohl, *Man Plus*, 1976

799

NANCY KRESS

Probability Sun

(New York: Tor, 2001)

Story type: Hard Science Fiction; Psychic Powers
Subject(s): Aliens
Major character(s): Lyle Kaufman, Military Personnel; Thomas Capelo, Scientist; Marbet Grant, Psychic
Time period(s): Indeterminate Future
Locale(s): World, Planet—Imaginary

Summary: An expedition is sent to the planet World to retrieve an alien artifact that might become a successful weapon against the bellicose Fallers. Removing it will do irreparable damage to the local inhabitants, however, whose society is dependent upon the field of shared consciousness, which originates in the device.

Where it's reviewed:
Science Fiction Chronicle, July 2001, page 42

Other books by the same author:
Probability Moon, 2000
Yanked, 1999
Beaker's Dozen, 1998
Maximum Light, 1998
Oaths and Miracles, 1996

Other books you might like:
Brian Ball, *Planet Probability*, 1973
Stephen Baxter, *The Ring*, 1995
Algis Budrys, *Rogue Moon*, 1960
Andre Norton, *Lord of Thunder*, 1962
Robert Silverberg, *Across a Billion Years*, 1969

800

PAUL LEVINSON

Borrowed Tides

(New York: Tor, 2001)

Story type: Space Colony
Subject(s): Space Exploration
Major character(s): Aaron Schoenfeld, Scientist, Spaceman; Jack Lumet, Scientist, Spaceman; Kathy Lotari, Doctor, Spacewoman
Time period(s): 21st century
Locale(s): Outer Space; N'Urth, Planet—Imaginary

Summary: The first voyage to another star system is launched from the planet Mars with a small crew, including two scientists already in their seventies. After reaching Alpha Centauri, the crew watches as a lifeless planet is quickly transformed into a mirror image of Earth, suitable for human colonization, and they set out to explore it.

Where it's reviewed:
Publishers Weekly, February 26, 2001, page 63
Science Fiction Chronicle, March 2001, page 43

Other books by the same author:
Paul Levinson's Bestseller, 1999
The Silk Code, 1999

Other books you might like:
Poul Anderson, *The Enemy Stars*, 1958
Gordon R. Dickson, *Mission to Universe*, 1965
Molly Gloss, *The Dazzle of Day*, 1997
Edmond Hamilton, *The Haunted Stars*, 1960
Alexei Panshin, *Rite of Passage*, 1968

801

SALLIE LOWENSTEIN

Focus

(Kensington, Maryland: Lion Stone, 2001)

Story type: Young Adult
Subject(s): Aliens; Genetic Engineering
Major character(s): Andrew Haldran, Teenager; Tomas Chalder, Miner
Time period(s): Indeterminate Future
Locale(s): Miners World, Planet—Imaginary

Summary: Young Andrew refuses genetic treatment which would concentrate his abilities in a single area and allow him to choose his profession. His family immigrates to a distant planet where mining fuels the economy, and there he solves the mystery of an enigmatic man, meets an alien being, and entertains his sister with a series of fairy stories. This is a first SF novel.

Where it's reviewed:
Science Fiction Chronicle, April 2001, page 37

Other books you might like:
Robert A.W. Lowndes, *The Mystery of the Third Mine*, 1953
Alan E. Nourse, *Scavengers in Space*, 1959
Charles Oberndorf, *Testing*, 1993
Jerry Pournelle, *Starswarm*, 1998
Charles Sheffield, *The Billion Dollar Boy*, 1997

802

SCOTT MACKAY

The Meek

(New York: Roc, 2001)

Story type: Genetic Manipulation
Subject(s): Genetic Engineering
Major character(s): Cody Wisner, Engineer; Deirdre Malvern, Engineer; Lulu, Mutant
Time period(s): Indeterminate Future

Locale(s): Ceres, Asteroid

Summary: An experiment in genetic engineering is terminated when the altered colonists of the asteroid Ceres prove to be chronically violent. Years later, engineers are sent to evaluate the supposedly dead colony for future use. They discover that some of the altered humans still survive, and have developed new abilities, including a form of telepathy.

Where it's reviewed:
Science Fiction Chronicle, March 2001, page 46

Other books by the same author:
Outpost, 1998

Other books you might like:
Poul Anderson, *The Snows of Ganymede*, 1958
Lois McMaster Bujold, *Falling Free*, 1988
Gordon R. Dickson, *The Space Swimmers*, 1967
David Gerrold, *Under the Eye of God*, 1993
Paul Preuss, *Human Error*, 1985

803

KEN MACLEOD

Cosmonaut Keep

(New York: Tor, 2001)

Story type: First Contact
Subject(s): Aliens
Major character(s): Matt Cairns, Computer Expert; Gregor Cairns, Fisherman
Time period(s): Indeterminate Future
Locale(s): Earth; Mingulay, Planet—Imaginary

Summary: The story alternates between two generations of the same human family. In one generation, the first contact is made with an alien race, with the usual problems and misunderstandings. In the other, the two races have learned to live in harmony, and humans and aliens now jointly colonize planets.

Where it's reviewed:
Booklist, April 15, 2001, page 1542
Locus, April 2001, page 29
Publishers Weekly, April 15, 2001, page 55

Other books by the same author:
The Sky Road, 1999
The Cassini Division, 1998
The Stone Canal, 1996
The Star Fraction, 1995

Other books you might like:
Hal Clement, *Cycle of Fire*, 1957
Gwyneth Jones, *White Queen*, 1991
Eric S. Nylund, *Signal to Noise*, 1998
Charles Pellegrino, *Flying to Valhalla*, 1993
Sheri S. Tepper, *The Fresco*, 2000

804

ANNE MCCAFFREY

The Skies of Pern

(New York: Ballantine Del Rey, 2001)

Story type: Space Colony

Series: Pern. Book 16
Subject(s): Space Colonies
Major character(s): Lessa, Leader; F'lar, Leader; F'Lessan, Warrior (dragonrider)
Time period(s): Indeterminate Future
Locale(s): Pern, Planet—Imaginary

Summary: The inhabitants of Pern have finally defeated the menace of the Thread. Just as it appears that they will be able to colonize the rest of the planet, conservative elements refuse to budge, and then a new menace appears requiring the dragonriders to act again.

Where it's reviewed:
Booklist, January 1, 2001, page 870
Library Journal, February 15, 2001, page 204
Locus, February 2001, page 27
Publishers Weekly, February 19, 2001, page 74

Other books by the same author:
Acorna's World, 2000
Pegasus in Space, 2000
Nimisha's Ship, 1999
Freedom's Challenge, 1998
The Masterharper of Pern, 1998

Other books you might like:
Brian W. Aldiss, *Helliconia Spring*, 1982
C.J. Cherryh, *Forty Thousand in Gehenna*, 1965
Frank Herbert, *Dune*, 1965
C.C. MacApp, *Prisoners of the Sky*, 1969
Robert Silverberg, *At Winter's End*, 1988

805

KEVIN MCCARTHY
DAVID B. SILVA, Co-Author

Special Effects

(New York: DAW, 2001)

Story type: Psychic Powers
Series: Family. Book 1
Subject(s): Extrasensory Perception
Major character(s): Michael Hastings, Scientist; Daniel Kaufman, Police Officer; Summer Mann, Psychic, Fugitive
Time period(s): 2000s (2001)
Locale(s): Los Angeles, California

Summary: Three young psychics are being studied by a secret government agency whose head wants to use them as assassins. One of the researchers arranges for them to escape and accompanies them to Los Angeles, where they all assume false identities. They are aided by a policeman, who requests in exchange that they help him investigate a series of murders. This is a first novel for McCarthy; David Silva has previously published in the horror field.

Where it's reviewed:
Science Fiction Chronicle, February 2001, page 46

Other books you might like:
John Farris, *The Fury*, 1976
Stephen King, *Firestarter*, 1980
Michael Kurland, *Psi Hunt*, 1980
Murray Leinster, *Talents, Inc.*, 1962

Dan Morgan, *Mind Trap*, 1970

806

ASHLEY MCCONNELL

The Morpheus Factor
(New York: Roc, 2001)

Story type: First Contact
Series: Stargate SG-1. Number 4
Subject(s): Space Exploration; Dreams and Nightmares
Major character(s): Jack O'Neil, Military Personnel; Samantha Carter, Scientist, Military Personnel; Daniel Jackson, Archaeologist
Time period(s): 21st century
Locale(s): P4V-837, Planet—Imaginary

Summary: A team of scientists and military personnel travel through a stargate which allows instantaneous transportation to other planets. They arrive on a mysterious planet whose natives seem to be friendly. Shortly after arriving, however, different members of the expedition begin to observe different realities, and they eventually discover that the locals use directed dreams to confuse intruders.

Where it's reviewed:
Science Fiction Chronicle, April 2001, page 40

Other books by the same author:
Stargate SG-1, 1998
The Courts of Sorcery, 1997
Scimitar, 1996
The Itinerant Exorcist, 1996
Too Close for Comfort, 1993

Other books you might like:
Keith Laumer, *Night of Delusions*, 1972
Ursula K. Le Guin, *The Word for the World Is Forest*, 1972
Bill McCay, *Resistance*, 1999
Jack McDevitt, *Ancient Shores*, 1996
Andre Norton, *Star Gate*, 1958

807

JACK MCDEVITT

Deepsix
(New York: Avon, 2001)

Story type: First Contact; Disaster
Subject(s): Aliens
Major character(s): Priscilla Hutchins, Spaceship Captain, Scientist; Kellie Collier, Spacewoman; Marcel Clairveau, Spaceship Captain
Time period(s): 23rd century (2223)
Locale(s): Maleiva III, Planet—Imaginary

Summary: Scientists are on hand to watch Maleiva III's destruction when a rogue planet enters the system, but at the last minute, signs of an ancient civilization are spotted on the planet's surface. A small group lands to investigate and is stranded with no way off the planet before the catastrophic collision occurs, unless the secret of an alien technology can be turned to their advantage.

Where it's reviewed:
Analog, April 2001, page 134
Booklist, February 15, 2001, page 1122
Locus, March 2001, page 23
Science Fiction Chronicle, February 2001, page 40

Other books by the same author:
Infinity Beach, 2000
Moonfall, 1998
Eternity Road, 1997
Ancient Shores, 1996
The Engines of God, 1994

Other books you might like:
Michael Bishop, *Transfigurations*, 1979
Edmond Hamilton, *The Haunted Stars*, 1960
Fritz Leiber, *The Wanderer*, 1964
Yvonne Navarro, *Final Impact*, 1997
Andre Norton, *Galactic Derelict*, 1959

808

DONNA MCMAHON

Dance of Knives
(New York: Tor, 2001)

Story type: Dystopian
Subject(s): Futuristic Fiction
Major character(s): Klale Renhardt, Entertainer; Cedar de Groot, Businessman; Toni, Saloon Keeper/Owner
Time period(s): 22nd century
Locale(s): Vancouver, British Columbia, Canada

Summary: An unemployed woman arrives in a future Vancouver and takes a job as an entertainer in a local bar. Shortly afterward, she is rescued from danger by a man, who supposedly has had his personality removed and is now a slave. She decides to repay him by securing his freedom, even though this pits her against some of the most powerful people in the city. This is a first novel.

Where it's reviewed:
Analog, October 2000, page 132
Magazine of Fantasy & Science Fiction, March 2001, page 104
Science Fiction Chronicle, July 2001, page 42

Other books you might like:
John Gregory Betancourt, *Johnny Zed*, 1988
Jerry Earl Brown, *Under the City of Angels*, 1981
Ron Goulart, *After Things Fell Apart*, 1977
Steven Gould, *Blind Waves*, 2000
K.W. Jeter, *Dr. Adder*, 1984

809

L.E. MODESITT JR.

The Octagonal Raven
(New York: Tor, 2001)

Story type: Mystery
Subject(s): Political Thriller
Major character(s): Daryn Alwyn, Consultant; Federico Pynia, Government Official; Eldyn Nyhal, Businessman

Time period(s): Indeterminate Future
Locale(s): Earth

Summary: In a far future Earth that only vaguely resembles ours, a genetically altered man designed to be one of society's leaders escapes a series of murder attempts. When his sister is killed, he conducts his own investigation and discovers a plot within certain elements of the government to reshape human society from within.

Where it's reviewed:
Booklist, January 1, 2001, page 928
Library Journal, February 15, 2001, page 205
New York Times Book Review, February 25, 2001, page 24
Science Fiction Chronicle, February 2001, page 42

Other books by the same author:
Timegods' World, 2000
Gravity Dreams, 1999
The Colors of Chaos, 1999
The Forever Hero, 1999
The White Order, 1998

Other books you might like:
Gordon R. Dickson, *Sleepwalker's World*, 1972
Robert A. Heinlein, *Beyond This Horizon*, 1942
Robert Sheckley, *The Status Civilization*, 1960
Brian Stableford, *The Architects of Emortality*, 1999
Jack Vance, *To Live Forever*, 1956

810

LYDA MOREHOUSE

Archangel Protocol

(New York: Roc, 2001)

Story type: Religious
Subject(s): Computers
Major character(s): Deidre McMannus, Detective—Private; Daniel Fitzpatrick, Prisoner; Michael Angelucci, Police Officer
Time period(s): 2070s (2076)
Locale(s): New York, New York

Summary: The United States has become a theocracy and religious fundamentalism controls most world governments. Deidre McMannus, a private detective, is excommunicated after her partner assassinates the Pope. She finds herself in fresh trouble when a police officer tells her that the religious manifestations on the Internet have been faked. This is a first novel.

Where it's reviewed:
Science Fiction Chronicle, April 2001, page 39

Other books you might like:
Kevin J. Anderson, *Resurrection Inc.*, 1988
Lester Del Rey, *The Eleventh Commandment*, 1962
Mick Farren, *The Armageddon Crazy*, 1989
Fritz Leiber, *Gather Darkness*, 1943
Gore Vidal, *Messiah*, 1954

811

MIKE MOSCOE

They Also Serve

(New York: Ace, 2000)

Story type: Lost Colony
Subject(s): Space Exploration
Major character(s): Ray Longknife, Military Personnel (colonel); Mary Rodrigo, Military Personnel (captain)
Time period(s): Indeterminate Future
Locale(s): Santa Maria, Planet—Imaginary

Summary: A starship inadvertently travels to the wrong destination and the crew finds itself on a lost colony that was inadvertently settled three centuries previously. Although everything seems to be peaceful on Santa Maria, the visitors begin to suspect something is amiss and eventually learn that an alien artificial intelligence has been awakened from an age long sleep.

Where it's reviewed:
Locus, February 2001, page 27
Science Fiction Chronicle, February 2001, page 46

Other books by the same author:
The Price of Peace, 2000
The First Casualty, 1999
Lost Days, 1998
Second Fire, 1997
First Dawn, 1996

Other books you might like:
Poul Anderson, *Let the Spacemen Beware!*, 1963
Michael Bishop, *Stolen Faces*, 1977
Jack L. Chalker, *Balshazzar's Serpent*, 2000
A. Bertram Chandler, *Spartan Planet*, 1969
Anne Gay, *Mindsail*, 1990

812

LINDA NAGATA

Limit of Vision

(New York: Tor, 2001)

Story type: Techno-Thriller
Subject(s): Scientific Experiments
Major character(s): Virgil Copeland, Scientist; Ela Suvanathat, Journalist; Randall Panwar, Scientist
Time period(s): 21st century
Locale(s): United States; Vietnam

Summary: Two scientists are performing illegal experiments involving a type of individually self-aware nanotech lifeforms when one of their co-workers dies, seemingly because of the experiment. Elsewhere, a journalist discovers a hidden cult that has extraordinary powers, apparently derived from their coexistence with the microscopic intelligences.

Where it's reviewed:
Locus, March 2001, page 21
Science Fiction Chronicle, March 2001, page 43

Other books by the same author:
Vast, 1998

Deception Well, 1997
Tech Heaven, 1995
The Bohr Maker, 1995

Other books you might like:
Greg Bear, *Queen of Angels*, 1990
Ben Bova, *Moonrise*, 1996
Tony Daniel, *Metaplanetary*, 2001
Don DeBrandt, *V.I.*, 2000
Michael Flynn, *The Nanotech Chronicles*, 1991

813

HUGH NISSENSON

The Song of the Earth

(Chapel Hill, North Carolina: Algonquin, 2001)

Story type: Genetic Manipulation
Subject(s): Genetic Engineering
Major character(s): John Firth Baker, Artist, Genetically Altered Being; Jeannette Baker, Historian; Sri Billy Lee Mookerjee, Religious
Time period(s): 21st century (2032-2059)
Locale(s): Norway; Japan

Summary: Jeannette Baker wants her son to be a superlative artist, so she travels to Japan for genetic alteration of her unborn child. The balance of the story is a biography of her son, who is murdered in 2059 after leading a controversial, productive, but strangely altered life. The narrative is a series of diary extracts, notes, letters, and other documents. This is the author's first science fiction novel.

Where it's reviewed:
Ecologist, June 2001, page 64
Publishers Weekly, April 30, 2001, page 56
Science Fiction Chronicle, June 2001, page 36

Other books you might like:
Greg Bear, *Sisters*, 1990
Hilari Bell, *Navohar*, 2000
Leigh Kennedy, *The Journal of Nicholas the American*, 1986
Pamela Sargent, *Cloned Lives*, 1976
Robert Silverberg, *Dying Inside*, 1972

814

ANDRE NORTON

Time Traders II

(New York: Baen, 2001)

Story type: Time Travel
Series: Time Traders
Subject(s): Aliens
Major character(s): Travis Fox, Time Traveler; Ross Murdock, Time Traveler; Gordon Ashe, Time Traveler
Time period(s): Indeterminate Future
Locale(s): Topaz, Planet—Imaginary; Hawaika, Planet—Imaginary

Summary: These are the third and fourth novels in the Time Traders series. In the first, agents have memories of their ancestors implanted in them so they can function on a distant world caught in the time war. In the second, they travel to a

water world to help its inhabitants avoid being conquered by agents of a galactic empire.

Other books by the same author:
The Scent of Magic, 1998
The Warding of Witch World, 1996
The Mirror of Destiny, 1995
The Hands of Llyr, 1994
Mark of the Cat, 1992

Other books you might like:
Poul Anderson, *Mayday Orbit*, 1961
John Brunner, *Bedlam Planet*, 1968
A. Bertram Chandler, *The Anarch Lords*, 1981
Keith Laumer, *Beyond the Imperium*, 1981
Jack Vance, *The Gray Prince*, 1974

815

PATRICK O'LEARY

Other Voices, Other Doors

(Auburn, Washington: Fairwood, 2001)

Story type: Collection
Subject(s): Short Stories

Summary: This collection consists of eight stories, eight essays, and a selection of poems. They are predominantly satirical, sometimes farcical, and involve alien visitors, alternate histories, a boy who suddenly becomes a genius, and other subjects. The stories were originally published during the 1990s.

Where it's reviewed:
Locus, January 2001, page 53

Other books by the same author:
The Gift, 1997
Door Number Three, 1995

Other books you might like:
Avram Davidson, *The Avram Davidson Treasury*, 1998
Paul Di Filippo, *Fractal Paisleys*, 1997
Mike Resnick, *In Space No One Can Hear You Laugh*, 2000
Robert Sheckley, *Collected Stories of Robert Sheckley*, 1992
Gene Wolfe, *Strange Travelers*, 2000

816

H. BEAM PIPER

The Complete Paratime

(New York: Ace, 2001)

Story type: Time Travel; Alternate Universe
Subject(s): Time Travel

Summary: All of the stories in Piper's Paratime series are collected in this omnibus volume. The Paratime Police travel through time to prevent anyone from changing the course of history. Generally they find discrepancies and have to act to restore the original time track. The stories were originally published between 1948 and the 1960s.

Other books by the same author:
Fuzzies and Other People, 1984
The Worlds of H. Beam Piper, 1984

Empire, 1981
Federation, 1981
The Other Human Race, 1964

Other books you might like:
Poul Anderson, *The Time Patrol*, 1991
Isaac Asimov, *The End of Eternity*, 1955
Sean Dalton, *Turncoat*, 1994
Fritz Leiber, *Changewar*, 1983
Andre Norton, *Crossroads of Time*, 1956

817

FREDERIK POHL, Editor

The SFWA Grand Masters: Volume Three
(New York: Tor, 2001)

Story type: Anthology
Subject(s): Short Stories

Summary: The volumes in this series highlight some of the best short fiction of major writers in the field. Those writers selected this time are A.E. van Vogt, Lester Del Rey, Frederik Pohl, Damon Knight, and Jack Vance. There are three to five stories by each, generally taken from early points in their respective careers.

Other books by the same author:
The Far Shore of Time, 1999
O Pioneer, 1998
The Siege of Eternity, 1997
The Other Side of Time, 1996
Mining the Oort, 1992

Other books you might like:
Lester Del Rey, *Nerves*, 1956
Damon Knight, *The Man in the Tree*, 1984
Frederik Pohl, *The Merchant's War*, 1984
A.E. van Vogt, *Away and Beyond*, 1952
Jack Vance, *The Worlds of Jack Vance*, 1973

818

MATT REILLY

Temple
(New York: St Martin's Press, 2001)

Story type: Espionage Thriller
Subject(s): Technology
Major character(s): William Race, Linguist; Dwayne Scott, Military Personnel; Francis Nash, Scientist
Time period(s): 2000s (2001)
Locale(s): Peru

Summary: Neo-Nazi terrorists and an American military expedition battle in the jungles of Peru, seeking an ancient idol manufactured from an element not native to Earth. There's a weapon powerful enough to destroy the planet, a plot to destroy the U.S. economy, and several other subplots as well, but most of the novel consists of one ongoing gunfight.

Where it's reviewed:
Science Fiction Chronicle, March 2001, page 43

Other books by the same author:
Ice Station, 1999

Other books you might like:
George Bartram, *The Sunset Gun*, 1983
Milan Chiba, *Noonblaze*, 1981
Michael Crichton, *Congo*, 1980
James Rollins, *Subterranean*, 1999
Ian Watson, *The Martian Inca*, 1977

819

MIKE RESNICK

The Outpost
(New York: Tor, 2001)

Story type: Humor
Subject(s): Aliens
Major character(s): Catastrophe Baker, Criminal; Billy Karma, Criminal; Johnny Testosterone, Criminal
Time period(s): Indeterminate Future
Locale(s): Henry II, Planet—Imaginary; Outer Space

Summary: A handful of the greatest criminals, thieves, swindlers, and assassins in the galaxy all wander to Outpost, a tavern on a remote world called Henry II. There they swap tall stories at great length before discovering the human space navy has been defeated by an alien invasion force now planning to add their refuge to its string of conquests.

Where it's reviewed:
Analog, May 2001, page 133
Science Fiction Chronicle, June 2001, page 37

Other books by the same author:
Tales of the Galactic Midway, 2001
In Space No One Can Hear You Laugh, 2000
A Hunger in the Soul, 1998
Kirinyaga, 1998
The Widowmaker Unleashed, 1998

Other books you might like:
Poul Anderson, *A Midsummer Tempest*, 1975
John Boyd, *The Andromeda Gun*, 1974
Arthur C. Clarke, *Tales from the White Hart*, 1957
L. Sprague de Camp, *Tales from Gavagan's Bar*, 1953
   Fletcher Pratt, co-author
Spider Robinson, *Callahan's Legacy*, 1996

820

MIKE RESNICK

Tales of the Galactic Midway
(New York: Farthest Star, 2001)

Story type: Humor
Subject(s): Aliens; Space Exploration; Circus
Major character(s): Thaddeus Flint, Entertainer; Mr. Ahasuerus, Entertainer; Billybuck Dancer, Entertainer
Time period(s): Indeterminate Future
Locale(s): Outer Space

Summary: The four novels gathered here were first published in the early 1980s. All four involve a circus that travels from

planet to planet, getting into trouble constantly because of misunderstandings about the nature of their acts. There's also an interstellar sharpshooting contest, an effort to replace terrestrial animal acts with aliens, and other humorous situations.

Other books by the same author:
The Outpost, 2001
In Space No One Can Hear You Laugh, 2000
A Hunger in the Soul, 1998
Kirinyaga, 1998
The Widowmaker Unleashed, 1998

Other books you might like:
Stephen Goldin, *The Imperial Stars*, 1976
Harry Harrison, *The Stainless Steel Rat Joins the Circus*, 1999
Keith Laumer, *Earthblood*, 1966
    Rosel George Brown, co-author
Barry Longyear, *Circus World*, 1980
George R.R. Martin, *Tuf Voyaging*, 1986

821

JOHN RINGO

Gust Front
(New York: Baen, 2001)

Story type: Invasion of Earth
Subject(s): Military Life; Aliens
Major character(s): Michael O'Neal, Military Personnel; Robert Duncan, Military Personnel
Time period(s): 2000s (2004)
Locale(s): Norway; Barwhon, Planet—Imaginary

Summary: The human race has agreed to send some of its military units as mercenaries in an interstellar war. This attracts the unwelcome attention of the other side, and a massive invasion force prepares to conquer the Earth. The invaders are unprepared for the ferocity and inventiveness of the human defenses in this military adventure. This is a sequel to *A Hymn Before Battle*.

Other books by the same author:
A Hymn Before Battle, 2000

Other books you might like:
Brian W. Aldiss, *Vanguard from Alpha*, 1959
John Brunner, *The Super Barbarians*, 1962
Alan Dean Foster, *A Call to Arms*, 1991
Harry Harrison, *Invasion: Earth*, 1982
Larry Niven, *Footfall*, 1985
    Jerry Pournelle, co-author

822

J.D. ROBB (Pseudonym of Nora Roberts)

Betrayal in Death
(New York: Berkley, 2001)

Story type: Mystery
Series: Eve Dallas. Book 12
Subject(s): Future; Mystery and Detective Stories

Major character(s): Eve Dallas, Detective—Homicide; Roarke, Businessman, Spouse (Eve's husband); Sylvester Yost, Criminal (assassin)
Time period(s): 2050s (2059)
Locale(s): New York, New York

Summary: A professional killer, who sometimes hides off Earth, has returned and is systematically and brutally murdering people who work for Eve Dallas' husband, Roarke. She has to overcome an interfering FBI agent, interpersonal conflicts among her staff, a visiting friend of doubtful character, and other distractions before finally capturing the culprit.

Where it's reviewed:
Locus, May 2001, page 29
Publishers Weekly, February 19, 2001, page 75
Science Fiction Chronicle, June 2001, page 40

Other books by the same author:
Judgment in Death, 2000 (Eve Dallas. Book 11)
Conspiracy in Death, 1999 (Eve Dallas. Book 8)
Loyalty in Death, 1999 (Eve Dallas. Book 9)
Holiday in Death, 1998 (Eve Dallas. Book 7)
Vengeance in Death, 1997 (Eve Dallas. Book 6)

Other books you might like:
George Foy, *The Shift*, 1996
Eric James Fullilove, *Circle of One*, 1996
Lynn Hightower, *Alien Rites*, 1995
Lee Killough, *Spider Play*, 1986
Richard Paul Russo, *Carlucci's Heart*, 1997

823

SPIDER ROBINSON

By Any Other Name
(New York: Baen, 2001)

Story type: Collection
Subject(s): Short Stories

Summary: This volume collects 18 stories originally published between 1976 and 2000. Some involve serious themes, but the individual tales are predominantly humorous, often using puns and farcical situations. Stranded time travelers, interplanetary conflicts, aliens, and other themes are all utilized.

Where it's reviewed:
Science Fiction Chronicle, June 2001, page 40

Other books by the same author:
User Friendly, 1998
Lifehouse, 1997
Callahan's Legacy, 1996
Lady Slings the Booze, 1993
Kill the Editor, 1991

Other books you might like:
Poul Anderson, *Explorations*, 1981
Gordon R. Dickson, *Beginnings*, 1988
Harry Harrison, *50 in 50*, 2001
Eric Frank Russell, *Major Ingredients*, 2000
Robert Sheckley, *Pilgrimage to Earth*, 1957

824

SPIDER ROBINSON

The Free Lunch

(New York: Tor, 2001)

Story type: Time Travel
Subject(s): Time Travel
Major character(s): Annie, Worker; Mike, Teenager; Alonzo Haines, Businessman
Time period(s): 2020s (2023)
Locale(s): United States

Summary: Mike is a runaway teen, who takes refuge in Dreamworld, a gigantic high tech amusement park of the future. He is assisted by Annie, who apparently works for the corporation. Together they investigate the fact that more costumed trolls leave the park every day than enter, and eventually discover it is a nexus for time travelers from the future.

Other books by the same author:
By Any Other Name, 2001
User Friendly, 1998
Lifehouse, 1997
Callahan's Legacy, 1996
Lady Slings the Booze, 1993

Other books you might like:
Joseph Addison, *Tesseract*, 1988
Peter Heath, *Assassins from Tomorrow*, 1967
Robert A. Heinlein, *The Door into Summer*, 1956
Charles Eric Maine, *Timeliner*, 1955
Clifford D. Simak, *Our Children's Children*, 1974

825

RICHARD PAUL RUSSO

Ship of Fools

(New York: Ace, 2001)

Story type: Generation Starship
Subject(s): Unexplained Phenomena; Aliens
Major character(s): Bartolomeo Aguilera, Spaceman; Nikos Costa, Spaceship Captain; Bernard Soldano, Religious (bishop)
Time period(s): Indeterminate Future
Locale(s): Antioch, Planet—Imaginary; *Argonos*, Spaceship

Summary: The *Argonos* has been in space for generations, and tensions are threatening to tear its society apart. Some want to abandon the ship and settle on a planet, others want to stay in space and shape the ship's mission to their own preferences. Then they find a colony whose people have been slaughtered, and a gigantic alien ship, apparently deserted and open for investigation.

Where it's reviewed:
Library Journal, January 1, 2001, page 163
Locus, February 2001, page 22
New York Times Book Review, January 21, 2001, page 16

Other books by the same author:
Terminal Visions, 2000
Carlucci's Heart, 1997

Carlucci's Edge, 1995
Destroying Angel, 1992
Inner Eclipse, 1988

Other books you might like:
Gregory Benford, *Artifact*, 1985
Arthur C. Clarke, *Rendezvous with Rama*, 1973
Jack McDevitt, *The Engines of God*, 1994
Anne Moroz, *No Safe Place*, 1986
Andre Norton, *Sargasso of Space*, 1955

826

PAMELA SARGENT

Child of Venus

(New York: Avon Eos, 2001)

Story type: Space Colony
Series: Venus. Book 3
Subject(s): Space Colonies
Major character(s): Mahala Liangharad, Teenager; Karin Mugabe, Teacher; Malik Haddad, Settler
Time period(s): Indeterminate Future
Locale(s): Venus

Summary: Humans have colonized Venus and made it marginally habitable. The growing population has reached an accord with Earth, but the bonds between the two cultures are growing thinner and there is reason to believe a break is inevitable. This leads to unrest among the Venusians, and a young girl with genetic enhancements finds herself in the middle of things.

Where it's reviewed:
Publishers Weekly, March 19, 2001, page 80

Other books by the same author:
Climb the Wind, 1999
The Alien Child, 1988
Venus of Shadows, 1988
The Shore of Women, 1986
Venus of Dreams, 1986

Other books you might like:
Greg Bear, *Moving Mars*, 1993
Ben Bova, *Venus*, 2000
Robert A. Heinlein, *Between Planets*, 1951
Paul Preuss, *Maelstrom*, 1988
Kim Stanley Robinson, *Red Mars*, 1993

827

JAMES H. SCHMITZ

The Hub: Dangerous Territory

(New York: Baen, 2001)

Story type: Collection
Subject(s): Short Stories
Locale(s): Outer Space

Summary: One novel and nine short stories, written between 1955 and 1969, are all set in the Hub, the central portion of the galaxy. Several characters are common to one or more stories,

most of which are space operas. There is also a guide to the characters and other commentary on the stories.

Where it's reviewed:
Science Fiction Chronicle, June 2001, page 40

Other books by the same author:
Trigger & Friends, 2001
Telzey Amberdon, 2000
The Eternal Frontiers, 1973
A Pride of Monsters, 1970
The Witches of Karres, 1966

Other books you might like:
A. Bertram Chandler, *The Anarch Lords*, 1981
Edmond Hamilton, *Star Wolf*, 1982
Keith Laumer, *The Glory Game*, 1973
Murray Leinster, *SOS from Three Worlds*, 1966
Robert Silverberg, *Collision Course*, 1959

828

JAMES H. SCHMITZ

Trigger & Friends

(New York: Baen, 2001)

Story type: Collection
Subject(s): Short Stories

Summary: This volume contains five short stories and a novel by the late James H. Schmitz, all set in the same universe. One was rewritten by another writer to make it fit better with the other stories in the book. They were originally published between 1958 and 1974, and are largely freewheeling space adventures, sometimes involving Schmitz's recurring character, Trigger Argee. Two non-fiction pieces about Schmitz are included.

Where it's reviewed:
Locus, March 2001, page 33
Science Fiction Chronicle, April 2001, page 39

Other books by the same author:
Telzey Amberdon, 2000
The Eternal Frontiers, 1973
The Telzey Toy, 1973
A Pride of Monsters, 1970
The Witches of Karres, 1966

Other books you might like:
Poul Anderson, *Agent of the Terran Empire*, 1965
Pauline Ashwell, *Unwillingly to Earth*, 1992
C.J. Cherryh, *Cyteen*, 1988
Keith Laumer, *Retief and the Rascals*, 1993
Timothy Zahn, *The Icarus Hunt*, 1999

829

CHARLES SHEFFIELD

Spheres of Heaven

(New York: Baen, 2001)

Story type: Space Opera
Subject(s): Aliens

Major character(s): Chan Dalton, Spaceman; Dougal McDougal, Diplomat (ambassador); Danny Casement, Spaceman
Time period(s): Indeterminate Future
Locale(s): Outer Space; *Mood Indigo*, Spaceship

Summary: The human race has been quarantined in the solar system ever since contacting galactic civilization. Now the aliens have summoned one specific human to represent the race at a meeting in outer space. He reluctantly accepts the job, and discovers that the consequences of failure will be catastrophic.

Where it's reviewed:
Booklist, February 15, 2001, page 1122
Library Journal, February 15, 2001, page 204
Locus, February 2001, page 23

Other books by the same author:
The Compleat McAndrew, 2000
The Cyborg from Earth, 1998
Putting Up Roots, 1997
Proteus in the Underworld, 1995
The Ganymede Club, 1995

Other books you might like:
Gordon R. Dickson, *The Star Road*, 1974
Irving A. Greenfield, *The Star Trial*, 1974
Alexander Jablokov, *Deepdrive*, 1998
Damon Knight, *The Sun Saboteurs*, 1961
Jack Williamson, *The Trial of Terra*, 1962

830

DAVID SHERMAN
DAN CRAGG, Co-Author

Hangfire

(New York: Ballantine Del Rey, 2001)

Story type: Military
Series: Starfist. Book 6
Subject(s): Military Life
Major character(s): Rachman Claypoole, Military Personnel; Joe Dean, Military Personnel; Theodosius Sturgeon, Military Personnel
Time period(s): Indeterminate Future
Locale(s): Havanagas, Planet—Imaginary; Thorsfinni's World, Planet—Imaginary; Earth

Summary: Three members of an elite corps of space marines are given a temporary assignment on a planet where organized crime has grown so powerful that it rivals the planetary government. Their job is to identify and capture the head of the mob in order to shift the balance of power to the authorities.

Other books by the same author:
Technokill, 2000
Blood Contact, 1999
School of Fire, 1998
Steel Gauntlet, 1998
First to Fight, 1997

Other books you might like:
Lois McMaster Bujold, *Cetaganda*, 1996

Chris Bunch, *The Last Legion*, 1999
Gordon R. Dickson, *Naked to the Stars*, 1961
W. Michael Gear, *Starstrike*, 1990
Roland Green, *On the Verge*, 1998

831

ROBERT SILVERBERG, Editor

Nebula Awards Showcase 2001
(New York: Harcourt, 2001)

Story type: Anthology
Subject(s): Short Stories

Summary: This is the retrospective best of the year for 1999 as chosen by the Science Fiction and Fantasy Writers of America. Included are all the short fiction winners and some of the also-rans, plus several essays and a complete listing of past winners in each category. The stories are by Ted Chiang, Mary A. Turzillo, Leslie What, Michael Swanwick, and others.

Other books by the same author:
Lord Prestimion, 1999
The Alien Years, 1998
The Sorcerers of Majipoor, 1997
Starborne, 1996
Hot Sky at Midnight, 1994

Other books you might like:
Isaac Asimov, *Isaac Asimov Presents the Great SF Stories 21 (1959)*, 1990
Ellen Datlow, *The Year's Best Fantasy and Horror: Sixth Annual Collection*, 1993
Gardner Dozois, *The Year's Best Science Fiction: Thirteenth Annual Collection*, 1996
David G. Hartwell, *Masterpieces of Fantasy and Wonder*, 1994
David G. Hartwell, *Year's Best SF*, 1996

832

BRIAN STABLEFORD

The Cassandra Complex
(New York: Tor, 2001)

Story type: Immortality; Mystery
Subject(s): Immortality
Major character(s): Lisa Friemann, Police Officer, Scientist; Morgan Miller, Scientist; Mike Grundy, Police Officer
Time period(s): 2040s (2041)
Locale(s): England

Summary: Mysterious figures kidnap a prominent scientist, assault two others, and destroy a long running experiment with mice. Subsequent investigation reveals they believe someone has discovered the key to human immortality. Corporations, activist groups, and government agencies all pursue the truth, but for very different reasons.

Where it's reviewed:
Publishers Weekly, March 5, 2001, page 67
Science Fiction Chronicle, April 2001, page 35

Other books by the same author:
The Fountains of Youth, 2000
The Architects of Emortality, 1999
Inherit the Earth, 1998
Chimera's Cradle, 1997
Salamander's Fire, 1995

Other books you might like:
Roger MacBride Allen, *The Modular Man*, 1992
Joe Haldeman, *Buying Time*, 1989
James Halperin, *The First Immortal*, 1998
Syd Logsdon, *A Fond Farewell to Dying*, 1981
Steve Perry, *The Forever Drug*, 1995

833

IAN STEWART

Flatterland
(Cambridge, Massachusetts: Perseus, 2001)

Story type: Satire
Subject(s): Virtual Reality
Major character(s): Victoria Line, Explorer; Space Hopper, Mythical Creature
Time period(s): Indeterminate
Locale(s): Flatterland, Alternate Universe

Summary: In this sequel to *Flatland* by Edwin Abbott, Victoria Line is a two dimensional being, who explores the third dimension, accompanied for much of the time by an unusual creature called the Space Hopper. This provides the means for some satirical commentary on the world, as well as introducing the reader to some very sophisticated discussions of the nature of space and the universe.

Where it's reviewed:
Publishers Weekly, April 2, 2001, page 43
Science Fiction Chronicle, June 2001, page 36

Other books you might like:
Edwin A. Abbott, *Flatland*, 1884
Stephen Baxter, *Raft*, 1992
Lewis Carroll, *The Annotated Alice*, 1960
Norton Juster, *The Phantom Tollbooth*, 1961
Christopher Priest, *The Inverted World*, 1974

834

S.M. STIRLING

T2: Infiltrator
(New York: HarperEntertainment, 2001)

Story type: Time Travel; Techno-Thriller
Subject(s): Computers
Major character(s): John Connor, Teenager; Dieter Von Rossbach, Spy; Roger Colvin, Businessman
Time period(s): 2020s (2021-2028)
Locale(s): Los Angeles, California; Sacramento, California; Paraguay

Summary: In this novel set in the universe of the two *Terminator* films, Sarah and John Connor are in hiding in Paraguay, even though they believe they have altered the course of time so that the computers of the future cannot send

any more terminators after them. They are wrong, however, and the newest time traveling assassin is far more intelligent and resourceful than any of those previously given the mission.

Where it's reviewed:
Science Fiction Chronicle, July 2001, page 44

Other books by the same author:
On the Oceans of Eternity, 2000
Against the Tide of Years, 1999
Island in the Sea of Time, 1998
Betrayals, 1996
Drakon, 1996

Other books you might like:
Martin Caidin, *The God Machine*, 1968
Philip K. Dick, *Vulcan's Hammer*, 1960
Randall Frakes, *The Terminator*, 1991
D.F. Jones, *Colossus*, 1966
Dean R. Koontz, *Lightning*, 1988

835

WILLIAM TENN

Immodest Proposals

(Framingham, Massachusetts: NESFA, 2001)

Story type: Collection
Subject(s): Short Stories

Summary: Most of these 33 short stories were published between 1947 and 1957, with a few that were written later. A large proportion of these contain elements of humor, often satiric or wry. They involve everything from time travel to alien invasions to the colonization of the planet Venus.

Where it's reviewed:
Booklist, April 15, 2001, page 1544

Other books by the same author:
The Seven Sexes, 1968
The Wooden Star, 1968
The Square Root of Man, 1968
Of Men and Monsters, 1963
Time in Advance, 1958

Other books you might like:
Avram Davidson, *Or All the Seas with Oysters*, 1962
Damon Knight, *Far Out*, 1961
Frederik Pohl, *The Day the Martians Came*, 1988
Robert Sheckley, *Notions Unlimited*, 1960
Theodore Sturgeon, *Thunder and Roses*, 1997

836

MATTHEW THOMAS

Terror Firma

(London: Harper, 2001)

Story type: Humor
Subject(s): Aliens; Extrasensory Perception
Major character(s): Dave Pierce, Paranormal Investigator; Frank MacIntyre, Pilot; Kate Jennings, Journalist
Time period(s): 2000s (2001)

Locale(s): Nevada; England

Summary: All of the weird things reported in the tabloids are true in this humorous spoof of the paranormal. UFO spotter Dave Pierce teams up with a pilot, who saw something he can't explain, and an investigative reporter to reveal the truth to the public, with frequently hilarious consequences.

Other books by the same author:
Before & After, 2000

Other books you might like:
Gary A. Braunbeck, *In Hollow Houses*, 2000
Avram Davidson, *Rork!*, 1965
Geoffrey Marsh, *The King of Satan's Eyes*, 1984
Mark Sumner, *The Monster of Minnesota*, 1997
G.W. Tirpa, *In Fluid Silence*, 2001

837

G.W. TIRPA

In Fluid Silence

(Renton, Washington: Wizards of the Coast, 2001)

Story type: Psychic Powers
Series: Dark Matter. Book 3
Subject(s): Espionage
Major character(s): Michael McCain, Government Official; Jane Meara, Government Official; Ngan Song Kun'dren, Spy
Time period(s): 2000s (2001)
Locale(s): Chicago, Illinois

Summary: Two government officials discover authorities have been concealing contact with aliens, and that many other things reported in the tabloids are actually true. In this adventure, McCain and Meara are involved in the attempt to hunt down the man who was occult advisor to Adolf Hitler. This is a first novel.

Where it's reviewed:
Science Fiction Chronicle, April 2001, page 38

Other books you might like:
Kevin J. Anderson, *Antibodies*, 1997
Ken Goddard, *First Evidence*, 1999
Charles L. Grant, *Goblins*, 1994
Ben Mezrich, *Skin*, 1999
Mark Sumner, *Insanity, Illinois*, 1998

838

JUDITH TRACY

Destiny's Door

(Farmingdale, New York: Padwolf, 2001)

Story type: Alternate Intelligence
Subject(s): Artificial Intelligence; Computers
Major character(s): Donald Thurman, Teenager, Computer Expert; Teresa Harding, Young Woman
Time period(s): 2000s (2001)
Locale(s): United States

Summary: A teenager discovers that artificial intelligences have become self-aware within the Internet. They advise him

that they wish to help people, and start by assisting a woman who is trying to find out why the government is concealing the truth about the man she loves. This is a first novel.

Where it's reviewed:
Science Fiction Chronicle, March 2001, page 44

Other books you might like:
Algis Budrys, *Michaelmas*, 1977
Bruce Coville, *Operation Sherlock*, 1986
Esther Friesner, *The Sherwood Game*, 1995
David Gerrold, *When Harlie Was One*, 1972
Thomas P. Ryan, *The Adolescence of P-1*, 1977

839

HARRY TURTLEDOVE

American Empire: Blood and Iron
(New York: Ballantine Del Rey, 2001)

Story type: Alternate Universe
Series: American Empire. Book 1
Subject(s): Alternate History
Major character(s): Jake Featherstone, Unemployed; Chester Martin, Worker; Lucien Galter, Farmer
Time period(s): 1920s
Locale(s): North America

Summary: This is the opening volume of a new series that follows the Great War sequence. The Confederacy won its independence and fought against the USA during the Great War. Now it appears likely to fall under the sway of a fascist demagogue, even as its northern neighbor is flirting with a socialist government. A large cast of characters reacts and interacts as the world lurches toward a new war.

Where it's reviewed:
Booklist, April 15, 2001, page 1510
Science Fiction Chronicle, July 2001, page 42

Other books by the same author:
Colonization: Aftershocks, 2001
Through the Darkness, 2001
Sentry Peak, 2000
Down in the Bottomlands, 1999
Between the Rivers, 1998

Other books you might like:
Brian W. Aldiss, *The Year Before Yesterday*, 1987
Harry Harrison, *Stars & Stripes Forever*, 1998
Jake Page, *Shatterhand*, 1996
David C. Poyer, *The Shiloh Project*, 1981
William Sanders, *The Wild Blue and the Gray*, 1991

840

HARRY TURTLEDOVE, Editor

The Best Military Science Fiction of the Twentieth Century
(New York: Ballantine Del Rey, 2001)

Story type: Anthology; Military
Subject(s): Short Stories; Military Life

Summary: This is a collection of 13 generally long stories in which military tactics or lifestyles are a major element. The stories were originally published between 1956 and 1985 and include contributions by Cordwainer Smith, Arthur C. Clarke, C.J. Cherryh, Philip K. Dick, Poul Anderson, and others.

Other books by the same author:
Colonization: Aftershocks, 2001
Darkness Descending, 2000
Sentry Peak, 2000
Second Contact, 1999
American Front, 1998

Other books you might like:
Orson Scott Card, *Ender's Game*, 1985
Gordon R. Dickson, *The Chantry Guild*, 1988
David Drake, *Lieutenant Leary Commanding*, 2000
Joe Haldeman, *The Forever War*, 1974
Anne McCaffrey, *Dragonflight*, 1968

841

HARRY TURTLEDOVE

Colonization: Aftershocks
(New York: Ballantine Del Rey, 2001)

Story type: Invasion of Earth
Series: Colonization. Book 3
Subject(s): Aliens
Major character(s): Sam Yeager, Military Personnel; Queek, Alien; Vyacheslav Molotov, Political Figure
Time period(s): 1960s (1960)
Locale(s): United States; Union of Soviet Socialist Republics; China

Summary: In the concluding volume of this trilogy, Earth is invaded by reptilian aliens during World War II. Although they establish a beachhead, much of the planet remains independent at the start of the 1960s. Then humans develop atomic weapons and the aliens must decide whether or not to pursue their conquest.

Where it's reviewed:
Booklist, November 15, 2000, page 588
Library Journal, February 15, 2001, page 205

Other books by the same author:
Darkness Descending, 2000
Sentry Peak, 2000
Into the Darkness, 1999
Second Contact, 1999
Between the Rivers, 1998

Other books you might like:
Brian W. Aldiss, *The Year Before Yesterday*, 1987
John Barnes, *Finity*, 1999
Ben Bova, *Triumph*, 1993
Brad Linaweaver, *Moon of Ice*, 1988
Fred Saberhagen, *A Century of Progress*, 1983

Science Fiction

842

S.L. VIEHL

Endurance

(New York: Roc, 2001)

Story type: Space Opera
Series: Stardoc. Book 3
Subject(s): Space Travel
Major character(s): Cherijo Torin, Doctor; Duncan Reever, Linguist; SrrokVar, Alien
Time period(s): Indeterminate Future
Locale(s): Outer Space; Catopsa, Planet—Imaginary

Summary: Dr. Cherijo Torin is betrayed by a man she trusts and becomes a slave to an alien race. Although the other slaves hate her, she quietly begins working to improve their lot, and ultimately makes enough allies so that she is intimately involved in a successful rebellion against the slaveholders.

Other books by the same author:
Beyond Varallan, 2000
Stardoc, 2000

Other books you might like:
Philip K. Dick, *Dr. Futurity*, 1960
Stephen Leigh, *Dark Water's Embrace*, 1998
Murray Leinster, *Quarantine World*, 1992
Alan E. Nourse, *Star Surgeon*, 1960
James White, *Final Diagnosis*, 1997

843

DAVID WEBER, Editor

Changer of Worlds

(New York: Baen, 2001)

Story type: Anthology
Series: Worlds of Honor. Book 3
Subject(s): Short Stories
Major character(s): Honor Harrington, Military Personnel (interstellar officer)

Summary: Four long stories chronicle part of the career of Honor Harrington, an interstellar military officer, featured in a number of the editor's novels. Three of the stories are by Weber himself, the fourth is by Eric Flint. All are original to this collection.

Where it's reviewed:
Publishers Weekly, February 19, 2001, page 74

Other books by the same author:
The Apocalypse Troll, 1999
Worlds of Honor, 1999
More than Honor, 1998
The War God's Own, 1998
In Enemy Hands, 1997

Other books you might like:
Lois McMaster Bujold, *Shards of Honor*, 1986
David Feintuch, *Challenger's Hope*, 1995
W. Michael Gear, *A Relic of Empire*, 1992
Roland Green, *The Peace Company*, 1985

John Ringo, *A Hymn Before Battle*, 2000

844

DAVID WEBER
JOHN RINGO, Co-Author

March Upcountry

(New York: Baen, 2001)

Story type: Military
Series: March. Book 1
Subject(s): Space Colonies
Major character(s): Roger MacClintock, Royalty (prince), Military Personnel; Eva Kosutic, Military Personnel; Captain Pahner, Military Personnel
Time period(s): Indeterminate Future
Locale(s): Marduk, Planet—Imaginary

Summary: Spoiled, inexperienced Prince Roger is sent on a ceremonial visit to a distant world, when sabotage and a hostile military force leave him stranded on another world entirely, with only a small contingent of guards. In that environment, he matures quickly and discovers he has a talent for war.

Where it's reviewed:
Booklist, April 15, 2001, page 1544
Publishers Weekly, April 16, 2001, page 49
Science Fiction Chronicle, July 2001, page 42

Other books by the same author:
Ashes of Victory, 2000
The Apocalypse Troll, 1999
More than Honor, 1998
The War God's Own, 1998
In Enemy Hands, 1997

Other books you might like:
Lois McMaster Bujold, *The Warrior's Apprentice*, 1986
Chris Bunch, *Firemask*, 2000
Michael Collins, *The Planets of Death*, 1970
David Drake, *Hammer's Slammers*, 1979
Roland Green, *On the Verge*, 1998

845

K.D. WENTWORTH

Stars over Stars

(New York: Baen, 2001)

Story type: Space Colony
Series: Heyoka Blackeagle. Book 2
Subject(s): Aliens
Major character(s): Heyoka Blackeagle, Military Personnel, Alien (hrinn); Mitsu, Military Personnel; Skal, Military Personnel, Alien (hrinn)
Time period(s): Indeterminate Future
Locale(s): Oleaaka, Planet—Imaginary

Summary: Heyoka Blackeagle is a hrinn, but he was raised by a human family and understands the values of both races, which are loosely allied against an aggressive interstellar empire. He is training a mixed group of both species on a

remote colony world, when it is cut off, and rather than leave his command, he stays behind to help them survive.

Where it's reviewed:
Science Fiction Chronicle, June 2001, page 40

Other books by the same author:
Black on Black, 1999
House of Moons, 1995
Moonspeaker, 1994
The Imperium Game, 1994

Other books you might like:
John Blair, *A Landscape of Darkness*, 1990
Lois McMaster Bujold, *Shards of Honor*, 1986
David Drake, *The Forlorn Hope*, 1984
Alan Dean Foster, *Dirge*, 2000
Jerry Pournelle, *Falkenberg's Legion*, 1990

846

LIZ WILLIAMS

The Ghost Sister
(New York: Bantam, 2001)

Story type: Psychic Powers
Subject(s): Aliens
Major character(s): Mevennen Ai Mordha, Alien; Eleres Ai Mordha, Alien; Sereth, Alien
Time period(s): Indeterminate Future
Locale(s): Monde D'Isle, Planet—Imaginary

Summary: On a distant planet, the local inhabitants share a common mind at times, and are subject to brief periods of mass violence. The protagonist is a young woman, who cannot maintain the necessary mental contact with the rest of her race, and who is therefore in danger of being killed because of xenophobia. Her devoted brother protects her through a series of adventures. This is a first novel.

Other books you might like:
Isaac Asimov, *Nightfall*, 1990
    Robert Silverberg, co-author
Michael Bishop, *Stolen Faces*, 1977
Nancy Kress, *Probability Moon*, 2000
Stephen Leigh, *Dark Water's Embrace*, 1998
Frederik Pohl, *Stopping at Slowyear*, 1991

847

SEAN WILLIAMS
SHANE DIX, Co-Author

A Dark Imbalance
(New York: Ace, 2001)

Story type: Post-Disaster; Space Opera
Series: Evergence. Book 3
Subject(s): Cloning
Major character(s): Morgan Roche, Spy; The Box, Artificial Intelligence; Adoni Cane, Clone
Time period(s): Indeterminate Future
Locale(s): Outer Space

Summary: Earth has been destroyed by an unknown enemy. Now a group of superwarriors has begun to infiltrate the solar system in an attempt to track down the humans who survived and eliminate them as well. Morgan Roche is a spy, who discovers the truth about a mysterious artificial intelligence and faces the threat of the cloned warriors.

Other books by the same author:
The Dying Light, 2000 (Shane Dix, co-author)
The Prodigal Sun, 1999 (Shane Dix, co-author)

Other books you might like:
Roger MacBride Allen, *The Ring of Charon*, 1990
Poul Anderson, *After Doomsday*, 1961
Roxann Dawson, *Entering Tenebrea*, 2001
    Daniel Graham, co-author
Alastair Reynolds, *Revelation Space*, 2000
Dan Simmons, *The Rise of Endymion*, 1997

848

JACK WILLIAMSON

Terraforming Earth
(New York: Tor, 2001)

Story type: Post-Disaster
Subject(s): Cloning; Ecothriller
Major character(s): Arne, Clone; Cleo, Clone; Casey, Clone
Time period(s): Indeterminate Future
Locale(s): Moon (Earth's); Earth

Summary: A large object from space strikes Earth, killing all human life and rendering the planet uninhabitable. The only survivors are a group of clones on the moon, a small society which preserves itself by continuing to clone each other as they slowly gain the resolve, and the knowledge, to begin altering Earth's atmosphere back to what it once was.

Other books by the same author:
The Silicon Dagger, 1999
The Black Sun, 1997
Beachhead, 1992
Mazeway, 1990
Lifeburst, 1984

Other books you might like:
Arthur C. Clarke, *The Hammer of God*, 1993
Elizabeth Hand, *Icarus Descending*, 1993
Donald Malcolm, *The Iron Rain*, 1976
Yvonne Navarro, *Final Impact*, 1997
Charles Sheffield, *Aftermath*, 1998

849

ROBERT CHARLES WILSON

The Chronoliths
(New York: Tor, 2001)

Story type: Time Travel
Subject(s): Disasters
Major character(s): Scott Warden, Computer Expert; Sulamith Chopra, Scientist; Hitch Paley, Drug Dealer
Time period(s): 21st century (2021-2075)
Locale(s): Minnesota; Thailand; Baltimore, Maryland

Science Fiction

Summary: A series of strange, seemingly indestructible monuments begin appearing in Asia, apparently sent back through time by a victorious warlord 20 years in the future. Efforts are made to prevent his rise to power, but many others become entranced with the idea and form cults to protect the enigmatic and unidentified figure.

Other books by the same author:
Bios, 2000
Darwinia, 1999
Mysterium, 1994
The Harvest, 1993
Gypsies, 1989

Other books you might like:
Joseph Addison, *Tesseract*, 1988
Stephen Baxter, *Manifold: Time*, 2000
Gregory Benford, *Timescape*, 1980
John Lymington, *Froomb!*, 1976
Wilson Tucker, *Time Bomb*, 1955

850

GENE WOLFE

Return to the Whorl

(New York: Tor, 2001)

Story type: Space Colony
Series: Book of the Short Sun. Book 3
Subject(s): Space Exploration
Major character(s): Horn, Traveler; Maytera Mint, Rebel; Hound, Businessman
Time period(s): Indeterminate Future
Locale(s): *Whorl*, Spaceship

Summary: Horn, as part of his quest to find Patera Silk, has been traveling from planet to planet and finally to the great starship that spread humanity to the stars. Now his identity may have merged with that of Silk, and he himself has become partially independent of time and space.

Where it's reviewed:
Booklist, February 15, 2001, page 1122
Library Journal, February 15, 2001, page 205
Locus, February 2001, page 21
Publishers Weekly, January 22, 2001, page 307

Other books by the same author:
In Green's Jungles, 2000
Litany of the Long Sun, 2000
Strange Travelers, 2000
On Blue's Waters, 1999
Castleview, 1990

Other books you might like:
Samuel R. Delany, *They Fly at Ciron*, 1993
L. Warren Douglas, *Glaice*, 1996
Molly Gloss, *The Dazzle of Day*, 1997
Stephen Leigh, *Dark Water's Embrace*, 1998
Frank M. Robinson, *The Dark Beyond the Stars*, 1991

851

SARAH ZETTEL

Kingdom of Cages

(New York: Warner, 2001)

Story type: Genetic Manipulation; Space Colony
Subject(s): Space Colonies; Genetic Engineering
Major character(s): Chena Trust, Genetically Altered Being; Teal Trust, Genetically Altered Being; Nan Elle, Scientist
Time period(s): Indeterminate Future
Locale(s): Pandora, Planet—Imaginary

Summary: Pandora is the only human colony world which is not slowly dying as mutating plagues and environmental disasters ravage all other settlements. When the other colonies demand the Pandorans explain their immunity, two young girls become refugees from their own people as they discover they are part of a sinister biological experiment.

Other books by the same author:
The Quiet Invasion, 2000
Playing God, 1998
Fool's War, 1997
Reclamation, 1996

Other books you might like:
Ray Aldridge, *The Emperor of Everything*, 1992
Sharon Baker, *Journey to Memblar*, 1987
Stanislaw Lem, *Eden*, 1989
Hugh Nissenson, *The Song of the Earth*, 2001
Vernor Vinge, *A Fire upon the Deep*, 1990

Historical Fiction in Review
by
Daniel S. Burt

istorical fiction in the first half of 2001 continues to enjoy something of a renaissance in which the past continues to exert a strong hold on both literary and genre writers. In the novels collected here, masters of the historical novel, such as Beryl Bainbridge and Mary Lee Settle, are represented, as are such historical novel stalwarts as Don Coldsmith, Bernard Cornwell, Thomas Fleming, Colleen McCullough, Jeff Shaara, Wilbur A. Smith, and Jack Whyte. All the major subgenres—fictional biography, historical mystery, and historical fantasy—are well represented, and the list includes several impressive first novels and accomplished follow-ups to heralded debut efforts.

Selection Criteria

Before surveying the novels that follow, it is necessary to outline the selection criteria used in compiling this list. The appeal of the past for the writer is a constant in all novels, with the exception of science fiction set in the future or fantasy novels set in an imagined, alternative world outside historical time. Yet not all novels set in the past are truly historical. Central to any workable definition of historical fiction is the degree to which the writer attempts not to recall the past but to recreate it. In some cases, the timeframe, setting, and customs of a novel's era are merely incidental to its action and characterization. In other cases, period details function as little more than a colorful backdrop for characters and situations that could as easily be played out in a different era with little alteration. So-called historical "costume dramas" could, to a greater or lesser degree, work as well with a change of costume in a different place and time. The novels that we can identify as historical attempt much more than incidental surface details or interchangeable historical eras. What justifies a designation as a historical novel is the writer's attempt at providing an accurate and full representation of a particular historical era. The writer of historical fiction shares with the historian an attempted truthful depiction of past events, lives, and customs. In historical fiction, the past itself becomes as much a subject for the novelist as the characters and action.

Most of us use the phrase "historical novel" casually, never really needing an exact definition to make ourselves understood. We just know it when we see it. This listing, however, requires a set of criteria to determine what's in and what's out. Otherwise the list has no boundaries. If the working definition of historical fiction is too loose, every novel set in a period before the present qualifies, and nearly every novel becomes a historical novel immediately upon publication. If the definition is so strict that only books set in a time before the author's birth, for example, make the cut, then countless works that critics, readers, librarians, and the authors themselves think of as historical novels would be excluded.

My challenge, therefore, was to fashion a definition or set of criteria flexible enough to include novels that passed what can be regarded as the litmus test for historical fiction: Did the author use his or her imagination—and often quite a bit of research—to evoke another and earlier time than the author's own? Walter Scott, who is credited with "inventing" the historical novel in the early nineteenth century, provided a useful criterion in the subtitle of *Waverley: Tis Sixty Years Since* his story of Scottish life at the time of the Jacobite Rebellion of 1745. This period of sixty years supplies a possible formula for separating the created past from the remembered past. What is unique and distinctive about the so-called historical novel is its attempt to imagine a distant period of time before the novelist's lifetime, a past not recalled but created. Scott's sixty-year span (the same, incidentally, used by Tolstoy in *War and Peace*) between a novel's composition and its imagined era offers an arbitrary but useful means to distinguish between the personal and the historical past. The distance of two generations or nearly a lifetime provides a necessary span for the past to emerge as history and forces the writer to rely on more than recollection to uncover the patterns and textures of the past. I

have, therefore, adopted Scott's formula but adjusted it to fifty years, including those books in which the significant portion of their plots is set in a period fifty years or more before the novel was written.

Because a rigid application of this fifty-year rule might rule out quite a few books intended by their authors, and regarded by their readers, to be historical novels, another test has been applied to books written about more recent eras: Did the author use actual historical figures and events while setting out to recreate a specific, rather than a general or incidental, historical period? Although it is, of course, risky to speculate about a writer's intention, it is possible by looking at the book's approach, its use of actual historical figures, and its emphasis on a distinctive time and place that enhances the reader's knowledge of past lives, events, and customs to detect when a book conforms to what most would consider a central preoccupation of the historical novel. By this test, Emma Tennant's *Sylvia and Ted*, which falls short in much of its coverage of the fifty-year barrier, was included because of its obvious attempt to portray the lives of writers Sylvia Plath and Ted Hughes.

I have tried to apply these criteria for the historical novel as a guide, not as an inflexible rule, and have allowed some exceptions when warranted by special circumstances. I hope I have been able to anticipate what most readers would consider historical novels, but I recognize that I may have overlooked some worthy representations of the past in the interest of dealing with a manageable list of titles. Finally, not every title in the Western, historical mystery, or historical romance genres has been included to avoid unnecessary duplication with the other sections of this book. I have included those novels that share characteristics with another genre—whether fantasy, Western, mystery, or romance—that seem to put the strongest emphasis on historical interest, detail, and accuracy.

Historical Fiction in 2001

Among the novels reviewed in this volume of *What Do I Read Next?*, fans of the historical novel have many strong choices, with most of the expected subgenres—sea stories, family sagas, historical mysteries, fictional biographies—well represented by familiar names and by promising newcomers. Virtually every conceivable historical era is treated, in various locations, from prehistory to Ancient Rome, from the Middle Ages through the Elizabethan and Victorian periods, and America from colonial days through World War II.

Highlights among the novels selected are Jeff Shaara's *Rise to Rebellion* which uses the methods previously employed by his father Michael Shaara in *The Killer Angels* (a book many critics rank as one of the greatest historical novels ever written). Jeff Shaara has also developed a style of his own, evident in his novels on the Civil War, the Mexican War and the American Revolution. *Rise to Rebellion* is the first novel of what is hoped to be an ongoing

series. Mary Lee Settle, author of a number of highly acclaimed historicals, returns with *I, Roger Williams*, an autobiographical treatment of the early American figure. The astonishly prolific historical mystery writer P.C. Doherty is represented by three mysteries, each from a different historical era—Ancient Egypt, Greece during the lifetime of Alexander the Great, and the Middle Ages. Finally, the list includes the last efforts (unfortunately) of a number of writers who have recently died. They include Malcolm Bradbury's *To the Hermitage*, Marion Zimmer Bradley's *Priestess of Avalon* (with Diana L. Paxson), Peter Everett's *Bellocq's Women*, and Wilder Perkins' *Hoare and the Matter of Treason*.

The list also includes a number of exciting debut efforts by Jane Alison (*The Love-Artist*), David Anthony Durham (*Gabriel's Story*), Douglas Galbraith (*The Rising Sun*), Ross King (*Ex-Libris*), Edie Meidav (*The Far Field*), Fidelis Morgan (*Unnatural Fire*), Elizabeth Redfern (*The Music of the Spheres*), Betsy Tobin (*Bone House*), Kate Walbert (*Gardens of Kyoto*), and Geling Yan (*The Lost Daughter of Happiness*). Other firsts include the beginnings of two promising projected series: Candace Robb's *A Trust Betrayed* (an historical mystery set in 13th century Scotland) and Julian Stockwin's *Kydd* (a naval adventure series set during the age of sail from the perspective of a common sailor). An intriguing first is veteran mystery writer Robert B. Parker's debut as a western writer (*Gunman's Rhapsody*). Traces of Boston's Spenser are evident in Parker's version of Wyatt Earp and the famous gunfight at the OK Corral. Impressive second efforts after promising debuts include Alys Clare's *Ashes of Elements*, Nicholas Griffin's *The House of Sight and Shadow*, Jan Needle's *The Wicked Trade*, and Jean-Christophe Rufin's *The Siege of Isfahan*.

Historical mysteries continue to be popular, representing the single largest subcategory of the genre. There is detection going on from Ancient Egypt (Doherty's *The Anubis Slayings* and Lynda S. Robinson's *Slayer of Gods*) to Ancient Rome (Lindsay Davis' *Ode to a Banker*), through Europe's Middle Ages (Sara Conway's *Murder on Good Friday*, Roberta Gellis' *A Personal Devil*, and Michael Jecks' *The Boy-Bishop's Glovemaker*), Medieval Japan (Laura Joh Rowland's *Blood Lotus*), the Elizabethan era (Karen Harper's *The Twylight Tower* and Edward Marston's *The Devil's Apprentice*), the Victorian Period (Anne Perry's *The Whitechapel Conspiracy*), and into the 20th century (Jeanne M. Dams' *Green Grow the Victims*, Gillian Linscott's *A Perfect Daughter*, Lise McClendon's *One O'Clock Jump*, and Elizabeth Peters' *Lord of the Silent*). Several historical mystery series offer new installments, including Barbara Hambly's *Die upon a Kiss*, Ann McMillan's *Civil Blood*, Max Allan Collins' *Angel in Black*, and Stuart M. Kaminsky's *A Few Minutes Past Midnight*. Some of the more intriguing historical sleuths are Beau Brummell (in Rosemary Stevens' *The Tainted Snuff Box*), Elizabeth I (in Karen Harper's *The Twylight Tower*), and Groucho Marx

(in Ron Goulart's *Groucho Marx and the Broadway Murders*).

Another major subcategory of historical fiction, fictional biography, was equally well-represented in the first half of 2001. A wide cast of historical personages are portrayed at full length or at significant moments in their lives. These include the Roman poet Ovid in Jane Alison's *The Love-Artist*, Cleopatra in Karen Essex's *Kleopatra*, Samuel Johnson in Beryl Bainbridge's *According to Queeney*, Billy the Kid in Bill Brooks' *The Stone Garden*, Doc Holliday in Bruce Olds' *Bucking the Tiger*, the Brothers Grimm in Haydn Middleton's *Grimm's Last Fairytale*, Alma Mahler in Max Phillips' *The Artist's Wife*. Such little known but intriguing historical figures as photographer E.J. Bellocq, in Peter Everett's *Bellocq's Women*, and artist Franz Marc, in Sheldon Greene's *Burnt Umber*, are also presented. Two of the more intriguing fictional biographies are Catherine Clement's look at the relationship between German philosopher Martin Heidegger and Hannah Arendt (*Martin and Hannah*) and Emma Tennant's view of the troubled marriage of poets Sylvia Plath and Ted Hughes (*Sylvia and Ted*).

A distinguished group of historical figures make appearances in several novels, including many of the founding fathers in Jeff Shaara's *Rise to Rebellion*. Tarnished images of the Revolutionary icons surface in Paul Lussier's irreverent *Last Refuge of a Scoundrel*. Louis XIV is glimpsed in Frederic Richaud's *Gardener to the King*. The life of pirate Anne Bonney is imagined in Elizabeth Garrett's *The Sweet Trade*. Martin Luther figures prominently in Reg Grant's *Storm*, and Michael Collins dominates Morgan Llywelyn's *1921*. Conspirator Guy Fawkes is brilliantly resurrected in Paul West's *Fifth of November*.

Several novels are built around actual historical events or based on true stories. The Tulsa race riots of 1921 are depicted in Rilla Askew's *Fire in Beulah*, the Donner Party disaster in James D. Houston's *Snow Mountain Passage*, the attempt of the first woman to navigate the Colorado River through the Grand Canyon in Lisa Michaels' *Grand Ambition*, and the experiences of a Russian ballet troupe stranded in Puerto Rico after the Russian Revolution in 1917 in Rosario Ferre's *Flight of the Swan*.

Finally, there are a number of unusual or at least uncommon treatments in the historical novels listed. The American West is examined from the perspective of black Americans in David Anthony Durham's *Gabriel's Story* and J.P. Sinclair's *Buffalo Gordon*; from the perspective of Jewish Americans in Harriet Rochlin's *On Her Way Home*; from a humorous perspective in Peter Bowen's *Kelly and the Three-Toed Horse*; and from the perspective of myth and legend in Aaron Latham's *Code of the West*, which overlays Arthurian legend on the western experience. Lisa E. Davis looks at the experiences of gays and lesbians in 1940s Greenwich Village in an imaginative mystery in *Under the Mink*, and James Runcie provides a marvelously inventive time-traveling story in *The Discovery of Chocolate*, which moves through the centuries exploring the cultural impact of chocolate. Sweet.

Recommendations

Here are my selections of the 20 most accomplished and interesting historical novels for the first half of 2001:

Jane Alison, *The Love-Artist*

Beryl Bainbridge, *According to Queeney*

Bernard Cornwell, *Sharpe's Trafalgar*

Emma Donoghue, *Slammerkin*

Louise Erdrich, *The Last Report on the Miracles at Little No Horse*

Thomas Fleming, *When This Cruel War Is Over*

Amitav Ghosh, *The Glass Palace*

Nicholas Griffin, *The House of Sight and Shadow*

James D. Houston, *Snow Mountain Passage*

Helen Humphreys, *Afterimage*

Ross King, *Ex-Libris*

Micheline Marcom, *Three Apples Fell from Heaven*

Bruce Olds, *Bucking the Tiger*

Richard Rayner, *The Cloud Sketcher*

Frederic Richaud, *Gardener to the King*

Mary Lee Settle, *I, Roger Williams*

Jeff Shaara, *Rise to Rebellion*

Lalita Tademy, *Cane River*

Betsy Tobin, *Bone House*

Paul West, *A Fifth of November*

For More Information about Historical Fiction

Printed Sources

Adamson, Lynda G. *American Historical Fiction: An Annotated Guide to Novels for Adults and Young Adults*. Phoenix: Oryx Press, 1999.

Adamson, Lynda G. *World Historical Fiction: An Annotated Guide to Novels for Adults and Young Adults*. Phoenix: Oryx Press, 1999.

Burt, Daniel S. *What Historical Fiction Do I Read Next?* Detroit: Gale, 1997.

Hartman, Donald K. *Historical Figures in Fiction*. Phoenix: Oryx Press, 1994.

Electronic Sources

The Historical Novel Society (http//www.historicalnovelsociety.com). Includes articles, interviews, and reviews of historical novels.

Of Ages Past: The Online Magazine of Historical Fiction (http://www.angelfire.com/il/ofagespast/). Includes

novel excerpts, short stories, articles, author profiles, and reviews.

Soon's Historical Fiction Site (http://www.uts.cc.utexas .edu/soon/histfiction/index.html) A rich source of infor-

mation on the historical novel genre, including links to more specialized sites on particular authors and types of historical fiction.

Historical Titles

852

JANE ALISON

The Love-Artist
(New York: Farrar, Straus & Giroux, 2001)

Story type: Historical/Ancient Rome
Subject(s): Roman Empire; Poetry; Witches and Witchcraft
Major character(s): Ovid, Historical Figure, Writer (poet); Xenia, Young Woman, Witch; Julia, Historical Figure (granddaughter of the emperor)
Time period(s): 1st century
Locale(s): Black Sea, Europe; Rome, Roman Empire

Summary: This novel imagines what might have caused the Roman poet Ovid's lifetime banishment by the Emperor Augustus in 8 A.D. In this version, Ovid, while on a trip to the Black Sea, meets a young beauty, Xenia, who becomes the poet's inspiration. In spite of the danger posed by Xenia's talent for witchcraft, Ovid takes her back to Rome with him. There he gains the patronage of the embittered granddaughter of Augustus, Julia, who has her own motives for befriending the acclaimed poet. This is an ingenious novel of romantic intrigue with authentic period flavor.

Where it's reviewed:
Booklist, February 1, 2001, page 1038
Kirkus Reviews, January 15, 2001, page 68
Library Journal, February 1, 2001, page 124
Publishers Weekly, March 5, 2001, page 124

Other books you might like:
Colin Falconer, *When We Were Gods*, 2000
Vintila Hora, *God Was Born in Exile*, 1961
David Malouf, *An Imaginary Life*, 1978
Allan Massie, *Augustus*, 1986
Vincent Panella, *Cutter's Island*, 2000

853

RILLA ASKEW

Fire in Beulah
(New York: Viking, 2001)

Story type: Historical/Roaring Twenties
Subject(s): Race Relations; Oil; Brothers and Sisters
Major character(s): Althea Dedham, Spouse (of Franklin); Franklin Dedham, Businessman (oil speculator); Graceful, Servant (maid)
Time period(s): 1920s (1920-1921)
Locale(s): Tulsa, Oklahoma

Summary: Set during the Oklahoma oil rush of the 1920s and culminating in the Tulsa race riot of 1921, this haunting novel concerns the relationship between an oil wildcatter's wife, Althea Dedham, and her black maid, Graceful. The sinister catalyst for the novel's action is Althea's troubled brother Japheth, who rapes Graceful and incites Althea's husband, Franklin, against his partner. The action forces Althea to become Graceful's ally, and her moral growth is set against a vivid period background of racial conflict that explodes into violence.

Where it's reviewed:
Kirkus Reviews, November 1, 2000, page 1500
Publishers Weekly, November 13, 2000, page 83

Other books by the same author:
The Mercy Seat, 1997
Strange Business, 1992

Other books you might like:
Kathleen Cambor, *In Sunlight, in a Beautiful Garden*, 2000
David Anthony Durham, *Gabriel's Story*, 2001
Aaron Roy Even, *Bloodroot*, 2000
Fred Harris, *Easy Pickin's*, 2000
Joe R. Lansdale, *The Bottoms*, 2000

BERYL BAINBRIDGE

According to Queeney
(New York: Carroll & Graf, 2001)

Story type: Historical/Georgian
Subject(s): Biography; Writing
Major character(s): Samuel Johnson, Historical Figure, Writer; Hester Thrale, Historical Figure; Queeney Thrale, Young Woman
Time period(s): 18th century
Locale(s): London, England

Summary: For this novel, Bainbridge, who specializes in inventive looks at historical figures and periods selects 18th century England and its literary giant, Dr. Samuel Johnson. The story of Johnson's relationship with his benefactress, Mrs. Hester Thrale, is portrayed from the vantage point of Thrale's daughter, Queeney. This is a believable portrait, both of Johnson and his era, supported by evident meticulous research and an imaginative ability to penetrate the psyche of the participants.

Other books by the same author:
Master Georgie, 1998
Every Man for Himself, 1996
The Birthday Boys, 1994
Watson's Apology, 1984
Young Adolf, 1979

Other books you might like:
Winifred Carter, *Dr. Johnson's Dear Mistress*, 1949
Sara George, *The Journal of Mrs. Pepys*, 1999
J.D. Landis, *Longing*, 2000
Charles Norman, *Mr. Oddity: Samuel Johnson, LL.D.*, 1951
Paul West, *A Fifth of November*, 2001

855

ROSANNE BITTNER

Mystic Warriors
(New York: Forge, 2001)

Story type: Historical/American West; Indian Culture
Series: Mystic Dreams. Book 3
Subject(s): Indians of North America
Major character(s): Buffalo Dreamer, Indian (Lakota), Spouse (of Rising Eagle); Rising Eagle, Spouse (of Buffalo Dreamer), Indian (Lakota)
Time period(s): 1850s (1855)
Locale(s): Lakota Nation, West

Summary: In the final book of Bittner's Mystic Dreams series, it is 1855 and white buffalo hunters steal the Lakota's most sacred talisman, the pelt of a white buffalo. The loss speeds their ill fortune as the whites gain power over them. The novel explores the tribe's encounters with the whites and the relationship between the Lakota holy woman, Buffalo Dreamer, and her husband, Rising Eagle, whose son by a former captive is one of the belligerent white soldiers.

Other books by the same author:
Mystic Visions, 2000

Mystic Dreamers, 1999
Texas Embrace, 1997
Tame the Wild Wind, 1996
Chase the Sun, 1995

Other books you might like:
Don Coldsmith, *The Spanish Bit Saga*, 1980-
W. Michael Gear, *The First North Americans Series*, 1990-
Kathleen O'Neal Gear, co-author
Pamela Jekel, *She Who Hears the Sun*, 1999
Vella Munn, *Blackfeet Season*, 1999
Janelle Taylor, *Lakota Dawn*, 1999

856

E.A. BLAIR

A Journey to the Interior
(Houston: Scrivenery, 2000)

Story type: Historical/American West
Subject(s): Fur Trade; American West; Frontier and Pioneer Life
Major character(s): Caleb Bring, Military Personnel (captain)
Time period(s): 1800s
Locale(s): Yellowstone Territory, Wyoming

Summary: Set in the early years of western exploration following the trailblazing of Lewis and Clark, this novel recounts the story of a fur-trading expedition by keelboat and horseback into the Yellowstone Territory of the Crow Indians. A diverse group of intrepid frontiersmen is led by Captain Caleb Bring, a gritty New Englander. The group must contend with privation, harsh weather, and Native Americans. The reliability of Blair's account is buttressed by details from the journal of English botanist John Bradbury.

Where it's reviewed:
Booklist, December 15, 2000, page 784
Publishers Weekly, November 13, 2000, page 88

Other books you might like:
Louis Charbonneau, *Trail*, 1989
David Nevins, *Eagle's Cry*, 2000
Donald Culross Peattie, *Forward the Nation*, 1942
James Alexander Thom, *Sign-Talker*, 2000
Dale Van Every, *The Shining Mountains*, 1948

857

PETER BOWEN

Kelly and the Three-Toed Horse
(New York: St. Martin's Press, 2001)

Story type: Historical/American West; Indian Culture
Series: Yellowstone Kelly. Number 4
Subject(s): Indians of North America; Fossils
Major character(s): Luther ''Yellowstone'' Kelly, Scout, Gunfighter; Alys de Bonneterre, Young Woman; Blue Fox, Indian (Cheyenne), Mentally Ill Person (psychopath)
Time period(s): 1870s
Locale(s): Wyoming

Summary: Yellowstone Kelly, Bowen's western gunfighter, scout, and adventurer, leads a party of academics into Wyo-

ming's Indian territory during the 1870s following the discovery of a fossil skeleton of a three-toed horse. While dealing with the tenderfeet, Kelly falls for the beautiful Alys de Bonneterre, while facing down the Dartmouth-educated Cheyenne warrior and psychopath, Blue Fox. This is an offbeat western adventure with a comic and irreverent take on the wild west.

Where it's reviewed:
Booklist, March 1, 2001, page 1225
Kirkus Reviews, February 1, 2001, page 123
Publishers Weekly, February 26, 2001, page 62

Other books by the same author:
Long Son, 1999
The Gabriel DuPre Series, 1996-
Imperial Kelly, 1992
Kelly Blue, 1991
Yellowstone Kelly, 1987

Other books you might like:
David Ballantine, *Chalk's Woman*, 2000
Thomas Berger, *The Return of Little Big Man*, 1999
Peter Carey, *True History of the Kelly Gang*, 2000
Larry McMurtry, *Boone's Lick*, 2000
James Welch, *Heartsong of Charging Elk*, 2000

858

MALCOLM BRADBURY

To the Hermitage
(Woodstock, New York: Overlook, 2001)

Story type: Historical/Exotic
Subject(s): Russian Empire; Travel
Major character(s): Denis Diderot, Philosopher, Historical Figure; Catherine the Great, Historical Figure, Ruler (Empress of Russia); Voltaire, Historical Figure, Writer
Time period(s): 1770s (1773); 1990s (1993)
Locale(s): St. Petersburg, Russia

Summary: The late novelist and critic's final work is a clever dual narrative that connects a group of Cambridge academics who journey to St. Petersburg in 1993, just as the military coup against Boris Yeltsin is unfolding, and a journey 220 years earlier of the French philosopher and encyclopedist Denis Diderot to the court of Catherine the Great for a series of discussions on the modern world during the Age of Reason. While the effort to connect the two eras is more witty than compelling, Bradbury's re-creation of the past is brimming with playful and entertaining ideas and details.

Where it's reviewed:
Booklist, March 1, 2001, page 1353
Kirkus Reviews, March 1, 2001, page 274
Library Journal, April 1, 2001, page 131
Publishers Weekly, March 26, 2001, page 60

Other books by the same author:
Doctor Criminale, 1992
Cuts, 1987
Rates of Exchange, 1983
The History Man, 1975
Eating People Is Wrong, 1959

Other books you might like:
Evelyn Anthony, *Royal Intrigue*, 1954
Guy Endore, *Voltaire! Voltaire!*, 1961
Romain Gary, *The Enchanters*, 1975
Victor Pelevin, *Buddha's Little Finger*, 2000
Francisco Rebolledo, *Rasero*, 1996

859

MARION ZIMMER BRADLEY
DIANA L. PAXSON, Co-Author

Priestess of Avalon
(New York: Viking, 2001)

Story type: Historical/Fantasy; Historical/Ancient Rome
Subject(s): Ancient History; Fantasy; Women
Major character(s): Helena, Royalty (British princess), Historical Figure; Flavius Constantius Chlorus, Ruler (Roman emperor), Historical Figure; Constantine, Ruler (Roman emperor), Historical Figure
Time period(s): 3rd century
Locale(s): England; Roman Empire

Summary: Bradley who died in 1999, is joined by veteran fantasy writer Paxson in a prequel to Bradley's acclaimed *The Mists of Avalon* (1982). It is the 3rd century, and a young British princess, Eilan, journeys to the Isle of Avalon to be educated in the Celtic goddess cult. When Flavius Constantius Chlorus and his Roman army threaten, Eilan, now known as Helena, weds Constantius, the future Roman emperor and has a son, Constantine, who later becomes emperor. At the seat of power, Helena draws on her goddess faith to deal with the challenges of ruling and to reconcile pagan beliefs with the new Christianity.

Where it's reviewed:
Booklist, April 15, 2001, page 1510
Kirkus Reviews, April 1, 2001, page 456
Publishers Weekly, April 30, 2001, page 62

Other books by the same author:
The Forest House, 1993
The Firebrand, 1987
The Mists of Avalon, 1982

Other books you might like:
Bernard Cornwell, *Stonehenge*, 2000
Louis De Wohl, *The Living Wood*, 1947
Judith Hand, *Voice of the Goddess*, 2001
Joan Dahr Lambert, *Circles of Stone*, 1997
Judith Tarr, *White Mare's Daughter*, 1998

860

BILL BROOKS

The Stone Garden
(New York: Forge, 2001)

Story type: Historical/American West
Subject(s): American West; Biography; Crime and Criminals
Major character(s): Billy the Kid, Historical Figure, Outlaw; Manuella, Young Woman; Pat Garrett, Lawman (sheriff), Historical Figure

Historical

Time period(s): 19th century; 1900s (1880s-1908)
Locale(s): New Mexico

Summary: What if Billy the Kid was not killed in an ambush by Pat Garrett in 1881? That is the intriguing premise of Brooks' revisionist take on the life and legend of America's most famous outlaw. In this version, Garrett shoots the wrong man and lies to cover it up. Billy's story continues into the first decade of the 20th century, told from Billy's own perspective and that of his long-time lover, Manuella. Vowing revenge on Garrett, Billy dreams of the good old days of the Lincoln County War, while the actual unsolved murder of Garrett in 1908 is given an intriguing solution.

Where it's reviewed:
Publishers Weekly, May 21, 2001, page 78

Other books by the same author:
Pistolero, 1998
Dust on the Wind, 1997
Deadwood, 1996
Old Times, 1995
The Last Law There Was, 1995

Other books you might like:
Edwin Corle, *Billy the Kid*, 1953
David Everitt, *The Story of Pat Garrett and Billy the Kid*, 1990
Elizabeth Fackler, *Billy the Kid*, 1995
Larry McMurtry, *Anything for Billy*, 1988
N. Scott Momaday, *The Ancient Child*, 1989

861

BARTLE BULL

The Devil's Oasis

(New York: Carroll & Graf, 2001)

Story type: Historical/World War II; Action/Adventure
Subject(s): Africa; World War II
Major character(s): Wellington Rider, Military Personnel (British officer); Anton Rider, Hunter; Ernst von Decken, Military Personnel (German soldier)
Time period(s): 1930s; 1940s (1939-1942)
Locale(s): Cairo, Egypt

Summary: Bull's action/adventure yarn featuring a large cast of repeated characters from *The White Rhino Hotel* and *A Cafe on the Nile* moves into World War II as the dashing hunter Anton Rider and his eldest son, Wellington, try to halt Rommel's Afrika Korps. Supporting the other side is Rider's German friend, Ernst von Decken. Fans of exotic adventure fiction will not be disappointed in this fast-paced novel with an authentic period flavor.

Where it's reviewed:
Kirkus Reviews, March 1, 2001, page 290
Library Journal, March 15, 2001, page 104
Publishers Weekly, February 26, 2001, page 57

Other books by the same author:
A Cafe on the Nile, 1998
The White Rhino Hotel, 1992

Other books you might like:
Noel Barber, *Sakkara*, 1984

Robert Beylen, *The Way to the Sun*, 1971
Len Deighton, *City of Gold*, 1992
Glenn Meade, *The Sands of Sakkara*, 1999
Michael Ondaatje, *The English Patient*, 1992

862

GERALDINE BURROWS

Miss Sedgewick and the Spy

(Unity, Maine: Five Star, 2000)

Story type: Historical/Napoleonic Wars; Romantic Suspense
Subject(s): Espionage
Major character(s): Drusilla Sedgewick, Spy; MacRory Holt, Military Personnel (colonel); Henry Lazare, Spy
Time period(s): 1810s (1814-1815)
Locale(s): France

Summary: Set on the eve of the battle of Waterloo, this Regency historical is the fanciful tale of young Drusilla Sedgewick, who is recruited as a spy. Paired with ace undercover agent Colonel MacRory Holt, Drusilla battles the wily French spymaster Henry Lazare while trying to prevent a plot to murder the Duke of Wellington. Less than believable, there is more history here than in many Regency romances, but far more make-believe than a historical novel purist demands.

Where it's reviewed:
Kirkus Reviews, December 1, 2000, page 1644

Other books by the same author:
Miss Thornrose and the Rake, 1999

Other books you might like:
Stephanie Barron, *The Jane Austen Series*, 1996-
Allan Mallinson, *A Close Run Thing*, 1999
Wilder Perkins, *The Captain Bartholomew Hoare Series*, 1998-2001
Amanda Quick, *Affair*, 1997
Joan Wolf, *The Gamble*, 1998

863

ANN CHAMBERLIN

The Merlin of the Oak Wood

(New York: Tor, 2001)

Story type: Historical/Fantasy; Historical/Medieval
Series: Joan of Arc Tapestries. Number 2
Subject(s): Middle Ages; Occult; Fantasy
Major character(s): Yann, Psychic, Witch; Joan of Arc, Historical Figure, Warrior; Gilles de Rais, Nobleman, Historical Figure
Time period(s): 15th century
Locale(s): France

Summary: Mixing history and fantasy, Chamberlin continues her account of the life of Joan of Arc. The soldier-witch Gilles de Rais continues to battle the English while dealing with betrayal all around him. Meanwhile, witch Yann learns the identity of France's savior, the peasant girl Jehannette d'Arc, later known as Joan of Arc. Joan eventually accepts her role as France's military leader, and at the novel's close she is shown gathering an army to relieve the siege of Orleans. Cutting

among several subplots, the novel is a rich mix of magic, realistic detail, and history shown in the original light of the uncanny.

Where it's reviewed:
Kirkus Reviews, April 15, 2001, page 548

Other books by the same author:
Leaving Eden, 1999
The Merlin of St. Gilles' Well, 1999
The Reign of the Favored Women, 1998
The Sultan's Daughter, 1997
Sofia, 1996

Other books you might like:
Marion Zimmer Bradley, *The Forest House*, 1993
Thomas Keneally, *Blood Red, Sister Rose*, 1974
Stephen R. Lawhead, *The Pendragon Cycle Series*, 1987-1996
Pamela Marcantel, *An Army of Angels*, 1997
Anna Lee Waldo, *Circle of Stones*, 1999

864

TIM CHAMPLIN

A Trail to Wounded Knee

(Thorndike: Five Star, 2001)

Story type: Historical/American West; Indian Culture
Subject(s): Indians of North America; American West; Frontier and Pioneer Life
Major character(s): Thaddeus Coyle, Military Personnel (lieutenant), Government Official (Bureau of Indian Affairs); Emma Coyle, Spouse (of Thaddeus)
Time period(s): 1870s
Locale(s): Dakota Territory, West

Summary: Champlin's look at pioneer life on the Western frontier is from the perspective of army Lieutenant Thaddeus Coyle, who is court-martialed and abandoned by his wife Emma, who decides that frontier life is not for her. Starting over, Coyle goes to work for the Bureau of Indian Affairs and is on hand for the ghost dance phenomenon that culminates in the massacre at Wounded Knee. Authentic in its historical detail, the novel is a competent recreation of its period and the conflict between settlers and Indians.

Where it's reviewed:
Booklist, April 15, 2001, page 1532

Other books by the same author:
Lincoln's Ransom, 2000
Swift Thunder, 2000
Tombstone Conspiracy, 1999
Staghorn, 1998
Deadly Season, 1997

Other books you might like:
Don Coldsmith, *Raven Mocker*, 2001
Terry C. Johnston, *Wind Walker*, 2001
Douglas C. Jones, *A Creek Called Wounded Knee*, 1978
J.P. Sinclair Lewis, *Buffalo Gordon*, 2001
Earl P. Murray, *Song of Wovoka*, 1992

865

ALYS CLARE

Ashes of the Elements

(New York: St. Martin's Minotaur, 2001)

Story type: Historical/Medieval; Mystery
Subject(s): Mystery and Detective Stories; Middle Ages
Major character(s): Helewise of Hawkenlye, Religious (abbess); Sir Josse d'Acquin, Knight
Time period(s): 12th century
Locale(s): England

Summary: Set during the reign of Richard the Lionheart, Clare's well-received historical mystery series features Abbess Helewise and her worldly partner, king's man Josse d'Acquin. The death of a poacher in Wealden Forest prompts their investigation. Are the mysterious Forest People responsible? Or does the death and a subsequent murder conceal a much more sinister conspiracy? Clare's specialty is an assured touch in delivering a strong medieval atmosphere. This is a worthy successor to the author's debut *Fortune Like the Moon*.

Where it's reviewed:
Kirkus Reviews, March 1, 2001, page 293
Publishers Weekly, April 2, 2001, page 43

Other books by the same author:
Fortune Like the Moon, 2000

Other books you might like:
P.C. Doherty, *The Matthew Jankyn Series*, 1988-
Ian Morson, *The Falconer Series*, 1994-
Sharan Newman, *To Wear the White Cloak*, 2000
Ellis Peters, *The Brother Cadfael Series*, 1977-1994
Peter Tremayne, *The Monk Who Vanished*, 2000

866

CATHERINE CLEMENT

Martin and Hannah

(Amherst, New York: Prometheus, 2001)

Story type: Historical/World War II
Subject(s): Biography; Philosophy; Nazis
Major character(s): Martin Heidegger, Historical Figure, Philosopher; Hannah Arendt, Historical Figure, Writer; Elfriede Heidegger, Historical Figure, Spouse (of Martin)
Time period(s): 20th century
Locale(s): Germany

Summary: The novel explores the triangular relationship among German philosopher Martin Heidegger, his wife, Elfriede, and his former student and lover, Hannah Arendt. In the 1970s, the three are reunited, and the novel looks back on their tangled lives with the question of Heidegger's betrayal by joining the Nazi party in the 1930s the crucial issue as each woman tries to assert her emotional claims over the aging and dying philosopher.

Where it's reviewed:
Booklist, March 1, 2001, page 1225
Publishers Weekly, March 12, 2001, page 64

Historical

Other books you might like:
Bruce Duffy, *The World as I Found It*, 1967
Terrence Eagleton, *Saints and Scholars*, 1987
Denise Giardina, *Saints and Villains*, 1998
David Farrell Krell, *Nietzsche*, 1996
Norma Rosen, *John and Anzia*, 1989

867
SUSANN COKAL
Mirabilis
(New York: Putnam, 2001)

Story type: Historical/Medieval
Subject(s): Middle Ages
Major character(s): Bonne Mirabilis, Care Giver (wet nurse); Godfridus, Artisan (carver); Radegonde Putemonnoie, Widow(er), Wealthy
Time period(s): 14th century
Locale(s): Villeneuve, France

Summary: This absorbing account of medieval life concerns the illegitimate daughter of a woman thought by the villagers of Villeneuve, France, to be miraculous but later imprisoned and burned. The daughter, Bonne, survives as a wet nurse who, though her own illegitimate child died six years before, manages to keep her milk flowing by suckling Godfridus, a journeyman church carver, is hired by the wealthy, pregnant widow Radegonde Putemonnoie. When the town is besieged by the English and the townspeople are starving, Radegonde refuses to help. Bonne realizes she can provide milk and finds herself elevated in the eyes of her neighbors by her capacity to feed them all. This is an fascinating look at medieval customs as bizarre as it is intriguing.

Where it's reviewed:
Kirkus Reviews, April 15, 2001, page 518
Publishers Weekly, June 11, 2001, page 56

Other books you might like:
Donna Woolfolk Cross, *Pope Joan*, 1996
Catherine Maccoun, *The Age of Miracles*, 1989
H.F.M. Prescott, *Son of Dust*, 1956
Barry Unsworth, *Morality Play*, 1995
Fritz Von Unruh, *The Saint*, 1950

868
DON COLDSMITH
The Long Journey Home
(New York: Forge, 2001)

Story type: Historical/American West; Indian Culture
Subject(s): Indians of North America; Olympics; Sports/Track
Major character(s): John Buffalo, Indian (Lakota Sioux), Sports Figure (track and field); Jim Thorpe, Historical Figure, Sports Figure (track and field); Bill Picket, Cowboy
Time period(s): 19th century; 20th century
Locale(s): United States; Europe

Summary: Coldsmith spins a rambling yarn about a Lakota Sioux athlete, John Buffalo, whose dreams of Olympic glory are spoiled by racial prejudice. Buffalo's career takes him across the United States and Europe and he encounters a wide selection of historical figures including Jim Thorpe, Jesse Owens, Will Rogers, and Theodore Roosevelt. Coldsmith offers convincing views of the flu epidemic of 1918 and early Hollywood as he chronicles a proud Native American forced to contend with modern culture that insists on assimilation and deference.

Where it's reviewed:
Booklist, March 15, 2001, page 1353
Library Journal, February 15, 2001, page 198
Publishers Weekly, December 11, 2000, page 63

Other books by the same author:
Raven Mocker, 2001
Southwind, 1998
Tallgrass, 1997
Runestone, 1995
The Spanish Bit Saga, 1980-

Other books you might like:
Win Blevins, *Stone Song*, 1995
David Anthony Durham, *Gabriel's Story*, 2001
Joyce R. Hudson, *Apalachee*, 2000
Andrew Huebner, *American by Blood*, 2000
James Welch, *Heartsong of Charging Elk*, 2000

869
DON COLDSMITH
Raven Mocker
(Norman: University of Oklahoma Press, 2001)

Story type: Indian Culture; Historical/American West
Series: Spanish Bit Saga
Subject(s): Indians of North America; Cultures and Customs
Major character(s): Corn Flower, Indian (Cherokee), Shaman
Time period(s): Indeterminate Past
Locale(s): Arkansas

Summary: This installment of Coldsmith's Spanish Bit Saga follows the career of an orphaned Cherokee girl, Corn Flower, who takes the name of the healer Snakewater who adopts her. Suspected of being the embodiment of a spiritual demon called the Raven Mocker who can steal years from others' lives, she flees west to Arkansas to settle with the Elk Dog people and plays a crucial role in their development of the annual Sun Dance. Coldsmith is accomplished in recreating Native American myths and culture.

Where it's reviewed:
Booklist, March 1, 2001, page 1225
Publishers Weekly, February 19, 2001, page 71

Other books by the same author:
The Long Journey Home, 2001
Tallgrass, 1997
Runestone, 1995
The Smoky Hill, 1989
The Spanish Bit Saga, 1980-

Other books you might like:
Joseph Bruchac, *Dawn Land*, 1993

W. Michael Gear, *The First North Americans Series*, 1990-
Kathleen O'Neal Gear, co-author
Pamela Jekel, *She Who Hears the Sun*, 1999
Vella Munn, *Blackfeet Season*, 1999
Linda Lay Shuler, *She Who Remembers*, 1988

█870█

MAX ALLAN COLLINS

Angel in Black

(New York: New American Library, 2001)

Story type: Mystery
Series: Nathan Heller
Subject(s): Mystery and Detective Stories; Crime and Criminals; Movie Industry
Major character(s): Nathan Heller, Detective—Private; Eliot Ness, Historical Figure, FBI Agent; Orson Welles, Historical Figure, Actor
Time period(s): 1940s (1947)
Locale(s): Los Angeles, California

Summary: Collins offers his unique take on the famous Black Dahlia case, one of Los Angeles' most famous unsolved mysteries. Chicago private detective Nathan Heller is in Los Angeles in 1947, and when a woman is found tortured, raped, cut in two, and drained of fluids, her identity is a mystery to all except the P.I. She is a woman that Heller had had a recent affair with, making him a prime suspect. Concealing his relationship with the victim, Heller assists in the investigation, pursuing a theory that the killing was not a sex crime but a Mob execution. To assist him, Heller calls on old friend Eliot Ness and makes contact with such Hollywood figures as Orson Welles.

Where it's reviewed:
Booklist, March 1, 2001, page 1225
Publishers Weekly, February 26, 2001, page 62

Other books by the same author:
The Hindenburg Murders, 2000
Majic Man, 1999
Flying Blind, 1998
Stolen Away, 1991
True Crime, 1984

Other books you might like:
James Ellroy, *The Black Dahlia*, 1987
Ron Goulart, *The Groucho Marx Series*, 1998-
Robert Lee Hall, *Murder at San Simeon*, 1988
Stuart M. Kaminsky, *The Toby Peters Series*, 1977-
Lise McClendon, *One O'Clock Jump*, 2001

█871█

SARA CONWAY

Murder on Good Friday

(Nashville: Cumberland House, 2001)

Story type: Historical/Medieval; Mystery
Series: Lord Godwin. Number 1
Subject(s): Mystery and Detective Stories; Middle Ages; Religious Conflict

Major character(s): Lord Godwin, Veteran (ex-crusader), Lawman (bailiff)
Time period(s): 13th century (1220)
Locale(s): Hexham, England

Summary: In the debut of a medieval mystery series, it is 1220 and in Hexham, England, a young boy is found strangled. It is revealed that the boy was killed on Good Friday, and his body has been marked in imitation of Christ's crucifixion wounds. The community suspects Jews as the culprits in a religiously motivated killing. Investigating is Hexham's bailiff, Lord Godwin, a disillusioned ex-crusader wracked with guilt over failing to protect a friend from death during the Crusades. Godwin tries to protect the town's Jews while attempting to discover who would have wanted the child to die and why.

Where it's reviewed:
Publishers Weekly, February 26, 2001, page 63

Other books you might like:
Alys Clare, *Ashes of the Elements*, 2001
P.C. Doherty, *The Demon Archer*, 2001
Roberta Gellis, *A Personal Devil*, 2001
Michael Jecks, *The Boy-Bishop's Glovemaker*, 2001
Edward Marston, *The Wildcats of Exeter*, 2001

█872█

CATHERINE COOKSON

Kate Hannigan's Girl

(New York: Simon & Schuster, 2001)

Story type: Historical/World War I
Subject(s): Country Life
Major character(s): Kate Hannigan, Spouse; Annie Hannigan, Bastard Daughter; Catherine Davidson, Young Woman
Time period(s): 1910s
Locale(s): Tyneside, England

Summary: Cookson's 100th novel, published posthumously, is set, like many of the author's books, in the north of England during the years following World War I. The story concerns earnest Annie Hannigan, who learns that she is illegitimate. Despite her mother's now respectable life, Annie is hounded by the sinister Catherine Davidson, who is bent on destroying any claims for happiness for Annie, who falls in love with a poor, Oxford educated young man. This is a fast-paced melodrama drawn from Cookson's patented sense of her imagined community's values.

Where it's reviewed:
Booklist, January 2001, page 869
Kirkus Reviews, February 15, 2001, page 200
Publishers Weekly, January 22, 2001, page 303

Other books by the same author:
The Desert Crop, 1999
The Maltese Angel, 1993
My Beloved Son, 1991
The Rag Nymph, 1991
The Love Child, 1990

Other books you might like:
Helen Dunmore, *A Spell of Winter*, 2001
Catherine Dupre, *Gentleman's Child*, 1990

Historical

Helen Humphreys, *Afterimage*, 2001
Jessica Stirling, *The Dark Pasture*, 1978
Jean Stubbs, *The Vivian Inheritance*, 1982

873

BERNARD CORNWELL

Sharpe's Trafalgar

(New York: HarperCollins, 2001)

Story type: Historical/Post-French Revolution; Military
Series: Richard Sharpe. Book 17
Subject(s): Sea Stories; Military Life; War
Major character(s): Richard Sharpe, Military Personnel (British army officer); Lady Grace Hale, Noblewoman
Time period(s): 1800s (1805)
Locale(s): *Calliope*, At Sea; *Revenant*, At Sea; *Pucelle*, At Sea

Summary: British infantryman Richard Sharpe ships out in this chapter of his military career. Newly promoted to the officer corps for saving Lord Arthur Wellesley's life in India, Sharpe sails home to England aboard an East India Company merchant ship. A shipboard romance with Lady Grace Hale is interrupted by the appearance of a French warship, and Sharpe becomes aware of the existence of a stolen treaty that could provoke India into a new war with Britain. Pursuit of the French leads Sharpe to the fateful battle at Trafalgar. Cornwell shows himself adept at rendering naval warfare, and his historically reliable account of Trafalgar is masterful.

Where it's reviewed:
Booklist, March 15, 2001, page 1332
Kirkus Reviews, March 15, 2001, page 363
Library Journal, April 15, 2001, page 131
Publishers Weekly, April 16, 2001, page 46

Other books by the same author:
Stonehenge, 2000
The Arthurian Warlord Trilogy, 1996-1998
The Starbuck Chronicles, 1993-
Redcoat, 1988
The Richard Sharpe Series, 1981-

Other books you might like:
Allan Mallinson, *Honorable Company*, 2000
Jan Needle, *The Wicked Trade*, 2001
Dudley Pope, *Ramage at Trafalgar*, 1986
Julian Stockwin, *Kydd*, 2001
Richard Woodman, *Decision at Trafalgar*, 1986

874

JEANNE M. DAMS

Green Grow the Victims

(New York: Walker, 2001)

Story type: Mystery; Historical/Victorian America
Series: Hilda Johansson. Number 3
Subject(s): Mystery and Detective Stories; Detection; Servants
Major character(s): Hilda Johansson, Servant, Detective—Amateur
Time period(s): 1900s

Locale(s): South Bend, Indiana

Summary: South Bend, Indiana's housekeeper-sleuth Hilda Johansson returns for her third investigation. Amidst well-researched and capably delivered period and regional details, Hilda is asked to locate a missing candidate for the city council who is suspected of murder. Physical evidence and an eye-witness both point to his guilt, but Hilda is not convinced, and she embarks on a revealing and entertaining tour of Americana at the turn of the century.

Where it's reviewed:
Booklist, May 1, 2001, page 1628
Publishers Weekly, April 16, 2001, page 47

Other books by the same author:
Red, White, and Blue Murder, 2000
Death in Lacquer Red, 1999
The Dorothy Martin Series, 1995-

Other books you might like:
Charlotte Vale Allen, *Mood Indigo*, 1998
Dianne Day, *The Fremont Jones Series*, 1995-
Annette Meyers, *Free Love*, 1999
Miriam Grace Monfredo, *The Seneca Falls Series*, 1992-
Marcella Thum, *Fernwood*, 1973

875

JOHN R. DANN

Song of the Axe

(New York: Forge, 2001)

Story type: Historical/Pre-history
Subject(s): Mythology; Legends
Major character(s): Agon, Prehistoric Human; Eena, Prehistoric Human; Ka, Prehistoric Human, Shaman
Time period(s): Indeterminate Past (circa 30,000 B.C.)
Locale(s): Earth (Eurasia continent)

Summary: This massive prehistoric tale set in Eurasia around 30,000 B.C., traces the relationship between Agon and Eena. Captured by a rival Neanderthal tribe led by the shaman Ka, Eena is rescued by Agon, who takes her as his wife. They try to settle in peace, but must contend with the vengeance of Ka's descendants. Both are sustained by their skill in battle, strength of character, and a faith in one another that humanizes an otherwise brutal and bloody landscape.

Where it's reviewed:
Kirkus Reviews, February 1, 2001, page 126
Library Journal, February 1, 2001, page 124
Publishers Weekly, March 12, 2001, page 63

Other books you might like:
Jean Auel, *The Clan of the Cave Bear*, 1980
W. Michael Gear, *People of the Earth*, 1992
    Kathleen O'Neal Gear, co-author
William Sarabande, *Beyond the Sea of Ice*, 1987
Judith Tarr, *Lady of Horses*, 2000
Joan Wolf, *The Reindeer Hunters*, 1994

876

CHARLES DAVIS

Allegiances

(Fort Lauderdale, Florida: Merriman, 2000)

Story type: Historical/American Civil War
Subject(s): Sea Stories; Civil War
Major character(s): Jonathan Wade, Military Personnel (Confederate naval officer)
Time period(s): 1860s
Locale(s): Virginia; *America*, At Sea

Summary: The often neglected naval history of the Civil War is the subject here in a nautical adventure featuring Confederate Naval Commander Jonathan Wade. When war breaks out, Wade reluctantly joins the Confederate navy and gains command of the dispatch vessel *America*, the winner of the first America's Cup yacht race in 1851. His mission to carry rebel agents to Britain becomes connected with a scheme to bring England into the war against the Union, as Wade dodges Union warships, penetrates blockaded ports, and deals with spies and Southern traitors.

Where it's reviewed:
Booklist, November 15, 2000, page 614
Publishers Weekly, January 29, 2001, page 64

Other books you might like:
George Fielding Eliot, *Caleb Pettengill, U.S.N.*, 1956
Noel B. Gerson, *Clear for Action!*, 1970
F. Van Wyck Mason, *Armored Giants*, 1980
David Poyer, *Fire on the Waters*, 2001
Don Tracy, *On the Midnight Tide*, 1957

877

LINDSEY DAVIS

Ode to a Banker

(New York: Mysterious, 2001)

Story type: Historical/Ancient Rome; Mystery
Series: Marcus Didius Falco. Number 13
Subject(s): Mystery and Detective Stories; Authors and Writers; Roman Empire
Major character(s): Marcus Didius Falco, Detective—Private, Spy; Aurelius Chrysippus, Banker, Publisher
Time period(s): 1st century (74)
Locale(s): Rome, Roman Empire

Summary: The murder of Aurelius Chrysippus, a banker and part-time publisher, provides the occasion for private detective Marcus Didius Falco's investigation among ancient Rome's literati and banking community. Meanwhile on the domestic front, an imperial spy that Falco does not trust is going out of his way to appeal to his mother and sister, while contractors hired to renovate his new home are robbing him blind. It's all in a day's work for ancient Rome's favorite gumshoe, or is it gumsandal?

Where it's reviewed:
Booklist, May 1, 2001, page 1628
Kirkus Reviews, April 15, 2001, page 544
Publishers Weekly, June 11, 2001, page 65

Other books by the same author:
One Virgin Too Many, 2000
Three Hands in the Fountain, 1999
Two for the Lions, 1999
A Dying Light in Corduba, 1998
Time to Depart, 1995

Other books you might like:
Jane Alison, *The Love-Artist*, 2001
Ron Burns, *Roman Shadows*, 1992
Colleen McCullough, *The Masters of Rome Series*, 1990-
John Maddox Roberts, *The SPQR Series*, 1990-
Steven Saylor, *The Roma Sub Rosa Series*, 1991-

878

LISA E. DAVIS

Under the Mink

(Los Angeles: Alyson, 2001)

Story type: Mystery; Lesbian/Historical
Subject(s): Homosexuality/Lesbianism; Mystery and Detective Stories
Major character(s): Blackie Cole, Singer, Lesbian
Time period(s): 1940s (1949)
Locale(s): New York, New York (Greenwich Village)

Summary: This attempt at a historical lesbian mystery series is set in 1949 Greenwich Village and involves struggling lesbian singer Blackie Cole. A witness to the murder of a young gay man at the Candy Box Club, Blackie is sworn to silence by her mobster boss. When she finally tells the victim's sister, whom Blackie falls for, the singer's life is endangered. This is a richly detailed evocation of the lesbian and gay subculture of New York in the pre-Stonewall era.

Where it's reviewed:
Booklist, March 15, 2001, page 1357
Library Journal, April 1, 2001, page 137
Publishers Weekly, March 12, 2001, page 65

Other books you might like:
Max Allan Collins, *Angel in Black*, 2001
Lauren Maddison, *Deceptions*, 1999
Lise McClendon, *One O'Clock Jump*, 2001
Annette Meyers, *Murder Me Now*, 2000
Abigail Padgett, *Blue*, 1998

879

P.C. DOHERTY

The Anubis Slayings

(New York: St. Martin's Minotaur, 2001)

Story type: Historical/Ancient Egypt; Mystery
Series: Ancient Egyptian Mysteries. Number 3
Subject(s): Mystery and Detective Stories; Egyptian Religion; Ancient History
Major character(s): Amerotke, Judge (Chief Judge of Egypt); Hatusu, Historical Figure, Ruler (pharaoh)
Time period(s): 15th century B.C. (1479 B.C.)
Locale(s): Egypt

Summary: Amerotke, judge and supporter of the female pharaoh Hatusu, must investigate the theft of a sacred amethyst and a series of grisly murders that occur within the inner sanctum of a heavily guarded temple. Hanging in the balance is war with the Mitanni of the north and a civil war that might topple Hatusu from power. Those with a particular interest in ancient Egypt will be enthralled; others will still enjoy a fast-paced, though bloody, mystery with an authentic period flavor.

Where it's reviewed:
Booklist, May 15, 2001, page 1736
Kirkus Reviews, May 1, 2001, page 628
Publishers Weekly, May 14, 2001, page 56

Other books by the same author:
The Horus Killings, 2000
The Mask of Ra, 1999
The Hugh Corbett Series, 1986-

Other books you might like:
Anna Apostolou, *A Murder in Thebes*, 1998
Pauline Gedge, *The Horus Road*, 2001
Lauren Haney, *A Vile Justice*, 1999
Lee Levin, *King Tut's Private Eye*, 1996
Lynda S. Robinson, *Slayer of Gods*, 2001

880

P.C. DOHERTY

The Demon Archer

(New York: St. Martin's Minotaur, 2001)

Story type: Historical/Medieval; Mystery
Series: Hugh Corbett
Subject(s): Mystery and Detective Stories; Middle Ages
Major character(s): Sir Hugh Corbett, Government Official, Investigator; Edward I, Ruler (King of England), Historical Figure; Lord Henry Fitzalan, Nobleman
Time period(s): 14th century (1303)
Locale(s): England

Summary: The death of the much-hated Lord Henry Fitzalan, shot through the heart with an arrow in England's Ashdown Forest in 1303, is the occasion for this installment of Doherty's accomplished historical mystery series featuring detective Hugh Corbett, Clerk of the Secret Seal. Dispatched by King Edward I to investigate, Corbett has no shortage of suspects and motives. An emissary of the king in arranging a state marriage, Lord Henry may have been killed for political reasons or the cause may be closer to home. Doherty is skilled in his period details, and readers will be delightfully and entertainingly transported back in time to watch a real pro in action.

Where it's reviewed:
Booklist, February 15, 2001, page 1118
Kirkus Reviews, January 1, 2001, page 82
Publishers Weekly, January 22, 2001, page 303

Other books by the same author:
The Horus Killings, 2000
The Devil's Hunt, 1998
The Song of a Dark Angel, 1994
The Masked Man, 1991

The Prince of Darkness, 1990

Other books you might like:
Alys Clare, *Ashes of the Elements*, 2001
Margaret Frazier, *The Squire's Tale*, 2000
Roberta Gellis, *A Personal Devil*, 2001
Simon Hawke, *A Mystery of Errors*, 2000
Edward Marston, *The Wildcats of Exeter*, 2001

881

P.C. DOHERTY

The House of Death

(New York: Carroll & Graf, 2001)

Story type: Historical/Ancient Greece; Mystery
Subject(s): Mystery and Detective Stories; Ancient History
Major character(s): Alexander the Great, Historical Figure, Ruler; Telamon, Doctor
Time period(s): 4th century B.C. (334 B.C.)
Locale(s): Greece; Persia

Summary: The prolific historical mystery master Doherty moves from medieval Britain and ancient Egypt to the court of Alexander the Great in 334 B.C. for this foray in the historical mystery genre. On the brink of invading Persia, Alexander is beset with a series of troubling murders that point to Persian spies and traitors in his camp. The young commander turns to his old friend, the physician Telamon, to solve the crimes and uncover the identity of a master spy. Details of everyday life and customs are ably displayed in this fast-paced mystery that builds to a climax at the epic battle of the Granicus and Alexander's victory over Persia's King Darius.

Where it's reviewed:
Booklist, May 1, 2001, page 1630
Kirkus Reviews, April 15, 2001, page 434
Publishers Weekly, May 7, 2001, page 227

Other books by the same author:
The Anubis Slayings, 2001
The Horus Killings, 2000
The Hugh Corbett Series, 1986-

Other books you might like:
Anna Apostolou, *A Murder in Macedon*, 1997
Anna Apostolou, *A Murder in Thebes*, 1998
Maurice Druon, *Alexander the God*, 1954
Harold Lamb, *Alexander of Macedon*, 1946
Mary Renault, *Fire from Heaven*, 1969

882

EMMA DONOGHUE

Slammerkin

(New York: Harcourt, 2001)

Story type: Historical/Georgian
Subject(s): Prostitution
Major character(s): Mary Saunders, Prostitute; Jane Jones, Gentlewoman; Doll Higgins, Prostitute
Time period(s): 18th century
Locale(s): London, England

Summary: Based on an actual English prostitute, this is a gripping and colorful depiction of the life and times of Mary Saunders. Born into grinding poverty on the mean streets of London, Mary's love for fine clothes leads her into prostitution. Instructed in the business by mentor Doll Higgins, Mary eventually finds refuge in the country home of clothiers Thomas and Jane Jones, where her resentment over her diminished prospects escalates into violence. Donoghue provides an authentic portrait of 18th century life while offering a thoughtful analysis of women's roles and the various compromises required to achieve independence.

Where it's reviewed:
Booklist, April 1, 2001, page 1451
Kirkus Reviews, April 1, 2001, page 434
Publishers Weekly, May 21, 2001, page 80

Other books by the same author:
Kissing the Witch, 1997
Hood, 1996
Stir-Fry, 1994

Other books you might like:
Margaret Atwood, *Alias Grace*, 1996
Nicholas Griffin, *The House of Sight and Shadow*, 2000
Sheri Holman, *The Dress Lodger*, 2000
David Liss, *A Conspiracy of Paper*, 2000
Betsy Tobin, *Bone House*, 2000

883

SYBIL DOWNING

The Binding Oath

(Boulder: University Press of Colorado, 2001)

Story type: Mystery; Historical/Roaring Twenties
Subject(s): Prohibition; Mystery and Detective Stories
Major character(s): Liz O'Brien, Journalist
Time period(s): 1920s (1922)
Locale(s): Denver, Colorado

Summary: This historical mystery features plucky reporter Liz O'Brien, who gets involved with two murders, a bootlegging operation, and a conspiracy by the Ku Klux Klan to take control of the state. O'Brien is an attractive, engaging sleuth and the setting is fresh.

Where it's reviewed:
Publishers Weekly, March 5, 2001, page 62

Other books by the same author:
Fire in the Hole, 1996

Other books you might like:
Max Allan Collins, *Angel in Black*, 2001
Lisa E. Davis, *Under the Mink*, 2001
Gillian Linscott, *The Perfect Daughter*, 2001
Lise McClendon, *One O'Clock Jump*, 2001
Annette Meyers, *Murder Me Now*, 2000

884

HELEN DUNMORE

A Spell of Winter

(New York: Atlantic Monthly, 2001)

Story type: Historical/World War I; Gothic
Subject(s): Brothers and Sisters; Family Relations
Major character(s): Catherine Allen, Narrator; Rob Allen, Young Man
Time period(s): 1910s
Locale(s): England

Summary: This dark, atmospheric gothic tale, set in the early years of the 20th century, concerns orphaned siblings Catherine and Rob Allen, who grow up in their grandfather's crumbling country estate in the English countryside. The Allens are haunted by family shame and secrets, and the novel follows their development in an uncanny atmosphere of madness, violence, and eroticism. Dunmore is expert in converting a classic gothic setting into a modern tale of forbidden passion, psychological obsession, and retribution.

Where it's reviewed:
Booklist, January 2001, page 915
Kirkus Reviews, December 1, 2000, page 1631

Other books by the same author:
Brother Brother, Sister Sister, 2000
With Your Crooked Heart, 2000
Bestiary, 1997
Talking to the Dead, 1996
Recovering a Body, 1994

Other books you might like:
Sheri Holman, *The Dress Lodger*, 2000
Kazuo Ishiguro, *When We Were Orphans*, 2000
Pierre Magnan, *The Murdered House*, 2000
Ann Victoria Roberts, *Moon Rising*, 2001
Christina Schwarz, *Drowning Ruth*, 2000

885

CAROLA DUNN

To Davy Jones Below

(New York: St. Martin's, 2001 Press)

Story type: Mystery; Historical/Roaring Twenties
Series: Daisy Dalrymple. Book 8
Subject(s): Mystery and Detective Stories; Cruise Ships
Major character(s): Daisy Dalrymple Fletcher, Journalist, Detective—Amateur; Alec Fletcher, Detective—Police (Scotland Yard), Spouse (of Daisy)
Time period(s): 1920s
Locale(s): London, England; *Talavera*, At Sea

Summary: On their honeymoon aboard the liner *Talavera*, bound for America, journalist Daisy Dalrymple and Scotland Yard detective Alec Fletcher encounter a series of accidents and murder. Despite a bout of seasickness, Alec is recruited to find out what caused a man to fall overboard. When another passenger is shot, the couple must learn who aboard is a killer and why.

Historical

Where it's reviewed:
Booklist, March 1, 2001, page 1230
Publishers Weekly, March 5, 2001, page 66

Other books by the same author:
Rattle His Bones, 2000
Styx and Stones, 1999
Dead in the Water, 1998
Damsel in Distress, 1997
Byron's Daughter, 1991

Other books you might like:
Conrad Allen, *Murder on the Mauretania*, 2000
Gillian Linscott, *The Nell Bray Series*, 1991-
Anne Perry, *The Thomas and Charlotte Pitt Series*, 1979-
Elizabeth Peters, *The Amelia Peabody Series*, 1975-
Jim Walker, *Murder on the Titanic*, 1998

886

DAVID ANTHONY DURHAM

Gabriel's Story

(New York: Doubleday, 2001)

Story type: Historical/Post-American Civil War; Historical/American West
Subject(s): Frontier and Pioneer Life; African Americans; Reconstruction
Major character(s): Gabriel Lynch, Teenager, Runaway; Marshall Hogg, Cowboy, Outlaw
Time period(s): 1870s
Locale(s): Kansas; Texas; Arizona

Summary: First time novelist Durham offers an able coming-of-age story set in the American West during the Reconstruction period of the 1870s and featuring a young African-American protagonist, Gabriel Lynch, who journeys from the urban North with his widowed mother to a sod house on the Kansas prairie. Dissatisfied with frontier life as a homesteader, Gabriel runs away from home to become a cowboy. He joins a group of cattle drovers led by Marshall Hogg, and Gabriel's adventure turns into a nightmare after Hogg accidentally murders a man causing the gang to flee from the law and pursue the outlaw's fate. Eventually, Gabriel manages to break free of his comrades, but the evil he has been exposed to follows him back home. Durham helps to document the hidden history of the American West in which a fourth of all cowboys were black. He also deals authentically with the racism black pioneers faced in trying to carve out a new life.

Where it's reviewed:
Booklist, December 15, 2000, page 788
Library Journal, November 1, 2000, page 101
New York Times Book Review, February 25, 2001, page 7
Publishers Weekly, December 4, 2000, page 54

Other books you might like:
Allen B. Ballard, *Where I'm Bound*, 2000
Aaron Roy Even, *Bloodroot*, 2000
J.P. Sinclair Lewis, *Buffalo Gordon*, 2001
Cormac McCarthy, *All the Pretty Horses*, 1992
Larry McMurtry, *Boone's Lick*, 2000

887

ARABELLA EDGE

Company: The Story of a Murderer

(New York: Simon & Schuster, 2001)

Story type: Historical/Seventeenth Century
Subject(s): Shipwrecks; Murder
Major character(s): Jeronimus Cornelisz, Apothecary
Time period(s): 17th century (1629)
Locale(s): *Batavia*, At Sea; Australia

Summary: This harrowing tale is based on the 1629 voyage of the Dutch East Indian flagship *Batavia* which is wrecked off the Australian coast. Among the survivors is Jeronimus Cornelisz, an apothecary, who instead of helping his fellow survivors becomes a murderous madman. Becoming the master of the island refuge, Cornelisz decides who should live and who should die in a bloody orgy of wicked mastery.

Other books you might like:
Douglas Galbraith, *The Rising Sun*, 2001
Nicholas Griffin, *The Requiem Shark*, 2000
Matthew Kneale, *English Passengers*, 2000
Nick P. Maginnis, *Antonia's Island*, 2001
Colleen McCullough, *Morgan's Run*, 2000

888

RANDY LEE EICKHOFF

The Destruction of the Inn

(New York: Forge, 2001)

Story type: Historical/Pre-history; Legend
Series: Ulster Cycle. Book 4
Subject(s): Mythology; Legends
Major character(s): Conaire, Royalty (king)
Time period(s): Indeterminate Past
Locale(s): Ireland

Summary: Eickhoff continues his modern adaptations of the ancient Irish Ulster Cycle, legendary tales translated from the Gaelic set in the distant past where history and fantasy meet. This installment follows the rise and fall of Conaire, the Irish king fathered by a bird-man. Alongside his three foster-brothers, he fills his youth with pranks until being called to rule. Jealousy causes his former companions to join forces with English raiders to terrorize the countryside.

Where it's reviewed:
Booklist, March 15, 2001, page 1353
Kirkus Reviews, February 1, 2001, page 143
Publishers Weekly, February 26, 2001, page 59

Other books by the same author:
The Feast, 1999
The Fourth Horseman, 1997
The Raid, 1997
The Gombeen Man, 1992
A Hand to Execute, 1987

Other books you might like:
Andrew M. Greeley, *The Magic Cup*, 1979
Cecelia Holland, *The Kings in Winter*, 1968

Morgan Llywelyn, *Finn Mac Cool*, 1994
Morgan Lylwelyn, *Red Branch*, 1989
Diana L. Paxson, *The Shield between the Worlds*, 1994

889

LOUISE ERDRICH

The Last Report on the Miracles at Little No Horse

(New York: HarperCollins, 2001)

Story type: Historical/American West; Indian Culture
Subject(s): Indians of North America; Religious Life
Major character(s): Damien Modeste, Religious (priest); Pauline Puyat, Religious (nun)
Time period(s): 20th century
Locale(s): North Dakota

Summary: Erdrich continues her remarkable animation of the world of an Ojibwe reservation in North Dakota. In this installment of her chronicle of the relationships among a number of families, the focus is on the secret identity of the resident priest, Father Damien Modeste. Father Damien is in fact Agnes DeWitt, whose secret is connected with that of Sister Leopolda, aka Pauline Puyat, who is being considered for sainthood. Details of Father Damien's life range over much of the 20th century, a compelling angle from which to view the intricate life and behavior in this unique slice of the American West.

Where it's reviewed:
Booklist, February 15, 2001, page 1088
Kirkus Reviews, February 1, 2001, page 127
Publishers Weekly, January 29, 2001, page 63

Other books by the same author:
The Antelope Wife, 1998
The Bingo Palace, 1994
Love Medicine, 1993
Tracks, 1988
The Beet Queen, 1986

Other books you might like:
Harold Adams, *A Way with Widows*, 1994
Willa Cather, *Death Comes for the Archbishop*, 1927
Mary Gardner, *Milkweed*, 1994
Harold B. Meyers, *Reservations*, 1999
Lauraine Snelling, *An Untamed Land*, 1996

890

KAREN ESSEX

Kleopatra

(New York: Warner, 2001)

Story type: Historical/Ancient Rome
Subject(s): Ancient History; Kings, Queens, Rulers, etc.; Biography
Major character(s): Kleopatra, Historical Figure, Ruler; Auletes, Historical Figure, Ruler; Julius Caesar, Historical Figure, Military Personnel
Time period(s): 1st century B.C.
Locale(s): Egypt; Rome, Roman Empire

Summary: This version of the life and times of the infamous Egyptian queen concentrates on her rise to the throne and her survival skills against adversaries close to home. The daughter of King Auletes, Kleopatra (the spelling emphasizes her Greek lineage) uses her wits, rather than her beauty, to withstand rivalries and plots among her siblings. Reaching the throne on the death of Auletes, Kleopatra recognizes that her and the kingdom's survival will depend on an alliance with Rome, and she sets her sights on Julius Caesar. This is a refreshing version of the familiar story, emphasizing the Egyptian queen's savvy over her sex appeal.

Where it's reviewed:
Kirkus Reviews, June 1, 2001, page 757

Other books you might like:
Colin Falconer, *When We Were Gods*, 2000
Margaret George, *The Memoirs of Cleopatra*, 1997
Kathleen Lindsay, *Enchantress of the Nile*, 1965
Martha Rofheart, *The Alexandrian*, 1974
Judith Tarr, *Throne of Isis*, 1994

891

LOREN D. ESTLEMAN

The Master Executioner

(New York: Forge, 2001)

Story type: Historical/American West
Subject(s): American West
Major character(s): Oscar Stone, Executioner (hangman); Gretchen Smollet, Young Woman
Time period(s): 19th century
Locale(s): West

Summary: Estleman chronicles the life and times of hangman Oscar Stone, who approaches his job with the professional skill of a master craftsman. As a young runaway, Oscar apprentices with the principal hangman of the Kansas frontier. He then courts Gretchen Smollet, and the pair lives together for a time until Gretchen, who can't bear Oscar's line of work, flees. Spending much of his life pursuing her, Oscar learns he may or may not have fathered a son whom he hanged as a murderer. Estleman is a master of his milieu, and this is a convincing reconstruction of its era and an unusual perspective on it.

Where it's reviewed:
Kirkus Reviews, April 1, 2001, page 436

Other books by the same author:
The Rocky Mountain Moving Picture Association, 1999
Thunder City, 1999
Edsel, 1995
Whiskey River, 1990
Motor City Blue, 1986

Other books you might like:
James D. Houston, *Snow Mountain Passage*, 2001
Andrew Huebner, *American by Blood*, 2000
Larry McMurtry, *Boone's Lick*, 2000
Bruce Olds, *Bucking the Tiger*, 2001
Robert B. Parker, *Gunman's Rhapsody*, 2001

Historical

892
PETER EVERETT

Bellocq's Women
(London: Cape, 2001)

Story type: Historical/Victorian America
Subject(s): Biography; Photography; Prostitution
Major character(s): E.J. Bellocq, Historical Figure, Photographer
Time period(s): 19th century; 20th century
Locale(s): New Orleans, Louisiana

Summary: E.J. Bellocq's series of photographs, taken in 1912, captured the women who worked in the brothels of New Orleans' notorious Storyville. Everett offers a look at the man behind the camera in a fictionalized biography of the photographer, tracing Bellocq's career as a youthful loner and habitue of New Orleans' barrooms, brothels, and rooming houses, as well as his relationships with several prostitutes. This is a seamy, though ultimately poetic and satisfying, look at the dark side of Storyville and its human cost.

Where it's reviewed:
Publishers Weekly, May 7, 2001, page 224

Other books you might like:
Nelson Algren, *A Walk on the Wild Side*, 1956
Lois Battle, *Storyville*, 1962
Barbara Hambly, *Die upon a Kiss*, 2001
Michael Ondaatje, *Coming through Slaughter*, 1976
Josh Russell, *Yellow Jack*, 1999

893
ROSARIO FERRE

Flight of the Swan
(New York: Farrar, Straus & Giroux, 2001)

Story type: Historical/Russian Revolution
Subject(s): Ballet; Revolution
Major character(s): Madame, Dancer (ballerina); Masha, Dancer (ballerina); Diamantino Marquez, Revolutionary
Time period(s): 1910s (1917)
Locale(s): San Juan, Puerto Rico

Summary: This novel is inspired by an actual historical event when ballerina Anna Pavlova and her troupe were stranded in Puerto Rico after the outbreak of the Russian Revolution in 1917. The legendary Pavlova is here identified as ''Madame'' by Masha, a member of the company who narrates. Madame falls in love with the revolutionary Diamantino Marquez as the company gets swept up in the Puerto Rican independence movement. Although full of dramatic potential, the book is more lifeless than it should be and less impressive than Ferre's earlier works.

Where it's reviewed:
Kirkus Reviews, April 15, 2001, page 519
Publishers Weekly, May 7, 2001, page 219

Other books by the same author:
Eccentric Neighborhoods, 1998
Sweet Diamond Dust, 1996

The House on the Lagoon, 1995
The Youngest Doll, 1991

Other books you might like:
Isabel Allende, *Daughter of Fortune*, 1999
Julia Alvarez, *In the Name of Salome*, 2000
Amy Ephron, *White Rose*, 1999
Mayra Montero, *The Messenger*, 1999
Manuel Vazquez Montalban, *Galindez*, 1992

894
THOMAS FLEMING

When This Cruel War Is Over
(New York: Forge, 2001)

Story type: Historical/American Civil War
Subject(s): Civil War; Espionage
Major character(s): Janet Todd, Southern Belle; Paul Stapleton, Military Personnel (Union major); Henry Gentry, Military Personnel (Union colonel), Historical Figure
Time period(s): 1860s (1864)
Locale(s): Indiana; Kentucky

Summary: Prolific historian and novelist Fleming departs from his more characteristic terrain of the American Revolution for this Civil War tale based on actual historical events. In the summer of 1864, hostility against the Union in the border state of Kentucky and neighboring Indiana gives birth to the Sons of Liberty, a secret insurrectionist group dedicated to the creation of the Northwest Confederacy. Colonel Henry Gentry recruits Union Major Paul Stapleton to spy on the Sons of Liberty and one of their staunchest supporters, southern belle Janet Todd. Complications develop when Stapleton falls in love with his quarry. Documentary evidence in the form of actual letters between Gentry and President Lincoln lends credibility here as do appearances by such historical figures as John Wilkes Booth and Mary Surratt.

Where it's reviewed:
Kirkus Reviews, January 1, 2001, page 17

Other books by the same author:
Dreams of Glory, 2000
Hours of Gladness, 1999
Remember the Morning, 1997
The Spoils of War, 1985
Liberty Tavern, 1976

Other books you might like:
Chris Adrian, *Gob's Grief*, 2000
John Calvin Batchelor, *American Falls*, 1985
John Jakes, *On Secret Service*, 2000
Michael Kilian, *A Killing at Ball's Bluff*, 2001
David Robertson, *Booth*, 1998

895
MICHAEL CURTIS FORD

The Ten Thousand
(New York: St. Martin's Press, 2001)

Story type: Historical/Ancient Greece
Subject(s): War; Ancient History; Biography

Major character(s): Xenophon, Historical Figure, Military Personnel; Themistogenes, Slave (former), Companion (of Xenophon)
Time period(s): 5th century B.C.
Locale(s): Persia

Summary: Based on Xenophon's *Anabasis*, this novel chronicles the maturation and military adventures of Xenophon from a pampered youth of privilege to his days as a mercenary soldier in the war with Persia. Set after Athens' defeat by Sparta, the novel is told from the perspective of Xenophon's alter-ego, Themistogenes. The story recounts how a Greek force of 10,000 is stranded behind enemy lines, necessitating Xenophon's leadership to save the soldiers. Ford offers a convincing reconstruction of the era's customs and military strategies.

Where it's reviewed:
Kirkus Reviews, April 15, 2001, page 520
Publishers Weekly, May 28, 2001, page 50

Other books you might like:
Gillian Bradshaw, *The Sand-Reckoner*, 2000
Ellen Gilchrist, *Anabasis: A Journey to the Interior*, 1994
Steven Pressfield, *Gates of Fire*, 1998
Steven Pressfield, *Tides of War*, 2000
Mary Renault, *The Last of the Wine*, 1956

896

KAREN JOY FOWLER

Sister Noon

(New York: Putnam, 2001)

Story type: Historical/American West Coast
Subject(s): American West; Women
Major character(s): Lizzie Hayes, Spinster, Volunteer; Mary Ellen Pleasant, Wealthy; Jenny Ijub, Orphan, Child
Time period(s): 1890s
Locale(s): San Francisco, California

Summary: Set in Gilded Age San Francisco during the 1890s, this intriguing novel looks at the growth and development of spinster Lizzie Hayes, who runs the Ladies' Relief and Protection Society Home for Girls. There she meets the enigmatic Mrs. Mary Ellen Pleasant from New Orleans, who may or may not be a former slave and voodoo queen. Mrs. Pleasant is accompanied by four-year-old Jenny Ijub, whose parentage serves as an important element of the novel's plot. The impact of both Mrs. Pleasant and Jenny on Lizzie is the focus here in a subtle look at women's lives in an interesting historical setting.

Where it's reviewed:
Kirkus Reviews, March 15, 2001, page 351
Publishers Weekly, April 9, 2001, page 48

Other books by the same author:
Black Glass, 1998
The Sweetheart Season, 1996
Sarah Canary, 1991

Other books you might like:
Carrie Brown, *The Hatbox Baby*, 2000

Louise Erdrich, *The Last Report on the Miracles at Little No Horse*, 2001
Helen Humphreys, *Afterimage*, 2001
Richard Rayner, *The Cloud Sketcher*, 2000
Geling Yan, *The Lost Daughter of Happiness*, 2001

897

DOUGLAS GALBRAITH

The Rising Sun

(New York: Atlantic Monthly, 2001)

Story type: Historical/Seventeenth Century
Subject(s): Sea Stories; Business Enterprises
Major character(s): William Paterson, Businessman; Roderick Mackenzie, Accountant (bookkeeper)
Time period(s): 17th century; 18th century (1698-1707)
Locale(s): *Rising Sun*, At Sea; Edinburgh, Scotland; Panama

Summary: This accomplished historical recreation chronicles the failed Darien Expedition of 1698, the brainchild of trader William Paterson to establish a Scottish trading colony on the Isthmus of Panama. As described by the company's superintendent of cargoes, Roderick Mackenzie, the adventures of the *Rising Sun* and her sister ships are dramatized through a grueling voyage and a yearlong struggle with the climate, disease, and wary and enigmatic natives. Galbraith manages to convincingly portray the era and the voice of an ambitious opportunist caught in an ill-fated scheme.

Where it's reviewed:
Booklist, November 15, 2000, page 618
Kirkus Reviews, December 1, 2000, page 1633
Library Journal, December 2000, page 53
New York Times, February 26, 2001, page E8
Publishers Weekly, January 15, 2001, page 53

Other books you might like:
Nicholas Griffin, *The Requiem Shark*, 2000
Gene Hackman, *The Wake of the Perdido Star*, 1999
    Daniel Lenihan, co-author
Matthew Kneale, *English Passengers*, 2000
Colleen McCullough, *Morgan's Run*, 2000
James L. Nelson, *The Blackbirder*, 2001

898

DOROTHY GARLOCK

The Edge of Town

(New York: Warner, 2001)

Story type: Historical/Roaring Twenties
Subject(s): Small Town Life; Farm Life; Romance
Major character(s): Julie Jones, Young Woman; Evan Johnson, Veteran (World War I)
Time period(s): 1920s
Locale(s): Missouri

Summary: This is a tender romantic story set in Missouri during the 1920s. Julie Jones is a country girl caring for her widowed father and five siblings, while dreaming of the arrival of Mr. Right. He comes in the form of Evan Johnson, the son of the Joneses' despised neighbor. The novel follows

the course of their romance while portraying the region and the era through a subplot involving the hunt for a rapist.

Where it's reviewed:
Publishers Weekly, April 2, 2001, page 39

Other books by the same author:
More than Memory, 2001
After the Parade, 2000
With Heart, 1999
With Song, 1999
Wayward Wind, 1998

Other books you might like:
Alice Adams, *After the War*, 2000
Kathleen Cambor, *In Sunlight, in a Beautiful Garden*, 2000
Brad Kessler, *Lick Creek*, 2001
Sarah Stonich, *These Granite Islands*, 2001
Jane Roberts Wood, *Grace*, 2001

899

ELIZABETH GARRETT

The Sweet Trade
(New York: Forge, 2001)

Story type: Historical/Colonial America
Subject(s): Sea Stories; Pirates; Biography
Major character(s): Anne Bonny, Historical Figure, Pirate; Mary Read, Historical Figure, Pirate; Calico Jack Rackam, Historical Figure, Pirate
Time period(s): 18th century
Locale(s): American Colonies; West Indies

Summary: Garrett constructs a rollicking adventure yarn out of the actual historical figures Anne Bonny and Mary Read, two women who become pirates in the 18th century. Anne is the headstrong daughter of a southern planter, who takes up piracy after a quarrel with her father; Mary is dressed as a boy early on by her mother. Mary joins forces with Anne and Calico Jack Rackam to terrorize merchant shipping in the West Indies until their inevitable capture. The novel is more colorful than believable, despite an effort to use actual records to document the heroines' lives.

Where it's reviewed:
Booklist, March 15, 2001, page 1354
Kirkus Reviews, February 15, 2001, page 201
Publishers Weekly, March 12, 2001, page 62

Other books you might like:
Tamara J. Eastman, *The Pirate Trial of Anne Bonny and Mary Read*, 2000
Chloe Gartner, *Anne Bonny*, 1977
Pamela Jekel, *Sea Star*, 1983
Alison MacLeod, *The Changeling*, 1996
Alison York, *The Fire and the Rope*, 1979

900

PAULINE GEDGE

The Horus Road
(New York: Soho, 2001)

Story type: Historical/Ancient Egypt
Series: Lords of the Two Lands Trilogy. Volume 3
Subject(s): Ancient History; Rebellions, Revolts, and Uprisings; Cultures and Customs
Major character(s): Apepa, Ruler (pharaoh), Historical Figure; Ahmose, Royalty, Historical Figure
Time period(s): 16th century B.C.
Locale(s): Egypt

Summary: Concluding her Lords of the Two Lands trilogy, Gedge continues the story of the rebellion against the tyrannical Pharaoh Apepa and the Hyksos dynasty by native Egyptians. Ahmose, the youngest son of Prince Seqenenra Tao, is given the responsibility of leading the Egyptian army against the Hyksos usurpers, but he depends on the women of his family to rally the rebels and organize resistance while he recovers from wounds caused by a would-be assassin. This is a satisfying conclusion to an adventure series supported by impressive historical research into the customs of ancient Egypt.

Where it's reviewed:
Kirkus Reviews, April 1, 2001, page 456

Other books by the same author:
The Hippopotamus Marsh, 2000
The Oasis, 2000
House of Illusion, 1997
Lady of the Reeds, 1995
Mirage, 1990

Other books you might like:
Allen Drury, *A God Against the Gods*, 1976
Jacquetta Hawkes, *King of the Two Lands*, 1966
Christian Jacq, *The Ramses Quintet*, 1997-1999
Naguib Mahfouz, *Akhenaten: Dweller in Truth*, 2000
Wilbur A. Smith, *Warlock*, 2001

901

ROBERTA GELLIS

A Personal Devil
(New York: Forge, 2001)

Story type: Historical/Medieval; Mystery
Series: Magdalene la Batarde. Number 2
Subject(s): Mystery and Detective Stories; Middle Ages
Major character(s): Magdalene la Batarde, Madam; Sir Bellamy of Itchen, Knight; Sabina, Prostitute, Handicapped (blind)
Time period(s): 12th century (1139)
Locale(s): London, England

Summary: Magdalene la Batarde, the madam of the Old Priory Guesthouse, and her gallant accomplice, Sir Bellamy of Itchen, come to the aid of one of Magdalene's former clients who has been charged in his wife's murder. His only alibi comes from his current mistress and former Old Priory

denizen, blind Sabina, who may be lying to protect the man she loves. Magdalene and Sir Bellamy take up the case which involves an interesting medieval version of forensics, a well-paced, suspenseful story, and some solid authentic period touches.

Where it's reviewed:
Booklist, March 15, 2001, page 1357
Kirkus Reviews, January 15, 2001, page 82
Publishers Weekly, February 12, 2001, page 187

Other books by the same author:
A Mortal Bane, 1999
A Silver Mirror, 1989
Masques of Gold, 1988
The Roselynde Chronicles, 1978-
The Dragon and the Rose, 1977

Other books you might like:
Fiona Buckley, *To Ruin a Queen*, 2000
P.F. Chisholm, *A Plague of Angels*, 1998
P.C. Doherty, *The Hugh Corbett Series*, 1986-
Ian Morson, *The William Falconer Series*, 1994-
Sharan Newman, *The Catherine LeVendeur Series*, 1993-

902

AMITAV GHOSH

The Glass Palace

(New York: Random House, 2001)

Story type: Historical/Victorian; Family Saga
Subject(s): Cultural Conflict; Family Relations
Major character(s): Rajkumar, Businessman; Dolly, Servant
Time period(s): 19th century; 20th century
Locale(s): India; Burma

Summary: Burma's troubled colonial past is the subject of this sweeping epic that presents events from the British invasion and seizure of Burma's capital in 1885 through World War II to the present state of affairs in Myanmar. Events are reflected through the life of a young Indian boy, Rajkumar, who gains a fortune in rubber and teak which he uses to help unite him with his beloved Dolly, a nursemaid, who follows the Burmese royal family into exile in India. The novel convincingly weaves a complex multigenerational family saga around the key events of over a century of momentous change.

Where it's reviewed:
Booklist, December 15, 2000, page 786
Kirkus Reviews, November 15, 2000, page 1561
Library Journal, February 1, 2001, page 125
New York Times Book Review, February 11, 2001, page 7
Publishers Weekly, November 13, 2000, page 82

Other books by the same author:
The Calcutta Chromosome, 1995
In an Antique Land, 1993
The Shadow Lines, 1989
The Circle of Reason, 1986

Other books you might like:
Stephen D. Becker, *The Blue-Eyed Shan*, 1983
Maurice Collis, *She Was a Queen*, 1962
Alexandra Jones, *Mandalay*, 1988

Karen Roberts, *The Flower Boy*, 2000
Rebecca Ryman, *Shalimar*, 1999

903

RON GOULART

Groucho Marx and the Broadway Murders

(New York: St. Martin's Minotaur, 2001)

Story type: Mystery
Series: Groucho Marx. Book 4
Subject(s): Mystery and Detective Stories; Theater
Major character(s): Groucho Marx, Historical Figure, Entertainer; Frank Denby, Journalist (former crime reporter), Writer
Time period(s): 1930s (1939)
Locale(s): New York, New York

Summary: In this installment of Goulart's amusing, pun-filled historical mystery series employing Groucho Marx as sleuth, mayhem aboard the *Super Chief* bound for New York leads to more opportunity for investigation on Broadway. At the premiere of *Make Mine Murder*, Groucho and his sidekick, Frank Denby, must deal with the discovery of a real corpse that halts the performance. More slapstick and fun than mystifying, mystery purists may demur but Groucho fans will applaud.

Where it's reviewed:
Kirkus Reviews, May 15, 2001, page 708

Other books by the same author:
Elementary, My Dear Groucho, 1999
Groucho Marx, Private Eye, 1999
Groucho Marx, Master Detective, 1998
Now He Thinks He's Dead, 1992
Even the Butler Was Poor, 1990

Other books you might like:
George Baxt, *The Noel Coward Murder Case*, 1992
Max Allan Collins, *Angel in Black*, 2001
Robert Lee Hall, *Murder at San Simeon*, 1988
Stuart M. Kaminsky, *A Few Minutes Past Midnight*, 2001
Stuart M. Kaminsky, *You Bet Your Life*, 1978

904

REG GRANT

Storm

(Colorado Springs: WaterBrook, 2001)

Story type: Historical/Renaissance
Subject(s): Biography; Religious Conflict
Major character(s): Martin Luther, Historical Figure, Religious (monk); Katharina von Bora, Historical Figure, Religious (former nun)
Time period(s): 16th century
Locale(s): Germany

Summary: The life and times of the father of Protestantism, Martin Luther, are chronicled in this vivid, but historically simplified work of biographical fiction. The history of the Reformation is glimpsed, as well as Luther's relationship with the former nun Katherina von Bora. To their story is linked the romantic complications of one of Luther's friends and a

Jew. This is far too propagandistic to be reliable as history, missing the complexity of either Luther's contradictory personality or the subtle and shifting challenges he faced.

Where it's reviewed:
Booklist, January 1, 2001, page 916
Publishers Weekly, February 5, 2001, page 69

Other books you might like:
Gladys Barr, *Monk in Armour*, 1950
William S. Davis, *The Friar of Wittenberg*, 1912
Serge Filippini, *The Man in Flames*, 2000
Charles Ludwig, *Queen of the Reformation*, 1986
Asta Scheib, *Children of Disobedience*, 2000

905

MICHAEL GREEN

Squire Haggard's Journal

(North Pomfret, Vermont: Trafalgar Square, 2001)

Story type: Historical/Georgian
Subject(s): Diaries
Major character(s): Amos Haggard, Landowner; Roderick Haggard, Gentleman; Fanny Foulacre, Gentlewoman
Time period(s): 18th century
Locale(s): Bath, England; London, England; Europe

Summary: To celebrate the 25th anniversary of this comic favorite, which first appeared as a regular column in a British newspaper, Green has updated his parody of an 18th century diary kept by Squire Amos Haggard. In financial distress after a lifetime of whoring, drunkenness, and gluttony, Haggard has great hopes for the marriage of his son Roderick to the fashionable and wealthy Fanny Foulacre. The comic misadventures of father and son take them from Bath, to London and then to the Continent for a witty survey of the Georgian scene. Historical figures such as Baron von Munchausen, the Marquis de Lafayette, and Samuel Johnson put in cameo appearances.

Where it's reviewed:
Kirkus Reviews, February 1, 2001, page 144
Publishers Weekly, January 22, 2001, page 303

Other books you might like:
Joan Aiken, *Lady Catherine's Necklace*, 2000
Joan Austen-Leigh, *A Visit to Highbury*, 1995
Julia Barrett, *Jane Austen's Charlotte*, 2000
James Fleming, *The Temple of Optimism*, 2000
Nicholas Griffin, *The House of Sight and Shadow*, 2000

906

SHELDON GREENE

Burnt Umber

(Wellfleet, Massachusetts: Leapfrog, 2001)

Story type: Historical/World War I; Arts
Subject(s): Artists and Art; War
Major character(s): Franz Marc, Historical Figure, Artist (painter); Harry Baer, Artist; Vasily Kandinsky, Historical Figure, Artist (painter)
Time period(s): 20th century

Locale(s): Europe

Summary: Greene connects the actual lives of two historical figures—German painter Franz Marc and American artist Harold Paris (here named Harry Baer)—while shuttling between World War I and II to explore the artistic sensibility and the historical moment. During World War II, Baer discovers Marc's lost sketchbook and the narrative shifts back to 1909 to chronicle Marc's relationship with modern art pioneer Vasily Kandinsky. Baer's postwar life is then viewed, as he teaches art at Berkeley and witnesses protests over Vietnam. More disjointed than seamless, the novel puts the 20th century into an only occasionally engaging artistic context.

Where it's reviewed:
Booklist, April 15, 2001, page 1533
Kirkus Reviews, March 15, 2001, page 353

Other books by the same author:
Lost & Found, 1980

Other books you might like:
Catherine Clement, *Martin and Hannah*, 2001
Peter Everett, *Bellocq's Women*, 2001
Gerhard Kopf, *Piranesi's Dream*, 2000
Max Phillips, *The Artist's Wife*, 2001
Emma Tennant, *Sylvia and Ted*, 2001

907

NICHOLAS GRIFFIN

The House of Sight and Shadow

(New York: Villard, 2000)

Story type: Historical/Georgian; Historical/Seventeenth Century
Subject(s): Medicine
Major character(s): Joseph Bendix, Doctor; Sir Edmund Calcraft, Doctor; Daniel Defoe, Historical Figure, Writer
Time period(s): 17th century; 18th century
Locale(s): London, England

Summary: Griffin follows his successful sea going historical, *The Requiem Shark*, with an equally strong performance in a story set in London during the late 17th and early 18th centuries. Young physician Joseph Bendix hopes to secure his fortune by attaching himself to the eminent London anatomist, Sir Edmund Calcraft, who conducts his medical experiments on hanged thieves, the corpses of which are clandestinely procured. Bendix becomes equally attached to Calcraft's daughter, whose unusual ailments and the search for a cure dominate the action, along with appearances by such historical figures as writer Daniel Defoe, and notorious criminals Jack Sheppard and Jonathan Wild. The ultimate star of the show, however, is period London itself, which is displayed in all its atmospheric period glory.

Where it's reviewed:
Booklist, March 1, 2001, page 1226
Kirkus Reviews, March 1, 2001, page 279
Publishers Weekly, March 19, 2001, page 76

Other books by the same author:
The Requiem Shark, 2000

Other books you might like:

Bruce Alexander, *The Sir John Fielding Series*, 1994-
Ross King, *Ex-Libris*, 2001
David Liss, *A Conspiracy of Paper*, 2000
Andrew Miller, *Ingenious Pain*, 1997
Iain Pears, *An Instance of the Fingerpost*, 1998

908

BARBARA HAMBLY

Die upon a Kiss

(New York: Bantam, 2001)

Story type: Mystery; Historical/Antebellum American South
Series: Benjamin January. Book 5
Subject(s): Mystery and Detective Stories; Opera; Theater
Major character(s): Benjamin January, Slave (former), Musician (pianist); Lorenzo Belaggio, Producer (opera impresario); John Davis, Producer (theatrical)
Time period(s): 1830s (1835)
Locale(s): New Orleans, Louisiana

Summary: It is Carnival, 1835, in ante-bellum New Orleans in this installment of Hambly's historical mystery series featuring former slave, Paris-educated surgeon, working musician, and sleuth Benjamin January. Opera impresario Lorenzo Belaggio has been invited to mount a production of *Othello*, and its interracial love story could be the reason behind a series of attacks on Belaggio's troupe. Suspicion, however, falls on a rival theatrical producer, January's friend John Davis, and January investigates in order to clear him. His search uncovers a large international conspiracy involving the slave trade.

Where it's reviewed:
Booklist, March 15, 2001, page 1333
Kirkus Reviews, April 15, 2001, page 545
Publishers Weekly, April 23, 2001, page 52

Other books by the same author:
Sold Down the River, 2000
Dragonshadow, 1999
Graveyard Dust, 1999
Fever Season, 1998
A Free Man of Color, 1997

Other books you might like:
Michael Kilian, *Murder at Manassas*, 2000
Ann McMillan, *The Civil War Mystery Series*, 1999-
Miriam Grace Monfredo, *Sisters of Cain*, 2000
Josh Russell, *Yellow Jack*, 1999
Penn Williamson, *Mortal Sins*, 2000

909

KAREN HARPER

The Twylight Tower

(New York: Delacorte, 2001)

Story type: Historical/Elizabethan; Mystery
Series: Elizabeth I. Number 3
Subject(s): Mystery and Detective Stories; Historical; Biography

Major character(s): Elizabeth I, Historical Figure, Ruler (Queen of England); Robert Dudley, Nobleman (Earl of Leicester), Historical Figure
Time period(s): 16th century (1560)
Locale(s): England

Summary: In this third outing employing Elizabeth I as sleuth, Harper uses the historical facts surrounding the queen's infatuation with Robert Dudley and the mysterious death of his wife as the occasion for detecting a conspiracy to wrest the throne from the young queen. Harper's Elizabeth emerges as far more modern than the historical Elizabeth in her values, particularly her latent feminism which exposes the double standard that allows a king's dalliance but disapproves of a queen's. Despite some missteps, this is an entertaining look at a colorful period of English history.

Where it's reviewed:
Booklist, February 15, 2001, page 1119
Library Journal, February 1, 2001, page 127
Publishers Weekly, February 26, 2001, page 62

Other books by the same author:
The Tidal Poole, 2000
The Poyson Garden, 1999
Empty Cradle, 1998
Black Orchid, 1996
Promises to Keep, 1994

Other books you might like:
Fiona Buckley, *To Ruin a Queen*, 2000
Kathy Lynn Emerson, *The Susanna, Lady Appleton Series*, 1997-
Robin Maxwell, *The Queen's Bastard*, 1999
Rosalind Miles, *I, Elizabeth*, 1994
Leonard Tourney, *The Matthew Stock Series*, 1980-

910

JOANNE HARRIS

Five Quarters of the Orange

(New York: Morrow, 2001)

Story type: Historical/World War II
Subject(s): Nazis; Food; Family Relations
Major character(s): Framboise Dartigen, Restaurateur (cafe owner); Mirabelle Dartigen, Cook
Time period(s): 1940s
Locale(s): Les Laveuses, France

Summary: The author of *Chocolat* continues her linking of human drama with food in this tale of French village life under the German occupation. Framboise Dartigen as a young girl tricks her mother and reveals secrets to the German soldiers. Tragedy follows and townspeople die while the Dartigens are branded collaborators. Years later Framboise returns to the village to open a cafe, having inherited her mother's treasured recipe book. Her recollections clarify a complex plot of family relations, the impact of the war, and provide mouth-watering descriptions of French delicacies.

Where it's reviewed:
Booklist, March 1, 2001, page 1188
Library Journal, April 1, 2001, page 132
Publishers Weekly, April 30, 2001, page 53

Historical

Other books by the same author:
Blackberry Wine, 2000
Chocolat, 1999

Other books you might like:
Joan Dial, *Echoes of War*, 1984
Sebastian Faulks, *Charlotte Gray*, 1999
Jonathan Hull, *Losing Julia*, 2000
Pierre Magnan, *The Murdered House*, 2000
Thomas Sanchez, *Day of the Bees*, 2000

911

WILLIAM HEFFERNAN

Beulah Hill
(New York: Simon & Schuster, 2000)

Story type: Historical/Depression Era; Mystery
Subject(s): Mystery and Detective Stories; Race Relations; Depression (Economic)
Major character(s): Jehiel Flood, Farmer; Samuel Bradley, Police Officer (constable); Elizabeth Flood, Teacher
Time period(s): 1930s
Locale(s): Vermont

Summary: Veteran thriller writer Heffernan ventures back in time to rural Vermont in the 1930s for a taut murder investigation that exposes deep-seated racial prejudice. When the son of a white racist patriarch is found pitchforked on the property of Jehiel Flood, the last black farmer on Beulah Hill, the investigating constable is Samuel Bradley. Though descended from slaves, Bradley is considered ''bleached'' due to interracial marriages among his ancestors and, therefore, white by Vermont racial law. Bradley, in love with Flood's schoolteacher daughter Elizabeth, finds himself with divided sympathies and caught between a racial divide. He tries to clear Jehiel of the murder while confronting his own past and the residual legacy of slavery and ongoing bigotry.

Where it's reviewed:
Kirkus Reviews, January 1, 2001, page 17
New York Times Book Review, March 4, 2001, page 25
Publishers Weekly, January 8, 2001, page 46

Other books by the same author:
Red Angel, 2000
Cityside, 1999
The Dinosaur Club, 1997
Winter's Gold, 1997
Blood Rose, 1991

Other books you might like:
Wendell Berry, *Jayber Crow*, 2000
Christopher Brookhouse, *Passing Game*, 2000
Josephine Humphreys, *Nowhere Else on Earth*, 2000
Joe R. Lansdale, *The Bottoms*, 2000
Jeffrey Lent, *In the Fall*, 2000

912

JAMES D. HOUSTON

Snow Mountain Passage
(New York: Knopf, 2001)

Story type: Historical/American West
Subject(s): Disasters; Pioneers; Frontier and Pioneer Life
Major character(s): James Frazier Reed, Pioneer, Historical Figure; Patty Reed, Relative (daughter of James), Historical Figure; John Sutter, Historical Figure
Time period(s): 1840s (1846)
Locale(s): Sierra Nevada Mountains, California; Nevada

Summary: Houston provides a vivid retelling of the harrowing Donner Party disaster in which a group of settlers heading for California were trapped by the snow in the Sierra Nevada Mountains and were forced into cannibalism to survive. The story is told from the perspective of James Frazier Reed, who, compelled to leave his family in Nevada, mounts a rescue mission to save them, and his daughter Patty's memories of the disaster. The double focus adds considerable suspense and human intensity to this defining mythic event in the history of western settlement.

Where it's reviewed:
Kirkus Reviews, February 15, 2001, page 203
New York Times Book Review, April 8, 2001, page 29
Publishers Weekly, March 19, 2001, page 77

Other books by the same author:
The Last Paradise, 1998
Love Life, 1985
Continental Drift, 1978
A Native Son of the Golden West, 1971

Other books you might like:
Hoffman Birney, *Grim Journey*, 1935
David Galloway, *Tamsen*, 1983
Peter R. Limburg, *Deceived: The Story of the Donner Party*, 1998
Richard Rhodes, *The Ungodly*, 1973
Ann T. Ross, *The Pilgrimage*, 1987

913

HELEN HUMPHREYS

Afterimage
(New York: Metropolitan, 2001)

Story type: Historical/Victorian; Gothic
Subject(s): Photography; Servants
Major character(s): Annie Phelan, Servant, Model; Isabelle Dashell, Spouse (of Eldon), Photographer; Eldon Dashell, Cartographer, Spouse (of Isabelle)
Time period(s): 1860s (1865)
Locale(s): England

Summary: Inspired by the Victorian photographer Julia Margaret Cameron, who specialized in posing her models in classical and literary costumes and attitudes, Humphreys explores an obsessive triangle when orphan Annie Phelan goes to work as a servant on an English country estate. Her mistress, Isabelle, is an intense photographer who recruits Annie as her

model. Her husband, Eldon, is preoccupied with Arctic exploration, and he also gets Annie to participate in his imaginary expeditions. The novel explores the mounting tension as the couple's obsessions are worked out in a competition for the young maid.

Where it's reviewed:
Booklist, March 1, 2001, page 1227
Kirkus Reviews, February 15, 2001, page 203
Library Journal, April 1, 2001, page 132
New York Times Book Review, April 15, 2001, page 29
Publishers Weekly, March 5, 2001, page 61

Other books by the same author:
Leaving Earth, 1998

Other books you might like:
Sarah Blake, *Grange House*, 2000
Helen Dunmore, *A Spell of Winter*, 2001
James Fleming, *The Temple of Optimism*, 2000
Sheri Holman, *The Dress Lodger*, 2000
Sarah Waters, *Affinity*, 2000

914

CAROLINE ROSE HUNT

Primrose Past

(New York: ReganBooks, 2000)

Story type: Historical/Victorian
Subject(s): Diaries
Major character(s): Cygnet, Teenager
Time period(s): 1840s (1848)
Locale(s): England

Summary: Daily life in Victorian England is the subject of this novel that takes the form of a diary kept by a 15-year-old girl identified only by her nickname, Cygnet. She records the English countryside, domestic routine, and the annoyances of her little brother. Circumstances become more dramatic due to the illness of her mother and her parents' sojourn in London. Hunt has done an admirable job of historical reconstruction.

Where it's reviewed:
Booklist, February 15, 2001, page 1116

Other books you might like:
David Anthony Durham, *Gabriel's Story*, 2001
Tony Earley, *Jim the Boy*, 2000
Brad Kessler, *Lick Creek*, 2001
Karen Roberts, *The Flower Boy*, 2000
Emma Tennant, *An Unequal Marriage*, 1994

915

SYLVIA IPARRAGUIRRE

Tierra del Fuego

(Willimantic, Connecticut: Curbstone, 2000)

Story type: Historical/Victorian
Subject(s): Indians of South America; Cultural Conflict

Major character(s): Jemmy Button, Indian (Yamana), Historical Figure; Robert Fitzroy, Historical Figure, Military Personnel (naval captain); John William Guevara, Sailor
Time period(s): 19th century (1830-1865)
Locale(s): Tierra del Fuego, Argentina; England; Falkland Islands

Summary: Argentinean writer Iparraguirre has constructed an intriguing drama about cultural conflict based on the historical facts surrounding a Yamana Indian, Jemmy Button, taken by British Captain Robert Fitzroy of Darwin's *Beagle* to be ''civilized'' in England before returning him to South America as an agent of civilization. Narrated by sailor John William Guevara, a man with an English father and Argentinean mother, the novel explores the tragic consequences of an arrogant experiment.

Where it's reviewed:
Booklist, January 2001, page 915
Library Journal, December 2000, page 189
Publishers Weekly, November 20, 2000, page 48

Other books you might like:
Arthur Japin, *The Two Hearts of Kwasi Boachi*, 2000
Roger McDonald, *Mr. Darwin's Shooter*, 1998
Irving Stone, *The Origin*, 1980
Benjamin Subercaseaux, *Jemmy Button*, 1954
James Welch, *Heartsong of Charging Elk*, 2000

916

CHRISTIAN JACQ

Paneb the Ardent

(New York: Pocket, 2001)

Story type: Historical/Ancient Egypt
Series: Stone of Light. Number 3
Subject(s): Egyptian Antiquities; Egyptian Religion; Ancient History
Major character(s): Paneb the Ardent, Artisan; Nefer, Artisan
Time period(s): 13th century B.C.
Locale(s): Egypt

Summary: This is the third volume of Jacq's series concerning the secret village dubbed the Place of Truth and populated by the Brotherhood, gifted craftsmen responsible for designing and building Egypt's monuments. In this installment, Nefer is appointed master of the Brotherhood and a resentful traitor pursues a plan to destroy his own community. The responsibility to protect the Brotherhood's precious Stone of Light falls on Nefer's adopted son, Paneb the Ardent.

Where it's reviewed:
Booklist, April 15, 2001, page 1451
Publishers Weekly, February 26, 2001, page 59

Other books by the same author:
The Wise Woman, 2000
Nefer the Silent, 1999
The Ramses Quintet, 1997-1999

Other books you might like:
P.C. Doherty, *The Ancient Egyptian Series*, 1999-
Pauline Gedge, *Child of the Morning*, 1977
Jacquetta Hawkes, *King of the Two Lands*, 1966

Historical

Naguib Mahfouz, *Akhenaten: Dweller in Truth*, 2000
Wilbur A. Smith, *Warlock*, 2001

917

CHRISTIAN JACQ

The Wise Woman

(New York: Pocket, 2000)

Story type: Historical/Ancient Egypt
Series: Stone of Light. Number 2
Subject(s): Egyptian Antiquities; Egyptian Religion; Ancient History
Major character(s): Mehy, Military Personnel (general); Ubekhet, Young Woman; Merenptah, Ruler (pharaoh), Historical Figure
Time period(s): 13th century B.C.
Locale(s): Egypt

Summary: Jacq continues his series concerning the secret village, the Place of Truth, populated by the best artisans, who protect the sacred Stone of Light that allows them to create Egypt's magnificent tombs and palaces. Ramses the Great has died, and his son, Merenptah, has succeeded him. Mehy, rebuffed in his desire to be accepted into the exclusive enclave of artisans, continues his campaign of vengeance against the Place of Truth, sowing distrust and unrest. One of the village's wise women, Ubekhet, must meet the challenge to protect the Stone of Light.

Other books by the same author:
Paneb the Ardent, 2001
Nefer the Silent, 1999
The Ramses Quintet, 1997-1999

Other books you might like:
P.C. Doherty, *The Anubis Slayings*, 2001
Pauline Gedge, *The Horus Road*, 2001
Anton Gill, *City of the Dead*, 1993
Norman Mailer, *Ancient Evenings*, 1983
Lynda S. Robinson, *The Lord Meren Series*, 1994-

918

MICHAEL JECKS

The Boy-Bishop's Glovemaker

(London: Headline, 2001)

Story type: Historical/Medieval; Mystery
Series: Medieval West Country. Number 10
Subject(s): Mystery and Detective Stories; Middle Ages
Major character(s): Sir Baldwin de Furnshill, Knight, Government Official (Keeper of the King's Peace); Simon Puttock, Lawman (bailiff); Ralph Glover, Artisan
Time period(s): 14th century (1321)
Locale(s): Exeter, England

Summary: In the English city of Exeter at Christmas time, festivities are underway to celebrate the election of a ''boy-bishop'' who will serve for a single day. When craftsman Ralph Glover, commissioned to make the gem-studded gloves for the occasion is found hanged, suspicion points to his apprentice. Sir Baldwin de Furnshill, Keeper of the King's

Peace, and Bailiff Simon Puttock pursue a different theory, uncovering a number of secrets in the cathedral town. Jecks' mysteries are packed with details of medieval life and customs, and this installment is no exception.

Where it's reviewed:
Kirkus Reviews, February 15, 2001, page 217
New York Times Book Review, April 22, 2001, page 17
Publishers Weekly, March 19, 2001, page 79

Other books by the same author:
Belladonna at Belstone, 2000
Squire Throwleigh's Heir, 2000
The Abbot's Gibbet, 1998
The Leper's Return, 1998
The Merchant's Partner, 1995

Other books you might like:
Susanna Gregory, *The Matthew Bartholomew Series*, 1996-
Ian Morson, *The William Falconer Series*, 1994-
Sharon Kay Penman, *The Justin de Quincy Series*, 1996-
Candace M. Robb, *The Owen Archer Series*, 1993-
Joan Wolf, *The Poisoned Serpent*, 2000

919

TERRY C. JOHNSTON

Wind Walker

(New York: Doubleday, 2001)

Story type: Historical/American West; Mountain Man
Series: Titus Bass
Subject(s): American West; Frontier and Pioneer Life; Indians of North America
Major character(s): Titus Bass, Mountain Man; Waits-by-the-Water, Indian (Crow), Spouse (of Titus)
Time period(s): 1840s; 1850s
Locale(s): Oregon Trail, West

Summary: Johnston brings to an elegiac conclusion his historical western series featuring intrepid mountain man Titus Bass. In the aftermath of the Taos Rebellion, depicted in the previous novel, *Death Rattle*, Bass heads north with his family to the home of his wife, Waits-by-the-Water, among the Crow. Bass confronts a changed western landscape threatened by settlers and the Mormons along the Oregon Trail. Family troubles, old adversaries, and the inevitability of time and change complicate Bass' waning years in which the closing of the American frontier is reflected in Bass' own end.

Where it's reviewed:
Booklist, January 2001, page 918
Publishers Weekly, February 5, 2001, page 70

Other books by the same author:
Death Rattle, 1999
Ride the Moon Down, 1998
Buffalo Palace, 1996
Dance on the Wind, 1995
Dream Catcher, 1994

Other books you might like:
Irwin R. Blacker, *Taos*, 1959
John Byrne Cooke, *The Snowblind Moon*, 1985
W. Michael Gear, *The Morning River*, 1996

R.C. House, *Warhawk*, 1993
Cameron Judd, *The Shadow Warriors*, 1997

920

JEANNE KALOGRIDIS

The Burning Times
(New York: Simon & Schuster, 2001)

Story type: Historical/Medieval; Historical/Fantasy
Subject(s): Fantasy; Witches and Witchcraft; Middle Ages
Major character(s): Marie Francoise, Religious (abbess); Michel, Religious (monk)
Time period(s): 14th century (1357)
Locale(s): France

Summary: Kalogridis' medieval fantasy concerns the investigation of an agent of the Inquisition, Brother Michel, who is charged with gaining a confession of heresy from a young abbess, Marie Francoise. She confesses to a pagan upbringing as a custodian of the cult of Diana. Fleeing from prosecution, Marie Francoise, a.k.a. Sybille, struggles to maintain her powers and the goddess cult in the face of changing times. Kalogridis balances fantasy with well-researched details from medieval history.

Where it's reviewed:
Kirkus Reviews, February 15, 2001, page 204
Library Journal, March 15, 2001, page 105
Publishers Weekly, February 12, 2001, page 182

Other books by the same author:
Lord of the Vampires, 1996
Lord of the Vampires, 1996
Children of the Vampire, 1995
Covenant with the Vampire, 1994

Other books you might like:
Marion Zimmer Bradley, *The Mists of Avalon*, 1982
Marion Zimmer Bradley, *Priestess of Avalon*, 2001
    Diana L. Paxson, co-author
Elizabeth Chadwick, *The Marsh King's Daughter*, 2000
Joan Dahr Lambert, *Circles of Stone*, 1997
Judith Tarr, *White Mare's Daughter*, 1998

921

STUART M. KAMINSKY

A Few Minutes Past Midnight
(New York: Carroll & Graf, 2001)

Story type: Mystery; Historical/World War II
Series: Toby Peters
Subject(s): Mystery and Detective Stories; Serial Killer; Movie Industry
Major character(s): Toby Peters, Detective—Private; Charlie Chaplin, Historical Figure, Actor
Time period(s): 1940s (1943)
Locale(s): Hollywood, California

Summary: Hollywood's most amusing vintage private eye, Toby Peters, is back on the case, hired by Charlie Chaplin, when the actor receives threats from a serial killer. The mystery is ingenious but only part of the appeal here. Kaminsky is

exuberant in his use of colorful eccentric characters and encyclopedic in his references, bringing the past era back to life.

Where it's reviewed:
Booklist, May 1, 2001, page 1634
Kirkus Reviews, June 1, 2001, page 775
Publishers Weekly, June 11, 2001, page 64

Other books by the same author:
A Fatal Glass of Beer, 1997
Tomorrow Is Another Day, 1995
Poor Butterfly, 1990
Smart Moves, 1986
Never Cross a Vampire, 1980

Other books you might like:
Michael Chabon, *The Amazing Adventures of Kavalier & Clay*, 2000
Max Allan Collins, *Angel in Black*, 2001
John Dunning, *Two O'Clock, Eastern Wartime*, 2001
Ron Goulart, *The Groucho Marx Series*, 1998-
Lise McClendon, *One O'Clock Jump*, 2001

922

N.M. KELBY

In the Company of Angels
(New York: Hyperion, 2001)

Story type: Historical/World War II
Subject(s): World War II; Holocaust; Gardens and Gardening
Major character(s): Marie Claire Durrieu, Orphan; Xavier, Religious (nun); Anne, Religious (nun)
Time period(s): 1940s
Locale(s): Tournai, Belgium

Summary: Kelby constructs a poetic and sometimes surrealistic religious fable set during World War II. Marie Claire Durrieu is a Jewish orphan, the lone survivor of a family of Belgian flower growers. Rescued by two nuns—Mother Xavier and the younger Sister Anne—Marie Claire is hidden in their convent and unusual things begin to occur. Complicating the rich texture of the novel is Mother Xavier's German parentage, and Anne's love for the German commander. The novel's climax is a crescendo of the symbolic that will either madden or inspire readers.

Where it's reviewed:
Kirkus Reviews, February 15, 2001, page 204
Publishers Weekly, February 26, 2001, page 56

Other books you might like:
Alice Adams, *After the War*, 2000
Pierre Magnan, *The Murdered House*, 2000
Alex Miller, *Conditions of Faith*, 2000
Catherine M. Rae, *Marike's World*, 2000
Helga Ruebsamen, *The Song and the Truth*, 2000

Historical

923

BRAD KESSLER

Lick Creek

(New York: Scribner, 2001)

Story type: Historical/Roaring Twenties
Subject(s): Miners and Mining; Rural Life
Major character(s): Emily Jenkins, Teenager; Joseph Gershon, Worker (lineman); Robert Daniels, Businessman
Time period(s): 1920s
Locale(s): West Virginia

Summary: In the remote mining country of West Virginia, teenager Emily Jenkins' father and brother are killed in a mine explosion. To make ends meet, she sells mushrooms, blackberries, and goat cheese in a neighboring town. Emily is seduced by a supervisor of the power company, Robert Daniels, who wishes to build power lines across the Jenkins' farm, she vows revenge by sabotaging the power company. When a young lineman, Joseph Gershon, is struck by lightning and is nursed on the Jenkins' farm, Emily and Joseph fall in love before a fateful climax at a celebration for the completion of the electrification project. Kessler does a fine job capturing the era and the region.

Where it's reviewed:
Booklist, January 2001, page 918
Kirkus Reviews, January 1, 2001, page 12
New York Times Book Review, April 1, 2001, page 19
Publishers Weekly, January 15, 2001, page 50

Other books you might like:
David Baldacci, *Wish You Well*, 2000
Wendell Berry, *Jayber Crow*, 2000
Christina Schwarz, *Drowning Ruth*, 2000
Mary Lee Settle, *The Scapegoat*, 1980
Lee Smith, *Family Linen*, 1996

924

ROSS KING

Ex-Libris

(New York: Walker, 2001)

Story type: Mystery; Historical/Seventeenth Century
Subject(s): Mystery and Detective Stories; Books and Reading; Civil War/English
Major character(s): Isaac Inchbold, Store Owner (bookshop); Althea Greatorex, Noblewoman (Lady Marchamont)
Time period(s): 17th century (1660)
Locale(s): London, England; Dorsetshire, England

Summary: King's gripping, literate historical thriller is set in Britain following the English Civil War. Lady Marchamont of Pontifex Hall in Dorsetshire summons London bookseller Isaac Inchbold to restore her library that has been ransacked during the struggle. Of particular interest is an antiquated, heretical volume, *The Labyrinth of the World*. The search for this book will place Inchbold's life in danger and uncover a fascinating hidden world of dark, arcane secrets and mixed, deadly motives.

Where it's reviewed:
Booklist, February 15, 2001, page 1120
Kirkus Reviews, December 15, 2000, page 1709
Library Journal, February 1, 2001, page 125
Publishers Weekly, December 11, 2000, page 52

Other books you might like:
Umberto Eco, *The Name of the Rose*, 1983
Sheri Holman, *The Dress Lodger*, 2000
David Liss, *A Conspiracy of Paper*, 2000
Iain Pears, *An Instance of the Fingerpost*, 1998
Betsy Tobin, *Bone House*, 2000

925

JANE KIRKPATRICK

No Eye Can See

(Colorado Springs, Colorado: WaterBrook, 2001)

Story type: Historical/American West; Religious
Series: Kinship and Courage. Book 2
Subject(s): Frontier and Pioneer Life; Women
Major character(s): Suzanne Cullver, Widow(er), Handicapped (blind)
Time period(s): 19th century
Locale(s): Oregon Trail, West; California

Summary: Christian writer Kirkpatrick offers a sequel to her novel *All Together in One Place*, continuing the story of a group of women who band together on the trek west after losing the men in their lives. The novel, centered on the experiences of blind and widowed Suzanne Cullver, traces the daily routine of life on the Oregon Trail enroute to California and a new life in a mining town. Good period details illustrate this inspiring story of starting over and persisting through considerable challenges.

Where it's reviewed:
Publishers Weekly, January 1, 2001, page 67

Other books by the same author:
All Together in One Place, 2000
A Gathering of Finches, 1997
Homestead, 1997
Love to Water My Soul, 1996

Other books you might like:
David Ballantine, *Chalk's Woman*, 2000
Terry Kay, *Taking Lottie Home*, 2000
Larry McMurtry, *Boone's Lick*, 2000
Richard S. Wheeler, *The Fields of Eden*, 2001

926

AARON LATHAM

Code of the West

(New York: Simon & Schuster, 2001)

Story type: Historical/American West; Legend
Subject(s): Arthurian Legend; American West; Cowboys/Cowgirls
Major character(s): Jimmy Goodnight, Captive, Cowboy; Revelie Sanborn, Young Woman; Jack Loving, Cowboy
Time period(s): 19th century (1860s-1890s)

Locale(s): Texas

Summary: Latham transplants the Arthurian legend to the Wild West. The Arthur stand-in is Texan orphan Jimmy Goodnight whose heroic lineage is announced when, at a county fair competition, he pulls an axe out of an anvil. His Guinevere is the Bostonian blue-blood Revelie Sanborn, and the Lancelot is Jimmy's best friend, Jack Loving. Action includes encounters with the ''Robbers' Roost'' Gang and doom from an evil son that Jimmy never knew he had fathered. The parallels are labored, and interest is intermittent in this too-often self-conscious pastiche.

Where it's reviewed:
Booklist, March 1, 2001, page 1120
Kirkus Reviews, February 15, 2001, page 207
Library Journal, March 15, 2001, page 105
Publishers Weekly, February 19, 2001, page 69

Other books by the same author:
The Ballad of Gussie and Clyde, 1997
Orchids for Mother, 1977

Other books you might like:
Chris Adrian, *Gob's Grief*, 2000
Mike Blakely, *Summer of Pearls*, 2000
Larry McMurtry, *Anything for Billy*, 1988
Larry McMurtry, *Boone's Lick*, 2000
Charles F. Price, *The Cock's Spur*, 2000

927

J.P. SINCLAIR LEWIS

Buffalo Gordon

(New York: Forge, 2001)

Story type: Historical/Post-American Civil War; Historical/American West
Subject(s): Reconstruction; African Americans; Military Life
Major character(s): Nate Gordon, Military Personnel (cavalry sergeant), Slave (former); Cougar Eyes, Indian (Cheyenne)
Time period(s): 1860s
Locale(s): Louisiana; Indian Territory

Summary: In the first novel of a projected series to chronicle western history from an African-American perspective, former runaway slave Nate Gordon returns to Louisiana as a cavalry sergeant given the task of recruiting members for the newly formed Ninth U.S. Negro Cavalry. He must contend with racist Union officers, ex-rebels, and internal dissent before heading off to Cheyenne Indian territory where he tangles with warrior chief Cougar Eyes, who gives his adversary the nickname ''Buffalo Gordon.'' Although supported by evident historical research, this is an overly earnest adventure series undermined by the superhuman perfection of the novel's title character and other narrative missteps.

Where it's reviewed:
Kirkus Reviews, December 15, 2000, page 1710
Publishers Weekly, December 18, 2000, page 54

Other books you might like:
Allen B. Ballard, *Where I'm Bound*, 2000
Mike Blakely, *Shortgrass Song*, 1994

David Anthony Durham, *Gabriel's Story*, 2001
John Prebble, *The Buffalo Soldiers*, 1959
Tom Willard, *Buffalo Soldiers*, 1996

928

MIRIAM STRIEZHEFF LEWIS

Departures

(Philadelphia: Xlibris, 2001)

Story type: Historical/Regency
Subject(s): Marriage; Gypsies; Jews
Major character(s): Jeannette Ballin, Young Woman; Iacob Abelscu, Businessman (fur merchant)
Time period(s): 1810s
Locale(s): Paris, France; Romania

Summary: Set in the early years of the 19th century, the novel concerns the difficulties faced by Parisienne Jeannette Ballin, who marries fur merchant Iacob Abelscu and moves to the wilds of Moldavia in what is now eastern Romania. There Turks battle Greeks and the Jewish and gypsy communities are both caught in the middle. The novel depicts a strong-willed woman who must deal with considerable challenges based on her religion and gender.

Other books you might like:
Meto Jovanovski, *Cousins*, 1987
Jeanne Mackin, *The Sweet By and By*, 2001
Herta Muller, *The Land of Green Plums*, 1996
Zaharia Stancu, *Barefoot*, 1972
Geling Yan, *The Lost Daughter of Happiness*, 2001

929

QIAO LI

Wintry Night

(New York: Columbia University Press, 2001)

Story type: Family Saga
Subject(s): Chinese; Family Relations; War
Major character(s): Dengmei, Spouse (of Liu Ahan); Liu Ahan, Spouse (of Dengmei); Liu Mingji, Military Personnel (Japanese conscript)
Time period(s): 1890s; 20th century (1890s-1940s)
Locale(s): Taiwan; Philippines

Summary: Volumes one and three of Li Qiao's massive Taiwanese epic are translated here; volume 2 has been omitted. The novel looks at the settlement of Taiwan in the 19th century through several generations of a northern migrant family, the Pengs. Young Dengmei has been purchased as a bride for the Pengs youngest son. When he dies, she is married to Liu Ahan, a soldier, and the first half of the novel concerns family relations and village life up to the Japanese invasion of Taiwan in 1895. In part two their son, who is conscripted into the Japanese army for their campaign in the Philippines during World War II, dominates the story.

Where it's reviewed:
Booklist, March 1, 2001, page 1227
Kirkus Reviews, March 15, 2001, page 364
Publishers Weekly, February 5, 2001, page 66

Historical

Other books you might like:
Lisa Huang Fleischman, *Dream of the Walled City*, 2000
Bette Bao Lord, *The Middle Heart*, 1996
Ruthanne Lum McCunn, *The Moon Pearl*, 2000
Mo Yan, *Red Sorghum*, 1993
Paul West, *The Tent of Orange Mist*, 1995

930

GILLIAN LINSCOTT

A Perfect Daughter

(New York: St. Martin's Press, 2001)

Story type: Historical/Edwardian; Mystery
Series: Nell Bray
Subject(s): Mystery and Detective Stories; Women's Rights
Major character(s): Nell Bray, Suffragette, Detective—
   Amateur; Verona North, Student (art)
Time period(s): 1910s (1914)
Locale(s): London, England; Devon, England

Summary: Suffragette and sleuth Nell Bray returns for a case set during the summer of 1914. While she is busy fighting for the vote, Nell is asked to keep an eye on her niece, Verona North, who is enrolled in a London art school. When this perfectly proper young woman is found hanged, pregnant, and drugged, Nell doubts a suicide verdict. Her investigation leads her to question Verona's friends and associates and uncover the troubling secret life of her niece. Meanwhile, Scotland Yard suspects Nell of harboring fugitive suffragettes. Linscott is an expert in weaving details of the era around her intrigue, and this is a fine addition to a successful series.

Where it's reviewed:
Kirkus Reviews, March 1, 2001, page 297
Library Journal, April 1, 2001, page 137
Publishers Weekly, March 26, 2001, page 66

Other books by the same author:
Absent Friends, 1999
Dance on Blood, 1998
Dead Man's Sweetheart, 1996
An Easy Day for a Lady, 1995
Crown Witness, 1995

Other books you might like:
Rennie Airth, *River of Darkness*, 1999
Dianne Day, *The Fremont Jones Series*, 1995-
Annette Meyers, *Murder Me Now*, 2000
Miriam Grace Monfredo, *The Seneca Falls Series*, 1992-
Charles Todd, *Search of the Dark*, 1999

931

ROBIN LIPPINCOTT

Our Arcadia

(New York: Viking, 2001)

Story type: Historical/Roaring Twenties
Subject(s): Homosexuality/Lesbianism; Friendship; Artists
   and Art
Major character(s): Nora Hartley, Divorced Person; Lark Martin, Homosexual

Time period(s): 20th century (1928-1943)
Locale(s): Truro, Massachusetts

Summary: Set on Cape Cod, Massachusetts, this engaging novel depicts an odd-couple-like pair and their bohemian household. Recently divorced Nora Hartley and homosexual Lark Martin buy a house together in Truro, and the novel describes their various relationships with the artistic community on Cape Cod during the next 15 years. Lippincott weaves a number of themes around his setting and the two central characters, and is particularly skilled in creating a sense of atmosphere and place.

Other books by the same author:
Mr. Dalloway, 1999
The Real, True Angel, 1996

Other books you might like:
Ann Howard Creel, *The Magic of Ordinary Days*, 2001
Dorothy Garlock, *The Edge of Town*, 2001
Helen Humphreys, *Afterimage*, 2001
Miranda Seymour, *The Summer of '39*, 1999
Sarah Stonich, *These Granite Islands*, 2001

932

GARY LIVINGSTON

Tears of Ice

(Philadelphia: Xlibris, 2001)

Story type: Coming-of-Age; Military
Subject(s): Jews; Child Abuse; Military Life
Major character(s): Poti Levin, Abuse Victim; Yuri Do-
   minkov, Military Personnel (Russian sergeant); Gai
   Bosha, Military Personnel (Russian private)
Time period(s): 1820s
Locale(s): Russia

Summary: Livingston dramatizes a largely forgotten historical event: the Rekruchina Decree of 1827 issued by Russia's Czar Nicholas I that forced 60,000 Jewish children into the army to promote the dissolution of Russian Jews. Poti Levin is a 12-year-old forced on a brutal journey with other boys to a military camp in the Russian interior. Beset by a cruel sergeant. Yuri Dominkov, and befriended by Private Gai Bosha, Levin and his peers are shown trying to survive.

Other books you might like:
Vassily Aksyonov, *Generations of Winter*, 1994
B. Bartos-Hoppner, *Storm over the Caucasus*, 1968
Abraham Cahan, *The White Terror and the Red*, 1905
Andrei Makine, *Confessions of a Fallen Standard Bearer*,
   2000
Bernard Malamud, *The Fixer*, 1966

933

MORGAN LLYWELYN

1921

(New York: Forge, 2001)

Story type: Historical/Roaring Twenties
Subject(s): Civil War; Irish Republican Army

Major character(s): Henry Mooney, Journalist; Ella Rutledge, Young Woman; Michael Collins, Historical Figure, Political Figure
Time period(s): 1910s; 1920s (1917-1921)
Locale(s): Ireland

Summary: Popular historical novelist and expert on Ireland Llywelyn, in a sequel to *1916*, offers a chronicle of modern Irish history from the aftermath of the Easter Rebellion in 1917 through the bloody war with Britain and the civil war that follows the peace treaty. This is a highly-documented account in which the historical events and major figures, such as Michael Collins, are reflected through the fictional perspective of journalist Henry Mooney and his relationship with Anglo-Irish Ella Rutledge.

Where it's reviewed:
Booklist, March 15, 2001, page 1354
Kirkus Reviews, January 1, 2001, page 18
Publishers Weekly, January 15, 2001, page 51

Other books by the same author:
1916, 1998
Pride of Lions, 1996
Strongbow, 1996
Brian Boru, Emperor of the Irish, 1995
Lion of Ireland, 1980

Other books you might like:
Roddy Doyle, *A Star Called Henry*, 1999
J.G. Farrell, *Troubles*, 1971
Constantine FitzGibbon, *High Heroic*, 1969
Thomas Flanagan, *The End of the Hunt*, 1994
Cathal Liam, *Consumed in Freedom's Flame*, 2000

934

PAUL LUSSIER

Last Refuge of Scoundrels
(New York: Warner, 2001)

Story type: Historical/American Revolution
Subject(s): Revolutionary War; Politics; War
Major character(s): John Lawrence, Military Personnel (aide-de-camp to Washington); Deborah Simpson, Spy, Prostitute (former); George Washington, Historical Figure, Military Personnel
Time period(s): 1770s; 1780s
Locale(s): United States

Summary: Revisionism reigns in this often delightful, sometimes heavy-handed, irreverent view of the American Revolution that succeeds despite the best efforts of the self-serving Founding Fathers to advance their own interests ahead of all others. The fictional story links young John Lawrence with the one-time whore and cagey spy, Deborah Simpson, working for George Washington. She is the real brains behind the successful prosecution of the war. In Lussier's interpretation, Samuel Adams is a thug; John Hancock is as ostentatious as his signature; and John Adams is a self-serving opportunist. With friends like these, the fledgling American republic doesn't need enemies, and the British, effete bumblers all, hardly qualify. The major events of the Revolutionary War—the Boston Massacre, the battles of

Lexington and Concord, and Valley Forge—are all depicted through Lussier's offbeat lens.

Where it's reviewed:
Booklist, November 15, 2000, page 610
Kirkus Reviews, November 15, 2000, page 1563
Library Journal, November 1, 2000, page 135
Publishers Weekly, December 4, 2000, page 52

Other books you might like:
William Eastlake, *The Long Naked Descent into Boston*, 1977
Thomas Fleming, *Dreams of Glory*, 2000
William Martin, *Citizen Washington*, 1999
William Safire, *Scandalmonger*, 2000
Gore Vidal, *Burr*, 1973

935

MALCOLM MACDONALD

Rose of Nancemillin
(New York: St. Martin's Press, 2001)

Story type: Historical/Edwardian
Subject(s): Servants; Actors and Actresses; Theater
Major character(s): Lucinda-Ella "Rose" Tremayne, Servant (lady's maid); Fenella Carclew, Teenager; Louis Redmile-Smith, Gentleman
Time period(s): 1910s (1912)
Locale(s): London, England; United States

Summary: The prolific MacDonald offers an Edwardian tale of theatrical success as Cornish housemaid Rose Tremayne perfects her talent at mimicry while in the service of teenager Fenella Carclew. When Rose goes to work backstage for a London company, she is pressed into emergency service on stage and her talent propels her to fame as a lead and a star in England and America. Her career complicates her on-again, off-again relationship with the genteel Louis Redmile-Smith, but the interest here is more on the details of Rose's career than her romances.

Where it's reviewed:
Booklist, April 1, 2001, page 1451
Kirkus Reviews, February 15, 2001, page 213
Publishers Weekly, March 12, 2001, page 63

Other books by the same author:
Tamsin Harte, 2000
Like a Diamond, 1999
Kernow and Daughter, 1996
The Trevarton Inheritance, 1996
All Desires Known, 1994

Other books you might like:
Helen Ashfield, *Emerald*, 1983
Catherine Cookson, *Kate Hannigan's Girl*, 2001
Emma Donoghue, *Slammerkin*, 2001
Jane Julian, *Ellen Bray*, 1985
Mary Lide, *Tregaran*, 1989

Historical

936

JEANNE MACKIN

The Sweet By and By

(New York: St. Martin's Press, 2001)

Story type: Historical/Victorian America; Ghost Story
Subject(s): Ghosts; Spiritualism
Major character(s): Helen West, Journalist; Maggie Fox, Historical Figure, Occultist; Leah Fox, Historical Figure, Occultist
Time period(s): 1990s; 19th century
Locale(s): New York

Summary: This intriguing story of spiritualism and obsession shuttles between the contemporary world of journalist Helen West, who is mourning the tragic death of her lover, and the historical story of Maggie and Leah Fox, whose spiritualism she is researching. The Foxes become famous as mediums, and despite West's skepticism of their methods, the journalist grows increasingly sympathetic to Maggie Fox's powers as she becomes convinced that the dead can indeed revisit the living. Mackin connects both contemporary and historical stories for a compelling modern ghost tale.

Where it's reviewed:
Booklist, February 1, 2001, page 1040
Kirkus Reviews, January 15, 2001, page 74
Library Journal, February 1, 2001, page 126
Publishers Weekly, January 15, 2001, page 52

Other books by the same author:
Dreams of Empire, 1996
The Queen's War, 1991
The Frenchwoman, 1989

Other books you might like:
Helen Humphreys, *Afterimage*, 2001
Meagan McKinney, *The Fortune Hunter*, 1998
Roberta Rogow, *The Problem of the Spiteful Spiritualist*, 1999
Katie Ross, *A Hint of Mischief*, 1998
Sarah Waters, *Affinity*, 2000

937

NICK P. MAGINNIS

Antonia's Island

(Saratoga, Florida: Pineapple, 2001)

Story type: Historical/Exotic
Subject(s): Survival; Mexicans; Islands
Major character(s): Rodrigo Vallerdas, Spouse (of Antonia); Antonia Vallerdas, Spouse (of Rodrigo)
Time period(s): 1910s (1914)
Locale(s): Mexico

Summary: Set during the Mexican Revolution, this interesting novel follows the Vallerdas family, who sets sail for a new life in California only to be shipwrecked on a desert island. Survivors include individuals from various social classes who replicate in miniature the revolutionary forces that have torn Mexican society apart. Haunting the scene is a mysterious and

charismatic loner known as El Diablo de Chiapas, who may be the castaways' savior or destroyer.

Other books you might like:
Michel Bernanos, *The Other Side of the Mountain*, 1968
Clare Coleman, *Daughter of the Reef*, 1992
Carlos Fuentes, *The Years with Laura Diaz*, 2000
Agustin Yanez, *The Edge of the Storm*, 1963
Norman Zollinger, *Not of War Only*, 1994

938

MICHELINE AHARONIAN MARCOM

Three Apples Fell from Heaven

(New York: Riverhead, 2001)

Story type: Historical/World War I
Subject(s): War; Massacres
Major character(s): Anaguil, Young Woman; Sargis, Writer (poet); Lucine, Servant
Time period(s): 1910s (1915-1917)
Locale(s): Turkey

Summary: One of the 20th century's greatest tragedies was the genocide committed by the Turkish government which systematically massacred nearly one million Armenians during World War I. Basing her story on the experiences of her grandmother, a survivor, Marcom gives voice to the unspeakable horror in a collection of vignettes from various perspectives, including Anaguil, an Armenian girl taken in by her Turkish neighbors after the death of her parents; Sargis, a young parent who hides in his mother's attic, dressed as a woman, who is slowly going mad; and Lucine, a servant at the American consulate, who is resented by her neighbors for her presumed privileges. This is a poetic and moving testimony to one of the darkest chapters of world history.

Where it's reviewed:
Booklist, March 15, 2001, page 1354
Kirkus Reviews, March 15, 2001, page 354
Library Journal, May 15, 2001, page 164
New York Times Book Review, April 22, 2001, page 26

Other books you might like:
Adam Bagdasarian, *The Forgotten Fire*, 2000
Carol Edgarian, *Rise the Euphrates*, 1994
Jack Hashian, *Mamigon*, 1982
Nancy Kricorian, *Zabelle*, 1998
Richard Reinhardt, *The Ashes of Smyrna*, 1970

939

EDWARD MARSTON

The Devil's Apprentice

(New York: St. Martin's Minotaur, 2001)

Story type: Historical/Elizabethan; Mystery
Series: Nicholas Bracewell. Number 11
Subject(s): Mystery and Detective Stories; Theater
Major character(s): Nicholas Bracewell, Producer (theatrical); Sir Michael Greenleaf, Landowner; Davy Stratton, Apprentice, Actor
Time period(s): 16th century

Locale(s): London, England; Essex, England

Summary: A bitter winter threatens to close down the Elizabethan theatrical company managed by Nicholas Bracewell and the Westfield Men agree to an offer from Sir Michael Greenleaf to perform in his warm manor house in Essex. The only catch is that they must agree to take on a new apprentice, Davy Stratton, who proves quarrelsome and disruptive. More menace follows when the lead actor succumbs to the same ailments that afflict his character in the play and when a prominent audience member dies during the opening night production. Nicholas must use all his wits and considerable resources to keep the troupe together and get to the bottom of the sinister forces at play.

Where it's reviewed:
Kirkus Reviews, May 15, 2001, page 713

Other books by the same author:
The Domesday Book Series, 1994-
The Nicholas Bracewell Series, 1988-

Other books you might like:
Stephanie Cowell, *The Players*, 1997
Simon Hawke, *A Mystery of Errors*, 2000
Robert Nye, *The Late Mr. Shakespeare*, 1999
Kate Sedley, *The Roger the Chapman Series*, 1992-
Leonard Tourney, *The Matthew Stock Series*, 1980-

940

LEE MARTIN

Quakertown

(New York: Dutton, 2001)

Story type: Historical/Roaring Twenties
Subject(s): African Americans; Family Relations
Major character(s): Little Washington Jones, Gardener; Andrew Bell, Banker
Time period(s): 1920s
Locale(s): Denton, Texas

Summary: Based on an actual episode in north Texas history from the 1920s, the novel looks at the consequences of racial conflict and segregation in Denton, Texas, in the interlocked relationships between two families. Little Washington Jones is an accomplished gardener and resident of the black community of Quakertown. He is asked by banker Andrew Bell to help smooth the racial division between the white and black neighborhoods, but there are disastrous consequences. Although the novel moves toward the melodramatic and sensational in its plot, the details are authentic and convincing.

Where it's reviewed:
Kirkus Reviews, May 15, 2001, page 611
Publishers Weekly, June 11, 2001, page 60

Other books by the same author:
From Our House, 2001
The Least You Need to Know, 1996
Bird in a Cage, 1995
Inherited Murder, 1994
The Day That Dusty Died, 1994

Other books you might like:
Rilla Askew, *Fire in Beulah*, 2001

Dorothy Garlock, *The Edge of Town*, 2001
William Heffernan, *Beulah Hill*, 2000
Lalita Tademy, *Cane River*, 2001
Jane Roberts Wood, *Grace*, 2001

941

ROBIN MAXWELL

Virgin

(New York: Arcade, 2001)

Story type: Historical/Elizabethan
Subject(s): Biography; Kings, Queens, Rulers, etc.
Major character(s): Elizabeth I, Historical Figure, Ruler (queen); Robert Dudley, Nobleman (Earl of Leicester), Historical Figure; Thomas Seymour, Historical Figure, Nobleman
Time period(s): 16th century (1540s)
Locale(s): England

Summary: Maxwell continues her chronicle of the life of Elizabeth I and the intrigue during the Tudor period with this depiction of the young princess' adolescence. After the death of Henry VIII, his widow, Catherine Parr, marries the Lord High Admiral, Thomas Seymour, whose designs on the throne include the seduction of the teenage Elizabeth. Considerable speculation fills the gap in the historical record in this account that alternates between breathless emotions and scholarly minutiae.

Where it's reviewed:
Kirkus Reviews, April 15, 2001, page 528
Library Journal, April 15, 2001, page 133
Publishers Weekly, June 4, 2001, page 59

Other books by the same author:
The Queen's Bastard, 1999
The Secret Diary of Anne Boleyn, 1997

Other books you might like:
Fiona Buckley, *To Shield the Queen*, 1997
Joanna Dessau, *The Red-Haired Brat*, 1978
Susan Kay, *Legacy*, 1986
Rosalind Miles, *I, Elizabeth*, 1994
Jean Plaidy, *Queen of This Realm*, 1984

942

LISE MCCLENDON

One O'Clock Jump

(New York: St. Martin's Press, 2001)

Story type: Mystery; Historical/Depression Era
Series: Dorie Lennox
Subject(s): Mystery and Detective Stories
Major character(s): Dorie Lennox, Detective—Private; Amos Haddam, Detective—Private, Veteran (World War I)
Time period(s): 1930s (1939)
Locale(s): Kansas City, Missouri

Summary: McClendon launches a new historical mystery series featuring PI Dorie Lennox in 1939 Kansas City. Hired to follow a meatpacker's girlfriend, Dorie witnesses her target jump to her death into the Missouri River. During her investi-

gation of the woman's suicide, Dorie stumbles into a tangle of deception and mixed motives, and the trail leads to her own boss, Amos Haddan, a troubled veteran of World War I. Dorie is a refreshing sleuth, and the novel offers a convincing portrait of the region and era, just before America's entry into World War II.

Where it's reviewed:
Booklist, January 2001, page 925
Library Journal, February 1, 2001, page 127
Publishers Weekly, February 12, 2001, page 187

Other books by the same author:
The Alix Thorssen Series, 1995-

Other books you might like:
Michael Chabon, *The Amazing Adventures of Kavalier & Clay*, 2001
John Dunning, *Two O'Clock, Eastern Wartime*, 2000
Fred Harris, *Easy Pickin's*, 2000
Stephen Hunter, *Hot Springs*, 2000
Annette Meyers, *Murder Me Now*, 2000

943

COLLEEN MCCULLOUGH

The Song of Troy

(London: Orion/Trafalgar, 2001)

Story type: Historical/Ancient Greece
Subject(s): War; Ancient History
Major character(s): Helen, Noblewoman; Achilles, Military Personnel (Greek military leader); Hektor, Military Personnel (Trojan military leader)
Time period(s): 12th century B.C.
Locale(s): Troy, Ancient Civilization

Summary: McCullough conjoins a number of classical sources, including Homer, Herodotus, and Sophocles, with a modern sensibility to retell the story of the Trojan War. Each chapter is told from the perspective of one of the famous principals, from Helen, whose lusts precipitate the combat, to the opposing leaders Achilles and Hektor, and others such as Odysseus and Klytemnestra. The multiple perspectives add depth and complexity of motive to the familiar story of passion and war.

Where it's reviewed:
Booklist, May 15, 2001, page 1708
Kirkus Reviews, May 15, 2001, page 704

Other books by the same author:
Morgan's Run, 2000
Fortune's Favorite, 1993
The First Man in Rome, 1990
The Ladies of Missalonghi, 1987
The Thorn Birds, 1977

Other books you might like:
John Erskine, *The Private Life of Helen of Troy*, 1925
Richard Matturro, *Troy*, 1989
Phillip Parotti, *The Greek Generals Talk*, 1986
Richard Powell, *Whom the Gods Would Destroy*, 1970

944

STEVE MCGIFFEN

Tennant's Rock

(New York: St. Martin's Press, 2001)

Story type: Historical/American West
Subject(s): Frontier and Pioneer Life
Major character(s): Sissy, Young Woman; Nate, Convict; Swann, Farmer
Time period(s): 1860s (post Civil War)
Locale(s): Sacramento Valley, California

Summary: This is a realistic look at frontier life in California following the Civil War. The story is narrated by Sissy, a young woman trying to survive after her father is killed by her brother, Nathan. Sissy and her mother nurse a wounded man, Swann, who repays their kindness by taking control of their farm and raping Sissy. Then Nathan returns from prison, but he is not the savior that Sissy has been waiting for, and ultimately she must rely on herself to get through the bleak times that seem to be her continual fate.

Where it's reviewed:
Booklist, April 15, 2001, page 1535
Kirkus Reviews, May 15, 2001, page 691

Other books you might like:
David Ballantine, *Chalk's Woman*, 2000
David Anthony Durham, *Gabriel's Story*, 2001
Brad Kessler, *Lick Creek*, 2001
Larry McMurtry, *Boone's Lick*, 2000
Alice Walker, *The Color Purple*, 1982

945

ANN MCMILLAN

Civil Blood

(New York: Viking, 2001)

Story type: Historical/American Civil War; Mystery
Series: Civil War Mystery. Number 3
Subject(s): Mystery and Detective Stories; Civil War; Diseases
Major character(s): Narcissa Powers, Nurse, Detective—Amateur; Judah Daniel, Healer (herbal), Slave (freed)
Time period(s): 1860s (1862)
Locale(s): Richmond, Virginia

Summary: In this installment of the author's Civil War era mystery series, a stolen officer's coat stuffed with money infected by smallpox is the stimulus for a dangerous quest by wartime nurse Narcissa Powers and her companion, former slave and herbal healer Judah Daniel. The bills could unleash an epidemic even more deadly to Richmond's population than the threatening Union troops. The pair try to find the items which have been stolen by one of Richmond's youth gangs, while a killer stalks anyone who has seen the coat. Their investigation takes them on a well-researched tour of wartime Richmond, full of twists and turns and not a few surprises.

Where it's reviewed:
Booklist, May 1, 2001, page 1637
Kirkus Reviews, April 15, 2001, page 546

Publishers Weekly, April 23, 2001, page 51

Other books by the same author:
Angel Trumpet, 1999
Dead March, 1998

Other books you might like:
Barbara Hambly, *The Benjamin January Series*, 1997-
Michael Kilian, *A Killing at Ball's Bluff*, 2001
Miriam Grace Monfredo, *Must the Maiden Die*, 1999
Anne Perry, *Slaves of Obsession*, 2000
Jim Walker, *Murder at Gettysburg*, 1999

946

EDIE MEIDAV

The Far Field

(Boston: Houghton Mifflin, 2001)

Story type: Historical/Exotic
Subject(s): Cultural Conflict; Buddhism
Major character(s): Henry Frye Gould, Settler; Nani, House-keeper
Time period(s): 1930s
Locale(s): Ceylon

Summary: Meidav's debut novel is a study of the colonial mentality, set in Ceylon during the 1930s. Henry Frye Gould leaves his wife and child in a spiritual search for an ideal community. A convert to Buddhism, Frye journeys to Ceylon to create a model Buddhist village. Aided by Nani, a beautiful housekeeper who becomes his lover, Frye makes initial progress in his scheme, but, inevitably, his plan goes awry and those he has trusted are revealed to be not who they appear. His eventual redemption comes from an unlikely source.

Where it's reviewed:
Kirkus Reviews, March 1, 2001, page 282
Publishers Weekly, February 12, 2001, page 182

Other books you might like:
Christopher Hudson, *Where the Rainbow Ends*, 1987
Barbara Kingsolver, *The Poisonwood Bible*, 1998
Peter Matthiessen, *At Play in the Fields of the Lord*, 1965
Karen Roberts, *The Flower Boy*, 2000
Shyam Selvadurai, *Cinnamon Gardens*, 1999

947

LISA MICHAELS

Grand Ambition

(New York: Norton, 2001)

Story type: Historical/Roaring Twenties; Historical/American West
Subject(s): Rivers; American West; Marriage
Major character(s): Bessie Hyde, Spouse (of Glen), Adventurer; Glen Hyde, Spouse (of Bessie), Adventurer
Time period(s): 1920s (1928)
Locale(s): Grand Canyon, Arizona; Colorado River, Arizona

Summary: This debut novel by Michaels is based on an actual historical event: the adventures of the first husband-and-wife team to take on the Colorado River and its dangerous rapids

through the Grand Canyon using a homemade scow. Their experiences test their endurance and resolve as the river takes its demanding toll on the couple. Michaels weaves a number of themes in this thoughtful adventure yarn that draws on its period to place the action in a believable, authentic context.

Where it's reviewed:
Booklist, April 15, 2001, page 1536
Kirkus Reviews, April 1, 2001, page 447
Publishers Weekly, June 11, 2001, page 58

Other books you might like:
James D. Houston, *Snow Mountain Passage*, 2001
Alison McLeay, *Passage Home*, 1990
Harold B. Meyers, *Reservations*, 1999
Peter Nichols, *Voyage to the North Star*, 1999
Diane Smith, *Letters from Yellowstone*, 1999

948

HAYDN MIDDLETON

Grimm's Last Fairytale

(New York: St. Martin's Press, 2001)

Story type: Historical/Fantasy
Subject(s): Biography; Fairy Tales; Writing
Major character(s): Jacob Grimm, Historical Figure, Writer; Wilhelm Grimm, Historical Figure, Writer
Time period(s): 19th century
Locale(s): Berlin, Germany; Hesse, Germany

Summary: This is a dense and multilayered novel that looks at the lives and times of the Brothers Grimm. In 1863, the last year of Jacob Grimm's life, he journeys from Berlin to his hometown of Hesse with his niece. Haunted by the death of his writing partner, Wilhelm, Jacob reflects on his past and manages a final, troubling rendition of the "Sleeping Beauty" fairy tale. The connections between the Grimms, their era, their creations, and the emergence of modern German history are intriguingly made in this inventive blend of biography and fantasy.

Where it's reviewed:
Booklist, March 15, 2001, page 1355
Kirkus Reviews, January 15, 2001, page 75
Publishers Weekly, January 22, 2001, page 301

Other books by the same author:
The Collapsing Castle, 1991
The Lie of the Land, 1989

Other books you might like:
Stephen Dobyns, *The Wrestler's Cruel Study*, 1993
Margaret Ann Hubbard, *Flight of the Swan*, 1946
J.D. Landis, *Longing*, 2000
Helga Ruebsamen, *The Song and the Truth*, 2000
Anthony Schmitz, *Darkest Desire*, 1998

Historical

949

FIDELIS MORGAN

Unnatural Fire

(New York: Morrow, 2001)

Story type: Historical/Seventeenth Century; Mystery
Series: Countess Ashby de la Zouche. Number 1
Subject(s): Mystery and Detective Stories
Major character(s): Lady Anastasia Ashby de la Zouche, Noblewoman (countess), Journalist; Alpiew, Servant
Time period(s): 17th century (1699)
Locale(s): London, England

Summary: Morgan launches a witty Restoration-era mystery featuring a down-at-the-heals former mistress of Charles II, Lady Ashby de la Zouche, and her former personal maid, Alpiew. To earn money, the pair join forces to write articles for a London scandal sheet and agree to follow a well-to-do merchant at the request of his suspicious wife. When they stumble on his murdered body one night in Covent Garden, the pair is launched on a rollicking investigation of complex villainy that makes full use of period details.

Where it's reviewed:
Publishers Weekly, February 26, 2001, page 63

Other books you might like:
Bruce Alexander, *The Color of Death*, 2000
Philippa Carr, *Daughters of England*, 1995
Ross King, *Ex-Libris*, 2001
Iain Pears, *An Instance of the Fingerpost*, 1998
Betsy Tobin, *Bone House*, 2000

950

JAN NEEDLE

The Wicked Trade

(Ithaca, New York: McBooks, 2001)

Story type: Historical/Georgian; Military
Series: William Bentley. Number 2
Subject(s): Sea Stories; Adventure and Adventurers
Major character(s): William Bentley, Military Personnel (British midshipman); Sam Holt, Military Personnel (British midshipman)
Time period(s): 1790s
Locale(s): London, England; *Biter*, At Sea

Summary: Needle continues his naval series involving midshipman William Bentley, who is posted aboard an impress ship, legally kidnapping seamen to fill the Royal Navy's warships during the conflict with France. The story continues the author's grimly realistic look at the age of sail as Bentley and his fellow midshipman Sam Holt are drawn into a far-reaching conspiracy while tackling the ''wicked trade'' of smuggling.

Where it's reviewed:
Publishers Weekly, March 19, 2001, page 77

Other books by the same author:
A Fine Boy for Killing, 2000

Other books you might like:
Alexander Kent, *The Richard Bolitho Series*, 1968-1986
Dewey Lambdin, *The Alan Lewrie Series*, 1989-
Patrick O'Brian, *The Aubrey-Maturin Series*, 1968-1999
Dudley Pope, *The Nicholas Ramage Series*, 1965-
Richard Woodman, *The Nathaniel Drinkwater Series*, 1984-

951

JAMES L. NELSON

The Blackbirder

(New York: Morrow, 2001)

Story type: Historical/Colonial America
Series: Brethren of the Coast Trilogy. Book 2
Subject(s): Sea Stories; Slavery; American Colonies
Major character(s): Thomas Marlowe, Pirate (former), Plantation Owner; King James, Slave (former)
Time period(s): 1700s (1702)
Locale(s): Williamsburg, Virginia, American Colonies; At Sea; Africa

Summary: In the second installment of Nelson's trilogy, former pirate Thomas Marlowe is struggling to live lawfully in Tidewater Virginia. Marlowe is dispatched to bring to justice his good friend King James, a freedman who has killed a slave ship's captain and has fled to Africa in the slave ship, the *Blackbirder*. In a series of high seas actions, Marlowe gives chase as far as West Africa and the slave port of Whydah. Not as accomplished nor as convincing as Patrick O'Brian's Aubrey/Maturin series, this is thinner historically with occasional anachronisms spoiling things, but Nelson can keep the action moving, and the era itself—colonial America and its sea history—makes for an engaging story.

Where it's reviewed:
Booklist, March 15, 2001, page 1355
Publishers Weekly, January 29, 2001, page 65

Other books by the same author:
The Guardship, 2000
Lords of the Ocean, 1999
The Continental Risque, 1998
The Maddest Idea, 1997
By Force of Arms, 1996

Other books you might like:
Ken Follett, *A Place Called Freedom*, 1995
Nicholas Griffin, *The Requiem Shark*, 2000
Gene Hackman, *The Wake of the Perdido Star*, 1999
   Daniel Lenihan, co-author
Thomas Hoover, *Caribbee*, 1985
Wilbur A. Smith, *Monsoon*, 1999

952

JAMYANG NORBU

Sherlock Holmes: The Missing Years

(New York: Bloomsbury, 2001)

Story type: Historical/Exotic; Mystery
Subject(s): Mystery and Detective Stories

Major character(s): Sherlock Holmes, Detective—Private; Huree Chunder Mookherjee, Scholar, Spy
Time period(s): 1890s (1891)
Locale(s): Tibet; India

Summary: After Sir Arthur Conan Doyle resurrected Holmes from his apparent death at the Reichenbach Falls in ''The Adventure of the Empty House,'' Holmes tells Watson that he has spent two years in Tibet. This inventive adaptation suggests what Holmes might have been up to during these missing years. Fleeing Moriarity's henchman, Holmes, accompanied by a Bengali scholar and spy, Huree Chunder Mookherjee, travels to Tibet where they meet the young Dalai Lama and must take on a Chinese-backed evil magician.

Where it's reviewed:
Booklist, December 1, 2000, page 697
Publishers Weekly, December 18, 2000, page 58

Other books you might like:
Laurie R. King, *The Mary Russell/Sherlock Holmes Series*, 1994-
Larry Millet, *The American Chronicles of John H. Watson, M.D.*, 1996-
Sena Jeter Naslund, *Sherlock in Love*, 1993
Roberta Rogow, *The Problem of the Spiteful Spiritualist*, 1999
Gerard Williams, *Dr. Mortimer and the Barking Man Mystery*, 2001

953

CHARLES O'BRIEN

Mute Witness
(Scottsdale, Arizona: Poisoned Pen, 2001)

Story type: Historical/Georgian; Mystery
Subject(s): Mystery and Detective Stories; Theater; Deafness
Major character(s): Anne Cartier, Actress, Teacher; Paul de Saint-Martin, Detective—Police
Time period(s): 1780s (1786)
Locale(s): London, England; Paris, France

Summary: This delightful debut historical mystery is set in Paris on the eve of the French Revolution. Young London actress Anne Cartier is called to Paris when her stepfather apparently murders his mistress and then takes his own life. Anne is not convinced and with the aid of Colonel Paul de Saint-Martin of the royal highway patrol, she employs skills developed from working as a teacher of the deaf. She faces the challenge of solving several murders, as well as discovering the identity of a jewel thief. The author, a former history professor, has converted considerable scholarship to craft a believable background for a convincing and entertaining mystery.

Where it's reviewed:
Booklist, May 1, 2001, page 1638
Publishers Weekly, April 30, 2000, page 60

Other books you might like:
Bruce Alexander, *The Color of Death*, 2000
Nicholas Griffin, *The House of Sight and Shadow*, 2000
Ross King, *Ex-Libris*, 2001
Anne Perry, *A Dish Taken Cold*, 2001

Elizabeth Redfern, *The Music of the Spheres*, 2001

954

BRUCE OLDS

Bucking the Tiger
(New York: Farrar, Straus & Giroux, 2001)

Story type: Historical/American West
Subject(s): Biography; Dentistry; American West
Major character(s): John Henry ''Doc'' Holliday, Gambler, Historical Figure; Wyatt Earp, Historical Figure, Lawman; Bat Masterson, Historical Figure, Lawman
Time period(s): 19th century
Locale(s): United States

Summary: Olds returns to his collage method presented in his debut novel about John Brown (*Raising Holy Hell*, 1995), weaving together poems, news accounts, song lyrics, photographs, and eyewitness testimony, to chronicle the life of western legend John Henry ''Doc'' Holliday. Diagnosed with fatal consumption, the Ivy League-educated dentist Holliday heads west to pursue a career as a gambler and gunman. Doc's path crosses those of such western icons as Billy the Kid, Wyatt Earp, and Bat Masterson, as well as the Clantons at the OK Corral. Olds provides a brilliant pastiche of voices and styles to capture the man and his era.

Where it's reviewed:
Kirkus Reviews, June 1, 2001, page 766

Other books by the same author:
Raising Holy Hell, 1995

Other books you might like:
Thomas Berger, *The Return of Little Big Man*, 1999
Jane Candia Coleman, *Doc Holliday's Woman*, 1995
Randy Lee Eickhoff, *The Fourth Horseman*, 1997
Paul West, *O.K.: The Corral, the Earps, and Doc Holliday*, 2000
Richard S. Wheeler, *Masterson*, 1999

955

ROBIN PAIGE (Pseudonym of William Albert and Susan Wittig Albert)

Death at Epsom Downs
(New York: Berkley Prime Crime, 2001)

Story type: Historical/Victorian; Mystery
Series: Victorian Mystery
Subject(s): Mystery and Detective Stories; Horse Racing
Major character(s): Lord Charles Sheridan, Nobleman, Photographer; Lady Kathryn ''Kate'' Ardleigh Sheridan, Noblewoman, Writer; Albert, Royalty (Prince of Wales), Historical Figure (later Edward VII)
Time period(s): 1890s (1899)
Locale(s): Epsom, England

Summary: It's Derby Day at Epsom Downs in this late Victorian era mystery involving high-born sleuths Lord Charles and Lady Kathryn Sheridan. When one of the thoroughbreds, Gladiator, goes berserk, killing his jockey and another horse, the Prince of Wales believes someone has

drugged Gladiator and asks Lord Charles to investigate. Meanwhile, Lady Kathryn learns that the famous actress Lillie Langtrey owes a fortune to a bookie who has been shot. It is up to the Sheridans to connect both cases.

Where it's reviewed:
Booklist, March 1, 2001, page 1231
Library Journal, February 1, 2001, page 127
Publishers Weekly, February 5, 2001, page 72

Other books by the same author:
Death at Whitechapel, 2000
Death at Rottingdean, 1999
Death at Daisy's Folly, 1997
Death at Gallows Green, 1995
Death at Bishop's Keep, 1994

Other books you might like:
William J. Palmer, *The Dons and Mr. Dickens*, 2000
Cynthia Peale, *Murder at Bertram's Bower*, 2001
Anne Perry, *The Thomas and Charlotte Pitt Series*, 1979-
Anne Perry, *The William Monk Series*, 1990-
Roberta Rogow, *The Problem of the Spiteful Spiritualist*, 1999

956

ROBERT B. PARKER

Gunman's Rhapsody

(New York: Putnam, 2001)

Story type: Historical/American West
Subject(s): American West; Frontier and Pioneer Life
Major character(s): Wyatt Earp, Historical Figure, Lawman; Josie Marcus, Historical Figure, Actress; Johnny Behan, Lawman
Time period(s): 1870s (1879)
Locale(s): Tombstone, Arizona

Summary: The author of the Spenser mystery series shifts locales from Boston to Tombstone for his first western, taking on the legendary Wyatt Earp and the infamous gunfight at the OK Corral. The Earp brothers abandon Dodge City for opportunities in Tombstone, where Wyatt falls for actress Josie Marcus who is attached to his lawman rival, Johnny Behan. Behan's animosity toward Wyatt provides the motive for the Clantons' ire, leading to the famous shootout. Parker breathes new life in the well-worked event, and his Spenser admirers will not be disappointed by the change of venue and era.

Where it's reviewed:
Booklist, March 15, 2001, page 1333
Kirkus Reviews, April 1, 2001, page 449
Publishers Weekly, May 14, 2001, page 51

Other books by the same author:
Paper Doll, 1993
Double Deuce, 1992
Pastime, 1991
Valediction, 1984
The Widening Gyre, 1983

Other books you might like:
Randy Lee Eickhoff, *The Fourth Horseman*, 1997
Loren D. Estleman, *Bloody Season*, 1988

Bruce Olds, *Bucking the Tiger*, 2001
Leslie Scott, *Tombstone Showdown*, 1957
Paul West, *O.K.: The Corral, the Earps, and Doc Holliday*, 2000

957

CYNTHIA PEALE (Pseudonym of Nancy Zaroulis)

Murder at Bertram's Bower

(New York: Doubleday, 2001)

Story type: Mystery; Historical/Victorian America
Series: Beacon Hill Mystery. Number 2
Subject(s): Mystery and Detective Stories; Brothers and Sisters
Major character(s): Addington Ames, Detective—Amateur; Caroline Ames, Detective—Amateur; Agatha Montgomery, Gentlewoman
Time period(s): 1890s (1892)
Locale(s): Boston, Massachusetts

Summary: Brother and sister sleuths Addington and Caroline Ames return for their second case in Peale's historical mystery series set in Victorian Boston. Panic strikes when it is feared that London's Jack the Ripper may have moved west after a young former prostitute is found slashed to death in an alley. The victim worked as a secretary at Bertram's Bower, a refuge for wayward women, run by Caroline's childhood friend, Agatha Montgomery. When another girl from the Bower is killed in the same manner, the Ameses take up the case. The mystery competes with the atmosphere here as the brother and sister team is launched across 1890s Boston from Beacon Hill to the gritty immigrant neighborhood of the South End.

Where it's reviewed:
Booklist, February 15, 2001, page 1120
Kirkus Reviews, January 15, 2001, page 84
Library Journal, March 1, 2001, page 133
Publishers Weekly, January 15, 2001, page 56

Other books by the same author:
The Death of Colonel Mann, 2000

Other books you might like:
Caleb Carr, *The Alienist*, 1994
Dianne Day, *Beacon Street Mourning*, 2000
Andrew M. Greeley, *Irish Lace*, 1996
Anne Perry, *The Thomas and Charlotte Pitt Series*, 1979-
Anne Perry, *The William Monk Series*, 1990-

958

WILDER PERKINS

Hoare and the Matter of Treason

(New York: St. Martin's Minotaur, 2001)

Story type: Historical/Napoleonic Wars; Mystery
Series: Captain Bartholomew Hoare
Subject(s): Mystery and Detective Stories; Espionage
Major character(s): Bartholomew Hoare, Military Personnel (British naval officer), Handicapped (crushed larynx); Eleanor Graves, Widow(er)

Time period(s): 1800s
Locale(s): Weymouth, England; London, England

Summary: Unfortunately, due to the death of the author, this is the last of Perkins' clever mysteries set during the reign of George III. Bartholomew Hoare commands the *Royal Duke*, a floating spy center whose crew includes an unorthodox mix of talented undercover operatives. Shortly after his marriage to the widow Eleanor Graves, Hoare is called to London to locate and retrieve stolen Admiralty papers. This is the beginning of an investigation uncovering treason that could bring down the government and a kidnapping of his new bride and adopted daughter. Perkins' accomplished period touches include appearances by both the historical Jane Austen and the fictional Horatio Hornblower.

Where it's reviewed:
Kirkus Reviews, February 1, 2001, page 147
Publishers Weekly, January 29, 2001, page 68

Other books by the same author:
Hoare and the Headless Captains, 2000
Hoare and the Portsmouth Atrocities, 1998

Other books you might like:
Bruce Alexander, *The Sir John Fielding Series*, 1994-
Stephanie Barron, *The Jane Austen Series*, 1996-
Allan Mallinson, *A Close Run Thing*, 1999
Patrick O'Brian, *The Aubrey-Maturin Series*, 1968-1999
Kate Ross, *The Julian Kestrel Series*, 1993-1997

959

ANNE PERRY

A Dish Taken Cold

(New York: Carroll & Graf, 2001)

Story type: Historical/French Revolution
Subject(s): Revolution; Revenge
Major character(s): Madame Anne-Louise-Germaine de Stael, Historical Figure, Noblewoman; Celie, Widow(er), Servant; Amandine, Young Woman
Time period(s): 1790s (1792)
Locale(s): Paris, France

Summary: Perry leaves the familiar English Victorian territory of her two detective series for a novella-length tale of vengeance set in revolutionary France. Celie is a young widowed servant in the employ of the historical figure Madame de Stael. Her baby son dies in his crib when Amandine, the woman to whom Celie entrusts him, leaves the child unattended while she slips out to meet her lover. Celie mounts a campaign of revenge that quickly escalates beyond anything she could have anticipated into treason charges as the Prussian army marches on Paris and the Reign of Terror takes its bloody toll.

Where it's reviewed:
Publishers Weekly, January 1, 2001, page 71

Other books by the same author:
The Whitechapel Conspiracy, 2001
Slaves of Obsession, 2000
The Twisted Root, 1999
A Breach of Promise, 1998

The Silent Cry, 1997

Other books you might like:
Susanne Alleyn, *A Far Better Rest*, 2000
Michele De Kretser, *The Rose Grower*, 2000
Alan Jolis, *Love and Terror*, 1998
Tanith Lee, *The Gods Are Thirsty*, 1996
Marge Piercy, *City of Darkness, City of Light*, 1996

960

ANNE PERRY

The Whitechapel Conspiracy

(New York: Ballantine, 2001)

Story type: Historical/Victorian; Mystery
Series: Thomas and Charlotte Pitt
Subject(s): Mystery and Detective Stories; Crime and Criminals
Major character(s): Thomas Pitt, Police Officer (inspector), Spouse (of Charlotte); Charlotte Pitt, Socialite, Spouse (of Thomas)
Time period(s): 1890s (1892)
Locale(s): London, England

Summary: When revenge over a murder conviction costs Inspector Thomas Pitt his command of the Bow Street station, he is forced to take up undercover work in the slums of Spitalfield pursuing anarchists. While Pitt's wife, Charlotte, attempts to restore her husband's good name, she uncovers a conspiracy at the highest reaches of power in Victorian England. Connected to the main event is a delightfully intriguing subplot in which the author offers her own original take on the Jack the Ripper case. Perry is very much back in form in this installment of her popular historical mystery series.

Where it's reviewed:
Booklist, October 15, 2000, page 390
Library Journal, February 1, 2001, page 128
Publishers Weekly, November 6, 2000, page 73

Other books by the same author:
A Dish Taken Cold, 2001
Half Moon Street, 2000
Slaves of Obsession, 2000
Bedford Square, 1999
The Twisted Root, 1999

Other books you might like:
Peter Ackroyd, *The Trial of Elizabeth Cree*, 1995
Laurie R. King, *The Mary Russell/Sherlock Holmes Series*, 1994-
Gillian Linscott, *The Nell Bray Series*, 1991-
William J. Palmer, *The Dons and Mr. Dickens*, 2000
Cynthia Peale, *Murder at Bertram's Bower*, 2001

961

ELIZABETH PETERS (Pseudonym of Barbara Mertz)

Lord of the Silent

(New York: Morrow, 2001)

Story type: Historical/World War I; Mystery
Series: Amelia Peabody. Number 13

Historical

Subject(s): Mystery and Detective Stories; Egyptian Antiquities; Archaeology
Major character(s): Amelia Peabody Emerson, Detective—Amateur, Archaeologist; Ramses Emerson, Archaeologist; Nefret Forth, Doctor, Spouse (of Ramses)
Time period(s): 1910s (1915)
Locale(s): Luxor, Egypt; Cairo, Egypt

Summary: It is 1915 and a new excavating season for the intrepid archaeologist-sleuth Amelia Peabody, who journeys to Egypt with her husband; their son, Ramses; and his new wife, Nefret. Amelia's main concern is to prevent the British War Office from recruiting Ramses for another dangerous spy mission. Tomb robbers in Luxor provide an excuse to get Ramses and Nefret out of harm's way but actually puts them in the midst of murder that escalates like the war that grips Northern Africa. Fans of the author's mystery series will be delighted by this installment, while new recruits will be captivated by the period details and a winning cast.

Where it's reviewed:
Booklist, March 1, 2001, page 1188
New York Times Book Review, June 10, 2001, page 28
Publishers Weekly, April 23, 2001, page 52

Other books by the same author:
He Shall Thunder in the Sky, 2000
The Falcon at the Portal, 1999
The Snake, the Crocodile, and the Dog, 1992
The Last Camel Died at Noon, 1991
The Mummy Case, 1985

Other books you might like:
Olivia Manning, *The Danger Tree*, 1977
Glenn Meade, *The Sands of Sakkara*, 1999
Michael Pearce, *The Mamur Zapt Series*, 1988-
Robert Sole, *The Photographer's Wife*, 1999
David Stevens, *The Waters of Babylon*, 2000

962

MAX PHILLIPS

The Artist's Wife

(New York: Holt, 2001)

Story type: Arts
Subject(s): Autobiography; Music and Musicians; Artists and Art
Major character(s): Alma Schindler, Historical Figure, Spouse (of Gustav Mahler); Gustav Mahler, Historical Figure, Composer; Franz Werfel, Historical Figure, Writer
Time period(s): 19th century; 20th century
Locale(s): Vienna, Austria; United States

Summary: The remarkable life and times of Alma Schindler, the daughter of a Viennese painter who becomes connected with some of the most famous artists of the 20th century, is chronicled here in a first-person memoir, narrated by Alma from the grave. She tells the story of her love for the painter Gustav Klimt, her marriage to composer/conductor Gustav Mahler, and subsequent relationships with architect Walter Gropius, painter Oskar Kokoschka, and writer Franz Werfel. A muse to all, Alma's enigmatic appeal is captured here, as well as a believable reconstruction of her era, including pre-

war Vienna, Germany during the Bauhaus Movement, Hitler's rise to power, and the expatriate Hollywood community.

Where it's reviewed:
Booklist, April 15, 2001, page 1452
Kirkus Reviews, May 1, 2001, page 615
Publishers Weekly, June 4, 2001, page 55

Other books by the same author:
Snakebite Sonnet, 1996

Other books you might like:
Susanne Keegan, *The Bride of the Wind*, 1991
J.D. Landis, *Longing*, 2000
Barbara Mujica, *Frida*, 2001

963

DAVID POYER

Fire on the Waters

(New York: Simon & Schuster, 2001)

Story type: Historical/American Civil War
Subject(s): War; Civil War; Sea Stories
Major character(s): Elisha Baker, Military Personnel; Captain Trezevant, Military Personnel; Lieutenant Claiborne, Military Personnel
Time period(s): 1860s (1861)
Locale(s): *Owanee*, At Sea

Summary: Civil War events that take place at sea have not received a fraction of the coverage given land battles by historical novelists, and Poyer fills the gap with this rousing nautical adventure set aboard the Navy sloop *Owanee* when war is declared. It's an occasion for divided loyalties for the ship's captain and executive officer. When Captain Trezevant leaves the ship for the Confederacy, Lieutenant Claiborne takes command, with young Elisha Baker as his gunnery officer.

Where it's reviewed:
Kirkus Reviews, April 15, 2001, page 533

Other books by the same author:
China Sea, 2000
Thunder on the Mountain, 1999
Tomahawk, 1998
As the Wolf Loves Winter, 1996
Down to a Sunless Sea, 1996

Other books you might like:
Robert S. MacDonald, *The Catherine*, 1982
F. Van Wyck Mason, *Proud New Flags*, 1951
Louise Meriwether, *Fragments of the Ark*, 1994
Christopher Nicole, *Iron Ships, Iron Men*, 1989
Willard M. Wallace, *The Raiders*, 1970

964

RICHARD RAYNER

The Cloud Sketcher

(New York: HarperCollins, 2000)

Story type: Historical/Roaring Twenties
Subject(s): Real Estate; Murder; Construction

Major character(s): Esko Vaananen, Architect, Immigrant; Katerina Malysheva, Immigrant; Andrew MacCormick, Businessman
Time period(s): 20th century (1901-1920s)
Locale(s): New York, New York; Finland

Summary: Ranging from the Arctic Circle in the early years of the 20th century through the Finnish Civil War and New York City during the Roaring Twenties, this is an impressive tale about Finnish architect Esko Vaananen who, inspired by the first elevator in his native country, aspires to build a ''cloud sketcher'' or skyscraper. His ambitions are connected by his hopeless love for the unattainable daughter of a Russian aristocrat, Katerina Malysheva. Coming to New York City, Esko works as a riveter on skyscrapers before realizing his architectural dreams. Katerina is also in New York, engaged to blueblood businessman Andrew MacCormick. After MacCormick is murdered, Esko is charged with the crime, and he is forced to resort to his underworld connections for assistance. Rayner provides a vivid introduction to Finnish culture and history, as well as an evocative look at Jazz Age New York in the midst of its real estate boom.

Where it's reviewed:
Booklist, November 15, 2000, page 588
Kirkus Reviews, November 15, 2000, page 1567
Library Journal, December 2000, page 192
Publishers Weekly, December 4, 2000, page 51

Other books by the same author:
Murder Book, 1997
The Blue Suit, 1995
The Elephant, 1992

Other books you might like:
Kevin Baker, *Dreamland*, 1999
Richard E. Crabbe, *Suspension*, 2000
E.L. Doctorow, *Billy Bathgate*, 1989
Amram Ducovny, *Coney*, 2000
Andrei Makine, *Confessions of a Fallen Standard Bearer*, 2000

965

JAMES REASONER

Battle Lines

(New York: Forge, 2001)

Story type: Historical/World War II
Subject(s): War; World War II; Military Life
Major character(s): Joe Parker, Writer, Military Personnel; Dale Parker, Mechanic, Military Personnel; Adam Bergman, Military Personnel
Time period(s): 1940s (1941)
Locale(s): United States

Summary: The author of the Civil War Battle Series fires the first salvo in a proposed series on World War II, introducing a number of characters, including brothers Joe and Dale Parker and their Jewish friend, Adam Bergman, who enlist largely because of Dale's affair with the wife of a powerful Chicago banker. Once in uniform, the stage is set for the wartime action of future volumes.

Where it's reviewed:
Booklist, May 15, 2001, page 1733

Other books by the same author:
Vicksburg, 2001
Antietam, 2000
Chancellorsville, 2000
Manassas, 1999
Shiloh, 1999

Other books you might like:
Ronald Florence, *The Last Season*, 2000
David L. Robbins, *The End of War*, 2000
Judith Saxton, *You Are My Sunshine*, 2000
Miranda Seymour, *The Summer of '39*, 1999
Herman Wouk, *The Winds of War*, 1971

966

JAMES REASONER

Vicksburg

(Nashville: Cumberland House, 2001)

Story type: Historical/American Civil War; Family Saga
Series: Civil War Battle. Book 5
Subject(s): Military Life; Civil War; Family Relations
Major character(s): Cory Brannon, Military Personnel (Confederate soldier); Lucille Farrell, Young Woman
Time period(s): 1860s (1862-1863)
Locale(s): Vicksburg, Mississippi

Summary: Reasoner's Civil War Battle series links historical events to the fictional Brannon family of Culpepper County, Virginia. The setting here is the pivotal siege of Vicksburg that will determine control of the Mississippi and possibly the outcome of the war. Cory Brannon is involved in the dangerous job of trying to keep Vicksburg supplied with food and arms by breaching the Union blockade. Cory's love, Lucille Farrell, is also one of Vicksburg's defenders, and the novel weaves the pair's fictional exploits around historical events and figures.

Where it's reviewed:
Publishers Weekly, April 2, 2001, page 41

Other books by the same author:
Battle Lines, 2001
Antietam, 2000
Chancellorsville, 2000
Manassas, 1999
Shiloh, 1999

Other books you might like:
Allen B. Ballard, *Where I'm Bound*, 2000
Thomas Fleming, *When This Cruel War Is Over*, 2001
John Jakes, *On Secret Service*, 2000
C.X. Moreau, *Promise of Glory*, 2000
Gerry Morrison, *Unvexed to the Sea*, 1961

967

ELIZABETH REDFERN

The Music of the Spheres

(New York: Putnam, 2001)

Story type: Historical/Georgian
Subject(s): Espionage; Astronomy
Major character(s): Jonathan Absey, Government Official (Home Office clerk); Alexander Wilmot, Homosexual
Time period(s): 1790s (1795)
Locale(s): London, England

Summary: This densely constructed historical thriller is set in 1795 in London when fears of invasion by the armies of Revolutionary France are rampant. Home Office clerk Jonathan Absey is given the task of rooting out French spies, who may be smuggling military information. He also must deal with the recent murder of his 18-year-old daughter and his quest to catch her killer. Absey recruits the help of Alexander Wilmot, his homosexual half brother, whose connections with a group of amateur astronomers lead to a complex conspiracy and a rich collection of vividly presented characters. Redfern takes her time to get things right, and the reader with patience will appreciate her efforts.

Where it's reviewed:
Booklist, May 1, 2001, page 1595
Kirkus Reviews, May 15, 2001, page 694
Publishers Weekly, May 28, 2001, page 45

Other books you might like:
Nicholas Griffin, *The House of Sight and Shadow*, 2000
Ross King, *Ex-Libris*, 2001
Matthew G. Kneale, *English Passengers*, 2000
Iain Pears, *An Instance of the Fingerpost*, 1998
Wilder Perkins, *Hoare and the Matter of Treason*, 2001

968

FREDERIC RICHAUD

Gardener to the King

(New York: Arcade, 2001)

Story type: Historical/Seventeenth Century
Subject(s): Kings, Queens, Rulers, etc.; Gardens and Gardening
Major character(s): Jean-Baptiste de La Quintinie, Gardener; Louis XIV, Royalty (King of France), Historical Figure
Time period(s): 17th century (1670s)
Locale(s): Versailles, France

Summary: The court world of the Sun King, Louis XIV, at Versailles is depicted from the perspective of the king's Steward of the Orchards and Kitchen Gardens, Jean-Baptiste de La Quintinie. Absorbed by his professional responsibilities, La Quintinie gradually grows disillusioned with Louis' arrogance and self-indulgence and the luxurious waste of his court. La Quintinie's essential natural rhythms derived from his gardens are contrasted with the artificial superficialities of the more glittering, shallow entourage surrounding the crown.

Where it's reviewed:
Kirkus Reviews, March 15, 2001, page 357

Other books you might like:
Louis Auchincloss, *The Cat and the King*, 1981
Mildred Allen Butler, *Ward of the Sun King*, 1970
Francoise d'Aubigne Chandernagor, *The King's Way*, 1984
Sylvia Pell, *The Shadow of the Sun*, 1978
Judith Merkle Riley, *The Oracle Glass*, 1994

969

ANDREA RITTER

Sunflower of the Third Reich

(Philadelphia: Xlibris, 2001)

Story type: Historical/World War II
Subject(s): War; Family Relations; Nazis
Major character(s): Heinz Stettner, Military Personnel (SS officer); Luise Stettner, Spouse (of Heinz); Marianne Stettner, Young Woman (daughter of Heinz and Luise)
Time period(s): 1940s (1943-1945)
Locale(s): Germany

Summary: World War II is told from the German perspective in this family chronicle of the Stettners, ordinary German citizens during the war. Heinz is a loyal SS officer fighting on the Russian front; his wife, Luise, struggles to protect her children at all costs. One daughter, Marianne, is selected to bear children for the Third Reich, and another, the rebellious Lilli has a romance with a Polish prisoner in one of the German labor camps, a dangerous affair that could imperil the entire family. The period details are convincing, and the perspective provides a refreshing look at the war.

Other books you might like:
Sheldon Greene, *Burnt Umber*, 2001
Gunnar Kopperud, *The Time of Light*, 2000
Helga Ruebsamen, *The Song and the Truth*, 2000
Paullina Simons, *The Bronze Horseman*, 2001
John Wray, *The Right Hand of Sleep*, 2001

970

MANUEL RIVAS

The Carpenter's Pencil

(Woodstock, New York: Overlook, 2001)

Story type: Psychological
Subject(s): Civil War/Spanish; Political Prisoners
Major character(s): Dr. Daniel Da Barca, Political Prisoner; Herbal, Guard (prison); Marisa Mallo, Young Woman
Time period(s): 1930s
Locale(s): Spain

Summary: Set during the Spanish Civil War, this is the story of Dr. Daniel Da Barca, a Republican captive in Franco's prison, whose fate is linked with that of the Falangist guard, Herbal, and of an unnamed painter who brings them together. The other significant character is Marisa Mallo, loved by both Da Barca and Herbal. Complex and demanding in its narrative shifts, the novel makes a powerful atmospheric presentation of the dehumanizing force of war and the essential human connections among opposites.

Where it's reviewed:
Library Journal, March 15, 2001, page 106
Publishers Weekly, May 14, 2001, page 54

Other books by the same author:
Butterfly, 2000

Other books you might like:
Camilo Jose Cela, *Mazurka for Two Dead Men*, 1992
Michel Del Castillo, *Child of Our Time*, 1958
Miguel Delibes, *The Stuff of Heroes*, 1990
Stephen Frances, *La Guerra: A Spanish Saga*, 1970
Bruce Palmer, *They Shall Not Pass*, 1971

971

CANDACE M. ROBB

A Trust Betrayed

(New York: Mysterious, 2001)

Story type: Mystery; Historical/Medieval
Series: Margaret Kerr
Subject(s): Mystery and Detective Stories; Middle Ages
Major character(s): Dame Margaret Kerr, Detective—Amateur, Spouse (of Roger); Roger Sinclair, Spouse (of Margaret), Businessman (merchant); Jack Sinclair, Young Man
Time period(s): 13th century (1297)
Locale(s): Edinburgh, Scotland; Perth, Scotland

Summary: Veteran historical mystery writer Robb initiates a new mystery series set in 13th century Scotland during the Wars of Independence against the English. When Margaret Kerr's husband, Roger, a merchant, goes missing and his cousin, Jack, who searches for him, turns up dead, Margaret sets out herself from Perth to Edinburgh to investigate. In a brilliantly re-created period Edinburgh, Margaret is plunged into a tangle of political intrigue that draws on the history of the era. This is an accomplished series debut that leaves a number of potential threads to follow in subsequent volumes.

Where it's reviewed:
Booklist, March 15, 2001, page 1359
Kirkus Reviews, February 15, 2001, page 220
Publishers Weekly, April 9, 2001, page 53

Other books by the same author:
The Owen Archer Series, 1993-

Other books you might like:
Alys Clare, *Ashes of the Elements*, 2001
P.C. Doherty, *The Demon Archer*, 2001
Margaret Frazer, *The Squire's Tale*, 2000
Edward Marston, *The Wildcats of Exeter*, 2001
Kate Sedley, *The Brothers of Glastonbury*, 2001

972

LYNDA S. ROBINSON

Slayer of Gods

(New York: Mysterious, 2001)

Story type: Historical/Ancient Egypt; Mystery
Series: Lord Meren. Number 6

Subject(s): Mystery and Detective Stories; Egyptian Religion
Major character(s): Lord Meren, Nobleman, Government Official
Time period(s): 14th century B.C.
Locale(s): Egypt

Summary: The historical circumstances surrounding the death of Queen Nefertiti drives this installment of the author's impressive historical mystery series involving Lord Meren, the counselor of the boy pharaoh, Tutankhamun. Lord Meren becomes convinced that the queen died not from the plague but from poison, and sets out to solve the crime in a dangerous investigation that will risk both his life and the lives of his family. The author provides enough essential information allowing readers new to the series to find their way through the novel's various relationships.

Where it's reviewed:
Kirkus Reviews, April 1, 2001, page 465
Publishers Weekly, April 1, 2001, page 137

Other books by the same author:
Drinker of Blood, 1998
Eater of Souls, 1997
Murder at the Feast of Rejoicing, 1996
Murder at the God's Gate, 1995
Murder at the Place of Anubis, 1994

Other books you might like:
Anna Apostolou, *A Murder in Thebes*, 1998
P.C. Doherty, *The Anubis Slayings*, 2001
Pauline Gedge, *The Horus Road*, 2001
Lauren Haney, *A Vile Justice*, 1999
Lee Levin, *King Tut's Private Eye*, 1996

973

HARRIET ROCHLIN

On Her Way Home

(Santa Barbara, California: Daniel & Daniel, 2001)

Story type: Historical/American West
Series: Desert Dwellers Trilogy. Book 3
Subject(s): Jews; American West; Sisters
Major character(s): Frieda Goldson, Young Woman; Ida Goldson, Teenager
Time period(s): 1880s
Locale(s): Arizona

Summary: This tale of the relationship between two sisters provides an interesting Jewish perspective on the American West. Set in the Arizona frontier in the 1880s, the story involves the challenges faced by Frieda Goldson when her sister, Ida, disappears on a trip through the desert only to return pregnant by the murderer of her companions. Frieda comes to her sister's defense while learning a lesson about family and forgiveness.

Where it's reviewed:
Booklist, March 1, 2001, page 1229

Other books by the same author:
The First Lady of Dos Cacahuates, 1998
The Reformer's Apprentice, 1996

Historical

Other books you might like:
David Anthony Durham, *Gabriel's Story*, 2001
Louise Erdrich, *The Last Report on the Miracles at Little No Horse*, 2001
Jane Kirkpatrick, *No Eye Can See*, 2001
Aaron Latham, *Code of the West*, 2001
Richard S. Wheeler, *The Fields of Eden*, 2001

974

HOZY ROSSI

Appointment with Il Duce

(New York: Welcome Rain, 2001)

Story type: Coming-of-Age
Subject(s): Music and Musicians; Dentistry
Major character(s): Beppe Arpino, Musician (cellist), Dentist
Time period(s): 1930s
Locale(s): Naples, Italy; Rome, Italy

Summary: This is a quirky version of Italy under Mussolini as dramatized through the career of Beppe Arpino, an impoverished boy from an isolated southern Italian town. He first achieves some acclaim for his musical talent as a cellist but eventually turns to dentistry. Under the tutelage of an eccentric doctor with a theory of holistic health, Beppe is convinced to bring his theory to the attention of Il Duce and becomes part of the new Fascist regime. This look at the era is alternately charming and maddening in its occasional descent into silliness.

Where it's reviewed:
Booklist, April 1, 2001, page 1454
Publishers Weekly, May 21, 2001, page 81

Other books you might like:
Giorgio Bassani, *The Garden of the Finzi-Continis*, 1965
Alan Gelb, *Mussolini*, 1985
Elsa Morante, *History*, 1977
Alberto Moravia, *1934*, 1983
Ignazio Silone, *Bread and Wine*, 1937

975

LAURA JOH ROWLAND

Black Lotus

(New York: St. Martin's Minotaur, 2001)

Story type: Mystery; Historical/Seventeenth Century
Series: Sano Ichiro. Number 6
Subject(s): Mystery and Detective Stories; Religious Communes; Samurai
Major character(s): Sano Ichiro, Detective—Police, Warrior (samurai); Reiko, Spouse (of Ichiro)
Time period(s): 17th century (1693)
Locale(s): Edo, Japan

Summary: The secrets that lurk inside a Buddhist temple and its secret cult following are the subjects for this installment of Rowland's highly-acclaimed mystery series set in Shogun-era Japan. What seems to be a clear-cut case of murder and arson by a teenage girl at the Black Lotus temple proves far more complicated for samurai detective Sano Ichiro and his wife,

Reiko. At the center of their investigation is the Buddhist sect that has generated great animosity, as well as sympathy among those in power at the shogun's court, and Sano must try to restrain his wife while preserving protocol in this well-represented view of life and customs in medieval Japan.

Where it's reviewed:
Booklist, January 2001, page 926
Kirkus Reviews, January 15, 2001, page 84
Library Journal, March 1, 2001, page 133
Publishers Weekly, January 29, 2001, page 68

Other books by the same author:
The Samurai's Wife, 2000
The Samurai's Wife, 2000
The Concubine's Tattoo, 1998
The Way of the Traitor, 1997
Bundori, 1996
Shinju, 1994

Other books you might like:
Dale Furutani, *Kill the Shogun*, 2000
Lucia St. Clair Robson, *The Tokaido Road*, 1991
Edward Tolosko, *Sakuran*, 1978
Ann Woodward, *The Exile Way*, 1996
Eiji Yoshikawa, *Musashi*, 1981

976

JEAN-CHRISTOPHE RUFIN

The Siege of Isfahan

(New York: Norton, 2001)

Story type: Historical/Exotic; Action/Adventure
Subject(s): Medicine
Major character(s): Jean-Baptiste Poncet, Apothecary; Juremi, Captive
Time period(s): 18th century
Locale(s): Russia; Isfahan, Persia; Afghanistan

Summary: Rufin's engaging sequel to the Prix Goncourt-winning *The Abyssinian* presents the further adventures of the 18th century French apothecary Jean-Baptiste Poncet in a series of exotic challenges. First he must escape from Isfahan, capital of Persia, to rescue his friend Juremi, who is imprisoned in Russia. Then they must deal with being sold as slaves in Afghanistan before getting back to rescue Poncet's wife and daughter in Isfahan, under siege by an Afghan army. This is colorful, fast-paced adventure in the Alexandre Dumas and Rafael Sabatini tradition that will appeal to readers of historical fiction who enjoy derring-do in a richly imagined past world.

Where it's reviewed:
Booklist, March 15, 2001, page 1355
Kirkus Reviews, March 15, 2001, page 365
New York Times Book Review, April 1, 2001, page 16
Publishers Weekly, February 12, 2001, page 186

Other books by the same author:
The Abyssinian, 1999

Other books you might like:
Madeleine Brent, *Stormswift*, 1985
Dorothy Dunnett, *Gemini*, 2000

George MacDonald Fraser, *Flashman*, 1969
Alan Scholfield, *The Hammer of God*, 1973
Mason McCann Smith, *When the Emperor Dies*, 1981

977

JAMES RUNCIE

The Discovery of Chocolate

(New York: HarperCollins, 2001)

Story type: Historical/Fantasy
Subject(s): Time Travel; Food
Major character(s): Diego de Godoy, Adventurer; Ignacia, Young Woman
Time period(s): Multiple Time Periods (16th-20th centuries)
Locale(s): Mexico; Europe; Spain

Summary: This inventive fantasy told in a series of vignettes spans four centuries with chocolate at the center of its action. Diego de Godoy leaves Spain in 1518 with Cortes for the conquest of Mexico. As a guest of Montezuma, he meets and falls in love with Ignacia who introduces him to *cacahuatl*, or chocolate. When the Spanish defeat Montezuma, Ignacia serves Diego a drink that makes him immortal, and he travels through the centuries, introducing chocolate to Europe, sharing chocolate creams with the Marquis de Sade, inventing the Sacher torte while getting analyzed by Sigmund Freud, and helping the Hershey Company develop the Kiss. This is a delightful fantasy for any historical novel reader with a sweet tooth and a taste for history delivered with a comic slant.

Where it's reviewed:
Booklist, February 15, 2001, page 1117
Kirkus Reviews, December 15, 2000, page 1714
Publishers Weekly, January 8, 2001, page 48

Other books you might like:
Timothy Findley, *Pilgrim*, 1999
Enid Futterman, *Bittersweet Journey*, 1998
Joanne Harris, *Chocolat*, 1999
Eduardo Squiglia, *Fordlandia*, 2000
Virginia Woolf, *Orlando*, 1928

978

ELENA SANTANGELO

Hang My Head and Cry

(New York: St. Martin's Minotaur, 2001)

Story type: Historical/Post-American Civil War; Mystery
Series: Pat Montella. Book 2
Subject(s): Mystery and Detective Stories; Time Travel; Psychic Powers
Major character(s): Pat Montella, Detective—Amateur, Psychic; Emancipation Jackson, Slave (former), Child
Time period(s): 2000s; 1870s
Locale(s): Virginia

Summary: The second volume in the author's paranormal mystery series featuring ghost detective Pat Montella takes place on a Civil War-era estate in Virginia. When a long-dead body is unearthed on the property, Pat's unique ability to go back in time allows her to see the 1870s and the conflict of

Reconstruction from the perspective of a 10-year-old former slave named Emancipation Jackson. Past events and present occurrences are woven together in this inventive mystery.

Where it's reviewed:
Kirkus Reviews, February 15, 2001, page 221
Publishers Weekly, February 5, 2001, page 70

Other books by the same author:
By Blood Possessed, 1999

Other books you might like:
Barbara Hambly, *Die upon a Kiss*, 2001
Michael Kilian, *A Killing at Ball's Bluff*, 2001
Ann McMillan, *Civil Blood*, 2001
Miriam Grace Monfredo, *Sisters of Cain*, 2000
Jim Walker, *Murder at Gettysburg*, 1999

979

MARY LEE SETTLE

I, Roger Williams

(New York: Norton, 2001)

Story type: Historical/Colonial America; Historical/Seventeenth Century
Subject(s): Autobiography; Puritans; Religious Conflict
Major character(s): Roger Williams, Historical Figure, Religious; Sir Edward Coke, Historical Figure, Judge
Time period(s): 17th century
Locale(s): London, England; Providence, Rhode Island, American Colonies; Salem, Massachusetts, American Colonies

Summary: Accomplished historical novelist Settle provides an autobiographical account of the important American colonial figure and advocate of religious and personal freedom, Roger Williams. Narrated at the end of his life, Williams chronicles his years in Jacobean London as clerk to the celebrated jurist Sir Edward Coke, court intrigue, and persecution. Fleeing to New England, Williams resists Puritan conformity and is banished by his fellow colonists, enduring years of exile among the Narragansett Indians before the founding of Providence, Rhode Island, dedicated to tolerance and freedom of conscience. This is an impressive impersonation of a remarkable American original.

Where it's reviewed:
New York Times Book Review, April 22, 2001, page 16

Other books by the same author:
Addie, 1998
Celebration, 1986
The Killing Ground, 1982
Blood Tie, 1977
Know Nothing, 1960

Other books you might like:
Barbara Dodge Borland, *The Great Hunger*, 1963
Marcy Moran Heidish, *Witnesses*, 1980
Gilbert Rees, *I Seek a City*, 1950
William Greenough Schofield, *Ashes in the Wilderness*, 1942

Historical

980

JEFF SHAARA

Rise to Rebellion

(New York: Ballantine, 2001)

Story type: Historical/American Revolution
Subject(s): American Colonies; Revolutionary War; War
Major character(s): Benjamin Franklin, Historical Figure, Political Figure; John Adams, Historical Figure, Political Figure; Thomas Gage, Historical Figure, Military Personnel (British general)
Time period(s): 1770s (1770-1776)
Locale(s): American Colonies

Summary: Shaara's books provide convincing recreations of crucial moments and individuals in American history. *Rise to Rebellion* chronicles the years from the opening conflicts of the Boston Massacre in 1770 through the signing of the Declaration of Independence in 1776. The major events in between—the Boston Tea Party; the first two Continental Congresses; Paul Revere's ride; the battles of Lexington, Concord, Bunker Hill, and Fort Ticonderoga—are covered from the perspective of their participants. The primary characters are Benjamin Franklin, John Adams, British general Thomas Gage, and colonial governor of Massachusetts Thomas Hutchinson, but portraits of such figures as Thomas Paine, John Hancock, and Thomas Jefferson are included as well. The result is alternatively diffusely expository and intimate in its portraiture, and fans of American history and the Shaaras' previous work will look forward to the continuation of the story.

Where it's reviewed:
Booklist, March 1, 2001, page 1188
Kirkus Reviews, April 15, 2001, page 535
Library Journal, March 15, 2001, page 106
Publishers Weekly, May 21, 2001, page 78

Other books by the same author:
Gone for Soldiers, 2000
The Last Full Measure, 1998
Gods and Generals, 1996

Other books you might like:
Thomas Fleming, *Dreams of Glory*, 2000
John Ensor Harr, *Dark Eagle*, 1999
Paul Lussier, *Last Refuge of Scoundrels*, 2001
William Martin, *Citizen Washington*, 1999
William Safire, *Scandalmonger*, 2000

981

PAULLINA SIMONS

The Bronze Horseman

(New York: Morrow, 2001)

Story type: Historical/World War II
Subject(s): War; Sisters; Russians
Major character(s): Tatiana Metanov, Worker (factory); Dasha Metanov, Young Woman; Alexander Belov, Military Personnel (Russian officer)
Time period(s): 1940s (1941)

Locale(s): Leningrad, Union of Soviet Socialist Republics

Summary: Set during the Nazi seige of Leningrad, this emotionally charged novel chronicles the travails of two sisters—Tatiana and Dasha Metanov—and their love for a Red Army officer, Alexander Belov. Courting Dasha, Alexander falls in love with Tatiana, and the couple comes together despite the deadly deprivations of the seige and Alexander's dangerous secret that threatens to explode. Despite over-idealized central characters and a tendency toward melodramatic excesses, this is a page-turner that works the historical details into a gripping story of love during wartime.

Where it's reviewed:
Kirkus Reviews, April 1, 2001, page 451
Publishers Weekly, May 28, 2001, page 48

Other books by the same author:
Eleven Hours, 1998
Red Leaves, 1996
Tully, 1994

Other books you might like:
Vassily Aksyonov, *Generations of Winter*, 1994
Gunnar Kopperud, *The Time of Light*, 2000
Andrei Makine, *Confessions of a Fallen Standard Bearer*, 2000
David L. Robbins, *War of the Rats*, 1999
Paul Watkins, *The Forger*, 2000

982

WILBUR A. SMITH

Warlock

(New York: St. Martin's Press, 2001)

Story type: Historical/Ancient Egypt; Action/Adventure
Subject(s): Ancient History
Major character(s): Nefer Memnon, Royalty (prince); Taita, Sorcerer; Naja, Ruler (pharaoh)
Time period(s): Indeterminate Past
Locale(s): Egypt

Summary: Smith brings back the sorcerer, Taita, who appeared in *River God* and *The Seventh Scroll*, for another turn in his epic action treatment of ancient Egypt. The legitimate rulers have been killed and the heir, Nefer Memnon, is being pursued by the false pharaoh, Lord Naja. To keep Nefer alive becomes the charge of Taita, who must outwit assassins and evil magicians, while raising an army for a final battle to decide the throne. Action lovers will relish Smith's fast-paced and vivid narrative, but this is not for the squeamish: blood flows freely here.

Where it's reviewed:
Booklist, March 1, 2001, page 1189
Kirkus Reviews, March 15, 2001, page 365
Library Journal, April 15, 2001, page 134
Publishers Weekly, April 9, 2001, page 49

Other books by the same author:
Monsoon, 1999
Birds of Prey, 1997
The Seventh Scroll, 1995
River God, 1994

The Burning Shore, 1985

Other books you might like:
Pauline Gedge, *The Horus Road*, 2001
Jacquetta Hawkes, *King of the Two Lands*, 1966
Christian Jacq, *Paneb the Ardent*, 2001
Naguib Mahfouz, *Akhenaten: Dweller in Truth*, 2000
Norman Mailer, *Ancient Evenings*, 1983

983

ROSEMARY STEVENS

The Tainted Snuff Box

(New York: Berkeley Prime Crime, 2001)

Story type: Historical/Regency; Mystery
Series: Beau Brummell. Number 2
Subject(s): Mystery and Detective Stories
Major character(s): George Bryan "Beau" Brummell, Historical Figure, Socialite; George, Prince of Wales, Royalty (later George IV), Historical Figure; Chakkri, Animal (Siamese cat)
Time period(s): 1800s (1805)
Locale(s): London, England; Brighton, England

Summary: In this Regency era mystery featuring Beau Brummell as sleuth, the Prince of Wales has retreated to Brighton after receiving threatening letters. Then the prince's food taster samples snuff from a nobleman's snuff box and is poisoned so the prince asks Brummell to find out who is responsible. Brummell's assistant is his pet, Chakkri, "the only Siamese cat in England." The author shows her expertise in the era in this intriguing mystery that features a colorful historical cast of characters.

Where it's reviewed:
Publishers Weekly, April 16, 2001, page 47

Other books by the same author:
Death on a Silver Tray, 2000
Lord and Master, 1997
Miss Pymbroke's Rules, 1997
A Crime of Manners, 1996

Other books you might like:
Bruce Alexander, *The Sir John Fielding Series*, 1994-
Stephanie Barron, *The Jane Austen Series*, 1996-
Molly Brown, *Invitation to a Funeral*, 1995
Richard Falkirk, *The Blackstone Series*, 1972-1974
Kate Ross, *The Julian Kestrel Series*, 1993-1997

984

JULIAN STOCKWIN

Kydd

(New York: Scribner, 2001)

Story type: Action/Adventure; Historical/Georgian
Subject(s): Sea Stories; War
Major character(s): Tom Kydd, Military Personnel (British sailor), Worker (wig maker); Nicholas Renzi, Military Personnel (British sailor)
Time period(s): 1790s (1793)
Locale(s): *Duke William*, At Sea

Summary: The author, a retired lieutenant commander in the British Navy, launches a new nautical series set during the age of sail. Stockwin's perspective, however, is not from the captain's quarter but the quarter-deck, following the progress of Thomas Kydd, a 20-year-old wig maker, who is impressed into service in 1793. Kydd is a landlubber, who must endure a sadistic boatswain, a shipwreck, a mutinous crew, and naval engagements against the French. His mentor is the mysterious Nicholas Renzi, whose full story will surely be featured in future installments. Negative comparisons with Patrick O'Brian notwithstanding, this is a strong debut with a fresh slant on a well-worked subject and era.

Where it's reviewed:
Booklist, April 1, 2001, page 1454
Kirkus Reviews, April 15, 2001, page 535
Publishers Weekly, June 4, 2001, page 59

Other books you might like:
Alexander Kent, *The Richard Bolitho Series*, 1968-1986
Dewey Lambdin, *The Alan Lewrie Series*, 1989-
Jan Needle, *The Wicked Trade*, 2001
Patrick O'Brian, *The Aubrey-Maturin Series*, 1968-1999
Dudley Pope, *The Nicholas Ramage Series*, 1965-

985

SARAH STONICH

These Granite Islands

(Boston: Little, Brown, 2001)

Story type: Historical/Americana
Subject(s): Depression (Economic); Lovers
Major character(s): Isobel Howard, Artisan (hat maker); Cathryn Malley, Heiress; Jack Reese, Ranger (forest)
Time period(s): 1930s (1936)
Locale(s): Cypress, Minnesota

Summary: Set in 1930s Minnesota during the Great Depression, this brooding story of love and betrayal concerns Isobel Howard, a hat maker living in the mining town of Cypress and her friendship with flamboyant Cathryn Malley. Both are unhappily married, and the two become close friends. Isobel helps cover for Cathryn in her affair with forest ranger Jack Reese, and when the couple disappear after a fire, Isobel broods for years trying to decipher what became of her friend until on her deathbed the truth is revealed at last.

Where it's reviewed:
Kirkus Reviews, December 15, 2000, page 1716
Publishers Weekly, January 8, 2001, page 45

Other books you might like:
Carrie Brown, *The Hatbox Baby*, 2000
Sandra Dallas, *Alice's Tulips*, 2000
Jeff Hutton, *Perfect Silence*, 2000
Alex Miller, *Conditions of Faith*, 2000
Christina Schwarz, *Drowning Ruth*, 2000

Historical

986

LALITA TADEMY

Cane River

(New York: Warner, 2001)

Story type: Family Saga; Historical/American Civil War
Subject(s): Civil War; American South; African Americans
Major character(s): Suzette, Slave; Philomene Daurat, Slave; Emily Fredieu, Slave
Time period(s): 19th century; 20th century (1830s-1930s)
Locale(s): Cane River, Louisiana

Summary: Based on the author's own ancestors, this family saga chronicles over 100 years in the lives of five generations of an African-American family living along the Cane River in Louisiana. Beginning in 1834, the house slave Suzette is forced to become the mistress of a French planter. Her daughter, Philomene, in turn becomes the mistress of a Creole planter, and her daughter, Emily, born a slave in 1861, struggles through Reconstruction. Written from a variety of perspectives, the novel offers a gripping, first-hand look at the impact of slavery and racial identity on a community through a significant portion of American history.

Where it's reviewed:
Booklist, February 15, 2001, page 1086
Kirkus Reviews, February 15, 2001, page 211
Publishers Weekly, March 12, 2001, page 62

Other books you might like:
Rilla Askew, *Fire in Beulah*, 2001
Edward Ball, *Slaves in the Family*, 1998
David Anthony Durham, *Gabriel's Story*, 2001
William Heffernan, *Beulah Hill*, 2001
Josephine Humphreys, *Nowhere Else on Earth*, 2000

987

EMMA TENNANT

Sylvia and Ted

(New York: Holt/Macrae, 2001)

Story type: Literary
Subject(s): Biography; Poetry; Marriage
Major character(s): Sylvia Plath, Historical Figure, Writer (poet); Ted Hughes, Historical Figure, Writer (poet); Assia Wevill, Lover (Ted's), Historical Figure
Time period(s): 1950s; 1960s
Locale(s): England

Summary: The passionate and troubled marriage of two poets—Sylvia Plath and Ted Hughes—is dramatized beginning with their first meeting and initially happy life together that turns bitter. One of the primary factors in the famous couple's estrangement was Hughes' mistress, Assia Wevill. Both Plath and Wevill eventually commit suicide, and the destructive triangle of three complex and talented individuals is chronicled from each of the participant's perspectives.

Where it's reviewed:
Booklist, March 15, 2001, page 1348
Library Journal, April 15, 2001, page 134
Publishers Weekly, April 16, 2001, page 43

Other books by the same author:
Burnt Diaries, 1999
Strangers: A Family Romance, 1999
Hooked Rugs, 1995
Pemberley, 1995
An Unequal Marriage, 1994

Other books you might like:
Jane Alison, *The Love-Artist*, 2001
Federico Andahazi, *The Merciful Women*, 2000
Catherine Clement, *Martin and Hannah*, 2001
J.D. Landis, *Longing*, 2000
Barbara Mujica, *Frida*, 2001

988

BODIE THOENE
BROCK THOENE, Co-Author

Jerusalem's Heart

(New York: Viking, 2001)

Story type: Military; Multicultural
Series: Zion Legacy. Book 3
Subject(s): War; Jews; Arab-Israeli Wars
Major character(s): Jacob Kalner, Military Personnel (Israeli soldier); Lori Kalner, Nurse; David Mayer, Military Personnel (Israeli), Pilot
Time period(s): 1940s (1948)
Locale(s): Jerusalem, Palestine

Summary: In the third installment of the Thoenes' chronicle of the birth of the modern state of Israel, bitter hand-to-hand combat is waged for control of Jerusalem as a beleaguered band of Jewish fighters are besieged by the Arabs and a desperate relief attempt is mounted using an ancient Roman road that might circumvent the Muslim forces. Characters from the previous volumes, including Jacob and Lori Kalner, are featured, as well as the airborne heroism of Israeli pilot David Mayer. This is a highly partisan view, and the authors' anti-Muslim bias distorts an otherwise fast-paced and well-researched drama.

Where it's reviewed:
Booklist, February 15, 2001, page 1086
Publishers Weekly, March 12, 2001, page 63

Other books by the same author:
All Rivers to the Sea, 2000
Thunder from Jerusalem, 2000
Jerusalem Vigil, 2000
In My Father's House, 1992
The Zion Covenant Series, 1986-1988

Other books you might like:
Jesse L. Lasky, *The Offer*, 1981
    Pat Silver, co-author
Meyer Levin, *The Harvest*, 1978
Leon Uris, *Exodus*, 1958
Morris L. West, *The Tower of Babel*, 1968
Herman Wouk, *The Hope*, 1993

989

BETSY TOBIN

Bone House

(New York: Scribner, 2000)

Story type: Historical/Seventeenth Century; Mystery
Subject(s): Mystery and Detective Stories; Country Life
Major character(s): Unnamed Character, Narrator, Servant (chambermaid); Dora, Prostitute, Crime Victim
Time period(s): 17th century
Locale(s): England

Summary: Set in rural England during the 17th century, this is a dark, brooding novel of suspense animated by the death of the local village prostitute, Dora. An unnamed chambermaid, who is determined to uncover the truth behind Dora's death, narrates the story and discovers the woman's complicated secret life. Her investigation affords a fascinating glimpse into ordinary affairs and beliefs during the period. Tobin expertly weaves her evident research into an exceptional exercise in re-animating the past.

Where it's reviewed:
Kirkus Reviews, December 15, 2000, page 1717
New York Times Book Review, February 25, 2001, page 30
Publishers Weekly, December 4, 2000, page 50

Other books you might like:
Tracy Chevalier, *Girl with a Pearl Earring*, 1999
Sheri Holman, *The Dress Lodger*, 2000
Ross King, *Ex-Libris*, 2001
David Liss, *A Conspiracy of Paper*, 2000
Iain Pears, *An Instance of the Fingerpost*, 1998

990

H.N. TURTELTAUB (Pseudonym of Harry Turtledove)

Over the Wine-Dark Sea

(New York: Forge, 2001)

Story type: Historical/Ancient Greece
Subject(s): Ancient History
Major character(s): Menedemos, Trader; Sostratos, Trader
Time period(s): 4th century B.C. (310 B.C.)
Locale(s): Rhodes, Greece; Asia Minor; Rome, Italy

Summary: Writing under the pseudonym H.N. Turteltaub, historical-fantasist Turtledove lays aside alternate history for a well-researched exploration of ancient Greece, circa 310 B.C. Cousins Menedemos and Sostratos set out on a trading journey from their native Rhodes to Asia Minor and to an obscure barbarian town in Italy, known as Rome. Their adventures provide the excuse for the author to document the customs, values, and beliefs of the Hellenistic world.

Where it's reviewed:
Kirkus Reviews, April 15, 2001, page 541
Library Journal, May 15, 2001, page 162

Other books by the same author:
Justinian, 1998
The Guns of the South, 1992

Other books you might like:
Gillian Bradshaw, *The Sand-Reckoner*, 2000
P.C. Doherty, *The House of Death*, 2001
Karen Essex, *Kleopatra*, 2001
Michael Curtis Ford, *The Ten Thousand*, 2001
Steven Pressfield, *Tides of War*, 2000

991

H.M. VAN DEN BRINK

On the Water

(New York: Grove, 2001)

Story type: Historical/World War II
Subject(s): Sports
Major character(s): Anton, Teenager; David, Teenager
Time period(s): 1930s; 1940s
Locale(s): Amsterdam, Netherlands

Summary: This is a sensitive story of a relationship forged in the teamwork of rowing and framed by the experiences of World War II. Anton is a teenager from a working-class Amsterdam family, who is paired with the self-assured and affluent David in the summer of 1939. Their relationship on the river as they perfect their rowing skills is juxtaposed with Anton's later recollections of events prior to Amsterdam's liberation by the Allies.

Where it's reviewed:
Kirkus Reviews, May 1, 2001, page 621
Publishers Weekly, April 2, 2001, page 40

Other books you might like:
Tessa De Loo, *The Twins*, 2000
Nomi Eve, *The Family Orchard*, 2000
Arthur Japin, *The Two Hearts of Kwasi Boachi*, 2000
Ella Leffland, *Breath and Shadows*, 1999
Helga Ruebsamen, *The Song and the Truth*, 2000

992

KATE WALBERT

Gardens of Kyoto

(New York: Scribner, 2001)

Story type: Historical/World War II; Historical/Korean War
Subject(s): War; Love
Major character(s): Ellen, Narrator, Young Woman; Randall, Military Personnel, Cousin (Ellen's); Henry, Military Personnel
Time period(s): 1940s; 1950s
Locale(s): Philadelphia, Pennsylvania

Summary: Award-winning short story writer Walbert's debut novel looks at relationships under wartime pressure. Ellen narrates the story of her passionate attachment to her cousin, Randall, that is tragically ended by his death during World War II. When his father sends her Randall's diary and a book called *The Gardens of Kyoto*, Ellen tries to reassemble the pieces of Randall's life and its connections to her own. As World War II gives way to the Korean War, Ellen falls in love again with a young soldier, Henry, who like her is actually in love with another.

Historical

Where it's reviewed:
New York Times Book Review, April 8, 2001, page 15
Publishers Weekly, March 12, 2001, page 60

Other books by the same author:
Where She Went, 1998

Other books you might like:
Alice Adams, *After the War*, 2000
Rona Jaffe, *The Road Taken*, 2000
Sharon Rolens, *Worthy's Town*, 2000
Christina Schwarz, *Drowning Ruth*, 2000
Judith H. Wall, *My Mother's Daughter*, 2000

993

PAUL WEST

A Fifth of November

(New York: New Directions, 2001)

Story type: Historical/Seventeenth Century
Subject(s): Religious Conflict; Catholicism; Conspiracies
Major character(s): Henry Garnet, Religious (Catholic priest); Anne Vaux, Noblewoman; Guy Fawkes, Historical Figure, Revolutionary
Time period(s): 17th century (1605)
Locale(s): England

Summary: West's novel is a remarkable recreation of the events and personalities surrounding the Gunpowder Plot of 1605, in which a group of Catholic conspirators led by Guy Fawkes attempted to blow up Parliament, King James I, and his chief ministers. Events are seen through the tortured conscience of Jesuit priest Henry Garnet, who is hidden in the secret recesses of Catholic noblewoman Anne Vaux's home. When the conspiracy is launched and foiled, the perspective widens to offer portraits of Guy Fawkes, Sir Robert Cecil, and Sir Edward Coke. This is a demanding but rewarding effort in historical animation.

Where it's reviewed:
Kirkus Reviews, May 1, 2001, page 622
Publishers Weekly, May 14, 2001, page 53

Other books by the same author:
Dry Danube, 2000
OK, 2000
Life with Swan, 1999
The Tent of Orange Mist, 1995
Lord Byron's Doctor, 1989

Other books you might like:
Robert Hugh Benson, *Come Rack! Come Rope!*, 1912
Patricia Finney, *Firedrake's Eye*, 1992
George P. Garrett, *The Succession*, 1983
Kate Kirby, *Scapegoat for a Stuart*, 1976
Jane Oliver, *Mine Is the Kingdom*, 1937

994

RICHARD S. WHEELER

The Fields of Eden

(New York: Forge, 2001)

Story type: Historical/American West; Historical/American West Coast
Subject(s): Pioneers; American West; Frontier and Pioneer Life
Major character(s): John McLoughlin, Businessman (head agent, Hudson Bay Co.); Garwood Reese, Political Figure; Jasper Constable, Religious (missionary)
Time period(s): 1840s
Locale(s): Oregon

Summary: Western master Wheeler dramatizes the struggle to possess the Oregon Territory in the 1840s by looking at the experiences of a large cast of individuals. The characters in the book include John McLoughlin, the head agent for the British Hudson Bay Company, who tries to halt American incursion; Garwood Reese, who hopes to drive out the British and become Oregon's first governor; Jasper Constable, a Methodist missionary; and a number of other pioneers who must contend with the harsh realities of frontier life.

Where it's reviewed:
Kirkus Reviews, April 1, 2001, page 458
Publishers Weekly, May 17, 2001, page 223

Other books by the same author:
Aftershocks, 1999
Masterson, 1999
Buffalo Commons, 1998
Second Lives, 1997
Dodging Red Cloud, 1989

Other books you might like:
Don Berry, *To Build a Ship*, 1963
James D. Houston, *Snow Mountain Passage*, 2001
Christian McCord, *Across the Shining Mountains*, 1986
Larry McMurtry, *Boone's Lick*, 2000
Dana Fuller Ross, *Oregon!*, 1980

995

JACK WHYTE

Uther

(New York: Forge, 2001)

Story type: Legend; Historical/Fantasy
Series: Camulod Chronicles. Book 7
Subject(s): Arthurian Legend; Dark Ages
Major character(s): Uther Pendragon, Ruler (King of Cambria); Caius Merlyn Britannicus, Sorcerer, Warrior; Ygraine, Bride (arranged marriage)
Time period(s): 5th century
Locale(s): England

Summary: Whyte continues his realistic retelling of the Arthurian legend with the story of Arthur's father and mother, Uther Pendragon and Ygraine of Ireland. When his father dies, Uther becomes King of Cambria, while his cousin Caius Merlyn Britannicus rules Camulod. Uther must battle King

Lot of Cornwall, who comes between Uther and his arranged bride, Ygraine. Whyte's version of the familiar legend is an intriguing reanimation that stresses the grim and violent basis for the often etherealized fantasy.

Where it's reviewed:
Publishers Weekly, March 19, 2001, page 78

Other books by the same author:
The Fort at River's Bend, 1999
The Sorcerer: Metamorphosis, 1999
The Saxon Shore, 1998
The Singing Sword, 1996
The Eagles' Brood, 1994

Other books you might like:
Catherine Christian, *The Pendragon*, 1979
Bernard Cornwell, *The Warlord Chronicles*, 1996-1998
John Gloag, *Artorius Rex*, 1977
Parke Godwin, *Firelord*, 1980
Joan Wolf, *The Road to Avalon*, 1988

996

GERARD WILLIAMS

Dr. Mortimer and the Barking Man Mystery

(New York: Carroll & Graf, 2001)

Story type: Historical/Victorian; Mystery
Series: Dr. James Mortimer
Subject(s): Mystery and Detective Stories
Major character(s): James Mortimer, Doctor, Spouse (of Violet); Violet Branscombe, Doctor, Spouse (of James); Iris Starr, Prostitute
Time period(s): 1890s (1891)
Locale(s): London, England

Summary: In yet another working on the fringe of the Sherlock Holmes canon, Sir Henry Baskerville's physician, James Mortimer, from Arthur Conan Doyle's *The Hound of the Baskervilles* is put into service as a sleuth in this late-Victorian mystery series. With his wife, Dr. Violet Branscombe, as his partner, Mortimer, at the urging of fallen woman Iris Starr, who once saved Violet's life, investigates the murder of a Russian general in a Soho brothel. Iris' sweetheart, a revolutionary agitator, who has been trailing the Russian is the obvious suspect, but Mortimer and Branscombe uncover more sinister suspects. The characterization here is not as strong as the late-Victorian atmosphere.

Where it's reviewed:
Kirkus Reviews, March 1, 2001, page 299

Other books by the same author:
Dr. Mortimer and the Aldgate Mystery, 2000

Other books you might like:
Peter Ackroyd, *The Trial of Elizabeth Cree*, 1995
Laurie R. King, *The Mary Russell/Sherlock Holmes Series*, 1994-
Gillian Linscott, *The Nell Bray Series*, 1991-
Anne Perry, *The Whitechapel Conspiracy*, 2001
M.J. Trow, *The Inspector Lestrade Series*, 1999-

997

JANE ROBERTS WOOD

Grace

(New York: Dutton, 2001)

Story type: Historical/World War II
Subject(s): Small Town Life; World War II
Major character(s): Grace Gillian, Teacher (high school); John Appleby, Widow(er); Dan Manning, Military Personnel
Time period(s): 1940s (1944)
Locale(s): Cold Springs, Texas

Summary: Small town life in east Texas during World War II is the subject in this story dramatizing the loves of Grace Gillian, the resident beauty of Cold Springs, Texas, whose husband has inexplicably left her. Her admirers include the widower John Appleby, a student in her English class and his father, and soldier Dan Manning, who vows to return for Grace by war's end. Around Grace's emotional life is woven a look at the personal cost of the war and the era's sexism, racism, and classism.

Where it's reviewed:
Booklist, April 15, 2001, page 1538
Kirkus Reviews, March 15, 2001, page 361
Publishers Weekly, March 19, 2001, page 75

Other books by the same author:
Dance a Little Longer, 1993
A Place Called Sweet Shrub, 1990
The Train to Estelline, 1987

Other books you might like:
Alice Adams, *After the War*, 2000
Rona Jaffe, *The Road Taken*, 2000
Sharon Rolens, *Worthy's Town*, 2000
Christina Schwarz, *Drowning Ruth*, 2000
Judith H. Wall, *My Mother's Daughter*, 2000

998

RICHARD WOODMAN

The Privateersman

(New York: Severn House, 2001)

Story type: Historical/American Revolution; Action/Adventure
Series: William Kite. Number 2
Subject(s): Sea Stories
Major character(s): William Kite, Widow(er), Sailor; Sarah Tyrrell, Widow(er)
Time period(s): 1770s
Locale(s): England; West Indies; Rhode Island, American Colonies

Summary: This second installment of Woodman's series on 17th century English sailor William Kite is set during the opening of the American Revolution. Kite is now a widower, betrayed by his trading partners, and off on a voyage to the West Indies and then to Rhode Island amidst growing tension between the crown and the colonies. Pursuing an old friend's widow after her husband is lynched as a Tory, Kite sets out to avenge himself on the rebels who have destroyed his ship.

Historical

Fans of nautical adventure will not be disappointed, and historical novel fans will be refreshed to see the colonists in the villain roles.

Where it's reviewed:
Booklist, February 15, 2001, page 1118

Other books by the same author:
Endangered Species, 2000
The Guineaman, 2000
The Darkening Sea, 2000
Wager, 1999
The Nathaniel Drinkwater Series, 1984-

Other books you might like:
Dewey Lambdin, *The Alan Lewrie Series*, 1989-
Jan Needle, *The Wicked Trade*, 2001
James L. Nelson, *The Blackbirder*, 2001
Dudley Pope, *The Nicholas Ramage Series*, 1965-
Julian Stockwin, *Kydd*, 2001

999

JOHN WRAY

The Right Hand of Sleep

(New York: Knopf, 2001)

Story type: Historical/World War I; Historical/World War II
Subject(s): War; Nazis
Major character(s): Oskar Voxlauer, Military Personnel (Austrian soldier), Veteran (World War I); Kurt Bauer, Military Personnel (Nazi soldier); Else Bauer, Young Woman
Time period(s): 20th century
Locale(s): Niessen, Austria

Summary: The continuity between the two world wars of the 20th century is the theme in this assured first novel that concerns Oskar Voxlauer, who leaves his family to join the Austrian army in 1917. His experiences lead to his desertion and exile in the Ukraine. In 1938 he returns home to Niessen as Hitler's war machine gathers steam. Oskar falls in love with a gamekeeper's daughter, Else Bauer, and his rival is Else's more-than-cousin, Kurt, who is the head of the Nazis in Niessen. This taut triangle escalates into violence as history pushes Oskar to take a stand.

Where it's reviewed:
Kirkus Reviews, March 1, 2001, page 289
Library Journal, February 1, 2001, page 126
New York Times Book Review, May 20, 2001, page 34
Publishers Weekly, March 5, 2001, page 61

Other books you might like:
Joanne Harris, *Five Quarters of the Orange*, 2001
Gunnar Kopperud, *The Time of Light*, 2000
Pierre Magnan, *The Murdered House*, 2000
Andrea Ritter, *The Flower of the Third Reich*, 2001
Thomas Sanchez, *Day of the Bees*, 2000

1000

PATRICIA WYNN

The Birth of Blue Satan

(Austin, Texas: Pemberley, 2001)

Story type: Historical/Georgian; Mystery
Subject(s): Mystery and Detective Stories
Major character(s): Gideon Viscount St. Mars, Nobleman, Highwayman; Isabella Mayfield, Young Woman; Hester Kean, Servant
Time period(s): 1710s (1715)
Locale(s): England

Summary: Romance writer Wynn attempts an historical mystery set in Georgian England in the first of a projected series involving young nobleman Gideon Viscount St. Mars. In this novel, Gideon is forced into disguise as the highwayman Blue Satan to save himself from a murder charge and a conspiracy that has ruined his family. Gideon is in love with Isabella Mayfield, who remains tantalizingly beyond his reach, but he gains the assistance of Hester Kean, serving woman of his intended. It's a bit over the top, but good fun the same.

Other books by the same author:
Capturing Annie, 2000
A Pair of Rogues, 1997
A Country Affair, 1996
The Christmas Spirit, 1996
The Bumblebroth, 1995

Other books you might like:
Bruce Alexander, *The Sir John Fielding Series*, 1994-
Helen Ashfield, *The Loving Highwayman*, 1983
Stephanie Barron, *The Jane Austen Series*, 1996-
Geraldine Burrows, *Miss Sedgewick and the Spy*, 2000
Wilder Perkins, *The Captain Bartholomew Hoare Series*, 1998-2001

1001

GELING YAN

The Lost Daughter of Happiness

(New York: Hyperion, 2001)

Story type: Historical/American West
Subject(s): Chinese; Prostitution
Major character(s): Fusang, Prostitute; Da Yong, Criminal; Chris, Businessman
Time period(s): 1870s
Locale(s): San Francisco, California

Summary: Set in San Francisco during the 1870s, the novel tells the story of Fusang, who is kidnapped from her Chinese village and sold as a prostitute in America. Her experiences chronicle the lot of Chinese immigrants, including slave auctions, mob riots, and violent attacks by whites. Through it all, Fusang's remarkable serenity saves her and attracts the attention of both the Chinese gangster Da Yong and Chris, a Caucasian boy who worships her. Fusang is based on a historical figure who remains shadowy and enigmatic, despite the author's skill in evoking her era.

Where it's reviewed:
Library Journal, February 15, 2001, page 203
Publishers Weekly, March 5, 2001, page 62

Other books you might like:
June Wyndham Davies, *Golden Destiny*, 1993

Maxine Hong Kingston, *Tripmaster Monkey*, 1989
Ruthanne Lum McCunn, *Thousand Pieces of Gold*, 1981
Fae Myenne Ng, *Bone*, 1994
Linda Ching Sledge, *A Map of Paradise*, 1997

Inspirational Fiction in Review
by
Melissa Hudak

Many types of genre fiction are known for their willingness to change, evolving to better reflect the times in which we live and better meet the needs of readers. For example, mystery fiction moved from straightforward puzzles in the Agatha Christie tradition to deeply involved character studies. Romances now run the gamut from the squeaky clean to racy, and include every possible option in-between. Inspirational fiction has not changed or evolved, nor has it given its readers much of an option in terms of content. A reader picking up an inspirational fiction title published in 1980 will find largely the same material in a book published in 2001. That content adheres to very strict guidelines of what is and is not allowable by the publishers, presumably in response to their readers' demands.

One very blatant example of this unwillingness to evolve has been the depiction of African Americans in inspirational fiction. For many years, the few African American characters that appeared in inspirational fiction books were relegated to supporting characters, such as the friend of the white lead or the devoted slave in Civil War era historical novels. Over the past two years, however, this situation is slowly changing, due in large part to the success of such African American authors as Sharon Ewell Foster and Angela Benson. Both women enjoyed well-deserved attention for their recent titles, Foster's *Passing by Samaria* and Benson's *Awakening Mercy*.

In addition, a new publishing imprint has appeared to give even more voice to African American writers of inspirational fiction. A prominent agent, Denise Stinson, aware of the lack of presence of African American authors and characters in the genre started her own publishing imprint. Walk Worthy Press, distributed by Warner Books, debuted in 2000 with the title *Temptation* by Victoria Christopher Murray. In many ways, the set-up of the plot line of *Temptation* mirrors the more conventional story lines used by the traditional Christian presses like Tyndale House or Multnomah Books. The book focuses on Kyla and Jefferson Blake and

their wonderful marriage, which is threatened by Kyla's friend, Jasmine. Jasmine thinks that since Jefferson is such a great husband, he'll be a great man for her as well. Wonderful marriages are common in inspirational fiction titles and threats to those marriages do occasionally appear. However, the sexual talk, innuendo, and action that appear in *Temptation* as Jasmine goes after Jefferson are things rarely, if ever, seen in the genre prior to this book's publication.

Walk Worthy Press followed *Temptation* with a novel called *Singsation*, by Jacquelin Thomas. While *Singsation*, the story of a young girl named Deborah Anne Peterson and her rise to musical stardom, has less sexual content than *Temptation*, it is still not a typical entry in the Christian fiction marketplace. The heroine, rather than living in the often unbelievably good world of the typical inspirational fiction book, is surrounded by people who swear, drink, and have sex outside of marriage, yet are not portrayed as evil but instead as fallible human beings. Some of the characters are even Christians who happen to make the occasional mistake. Deborah herself finds that her once strong faith isn't quite as powerful as she thought it was before her glimpse of the glamorous life and all it offers her. Her struggles to keep her faith alive while she experiences everything the material world has to offer are portrayed in a believable and sympathetic manner.

Michele Andrea Bowen's *Church Folk* is another Walk Worthy title that pushes the envelope of how characters in inspirational fiction books should or should not act. Reading a brief synopsis of the plot might lead readers to believe *Church Folk* is a homespun look at the life of a minister and his new wife. On the surface, that is what the book is about. Young Essie Lee Lane marries pastor Theophilus Simmons and they start their new life together ministering at the Greater Hope Gospel United Church. Shades of Jan Karon's popular Mitford series featuring Father Timothy Kavanagh? Definitely not! Timothy Kavanagh and his girlfriend/bride Cynthia never had to cope with the things Essie Lee and

Theophilus face. For one thing, the church leadership is involved in the running of a call girl service. And Theophilus is regretting an affair with Glodean, a member of the congregation who has had numerous flings with pastors and sees nothing wrong with it. Take those plot lines and combine them with some of the saltiest language ever to appear in a book marketed as inspirational fiction and you arrive with a book that is something the average reader of this genre will find a radical departure, to say the least.

All that said, the Walk Worthy titles are compulsively readable, with largely three-dimensional characters who are not portrayed as inherently evil just because they are flawed. Instead, they come across as real human beings who, although Christians, make mistakes, question their beliefs, and often wonder just what God is planning for them. Only time will tell if the traditionally conservative inspirational fiction readership will accept the Walk Worthy books, but hopefully the solid characterization and plotting of the books will make acceptance more palatable.

The Walk Worthy Press books were of special interest because the majority of the remaining titles published within the genre in the past few months stuck largely with the status quo. In other words, more historical fiction, more romances involving largely predictable outcomes, and the occasional futuristic or science fiction novel to spice up the genre just a bit. A few authors are tackling subjects that were once taboo in inspirational fiction, such as domestic abuse and infertility, but they are few and far between.

One of these authors is Linda Hall, who writes a touching story about a young wife and mother named Sadie who is abused by her husband in *Sadie's Song*. Although not the first inspirational writer to tackle this issue, Hall does a good job of portraying Sadie and explaining why she stays with a man who not only abuses her, but may also be involved in the disappearance of a young girl. Although Hall's book doesn't quite reach the powerful heights of Vinita Hampton Wright's *Velma Still Cooks in Leeway* or Bette Nordberg's *Serenity Bay*, two recent titles that also deal with domestic abuse, it is still a strong look at a topic once considered off-limits for writers of inspirational fiction.

Another plot line that has rarely appeared in inspirational fiction until recently is that of infertility. In the first half of 2001, two authors tackled this subject. Joseph Bentz' *Cradle of Dreams* tells the story of Paul and Laura Phillips, a young couple who get married, settle into a house, and begin planning for their children. The children fail to arrive as the months pass, and their marriage is strained while they undergo tests and surgical procedures in a desperate attempt to conceive. While the ending is predictable, it is still noteworthy that this topic is discussed at all in the genre.

A similar story to Bentz' is told in Tracie Peterson's *The Long Awaited Child*. Tess Holbrook has always dreamed of having a child, but after ten years of trying she finally has to concede that she will not get pregnant. Because she herself was adopted, Tess had always wanted a child of her own bloodline, so she would have somebody who was truly related to her. However, with that dream shattered, Tess finally decides that perhaps adoption would at least give her a child to love, even if that child were not of her own blood. Like the Bentz book, *The Long Awaited Child* doesn't contain any huge surprises in terms of plot resolution. However, both are interesting looks at the emotional tumult suffered by couples facing infertility.

Following more traditional paths, some of the most popular writers in the inspirational fiction genre had new releases in 2001, including Stephen A. Bly, Gilbert Morris, and Janette Oke. Bly, a prolific writer of western-themed stories, is continuing three series in 2001. His The Belles of Lordsburg series is highly enjoyable, and the second entry in the series, *The General's Notorious Widow*, is a charming story reminiscent of Bly's Heroines of the Golden West Series of the late 1990s. Bly's other two current series, Fortunes of the Black Hills and Skinners of Goldfield, also had new installments published in 2001. None of the three contain any surprises for Bly's growing fan base, but they are all enjoyable to read.

Gilbert Morris also has three series with new entries in 2001. His long-running House of Winslow series is now up to 25 titles with *The Amazon Quest*, taking the adventurous Winslow clan past World War I. The 26th title in the series, *The Golden Angel*, will be released in the last half of 2001. Morris is also re-releasing a series of mysteries originally published in the 1980s. While the Dani Ross series doesn't contain an exceptional group of titles, the books are of interest to Morris' many fans since they have been out of print for many years. Morris' perhaps best-loved series is the one he has co-written with his daughter, Lynn, since 1994. The Cheney Duvall series has followed the young doctor from her graduation from medical school just after the Civil War through positions in the Ozark Mountains, New Orleans, San Francisco, Hawaii, and various other locales. She has struggled through cholera epidemics, distrust of female doctors by the medical establishment, lost loves, and numerous other traumas. When the series finally wrapped up with its eighth book (*Driven with the Wind*) in late 2000, many readers were probably disappointed that the series was seemingly ending its run. But in 2001 came *Where Two Seas Met*, the first in the Cheney and Shiloh series, which follows the intrepid doctor and her new husband and longtime friend, Shiloh Irons, as they honeymoon on a shipboard voyage and immediately run into a storm and a mysterious epidemic on an island. The fact that Cheney's adventures will continue on after her marriage will probably please Morris' many fans.

Janette Oke is usually as prolific as Bly and Morris, but 2001 saw her release just two titles, one co-written with her daughter, Laurel Oke Logan. That title is a bit of a departure for Oke, who is best known for her historical romances. Instead of a historical love story, *Dana's Valley* tells the

story of Dana Walsh, a young girl stricken with leukemia, and the effects her illness and eventual death have on her family. While at times the story seems pat and overly simplistic, the authors do bring a measure of realism to what could have been a treacly sweet story. Oke's only solo work to be published in 2001 will be a return to the historicals, in this case a follow-up to her 2000 title, *Beyond the Gathering Storm* entitled *When Tomorrow Comes*.

Whether inspirational fiction ever grows beyond its self-imposed content guidelines remains to be seen, but a few authors are attempting to break out. Only time (and sales) will prove if this small trend is acceptable to the genre readership at large, and if the trend will continue.

Recommended Titles

Listed below are my choices for the best inspirational books in this volume.

Hidden Places by Lynn N. Austin

Little White Lies by Ron and Janet Benry

Abiding Hope by Angela Benson

Cradle of Dreams by Joseph Bentz

Pathways by Lisa Tawn Bergren

The General's Notorious Widow by Stephen A. Bly

Church Folk by Michele Andrea Bowen

The Champion by Carman

Grace in Autumn by Lori Copeland and Angela Elwell Hunt

True Believers by Linda Dorrell

Clouds Without Rain by P.L. Gaus

Just Shy of Harmony by Philip Gulley

Sadie's Song by Linda Hall

Hidden Gifts by Rick Hamlin

The Truth Seeker by Dee Henderson

Times and Seasons by Beverly LaHaye and Terri Blackstock

Valley of Promises by Bonnie Leon

Where Two Seas Met by Lynn and Gilbert Morris

The Swan House by Elizabeth Musser

Freedom's Shadow by Marlo Schalesky

The Amber Photograph by Penelope J. Stokes

Singsation by Jacquelin Thomas

The Winter Garden by Johanna Verweerd

Edge of the Wilderness by Stephanie Grace Whitson

The Devil's Mouth by Thomas Williams

Inspirational Titles

1002

CAROLYNE AARSEN

A Hero for Kelsey
(New York: Steeple Hill, 2001)

Story type: Romance
Subject(s): Widows
Major character(s): Kelsey Swain, Single Parent, Widow(er); Will Dempsey, Businessman (owner, road construction firm)
Time period(s): 2000s
Locale(s): United States

Summary: Single mother Kelsey Swain is struggling to make ends meet when she runs into Will Dempsey, a friend of her late husband. Since her marriage convinced her that heroes no longer exist, Kelsey isn't much interested in romance. Neither is Will, for that matter, especially when the romance comes with a ready-made family. However, the two share a past that makes them realize they just might have a future together.

Other books by the same author:
A Family at Last, 2000
A Mother at Last, 2000
A Bride at Last, 1999
A Family-Style Christmas, 1999
The Cowboy's Bride, 1999

Other books you might like:
Irene Brand, *The Test of Love*, 2000
Valerie Hansen, *The Perfect Couple*, 2000
Debra Kastner, *The Forgiving Heart*, 2000
Kate Welsh, *Their Forever Love*, 2000
Cheryl Wolverton, *Healing Hearts*, 2000

1003

GINNY AIKEN

Camellia
(Wheaton, Illinois: Tyndale House, 2001)

Story type: Romance
Series: Bellamy's Blossoms. Book 3
Subject(s): Pregnancy; Widows
Major character(s): Camellia Bellamy Sprague, Widow(er), Single Parent (pregnant); Stephen Hardesty, Doctor
Time period(s): 2000s
Locale(s): Bellamy, Virginia

Summary: Widowed and pregnant, Camellia Bellamy Sprague is anxiously awaiting the birth of her child when her doctor suddenly retires. In her final trimester, Camellia has no choice but to accept the care of Dr. Stephen Hardesty, her physician's replacement. Camellia thinks Dr. Hardesty is too young to trust, but eventually she grows to accept the new doctor, who left a lucrative city practice to settle in the small town of Bellamy, Virginia. As time goes on, the two not only develop a friendship, but also fall in love.

Other books by the same author:
Lark, 2000
Magnolia, 2000
County Fair, 1997
Crystal Memories, 1997
Candy Kiss, 1996

Other books you might like:
Mary Carlson, *The Whispering Pines Series*, 1999-
Robin Jones Gunn, *The Glenbrooke Series*, 1995-
Annie Jones, *Deep Dixie*, 1999
Tracie Peterson, *The Long Awaited Child*, 2001
Augusta Trobaugh, *Praise Jerusalem*, 1997

1004

RANDY C. ALCORN
ANGELA ALCORN, Co-Author
KARINA ALCORN, Co-Author

The Ishbane Conspiracy

(Sisters, Oregon: Multnomah, 2001)

Story type: Contemporary/Fantasy
Series: Foulgrin's Letters. Book 2
Subject(s): Good and Evil
Major character(s): Ishbane, Demon; Lord Foulgrin, Demon
Time period(s): 2000s
Locale(s): United States; Hell

Summary: Demons Foulgrin and Ishbane conspire to win the souls of four young college students. Jillian, who recently lost her father in a car accident, lives an otherwise picture perfect life. However, her grief over her loss and her shaky spiritual life make her a suitable candidate for the demons' attention. Jillian's friend Brittany is outwardly tough, but inwardly uncertain of her place in life. Ian is an athlete who has recently begun dabbling in the occult. Rob, a former gang member trying to go straight, is a devout Christian, but even he has his doubts. All four friends soon find themselves fighting the demons that hope to lure them to the evil side. Randy Alcorn, the author of *Lord Foulgrin's Letters* wrote this sequel.

Other books by the same author:
Lord Foulgrin's Letters, 2000

Other books you might like:
T. Davis Bunn, *The Messenger*, 1995
Roger Elwood, *The Angelwalk Series*, 1989-
Joseph F. Girzone, *The Joshua Series*, 1987-
F. Parker Hudson, *On the Edge*, 1998
Nancy Moser, *The Mustard Seed Series*, 1998-

1005

RANDY C. ALCORN

Safely Home

(Wheaton, Illinois: Tyndale House, 2001)

Story type: Contemporary
Subject(s): China; Communism
Major character(s): Ben Fielding, Businessman; Li Quan, Teacher
Time period(s): 2000s
Locale(s): Portland, Oregon; China

Summary: Ben Fielding, a successful businessman who has no time in his busy schedule for religion, travels to China in an attempt to shore up his company's assets in that country. He is reunited with his college roommate, Li Quan, who has the deep devotion to God that Ben lacks. However, due to his country's Communist status, Li Quan is forced to keep his spiritual beliefs a secret. As the two men become reacquainted, they both grow closer to God.

Other books by the same author:
Lord Foulgrin's Letters, 2000
Edge of Eternity, 1998
Dominion, 1996

Deadline, 1994

Other books you might like:
T. Davis Bunn, *The Great Divide*, 2000
Donna Fletcher Crow, *Where Love Calls*, 1998
Rene Gutteridge, *Ghost Writer*, 2000
Jon Henderson, *Tigers and Dragons*, 1993
Barbara Jean Hicks, *China Doll*, 1998

1006

LYNN N. AUSTIN

Hidden Places

(Minneapolis: Bethany House, 2001)

Story type: Contemporary
Subject(s): Depression (Economic); Farm Life; Widows
Major character(s): Eliza Wyatt, Widow(er)
Time period(s): 1930s
Locale(s): United States

Summary: Recent widow Eliza Wyatt is still struggling with the loss of her husband and the newfound responsibilities of running an orchard and raising her children by herself when a mysterious stranger arrives at her farm. He offers to work in exchange for food and Eliza, always willing to help those in need during the difficult times of the Great Depression, allows him to stay. The man proves to be a godsend, but Eliza soon begins to wonder about him. Something in his demeanor seems to be odd and she wonders if she can fully trust him.

Other books by the same author:
Wings of Refuge, 2000
Eve's Daughters, 1999
Among the Gods, 1998
My Father's God, 1997
Fly Away, 1996

Other books you might like:
Robin Lee Hatcher, *The Shepherd's Voice*, 2000
Bonnie Leon, *The Matanuska Series*, 2001-
Lorena McCourtney, *Escape*, 1996
Ann Tatlock, *A Room of My Own*, 1998
Bodie Thoene, *Shiloh Autumn*, 1996

1007

JUDY BAER

Libby's Story

(Wheaton, Illinois: Tyndale House, 2001)

Story type: Contemporary
Series: Three Lifelong Friends. Book 2
Subject(s): Aging; Illness
Major character(s): Libby Morrison, Care Giver (of parents); Reese Reynolds, Handicapped (paralyzed), Police Officer
Time period(s): 2000s
Locale(s): Oakview, Minnesota

Summary: Libby Morrison is an attractive young woman with a lot of love to give, but she has devoted her life to caring for her aging parents. Her mother, a victim of Alzheimer's disease, is a deep concern. Although she has the support of her church and her two best friends, Libby is slowly losing

control of her life. When she meets Reese Reynolds, a man left bitter after being paralyzed by a gunshot wound, the two unexpectedly find solace in one another's company and begin to fall in love. Judy Baer is also the author of numerous titles for teenagers.

Other books by the same author:
Jenny's Story, 2000

Other books you might like:
Lori Copeland, *The Heavenly Daze Series*, 2001-
Philip Gulley, *The Harmony Series*, 2000-
Robin Jones Gunn, *The Glenbrooke Series*, 1995-
Beverly LaHaye, *The Seasons under Heaven Series*, 1999-
Vinita Hampton Wright, *Velma Still Cooks in Leeway*, 2000

1008

JUDY BAER

Tia's Story

(Wheaton, Illinois: Tyndale House, 2001)

Story type: Contemporary
Series: Three Lifelong Friends. Book 3
Subject(s): Business; Volunteerism
Major character(s): Tia Warden, Store Owner
Time period(s): 2000s
Locale(s): Minnesota

Summary: Tia Warden has spent the past few years of her life concentrating on building a successful business. Now that her store, Tia's Attic, is a runaway success, she has time to sit back and contemplate her life. To her surprise, Tia discovers that something is missing and she sets out to find fulfillment from things other than business.

Other books by the same author:
Libby's Story, 2001
Jenny's Story, 2000

Other books you might like:
Karen Ball, *Reunion*, 1999
Terri Blackstock, *The Second Chances Series*, 1996-
Robin Jones Gunn, *The Glenbrooke Series*, 1995-
Annie Jones, *The Double Heart Diner*, 1999
Shari MacDonald, *The Salinger Sisters Series*, 1998-

1009

JAMES SCOTT BELL

The Nephilim Seed

(Nashville: Broadman & Holman, 2001)

Story type: Contemporary
Subject(s): Ethics; Kidnapping; Medical Thriller
Major character(s): Janice Ramsey, Lawyer, Single Parent
Time period(s): 2000s
Locale(s): Chicago, Illinois

Summary: Lawyer Janice Ramsey is doing her best to juggle her career and her family life. Then Janice's ten-year-old daughter is kidnapped. To her horror, Janice discovers that her ex-husband is involved in the crime, though not due to a parental dispute. Instead, her daughter is being used as a pawn

in an evil man's plot to control the human race by developing a technology that controls human emotion.

Other books by the same author:
Blind Justice, 2000
Final Witness, 1999
Circumstantial Evidence, 1997
The Darwin Conspiracy, 1995

Other books you might like:
T. Davis Bunn, *The Presence*, 1990
Larry Burkett, *Kingdom Come*, 2001
Michael Farris, *Guilty by Association*, 1997
Dee Henderson, *Danger in the Shadows*, 1999
Robert Whitlow, *The List*, 2000

1010

CARRIE BENDER

Lilac Blossom Time

(Scottdale, Pennsylvania: Herald, 2001)

Story type: Contemporary
Series: Dora's Diary. Book 2
Subject(s): Amish
Major character(s): Dora Kauffman, Servant (hired girl), Companion; Matthew, Boyfriend; Mrs. Worthington, Employer
Time period(s): 2000s
Locale(s): Minnesota; Pennsylvania

Summary: Young Dora Kauffman is enjoying her single life, even under the strict rules of her Amish lifestyle. She has been living in Minnesota for some time, far away from her parents in Pennsylvania. Once seriously considering marriage to a young man named Matthew, Dora is upset when he moves to California. After working as a *Maad* (hired girl) to a large family, Dora decides she needs a change, so she returns to Pennsylvania and takes a job as a companion to well-to-do Mrs. Worthington. Dora accompanies her employer on a trip to California, where she meets up with Matthew and rekindles their romance.

Other books by the same author:
Woodland Dell's Secret, 2001
Hemlock Hill Hideaway, 2000
Birch Hollow Schoolmarm, 1999
Chestnut Ridge Acres, 1997
A Treasured Friendship, 1996

Other books you might like:
Lori Copeland, *The Heavenly Daze Series*, 2001-
Philip Gulley, *The Harmony Series*, 2000-
Jan Karon, *The Mitford Years Series*, 1994-
Beverly Lewis, *The Heritage of Lancaster County Series*, 1997-
Gayle G. Roper, *The Document*, 1998

Inspirational

1011

RON BENREY
JANET BENREY, Co-Author

Little White Lies

(Nashville: Broadman & Holman, 2001)

Story type: Mystery
Subject(s): Business; Murder
Major character(s): Pippa Hunnechurch, Businesswoman (executive headhunter)
Time period(s): 2000s
Locale(s): Ryde, Maryland

Summary: Pippa Hunnechurch is running a one-woman business, working as a headhunter finding executives for corporations. The recession hits her business hard and she begins to have serious concerns for the future. Hoping to jumpstart the business, Pippa attends a Chamber of Commerce meeting where she meets Marsha Morgan, who helps her land a dream assignment. Soon afterward, Marsha drowns mysteriously. When the police write the death off as an accident, Pippa decides to investigate what she believes was murder. First novel from a husband and wife team.

Other books you might like:
Terri Blackstock, *The Sun Coast Chronicles*, 1995-
Kathi Mills-Macias, *Obsession*, 2001
Gilbert Morris, *The Dani Ross Series*, 2000-
Gayle Roper, *The Amhearst Series*, 1997-
Patricia H. Rushford, *The Helen Bradley Series*, 1997-

1012

ANGELA BENSON

Abiding Hope

(Wheaton, Illinois: Tyndale House, 2001)

Story type: Contemporary
Series: Genesis House. Book 2
Subject(s): African Americans; Grief; Marriage
Major character(s): Shay Taylor, Spouse; Marvin Taylor, Spouse
Time period(s): 2000s
Locale(s): Odessa, Mississippi

Summary: After their young son dies, Shay and Marvin Taylor are so wrapped up in their grief they can't concentrate on their jobs or their marriage. As a result, they lose their positions with Genesis House, a charitable organization in Atlanta, and nearly lose their marriage as well. The Taylors hope to put their lives back together. They accept new jobs in Odessa, Mississippi and are determined to make their marriage work. However, Shay desperately wants to have another baby and Marvin isn't willing to risk the heartache of losing another child. Can their marriage withstand this very important difference of opinion?

Other books by the same author:
Awakening Mercy, 2000
A Family Wedding, 1997
Second Chance Dad, 1997
The Nicest Guy in America, 1997

The Way Home, 1997

Other books you might like:
Michele Andrea Bowen, *Church Folk*, 2001
Linda Dorrell, *True Believers*, 2001
Sharon Ewell Foster, *Ain't No River*, 2001
Victoria Christopher Murray, *Temptation*, 2000
Jacquelin Thomas, *Singsation*, 2001

1013

JOSEPH BENTZ

Cradle of Dreams

(Minneapolis: Bethany House, 2001)

Story type: Contemporary
Subject(s): Adoption; Infertility
Major character(s): Paul Phillips, Professor; Laura Phillips, Nurse
Time period(s): 2000s
Locale(s): Pasadena, California

Summary: Paul and Laura Phillips marry with the hopes of having a large family, but as the months go by and Laura doesn't become pregnant, they begin to worry. The two undergo fertility testing and when it appears as if Paul may be unable to father a child, they decide to pursue other options, including adoption. Laura, however, becomes obsessed with having a child and Paul soon begins to wonder if their lives will ever be normal again.

Where it's reviewed:
Publishers Weekly, May 14, 2001, page 51

Other books by the same author:
A Son Comes Home, 1999
Song of Fire, 1995

Other books you might like:
Shirlee Evans, *A Life Apart*, 1990
Barbara Jean Hicks, *China Doll*, 1998
Tracie Peterson, *The Long Awaited Child*, 2001
Lois Richer, *Mother's Day Miracle*, 2000
Cheryl Wolverton, *A Father's Love*, 1998

1014

EILEEN BERGER

A Special Kind of Family

(New York: Steeple Hill, 2001)

Story type: Romance
Subject(s): Unmarried Mothers
Major character(s): Vanessa McHenry, Child-Care Giver; Rob Corland, Health Care Professional (paramedic), Boyfriend (Vanessa's ex)
Time period(s): 2000s
Locale(s): United States

Summary: Vanessa McHenry's life is thrown into turmoil when her beloved grandmother falls and breaks her hip. With Gran in the hospital, Vanessa must move into her house and take over as caregiver to the five pregnant teenagers in Gran's care. Trying to juggle work and the girls proves more difficult

than Vanessa had imagined. Luckily, her one-time boyfriend Rob Corland is around to help her out.

Other books by the same author:
Reunions, 2000
The Missing Hydrangeas, 2000
The Highly Suspicious Halo, 2000
A Family for Andi, 1999
To Galilee with Love, 1999

Other books you might like:
Lynn Bulock, *Gifts of Grace*, 1999
Valerie Hansen, *The Wedding Arbor*, 1999
Lois Richer, *Wedding on the Way*, 1999
Janet Tronstad, *An Angel for Dry Creek*, 1999
Lenora Worth, *His Brother's Wife*, 1999

`1015`
LISA TAWN BERGREN

Pathways
(Colorado Springs, Colorado: WaterBrook, 2001)

Story type: Contemporary
Series: Full Circle. Book 3
Subject(s): Airplane Accidents; Survival
Major character(s): Bryn Bailey, Doctor, Survivor; Eli Pierce, Pilot (bush), Survivor
Time period(s): 2000s
Locale(s): Alaska

Summary: When Bryn Bailey visited Alaska as a young woman, she fell in love with Eli Pierce. Unfortunately, Bryn didn't share Eli's deep faith so the romance broke up. Now, ten years later, Bryn returns to Alaska and once again meets Eli, now a bush pilot. To her surprise, not only does she still have deep feelings for him, but she is also beginning to share his faith. When their plane goes down during a sudden storm, Bryn and Eli fight to survive in the Alaskan wilderness. This title is part of a six book series, five of which were published previously. *Pathways*, however, is a new title and has not been published before.

Other books by the same author:
Midnight Sun, 2000
The Bridge, 2000
Deep Harbor, 1999
The Captain's Bride, 1998
Firestorm, 1996

Other books you might like:
Karen Ball, *Wilderness*, 1999
Roger Elwood, *Survival in the Wilderness*, 2000
Marilyn Kok, *On Assignment*, 1999
Karen Rispin, *Summit*, 1999
Elaine Schulte, *Voyage*, 1996

`1016`
TERRI BLACKSTOCK

Seaside
(Grand Rapids, Michigan: Zondervan, 2001)

Story type: Contemporary

Subject(s): Mothers and Daughters
Major character(s): Maggie Downing, Photographer, Parent (of Sarah and Corinne); Sarah, Volunteer; Corinne, Businesswoman
Time period(s): 2000s
Locale(s): Florida

Summary: Sarah and Corinne are a little shocked when they are invited to spend the week at a beach in Florida by their mother, a famous photographer. Reluctant to put aside their busy lives, both women eventually do travel to the seaside for the family reunion. Soon they learn their mother has some sad news to impart, and the family which was never close, begins to bond.

Other books by the same author:
Trial by Fire, 2000
Word of Honor, 1999
Broken Wings, 1998
Private Justice, 1998
Shadow of Doubt, 1998

Other books you might like:
Lynn N. Austin, *Eve's Daughters*, 1999
Jerry B. Jenkins, *Though None Go with Me*, 2000
Tracie Peterson, *A Slender Thread*, 2000
Francine Rivers, *Leota's Garden*, 1999
Penelope J. Stokes, *The Amethyst Heart*, 2000

`1017`
LAURALEE BLISS
PAMELA GRIFFIN, Co-Author
DINA LEONHARDT KOEHLY, Co-Author
GAIL SATTLER, Co-Author

Tails of Love
(Uhrichsville, Ohio: Barbour, 2001)

Story type: Anthology; Romance
Subject(s): Pets
Time period(s): 2000s

Summary: This anthology of four romantic stories all involve couples brought together by their pets. In Lauralee Bliss' "Ark of Love," Brian loses his pet store to a friend who betrays him, making him unwilling to trust again. Gail Sattler tells the story of Fido and Fluffy in "Neighbor's Fence." The dogs hate each other and so do their owners, but somehow the dogs and people eventually work things out. The other stories are "Walk, Don't Run" by Pamela Griffin and "Dog Park" by Dina Leonhardt Koehly.

Other books you might like:
Ginny Aiken, *A Bouquet of Love*, 1999
Lisa Tawn Bergren, *Porch Swings and Picket Fences*, 1999
Kristin Billerbeck, *Forever Friends*, 2000
Kimberley Comeaux, *Love Afloat*, 2001
Peggy Darty, *Getaways*, 2000

Inspirational

1018

STEPHEN A. BLY

The General's Notorious Widow

(Wheaton, Illinois: Crossway, 2001)

Story type: Historical/American West
Series: Belles of Lordsburg
Subject(s): Scandal; Widows
Major character(s): Lixie Miller, Widow(er)
Time period(s): 1880s
Locale(s): Lordsburg, New Mexico

Summary: Lixie Miller is deeply grieved when her husband dies under scandalous circumstances. Hoping to put the past behind her, Lixie travels to Lordsburg, New Mexico to find some solitude. Unfortunately, the dull routine just gives Lixie more time to brood. Then an attorney's visit brings her out of her shell. After he leaves town, Lixie becomes involved in the social life of Lordsburg and even begins to take care of an injured Indian girl. Little by little, Lixie begins to leave her old life behind as she finds happiness.

Other books by the same author:
Picture Rock, 2001
The Long Trail Home, 2001
The Senator's Other Daughter, 2001
Fool's Gold, 2000
Proud Quail of the San Joaquin, 2000

Other books you might like:
Kristen Heitzmann, *The Rocky Mountain Legacy Series*, 1998-
Janette Oke, *The Women of the West Series*, 1990-
Judith Pella, *The Ribbons of Steel Series*, 1997-
Tracie Peterson, *The Westward Chronicles*, 1998-
Stephanie Grace Whitson, *The Keepsake Legacies Series*, 1998-

1019

STEPHEN A. BLY

The Long Trail Home

(Nashville: Broadman & Holman, 2001)

Story type: Historical/American West
Series: Fortunes of the Black Hills. Book 3
Subject(s): Crime and Criminals; Fathers and Sons
Major character(s): Samuel Fortune, Drifter, Criminal
Time period(s): 1880s
Locale(s): West

Summary: Samuel Fortune has never quite fit into his family, finding their Christian beliefs too difficult to live up to. As a result, Samuel drifts away from them and ends up in Texas, where he gets into trouble with the law. After being released from prison, Samuel returns home to the Dakota Territory where his father and brother live. Both men want to help Samuel, but he insists on going his own way. Hunted by former partners who think he cheated them, Samuel must face his past before he can begin again.

Other books by the same author:
Picture Rock, 2001

The Senator's Other Daughter, 2001
Fool's Gold, 2000
Hidden Treasure, 2000
Proud Quail of the San Joaquin, 2000

Other books you might like:
Dianna Crawford, *The Frontier Women Series*, 2000-
Kristen Heitzmann, *The Rocky Mountain Legacy Series*, 1998-
Al Lacy, *The Journeys of the Stranger Series*, 1994-
Gilbert Morris, *The Reno Saga*, 1992-
Jim Walker, *The Wells Fargo Trail Series*, 1994-

1020

STEPHEN A. BLY

Picture Rock

(Wheaton, Illinois: Crossway, 2001)

Story type: Historical/American West
Series: Skinners of Goldfield. Book 3
Subject(s): Gold
Major character(s): O.T. Skinner, Clerk (in assay office); Dola Mae Skinner, Restaurateur
Time period(s): 1900s
Locale(s): Goldfield, Nevada

Summary: The Skinner family had planned to stay in Goldfield, Nevada only long enough to replenish their supplies for a trip to California. However, the gold boom continues, keeping Dola Mae Skinner's cafe prosperous. Her husband, O.T., has earned enough money from his job in the town's assay office to buy his long-dreamed of vineyard in California. When a union organization leads to violence, the Skinners believe it is time to move on, but their unrealized love for Goldfield just may change their minds and convince them to stay.

Other books by the same author:
The Long Trail Home, 2001
The Senator's Other Daughter, 2001
Fool's Gold, 2000
Hidden Treasure, 2000
Proud Quail of the San Joaquin, 2000

Other books you might like:
Lisa Tawn Bergren, *The Northern Lights Series*, 1998-
Lynn Morris, *The Cheney Duvall Series*, 1994-
Catherine Palmer, *The Town Called Hope Series*, 1997-
Judith Pella, *The Ribbons of Steel Series*, 1997-
Lori Wick, *The Californians Series*, 1992-

1021

MICHELE ANDREA BOWEN

Church Folk

(New York: Walk Worthy, 2001)

Story type: Contemporary
Subject(s): African Americans; Religious Life
Major character(s): Essie Lee Lane Simmons, Spouse; Theophilius Henry Simmons, Religious (pastor)
Time period(s): 1960s

Locale(s): Charleston, Mississippi

Summary: When handsome pastor Theophilius Simmons arrives at his new ministry in Charleston, Mississippi, nearly every single young woman in town has their eye on him. To the surprise of the town's residents, Theophilius begins courting quiet Essie Lee Lane. Even more surprisingly, the pastor marries Essie. As the two begin their married life together, they face some difficult issues, including the presence of one of Theophilius' former loves in his congregation. A warning: this book contains sexual situations and language some may find offensive. First novel.

Where it's reviewed:
Booklist, May 15, 2001, page 1730
Publishers Weekly, May 14, 2001, page 50

Other books you might like:
Angela Benson, *Awakening Mercy*, 2000
Linda Dorrell, *True Believers*, 2001
Sharon Ewell Foster, *Ain't No River*, 2001
Lisa E. Samson, *The Church Ladies*, 2001
Jacquelin Thomas, *Singsation*, 2001

1022

DEAN BRIGGS

The Most Important Little Boy in the World

(Nashville: Word, 2001)

Story type: Contemporary/Fantasy
Subject(s): Healing
Major character(s): Joshua Chisom, Child, Healer
Time period(s): 2000s
Locale(s): United States

Summary: An unknown virus is threatening to wipe out the entire human race, and doctors and scientists are powerless in their attempts to stop it. The world's only hope is an eight-year-old boy—a boy with magical gifts of healing powers and a strange resistance to the virus. But can one little boy save the world?

Other books by the same author:
The God Spot, 1999

Other books you might like:
Larry Burkett, *Kingdom Come*, 2001
Alton Gansky, *By My Hands*, 1996
Angela Elwell Hunt, *The Immortal*, 2000
Nancy Moser, *The Mustard Seed Series*, 1998-
Bill Myers, *Eli*, 2000

1023

LYNN BULOCK

The Prodigal's Return

(New York: Steeple Hill, 2001)

Story type: Romance
Subject(s): Aging
Major character(s): Laurel Harrison, Care Giver; Tripp Jordan, Police Officer (deputy sheriff)

Time period(s): 2000s
Locale(s): Missouri

Summary: Laurel Harrison has spent most of her adult life living in California, but when her aging father needs her help she returns to her Missouri hometown to take care of him. No sooner is Laurel settled in than she meets handsome deputy sheriff Tripp Jordan. Sparks fly between the two, but Laurel is uncertain if she is ready for commitment, especially when the commitment means staying in Missouri and leaving California for good.

Other books by the same author:
Walls of Jericho, 2001
Looking for Miracles, 2000
Gifts of Grace, 1999
Island Breeze, 1999
Dalton's Dilemma, 1998

Other books you might like:
Kathryn Alexander, *Heart of a Husband*, 2000
Valerie Hansen, *The Perfect Couple*, 2000
Janet Tronstad, *An Angel for Dry Creek*, 1999
Kate Welsh, *Their Forever Love*, 2000
Cheryl Wolverton, *For Love of Hawk*, 1999

1024

LYNN BULOCK

Walls of Jericho

(New York: Steeple Hill, 2001)

Story type: Romance
Subject(s): Family Life
Major character(s): Claire Jericho, Housewife; Ben Jericho, Spouse (of Claire)
Time period(s): 2000s
Locale(s): United States

Summary: Claire Jericho has been married for nearly 20 years to her childhood sweetheart, Ben. On the whole, they have been happy. When her children no longer need her, Claire begins to wonder what life would have been like if she had pursued a career outside the home. Deciding to see if there is more to life than cooking and cleaning, Claire begins to live out some of her dreams, leaving Ben wondering what happened to the contented housewife he married.

Other books by the same author:
Looking for Miracles, 2000
Gifts of Grace, 1999
Island Breeze, 1999
Dalton's Dilemma, 1998
Surrender, 1997

Other books you might like:
Peggy Darty, *Promises*, 1997
Karen Kingsbury, *A Time to Dance*, 2001
Jane Peart, *Promises to Keep*, 1998
Deborah Raney, *A Vow to Cherish*, 1996
Lenora Worth, *Logan's Child*, 1998

1025

MELODY CARLSON

Blood Sisters

(Eugene, Oregon: Harvest House, 2001)

Story type: Contemporary
Subject(s): Depression; Friendship
Major character(s): Judith Blackwell, Widow(er)
Time period(s): 2000s
Locale(s): United States

Summary: After losing her husband and her son, Judith Blackwell is overwhelmed by depression. On the brink of suicide, Judith receives a mysterious envelope containing the obituary of her childhood best friend, Jasmine Morrison. Wondering who sent it to her, Judith returns to her hometown to learn more about Jasmine's death and to try to find the person who sent the obituary.

Other books by the same author:
Someone to Belong To, 2001
Everything I Long For, 2000
Looking for You All My Life, 2000
A Place to Come Home To, 1999
Shades of Light, 1998

Other books you might like:
Judy Baer, *Jenny's Story*, 2000
Irene Brand, *Tender Love*, 2000
Dee Henderson, *True Devotion*, 2000
Karen Kingsbury, *Waiting for Morning*, 1999
Beverly Lewis, *The Postcard*, 1999

1026

CARMAN

The Champion

(Nashville: Thomas Nelson, 2001)

Story type: Contemporary
Subject(s): Sports/Boxing
Major character(s): Orlando Leone, Sports Figure (boxer), Religious (youth minister)
Time period(s): 2000s
Locale(s): United States

Summary: After a difficult and troubled youth, things are finally looking up for Orlando Leone. His boxing career, which led to nothing but trouble, is behind him. Orlando has found personal satisfaction working as a minister at a youth center during the day and as a security guard at a hotel at night. Then he knocks out the current heavyweight champion during an altercation at the hotel. The resulting publicity leads to Orlando's return to the ring. It also leads to the same pressures that caused his failure before and Orlando is uncertain that his newfound faith will be strong enough to withstand the pressure of a celebrity lifestyle. This novel was written by Christian singer Carman and inspired the movie of the same title.

Other books you might like:
Steven Chapman, *The Hunter*, 2001
Robin Lee Hatcher, *Whispers from Yesterday*, 1999

Beverly LaHaye, *Times and Seasons*, 2001
Roy Minor, *In the Fall*, 1999
Ken Stuckey, *Conflict in California*, 2001

1027

LINDA CHAIKIN

Thursday's Child

(Eugene, Oregon: Harvest House, 2001)

Story type: Historical/World War II
Series: Day to Remember. Book 4
Subject(s): World War II
Major character(s): Laura Holden, Spouse
Time period(s): 1940s
Locale(s): Greece

Summary: Laura Holden has spent the majority of World War II in relative safety. Her only concern is the welfare of her husband, whom she has not seen for some time. Learning that he is in Greece, Laura decides to go there to meet him, even though she realizes that the journey will be a perilous one. However, she feels the reconciliation is necessary to keep her marriage alive.

Other books by the same author:
Tuesday's Child, 2000
Wednesday's Child, 2000
For Whom the Stars Shine, 1999
Island Bride, 1999
Monday's Child, 1999

Other books you might like:
Elyse Larson, *The Women of Valor Series*, 2000-
Jane Peart, *Courageous Bride*, 1998
Michael Phillips, *The Stonewycke Legacy Series*, 1997-
Noreen Riols, *The House of Annanbrae Series*, 1994-
Penelope J. Stokes, *The Faith on the Homefront Series*, 1996-

1028

LORI COPELAND

Child of Grace

(Wheaton, Illinois: Tyndale House, 2001)

Story type: Contemporary
Subject(s): Business; Pregnancy
Major character(s): E.J. Roberts, Businesswoman
Time period(s): 2000s
Locale(s): Cullen's Corner, North Carolina

Summary: When her business takes a sudden downturn, E.J. Roberts returns to her hometown of Cullen's Corner, North Carolina in an attempt to put her life back together. She and a friend had built Kilgore's Kosmetics into a thriving enterprise and the thought of losing the business has her rattled. To make matters worse, the single E.J. is pregnant. Staying with her beloved Grams, E.J. can almost convince herself that everything will work out, but soon reality steps in and she has to make some serious decisions about her life.

Other books by the same author:
Christmas Vows: $5.00 Extra, 2001
Glory, 2000

Marrying Walker McKay, 2000
Hope, 1999
June, 1999

Other books you might like:
Ginny Aiken, *Camellia*, 2001
Joseph Bentz, *Cradle of Dreams*, 2001
Robin Jones Gunn, *The Glenbrooke Series*, 1995-
Tracie Peterson, *The Long Awaited Child*, 2001
Francine Rivers, *The Atonement Child*, 1999

1029

LORI COPELAND
ANGELA ELWELL HUNT, Co-Author

Grace in Autumn

(Nashville: Word, 2001)

Story type: Contemporary
Series: Heavenly Daze. Book 2
Subject(s): Islands
Major character(s): Charles Graham, Art Dealer (gallery owner), Writer (unpublished novelist); Babette Graham, Art Dealer (gallery owner)
Time period(s): 2000s
Locale(s): Heavenly Daze, Maine

Summary: As the citizens of the tiny island of Heavenly Daze off the coast of Maine prepare for winter, Charles and Babette Graham face a difficult time. They had opened their art gallery with high hopes, but with the tourist trade leaving along with the warm weather, the Grahams' finances become precarious. When their roof begins to leak, it looks as if the Grahams' dreams of business ownership may be coming to an end unless they can find some money fast.

Other books by the same author:
The Island of Heavenly Daze, 2000

Other books you might like:
Mary Carlson, *The Whispering Pines Series*, 1999-
Philip Gulley, *The Harmony Series*, 2000-
Barbara Jean Hicks, *Loves Me, Loves Me Not*, 2000
Jan Karon, *The Mitford Years Series*, 1994-
Bonnie Leon, *A Sacred Place*, 2000

1030

LYN COTE

Finally Home

(New York: Steeple Hill, 2001)

Story type: Romance
Subject(s): Construction
Major character(s): Hannah Kirkland, Fiance(e) (former); Guthrie Thomas, Carpenter
Time period(s): 2000s
Locale(s): Wisconsin

Summary: Jilted bride Hannah Kirkland travels to the small town in Wisconsin where her parents are building their dream home. Her main intent is to help her parents settle into their new house, but she also hopes the different setting will help her mend her broken heart. When Hannah meets Guthrie

Thomas, the carpenter working on the house, she soon has a new love in her life. However, Guthrie's past threatens to keep them apart.

Other books by the same author:
Echoes of Mercy, 2000
Hope's Garden, 2000
Lost in His Love, 2000
New Man in Town, 1999
Whispers of Love, 1999

Other books you might like:
Irene Hannon, *A Family to Call Her Own*, 1998
Susan Kirby, *Love Sign*, 2001
Sara Mitchell, *Shelter of His Arms*, 1998
Carole Gift Page, *Rachel's Hope*, 1998
Jane Peart, *Promises to Keep*, 1998

1031

LINDA DORRELL

True Believers

(Grand Rapids, Michigan: Baker, 2001)

Story type: Contemporary
Subject(s): Charity
Major character(s): Peggy Nickles, Heiress
Time period(s): 1950s (1954)
Locale(s): Bonham, South Carolina

Summary: In the summer of 1954, cotton heiress Peggy Nickles buys a dilapidated rural church, intending to fix it up then turn the deed over to a black congregation that has nowhere else to meet. However, the white residents of the small southern community of Bonham, South Carolina see nothing noble or charitable about Peggy's intentions. Facing the hatred of their community, Peggy, a minister, and an itinerant carpenter band together to rebuild the church. First novel.

Other books you might like:
Sigmund Brouwer, *Out of the Shadows*, 2001
Sharon Ewell Foster, *Passing by Samaria*, 2000
Laurel Schunk, *Black and Secret Midnight*, 1998
Ann Tatlock, *A Room of My Own*, 1998
Augusta Trobaugh, *Resting in the Bosom of the Lamb*, 1999

1032

BIRDIE L. ETCHISON

Oregon

(Uhrichsville, Ohio: Barbour, 2001)

Story type: Collection
Subject(s): Romance
Locale(s): Oregon

Summary: This collection of four romantic stories follows the lives of the four Galloway siblings as they find love and romance in turn of the century Oregon. The stories are ''The Heart Has Its Reasons,'' ''Love Shall Come Again,'' ''Love's Tender Path,'' and ''Anna's Hope.''

Inspirational

Other books by the same author:
The Sea Beckons, 2000
A Tender Melody, 1999
Finding Courtney, 1999
Albert's Destiny, 1998

Other books you might like:
Ann Bell, *Montana*, 2000
Mary Hawkins, *Australia*, 2000
Melanie Panagiotopoulos, *Greece*, 2000
Tracie Peterson, *Alaska*, 1998
Lauraine Snelling, *Dakota*, 1998

1033

EVA MARIE EVERSON
G.W. FRANCIS CHADWICK, Co-Author

Shadow of Dreams
(Uhrichsville, Ohio: Promise Press, 2001)

Story type: Contemporary
Subject(s): Prostitution
Major character(s): Katie Morgan Webster, Spouse, Wealthy; Ben Webster, Hotel Owner, Spouse
Time period(s): 2000s
Locale(s): New York, New York; Brooksboro, Georgia

Summary: On the surface, Katie Morgan Webster seems to have it all. Not only is she beautiful and intelligent, she is also married to handsome and wealthy hotelier Ben Webster. However, Katie is hiding a terrible secret from her past. Fleeing from a destructive home life as a teenager, Katie had ended up in New York City living a life surrounded by drugs and prostitution. Not even Ben knows the full truth of what went on in Katie's life years before. Now elements from her past have turned up to haunt her and they may just destroy Katie's life.

Other books you might like:
Randy C. Alcorn, *The Foulgrin's Letters Series*, 2000-
Joseph Bentz, *A Son Comes Home*, 1999
Shaunti Feldhahn, *The Veritas Conflict*, 2001
D.S. Lliteras, *613 West Jefferson*, 2001
Francine Rivers, *Leota's Garden*, 1999

1034

SHAUNTI FELDHAHN

The Veritas Conflict
(Sisters, Oregon: Multnomah, 2001)

Story type: Contemporary/Fantasy
Subject(s): Good and Evil
Major character(s): Claire Rivers, Student—College
Time period(s): 2000s
Locale(s): Cambridge, Massachusetts; Heaven; Hell

Summary: Claire Rivers is thrilled to be studying at Harvard University, not realizing that God has placed her at the college for reasons other than her academic career. The university has become the battleground for a fight of dominance between Satan and God. Now Claire, a Christian, has become the focal

point of this war and Satan will stop at nothing to destroy her faith in God. First novel.

Other books you might like:
Randy C. Alcorn, *Lord Foulgrin's Letters*, 2000
Angela Elwell Hunt, *The Immortal*, 2000
Shane Johnson, *The Last Guardian*, 2001
Nancy Moser, *The Mustard Seed Series*, 1998-
Bill Myers, *Eli*, 2000

1035

P.L. GAUS

Clouds Without Rain
(Athens: Ohio University Press, 2001)

Story type: Mystery
Series: Michael Branden. Book 3
Subject(s): Amish
Major character(s): Michael Branden, Professor, Detective—Amateur
Time period(s): 2000s
Locale(s): Holmes County, Ohio

Summary: An Amish man dies in what appears to be the accidental collision of a horse and buggy with a semi truck. However, Professor Michael Branden grows suspicious over some aspects of the supposed accident. When the trustee of the dead man's estate disappears, Branden realizes there is more to the situation than meets the eye and decides to investigate further.

Where it's reviewed:
Booklist, May 1, 2001, page 1632
Publishers Weekly, May 21, 2001, page 83

Other books by the same author:
Broken English, 2000
Blood of the Prodigal, 1999

Other books you might like:
Dudley J. Delffs, *The Father Grif Series*, 1998-
Robert Funderburk, *The Dylan St. John Series*, 1996-
Beverly Lewis, *The Heritage of Lancaster County Series*, 1997-
Gayle G. Roper, *The Document*, 1998
Audrey Stallsmith, *The Thyme Will Tell Series*, 1998-

1036

JOSEPH F. GIRZONE

The Parables of Joshua
(New York: Doubleday, 2001)

Story type: Collection
Subject(s): Bible
Major character(s): Joshua, Religious
Time period(s): 2000s
Locale(s): United States

Summary: Author Girzone returns with more stories about Joshua, his modern day version of Jesus. This collection of stories draws parallels between New Testament parables and present day concerns. Among the stories are ''The Parable of

the Criminal and the Righteous Politician,'' about capital punishment, and ''The Parable of the Precious Seed,'' about abortion.

Other books by the same author:
Joshua: The Homecoming, 1999
Joshua and the Shepherd, 1996
Joshua and the City, 1995
Joshua in the Holy Land, 1992
Joshua and the Children, 1989

Other books you might like:
Joan Brady, *God on a Harley*, 1995
T. Davis Bunn, *The Messenger*, 1995
Roger Elwood, *The Angelwalk Series*, 1989-
Nancy Moser, *The Mustard Seed Series*, 1998-
Elmer L. Towns, *The Son*, 1999

1037

PHILIP GULLEY

Just Shy of Harmony

(Sisters, Oregon: Multnomah, 2001)

Story type: Contemporary
Series: Harmony. Book 2
Subject(s): Small Town Life
Major character(s): Sam Gardner, Religious (minister); Jessie Peacock, Wealthy (wins lottery); Wayne Fleming, Neighbor (of Sam)
Time period(s): 2000s
Locale(s): Harmony, Indiana

Summary: The citizenry of Harmony, Indiana continue to live their quiet, but eventful, lives in their beloved small town. Pastor Sam Gardner, still fairly new to the ministry, struggles with his faith. His neighbor, Wayne Fleming, must decide whether to take his wife back when she returns to him after having left him for another man. Meanwhile, Jessie Peacock wins five million dollars in the lottery. Heartwarming stories in the tradition of Jan Karon.

Other books by the same author:
Home to Harmony, 2000
Home Town Tales, 1998
Front Porch Tales, 1997

Other books you might like:
Lori Copeland, *The Heavenly Daze Series*, 2001-
Robert Funderburk, *The Innocent Years Series*, 1994-
Robin Jones Gunn, *The Glenbrooke Series*, 1995-
James Calvin Schaap, *The Secrets of Barneveld Calvary*, 1997
Lance Wubbels, *The Gentle Hills Series*, 1994-

1038

LINDA HALL

Sadie's Song

(Sisters, Oregon: Multnomah, 2001)

Story type: Contemporary
Subject(s): Abuse; Missing Persons
Major character(s): Sadie, Abuse Victim

Time period(s): 2000s
Locale(s): Coffin's Reach, Maine

Summary: Sadie married her husband Troy after being drawn to his strong religious beliefs. Now, after five children, Sadie is finding it more and more difficult to reconcile her husband's violent outbursts with their shared faith. Then a little girl disappears from their hometown. To her horror, Sadie finds some of the girl's drawings among her husband's possessions. Could it be that her abusive husband has become a child killer?

Where it's reviewed:
Publishers Weekly, April 30, 2001, page 51

Other books by the same author:
Katheryn's Secret, 2000
Island of Refuge, 1999
Margaret's Peace, 1998
April Operation, 1997
November Veil, 1996

Other books you might like:
Terri Blackstock, *Presumption of Guilt*, 1997
Beverly Bush, *Wings of a Dove*, 1996
Bette Nordberg, *Serenity Bay*, 2000
Steven W. Wise, *Chambers*, 1994
Vinita Hampton Wright, *Velma Still Cooks in Leeway*, 2000

1039

RICK HAMLIN

Hidden Gifts

(Minneapolis: Bethany House, 2001)

Story type: Contemporary
Series: First Church. Book 2
Subject(s): Singing
Major character(s): Roger Kimmelman, Singer
Time period(s): 2000s
Locale(s): United States

Summary: Roger Kimmelman has achieved success beyond his wildest dreams. His singing has made him one of the hottest musical acts in the country and he is in demand for concerts around the world. Deciding to take a break, he agrees to give a Christmas concert in his hometown. Once he arrives though, Roger begins to realize that success and the material possessions it brings cannot guarantee happiness. Knowing there is a void in his life, Roger decides to renew his commitment to God in hopes of finding true peace.

Other books by the same author:
Mixed Blessings, 2000

Other books you might like:
Annie Jones, *The Snowbirds*, 2001
Paul McCusker, *Epiphany*, 1998
Carole Gift Page, *Cassandra's Song*, 2001
Jacquelin Thomas, *Singsation*, 2001
Kathleen Yapp, *A New Song*, 1994

Inspirational

1040

VALERIE HANSEN

Second Chances

(New York: Steeple Hill, 2001)

Story type: Romance
Subject(s): Reunions
Major character(s): Belinda Carnes, Young Woman, Girl-friend; Paul Randall, Lawyer, Boyfriend
Time period(s): 2000s
Locale(s): United States

Summary: Belinda Carnes and Paul Randall were teenage sweethearts even though Belinda's minister father didn't approve of the young rebel romancing his daughter. Then one night, after Belinda's father got into an argument with Paul, the church caught fire and Paul was blamed for it. Angry when even Belinda turned on him, Paul left town. Now, years later, he is back. Although a successful lawyer, Paul is still hurt over Belinda's treatment of him so many years before. However, he has put his feelings aside in order to help her aunts, who are being swindled. To his shock, the man who is cheating the elderly women is also dating Belinda.

Other books by the same author:
The Perfect Couple, 2000
The Troublesome Angel, 2000
The Wedding Arbor, 1999

Other books you might like:
Carolyne Aarsen, *A Hero for Kelsey*, 2001
Leona Karr, *Rocky Mountain Miracle*, 2001
Loree Lough, *Suddenly Home*, 2001
Ruth Scofield, *Wonders of the Heart*, 2001
Lenora Worth, *Logan's Child*, 1998

1041

JILLIAN HART

Heaven Sent

(New York: Steeple Hill, 2001)

Story type: Romance
Subject(s): Triplets
Major character(s): Hope Ashton, Photographer; Matthew Shaw, Widow(er)
Time period(s): 2000s
Locale(s): Montana

Summary: Hope Ashton has traveled the world working as a photographer. Matthew Shaw is a widower struggling to raise his triplet sons on his own in Montana. When the two meet, they feel an immediate attraction. Hope, however, isn't certain she is ready to settle down to a domestic routine and Matthew doesn't want to commit to a relationship unless Hope is ready to be a mother.

Other books by the same author:
Night Hawk's Bride, 2001
Malcolm's Honor, 2000
Montana Man, 2000
Cooper's Wife, 1999
Last Chance Bride, 1998

Other books you might like:
Carolyne Aarsen, *A Family at Last*, 2000
Kathryn Alexander, *Twin Wishes*, 2000
Irene Hannon, *A Family to Call Her Own*, 1998
Arlene James, *With Baby in Mind*, 1998
Loree Lough, *Suddenly Mommy*, 1998

1042

ROBIN LEE HATCHER

In His Arms

(Grand Rapids, Michigan: Zondervan, 2001)

Story type: Historical/American West; Romance
Series: Coming to America. Book 3
Subject(s): Crime and Criminals; Emigration and Immigration
Major character(s): Mary Malone, Immigrant, Accountant (bookkeeper)
Time period(s): 1890s
Locale(s): Whistle Stop, Idaho

Summary: Young Mary Malone immigrates to the United States from Ireland with high expectations. However, her life in America forces her to confront the brutal realities a young woman on her own must deal with in the 1890s. After taking a job with a wealthy society man, Mary is forced to hit him on the head in order to escape his advances. Realizing nobody will believe she acted in self-defense, Mary leaves him for dead and takes the first train heading west. She meets saloon owner Blanche Loraine, who offers her a job as a bookkeeper. Mary settles into a calmer life in Whistle Stop, Idaho, and begins to fall in love with the local sheriff. However, she realizes it is only a matter of time before her past catches up with her. This is a title rewritten for the inspirational fiction market. It was published under the same title in 1998 by HarperPaperbacks.

Other books by the same author:
Patterns of Love, 2001
Ribbon of Years, 2001
Daddy Claus, 2000
Dear Lady, 2000
The Shepherd's Voice, 2000

Other books you might like:
Lisa Tawn Bergren, *The Northern Lights Series*, 1998-
Stephen A. Bly, *The Heroines of the Golden West Series*, 1998-
Lori Copeland, *The Brides of the West Series*, 1998-
Catherine Palmer, *The Town Called Hope Series*, 1997-
Jane Peart, *The Westward Dreams Series*, 1994-

1043

ROBIN LEE HATCHER

Ribbon of Years

(Wheaton, Illinois: Tyndale House, 2001)

Story type: Contemporary
Subject(s): Memory
Major character(s): Miriam Gresham, Young Woman; Julianna Crosby, Spouse

Time period(s): 20th century; 21st century (1936-2001)
Locale(s): Idaho

Summary: For some time, Julianna Crosby has been depressed and unsatisfied with her life. One day she attends an estate sale where she finds a box labeled "my life." The contents seem so ordinary and uninteresting that Julianna is both perplexed and intrigued. Then she meets an elderly man who tells her about the owner of the box, Miriam Gresham. Through Miriam's story, Julianna gains a new appreciation for life.

Where it's reviewed:
Publishers Weekly, May 28, 2001, page 46

Other books by the same author:
In His Arms, 2001
Patterns of Love, 2001
Daddy Claus, 2000
Dear Lady, 2000
The Shepherd's Voice, 2000

Other books you might like:
Linda Hall, *Margaret's Peace*, 1998
Gary E. Parker, *Highland Hopes*, 2001
Tracie Peterson, *A Slender Thread*, 2000
Penelope J. Stokes, *The Amethyst Heart*, 2000
Augusta Trobaugh, *Resting in the Bosom of the Lamb*, 1999

1044

KRISTEN HEITZMANN

Sweet Boundless

(Minneapolis: Bethany House, 2001)

Story type: Historical/American West
Series: Diamond of the Rockies. Book 2
Subject(s): Miners and Mining
Major character(s): Carina DiGratia Shephard, Spouse (of Quillan); Quillan Shephard, Mine Owner
Time period(s): 1880s
Locale(s): Crystal, Colorado

Summary: Newly married, Carina DiGratia Shephard is anxious to settle down and enjoy her new life as a bride. Her husband, Quillan, however, is facing emotional problems that keep him from bonding with his wife. When remembrances of his troubled childhood become too much to bear, Quillan leaves town. With her husband's mine now her responsibility, Carina soon finds herself in unexpected danger.

Other books by the same author:
Honor's Reward, 2000
The Rose Legacy, 2000
Honor's Disguise, 1999
Honor's Price, 1998
Honor's Quest, 1998

Other books you might like:
Stephen A. Bly, *The Heroines of the Golden West Series*, 1998-
Ruth Glover, *The Wildrose Series*, 1994-
Kathleen Morgan, *The Brides of Culdee Creek Series*, 1999-
Jane Peart, *The American Quilt Series*, 1996-
Stephanie Grace Whitson, *The Dakota Moons Series*, 2001-

1045

DEE HENDERSON

The Truth Seeker

(Sisters, Oregon: Multnomah, 2001)

Story type: Mystery
Series: O'Malley. Book 3
Subject(s): Crime and Criminals
Major character(s): Quinn Diamond, Lawman (U.S. Marshal); Lisa O'Malley, Scientist (forensic pathologist)
Time period(s): 2000s
Locale(s): Chicago, Illinois

Summary: Forensic pathologist Lisa O'Malley is investigating a series of murders involving the discovery of numerous female skeletons. Both her work and her life are complicated by the reappearance of U.S. Marshal Quinn Diamond. Quinn is on the trail of a woman who disappeared from Montana 20 years earlier, soon after the murder of Quinn's father. Thinking the woman is somehow involved in his father's death, Quinn has made it his mission to find her. Then Lisa disappears and Quinn must put the past behind him in order to save her life.

Other books by the same author:
The Guardian, 2001
The Negotiator, 2000
True Devotion, 2000
Danger in the Shadows, 1999
God's Gift, 1998

Other books you might like:
Terri Blackstock, *The Newpointe 911 Series*, 1998-
Lynn Bulock, *Island Breeze*, 1999
B.J. Hoff, *The Daybreak Series*, 1995-
Gayle Roper, *The Key*, 1998
Ellen Vaughn, *The Strand*, 1997

1046

LIZ CURTIS HIGGS
CAROLYN ZANE, Co-Author
KAREN BALL, Co-Author

Three Weddings and a Giggle

(Sisters, Oregon: Multnomah, 2001)

Story type: Anthology
Subject(s): Love
Time period(s): 2000s

Summary: This light-hearted anthology presents three romantic novellas. In Liz Curtis Higgs' *Fine Print*, a businessman hires a speech coach to help him overcome his stage fright, little realizing his father is playing matchmaker. *Sweet Chariot* by Carolyn Zane, has octogenarians Opal and Eunice buying a motor home, which they intend to drive from Montana to Washington. Horrified, Opal's granddaughter, Lexie, and Eunice's grandson, Jake, come along for the ride. The title character of Karen Ball's *Bride on the Run* is heiress Alexandria Wingate. Alexandria's father insists she marry a man she doesn't love, so an hour before the ceremony she climbs out a window and heads for Oregon.

Inspirational

Other books you might like:
Ginny Aiken, *Dream Vacation*, 2000
Eileen Berger, *Reunions*, 2000
Lisa Tawn Bergren, *Porch Swings and Picket Fences*, 1999
Kristin Billerbeck, *Forever Friends*, 2000
Veda Boyd Jones, *Summer Dreams*, 1997

1047

ANGELA ELWELL HUNT
BILL MYERS, Co-Author

Then Comes Marriage

(Grand Rapids, Michigan: Zondervan, 2001)

Story type: Contemporary
Subject(s): Marriage
Major character(s): Heather Stone, Spouse (of Kurt); Kurt Stone, Spouse (of Heather)
Time period(s): 2000s
Locale(s): Illinois

Summary: On their first wedding anniversary, Kurt and Heather Stone get into a fight over the gifts they give to one another. Deciding Kurt just doesn't understand her, Heather runs off to her mother's house, while Kurt takes out his frustrations on the racquetball court. Told from alternating male/female viewpoints, the story tells how the young couple eventually reaches a new level in their relationship.

Other books you might like:
T. Davis Bunn, *The Book of Hours*, 2000
Linda Hall, *Margaret's Peace*, 1998
Rick Hamlin, *Mixed Blessings*, 2000
Robin Lee Hatcher, *The Forgiving Hour*, 1999
Jerry B. Jenkins, *Though None Go with Me*, 2000

1048

ANNIE JONES

The Snowbirds

(Sisters, Oregon: Multnomah, 2001)

Story type: Contemporary
Subject(s): Christmas; Family Relations
Major character(s): Nicolette Dorsey, Parent
Time period(s): 2000s
Locale(s): Persuasion, Alabama

Summary: Nicolette Dorsey's greatest pride in her troubled life is her daughter, Willa. Nicolette's life is complicated by her sisters, Collier and Petie, who believe their love for their sister gives them permission to interfere in her life. When the three sisters return to their hometown of Persuasion, Alabama, for Christmas, Nicolette is prepared for some meddling and unsolicited advice. What she is not prepared for is her aunt's new boarder, Sam Moss. Sam is somebody from Nicolette's past whom she would rather not see again, especially within the confines of her meddling family.

Other books by the same author:
Lost Romance Ranch, 2000
Cupid's Corner, 1999
Deep Dixie, 1999

The Double Heart Diner, 1999
Saving Grace, 1998

Other books you might like:
Terri Blackstock, *The Second Chances Series*, 1996-
T. Davis Bunn, *The Gift*, 1994
Shari MacDonald, *The Salinger Sisters Series*, 1998-
Suzy Pizzuti, *The Halo Hattie's Boarding House Series*, 1998-
Penelope J. Stokes, *The Amethyst Heart*, 2000

1049

LEONA KARR

Rocky Mountain Miracle

(New York: Steeple Hill, 2001)

Story type: Romance
Subject(s): Camps and Camping
Major character(s): Allie Lindsey, Counselor; Scott Davidson, Businessman
Time period(s): 2000s
Locale(s): Colorado

Summary: Allie Lindsey has never forgotten Scott Davidson, her first love. Meeting him again, she is dismayed to discover he has changed into a money hungry businessman who plans to close down Rainbow Camp in Colorado. Allie had hoped to bring some troubled children there for a vacation, but Scott's plans will end those dreams unless she can convince him that there are more important things in the world than money.

Other books by the same author:
Innocent Witness, 2000
Follow Me Home, 1998
Mystery Dad, 1998
The Charmer, 1997
Bodyguard, 1995

Other books you might like:
Carolyne Aarsen, *A Hero for Kelsey*, 2001
Irene Brand, *The Test of Love*, 2000
Valerie Hansen, *The Perfect Couple*, 2000
Robin Lee Hatcher, *Whispers from Yesterday*, 1999
Cynthia Rutledge, *The Marrying Kind*, 2001

1050

DEB KASTNER

A Daddy at Heart

(New York: Steeple Hill, 2001)

Story type: Romance
Subject(s): Abuse
Major character(s): Glory Weston, Administrator (runs a women's shelter); Ethan Wheeler, Lawyer
Time period(s): 2000s
Locale(s): Seattle, Washington

Summary: When lawyer Ethan Wheeler turns up at her women's shelter offering to make a large gift, Glory Weston is both surprised and confused. Usually she has to beg people to donate. As Glory begins to know Ethan better, she soon

begins to fall in love with the jaded lawyer and his little daughter.

Other books by the same author:
Black Hills Bride, 2000
The Forgiving Heart, 2000
Daddy's Home, 1999
Fool's Gold, 1999
A Holiday Prayer, 1998

Other books you might like:
Carolyne Aarsen, *A Family at Last*, 2000
Valerie Hansen, *Second Chances*, 2001
Jillian Hart, *Heaven Sent*, 2001
Marta Perry, *Father Most Blessed*, 2001
Cheryl Wolverton, *A Husband to Hold*, 2001

1051
SUSAN KIRBY

Love Sign
(New York: Steeple Hill, 2001)

Story type: Romance
Subject(s): Accidents
Major character(s): Shelby Taylor, Writer; Jake Jackson, Businessman
Time period(s): 2000s
Locale(s): Liberty Flats, Illinois

Summary: Jilted bride Shelby Taylor runs away from her embarrassing situation only to land in a worse one. While taking a break in Liberty Flats, Illinois, her car is crushed by a sign maker's truck. Stuck in the small town until her car is fixed, Shelby soon grows attached to Jake Jackson, owner of the crane that wrecked her car. Soon Shelby forgets all about her fiance and just might forget about leaving Liberty Flats as well.

Other books by the same author:
Your Dream and Mine, 1999
As the Lily Grows, 1997
When the Lilacs Bloom, 1997
Prairie Rose, 1997
My Secret Heart, 1995

Other books you might like:
Kathryn Alexander, *The Forever Husband*, 1999
Dee Henderson, *The Marriage Wish*, 1998
Ruth Scofield, *The Perfect Groom*, 1999
Kate Welsh, *Their Forever Love*, 2000
Cheryl Wolverton, *For Love of Hawk*, 1999

1052
AL LACY
JOANNA LACY, Co-Author

Let Freedom Ring
(Sisters, Oregon: Multnomah, 2001)

Story type: Historical
Series: Shadow of Liberty. Book 1
Subject(s): Emigration and Immigration; Russians
Major character(s): Vladimir Petrovna, Farmer

Time period(s): 1880s
Locale(s): Russia

Summary: Farmer Vladimir Petrovna and his family are living in near poverty, but they find great comfort in their faith in God. However, their religion is outlawed in czarist Russia and the Petrovnas find themselves facing possible arrest. Vladimir believes his only hope is to immigrate to America, where they will be able to worship freely. However, he has no idea how to earn the money so the family can make the journey.

Other books by the same author:
Damascus Journey, 2001
The Secret Place, 2001
Sincerely Yours, 2001
Ransom of Love, 2000
Until the Daybreak, 2000

Other books you might like:
T. Davis Bunn, *Winter Palace*, 1993
B.J. Hoff, *The Song of Erin Series*, 1997-
Bonnie Leon, *The Sowers Trilogy*, 1998-
Michael Phillips, *The Russians Series*, 1991-
Lauraine Snelling, *The Red River of the North Series*, 1996-

1053
BEVERLY LAHAYE
TERRI BLACKSTOCK, Co-Author

Times and Seasons
(Grand Rapids, Michigan: Zondervan, 2001)

Story type: Contemporary
Series: Seasons under Heaven. Book 3
Subject(s): Crime and Criminals; Remarriage
Major character(s): Cathy Flaherty, Single Parent (of Mark); Steve Bennett, Fiance(e) (of Cathy); Mark Flaherty, Teenager, Criminal (drugs)
Time period(s): 2000s
Locale(s): Cedar Circle, Tennessee

Summary: Cathy Flaherty's 15-year-old son Mark is arrested on drug charges, leaving her questioning her parenting abilities. When Mark is sentenced to a year in a juvenile detention facility, Cathy cancels her plans to wed Steve Bennett, much to Steve's dismay. Trying to convince Cathy that she is a good mother, Steve does his best to bond with Mark, only to begin to doubt his own potential as a stepfather.

Other books by the same author:
Showers in Season, 2000
Seasons under Heaven, 1999

Other books you might like:
Mary Carlson, *The Whispering Pines Series*, 1999-
Robin Jones Gunn, *The Glenbrooke Series*, 1995-
Karen Kingsbury, *A Moment of Weakness*, 2000
Ellen Vaughn, *The Strand*, 1997
Vinita Hampton Wright, *Velma Still Cooks in Leeway*, 2000

Inspirational

1054
BOB LARSON

Shock Talk
(Nashville: Thomas Nelson, 2001)

Story type: Contemporary
Subject(s): Mothers and Daughters; Television
Major character(s): Jenny Owens, Parent (of Allison); Allison Owens, Parent (of two-year-old); Billy McBride, Television Personality (talk show host)
Time period(s): 2000s
Locale(s): United States

Summary: Billy McBride is the host of one of television's most outrageous and controversial talk shows. He seemingly delights in the embarrassment of his guests, and pursues more and more controversy in hopes of higher ratings. Estranged mother and daughter Jenny and Allison Owens appear on Billy's show in hopes of repairing their damaged relationship, but instead become the victims of demonic possession. For once repulsed by the trouble his show has caused, Billy attempts to help the women, even resorting to exorcism to try to free them from possession. Author Bob Larson is the host of a radio talk show.

Other books by the same author:
The Senator's Agenda, 1995
Abaddon, 1993
Dead Air, 1991

Other books you might like:
Stanley Baldwin, *1999*, 1994
John Culea, *Light the Night*, 1997
Clay Jacobsen, *The Lasko Interview*, 1998
Bill Myers, *Eli*, 2000
Frank Peretti, *Prophet*, 1992

1055
ELYSE LARSON

So Shall We Stand
(Minneapolis: Bethany House, 2001)

Story type: Historical/World War II
Series: Women of Valor. Book 2
Subject(s): Murder; World War II
Major character(s): Nella Killian, Widow(er)
Time period(s): 1940s
Locale(s): Wales

Summary: Nella Killian is distraught when her husband's plane is shot down, so she and her daughter retreat to the relative tranquility of Wales. However, the realities of life in Great Britain during World War II won't let Nella escape entirely. She inadvertently uncovers proof that an American soldier's death was not what it appears to be; in fact, it might have been murder. As Nella begins to investigate, she becomes the killer's next target.

Other books by the same author:
For Such a Time, 2000

Other books you might like:
T. Davis Bunn, *The Rendezvous with Destiny Series*, 1993-
Linda Chaikin, *The Day to Remember Series*, 1999-
Jane Peart, *Courageous Bride*, 1998
Michael Phillips, *The Secret of the Rose Series*, 1993-
Penelope J. Stokes, *The Faith on the Homefront Series*, 1996-

1056
BONNIE LEON

Valley of Promises
(Nashville: Broadman & Holman, 2001)

Story type: Contemporary
Series: Matanuska. Book 1
Subject(s): Depression (Economic); Farm Life
Major character(s): Will Hasper, Farmer
Time period(s): 1930s
Locale(s): Matanuska Valley, Alaska

Summary: Many of the farmers in America are hit hard by a drought during the 1930s, with most of them left struggling to survive. Will Hasper and his family are on the verge of losing their Wisconsin farm when they are offered the chance to relocate to Matanuska Valley in Alaska. Once they arrive, however, the Haspers realize the earlier settlers aren't welcoming the newcomers. With no other choice but to stay, the Haspers do their best to settle into their new life.

Other books by the same author:
A Sacred Place, 2000
Harvest of Truth, 2000
In Fields of Freedom, 1999
Where Freedom Grows, 1998
Return to the Misty Shore, 1997

Other books you might like:
Robin Lee Hatcher, *The Shepherd's Voice*, 2000
Lorena McCourtney, *Escape*, 1996
Calvin Miller, *Snow*, 1998
Bodie Thoene, *Shiloh Autumn*, 1996
Lance Wubbels, *The Gentle Hills Series*, 1994-

1057
D.S. LLITERAS

613 West Jefferson
(Charlottesville, Virginia: Hampton Roads, 2001)

Story type: Contemporary
Subject(s): Drugs; Vietnam War
Major character(s): Richard Santo, Veteran (Vietnam War)
Time period(s): 1970s
Locale(s): Tallahassee, Florida

Summary: Still haunted by his experiences during combat, Vietnam veteran Richard Santo returns to the United States unsure of what the future holds. Living in his car, Richard ends up in Tallahassee, where he meets three men and a woman who live in a run down house near the Florida State University campus. Invited to come live with them, Richard is soon drawn into their world of drugs and prostitution. Wanting to fit in, Richard agrees to go along on a drug run to

Panama City. The run ends badly, but Richard hopes to use the experience to find the strength to move on with his life.

Where it's reviewed:
Booklist, March 15, 2001, page 1354
Publishers Weekly, February 26, 2001, page 60

Other books by the same author:
Judas the Gentile, 1999
The Thieves of Golgotha, 1998
Half Hidden by Twilight, 1994
Into the Ashes, 1993
In the Heart of Things, 1992

Other books you might like:
Jack Cavanaugh, *The Peacemakers*, 1999
Ted Dekker, *The Martyr's Song Series*, 2000-
Robert Funderburk, *The Rainbow's End*, 1997
Dee Henderson, *The O'Malley Series*, 2000-
Carole Gift Page, *A Locket for Maggie*, 2000

1058
LOREE LOUGH

Suddenly Home
(New York: Steeple Hill, 2001)

Story type: Romance
Subject(s): Airplane Accidents
Major character(s): Taylor Griffith, Musician, Teacher; Alex Van Buren, Pilot
Time period(s): 2000s
Locale(s): United States

Summary: Alex Van Buren and Taylor Griffith are both suffering from events in their past. In Alex's case, it was the crash of an airplane he was testing that causes him pain, both emotional and physical. Taylor's pain is all emotional. She lost her mother in a car accident and feels racked with guilt because, not realizing its importance, she didn't take the phone call telling her that her mother was in the hospital. Together, the two bond as they fight their personal demons and try to move on with their lives.

Other books by the same author:
Suddenly Reunited, 2000
Jake Walker's Wife, 1999
Lone Wolf, 1999
Sealed with a Kiss, 1999
The Wedding Wish, 1998

Other books you might like:
Irene Brand, *The Test of Love*, 2000
Lynn Bulock, *Looking for Miracles*, 2000
Irene Hannon, *The Way Home*, 2000
Patt Marr, *Angel in Disguise*, 2000
Ruth Scofield, *Whispers of the Heart*, 2000

1059
JAMES R. LUCAS

A Perfect Persecution
(Nashville: Broadman & Holman, 2001)

Story type: Fantasy
Subject(s): Abortion
Major character(s): Leslie Adams, Resistance Fighter
Time period(s): Indeterminate Future
Locale(s): Alternate Earth

Summary: In a future world, babies are aborted when they do not meet specific criteria deemed necessary by government leaders. Some people are horrified at this terrifying development and soon a small underground resistance movement springs up to rescue as many babies as possible. Among the resistance fighters is Leslie Adams, who has a very personal reason for her devotion to the cause.

Other books by the same author:
Noah: Voyage to a New Earth, 1991

Other books you might like:
Beverly LaHaye, *Showers in Season*, 2000
Nancy Moser, *The Mustard Seed Series*, 1998-
Frank Peretti, *The Visitation*, 1999
Francine Rivers, *The Atonement Child*, 1999
Ed Stewart, *Terminal Mercy*, 1999

1060
CINDY MCCORMICK MARTINUSEN

Blue Night
(Wheaton, Illinois: Tyndale House, 2001)

Story type: Contemporary
Series: Winter Passing. Book 2
Subject(s): Missing Persons; World War II
Major character(s): Kate Porter, Spouse
Time period(s): 1940s; 2000s
Locale(s): Austria; Italy

Summary: Kate Porter is vacationing with her husband Jack in Venice, Italy. Returning to their hotel, Kate is horrified to discover Jack is missing. Her only clue to his disappearance is a mysterious blue ceramic tile left behind in their room. Determined to find Jack, Kate investigates and soon learns the disappearance is somehow connected to the death of a young woman in Austria during World War II.

Other books by the same author:
Winter Passing, 2000

Other books you might like:
Lisa Tawn Bergren, *Midnight Sun*, 2000
Linda Chaikin, *The Day to Remember Series*, 1999-
Linda Hall, *Margaret's Peace*, 1998
Elyse Larson, *The Women of Valor Series*, 2000-
Robert L. Wise, *Be Not Afraid*, 2001

Inspirational

1061

SARA MITCHELL

Shenandoah Home

(Colorado Springs, Colorado: WaterBrook, 2001)

Story type: Historical
Series: Sinclair Legacy. Book 1
Subject(s): Sisters
Major character(s): Garnet Sinclair, Artist; Meredith Sinclair, Businesswoman
Time period(s): 1880s
Locale(s): Shenandoah Valley, Virginia

Summary: When his daughters are young, master craftsman Jacob Sinclair builds each girl a wooden chest in which he places an object he believes captures the child's essence. Now grown, Meredith and Garnet Sinclair find out how perceptive their father was as they try to find love and happiness. Garnet, an artist, falls in love with a man who has a troubled past. Meredith, meanwhile, finds success in the business world, quite a feat for a woman in the 1880s. Her financial success, however, has not led to personal fulfillment.

Other books by the same author:
Ransomed Heart, 1999
Montclair, 1997
In the Midst of Lions, 1996
Trial of the Innocent, 1995
A Deadly Snare, 1990

Other books you might like:
Stephen A. Bly, *The Heroines of the Golden West Series*, 1998-
T. Davis Bunn, *One Shenandoah Winter*, 1998
B.J. Hoff, *The Song of Erin Series*, 1997-
Catherine Palmer, *The Town Called Hope Series*, 1997-
Stephanie Grace Whitson, *The Keepsake Legacies Series*, 1998-

1062

GILBERT MORRIS

The Amazon Quest

(Minneapolis: Bethany House, 2001)

Story type: Family Saga
Series: House of Winslow. Book 25
Subject(s): Adventure and Adventurers; Rain Forest
Major character(s): Emily Winslow, Writer; James Parker, Imposter
Time period(s): 1910s
Locale(s): South America

Summary: When her beloved brother, Jared, is killed in combat during the Great War, Emily Winslow grieves deeply. Her sorrow lifts a bit when James Parker, a handsome stranger claiming to have been a comrade of Jared's, arrives at the Winslow house. Caught up in his tales of her brother's heroism, Emily slowly grows to love James. When James is revealed to be a liar, Emily is horrified and breaks off their engagement. Hurt by the deception, Emily decides to accompany her photographer brother, Wes, on a trip to the Amazon rain forest, where the two intend to write an article for *National Geographic*. When another man comes into Emily's life, she is unwilling to trust so easily.

Other books by the same author:
Four of a Kind, 2001
Jacob's Way, 2001
The End of Act Three, 2001
And Then There Were Two, 2000
Covenant of Love, 2000

Other books you might like:
Lawana Blackwell, *The Gresham Chronicles*, 1998-
Jack Cavanaugh, *The American Family Portrait Series*, 1994-
Diane Noble, *The California Chronicles*, 1999-
Jane Peart, *The Brides of Montclair Series*, 1989-
Michael Phillips, *The Heathersleigh Hall Series*, 1998-

1063

GILBERT MORRIS

Four of a Kind

(Wheaton, Illinois: Crossway, 2001)

Story type: Mystery
Series: Dani Ross. Book 4
Subject(s): Crime and Criminals
Major character(s): Dani Ross, Detective—Private; Alvin Flatt, Religious (minister); T. Valentine, Organized Crime Figure
Time period(s): 2000s
Locale(s): New Orleans, Louisiana

Summary: When Reverend Alvin Flatt is being threatened, he turns to private investigator Dani Ross for help. The minister's church is, unfortunately, in a building that mobster T. Valentine wants, and Valentine usually gets his way. Flatt, however, doesn't want to lose his church without a fight and he is certain that with Dani's help, good will prevail over evil. Valentine doesn't give up and it soon appears he may win out over the forces of good. This is a rewritten version of *Deadly Deception* (1992).

Other books by the same author:
Jacob's Way, 2001
The Amazon Quest, 2001
The End of Act Three, 2001
And Then There Were Two, 2000
Covenant of Love, 2000

Other books you might like:
Athol Dickson, *The Garr Reed Series*, 1996-
Robert Funderburk, *The Dylan St. John Series*, 1996-
B.J. Hoff, *The Daybreak Series*, 1995-
Gayle Roper, *The Amhearst Series*, 1997-
Patricia H. Rushford, *The Helen Bradley Series*, 1997-

1064

LYNN MORRIS
GILBERT MORRIS, Co-Author

Where Two Seas Met

(Minneapolis: Bethany House, 2001)

Story type: Historical/Post-American Civil War
Series: Cheney and Shiloh: The Inheritance. Book 1
Subject(s): Illness; Islands
Major character(s): Cheney Duvall Irons, Doctor; Shiloh Irons, Spouse (newlywed)
Time period(s): 1860s
Locale(s): At Sea; Tropical Island

Summary: In this continuation of the long-running Dr. Cheney Duvall series, Cheney has finally married her long-time love, Shiloh Irons. The two are enjoying a shipboard honeymoon when a sudden storm forces them to take shelter on an island being plagued by a mysterious epidemic. In an attempt to stop the spread of the disease, Cheney quarantines the island and the ship until the illness abates.

Other books by the same author:
Driven with the Wind, 2000
Island of the Innocent, 1998
In the Twilight, in the Evening, 1997
Secret Place of Thunder, 1996
Toward the Sunrising, 1996

Other books you might like:
Lawana Blackwell, *The Victorian Serenade Series*, 1995-
Linda L. Chaikin, *The Jewel of the Pacific Series*, 1999-
Catherine Palmer, *The Town Called Hope Series*, 1997-
Michael Phillips, *The Journals of Corrie Belle Hollister Series*, 1990-
Peggy Stoks, *Olivia's Touch*, 2000

1065

VICTORIA CHRISTOPHER MURRAY

Joy

(New York: Walk Worthy, 2001)

Story type: Contemporary
Subject(s): African Americans; Rape
Major character(s): Anya Mitchell, Businesswoman
Time period(s): 2000s
Locale(s): Los Angeles, California

Summary: Anya Mitchell has everything she could dream of. Her financial services company is a big success, her fiance is wonderful and loving, and her faith is strong and unwavering. Then Anya is attacked and raped in her office. Although her fiance's strength and her own faith see her through the horrors of the attack's aftermath, Anya soon learns her trials are not yet over.

Other books by the same author:
Temptation, 2000

Other books you might like:
Angela Benson, *The Genesis House Series*, 2000-
Michele Andrea Bowen, *Church Folk*, 2001

Lori Copeland, *Child of Grace*, 2001
Francine Rivers, *The Atonement Child*, 1999
Jacquelin Thomas, *Singsation*, 2001

1066

ELIZABETH MUSSER

The Swan House

(Minneapolis: Bethany House, 2001)

Story type: Contemporary
Subject(s): Grief; Race Relations
Major character(s): Mary Swan Middleton, Volunteer, Wealthy
Time period(s): 1960s
Locale(s): Atlanta, Georgia

Summary: Teenager Mary Swan Middleton is living a life of sheltered luxury when her mother is killed in a plane crash and torn apart by grief, Mary is unable to cope with the tragedy. Her maid encourages Mary to do volunteer work as a way to take her mind off her troubles. Reluctantly, she agrees and finds a very different world outside her circle of wealth and privilege. When Mary meets a young man named Carl, her once complacent view of life is shattered again as he opens her eyes to what life is like for a young black man like himself in Atlanta, Georgia, during the 1960s.

Where it's reviewed:
Publishers Weekly, June 4, 2001, page 53

Other books by the same author:
Two Testaments, 1997
Two Crosses, 1996

Other books you might like:
Angela Benson, *Awakening Mercy*, 2000
Linda Dorrell, *True Believers*, 2001
Sharon Ewell Foster, *Passing by Samaria*, 2000
Laurel Schunk, *Black and Secret Midnight*, 1998
Denise Williamson, *The Roots of Faith Series*, 1999-

1067

BETTE NORDBERG

Pacific Hope

(Minneapolis: Bethany House, 2001)

Story type: Contemporary
Subject(s): Marriage; Sailing
Major character(s): Kate Langston, Spouse; Mike Langston, Spouse
Time period(s): 2000s
Locale(s): Hawaii; At Sea

Summary: Kate Langston has decided there is no reason to continue her long marriage to her husband, Mike, since the two have grown so far apart. Hoping to convince her otherwise, Mike agrees to a divorce on one condition: that Kate help him sail their boat to Hawaii. Mike hopes the time alone will help them mend their broken relationship. Kate, believing the trip will do no good, but wanting her divorce, agrees. The two set sail only to soon realize they are being pursued by criminals.

Inspirational (side margin)

Other books by the same author:
Serenity Bay, 2000

Other books you might like:
Lynn Bulock, *Island Breeze*, 1999
Dee Henderson, *True Devotion*, 2000
Angela Elwell Hunt, *Then Comes Marriage*, 2001
Karen Kingsbury, *A Time to Dance*, 2001
Deborah Raney, *A Vow to Cherish*, 1996

1068

JANETTE OKE
LAUREL OKE LOGAN, Co-Author

Dana's Valley

(Minneapolis: Bethany House, 2001)

Story type: Contemporary
Subject(s): Cancer; Illness
Major character(s): Dana Walsh, Student—Elementary School; David Walsh, Parent; Angela Walsh, Parent
Time period(s): 2000s
Locale(s): United States

Summary: David and Angela Walsh are a happy, contented couple doing their best to raise their four children in a loving environment. Then their oldest daughter, Dana, changes. The once cheerful and happy girl is always tired and seems to suffer from flu-like symptoms on a never-ending basis. To their horror, the Walshes soon learn Dana has leukemia. Their once complacent life is turned upside down as the family adjusts to the realities of chemotherapy treatments and medical crises. As the situation grows more and more life threatening, the family members begin to wonder why God has put their daughter and sister through this terrible situation.

Where it's reviewed:
Library Journal, April 1, 2001, page 86

Other books you might like:
Joseph Bentz, *A Son Comes Home*, 1999
Angela Elwell Hunt, *Gentle Touch*, 1997
Beverly LaHaye, *Seasons under Heaven*, 1999
Gayle Roper, *Spring Rain*, 2001
Ann Tatlock, *A Place Called Morning*, 1998

1069

JOHN OLSON
RANDALL INGERMANSON, Co-Author

Oxygen

(Minneapolis: Bethany House, 2001)

Story type: Science Fiction
Subject(s): Space Travel
Major character(s): Valkerie Jansen, Scientist (microbial ecologist), Astronaut
Time period(s): Indeterminate Future
Locale(s): Spaceship

Summary: In the not too distant future, Valkerie Jansen unexpectedly becomes a member of a NASA astronaut crew. Through her work in space as a microbial ecologist, Valkerie hopes to conduct some research that will lead to scientific advances. However, her hopes for the future are dashed when an explosion cripples the spacecraft. Since it appears as if sabotage was involved, the crew immediately become suspects. Their only hope for survival is to work together as a team, but first they must discover who among them is the saboteur.

Other books you might like:
Larry Burkett, *Kingdom Come*, 2001
Dee Henderson, *True Devotion*, 2000
Robert Don Hughes, *The Fallen*, 1995
Shane Johnson, *The Last Guardian*, 2001
L.A. Mazulli, *Nephilim*, 1999

1070

CAROLE GIFT PAGE

Cassandra's Song

(New York: Steeple Hill, 2001)

Story type: Romance
Subject(s): Music and Musicians; Parenthood
Major character(s): Cassandra Rowlands, Musician (pianist); Antonio Pagliarulo, Singer (tenor)
Time period(s): 2000s
Locale(s): United States

Summary: Concert pianist Cassandra Rowlands is growing increasingly worried over her widowed father. He seems so lonely, she decides some matchmaking is in order. Finding a woman she considers the perfect match for her father, Cassandra is surprised when another relationship develops instead of the one she had intended. She falls in love with the woman's handsome son, tenor Antonio Pagliarulo.

Other books by the same author:
A Family to Cherish, 2000
A Locket for Maggie, 2000
A Rose for Jenny, 1999
Rachel's Hope, 1998
Storms over Willowbrook, 1998

Other books you might like:
Rick Hamlin, *Hidden Gifts*, 2001
Sara Mitchell, *Night Music*, 1998
Janette Oke, *The Matchmakers*, 1997
Patricia H. Rushford, *Morningstar*, 1998
Jacquelin Thomas, *Singsation*, 2001

1071

CATHERINE PALMER
KRISTIN BILLERBECK, Co-Author
GINNY AIKEN, Co-Author

Victorian Christmas Keepsake

(Wheaton, Illinois: Tyndale House, 2001)

Story type: Anthology; Romance
Subject(s): Victorian Period; Short Stories

Summary: These three romantic novellas are set in the Victorian era. Among them is Kristin Billerbeck's *Far Above Rubies*, in which a young woman named Emma, who has always felt inferior to her beautiful sister, is sent out west to

marry her sister's fiance. The other stories are *Behold the Lamb* by Catherine Palmer and *Memory to Keep* by Ginny Aiken.

Other books you might like:
Lawana Blackwell, *The Victorian Serenade Series*, 1995-
Donna Fletcher Crow, *The Cambridge Chronicles*, 1994-
Linda Ford, *Prairie Brides*, 2000
Jane Peart, *The Edgecliffe Manor Series*, 1996-
Colleen L. Reece, *Frontiers*, 2000

1072

JANE PEART

A Tangled Web

(Grand Rapids, Michigan: Zondervan, 2001)

Story type: Historical/American West
Series: Westward Dreams. Book 6
Subject(s): Restaurants
Major character(s): Darcy Welburne, Waiter/Waitress
Time period(s): 1900s
Locale(s): Juniper Junction, Arizona

Summary: Darcy hates politics with a passion, so when her fiance Grady decides to run for sheriff, she runs off for Juniper Junction, Arizona. The only job she can find is as a waitress, something Darcy considers demeaning. To make everybody back home think she is a huge success, Darcy begins to lie in her letters. Then the lies get out of control and, when Grady comes to town for a visit, Darcy has some explaining to do.

Other books by the same author:
A Sinister Silence, 2001
A Montclair Homecoming, 2000
Circle of Love, 2000
Undaunted Spirit, 1999
Promises to Keep, 1998

Other books you might like:
Kathleen Morgan, *The Brides of Culdee Creek Series*, 1999-
Lynn Morris, *The Cheney Duvall Series*, 1994-
Judith Pella, *The Ribbons of Steel Series*, 1997-
Tracie Peterson, *The Westward Chronicles*, 1998-
Lori Wick, *The Californians Series*, 1992-

1073

TRACIE PETERSON
JAMES SCOTT BELL, Co-Author

Angels Flight

(Minneapolis: Bethany House, 2001)

Story type: Historical
Series: Shannon Saga. Book 2
Subject(s): Law; Racial Conflict
Major character(s): Kit Shannon, Lawyer
Time period(s): 1900s
Locale(s): Los Angeles, California

Summary: Female lawyers may not be common in the early 1900s, but Kit Shannon is determined to prove that a woman can be as good a lawyer as a man. Her first court cases prove successful and she is well on her way to establishing herself.

Then Kit accepts a case with racial overtones that threatens to tear the city apart. She soon finds herself not only fighting for her client, but for her career as well when well-meaning friends and relatives urge her to drop the case before it ruins her life.

Other books by the same author:
City of Angels, 2001

Other books you might like:
Stephen A. Bly, *The Old California*, 1999-
Kristen Heitzmann, *The Rocky Mountain Legacy Series*, 1998-
Diane Noble, *The California Chronicles*, 1999-
Michael Phillips, *The Mercy and Eagleflight Series*, 1996-
Lori Wick, *The Californians Series*, 1992-

1074

TRACIE PETERSON

Ashes and Ice

(Minneapolis: Bethany House, 2001)

Story type: Historical
Series: Yukon Quest. Book 2
Subject(s): Courage; Gold Discoveries
Major character(s): Karen Pierce, Adventurer; Adrik Ivanov, Guide
Time period(s): 1890s
Locale(s): Alaska

Summary: When tragedy suddenly strikes Karen Pierce's life, her once calm existence begins to spin out of control. Hoping to regain control of her destiny, Karen, now in charge of two young adults, decides her best option is to continue their planned journey to the gold fields of Alaska. Their guide is Adrik Ivanov, who is in love with Karen, though she spurns his advances. During the journey, Karen thrives under the rigorous conditions and even begins to believe love with Adrik may have a place in her life after all.

Other books by the same author:
The Long Awaited Child, 2001
Treasures of the North, 2001
A Slender Thread, 2000
Tidings of Peace, 2000
A Veiled Reflection, 2000

Other books you might like:
Lisa Tawn Bergren, *Midnight Sun*, 2000
Stephen A. Bly, *The Heroines of the Golden West Series*, 1998-
Bonnie Leon, *A Sacred Place*, 2000
Bonnie Leon, *Valley of Promises*, 2001
Alan Morris, *The Guardians of the North Series*, 1996-
Jim Walker, *The Ice Princess*, 1998

1075

TRACIE PETERSON

The Long Awaited Child

(Minneapolis: Bethany House, 2001)

Story type: Contemporary

Inspirational

Subject(s): Infertility
Major character(s): Tess Holbrook, Spouse
Time period(s): 2000s
Locale(s): Miami, Florida

Summary: Tess Holbrook has dreamed of having a baby for as long as she can remember, but after years of fertility treatments she finally has to face the fact that she cannot conceive. Struggling with what she sees as her own inadequacies, Tess is hesitant to try adoption since she herself was adopted and she has mixed feelings about the process. Then Tess meets a pregnant teenager named Sherry, who doesn't want her baby. Thinking her prayers for a family have finally been answered, Tess bonds with Sherry only to once again have her hopes dashed.

Other books by the same author:
Colorado Wings, 2001
Treasures of the North, 2001
A Slender Thread, 2000
Tidings of Peace, 2000
A Veiled Reflection, 2000

Other books you might like:
Kathryn Alexander, *Twin Wishes*, 2000
Joseph Bentz, *Cradle of Dreams*, 2001
Barbara Jean Hicks, *China Doll*, 1998
Beverly LaHaye, *The Seasons under Heaven Series*, 1999-
Francine Rivers, *The Atonement Child*, 1999

1076

MICHAEL PHILLIPS

A New Dawn over Devon

(Minneapolis: Bethany House, 2001)

Story type: Family Saga
Series: Heathersleigh Hall. Book 4
Subject(s): Family Life; Secrets
Major character(s): Lady Amanda Rutherford, Noblewoman
Time period(s): 1910s; 1920s (1915-1923)
Locale(s): Devonshire, England

Summary: With the Great War over, life in England is beginning to return to a sense of normalcy. As the soldiers return home, so does Amanda Rutherford, who spent most of the war years rebelling against her deeply Christian family, and getting herself into a lot of trouble in the process. Now repentant of her past mistakes, Amanda settles in at Heathersleigh Hall, hoping for a new start in life. This is the fourth and final installment in the Heathersleigh Hall series.

Other books by the same author:
A Rift in Time, 2000
An Ancient Strife, 2000
Hidden in Time, 2000
Heathersleigh Homecoming, 1999
Wayward Winds, 1999

Other books you might like:
Linda Chaikin, *Valiant Hearts*, 1998
B.J. Hoff, *The Song of Erin Series*, 1997-
Gilbert Morris, *The House of Winslow Series*, 1986-
Jane Peart, *The Edgecliffe Manor Series*, 1996-
Jake Thoene, *The Portraits of Destiny Series*, 1998-

1077

DEBORAH RANEY

Beneath a Southern Sky

(Colorado Springs, Colorado: WaterBrook, 2001)

Story type: Contemporary
Subject(s): Remarriage
Major character(s): Daria Camfield, Religious (missionary), Widow(er); Nathan "Nate" Camfield, Spouse (Daria's, presumed dead); Colson Hunter, Spouse (of Daria), Veterinarian
Time period(s): 2000s
Locale(s): United States; South America

Summary: Daria Camfield returns to the United States after serving as a missionary in South America. During her time abroad, Daria's husband was reported killed, leaving her pregnant and alone. After giving birth to a daughter, Daria slowly begins to recover from her loss. Although everything tells her it is too soon, Daria falls in love with veterinarian Colson Hunter. Knowing she should wait until she is more adjusted to her widowhood, Daria goes ahead and marries Colson anyway. Then her first husband is found alive, and Daria has some serious decisions to make.

Other books by the same author:
Kindred Bond, 1998
In the Still of the Night, 1997
A Vow to Cherish, 1996

Other books you might like:
Sandy Gills, *Mr. Francis' Wife*, 1998
Karen Kingsbury, *A Moment of Weakness*, 2000
Lorena McCourtney, *Searching for Stardust*, 1999
Karen Rispin, *Summit*, 1999
Linda Windsor, *Hi Honey, I'm Home*, 1999

1078

KAY D. RIZZO

Annie's Trust

(Nashville: Broadman & Holman, 2001)

Story type: Historical/American Civil War
Series: Serenity Inn. Book 6
Subject(s): Abolition; Underground Railroad
Major character(s): Annie Hawkins Ward, Spouse, Slave (freed); Ned Ward, Spouse, Slave (freed)
Time period(s): 1860s
Locale(s): Independence, Missouri; Kansas

Summary: Annie Hawkins wants to live a quiet, peaceful life, but that is an impossibility for a freed slave living in Missouri just prior to the Civil War. When Annie marries Ned Ward, another freed slave who works for the Underground Railroad, she knows his actions can cause problems for them both. Attacked by members of the Cranston Gang, a pro-slavery group, Ned is more determined than ever to fight for the abolitionist cause. He decides to go to Kansas to recruit supporters and although she is pregnant, Annie insists on coming along. The Cranston Gang attacks again, leading Annie to miscarry. Depressed and upset by everything that

has happened, Annie begins to question both the possible success of her marriage and the existence of God.

Other books by the same author:
Abigail's Dream, 2000
Josephine's Fortune, 1999
The Secret Dreams of Dolly Spencer, 1999
Lilia's Haven, 1999
Serenity's Quest, 1998

Other books you might like:
Sharon Ewell Foster, *Passing by Samaria*, 2000
Virginia Gaffney, *The Richmond Chronicles*, 1996-
Judith Pella, *Texas Angel*, 1999
Denise Williamson, *The Roots of Faith Series*, 1999-
P.B. Wilson, *Night Come Swiftly*, 1997

1079

GAYLE ROPER

Spring Rain

(Sisters, Oregon: Multnomah, 2001)

Story type: Contemporary
Series: Seaside Season. Book 1
Subject(s): AIDS (Disease)
Major character(s): Leigh Spenser, Teacher, Single Parent; Clay Wharton, Parent (of Leigh's child)
Time period(s): 2000s
Locale(s): Seaside, New Jersey

Summary: Leigh Spenser is living a quiet life in Seaside, New Jersey, concentrating on her work as a teacher and caring for her son, Billy. Then Billy's father, Clay Wharton, comes to town to visit his twin brother, Ted, who is dying of AIDS. As Clay tries to reconcile his ambivalent feelings about his brother, he also attempts to find some ties with his son.

Other books by the same author:
Caught in a Bind, 2000
The Decision, 1999
Caught in the Act, 1998
The Document, 1998
The Key, 1998

Other books you might like:
Joseph Bentz, *A Son Comes Home*, 1999
Sigmund Brouwer, *Out of the Shadows*, 2001
Linda Hall, *Margaret's Peace*, 1998
James Calvin Schaap, *In the Silence There Are Ghosts*, 1995
Penelope J. Stokes, *The Amethyst Heart*, 2000

1080

NANCY RUE

Pascal's Wager

(Sisters, Oregon: Multnomah, 2001)

Story type: Contemporary
Subject(s): Aging; Illness
Major character(s): Jill McGavock, Professor; Sam Hunt, Philosopher, Professor
Time period(s): 2000s
Locale(s): United States

Summary: Jill McGavock feels helpless. Her once brilliant mother's mind is deteriorating and Jill can do nothing to stop the process. In desperation, she goes to her colleague, philosophy professor Sam Hunt, for advice. He suggests she accept "Pascal's Wager:" to bet that God exists by living as if he does. Jill, an atheist, agrees to the experiment in hopes of finding some comfort over her mother's condition.

Other books by the same author:
Retreat to Love, 1996

Other books you might like:
Lynn N. Austin, *Eve's Daughters*, 1999
Judy Baer, *Libby's Story*, 2001
Beverly Lewis, *The Sunroom*, 1998
Francine Rivers, *Leota's Garden*, 1999
Johanna Verweerd, *The Winter Garden*, 2001

1081

CYNTHIA RUTLEDGE

The Marrying Kind

(New York: Steeple Hill, 2001)

Story type: Romance
Subject(s): Unemployment
Major character(s): Taylor Rollins, Fiance(e) (pretend); Nick Langan, Businessman
Time period(s): 2000s
Locale(s): United States

Summary: When Taylor Rollins' job is eliminated, more than her own future is at stake. Taylor is the sole support of her grandparents and now they face an uncertain future. Hoping to somehow get her position back, Taylor goes to CEO Nick Langan to beg him to reconsider. Nick has his own problem, though. A potential partner will send a lot of business Nick's way—if Nick reconsiders his decision to date the man's daughter. So while Nick can't give Taylor her old job back, he is willing to give her a new one as his pretend fiancee, at least until his business deal goes through.

Other books by the same author:
Undercover Angel, 2000
Unforgettable Faith, 2000

Other books you might like:
Kathryn Alexander, *Heart of a Husband*, 2000
Eileen Berger, *A Special Kind of Family*, 2001
Valerie Hansen, *The Perfect Couple*, 2000
Lois Richer, *His Answered Prayer*, 2000
Janet Tronstad, *A Gentleman for Dry Creek*, 2000

1082

LISA E. SAMSON

The Church Ladies

(Sisters, Oregon: Multnomah, 2001)

Story type: Contemporary
Subject(s): Christian Life; Small Town Life
Major character(s): Poppy Fraser, Spouse (minister's wife)
Time period(s): 2000s
Locale(s): Mount Oak, North Carolina

Inspirational (side margin)

Summary: Poppy Fraser loves her minister husband dearly, and followed him halfway across the country to the seminary, then to the southern town of Mount Oak, leaving her beloved Maryland behind. Still, every once in a while, the pressures of being a minister's wife become a bit much for Poppy. However, when tragedy strikes the small southern town, Poppy realizes just how strong the women of her church and the other churches in town are, as they band together to help those in need.

Other books by the same author:
Crimson Skies, 2000
Fields of Gold, 2000
Indigo Waters, 1999
The Moment I Saw You, 1998
The Warrior's Bride, 1997

Other books you might like:
Ginny Aiken, *The Bellamy's Blossoms Series*, 2000-
Thomas J. Davis, *The Christmas Quilt*, 2000
Robin Jones Gunn, *The Glenbrooke Series*, 1995-
Annie Jones, *Deep Dixie*, 1999
James Calvin Schaap, *The Secrets of Barneveld Calvary*, 1997

1083

MARLO M. SCHALESKY

Freedom's Shadow

(Wheaton, Illinois: Crossway, 2001)

Story type: Historical/Colonial America
Series: Winds of Freedom. Book 2
Subject(s): French and Indian War
Major character(s): White Wolf, Indian; Jonathan Grant, Frontiersman; Annie Hill, Young Woman
Time period(s): 1750s
Locale(s): East, American Colonies

Summary: White Wolf leaves his tribe behind in order to escape from the past that haunts him, only to get caught up in the horrors of the French and Indian War. Meanwhile, frontiersman Jonathan Grant leaves the colonies to return home to England to confront his own past. The two men and a headstrong young woman named Annie Hill find their lives crossing as they each try to fight the inner demons that haunt them.

Other books by the same author:
Cry Freedom, 2000

Other books you might like:
Dianna Crawford, *The Frontier Women Series*, 2000-
Sally Laity, *The Freedom's Holy Light Series*, 1994-
Gilbert Morris, *The Liberty Bell Series*, 1995-
Linda Rae Rao, *The Eagle Wings Series*, 1995-
Stephanie Grace Whitson, *The Dakota Moons Series*, 2001-

1084

LAUREL SCHUNK

A Clear North Light

(Wichita, Kansas: St. Kitts, 2001)

Story type: Mystery

Series: Lithuanian Trilogy. Book 1
Subject(s): Nazis
Major character(s): Petras Simonaitis, Artisan (glassmaker), Apprentice
Time period(s): 1930s
Locale(s): Lithuania

Summary: Petras Simonaitis is working as an apprentice to a glassmaker when the Nazis begin their rise to power in Lithuania. Being the sole support of his mother and sister, Petras feels he has no choice but to go along with some of the Nazis' rulings, no matter how he truly feels about their beliefs. When his sister is selected for breeding purposes by a wealthy nobleman who wishes to have Aryan children, Petras feels powerless to oppose him. Then his sister is found dead and Petras is horrified at what his weakness has caused. After his girlfriend is selected for breeding, he decides to stop at nothing in order to save her from the same fate his sister suffered.

Other books by the same author:
Black and Secret Midnight, 1998
Death in Exile, 1998
The Voice He Loved, 1995

Other books you might like:
Linda Chaikin, *The Day to Remember Series*, 1999-
Anne DeGraaf, *Bread upon the Waters*, 1995
Michael R. Joens, *Triumph of the Soul*, 1999
Michael Phillips, *The Secret of the Rose Series*, 1993-
Frank Simon, *Trial by Fire*, 1999

1085

FRANK SIMON

The Raptor Virus

(Nashville: Broadman & Holman, 2001)

Story type: Contemporary
Subject(s): Computers
Major character(s): Hanna Flaherty, Spouse, Computer Expert; Russell Flaherty, Spouse, Computer Expert
Time period(s): 2000s
Locale(s): United States

Summary: Russell and Hanna Flaherty begin their married life with big trouble. Having helped prevent the Y2K bug from throwing the world into chaos, the Flahertys now discover that the United States is facing another potential computer attack. A virus known as the Raptor has been placed into computer chips throughout the country and will wipe out computer systems nationwide. When it is discovered that the Flahertys know of the virus, enemies of the United States will stop at nothing to prevent them from fixing the Raptor Virus.

Other books by the same author:
The Y2K Bug, 1999
Trial by Fire, 1999
Walls of Terror, 1997
Veiled Threats, 1996

Other books you might like:
T. Davis Bunn, *The Dream Voyagers*, 1999
Larry Burkett, *Kingdom Come*, 2001
Grant F. Jeffrey, *Flee the Darkness*, 1998
Stephen R. Lawhead, *Dream Thief*, 1996

William Proctor, *The Last Star*, 2000

1086

SHARON SNOW SIROIS

Sawyer's Crossing

(Hartford, Connecticut: Lighthouse, 2001)

Story type: Mystery
Subject(s): Crime and Criminals
Major character(s): Kelly Douglas, Police Officer; Mark Mitchell, Police Officer (new police chief)
Time period(s): 2000s
Locale(s): Sawyer's Crossing, Vermont

Summary: Kelly Douglas has dreamed for years of being able to return to her hometown of Sawyer's Crossing, Vermont, to work as a police officer. After years of hard work, her dream is finally realized. There are a few setbacks, however. The town's police chief, who wholeheartedly supported Kelly's dreams, decides to retire, leaving a younger and handsome officer as the new chief. The potential romantic complications do little to deter Kelly from her main goal: to find the person responsible for the murder of her own parents years before.

Other books you might like:
Terri Blackstock, *The Newpointe 911 Series*, 1998-
Athol Dickson, *The Garr Reed Series*, 1996-
B.J. Hoff, *The Daybreak Series*, 1995-
Gayle G. Roper, *The Amhearst Series*, 1997-
Audrey Stallsmith, *The Thyme Will Tell Series*, 1998-

1087

DEBRA WHITE SMITH

A Shelter in the Storm

(Eugene, Oregon: Harvest House, 2001)

Story type: Romance; Mystery
Series: Seven Sisters. Book 3
Subject(s): Murder
Major character(s): Sonsee LeBlanc, Veterinarian; Taylor Delaney, Rancher
Time period(s): 2000s
Locale(s): New Orleans, Louisiana

Summary: Sonsee LeBlanc secretly loves her best friend, Taylor Delaney, but since he has made it clear that he has no intention of marrying, she does her best to think of him only as a friend. Then her father is murdered and, to Sonsee's horror, the chief suspect is none other than Taylor Delaney. The evidence against Taylor is abundant, but Sonsee is sure there is no way he could have committed such a crime. Anxious to prove him innocent, she begins to investigate the murder on her own.

Other books by the same author:
Second Chances, 2000
The Awakening, 2000
Best Friends, 1999
Texas Rose, 1999
Texas Honor, 1998

Other books you might like:
Ron Benrey, *Little White Lies*, 2001
Terri Blackstock, *The Newpointe 911 Series*, 1998-
B.J. Hoff, *The Daybreak Series*, 1995-
Gilbert Morris, *The Dani Ross Series*, 2000-
Gayle G. Roper, *The Amhearst Series*, 1997-

1088

LAURAINE SNELLING

The Long Way Home

(Minneapolis: Bethany House, 2001)

Story type: Historical/American Civil War
Series: Secret Refuge. Book 3
Subject(s): Civil War
Major character(s): Jesselynn Highwood, Pioneer; Louisa Highwood, Nurse
Time period(s): 1860s
Locale(s): West; Richmond, Virginia

Summary: Jesselynn Highwood escapes the ravages of the Civil War at great cost. With her family home destroyed, Jesselynn heads west with some family members and former slaves. The small group hopes to reach Oregon, but find life on the trail to be a long and difficult one. Meanwhile, Jesselynn's sister, Louisa, and brother, Zachary, remain in Virginia and try desperately to obtain much needed medical supplies for an Army hospital.

Other books by the same author:
Daughter of Twin Oaks, 2000
Sisters of the Confederacy, 2000
Blessing in Disguise, 1999
Hawaiian Sunrise, 1999
Tender Mercies, 1999

Other books you might like:
Jack Cavanaugh, *The Adversaries*, 1996
Roger Elwood, *The Plantation Letters Series*, 1997-
Virginia Gaffney, *The Richmond Chronicles*, 1996-
Gilbert Morris, *The Bonnets and Bugles Series*, 1995-
Jane Orcutt, *The Fugitive Heart*, 1998

1089

CAROL STEWARD

Courting Katarina

(New York: Steeple Hill, 2001)

Story type: Romance
Subject(s): Love
Major character(s): Katarina Berthoff, Businesswoman; Alex MacIntyre, Fire Fighter
Time period(s): 2000s
Locale(s): United States

Summary: When Katarina Berthoff and Alex MacIntyre become reacquainted at the wedding of her sister and his brother, sparks fly. When she was in high school, Katarina thought Alex was the greatest and regretted the fact that she never got to know him better. Now, unfortunately, Katarina is practically engaged to somebody else so even though she still

thinks Alex is wonderful, nothing can come of their attraction. That is, unless Alex can convince her otherwise.

Other books by the same author:
Second Time Around, 2000
Her Kind of Hero, 1999
There Comes a Season, 1998

Other books you might like:
Kathryn Alexander, *A Wedding in the Family*, 1998
Lyn Cote, *Hope's Garden*, 2000
Martha Mason, *Two Rings, One Heart*, 1998
Lois Richer, *Wedding on the Way*, 1999
Cheryl Wolverton, *A Matter of Trust*, 1997

1090

PENELOPE J. STOKES

The Amber Photograph

(Nashville: Word, 2001)

Story type: Contemporary
Subject(s): Secrets
Major character(s): Diedre McAlister, Photographer
Time period(s): 2000s
Locale(s): North Carolina

Summary: After her mother's death from cancer, Diedre McAlister is sorting through some of her possessions, when she comes across a box containing some secrets from her mother's past. Not only is Diedre not the biological daughter of the man she thought was her father, but she also has an older sister she's never heard about. Determined to track the woman down, Diedre's only clue is a yellowing photograph.

Other books by the same author:
The Amethyst Heart, 2000
The Blue Bottle Club, 1999
Remembering You, 1997
Till We Meet Again, 1997
Home Fires Burning, 1996

Other books you might like:
Lynn N. Austin, *Eve's Daughters*, 1999
Joseph Bentz, *A Son Comes Home*, 1999
Linda Hall, *Margaret's Peace*, 1998
Tracie Peterson, *A Slender Thread*, 2000
Francine Rivers, *Leota's Garden*, 1999

1091

BODIE THOENE
BROCK THOENE, Co-Author

Jerusalem's Heart

(New York: Viking, 2001)

Story type: Contemporary
Series: Zion Legacy. Book 3
Subject(s): War
Major character(s): Jacob Kalner, Military Personnel; David Mayer, Military Personnel, Pilot; Lori Kalner, Nurse
Time period(s): 1940s (1948)
Locale(s): Israel

Summary: It is May of 1948 and the Jewish settlers of Israel try to keep their fragile hold on their new country. Lori and Jacob Kalner, new immigrants to the area, continue to work for Israel's freedom. Jacob becomes a hero after leading a fight defending Jerusalem from aggressors. Another Israeli hero is David Mayer, who flies the country's only Messerschmitt airplane. With the other Israelis, they are willing to give their lives to have their country remain free.

Other books by the same author:
All Rivers to the Sea, 2000
Jerusalem Vigil, 2000
Thunder from Jerusalem, 2000
Ashes of Remembrance, 1999
Winds of the Cumberland, 1999

Other books you might like:
Lynn N. Austin, *Wings of Refuge*, 2000
Kathy Hawkins, *The Heart of Zion Series*, 1996-
Michael Phillips, *The Russians Series*, 1991-
Francine Rivers, *The Mark of the Lion Series*, 1993-
Robert Stone, *Damascus Gate*, 1998

1092

JACQUELIN THOMAS

Singsation

(New York: Walk Worthy, 2001)

Story type: Contemporary
Subject(s): Singing
Major character(s): Deborah Anne Peterson, Singer
Time period(s): 2000s
Locale(s): United States

Summary: Deborah Anne Peterson sings in the church choir, but dreams of making it big. When rap star Triage Blue visits the church with his grandmother and is impressed by Deborah's talent, he tells her he can make her a star. Triage Blue gets her a job as a backup singer with a band and soon Deborah is on her way to stardom. However, as Deborah's star climbs, her once strong faith begins to crumble and she must decide if fame is worth giving up her devotion to God, or if she can somehow hold onto her faith and still be famous.

Where it's reviewed:
Booklist, March 1, 2001, page 1228
Library Journal, April 1, 2001, page 88
Publishers Weekly, April 2, 2001, page 39

Other books by the same author:
Undeniably Yours, 2001
Family Ties, 2000
Love's Miracle, 2000
Forever Always, 1999
Someone Like You, 1999

Other books you might like:
Reed Arvin, *Wind in the Wheat*, 1994
Angela Benson, *Awakening Mercy*, 2000
Michele Andrea Bowen, *Church Folk*, 2001
Sharon Ewell Foster, *Ain't No River*, 2001
Victoria Christopher Murray, *Temptation*, 2000

1093

ELLEN GUNDERSON TRAYLOR

The Oracle

(Nashville: Word, 2001)

Story type: Contemporary
Series: David Rothmeyer Adventures. Book 2
Subject(s): Archaeology; Murder
Major character(s): David Rothmeyer, Archaeologist
Time period(s): 2000s
Locale(s): Middle East; England; United States

Summary: When a prominent United States senator involved in Middle Eastern politics is assassinated, the world is thrown into chaos. Then some ancient artifacts that appear to have a connection to the troubles are discovered and archaeologist David Rothmeyer is drawn into the conflict. His search for answers takes him from the Middle East, to England, then to America before he can finally begin to unravel the truth behind the situation.

Other books by the same author:
The Priest, 1998
Melchizedek, 1997
Jerusalem: The City of God, 1995
Esther, 1994
Joshua, 1994

Other books you might like:
Lisa Tawn Bergren, *Chosen*, 1996
T. Davis Bunn, *Riders of the Pale Horse*, 1994
Christopher A. Lane, *Eden's Gate*, 1998
Michael Phillips, *The Rift in Time Series*, 1997-
Frank Simon, *Walls of Terror*, 1997

1094

JANET TRONSTAD

A Bride for Dry Creek

(New York: Steeple Hill, 2001)

Story type: Romance
Subject(s): Reunions
Major character(s): Francis Elkton, Civil Servant; Flint Harris, FBI Agent
Time period(s): 2000s
Locale(s): Dry Creek, Montana

Summary: Francis Elkton and Flint Harris impulsively eloped to Las Vegas on their prom night, but haven't seen each other since. Told that a legal loophole made the marriage invalid, neither one bothered to obtain an annulment. Now, 20 years later, the two are suddenly reunited in their hometown of Dry Creek, Montana, and they learn their marriage was legal all along. For Flint, who has been carrying a torch for Francis for years, this is good news, but she isn't so sure marriage to him is what she wants.

Other books by the same author:
A Gentleman for Dry Creek, 2000
An Angel for Dry Creek, 1999

Other books you might like:
Lyn Cote, *Finally Home*, 2001
Dee Henderson, *The O'Malley Series*, 2000-
Cynthia Rutledge, *The Marrying Kind*, 2001
Carol Steward, *Courting Katarina*, 2001
Cheryl Wolverton, *A Husband to Hold*, 2001

1095

JOHANNA VERWEERD

The Winter Garden

(Minneapolis: Bethany House, 2001)

Story type: Contemporary
Subject(s): Illness; Mothers and Daughters
Major character(s): Ika Boerema, Landscaper
Time period(s): 2000s
Locale(s): Netherlands

Summary: Born out of wedlock, Ika Boerema grows up as an outcast who endures cruel teasing from her schoolmates and icy indifference from her mother. Ika's only friend is a young boy named Bart who works at the local nursery and encourages her love of horticulture. After she is grown, Ika leaves her hometown and pursues a career as a landscape architect. When her mother becomes ill, Ika reluctantly returns home to care for her, but her childhood still haunts her as she must face her mother's continuing coldness.

Other books you might like:
Lynn N. Austin, *Eve's Daughters*, 1999
Terri Blackstock, *Seaside*, 2001
Paul McCusker, *Epiphany*, 1998
Tracie Peterson, *A Slender Thread*, 2000
Francine Rivers, *Leota's Garden*, 1999

1096

STEPHANIE GRACE WHITSON

Edge of the Wilderness

(Nashville: Thomas Nelson, 2001)

Story type: Historical/American West
Series: Dakota Moons. Book 2
Subject(s): Indians of North America
Major character(s): Genevieve LaCroix Dane, Spouse, Indian; Simon Dane, Religious (minister)
Time period(s): 1860s
Locale(s): West

Summary: After surviving the Dakota Sioux uprising of 1862, Genevieve LaCroix marries her widowed employer, Reverend Simon Dane. Because of her mixed racial heritage, Genevieve has faced prejudice from other white settlers in the past, but her life becomes more difficult when she and her husband move to a prison camp to counsel captured Sioux. With the white settlers wanting revenge, the Danes must convince them that not all Indians are evil.

Other books by the same author:
Valley of the Shadow, 2001
Karyn's Memory Box, 1999
Nora's Ribbon of Memories, 1999

Inspirational

Sarah's Patchwork, 1998
Red Bird, 1997

Other books you might like:
Lisa Tawn Bergren, *The Northern Lights Series*, 1998-
Janette Oke, *Drums of Change*, 1996
Catherine Palmer, *The Town Called Hope Series*, 1997-
Michael Phillips, *The Mercy and Eagleflight Series*, 1996-
Marlo M. Schalesky, *Cry Freedom*, 2000

1097

LORI WICK

City Girl

(Eugene, Oregon: Harvest House, 2001)

Story type: Historical/American West
Series: Yellow Rose Trilogy. Book 3
Subject(s): Ranch Life
Major character(s): Reagan Sullivan, Child-Care Giver (nanny)
Time period(s): 1880s
Locale(s): Texas

Summary: Reagan Sullivan grows up in New York City and has little idea of what life on a ranch entails. So when she gives up a factory job to work as a nanny in Texas, Reagan has some surprises waiting for her. However, she soon grows to love country life and a handsome rancher named Cash, so the city girl may soon make her move to the country a permanent one.

Other books by the same author:
Bamboo and Lace, 2001
A Texas Sky, 2000
Every Little Thing about You, 1999
The Princess, 1999
Pretense, 1998

Other books you might like:
Lori Copeland, *Faith*, 1998
Dianna Crawford, *The Frontier Women Series*, 2000-
Kristen Heitzmann, *The Rocky Mountain Legacy Series*, 1998-
Al Lacy, *The Mail Order Bride Series*, 1998-
Judith Pella, *Texas Angel*, 1999

1098

THOMAS WILLIAMS

The Devil's Mouth

(Nashville: Word, 2001)

Story type: Fantasy
Series: Seven Kingdoms Chronicles. Book 2
Subject(s): Good and Evil
Major character(s): Lanson, Royalty (prince)
Time period(s): Indeterminate
Locale(s): Lochlaund, Mythical Place

Summary: When his father is murdered, Prince Lanson flees the castle in fear for his life. While hiding, he meets a beautiful tavern maid, also in hiding. However, she is running from the powerful church of Lochlaund. Falling in love with

her, Lanson's only hope of saving her life is to marry her, but to do so will expose him to his political enemies.

Other books by the same author:
The Crown of Eden, 1999

Other books you might like:
Randy C. Alcorn, *Lord Foulgrin's Letters*, 2000
Stephen R. Lawhead, *Dream Thief*, 1996
Nancy Moser, *The Mustard Seed Series*, 1998-
Michael Phillips, *The Caledonia Series*, 1999-
Kathy Tyers, *The Firebird Trilogy*, 1999-

1099

LINDA WINDSOR

It Had to Be You

(Sisters, Oregon: Multnomah, 2001)

Story type: Romance
Subject(s): Cruise Ships
Major character(s): Dan Jarrett, Rancher; Sunny Elders, Nurse
Time period(s): 2000s
Locale(s): At Sea

Summary: Rancher Dan Jarrett is convinced his new stepfather is a con artist, so he reluctantly accompanies his family on a cruise in order to find out the truth about the man. On the ship, Dan encounters sweet emergency room nurse Sunny Elders, who soon has him forgetting about his mother's romantic life and concentrating on his own.

Other books by the same author:
Maire, 2000
Not Exactly Eden, 2000
Hi Honey, I'm Home, 1999
Border Rose, 1998
Winter Rose, 1997

Other books you might like:
Terri Blackstock, *The Second Chances Series*, 1996-
Mary Davis, *Newlywed Games*, 2000
Robin Jones Gunn, *The Glenbrooke Series*, 1995-
Annie Jones, *The Route 66 Series*, 1999-
Shari MacDonald, *The Salinger Sisters Series*, 1998-

1100

ROBERT L. WISE

The Empty Coffin

(Nashville: Broadman & Holman, 2001)

Story type: Mystery
Series: Sam and Vera Sloan. Book 1
Subject(s): Crime and Criminals
Major character(s): Sam Sloan, Detective; Vera Sloan, Spouse
Time period(s): 2000s
Locale(s): United States

Summary: Working as a detective can be difficult, especially for a Christian. Having to face brutal and debased behavior every day, Sam Sloan often finds himself wondering where God is when people are acting their worst. Facing the challenge of an especially difficult murder case, Sam turns to God

and his wife, Vera, to find the courage to solve the case and keep his faith alive.

Other books by the same author:
Be Not Afraid, 2001
All That Remains, 1995
The Fall of Jerusalem, 1994
The Exiles, 1993
The Dawning, 1991

Other books you might like:
W.E. Davis, *The Gil Beckman Series*, 1994-
Athol Dickson, *The Garr Reed Series*, 1996-
Robert Funderburk, *The Dylan St. John Series*, 1996-
B.J. Hoff, *The Daniel and Jennifer Kaine Series*, 1986-
Sally S. Wright, *The Ben Reese Series*, 1997-

1101

CHERYL WOLVERTON

A Husband to Hold

(New York: Steeple Hill, 2001)

Story type: Romance
Series: Hill Creek, Texas

Subject(s): Secrets
Major character(s): Leah Thomas, Teacher; Mark Walker, Cowboy
Time period(s): 2000s
Locale(s): Hill Creek, Texas

Summary: Leah Thomas comes to Hill Creek, Texas hoping to escape from her troubled past. She meets Mark Walker, who is intrigued by Leah's quiet beauty. However, the past has a way of catching up with people, and Leah's past soon returns to haunt her. Together, though, the couple tries to find solutions that will help them move on with their lives.

Other books by the same author:
For Love of Mitch, 2000
Healing Hearts, 2000
What the Doctor Ordered, 2000
For Love of Hawk, 1999
For Love of Zach, 1999

Other books you might like:
Carolyne Aarsen, *A Hero for Kelsey*, 2001
Valerie Hansen, *The Perfect Couple*, 2000
Susan Kirby, *Love Sign*, 2001
Cynthia Rutledge, *The Marrying Kind*, 2001
Lenora Worth, *Logan's Child*, 1998

Inspirational

Popular Fiction in Review
by
Tom Barton

The popular fiction genre has continued to enjoy wide-spread acceptance and provides enjoyment for millions of readers. Attempting to reach readers, both those new to the genre and long-time fans, publishers have become more sophisticated in their distribution tactics, and advertising has played a key role. Also, technology, both new and old, has helped punch up sales. Television programs, such as *Oprah*, which devote time to promoting books have had a dramatic impact. A book that perhaps would enjoy modest success on its own, if selected by Oprah Winfrey can show a dramatic sales increase.

Some people believe that technology is about to revolutionize the publishing industry. Jason Epstein argues that the revolution is necessary. A former editor for writers such as Norman Mailer, Philip Roth, Gore Vidal and E.L. Doctorow, and co-founder of the *New York Review of Books*, Epstein has written a book, *Book Business* (Norton, 2001), on the subject. He says that publishing has changed from a cottage industry into big business. Publishing companies, through mergers and acquisitions, are now giant corporations more interested in the bottom line than publishing books. The booksellers have changed, too. When people moved to the suburbs, the bookstores followed, and rented space in expensive malls. Consequently, publishers and booksellers are under intense pressure because of costs, forcing them to seek only bestsellers which makes it difficult for new authors and authors not on the bestseller lists. Publishers are reluctant to cover production costs for an unknown author and booksellers can't afford to stock a book with an unknown sales potential. Epstein says the answer is the electronic book. An e-book can be stored on a publisher's hard drive until a reader offers to buy it.

Sales of electronic books are expected to increase dramatically over the next several years. However, there are some questions of a technical nature that must be solved before this revolution happens. For one thing, there are several formats available and it's not clear which, computers or portable reading devices, will emerge as the technology of choice.

Of course, computers already play a part in today's publishing. Readers with a personal computer and telephone modem hooked-up to the Internet can access information on most books in print from the publisher, the bookseller, or directly from the author. Readers can do this from the comfort of their homes at any time, day or night. Using this same Internet access, readers can make an online book purchase for themselves or a friend or search a library catalog for a book. Readers also can obtain book reviews and author interviews, and can participate in book discussion groups with other readers. Generally, the process is facilitated through websites, which are maintained by booksellers, publishers, authors, libraries, newspapers, magazines, and interested readers. One site, The *New York Times* Book Pages (www.nytimes.com/books), allows readers to browse the first chapter of a bestseller by reading it online, printing it or downloading it. The *Wall Street Journal* (www.opinionjournal.com) has provided an online serial with a new chapter offered each week. While the *Wall Street Journal* no doubt is interested in boosting subscriptions, the idea of offering fiction as a serial brings to mind three authors featured in this volume: Helen Fielding, John Grisham, and Stephen King.

In 1998, Helen Fielding wrote the bestseller *Bridget Jones's Diary*, about a 30-something professional woman, struggling with a weight problem and her unmarried status. Reportedly the idea for the novel came from a column Fielding penned for a London newspaper. The assignment caught on and it became the basis for the bestselling book. The book was so successful that it became a movie starring Renee Zellweger. Fielding's featured selection in this volume of *What Do I Read Next?*, *Cause Celeb*, was released this year in the United States, though it was published in England before *Bridget Jones's Diary*. While featuring some of Fielding's humorous wit, the book deals with

starvation, fund raising, and celebrity. This book, too, may be made into a movie.

No one will be surprised if John Grisham's book *A Painted House* is made into a movie. What's unusual is that the book first appeared in serialized installments in the *Oxford American* magazine. As the number one bestselling author since 1994, Grisham usually writes two thrillers a year. However, *A Painted House* isn't a thriller. The book is about an only child, Luke Chandler, growing up on a farm in Arkansas. Luke and his family follow the St. Louis Cardinals on the radio, while taking a break from their struggles to save a cotton crop threatened by extreme heat and heavy rains.

While elements of the book are straight from Grisham's childhood, living on a farm in Arkansas until the age of seven and dreaming of playing for the St. Louis Cardinals, the book is not a fictionalized autobiography. Set in the early 1950s, the story also deals with a family's anxiety about one of their members serving in the Korean War, a war that ended before Grisham was born. In the book, Luke's mother fosters in her son the dream of going to college as a way of escaping farm life. Grisham has admitted that his only interest in going to college was to play baseball, a short-lived career. Supposedly, Grisham was cut from the team when his coach learned he couldn't hit a curve ball or a fast ball. Fortunately, he discovered he has other talents. Whether Grisham will go back to his two-thriller formula or continue exploring other avenues, including serialization, remains to be seen.

Stephen King took serialization one step further than Grisham. King offered the first four chapters of his novel *The Plant* online. The project hit a snag because of problems with revenue collection, which relied on the honor system. For a dollar, readers could download a chapter. For the most part, the public cooperated with this arrangement, at least for the first couple of chapters. However, cooperation lagged noticeably by the fourth chapter and King finally suspended publication when paid readership increasingly declined.

Obviously, his Internet experience hasn't soured him on experimenting with new technology. Excerpts from his latest novel, *Dreamcatcher* have appeared on *Time* magazine's website. The novel, some say, marks a return to King's tried and true formula, telling a good story. The expectation is that the book will be a bestseller.

Worthy books published this year by established writers include those by Walter Mosley, Colson Whitehead, Lee Durkee, Anne Tyler, Amy Tan, Jan Karon, Richard Russo, and a posthumously published work by Willie Morris. Authors making noteworthy debuts include Manil Suri and Ana Menendez.

Walter Mosley struck out in a different direction in his new book *Fearless Jones*. Amateur detective Easy Rawlins, who readers first met in *Devil in the Blue Dress* and which was made into a movie starring Denzel Washington, is not featured. His new novel introduces readers to Paris Minton, a mild-mannered, relatively civilized man who becomes the target of some nasty people. Minton summons his life-long friend, Fearless Jones, a decorated war hero, to deal with the bad guys.

While many have characterized him as a mystery writer, in my opinion Mosley is more than that. For instance, if you want a sense of what life was like in the inner city for African Americans post World War II, Mosley's books are a good place to start. His settings make a reader feel like a fly on the wall. His characters are colorful and his stories are interesting, and he never avoids the complexity of race.

Another African American, Colson Whitehead, has just published his second book, *John Henry Days*. His first novel *The Intuitionist* attracted an audience that included science fiction and comic book fans. His latest book appeals to a more middle-class audience. One explanation could be the subject matter; in *John Henry Days* Whitehead tackles the plight of middle class African Americans searching for more in life than materialism.

The book treats African American folk hero John Henry, the ''steel driving man,'' as a man rather than as a super man. He has human feelings and he's not eager to match his mortal strength against a steam drill. Of course, he does, and he wins, but the contest kills him. A parallel story in the book is about a contemporary hack journalist. The intersection of the two stories gives added meaning to both.

Despite traveling to the South to do research for his book, which is set in West Virginia, Whitehead, a life-long New Yorker, isn't likely to be moving south anytime soon. This is just the opposite of the path Willie Morris' career followed. Morris, a white southerner, grew up in Yazoo City, Mississippi. He left the South and moved to the North, becoming the youngest editor-in-chief of *Harper's* magazine. While his most famous book, *North Toward Home*, is a non-fiction autobiography, Morris' last book, *Taps*, which was published posthumously (Morris died in 1999), is a fictional account of growing up in a small southern town at the beginning of the Korean War. In his writing, Morris is known for reflecting his experience of growing up in the South, with all its traditions and its problems.

Another Southern writer from Mississippi, Lee Durkee, also left the South to become a writer; or, at least he wrote his first novel in New England. He also has a connection to *Harper's*. The magazine has published some of his short fiction. Durkee's first novel, *Rides of the Midway*, is a coming- of-age novel set in Mississippi. The Vietnam War casts a large shadow over this story; the main character's father gets on a plane to Vietnam and never returns.

Durkee's unsentimental and humorous prose is reminiscent of Anne Tyler. While Tyler lives in and writes mostly about Baltimore, Maryland, her characters and her gentle style in some respects seem to defy a regional designation. Tyler writes about everyday people, not the cookie-cutter

kind one finds on television, but the kind with real lives, large extended families, and complicated relationships that have somehow gotten mixed up. Although her stories are accessible and gentle, there is an incremental poetic element to them that can draw tears from an unsuspecting reader. Tyler's latest book, *Back When We Were Grownups*, deals with the ''what if'' question most middle-aged people ask themselves from time-to-time. The main character, a woman who heads a very large, disjointed, extended family, wonders what her life would have been like if she had married her college boyfriend.

Another author who rises above categorization is Amy Tan. A Chinese American, Tan writes about cross-cultural tensions. Her work reflects her family experience and her Chinese ancestry. In her latest book, *The Bonesetter's Daughter*, an unresolved conflict between a daughter and her immigrant mother becomes an issue when the mother becomes dependent on her daughter. The book probably would have been released in 1999, but Tan decided to rewrite it when her mother died that year after a four-year bout with Alzheimer's disease. After her mother's death, Tan learned new information: Tan did not know that when her mother came to this country, she left behind her first husband and children; she learned that her grandmother committed suicide in China; and finally, Tan learned her mother's real name. As a result, Tan felt compelled to rewrite *The Bonesetter's Daughter*, which has been described as a fictional autobiography.

Despite her subjects, calling Tan a Chinese American writer is much too narrow. Practically speaking, her work has a very broad appeal. Her stories deal with adjustment to cultural conflicts and acculturation into American society, making her a favorite with a multicultural audience across the country.

A new voice, Manil Suri, also taps into his family's experience. He makes his debut with the multicultural novel *The Death of Vishnu*, which is set in Bombay, India. Despite this recent success, when it comes to fiction, Suri isn't a new kid on the block. He has been collecting rejection notices for many years. A university professor, Suri makes a living teaching mathematics in Maryland. Until this book, his only published literary work appeared in an obscure Bulgarian journal that Suri couldn't read because, of course, it was printed in Bulgarian.

The Death of Vishnu draws heavily on his experiences growing up in a one-room apartment in Bombay. Sharing a kitchen and bathroom with other families helped develop his imagination. Despite the novel's outward morbidity, the death of a drunken homeless man, the story has been characterized as humorous, which no doubt is a tribute to Suri's ability with the English language.

While his writing has religious elements to it, he prefers religion's intellectual side rather than its mystical side. His characters, both Hindu and Muslim, view themselves as religiously moral. Their actions are motivated by their imperfect intellectual understanding of religious theology. This interplay between the characters and their beliefs gives Suri's book a humanistic and humorous flavor.

Another new voice, Ana Menendez, a Cuban American, has written a multicultural collection, *In Cuba I Was a German Shepherd*, about exile and loss. A former journalist and winner of the Pushcart Prize (2000) for short fiction, Menendez lived in India for a time. She was born in the United States but both her parents are Cuban exiles. Though her stories are about Cuban and Dominican exiles, they offer insight into the immigrant experience and the bittersweet feelings it produces. Adjusting and acculturation in a new country are difficult processes for everyone. Menendez's treatment is humorous and sensitive.

Another author who writes with a sense of humor is Richard Russo. The author of five novels, Russso's latest, *Empire Falls*, is set in a small town in Maine. The town is economically depressed, as are the small towns in upstate New York which provide the settings for three of his other books, *Mohawk*, *The Risk Pool*, and *Nobody's Fool*, which was made into a movie starring Paul Newman and Melanie Griffith. In those three earlier works, Russo has dealt with father-son relationships. In *Empire Falls*, Russo looks at a father-daughter relationship. The book evolved into a story about the changing face of America at the end of the 20th century. His light, witty, insightful style has drawn comparisons with John Irving, Mark Twain, and Richard Yates.

While Jan Karon will never be compared with Mark Twain, she does write about pure Americana. Her latest book, *A Common Life*, the sixth of the Mitford Years series, chronicles life in a small idyllic town in the mountains of North Carolina. The novel is about Episcopal priest Tim Kavanagh's marriage to Cynthia Coppersmith. Despite a Christian theme of God's love and the basic decency of her characters, Karon's work hasn't been limited to the religious market.

My intention has been to draw a thumbnail sketch of trends and voices that are contributing to the current popular fiction scene. While sketches are always a bit incomplete, my hope is that readers will find these observations helpful. I don't mind saying that I'm very enthusiastic about popular fiction and my hope is that this essay reflects that. Before closing, I'd like to share the following anecdote, which I think supports the reason for my enthusiasm. Recently, a student asked for something to read. When I suggested something from the popular fiction collection, she shook her head. ''Don't you like stories?,'' I asked. ''Yes, but only if they're true,'' she responded. ''Too bad. You're limiting yourself,'' I said. ''Why?'' I mentioned Gao Xingjian's comments when he accepted the Nobel Prize for literature in 2000. Commenting on the importance of history, as well as literature, he remarked that though the characters in literary works are products of the imagination, they maintain a sureness of their own self worth.

His observation got the student's attention. For the next five or ten minutes, we talked about Gao Xingjian's comments. The following is a paraphrase of some of the points we discussed.

When one looks for the truth, objective facts often aren't enough. They limit a reader to outward appearances. If one wants to know motives and feelings, one looks for a good story.

There is much more to a good story than duplicating reality. A good story allows readers to see from the inside out as well as the outside in. He or she becomes aware of other possibilities, other points of view.

Characters reveal what they are thinking and why they are thinking it. For instance, a character is engaged to Mary but he loves Sue. Or a character loves John but she's going to marry Tom. Situations like this deal with the uniqueness of being human.

A good story allows readers to become part of the story via their experiences and imaginations. Consequently, cultural fashions and national identities become of little importance, if the writer gets it right. Yes, of course, an author does make things up, but a good story requires more. Emotion and valid life experiences are necessary, too. When imagination is combined properly with feelings and life situations, language transforms the end product into something magical for the reader. In short, a good story touches the mystery of being and reaffirms human existence.

When we completed our conversation, the student headed toward the popular fiction section. She was smiling. One could argue that the difference between popular fiction and literature is longevity. Only time will tell which of today's popular books will be considered literature tomorrow. While we're waiting for the votes to determine which will be literature and which will not, this is a really good time to be a reader.

Recommended Titles

Back When We Were Grownups by Anne Tyler

Big as Life by Maureen Howard

The Biographer's Tale by A.S. Byatt

The Bonesetter's Daughter by Amy Tan

Carry Me Across the Water by Ethan C. Canin

Cause Celeb by Helen Fielding

A Common Life by Jan Karon

Crawling at Night by Nani Power

The Death of Vishnu by Manil Suri

Dreamcatcher by Stephen King

The Dying Animal by Philip Roth

Empire Falls by Richard Russo

Faithless by Joyce Carol Oates

Fearless Jones by Walter Mosley

The Gardens of Kyoto by Kate Walbert

In Cuba I Was a German Shepherd by Ana Menendez

Love, Etc. by Julian Barnes

Martyrs' Crossing by Amy Wilentz

Motherland by Vineeta Vijayaraghavan

A Painted House by John Grisham

The Peppered Moth by Margaret Drabble

Rides of the Midway by Lee Durkee

Taps by Willie Morris

The Torturer's Apprentice by John Biguenet

Popular Fiction Titles

1102

CHRIS ADRIAN

Gob's Grief
(New York: Broadway, 2000)

Story type: Historical; Satire
Subject(s): Civil War; Ghosts; Brothers
Major character(s): Gob Woodhull, Scientist (wants to resurrect the dead), Twin (of Tomo); Maci Trufant, Lover (of Gob), Secretary (for Gob's mother); Tomo Woodhull, Military Personnel, Twin (of Gob)
Time period(s): 1860s; 1870s (1861-1875)
Locale(s): United States

Summary: Adrian combines historical characters with magic realism to tell a story of longing, grief, and madness in the aftermath of the Civil War. Gob, the fictional son of suffragette Victoria Woodhull, invents a machine to bring back Tomo, his twin who was killed at the battle of Chickamauga. He is aided by Maci, who converses with her brother, also killed in the war. Appearances by historical figures keep the story lively.

Where it's reviewed:
Booklist, December 1, 2000, page 675
Library Journal, January 1, 2001, page 151
New York Times Book Review, February 4, 2001, page 31

Other books you might like:
Lisa Carey, *Country of the Young*, 2000
Max Allan Collins, *Regeneration*, 1999
  Barbara Collins, co-author
Rhian Ellis, *After Life*, 2000
James Hynes, *The Lecturer's Tale*, 2001
Powell Padgett, *Mrs. Hollingsworth's Men*, 2000

1103

JANE ALISON

The Love-Artist
(New York: Farrar, Straus & Giroux, 2001)

Story type: Historical/Ancient Rome; Literary
Subject(s): Roman Empire; Exile; Love
Major character(s): Ovid, Historical Figure, Writer (poet banished from Rome); Xenia, Young Woman, Witch (a healer, predicts future)
Time period(s): 1st century
Locale(s): Rome, Roman Empire; Black Sea, Europe

Summary: Banished during the emperor's campaign to restore morality, the Roman poet Ovid meets Xenia, an "Amazon," a woman possessing spirituality, sensitivity, beauty, and physical strength. He is enthralled by her and she accompanies him when he returns to Rome. He intends for her to be his muse for a great poetic work but things end badly as he falls victim to greed, selfishness, and other masculine shortcomings.

Where it's reviewed:
Library Journal, February 1, 2001, page 124
Publishers Weekly, March 5, 2001, page 61

Other books you might like:
A.S. Byatt, *Possession*, 1990
Joyce Carol Oates, *Unholy Loves*, 1979
J.D. Salinger, *Raise High the Roof Beam, Carpenters; and Seymour*, 1963
Muriel Spark, *The Girls of Slender Means*, 1963
Romain Wilhelmsen, *The Curse of Destiny*, 2000

1104

BENJAMIN ANASTAS

The Faithful Narrative of a Pastor's Disappearance

(New York: Farrar, Straus & Giroux, 2001)

Story type: Psychological; Satire
Subject(s): African Americans; Clergy; Missing Persons
Major character(s): Bethany Caruso, Parent (of two children); Thomas Moser, Religious (reverend), Lover (of Bethany); Martha Howard, Real Estate Agent
Time period(s): 2000s (2001)
Locale(s): Boston, Massachusetts (suburban)

Summary: A Puritan church in suburban Boston recruits Rev. Thomas Moser, a black intellectual to be its pastor. Finding himself emotionally isolated from his white congregation, he soon falls into a relationship with Bethany Caruso, a beautiful, sensitive, married woman. When Thomas disappears one day, the church council tries to find out what happened to him. Church council member Martha Howard, a successful businesswoman, who is bitter and disappointed in her personal life, tries to pin the disappearance on Bethany.

Where it's reviewed:
Booklist, March 1, 2001, page 1224
Kirkus Reviews, February 15, 2001, page 198
Library Journal, March 1, 2001, page 130
New York Times Book Review, May 20, 2001, page 6
Publishers Weekly, April 23, 2001, page 48

Other books by the same author:
An Underachiever's Diary, 1998

Other books you might like:
Michele Andrea Bowen, *Church Folk*, 2001
Ralph Ellison, *Juneteenth*, 1999
Terry McMillan, *A Day Late and a Dollar Short*, 2001
Alice Walker, *The Way Forward Is with a Broken Heart*, 2000
John Edgar Wideman, *The Cattle Killing*, 1996

1105

SARA BACKER

American Fuji

(New York: Putnam, 2001)

Story type: Romance; Multicultural
Subject(s): Cultural Conflict; Women; Death
Major character(s): Gabriela "Gabby" Stanton, Professor (unexpectedly fired), Clerk (works for Mr. Eguchi); Mr. Eguchi, Undertaker (sells fantasy funerals); Alex Thorn, Parent
Time period(s): 2000s (2001)
Locale(s): Japan

Summary: In her first novel, Sara Backer explores cultural differences. Gabriela "Gabby" Stanton, 36, lives in Japan and after being fired from her teaching job, she's hired by Mr. Eguchi, a kind of undertaker. Alex Thorn, a middle-aged American, wants information about the death of his son, Cody, who died in a motorcycle accident while attending the school at which Gabby taught. Alex's search leads him to Gabby who reluctantly agrees to help. In the end, they're surprised at what they find.

Where it's reviewed:
Booklist, March 1, 2001, page 1224
Chicago Tribune Books, April 22, 2001, page 2
Library Journal, February 1, 2001, page 124
New York Times Book Review, March 25, 2001, page 20
Publishers Weekly, January 8, 2001, page 44

Other books you might like:
Alan Brown, *Audrey Hepburn's Neck*, 1996
Louise Erdrich, *The Last Report on the Miracles at Little No Horse*, 2001
Anna Esaki-Smith, *Meeting Luciano*, 1999
John Burnham Schwartz, *Bicycle Days*, 1989
Onoto Watanna, *The Heart of Hyacinth*, 2000

1106

JULIANNA BAGGOTT

Girl Talk

(New York: Pocket, 2001)

Story type: Coming-of-Age; Contemporary
Subject(s): Single Parent Families; Pregnancy; Mothers and Daughters
Major character(s): Lissy Jablonski, Advertising, Young Woman (unmarried and pregnant); Dotty Jablonski, Parent (Lissy's mother); Anthony Pantuliano, Parent (Lissy's father)
Time period(s): 1980s (1985); 2000s (2000)
Locale(s): New Hampshire; Bayonne, New Jersey

Summary: Poet and short story writer Julianna Baggott's debut novel explores the emotional bonds between mothers and daughters. Lissy, 30, is pregnant and unmarried. She thinks about the summer 15 years before when her father ran off with another woman and Lissy almost came unhinged. She and her mother took a trip during which Lissy lost her virginity, learned her father was not really her father and that her grandmother wasn't dead after all.

Where it's reviewed:
Booklist, November 15, 2000, page 621
Library Journal, November 15, 2000, page 95
New York Times Book Review, April 1, 2001, page 16
Publishers Weekly, November 20, 2000, page 43

Other books you might like:
Elizabeth Berg, *Open House*, 2000
India Knight, *My Life on a Plate*, 2000
Amy Tan, *The Bonesetter's Daughter*, 2001
John Updike, *Licks of Love*, 2000
Fay Weldon, *Rhode Island Blues*, 2000

1107

JOHN BANVILLE

Eclipse

(Thorndike, Maine: Thorndike, 2001)

Story type: Psychological; Literary
Subject(s): Acting; Ghosts; Self-Awareness
Major character(s): Alexander Cleve, Actor; Quirke, Maintenance Worker; Lily Cleve, Teenager (Cleve's daughter)
Time period(s): 2000s (2001)
Locale(s): Ireland

Summary: Alexander Cleve is a successful actor who is experiencing a mid-life crisis. Unable to separate himself from the roles he plays, he withdraws to his boyhood home to work through his dilemma. There he mulls over his past with the ghosts of his parents and others he may or may not have known. Meanwhile, the real world keeps spinning, and Cleve finds himself estranged from his wife and unable to help his troubled daughter.

Where it's reviewed:
Booklist, February 1, 2001, page 1039
Library Journal, February 1, 2001, page 124
Publishers Weekly, December 18, 2000, page 54

Other books by the same author:
The Untouchable, 1997
Althena, 1995
Ghosts, 1993
Mefisto, 1989
The Book of Evidence, 1989

Other books you might like:
Linda Barnes, *Dead Heat*, 1984
Elia Kazan, *The Understudy*, 1975
Iris Murdoch, *Sea the Sea*, 1978
Susan Richards Shreve, *Train Home*, 1994
Sarah Willis, *Rehearsal*, 2001

1108

PAT BARKER

Border Crossing

(New York: Farrar Straus & Giroux, 2001)

Story type: Psychological; Contemporary
Subject(s): Lifesaving; Murder; Children
Major character(s): Tom Seymour, Doctor (psychiatrist), Spouse (of Lauren); Danny Miller, Murderer (killed an old woman as a child), Convict (on parole)
Time period(s): 2000s (2001)
Locale(s): Newcastle, England

Summary: While out for a stroll, Tom Seymour sees a man attempt suicide by jumping into the river. A psychiatrist, Tom, saves the man, who turns out to be Danny Miller, a paroled convict. Tom's testimony convicted Danny of murder when he was a child. Now a young adult, Danny turns to Tom for help resolving his problematic childhood. During treatment, Danny reveals an uncanny ability for getting others to cross moral borders.

Where it's reviewed:
New York Times Book Review, March 18, 2001, page 10
Newsweek, March 5, 2001, page 58
Publishers Weekly, January 22, 2001, page 300

Other books by the same author:
Another World, 1998
Ghost Road, 1995
Eye in the Door, 1994
Regeneration, 1991
Blow Your House Down, 1984

Other books you might like:
Deepak Chopra, *Soulmate*, 2001
Nick Earls, *Bachelor Kisses*, 1998
F. Scott Fitzgerald, *Tender Is the Night*, 1934
Mark Salzman, *Lying Awake*, 2000

1109

JULIAN BARNES

Love, Etc.

(New York: Knopf, 2001)

Story type: Literary; Psychological
Subject(s): Friendship; Love; Men
Major character(s): Oliver Russell, Spouse (of Gillian), Friend (of Stuart); Stuart Hughes, Friend (of Oliver), Divorced Person (from Gillian); Gillian Russell, Spouse (of Oliver), Divorced Person (from Stuart)
Time period(s): 2000s (2001)
Locale(s): England

Summary: This story is about love and the blurred line that separates it from friendship. As Oliver, Gillian and Stuart approach middle age, they have some regrets about the choices made in their youth. Oliver, who is married to Gillian, stole her from his former best friend, Stuart. In the novel, each recall encounters and decisions they made in their lives. The story could be viewed as a sequel to the author's earlier novel, *Talking It Over*.

Where it's reviewed:
Booklist, November 15, 2000, page 586
Library Journal, December 2000, page 184
New York Times Book Review, February 25, 2001, page 8
Publishers Weekly, December 18, 2000, page 53

Other books by the same author:
England, England, 1999
Cross Channel, 1996
Porcupine, 1992
Talking It Over, 1991
A History of the World in 10 1/2 Chapters, 1989

Other books you might like:
John Biguenet, *The Torturer's Apprentice*, 2001
A.S. Byatt, *The Biographer's Tale*, 2001
Isabel Colegate, *Winter Journey*, 2001
William Gay, *Long Home*, 1999
Ha Jin, *Waiting*, 1999
Alan Lightman, *Diagnosis*, 2000

Popular Fiction

ANN BEATTIE

Perfect Recall
(New York: Scribner, 2001)

Story type: Collection; Satire
Subject(s): Social Conditions; Relationships; Family Life
Time period(s): 2000s (2001)
Locale(s): United States

Summary: In this collection of 11 short stories, Ann Beattie demonstrates her ability to place readers in living rooms and back yards, where her characters let their hair down, eat, drink, make merry, and above all, complain. Her colorful cast of characters, including a down in the mouth veteran, a famous cook, senior citizens, in-laws, and outlaws, strive for perfection and face tragedy. The author explores cultural trends with a deft touch.

Where it's reviewed:
Library Journal, December 2000, page 194
New York Times Book Review, January 14, 2001, page 7
Publishers Weekly, November 20, 2000, page 44

Other books by the same author:
Park City, 1998
Secrets and Surprises, 1991
What Was Mine, 1991
Picturing Will, 1989
Burning House, 1982

Other books you might like:
A.S. Byatt, *Elementals*, 1998
Penelope Fitzgerald, *The Means of Escape*, 2000
Ellen Gilchrist, *The Cabal*, 2000
William Trevor, *Death in Summer*, 1998

1111

DAVID BENIOFF

The 25th Hour
(New York: Carroll & Graf, 2001)

Story type: Contemporary Realism; Adult
Subject(s): Crime and Criminals; Drugs
Major character(s): Monty Brogan, Drug Dealer (heroin), Convict (gets a seven-year sentence); Frank Slattery, Businessman (bond trader), Friend (of Monty); Jakob Elinsky, Teacher (of high school English), Friend (of Monty)
Time period(s): 2000s (2001)
Locale(s): New York, New York

Summary: In Benioff's debut novel, characterization drives the story. Monty Brogan, an attractive, likable, slick drug dealer, has been sentenced to seven years hard time. Neither he nor his friends believe he can serve the sentence. On his last night of freedom, Monty and his friends party at a nightclub operated by Uncle Blue, a Russian gangster and Monty's former boss. Predictably, Uncle Blue wonders if Monty plans to snitch on him. A surprise ending adds to the fun.

Where it's reviewed:
Booklist, November 15, 2000, page 611
New York Times, January 22, 2001, page B11
Publishers Weekly, November 20, 2000, page 46

Other books you might like:
John Grisham, *The Partner*, 1997
George V. Higgins, *The Friends of Eddie Coyle*, 1972
Tom Perrotta, *Joe College*, 2000
Scott Phillips, *Ice Harvest*, 2000
Charles Willeford, *Miami Blues*, 1984

1112

ELIZABETH BERG

Never Change
(New York: Pocket, 2001)

Story type: Psychological
Subject(s): Women; Illness; Death
Major character(s): Myra Lipinski, Nurse (visits patients at home); Chip Reardon, Patient (terminally ill)
Time period(s): 2000s (2001)
Locale(s): Boston, Massachusetts

Summary: Myra Lipinski, 51, a nurse, unmarried and resigned to quiet desperation visits Chip Reardon, a terminally ill patient. They attended the same high school, but didn't run in the same circles—Chip, good looking and popular, was a star athlete, while Myra has always been homely and unattractive. Gradually, their relationship becomes personal out of their mutual need to overcome loneliness.

Where it's reviewed:
Atlantic Monthly, June 2001, page 104
Booklist, April 2001, page 1428
Chicago Tribune Books, June 17, 2001, page 1
Library Journal, April 15, 2001, page 130
Publishers Weekly, May 14, 2001, page 50

Other books by the same author:
Open House, 2000
What We Keep, 1998
The Pull of the Moon, 1996
Range of Motion, 1995
Durable Goods, 1993

Other books you might like:
Candace Bushnell, *Four Blondes*, 2000
Helen Fielding, *Bridget Jones's Diary*, 1996
Marilyn French, *The Women's Room*, 1993
Molly Giles, *Iron Shoes*, 2000
Doris Lessing, *Love, Again*, 1996

BETSY BERNE

Bad Timing
(New York: Villard, 2001)

Story type: Coming-of-Age
Subject(s): Pregnancy; Infidelity; Music and Musicians

Major character(s): Unnamed Character, Writer, Narrator; Joseph Pendleton, Businessman (nightclub owner), Lover (of narrator)
Time period(s): 2000s (2001)
Locale(s): New York, New York (Manhattan)

Summary: In Betsy Berne's debut novel, the unnamed white woman narrator tells the story of her one-night stand with a black man she meets at a glitzy Manhattan party. She becomes pregnant and eventually decides to terminate the pregnancy. When her lover learns about her decision, their relationship sort of evolves into an affair. Berne keeps the story interesting with insider knowledge of the hip Manhattan scene and her keen eye for graphic details.

Where it's reviewed:
Chicago Tribune Books, June 10, 2001, page 2
Library Journal, December 2000, page 184
New York Times Book Review, February 25, 2001, page 18
Publishers Weekly, November 27, 2000, page 50

Other books you might like:
Dorothy Cannell, *Mum's the Word*, 1990
Stanley Crouch, *Don't the Moon Look Lonesome*, 2000
Carrie Fisher, *Delusions of Grandma*, 1994
Hester Kaplan, *Kinship Theory*, 2001
Edna O'Brien, *Down by the River*, 1997

1114

SUZANNE BERNE

A Perfect Arrangement
(Chapel Hill, North Carolina: Algonquin Books of Chapel Hill, 2001)

Story type: Psychological; Modern
Subject(s): Careers; Marriage; Children
Major character(s): Mirella Cook-Goldman, Lawyer, Parent (of Jacob and Pearl); Randi Gill, Child-Care Giver (hired by Mirella); Howard Goldman, Spouse (of Mirella), Architect
Time period(s): 2000s (2001)
Locale(s): New Aylesbury, Massachusetts

Summary: Berne's novel deals with marital stress and difficulties related to child care in two-career families. Mirella, a lawyer, and Howard, an architect, have two children but little time for them, so they hire Randi, a nanny, who on the surface appears ideal. As the story unfolds, Mirella and Howard learn appearances aren't always what they seem. The couple is forced to wrestle with some tough emotional issues about themselves and each other.

Where it's reviewed:
Chicago Tribune Books, June 17, 2001, page 5
Library Journal, May 1, 2001, page 125
New York Times Book Review, May 27, 2001, page 6
People, June 11, 2001, page 43
Publishers Weekly, April 16, 2001, page 45

Other books by the same author:
A Crime in the Neighborhood, 1997

Other books you might like:
Faith Baldwin, *The Moon's Our Home*, 1973
Sandra Brown, *The Witness*, 1995

Mary Higgins Clark, *Let Me Call You Sweetheart*, 1995
Robin Cook, *Fatal Cure*, 1993
Richard North Patterson, *Dark Lady*, 1999

1115

JOHN BIGUENET

The Torturer's Apprentice
(New York: Ecco, 2001)

Story type: Collection; Literary
Subject(s): Slavery; Morality; Short Stories

Summary: John Biguenet, an O. Henry Award winner, presents a short story collection built around offbeat characters. Each in their own way has an unattractive social quality that the author mines to explore the moral complexities they face. The story from the book's title deals with a free lance torturer, a man hired to extract confessions. He hauls heavy torture equipment from town to town in medieval Europe over very poor roads.

Where it's reviewed:
Library Journal, February 15, 2001, page 204
New York Times Book Review, February 4, 2001, page 33
Publishers Weekly, February 12, 2001, page 186

Other books you might like:
Julian Barnes, *Love, Etc.*, 2001
Ann Beattie, *Perfect Recall*, 2001
A.S. Byatt, *The Biographer's Tale*, 2001
Isabel Colegate, *Winter Journey*, 2001
Don DeLillo, *The Body Artist*, 2001

1116

CARMEN BOULLOSA

Leaving Tabasco
(New York: Grove/Atlantic, 2001)

Story type: Coming-of-Age
Subject(s): Love; Violence; Imagination
Major character(s): Delmira Ulloa, Writer (of magical realism)
Time period(s): 1960s
Locale(s): Agustini, Mexico

Summary: In her latest book, Carmen Boullosa tells the story of Delmira Ulloa. As a child, Delmira grows up in a house with only women and her mother ignores her, while carrying on with a priest. Inspiring the girl's imagination, Delmira's grandmother tells her many magical and fantastic stories. Then as a teenager, Delmira gets involved in politics and is forced into exile. She never returns to her village but writes about her wonderful childhood.

Where it's reviewed:
Booklist, February 15, 2001, page 1114
Kirkus Reviews, February 1, 2001, page 123
Library Journal, January 1, 2001, page 151
New York Times Book Review, May 13, 2001, page 16

Other books by the same author:
They're Cows, We're Pigs, 2001

Popular Fiction

Other books you might like:
Isabel Allende, *The Stories of Eva Luna*, 1991
Sandra Cisneros, *The House on Mango Street*, 1994
Gabriel Garcia Marquez, *Love in the Time of Cholera*, 1988
V.S. Naipaul, *A Way in the World*, 1994
Marge Piercy, *Woman on the Edge of Time*, 1976

1117

CLARE BOYLAN

Beloved Stranger

(Washington, D.C.: Counterpoint, 2001)

Story type: Contemporary; Psychological
Subject(s): Marriage; Aging; Mental Illness
Major character(s): Dick Butler, Spouse (of Lily), Mentally Ill Person (bipolar disorder); Lily Butler, Spouse (of Dick), Parent (of Ruth); Tim Walcott, Doctor
Time period(s): 2000s (2001)
Locale(s): Dublin, Ireland

Summary: Dick and Lily Butler have been married for 50 years and for the most part, life has been good. Life takes a dramatic twist when Dick's behavior becomes erratic, ranging from mood swings to irrational spending sprees to gun-toting paranoid sieges. Lily is forced to take action and ultimately, Dick is institutionalized. The story, which is leavened with humor, deals with the difficulties faced by family members.

Where it's reviewed:
Library Journal, December 2000, page 184
Publishers Weekly, January 8, 2001, page 44

Other books by the same author:
Collected Stories, 2000
Another Family Christmas, 1997
Room for a Single Lady, 1997
That Bad Woman, 1995
11 Edward Street, 1992

Other books you might like:
Alice Adams, *Almost Perfect*, 1993
Russell Banks, *Affliction*, 1989
Ken Kesey, *One Flew over the Cuckoo's Nest*, 1962
Leone Ross, *Orange Laughter*, 2000
Anne Tyler, *Clock Winder*, 1981

1118

MALCOLM BRADBURY

To the Hermitage

(Woodstock, New York: Overlook, 2001)

Story type: Historical; Political
Subject(s): Biography; Authors and Writers; Academia
Major character(s): Unnamed Character, Professor (of English); Denis Diderot, Philosopher (French rationalism), Historical Figure; Catherine the Great, Historical Figure, Ruler (Empress of Russia)
Time period(s): 1990s (1993); 18th century (1713-1784)
Locale(s): St. Petersburg, Russia

Summary: Malcolm Bradbury's novel takes readers on an historical, gossipy, literary, Russian journey, weaving to-

gether visits to St. Petersburg separated by more than 200 years. In one visit, a delegation of contemporary academics attends a conference as Boris Yeltsin's enemies attempt to overthrow the government. During the 18th century the French philosopher Denis Diderot visits Empress Catherine the Great. The delegation's academic bickering and Diderot's witty conversations with the empress keep things very lively. An unnamed professor bridges the gaps for readers.

Where it's reviewed:
Atlantic Monthly, April 2001, page 107
Booklist, March 15, 2001, page 1353
Library Journal, April 1, 2001, page 131
New York Times Book Review, April 1, 2001, page 11

Other books by the same author:
Doctor Criminale, 1992
The History Man, 1975
Stepping Westward, 1965

Other books you might like:
John Barth, *Once upon a Time*, 1994
Frederick Busch, *The Mutual Friend*, 1978
A.S. Byatt, *The Biographer's Tale*, 2001
Stephen King, *Misery*, 1987
Philip Roth, *Zuckerman Unbound*, 1981

1119

BARBARA TAYLOR BRADFORD

The Triumph of Katie Byrne

(New York: Doubleday, 2001)

Story type: Psychological Suspense
Subject(s): Actors and Actresses; Friendship; Women
Major character(s): Katie Byrne, Actress (aspires to act on Broadway); Denise, Friend (of Katie), Crime Victim (murdered); Mac MacDonald, Detective—Police
Time period(s): 2000s (2001)
Locale(s): Connecticut; London, England; New York, New York

Summary: As teenagers, Katie Byrne and her friends Denise and Carly aspire to be successful Broadway actresses. When Denise is killed and Carly is left in a coma, the criminal is never caught. Almost undone. Katie leaves the country and works on the London stage. When she is offered a role on Broadway, Katie hesitates to accept since the attack on her friends still haunts her. Intent on catching the bad guy, Detective Mac MacDonald gives Katie moral support.

Where it's reviewed:
Publishers Weekly, February 26, 2001, page 57

Other books by the same author:
Her Own Rules, 1996
Dangerous to Know, 1995
Love in Another Town, 1995
Angel, 1993
Everything to Gain, 1992

Other books you might like:
Faith Baldwin, *The Moon's Our Home*, 1973
Judith Krantz, *The Jewels of Tessa Kent*, 1998
Ronald Levitsky, *The Innocence That Kills*, 1994

Sidney Sheldon, *A Stranger in the Mirror*, 1976
Susan Sontag, *In America*, 2000

1120

ANITA BROOKNER

The Bay of Angels

(New York: Random House, 2001)

Story type: Coming-of-Age
Subject(s): Mothers and Daughters; Widows; Relationships
Major character(s): Zoe Cunningham, Young Woman (seeking independence), Editor (freelance); Simon Gould, Step-Parent (of Zoe), Spouse (of Anne); Anne Gould, Parent (Zoe's mother), Widow(er) (when Simon dies suddenly)
Time period(s): 2000s (2001)
Locale(s): London, England; Nice, France

Summary: When Zoe Cunningham's widowed mother marries wealthy Simon Gould and moves to the south of France, life couldn't be better. After years as the dutiful daughter, Zoe is still young, single, and professional, with her own flat in London. Then, the bottom drops out. Simon dies, his wealth evaporates, and Zoe's mother has a nervous breakdown and is hospitalized. Zoe must examine the meaning of personal freedom, commitment, security, happiness, and loneliness.

Where it's reviewed:
Atlantic Monthly, June 2001, page 107
Book, May 2001, page 64
Booklist, March 1, 2001, page 1187
Library Journal, March 15, 2001, page 104
Publishers Weekly, April 2, 2001, page 36

Other books by the same author:
Undue Influence, 1999
Falling Slowly, 1998
Visitors, 1998
Altered States, 1996
Incidents in the Rue Laugier, 1996

Other books you might like:
Julia Alvarez, *In the Name of Salome*, 2000
V.C. Andrews, *End of the Rainbow*, 2001
Elizabeth Berg, *What We Keep*, 1998
Maeve Binchy, *Glass Lake*, 1995
Amy Tan, *The Joy Luck Club*, 1989

1121

SYLVIA BROWNRIGG

Pages for You

(New York: Farrar Straus & Giroux, 2001)

Story type: Gay/Lesbian Fiction; Romance
Subject(s): Women; College Life
Major character(s): Flannery Jansen, Student—College (freshman), Lesbian; Anne Arden, Student—Graduate (teaching assistant), Lesbian
Time period(s): 2000s (2001)
Locale(s): East Coast

Summary: In this novel, Sylvia Brownrigg tells a story of first love. Flannery Jansen, 17, grows up on the West Coast, but she enrolls in an elite East Coast university where she falls in love with a teaching assistant, Anne. The story details her emotional highs and lows from first kiss to first betrayal. The author keeps the story from falling into a sentimental trap with humor.

Where it's reviewed:
Booklist, March 1, 2001, page 1225
Publishers Weekly, February 19, 2001, page 67

Other books by the same author:
The Metaphysical Touch, 1999

Other books you might like:
Rita Mae Brown, *Rubyfruit Jungle*, 1983
Mary Beth Cashetta, *Lucy on the West Coast*, 1997
Gale Zoe Garnett, *Visible Amazement*, 2001
Allegra Goodman, *Paradise Park*, 2001
Sarah Waters, *Tipping the Velvet*, 1999

1122

MELVIN JULES BUKIET

Strange Fire

(New York: Norton, 2001)

Story type: Political; Gay/Lesbian Fiction
Subject(s): Blind; Political Thriller; Conspiracies
Major character(s): Nathan Kazakov, Writer (of political speeches), Handicapped (blind); Gabriel Ben Levi, Relative (the prime minister's son)
Time period(s): 2000s (2001)
Locale(s): Tel Aviv, Israel; Jerusalem, Israel

Summary: Set in the Middle East, the story centers around conspiracy and violence. Nathan Kazakov, a gay, blind veteran, is a speechwriter for the Israeli prime minister, a hard-line hawk. An assassination attempt by a Jewish fanatic prompts Nathan to begin an investigation that takes him to historical and holy places including the Dead Sea and the Dome of the Rock. He finds evidence of a conspiracy that may involve Gabriel, the prime minister's son.

Where it's reviewed:
Booklist, April 15, 2001, page 1533
Chicago Tribune Books, April 29, 2001, page 3
Kirkus Reviews, April 1, 2001, page 431
Publishers Weekly, May 21, 2001, page 82

Other books by the same author:
Signs and Wonders, 1999
After, 1996
While the Messiah Tarries, 1995
Stories of an Imaginary Childhood, 1992
Sandman's Dust, 1985

Other books you might like:
David Baldacci, *Saving Faith*, 1999
Saul Bellow, *The Dean's December*, 1982
Tom Clancy, *The Bear and the Dragon*, 2000
Frederick Forsyth, *The Day of the Jackal*, 1972
Jack Higgins, *Edge of Danger*, 2001

1123

RAINELLE BURTON

The Root Worker

(Woodstock, New York: Overlook, 2001)

Story type: Coming-of-Age; Ethnic

Subject(s): Mothers and Daughters; Voodoo; African Americans

Major character(s): Ellen, Child (troubled, abused by her family); Barbara, Young Woman (befriends Ellen)

Time period(s): 1960s

Locale(s): Detroit, Michigan

Summary: In her first book, Rainelle Burton provides readers with insight into growing up in a dysfunctional inner-city family that relies on hoodoo, a conjuring art, for guidance. For some reason, Ellen, 11, is singled out by her mother as a scapegoat for the family's misfortunes. Her mother orchestrates the physical and emotional abuse that Ellen suffers. The battering continues until Barbara, an educated woman who moves into the neighborhood, intervenes on the child's behalf.

Where it's reviewed:

Booklist, May 1, 2001, page 1664

Chicago Tribune Books, June 17, 2001, page 2

Publishers Weekly, January 15, 2001, page 47

Other books you might like:

Pat Conroy, *The Prince of Tides*, 1986

Anita Desai, *Fasting, Feasting*, 1999

Helen Dunmore, *A Spell of Winter*, 2001

Toni Morrison, *The Bluest Eye*, 1970

Sapphire, *Push*, 1996

1124

A.S. BYATT

The Biographer's Tale

(New York: Knopf, 2001)

Story type: Psychological; Coming-of-Age

Subject(s): Biography; Literature; Mystery

Major character(s): Phineas C. Nanson, Critic; Vera, Young Woman (works in a hospital), Relative (of biographer Destry-Scholes); Fulla, Scientist (bee taxonomist)

Time period(s): 2000s (2001)

Locale(s): England

Summary: This is a detective story with intellectual and literary twists. Phineas C. Nanson abandons literary criticism to become a biographer. While writing about another famous biographer, Phineas discovers his subject has played fast and loose with facts and has invented incidents. Along the way, Phineas falls in love with two women, one of whom is related to the man he is writing about.

Where it's reviewed:

Booklist, November 15, 2000, page 587

Library Journal, December 2000, page 186

New York Times Book Review, March 18, 2001, page 6

Publishers Weekly, November 6, 2000, page 70

Other books by the same author:

Elementals, 1998

Babel Tower, 1996

Still Life, 1996

Matisse Stories, 1993

Angels & Insects, 1992

Other books you might like:

Jonathan Carroll, *The Land of Laughs*, 2001

Alain De Botton, *Kiss & Tell*, 1996

Andrea Goldsmith, *Under the Knife*, 1998

Jane Rogers, *Promised Lands*, 1995

Evelyn Toynton, *Modern Art*, 2000

1125

ETHAN C. CANIN

Carry Me Across the Water

(New York: Random House, 2001)

Story type: Psychological; Historical/World War II

Subject(s): Emigration and Immigration; Jews; Quest

Major character(s): August Kleinman, Businessman (beer brewer)

Time period(s): 20th century (1930-1990)

Locale(s): New York, New York; Pittsburgh, Pennsylvania; Boston, Massachusetts

Summary: Ethan C. Canin delves into the indomitable spirit of 78-year-old August Kleinman. He escapes Hitler's Germany with his mother, survives the fighting on Okinawa in the Pacific, marries after the war, becomes a successful businessman, and raises three children. At the end of his life, he is haunted by a face-to-face encounter during the war with a Japanese soldier and sets out to make things right.

Where it's reviewed:

Booklist, March 1, 2001, page 1187

New York Times Book Review, May 6, 2001, page 8

Publishers Weekly, April 30, 2001, page 53

Other books by the same author:

For Kings and Planets, 1998

The Palace Thief, 1994

Blue River, 1991

Emperor of the Air, 1989

Other books you might like:

Lionel Abrahams, *The Celibacy of Felix Greenspan*, 1993

Saul Bellow, *Mr. Sammler's Planet*, 1970

E.L. Doctorow, *Ragtime*, 1975

Joseph Heller, *Good as Gold*, 1979

John Updike, *Bech*, 1970

1126

STEPHEN J. CANNELL

The Tin Collector

(New York: St. Martin's Press, 2001)

Story type: Contemporary Realism

Subject(s): Police Procedural; Mystery; Political Crimes and Offenses

Major character(s): Shane Scully, Detective—Police (sergeant, LAPD), Crime Suspect (in a murder); Alexa Hamilton, Police Officer (Internal Affairs); Sandy Sandoval, Prostitute (a police informant), Parent (of a 15-year-old boy)
Time period(s): 2000s (2001)
Locale(s): Los Angeles, California

Summary: Stephen J. Cannell, award winning TV writer, focuses on high-level corruption in the Los Angeles Police Department. Sgt. Shane Scully gets embroiled in controversy when he responds to an ex-girlfriend's plea for help. Her husband, Ray Molar, is trying to kill her. After Shane rushes to the scene and is forced to kill Ray, he becomes the object of an internal affairs investigation. Alexa Hamilton, known as the tin collector, sets her sights on Shane's badge.

Where it's reviewed:
Booklist, November 15, 2000, page 587
Publishers Weekly, November 27, 2000, page 51

Other books by the same author:
Devil's Workshop, 1999
Riding a Snake, 1998
King Con, 1997
Final Victim, 1996
The Plan, 1995

Other books you might like:
Michael Connelly, *A Darkness More than Night*, 2001
Nelson DeMille, *The Gold Coast*, 1990
George V. Higgins, *Bomber's Law*, 1993
Dennis Lehane, *Mystic River*, 2001

1127

KEVIN CANTY

Honeymoon & Other Stories

(New York: Talese/Doubleday, 2001)

Story type: Collection
Subject(s): Love
Time period(s): 2000s (2001)
Locale(s): East Coast

Summary: Kevin Canty's collection of 11 short stories features a cast of eccentric characters attempting to make sense of an incomprehensible world. The sojourn from immaturity to adulthood can be painful. Some people just don't make the cut, but their efforts can be instructive and worth reading. In the author's deft hands, twisted realities appear somewhat normal. Topics include incest, drug addiction, therapy, appetites, affection, terminal illness, and grief.

Where it's reviewed:
Booklist, April 1, 2001, page 1447
Library Journal, April 1, 2001, page 135
Publishers Weekly, April 9, 2001, page 52

Other books by the same author:
Nine Below Zero, 1999
Rounders, 1998
Into the Great Wide Open, 1996
A Stranger in This World, 1994

Other books you might like:
Joan Connor, *We Who Live Apart*, 2000
Katherine Ann Douglas, *Short Stories for Long Rainy Days*, 1998
Ha Jin, *The Bridegroom*, 2000
Patricia Preciado Martin, *Amor Eterno*, 2000
Nora Roberts, *From the Heart*, 2000

1128

JONATHAN CARROLL

The Wooden Sea

(New York: Tor, 2001)

Story type: Contemporary/Fantasy
Subject(s): Animals/Dogs; Mystery; Time Travel
Major character(s): Francis "Frannie" McCabe, Police Officer (chief); Magda McCabe, Spouse (of Francis); Astropel, Alien (guides McCabe)
Time period(s): 1960s; 1980s
Locale(s): Crane's View, New York

Summary: In this interesting mixture of fantasy and science fiction, Police Chief Francis McCabe of Crane's View becomes the key to a cosmic puzzle. McCabe adopts a three-legged dog which soon dies. McCabe buries it, but the next day finds the dog's body in his wife's car. Then a couple in town disappears without a trace. McCabe's delinquent youthful self shows up to introduce his older self to Astropel, a black extraterrestrial. Astropel shuttles McCabe through time looking for clues to the puzzle.

Where it's reviewed:
Booklist, December 15, 2000, page 785
New York Times Book Review, February 11, 2001, page 15
Publishers Weekly, January 8, 2001, page 47

Other books by the same author:
The Land of Laughs, 2001
The Marriage Sticks, 1999
Kissing the Beehive, 1998
Panic at Hand, 1995
From the Teeth of Angels, 1994

Other books you might like:
Peter Benchley, *Jaws*, 1974
Stephen King, *Dreamcatcher*, 2001
Susan Oleksiw, *Family Album*, 1995
Padgett Powell, *Mrs. Hollingsworth's Men*, 2000
Audrey Stallsmith, *Marigolds for Mourning*, 1999

1129

MAUD CASEY

The Shape of Things to Come

(New York: Morrow, 2001)

Story type: Satire; Psychological
Subject(s): Mothers and Daughters; Secrets; Dating (Social Customs)
Major character(s): Isabelle, Young Woman; Adeline, Divorced Person (still looking for Mr. Right), Parent (Isa-

belle's mother); Raymond, Neighbor (lives across the street), Aged Person
Time period(s): 2000s (2001)
Locale(s): Standardsville, Illinois

Summary: Maud Casey looks at unhappiness and self-pity amid modern conveniences and pop culture clutter. Isabelle, a single and unhappy college graduate, returns to the Midwest from San Francisco. While her mother Adeline is divorced, she is hopeful and still dates. Meanwhile, Isabelle gets work via a temporary employment agency and hangs around with the elderly man who lives across the street. When a boyfriend from high school re-enters her life, Isabelle renews a relationship with him.

Where it's reviewed:
Chicago Tribune Books, May 13, 2001, page 2
Kirkus Reviews, February 1, 2001, page 124
New York Times Book Review, May 6, 2001, page 22
Publishers Weekly, February 26, 2001, page 56

Other books by the same author:
Over the Water, 1994

Other books you might like:
Julianna Baggott, *Girl Talk*, 2001
Cheryl Benard, *Turning on the Girls*, 2001
Barbara Kingsolver, *Pigs in Heaven*, 1993
Larry McMurtry, *Buffalo Girls*, 1990
Amy Tan, *The Joy Luck Club*, 1989

1130

DAN CHAON

Among the Missing

(New York: Ballantine, 2001)

Story type: Collection
Subject(s): Relationships; Family Problems; Secrets
Time period(s): 2000s (2001)

Summary: The characters in this 12 story collection examine past events, hoping to understand reasons for the way things are in the present. In one, a man reflects on his childhood in which an elaborate fantasy world and periodic blackouts help him survive. He can't relate to the horror his brother reminds him about because he doesn't remember. In another, a son discusses the reasons a family drove into a lake, but never his own family's problems.

Where it's reviewed:
Chicago Tribune Books, June 24, 2001, page 1
Library Journal, April 1, 2001, page 136
Publishers Weekly, October 9, 2001, page 78

Other books by the same author:
Fitting Ends, 1995

Other books you might like:
T. Coraghessan Boyle, *Without a Hero*, 1994
Ellen Gilchrist, *The Cabal*, 2000
Irene Mock, *Inappropriate Behavior*, 2000
Helen Simpson, *Getting a Life*, 2001
John Updike, *Licks of Love*, 2000

1131

DENISE CHAVEZ

Loving Pedro Infante

(New York: Farrar, Straus & Giroux, 2001)

Story type: Humor; Multicultural
Subject(s): Relationships; Actors and Actresses; Mexican Americans
Major character(s): Tere Avila, Narrator; Irma Granados, Friend (of Tere); Graciela Vallejos, Cousin (of Irma)
Time period(s): 2000s (2001)
Locale(s): Cabritoville, New Mexico

Summary: In this humorous novel, Denise Chavez follows members of the Pedro Infante Fan Club. Infante, a Mexican movie star of the 1950s, fuels their hunger for romance and escape from Cabritoville, New Mexico. Club members watch his movies over and over because they aren't having much success in their own lives. The narrator of the story, Tere Avila, clings to a married man, despite advice from her best friend, Irma. The members' hilarious and slightly bawdy conversations keep things lively.

Where it's reviewed:
Booklist, April 15, 2001, page 1532
Library Journal, April 1, 2001, page 132
New York Times Book Review, May 13, 2001, page 17
Publishers Weekly, March 26, 2001, page 60

Other books by the same author:
Face of an Angel, 1994
The Last of the Menu Girls, 1986

Other books you might like:
Alex Abella, *Final Acts*, 2000
John Gregory Dunne, *Playland*, 1994
Maria Amparo Escandon, *Esperanza's Box of Saints*, 1999
John Jakes, *American Dreams*, 1998
Stephen King, *Misery*, 1987

1132

JAIME CLARKE

We're So Famous

(New York: Bloomsbury, 2001)

Story type: Adventure; Contemporary
Subject(s): Music and Musicians; Women
Major character(s): Paque, Teenager, Friend (of Daisy); Daisy, Teenager, Friend (of Stella); Stella, Teenager, Friend (of Paque)
Locale(s): Phoenix, Arizona; Hollywood, California

Summary: In his debut, Jaime Clarke, shows his knowledge of contemporary pop culture. Paque and Daisy grow up in Phoenix and are obsessed with MTV and its associated lifestyles. They drop out of high school and split to Hollywood. There they meet Stella, a kindred spirit, who is obsessed with movie stars. The three set out to live a life filled with pool parties and stretch limos but their plans take a different turn.

Where it's reviewed:
Kirkus Reviews, February 1, 2001, page 125

New York Times Book Review, April 29, 2001, page 20
Publishers Weekly, February 19, 2001, page 68

Other books you might like:
Jonathan Baird, *Songs from Nowhere Near the Heart*, 2001
Emma Bull, *War for the Oaks*, 1987
Stella Duffy, *Beneath the Blonde*, 2000
Genni Gunn, *The Road*, 1991
Linda Jaivin, *Rock 'n' Roll Babes from Outer Space*, 1998

1133

ROBERT COHEN

Inspired Sleep

(New York: Scribner, 2001)

Story type: Psychological; Satire
Subject(s): Sleep; Women; Single Parent Families
Major character(s): Bonnie Saks, Single Parent (raising two boys), Student—Graduate (working on dissertation); Ian Ogelvie, Researcher (sleep disorders)
Time period(s): 2000s (2001)
Locale(s): Boston, Massachusetts

Summary: Bonnie Saks, 39, is a single parent raising two sons. While working on her doctorate, she is barely making ends meet with a stopgap job teaching writing. When Bonnie becomes pregnant, she decides against abortion, but the emotional stress leads to sleep deprivation. Seeking help, she becomes part of a sleep research project. Her experience explores the relationship between research, drug companies, managed care, and the business world. Humor and intelligent observations keep things lively.

Where it's reviewed:
Booklist, December 15, 2000, page 785
Library Journal, December 2000, page 186
New York Times Book Review, January 21, 2001, page 9
Publishers Weekly, October 30, 2000, page 43

Other books by the same author:
Here and Now, 1996
The Organ Builder, 1988

Other books you might like:
Elizabeth Berg, *Open House*, 2000
Molly Gloss, *Wild Life*, 2000
John Grisham, *The Client*, 1993
Caroline Preston, *Lucy Crocker 2.0*, 2000
Alice Walker, *The Way Forward*, 2000

1134

SUSAN COLL

Karlmarx.com

(New York: Simon & Schuster, 2001)

Story type: Humor; Contemporary
Subject(s): Relationships; Self-Perception; Women
Major character(s): Ella Kennedy, Student—Graduate (doctoral candidate); Nigel, Boyfriend (of Ella)
Time period(s): 2000s (2001)
Locale(s): Washington, District of Columbia

Summary: In this humorous novel, Ella Kennedy works for a think tank, Neoclassicists of Universal Thought (NUTS), which turns out to be a front for the Russian Mafia. Ella's love life becomes complicated when her married lover quits his job and moves in with her, a situation that mirrors her doctoral reasearch. Her subject, Eleanor Marx, lived with a married man and died unhappy. However, everything works out in the end.

Where it's reviewed:
Booklist, March 1, 2001, page 1225
Kirkus Reviews, February 15, 2001, page 125
Publishers Weekly, April 2, 2001, page 39

Other books you might like:
Elizabeth Berg, *Never Change*, 2001
Sylvia Brownrigg, *The Metaphysical Touch*, 1999
Helen Fielding, *Bridget Jones's Diary*, 1996
Kirin Narayan, *Love, Stars and All That*, 1994

1135

MICHAEL CONNELLY

A Darkness More than Night

(Boston: Little Brown, 2001)

Story type: Contemporary Realism
Subject(s): Police Procedural; Serial Killer; Mystery
Major character(s): Terry McCaleb, FBI Agent (retired crime profiler), Consultant (to Los Angeles P.D.); Harry Bosch, Detective—Homicide (Los Angeles P.D.); David Storey, Director (of movies), Crime Suspect (of murder)
Time period(s): 2000s (2001)
Locale(s): Los Angeles, California

Summary: Michael Connelly sets two characters on a collision course in this thriller. Terry McCaleb, a former FBI crime profiler, is called in to help the LA police solve the grisly murder of a young starlet. McCaleb, who runs a charter fishing business since a heart transplant forced his early retirement, eagerly pursues the case. The yarn gets added zest when the evidence points to Harry Bosch, the hard-bitten detective hero from some of the author's other novels.

Where it's reviewed:
Book, January 2001, page 68
Booklist, September 1, 2000, page 6
Library Journal, November 1, 2000, page 132
Publishers Weekly, October 23, 2000, page 56

Other books by the same author:
Angels Flight, 1999
Void Moon, 1999
Blood Work, 1998
Trunk Music, 1997
The Poet, 1996

Other books you might like:
Kenneth Abel, *Cold Steel Rain*, 2000
Stephen J. Cannell, *The Tin Collector*, 2001
George V. Higgins, *At End of Day*, 2000
Dennis Lehane, *Mystic River*, 2001
Richard North Patterson, *Protect and Defend*, 2000

1136

JUSTIN CRONIN

Mary and O'Neil

(New York: Dial, 2001)

Story type: Collection; Romance
Subject(s): Marriage; Teachers; Abortion
Major character(s): O'Neil Burke, Relative (of Kay), Teacher (high school English); Kay Burke, Relative (O'Neil's older sister); Mary, Spouse (of O'Neil), Teacher (high school English)
Time period(s): 20th century (1979-2000)
Locale(s): Philadelphia, Pennsylvania

Summary: Justin Cronin's collection, consisting of eight short stories, follows O'Neil Burke and his family for about 21 years. At 19, the world seems to be at his feet: he's in love, he's in college, and he has the loving emotional support of his parents and his older sister, Kay. At book's end, youthful possibilities have turned into adult reality. His parents die suddenly, his sister marries unhappily and dies at age 39, and he finds Mary.

Where it's reviewed:
Booklist, January 1, 2001, page 914
Library Journal, January 1, 2001, page 152
New York Times Book Review, February 18, 2001, page 14
Publishers Weekly, December 11, 2000, page 63

Other books by the same author:
A Short History of the Long Ball, 1990

Other books you might like:
Isabel Colegate, *Winter Journey*, 2001
Sarah Dunant, *Mapping the Edge*, 2001
Stewart O'Nan, *Snow Angels*, 1994
Annie Proulx, *Heart Songs and Other Stories*, 1988
Ben Rice, *Pobby and Dingan*, 2000

1137

ANDREW CRUMEY

Mr. Mee

(New York: Picador, 2001)

Story type: Literary; Humor
Subject(s): Internet; Philosophy; Quest
Major character(s): Mr. Mee, Collector (of books); Catriona, Scientist ("life scientist"); Dr. Petrie, Professor (of French Literature)
Time period(s): 2000s (2001)
Locale(s): England

Summary: Mr. Mee, a slightly nutty book collector, is on a quest to find a 200-year-old French text that challenges the existence of the universe. In his search, he uses the Internet and discovers a few things besides the text. When he meets up with Catriona, she introduces him to the pleasures of the flesh. The narration of the book alternates between Mr. Mee, Dr. Petrie, and the slapstick Ferrand and Minard.

Where it's reviewed:
Library Journal, January 1, 2001, page 152

New York Times Book Review, April 1, 2001, page 6
Publishers Weekly, January 29, 2001, page 62

Other books by the same author:
Pfitz, 1997
Alembert's Principle, 1996
Music in a Foreign Language, 1996

Other books you might like:
John Banville, *The Newton Letter*, 1987
Julian Barnes, *Flaubert's Parrot*, 1984
Saul Bellow, *Ravelstein*, 2000
A.S. Byatt, *The Biographer's Tale*, 2001
A.N. Wilson, *A Watch in the Night*, 1996

1138

DON DELILLO

The Body Artist

(New York: Scribner, 2001)

Story type: Contemporary/Fantasy; Literary
Subject(s): Suicide; Relationships; Memory
Major character(s): Rey Robles, Director (film), Spouse (of Lauren); Lauren Hartke, Artist, Spouse (of Rey)
Time period(s): 1970s
Locale(s): New York, New York (Manhattan); East Coast

Summary: The story occurs within the mind of Lauren, a body artist, a person who uses gestures while shaping her body into artistic postures. Her husband, Rey, commits suicide in the apartment of his first wife. Lauren, Rey's third wife, takes in a strange man who recites phrases from her past conversations with her husband. She tries to decipher the phrases while performing her exercises. The story examines the nature of time, personal connections, grief, memory, creativity, and existence.

Where it's reviewed:
Booklist, October 1, 2000, page 292
Library Journal, January 1, 2001, page 152
New York Times Book Review, February 4, 2001, page 12
Publishers Weekly, November 20, 2000, page 43
Time, January 29, 2001, page 65

Other books by the same author:
Underworld, 1997
Mao II, 1991
Libra, 1988
White Noise, 1985
The Names, 1982

Other books you might like:
John Biguenet, *The Torturer's Apprentice*, 2001
Milan Kundera, *The Unbearable Lightness of Being*, 1984
David Mitchell, *Ghostwritten*, 2000
Rick Moody, *Demonology*, 2001

1139

TERRY DEVANE

Uncommon Justice

(New York: Putnam, 2001)

Story type: Contemporary Realism
Subject(s): Law; Trials; Homelessness
Major character(s): Mairead O'Clare, Lawyer (gets fired for honesty); Sheldon A. Gold, Lawyer (hires Mairead); Alpha, Streetperson (accused of murder)
Time period(s): 2000s (2001)
Locale(s): Boston, Massachusetts

Summary: This legal thriller focuses on the efforts of a smart scrappy female lawyer to get justice for a homeless man accused of murder. The lawyer, Mairead O'Clare, knows about disadvantage. Orphaned and disfigured, her lower body is covered with reddish marks known as hemangioma. O'Clare works with Sheldon Gold, a man also familiar with the world's troubles. Together, Gold and O'Clare keep the story interesting and fun.

Where it's reviewed:
Booklist, March 1, 2001, page 1230
Kirkus Reviews, February 15, 2001, page 200
Publishers Weekly, February 19, 2001, page 68

Other books you might like:
Reed Arvin, *The Will*, 2000
Margaret Atwood, *Alias Grace*, 1996
Russell Banks, *Rule of the Bone*, 1995
John Grisham, *The Rainmaker*, 1995
Robert Traver, *Anatomy of a Murder*, 1958

1140

JUDE DEVERAUX

The Summerhouse

(New York: Pocket, 2001)

Story type: Psychological; Contemporary/Fantasy
Subject(s): Divorce; Women; Friendship
Major character(s): Ellie, Writer (with writer's block); Leslie, Dancer (gave it up for marriage); Madison, Model (leaves career for husband)
Time period(s): 1980s; 1990s (1980-1999)
Locale(s): New York, New York; Maine

Summary: Leslie, Madison, and Ellie meet while waiting to renew their driver's licenses. Some 20 years later, they meet to compare notes about the choices they made and how their lives turned out. The fun starts when a fortune teller offers them a chance to rearrange three weeks of their past. Each woman must decide if such a change is worth the risk. Changing a portion changes the whole, but there's no telling how much.

Where it's reviewed:
Booklist, April 1, 2001, page 1428
Kirkus Reviews, April 1, 2001, page 434
Publishers Weekly, April 16, 2001, page 45

Other books by the same author:
Temptation, 2000
High Tide, 1999
An Angel for Emily, 1998
Legend, 1996
The Heiress, 1995

Other books you might like:
Elizabeth Berg, *Open House*, 2000
Barbara Taylor Bradford, *Love in Another Town*, 1995
Michael Chabon, *Werewolves in Their Youth*, 2000
Carol Dawson, *The Mother-in-Law Diaries*, 1999
Susan Minot, *Evening*, 1998

1141

MICHAEL DIBDIN

Thanksgiving

(New York: Pantheon, 2001)

Story type: Psychological Suspense
Subject(s): Journalism; Remarriage; Secrets
Major character(s): Anthony, Widow(er) (wife killed in a plane crash); Lucy, Spouse (of Anthony), Parent (mother of two); Darryl Bob Allen, Divorced Person (formerly married to Lucy)
Time period(s): 2000s (2001)
Locale(s): Seattle, Washington; Nevada

Summary: Examined in this novel are the complications that can arise when obsession is mixed with grief. After Anthony's wife dies, he becomes obsessed with finding out about her life before she married him. Traveling to Las Vegas, he meets despicable Darryl, Lucy's first husband. Darryl gives Anthony details about Lucy's sexual past that include multiple partners and pornographic photos. When Darryl is shot to death, Anthony is charged with murder.

Where it's reviewed:
Booklist, March 1, 2001, page 1226
Kirkus Reviews, January 15, 2001, page 70
New York Times Book Review, April 29, 2001, page 20
Publishers Weekly, January 29, 2001, page 62

Other books by the same author:
A Rich Full Death, 1999
Blood Rain, 1999
A Long Finish, 1998
Cosi Fan Tutti, 1997
Dead Lagoon, 1994

Other books you might like:
Frederick Barthelme, *Second Marriage*, 1984
Joy Fielding, *The Other Woman*, 1983
Stephen King, *Bag of Bones*, 1998
Nicholas Sparks, *Message in a Bottle*, 1998
John Updike, *Gertrude and Claudius*, 2000

1142

MARGARET DRABBLE

The Peppered Moth

(New York: Harcourt, 2001)

Story type: Family Saga; Literary
Subject(s): Family Relations; Genealogy; Mothers and Daughters
Major character(s): Bessie Bawtry, Parent (of Chrissie); Chrissie, Parent (of Faro); Faro Gaulden, Relative (Bessie's granddaughter)
Time period(s): 20th century
Locale(s): Breaseborough, England

Summary: Margaret Drabble chronicles a three-generation journey to middle class respectability. Grandmother Bessie Bawtry possesses brains and beauty and is the first from her family to be sent to college. Her daughter, Chrissie, has brains and passion, while her granddaughter, Faro, reaps benefits from both women. Some discussion of matrilineal DNA in humans and the evolutionary adaptations in the peppered moth adds intellectual heft to a story that is told with humor and insight.

Where it's reviewed:
Booklist, February 15, 2001, page 1084
Library Journal, February 1, 2001, page 125
New Yorker, April 16, 2001, page 87
Publishers Weekly, February 26, 2001, page 55

Other books by the same author:
A Natural Curiosity, 1989
The Radiant Way, 1987
The Ice Age, 1977
The Realms of Gold, 1975
The Needle's Eye, 1972

Other books you might like:
Lois Battle, *Southern Women*, 1984
Frederick Busch, *Long Way from Home*, 1993
Marek Halter, *The Book of Abraham*, 1986
Sue Miller, *Family Pictures*, 1990
Amy Tan, *The Joy Luck Club*, 1989

1143

SARAH DUNANT

Mapping the Edge

(New York: Random House, 2001)

Story type: Psychological
Subject(s): Mothers and Daughters; Missing Persons; Single Parent Families
Major character(s): Anna Franklin, Single Parent (of a six-year-old girl), Journalist (disappears on vacation); Estella, Friend (of Anna), Lawyer; Lily Franklin, Child (Anna's daughter)
Time period(s): 2000s (2001)
Locale(s): London, England; Florence, Italy

Summary: Sarah Dunant's novel explores the emotions of family and friends when a loved one suddenly disappears. Anna goes off on a short vacation, leaving daughter with

friends. When Anna doesn't return, everyone waits and wonders. The author poses two different scenarios: in one, Anna is staying with a secret lover; in the other, she is kidnapped by a psychopath. The two different scenarios enlarge the reader's view of Anna and her motivations. Suspense makes this a page turner.

Where it's reviewed:
Booklist, November 1, 2000, page 520
Library Journal, November 15, 2000, page 96
New York Times Book Review, February 18, 2001, page 34
Publishers Weekly, November 20, 2000, page 44

Other books by the same author:
Transgressions, 1997
Under My Skin, 1995
Flatlands, 1994
Birth Marks, 1991

Other books you might like:
Terri Blackstock, *Blind Trust*, 1997
Arthur Randall, *Betrayal*, 1999
Nan Ryan, *Wanting You*, 1999
Muriel Spark, *Aiding & Abetting*, 2001
Lucy Wadham, *Lost*, 2000

1144

HELEN DUNMORE

A Spell of Winter

(New York: Atlantic Monthly, 2001)

Story type: Adult; Coming-of-Age
Subject(s): Brothers and Sisters; Secrets; Love
Major character(s): Catherine Allen, Narrator (abandoned at a young age); Rob Allen, Young Man (abandoned at young age); Kate, Servant
Time period(s): 1900s; 1910s (1900-1918)
Locale(s): England

Summary: Cathy, the narrator, and her brother, Rob, are abandoned as small children when their mother runs off and their father is institutionalized. They grow up on their grandfather's dilapidated estate where their only positive interaction is with Kate, a maid. To survive, they become very close to each other, well beyond normal socially accepted boundaries. There are hints of other secrets, too. Then World War I intrudes, leaving Cathy alone with her failing grandfather.

Where it's reviewed:
Booklist, January 2, 2001, page 915
Library Journal, December 2000, page 187
New York Times Book Review, February 25, 2001, page 27

Other books by the same author:
With a Crooked Heart, 1999
Your Blue-Eyed Boy, 1998
Bestiary, 1997
Love of Fat Men, 1997
Talking to the Dead, 1996

Other books you might like:
Isabel Colegate, *Winter Journey*, 2001
Pat Conroy, *The Prince of Tides*, 1986
Doris Lessing, *Mara and Dann*, 1999

Mary Morris, *Waiting Room*, 1989
Edna O'Brien, *Wild December*, 2000

1145

DAVID ANTHONY DURHAM

Gabriel's Story

(New York: Doubleday, 2001)

Story type: Multicultural; Coming-of-Age
Subject(s): African Americans; Family Relations; Cowboys/
Cowgirls
Major character(s): Gabriel Lynch, Teenager, Runaway;
Eliza, Parent (of Gabriel), Widow(er); James, Teenager,
Friend (of Gabriel's)
Time period(s): 1870s (1871)
Locale(s): Crownsville, Kansas

Summary: Gabriel Lynch wants to be a doctor, not the homesteader and farmer his mother wants him to be. When he
meets James, who is also restless, they run away from home.
Hooking up with a band of renegade cowboys, they head west
only to discover a violent country and that their companions
are running from personal demons. When Gabriel returns
home, he has learned his parents are not as harsh as he once
thought.

Where it's reviewed:
Booklist, December 15, 2000, page 788
Library Journal, November 1, 2000, page 101
New York Times Book Review, February 15, 2001, page 7
New Yorker, March 19, 2001, page 152

Other books you might like:
Russell Banks, *Rule of the Bone*, 1995
Elmer Kelton, *Wagontongue*, 1996
Cormac McCarthy, *Blood Meridian*, 1985
Larry McMurtry, *Lonesome Dove*, 1985
Ishmael Reed, *Yellow Back Radio Broke-Down*, 1988

1146

LEE DURKEE

Rides of the Midway

(New York: Norton, 2001)

Story type: Coming-of-Age; Contemporary
Subject(s): Adolescence; American South; Small Town Life
Major character(s): Noel Weatherspoon, Young Man (prone
to trouble); Matt Weatherspoon, Relative (Noel's younger
brother); Ben, Relative (stepbrother of Noel and Matt)
Time period(s): 1970s; 1980s
Locale(s): Hattiesburg, Mississippi

Summary: Peppered with dark humor and down-home religion, Durkee's first novel follows the antics of Noel Weatherspoon. At age ten, he is robbed of becoming a hero, despite
scoring the winning run in a baseball game, when his slide
into home plate puts the opposing catcher into a coma. After
his father is killed in Vietnam, his mother remarries and Noel
passes through high school in a drug and alcohol induced
haze.

Where it's reviewed:
Booklist, December 15, 2000, page 785
New York Times Book Review, February 25, 2001, page 15
Publishers Weekly, December 11, 2000, page 61
Time, February 12, 2001, page 88

Other books you might like:
Tom Coyne, *Gentleman's Game*, 2001
Amram Ducovny, *Coney*, 2000
Judith Guest, *Ordinary People*, 1976
Jane Hamilton, *Disobedience*, 2000
Michael Lund, *Growing Up on Route 66*, 2000

1147

JEAN ECHENOZ

I'm Gone

(New York: New Press, 2001)

Story type: Adult; Psychological
Subject(s): Art; Self-Perception; Mystery
Major character(s): Felix Ferrer, Art Dealer (owns an art gal-
lery), Spouse (walks out on his wife); Jean-Philippe
Delahaye, Art Dealer (gallery assistant)
Time period(s): 1990s (1999)
Locale(s): Paris, France

Summary: Jean Echenoz won France's Prix Goncourt Prize in
1999 with this novel. The story revolves around Felix Ferrer,
a Paris art dealer experiencing a mid-life crisis. Ferrer leaves
his wife and embarks on an expedition to recover art treasures
from a shipwreck. He succeeds, only to have the treasure,
stolen from his gallery. After a heart attack, he has bypass
surgery and also has several affairs. Translated by Mark
Polizzotti.

Where it's reviewed:
Booklist, February 1, 2001, page 1038
Library Journal, January 1, 2001, page 152
Los Angeles Times Book Review, March 4, 2001, page 11
New York Times Book Review, March 25, 2001, page 22

Other books by the same author:
Big Blondes, 1997
Cherokee, 1994
Double Jeopardy, 1993

Other books you might like:
Alev Lytle Croutier, *The Palace of Tears*, 2000
Erica Jong, *Fear of Flying*, 1973
John L'Heureux, *Having Everything*, 1999

1148

JAMES ELLROY

The Cold Six Thousand

(New York: Knopf, 2001)

Story type: Political; Contemporary Realism
Subject(s): Violence; Crime and Criminals; Conspiracies
Major character(s): Wayne Tedrow Jr., Police Officer (Las
Vegas P.D.), Murderer (contract killer); Pete Bondurant,
Spy (ex-CIA), Criminal (ties to underworld); Ward Littel
Jr., FBI Agent (former), Lawyer

Time period(s): 1960s (1963-1968)
Locale(s): Las Vegas, Nevada; Dallas, Texas

Summary: Ellroy tells stories that combine imagination with historical facts. The book begins in 1963 on the day John F. Kennedy is assassinated. Wayne Tedrow, Jr., a Las Vegas cop and contract killer, sets out to execute a pimp. Readers follow Wayne as, unable to complete the contract, he meets characters who provide insight into the assassinations of JFK, his brother, Robert, and Martin Luther King, Jr.; the Vietnam War; drugs; gambling money; and Las Vegas.

Where it's reviewed:
Book, May 2001, page 72
Booklist, May 15, 2001, page 1332
Los Angeles Times Book Review, May 13, 2001, page 2
New York Times Book Review, May 20, 2001, page 9

Other books by the same author:
Crime Wave, 1999
American Tabloid, 1998
L.A. Noir, 1998
Brown's Requiem, 1994
White Jazz, 1992

Other books you might like:
Peter Abrahams, *Hard Rain*, 1988
Don DeLillo, *Libra*, 1988
Frederick Forsyth, *The Negotiator*, 1989
John Grisham, *The Pelican Brief*, 1992
Tom Wolfe, *A Man in Full*, 1998

1149

LOUISE ERDRICH

The Last Report on the Miracles at Little No Horse

(New York: HarperCollins, 2001)

Story type: Historical/American West; Indian Culture
Subject(s): Indians of North America; Religious Life
Major character(s): Agnes DeWitt, Spouse (common law), Imposter (poses as a priest); Berndt Vogel, Farmer (murdered), Spouse (of Agnes)
Time period(s): 20th century (1912-1992)
Locale(s): Ojibwe Reservation, North Dakota

Summary: Faith, deception, and absolution are themes explored in Louise Erdrich's novel. When her husband is murdered, Agnes assumes the identity of a priest. She becomes Father Damien, ministering to Native Americans on the Ojibwe Reservation. Now, at the age of 90, Father Damien is on his deathbed and explaining to a young priest why Sister Leopolda shouldn't be canonized. What unfolds is an epic tale that in fact is a history of many Native American clans.

Where it's reviewed:
Booklist, February 15, 2001, page 1085
Publishers Weekly, January 29, 2001, page 63

Other books by the same author:
The Birchbark House, 1999
Antelope Wife, 1998
Tales of Burning Love, 1996
Blue Jay's Dance, 1995

The Bingo Palace, 1994

Other books you might like:
Jim Harrison, *Dalva*, 1988
Janet Lewis, *Invasion*, 2000
Lee Maracie, *Sundogs*, 1992
Brian Moore, *Black Robe*, 1985

1150

HELEN FIELDING

Cause Celeb

(New York: Viking, 2001)

Story type: Contemporary; Satire
Subject(s): Africa; Charity; Social Issues
Major character(s): Rosie Richardson, Public Relations (for a publisher), Administrator (of refugee camp); Oliver, Television Personality, Boyfriend (of Rosie)
Time period(s): 2000s (2001)
Locale(s): London, England; Nambula, Africa

Summary: Helen Fielding's first novel (1995) has now been published in the U.S. taking aim at celebrity obsession and relief administration, the story is satirically funny, but the picture isn't pretty. Rosie Richardson quits her job as a publicist after a falling-out with her boyfriend, Oliver. She takes a job as an administrator of a refugee camp in Africa. When disaster strikes, causing UN food supplies to bog down, she returns to London to organize a celebrity benefit that will save thousands from starvation. The problem is—her celebrity contacts are through Oliver.

Where it's reviewed:
Booklist, December 1, 2000, page 675
Library Journal, December 2000, page 187
New York Times Book Review, February 25, 2001, page 20
Publishers Weekly, December 11, 2000, page 61

Other books by the same author:
Bridget Jones Diary, 1999

Other books you might like:
Gloria Emerson, *Loving Graham Greene*, 2000
Dorothy Gilman, *Caravan*, 1992
Bertrice Small, *A Memory of Love*, 2000

1151

RICHARD FLANAGAN

Death of a River Guide

(New York: Grove, 2001)

Story type: Psychological; Saga
Subject(s): Family Relations; Ancestors; Rafting
Major character(s): Jason Krezwa, Guide (river rafting), Companion (of Aljaz); Aljaz Cosini, Guide (river rafting), Accident Victim (drowns in river); Harry Cosini, Parent (of Aljaz)
Time period(s): 2000s (2001)
Locale(s): Tasmania, Australia (Franklin River)

Summary: In Richard Flanagan's second novel, he explores Australia's racial heritage. Jason and Aljaz are river guides on

Tasmania's Franklin River. On a rafting trip, the river floods and Aljaz gets trapped underwater. As he drowns, his life and the lives of his ancestors pass before him. His family makeup mirrors that of his country: his great-grandfather, a convict, ran from his captors and died in the wilderness; his great-grandmother was an aborigine; and his mother was Italian. Life has not been easy for any of them.

Where it's reviewed:
Booklist, November 15, 2000, page 615
Library Journal, January 1, 2001, page 153
New York Times Book Review, April 8, 2001, page 27
Publishers Weekly, January 15, 2001, page 51

Other books by the same author:
Sound of One Hand Clapping, 2001
The Hunting Variety, 1973

Other books you might like:
Rick Bass, *Where the Sea Used to Be*, 1998
Peter Carey, *True History of the Kelly Gang*, 2000
Douglas Galbraith, *The Rising Sun*, 2001
Julia Leigh, *Hunter*, 2000
Colleen McCullough, *Morgan's Run*, 2000

1152

MARJORIE LEET FORD

Do Try to Speak as We Do
(New York: St. Martin's Press, 2001)

Story type: Coming-of-Age
Subject(s): Au Pairs; Cultural Conflict; Women
Major character(s): Melissa, Child-Care Giver; Ted, Fiance(e) (of Melissa); Mrs. Haig-Ereildoun, Employer (of Melissa)
Time period(s): 2000s (2001)
Locale(s): London, England; Troonafchan, Scotland (coastal Hebrides)

Summary: Marjorie L. Ford makes her fiction debut with the diary of an American woman forced by economic circumstances to take a job caring for children of an upper-class English family. Unsuspecting Melissa is like a ship sailing in uncharted waters, waiting to run aground. Long hours, needy children, constant travel, and emotional abuse at the hands of her employer, who isn't above seducing Melissa's boyfriend, bring this nightmare to life. Wit and sensitivity keep things light.

Where it's reviewed:
Booklist, November 15, 2000, page 615
Library Journal, January 1, 2001, page 153
Publishers Weekly, February 26, 2001, page 59

Other books you might like:
V.C. Andrews, *Lightning Strikes*, 2000
Rachel Cusk, *The Country Life*, 1997
Helen DeWitt, *The Last Samurai*, 2000
Helen Fielding, *Cause Celeb*, 2001
Leslie Forbes, *Fish, Blood and Bone*, 2001

1153

LEON FORREST

Meteor in the Madhouse
(Evanston, Illinois: TriQuarterly, 2001)

Story type: Multicultural; Psychological
Subject(s): African Americans; Authors and Writers; Civil Rights Movement
Major character(s): Joubert Antoine Jones, Professor (successful dramatist), Narrator; Marvella Gooseberry, Neighbor (of Joubert's grandparent); Gram Gussie Jones, Grandparent (adopted Joubert)
Time period(s): 20th century (1972-1992)
Locale(s): Forest County, Illinois (Chicago); Forest County, Mississippi

Summary: Professor Joubert Jones, a character from *Divine Days*, narrates these five interconnected stories that unfold with humor and sensitivity. Set in fictional Forest County, a mirror image of Chicago's South Side, we learn about the misadventures and good fortunes of the professor's friends and relatives as they move north from Forest County, Mississippi. In the final episode, the professor himself is shot and killed in a drive-by shooting.

Where it's reviewed:
Booklist, February 15, 2001, page 1105
Chicago Tribune Books, April 15, 2001, page 1
Publishers Weekly, February 12, 2001, page 184

Other books by the same author:
Divine Days, 1993
Two Wings to Veil My Face, 1983
The Bloodworth Orphans, 1977
There Is a Tree More Ancient than Eden, 1973

Other books you might like:
Clare Boylan, *Beloved Stranger*, 2001
Ken Kesey, *One Flew over the Cuckoo's Nest*, 1962
Tim Parks, *Family Planning*, 1989
John A. Williams, *The Man Who Cried I Am*, 1967
Shay Youngblood, *Black Girl in Paris*, 2000

1154

KAREN JOY FOWLER

Sister Noon
(New York: Putnam, 2001)

Story type: Historical; Coming-of-Age
Subject(s): Social Conditions; Women; Adoption
Major character(s): Lizzie Hayes, Spinster (from a good family), Volunteer (keeps books for an orphanage); Mary Ellen Pleasant, Wealthy (mysterious)
Time period(s): 1890s
Locale(s): San Francisco, California

Summary: Fact and fancy are mixed in a story about 1890s San Francisco. Lizzie Hayes, a matronly, respectable spinster, is helping to run a home for girls, when Mrs. Pleasant, a housekeeper with a reputation for hosting wild parties, leaves a girl there. A man tries to adopt the child and Lizzie having a bad

Popular Fiction

feeling about him, hides her. Then the man reveals the child's identity and tries to blackmail the orphanage.

Where it's reviewed:
New York Times Book Review, May 20, 2001, page 40
Publishers Weekly, April 9, 2001, page 48
USA Today, May 31, 2001, page 9D

Other books by the same author:
Black Glass, 1998
The Sweetheart Season, 1996
Sarah Canary, 1991

Other books you might like:
Alice Adams, *Almost Perfect*, 1993
Gina Berriault, *The Lights of Earth*, 1984
Christopher Moore, *Bloodsucking Fiends*, 1995
Darcey Steinke, *Suicide Blonde*, 1994

1155

JEFFREY FRANK

The Columnist

(New York: Simon & Schuster, 2001)

Story type: Political; Satire
Subject(s): Journalism; News; Blackmail
Major character(s): Brandon Sladder, Journalist (columnist)
Time period(s): 20th century; 2000s (1960-2000)
Locale(s): Washington, District of Columbia

Summary: This book takes a satirical look at the big-time media that covers big-time government. Told as the memoirs of Brandon Sladder, the story chronicles his journalistic career covering American politics. Starting as a reporter in upstate New York, he ruthlessly moves up the career ladder, resorting to blackmail whenever necessary, until he becomes a columnist. The author's humor softens Sladder, a man who uses everyone, and makes him likable.

Where it's reviewed:
Booklist, April 15, 2001, page 1533
Kirkus Reviews, April 1, 2001, page 436
Library Journal, April 15, 2001, page 131
New York Times Book Review, June 3, 2001, page 35

Other books by the same author:
The Creep, 1968

Other books you might like:
V.C. Andrews, *Rain*, 2000
Anonymous, *Primary Colors*, 1996
David Baldacci, *The Simple Truth*, 1999
Larry McMurtry, *Cadillac Jack*, 1982
James Patterson, *Roses Are Red*, 2000

1156

LAURA FURMAN

Drinking with the Cook

(Houston: Windale, 2001)

Story type: Collection
Subject(s): Customs; Social Conditions; Women

Summary: Laura Furman focuses on the inner lives of her characters in this collection of 13 stories. Set in the suburbs and cities of Texas or New England, the stories involve mostly, female characters who deal with longing and loss as they face an unclear future. In one tale, a woman remembers a time when she lived in Sweden among draft dodgers. In another, a woman seeks pointers about her career, but makes a more important discovery. Each provides her own truths.

Where it's reviewed:
New York Times Book Review, June 3, 2001, page 53
Publishers Weekly, March 19, 2001, page 76

Other books by the same author:
Tuxedo Park, 1986
Watch Time Fly, 1983
The Shadow Line, 1982
The Glass House, 1980

Other books you might like:
Frederick Barthelme, *The Law of Averages*, 2000
Ann Beattie, *Perfect Recall*, 2001
T. Coraghessan Boyle, *After the Plague*, 2001
Raymond Carver, *Will You Please Be Quiet, Please?*, 1976
Michael Chabon, *Werewolves in Their Youth*, 2000

1157

ALAN FURST

Kingdom of Shadows

(New York: Random House, 2001)

Story type: Historical/World War II; Adult
Subject(s): Espionage; Politics; Nazis
Major character(s): Nicholas Morath, Spy, Nobleman (Hungarian aristocrat)
Time period(s): 1930s (1938-1939)
Locale(s): Paris, France; Budapest, Hungary

Summary: Alan Furst's novel makes ample use of moral ambiguity in his story of prewar Europe. The main character, Hungarian-born playboy Nicholas Morath, is busy enjoying the good life in Paris when his diplomat uncle recruits him for a secret mission. Morath gradually gets pulled into a web of intrigue while working to help those fleeing Nazi oppression. A colorful cast of characters and a vivid description of the physical and emotional landscape makes the book interesting.

Where it's reviewed:
Booklist, November 15, 2000, page 623
Library Journal, December 2000, page 187
Publishers Weekly, November 6, 2000, page 67
Time, March 12, 2001, page 89

Other books by the same author:
Red Gold, 1999
The World at Night, 1996
The Polish Officer, 1995
Dark Star, 1991
Night Soldiers, 1988

Other books you might like:
Michael Chabon, *The Amazing Adventures of Kavalier & Clay*, 2000
Ken Follett, *The Eye of the Needle*, 1978

John Grisham, *The Rainmaker*, 1995
John Le Carre, *The Spy Who Came in from the Cold*, 1964
Lee Roddy, *Days of Deception*, 1998

1158

DOUGLAS GALBRAITH

The Rising Sun

(New York: Atlantic Monthly, 2001)

Story type: Historical/Seventeenth Century; Quest
Subject(s): Voyages and Travels; Adventure and Adventurers
Major character(s): Robert Mackenzie, Administrator (of a cargo ship)
Time period(s): 17th century (1698)
Locale(s): Edinburgh, Scotland; Darien, Panama

Summary: In his first novel, Douglas Galbraith turns the clock back to the 17th century when the English, Dutch, and Spanish were building colonial empires. An expedition, aimed at starting an empire for Scotland, sets sail for what is modern day Panama. Known as the Darien Scheme, the venture is ill-fated. Trying to establish a colony, the men soon realize that they are not equipped to deal with a hostile environment.

Where it's reviewed:
Booklist, November 15, 2000, page 618
Library Journal, December 2000, page 187
New York Times Book Review, February 11, 2001, page 22
Publishers Weekly, January 15, 2001, page 53

Other books you might like:
Madison Smartt Bell, *Master of the Crossroads*, 2000
Peter Carey, *True History of the Kelly Gang*, 2000
Colleen McCullough, *Morgan's Run*, 2000
Patrick McGrath, *Martha Peake*, 2000
Gore Vidal, *The Golden Age*, 2000

1159

KATHLEEN GEORGE

Taken

(New York: Delacorte, 2001)

Story type: Adventure; Contemporary
Subject(s): Kidnapping; Mystery; Adoption
Major character(s): Marina Benedict, Actress (aspiring), Crime Victim (shot by kidnappers); Richard Christie, Detective—Police; Manny, Lawyer (runs an adoption ring)
Time period(s): 2000s (2001)
Locale(s): Pittsburgh, Pennsylvania

Summary: *Taken* concerns an adoption ring that uses kidnapping to provide babies for people willing to pay. On a hunch one day, Marina Benedict, an aspiring actress, follows an unsavory character carrying an infant. Her intuition proves to be correct: the man is a kidnapper. For her trouble, Marina is shot and left for dead. While recovering, she meets Detective Rich Christie and working together they rescue the child.

Where it's reviewed:
Chicago Tribune Books, June 3, 2001, page 2
Publishers Weekly, April 16, 2001, page 44

Other books by the same author:
Man in the Buick, 1999

Other books you might like:
William Faulkner, *Sanctuary*, 1972
John Fowles, *The Collector*, 1982
Graham Greene, *The Honorary Consul*, 1974
Mario Puzo, *The Fourth K*, 1991
Marilyn Wallace, *Lost Angel*, 1996

1160

AMITAV GHOSH

The Glass Palace

(New York: Random House, 2001)

Story type: Historical; Multicultural
Subject(s): Love; Exile; Conquest
Major character(s): Rajkumar, Businessman (teak trader); Dolly, Servant (of Second Princess); Thebaw, Ruler (Burma's last king), Expatriate (exiled by the British)
Time period(s): 1880s (1885); 20th century (1900-1999)
Locale(s): Mandalay, Burma; Ratnagiri, India

Summary: Amitav Ghosh's epic novel about Burma and Malaya covers a 115-year span. Rajkumar is a mere boy when he meets Dolly in the marketplace just as people begin to panic when they realize that the loud noises in the distance are British cannon. While the crowd turns to looting, Rajkumar locks Dolly's image into his memory. Subsequently, she is taken into exile with the royal family and he grows up to be a rich and famous teak dealer.

Where it's reviewed:
Library Journal, February 1, 2001, page 125
New York Times Book Review, February 11, 2001, page 7
Publishers Weekly, November 13, 2000, page 82

Other books by the same author:
The Calcutta Chromosome, 1995
The Shadow Lines, 1988

Other books you might like:
Peggy Payne, *Sister India*, 2001
Manil Suri, *The Death of Vishnu*, 2001
Amy Tan, *The Bonesetter's Daughter*, 2001
Ludmila Ulitskaya, *The Funeral Party*, 2001
Vineeta Vijayaraghavan, *Motherland*, 2001

1161

ANTHONY GIARDINA

Recent History

(New York: Random House, 2001)

Story type: Gay/Lesbian Fiction; Psychological
Subject(s): Italian Americans; Sexuality; Social Classes
Major character(s): Luca Carcera, Young Man (doubts his sexuality), Spouse (of Gina); Gina Carcera, Spouse (of Luca)
Time period(s): 1960s; 1970s
Locale(s): Massachusetts

Popular Fiction

Summary: As a sensitive only child, Luca's world gets turned upside down when his beloved father abandons his family for another man. Confused all through school, Luca never resolves the situation in his own mind, nor does he understand his own sexuality. Later, when he is married, the issue haunts him and threatens his happiness. In order to resolve this problem, Luca must first understand his family history.

Where it's reviewed:

Booklist, February 1, 2001, page 1039
Chicago Tribune Books, March 18, 2001, page 3
Library Journal, January 1, 2001, page 153
New York Times Book Review, March 11, 2001, page 31
Publishers Weekly, January 15, 2001, page 52

Other books you might like:

Jim Harrison, *Legend of the Fall*, 1989
Mario Puzo, *The Last Don*, 1996
Richard Russo, *Nobody's Fool*, 1993
William Styron, *Tidewater Morning*, 1993

1162

ALLEGRA GOODMAN

Paradise Park

(New York: Dial, 2001)

Story type: Coming-of-Age; Humor
Subject(s): Women; Jews; Quest
Major character(s): Sharon Spiegelman, Student—College (dropped out); Gary, Boyfriend (leaves Sharon)
Time period(s): 1970s (1974)

Summary: Sharon Spiegelman takes risks, asks questions, makes mistakes, and suffers, but she is never boring. Dropping out of college, where her father is a dean, she sets out for Hawaii with her 35-year-old boyfriend. He abandons her, leaving her with the hotel bill, no money, and nothing but a guitar. She dabbles with some new age religions, acquires another boyfriend, and sees God. Goodman keeps the story lively and entertaining with copious amounts of humor.

Where it's reviewed:

Booklist, February 1, 2001, page 72
Library Journal, January 1, 2001, page 154
New Yorker, April 2, 2001, page 87
Time, March 26, 2001, page 72

Other books by the same author:

Kaaterskill Falls, 1998
Family Markowitz, 1996
Total Immersion, 1989

Other books you might like:

Bliss Broyard, *My Father, Dancing*, 1999
Sarah Dunant, *Mapping the Edge*, 2001
Philip Roth, *Portnoy's Complaint*, 1969
Wendy Wasserstein, *An American Daughter*, 1997

1163

JOHN GRIESEMER

No One Thinks of Greenland

(New York: Picador, 2001)

Story type: Humor; Coming-of-Age
Subject(s): Military Bases; Hospitals
Major character(s): Colonel Lane Woolwrap, Military Personnel (slightly crazy bureaucrat); Corporal Rudy Spruance, Military Personnel (assigned to hospital newspaper); Sergeant Irene Teal, Military Personnel (Woolwrap's aide), Girlfriend (of Rudy)
Time period(s): 1950s (1959)
Locale(s): Quagattarsa, Greenland

Summary: In his debut novel, John Griesemer enters the madcap world of a remote U.S. Army base in Greenland. Corporal Rudy Spruance wakes up in the hospital after a swarm of mosquitoes attacks him. There he meets the eccentric Col. Lane Woolwrap and becomes a journalist when the colonel decides a newspaper is needed to boost morale. Rudy tackles the job with too much enthusiasm and begins to uncover embarrassing facts.

Where it's reviewed:

Booklist, March 1, 2001, page 1226
Kirkus Reviews, May 15, 2001, page 705
New York Times Book Review, July 1, 2001, page 22
Publishers Weekly, April 9, 2001, page 52

Other books you might like:

Robert Crichton, *The Secret of Santa Vittoria*, 1966
Joseph Heller, *Catch-22*, 1961
Carl Hiaasen, *Native Tongue*, 1991
Richard Hooker, *MASH*, 1968
Ken Kesey, *One Flew over the Cuckoo's Nest*, 1962

1164

MICHAEL GRIFFITH

Spikes

(New York: Arcade, 2001)

Story type: Humor; Literary
Subject(s): Sports/Golf; Self-Awareness; Self-Confidence
Major character(s): Brian Schwan, Sports Figure (struggling pro golfer); Bird Soulsby, Sports Figure (pro golfer paired with Schwan); Rosa Schwan, Spouse (of Brian)
Time period(s): 1990s (1990)
Locale(s): Charleston, South Carolina

Summary: Michael Griffith's first novel is about sports, but it avoids excessive sports jargon. The main character, Brian Schwan, 26 and struggling on the lowest rung of the professional golf tour, analyses his life as he walks through a do-or-die round. Brian is torn between satisfying his parents, his wife, and/or himself. These internal conflicts undermine his confidence, which is reflected in his golf scores.

Where it's reviewed:

Booklist, September 1, 2000, page 50
Library Journal, December 2000, page 188
New York Times Book Review, March 25, 2001, page 15

Other books you might like:
Mark Harris, *The Southpaw*, 1953
John Irving, *The World According to Garp*, 1978
Stephen King, *The Girl Who Loved Tom Gordon*, 1999
Nicholas Sparks, *A Walk to Remember*, 1999
Alan Watt, *Diamond Dog*, 2000

1165

JOHN GRISHAM

A Painted House

(New York: Doubleday, 2001)

Story type: Coming-of-Age; Family Saga
Subject(s): Farm Life; Family Relations; Migrant Labor
Major character(s): Luke Chandler, Child (of cotton farmers), Narrator; Eli Chandler, Grandparent (of Luke), Farmer (cotton); Tally Spruill, Migrant Worker (works for the Chandlers)
Time period(s): 1950s (1952)
Locale(s): Black Oak, Arkansas

Summary: In this book, Grisham trades courtrooms and lawyers for cotton fields and farmers. He introduces us to the Chandlers, who are struggling to make a living from their land. Told through the eyes of seven-year-old Luke, the story details how the family hires migrant labor, copes with the fickleness of the weather, and passes time listening to baseball on the radio, and writing letters to a beloved son fighting in the Korean War. Floods, murder, and trips to town make this a very lively story.

Where it's reviewed:
Booklist, February 1, 2001, page 1020
Library Journal, March 1, 2001, page 131
Publishers Weekly, January 22, 2001, page 302
Time, February 26, 2001, page 72

Other books by the same author:
The Brethren, 2000
The Partner, 1997
The Rainmaker, 1995
The Chamber, 1994
The Client, 1993

Other books you might like:
Bonnie Burnard, *A Good House*, 2000
William Gay, *Provinces of Night*, 2000
Alice Lichtenstein, *Genius of the World*, 2000
Frederick Reiken, *Lost Legends of New Jersey*, 2000
Henry Roth, *Call It Sleep*, 1934

1166

GWENDOLEN GROSS

Field Guide

(New York: Holt, 2001)

Story type: Psychological; Contemporary
Subject(s): Missing Persons; Grief; Rain Forest
Major character(s): Annabel Mendelssohn, Student—Graduate (of science); John Goode, Professor (of science); Leon Goode, Relative (John's son)

Time period(s): 2000s (2001)
Locale(s): Townsville, Australia

Summary: In her first novel, Gwendolen Gross takes readers into the Australian outback for scientific discovery and self-renewal. American Annabel Mendelssohn, a graduate student, chooses Australia for fieldwork. Aside from professional considerations, she seeks distance from her brother's death. Her fieldwork blossoms while working closely with Professor John Goode, then the professor mysteriously disappears and his son Leon organizes a search. Annabel joins the effort and she makes a connection with Leon.

Where it's reviewed:
Booklist, February 15, 2001, page 1116
Chicago Tribune Books, May 13, 2001, page 2
Kirkus Reviews, February 1, 2001, page 129
Library Journal, April 15, 2001, page 131
Publishers Weekly, February 19, 2001, page 67

Other books you might like:
Isabel Allende, *Of Love and Shadows*, 1987
V.C. Andrews, *Runaways*, 1998
Michael Crichton, *Jurassic Park*, 1990
Joan Didion, *A Book of Common Prayer*, 1977
W.H. Hudson, *Green Mansions*, 1935

1167

PEDRO JUAN GUTIERREZ

Dirty Havana Triology

(New York: Farrar Straus & Giroux, 2001)

Story type: Literary; Multicultural
Subject(s): Alcoholism; Drugs; Sexual Behavior
Major character(s): Pedro Juan, Journalist
Time period(s): 1990s (1994)
Locale(s): Havana, Cuba

Summary: A Cuban p oet, Gutierrez writes on one level about city life in a country with a dying economy, but on another level about hopelessness without intellectual or creative incentives. Pedro Juan, a burned-out journalist, makes a living with menial jobs and petty crimes. He resists pressures to immigrate and embraces a meaningless life of chasing women, drinking rum, and smoking dope. Sex scenes are explicit and plentiful. Natasha Wimmer did the translation.

Where it's reviewed:
Library Journal, November 1, 2000, page 133
Publishers Weekly, October 16, 2000, page 46

Other books you might like:
Reinaldo Arenas, *Color of Summer*, 2000
Al Azevedo, *Slum*, 2000
J.D. Landis, *Longing*, 2000
Mayra Montero, *Last Night I Spent with You*, 2000

1168

ELIZABETH HAY

A Student of Weather

(Washington, D.C.: Counterpoint, 2001)

Story type: Coming-of-Age
Subject(s): Sibling Rivalry; Rural Life; Sisters
Major character(s): Lucinda Hardy, Relative (Norma Joyce's sister), Teenager; Maurice Dove, Scientist (studies weather patterns); Norma Joyce Hardy, Relative (Lucinda's sister), Child
Time period(s): 20th century (1930s-1950s)
Locale(s): Saskatchewan, Canada; Ottawa, Ontario, Canada; New York, New York

Summary: Maurice Dove, a young scientist, arrives to study the weather in the drought-ridden Canadian countryside. Dove himself is studied by two sisters. Lucinda, 17, is thoughtful and quiet; her sister, Norma Joyce, 8, is brash and aggressive. When Dove goes back to Ottawa, a coincidence moves the sisters to a house on the same block. The story follows them from puberty to adulthood as they deal with their emotions toward Dove and each other.

Where it's reviewed:
Booklist, November 15, 2000, page 614
Library Journal, March 1, 2001, page 131
New York Times Book Review, February 11, 2001, page 23
Publishers Weekly, December 11, 2000, page 63

Other books by the same author:
Small Change, 1997
Captivity Tales, 1993
Only Snow in Havana, 1992

Other books you might like:
Lisa Tawn Bergren, *Deep Harbor*, 1999
Bonnie Burnard, *A Good House*, 2000
Isabel Colegate, *Winter Journey*, 2001
Molly Gloss, *Wild Life*, 2000
Eileen Goudge, *One Last Dance*, 2000

1169

MELINDA HAYNES

Chalktown

(New York: Hyperion, 2001)

Story type: Gothic; Saga
Subject(s): Race Relations; Religion; Violence
Major character(s): Hezekiah Sheehand, Teenager (16-year-old), Runaway; Yellababy Sheehand, Child (5-year-old), Handicapped (mentally retarded); Cathy, Teenager (14-year-old), Runaway
Time period(s): 1950s; 1960s (1955-1961)
Locale(s): Chalktown, Mississippi

Summary: In 1960s Mississippi, Hezekiah Sheehand, leaves home, escaping an abusive dysfunctional family. Hez finds a new family in his retarded brother Yellababy, and Cathy, a runaway. They settle in Chalktown, where everyone has pain in their past and communicates by writing on chalk boards. A death occurred in the abandoned house Hez moves into, a death that gradually merges with his story.

Where it's reviewed:
Kirkus Reviews, February 15, 2001, page 201
Library Journal, April 15, 2001, page 132
Publishers Weekly, April 30, 2001, page 51

Other books by the same author:
Mother of Pearl, 1999

Other books you might like:
Lee Durkee, *Rides of the Midway*, 2001
Judith Guest, *Ordinary People*, 1976
Cormac McCarthy, *Blood Meridian*, 1985
Larry McMurtry, *The Last Picture Show*, 1966
Stewart O'Nan, *Everyday People*, 2001

1170

SHELBY HEARON

Ella in Bloom

(New York: Knopf, 2001)

Story type: Contemporary/Mainstream
Subject(s): Mothers and Daughters; Single Parent Families; Secrets
Major character(s): Agatha, Parent (of Terrell and Ella), Housewife; Ella, Single Parent (of teenager, Birdie); Terrell, Spouse (of Rufus Hall), Parent (of teenagers)
Time period(s): 2000s (2000)
Locale(s): Austin, Texas; Old Metairie, Louisiana

Summary: Hearon's sixteenth novel revolves around the strategies siblings choose to placate parents while making their own way. Mother Agatha is obsessed with propriety. Terrell, the oldest and favored daughter, conforms publicly, and marries a successful lawyer, while hiding her own agenda. Ella, who can't compromise, elopes and leaves town. After being widowed, Ella struggles to raise her daughter. When Terrell is killed in an airplane crash, the wheels of reconciliation begin to turn. The author keeps it interesting.

Where it's reviewed:
Booklist, January 1, 2001, page 915
Chicago Tribune Book Review, January 7, 2001, page 7
Library Journal, December 2000, page 188
New York Times Book Review, February 11, 2001, page 20
Publishers Weekly, November 13, 2000, page 86

Other books by the same author:
Footprints, 1996
Life Estates, 1994
Hug Dancing, 1992
Owning Jolene, 1988
Five-Hundred Scorpions, 1987

Other books you might like:
Trezza Azzopardi, *The Hiding Place*, 2000
Heidi Julavits, *Mineral Palace*, 2000
Marge Piercy, *The Longings of Women*, 1995
Elizabeth Strout, *Amy and Isabelle*, 1998

1171

ALICE HOFFMAN

Blue Diary

(New York: Putnam, 2001)

Story type: Contemporary Realism
Subject(s): Murder; Trials; Small Town Life
Major character(s): Ethan Ford, Crime Suspect (in murder), Contractor; Jorie Ford, Spouse (of Ethan); Rachel Morris, Crime Victim (raped and murdered)
Time period(s): 2000s (2001)
Locale(s): Monroe, Massachusetts; Maryland

Summary: Ethan and Jorie Ford's idyllic life is tested when a photo of the man wanted for a murder and rape committed in Maryland 15 years ago is broadcast on TV. A viewer identifies the suspect as Ethan and he is arrested. As his friends raise money for his defense, Jorie seeks information about the victim, Rachel Morris. After reading Rachel's diary, Jorie begins to wonder about Ethan.

Where it's reviewed:
Kirkus Reviews, May 15, 2001, page 685

Other books by the same author:
The Drowning Season, 2000
The River King, 2000
Local Girls, 1999
White Horses, 1999
Here on Earth, 1997

Other books you might like:
Margaret Atwood, *Alias Grace*, 1996
James Lee Burke, *Cimarron Rose*, 1997
John Grisham, *A Time to Kill*, 1989
Phillip Margolin, *After Dark*, 1995
Robert Traver, *Anatomy of a Murder*, 1958

1172

JAMES D. HOUSTON

Snow Mountain Passage

(New York: Knopf, 2001)

Story type: Historical; Saga
Subject(s): Pioneers; Wilderness Survival; Guilt
Major character(s): James Frazier Reed, Pioneer, Historical Figure; Patty Reed, Relative (James' youngest daughter), Historical Figure
Time period(s): 1840s (1846)
Locale(s): Sierra Nevada Mountains, California

Summary: This is a haunting fictionalized account of the Donner Party, a group of settlers who resorted to cannibalism in order to survive after being trapped in the mountains by harsh winter weather. The story's perspective shifts between James Frazier Reed, who is trying to rescue the party, and his youngest daughter, Patty, who is trapped with the settlers. The author describes the pettiness, greed, and opportunism that hampers the rescue efforts and the anger, hunger, and despair felt by those who are trapped.

Where it's reviewed:
New York Times Book Review, March 19, 2001, page 77
Publishers Weekly, March 19, 2001, page 77

Other books you might like:
Molly Gloss, *Wild Life*, 2000
Ken Kesey, *Sometimes a Great Notion*, 1964
Larry McMurtry, *Lonesome Dove*, 1985
James A. Michener, *Centennial*, 1974
James Alexander Thom, *From Sea to Shining Sea*, 1984

1173

MAUREEN HOWARD

Big as Life

(New York: Viking, 2001)

Story type: Collection
Subject(s): Spring; Relationships; Social Classes
Locale(s): United States

Summary: Maureen Howard's collection of three novellas celebrates spring, life, and renewal. In *Children with Matches*, Marie Claude recalls her magical childhood living with eccentric aunts. In the second, *The Magdalene*, Irish beauty Nell Boyle is sent to America to live with wealthy relatives, who don't welcome her with open arms. The third story, *Big as Life*, follows the career of naturalist John James Audubon from the point of view of his wife, Lucy.

Where it's reviewed:
Booklist, April 15, 2001, page 1534
Kirkus Reviews, April 1, 2001, page 440
Library Journal, May 1, 2001, page 129
New York Times Book Review, July 1, 2001, page 11
Publishers Weekly, April 23, 2001, page 48

Other books by the same author:
A Lovers Almanac, 1998
Natural History, 1992
Expensive Habits, 1986
Facts of Life, 1978
Bridgeport Bus, 1965

Other books you might like:
Penelope Fitzgerald, *The Means of Escape*, 2000
Rebecca Goldstein, *Properties of Light*, 2000
Erika Krouse, *Come Up and See Me Sometime*, 2001
David Schickler, *Kissing in Manhattan*, 2001
Helen Simpson, *Getting a Life*, 2001

1174

HELEN HUMPHREYS

Afterimage

(New York: Metropolitan, 2001)

Story type: Historical; Gay/Lesbian Fiction
Subject(s): Photography; Models; Social Classes
Major character(s): Annie Phelan, Servant (orphaned by the Irish famine), Model (for Isabelle); Isabelle Dashell, Spouse (of Eldon), Photographer (of servants in costume); Eldon Dashell, Cartographer (plans to explore the world), Spouse (of Isabelle)

Popular Fiction

Time period(s): 1850s
Locale(s): England (Middle Road Farm)

Summary: Young, innocent servant girl Annie Phelan arrives at Middle Road Farm. Isabelle, the mistress of the manor, is a photographer and Annie soon becomes Isabelle's favorite model. Eldon, the man of the house, lends Annie books to read while developing an attachment to her. The three become involved in a love triangle. The author's deft description of life in the mid-19th century English countryside keeps the story interesting.

Where it's reviewed:
Booklist, March 1, 2001, page 1227
New York Times Book Review, April 15, 2001, page 29
Publishers Weekly, March 5, 2001, page 61

Other books by the same author:
Leaving Earth, 1998
The Perils of Geography, 1995
Ethel on Fire, 1991
Gods and Other Mortals, 1986

Other books you might like:
Frederick Barthelme, *Tracer*, 2001
Virginia Coffman, *Fire Dawn*, 1977
Anne Deveson, *Lines in the Sand*, 2000
Anna Gilber, *Miss Bede Is Staying*, 1983
Henry James, *Wings of the Dove*, 1970

1175

ANGELA HUTH

Easy Silence

(New York: St. Martin's Press, 2001)

Story type: Satire; Humor
Subject(s): Relationships; Music and Musicians; Marriage
Major character(s): William Handle, Musician (string quartet), Spouse (of Grace); Grace Handle, Artist (illustrates children's books)
Time period(s): 2000s (2001)
Locale(s): England

Summary: Angela Huth explores the knee jerk compromises, adjustments, denials, and acceptances that foster daily existence. William and Grace are a happily married middle-aged couple until William decides to kill Grace in order to run off with a younger woman. Grace doesn't notice as she is infatuated with a younger man. It turns out that the woman isn't interested in William and Grace's man is unstable. The author's sense of good manners and humor keeps it lively.

Where it's reviewed:
Library Journal, February 15, 2001, page 202
New York Times Book Review, April 1, 2001, page 16

Other books by the same author:
Wives and Fisherman, 1998
Land Girls, 1994
Invitation to the Married Life, 1991
Wanting, 1984
Somehow I Had a Brass Band, 1970

Other books you might like:
Kingsley Amis, *Difficulties with Girls*, 1988

Amanda Coe, *Whore in the Kitchen*, 2000
Keith Martin, *Absolute Bottom*, 1999
Will Self, *Tough Tough Toys for Tough Tough Boys*, 1998

1176

JAMES HYNES

The Lecturer's Tale

(New York: Picador, 2001)

Story type: Satire; Gothic
Subject(s): Psychological; Academia; Humor
Major character(s): Nelson Humboldt, Professor
Time period(s): 2000s (2001)
Locale(s): Midwest

Summary: Nelson Humboldt, a college lecturer at a prestigious school, falls victim to the maxim: publish or perish. Shortly after his dismissal, he obtains magical powers that make people give him what he wants. He gets his job back and more. The story explores paranoia and pretension, while skewering various critical theories, which include postmodernists and deconstructionists, as well as current theories about gender.

Where it's reviewed:
Booklist, January 1, 2001, page 915
Chicago Tribune Books, April 8, 2001, page 2
Library Journal, December 2000, page 189
New York Times Book Review, January 21, 2001, page 30

Other books by the same author:
Publish and Perish, 1997
Wild Colonial Boy, 1992

Other books you might like:
Ann Beattie, *Another You*, 1995
Amanda Cross, *Honest Doubt*, 2000
A.O. Faniran, *Taste of Injustice*, 1998
Maribeth Fischer, *Language of Good-Bye*, 2001
Maeve Flanagan, *Nell's Novel*, 1999

1177

LIDIA JORGE

The Painter of Birds

(New York: Harcourt, 2001)

Story type: Multicultural; Adult
Subject(s): Secrets; Fathers and Daughters; Emigration and Immigration
Major character(s): Walter Dias, Artist (sketches birds), Drifter (seduces women); Custodio Dias, Relative (Walter's brother), Spouse (of Walter's pregnant lover)
Time period(s): 20th century (1945-1999)
Locale(s): Portugal

Summary: Lidia Jorge won the City of Lisbon Prize for this, her second novel. Walter Dias' daughter, who remains unnamed in the book, longs for her father to claim her as his child but he never does. Walter travels the world, loving women and sketching birds. His brother, Custodio, married Walter's pregnant lover and so his daughter has a claim to

legitimacy, but everyone knows that she is Walter's illegitimate child. Translated by Margaret J. Costa.

Where it's reviewed:
Booklist, February 1, 2001, page 1040
Library Journal, January 1, 2001, page 154
Los Angeles Times Book Review, April 1, 2001, page 2

Other books by the same author:
Murmuring Coast, 1995

Other books you might like:
Maryse Conde, *Desirada*, 2000
Jenny Diski, *The Dream Mistress*, 1999
Gilbert Morris, *All That Glitters*, 1999
Ludmila Ulitskaya, *The Funeral Party*, 2001
John Updike, *Licks of Love*, 2000

1178

HESTER KAPLAN

Kinship Theory
(Boston: Little, Brown, 2001)

Story type: Contemporary; Modern
Subject(s): Mothers and Daughters; Pregnancy; Family Relations
Major character(s): Maggie Crown, Parent (agrees to be surrogate mother), Divorced Person; Dale, Young Woman (can't get pregnant), Relative (Maggie's daughter); Ben Wakem, Spouse (of Maggie's best friend), Lover (of Maggie)
Time period(s): 2000s (2001)
Locale(s): United States

Summary: Good intentions and hormonal swings make life challenging in this story about the complications arising from surrogate motherhood. Feeling guilty about her daughter Dale's infertility, Maggie Crown, 48, agrees to carry a baby for her. When her husband has an affair, Dale experiences marital difficulties. Then Maggie becomes attached to the baby and decides to keep it, while Ben, her boss, leaves his wife and moves in with her.

Where it's reviewed:
Book, January 2001, page 74
Booklist, November 15, 2000, page 618
Library Journal, November 1, 2000, page 135
New York Times Book Review, April 29, 2001, page 20

Other books by the same author:
The Edge of Marriage, 1999

Other books you might like:
Julianna Baggott, *Girl Talk*, 2001
Elizabeth Berg, *What We Keep*, 1998
Sarah Bird, *The Mommy Club*, 1991
Edna O'Brien, *Down by the River*, 1997
Amy Yurk, *The Kind of Love That Saves You*, 2000

1179

JAN KARON

A Common Life
(New York: Viking, 2001)

Story type: Inspirational; Americana
Series: Mitford Years
Subject(s): Customs; Weddings; Mountain Life
Major character(s): Timothy Kavanaugh, Bridegroom, Religious (reverend); Cynthia Coppersmith, Bride
Time period(s): 1990s (1995)
Locale(s): Mitford, North Carolina

Summary: The Mitford saga continues in this volume set between *A Light in the Window* and *These High, Green Hills* and focusing on Father Tim Kavanaugh and Cynthia Coppersmith's down-home wedding. In addition to tapping into the usual anxieties such social events often raise, the author allows her characters to reminisce about the weddings in their own lives, too. A sermon on sex is included, along with the recipe for the orange marmalade wedding cake.

Where it's reviewed:
Booklist, February 15, 2001, page 1084
Library Journal, February 1, 2001, page 77
Publishers Weekly, March 19, 2001, page 77

Other books by the same author:
A New Song, 1999
Out to Canaan, 1997
These High, Green Hills, 1996
A Light in the Window, 1995
At Home in Mitford, 1994

Other books you might like:
Jenny Colgan, *Amanda's Wedding*, 2001
Catherine Cookson, *Years of the Virgins*, 1993
Kaye Gibbons, *Charms for the Easy Life*, 1993
Anne Tyler, *Slipping-Down Life*, 1970
Eudora Welty, *Delta Wedding*, 1946

1180

STEPHEN KING

Dreamcatcher
(New York: Scribner, 2001)

Story type: Gothic; Psychological
Subject(s): Science Fiction; Mental Telepathy; Friendship
Major character(s): Pete, Hunter; Beaver, Hunter; Henry, Hunter
Time period(s): 2000s (2001)
Locale(s): Derry, Maine

Summary: Four friends, Pete, Beaver, Henry, and Jonesy, are on their annual hunting trip when they uncover a plot by aliens to take over the world. Three different kinds of aliens are involved, one that attacks the bowels, one a human look-alike, and the third a parasitic growth. The odds appear overwhelming, but the alien presence fosters telepathic communication among earthlings. With Stephen King, the yarn is not only frightening but seems plausible.

Where it's reviewed:
Library Journal, March 1, 2001, page 131
Publishers Weekly, February 12, 2001, page 184

Other books by the same author:
Bag of Bones, 1998
Green Mile, 1997
Delores Claiborne, 1992
Stand, 1978
Shining, 1977

Other books you might like:
Karla Andersdatter, *Woman Who Was Wild and Other Tales*, 1995
Michael Chabon, *Werewolves in Their Youth*, 2000
A.M. Homes, *Safety of Objects*, 1990
Joyce Carol Oates, *Goddess and Other Women*, 1974
Peter Straub, *Magic Terror*, 2000

1181

ERIKA KROUSE

Come Up and See Me Sometime

(New York: Scribner, 2001)

Story type: Collection
Subject(s): Social Conditions; Relationships

Summary: In her debut, Erika Krouse presents a collection of 13 stories. The subjects covered include drug addiction, battered women, lesbianism, abortion, infidelity, self-image, poverty, and romance. A colorful cast of characters deals with life's vagaries, which can be humorous, titillating, and nerve wracking. Stories include ''Husband,'' ''No Universe,'' ''Drugs and You,'' ''Mercy,'' ''Too Big to Float,'' ''Impersonators,'' and ''Other People's Mothers.''

Where it's reviewed:
Booklist, May 1, 2001, page 1666
Kirkus Reviews, February 15, 2001, page 206
New York Times Book Review, July 1, 2001, page 6
Publishers Weekly, May 14, 2001, page 52

Other books you might like:
Raymond Carver, *Where I'm Calling From*, 1988
Isak Dinesen, *Winter Tales*, 1942
Ellen Gilchrist, *The Cabal*, 2000
Barbara Kingsolver, *Prodigal Summer*, 2000
Flannery O'Connor, *A Good Man Is Hard to Find*, 1955

1182

JAKE LAMAR

If 6 Were 9

(New York: Crown, 2001)

Story type: Satire; Contemporary
Subject(s): Academia; African Americans; Murder
Major character(s): Reggie Brogus, Professor (of African American studies), Activist (former black militant); Clay Robinette, Professor (of journalism); Jennifer Wolfsheim, Crime Victim (murdered), Student—College
Time period(s): 2000s (2001)
Locale(s): Ohio

Summary: Clay Robinette, a professor of journalism, is settling into a career in academia when Reggie Brogus, a former black militant, knocks on his door. A visiting professor, Brogus asks if Robinette will come to his office where there is a dead body, that of Jennifer Wolfsheim, a white coed. Brogus asks Robinette to provide an alibi for him. Robinette reluctantly agrees, then becomes a prime suspect because of an affair he had with Wolfsheim.

Where it's reviewed:
Booklist, December 1, 2000, page 696
Chicago Tribune Book Review, April 1, 2001, page 7
Library Journal, November 1, 2000, page 101

Other books by the same author:
Close to the Bone, 1998
Last Integrationist, 1996

Other books you might like:
Parry Brown, *The Shirt Off His Back*, 1998
John Grisham, *A Time to Kill*, 1989
Chester B. Himes, *If He Hollers Let Him Go*, 1945
Walter Mosley, *Always Outnumbered, Always Outgunned*, 1998
Nichelle D. Tramble, *The Dying Ground*, 2001

1183

DENNIS LEHANE

Mystic River

(New York: Morrow, 2001)

Story type: Contemporary Realism; Psychological
Subject(s): Crime and Criminals; Murder; Friendship
Major character(s): Sean Devine, Police Officer; Jimmy Marcus, Convict (ex-con), Parent (of Katie, who was murdered); Dave Boyle, Abuse Victim, Crime Suspect (in Katie's murder)
Time period(s): 2000s (2001)
Locale(s): Boston, Massachusetts

Summary: Dennis Lehane's sixth novel examines the complexity of human motivation. The story revolves around the murder of 19-year-old Katie Marcus. Her father, Jimmy, grew up with the police officer assigned to investigate the case, Sean Devine. Dave Boyle, who is a suspect in the murder, also grew up with Jimmy and Sean. While not close, a common experience keeps them connected—Sean and Jimmy feel guilty about Dave's kidnap and sexual abuse by a phony cop some 25 years ago.

Where it's reviewed:
Booklist, November 15, 2000, page 588
Library Journal, December 2000, page 189

Other books by the same author:
Prayers for Rain, 1999
Gone, Baby, Gone, 1998
Sacred, 1997
Darkness, Take My Hand, 1996
Drink Before the War, 1994

Other books you might like:
Michael Connelly, *A Darkness More than Night*, 2001
George V. Higgins, *At End of Day*, 2000

James Patterson, *Kiss the Girls*, 1995
Jodi Picoult, *Salem Falls*, 2001
Scott Turow, *Presumed Innocent*, 1987

1184

BRAD LEITHAUSER

A Few Corrections

(New York: Knopf, 2001)

Story type: Psychological; Family Saga
Subject(s): Secrets; Business; Family Relations
Major character(s): Luke Palmer, Relative (Wes' son), Young Man; Wesley Cross Sultan, Businessman, Rake; Conrad Sultan, Relative (Wes' brother)
Time period(s): 2000s (2001)
Locale(s): Restoration, Michigan

Summary: In his fifth novel, Leithauser describes the life of Wesley Sultan, average Midwestern businessman, through his obituary, which changes with each chapter. His son interviews relatives, friends, lovers, and enemies to tell the story. The information gathered reveals the strategies and actions producing both success and failure in Sultan's life. At the end, readers come away with a picture of a man who wasn't as straitlaced or uptight as he appeared.

Where it's reviewed:
Book, May 2001, page 72
Booklist, April 15, 2001, page 1535
Chicago Tribune Books, April 22, 2001, page 1
New York Times Book Review, May 13, 2001, page 27

Other books by the same author:
The Friends of Freeland, 1997
Seaward, 1993
Hence, 1989
Equal Distance, 1985

Other books you might like:
Saul Bellow, *The Actual*, 1997
David Dorsey, *The Cost of Living*, 1997
Stanley Elkin, *The Franchiser*, 1976
Joanna Elm, *Delusion*, 1997
Harold Robbins, *Never Leave Me*, 1954

1185

DAVID L. LINDSEY

Animosity

(New York: Warner, 2001)

Story type: Psychological Suspense
Subject(s): Sculptors and Sculpting; Relationships; Models
Major character(s): Ross Marteau, Artist (sculpts from live models); Celeste Lacan, Benefactor; Leda Lacan, Relative (Celeste's sister), Model (for Ross)
Time period(s): 2000s (2001)
Locale(s): Paris, France; San Rafael, Texas

Summary: Lindsey's latest book is a psychological thriller. Ross Marteau is a successful sculptor who avoids controversy, while cultivating affluent clients. His life plan calls for him to pull all the strings. Then he meets the lovely Celeste

Lacan, who hires him to sculpt her sister, Leda, in the nude. Although he knows the assignment will be controversial, he just can't refuse Celeste anything. Murder, blackmail, and revenge follow and Ross finds himself caught in the middle.

Where it's reviewed:
Chicago Tribune Books, June 3, 2001, page 2
Kirkus Reviews, April 1, 2001, page 444

Other books by the same author:
The Color of Night, 1999
Requiem for a Glass Heart, 1996
An Absence of Light, 1994
Body of Truth, 1992
Mercy, 1990

Other books you might like:
Margaret Atwood, *The Edible Woman*, 1969
Ann Beattie, *Falling in Place*, 1991
Anita Brookner, *The Misalliance*, 1986
A.S. Byatt, *The Virgin in the Garden*, 1978
Tracy Chevalier, *Girl with a Pearl Earring*, 1999

1186

ELINOR LIPMAN

The Dearly Departed

(New York: Random House, 2001)

Story type: Psychological; Humor
Subject(s): Mothers; Death; Brothers and Sisters
Major character(s): Sunny Batten, Young Woman (whose mother dies); Fletcher Finn, Young Man (whose father dies)
Time period(s): 2000s (2001)
Locale(s): King George, New Hampshire

Summary: In Elinor Lipman's novel, adult children discover their parents' secret lives, after a faulty furnace kills them. Margaret Batten and Miles Finn have been secret lovers for 30 years. When their children come home for the funerals, they are shocked by the revelation. Having grown up in a single-parent household, Sunny can't get over how much Fletcher resembles her. Other people make the observation, too.

Where it's reviewed:
Atlantic Monthly, June 2001, page 105
Booklist, May 15, 2001, page 1732
Chicago Tribune Books, June 17, 2001, page 1
Library Journal, May 15, 2001, page 163
Publishers Weekly, May 14, 2001, page 50

Other books by the same author:
The Ladies' Man, 1999
The Inn at Lake Devine, 1998
Isabel's Bed, 1995
The Way Men Act, 1992
Then She Found Me, 1990

Other books you might like:
Anita Brookner, *Undue Influence*, 1999
James Lee Burke, *Purple Cane Road*, 2000
Louise Erdrich, *Tales of Burning Love*, 1996
Carol Muske-Dukes, *Life After Death*, 2001
Anne Tyler, *Dinner at the Homesick Restaurant*, 1982

Popular Fiction

1187

DAVID LODGE

Thinks. . .

(New York: Viking, 2001)

Story type: Literary; Contemporary
Subject(s): Humor; Art; Science
Major character(s): Helen Reed, Writer (of novels), Professor (of literature); Ralph Messenger, Professor (of science)
Time period(s): 2000s (2001)
Locale(s): Gloucester, England (University of Gloucester)

Summary: The author, known for mining the interplay of emotion and rationality in the human condition, focuses on art and science in this novel. Helen Reed, a writer-in-residence and an admirer of Henry James, goes toe-to-toe with Ralph Messenger, the head of the university's science department. During witty, verbal sword fights, Ralph, a married man with a reputation for philandering, resorts to sexual propositions but Helen, a widow with a moral conscience, holds her own.

Where it's reviewed:
Atlantic Monthly, June 2001, page 104
Booklist, April 1, 2001, page 1428
Kirkus Reviews, April 1, 2001, page 445
New York Times, June 5, 2001, page B7

Other books by the same author:
Home Truths, 2000
Therapy, 1995
Paradise News, 1991
Nice Work, 1988
Small World, 1984

Other books you might like:
Saul Bellow, *Ravelstein*, 2000
Don DeLillo, *White Noise*, 1985
Mark Harris, *The Tale Maker*, 1994
Iris Murdoch, *The Book and the Brotherhood*, 1988
Philip Roth, *The Breast*, 1985

1188

GOLDBERRY LONG

Juniper Tree Burning

(New York: Simon & Schuster, 2001)

Story type: Psychological; Quest
Subject(s): Brothers and Sisters; Suicide; Family Problems
Major character(s): Juniper Tree Burning ''Jennie'', Young Woman (child of hippie parents), Student (med school); Sunny Boy Blue, Relative (Jennie's younger brother)
Time period(s): 20th century (1966-1992)
Locale(s): Santa Fe, New Mexico

Summary: This novel examines how children can inherit problems from their families. Juniper's hippie parents, members of a back-to-nature group, raised her and her brother in an impoverished rural setting without running water. Her mother openly dislikes Juniper, citing misguided spiritual beliefs. Despite these difficulties, Juniper works hard, eventually finding her way to medical school. When her brother commits

suicide, she is forced to find out about his death and confront her past. First novel.

Where it's reviewed:
Booklist, May 15, 2001, page 1732
Chicago Tribune Books, May 27, 2001, page 5
Kirkus Reviews, April 15, 2001, page 527
Library Journal, May 15, 2001, page 164
Publishers Weekly, May 28, 2001, page 49

Other books you might like:
Martin Amis, *Night Train*, 1997
Madison Smartt Bell, *Years of Silence*, 1987
Carson McCullers, *The Heart Is a Lonely Hunter*, 1940
Tim Parks, *Destiny*, 1999
Anne Tyler, *Saint Maybe*, 1991

1189

LAURA GLEN LOUIS

Talking in the Dark

(New York: Harcourt, 2001)

Story type: Collection
Subject(s): Love; Chinese Americans; Loneliness
Time period(s): 2000s (2001)

Summary: In her first book, Laura Glen Louis, who won the Katherine Anne Porter Prize for her first short story, gives us a collection of eight short stories with characters wrestling with the existential angst of an aching heart. Many, but not all, of her characters are Chinese American and they include teenagers, abandoned wives and mothers, widowers, and divorced people. Themes include obsession, seduction, gold-digging, exploitation, extramarital sex, guilt, and self-recrimination. Loneliness can make even the strongest character vulnerable and sometimes unconventional.

Where it's reviewed:
Kirkus Reviews, February 1, 2001, page 133
Library Journal, January 1, 2001, page 160
Publishers Weekly, February 19, 2001, page 67

Other books you might like:
A.S. Byatt, *Possession*, 1990
Bobbie Ann Mason, *Love Life*, 1989
Alice Munro, *Open Secrets*, 1994
Katherine Anne Porter, *The Collected Short Stories of Katherine Anne Porter*, 1965
Amy Tan, *The Kitchen God's Wife*, 1991

1190

JONATHAN LOWY

Elvis and Nixon

(New York: Crown, 2001)

Story type: Contemporary/Fantasy; Humor
Subject(s): Presidents; Music and Musicians
Major character(s): Elvis Presley, Musician (king of rock 'n' roll), Historical Figure; Richard Nixon, Political Figure (president), Historical Figure
Time period(s): 1970s (1970)

Locale(s): Washington, District of Columbia; Las Vegas, Nevada

Summary: Jonathan Lowy's first novel, loosely based on an historical event, is told with tongue firmly in cheek. Elvis Presley has a mid-life crisis and sets out to find meaning. Presley, a narcotics addict, decides to help in the war on drugs, so he drives to the White House and offers his services to President Richard Nixon. Lowy adds a few spins to the yarn and tells it against a backdrop of other sensational events from the era.

Where it's reviewed:
Booklist, January 1, 2001, page 919
Library Journal, February 1, 2001, page 126
New York Times Book Review, March 4, 2001, page 7

Other books you might like:
William F. Buckley, *Elvis in the Morning*, 2001
Les Fox, *Return to Sender*, 1996
Robert Graham, *Elvis*, 1997
David M. Klein, *Kill Me Tender*, 2000
Robert S. Levinson, *Elvis and Marilyn Affair*, 1999

1191

GILA LUSTIGER

The Inventory
(New York: Arcade, 2001)

Story type: Historical/World War II
Subject(s): Holocaust; Nazis; Violence
Time period(s): 1930s; 1940s
Locale(s): Germany

Summary: In her first novel, Lustiger weaves a series of vignettes into a story of 1930s-1940s German society. Men, women, and children from all walks of life move to center stage to bear witness. Fear, violence and intimidation are rampant. The effect is to put the reader on the scene as the social, economic, political, racial, and religious tensions push the social fabric over the edge. Rebecca Morrison did the translation.

Where it's reviewed:
Booklist, November 15, 2000, page 619
Library Journal, December 2000, page 190
New York Times Book Review, January 7, 2001, page 14

Other books you might like:
S.Y. Agnon, *Only Yesterday*, 2000
Frank Simon, *Trial by Fire*, 1999
William Styron, *Sophie's Choice*, 1979
Simone Zelitch, *Louisa*, 2000

1192

ALISTAIR MACLEOD

Island
(New York: Norton, 2001)

Story type: Collection
Subject(s): Islands; Fishing; Family Relations
Locale(s): Cape Breton Island, Nova Scotia, Canada

Summary: In this critically acclaimed collection, which was first published in Canada, MacLeod returns to his beloved Cape Breton Island, just off the coast of Nova Scotia, to mine cultural gold. His stories explore coming-of-age, lobster fishing, family relationships, and superstition against a backdrop of harsh cold winters and the gray waves of the Atlantic Ocean. A pronounced Scottish cultural twist adds charm to the narrative.

Where it's reviewed:
Booklist, January 1, 2001, page 919
Library Journal, January 1, 2001, page 159
New York Times Book Review, February 18, 2001, page 6
Publishers Weekly, December 18, 2000, page 54

Other books by the same author:
No Great Mischief, 1999
As Birds Bring Forth the Sun, 1986
The Lost Salt Gift of Blood, 1976

Other books you might like:
Joan Connor, *We Who Live Apart*, 2000
Ellen Gilchrist, *The Cabal*, 2000
Josephine Humphreys, *Nowhere Else on Earth*, 2000
William Trevor, *The Hill Bachelors*, 2000

1193

MICHELINE AHARONIAN MARCOM

Three Apples Fell from Heaven
(New York: Riverhead, 2001)

Story type: Historical; Ethnic
Subject(s): Massacres; Violence; Refugees
Major character(s): Anaguil, Young Woman (watches her father jailed); Leslie Davis, Diplomat (American consul); Sargis, Writer (poet)
Time period(s): 1900s; 1910s (1909-1918)
Locale(s): Armenia

Summary: In her debut novel, Micheline Aharonian Marcom examines the mass murders of more than a million Armenians at the hands of Turks during World War I. The victims describe the madness they experienced in vignettes. The incessant brutality, graphically described, committed against neighbors, customers and other acquaintances foreshadows the recent troubles in the Balkans.

Where it's reviewed:
Booklist, March 15, 2001, page 1354
Library Journal, May 15, 2001, page 164
New York Times Book Review, April 22, 2001, page 26

Other books you might like:
Antranig Antreassian, *Death and Resurrection*, 1988
Nelson DeMille, *Word of Honor*, 1985
Carol Edgarian, *Rise the Euphrates*, 1994
Franz Werfel, *The Forty Days of Musa Dagh*, 1934
Elie Wiesel, *The Forgotten*, 1992

1194

DANIEL MARSHALL

Still Can't See Nothing Coming

(New York: HarperCollins, 2001)

Story type: Psychological; Coming-of-Age
Subject(s): Drugs; Violence; Alcoholism
Major character(s): Jim Drake, Teenager (does drugs and alcohol), Relative (Mandy's younger brother); Mandy Drake, Teenager (commits suicide), Abuse Victim (by her father)
Time period(s): 1990s
Locale(s): Madison, Wisconsin

Summary: Daniel Marshall's first novel deals with teenage alienation and self-destruction. The story revolves around the sibling relationship of Mandy and Jim. Coming from an abusive home, the two find emotional support in drugs, alcohol and mutual friends. When Mandy commits suicide, Jim is blamed and forced to leave home, he drops out of school and becomes a petty criminal. After robbing a local drug lord, he gets caught in another armed robbery. A few surprises keep it interesting.

Where it's reviewed:
Booklist, February 15, 2001, page 1116
Chicago Tribune Books, June 10, 2001, page 2
Kirkus Reviews, February 1, 2001, page 134
Publishers Weekly, February 5, 2001, page 65

Other books you might like:
Jane Hamilton, *Disobedience*, 2000
Melinda Haynes, *Chalktown*, 2001
Cormac McCarthy, *Blood Meridian*, 1985
Alice Munro, *Lives of Girls & Women*, 1971
J.D. Salinger, *Catcher in the Rye*, 1951

1195

SIMON MAWER

The Gospel of Judas

(Boston: Little, Brown, 2001)

Story type: Mystical; Literary
Subject(s): Love; Gospels; Death
Major character(s): Leo Newman, Religious (Catholic priest), Scholar (of ancient texts); Madeleine Brewer, Lover (of Leo), Spouse (of a diplomat)
Time period(s): 2000s (2001)
Locale(s): Rome, Italy

Summary: Mawer's book looks at life, love, and the existence of God. Leo Newman lives, not without effort, in a world insulated from reality. The story revolves around questions that challenge his vocation as a priest and his faith as a Christian. Newman strikes up a friendship with a married woman with whom he has an affair. Then he is called upon to translate an ancient text that denies Christ rose from the dead.

Where it's reviewed:
Atlantic Monthly, June 2001, page 106
Booklist, May 1, 2001, page 1667
Kirkus Reviews, April 15, 2001, page 528

Library Journal, April 1, 2001, page 133
Publishers Weekly, April 9, 2001, page 48

Other books by the same author:
Mendel's Dwarf, 1998
A Jealous God, 1996
Chimera, 1989

Other books you might like:
Umberto Eco, *The Name of the Rose*, 1983
Andrew M. Greeley, *Fall from Grace*, 1993
Malachi Martin, *Vatican*, 1986
Colleen McCullough, *The Thorn Birds*, 1977
Morris L. West, *Eminence*, 1998

1196

PATRICK MCCABE

Emerald Germs of Ireland

(New York: HarperCollins, 2001)

Story type: Psychological; Gothic
Subject(s): Serial Killer; Mothers and Sons; Humor
Major character(s): Pat McNab, Singer, Serial Killer
Time period(s): 2000s (2001)
Locale(s): Gullytown, Ireland

Summary: Pat McNab, 45, lives with his mother, an embittered woman who blames the world for her husband's desertion. Her off-key scolding pushes Pat over the edge and he clouts her with a frying pan, dispatching her from this world. However, she returns for periodic conversations with Pat as he sets out on a murderous career, dispatching victims to the tune of various popular songs. The story's humorous style and cutting social observations neutralize the bloodshed.

Where it's reviewed:
Booklist, January 1, 2001, page 870
Library Journal, February 1, 2001, page 126
Publishers Weekly, March 5, 2001, page 64

Other books by the same author:
Mondo Desperado, 1999
Breakfast on Pluto, 1998
Carn, 1997
Dead School, 1995
The Butcher Boy, 1993

Other books you might like:
Tibor Fischer, *I Like Being Killed*, 2000
Penelope Fitzgerald, *Human Voices*, 1999
Jonathan Lowy, *Elvis and Nixon*, 2001
Sue Miller, *The Good Mother*, 1986
Joyce Carol Oates, *Broke Heart Blues*, 1999

1197

SHARYN MCCRUMB

The Songcatcher

(New York: Dutton, 2001)

Story type: Family Saga
Subject(s): Mountain Life; Country Music; Women

Major character(s): Linda Walker, Singer (country music), Relative (estranged daughter); John Walker, Parent (of Linda), Aged Person (on death bed); Malcolm McCourry, Pioneer (of North Carolina), Relative (on Linda's maternal side)

Time period(s): Multiple Time Periods

Locale(s): Tennessee; North Carolina; Islay, Scotland

Summary: Sharyn McCrumb's novel, which has ties to her Ballad mystery series, is a family saga about a song. In 1751, Malcolm McCourry arrives in America with a special song and little else. The song has been handed down for generations. Now, a relative, Linda Walker, whose professional name is Lark McCourry, wants to sing the song but can't find the words. Meanwhile, Linda's estranged father Judge John Walker is dying. She attempts to be with him, but her plane crashes, stranding her in the wilderness.

Where it's reviewed:
Kirkus Reviews, April 15, 2001, page 546
Publishers Weekly, May 14, 2001, page 51

Other books by the same author:
The Ballad of Frankie Silver, 1998
Foggy Mountain Breakdown, 1997
The Rosewood Casket, 1996
If I'd Killed Him When I Met Him, 1995
She Walks These Hills, 1994

Other books you might like:
Larry Brown, *Fay*, 2000
James Lee Burke, *To the Bright and Shining Sun*, 1970
Willa Cather, *Novels & Stories 1905-1918*, 1999
William Gay, *Provinces of Night*, 2000
Thomas Wolfe, *Look Homeward, Angel*, 1929

1198

BERNICE L. MCFADDEN

The Warmest December

(New York: Dutton, 2001)

Story type: Psychological; Multicultural

Subject(s): African Americans; Alcoholism; Fathers and Daughters

Major character(s): Kenzie Lowe, Narrator, Abuse Victim; Hyman "Hy-Lo" Lowe, Parent (of Kenzie), Alcoholic (dying of liver disease)

Time period(s): 2000s (2001)

Locale(s): New York, New York (Brooklyn)

Summary: Bernice L. McFadden's novel chronicles an African American woman's painful journey to forgiveness and recovery. Abused physically and emotionally by her alcoholic father and neglected by her passive mother, Kenzie Lowe turned to drugs and alcohol for pain medication. Now in her 30s and on welfare, Kenzie must deal with her past when her dying father is hospitalized. She is able to move on with her own life after learning about her father's childhood.

Where it's reviewed:
Booklist, January 1, 2001, page 919
Kirkus Reviews, November 15, 2000, page 1565
Library Journal, November 1, 2000, page 101
Publishers Weekly, November 13, 2000, page 86

Other books by the same author:
Sugar, 2000

Other books you might like:
Margaret Atwood, *Surfacing*, 1972
Elizabeth Berg, *Durable Goods*, 1993
Maxine Clair, *October Suite*, 2001
Stewart O'Nan, *Everyday People*, 2001
Alice Walker, *The Color Purple*, 1982

1199

DENNIS MCFARLAND

Singing Boy

(New York: Holt, 2001)

Story type: Psychological; Contemporary Realism

Subject(s): Mothers and Sons; Widows; Grief

Major character(s): Malcolm Vaughn, Spouse (of Sarah), Parent (of Harry); Sarah Vaughn, Spouse (of Malcolm), Parent (of Harry); Deckard Jones, Friend (of Malcolm), Addict (recovered from drug abuse)

Time period(s): 2000s (2001)

Locale(s): Boston, Massachusetts

Summary: Dennis McFarland explores the subject of when bad things happen to good people. Driving home one night with his wife and son, Malcolm gets into a traffic altercation and is shot dead. The story follows his wife, Sarah, and his eight-year-old son, Harry, as they try to put their lives back together. Malcolm's best friend, Deckard Jones, attempts to help Sarah and Harry, while wrestling with his own demons.

Where it's reviewed:
Booklist, February 1, 2001, page 1040
Library Journal, January 1, 2001, page 155
New York Times Book Review, March 4, 2001, page 8

Other books by the same author:
Face at the Window, 1997
School for the Blind, 1994
Music Room, 1990

Other books you might like:
David Baldacci, *Wish You Well*, 2000
Eric Bogosian, *The Mall*, 2000
T.C. Boyle, *A Friend of the Earth*, 2000
Barry Gifford, *Wyoming*, 2000
Joyce Carol Oates, *Broke Heart Blues*, 1999

1200

TERRY MCMILLAN

A Day Late and a Dollar Short

(New York: Viking, 2001)

Story type: Family Saga; Multicultural

Subject(s): African Americans; Women; Family

Major character(s): Viola Price, Parent; Cecil Price, Spouse (driven away by Viola); Paris Price, Businesswoman, Addict (of painkillers)

Time period(s): 2000s (2001)

Locale(s): Chicago, Illinois; Los Angeles, California; Las Vegas, Nevada

Popular Fiction

Summary: Modern life poses many difficulties in maintaining personal and family relationships. After 40 years of marriage, Viola has driven her husband, Cecil, out of the house and into the arms of his girlfriend. Their children fare no better: Charlotte, the only daughter in town, doesn't get along with her mother; Paris has a successful career but is painfully lonely; Lewis, the only son, is an alcoholic; and Janelle, the youngest, finds out her second husband is molesting her daughter.

Where it's reviewed:
Booklist, November 15, 2000, page 588
Library Journal, January 1, 2001, page 155
Publishers Weekly, December 11, 2000, page 65
Time, January 29, 2001, page 68

Other books by the same author:
How Stella Got Her Groove Back, 1996
Disappearing Acts, 1993
Waiting to Exhale, 1992
Mama, 1987

Other books you might like:
Daniel Alef, *Pale Truth*, 2000
Tajuana Butler, *Sorority Sisters*, 2000
Pearl Cleage, *I Wish I Had a Red Dress*, 2001
J. California Cooper, *Future Has a Past*, 2000
Alice Walker, *The Way Forward*, 2000

1201

EDIE MEIDAV

The Far Field

(Boston: Houghton Mifflin, 2001)

Story type: Multicultural; Historical
Subject(s): Psychological; Cultural Conflict; Quest
Major character(s): Henry Frye Gould, Settler; Johnny, Assistant (Henry's), Spy (for the British); Nani, Housekeeper (maid)
Time period(s): 1930s (1936)
Locale(s): Rojottama, Ceylon

Summary: In Ceylon, now Sri Lanka, an island off the coast of India. Henry Frye Gould, a spiritual con man of sorts, attempts to build a religious community. Abandoning his wife and two children in New York along with his first name, Frye becomes an anti-missionary, combining eastern and western spiritual beliefs. A series of missteps, interference by the British, and local opposition doom Frye's efforts.

Where it's reviewed:
Booklist, April 1, 2001, page 1451
Library Journal, May 15, 2001, page 164
New York Times Book Review, April 29, 2001, page 15
Publishers Weekly, February 12, 2001, page 182

Other books you might like:
Reginald Dias, *The Orphan*, 1999
Barbara Kingsolver, *Prodigal Summer*, 2000
Michael Ondaatje, *Anil's Ghost*, 2000
Shyam Selvadurai, *Cinnamon Gardens*, 1999
Rose Swan, *Message of Love*, 2001

1202

ANA MENENDEZ

In Cuba I Was a German Shepherd

(New York: Grove, 2001)

Story type: Collection
Subject(s): Cuban Americans; Social Conditions; Memory
Time period(s): 2000s (2001)
Locale(s): Miami, Florida

Summary: In her first book, a collection of short stories, Ana Menendez explores the culture shock experienced by many Cubans and Cuban Americans now living in Miami. Her colorful cast of characters makes humorous, painful, and insightful observations comparing their current realities with the past. While many have done well, their common history and ties to Cuba make assimilation a bittersweet proposition. Their imaginations give life to memories of wealth, friendships, and status.

Where it's reviewed:
Booklist, April 15, 2001, page 1536
Library Journal, April 15, 2001, page 135
Publishers Weekly, May 5, 2001, page 221

Other books you might like:
Oscar Cisneros, *Empress of the Splendid Season*, 1999
Sandra Cisneros, *The House on Mango Street*, 1994
J. Joaquin Fraxedas, *The Lonely Crossing of Juan Cabrera*, 1993
Esmeralda Santiago, *Almost a Woman*, 1999
Ana Veciana-Suarez, *The Chin Kiss King*, 1997

1203

JACQUELYN MITCHARD

A Theory of Relativity

(New York: HarperCollins, 2001)

Story type: Contemporary/Mainstream
Subject(s): Traffic Accidents; Orphans; Grandparents
Major character(s): Keefer Nye, Orphan (parents killed in a car crash); Gordon Mckenna, Relative (Keefer's uncle), Adoptee
Time period(s): 2000s (2001)
Locale(s): Tall Trees, Wisconsin

Summary: Keefer Nye, an infant girl, is orphaned when her parents are killed in an auto accident. A custody battle ensues between her maternal uncle, Gordon McKenna, and her paternal grandparents, who believe she should go to their niece. The court rules in favor of the grandparents because Gordon was adopted and, under the law, is not considered to be a blood relative. However, the way is left open for an appeal of the case.

Where it's reviewed:
Booklist, April 1, 2001, page 1429
Kirkus Reviews, April 15, 2001, page 529
Library Journal, May 1, 2001, page 127
Publishers Weekly, April 23, 2001, page 45

Other books by the same author:
The Most Wanted, 1998
The Rest of Us, 1997
The Deep End of the Ocean, 1996

Other books you might like:
James Agee, *A Death in the Family*, 1967
David Baldacci, *Wish You Well*, 2000
Amit Chandhuri, *New World*, 2000
Avery Corman, *Kramer Versus Kramer*, 1977
Sue Miller, *The Good Mother*, 1986

1204

RICK MOODY

Demonology
(Boston: Little Brown, 2001)

Story type: Collection
Subject(s): Short Stories

Summary: This collection of Rick Moody's short stories has some experimental elements. Two stories contain one sentence each, although one is a little over two pages, while the other is 16 pages. In Moody's capable hands, the reader may not notice. Rock 'n' roll as a benchmark for life, psychics, a sibling's death, a drive-by shooting, a failed ostrich ranch, rare books, a man in a chicken mask, love, a Halloween party, a performing monkey, and the Shah of Iran are all topics that occur in these tales.

Where it's reviewed:
New York Times Book Review, February 25, 2001, page 12
Publishers Weekly, December 11, 2000, page 64

Other books by the same author:
Garden State, 1997
Purple America, 1997
Ring of Brightest Angels around Heaven, 1995
Ice Storm, 1994

Other books you might like:
John Biguenet, *The Torturer's Apprentice*, 2001
Frederick Busch, *Don't Tell Anyone*, 2000
A.S. Byatt, *Elementals*, 1998
Don DeLillo, *The Body Artist*, 2001
Peter Handke, *On a Dark Night I Left My Silent House*, 2000

1205

WILLIE MORRIS

Taps
(Boston: Houghton Mifflin, 2001)

Story type: Coming-of-Age; Historical
Subject(s): Adolescence; Small Town Life; Korean War
Major character(s): Swayze Barksdale, Teenager (16-year-old), Musician (at military funerals); Luke Cartwright, Store Owner (hardware store), Hero (of World War II); Arch, Friend (of Swayze), Musician (at military funerals)
Time period(s): 1950s (1950-1953)
Locale(s): Fisk's Landing, Mississippi

Summary: Willie Morris brings readers to Fisk's Landing, Mississippi, during the Korean War. Swayze Barksdale, 16, and his pal, Arch, are recruited to play ''Taps'' at the town's first military funeral. From then on, they play ''Taps'' each time a coffin returns. Before the summer is over, Swayze will learn about friendship, loss, infidelity, and violence, as well as love and sex. Morris provides a colorful cast to move the story forward.

Where it's reviewed:
Booklist, February 15, 2001, page 1084
Kirkus Reviews, February 15, 2001, page 209
New York Times Book Review, April 22, 2001, page 23
Publishers Weekly, February 26, 2001, page 55

Other books by the same author:
The Last of the Southern Girls, 1973

Other books you might like:
Larry Brown, *Father and Son*, 1996
Lee Durkee, *Rides of the Midway*, 2001
John Grisham, *A Time to Kill*, 1989
William Styron, *The Long March*, 1952
Dan Wakefield, *Going All the Way*, 1989

1206

WALTER MOSLEY

Fearless Jones
(Boston: Little, Brown, 2001)

Story type: Adventure; Saga
Subject(s): African Americans; Mystery; Nazis
Major character(s): Paris Minton, Store Owner (bookstore), Crime Victim (of arson); Fearless Jones, Veteran (World War II), Friend (of Paris); Leon Douglas, Convict, Criminal
Time period(s): 1950s (1954)
Locale(s): Los Angeles, California (Watts)

Summary: Mosley again returns to Watts circa the 1950s, but this time he introduces a new set of characters. Paris Minton owns a bookstore, but he misses the sense of belonging he felt in the small all-black town where he grew up. When Paris' store burns down, he turns to Fearless Jones for help. The plot thickens as the two encounter numerous white people determined to obtain a cache of stolen money.

Where it's reviewed:
Booklist, May 1, 2001, page 1636
Kirkus Reviews, April 1, 2001. page 464
Library Journal, June 1, 2001, page 224
New York Times Book Review, June 10, 2001, page 24
Publishers Weekly, May 28, 2001, page 53

Other books by the same author:
Walkin' the Dog, 1999
Blue Light, 1998
RL's Dream, 1995
White Butterfly, 1992
Devil in a Blue Dress, 1990

Other books you might like:
Anita Brookner, *A Friend from England*, 1989
Penelope Fitzgerald, *The Bookshop*, 1965

Langston Hughes, *Simple's Uncle Sam*, 1978
Terry McMillan, *Waiting to Exhale*, 1992
Richard Wright, *Eight Men*, 1961

1207

BARBARA MUJICA

Frida

(Woodstock, New York: Overlook, 2001)

Story type: Historical
Subject(s): Biography; Art; Relationships

Summary: Precocious, intelligent, talented, beautiful, and sexually experienced are just a few of the adjectives that are used to describe Frida Kahlo. This is a fictional account of the life, art, and pain experienced by the woman who was married to the Mexican painter Diego Rivera. The story is narrated by Frida's younger sister, Christina, and readers get a bird's-eye view of the glitterati of the era as Frida rubs elbows with the likes of Leon Trotsky and Paulette Goddard.

Where it's reviewed:
Booklist, January 1, 2001, page 920
Library Journal, November 15, 2000, page 97
New York Times Book Review, January 1, 2001, page 18
Publishers Weekly, October 30, 2000, page 44

Other books by the same author:
Sanchez Across the Street, 1997
The Deaths of Don Bernardo, 1990

Other books you might like:
Margaret Atwood, *Cat's Eye*, 1988
Rita Dove, *Through the Ivory Gate*, 1992
Helen Humphreys, *Afterimage*, 2001
J.D. Landis, *Longing*, 2000
Anita Shreve, *The Weight of Water*, 1997

1208

HARUKI MURAKAMI

The Sputnik Sweetheart

(New York: Knopf, 2001)

Story type: Multicultural; Romance
Subject(s): Relationships; Loneliness; Psychological
Major character(s): Unnamed Character, Professor (in love with Sumire), Narrator; Sumire, Student—College (devoted to Beat poets); Miu, Businesswoman (employer of Sumire)
Time period(s): 1950s (1957)
Locale(s): Tokyo, Japan; Greece

Summary: Three characters search for meaning in human connections in Murakami's seventh novel: the narrator, a teacher in Tokyo; Sumire, an aspiring writer; and Miu a married businesswoman. While vacationing on an island with Miu, Sumire disappears, the narrator sets out to find her. After discovering why Sumire loves Miu and a secret that makes Miu remote he returns to Tokoyo depressed. Murakami's sensitive touch makes it all make sense. Philip Gabriel provides the translation.

Where it's reviewed:
Booklist, January 15, 2001, page 870
Kirkus Reviews, January 15, 2001, page 75
Library Journal, January 2001, page 156
New York Times Book Review, June 10, 2001, page 13
Publishers Weekly, March 19, 2001, page 73

Other books by the same author:
Norwegian Wood, 2000
South of the Border, West of the Sun, 1999
Dance, Dance, Dance, 1994
The Elephant Vanishes, 1993
Hard-Boiled Wonderland and the End of the World, 1991

Other books you might like:
Julie Cannon, *Truelove & Homegrown Tomatoes*, 2001
Lucy Ellman, *Man or Mango*, 1998
Ishiguro Kazuo, *The Remains of the Day*, 1989
Judith Rossner, *Looking for Mr. Goodbar*, 1975
Anne Tyler, *The Accidental Tourist*, 1985

1209

CAROL MUSKE-DUKES

Life After Death

(New York: Random House, 2001)

Story type: Psychological
Subject(s): Widows; Mothers and Daughters; Grief
Major character(s): Boyd Schaeffer, Widow(er) (of Russell), Doctor (former); Russell Schaeffer, Spouse (of Boyd), Wealthy (dies suddenly); Will Youngren, Undertaker (buries Russell)
Time period(s): 2000s (2001)
Locale(s): St. Paul, Minnesota

Summary: Carol Muske-Dukes looks at grief and survival when a family member passes away suddenly. Russell Schaeffer dies shortly after an argument with his wife, Boyd. His death forces her to confront her own demons, as well as the notion that a curse uttered in anger caused Russell's death. She finds support in the unlikely company of Will Youngren, the undertaker who buries Russell. Will is also dealing with grief from his twin sister's death.

Where it's reviewed:
Booklist, May 15, 2001, page 1735
Library Journal, June 1, 2001, page 218
Los Angeles Times Book Review, May 30, 2001, page 1
New York Times Book Review, June 17, 2001, page 30
Publishers Weekly, April 23, 2001, page 48

Other books by the same author:
Saving St. Germ, 1993
Dear Digby, 1991

Other books you might like:
Alice Adams, *Medicine Men*, 1997
Margaret Atwood, *The Blind Assassin*, 2000
Judy Baer, *Jenny's Story*, 2000
David Baldacci, *Total Control*, 1997
Anita Brookner, *The Bay of Angels*, 2001

1210

AMELIE NOTHOMB

Fear and Trembling

(New York: St. Martin's Press, 2001)

Story type: Satire; Multicultural
Subject(s): Social Conditions; Gender Roles; Racism
Major character(s): Amelie, Businesswoman; Fubuki Mori, Businesswoman (Amelie's boss); Mr. Omochi, Businessman (Fubuki's boss)
Time period(s): 2000s (2001)
Locale(s): Japan

Summary: Belgian writer Amelie Nothomb puts a multicultural twist on conventional notions of the corporate glass ceiling. The story follows a young European woman living in Japan and working for the Yumimoto Corporation. She is ordered to speak English because her ability to speak Japanese threatens her male bosses. When she misses a deadline for a project, she is sent to clean restrooms by her supervisor, a woman. Humor keeps a potential for heavy-handedness in check. Translated by Adriana Hunter.

Where it's reviewed:
Booklist, February 15, 2001, page 1117
Library Journal, February 1, 2001, page 126
New York Times Book Review, March 25, 2001, page 20
Publishers Weekly, January 15, 2001, page 52

Other books by the same author:
Loving Sabotage, 2000

Other books you might like:
Isabel Allende, *Daughter of Fortune*, 1999
Louise Erdrich, *The Last Report on the Miracles at Little No Horse*, 2001
Karen Karbo, *Motherhood Made a Man out of Me*, 200
Amy Tan, *The Bonesetter's Daughter*, 2001

1211

JOYCE CAROL OATES

Faithless

(New York: Ecco, 2001)

Story type: Collection; Gothic
Subject(s): Social Conditions
Time period(s): 2000s (2001)

Summary: Joyce Carol Oates' collection of 21 short stories deals first and foremost with transgressions. Oates dramatizes daily activities while adding a grotesque spin. Subjects discussed include self-image, love, lust, revenge, assault, rape, passion, identity erosion, gun ownership, female alienation, fatal attraction, suicide, matricide, and euthanasia. The author gets readers' attention with these grim tales of polite and impolite terrors committed against the self and others.

Where it's reviewed:
Booklist, February 1, 2001, page 1020
New York Times Book Review, March 25, 2001, page 5

Other books by the same author:
Blonde, 2000

Broke Heart Blues, 1999
My Heart Laid Bare, 1998
Man Crazy, 1997
We Were the Mulvaneys, 1996

Other books you might like:
Alice Adams, *Last Lovely City*, 1999
Dwight Allen, *Green Suit*, 2000
Frederick Barthelme, *Moon Deluxe*, 1983

1212

STEWART O'NAN

Everyday People

(New York: Grove, 2001)

Story type: Multicultural; Contemporary
Subject(s): African Americans; City Life; Accidents
Major character(s): Chris Tolbert, Artist (graffiti), Handicapped (paralyzed from a fall); Eugene Tolbert, Convict (trying to go straight), Relative (Chris' brother); Harold Tolbert, Parent (of Chris and Eugene), Homosexual
Time period(s): 1990s (1998)
Locale(s): Pittsburgh, Pennsylvania

Summary: Stewart O'Nan writes about the trials and tribulations of an African-American family. Living in an economically impoverished neighborhood, the Tolberts are besieged by social pathologies, racial bias, gangs, drugs, and violent crime. Chris, 18, is confined to a wheelchair after falling off an overpass; his brother, Eugene, recently released from prison, has gotten religion and struggles to go straight; and Harold, the father knows his family needs him, but wants to leave them for his gay lover.

Where it's reviewed:
Booklist, December 1, 2000, page 676
Library Journal, November 15, 2000, page 97
New York Times Book Review, February 25, 2001, page 9
Publishers Weekly, November 20, 2000, page 43

Other books by the same author:
Prayer for Dying, 2000
World Away, 1998
Speed Queen, 1997
The Names of the Dead, 1996
Snow Angels, 1994

Other books you might like:
Beverly Clark, *Bound by Love*, 2000
Rhodesia Jackson, *Three Times Sweeter*, 2000
Debra Phillips, *Kiss or Keep*, 1999
Carl Weber, *Lookin' for Luv*, 2000

1213

HAN ONG

Fixer Chao

(New York: Farrar Straus & Giroux, 2001)

Story type: Satire; Multicultural
Subject(s): Social Classes; Racism; City Life
Major character(s): Shem C, Writer (embittered and unsuccessful); William Narciso Paulinha, Prostitute

Time period(s): 2000s (2001)
Locale(s): New York, New York (Manhattan)

Summary: Playwright Han Ong's first novel starts with a simple scam and builds it into a satirical tour de force, aimed at Manhattan's upper echelon. Shem C wants revenge for the poor reception his writing has received. He sets out to use *feng shui*, the Chinese art of arranging space for good luck, to get access to rich people. As part of the Scam, Shem C recruits William Paulinha and transforms him into Master Chao, a *feng shui* expert, who will advise upper class clients and then rob them.

Where it's reviewed:
Library Journal, February 15, 2001, page 202
Publishers Weekly, March 12, 2001, page 61

Other books you might like:
Don Lee, *Yellow*, 2001
Russell Charles Leong, *Phoenix Eyes and Other Stories*, 2001
Jim Thompson, *Grifters*, 1985

1214

CHUCK PALAHNIUK

Choke

(New York: Doubleday, 2001)

Story type: Psychological; Satire
Subject(s): Sexual Behavior; Old Age; Mothers and Sons
Major character(s): Victor Mancini, Addict (sex addict), Student—Graduate (medical school dropout); Ida Mancini, Aged Person (has Alzheimer's), Parent (of Victor)
Time period(s): 2000s (2001)
Locale(s): United States

Summary: Victor Mancini is simultaneously disgusting and outrageous but he's good to his mother. A med-school dropout, he works at an 18th century theme park and also earns money by faking choking epidsodes at fine restaurants. When an unsuspecting person "saves" him, Victor hits on him/her for money, which he uses to care for his mother, who is suffering from Alzheimer's disease. For entertainment, Victor likes quick, kinky sex with women during bathroom breaks at sexual addiction meetings.

Where it's reviewed:
Book, May 2001, page 71
Booklist, March 15, 2001, page 1355
Library Journal, March 1, 2001, page 132
New York Times Book Review, May 27, 2001, page 16
Publishers Weekly, April 2, 2001, page 37

Other books by the same author:
Invisible Monsters, 1999
Survivor, 1999
Fight Club, 1996

Other books you might like:
Djuna Barnes, *Nightwood*, 2000
Carrie Fisher, *Delusions of Grandma*, 1994
M.A. Harper, *The Worst Day of My Life, So Far*, 2001
Patrick McGrath, *Asylum*, 1997
Philip Roth, *The Dying Animal*, 2001

1215

MICHAEL PARKER

Towns Without Rivers

(New York: Morrow, 2001)

Story type: Psychological; Gothic
Subject(s): Brothers and Sisters; Quest
Major character(s): Eureka "Reka" Speight, Convict (falsely imprisoned); Randall Speight, Relative (Reka's kid brother), Model (nude)
Locale(s): Trent, North Carolina; Chicago, Illinois; Montana

Summary: Eureka "Reka" Speight is sent to prison for a crime she didn't commit. When released from prison, Reka leaves home and heads for Montana. She leaves an address for her brother Randall, but their father withholds it. Working as a nude art model, Randall wanders around the country looking for his sister. Meanwhile, Reka finds love and becomes pregnant. Eventually, both Reka and Randall return home to Trent, North Carolina.

Where it's reviewed:
Kirkus Reviews, April 15, 2001, page 531
Library Journal, May 15, 2001, page 164

Other books by the same author:
The Geographical Cure, 1994
Hello Down There, 1993

Other books you might like:
Isabel Colegate, *Winter Journey*, 2001
Pat Conroy, *The Prince of Tides*, 1986
Helen Dunmore, *A Spell of Winter*, 2001
Goldberry Long, *Juniper Tree Burning*, 2001
Joyce Carol Oates, *Angel of Light*, 1981

1216

TIM PARKS

Mimi's Ghost

(New York: Arcade, 2001)

Story type: Contemporary/Fantasy; Humor
Subject(s): Adventure and Adventurers; Ghosts; Crime and Criminals
Major character(s): Morris Duckworth, Con Artist, Serial Killer; Mimi Trevisan, Heiress (murdered by Duckworth), Spirit; Paola Trevisan, Spouse (of Duckworth), Relative (Mimi's sister)
Time period(s): 2000s (2001)
Locale(s): Verona, Italy

Summary: Parks' facile writing and offbeat sense of humor make this book about a serial killer interesting. Morris Duckworth kidnapped and murdered heiress Mimi Trevesan. Now married to her older sister, Paola, he is convinced that Mimi has forgiven him. As he schemes to gain control of the family fortune, Mimi's ghost visits him frequently and talks to him via a cell phone, and offers him advice. Originally published in 1995 in London.

Where it's reviewed:
Booklist, February 1, 2001, page 1042

Chicago Tribune Books, January 21, 2001, page 2
New York Times Book Review, January 14, 2001, page 13
Publishers Weekly, November 27, 2000, page 50

Other books by the same author:
Adultery, 1999
Destiny, 1999
Europa, 1997
Juggling, 1993
Shear, 1993

Other books you might like:
Isabel Colegate, *Winter Journey*, 2001
Kinky Friedman, *Mile High Club*, 2000
Jane Rogers, *Island*, 2000
Laurence Shames, *Welcome to Paradise*, 1999

1217

ANN PATCHETT

Bel Canto

(New York: HarperCollins, 2001)

Story type: Romance; Political
Subject(s): Hostages; Art; Terrorism
Major character(s): Roxane Coss, Singer (opera); Mr. Hosokawa, Businessman (builds factories), Wealthy
Time period(s): 2000s (2001)
Locale(s): South America

Summary: Ann Patchett's tale starts with economics and politics, adds opera, and stirs in terrorism. Officials in an unnamed South American country want Japanese businessman Mr. Hosokawa to build a factory in their country. They throw a birthday concert for him and invite his favorite opera singer, the American Roxane Coss. As the concert ends, terrorists burst in the building to take the country's president hostage, but he stayed home to watch his favorite soap opera.

Where it's reviewed:
Chicago Tribune Books, May 27, 2001, page 1
Kirkus Reviews, April 15, 2001, page 531
New York Times Book Review, June 10, 2001, page 37
New Yorker, June 18, 2001, page 164
Publishers Weekly, April 16, 2001, page 42

Other books by the same author:
The Magician's Assistant, 1997

Other books you might like:
Stanley Crouch, *Don't the Moon Look Lonesome*, 2000
Joan Didion, *The Last Thing He Wanted*, 1996
Doris Lessing, *The Good Terrorist*, 1985
Anne Tyler, *Earthly Possessions*, 1977
Lucy Wadham, *Lost*, 2000

1218

PEGGY PAYNE

Sister India

(New York: Riverhead, 2001)

Story type: Multicultural; Modern
Subject(s): Religious Conflict; Travel; Boarding Houses

Major character(s): Madame Natraja, Innkeeper (of the Saraswati Guest House), Expatriate (American); Ramesh, Cook (at the guest house)
Time period(s): 2000s (2001)
Locale(s): Varanasi, India

Summary: Western tourists visiting the most holy Hindu city find themselves interned in their guest house when violence erupts between the Hindu and Muslim factions. The guest house is run by a surly obese woman, an American who has changed her name from Estelle to Natraja. The tourists find themselves on an emotional roller coaster as the sights and sounds of chanting religious pilgrims, burning funeral pyres, poverty, and religious intolerance almost overwhelm them.

Where it's reviewed:
Booklist, January 1, 2001, page 920
New York Times Book Review, February 4, 2001, page 11

Other books by the same author:
Revelation, 1995

Other books you might like:
Amitav Ghosh, *The Glass Palace*, 2001
Manil Suri, *The Death of Vishnu*, 2001
Amy Tan, *The Bonesetter's Daughter*, 2001
Ludmila Ulitskaya, *The Funeral Party*, 2001
Vineeta Vijayaraghavan, *Motherland*, 2001

1219

NANI POWER

Crawling at Night

(New York: Atlantic Monthly, 2001)

Story type: Multicultural; Adult
Subject(s): Relationships; Sexual Behavior; Restaurants
Major character(s): Ito, Cook (sushi), Widow(er); Marianne, Waiter/Waitress (works with Ito), Parent
Time period(s): 2000s (2001)
Locale(s): New York, New York

Summary: In her first novel, Nani Power explores relationships developing from loneliness and desperation. A Japanese chef, Ito, alone with only a pornography collection, is attracted to Marianne, a waitress, who uses alcohol to cope with separation from her infant daughter. When Marianne gets fired, Ito wants to rescue her. He offers to take care of her and reunite her with her child, but life is rarely that simple. A colorful supporting cast adds to the story.

Where it's reviewed:
Library Journal, April 1, 2001, page 134
New York Times Book Review, April 29, 2001, page 7
Publishers Weekly, March 5, 2001, page 60

Other books you might like:
Isaac Adamson, *Tokyo Suckerpunch*, 2000
Marie Hara, *Bananaheart & Other Stories*, 1994
Toshio Mori, *Unfinished Message*, 2000
Yoshiko Uchida, *Picture Bride*, 1987
Lois-Ann Yamanaka, *Heads by Harry*, 1999

Popular Fiction

1220

TIM POWERS

Declare

(New York: Morrow, 2001)

Story type: Political; Contemporary/Fantasy
Subject(s): Spies; Supernatural; Espionage
Major character(s): Andrew Hale, Professor (at Oxford), Spy (retired); James Theodora, Spy (Hale's superior); Hakob Mammalian, Spy (Armenian powerbroker)
Time period(s): 20th century; 2000s (1948-2000)
Locale(s): London, England; Berlin, Germany; Paris, France

Summary: Powers serves up an old-fashioned Cold War espionage story with one extra ingredient: a supernatural power. Andrew Hale, summoned from retirement, sets out to remove this power, which is protecting the Soviet Union. Key elements to the plot are Mount Ararat, Noah's Ark, and the notorious Kim Philby, a British spy who worked for the Russians. While sounding incredible, in Powers' able hands, the story, which leans on 20-20 hindsight, becomes plausible.

Where it's reviewed:
Library Journal, November 15, 2000, page 97
Publishers Weekly, November 27, 2000, page 51

Other books by the same author:
The Drawing of the Dark, 1999
Earthquake Weather, 1997
Expiration Date, 1995
Last Call, 1992
The Stress of Her Regard, 1989

Other books you might like:
John Banville, *The Untouchable*, 1997
Stephen King, *Dreamcatcher*, 2001
John Le Carre, *The Russia House*, 1989
Robert Ludlum, *The Bourne Identity*, 1980
Thomas Pynchon, *Gravity's Rainbow*, 1973

1221

RICHARD RAYNER

The Cloud Sketcher

(New York: HarperCollins, 2000)

Story type: Historical; Romance
Subject(s): Emigration and Immigration; Prohibition; Crime and Criminals
Major character(s): Esko Vaananen, Architect (builder of skyscrapers), Immigrant (from Finland); Katerina Malysheva, Immigrant (from Russia); Paul Mantilini, Organized Crime Figure
Time period(s): 1920s (1929)
Locale(s): New York, New York

Summary: Esko Vaananen, a well-known architect, survives Russian political oppression in his native Finland, but cannot escape his love for Katerina, a Russian woman. They meet in New York City, where Prohibition is law and jazz is flourishing. Their love blossoms while he pursues his passion for building skyscrapers, but not before he is accused of murder.

A colorful cast, which includes gangsters and capitalists, keeps the story lively.

Where it's reviewed:
Booklist, November 15, 2000, page 588
Chicago Tribune Books, January 28, 2001, page 1
Library Journal, December 2000, page 192

Other books you might like:
Geoff Nicholson, *Female Ruins*, 2000
Ayn Rand, *The Fountainhead*, 1943
Francoise Sagan, *Fleeting Sorrow*, 1995
Frank Simon, *Trial by Fire*, 1999
Jane Vandenburgh, *Physics of Sunset*, 1999

1222

EMMA RICHLER

Sister Crazy

(New York: Pantheon, 2001)

Story type: Collection; Psychological
Subject(s): Brothers and Sisters; Women; Mental Illness
Major character(s): Jemina Weiss, Young Woman (middle child of five), Narrator; Ben Weiss, Young Man (oldest family member); Gus Weiss, Young Man (youngest family member)
Time period(s): 20th century; 2000s (1963-2000)
Locale(s): London, England; Canada

Summary: In her debut, Emma Richler has written a collection of loosely-linked stories following the exploits of the Weiss family. Headed by a Jewish sportwriter father and a protestant princess mother, the family moves from London to Canada. Narrated by the middle child, Jemina, the stories unfold as a stream of consciousness, as she connects various facts. Her humorous, deadpan delivery and her rapid-fire one-liners allow readers to overlook and to rationalize some inherent craziness.

Where it's reviewed:
Booklist, April 15, 2001, page 1537
New York Times Book Review, May 6, 2001, page 7
Publishers Weekly, April 16, 2001, page 43

Other books you might like:
Isabel Colegate, *Winter Journey*, 2001
Pat Conroy, *The Prince of Tides*, 1986
Anita Desai, *Fasting, Feasting*, 1999
Raj Kamal Jha, *The Blue Bedspread*, 1999
Catherine Ryan, *Funerals for Horses*, 1997

1223

PHILIP ROTH

The Dying Animal

(Boston: Houghton Mifflin, 2001)

Story type: Adult; Psychological
Series: David Kepesh
Subject(s): Erotica; Students; Teachers
Major character(s): David Kepesh, Professor (of social mores), Parent; Consuela Castillo, Lover (of Kepesh)
Time period(s): 2000s (2001)

Summary: The main character, David Kepesh, is a not quite doddering 70-year-old college lecturer. When Consuela contacts him, Kepesh recalls their unsettling and very torrid love affair eight years previously when she was a 24-year-old graduate student. Consuela wants to share some news with him and perhaps more. The sex is graphic as Roth uses his characters to examine Eros and mortality.

Where it's reviewed:
Chicago Tribune Books, April 22, 2001, page 3
Library Journal, May 1, 2001, page 128
New Republic, May 21, 2001, page 39
Publishers Weekly, March 26, 2001, page 59

Other books by the same author:
The Human Stain, 2000
I Married a Communist, 1998
American Pastoral, 1997
Deception, 1990
The Anatomy Lesson, 1983

Other books you might like:
Willa Cather, *The Professor's House*, 1925
Catherine Ryan Hyde, *Pay It Forward*, 1999
David Leavitt, *Martin Bauman*, 2000
Tucker Malarkey, *The Obvious Enchantment*, 2000
Lisa Shapiro, *The Color of Winter*, 1996

1224

RICHARD RUSSO

Empire Falls

(New York: Knopf, 2001)

Story type: Satire; Contemporary/Mainstream
Subject(s): City Life; Social Conditions; Relationships
Major character(s): Miles Roby, Restaurateur (runs the Empire Grill); Francine Whiting, Widow(er), Restaurateur (owns Empire Grill); Janine Roby, Spouse (divorcing Miles)
Time period(s): 2000s (2001)
Locale(s): Empire Falls, Maine

Summary: Miles Roby is in the midst of a mid-life crisis. Having left college without graduating, Miles' prospects appear to match those of the once thriving, now declining mill town where he lives. His wife, in the process of divorcing him, has taken up with an older man who, insists on eating at the grill Miles manages. On top of that, his teenage daughter, who is trying to dump her creepy boyfriend, attracts the attentions of a disturbed boy.

Where it's reviewed:
Booklist, April 1, 2001, page 1429
Chicago Tribune Books, May 27, 2001, page 1
Publishers Weekly, April 9, 2001, page 48

Other books by the same author:
Straight Man, 1997
Nobody's Fool, 1993
The Risk Pool, 1988
Mohawk, 1986

Other books you might like:
Donald Barthelme, *Paradise*, 1986

Ann Beattie, *Picturing Will*, 1989
Hilary Masters, *Hammertown Tales*, 1986
Joyce Carol Oates, *Broke Heart Blues*, 1999
Grace Paley, *Later the Same Day*, 1985

1225

BART SCHNEIDER

Secret Love

(New York: Viking, 2001)

Story type: Gay/Lesbian Fiction; Romance
Subject(s): Interracial Dating; Cultural Conflict; Family Problems
Major character(s): Jake Roseman, Lawyer, Activist (civil rights leader); Inez Roseman, Spouse (of Jake), Musician (concert violinist); Nisa Bohem, Activist (civil rights), Lover (of Jake)
Time period(s): 1960s (1964)
Locale(s): San Francisco, California

Summary: Bart Schneider's novel explores an interracial relationship against a background of 1960s civil rights demonstrations. Jake Roseman, 45, a successful Jewish lawyer, loves Nisa Bohem, a black actress he meets at a civil rights demonstration. Jake is afraid to introduce her to his family. His two children are mourning their mother, who committed suicide, and his father is a racist. Meanwhile, Nisa's actor friend, Peter, is having a homosexual affair with a white actor. Peter must reconcile his homosexuality with his Baptist upbringing and his commitment to the Nation of Islam.

Where it's reviewed:
Booklist, February 15, 2001, page 1117
New York Times Book Review, April 15, 2001, page 15
Publishers Weekly, February 26, 2001, page 58

Other books by the same author:
Blue Bossa, 1998

Other books you might like:
Ann Fairbairn, *Five Smooth Stones*, 1966
Sandra Kitt, *The Color of Love*, 1995
Stewart O'Nan, *Everyday People*, 2001
Leone Ross, *Orange Laughter*, 2000
Shawn Wong, *American Knees*, 1995

1226

DIANE SCHOEMPERLEN

Our Lady of the Lost and Found

(New York: Viking, 2001)

Story type: Inspirational; Contemporary/Fantasy
Subject(s): Religious Traditions; Saints; Miracles
Major character(s): Unnamed Character, Narrator (shares spiritual beliefs); Mary, Mother of God, Saint
Time period(s): 2000s (2001)
Locale(s): North

Summary: Schoemperlen's novel abandons conventional form for a series of reflections about human faith. An emotionally exhausted Virgin Mary arrives unannounced on the nameless narrator's doorstep and asks if she can stay for a few days.

Popular Fiction

The woman agrees and their subsequent conversations discuss spiritual beliefs and the various appearances Mary has made during the past 2,000 years.

Where it's reviewed:
Booklist, May 15, 2001, page 1734
Library Journal, April 1, 2001, page 134
Publishers Weekly, April 30, 2001, page 54

Other books by the same author:
In the Language of Love, 1994
The Man of My Dreams, 1990
Frogs and Other Stories, 1986

Other books you might like:
Louise Erdrich, *The Last Report on the Miracles at Little No Horse*, 2001
Andrew M. Greeley, *The Bishop and the Beggar Girl of St. Germain*, 2001
James A. Michener, *Miracle in Seville*, 1995
John Rechy, *The Miraculous Day of Amalia Gomez*, 1991
Josef Skvorecky, *The Miracle Game*, 1991

1227

ANITA SHREVE

The Last Time They Met

(Thorndike, Maine: Thorndike, 2001)

Story type: Psychological; Adult
Subject(s): Marriage; Women; Forgiveness
Major character(s): Linda Fallon, Writer (poet), Lover; Thomas Janes, Writer (poet), Lover; Regina Janes, Spouse (of Thomas), Narrator
Time period(s): 20th century; 2000s (1970-2000)
Locale(s): Toronto, Ontario, Canada; Kenya; New England

Summary: *The Last Time They Met* seamlessly goes back and forth between the past and the present. Linda and Thomas are first attracted to each other in high school when she is wild and he is conservative. In their 20s, they meet in Africa where they fall into bed with each other, despite being married to other people. It ends badly. Later, when they are older, they encounter each other again at a literary conference. Passion and human frailties are a volatile combination.

Where it's reviewed:
Atlantic Monthly, April 2001, page 105
Booklist, February 1, 2001, page 1020
Library Journal, February 15, 2001, page 203
Publishers Weekly, March 19, 2001, page 74

Other books by the same author:
The Pilot's Wife, 1998
The Weight of Water, 1997
Resistance, 1995
Where or When, 1993
Strange Fits of Passion, 1991

Other books you might like:
Barbara Taylor Bradford, *Power of a Woman*, 1997
Kate Chopin, *The Awakening*, 1899
Jamie Fuller, *The Diary of Emily Dickinson*, 1993
Jane Hamilton, *Disobedience*, 2000
Ying Hong, *Summer of Betrayal*, 1997

1228

JOSEF SKVORECKY

Two Murders in My Double Life

(New York: Farrar, Straus & Giroux, 2001)

Story type: Satire; Literary
Subject(s): Political Crimes and Offenses; Teachers; Murder
Major character(s): Danny Smiricky, Expatriate (living in Canada), Spouse (of Sidonia); Sidonia Smiricky, Publisher (of dissident writing), Crime Suspect (for informing on a friend); Raymond Hammett, Professor, Crime Victim (found strangled)
Time period(s): 2000s (2001)
Locale(s): Toronto, Ontario, Canada; Czech Republic

Summary: In his first book written in English, Josef Skvorecky, a prolific Czech writer, weaves together two tales that contrast the notions of political correctness in the West with those in the East. On a campus in Canada, an unnamed professor describing social customs between the sexes when another professor is murdered. The story then switches to the difficulty the first professor's wife experiences in the Czech Republic as her enemies identify her when a political informer.

Where it's reviewed:
Library Journal, April 15, 2001, page 133
New York Times Book Review, May 20, 2001, page 221
Publishers Weekly, May 7, 2001, page 221

Other books by the same author:
The Tenor Saxophonist's Story, 1997
The Bride of Texas, 1996
The Miracle Game, 1991
Dvorak in Love, 1987
The Engineer of Human Souls, 1984

Other books you might like:
Saul Bellow, *Ravelstein*, 2000
A.S. Byatt, *The Biographer's Tale*, 2001
John Cheever, *Falconer*, 1977
Don DeLillo, *White Noise*, 1985
Milan Kundera, *The Unbearable Lightness of Being*, 1984

1229

MURIEL SPARK

Aiding & Abetting

(New York: Doubleday, 2001)

Story type: Psychological; Historical
Subject(s): Murder; Missing Persons; Secrets
Major character(s): Hildegard Wolf, Doctor (treats emotional problems), Imposter (convicted of fraud); Robert Walker, Imposter (posing as Lord Lucan); Lord Lucan, Fugitive, Murderer (killed family nanny)
Time period(s): 1970s (1974); 2000s (2001)
Locale(s): England; Paris, France

Summary: The author uses an historical event to explore identity and deception. In an attempt to murder his wife, the 7th Earl of Lucan kills the family nanny by mistake then wounds his wife before escaping. Several years later, two men

seek treatment from Dr. Hildegard Wolf, both claiming to be the fugitive lord. Things get really interesting when one of the men discovers the good doctor has some secrets of her own.

Where it's reviewed:
Booklist, October 1, 2000, page 292
Library Journal, October 15, 2000, page 105
New York Times Book Review, March 11, 2001, page 14
Publishers Weekly, November 20, 2000, page 44
Time, March 12, 2001, page 90

Other books by the same author:
Open to the Public, 1997
Reality and Dreams, 1996
The Girls of Slender Means, 1963
The Public Image, 1963
The Prime of Miss Jean Brodie, 1961

Other books you might like:
S.Y. Agnon, *Only Yesterday*, 2000
A.S. Byatt, *The Biographer's Tale*, 2001
Kazuo Ishiguro, *When We Were Orphans*, 2000
Salman Rushdie, *The Ground Beneath Her Feet*, 1999
Rose Tremain, *Music and Silence*, 2000

1230

SARAH STONICH

These Granite Islands
(Boston: Little, Brown, 2001)

Story type: Psychological; Romance
Subject(s): Friendship; Women; Illness
Major character(s): Isobel Howard, Artisan (hat maker); Cathryn Malley, Heiress; Liam Malley, Spouse (of Cathryn)
Time period(s): 2000s (2001); 1930s (1936)
Locale(s): Cypress, Minnesota

Summary: Stonich's first novel weaves a tale of romance and mystery. On her deathbed, Isobel Howard, 99, tells the story of Cathryn Malley, an heiress who disappeared in the 1930s. The young women became friends, making hats together. Cathryn confides in Isobel about her affair with Jack Reese. While morally troubled by this, Isobel smoothes things over when Cathryn's husband Liam asked questions. Then, one day Jack's cabin burns down and the two lovers are never seen again.

Where it's reviewed:
Booklist, November 1, 2000, page 68
Chicago Tribune Books, June 10, 2001, page 2
Library Journal, December 20, 2000, page 193
Publishers Weekly, January 8, 2001, page 45

Other books you might like:
Helen Benedict, *The Sailor's Wife*, 2000
Dermot Bolger, *Temptation*, 2000
Willa Cather, *My Antonia*, 1918
Kate Chopin, *The Awakening*, 1899
Jude Deveraux, *The Summerhouse*, 2001

1231

MANIL SURI

The Death of Vishnu
(New York: Norton, 2001)

Story type: Multicultural; Satire
Subject(s): Social Classes; Apartments; Servants
Major character(s): Vishnu, Alcoholic, Servant; Samil Jahal, Young Man (a Muslim), Boyfriend (of Kavita); Kavita Asrani, Young Woman (a Hindu), Girlfriend (of Samil)
Time period(s): 2000s (2001)
Locale(s): Bombay, India

Summary: In his first novel, Manil Suri examines the multilayered complexity of human existence. The story occurs over a 24-hour period in an apartment building. Vishnu, the drunken house boy, lies dying on the stairs, while the residents argue over him. Mrs. Pathak and Mrs. Asrani, both Hindus, only agree on prejudice against their Muslim neighbors, the Jahals. As they bicker, Samil Jahal makes plans to elope with Kavita Asrani. Meanwhile, Vishnu drifts off into eternity.

Where it's reviewed:
Booklist, November 15, 2000, page 620
Library Journal, December 2000, page 193
Los Angeles Times Book Review, February 4, 2001, page 3
New York Times Book Review, January 28, 2001, page 8
Publishers Weekly, November 6, 2000, page 68

Other books you might like:
Amitav Ghosh, *The Glass Palace*, 2001
Peggy Payne, *Sister India*, 2001
Amy Tan, *The Bonesetter's Daughter*, 2001
Ludmila Ulitskaya, *The Funeral Party*, 2001
Vineeta Vijayaraghavan, *Motherland*, 2001

1232

TERESE SVOBODA

Trailer Girl
(Washington, D.C.: Counterpoint, 2001)

Story type: Collection; Gothic
Subject(s): Short Stories
Time period(s): 2000s (2001)
Locale(s): United States

Summary: Terese Svoboda's collection contains 14 short stories. The title story is a novella with a nameless woman as the main character. An abused product of foster homes, the woman lives in a seedy trailer park haunted by a wild child. It's up to the reader to determine if the child is real or a figment of the woman's imagination. In another tale, a psychic shakes down a client who is a murderer. These are upsetting, haunting, but poetic stories.

Where it's reviewed:
Library Journal, January 1, 2001, page 160
New York Times Book Review, March 11, 2001, page 20
Publishers Weekly, February 12, 2001, page 184

Other books by the same author:
A Drink Called Paradise, 1999
Cannibal, 1994

Other books you might like:
Mitch Cullen, *Tideland*, 2000
Helen Dunmore, *A Spell of Winter*, 2001
William Gay, *Provinces of Night*, 2000
Joy Williams, *The Quick and the Dead*, 2000

1233

AMY TAN

The Bonesetter's Daughter

(New York: Putnam, 2001)

Story type: Multicultural; Family Saga
Subject(s): Mothers and Daughters; Chinese Americans; Family Relations
Major character(s): Ruth Young, Writer (self-help books), Relative (daughter of LuLing); LuLing, Artist (calligraphy), Relative (daughter of Precious Auntie); Precious Auntie, Healer (the bonesetter's daughter), Grandparent (of Ruth)
Time period(s): 20th century (1900-1999)
Locale(s): United States; China

Summary: Chinese-American Ruth, a ghost writer in her mid-forties, is called home to care for her aged mother who suffers from Alzheimer's. While caring for her, Ruth begins to examine her unsatisfying relationships with her mother and her live-in boyfriend. When she finds a manuscript in her mother's handwriting that tells her mother's life story, a light goes on and Ruth begins to develop insight into her cultural heritage, her family, and her personal relationships.

Where it's reviewed:
Booklist, December 1, 2000, page 676
Library Journal, February 1, 2001, page 126
New York Times Book Review, February 18, 2001, page 9

Other books by the same author:
Hundred Secret Senses, 1995
The Kitchen God's Wife, 1991
The Joy Luck Club, 1989

Other books you might like:
Amitav Ghosh, *The Glass Palace*, 2001
Peggy Payne, *Sister India*, 2001
Manil Suri, *The Death of Vishnu*, 2001
Ludmila Ulitskaya, *The Funeral Party*, 2001
Vineeta Vijayaraghavan, *Motherland*, 2001

1234

JAMES THACKARA

America's Children

(Woodstock, New York: Overlook, 2001)

Story type: Historical/World War II
Subject(s): Physics; Nuclear Weapons; Politics
Major character(s): J. Robert Oppenheimer, Scientist (building the A-bomb), Historical Figure; Colonel Leslie Groves, Military Personnel (liaison with scientists)

Time period(s): 1940s; 1950s (1942-1953)
Locale(s): Los Alamos, New Mexico

Summary: This is the first American edition of Thackara's fictional account of the rise and fall of J. Robert Oppenheimer, head of the Manhattan Project. Originally published in 1984, the book details Oppenheimer's struggle to recruit the scientific talent necessary to build an atomic bomb. However, the very skills that are crucial to building the A-bomb, intellectual brilliance and social sensitivity, become liabilities when the political climate shifts and the Cold War starts. A complex but interesting story.

Where it's reviewed:
Booklist, March 1, 2001, page 1229
Library Journal, February 15, 2001, page 203

Other books by the same author:
Book of Kings, 1999

Other books you might like:
Pat Frank, *Alas, Babylon*, 1999
Rebecca Goldstein, *Properties of Light*, 2000
John Le Carre, *The Spy Who Came in from the Cold*, 1964
Donald Edwin Nuechterlein, *A Cold War Odyssey*, 1997
Jill Paton Walsh, *Desert in Bohemia*, 2000

1235

PAUL THEROUX

Hotel Honolulu

(Boston: Houghton Mifflin, 2001)

Story type: Literary; Adult
Subject(s): Hotels, Motels; Satire; Human Behavior
Major character(s): Buddy Hamstra, Hotel Owner (of Hotel Honolulu); Leon Edel, Scholar (studies James Joyce)
Time period(s): 2000s (2001)
Locale(s): Honolulu, Hawaii

Summary: Theroux himself makes an appearance in this novel, which is a series of detailed character sketches loosely connected around a seedy hotel that is managed by an unnamed writer who is suffering from writer's block. Mystery, sexual obsessions, child abuse, incest, infidelity, murder, and suicide flourish in this sordid tale. A colorful cast, including the daughter of a Chinese Hawaiian whore and JFK, and a gossip columnist involved with her son's homosexual lover, keep things lively.

Where it's reviewed:
Book, May 2001, page 71
Booklist, March 1, 2001, page 1189
Library Journal, March 15, 2001, page 108
Publishers Weekly, April 2, 2001, page 36

Other books by the same author:
Kowloon Tong, 1997
My Other Life, 1996
My Secret History, 1989
O-Zone, 1986
The Mosquito Coast, 1981

Other books you might like:
John Biguenet, *The Torturer's Apprentice*, 2001
Allegra Goodman, *Paradise Park*, 2001

William Trevor, *Mrs. Eckdorf in O'Neill's Hotel*, 1995
Kurt Vonnegut, *Deadeye Dick*, 1982
Herman Wouk, *Don't Stop the Carnival*, 1987

1236

BETSY TOBIN

Bone House

(New York: Scribner, 2000)

Story type: Historical/Seventeenth Century
Subject(s): Prostitution; Women; Rural Life
Major character(s): Unnamed Character, Narrator, Servant (chambermaid); Dora, Prostitute, Crime Victim (found frozen to death)
Time period(s): 17th century
Locale(s): England

Summary: In her first novel, Betsy Tobin, has written a mystery that paints a fascinating, but stark picture of life in the 17th century English countryside. When Dora, the local whore, is found frozen to death at the bottom of a ravine, local villagers almost come unglued. Dora's relations with men and her counseling of women makes almost everyone a suspect. A young chambermaid, herself the bastard child of the local midwife, narrates the story.

Where it's reviewed:
Booklist, January 1, 2001, page 925
Library Journal, January 1, 2001, page 158
New York Times Book Review, February 25, 2001, page 30

Other books you might like:
Alev Lytle Croutier, *The Palace of Tears*, 2000
James Elliot, *Nowhere to Hide*, 1997
Roberta Gellis, *Personal Devil*, 2001
Sheri Holman, *The Dress Lodger*, 2000

1237

ANNE TYLER

Back When We Were Grownups

(New York: Knopf, 2001)

Story type: Contemporary; Psychological
Subject(s): Women; Widows; Family Life
Major character(s): Rebecca ''Beck'' Davitch, Widow(er) (head of large extended family); Joe Davitch, Spouse (of Rebecca), Parent (four girls, one with Rebecca); Will, Boyfriend
Time period(s): 20th century; 2000s (1968-2000)
Locale(s): Baltimore, Maryland

Summary: Rebecca ''Beck'' Davitch leaves college at 19 to marry Joe, an older man with three children and a family business. By age 25, Beck is a widow with four daughters to raise and a business to run, as well as various in-laws to look after. At age 53, Beck wonders what life might have been like if she had married Will, her old boyfriend, instead.

Where it's reviewed:
Book, May 2001, page 63
Booklist, March 1, 2001, page 1189
Library Journal, March 15, 2001, page 108

New Yorker, May 14, 2001, page 107
Publishers Weekly, April 9, 2001, page 51

Other books by the same author:
A Patchwork Planet, 1998
Ladder of Years, 1995
Saint Maybe, 1991
Breathing Lessons, 1988
The Accidental Tourist, 1985

Other books you might like:
Alice Adams, *Medicine Men*, 1997
Margaret Atwood, *The Blind Assassin*, 2000
Penelope Fitzgerald, *The Bookshop*, 1978
Dennis McFarland, *Singing Boy*, 2001
Anita Shreve, *The Pilot's Wife*, 1998

1238

LUDMILA ULITSKAYA

The Funeral Party

(New York: Schocken, 2001)

Story type: Contemporary; Multicultural
Subject(s): Emigration and Immigration; Relationships; Love
Major character(s): Alik, Expatriate (Russian), Artist; Nina, Spouse (of Alik), Model (unemployed); Maika, Teenager (daughter of Alik's ex-lover)
Time period(s): 1990s (1991)
Locale(s): New York, New York (Manhattan)

Summary: Accomplished Russian writer Ludmila Ulitskaya makes her American debut with this novel. The story revolves around the deathbed of Alik, an expatriate Russian artist now living in Manhattan. As friends and relatives gather at his apartment, they reminisce about their connection to Alik and to each other. The author's deft touch for detail and nuance shifts the focus of the story from death to life.

Where it's reviewed:
Booklist, January 1, 2001, page 919
Library Journal, January 1, 2001, page 158
New York Times Book Review, February 11, 2001, page 19
Publishers Weekly, December 18, 2000, page 57

Other books you might like:
John Baneville, *Eclipse*, 2001
Nina Berberova, *The Book of Happiness*, 1999
Jhumpa Lahiri, *Interpreter of Maladies*, 1999
Elena Lappin, *Foreign Brides*, 1999
Manil Suri, *The Death of Vishnu*, 2001

1239

VINEETA VIJAYARAGHAVAN

Motherland

(New York: Soho, 2001)

Story type: Coming-of-Age; Multicultural
Subject(s): Adolescence; Women; Gender Roles
Major character(s): Maya, Teenager; Ammamma, Grandparent (of Maya); Reema, Relative (Maya's aunt), Spouse (of Sanjay)
Time period(s): 1990s (1991)

Locale(s): New York, New York; Coimbatore, India

Summary: This insightful first novel follows Maya, an American teenager as she spends the summer with relatives in India. At 15, Maya has issues with her parents and they are having marital difficulties. The visit to her birth country is an eye-opener as Maya is exposed to cultural, gender, generational, family, and individual differences. She returns with a new understanding of herself, her parents, and her heritage.

Where it's reviewed:
Booklist, November 15, 2000, page 622
Library Journal, December 2000, page 193
New York Times Book Review, January 14, 2001, page 19
Publishers Weekly, November 13, 2000, page 84

Other books you might like:
Amitav Ghosh, *The Glass Palace*, 2001
Peggy Payne, *Sister India*, 2001
Manil Suri, *The Death of Vishnu*, 2001
Amy Tan, *The Bonesetter's Daughter*, 2001
Ludmila Ulitskaya, *The Funeral Party*, 2001

1240

KATE WALBERT

The Gardens of Kyoto
(New York: Scribner, 2001)

Story type: Romance; Historical/World War II
Subject(s): Mothers and Daughters
Major character(s): Ellen, Narrator, Young Woman (in love with Randall); Randall, Military Personnel (killed in war), Cousin (Ellen's)
Time period(s): 20th century (1939-1953)
Locale(s): United States

Summary: In her debut novel, Kate Walbert, a Pushcart and O. Henry Prize winner, explores unrequited love and how war affects men and women differently. Ellen is a shy, retiring young woman, who is deeply in love with her cousin, Randall. When Randall is killed in World War II, his father sends Ellen his diary. She becomes increasingly obsessed and falls deeper in love with him. Later, she falls in love with a man named Henry, confusing him with Randall.

Where it's reviewed:
Booklist, February 15, 2001, page 1117
Library Journal, February 1, 2001, page 126
New York Times Book Review, April 8, 2001, page 15
Publishers Weekly, March 12, 2001, page 60

Other books you might like:
John Fowles, *The French Lieutenant's Woman*, 1969
David Hill, *Butterfly Sunday*, 2000
James A. Michener, *Sayonara*, 1954
Erich Segal, *Love Story*, 1970
Alice Walker, *The Way Forward Is with a Broken Heart*, 2000

1241

JENNIFER WEINER

Good in Bed
(New York: Pocket, 2001)

Story type: Humor
Subject(s): Women; Journalism; Obesity
Major character(s): Candace "Cannie" Shapiro, Journalist (newspaper), Young Woman (has a weight problem); Bruce Guberman, Boyfriend (dumps Candace), Journalist
Time period(s): 2000s (2001)
Locale(s): Philadelphia, Pennsylvania

Summary: The author uses humor and snappy dialogue to examine poor body image and other problems faced by many young women. The main character, Candace Shapiro, 28, is a reporter with a weight problem. Cannie and her sister, Lucy, were emotionally abused by their father and when he left, their mother took up with another woman. Lucy tries phone sex and striptease without success. Meanwhile, Cannie's ex-boyfriend decides to write about their sex life in his new column.

Where it's reviewed:
Publishers Weekly, April 9, 2001, page 50

Other books you might like:
Alice Adams, *Almost Perfect*, 1993
Margaret Atwood, *Bodily Harm*, 1981
Joan Didion, *The Last Thing He Wanted*, 1996
Ellen Gilchrist, *Sarah Conley*, 1997
Peggy Payne, *Sister India*, 2001

1242

W.D. WETHERELL

Morning
(New York: Pantheon, 2001)

Story type: Psychological; Contemporary/Mainstream
Subject(s): Television; Biography; Murder
Major character(s): Alec Brown, Relative (Chet's son), Writer (tells of McGowan's murder); Alec McGowan, Television Personality (host of a morning show), Crime Victim (murdered during a broadcast); Chet Standish, Murderer (of McGowan)
Time period(s): 1950s (1954); 2000s (2000)

Summary: In this novel, W.D. Wetherell uses familiar personalities of 1950s television as a backdrop for a murder occurring during a morning show broadcast. Host Alec McGowan, a rising star in the new medium, is shot and killed in 1954 by a colleague, Chet Standish. In the year 2000, Standish is dying of cancer and has been released from prison. For the first time, Standish meets his son, biographer Alec Brown, who is researching the story.

Where it's reviewed:
New York Times Book Review, April 27, 2001, page 39
Publishers Weekly, February 19, 2001, page 67

Other books by the same author:
Wherever That Great Heart May Be, 1996

The Wisest Man in America, 1995
Chekhov's Sister, 1990
Hyannis Boat and Other Stories, 1989
The Man Who Loved Levittown, 1985

Other books you might like:
William Harrington, *The Game Show Killer*, 1996
    Columbo series
Karin Kallmaker, *Making Up for Lost Time*, 1998
Bob Larson, *Shock Talk*, 2001
Frank M. Robinson, *Waiting*, 1999
Dorothy J. Samuels, *Filthy Rich*, 2001

1243

COLSON WHITEHEAD

John Henry Days

(New York: Doubleday, 2001)

Story type: Contemporary; Multicultural
Subject(s): Legends; African Americans; Fairs
Major character(s): J. Sutter, Journalist (freelance), Drifter;
    Pamela Street, Young Woman (grieving)
Time period(s): 2000s (2001)
Locale(s): Talcott, West Virginia

Summary: Whitehead's novel looks at the difference between
surviving with dignity and just surviving. Folk hero John
Henry, an African American railroad worker, who whipped a
jackhammer in a one-on-one contest, provides the story with a
backdrop. At a John Henry fair, we meet J. Sutter, an African
American journalist who travels from festival to festival, writing mindless articles while freeloading on expense accounts.
The festival ends with violence, but Sutter meets Pamela
Street giving him opportunity to find meaning in his life.

Where it's reviewed:
Library Journal, April 1, 2001, page 135
Newsweek, May 21, 2001, page 59
Publishers Weekly, April 16, 2001, page 43
Time, May 21, 2001, page 91

Other books by the same author:
The Intuitionist, 1999

Other books you might like:
Benjamin Anastas, *The Faithful Narrative of a Pastor's Dis-
    appearance*, 2001
Tananarive Due, *The Black Rose*, 2000
Ann Fairbairn, *Five Smooth Stones*, 1966
Jake Lamar, *If 6 Were 9*, 2001
Tom Wolfe, *A Man in Full*, 1998

1244

AMY WILENTZ

Martyrs' Crossing

(New York: Simon & Schuster, 2001)

Story type: Political; Historical
Subject(s): Mothers and Sons; Fathers and Daughters; Death
Major character(s): Marina Raad Hajimi, Parent (of a sick
    child), Spouse (of Palestinian leader); Hassan Hajimi,
    Spouse (of Marina), Political Prisoner (jailed for terror-

ism); George Raad, Parent (of Marina), Doctor (cardiolo-
    gist)
Time period(s): 2000s (2001)
Locale(s): Jerusalem, Israel; Ramallah, Palestine

Summary: Amy Wilentz uses her experience as a journalist in
this skillful story set in the Middle East. Marina needs to cross
the border into Israel to obtain treatment for her child. After
Marina is denied permission to enter the country because her
husband has been jailed for terrorism, the child dies. Various
factions plot to manipulate the incident for their own ends.
Meanwhile, the guilt-ridden Israeli officer who denied Marina
passage through the checkpoint seeks her forgiveness.

Where it's reviewed:
Booklist, January 1, 2001, page 922
Library Journal, January 1, 2001, page 158
New York Times Book Review, March 11, 2001, page 6
Publishers Weekly, January 15, 2001, page 53
Time, April 2, 2001, page 71

Other books you might like:
J.M. Coetzee, *Disgrace*, 1999
Nomi Eve, *The Family Orchard*, 2000
Gale Zoe Garnett, *Visible Amazement*, 2001
Linda Grant, *When I Lived in Modern Times*, 2001
Katie Schneider, *All We Know of Love*, 2000

1245

MARK WINEGARDNER

Crooked River Burning

(New York: Harcourt, 2001)

Story type: Historical; Contemporary
Subject(s): City Life; Politics; Journalism
Major character(s): David Zielinsky, Activist (political), Rela-
    tive (son of corrupt union official); Anne O'Connor, Jour-
    nalist (television), Relative (daughter of former mayor)
Time period(s): 20th century (1948-1969)
Locale(s): Cleveland, Ohio

Summary: Mark Winegardner's novel is organized around a
love story between David Zielinsky and Anne O'Connor who
meet at a summer resort and fall in love. However, they must
love from a distance as their lives are set on different paths.
He goes into politics; she goes into journalism. The city of
Cleveland provides a vivid backdrop to the story, including
baseball with the Indians, the birth of rock 'n' roll, the Sam
Sheppard trial, race riots, the administration of the first black
mayor, and industrial pollutants setting the Cuyahoga River
on fire.

Where it's reviewed:
Booklist, January 1, 2001, page 922
Library Journal, December 2000, page 193
New York Times Book Review, January 21, 2001, page 18
Publishers Weekly, November 20, 2000, page 45

Other books by the same author:
The Veracruz Blues, 1996

Other books you might like:
Carrie Brown, *The Hatbox Baby*, 2000
E.L. Doctorow, *City of God*, 2000

Popular Fiction

Jonathan Franzen, *The Twenty-Seventh City*, 1988
Jeannette Haien, *Matters of Chance*, 1997
Sharon Mitchell, *Sheer Necessity*, 1999

Catherine Palmer, *Prairie Storm*, 1999
Akhil Sharma, *An Obedient Father*, 2000
Joy Williams, *Quick and the Dead*, 2000

1246

LOIS-ANN YAMANAKA

Father of the Four Passages

(New York: Farrar Straus & Giroux, 2001)

Story type: Multicultural; Contemporary Realism
Subject(s): Single Parent Families; Fathers and Daughters; Mothers and Sons
Major character(s): Sonia Kurisu, Single Parent (of an autistic boy); Solomon ''Sonny Boy'' Kurisu, Child (of Sonia), Handicapped (autistic); Celeste, Relative (Sonia's sister)
Time period(s): 2000s (2001)
Locale(s): Hawaii; Las Vegas, Nevada

Summary: The story deals with the survival strategies of the down but not out. After her parents desert her and her sister, their mother emotionally and their father physically, Sonia chooses alcohol, drugs, and sex as a means of escape from the realities of her life. Haunted by feelings about her three abortions and now pregnant for a fourth time, she has the child, who turns out to be autistic. Sonia copes by physically abusing her son. The story is bleak but Sonia doesn't give up.

Where it's reviewed:
Booklist, December 1, 2000, page 694
Library Journal, October 15, 2000, page 105
New York Times Book Review, February 25, 2001, page 16
Publishers Weekly, October 30, 2000, page 45
Time, February 5, 2001, page 78

Other books by the same author:
Heads by Harry, 1999
Name Me Nobody, 1999
Blu's Hanging, 1997
Wild Meat and Bully Burgers, 1996

Other books you might like:
Trezza Azzopardi, *The Hiding Place*, 2000
Mitch Cullen, *Tideland*, 2000

1247

RICHARD YATES

The Collected Stories of Richard Yates

(New York: Holt, 2001)

Story type: Collection; Adult
Subject(s): Cultures and Customs; Loneliness; Self-Perception

Summary: This collection of works by Richard Yates, who died in 1992, contains seven unpublished stories. Some selections include autobiographical threads and some rely on characterization and subtext rather than structure. Story subjects include writers, the end of World War II, alcoholism, navy wives, tuberculosis patients, and relationships. Themes involve loneliness, failure, and emotional dissatisfaction. While commercial success eluded him, Yates is considered by many to have been one of the more influential writers of his generation.

Where it's reviewed:
Booklist, March 1, 2001, page 1230
Library Journal, March 15, 2001, page 108
New York Times Book Review, April 29, 2001, page 10
Publishers Weekly, March 5, 2001, page 60

Other books by the same author:
Liars in Love, 1981
A Good School, 1978
The Easter Parade, 1976
Disturbing the Peace, 1975
Eleven Kinds of Loneliness, 1962

Other books you might like:
Alice McDermott, *At Weddings and Wakes*, 1992
Susan Merrell, *A Member of the Family*, 2000
John O'Hara, *The Collected Stories of John O'Hara*, 1958
Clarissa Ross, *Beware the Kindly Stranger*, 2000
Meg Wolitzer, *Surrender, Dorothy*, 1999

Series Index

This index alphabetically lists series to which books featured in the entries belong. Beneath each series name, book titles are listed alphabetically with author names and genre codes. The genre codes are as follows: *c* Popular Fiction, *f* Fantasy, *h* Horror, *i* Inspirational, *m* Mystery, *r* Romance, *s* Science Fiction, *t* Historical, and *w* Western. Numbers refer to the entries that feature each title.

Time Period Index

This index chronologically lists the time settings in which the featured books take place. Main headings refer to a century; where no specific time is given, the headings MULTIPLE TIME PERIODS, INDETERMINATE PAST, INDETERMINATE FUTURE, and INDETERMINATE are used. The 18th through 21st centuries are broken down into decades when possible. (Note: 1800s, for example, refers to the first decade of the 19th century.) Featured titles are listed alphabetically beneath time headings, with author names and genre codes. The genre codes are as follows: *c* Popular Fiction, *f* Fantasy, *h* Horror, *i* Inspirational, *m* Mystery, *r* Romance, *s* Science Fiction, *t* Historical, and *w* Western. Numbers refer to the entries that feature each title.

MULTIPLE TIME PERIODS

The Awakening Land - James M. Vesely   *w*   545
The Discovery of Chocolate - James Runcie   *t*   977
The Graveyard Game - Kage Baker   *s*   755
Seasons of Harvest - James M. Vesely   *w*   546
The Songcatcher - Sharyn McCrumb   *c*   1197

INDETERMINATE PAST

The Destruction of the Inn - Randy Lee
   Eickhoff   *t*   888
Exiled from Camelot - Cherith Baldry   *f*   555
God of the Golden Fleece - Fred Saberhagen   *f*   630
Raven Mocker - Don Coldsmith   *t*   869
The Scarletti Curse - Christine Feehan   *r*   266
Son of the Shadows - Juliet Marillier   *f*   608
Song of the Axe - John R. Dann   *t*   875
Warlock - Wilbur A. Smith   *t*   982

16th CENTURY B.C.

The Horus Road - Pauline Gedge   *t*   900

15th CENTURY B.C.

The Anubis Slayings - P.C. Doherty   *m*   40
The Anubis Slayings - P.C. Doherty   *t*   879

14th CENTURY B.C.

Slayer of Gods - Lynda S. Robinson   *m*   160
Slayer of Gods - Lynda S. Robinson   *t*   972

13th CENTURY B.C.

Paneb the Ardent - Christian Jacq   *t*   916
The Wise Woman - Christian Jacq   *t*   917

12th CENTURY B.C.

The Song of Troy - Colleen McCullough   *t*   943

5th CENTURY B.C.

The Ten Thousand - Michael Curtis Ford   *t*   895

4th CENTURY B.C.

The House of Death - P.C. Doherty   *m*   42
The House of Death - P.C. Doherty   *t*   881
Over the Wine-Dark Sea - H.N. Turteltaub   *t*   990

2nd CENTURY B.C.

The Veil of Years - L. Warren Douglas   *f*   572

1st CENTURY B.C.

Kleopatra - Karen Essex   *t*   890

1st CENTURY

Devil's Sea - Greg Donegan   *s*   774
The Love-Artist - Jane Alison   *t*   852
The Love-Artist - Jane Alison   *c*   1103
Ode to a Banker - Lindsey Davis   *m*   35
Ode to a Banker - Lindsey Davis   *t*   877

3rd CENTURY

Priestess of Avalon - Marion Zimmer
   Bradley   *t*   859

5th CENTURY

Uther - Jack Whyte   *f*   650
Uther - Jack Whyte   *t*   995

6th CENTURY

The Tide of Victory - Eric Flint   *s*   781

12th CENTURY

Ashes of the Elements - Alys Clare   *m*   23
Ashes of the Elements - Alys Clare   *t*   865
The Beauty - Claire Delacroix   *r*   253
His Fair Lady - Kathleen Kirkwood   *r*   335
The Holding - Claudia Dain   *r*   250
Intimate Enemies - Shana Abe   *r*   201
Irish Hope - Donna Fletcher   *r*   269
Knave of Hearts - Shari Anton   *r*   210
The Knight - Juliana Garnett   *r*   277
Master of Desire - Kinley MacGregor   *r*   358
A Personal Devil - Roberta Gellis   *m*   59

A Personal Devil - Roberta Gellis   *t*   901
The Stone Maiden - Susan King   *r*   331

13th CENTURY

His Fair Lady - Kathleen Kirkwood   *r*   335
Ice Maiden - Debra Lee Brown   *r*   231
Murder on Good Friday - Sara Conway   *m*   26
Murder on Good Friday - Sara Conway   *t*   871
Secret Vows - Mary Reed McCall   *r*   368
The Swan Maiden - Susan King   *r*   332
The Truest Heart - Samantha James   *r*   316
A Trust Betrayed - Candace M. Robb   *t*   971
A Trust Betrayed - Candace M. Robb   *m*   157
Warrior's Song - Catherine Coulter   *r*   246

14th CENTURY

The Boy-Bishop's Glovemaker - Michael
   Jecks   *t*   918
The Burning Times - Jeanne Kalogridis   *t*   920
By Design - Madeline Hunter   *r*   310
The Demon Archer - P.C. Doherty   *m*   41
The Demon Archer - P.C. Doherty   *t*   880
The Highland Wife - Lyn Stone   *r*   437
Mirabilis - Susann Cokal   *t*   867
The Secret Swan - Shana Abe   *r*   202
The Swan Maiden - Susan King   *r*   332
The Temple and the Crown - Katherine Kurtz   *f*   600

15th CENTURY

His Stolen Bride - Shelley Bradley   *r*   226
The Merlin of the Oak Wood - Ann
   Chamberlin   *t*   863
The Merlin of the Oak Wood - Ann
   Chamberlin   *f*   563
Summer's Bride - Catherine Archer   *r*   211

16th CENTURY

Border Lord - Haywood Smith   *r*   431
Border Storm - Amanda Scott   *r*   421
The Devil's Apprentice - Edward Marston   *t*   939
The Dreamer - May McGoldrick   *r*   372
Forever, My Lady - Jen Holling   *r*   307
The Fraser Bride - Lois Greiman   *r*   289
Guardian of the Vision - Irene Radford   *f*   621
His Betrothed - Gayle Callen   *r*   235
One Knight in Venice - Tori Phillips   *r*   393
The Prize - Martine Berne   *r*   218

22nd CENTURY

23rd CENTURY

24th CENTURY

30th CENTURY

INDETERMINATE FUTURE

INDETERMINATE

Geographic Index

This index provides access to all featured books by geographic settings—such as countries, continents, oceans, and planets. States and provinces are indicated for the United States and Canada. Also interfiled are headings for fictional place names (Spaceships, Imaginary Planets, etc.). Sections are further broken down by city or the specific name of the imaginary locale. Book titles are listed alphabetically under headings, with author names and genre codes. The genre codes are as follows: *c* Popular Fiction, *f* Fantasy, *h* Horror, *i* Inspirational, *m* Mystery, *r* Romance, *s* Science Fiction, *t* Historical, and *w* Western. Numbers refer to the entries that feature each title.

AFGHANISTAN

The Siege of Isfahan - Jean-Christophe Rufin   *t*   976

AFRICA

The Blackbirder - James L. Nelson   *t*   951
Lioness - Nell Brien   *r*   227

Nambula
Cause Celeb - Helen Fielding   *c*   1150

Tunis
Warrior's Song - Catherine Coulter   *r*   246

ALTERNATE EARTH

The Eyre Affair - Jasper Fforde   *s*   780
A Perfect Persecution - James R. Lucas   *i*   1059
The Shadows of God - J. Gregory Keyes   *f*   595
The Storm of Heaven - Thomas Harlan   *f*   587

Africa
Pashazade: The First Arabesk - Jon Courtenay Grimwood   *s*   792

New Orleans
Leopard in Exile - Andre Norton   *f*   619

Paris
Leopard in Exile - Andre Norton   *f*   619

ALTERNATE UNIVERSE

DoOon Mode - Piers Anthony   *f*   553
Illumination - Terry McGarry   *f*   609

Aachim
A Shadow on the Glass - Ian Irvine   *f*   592

Azeroth
Day of the Dragon - Richard A. Knaak   *f*   597

Discworld
Thief of Time - Terry Pratchett   *f*   620

Faellem
A Shadow on the Glass - Ian Irvine   *f*   592

Flatterland
Flatterland - Ian Stewart   *s*   833

Majipoor
The King of Dreams - Robert Silverberg   *f*   635

Otherland
Sea of Silver Light - Tad Williams   *f*   651

Overworld
Blade of Tyshalle - Matthew Stover   *f*   639

Sutra
Talisker - Miller Lau   *f*   603

AMERICAN COLONIES

Rise to Rebellion - Jeff Shaara   *t*   980
The Sweet Trade - Elizabeth Garrett   *t*   899

EAST
Freedom's Shadow - Marlo M. Schalesky   *i*   1083

MASSACHUSETTS

Bracebridge
A Mischief in the Snow - Margaret Miles   *m*   121

Salem
I, Roger Williams - Mary Lee Settle   *t*   979

RHODE ISLAND

The Privateersman - Richard Woodman   *t*   998

Providence
I, Roger Williams - Mary Lee Settle   *t*   979

VIRGINIA

Williamsburg
The Blackbirder - James L. Nelson   *t*   951

ANCIENT CIVILIZATION

Sumer
Destiny - Maggie Shayne   *r*   425

Troy
The Song of Troy - Colleen McCullough   *t*   943

ARGENTINA

Tierra del Fuego
Tierra del Fuego - Sylvia Iparraguirre   *t*   915

ARMENIA

Three Apples Fell from Heaven - Micheline Aharonian Marcom   *c*   1193

ASIA MINOR

The House of Death - P.C. Doherty   *m*   42
Over the Wine-Dark Sea - H.N. Turteltaub   *t*   990

ASTEROID

The Precipice - Ben Bova   *s*   761

Ceres
The Meek - Scott Mackay   *s*   802

AT SEA

The Blackbirder - James L. Nelson   *t*   951
It Had to Be You - Linda Windsor   *i*   1099
My Lady Pirate - Elizabeth Doyle   *r*   260
Pacific Hope - Bette Nordberg   *i*   1067
Where Two Seas Met - Lynn Morris   *i*   1064

America
Allegiances - Charles Davis   *t*   876

Batavia
Company: The Story of a Murderer - Arabella Edge   *t*   887

Biter
The Wicked Trade - Jan Needle   *t*   950

Briarwind
Summer's Bride - Catherine Archer   *r*   211

Calliope
Sharpe's Trafalgar - Bernard Cornwell   *t*   873

Dark Fury
My Lord Pirate - Laura Renken   *r*   403

Duke William
Kydd - Julian Stockwin   *t*   984

Owanee
Fire on the Waters - David Poyer   *t*   963

Pucelle
Sharpe's Trafalgar - Bernard Cornwell   *t*   873

Revenant
Sharpe's Trafalgar - Bernard Cornwell   *t*   873

ETHIOPIA

EUROPE

FALKLAND ISLANDS

FICTIONAL CITY

FICTIONAL COUNTRY

Genre Index

This index lists the books featured as main entries in *What Do I Read Next?* by genre and story type within each genre. Beneath each of the nine genres, the story types appear alphabetically, and titles appear alphabetically under story type headings. The name of the primary author, genre code and the book entry number also appear with each title. The genre codes are as follows: *c* Popular Fiction, *f* Fantasy, *h* Horror, *i* Inspirational, *m* Mystery, *r* Romance, *s* Science Fiction, *t* Historical, and *w* Western. For definitions of the story types, see the "Key to Genre Terms" following the Introduction.

FANTASY

Adventure

Corsair - Chris Bunch   f   560

Alternate History

The Storm of Heaven - Thomas Harlan   f   587

Alternate Universe

The Emerald Burrito of Oz - John Skipp   f   636
The King of Dreams - Robert Silverberg   f   635
Leopard in Exile - Andre Norton   f   619
Sea of Silver Light - Tad Williams   f   651
The Shadows of God - J. Gregory Keyes   f   595

Alternate World

Blade of Tyshalle - Matthew Stover   f   639
Perdido Street Station - China Mieville   f   611
Point of Dreams - Melissa Scott   f   632
Sir Apropos of Nothing - Peter David   f   569
Tails You Lose - Lisa Smedman   f   637

Anthology

Oceans of Magic - Brian M. Thomsen   f   642
Out of Avalon - Jennifer Roberson   f   624
Starlight 3 - Patrick Nielsen-Hayden   f   615
Sword and Sorceress XVIII - Marion Zimmer
   Bradley   f   557

Collection

Dossier - Stepan Chapman   f   564
Meet Me in the Moon Room - Ray
   Vukcevich   f   646
Redgunk Tales - William R. Eakin   f   575
Stories for an Enchanted Afternoon - Kristine Kathryn
   Rusch   f   628
Stranger Things Happen - Kelly Link   f   606
Tales from Earthsea - Ursula K. Le Guin   f   604

Contemporary

American Gods - Neil Gaiman   f   583
The Dark Remains - Mark Anthony   f   552
The Dragon Charmer - Jan Siegel   f   634
Hell on Earth - Michael Reaves   f   622
Nothing but Blue Skies - Tom Holt   f   589

Past the Size of Dreaming - Nina Kiriki
   Hoffman   f   588
St. Patrick's Gargoyle - Katherine Kurtz   f   599
The Second Summoning - Tanya Huff   f   590
Talisker - Miller Lau   f   603
The Wooden Sea - Jonathan Carroll   f   562

Historical

Guardian of the Vision - Irene Radford   f   621
The Merlin of the Oak Wood - Ann
   Chamberlin   f   563
The Serpent's Shadow - Mercedes Lackey   f   602
Son of the Shadows - Juliet Marillier   f   608
Son of the Sword - J. Ardian Lee   f   605
The Temple and the Crown - Katherine Kurtz   f   600

Humor

Artemis Fowl - Eoin Colfer   f   566
Not Quite Scaramouche - Joel Rosenberg   f   626
Nothing but Blue Skies - Tom Holt   f   589
The Philosophical Strangler - Eric Flint   f   580
Thief of Time - Terry Pratchett   f   620

Legend

God of the Golden Fleece - Fred Saberhagen   f   630
Uther - Jack Whyte   f   650

Light Fantasy

Murphy's Lore: Fools' Day - Patrick Thomas   f   641
Summers at Castle Auburn - Sharon Shinn   f   633

Literary

The Beyond - Jeffrey Ford   f   581

Magic Conflict

Ascendance - R.A. Salvatore   f   631
Battleaxe - Sara Douglass   f   573
Beyond World's End - Mercedes Lackey   f   601
The Curer - Adam Nichols   f   614
Dragons of a Lost Star - Margaret Weis   f   647
Enemy Glory - Karen Michalson   f   610
The Fire Dragon - Katharine Kerr   f   594
The Floodgate - Elaine Cunningham   f   567
Johan - Clayton Emery   f   577
Knight or Knave - Andre Norton   f   618

Knight's Dawn - Kim Hunter   f   591
Krondor: Tear of the Gods - Raymond E.
   Feist   f   579
Kushiel's Dart - Jacqueline Carey   f   561
The Mask and the Sorceress - Dennis Jones   f   593
The One Kingdom - Sean Russell   f   629
The Queen's Necklace - Teresa Edgerton   f   576
Ravenheart - David Gemmell   f   584
The Ring of Five Dragons - Eric Van
   Lustbader   f   645
St. Patrick's Gargoyle - Katherine Kurtz   f   599
The Saints of the Sword - John Marco   f   607
Sea of Sorrows - Michelle West   f   649
A Shadow on the Glass - Ian Irvine   f   592
The Shadow Sorceress - L.E. Modesitt Jr.   f   612
Shapechanger's Song - Jennifer Roberson   f   625
The Shasht War - Christopher Rowley   f   627
The Storm of Heaven - Thomas Harlan   f   587
Summerblood - Tom Deitz   f   570
The Summoning - Troy Denning   f   571
The Sword in the Storm - David Gemmell   f   585
The Thirteenth Legion - Gav Thorpe   f   643
The Thirteenth Scroll - Rebecca Neason   f   613
Through the Darkness - Harry Turtledove   f   644
The Vacant Throne - Ed Greenwood   f   586
Wizardborn - David Farland   f   578
Yesterday's Kings - Angus Wells   f   648

Mystery

License Invoked - Robert Asprin   f   554
Point of Dreams - Melissa Scott   f   632
Talisker - Miller Lau   f   603

Political

The Curse of Chalion - Lois McMaster
   Bujold   f   559

Quest

DoOon Mode - Piers Anthony   f   553
Exiled from Camelot - Cherith Baldry   f   555
The Ill-Made Mute - Cecilia Dart-Thornton   f   568
Illumination - Terry McGarry   f   609
Issola - Steven Brust   f   558
Kingdoms of Light - Alan Dean Foster   f   582
Not Quite Scaramouche - Joel Rosenberg   f   626
Sea of Sorrows - Michelle West   f   649
The Veil of Years - L. Warren Douglas   f   572

465

HORROR

INSPIRATIONAL

POPULAR FICTION

ROMANCE

Anthology

Contemporary

Subject Index

This index lists subjects which are covered in the featured titles. Beneath each subject heading, titles are arranged alphabetically with the author names, genre codes, and entry numbers also indicated. The genre codes are as follows: *c* Popular Fiction, *f* Fantasy, *h* Horror, *i* Inspirational, *m* Mystery, *r* Romance, *s* Science Fiction, *t* Historical, and *w* Western.

Subject Index

Courtship

Be My Valentine - Sheila Rabe   *r*   399
Enchanting Pleasures - Eloisa James   *r*   315
An English Rose - Debra Satinwood   *r*   419
His Blushing Bride - Elena Greene   *r*   287
His Lordship's Swan - Martha Kirkland   *r*   334
The Marriage Lesson - Victoria Alexander   *r*   206
The Matchmaker - Rexanne Becnel   *r*   215
An Offer from a Gentleman - Julia Quinn   *r*   398
The Painted Lady - Barbara Metzger   *r*   378
Valentine Rogues - Cindy Holbrook   *r*   306

Cowboys/Cowgirls

Code of the West - Aaron Latham   *t*   926
Gabriel's Story - David Anthony Durham   *c*   1145

Crafts

Uncommon Clay - Margaret Maron   *m*   109

Creative Writing

The Merciful Women - Federico Andahazi   *h*   652

Crime and Criminals

The 25th Hour - David Benioff   *c*   1111
.44 - H.A. DeRosso   *w*   476
Angel in Black - Max Allan Collins   *t*   870
Bad News - Donald E. Westlake   *m*   192
Beyond Contentment - Glen Onley   *w*   515
Beyond the Outposts - Max Brand   *w*   458
Bitterroot - James Lee Burke   *w*   465
Blue Horizons - Irene Bennett Brown   *w*   464
Bone Island Mambo - Tom Corcoran   *m*   27
The Cloud Sketcher - Richard Rayner   *c*   1221
Cold Hands - Clare Curzon   *m*   31
The Cold Six Thousand - James Ellroy   *c*   1148
Concrete Desert - Jon Talton   *w*   542
Cow Thief Trail - Bennett Foster   *w*   482
The Devil's Shadow - Hugh Holton   *m*   83
The Doomsday Marshal and the Mountain Man - Ray Hogan   *w*   492
The Empty Coffin - Robert L. Wise   *i*   1100
Fearless Jones - Walter Mosley   *m*   126
Four of a Kind - Gilbert Morris   *i*   1063
Ghost Town - Ed Gorman   *w*   487
A Golden Trail of Murder - John Paxson   *w*   523
Grift Sense - James Swain   *m*   180
Gunman's Rhapsody - Robert B. Parker   *w*   520
Hangman - Michael Slade   *h*   738
The Hunting Wind - Steve Hamilton   *m*   75
In His Arms - Robin Lee Hatcher   *i*   1042
Johnny Blue and the Hanging Judge - Joseph A. West   *w*   548
K Falls - Skye Kathleen Moody   *w*   509
The Killer Gun - Lauran Paine   *w*   519
The Long Trail Home - Stephen A. Bly   *i*   1019
The Masked Gun - Barry Cord   *w*   469
The Master Executioner - Loren D. Estleman   *w*   479
Men Beyond the Law - Max Brand   *w*   459
Mimi's Ghost - Tim Parks   *c*   1216
Mystic River - Dennis Lehane   *c*   1183
Panicking Ralph - Bill James   *m*   86
Perhaps She'll Die - M.K. Preston   *w*   526
Reinventing Romeo - Connie Lane   *r*   343
Ring of Truth - Nancy Pickard   *m*   149
Sawyer's Crossing - Sharon Snow Sirois   *i*   1086
The Seeds of Time - Carol Cail   *w*   466
Seven Up - Janet Evanovich   *m*   50
Shannon: US Marshal - Charles E. Friend   *w*   484
Shooting Chant - Aimee Thurlo   *w*   543
The Stone Garden - Bill Brooks   *w*   860
The Stone Garden - Bill Brooks   *w*   461
Thunder Voice - Sigmund Brouwer   *w*   462

Times and Seasons - Beverly LaHaye   *i*   1053
The Truth Seeker - Dee Henderson   *i*   1045
The Ultimate Havana - John Lantigua   *m*   101
Under the Color of Law - Michael McGarrity   *w*   505
The Virginian - Owen Wister   *w*   549
West Texas - Al Sarrantonio   *w*   535
The Whitechapel Conspiracy - Anne Perry   *t*   960
A Woman of Virtue - Liz Carlyle   *r*   239

Cruise Ships

Birds of Prey - J.A. Jance   *m*   89
It Had to Be You - Linda Windsor   *i*   1099
To Davy Jones Below - Carola Dunn   *t*   885

Crusades

His Fair Lady - Kathleen Kirkwood   *r*   335

Cuban Americans

In Cuba I Was a German Shepherd - Ana Menendez   *c*   1202
The Ultimate Havana - John Lantigua   *m*   101

Cults

Balak - Stephen Mark Rainey   *h*   727
Black Lotus - Laura Joh Rowland   *m*   161
The Death of an Irish Sinner - Bartholomew Gill   *m*   61
Gemini Rising - Brian McNaughton   *h*   709

Cultural Conflict

American Fuji - Sara Backer   *c*   1105
The Bad Luck Wedding Night - Geralyn Dawson   *r*   252
Do Try to Speak as We Do - Marjorie Leet Ford   *c*   1152
The Far Field - Edie Meidav   *c*   1201
The Far Field - Edie Meidav   *t*   946
The Glass Palace - Amitav Ghosh   *t*   902
Heart of a Warrior - Johanna Lindsey   *r*   352
The Prize - Martine Berne   *r*   218
Secret Love - Bart Schneider   *c*   1225
Tierra del Fuego - Sylvia Iparraguirre   *t*   915
Water Touching Stone - Eliot Pattison   *m*   144

Cultures and Customs

Clouds Without Rain - P.L. Gaus   *m*   58
The Collected Stories of Richard Yates - Richard Yates   *c*   1247
The Horus Road - Pauline Gedge   *t*   900
Raven Mocker - Don Coldsmith   *t*   869

Customs

A Common Life - Jan Karon   *c*   1179
Drinking with the Cook - Laura Furman   *c*   1156

Cyborgs

Edward Maret - Robert L. Katz   *s*   798

Dancing

Considering Kate - Nora Roberts   *r*   411
Corpse de Ballet - Ellen Pall   *m*   141

Dark Ages

Uther - Jack Whyte   *t*   995

Dating (Social Customs)

Bad Boy - Olivia Goldsmith   *r*   278
Dawn in Eclipse Bay - Jayne Ann Krentz   *r*   337
The Shape of Things to Come - Maud Casey   *c*   1129

Deafness

Blind Side - Penny Warner   *m*   189
The Highland Wife - Lyn Stone   *r*   437
His Lordship's Swan - Martha Kirkland   *r*   334
Mute Witness - Charles O'Brien   *m*   134
Mute Witness - Charles O'Brien   *t*   953

Death

American Fuji - Sara Backer   *c*   1105
Dark Undertakings - Rebecca Tope   *m*   184
Deadfellas - David Whitman   *h*   748
The Dearly Departed - Elinor Lipman   *c*   1186
The Gospel of Judas - Simon Mawer   *c*   1195
Martyrs' Crossing - Amy Wilentz   *c*   1244
Never Change - Elizabeth Berg   *c*   1112

Demons

Declare - Tim Powers   *h*   723

Dentistry

Appointment with Il Duce - Hozy Rossi   *t*   974
Bucking the Tiger - Bruce Olds   *t*   954

Depression

Blood Sisters - Melody Carlson   *i*   1025
Breakaway - Laura Crum   *m*   30

Depression (Economic)

Beulah Hill - William Heffernan   *t*   911
Hidden Places - Lynn N. Austin   *i*   1006
These Granite Islands - Sarah Stonich   *t*   985
Valley of Promises - Bonnie Leon   *i*   1056

Detection

Almost a Lady - Heidi Betts   *r*   219
Green Grow the Victims - Jeanne M. Dams   *t*   874
Sleepeasy - T.M. Wright   *h*   751
Wire Mesh Mothers - Elizabeth Massie   *h*   705

Diaries

Primrose Past - Caroline Rose Hunt   *t*   914
Squire Haggard's Journal - Michael Green   *t*   905

Difference

In Praise of Younger Men - Jo Beverley   *r*   224

Disasters

The Chronoliths - Robert Charles Wilson   *s*   849
Falling Stars - Michael Flynn   *s*   782
Fatal Voyage - Kathy Reichs   *m*   153
Hammerfall - C.J. Cherryh   *s*   765
Snow Mountain Passage - James D. Houston   *t*   912

Diseases

Civil Blood - Ann McMillan   *t*   945

Horse Racing

Hospitals

Hostages

Hotels, Motels

Human Behavior

Humor

Hunting

Hurricanes

Identity

Identity, Concealed

Illness

Imagination

Immortality

Independence

Indian Reservations

Indians of North America

Indians of South America

Infertility

Infidelity

Subject Index

Subject Index

Writing

Character Name Index

This index alphabetically lists the major characters in each featured title. Each character name is followed by a description of the character. Citations also provide titles of the books featuring the character, listed alphabetically if there is more than one title; author names and genre codes. The genre codes are as follows: *c* Popular Fiction, *f* Fantasy, *h* Horror, *i* Inspirational, *m* Mystery, *r* Romance, *s* Science Fiction, *t* Historical, and *w* Western. Numbers refer to the entries that feature each title.

A

Abbott, Ellie (Writer)
The Summerhouse - Jude Deveraux   *r*   256

Abelscu, Iacob (Businessman)
Departures - Miriam Striezheff Lewis   *t*   928

Absey, Jonathan (Government Official)
The Music of the Spheres - Elizabeth Redfern   *t*   967

Achilles (Military Personnel)
The Song of Troy - Colleen McCullough   *t*   943

Ackroyd, Laura (Journalist)
Dead on Arrival - Patricia Hall   *m*   72

Adair, Mark (Military Personnel; Nobleman)
Lord Harry's Daughter - Evelyn Richardson   *r*   406

Adaiz (Alien; Spy)
Resurrection - Arwen Elys Dayton   *s*   771

Adamov, Augustus (Ruler)
Royal Bride - Joan Wolf   *r*   450

Adams, Abigail (Historical Figure)
Rise to Rebellion - Jeff Shaara   *w*   539

Adams, Carrie (Spouse)
Longshadow's Woman - Bronwyn Williams   *r*   448

Adams, Constance (Real Estate Agent)
The Lawman Meets His Bride - Meagan
  McKinney   *r*   374

Adams, John (Historical Figure; Political Figure)
Rise to Rebellion - Jeff Shaara   *w*   539
Rise to Rebellion - Jeff Shaara   *t*   980

Adams, Leslie (Resistance Fighter)
A Perfect Persecution - James R. Lucas   *i*   1059

Adams, Liz Hampton (Spouse)
The Hampton Passion - Julie Ellis   *r*   264

Adams, Victor (Doctor)
The Hampton Passion - Julie Ellis   *r*   264

Adeline (Divorced Person; Parent)
The Shape of Things to Come - Maud
  Casey   *c*   1129

Adkins, Becky (Child; Survivor)
Beyond Contentment - Glen Onley   *w*   515

Adrianna (Noblewoman)
The Prize - Martine Berne   *r*   218

Agatha (Parent; Housewife)
Ella in Bloom - Shelby Hearon   *c*   1170

Agon (Prehistoric Human)
Song of the Axe - John R. Dann   *t*   875

Aguilera, Bartolomeo (Spaceman)
Ship of Fools - Richard Paul Russo   *s*   825

Ahasuerus (Entertainer)
Tales of the Galactic Midway - Mike
  Resnick   *s*   820

Ahmose (Royalty; Historical Figure)
The Horus Road - Pauline Gedge   *t*   900

Ahten, Raj (Warrior)
Wizardborn - David Farland   *f*   578

Ahvren (Military Personnel)
A Matter of Profit - Hilari Bell   *s*   757

Ai Mordha, Eleres (Alien)
The Ghost Sister - Liz Williams   *s*   846

Ai Mordha, Mevennen (Alien)
The Ghost Sister - Liz Williams   *s*   846

Ainsley, Valoree (Pirate; Heiress)
Lady Pirate - Lynsay Sands   *r*   418

Ainsworth, Marcel (Sea Captain; Nobleman)
Summer's Bride - Catherine Archer   *r*   211

Aislinn of Amberlea (Noblewoman)
The Knight - Juliana Garnett   *r*   277

Akhlaur (Wizard)
The Floodgate - Elaine Cunningham   *f*   567

al-Mansur, Ashraf (Nobleman; Fugitive)
Pashazade: The First Arabesk - Jon Courtenay
  Grimwood   *s*   792

Albert (Royalty; Historical Figure)
Death at Epsom Downs - Robin Paige   *t*   955

Albert (Slave)
The Magic Wagon - Joe R. Lansdale   *w*   499

Albertson, Bobby (Director)
Bobby's Girl - J.D. Austin   *s*   754

Alea (Spacewoman)
A Wizard in a Feud - Christopher Stasheff   *f*   638

Alethea (Artist)
Metaplanetary - Tony Daniel   *s*   767

Alexander the Great (Historical Figure; Ruler)
The House of Death - P.C. Doherty   *m*   42
The House of Death - P.C. Doherty   *t*   881

Alfonsa de las Fuentes, Margarita (Young Woman;
Spy)
The Spy Who Loved Him - Merline Lovelace   *r*   357

Ali, Sher (Military Personnel; Royalty)
The Long Love - Katharine Gordon   *r*   279

Alice (Servant)
A Fragment of Life - Arthur Machen   *h*   704

Alik (Expatriate; Artist)
The Funeral Party - Ludmila Ulitskaya   *c*   1238

Alix (Mythical Creature)
Shapechanger's Song - Jennifer Roberson   *f*   625

Allen, Catherine (Narrator)
A Spell of Winter - Helen Dunmore   *t*   884
A Spell of Winter - Helen Dunmore   *c*   1144

Allen, Darryl Bob (Divorced Person)
Thanksgiving - Michael Dibdin   *c*   1141

Allen, Rob (Young Man)
A Spell of Winter - Helen Dunmore   *c*   1144
A Spell of Winter - Helen Dunmore   *t*   884

Alpha (Streetperson)
Uncommon Justice - Terry Devane   *c*   1139

Alpiew (Servant)
Unnatural Fire - Fidelis Morgan   *m*   125
Unnatural Fire - Fidelis Morgan   *t*   949

Alvarez (Police Officer)
The Ambiguity of Murder - Roderic Jeffries   *m*   90

Alvarez, Charlotte (Rancher)
Shannon: US Marshal - Charles E. Friend   *w*   484

Alvarez, David (Police Officer)
Rosewood's Ashes - Aileen Schumacher   *m*   166

Alwyn, Daryn (Consultant)
The Octagonal Raven - L.E. Modesitt Jr.   *s*   809

Alys (Archaeologist)
Kelly and the Three-Toed Horse - Peter
  Bowen   *w*   456

Amandine (Young Woman)
A Dish Taken Cold - Anne Perry   *t*   959

Ambler, Jack (Pioneer; Farmer)
Blue Horizons - Irene Bennett Brown   *w*   464

Amelie (Businesswoman)
Fear and Trembling - Amelie Nothomb   *c*   1210

Amerotke (Judge)
The Anubis Slayings - P.C. Doherty   *t*   879
The Anubis Slayings - P.C. Doherty   *m*   40

Ames (Ruler)
Metaplanetary - Tony Daniel   *s*   767

Ames, Addington (Detective—Amateur)
Murder at Bertram's Bower - Cynthia Peale   *m*   145

Murder at Bertram's Bower - Cynthia Peale *t* 957

Ames, Caroline (Detective—Amateur)
Murder at Bertram's Bower - Cynthia Peale *m* 145
Murder at Bertram's Bower - Cynthia Peale *t* 957

Ammamma (Grandparent)
Motherland - Vineeta Vijayaraghavan *c* 1239

Anaguil (Young Woman)
Three Apples Fell from Heaven - Micheline Aharonian Marcom *t* 938
Three Apples Fell from Heaven - Micheline Aharonian Marcom *c* 1193

Anders, D.P. (Police Officer)
The Wooden Leg of Inspector Anders - Marshall Browne *m* 15

Anderson, Elizabeth (Mail Order Bride; Southern Belle)
The Outlaw Takes a Wife - Sylvia McDaniel *r* 370

Anderson, Sunny (Artist)
Just the Way You Aren't - Lynda Simmons *r* 426

Andris (Warrior)
The Floodgate - Elaine Cunningham *f* 567

Angelucci, Michael (Police Officer)
Archangel Protocol - Lyda Morehouse *s* 810

Anne (Religious)
In the Company of Angels - N.M. Kelby *t* 922

Annie (Worker)
The Free Lunch - Spider Robinson *s* 824

Anthem, Billy (Relative)
Texas Born - Kerry Newcomb *w* 512

Anthem, Cole (Relative)
Texas Born - Kerry Newcomb *w* 512

Anthem, John (Rancher)
Texas Born - Kerry Newcomb *w* 512

Anthony (Widow(er))
Thanksgiving - Michael Dibdin *c* 1141

Anton (Teenager)
On the Water - H.M. van den Brink *t* 991

Antonina (Noblewoman)
The Tide of Victory - Eric Flint *s* 781

Apepa (Ruler; Historical Figure)
The Horus Road - Pauline Gedge *t* 900

Apodaca, Joe (Military Personnel)
Shadows on the Land - James M. Vesely *w* 547

Apodaca, Miguel (Military Personnel)
Seasons of Harvest - James M. Vesely *w* 546

Apodaca, Primitivo (Military Personnel)
Seasons of Harvest - James M. Vesely *w* 546

Apodaca, Rueben (Handicapped)
Shadows on the Land - James M. Vesely *w* 547

Applebaum, Juliet (Parent; Lawyer)
The Big Nap - Ayelet Waldman *m* 188

Appleby, John (Widow(er))
Grace - Jane Roberts Wood *t* 997

Appleby, Madison (Model)
The Summerhouse - Jude Deveraux *r* 256

Apropos (Thief; Abuse Victim)
Sir Apropos of Nothing - Peter David *f* 569

Arburg, Whitey (Lawman)
Cow Thief Trail - Bennett Foster *w* 482

Arch (Friend; Musician)
Taps - Willie Morris *c* 1205

Archer, Grant (Scientist)
Jupiter - Ben Bova *s* 760

Archer, Morse (Military Personnel; Imposter)
The Wedding Wager - Deborah Hale *r* 292

Arden, Anne (Student—Graduate; Lesbian)
Pages for You - Sylvia Brownrigg *c* 1121

Arendt, Hannah (Historical Figure; Writer)
Martin and Hannah - Catherine Clement *t* 866

Arkanian, Petra (Military Personnel)
Shadow of the Hegemon - Orson Scott Card *s* 763

Armstrong, Catherine (Crime Victim)
Border Lord - Haywood Smith *r* 431

Arne (Clone)
Terraforming Earth - Jack Williamson *s* 848

Arnette, Cal (Lawman)
Twice Dead - Elizabeth Dearl *w* 475

Arnold, Jessie (Detective—Amateur)
Dead North - Sue Henry *m* 80
Dead North - Sue Henry *w* 490

Arpino, Beppe (Musician; Dentist)
Appointment with Il Duce - Hozy Rossi *t* 974

Arutha (Ruler)
Krondor: Tear of the Gods - Raymond E. Feist *f* 579

Asdeon (Demon)
Hell on Earth - Michael Reaves *f* 622

Ashborn, Lydia (Student)
Beyond World's End - Mercedes Lackey *f* 601

Ashby de la Zouche, Anastasia (Noblewoman; Journalist)
Unnatural Fire - Fidelis Morgan *m* 125
Unnatural Fire - Fidelis Morgan *t* 949

Ashcroft, Howard (Occultist)
Worse Things Waiting - Brian McNaughton *h* 711

Ashe, Gordon (Time Traveler)
Time Traders II - Andre Norton *s* 814

Ashera, Eleusis (Government Official)
The Ring of Five Dragons - Eric Van Lustbader *f* 645

Ashford, Charles "Chas" Harrison (Nobleman)
Miss Westlake's Windfall - Barbara Metzger *r* 377

Ashton, Hope (Photographer)
Heaven Sent - Jillian Hart *i* 1041

Asrani, Kavita (Young Woman; Girlfriend)
The Death of Vishnu - Manil Suri *c* 1231

Astropel (Alien)
The Wooden Sea - Jonathan Carroll *c* 1128

Aten, Nick (Teenager)
Blood Crazy - Simon Clark *h* 666

Atherton, Thomas (Cowboy)
The Buffalo Hunters - Gary McCarthy *w* 504

Atkins, Jessica (Child; Handicapped)
The Christmas Thingy - F. Paul Wilson *h* 749

Attla, Raymond (Police Officer)
Silent as the Hunter - Christopher Lane *m* 100

August, Billie (Detective—Private)
Whatever Doesn't Kill You - Gillian Roberts *m* 158

August, Shelby (Accountant)
Nighttime Guardian - Amanda Stevens *r* 435

Auletes (Historical Figure; Ruler)
Kleopatra - Karen Essex *t* 890

Aurya (Sorceress)
The Thirteenth Scroll - Rebecca Neason *f* 613

Austin (Animal)
The Second Summoning - Tanya Huff *f* 590

Avall (Ruler)
Summerblood - Tom Deitz *f* 570

Avantar (Guard)
Sea of Sorrows - Michelle West *f* 649

Avenel, Gawain (Knight; Imposter)
The Swan Maiden - Susan King *r* 332

Averan (Young Woman)
Wizardborn - David Farland *f* 578

Avila, Tere (Narrator)
Loving Pedro Infante - Denise Chavez *c* 1131

Axis (Nobleman)
Battleaxe - Sara Douglass *f* 573

Aydrian (Sorcerer)
Ascendance - R.A. Salvatore *f* 631

B

Babcock, Lydia Arlington (Environmentalist)
The Voice of the Butterfly - John Nichols *w* 513

Baca, Iggy (Lawyer)
Carreta de la Muerte (Cart of Death) - Mari Ulmer *w* 544

Baer, Harry (Artist)
Burnt Umber - Sheldon Greene *t* 906

Bahr, Marshall "Mars" (Detective—Police)
Third Person Singular - K.J. Erickson *m* 49

Bailey, Bryn (Doctor; Survivor)
Pathways - Lisa Tawn Bergren *i* 1015

Bailey, Joe (Detective—Police; Magician)
Beyond Belief - Roy Johansen *h* 690

Bainbridge, Gabriel (Nobleman)
Intrigued - Bertrice Small *r* 429

Baker, Catastrophe (Criminal)
The Outpost - Mike Resnick *s* 819

Baker, Elisha (Military Personnel)
Fire on the Waters - David Poyer *t* 963

Baker, Jeannette (Historian)
The Song of the Earth - Hugh Nissenson *s* 813

Baker, John Firth (Artist; Genetically Altered Being)
The Song of the Earth - Hugh Nissenson *s* 813

Baldwin de Furnshill (Knight; Government Official)
The Boy-Bishop's Glovemaker - Michael Jecks *t* 918

Ballin, Jeannette (Young Woman)
Departures - Miriam Striezheff Lewis *t* 928

Ballinger, Trace (Lawyer)
Lip Service - Suzanne Simmons *r* 427

Bane, Grimwar (Mythical Creature)
The Messenger - Douglas Niles *f* 616

Banning, Gabriella (Noblewoman; Impoverished)
Scandalous - Karen Robards *r* 408

Banning, Marcus (Nobleman; Imposter)
Scandalous - Karen Robards *r* 408

Bannister, Lilyanne (Gentlewoman)
The Painted Lady - Barbara Metzger *r* 378

Banouin (Trader)
The Sword in the Storm - David Gemmell *f* 585

Banqueros, Felix (Teacher)
The View from Hell - John Shirley *h* 736

Banyon, Eric (Student)
Beyond World's End - Mercedes Lackey *f* 601

Barbara (Young Woman)
The Root Worker - Rainelle Burton *c* 1123

Bardolph, Francis (Nobleman; Spy)
One Knight in Venice - Tori Phillips *r* 393

Barksdale, Swayze (Teenager; Musician)
Taps - Willie Morris *c* 1205

Barnette, E.T. (Banker; Landowner)
The Wolf's Pack - Richard Parry *w* 521

Barr, Temple (Public Relations)
Cat in a Leopard Spot - Carole Nelson
Douglas *m* 44

Barrett, Shelby (Actress; Office Worker)
Be My Valentine - Sheila Rabe *r* 399

Barrington, Stone (Detective—Private; Lawyer)
Cold Paradise - Stuart Woods *m* 198

Barry, Brette (Single Parent; Postal Worker)
Dead End - Helen R. Myers *r* 389

Barton, Rachel (Heiress; Businesswoman)
The Yorkshire Lady - Nadine Miller *r* 383

Bartram (Nobleman)
Yesterday's Kings - Angus Wells *f* 648

Bass, Titus (Mountain Man)
Wind Walker - Terry C. Johnston *t* 919

Basspriot, Faubon (Police Officer)
Fool Me Twice - Matthew Hughes *s* 795

Batten, Sunny (Young Woman)
The Dearly Departed - Elinor Lipman *c* 1186

Bauer, Else (Young Woman)
The Right Hand of Sleep - John Wray *t* 999

Bauer, Kurt (Military Personnel)
The Right Hand of Sleep - John Wray *t* 999

Bawtry, Bessie (Parent)
The Peppered Moth - Margaret Drabble *c* 1142

Bayguard, Moreen (Warrior; Hunter)
The Messenger - Douglas Niles *f* 616

BB (Sidekick)
The Last Blue Plate Special - Abigail
Padgett *m* 138

Bean (Military Personnel)
Shadow of the Hegemon - Orson Scott Card *s* 763

Bean, Madeline (Caterer; Detective—Amateur)
Dim Sum Dead - Jerrilyn Farmer *m* 52

Beaudry, Clint (Lawman; Gunfighter)
Outlaw's Bride - Maureen McKade *r* 373

Beaufort, Charity (Royalty; Bride)
Royal Bride - Joan Wolf *r* 450

Beaumont, J.P. (Police Officer)
Birds of Prey - J.A. Jance *m* 89

Beaver (Hunter)
Dreamcatcher - Stephen King *c* 1180

Beck, David (Doctor)
Tell No One - Harlan Coben *m* 24

Beckett, Grace (Doctor)
The Dark Remains - Mark Anthony *f* 552

Beckett, Sophia Maria "Sophie" (Bastard Daughter;
Ward)
An Offer from a Gentleman - Julia Quinn *r* 398

Bedford-Browne, Lydia Jane (Noblewoman)
The Indiscretion - Judith Ivory *r* 311

Begum, Arina (Fiance(e))
The Long Love - Katharine Gordon *r* 279

Behan, Johnny (Lawman)
Gunman's Rhapsody - Robert B. Parker *t* 956

Belaggio, Lorenzo (Producer)
Die upon a Kiss - Barbara Hambly *t* 908

Belisarius (Military Personnel)
The Tide of Victory - Eric Flint *s* 781

Bell, Andrew (Banker)
Quakertown - Lee Martin *w* 503
Quakertown - Lee Martin *t* 940

Bellamy of Itchen (Knight)
A Personal Devil - Roberta Gellis *m* 59

A Personal Devil - Roberta Gellis *t* 901

Bellocq, E.J. (Historical Figure; Photographer)
Bellocq's Women - Peter Everett *t* 892

Belov, Alexander (Military Personnel)
The Bronze Horseman - Paullina Simons *t* 981

Beltran (Knight)
The Dark Remains - Mark Anthony *f* 552

Ben (Relative)
Rides of the Midway - Lee Durkee *c* 1146

Ben Levi, Gabriel (Relative)
Strange Fire - Melvin Jules Bukiet *c* 1122

Bendix, Joseph (Doctor)
The House of Sight and Shadow - Nicholas
Griffin *t* 907

Benedict, Marina (Actress; Crime Victim)
Taken - Kathleen George *c* 1159

Bennett, Allie (Accountant; Volunteer)
Unbreak My Heart - Teresa Hill *r* 304

Bennett, Steve (Fiance(e))
Times and Seasons - Beverly LaHaye *i* 1053

Benny (Criminal)
Deadfellas - David Whitman *h* 748

Bent, Charles (Trader; Historical Figure)
Moon Medicine - Mike Blakely *w* 453

Bentley, William (Military Personnel)
The Wicked Trade - Jan Needle *t* 950

Benton, Reed (Lawman; Rancher)
Summer Moon - Jill Marie Landis *r* 342

Bergman, Adam (Military Personnel)
Battle Lines - James Reasoner *t* 965

Bernier, Alex (Journalist; Detective—Amateur)
The Fourth Wall - Beth Saulnier *m* 164

Berthoff, Katarina (Businesswoman)
Courting Katarina - Carol Steward *i* 1089

Beryl (Mythical Creature; Ruler)
Dragons of a Lost Star - Margaret Weis *f* 647

Bex, Lucy (Gardener; Detective—Amateur)
Common or Garden Crime - Sheila Pim *m* 150

Billy the Kid (Historical Figure; Outlaw)
The Stone Garden - Bill Brooks *t* 860

Biscara (Landowner)
The Cavan Breed - Les Savage Jr. *w* 537

Bishop, Frank (Police Officer)
The Blue Nowhere - Jeffery Deaver *m* 37

B'Kah, Romlijhian (Alien; Royalty)
The Star King - Susan Grant *r* 282

Black, Aiden (Nobleman)
The Marriage Contract - Cathy Maxwell *r* 365

Black, Matilda (Witch)
Past the Size of Dreaming - Nina Kiriki
Hoffman *f* 588

Blackburn, Kee (Indian; Investigator)
Raven - Laura Baker *r* 213

Blackeagle, Heyoka (Military Personnel; Alien)
Stars over Stars - K.D. Wentworth *s* 845

Blackeye, Khurdis (Sorcerer)
The Curer - Adam Nichols *f* 614

Blackstock, Dorothy "Dodie" (Editor)
Dying Voices - Laura Wilson *m* 197

Blackthorne, Gideon (Nobleman)
Devil in the Dark - Evelyn Rogers *r* 413

Blackthorne, Richard (Businessman; Recluse)
Taming the Beast - Amy J. Fetzer *r* 268

Blackwell, Judith (Widow(er))
Blood Sisters - Melody Carlson *i* 1025

Blakewell, Claire (Gentlewoman)
A Bride for Lord Challmond - Debbie
Raleigh *r* 400

Blaylock, Nathan (Gunfighter; Gambler)
The Wolf's Pack - Richard Parry *w* 521

Blocker, Ab (Cowboy)
Get Along, Little Dogies - Lisa Waller
Rogers *w* 533

Blue, Carolyn (Journalist)
Crime Brulee - Nancy Fairbanks *m* 51

Blue, Jason (Professor)
Crime Brulee - Nancy Fairbanks *m* 51

Blue Fox (Indian; Mentally Ill Person)
Kelly and the Three-Toed Horse - Peter
Bowen *t* 857
Kelly and the Three-Toed Horse - Peter
Bowen *w* 456

Blythe, Richard (Writer; Nobleman)
A Rogue's Embrace - Margaret Moore *r* 386

Bodine, Juliet (Writer; Professor)
Corpse de Ballet - Ellen Pall *m* 141

Boerema, Ika (Landscaper)
The Winter Garden - Johanna Verweerd *i* 1095

Bohem, Nisa (Activist; Lover)
Secret Love - Bart Schneider *c* 1225

Bonderoff, Jim (Wealthy; Computer Expert)
Excuse Me? Whose Baby? - Jacqueline
Diamond *r* 258

Bondurant, Pete (Spy; Criminal)
The Cold Six Thousand - James Ellroy *c* 1148

Bonneau, Louis (Immigrant)
The Awakening Land - James M. Vesely *w* 545

Bonneaux, Julia (Southern Belle; Impoverished)
The Horse Soldier - Merline Lovelace *r* 355

Bonneterre, Alys de (Young Woman)
Kelly and the Three-Toed Horse - Peter
Bowen *t* 857

Bonney, Billy (Outlaw; Historical Figure)
The Stone Garden - Bill Brooks *w* 461

Bonny, Anne (Historical Figure; Pirate)
The Sweet Trade - Elizabeth Garrett *t* 899

Boone, Roy (Drifter)
The Gallows Land - Bill Pronzini *w* 527

Bora, Katharina von (Historical Figure; Religious)
Storm - Reg Grant *t* 904

Bosch, Harry (Detective—Homicide)
A Darkness More than Night - Michael
Connelly *c* 1135

Bosha, Gai (Military Personnel)
Tears of Ice - Gary Livingston *t* 932

Boswell, Jasmine (Military Personnel; Space
Explorer)
The Star King - Susan Grant *r* 282

Bouchie, Roxanne (Doctor; Lesbian)
The Last Blue Plate Special - Abigail
Padgett *m* 138

Boudreaux, Chantz (Bastard Son; Overseer)
Fever - Katherine Sutcliffe *r* 438

Box (Artificial Intelligence)
A Dark Imbalance - Sean Williams *s* 847

Boyle, Dave (Abuse Victim; Crime Suspect)
Mystic River - Dennis Lehane *c* 1183
Mystic River - Dennis Lehane *m* 102

Boyle, Emma (Police Officer)
Candyland - Evan Hunter *m* 84

Bracewell, Nicholas (Producer)
The Devil's Apprentice - Edward Marston *t* 939

Brackley, Camden Thurston (Nobleman; Fiance(e))
Never a Bride - Amelia Grey   r   290

Bradley, Samuel (Police Officer)
Beulah Hill - William Heffernan   t   911

Bragg, Rick (Police Officer)
Deadly Love - B.D. Joyce   r   325

Brakeburn-Blackheart, Lilliana (Noblewoman)
The Queen's Necklace - Teresa Edgerton   f   576

Bran (Warrior)
Son of the Shadows - Juliet Marillier   f   608

Branden, Michael (Professor; Detective—Amateur)
Clouds Without Rain - P.L. Gaus   i   1035
Clouds Without Rain - P.L. Gaus   m   58

Brannick, Jim (Farmer; Lawman)
Brannick: And the Untamed West - Harold G.
    Ross   w   534

Brannon, Cory (Military Personnel)
Vicksburg - James Reasoner   t   966

Branscombe, Violet (Doctor; Spouse)
Dr. Mortimer and the Barking Man Mystery - Gerard
    Williams   m   195
Dr. Mortimer and the Barking Man Mystery - Gerard
    Williams   t   996

Brave Horse (Relative; Indian)
Mystic Warriors - Rosanne Bittner   w   452

Bray, Nell (Suffragette; Detective—Amateur)
The Perfect Daughter - Gillian Linscott   m   105
A Perfect Daughter - Gillian Linscott   t   930

Brennan, Daniel (Businessman)
A Notorious Love - Sabrina Jeffries   r   317

Brennan, Kelly (Time Traveler; Widow(er))
Time After Time - Constance O'Day-Flannery   r   391

Brennan, Temperance (Anthropologist)
Fatal Voyage - Kathy Reichs   m   153

Brennon, Meg (Pioneer; Abuse Victim)
Blue Horizons - Irene Bennett Brown   w   464

Brewer, Madeleine (Lover; Spouse)
The Gospel of Judas - Simon Mawer   c   1195

Bridge, Nora (Radio Personality; Journalist)
Summer Island - Kristin Hannah   r   293

Bridge, Ruby (Entertainer; Writer)
Summer Island - Kristin Hannah   r   293

Bridgerton, Benedict (Nobleman)
An Offer from a Gentleman - Julia Quinn   r   398

Briggs, Cady (Heiress; Businesswoman)
Lost and Found - Jayne Ann Krentz   r   338

Briggs, Harry (Detective—Private; Teacher)
Sleepeasy - T.M. Wright   h   751

Briggs, Lamar (Detective—Police)
Judas Eyes - Barry Hoffman   h   688

Bright, Anthea (Teacher; Gentlewoman)
The Bad Man's Bride - Susan Kay Law   r   348

Bring, Caleb (Military Personnel)
A Journey to the Interior - E.A. Blair   t   856

Brisane (Sorceress)
Exiled from Camelot - Cherith Baldry   f   555

Britannicus, Caius Merlyn (Sorcerer; Warrior)
Uther - Jack Whyte   f   650
Uther - Jack Whyte   f   995

Brogan, Monty (Drug Dealer; Convict)
The 25th Hour - David Benioff   c   1111

Brogus, Reggie (Professor; Activist)
If 6 Were 9 - Jake Lamar   c   1182

Brooks, Christine Bennett (Housewife; Teacher)
The April Fool's Day Murder - Lee Harris   m   77

Brooks, Melanie (Teacher)
Follow That Baby! - Isabel Sharpe   r   423

Broussard, Juliette (Orphan; Heiress)
Fever - Katherine Sutcliffe   r   438

Brown, Alec (Relative; Writer)
Morning - W.D. Wetherell   c   1242

Brown, Jedidiah (Lawman)
The Lawmans Surrender - Debra Mullins   r   388

Brownley, Lauren (Musician)
The Witness - Ginna Gray   r   285

Bruce, Robert (Leader)
The Temple and the Crown - Katherine Kurtz   f   600

Brummell, George Bryan "Beau" (Historical Figure;
Socialite)
The Tainted Snuff Box - Rosemary Stevens   m   178
The Tainted Snuff Box - Rosemary Stevens   t   983

Bryan (Royalty)
Summers at Castle Auburn - Sharon Shinn   f   633

Brynmaur (Healer)
The Curer - Adam Nichols   f   614

Buckner, Tish (Young Woman; Spy)
The Way We Wed - Pat Warren   r   445

Buffalo, John (Indian; Sports Figure)
The Long Journey Home - Don Coldsmith   t   868

Buffalo Dreamer (Indian; Spouse)
Mystic Warriors - Rosanne Bittner   w   452
Mystic Warriors - Rosanne Bittner   t   855

Bugg, Konstanze (Runaway; Singer)
The Mermaid of Penperro - Lisa Cach   r   234

Burbank, George (Rancher)
The Power of the Dog - Thomas Savage   w   538

Burbank, Phil (Rancher; Relative)
The Power of the Dog - Thomas Savage   w   538

Burbrooke, Edward (Nobleman)
Beyond Innocence - Emma Holly   r   308

Burbrooke, Freddie (Nobleman)
Beyond Innocence - Emma Holly   r   308

Burgess (Alien)
DoOon Mode - Piers Anthony   f   553

Burke, Jessica (Scientist; Student)
Someone to Watch over Her - Margaret
    Watson   r   446

Burke, Kay (Relative)
Mary and O'Neil - Justin Cronin   c   1136

Burke, O'Neil (Relative; Teacher)
Mary and O'Neil - Justin Cronin   c   1136

Burkhart, Zack (Rancher; Single Parent)
Catch a Dream - Mary Jane Meier   r   376

Burne (Warrior)
The Temple of Elemental Evil - Thomas M.
    Reid   f   623

Burnett, Anne (Gentlewoman; Bride)
The Marriage Contract - Cathy Maxwell   r   365

Burnett, Tanner (Veteran; Outlaw)
The Outlaw Takes a Wife - Sylvia McDaniel   r   370

Burns, Marty (Detective—Private; Actor)
Greed & Stuff - Jay Russell   m   162

Burrack, Samuel (Lawman; Adventurer)
Blood Rock - Ralph Cotton   w   470

Burroughs, Vivienne (Orphan; Noblewoman)
His Forbidden Kiss - Margaret Moore   r   385

Butler (Servant)
Artemis Fowl - Eoin Colfer   f   566

Butler, Dick (Spouse; Mentally Ill Person)
Beloved Stranger - Clare Boylan   c   1117

Butler, Lily (Spouse; Parent)
Beloved Stranger - Clare Boylan   c   1117

Butler, Ples (Gunfighter)
Broken Ranks - Hiram King   w   497

Button, Jemmy (Indian; Historical Figure)
Tierra del Fuego - Sylvia Iparraguirre   t   915

Byrde, Olivia (Gentlewoman)
The Matchmaker - Rexanne Becnel   r   215

Byrne, Katie (Actress)
The Triumph of Katie Byrne - Barbara Taylor
    Bradford   c   1119

Byrne, Rowan (Artist)
This Flesh Unknown - Gary A. Braunbeck   h   659

Byron, George Gordon (Writer; Historical Figure)
The Merciful Women - Federico Andahazi   h   652

C

Caballeros, Carlos (Political Figure; Military
Personnel)
The Spy Who Loved Him - Merline Lovelace   r   357

Caddrick, John (Political Figure)
The House That Jack Built - Robert Asprin   s   753

Caesar, Julius (Historical Figure; Military Personnel)
Kleopatra - Karen Essex   t   890

Cahill, Francesca (Activist; Gentlewoman)
Deadly Love - B.D. Joyce   r   325

Caine, John (Detective—Private)
Silversword - Charles Knief   m   97

Cairns, Gregor (Fisherman)
Cosmonaut Keep - Ken MacLeod   s   803

Cairns, Matt (Computer Expert)
Cosmonaut Keep - Ken MacLeod   s   803

Calcraft, Edmund (Doctor)
The House of Sight and Shadow - Nicholas
    Griffin   t   907

Caldwell, Patrick "Trick" (Highwayman;
Nobleman)
Amber - Lauren Royal   r   416

Calhoun, Susannah (Young Woman; Prisoner)
The Lawmans Surrender - Debra Mullins   r   388

Callaghan, Brittany (Construction Worker)
Heart of a Warrior - Johanna Lindsey   r   352

Callahan, Nita (Teenager; Wizard)
The Wizard's Dilemma - Diane Duane   f   574

Cambian, Della Joan (Teenager; Vampire)
Red Moon Rising - Billie Sue Mosiman   h   712

Cambridge, Laura (Child-Care Giver)
Taming the Beast - Amy J. Fetzer   r   268

Camfield, Daria (Religious; Widow(er))
Beneath a Southern Sky - Deborah Raney   i   1077

Camfield, Nathan "Nate" (Spouse)
Beneath a Southern Sky - Deborah Raney   i   1077

Campbell, Averyl (Noblewoman)
His Stolen Bride - Shelley Bradley   r   226

Campbell, Charles (Real Estate Agent)
The Haunting of Hip Hop - Bertice Barry   h   655

Campbell, Dan (Guide)
Lioness - Nell Brien   r   227

Campbell, James (Government Official)
Stark's Command - John G. Hemry   s   794

Campbell, Janet Leslie (Noblewoman; Widow(er))
The Heart Queen - Patricia Potter   r   396

Campbell, Leith (Laird)
The Prize - Martine Berne   r   218

Cane, Adoni (Clone)
A Dark Imbalance - Sean Williams   s   847

Cantares, Rodrigo (Military Personnel)
Messenger on the Battlefield - Melinda Rice *w* 531

Capel, Fern (Witch)
The Dragon Charmer - Jan Siegel *f* 634

Capelo, Thomas (Scientist)
Probability Sun - Nancy Kress *s* 799

Capillupo, Frank (Pilot)
The Binding Oath - Sybil Downing *w* 477

Carcera, Gina (Spouse)
Recent History - Anthony Giardina *c* 1161

Carcera, Luca (Young Man; Spouse)
Recent History - Anthony Giardina *c* 1161

Carclew, Fenella (Teenager)
Rose of Nancemillin - Malcolm MacDonald *t* 935

Cardinella, Sofia (Young Woman; Businesswoman)
Fly Me to the Moon - Kylie Adams *r* 203

Carillon (Ruler)
Shapechanger's Song - Jennifer Roberson *f* 625

Carnes, Belinda (Young Woman; Girlfriend)
Second Chances - Valerie Hansen *i* 1040

Carpenter, Ernestine "Ernie" (Teacher; Detective—Amateur)
Closer than the Bones - Dean James *m* 87

Carpenter, Luke (Businessman)
Sweet Annie - Cheryl St. John *r* 433

Carr, Anthony (Government Official)
Children of Hope - David Feintuch *s* 779

Carr, Randall (Teenager)
Children of Hope - David Feintuch *s* 779

Carrier, Judy (Lawyer)
The Vendetta Defense - Lisa Scottoline *m* 167

Carrington, Savannah (Heiress)
Hero for Hire - Sheridon Smythe *r* 432

Carson, Kit (Time Traveler)
The House That Jack Built - Robert Asprin *s* 753

Carson, Roberta (Writer)
Falling Stars - Michael Flynn *s* 782

Carstairs, Jack (Military Personnel)
Gallant Waif - Ann Gracie *r* 281

Carter, Samantha (Scientist; Military Personnel)
The Morpheus Factor - Ashley McConnell *s* 806

Cartier, Anne (Actress; Teacher)
Mute Witness - Charles O'Brien *m* 134
Mute Witness - Charles O'Brien *t* 953

Cartland, Kennard Wyndgate "Kasey" (Nobleman; Artist)
The Painted Lady - Barbara Metzger *r* 378

Cartwright, April (Single Parent)
Man on a Mission - Carla Cassidy *r* 243

Cartwright, Luke (Store Owner; Hero)
Taps - Willie Morris *c* 1205

Caruso, Bethany (Parent)
The Faithful Narrative of a Pastor's Disappearance - Benjamin Anastas *c* 1104

Carver, J.D. (Construction Worker; Hotel Owner)
All Shook Up - Susan Andersen *r* 207

Casement, Danny (Spaceman)
Spheres of Heaven - Charles Sheffield *s* 829

Casey (Clone)
Terraforming Earth - Jack Williamson *s* 848

Castillo, Consuela (Lover)
The Dying Animal - Philip Roth *c* 1223

Catherine of Somerset (Noblewoman; Imposter)
Secret Vows - Mary Reed McCall *r* 368

Catherine the Great (Historical Figure; Ruler)
To the Hermitage - Malcolm Bradbury *c* 1118

To the Hermitage - Malcolm Bradbury *t* 858

Cathryn of Greneforde (Noblewoman; Abuse Victim)
The Holding - Claudia Dain *r* 250

Cathy (Teenager; Runaway)
Chalktown - Melinda Haynes *c* 1169

Catriona (Scientist)
Mr. Mee - Andrew Crumey *c* 1137

Cavaco, Mike (Cook; Taxi Driver)
Making over Mike - Lisa Plumley *r* 394

Cavan, Teresa (Servant; Heroine)
The Cavan Breed - Les Savage Jr. *w* 537

Cavendish, Beatrice (Heiress)
All a Woman Wants - Patricia Rice *r* 404

Celeste (Relative)
Father of the Four Passages - Lois-Ann Yamanaka *c* 1246

Celie (Widow(er); Servant)
A Dish Taken Cold - Anne Perry *t* 959

Cellars, Colin (Detective—Police)
Outer Perimeter - Ken Goddard *s* 790

Celsa (Girlfriend)
The Stone Garden - Bill Brooks *w* 461

Ceniza-Bendiga, Elena Teresa (Spy)
Declare - Tim Powers *h* 723

Cezer (Animal)
Kingdoms of Light - Alan Dean Foster *f* 582

Chakkri (Animal)
The Tainted Snuff Box - Rosemary Stevens *t* 983

Chalder, Tomas (Miner)
Focus - Sallie Lowenstein *s* 801

Challis, Claire (Artist)
Balak - Stephen Mark Rainey *h* 727

Chambers, Vivian (Bodyguard)
When the Cold Wind Blows - Charles L. Grant *h* 682

Chandler, Eli (Grandparent; Farmer)
A Painted House - John Grisham *c* 1165

Chandler, Luke (Child; Narrator)
A Painted House - John Grisham *c* 1165

Chandler, Susan "Sunny" Hadden (Heiress)
Walk on the Wild Side - Donna Kauffman *r* 326

Chandler, Zinc (Detective—Police)
Hangman - Michael Slade *h* 738

Chaplin, Alessandro (Detective—Police)
Talisker - Miller Lau *f* 603

Chaplin, Charlie (Historical Figure; Actor)
A Few Minutes Past Midnight - Stuart M. Kaminsky *m* 91
A Few Minutes Past Midnight - Stuart M. Kaminsky *t* 921

Chapman, Michael (Photographer)
The Midnight Side - Natasha Mostert *h* 713

Char (Mythical Creature)
The Inheritance - Nancy Varian Berberick *f* 556

Charnock, Jack (Scientist; Terrorist)
A River out of Eden - John Hockenberry *w* 491

Chase (Amnesiac)
Back in Baby's Arms - Tina Wainscott *r* 443

Chase, Kendra (Noblewoman)
Amber - Lauren Royal *r* 416

Chastain, Alexis (Royalty; Teacher)
The Runaway Princess - Patricia Forsythe *r* 270

Cheng-Ming (Student)
The Hell Screens - Alvin Lu *h* 700

Chessman, Jack (Police Officer)
Alyssa Again - Sylvie Kurtz *r* 341

Child-of-the-Waters (Indian)
The Hidden Treasure of the Chisos - Patrick Dearen *w* 473

Chisom, Joshua (Child; Healer)
The Most Important Little Boy in the World - Dean Briggs *i* 1022

Chopra, Sulamith (Scientist)
The Chronoliths - Robert Charles Wilson *s* 849

Chris (Businessman)
The Lost Daughter of Happiness - Geling Yan *w* 551
The Lost Daughter of Happiness - Geling Yan *t* 1001

Chrissie (Parent)
The Peppered Moth - Margaret Drabble *c* 1142

Christian, Arthur (Nobleman)
The Beautiful Stranger - Julia London *r* 353

Christie, Richard (Detective—Police)
Taken - Kathleen George *c* 1159

Christina (Royalty; Spouse)
Tempting - Susan Johnson *r* 321

Chrysippus, Aurelius (Banker; Publisher)
Ode to a Banker - Lindsey Davis *t* 877

Clah, Clifford (Indian; Shaman)
Shooting Chant - Aimee Thurlo *w* 543

Clah, Ella (Police Officer; Indian)
Red Mesa - Aimee Thurlo *m* 183
Shooting Chant - Aimee Thurlo *w* 543

Claiborne (Military Personnel)
Fire on the Waters - David Poyer *t* 963

Clairveau, Marcel (Spaceship Captain)
Deepsix - Jack McDevitt *s* 807

Clark, Megan (Librarian; Anthropologist)
Murder Past Due - D.R. Meredith *m* 119

Claudius (Animal)
Wolf in Sheep's Clothing - Ann Campbell *m* 20

Claypoole, Rachman (Military Personnel)
Hangfire - David Sherman *s* 830

Clayton, Jessica (Store Owner)
The Perfect Family - Patricia Potter *r* 397

Clayton, Randall (Nobleman)
Perfect Sin - Kat Martin *r* 363

Cleo (Clone)
Terraforming Earth - Jack Williamson *s* 848

Cleve, Alexander (Actor)
Eclipse - John Banville *c* 1107

Cleve, Lily (Teenager)
Eclipse - John Banville *c* 1107

Cley (Religious)
The Beyond - Jeffrey Ford *f* 581

Codine, Ben (Outlaw)
The Masked Gun - Barry Cord *w* 469

Cody, Buffalo Bill (Historical Figure)
The Buffalo Hunters - Gary McCarthy *w* 504

Cody, Samuel (Businessman; Diplomat)
The Indiscretion - Judith Ivory *r* 311

Coffey, Jack (Detective—Private)
Just One Kiss - Carla Cassidy *r* 242

Coke, Edward (Historical Figure; Judge)
I, Roger Williams - Mary Lee Settle *t* 979

Cole, Blackie (Singer; Lesbian)
Under the Mink - Lisa E. Davis *t* 878

Cole, Larry (Police Officer)
The Devil's Shadow - Hugh Holton *m* 83

Colin (Orphan)
Hell on Earth - Michael Reaves   *f*   622

Colin of Shanekill (Warrior)
Irish Hope - Donna Fletcher   *r*   269

Colleen (Young Woman)
DoOon Mode - Piers Anthony   *f*   553

Collier, Kellie (Spacewoman)
Deepsix - Jack McDevitt   *s*   807

Collins, Brad (Cowboy)
Brannick: And the Untamed West - Harold G.
    Ross   *w*   534

Collins, Cassie (Single Parent)
Do You Take This Rebel? - Sherryl Woods   *r*   451

Collins, Michael (Historical Figure; Political Figure)
1921 - Morgan Llywelyn   *t*   933

Colvin, Roger (Businessman)
T2: Infiltrator - S.M. Stirling   *s*   834

Compton, Bill (Vampire)
Dead Until Dark - Charlaine Harris   *h*   685

Conaire (Royalty)
The Destruction of the Inn - Randy Lee
    Eickhoff   *t*   888

Connavar (Warrior)
The Sword in the Storm - David Gemmell   *f*   585

Connor, Amanda (Businesswoman)
Making over Mike - Lisa Plumley   *r*   394

Connor, John (Teenager)
T2: Infiltrator - S.M. Stirling   *s*   834

Connors, Beatrice "Birdie" (Relative; Doctor)
The Four Seasons - Mary Alice Monroe   *r*   384

Conor (Religious)
Son of the Shadows - Juliet Marillier   *f*   608

Conroy, Sara (Single Parent; Divorced Person)
Loving a Lonesome Cowboy - Debbi Rawlins   *r*   402

Constable, Jasper (Religious)
The Fields of Eden - Richard S. Wheeler   *t*   994

Constantine (Ruler; Historical Figure)
Priestess of Avalon - Marion Zimmer
    Bradley   *t*   859

Constantius Chlorus, Flavius (Ruler; Historical
    Figure)
Priestess of Avalon - Marion Zimmer
    Bradley   *t*   859

Cook-Goldman, Mirella (Lawyer; Parent)
A Perfect Arrangement - Suzanne Berne   *c*   1114

Cooper, Donna (Rodeo Rider; Heroine)
Queen of the Rodeo - Michael Little   *w*   501

Copeland, Virgil (Scientist)
Limit of Vision - Linda Nagata   *s*   812

Coper, Henry (Villain)
Man from Wolf River - John D. Nesbitt   *w*   511

Coppersmith, Cynthia (Bride)
A Common Life - Jan Karon   *c*   1179

Corbett, Hugh (Government Official; Investigator)
The Demon Archer - P.C. Doherty   *m*   41
The Demon Archer - P.C. Doherty   *t*   880

Corbin, Jeff (Lawyer)
Girl of the Manzanos - Barbara Spencer
    Foster   *w*   481

Cord, Mackenzy "Mac" (Bounty Hunter)
Hero for Hire - Sheridon Smythe   *r*   432

Corey, Steve (Veteran)
The Seduction of Ellen - Nan Ryan   *r*   417

Corinne (Businesswoman)
Seaside - Terri Blackstock   *i*   1016

Corland, Rob (Health Care Professional; Boyfriend)
A Special Kind of Family - Eileen Berger   *i*   1014

Corn Flower (Indian; Shaman)
Raven Mocker - Don Coldsmith   *t*   869
Raven Mocker - Don Coldsmith   *w*   467

Cornelisz, Jeronimus (Apothecary)
Company: The Story of a Murderer - Arabella
    Edge   *t*   887

Cornelius, Ellen (Care Giver; Single Parent)
The Seduction of Ellen - Nan Ryan   *r*   417

Corso, Frank (Journalist)
Fury - G.M. Ford   *m*   55

Cortez, Rebecca (Military Personnel; Doctor)
Operation Sierra-75 - Thomas S. Gressman   *s*   791

Cosini, Aljaz (Guide; Accident Victim)
Death of a River Guide - Richard Flanagan   *c*   1151

Cosini, Harry (Parent)
Death of a River Guide - Richard Flanagan   *c*   1151

Coss, Roxane (Singer)
Bel Canto - Ann Patchett   *c*   1217

Costa, Nikos (Spaceship Captain)
Ship of Fools - Richard Paul Russo   *s*   825

Cougar Eyes (Indian)
Buffalo Gordon - J.P. Sinclair Lewis   *t*   927

Coulter, Bethany (Handicapped)
Phantom Waltz - Catherine Anderson   *r*   208

Courbet, Jean Luc "Jack" (Writer; Vampire)
Bound in Blood - Thomas Lord   *h*   699

Courbet, Noel (Actress; Vampire)
Bound in Blood - Thomas Lord   *h*   699

Covington, Grace "Candi" (Social Worker;
    Detective—Amateur)
Mama Cracks a Mask of Innocence - Nora
    DeLoach   *m*   39

Covington, Simone (Paralegal)
Mama Cracks a Mask of Innocence - Nora
    DeLoach   *m*   39

Cox, Luther (Detective—Police)
Natural Law - D.R. Schanker   *m*   165

Coyle, Emma (Spouse)
A Trail to Wounded Knee - Tim Champlin   *t*   864

Coyle, Thaddeus (Military Personnel; Government
    Official)
A Trail to Wounded Knee - Tim Champlin   *t*   864

Craer (Thief)
The Vacant Throne - Ed Greenwood   *f*   586

Craig, Clare (Divorced Person; Single Parent)
Thursdays at Eight - Debbie Macomber   *r*   360

Cranford, Peregrine (Gentleman; Twin)
The Riddle of the Shipwrecked Spinster - Patricia
    Veryan   *r*   441

Cranford, Piers (Nobleman; Twin)
The Riddle of the Shipwrecked Spinster - Patricia
    Veryan   *r*   441

Creeper (Murderer)
Concrete Desert - Jon Talton   *w*   542

Creighton, Ken (Architect)
Gemini Rising - Brian McNaughton   *h*   709

Creighton, Marcia (Journalist)
Gemini Rising - Brian McNaughton   *h*   709

Creighton, Melody (Teenager)
Gemini Rising - Brian McNaughton   *h*   709

Crepsley, Larten (Vampire)
Cirque Du Freak - Darren Shan   *h*   734

Cristo (Religious)
Enemy Glory - Karen Michalson   *f*   610

Criswell, Marissa (Single Parent; Health Care
    Professional)
Just One Kiss - Carla Cassidy   *r*   242

Crosby, Julianna (Spouse)
Ribbon of Years - Robin Lee Hatcher   *i*   1043

Crown, Maggie (Parent; Divorced Person)
Kinship Theory - Hester Kaplan   *c*   1178

Cuesta, Willie (Detective—Private)
The Ultimate Havana - John Lantigua   *m*   101

Cullinane, Jason (Nobleman)
Not Quite Scaramouche - Joel Rosenberg   *f*   626

Cullver, Suzanne (Widow(er); Handicapped)
No Eye Can See - Jane Kirkpatrick   *t*   925

Cullyn (Woodsman)
Yesterday's Kings - Angus Wells   *f*   648

Culpepper, Jett (Detective—Private)
Scent of Murder - Cynthia G. Alwyn   *m*   2

Cunningham, Zoe (Young Woman; Editor)
The Bay of Angels - Anita Brookner   *c*   1120

Custer, George Armstrong (Military Personnel;
    Historical Figure)
American Woman - R. Garcia y Robertson   *w*   485

Custer, George Armstrong Jr. (Military Personnel)
The Year the Cloud Fell - Kurt R.A.
    Giambastini   *s*   788

Cutler, Patrick (Teenager; Runaway)
Dead North - Sue Henry   *w*   490
Dead North - Sue Henry   *m*   80

Cutter, Jake (Spy)
Avengers - Brian Lumley   *h*   702

Cygnet (Teenager)
Primrose Past - Caroline Rose Hunt   *t*   914

Cynster, Alasdair Reginald "Lucifer" (Gentleman;
    Collector)
All about Love - Stephanie Laurens   *r*   346

Cyrion, Philipa (Astrologer)
Heart of Stone - Denny DeMartino   *s*   772

D

Da Barca, Daniel (Political Prisoner)
The Carpenter's Pencil - Manuel Rivas   *t*   970

Da Yong (Criminal)
The Lost Daughter of Happiness - Geling
    Yan   *t*   1001
The Lost Daughter of Happiness - Geling
    Yan   *w*   551

d'Acquin, Josse (Knight)
Ashes of the Elements - Alys Clare   *m*   23
Ashes of the Elements - Alys Clare   *t*   865

Dahak (Sorcerer)
The Storm of Heaven - Thomas Harlan   *f*   587

Dain (Mythical Creature; Nobleman)
The Chalice - Deborah Chester   *f*   565

Daisy (Teenager; Friend)
We're So Famous - Jaime Clarke   *c*   1132

Dale (Young Woman; Relative)
Kinship Theory - Hester Kaplan   *c*   1178

Dalemwood, George (Writer)
The Wooden Sea - Jonathan Carroll   *f*   562

Dalgliesh, Adam (Police Officer)
Death in Holy Orders - P.D. James   *m*   88

Dallas, Eve (Detective—Homicide)
Betrayal in Death - J.D. Robb   *s*   822
Seduction in Death - J.D. Robb   *r*   410

Dallas, Nathan (Journalist)
Nighttime Guardian - Amanda Stevens   *r*   435

E

Found, Michael (Professor)
Thoroughly Kissed - Kristine Grayson   *r*   286

Fowl, Artemis (Thief; Child)
Artemis Fowl - Eoin Colfer   *f*   566

Fox, Charlie (Cowboy; Actor)
Cowboy for Hire - Alice Duncan   *r*   261

Fox, Leah (Historical Figure; Occultist)
The Sweet By and By - Jeanne Mackin   *t*   936

Fox, Maggie (Historical Figure; Occultist)
The Sweet By and By - Jeanne Mackin   *t*   936

Fox, Travis (Time Traveler)
Time Traders II - Andre Norton   *s*   814

Franklin, Anna (Single Parent; Journalist)
Mapping the Edge - Sarah Dunant   *c*   1143

Franklin, Benjamin (Historical Figure; Political
Figure)
Rise to Rebellion - Jeff Shaara   *t*   980
The Shadows of God - J. Gregory Keyes   *f*   595

Franklin, Lily (Child)
Mapping the Edge - Sarah Dunant   *c*   1143

Franks, Joseph (Detective—Police)
Holy Rollers - J. Newman   *h*   714

Franx (Military Personnel; Convict)
The Thirteenth Legion - Gav Thorpe   *f*   643

Fraser, Anora "Mary" (Noblewoman)
The Fraser Bride - Lois Greiman   *r*   289

Fraser, Cleopatra "Cleo" (Archaeologist)
The Price of Passion - Susan Sizemore   *r*   428

Fraser, Poppy (Spouse)
The Church Ladies - Lisa E. Samson   *i*   1082

Frazer, Byron (Psychologist; Widow(er))
Finding Ian - Stella Cameron   *r*   237

Fredieu, Emily (Slave)
Cane River - Lalita Tademy   *t*   986

Freemantle, Leonora (Gentlewoman; Teacher)
The Wedding Wager - Deborah Hale   *r*   292

Friemann, Lisa (Police Officer; Scientist)
The Cassandra Complex - Brian Stableford   *s*   832

Frisch, Nettie (Police Officer; Computer Expert)
Third Person Singular - K.J. Erickson   *m*   49

Frost, Gunny (Military Personnel)
Operation Sierra-75 - Thomas S. Gressman   *s*   791

Fulla (Scientist)
The Biographer's Tale - A.S. Byatt   *c*   1124

Fuller, Josephine "Jo" (Investigator; Divorced
Person)
At Large - Lynne Murray   *m*   130

Fusang (Prostitute)
The Lost Daughter of Happiness - Geling
Yan   *w*   551
The Lost Daughter of Happiness - Geling
Yan   *t*   1001

G

Gage, Thomas (Historical Figure; Military
Personnel)
Rise to Rebellion - Jeff Shaara   *t*   980

Gallagher, Dan (Journalist; Critic)
The Trouble with Mary - Millie Criswell   *r*   248

Galter, Lucien (Farmer)
American Empire: Blood and Iron - Harry
Turtledove   *s*   839

Garcia y Grant, Christina (Lawyer; Innkeeper)
Carreta de la Muerte (Cart of Death) - Mari
Ulmer   *w*   544
Carreta de la Muerte (Cart of Death) - Mari
Ulmer   *m*   185

Gardner, Sam (Religious)
Just Shy of Harmony - Philip Gulley   *i*   1037

Gareth of Summerfield (Nobleman; Criminal)
The Truest Heart - Samantha James   *r*   316

Garland, Ed (Rancher)
The Bloody Quarter - Les Savage Jr.   *w*   536

Garnet, Henry (Religious)
A Fifth of November - Paul West   *t*   993

Garrett, Andrew (Military Personnel; Veteran)
The Horse Soldier - Merline Lovelace   *r*   355

Garrett, Pat (Lawman; Historical Figure)
The Stone Garden - Bill Brooks   *w*   461
The Stone Garden - Bill Brooks   *t*   860

Garth, Isabel (Teacher; Artist)
The Gripping Beast - Margot Wadley   *m*   187

Garvey, Flynn (Bastard Son)
Sweethearts of the Twilight Lanes - Luanne
Jones   *r*   324

Garvey, Hannah (Businesswoman)
South of Sanity - Suzann Ledbetter   *r*   349

Gary (Boyfriend)
Paradise Park - Allegra Goodman   *c*   1162

Gaulden, Faro (Relative)
The Peppered Moth - Margaret Drabble   *c*   1142

Gavril (Royalty)
The Chalice - Deborah Chester   *f*   565

Gayle, Tassis (Ruler)
The Saints of the Sword - John Marco   *f*   607

Genevieve of Harwick (Noblewoman; Stowaway)
Summer's Bride - Catherine Archer   *r*   211

Gentry, Henry (Military Personnel; Historical
Figure)
When This Cruel War Is Over - Thomas
Fleming   *t*   894

George, Prince of Wales (Royalty; Historical Figure)
The Tainted Snuff Box - Rosemary Stevens   *t*   983

Geraint, Tristan (Nobleman)
The Secret Swan - Shana Abe   *r*   202

Gerald (Terrorist)
K Falls - Skye Kathleen Moody   *w*   509

Gerrard (Warrior)
Planeshift - J. Robert King   *f*   596

Gershon, Joseph (Worker)
Lick Creek - Brad Kessler   *t*   923

Getz, Julie (Child)
Ordinary Horror - David Searcy   *h*   733

Getz, Mike (Salesman)
Ordinary Horror - David Searcy   *h*   733

Giambelli, Sophia (Public Relations; Heiress)
The Villa - Nora Roberts   *r*   412

Gibson, Carole Ann (Detective—Private; Lawyer)
Paradise Interrupted - Penny Mickelbury   *m*   120

Gill, Randi (Child-Care Giver)
A Perfect Arrangement - Suzanne Berne   *c*   1114

Gillette, Wyatt (Computer Expert)
The Blue Nowhere - Jeffery Deaver   *m*   37

Gillian, Bucy (Spouse)
Grace - Jane Roberts Wood   *w*   550

Gillian, Grace (Teacher)
Grace - Jane Roberts Wood   *w*   550
Grace - Jane Roberts Wood   *t*   997

Gillian of Westerbrook (Noblewoman; Fugitive)
The Truest Heart - Samantha James   *r*   316

Gillo, Thru (Military Personnel)
The Shasht War - Christopher Rowley   *f*   627

Gilmore, Daniel (Widow(er); Gentleman)
Time After Time - Constance O'Day-Flannery   *r*   391

Gilmore, Truman (Salesman)
Duet for the Devil - T. Winter-Damon   *h*   750

Giraldus (Nobleman)
The Thirteenth Scroll - Rebecca Neason   *f*   613

Glendenning (Nobleman)
Lady of Skye - Patricia Cabot   *r*   233

Glitsky, Abe (Detective—Homicide)
The Hearing - John Lescroart   *m*   103

Glover, Ralph (Artisan)
The Boy-Bishop's Glovemaker - Michael
Jecks   *t*   918

Godfridus (Artisan)
Mirabilis - Susann Cokal   *t*   867

Godoy, Diego de (Adventurer)
The Discovery of Chocolate - James Runcie   *t*   977

Godwin (Veteran; Lawman)
Murder on Good Friday - Sara Conway   *m*   26
Murder on Good Friday - Sara Conway   *t*   871

Gold, Sheldon A. (Lawyer)
Uncommon Justice - Terry Devane   *c*   1139

Goldman, Howard (Spouse; Architect)
A Perfect Arrangement - Suzanne Berne   *c*   1114

Goldson, Frieda (Young Woman)
On Her Way Home - Harriet Rochlin   *t*   973

Goldson, Ida (Teenager)
On Her Way Home - Harriet Rochlin   *t*   973

Goode, John (Professor)
Field Guide - Gwendolen Gross   *c*   1166

Goode, Leon (Relative)
Field Guide - Gwendolen Gross   *c*   1166

Goodlow, Sam (Detective—Private)
Sleepeasy - T.M. Wright   *h*   751

Goodnight, Jimmy (Captive; Cowboy)
Code of the West - Aaron Latham   *w*   500
Code of the West - Aaron Latham   *t*   926

Goodnight, Revelie (Spouse)
Code of the West - Aaron Latham   *w*   500

Gooseberry, Marvella (Neighbor)
Meteor in the Madhouse - Leon Forrest   *c*   1153

Gordon, Nate (Military Personnel; Slave)
Buffalo Gordon - J.P. Sinclair Lewis   *t*   927

Gordon, Rose (Widow(er))
The Power of the Dog - Thomas Savage   *w*   538

Gorgrael (Sorcerer)
Battleaxe - Sara Douglass   *f*   573

Gould, Anne (Parent; Widow(er))
The Bay of Angels - Anita Brookner   *c*   1120

Gould, Henry Frye (Settler)
The Far Field - Edie Meidav   *c*   1201
The Far Field - Edie Meidav   *t*   946

Gould, Simon (Step-Parent; Spouse)
The Bay of Angels - Anita Brookner   *c*   1120

Gourmet Detective (Consultant; Detective—
Amateur)
Eat, Drink, and Be Buried - Peter King   *m*   95

Graceful (Servant)
Fire in Beulah - Rilla Askew   *t*   853

Grady, Jake (Rancher)
The Masked Gun - Barry Cord   *w*   469

Character Name Index

Johansson, Hilda (Servant; Detective—Amateur)
Green Grow the Victims - Jeanne M. Dams   *m*   33
Green Grow the Victims - Jeanne M. Dams   *t*   874

Johnny (Assistant; Spy)
The Far Field - Edie Meidav   *c*   1201

Johnson, Alma (Security Officer)
Tails You Lose - Lisa Smedman   *f*   637

Johnson, Evan (Veteran)
The Edge of Town - Dorothy Garlock   *t*   898

Johnson, Samuel (Historical Figure; Writer)
According to Queeney - Beryl Bainbridge   *t*   854

Jonas, Paul (Military Personnel)
Sea of Silver Light - Tad Williams   *f*   651

Jones, Aurora Q. (Businesswoman)
The Emerald Burrito of Oz - John Skipp   *f*   636

Jones, Camellia (Relative)
Quakertown - Lee Martin   *w*   503

Jones, Cami (Librarian)
Overnight Cinderella - Katherine Garbera   *r*   275

Jones, Casey (Detective—Private)
Better Off Dead - Katy Munger   *m*   128

Jones, David (Consultant; Businessman)
Be My Valentine - Sheila Rabe   *r*   399

Jones, Deckard (Friend; Addict)
Singing Boy - Dennis McFarland   *c*   1199

Jones, Fearless (Veteran; Friend)
Fearless Jones - Walter Mosley   *m*   126
Fearless Jones - Walter Mosley   *c*   1206

Jones, Gram Gussie (Grandparent)
Meteor in the Madhouse - Leon Forrest   *c*   1153

Jones, Jane (Gentlewoman)
Slammerkin - Emma Donoghue   *t*   882

Jones, Joubert Antoine (Professor; Narrator)
Meteor in the Madhouse - Leon Forrest   *c*   1153

Jones, Julie (Young Woman)
The Edge of Town - Dorothy Garlock   *t*   898

Jones, Kalem (Military Personnel)
Broken Ranks - Hiram King   *w*   497

Jones, Lena (Detective—Private; Police Officer)
Desert Noir - Betty Webb   *m*   190

Jones, Little Washington (Gardener)
Quakertown - Lee Martin   *t*   940
Quakertown - Lee Martin   *w*   503

Jones, Renie (Cousin)
Suture Self - Mary Daheim   *m*   32

Jordan, Tripp (Police Officer)
The Prodigal's Return - Lynn Bulock   *i*   1023

Jordon, Doris (Sidekick; Lawyer)
Carreta de la Muerte (Cart of Death) - Mari Ulmer   *w*   544

Jorth, Ellen (Young Woman)
To the Last Man - Zane Grey   *w*   488

Jose (Military Personnel)
Victor Lopez at the Alamo - James Rice   *w*   529

Joseph (Time Traveler)
The Graveyard Game - Kage Baker   *s*   755

Joshua (Religious)
The Parables of Joshua - Joseph F. Girzone   *i*   1036

Joy, Otis (Religious; Imposter)
The Reaper - Peter Lovesey   *m*   107

Julia (Historical Figure)
The Love-Artist - Jane Alison   *t*   852

Juniper Tree Burning "Jennie" (Young Woman; Student)
Juniper Tree Burning - Goldberry Long   *c*   1188

Junzo (Wizard)
The Phoenix - Stephen D. Sullivan   *f*   640

Juremi (Captive)
The Siege of Isfahan - Jean-Christophe Rufin   *t*   976

K

Ka (Prehistoric Human; Shaman)
Song of the Axe - John R. Dann   *t*   875

Kage (Military Personnel; Convict)
The Thirteenth Legion - Gav Thorpe   *f*   643

Kahlo, Christina (Historical Figure; Narrator)
Frida - Barbara Mujica   *c*   1207

Kahlo, Frida (Artist; Historical Figure)
Frida - Barbara Mujica   *c*   1207

Kaia (Nobleman)
Devil's Sea - Greg Donegan   *s*   774

Kalner, Jacob (Military Personnel)
Jerusalem's Heart - Bodie Thoene   *i*   1091
Jerusalem's Heart - Bodie Thoene   *t*   988

Kalner, Lori (Nurse)
Jerusalem's Heart - Bodie Thoene   *t*   988
Jerusalem's Heart - Bodie Thoene   *i*   1091

Kandinsky, Vasily (Historical Figure; Artist)
Burnt Umber - Sheldon Greene   *t*   906

Karan (Psychic)
A Shadow on the Glass - Ian Irvine   *f*   592

Karen (Mythical Creature; Real Estate Agent)
Nothing but Blue Skies - Tom Holt   *f*   589

Karlstad, Egon (Scientist)
Jupiter - Ben Bova   *s*   760

Karma, Billy (Criminal)
The Outpost - Mike Resnick   *s*   819

Kate (Servant)
A Spell of Winter - Helen Dunmore   *c*   1144

Kati (Ruler)
Empress of Light - James C. Glass   *s*   789

Katz, Phil (Doctor)
Eternity - Tamara Thorne   *h*   743

Kauffman, Dora (Servant; Companion)
Lilac Blossom Time - Carrie Bender   *i*   1010

Kaufman, Daniel (Police Officer)
Special Effects - Kevin McCarthy   *s*   805

Kaufman, Lyle (Military Personnel)
Probability Sun - Nancy Kress   *s*   799

Kavanaugh, Timothy (Bridegroom; Religious)
A Common Life - Jan Karon   *c*   1179

Kay (Knight)
Exiled from Camelot - Cherith Baldry   *f*   555

Kazakov, Nathan (Writer; Handicapped)
Strange Fire - Melvin Jules Bukiet   *c*   1122

Kean, Hester (Servant)
The Birth of Blue Satan - Patricia Wynn   *m*   200
The Birth of Blue Satan - Patricia Wynn   *t*   1000

Keaton, Sam (Lawman)
Thunder Voice - Sigmund Brouwer   *w*   462

Keegan, Phil (Police Officer)
Triple Pursuit - Ralph McInerny   *m*   116

Keene, Bryce (Widow(er); Nobleman)
A Proper Affair - Victoria Malvey   *r*   362

Kelly, Irene (Journalist)
Flight - Jan Burke   *m*   19

Kelly, Luther "Yellowstone" (Scout; Gunfighter)
Kelly and the Three-Toed Horse - Peter Bowen   *t*   857

Kelly and the Three-Toed Horse - Peter Bowen   *w*   456

Kelsey, Andrew (Historical Figure; Settler)
An Ordinary Woman - Cecelia Holland   *w*   493

Kelsey, Ben (Historical Figure; Settler)
An Ordinary Woman - Cecelia Holland   *w*   493

Kelsey, Nancy (Settler; Historical Figure)
An Ordinary Woman - Cecelia Holland   *w*   493

Kendall, Alice (Lawyer; Gentlewoman)
Nightingale's Gate - Linda Francis Lee   *r*   350

Kendall, Annie (Con Artist)
Too Good to Be True - Kasey Michaels   *r*   382

Kendrick, Ryan (Rancher; Wealthy)
Phantom Waltz - Catherine Anderson   *r*   208

Kenmare, Fionna (Singer)
License Invoked - Robert Asprin   *f*   554

Kennedy, Agnes (Criminal)
Water of Death - Paul Johnston   *s*   797

Kennedy, Dillon "Duck" (Detective—Police)
Killer Riches - Chassie West   *m*   191

Kennedy, Ella (Student—Graduate)
Karlmarx.com - Susan Coll   *t*   1134

Kent, Alexander "Alex" (Doctor)
The Colors of Love - Vanessa Grant   *r*   283

Kentraine, Beth (Student)
Beyond World's End - Mercedes Lackey   *f*   601

Kenyon, Liz (Widow(er))
Thursdays at Eight - Debbie Macomber   *r*   360

Kepesh, David (Professor; Parent)
The Dying Animal - Philip Roth   *c*   1223

Kerney, Kevin (Police Officer)
Under the Color of Law - Michael McGarrity   *w*   505
Under the Color of Law - Michael McGarrity   *m*   114

Kerr, Margaret (Detective—Amateur; Spouse)
A Trust Betrayed - Candace M. Robb   *m*   157
A Trust Betrayed - Candace M. Robb   *t*   971

Kerslake, Susan (Housekeeper; Smuggler)
The Dragon's Bride - Jo Beverley   *r*   223

Kethol (Warrior)
Not Quite Scaramouche - Joel Rosenberg   *f*   626

Kethrenan (Royalty)
The Inheritance - Nancy Varian Berberick   *f*   556

Kilbourn, Joanne (Professor; Detective—Amateur)
Burying Ariel - Gail Bowen   *m*   10

Killian, Nella (Widow(er))
So Shall We Stand - Elyse Larson   *i*   1055

Kills Crow, Kole (Fugitive; Indian)
You Never Can Tell - Kathleen Eagle   *r*   263

Kilory, Sarah (Spouse)
American Woman - R. Garcia y Robertson   *w*   485

Kimball, Kate Stanislaski (Dancer; Teacher)
Considering Kate - Nora Roberts   *r*   411

Kimmelman, Roger (Singer)
Hidden Gifts - Rick Hamlin   *i*   1039

Kincaid, Duncan (Police Officer)
A Finer End - Deborah Crombie   *m*   29

Kincaid, Rory (Businessman; Political Figure)
This Perfect Kiss - Christie Ridgway   *r*   407

King, Darryl (Villain)
Queen of the Rodeo - Michael Little   *w*   501

King, Nathan "Eannatum" (Witch; Immortal)
Destiny - Maggie Shayne   *r*   425

King James (Slave)
The Blackbirder - James L. Nelson   *t*   951

Liu Ahan (Spouse)
Wintry Night - Qiao Li   t   929

Liu Mingji (Military Personnel)
Wintry Night - Qiao Li   t   929

Llewelyn (Religious; Magician)
Enemy Glory - Karen Michalson   f   610

Llian (Historian)
A Shadow on the Glass - Ian Irvine   f   592

Lloyd (Police Officer)
Scene of Crime - Jill McGown   m   115

Lloyd, Hunter (Lawyer)
7B - Stella Cameron   r   236

Lobsang (Religious)
Thief of Time - Terry Pratchett   f   620

Lockhart, Olivia (Judge)
16 Lighthouse Road - Debbie Macomber   r   359

Loholt (Young Man)
Exiled from Camelot - Cherith Baldry   f   555

Lone Hawk (Indian; Warrior)
Cheyenne Summer - Vella Munn   w   510

Longbourne, Elissa (Noblewoman; Parent)
A Rogue's Embrace - Margaret Moore   r   386

Longbourne, Will (Child)
A Rogue's Embrace - Margaret Moore   r   386

Longfellow, Richard (Farmer)
A Mischief in the Snow - Margaret Miles   m   121

Longknife, Ray (Military Personnel)
They Also Serve - Mike Moscoe   s   811

Longshadow, Jonah (Convict; Horse Trainer)
Longshadow's Woman - Bronwyn Williams   r   448

Lopez, Victor (Child)
Victor Lopez at the Alamo - James Rice   w   529

Lost, Emma (Professor; Writer)
Thoroughly Kissed - Kristine Grayson   r   286

Lotari, Kathy (Doctor; Spacewoman)
Borrowed Tides - Paul Levinson   s   800

Lou (Saloon Keeper/Owner)
The Pickup Artist - Terry Bisson   s   759

Loudon, Gabriel (Nobleman; Spy)
Fallen - Emma Jensen   r   318

Loudon, Quinn (Lawyer; Fugitive)
The Lawman Meets His Bride - Meagan
   McKinney   r   374

Louis XIV (Royalty; Historical Figure)
Gardener to the King - Frederic Richaud   t   968

Lovell, John Henry (Diplomat; Knight)
Lilies on the Lake - Katherine Kingsley   r   333

Lovell, Pierre (Trapper)
Bodie Gone - Bill Hyde   w   495

Loving, Jack (Cowboy)
Code of the West - Aaron Latham   t   926
Code of the West - Aaron Latham   w   500

Lowe, Hyman "Hy-Lo" (Parent; Alcoholic)
The Warmest December - Bernice L.
   McFadden   c   1198

Lowe, Kenzie (Narrator; Abuse Victim)
The Warmest December - Bernice L.
   McFadden   c   1198

Lu, Che (Military Personnel)
Area 51: The Grail - Robert Doherty   s   773

Lu-Tze (Religious)
Thief of Time - Terry Pratchett   f   620

Lucan (Fugitive; Murderer)
Aiding & Abetting - Muriel Spark   c   1229

Lucas, Billy (Bodyguard)
The Heiress and the Bodyguard - Ryanne
   Corey   r   244

Lucia, Anthony "Pigeon Tony" (Murderer)
The Vendetta Defense - Lisa Scottoline   m   167

Lucia, Frank (Relative)
The Vendetta Defense - Lisa Scottoline   m   167

Lucine (Servant)
Three Apples Fell from Heaven - Micheline Aharonian
   Marcom   t   938

Lucy (Spouse; Parent)
Thanksgiving - Michael Dibdin   c   1141

LuLing (Artist; Relative)
The Bonesetter's Daughter - Amy Tan   c   1233

Lulu (Mutant)
The Meek - Scott Mackay   s   802

Lumet, Jack (Scientist; Spaceman)
Borrowed Tides - Paul Levinson   s   800

Lumsey, Nora (Lawyer)
Natural Law - D.R. Schanker   m   165

Luther, Martin (Historical Figure; Religious)
Storm - Reg Grant   t   904

Ly-San-Ter, Dalden (Warrior)
Heart of a Warrior - Johanna Lindsey   r   352

Lyles, Garrett (Murderer)
Beyond Belief - Roy Johansen   h   690

Lynch, Gabriel (Teenager; Runaway)
Gabriel's Story - David Anthony Durham   c   1145
Gabriel's Story - David Anthony Durham   t   886

Lynley, Thomas (Police Officer)
A Traitor to Memory - Elizabeth George   m   60

Lynx, Mahmahmi (Businesswoman)
Reunion - Alan Dean Foster   s   784

Lynx, Philip (Space Explorer)
Reunion - Alan Dean Foster   s   784

Lysandra (Healer)
The Thirteenth Scroll - Rebecca Neason   f   613

Lytton, Tafaline "Taffy" (Photographer; Time
   Traveler)
Night Visitor - Melanie Jackson   r   313

M

Mabry, Bubba (Detective—Private)
Crazy Love - Steve Brewer   m   13

MacBain, Robert "Rob" (Nobleman; Handicapped)
The Highland Wife - Lyn Stone   r   437

Macbeth, Hamish (Police Officer)
Death of a Dustman - M.C. Beaton   m   6

MacCade, Shaw (Miner; Mountain Man)
The Taming of Shaw MacCade - Judith E.
   French   r   274

MacClintock, Roger (Royalty; Military Personnel)
March Upcountry - David Weber   s   844

MacCormick, Andrew (Businessman)
The Cloud Sketcher - Richard Rayner   t   964

MacDonald, Mac (Detective—Police)
The Triumph of Katie Byrne - Barbara Taylor
   Bradford   c   1119

MacGillivray, Angus (Knight; Kidnapper)
The Beauty - Claire Delacroix   r   253

MacGowan, Ramsay (Nobleman; Rogue)
The Fraser Bride - Lois Greiman   r   289

Macgrath, Kacy (Artist)
After Twilight - Dee Davis   r   251

MacGregor, Hugh Redmond (Rancher)
MacGregor's Lantern - Corinne Joy Brown   w   463

MacGregor, Jamie (Detective—Police; Time
   Traveler)
Highland Dream - Tess Mallory   r   361

Machen, Tim (Criminal)
Deadfellas - David Whitman   h   748

MacInness, Mairi (Noblewoman)
The Highland Wife - Lyn Stone   r   437

MacIntyre, Alex (Fire Fighter)
Courting Katarina - Carol Steward   i   1089

MacIntyre, Frank (Pilot)
Terror Firma - Matthew Thomas   s   836

MacIntyre, Malcolm (Hero; Spirit)
Night Visitor - Melanie Jackson   r   313

MacKenzie, Blake (Businessman)
Seeing Stars - Vanessa Grant   r   284

MacKenzie, John Alexander (Doctor)
Murder at Bertram's Bower - Cynthia Peale   m   145

Mackenzie, Robert (Administrator)
The Rising Sun - Douglas Galbraith   c   1158

Mackenzie, Roderick (Accountant)
The Rising Sun - Douglas Galbraith   t   897

MacLaren, Alainna (Laird; Artisan)
The Stone Maiden - Susan King   r   331

MacLeod, Malky (Warrior)
Talisker - Miller Lau   f   603

MacLeod, Margaret "Maggie" (Herbalist)
Fallen - Emma Jensen   r   318

MacLeod, Ross (Foreman)
The Perfect Family - Patricia Potter   r   397

MacMillan, Tyler (Vintner; Heir)
The Villa - Nora Roberts   r   412

MacRae, Lauren (Warrior; Laird)
Intimate Enemies - Shana Abe   r   201

MacTavish (Guard)
The Last Harbor - George Foy   s   785

MacTavish, Lachlan (Businessman; Kidnapper)
All a Woman Wants - Patricia Rice   r   404

Madame (Dancer)
Flight of the Swan - Rosario Ferre   t   893

Madaris, Jacob "Jake" (Rancher)
Secret Love - Brenda Jackson   r   312

Madison (Model)
The Summerhouse - Jude Deveraux   c   1140

Madison, Gabe (Businessman)
Dawn in Eclipse Bay - Jayne Ann Krentz   r   337

Madison, Taylor (Detective—Amateur; Writer)
Twice Dead - Elizabeth Dearl   w   475

Maelwaedd, Rhodry (Nobleman)
The Fire Dragon - Katharine Kerr   f   594

Mahler, Gustav (Historical Figure; Composer)
The Artist's Wife - Max Phillips   t   962

Maika (Teenager)
The Funeral Party - Ludmila Ulitskaya   c   1238

Majere, Palin (Warrior)
Dragons of a Lost Star - Margaret Weis   f   647

Makarova, Xenia (Scientist)
Manifold: Space - Stephen Baxter   s   756

Makri, Hati (Warrior)
Hammerfall - C.J. Cherryh   s   765

Maldon, Abigail Backworth (Widow(er);
   Matchmaker)
Someone to Love - Kasey Michaels   r   381

Maldoror (Serial Killer)
Duet for the Devil - T. Winter-Damon   h   750

Malenfant, Reid (Space Explorer)
Manifold: Space - Stephen Baxter   s   756

Malevolyn, Augustus (Military Personnel)
Legacy of Blood - Richard A. Knaak   f   598

Malinari, Nephran (Vampire)
Avengers - Brian Lumley   h   702

Malley, Cathryn (Heiress)
These Granite Islands - Sarah Stonich   c   1230
These Granite Islands - Sarah Stonich   t   985

Malley, Liam (Spouse)
These Granite Islands - Sarah Stonich   c   1230

Mallo, Marisa (Young Woman)
The Carpenter's Pencil - Manuel Rivas   t   970

Mallory, Guinevere (Noblewoman; Widow(er))
The Widow's Kiss - Jane Feather   r   265

Malloy, Ted (Spouse)
Blue Horizons - Irene Bennett Brown   w   464

Malone, Cash (Thief)
Gunning for Regret - Wolf MacKenna   w   502

Malone, Mary (Immigrant; Accountant)
In His Arms - Robin Lee Hatcher   i   1042

Malvern, Deirdre (Engineer)
The Meek - Scott Mackay   s   802

Malwa (Alien)
The Tide of Victory - Eric Flint   s   781

Malysheva, Katerina (Immigrant)
The Cloud Sketcher - Richard Rayner   c   1221
The Cloud Sketcher - Richard Rayner   t   964

Mammalian, Hakob (Spy)
Declare - Tim Powers   c   1220

Mancini, Ida (Aged Person; Parent)
Choke - Chuck Palahniuk   c   1214

Mancini, Munch (Mechanic; Addict)
Unfinished Business - Barbara Seranella   m   168

Mancini, Victor (Addict; Student—Graduate)
Choke - Chuck Palahniuk   c   1214

Mandeville, Juliana "Ana" (Noblewoman; Orphan)
His Fair Lady - Kathleen Kirkwood   r   335

Mann, Summer (Psychic; Fugitive)
Special Effects - Kevin McCarthy   s   805

Manning, Connor (Rake; Landowner)
A Scarlet Bride - Sylvia McDaniel   r   371

Manning, Dan (Military Personnel)
Grace - Jane Roberts Wood   t   997

Manny (Lawyer)
Taken - Kathleen George   c   1159

Manoso, Ricardo Carlos "Ranger" (Bounty Hunter)
Seven Up - Janet Evanovich   m   50

Mantilini, Paul (Organized Crime Figure)
The Cloud Sketcher - Richard Rayner   c   1221

Manuella (Young Woman)
The Stone Garden - Bill Brooks   t   860

Mapstone, David (Professor)
Concrete Desert - Jon Talton   m   182
Concrete Desert - Jon Talton   w   542

Marc, Franz (Historical Figure; Artist)
Burnt Umber - Sheldon Greene   t   906

Marche, Rebecca (Wealthy)
Mightier than the Sword - Peggy Waide   r   442

Marcus, Jimmy (Convict; Parent)
Mystic River - Dennis Lehane   c   1183
Mystic River - Dennis Lehane   m   102

Marcus, Josie (Historical Figure; Actress)
Gunman's Rhapsody - Robert B. Parker   w   520
Gunman's Rhapsody - Robert B. Parker   t   956

Maret, Edward (Cyborg)
Edward Maret - Robert L. Katz   s   798

Margal (Sorcerer)
The Evil Returns - Hugh B. Cave   h   664

Marianne (Waiter/Waitress; Parent)
Crawling at Night - Nani Power   c   1219

Marie Francoise (Religious)
The Burning Times - Jeanne Kalogridis   t   920

Markham, Julia (Abuse Victim)
On the Strength of Wings - Marthayn
   Pelegrimas   w   524

Markham-Sands, Cecilia (Noblewoman)
A Woman of Virtue - Liz Carlyle   r   239

Marlowe, Thomas (Pirate; Plantation Owner)
The Blackbirder - James L. Nelson   t   951

Marquez, Diamantino (Revolutionary)
Flight of the Swan - Rosario Ferre   t   893

Mars, George Washington (Businessman; Veteran)
The Killer Gun - Lauran Paine   w   519

Marteau, Ross (Artist)
Animosity - David L. Lindsey   c   1185

Martin, Chester (Worker)
American Empire: Blood and Iron - Harry
   Turtledove   s   839

Martin, Lark (Homosexual)
Our Arcadia - Robin Lippincott   t   931

Martingale, Lili (Orphan; Noblewoman)
The Unsuitable Miss Martingale - Barbara
   Hazard   r   296

Marx, Groucho (Historical Figure; Entertainer)
Groucho Marx and the Broadway Murders - Ron
   Goulart   m   65
Groucho Marx and the Broadway Murders - Ron
   Goulart   t   903

Mary (Spouse; Teacher)
Mary and O'Neil - Justin Cronin   c   1136

Mary, Mother of God (Saint)
Our Lady of the Lost and Found - Diane
   Schoemperlen   c   1226

Maryn (Royalty)
The Fire Dragon - Katharine Kerr   f   594

Masha (Dancer)
Flight of the Swan - Rosario Ferre   t   893

Massey, Elizabeth (Noblewoman; Widow(er))
Seductive - Thea Devine   r   257

Massey, Nicholas (Nobleman; Heir)
Seductive - Thea Devine   r   257

Massey, Sam (Mine Owner)
Death Rides the Denver Stage - Lewis B.
   Patten   w   522

Masters, Molly (Artist; Writer)
When the Fax Lady Sings - Leslie O'Kane   m   135

Masterson, Bat (Historical Figure; Lawman)
Bucking the Tiger - Bruce Olds   t   954

Matheson, Cait (Young Woman)
Son of the Sword - J. Ardian Lee   f   605

Matheson, Dylan (Time Traveler; Martial Arts
   Expert)
Son of the Sword - J. Ardian Lee   f   605

Matlock, Joni (Pharmacist)
A January Chill - Rachel Lee   r   351

Matteo (Wizard)
The Floodgate - Elaine Cunningham   f   567

Matthew (Boyfriend)
Lilac Blossom Time - Carrie Bender   i   1010

Matthews, Chance (Scientist; Psychic)
Threshold - Caitlin R. Kiernan   h   693

Maxian (Royalty)
The Storm of Heaven - Thomas Harlan   f   587

Maxwell, Duncan "Black Bastard" (Outlaw)
Border Lord - Haywood Smith   r   431

Maxwell, Marlena (Young Woman)
The Impossible Texan - Allie Shaw   r   424

Maya (Teenager)
Motherland - Vineeta Vijayaraghavan   c   1239

Mayer, David (Military Personnel; Pilot)
Jerusalem's Heart - Bodie Thoene   t   988
Jerusalem's Heart - Bodie Thoene   i   1091

Mayfield, Elizabeth (Government Official)
License Invoked - Robert Asprin   f   554

Mayfield, Isabella (Young Woman)
The Birth of Blue Satan - Patricia Wynn   t   1000

McAlister, Diedre (Photographer)
The Amber Photograph - Penelope J. Stokes   i   1090

McAllister, Cassidy "Cass" Rose (Pioneer)
Jezebel's Sister - Emily Carmichael   r   240

McAvoy, Ed (Police Officer)
Stream of Death - Bill Stackhouse   m   176

McBride, Billy (Television Personality)
Shock Talk - Bob Larson   i   1054

McCabe, Francis "Frannie" (Police Officer)
The Wooden Sea - Jonathan Carroll   f   562
The Wooden Sea - Jonathan Carroll   c   1128

McCabe, Magda (Spouse)
The Wooden Sea - Jonathan Carroll   c   1128

McCabe, Thomas (Government Official)
Cheyenne Raiders - Jackson O'Reilly   w   516

McCain, Michael (Government Official)
In Fluid Silence - G.W. Tirpa   s   837

McCain, Sam (Lawyer; Detective—Private)
Will You Still Love Me Tomorrow? - Ed
   Gorman   m   63

McCaleb, Terry (FBI Agent; Consultant)
A Darkness More than Night - Michael
   Connelly   c   1135

McCarron, Blue (Psychologist; Lesbian)
The Last Blue Plate Special - Abigail
   Padgett   m   138

McCarthy, Gail (Veterinarian; Detective—Amateur)
Breakaway - Laura Crum   m   30

McClintoch, Lara (Antiques Dealer; Detective—
   Amateur)
The African Quest - Lyn Hamilton   m   74

McCourry, Lark (Musician)
The Songcatcher - Sharyn McCrumb   m   113

McCourry, Malcolm (Pioneer; Relative)
The Songcatcher - Sharyn McCrumb   c   1197

McCracken, Charles (Relative; Handicapped)
Beneath a Whiskey Sky - Tracy Knight   w   498

McCracken, Sim (Gunfighter; Drifter)
Beneath a Whiskey Sky - Tracy Knight   w   498

McDolen, Kate (Teacher)
Wire Mesh Mothers - Elizabeth Massie   h   705

McDougal, Dougal (Diplomat)
Spheres of Heaven - Charles Sheffield   s   829

McDougall, Drake Thornton (Laird; Murderer)
His Stolen Bride - Shelley Bradley   r   226

McFaile, Korine (Landscaper; Detective—Amateur)
Three Dirty Women and the Bitter Brew - Julie Wray
   Herman   m   81

McFarland, Charlie (Hippie; Environmentalist)
The Voice of the Butterfly - John Nichols   w   513

McGarr, Peter (Police Officer)
The Death of an Irish Sinner - Bartholomew
Gill   *m*   61

McGavock, Jill (Professor)
Pascal's Wager - Nancy Rue   *i*   1080

McGowan, Alec (Television Personality; Crime
Victim)
Morning - W.D. Wetherell   *c*   1242

McHenry, Vanessa (Child-Care Giver)
A Special Kind of Family - Eileen Berger   *i*   1014

Mckenna, Gordon (Relative; Adoptee)
A Theory of Relativity - Jacquelyn Mitchard   *c*   1203

McKennon, Kerr (Rancher)
MacGregor's Lantern - Corinne Joy Brown   *w*   463

McKinnon, Kerry MacGregor (Widow(er))
The Beautiful Stranger - Julia London   *r*   353

McKnight, Alex (Detective—Private; Police Officer)
The Hunting Wind - Steve Hamilton   *m*   75

McLain, Daniel (Religious; Widow(er))
To Wed in Texas - Jodi Thomas   *r*   439

McLeod, Angus (Sidekick; Cowboy)
The O'Keefe Empire - Jane Candia Coleman   *w*   468

McLoughlin, John (Businessman)
The Fields of Eden - Richard S. Wheeler   *t*   994

McMannus, Deidre (Detective—Private)
Archangel Protocol - Lyda Morehouse   *s*   810

McNab, Pat (Singer; Serial Killer)
Emerald Germs of Ireland - Patrick
McCabe   *c*   1196

McNabb, Maxie (Widow(er))
Dead North - Sue Henry   *w*   490

McNaughton, Alexander "Zan" (Vintner)
A Lovely Illusion - Tessa Barclay   *r*   214

McPherson, Kate (Tour Guide)
Eternity - Tamara Thorne   *h*   743

McRay, Dillon (Rodeo Rider)
Dangerous Moves - Mary Morgan   *r*   387

McSwain, Diamond (Actress)
Secret Love - Brenda Jackson   *r*   312

McTaggart, Jace (Rancher; Political Figure)
The Runaway Princess - Patricia Forsythe   *r*   270

McVicar, Brianna (Young Woman)
In the Blood - Stephen Gresham   *h*   683

Meara, Jane (Government Official)
In Fluid Silence - G.W. Tirpa   *s*   837

Medea (Ruler)
God of the Golden Fleece - Fred Saberhagen   *f*   630

Mee (Collector)
Mr. Mee - Andrew Crumey   *c*   1137

Mehy (Military Personnel)
The Wise Woman - Christian Jacq   *t*   917

Melissa (Child-Care Giver)
Do Try to Speak as We Do - Marjorie Leet
Ford   *c*   1152

Mendark (Sorcerer)
A Shadow on the Glass - Ian Irvine   *f*   592

Mendelssohn, Annabel (Student—Graduate)
Field Guide - Gwendolen Gross   *c*   1166

Menedemos (Trader)
Over the Wine-Dark Sea - H.N. Turteltaub   *t*   990

Mentor (Vampire)
Red Moon Rising - Billie Sue Mosiman   *h*   712

Merchon, Duke (Businessman)
Overnight Cinderella - Katherine Garbera   *r*   275

Meren (Nobleman; Government Official)
Slayer of Gods - Lynda S. Robinson   *m*   160

Slayer of Gods - Lynda S. Robinson   *t*   972

Merenptah (Ruler; Historical Figure)
The Wise Woman - Christian Jacq   *t*   917

Meria (Housewife)
The Sword in the Storm - David Gemmell   *f*   585

Merriem, Portia "Pip" (Noblewoman; Scholar)
Lilies on the Lake - Katherine Kingsley   *r*   333

Merriman, Emily (Gentlewoman)
Bewitched - Heather Cullman   *r*   249

Merriton, Cressida (Gentlewoman)
The Lady from Lisbon - Sheila Walsh   *r*   444

Merrydown, Conan (Gentleman)
Breaking the Rules - Sandra Heath   *r*   298

Merryn (Noblewoman)
Summerblood - Tom Deitz   *f*   570

Messenger, Ralph (Professor)
Thinks. . . - David Lodge   *c*   1187

Metaire, Gil (Military Personnel)
Once They Wore the Gray - Johnny D.
Boggs   *w*   455

Metanov, Dasha (Young Woman)
The Bronze Horseman - Paullina Simons   *t*   981

Metanov, Tatiana (Worker)
The Bronze Horseman - Paullina Simons   *t*   981

Mhulhar, Ket (Alien; Fugitive)
Bobby's Girl - J.D. Austin   *s*   754

Michaels, Elena (Journalist; Werewolf)
Bitten - Kelley Armstrong   *h*   653

Michaelson, Hari (Actor)
Blade of Tyshalle - Matthew Stover   *f*   639

Michel (Religious)
The Burning Times - Jeanne Kalogridis   *t*   920

Michelet, Ariana (Scientist)
Devil's Sea - Greg Donegan   *s*   774

Middleton, Mary Swan (Volunteer; Wealthy)
The Swan House - Elizabeth Musser   *i*   1066

Midnight, Brenda (Designer)
Murder and the Mad Hatter - Barbara Jaye
Wilson   *m*   196

Midnight Louie (Animal; Detective—Amateur)
Cat in a Leopard Spot - Carole Nelson
Douglas   *m*   44

Mike (Teenager)
The Free Lunch - Spider Robinson   *s*   824

Miller, Danny (Murderer; Convict)
Border Crossing - Pat Barker   *c*   1108

Miller, Lixie (Widow(er))
The General's Notorious Widow - Stephen A.
Bly   *i*   1018

Miller, Morgan (Scientist)
The Cassandra Complex - Brian Stableford   *s*   832

Miller, Sara (Child)
The Colors of Love - Vanessa Grant   *r*   283

Millhone, Kinsey (Detective—Private; Divorced
Person)
P Is for Peril - Sue Grafton   *m*   66

Mina (Warrior)
Dragons of a Lost Star - Margaret Weis   *f*   647

Miniter, Amy (Real Estate Agent)
Worse Things Waiting - Brian McNaughton   *h*   711

Miniter, Jane (Teenager)
Downward to Darkness - Brian McNaughton   *h*   708

Minogue, Matt (Police Officer)
A Carra King - John Brady   *m*   12

Mint, Maytera (Rebel)
Return to the Whorl - Gene Wolfe   *s*   850

Minton, Paris (Store Owner; Crime Victim)
Fearless Jones - Walter Mosley   *m*   126
Fearless Jones - Walter Mosley   *c*   1206

Mirabilis, Bonne (Care Giver)
Mirabilis - Susann Cokal   *t*   867

Misrix (Demon)
The Beyond - Jeffrey Ford   *f*   581

Mitchell, Anya (Businesswoman)
Joy - Victoria Christopher Murray   *i*   1065

Mitchell, Joseph (Religious)
Under the Color of Law - Michael
McGarrity   *w*   505

Mitchell, Mark (Police Officer)
Sawyer's Crossing - Sharon Snow Sirois   *i*   1086

Mitsu (Military Personnel)
Stars over Stars - K.D. Wentworth   *s*   845

Miu (Businesswoman)
The Sputnik Sweetheart - Haruki Murakami   *c*   1208

Moberley, Gaynor (Businessman)
The Dragon Charmer - Jan Siegel   *f*   634

Moberly, Hugh (Rancher)
Hearn's Valley - Wayne D. Overholser   *w*   517

Modeste, Damien (Religious)
The Last Report on the Miracles at Little No Horse -
Louise Erdrich   *t*   889

Moira (Young Woman)
A Wizard in a Feud - Christopher Stasheff   *f*   638

Molotov, Vyacheslav (Political Figure)
Colonization: Aftershocks - Harry Turtledove   *s*   841

Monahan, Rory (Professor)
The Temptation of Rory Monahan - Elizabeth
Bevarly   *r*   221

Monahan, Tess (Teacher)
First Comes Love - Elizabeth Bevarly   *r*   220

Montana, Dylan (Detective—Police)
Remember Your Lies - Jill Jones   *r*   323

Montella, Pat (Detective—Amateur; Psychic)
Hang My Head and Cry - Elena Santangelo   *t*   978

Montero, Britt (Journalist; Detective—Amateur)
You Only Die Twice - Edna Buchanan   *m*   16

Montford, Jack (Architect; Cousin)
A Finer End - Deborah Crombie   *m*   29

Montgomery, Agatha (Gentlewoman)
Murder at Bertram's Bower - Cynthia Peale   *t*   957

Montgomery, Athena (Gentlewoman)
Athena's Conquest - Catherine Blair   *r*   225

Montgomery, Christian "Kit" (Nobleman; Lawman)
Never Marry a Cowboy - Lorraine Heath   *r*   297

Montgomery, Maddie (Counselor; Femme Fatale)
Messing around with Max - Lori Foster   *r*   272

Montoya, Feliciana (Relative)
Messenger on the Battlefield - Melinda Rice   *w*   531

Montoya, Isabelina (Child)
Messenger on the Battlefield - Melinda Rice   *w*   531

Mookerjee, Sri Billy Lee (Religious)
The Song of the Earth - Hugh Nissenson   *s*   813

Mookherjee, Huree Chunder (Scholar; Spy)
Sherlock Holmes: The Missing Years - Jamyang
Norbu   *t*   952

Mooney, Henry (Journalist)
1921 - Morgan Llywelyn   *t*   933

Moore, Bobby (Teenager)
Grace - Jane Roberts Wood   *w*   550

Moore, Jack (Highwayman; Amnesiac)
No Other Love - Candace Camp   *r*   238

Moore, Meg (Linguist)
The Defiant Hero - Suzanne Brockmann   *r* 229

Morath, Nicholas (Spy; Nobleman)
Kingdom of Shadows - Alan Furst   *c* 1157
Kingdom of Shadows - Alan Furst   *m* 57

Mordant, Frank (Businessman)
The Doorkeepers - Graham Masterton   *h* 706

Morelli, Joe (Police Officer)
Seven Up - Janet Evanovich   *m* 50

Moreston, Pearl (Noblewoman; Scholar)
Rogue's Honor - Brenda Hiatt   *r* 303

Morgan, Billy (Relative)
Return to Ithaca - Randy Lee Eickhoff   *w* 478

Morgan, Henry (Military Personnel)
Return to Ithaca - Randy Lee Eickhoff   *w* 478

Morgan, Kelly (Mountain Man)
The Cavan Breed - Les Savage Jr.   *w* 537

Morgan, Steve (Diplomat; Wealthy)
Savage Desire - Rosemary Rogers   *r* 414

Morgan, Virginia "Ginny" Brandon (Adventurer; Spouse)
Savage Desire - Rosemary Rogers   *r* 414

Morgette, Dolf (Miner)
Morgette in the Yukon - G.G. Boyer   *w* 457

Mori, Fubuki (Businesswoman)
Fear and Trembling - Amelie Nothomb   *c* 1210

Moriarty, James (Scientist; Criminal)
The Great Game - Michael Kurland   *m* 99

Morning Sky (Indian; Captive)
The Doomsday Marshal and the Mountain Man - Ray Hogan   *w* 492

Morrell, Chantalene (Detective—Amateur; Gypsy)
Perhaps She'll Die - M.K. Preston   *w* 526

Morris, Jack (Spouse)
Holy Rollers - J. Newman   *h* 714

Morris, Mary (Housewife)
Holy Rollers - J. Newman   *h* 714

Morris, Rachel (Crime Victim)
Blue Diary - Alice Hoffman   *c* 1171

Morrison, Libby (Care Giver)
Libby's Story - Judy Baer   *i* 1007

Mortimer, James (Doctor; Spouse)
Dr. Mortimer and the Barking Man Mystery - Gerard Williams   *m* 195
Dr. Mortimer and the Barking Man Mystery - Gerard Williams   *t* 996

Mortmain, Rafe (Government Official; Villain)
Midnight Bride - Susan Carroll   *r* 241

Moseby, Frankie (Young Man)
Girl of the Manzanos - Barbara Spencer Foster   *w* 481

Moser, Thomas (Religious; Lover)
The Faithful Narrative of a Pastor's Disappearance - Benjamin Anastas   *c* 1104

Motley (Criminal)
Perdido Street Station - China Mieville   *f* 611

Mrs. Murphy (Animal)
Claws and Effect - Rita Mae Brown   *m* 14

Mugabe, Karin (Teacher)
Child of Venus - Pamela Sargent   *s* 826

Mulholland, Petey (Gambler)
The Haunting of Hood Canal - Jack Cady   *h* 662

Mullins, Thomas (Military Personnel)
West Texas - Al Sarrantonio   *w* 535

Murchison, Julia (Housewife; Parent)
Thursdays at Eight - Debbie Macomber   *r* 360

Murdock, Ross (Time Traveler)
Time Traders II - Andre Norton   *s* 814

Murgatroyd (Housekeeper)
The Christmas Thingy - F. Paul Wilson   *h* 749

Murkin, Marie (Housekeeper)
Triple Pursuit - Ralph McInerny   *m* 116

Murphy, John (Saloon Keeper/Owner)
Murphy's Lore: Fools' Day - Patrick Thomas   *f* 641

N

Nagel, Jerry (Spaceman)
Melchior's Fire - Jack L. Chalker   *s* 764

Nailor, John (Detective—Homicide)
Film Strip - Nancy Bartholomew   *m* 5

Naja (Ruler)
Warlock - Wilbur A. Smith   *t* 982

Nani (Housekeeper)
The Far Field - Edie Meidav   *c* 1201
The Far Field - Edie Meidav   *t* 946

Nanson, Phineas C. (Critic)
The Biographer's Tale - A.S. Byatt   *c* 1124

Nash, Francis (Scientist)
Temple - Matt Reilly   *s* 818

Nate (Convict)
Tennant's Rock - Steve McGiffen   *t* 944

Natraja (Innkeeper; Expatriate)
Sister India - Peggy Payne   *c* 1218

Navarre, Jackson "Tres" (Detective—Private; Professor)
The Devil Went Down to Austin - Rick Riordan   *m* 156

Naylor, Jacob Alistair (Activist)
Hush - Tim Lebbon   *h* 697

Nefer (Artisan)
Paneb the Ardent - Christian Jacq   *t* 916

Nefer Memnon (Royalty)
Warlock - Wilbur A. Smith   *t* 982

Nemoto (Scientist)
Manifold: Space - Stephen Baxter   *s* 756

Neska (Indian)
Seasons of Harvest - James M. Vesely   *w* 546

Ness, Eliot (Historical Figure; FBI Agent)
Angel in Black - Max Allan Collins   *t* 870

Newberry, Guy (Journalist)
Point Deception - Marcia Muller   *m* 127

Newborn, Rae (Artisan; Mentally Ill Person)
Folly - Laurie R. King   *m* 94

Newman, Leo (Religious; Scholar)
The Gospel of Judas - Simon Mawer   *c* 1195

Newton, Elizabeth (Housewife)
Darkness Demands - Simon Clark   *h* 667

Newton, John (Writer)
Darkness Demands - Simon Clark   *h* 667

Newton, Paul (Teenager)
Darkness Demands - Simon Clark   *h* 667

Next, Thursday (Police Officer)
The Eyre Affair - Jasper Fforde   *s* 780

Nicholet, Napoleon (Lawyer)
The Bloody Quarter - Les Savage Jr.   *w* 536

Nicholls, Faith (Art Dealer)
Nobody's Angel - Patricia Rice   *r* 405

Nicholson, Josephine (Military Personnel; Pilot)
Secrets in the Sky - Melinda Rice   *w* 532

Nicholson, March (Government Official)
The Time It Never Rained - Elmer Kelton   *w* 496

Nickles, Peggy (Heiress)
True Believers - Linda Dorrell   *i* 1031

Nicoletta (Healer; Herbalist)
The Scarletti Curse - Christine Feehan   *r* 266

Nidaba (Witch; Immortal)
Destiny - Maggie Shayne   *r* 425

Nigel (Boyfriend)
Karlmarx.com - Susan Coll   *c* 1134

Night Bird Woman (Indian)
Cheyenne Raiders - Jackson O'Reilly   *w* 516

Nihmedu, Galaeron (Mythical Creature)
The Summoning - Troy Denning   *f* 571

Nilsson, John (Military Personnel)
The Defiant Hero - Suzanne Brockmann   *r* 229

Nina (Spouse; Model)
The Funeral Party - Ludmila Ulitskaya   *c* 1238

Nixon, Richard (Political Figure; Historical Figure)
Elvis and Nixon - Jonathan Lowy   *c* 1190

no Delaunay, Phedre (Slave)
Kushiel's Dart - Jacqueline Carey   *f* 561

North, Verona (Student)
A Perfect Daughter - Gillian Linscott   *t* 930

Norton, Kiru (Tourist)
Space Wasters - David Garnett   *s* 786

Norton, Wayne (Tourist)
Space Wasters - David Garnett   *s* 786

Nye, Keefer (Orphan)
A Theory of Relativity - Jacquelyn Mitchard   *c* 1203

Nyhal, Eldyn (Businessman)
The Octagonal Raven - L.E. Modesitt Jr.   *s* 809

O

O'Brien, Kali (Lawyer)
Witness for the Defense - Jonnie Jacobs   *m* 85

O'Brien, Liz (Journalist)
The Binding Oath - Sybil Downing   *m* 45
The Binding Oath - Sybil Downing   *t* 883
The Binding Oath - Sybil Downing   *w* 477

O'Clare, Mairead (Lawyer)
Uncommon Justice - Terry Devane   *c* 1139

O'Connell, Alex (Child)
The Mummy Returns - Max Allan Collins   *h* 668

O'Connell, Brody (Contractor; Single Parent)
Considering Kate - Nora Roberts   *r* 411

O'Connell, Evelyn (Archaeologist)
The Mummy Returns - Max Allan Collins   *h* 668

O'Connell, Richard (Mercenary)
The Mummy Returns - Max Allan Collins   *h* 668

O'Connor, Anne (Journalist; Relative)
Crooked River Burning - Mark Winegardner   *c* 1245

O'Connor, Cork (Detective—Private; Indian)
Purgatory Ridge - William Kent Krueger   *m* 98

O'Connor, Francis (Criminal)
Deadfellas - David Whitman   *h* 748

Oddie, Mike (Police Officer)
Unholy Dying - Robert Barnard   *m* 4

O'Donnell, Maureen (Social Worker; Detective—Amateur)
Exile - Denise Mina   *m* 122

O'Dwyer Collins, Henrietta (Widow(er); Journalist)
Resort to Murder - Carolyn Hart   *m* 78

Ogelvie, Ian (Researcher)
Inspired Sleep - Robert Cohen   c   1133

O'Hara, Annie (Antiques Dealer; Detective—
Amateur)
Wolf in Sheep's Clothing - Ann Campbell   m   20

O'Hara, Elaine (Scientist)
Jupiter - Ben Bova   s   760

O'Hara, Maeve (Student—College)
Adams Fall - Sean Desmond   h   671

O'Keefe, Alex (Rancher)
The O'Keefe Empire - Jane Candia Coleman   w   468

O'Keefe, Joanna (Spouse; Rancher)
The O'Keefe Empire - Jane Candia Coleman   w   468

Oliver (Television Personality; Boyfriend)
Cause Celeb - Helen Fielding   c   1150

O'Malley, Lisa (Scientist)
The Truth Seeker - Dee Henderson   i   1045

O'Malley, Marcus (Lawman)
The Guardian - Dee Henderson   r   299

Omochi (Businessman)
Fear and Trembling - Amelie Nothomb   c   1210

O'Neal, Michael (Military Personnel)
Gust Front - John Ringo   s   821

O'Neil, Jack (Military Personnel)
The Morpheus Factor - Ashley McConnell   s   806

O'Netti, Neil (Writer)
Father Panic's Opera Macabre - Thomas
Tessier   h   742

Oppenheimer, J. Robert (Scientist; Historical Figure)
America's Children - James Thackara   c   1234

Ortiz, Manuel (Fugitive; Murderer)
The Killer Gun - Lauran Paine   w   519

Oskar (Animal)
Kingdoms of Light - Alan Dean Foster   f   582

Ovid (Historical Figure; Writer)
The Love-Artist - Jane Alison   t   852
The Love-Artist - Jane Alison   c   1103

Owens, Allison (Parent)
Shock Talk - Bob Larson   i   1054

Owens, Jenny (Parent)
Shock Talk - Bob Larson   i   1054

Ozma (Royalty)
The Emerald Burrito of Oz - John Skipp   f   636

P

Paddy (Mythical Creature)
St. Patrick's Gargoyle - Katherine Kurtz   f   599

Paget, Neil (Police Officer)
Thread of Evidence - Frank Smith   m   172

Pagliarulo, Antonio (Singer)
Cassandra's Song - Carole Gift Page   i   1070

Pahner (Military Personnel)
March Upcountry - David Weber   s   844

Paige, Martin (Writer)
Worse Things Waiting - Brian McNaughton   h   711

Paley, Hitch (Drug Dealer)
The Chronoliths - Robert Charles Wilson   s   849

Palmer, Luke (Relative; Young Man)
A Few Corrections - Brad Leithauser   c   1184

Pan (Deity)
Murphy's Lore: Fools' Day - Patrick Thomas   f   641

Paneb the Ardent (Artisan)
Paneb the Ardent - Christian Jacq   t   916

Panfilo (Military Personnel)
Through the Darkness - Harry Turtledove   f   644

Panic, Anton (Religious)
Father Panic's Opera Macabre - Thomas
Tessier   h   742

Panic, Marisa (Young Woman)
Father Panic's Opera Macabre - Thomas
Tessier   h   742

Pantuliano, Anthony (Parent)
Girl Talk - Julianna Baggott   c   1106

Panwar, Randall (Scientist)
Limit of Vision - Linda Nagata   s   812

Paque (Teenager; Friend)
We're So Famous - Jaime Clarke   c   1132

Pardoe, Christopher (Religious)
Unholy Dying - Robert Barnard   m   4

Parker, Bethany (Child)
Secrets in the Sky - Melinda Rice   w   532

Parker, Claire (Detective—Homicide)
Funny Money - Laurence Gough   m   64

Parker, Dale (Mechanic; Military Personnel)
Battle Lines - James Reasoner   t   965

Parker, Emmett Quanah (Police Officer; Indian)
Ancient Ones - Kirk Mitchell   m   123
Ancient Ones - Kirk Mitchell   w   507
Spirit Sickness - Kirk Mitchell   w   508

Parker, James (Imposter)
The Amazon Quest - Gilbert Morris   i   1062

Parker, Joe (Writer; Military Personnel)
Battle Lines - James Reasoner   t   965

Parrish, James (Veteran; Rancher)
Shadows on the Land - James M. Vesely   w   547

Parrish, Owen Forbes (Rancher)
The Awakening Land - James M. Vesely   w   545

Partlett, Maggie (Waiter/Waitress)
The Skeleton in the Closet - M.C. Beaton   m   7

Paterson, William (Businessman)
The Rising Sun - Douglas Galbraith   t   897

Paulinha, William Narciso (Prostitute)
Fixer Chao - Han Ong   c   1213

Pawli (Teenager)
The Curer - Adam Nichols   f   614

Peace, Charlie (Police Officer)
Unholy Dying - Robert Barnard   m   4

Peacock, Jessie (Wealthy)
Just Shy of Harmony - Philip Gulley   i   1037

Pedro (Military Personnel)
Victor Lopez at the Alamo - James Rice   w   529

Pedro Juan (Journalist)
Dirty Havana Triology - Pedro Juan
Gutierrez   c   1167

Pell, Amos (Rancher)
Beneath a Whiskey Sky - Tracy Knight   w   498

Pellam, John (Filmmaker; Detective—Amateur)
Hell's Kitchen - Jeffery Deaver   m   38

Pencarreth, Erica (Museum Curator)
A Lovely Illusion - Tessa Barclay   r   214

Pendleton, Joseph (Businessman; Lover)
Bad Timing - Betsy Berne   c   1113

Pendleton, Lucas (Businessman)
My True Love - Cheryl Holt   r   309

Pendragon, Uther (Ruler)
Uther - Jack Whyte   t   995
Uther - Jack Whyte   f   650

Percy, Catherine (Fugitive)
The Dreamer - May McGoldrick   r   372

Perna, Gaetano (Immigrant)
The Awakening Land - James M. Vesely   w   545

Perron, Jade (Businesswoman; Divorced Person)
Finding Ian - Stella Cameron   r   237

Persimmons (Government Official)
The Diplomatic Touch - David Bischoff   s   758

Pete (Hunter)
Dreamcatcher - Stephen King   c   1180

Peters, Mido (Lawman)
The Masked Gun - Barry Cord   w   469

Peters, Toby (Detective—Private)
A Few Minutes Past Midnight - Stuart M.
Kaminsky   m   91
A Few Minutes Past Midnight - Stuart M.
Kaminsky   t   921

Peterson, Deborah Anne (Singer)
Singsation - Jacquelin Thomas   i   1092

Peterson, Wesley (Police Officer; Archaeologist)
An Unhallowed Grave - Kate Ellis   m   48

Petinske, Angela "Tony" (Teenager)
Wire Mesh Mothers - Elizabeth Massie   h   705

Petrie (Professor)
Mr. Mee - Andrew Crumey   c   1137

Petrovna, Vladimir (Farmer)
Let Freedom Ring - Al Lacy   i   1052

Petrungero, Pietro (Singer)
Never Call It Loving - Ellen Ramsay   r   401

Pewter (Animal)
Claws and Effect - Rita Mae Brown   m   14

Phelan, Annie (Servant; Model)
Afterimage - Helen Humphreys   t   913
Afterimage - Helen Humphreys   c   1174

Phenesa (Royalty)
The Chalice - Deborah Chester   f   565

Philby, Kim (Spy; Historical Figure)
Declare - Tim Powers   h   723

Phillips, Laura (Nurse)
Cradle of Dreams - Joseph Bentz   i   1013

Phillips, Paul (Professor)
Cradle of Dreams - Joseph Bentz   i   1013

Picket, Bill (Cowboy)
The Long Journey Home - Don Coldsmith   t   868

Pickett, Mel (Police Officer; Detective—Amateur)
Death of a Hired Man - Eric Wright   m   199

Pierce, Dave (Paranormal Investigator)
Terror Firma - Matthew Thomas   s   836

Pierce, Eli (Pilot; Survivor)
Pathways - Lisa Tawn Bergren   i   1015

Pierce, Karen (Adventurer)
Ashes and Ice - Tracie Peterson   i   1074

Pierette (Witch)
The Veil of Years - L. Warren Douglas   f   572

Pike, Gar (Spaceman)
A Wizard in a Feud - Christopher Stasheff   f   638

Pike, Rounder (Rancher)
The Time It Never Rained - Elmer Kelton   w   496

Pippard, Dougald (Nobleman)
Rules of Attraction - Christina Dodd   r   259

Pitman, Delia (Prostitute; Dancer)
The Seeds of Time - Carol Cail   w   466

Pitt, Charlotte (Socialite; Spouse)
The Whitechapel Conspiracy - Anne Perry   t   960

Pitt, Thomas (Police Officer; Spouse)
The Whitechapel Conspiracy - Anne Perry   t   960

Plath, Sylvia (Historical Figure; Writer)
Sylvia and Ted - Emma Tennant   t   987

S

St. Clare, Amiranth (Noblewoman)
The Secret Swan - Shana Abe   r   202

St. Clare, Arden (Time Traveler; Heiress)
To Tame a Rogue - Linda Kay   r   328

St. James, Beau (Lawyer; Single Parent)
An English Rose - Debra Satinwood   r   419

St. John, Mace (Detective—Homicide)
Unfinished Business - Barbara Seranella   m   168

St. John, Trevor (Nobleman; Wealthy)
A Matter of Pride - Gabriella Anderson   r   209

St. Leger, Valentine (Doctor)
Midnight Bride - Susan Carroll   r   241

St. Mars, Gideon Viscount (Nobleman; Highwayman)
The Birth of Blue Satan - Patricia Wynn   m   200
The Birth of Blue Satan - Patricia Wynn   t   1000

Saint-Martin, Paul de (Detective—Police)
Mute Witness - Charles O'Brien   s   953

St. Vallier, Stella (Professor)
Still of the Night - Meagan McKinney   r   375

Saks, Bonnie (Single Parent; Student—Graduate)
Inspired Sleep - Robert Cohen   c   1133

Sally (Outcast; Thief)
The Buffalo Hunters - Gary McCarthy   w   504

Sameth (Royalty)
Lirael - Garth Nix   f   617

Samuels, Rheada (Indian; Tour Guide)
Raven - Laura Baker   r   213

Sanborn, Revelie (Young Woman)
Code of the West - Aaron Latham   t   926

Sandoval, Sandy (Prostitute; Parent)
The Tin Collector - Stephen J. Cannell   c   1126

Santana, Marques (Pirate)
My Lady Pirate - Elizabeth Doyle   r   260

Santo, Richard (Veteran)
613 West Jefferson - D.S. Lliteras   i   1057

Sarah (Volunteer)
Seaside - Terri Blackstock   i   1016

Sarasper (Healer)
The Vacant Throne - Ed Greenwood   f   586

Sargis (Writer)
Three Apples Fell from Heaven - Micheline Aharonian Marcom   t   938
Three Apples Fell from Heaven - Micheline Aharonian Marcom   c   1193

Saunders, Mary (Prostitute)
Slammerkin - Emma Donoghue   t   882

Sawyers, Annie (Store Owner)
Annie, Get Your Guy - Lori Foster   r   271

Sawyers, Max (Businessman)
Messing around with Max - Lori Foster   r   272

Sazes, Clyde (Lawman)
Blood Rock - Ralph Cotton   w   470

Scarletti, Giovanni (Nobleman)
The Scarletti Curse - Christine Feehan   r   266

Schaeffer, Boyd (Widow(er); Doctor)
Life After Death - Carol Muske-Dukes   c   1209

Schaeffer, Maddie (Widow(er); Businesswoman)
Back in Baby's Arms - Tina Wainscott   r   443

Schaeffer, Russell (Spouse; Wealthy)
Life After Death - Carol Muske-Dukes   c   1209

Schilling, Charlie (Police Officer)
The Lost - Jack Ketchum   h   692

Schindler, Alma (Historical Figure; Spouse)
The Artist's Wife - Max Phillips   t   962

Schoenfeld, Aaron (Scientist; Spaceman)
Borrowed Tides - Paul Levinson   s   800

Schulz, Goldy Bear (Caterer; Detective—Amateur)
Sticks & Scones - Diane Mott Davidson   m   34

Schwan, Brian (Sports Figure)
Spikes - Michael Griffith   c   1164

Schwan, Rosa (Spouse)
Spikes - Michael Griffith   c   1164

Scott, Brenna (Animal Trainer)
Scent of Murder - Cynthia G. Alwyn   m   2

Scott, Dwayne (Military Personnel)
Temple - Matt Reilly   s   818

Scott, Nicolette "Nick" (Archaeologist; Detective—Amateur)
The Return of the Spanish Lady - Val Davis   m   36

Scott, Peter (Nobleman)
The Serpent's Shadow - Mercedes Lackey   f   602

Scully, Shane (Detective—Police; Crime Suspect)
The Tin Collector - Stephen J. Cannell   c   1126

Seafort, Nicholas (Spaceship Captain)
Children of Hope - David Feintuch   s   779

Season, Jillian (Relative; Model)
The Four Seasons - Mary Alice Monroe   r   384

Season, Rose (Relative)
The Four Seasons - Mary Alice Monroe   r   384

Seavers (Military Personnel)
West Texas - Al Sarrantonio   w   535

Secca (Sorceress; Noblewoman)
The Shadow Sorceress - L.E. Modesitt Jr.   f   612

Sedgwick, Drusilla (Spy)
Miss Sedgewick and the Spy - Geraldine Burrows   t   862

Selby, Mike (Paralegal)
Balak - Stephen Mark Rainey   h   727

Sereth (Alien)
The Ghost Sister - Liz Williams   s   846

Servi, Anita (Social Worker; Detective—Amateur)
Guilty Mind - Irene Marcuse   m   108

Setterington, Hannah (Businesswoman; Companion)
Rules of Attraction - Christina Dodd   r   259

Seymour, Thomas (Historical Figure; Nobleman)
Virgin - Robin Maxwell   t   941

Seymour, Tom (Doctor; Spouse)
Border Crossing - Pat Barker   c   1108

Shaddler, Alterith (Teacher)
Ravenheart - David Gemmell   f   584

Shadow (Convict)
American Gods - Neil Gaiman   f   583

Shan, Darren (Child)
Cirque Du Freak - Darren Shan   h   734

Shanhaevel (Mythical Creature)
The Temple of Elemental Evil - Thomas M. Reid   f   623

Shannon, Clay (Lawman)
Shannon: US Marshal - Charles E. Friend   w   484

Shannon, Kit (Lawyer)
Angels Flight - Tracie Peterson   i   1073

Shapiro, Candace "Cannie" (Journalist; Young Woman)
Good in Bed - Jennifer Weiner   c   1241

Shapiro, Desiree (Detective—Private)
Murder Can Upset Your Mother - Selma Eichler   m   47

Shapiro, Hank (Government Official)
The Pickup Artist - Terry Bisson   s   759

Shapiro, Virginia "Ginny" (Journalist; Fugitive)
Storm Warning - Dinah McCall   r   367

Sharpe, Richard (Military Personnel)
Sharpe's Trafalgar - Bernard Cornwell   t   873

Shaw, Garrett (Lawman)
Still of the Night - Meagan McKinney   r   375

Shaw, Matthew (Widow(er))
Heaven Sent - Jillian Hart   i   1041

Sheehand, Hezekiah (Teenager; Runaway)
Chalktown - Melinda Haynes   c   1169

Sheehand, Yellababy (Child; Handicapped)
Chalktown - Melinda Haynes   c   1169

Shelton, Marianne (Noblewoman; Writer)
The Marriage Lesson - Victoria Alexander   r   206

Shem C (Writer)
Fixer Chao - Han Ong   c   1213

Shen-oh-way, Charley (Parent; Murderer)
A River out of Eden - John Hockenberry   w   491

Shepard, Lucas (Scientist)
The Living Blood - Tananarive Due   h   672

Shephard, Carina DiGratia (Spouse)
Sweet Boundless - Kristen Heitzmann   i   1044

Shephard, Quillan (Mine Owner)
Sweet Boundless - Kristen Heitzmann   i   1044

Sherard, Tom (Spy)
The Fury and the Terror - John Farris   h   676

Sherbrooke, Mary Rose (Bastard Daughter; Bride)
The Scottish Bride - Catherine Coulter   r   245

Sherbrooke, Tysen (Nobleman; Religious)
The Scottish Bride - Catherine Coulter   r   245

Sheridan, Charles (Nobleman; Photographer)
Death at Epsom Downs - Robin Paige   m   140
Death at Epsom Downs - Robin Paige   t   955

Sheridan, Kathryn "Kate" Ardleigh (Noblewoman; Writer)
Death at Epsom Downs - Robin Paige   m   140
Death at Epsom Downs - Robin Paige   t   955

Sherman, Roger (Military Personnel)
Metaplanetary - Tony Daniel   s   767

Short, Holly (Mythical Creature)
Artemis Fowl - Eoin Colfer   f   566

Shugak, Kate (Detective—Private)
The Singing of the Dead - Dana Stabenow   m   175

Silva, Joe (Police Officer)
Friends and Enemies - Susan Oleksiw   m   136

Silvey, Deacon (Worker; Psychic)
Threshold - Caitlin R. Kiernan   h   693

Simmons, Essie Lee Lane (Spouse)
Church Folk - Michele Andrea Bowen   i   1021

Simmons, Theophilius Henry (Religious)
Church Folk - Michele Andrea Bowen   i   1021

Simona (Young Woman)
The Shasht War - Christopher Rowley   f   627

Simonaitis, Petras (Artisan; Apprentice)
A Clear North Light - Laurel Schunk   i   1084

Simpson, Deborah (Spy; Prostitute)
Last Refuge of Scoundrels - Paul Lussier   t   934

Simpson, Sarah (Noblewoman; Businesswoman)
The Bad Luck Wedding Night - Geralyn Dawson   r   252

Sinann (Mythical Creature)
Son of the Sword - J. Ardian Lee   f   605

Sinclair, Garnet (Artist)
Shenandoah Home - Sara Mitchell   i   1061

Sinclair, Ian (Military Personnel; Guardian)
Anne's Perfect Husband - Gayle Wilson   r   449

Sinclair, Jack (Young Man)
A Trust Betrayed - Candace M. Robb   *t*   971

Sinclair, Meredith (Businesswoman)
Shenandoah Home - Sara Mitchell   *i*   1061

Sinclair, Reese (Saloon Keeper/Owner)
Reese's Wild Wager - Barbara McCauley   *r*   369

Sinclair, Roger (Spouse; Businessman)
A Trust Betrayed - Candace M. Robb   *t*   971

Singleton, Ray (Farmer)
The Magic of Ordinary Days - Ann Howard
    Creel   *w*   471

Sisay (Warrior)
Planeshift - J. Robert King   *f*   596

Sissy (Young Woman)
Tennant's Rock - Steve McGiffen   *t*   944

Skal (Military Personnel; Alien)
Stars over Stars - K.D. Wentworth   *s*   845

Skeehan, Georgia (Fire Fighter; Single Parent)
The Fourth Angel - Suzanne Chazin   *m*   21

Skinner, Dola Mae (Restaurateur)
Picture Rock - Stephen A. Bly   *i*   1020

Skinner, O.T. (Clerk)
Picture Rock - Stephen A. Bly   *i*   1020

Skullcrusher, Nekros (Mythical Creature)
Day of the Dragon - Richard A. Knaak   *f*   597

Skye, Jilly (Businesswoman)
This Perfect Kiss - Christie Ridgway   *r*   407

Skye, Sunni (Prostitute; Murderer)
Natural Law - D.R. Schanker   *m*   165

Sladder, Brandon (Journalist)
The Columnist - Jeffrey Frank   *c*   1155

Slade, Ethan (Widow(er); Rancher)
Loving a Lonesome Cowboy - Debbi Rawlins   *r*   402

Slatter, Tug (Teenager)
Blood Crazy - Simon Clark   *h*   666

Slattery, Frank (Businessman; Friend)
The 25th Hour - David Benioff   *c*   1111

Sloan, C.D. "Seedy" (Police Officer)
Little Knell - Catherine Aird   *m*   1

Sloan, Dean (Businessman; Wealthy)
Summer Island - Kristin Hannah   *r*   293

Sloan, Melisande (Young Woman)
The Last Harbor - George Foy   *s*   785

Sloan, Sam (Detective)
The Empty Coffin - Robert L. Wise   *i*   1100

Sloan, Vera (Spouse)
The Empty Coffin - Robert L. Wise   *i*   1100

Sloane, Sydney (Detective—Private; Lesbian)
East of Niece - Randye Lordon   *m*   106

Sloane, Todd (Publisher; Journalist)
Looking for Laura - Judith Arnold   *r*   212

Slocombe, Drew (Undertaker; Nurse)
Dark Undertakings - Rebecca Tope   *m*   184

Slocum (Businessman; Unemployed)
The Last Harbor - George Foy   *s*   785

Smelt, Gordon (Entertainer)
Nothing but Blue Skies - Tom Holt   *f*   589

Smiles, Sibyl (Gentlewoman)
7B - Stella Cameron   *r*   236

Smiricky, Danny (Expatriate; Spouse)
Two Murders in My Double Life - Josef
    Skvorecky   *c*   1228

Smiricky, Sidonia (Publisher; Crime Suspect)
Two Murders in My Double Life - Josef
    Skvorecky   *c*   1228

Smith, Dan (Detective—Private; Boyfriend)
Blind Side - Penny Warner   *m*   189

Smith, Orpheus Beauregard "Bo" (Restaurateur)
In the Blood - Stephen Gresham   *h*   683

Smith, Sloane (Sidekick)
The Weeping Woman - Michael Kilian   *m*   93

Smith, Sugar Bear (Blacksmith)
The Haunting of Hood Canal - Jack Cady   *h*   662

Smith, Zoe (Librarian)
Aphrodite's Kiss - Julie Kenner   *r*   330

Smohalla, Francine (Scientist)
A River out of Eden - John Hockenberry   *w*   491

Smollet, Gretchen (Young Woman)
The Master Executioner - Loren D. Estleman   *t*   891

Snakewater (Shaman)
Raven Mocker - Don Coldsmith   *w*   467

Snowden, Brooke (Teacher)
Alyssa Again - Sylvie Kurtz   *r*   341

Soak, Ronnie (Businessman)
Thief of Time - Terry Pratchett   *f*   620

Solage, Dominic (Courier)
Athena's Conquest - Catherine Blair   *r*   225

Soldano, Bernard (Religious)
Ship of Fools - Richard Paul Russo   *s*   825

Soldier (Knight; Amnesiac)
Knight's Dawn - Kim Hunter   *f*   591

Somerford, George Connaught "Con" (Nobleman)
The Dragon's Bride - Jo Beverley   *r*   223

Song, Louie (Government Official)
K Falls - Skye Kathleen Moody   *m*   124

Sorenson, Michael (Doctor)
Plain Jane - Fern Michaels   *r*   380

Sostratos (Trader)
Over the Wine-Dark Sea - H.N. Turteltaub   *t*   990

Soulsby, Bird (Sports Figure)
Spikes - Michael Griffith   *c*   1164

Space Hopper (Mythical Creature)
Flatterland - Ian Stewart   *s*   833

Spagg (Businessman)
Knight's Dawn - Kim Hunter   *f*   591

Speaks While Leaving (Young Woman)
The Year the Cloud Fell - Kurt R.A.
    Giambastini   *s*   788

Speight, Eureka "Reka" (Convict)
Towns Without Rivers - Michael Parker   *c*   1215

Speight, Randall (Relative; Model)
Towns Without Rivers - Michael Parker   *c*   1215

Speilman, Gene (Immigrant)
The Emerald Burrito of Oz - John Skipp   *f*   636

Spencer, Hope (Journalist)
True Confessions - Rachel Gibson   *w*   486

Spenser (Detective—Private)
Potshot - Robert B. Parker   *m*   142

Spenser, Leigh (Teacher; Single Parent)
Spring Rain - Gayle Roper   *i*   1079

Spenser, Mardee (Heroine)
Girl of the Manzanos - Barbara Spencer
    Foster   *w*   481

Spiegelman, Sharon (Student—College)
Paradise Park - Allegra Goodman   *c*   1162

Spivey, Septimus (Spirit)
7B - Stella Cameron   *r*   236

Spotted Fox (Indian)
Cheyenne Raiders - Jackson O'Reilly   *w*   516

Sprague, Camellia Bellamy (Widow(er); Single Parent)
Camellia - Ginny Aiken   *i*   1003

Spring, Ian (Teenager)
Finding Ian - Stella Cameron   *r*   237

Spruance, Rudy (Military Personnel)
No One Thinks of Greenland - John
    Griesemer   *c*   1163

Spruill, Tally (Migrant Worker)
A Painted House - John Grisham   *c*   1165

S'ree (Animal; Wizard)
The Wizard's Dilemma - Diane Duane   *f*   574

SrrokVar (Alien)
Endurance - S.L. Viehl   *s*   842

Stackhouse, Jason (Foreman)
Dead Until Dark - Charlaine Harris   *h*   685

Stackhouse, Sookie (Waiter/Waitress)
Dead Until Dark - Charlaine Harris   *h*   685

Stael, Anne-Louise-Germaine de (Historical Figure; Noblewoman)
A Dish Taken Cold - Anne Perry   *t*   959

Standish, Chet (Murderer)
Morning - W.D. Wetherell   *c*   1242

Stansbury, Cordelia "Mary Westerman" (Runaway; Imposter)
The Riddle of the Shipwrecked Spinster - Patricia
    Veryan   *r*   441

Stanton, Cat (Twin; Architect)
Lioness - Nell Brien   *r*   227

Stanton, Gabriela "Gabby" (Professor; Clerk)
American Fuji - Sara Backer   *c*   1105

Stanton, Reilly (Nobleman; Doctor)
Lady of Skye - Patricia Cabot   *r*   233

Stapleton, Paul (Military Personnel)
When This Cruel War Is Over - Thomas
    Fleming   *t*   894

Stark, Ethan (Military Personnel)
Stark's Command - John G. Hemry   *s*   794

Starr, Iris (Prostitute)
Dr. Mortimer and the Barking Man Mystery - Gerard
    Williams   *t*   996

Starr, Matt (Businessman)
Charming Lily - Fern Michaels   *r*   379

Steele (Miner; Rancher)
Steele - Robert H. Redding   *w*   528

Stella (Teenager; Friend)
We're So Famous - Jaime Clarke   *c*   1132

Stenson, Dorothy (Neighbor)
Twice Dead - Elizabeth Dearl   *w*   475

Stephen of Wilmont (Nobleman)
Knave of Hearts - Shari Anton   *r*   210

Sterling, Grant (Lawyer)
I Do, but Here's the Catch - Pamela Burford   *r*   232

Stettner, Heinz (Military Personnel)
Sunflower of the Third Reich - Andrea Ritter   *t*   969

Stettner, Luise (Spouse)
Sunflower of the Third Reich - Andrea Ritter   *t*   969

Stettner, Marianne (Young Woman)
Sunflower of the Third Reich - Andrea Ritter   *t*   969

Stevenson, Brooke (Health Care Professional)
Dangerous Moves - Mary Morgan   *r*   387

Stewart, John (Laird; Nobleman)
The Dreamer - May McGoldrick   *r*   372

Stodla, Frank (Outlaw; Thief)
Ghost Town - Ed Gorman   *w*   487

Character Name Index

Thornton, Spencer (Nobleman; Spy)
His Betrothed - Gayle Callen   *r*   235

Thorpe, Benjamin (Architect)
Candyland - Evan Hunter   *m*   84

Thorpe, Jim (Historical Figure; Sports Figure)
The Long Journey Home - Don Coldsmith   *t*   868

Thorssen, Alix (Art Dealer; Detective—Amateur)
Blue Wolf - Lise McClendon   *m*   111

Thrale, Hester (Historical Figure)
According to Queeney - Beryl Bainbridge   *t*   854

Thrale, Queeney (Young Woman)
According to Queeney - Beryl Bainbridge   *t*   854

Three Fingers (Chieftain)
Raven Mocker - Don Coldsmith   *w*   467

Thurborne, Daniel (Nobleman; Heir)
Lady Pirate - Lynsay Sands   *r*   418

Thurman, Donald (Teenager; Computer Expert)
Destiny's Door - Judith Tracy   *s*   838

Thurston, Alexandra Halsted (Socialite; Divorced Person)
A Scarlet Bride - Sylvia McDaniel   *r*   371

Tibibnia, Ellen (Psychic)
The Doorkeepers - Graham Masterton   *h*   706

Tippins, Jake (Detective—Police)
Have Gown, Need Groom - Rita Herron   *r*   302

Tiptree, Jacobia "Jake" (Single Parent; Stock Broker)
Repair to Her Grave - Sarah Graves   *m*   67

Tiresias, Dog (Indian; Cowboy)
Return to Ithaca - Randy Lee Eickhoff   *w*   478

Todd, Janet (Southern Belle)
When This Cruel War Is Over - Thomas Fleming   *t*   894

Todd, Jennifer (Abuse Victim; Pioneer)
The Gallows Land - Bill Pronzini   *w*   527

Todd, Mase (Villain)
The Gallows Land - Bill Pronzini   *w*   527

Tolbert, Chris (Artist; Handicapped)
Everyday People - Stewart O'Nan   *c*   1212

Tolbert, Eugene (Convict; Relative)
Everyday People - Stewart O'Nan   *c*   1212

Tolbert, Harold (Parent; Homosexual)
Everyday People - Stewart O'Nan   *c*   1212

Tolton, Garth (Nobleman)
The Missing Grooms - Cindy Holbrook   *r*   305

Tomlinson (Genius; Philosopher)
Shark River - Randy Wayne White   *m*   193

Toni (Saloon Keeper/Owner)
Dance of Knives - Donna McMahon   *s*   808

Torin, Cherijo (Doctor)
Endurance - S.L. Viehl   *s*   842

Torquil (Religious)
The Temple and the Crown - Katherine Kurtz   *f*   600

Touches the Wind (Indian)
Cheyenne Summer - Vella Munn   *w*   510

Townley, Willard (Art Dealer)
A Lovely Illusion - Tessa Barclay   *r*   214

Townsled, Simon (Nobleman)
A Bride for Lord Challmond - Debbie Raleigh   *r*   400

Tracker, Jacob (Clerk)
In the Blood - Stephen Gresham   *h*   683

Trampas (Outlaw; Outcast)
The Virginian - Owen Wister   *w*   549

Trask, Ben (Spy)
Avengers - Brian Lumley   *h*   702

Trask, Miles (Cowboy; Outcast)
Cow Thief Trail - Bennett Foster   *w*   482

Travers, Tory (Engineer; Single Parent)
Rosewood's Ashes - Aileen Schumacher   *m*   166

Tremayne, Lucinda-Ella "Rose" (Servant)
Rose of Nancemillin - Malcolm MacDonald   *t*   935

Trench, Mark (Businessman)
The House in the High Wood - Jeffrey Barlough   *h*   654

Trent, Delilah Haskell (Heiress)
The Wolf of Haskell Hall - Colleen Shannon   *r*   422

Trent, Evan (Nobleman)
His Lordship's Swan - Martha Kirkland   *r*   334

Trent, Michael (Military Personnel)
A Husband by Law - Cynthia Sterling   *r*   434

Trevain, Nathan (Gentleman; Spy)
Enchanted by Your Kisses - Pamela Britton   *r*   228

Trevisan, Mimi (Heiress; Spirit)
Mimi's Ghost - Tim Parks   *c*   1216

Trevisan, Paola (Spouse; Relative)
Mimi's Ghost - Tim Parks   *c*   1216
Mimi's Ghost - Tim Parks   *h*   717

Trewella, Tom (Banker; Smuggler)
The Mermaid of Penperro - Lisa Cach   *r*   234

Trezevant (Military Personnel)
Fire on the Waters - David Poyer   *t*   963

Trijn (Police Officer)
Point of Dreams - Melissa Scott   *f*   632

Trin, Marak (Warrior)
Hammerfall - C.J. Cherryh   *s*   765

Tripp, Ben (Detective—Private)
A Golden Trail of Murder - John Paxson   *w*   523

Trona, Joe (Police Officer)
Silent Joe - T. Jefferson Parker   *m*   143

Trufant, Maci (Lover; Secretary)
Gob's Grief - Chris Adrian   *c*   1102

Trumbull, Victoria (Writer; Aged Person)
Deadly Nightshade - Cynthia Riggs   *m*   155

Trust, Chena (Genetically Altered Being)
Kingdom of Cages - Sarah Zettel   *s*   851

Trust, Teal (Genetically Altered Being)
Kingdom of Cages - Sarah Zettel   *s*   851

Tryst, Sadun (Warrior)
Legacy of Blood - Richard A. Knaak   *f*   598

Tully, Zach (Police Officer)
Eternity - Tamara Thorne   *h*   743

Turcotte, Mike (Military Personnel)
Area 51: The Grail - Robert Doherty   *s*   773

Turnipseed, Anna (FBI Agent; Indian)
Ancient Ones - Kirk Mitchell   *w*   507
Ancient Ones - Kirk Mitchell   *w*   123
Spirit Sickness - Kirk Mitchell   *w*   508

Two Dogs (Indian; Chieftain)
Steele - Robert H. Redding   *w*   528

Tyrrell, Sarah (Widow(er))
The Privateersman - Richard Woodman   *t*   998

U

Ubekhet (Young Woman)
The Wise Woman - Christian Jacq   *t*   917

Ulloa, Delmira (Writer)
Leaving Tabasco - Carmen Boullosa   *c*   1116

Ulrika "Rika" (Warrior; Abuse Victim)
Ice Maiden - Debra Lee Brown   *r*   231

Underwood, Ben (Detective—Private)
An Uncommon Hero - Marie Ferrarella   *r*   267

Unnamed Character (Narrator; Student—College)
Adams Fall - Sean Desmond   *h*   671

Unnamed Character (Writer; Narrator)
Bad Timing - Betsy Berne   *c*   1113

Unnamed Character (Narrator; Servant)
Bone House - Betsy Tobin   *c*   1236
Bone House - Betsy Tobin   *t*   989

Unnamed Character (Narrator)
Johnny Blue and the Hanging Judge - Joseph A. West   *w*   548
Our Lady of the Lost and Found - Diane Schoemperlen   *c*   1226

Unnamed Character (Professor; Narrator)
The Sputnik Sweetheart - Haruki Murakami   *c*   1208

Unnamed Character (Professor)
To the Hermitage - Malcolm Bradbury   *c*   1118

Upton, Charles (Businessman; Wealthy)
Red Moon Rising - Billie Sue Mosiman   *h*   712

V

Vaananen, Esko (Architect; Immigrant)
The Cloud Sketcher - Richard Rayner   *c*   1221
The Cloud Sketcher - Richard Rayner   *t*   964

Val Orden, Gaborn (Nobleman)
Wizardborn - David Farland   *f*   578

Vala (Warrior)
The Summoning - Troy Denning   *f*   571

Valentin, Sebastien (Mythical Creature; Matchmaker)
Your Wish Is My Command - Donna Kauffman   *r*   327

Valentine, T. (Organized Crime Figure)
Four of a Kind - Gilbert Morris   *i*   1063

Valentine, Tony (Consultant; Police Officer)
Grift Sense - James Swain   *m*   180

Valentino, Eddie (Detective—Private)
Louisiana Hotshot - Julie Smith   *m*   173

Vallejos, Graciela (Cousin)
Loving Pedro Infante - Denise Chavez   *c*   1131

Vallerdas, Antonia (Spouse)
Antonia's Island - Nick P. Maginnis   *t*   937

Vallerdas, Rodrigo (Spouse)
Antonia's Island - Nick P. Maginnis   *t*   937

Van Buren, Alex (Pilot)
Suddenly Home - Loree Lough   *i*   1058

Van Cise, Phil (Lawyer)
The Binding Oath - Sybil Downing   *m*   45
The Binding Oath - Sybil Downing   *w*   477

Van Dusen, Charles (FBI Agent)
Cruzatte and Maria - Peter Bowen   *m*   11

Van Huyten, Mariesa (Businesswoman)
Falling Stars - Michael Flynn   *s*   782

Vane, Adeline (Noblewoman)
Bewitched - Heather Cullman   *r*   249

Vane, Michael (Nobleman; Recluse)
Bewitched - Heather Cullman   *r*   249

Vaughn, Malcolm (Spouse; Parent)
Singing Boy - Dennis McFarland   *c*   1199

Vaughn, Sarah (Spouse; Parent)
Singing Boy - Dennis McFarland   *c*   1199

Vaux, Anne (Noblewoman)
A Fifth of November - Paul West   *t*   993

Character Description Index

This index alphabetically lists descriptions of the major characters in featured titles. The descriptions may be occupations (astronaut, lawyer, etc.) or may describe persona (amnesiac, runaway, teenager, etc.). For each description, character names are listed alphabetically. Also provided are book titles, author names, genre codes and entry numbers. The genre codes are as follows: *c* Popular Fiction, *f* Fantasy, *h* Horror, *i* Inspirational, *m* Mystery, *r* Romance, *s* Science Fiction, *t* Historical, and *w* Western.

ABUSE VICTIM

Apropos
Sir Apropos of Nothing - Peter David *f* 569

Boyle, Dave
Mystic River - Dennis Lehane *c* 1183
Mystic River - Dennis Lehane *m* 102

Brennon, Meg
Blue Horizons - Irene Bennett Brown *w* 464

Cathryn of Greneforde
The Holding - Claudia Dain *r* 250

Drake, Mandy
Still Can't See Nothing Coming - Daniel Marshall *c* 1194

Henderson, Mistie Dawn
Wire Mesh Mothers - Elizabeth Massie *h* 705

Levin, Poti
Tears of Ice - Gary Livingston *t* 932

Lowe, Kenzie
The Warmest December - Bernice L. McFadden *c* 1198

Markham, Julia
On the Strength of Wings - Marthayn Pelegrimas *w* 524

Sadie
Sadie's Song - Linda Hall *i* 1038

Todd, Jennifer
The Gallows Land - Bill Pronzini *w* 527

Ulrika "Rika"
Ice Maiden - Debra Lee Brown *r* 231

ACCIDENT VICTIM

Cosini, Aljaz
Death of a River Guide - Richard Flanagan *c* 1151

ACCOUNTANT

August, Shelby
Nighttime Guardian - Amanda Stevens *r* 435

Bennett, Allie
Unbreak My Heart - Teresa Hill *r* 304

Hawthorne, Simon
Making Mr. Right - Jamie Denton *r* 254

Mackenzie, Roderick
The Rising Sun - Douglas Galbraith *t* 897

Malone, Mary
In His Arms - Robin Lee Hatcher *i* 1042

ACTIVIST

Bohem, Nisa
Secret Love - Bart Schneider *c* 1225

Brogus, Reggie
If 6 Were 9 - Jake Lamar *c* 1182

Cahill, Francesca
Deadly Love - B.D. Joyce *r* 325

Naylor, Jacob Alistair
Hush - Tim Lebbon *h* 697

Roseman, Jake
Secret Love - Bart Schneider *c* 1225

Zielinsky, David
Crooked River Burning - Mark Winegardner *c* 1245

ACTOR

Burns, Marty
Greed & Stuff - Jay Russell *m* 162

Chaplin, Charlie
A Few Minutes Past Midnight - Stuart M. Kaminsky *t* 921
A Few Minutes Past Midnight - Stuart M. Kaminsky *m* 91

Cleve, Alexander
Eclipse - John Banville *c* 1107

Fox, Charlie
Cowboy for Hire - Alice Duncan *r* 261

Halloran, Claude
Bound in Blood - Thomas Lord *h* 699

Michaelson, Hari
Blade of Tyshalle - Matthew Stover *f* 639

Revill, Nick
Death of Kings - Philip Goodin *m* 62

Stratton, Davy
The Devil's Apprentice - Edward Marston *t* 939

Welles, Orson
Angel in Black - Max Allan Collins *t* 870

ACTRESS

Barrett, Shelby
Be My Valentine - Sheila Rabe *r* 399

Benedict, Marina
Taken - Kathleen George *c* 1159

Byrne, Katie
The Triumph of Katie Byrne - Barbara Taylor Bradford *c* 1119

Cartier, Anne
Mute Witness - Charles O'Brien *m* 134
Mute Witness - Charles O'Brien *t* 953

Courbet, Noel
Bound in Blood - Thomas Lord *h* 699

Langtry, Lillie
Death at Epsom Downs - Robin Paige *m* 140

Marcus, Josie
Gunman's Rhapsody - Robert B. Parker *t* 956
Gunman's Rhapsody - Robert B. Parker *w* 520

McSwain, Diamond
Secret Love - Brenda Jackson *r* 312

Watson, Alice
If You Want Me - Kayla Perrin *r* 392

Wilkes, Amy
Cowboy for Hire - Alice Duncan *r* 261

ADDICT

Jones, Deckard
Singing Boy - Dennis McFarland *c* 1199

Mancini, Munch
Unfinished Business - Barbara Seranella *m* 168

Mancini, Victor
Choke - Chuck Palahniuk *c* 1214

Price, Paris
A Day Late and a Dollar Short - Terry McMillan *c* 1200

ADMINISTRATOR

Mackenzie, Robert
The Rising Sun - Douglas Galbraith *c* 1158

Richardson, Rosie
Cause Celeb - Helen Fielding *c* 1150

Weston, Glory
A Daddy at Heart - Deb Kastner *i* 1050

ARCHITECT

ART DEALER

ARTIFICIAL INTELLIGENCE

ARTISAN

ARTIST

ASSISTANT

ASTROLOGER

ASTRONAUT

BAKER

BANKER

BASTARD DAUGHTER

Beckett, Sophia Maria "Sophie"
An Offer from a Gentleman - Julia Quinn   *r*   398

Hannigan, Annie
Kate Hannigan's Girl - Catherine Cookson   *t*   872

James, Taylor Christie
Wild Flower - Cheryl Anne Porter   *r*   395

Sherbrooke, Mary Rose
The Scottish Bride - Catherine Coulter   *r*   245

BASTARD SON

Boudreaux, Chantz
Fever - Katherine Sutcliffe   *r*   438

Garvey, Flynn
Sweethearts of the Twilight Lanes - Luanne Jones   *r*   324

BEACHCOMBER

Jackson, J.W.
Vineyard Shadows - Philip R. Craig   *m*   28

BENEFACTOR

Lacan, Celeste
Animosity - David L. Lindsey   *c*   1185

BLACKSMITH

Smith, Sugar Bear
The Haunting of Hood Canal - Jack Cady   *h*   662

BODYGUARD

Chambers, Vivian
When the Cold Wind Blows - Charles L. Grant   *h*   682

Lancet, Marisa
A True Prince - Veronica Sattler   *r*   420

Lucas, Billy
The Heiress and the Bodyguard - Ryanne Corey   *r*   244

Raith
The Queen's Necklace - Teresa Edgerton   *f*   576

Sullivan, Grady
Too Good to Be True - Kasey Michaels   *r*   382

BOUNTY HUNTER

Cord, Mackenzy "Mac"
Hero for Hire - Sheridon Smythe   *r*   432

Manoso, Ricardo Carlos "Ranger"
Seven Up - Janet Evanovich   *m*   50

Plum, Stephanie
Seven Up - Janet Evanovich   *m*   50

BOYFRIEND

Corland, Rob
A Special Kind of Family - Eileen Berger   *i*   1014

Gary
Paradise Park - Allegra Goodman   *c*   1162

Guberman, Bruce
Good in Bed - Jennifer Weiner   *c*   1241

Jahal, Samil
The Death of Vishnu - Manil Suri   *c*   1231

Matthew
Lilac Blossom Time - Carrie Bender   *i*   1010

Nigel
Karlmarx.com - Susan Coll   *c*   1134

Oliver
Cause Celeb - Helen Fielding   *c*   1150

Randall, Paul
Second Chances - Valerie Hansen   *i*   1040

Smith, Dan
Blind Side - Penny Warner   *m*   189

Will
Back When We Were Grownups - Anne Tyler   *c*   1237

BRIDE

Beaufort, Charity
Royal Bride - Joan Wolf   *r*   450

Burnett, Anne
The Marriage Contract - Cathy Maxwell   *r*   365

Coppersmith, Cynthia
A Common Life - Jan Karon   *c*   1179

Rawlings, Francesca
All about Passion - Stephanie Laurens   *r*   347

Sherbrooke, Mary Rose
The Scottish Bride - Catherine Coulter   *r*   245

Winthrop, Ellen
A Husband by Law - Cynthia Sterling   *r*   434

Ygraine
Uther - Jack Whyte   *f*   650
Uther - Jack Whyte   *t*   995

BRIDEGROOM

Kavanaugh, Timothy
A Common Life - Jan Karon   *c*   1179

BUSINESSMAN

Abelscu, Iacob
Departures - Miriam Striezheff Lewis   *t*   928

Blackthorne, Richard
Taming the Beast - Amy J. Fetzer   *r*   268

Brennan, Daniel
A Notorious Love - Sabrina Jeffries   *r*   317

Carpenter, Luke
Sweet Annie - Cheryl St. John   *r*   433

Chris
The Lost Daughter of Happiness - Geling Yan   *t*   1001
The Lost Daughter of Happiness - Geling Yan   *w*   551

Cody, Samuel
The Indiscretion - Judith Ivory   *r*   311

Colvin, Roger
T2: Infiltrator - S.M. Stirling   *s*   834

Daniels, Robert
Lick Creek - Brad Kessler   *t*   923

Darrow, Will
First Comes Love - Elizabeth Bevarly   *r*   220

Davidson, Scott
Rocky Mountain Miracle - Leona Karr   *i*   1049

de Floon, Caz
The Wooden Sea - Jonathan Carroll   *f*   562

de Groot, Cedar
Dance of Knives - Donna McMahon   *s*   808

Dedham, Franklin
Fire in Beulah - Rilla Askew   *t*   853

Dempsey, Will
A Hero for Kelsey - Carolyne Aarsen   *i*   1002

Donovan, Guy
Annie, Get Your Guy - Lori Foster   *r*   271

Easton, Mack
Lost and Found - Jayne Ann Krentz   *r*   338

Eckman, Hank
The View from Hell - John Shirley   *h*   736

Fielding, Ben
Safely Home - Randy C. Alcorn   *i*   1005

Fitzmichael, Vincent
Edward Maret - Robert L. Katz   *s*   798

Gray Squirrel
Tails You Lose - Lisa Smedman   *f*   637

Haines, Alonzo
The Free Lunch - Spider Robinson   *s*   824

Hawthorne, Lucas
Nightingale's Gate - Linda Francis Lee   *r*   350

Hosokawa
Bel Canto - Ann Patchett   *c*   1217

Hound
Return to the Whorl - Gene Wolfe   *s*   850

Humphries, Martin
The Precipice - Ben Bova   *s*   761

Jackson, Jake
Love Sign - Susan Kirby   *i*   1051

Jones, David
Be My Valentine - Sheila Rabe   *r*   399

Kincaid, Rory
This Perfect Kiss - Christie Ridgway   *r*   407

Kleinman, August
Carry Me Across the Water - Ethan C. Canin   *c*   1125

Langan, Nick
The Marrying Kind - Cynthia Rutledge   *i*   1081

MacCormick, Andrew
The Cloud Sketcher - Richard Rayner   *t*   964

MacKenzie, Blake
Seeing Stars - Vanessa Grant   *r*   284

MacTavish, Lachlan
All a Woman Wants - Patricia Rice   *r*   404

Madison, Gabe
Dawn in Eclipse Bay - Jayne Ann Krentz   *r*   337

Mars, George Washington
The Killer Gun - Lauran Paine   *w*   519

McLoughlin, John
The Fields of Eden - Richard S. Wheeler   *t*   994

Merchon, Duke
Overnight Cinderella - Katherine Garbera   *r*   275

Moberley, Gaynor
The Dragon Charmer - Jan Siegel   *f*   634

Mordant, Frank
The Doorkeepers - Graham Masterton   *h*   706

Nyhal, Eldyn
The Octagonal Raven - L.E. Modesitt Jr.   *s*   809

Omochi
Fear and Trembling - Amelie Nothomb   *c*   1210

Paterson, William
The Rising Sun - Douglas Galbraith   *t*   897

Pendleton, Joseph
Bad Timing - Betsy Berne   *c*   1113

Pendleton, Lucas
My True Love - Cheryl Holt   *r*   309

Posenato, Bobo
Mimi's Ghost - Tim Parks   *h*   717

Quinn, Adrian
Nobody's Angel - Patricia Rice   *r*   405

Shadow
American Gods - Neil Gaiman   *f*   583

Speight, Eureka "Reka"
Towns Without Rivers - Michael Parker   *c*   1215

Tolbert, Eugene
Everyday People - Stewart O'Nan   *c*   1212

COOK

Cavaco, Mike
Making over Mike - Lisa Plumley   *r*   394

Dartigen, Mirabelle
Five Quarters of the Orange - Joanne Harris   *t*   910

Ito
Crawling at Night - Nani Power   *c*   1219

Ramesh
Sister India - Peggy Payne   *c*   1218

Wilde, Max
Born to Be Wild - Patti Berg   *r*   217

COUNSELOR

Lindsey, Allie
Rocky Mountain Miracle - Leona Karr   *i*   1049

Montgomery, Maddie
Messing around with Max - Lori Foster   *r*   272

COURIER

Solage, Dominic
Athena's Conquest - Catherine Blair   *r*   225

COUSIN

Jones, Renie
Suture Self - Mary Daheim   *m*   32

Montford, Jack
A Finer End - Deborah Crombie   *m*   29

Randall
The Gardens of Kyoto - Kate Walbert   *c*   1240
Gardens of Kyoto - Kate Walbert   *t*   992

Rawlings, Gid
Comanche Peace Pipe - Patrick Dearen   *w*   472
The Hidden Treasure of the Chisos - Patrick
  Dearen   *w*   473
On the Pecos Trail - Patrick Dearen   *w*   474

Vallejos, Graciela
Loving Pedro Infante - Denise Chavez   *c*   1131

COWBOY

Atherton, Thomas
The Buffalo Hunters - Gary McCarthy   *w*   504

Blocker, Ab
Get Along, Little Dogies - Lisa Waller
  Rogers   *w*   533

Collins, Brad
Brannick: And the Untamed West - Harold G.
  Ross   *w*   534

Dupree, Johnny Blue
Johnny Blue and the Hanging Judge - Joseph A.
  West   *w*   548

Fahr, Clee
Death Rides the Denver Stage - Lewis B.
  Patten   *w*   522

Felver, Owen
Man from Wolf River - John D. Nesbitt   *w*   511

Fox, Charlie
Cowboy for Hire - Alice Duncan   *r*   261

Goodnight, Jimmy
Code of the West - Aaron Latham   *t*   926
Code of the West - Aaron Latham   *w*   500

Hogg, Marshall
Gabriel's Story - David Anthony Durham   *t*   886

Loving, Jack
Code of the West - Aaron Latham   *t*   926
Code of the West - Aaron Latham   *w*   500

McLeod, Angus
The O'Keefe Empire - Jane Candia Coleman   *w*   468

Picket, Bill
The Long Journey Home - Don Coldsmith   *t*   868

Tiresias, Dog
Return to Ithaca - Randy Lee Eickhoff   *w*   478

Trask, Miles
Cow Thief Trail - Bennett Foster   *w*   482

Virginian
The Virginian - Owen Wister   *w*   549

Walker, Mark
A Husband to Hold - Cheryl Wolverton   *i*   1101

CRIME SUSPECT

Boyle, Dave
Mystic River - Dennis Lehane   *m*   102
Mystic River - Dennis Lehane   *c*   1183

Ford, Ethan
Blue Diary - Alice Hoffman   *c*   1171

Hawthorne, Lucas
Nightingale's Gate - Linda Francis Lee   *r*   350

Scully, Shane
The Tin Collector - Stephen J. Cannell   *c*   1126

Smiricky, Sidonia
Two Murders in My Double Life - Josef
  Skvorecky   *c*   1228

Storey, David
A Darkness More than Night - Michael
  Connelly   *c*   1135

CRIME VICTIM

Armstrong, Catherine
Border Lord - Haywood Smith   *r*   431

Benedict, Marina
Taken - Kathleen George   *c*   1159

Denise
The Triumph of Katie Byrne - Barbara Taylor
  Bradford   *c*   1119

Dora
Bone House - Betsy Tobin   *c*   1236
Bone House - Betsy Tobin   *t*   989

Hammett, Raymond
Two Murders in My Double Life - Josef
  Skvorecky   *c*   1228

McGowan, Alec
Morning - W.D. Wetherell   *c*   1242

Minton, Paris
Fearless Jones - Walter Mosley   *c*   1206
Fearless Jones - Walter Mosley   *m*   126

Morris, Rachel
Blue Diary - Alice Hoffman   *c*   1171

Westmoreland, Penelope
My True Love - Cheryl Holt   *r*   309

Wolfsheim, Jennifer
If 6 Were 9 - Jake Lamar   *c*   1182

CRIMINAL

Baker, Catastrophe
The Outpost - Mike Resnick   *s*   819

Benny
Deadfellas - David Whitman   *h*   748

Bondurant, Pete
The Cold Six Thousand - James Ellroy   *c*   1148

Da Yong
The Lost Daughter of Happiness - Geling
  Yan   *t*   1001
The Lost Daughter of Happiness - Geling
  Yan   *w*   551

Dixon, Wyatt
Bitterroot - James Lee Burke   *w*   465

Douglas, Leon
Fearless Jones - Walter Mosley   *c*   1206

Flaherty, Mark
Times and Seasons - Beverly LaHaye   *i*   1053

Fortune, Samuel
The Long Trail Home - Stephen A. Bly   *i*   1019

Gareth of Summerfield
The Truest Heart - Samantha James   *r*   316

Greenstreet, Sidney
Sleepeasy - T.M. Wright   *h*   751

Greyboar
The Philosophical Strangler - Eric Flint   *f*   580

Hades, Acheron
The Eyre Affair - Jasper Fforde   *s*   780

Holloway, Jon
The Blue Nowhere - Jeffery Deaver   *m*   37

Ignace
The Philosophical Strangler - Eric Flint   *f*   580

Karma, Billy
The Outpost - Mike Resnick   *s*   819

Kennedy, Agnes
Water of Death - Paul Johnston   *s*   797

Machen, Tim
Deadfellas - David Whitman   *h*   748

Moriarty, James
The Great Game - Michael Kurland   *m*   99

Motley
Perdido Street Station - China Mieville   *f*   611

O'Connor, Francis
Deadfellas - David Whitman   *h*   748

Taltos, Vlad
Issola - Steven Brust   *f*   558

Testosterone, Johnny
The Outpost - Mike Resnick   *s*   819

Yost, Sylvester
Betrayal in Death - J.D. Robb   *s*   822

CRITIC

Gallagher, Dan
The Trouble with Mary - Millie Criswell   *r*   248

Nanson, Phineas C.
The Biographer's Tale - A.S. Byatt   *c*   1124

CYBORG

Maret, Edward
Edward Maret - Robert L. Katz   *s*   798

DANCER

Kimball, Kate Stanislaski
Considering Kate - Nora Roberts   *r*   411

Chaplin, Alessandro
Talisker - Miller Lau   *f*   603

Christie, Richard
Taken - Kathleen George   *c*   1159

Cox, Luther
Natural Law - D.R. Schanker   *m*   165

Dalrymple, Quintillian
Water of Death - Paul Johnston   *s*   797

Fletcher, Alec
To Davy Jones Below - Carola Dunn   *m*   46
To Davy Jones Below - Carola Dunn   *t*   885

Franks, Joseph
Holy Rollers - J. Newman   *h*   714

Halford, Daniel
Mother Tongue - Teri Holbrook   *m*   82

Ichiro, Sano
Black Lotus - Laura Joh Rowland   *t*   975

Kennedy, Dillon "Duck"
Killer Riches - Chassie West   *m*   191

MacDonald, Mac
The Triumph of Katie Byrne - Barbara Taylor
   Bradford   *c*   1119

MacGregor, Jamie
Highland Dream - Tess Mallory   *r*   361

Montana, Dylan
Remember Your Lies - Jill Jones   *r*   323

Potter, Ingram
Balak - Stephen Mark Rainey   *h*   727

Rathe, Nicolas
Point of Dreams - Melissa Scott   *f*   632

Raye, Winona
Millionaire M.D. - Jennifer Greene   *r*   288

Saint-Martin, Paul de
Mute Witness - Charles O'Brien   *t*   953

Scully, Shane
The Tin Collector - Stephen J. Cannell   *c*   1126

Thorne, Maddy
Hangman - Michael Slade   *h*   738

Tippins, Jake
Have Gown, Need Groom - Rita Herron   *r*   302

DETECTIVE—PRIVATE

August, Billie
Whatever Doesn't Kill You - Gillian Roberts   *m*   158

Barrington, Stone
Cold Paradise - Stuart Woods   *m*   198

Briggs, Harry
Sleepeasy - T.M. Wright   *h*   751

Burns, Marty
Greed & Stuff - Jay Russell   *m*   162

Caine, John
Silversword - Charles Knief   *m*   97

Coffey, Jack
Just One Kiss - Carla Cassidy   *r*   242

Cuesta, Willie
The Ultimate Havana - John Lantigua   *m*   101

Culpepper, Jett
Scent of Murder - Cynthia G. Alwyn   *m*   2

Falco, Marcus Didius
Ode to a Banker - Lindsey Davis   *m*   35
Ode to a Banker - Lindsey Davis   *t*   877

Farris, Shara
Judas Eyes - Barry Hoffman   *h*   688

Gibson, Carole Ann
Paradise Interrupted - Penny Mickelbury   *m*   120

Goodlow, Sam
Sleepeasy - T.M. Wright   *h*   751

Grayson, Cole
Private Vows - Sally Steward   *r*   436

Haddam, Amos
One O'Clock Jump - Lise McClendon   *m*   112
One O'Clock Jump - Lise McClendon   *t*   942

Hastings, Stanley
Cozy - Parnell Hall   *m*   71

Hawkes, Frank
Duet for the Devil - T. Winter-Damon   *h*   750

Heller, Nathan
Angel in Black - Max Allan Collins   *t*   870
Angel in Black - Max Allan Collins   *m*   25

Holmes, Sherlock
The Great Game - Michael Kurland   *m*   99
Sherlock Holmes: The Missing Years - Jamyang
   Norbu   *t*   952

Howe, Emma
Whatever Doesn't Kill You - Gillian Roberts   *m*   158

Jacovich, Milan
The Dutch - Les Roberts   *m*   159

Jantzen, Joe
Follow That Baby! - Isabel Sharpe   *r*   423

Jones, Casey
Better Off Dead - Katy Munger   *m*   128

Jones, Lena
Desert Noir - Betty Webb   *m*   190

Lennox, Dorie
One O'Clock Jump - Lise McClendon   *m*   112
One O'Clock Jump - Lise McClendon   *t*   942

Liffey, Jack
The Orange Curtain - John Shannon   *m*   169

Light, Robin
Blowing Smoke - Barbara Block   *m*   8

Mabry, Bubba
Crazy Love - Steve Brewer   *m*   13

McCain, Sam
Will You Still Love Me Tomorrow? - Ed
   Gorman   *m*   63

McKnight, Alex
The Hunting Wind - Steve Hamilton   *m*   75

McMannus, Deidre
Archangel Protocol - Lyda Morehouse   *s*   810

Millhone, Kinsey
P Is for Peril - Sue Grafton   *m*   66

Navarre, Jackson "Tres"
The Devil Went Down to Austin - Rick
   Riordan   *m*   156

O'Connor, Cork
Purgatory Ridge - William Kent Krueger   *m*   98

Peters, Toby
A Few Minutes Past Midnight - Stuart M.
   Kaminsky   *t*   921
A Few Minutes Past Midnight - Stuart M.
   Kaminsky   *m*   91

Principal, Laura
In the Midnight Hour - Michelle Spring   *m*   174

Reid, Savannah
Sour Grapes - G.A. McKevett   *m*   117

Roberts, Mitch
Samedi's Knapsack - Gaylord Dold   *m*   43

Ross, Dani
Four of a Kind - Gilbert Morris   *i*   1063

Shapiro, Desiree
Murder Can Upset Your Mother - Selma
   Eichler   *m*   47

Shugak, Kate
The Singing of the Dead - Dana Stabenow   *m*   175

Sloane, Sydney
East of Niece - Randye Lordon   *m*   106

Smith, Dan
Blind Side - Penny Warner   *m*   189

Spenser
Potshot - Robert B. Parker   *m*   142

Strange, Derek
Right as Rain - George P. Pelecanos   *m*   146

Taylor, George Bailey
Aphrodite's Kiss - Julie Kenner   *r*   330

Tripp, Ben
A Golden Trail of Murder - John Paxson   *w*   523

Underwood, Ben
An Uncommon Hero - Marie Ferrarella   *r*   267

Valentino, Eddie
Louisiana Hotshot - Julie Smith   *m*   173

Wallace, Talba
Louisiana Hotshot - Julie Smith   *m*   173

DIPLOMAT

Cody, Samuel
The Indiscretion - Judith Ivory   *r*   311

Davis, Leslie
Three Apples Fell from Heaven - Micheline Aharonian
   Marcom   *c*   1193

Diadem, Sarah
The Diplomatic Touch - David Bischoff   *s*   758

Diadem, Thomas
The Diplomatic Touch - David Bischoff   *s*   758

Lovell, John Henry
Lilies on the Lake - Katherine Kingsley   *r*   333

McDougal, Dougal
Spheres of Heaven - Charles Sheffield   *s*   829

Morgan, Steve
Savage Desire - Rosemary Rogers   *r*   414

Raithe, Pallas
Blade of Tyshalle - Matthew Stover   *f*   639

DIRECTOR

Albertson, Bobby
Bobby's Girl - J.D. Austin   *s*   754

Robles, Rey
The Body Artist - Don DeLillo   *c*   1138

Storey, David
A Darkness More than Night - Michael
   Connelly   *c*   1135

Thorn, Cordelia
The Merchant of Venus - Ellen Hart   *m*   79

DISSIDENT

Yun, Shan Tao
Water Touching Stone - Eliot Pattison   *m*   144

DIVORCED PERSON

Adeline
The Shape of Things to Come - Maud
   Casey   *c*   1129

Allen, Darryl Bob
Thanksgiving - Michael Dibdin   *c*   1141

Conroy, Sara
Loving a Lonesome Cowboy - Debbi Rawlins   *r*   402

Craig, Clare
Thursdays at Eight - Debbie Macomber   r   360

Crown, Maggie
Kinship Theory - Hester Kaplan   c   1178

Fuller, Josephine "Jo"
At Large - Lynne Murray   m   130

Hartley, Nora
Our Arcadia - Robin Lippincott   t   931

Hughes, Stuart
Love, Etc. - Julian Barnes   c   1109

Millhone, Kinsey
P Is for Peril - Sue Grafton   m   66

Perron, Jade
Finding Ian - Stella Cameron   r   237

Russell, Gillian
Love, Etc. - Julian Barnes   c   1109

Thurston, Alexandra Halsted
A Scarlet Bride - Sylvia McDaniel   r   371

DOCTOR

Adams, Victor
The Hampton Passion - Julie Ellis   r   264

Bailey, Bryn
Pathways - Lisa Tawn Bergren   i   1015

Beck, David
Tell No One - Harlan Coben   m   24

Beckett, Grace
The Dark Remains - Mark Anthony   f   552

Bendix, Joseph
The House of Sight and Shadow - Nicholas
   Griffin   t   907

Bouchie, Roxanne
The Last Blue Plate Special - Abigail
   Padgett   m   138

Branscombe, Violet
Dr. Mortimer and the Barking Man Mystery - Gerard
   Williams   m   195
Dr. Mortimer and the Barking Man Mystery - Gerard
   Williams   t   996

Calcraft, Edmund
The House of Sight and Shadow - Nicholas
   Griffin   t   907

Connors, Beatrice "Birdie"
The Four Seasons - Mary Alice Monroe   r   384

Cortez, Rebecca
Operation Sierra-75 - Thomas S. Gressman   s   791

Donivan, Molly
Twilight in Texas - Jodi Thomas   r   440

Filek
The Shasht War - Christopher Rowley   f   627

Forth, Nefret
Lord of the Silent - Elizabeth Peters   m   148
Lord of the Silent - Elizabeth Peters   t   961

Hardesty, Stephen
Camellia - Ginny Aiken   i   1003

Howell, Hannah
Have Gown, Need Groom - Rita Herron   r   302

Irons, Cheney Duvall
Where Two Seas Met - Lynn Morris   i   1064

Katz, Phil
Eternity - Tamara Thorne   h   743

Kent, Alexander "Alex"
The Colors of Love - Vanessa Grant   r   283

Kirby, Jeff
The Way We Wed - Pat Warren   r   445

Lewis, Jane
Plain Jane - Fern Michaels   r   380

Lotari, Kathy
Borrowed Tides - Paul Levinson   s   800

MacKenzie, John Alexander
Murder at Bertram's Bower - Cynthia Peale   m   145

Mortimer, James
Dr. Mortimer and the Barking Man Mystery - Gerard
   Williams   m   195
Dr. Mortimer and the Barking Man Mystery - Gerard
   Williams   t   996

Polidori, John
The Merciful Women - Federico Andahazi   h   652

Purdue, Thomas
The Midnight Special - Larry Karp   m   92

Raad, George
Martyrs' Crossing - Amy Wilentz   c   1244

St. Leger, Valentine
Midnight Bride - Susan Carroll   r   241

Schaeffer, Boyd
Life After Death - Carol Muske-Dukes   c   1209

Seymour, Tom
Border Crossing - Pat Barker   c   1108

Sorenson, Michael
Plain Jane - Fern Michaels   r   380

Stanton, Reilly
Lady of Skye - Patricia Cabot   r   233

Telamon
The House of Death - P.C. Doherty   m   42
The House of Death - P.C. Doherty   t   881

Torin, Cherijo
Endurance - S.L. Viehl   s   842

Voss, Tobin
Bitterroot - James Lee Burke   w   465

Walcott, Tim
Beloved Stranger - Clare Boylan   c   1117

Webb, Justin
Millionaire M.D. - Jennifer Greene   r   288

Witherspoon, Maya
The Serpent's Shadow - Mercedes Lackey   f   602

Wolf, Hildegard
Aiding & Abetting - Muriel Spark   c   1229

DRIFTER

Boone, Roy
The Gallows Land - Bill Pronzini   w   527

Dawson, Adam
There Came a Stranger - Andrew J. Fenady   w   480

Dias, Walter
The Painter of Birds - Lidia Jorge   c   1177

Fahr, Clee
Death Rides the Denver Stage - Lewis B.
   Patten   w   522

Felver, Owen
Man from Wolf River - John D. Nesbitt   w   511

Fogg, Buster
The Magic Wagon - Joe R. Lansdale   w   499

Fortune, Samuel
The Long Trail Home - Stephen A. Bly   i   1019

McCracken, Sim
Beneath a Whiskey Sky - Tracy Knight   w   498

Reacher, Jack
Echo Burning - Lee Child   m   22

Sutter, J.
John Henry Days - Colson Whitehead   c   1243

DRUG DEALER

Brogan, Monty
The 25th Hour - David Benioff   c   1111

Paley, Hitch
The Chronoliths - Robert Charles Wilson   s   849

EDITOR

Blackstock, Dorothy "Dodie"
Dying Voices - Laura Wilson   m   197

Cunningham, Zoe
The Bay of Angels - Anita Brookner   c   1120

Ferrenzo, Natalie
The Other Woman - Patricia Kay   r   329

Rawlings, Claire
Who Killed Mona Lisa? - Carole Bugge   m   17

Redding, Theresa Jo "Tess"
Sweethearts of the Twilight Lanes - Luanne
   Jones   r   324

EMPLOYER

Haig-Ereildoun
Do Try to Speak as We Do - Marjorie Leet
   Ford   c   1152

Worthington
Lilac Blossom Time - Carrie Bender   i   1010

ENGINEER

Malvern, Deirdre
The Meek - Scott Mackay   s   802

Travers, Tory
Rosewood's Ashes - Aileen Schumacher   m   166

Wisner, Cody
The Meek - Scott Mackay   s   802

ENTERTAINER

Ahasuerus
Tales of the Galactic Midway - Mike
   Resnick   s   820

Bridge, Ruby
Summer Island - Kristin Hannah   r   293

Dancer, Billybuck
Tales of the Galactic Midway - Mike
   Resnick   s   820

Flint, Thaddeus
Tales of the Galactic Midway - Mike
   Resnick   s   820

Hastings, Willow
Almost a Lady - Heidi Betts   r   219

Marx, Groucho
Groucho Marx and the Broadway Murders - Ron
   Goulart   m   65
Groucho Marx and the Broadway Murders - Ron
   Goulart   t   903

Renhardt, Klale
Dance of Knives - Donna McMahon   s   808

Smelt, Gordon
Nothing but Blue Skies - Tom Holt   f   589

ENVIRONMENTALIST

Babcock, Lydia Arlington
The Voice of the Butterfly - John Nichols   w   513

McFarland, Charlie
The Voice of the Butterfly - John Nichols   w   513

EXECUTIONER

Rudd, Fabian
The Master Executioner - Loren D. Estleman   *w*   479

Stone, Oscar
The Master Executioner - Loren D. Estleman   *t*   891
The Master Executioner - Loren D. Estleman   *w*   479

EXPATRIATE

Alik
The Funeral Party - Ludmila Ulitskaya   *c*   1238

Doolittle, Delilah
Delilah Doolittle and the Canine Chorus - Patricia Guiver   *m*   69

Natraja
Sister India - Peggy Payne   *c*   1218

Smiricky, Danny
Two Murders in My Double Life - Josef Skvorecky   *c*   1228

Thebaw
The Glass Palace - Amitav Ghosh   *c*   1160

EXPLORER

Line, Victoria
Flatterland - Ian Stewart   *s*   833

FARMER

Ambler, Jack
Blue Horizons - Irene Bennett Brown   *w*   464

Brannick, Jim
Brannick: And the Untamed West - Harold G. Ross   *w*   534

Chandler, Eli
A Painted House - John Grisham   *c*   1165

Flood, Jehiel
Beulah Hill - William Heffernan   *t*   911

Galter, Lucien
American Empire: Blood and Iron - Harry Turtledove   *s*   839

Hanson, Lute
More than Memory - Dorothy Garlock   *r*   276

Hasper, Will
Valley of Promises - Bonnie Leon   *i*   1056

Jackson, Gabriel
The Bad Man's Bride - Susan Kay Law   *r*   348

Longfellow, Richard
A Mischief in the Snow - Margaret Miles   *m*   121

Petrovna, Vladimir
Let Freedom Ring - Al Lacy   *i*   1052

Singleton, Ray
The Magic of Ordinary Days - Ann Howard Creel   *w*   471

Swann
Tennant's Rock - Steve McGiffen   *t*   944

Vogel, Berndt
The Last Report on the Miracles at Little No Horse - Louise Erdrich   *c*   1149

Willett, Charlotte
A Mischief in the Snow - Margaret Miles   *m*   121

FBI AGENT

Dean, Sullivan "Sully"
Storm Warning - Dinah McCall   *r*   367

Demarkian, Gregor
True Believers - Jane Haddam   *m*   70

Ellison, Kathleen "Kate"
Reinventing Romeo - Connie Lane   *r*   343

Harris, Flint
A Bride for Dry Creek - Janet Tronstad   *i*   1094

Littel, Ward Jr.
The Cold Six Thousand - James Ellroy   *c*   1148

McCaleb, Terry
A Darkness More than Night - Michael Connelly   *c*   1135

Ness, Eliot
Angel in Black - Max Allan Collins   *t*   870

Rawlins, Sam "Grey Wolf"
The Witness - Ginna Gray   *r*   285

Turnipseed, Anna
Ancient Ones - Kirk Mitchell   *m*   123
Ancient Ones - Kirk Mitchell   *w*   507
Spirit Sickness - Kirk Mitchell   *w*   508

Van Dusen, Charles
Cruzatte and Maria - Peter Bowen   *m*   11

FEMME FATALE

Montgomery, Maddie
Messing around with Max - Lori Foster   *r*   272

FIANCE(E)

Begum, Arina
The Long Love - Katharine Gordon   *r*   279

Bennett, Steve
Times and Seasons - Beverly LaHaye   *i*   1053

Brackley, Camden Thurston
Never a Bride - Amelia Grey   *r*   290

Jerningham, Gabrielle "Gabby"
Enchanting Pleasures - Eloisa James   *r*   315

Kirkland, Hannah
Finally Home - Lyn Cote   *i*   1030

Rollins, Taylor
The Marrying Kind - Cynthia Rutledge   *i*   1081

Ted
Do Try to Speak as We Do - Marjorie Leet Ford   *c*   1152

Whittingham, Mirabella
Never a Bride - Amelia Grey   *r*   290

FILMMAKER

Fatty
The Hell Screens - Alvin Lu   *h*   700

Pellam, John
Hell's Kitchen - Jeffery Deaver   *m*   38

FIRE FIGHTER

MacIntyre, Alex
Courting Katarina - Carol Steward   *i*   1089

Skeehan, Georgia
The Fourth Angel - Suzanne Chazin   *m*   21

FISHERMAN

Cairns, Gregor
Cosmonaut Keep - Ken MacLeod   *s*   803

FOREMAN

MacLeod, Ross
The Perfect Family - Patricia Potter   *r*   397

Stackhouse, Jason
Dead Until Dark - Charlaine Harris   *h*   685

FRIEND

Arch
Taps - Willie Morris   *c*   1205

Daisy
We're So Famous - Jaime Clarke   *c*   1132

Denise
The Triumph of Katie Byrne - Barbara Taylor Bradford   *c*   1119

Elinsky, Jakob
The 25th Hour - David Benioff   *c*   1111

Estella
Mapping the Edge - Sarah Dunant   *c*   1143

Granados, Irma
Loving Pedro Infante - Denise Chavez   *c*   1131

Hughes, Stuart
Love, Etc. - Julian Barnes   *c*   1109

James
Gabriel's Story - David Anthony Durham   *c*   1145

Jones, Deckard
Singing Boy - Dennis McFarland   *c*   1199

Jones, Fearless
Fearless Jones - Walter Mosley   *m*   126
Fearless Jones - Walter Mosley   *c*   1206

Paque
We're So Famous - Jaime Clarke   *c*   1132

Russell, Oliver
Love, Etc. - Julian Barnes   *c*   1109

Slattery, Frank
The 25th Hour - David Benioff   *c*   1111

Stella
We're So Famous - Jaime Clarke   *c*   1132

FRONTIERSMAN

Dorset, Lew
Beyond the Outposts - Max Brand   *w*   458

Grant, Jonathan
Freedom's Shadow - Marlo M. Schalesky   *i*   1083

Limousin, Jean
The Tyrant - Max Brand   *w*   460

FUGITIVE

al-Mansur, Ashraf
Pashazade: The First Arabesk - Jon Courtenay Grimwood   *s*   792

DeCarlo, Anna
Bride on the Run - Elizabeth Lane   *r*   344

Gillian of Westerbrook
The Truest Heart - Samantha James   *r*   316

Hawksmore, Adam
Mightier than the Sword - Peggy Waide   *r*   442

Kills Crow, Kole
You Never Can Tell - Kathleen Eagle   *r*   263

Loudon, Quinn
The Lawman Meets His Bride - Meagan McKinney   *r*   374

Lucan
Aiding & Abetting - Muriel Spark   *c*   1229

HISTORIAN

HISTORICAL FIGURE

Joan of Arc
The Merlin of the Oak Wood - Ann
   Chamberlin   *f* 563
The Merlin of the Oak Wood - Ann
   Chamberlin   *t* 863

Johnson, Samuel
According to Queeney - Beryl Bainbridge *t* 854

Julia
The Love-Artist - Jane Alison *t* 852

Kahlo, Christina
Frida - Barbara Mujica *c* 1207

Kahlo, Frida
Frida - Barbara Mujica *c* 1207

Kandinsky, Vasily
Burnt Umber - Sheldon Greene *t* 906

Kelsey, Andrew
An Ordinary Woman - Cecelia Holland *w* 493

Kelsey, Ben
An Ordinary Woman - Cecelia Holland *w* 493

Kelsey, Nancy
An Ordinary Woman - Cecelia Holland *w* 493

Kleopatra
Kleopatra - Karen Essex *t* 890

Langtry, Lillie
Death at Epsom Downs - Robin Paige *m* 140

Louis XIV
Gardener to the King - Frederic Richaud *t* 968

Luther, Martin
Storm - Reg Grant *t* 904

Mahler, Gustav
The Artist's Wife - Max Phillips *t* 962

Marc, Franz
Burnt Umber - Sheldon Greene *t* 906

Marcus, Josie
Gunman's Rhapsody - Robert B. Parker *t* 956
Gunman's Rhapsody - Robert B. Parker *w* 520

Marx, Groucho
Groucho Marx and the Broadway Murders - Ron
   Goulart *m* 65
Groucho Marx and the Broadway Murders - Ron
   Goulart *t* 903

Masterson, Bat
Bucking the Tiger - Bruce Olds *t* 954

Merenptah
The Wise Woman - Christian Jacq *t* 917

Ness, Eliot
Angel in Black - Max Allan Collins *t* 870

Nixon, Richard
Elvis and Nixon - Jonathan Lowy *c* 1190

Oppenheimer, J. Robert
America's Children - James Thackara *c* 1234

Ovid
The Love-Artist - Jane Alison *t* 852
The Love-Artist - Jane Alison *c* 1103

Philby, Kim
Declare - Tim Powers *h* 723

Plath, Sylvia
Sylvia and Ted - Emma Tennant *t* 987

Presley, Elvis
Elvis and Nixon - Jonathan Lowy *c* 1190

Rackam, Calico Jack
The Sweet Trade - Elizabeth Garrett *t* 899

Rais, Gilles de
The Merlin of the Oak Wood - Ann
   Chamberlin   *f* 563
The Merlin of the Oak Wood - Ann
   Chamberlin   *t* 863

Read, Mary
The Sweet Trade - Elizabeth Garrett *t* 899

Reed, James Frazier
Snow Mountain Passage - James D. Houston *t* 912
Snow Mountain Passage - James D.
   Houston *c* 1172
Snow Mountain Passage - James D.
   Houston *w* 494

Reed, Patty
Snow Mountain Passage - James D.
   Houston *w* 494
Snow Mountain Passage - James D.
   Houston *c* 1172
Snow Mountain Passage - James D. Houston *t* 912

Schindler, Alma
The Artist's Wife - Max Phillips *t* 962

Seymour, Thomas
Virgin - Robin Maxwell *t* 941

Stael, Anne-Louise-Germaine de
A Dish Taken Cold - Anne Perry *t* 959

Sutter, John
Snow Mountain Passage - James D. Houston *t* 912

Thorpe, Jim
The Long Journey Home - Don Coldsmith *t* 868

Thrale, Hester
According to Queeney - Beryl Bainbridge *t* 854

Voltaire
To the Hermitage - Malcolm Bradbury *t* 858

Washington, George
Last Refuge of Scoundrels - Paul Lussier *t* 934
Rise to Rebellion - Jeff Shaara *w* 539

Welles, Orson
Angel in Black - Max Allan Collins *t* 870

Werfel, Franz
The Artist's Wife - Max Phillips *t* 962

Wevill, Assia
Sylvia and Ted - Emma Tennant *t* 987

Williams, Roger
I, Roger Williams - Mary Lee Settle *t* 979

Xenophon
The Ten Thousand - Michael Curtis Ford *t* 895

HOMOSEXUAL

Martin, Lark
Our Arcadia - Robin Lippincott *t* 931

Rios, Henry
Rag and Bone - Michael Nava *m* 133

Tolbert, Harold
Everyday People - Stewart O'Nan *c* 1212

Wilmot, Alexander
The Music of the Spheres - Elizabeth Redfern *t* 967

HORSE TRAINER

Dante, Cliff
The Marquis of Fraud - Philip Reed *m* 152

Longshadow, Jonah
Longshadow's Woman - Bronwyn Williams *r* 448

HOTEL OWNER

Carver, J.D.
All Shook Up - Susan Andersen *r* 207

Hamstra, Buddy
Hotel Honolulu - Paul Theroux *c* 1235

Lawrence, Dru
All Shook Up - Susan Andersen *r* 207

Webster, Ben
Shadow of Dreams - Eva Marie Everson *i* 1033

HOTEL WORKER

Pye, Ray
The Lost - Jack Ketchum *h* 692

HOUSEKEEPER

Kerslake, Susan
The Dragon's Bride - Jo Beverley *r* 223

Murgatroyd
The Christmas Thingy - F. Paul Wilson *h* 749

Murkin, Marie
Triple Pursuit - Ralph McInerny *m* 116

Nani
The Far Field - Edie Meidav *t* 946
The Far Field - Edie Meidav *c* 1201

HOUSEWIFE

Agatha
Ella in Bloom - Shelby Hearon *c* 1170

Brooks, Christine Bennett
The April Fool's Day Murder - Lee Harris *m* 77

Darnell, Mary
A Fragment of Life - Arthur Machen *h* 704

Dawson, Sandra
The Evil Returns - Hugh B. Cave *h* 664

Headrick, Leslie
The Summerhouse - Jude Deveraux *r* 256

Isawa Kaede
The Phoenix - Stephen D. Sullivan *f* 640

Jericho, Claire
Walls of Jericho - Lynn Bulock *i* 1024

Meria
The Sword in the Storm - David Gemmell *f* 585

Morris, Mary
Holy Rollers - J. Newman *h* 714

Murchison, Julia
Thursdays at Eight - Debbie Macomber *r* 360

Newton, Elizabeth
Darkness Demands - Simon Clark *h* 667

HUNTER

Bayguard, Moreen
The Messenger - Douglas Niles *f* 616

Beaver
Dreamcatcher - Stephen King *c* 1180

Henry
Dreamcatcher - Stephen King *c* 1180

Pete
Dreamcatcher - Stephen King *c* 1180

Rider, Anton
The Devil's Oasis - Bartle Bull *t* 861

IMMIGRANT

Bonneau, Louis
The Awakening Land - James M. Vesely *w* 545

Malone, Mary
In His Arms - Robin Lee Hatcher *i* 1042

Malysheva, Katerina
The Cloud Sketcher - Richard Rayner *c* 1221
The Cloud Sketcher - Richard Rayner *t* 964

MINE OWNER

Massey, Sam
Death Rides the Denver Stage - Lewis B. Patten   *w*   522

Shephard, Quillan
Sweet Boundless - Kristen Heitzmann   *i*   1044

MINER

Chalder, Tomas
Focus - Sallie Lowenstein   *s*   801

MacCade, Shaw
The Taming of Shaw MacCade - Judith E. French   *r*   274

Morgette, Dolf
Morgette in the Yukon - G.G. Boyer   *w*   457

Quillen, Jack
Morgette in the Yukon - G.G. Boyer   *w*   457

Quinn, Peter
Bodie Gone - Bill Hyde   *w*   495

Steele
Steele - Robert H. Redding   *w*   528

MODEL

Appleby, Madison
The Summerhouse - Jude Deveraux   *r*   256

Halloran, Claude
Bound in Blood - Thomas Lord   *h*   699

Lacan, Leda
Animosity - David L. Lindsey   *c*   1185

Madison
The Summerhouse - Jude Deveraux   *c*   1140

Nina
The Funeral Party - Ludmila Ulitskaya   *c*   1238

Phelan, Annie
Afterimage - Helen Humphreys   *t*   913
Afterimage - Helen Humphreys   *c*   1174

Season, Jillian
The Four Seasons - Mary Alice Monroe   *r*   384

Speight, Randall
Towns Without Rivers - Michael Parker   *c*   1215

MOUNTAIN MAN

Bass, Titus
Wind Walker - Terry C. Johnston   *t*   919

MacCade, Shaw
The Taming of Shaw MacCade - Judith E. French   *r*   274

Morgan, Kelly
The Cavan Breed - Les Savage Jr.   *w*   537

Wilkinson, Hode
The Doomsday Marshal and the Mountain Man - Ray Hogan   *w*   492

MOUNTAINEER

Harper, Lily
Charming Lily - Fern Michaels   *r*   379

MURDERER

Creeper
Concrete Desert - Jon Talton   *w*   542

Lake, Junior
Blood Rock - Ralph Cotton   *w*   470

Lucan
Aiding & Abetting - Muriel Spark   *c*   1229

Lucia, Anthony "Pigeon Tony"
The Vendetta Defense - Lisa Scottoline   *m*   167

Lyles, Garrett
Beyond Belief - Roy Johansen   *h*   690

McDougall, Drake Thornton
His Stolen Bride - Shelley Bradley   *r*   226

Miller, Danny
Border Crossing - Pat Barker   *c*   1108

Ortiz, Manuel
The Killer Gun - Lauran Paine   *w*   519

Shen-oh-way, Charley
A River out of Eden - John Hockenberry   *w*   491

Skye, Sunni
Natural Law - D.R. Schanker   *m*   165

Standish, Chet
Morning - W.D. Wetherell   *c*   1242

Tedrow, Wayne Jr.
The Cold Six Thousand - James Ellroy   *c*   1148

MUSEUM CURATOR

Harper, Benni
Arkansas Traveler - Earlene Fowler   *m*   56

Howe, Vanessa
This Flesh Unknown - Gary A. Braunbeck   *h*   659

Pencarreth, Erica
A Lovely Illusion - Tessa Barclay   *r*   214

MUSICIAN

Arch
Taps - Willie Morris   *c*   1205

Arpino, Beppe
Appointment with Il Duce - Hozy Rossi   *t*   974

Barksdale, Swayze
Taps - Willie Morris   *c*   1205

Brownley, Lauren
The Witness - Ginna Gray   *r*   285

du Pre, Gabriel
Cruzatte and Maria - Peter Bowen   *m*   11

Griffith, Taylor
Suddenly Home - Loree Lough   *i*   1058

Handle, William
Easy Silence - Angela Huth   *c*   1175

Hudson, Harry
The Haunting of Hip Hop - Bertice Barry   *h*   655

January, Benjamin
Die upon a Kiss - Barbara Hambly   *m*   73
Die upon a Kiss - Barbara Hambly   *t*   908

McCourry, Lark
The Songcatcher - Sharyn McCrumb   *m*   113

Presley, Elvis
Elvis and Nixon - Jonathan Lowy   *c*   1190

Roseman, Inez
Secret Love - Bart Schneider   *c*   1225

Rossi, Carlotta "Charli"
I Do, but Here's the Catch - Pamela Burford   *r*   232

Rowlands, Cassandra
Cassandra's Song - Carole Gift Page   *i*   1070

MUTANT

Lulu
The Meek - Scott Mackay   *s*   802

MYTHICAL CREATURE

Alix
Shapechanger's Song - Jennifer Roberson   *f*   625

Bane, Grimwar
The Messenger - Douglas Niles   *f*   616

Beryl
Dragons of a Lost Star - Margaret Weis   *f*   647

Char
The Inheritance - Nancy Varian Berberick   *f*   556

Dain
The Chalice - Deborah Chester   *f*   565

De'Unnero
Ascendance - R.A. Salvatore   *f*   631

Eldest Brother
Tails You Lose - Lisa Smedman   *f*   637

Fallabaine, Kerrick
The Messenger - Douglas Niles   *f*   616

Jaeger
Johan - Clayton Emery   *f*   577

Karen
Nothing but Blue Skies - Tom Holt   *f*   589

Nihmedu, Galaeron
The Summoning - Troy Denning   *f*   571

Paddy
St. Patrick's Gargoyle - Katherine Kurtz   *f*   599

Shanhaevel
The Temple of Elemental Evil - Thomas M. Reid   *f*   623

Short, Holly
Artemis Fowl - Eoin Colfer   *f*   566

Sinann
Son of the Sword - J. Ardian Lee   *f*   605

Skullcrusher, Nekros
Day of the Dragon - Richard A. Knaak   *f*   597

Space Hopper
Flatterland - Ian Stewart   *s*   833

Sungold, Elansa
The Inheritance - Nancy Varian Berberick   *f*   556

Valentin, Sebastien
Your Wish Is My Command - Donna Kauffman   *r*   327

Wednesday
American Gods - Neil Gaiman   *f*   583

NARRATOR

Allen, Catherine
A Spell of Winter - Helen Dunmore   *c*   1144
A Spell of Winter - Helen Dunmore   *t*   884

Avila, Tere
Loving Pedro Infante - Denise Chavez   *c*   1131

Chandler, Luke
A Painted House - John Grisham   *c*   1165

Ellen
Gardens of Kyoto - Kate Walbert   *t*   992
The Gardens of Kyoto - Kate Walbert   *c*   1240

Janes, Regina
The Last Time They Met - Anita Shreve   *c*   1227

Jones, Joubert Antoine
Meteor in the Madhouse - Leon Forrest   *c*   1153

Kahlo, Christina
Frida - Barbara Mujica   *c*   1207

Lowe, Kenzie
The Warmest December - Bernice L. McFadden   *c*   1198

NEIGHBOR

NOBLEMAN

Halliot, Laurie
Border Storm - Amanda Scott   *r*   421

Rose
The Magic of Ordinary Days - Ann Howard Creel   *w*   471

PRIVATEER

Lambert, Bethany
The Sea Nymph - Ruth Langan   *r*   345

PRODUCER

Belaggio, Lorenzo
Die upon a Kiss - Barbara Hambly   *t*   908

Bracewell, Nicholas
The Devil's Apprentice - Edward Marston   *t*   939

Davis, John
Die upon a Kiss - Barbara Hambly   *t*   908

Younger, Jack
The View from Hell - John Shirley   *h*   736

PROFESSOR

Blue, Jason
Crime Brulee - Nancy Fairbanks   *m*   51

Bodine, Juliet
Corpse de Ballet - Ellen Pall   *m*   141

Branden, Michael
Clouds Without Rain - P.L. Gaus   *m*   58
Clouds Without Rain - P.L. Gaus   *i*   1035

Brogus, Reggie
If 6 Were 9 - Jake Lamar   *c*   1182

Dennistoun
Degrees of Fear - William I.I. Read   *h*   730

Found, Michael
Thoroughly Kissed - Kristine Grayson   *r*   286

Goode, John
Field Guide - Gwendolen Gross   *c*   1166

Hale, Andrew
Declare - Tim Powers   *h*   723
Declare - Tim Powers   *c*   1220

Hammett, Raymond
Two Murders in My Double Life - Josef Skvorecky   *c*   1228

Humboldt, Nelson
The Lecturer's Tale - James Hynes   *c*   1176

Hunt, Sam
Pascal's Wager - Nancy Rue   *i*   1080

Jones, Joubert Antoine
Meteor in the Madhouse - Leon Forrest   *c*   1153

Kepesh, David
The Dying Animal - Philip Roth   *c*   1223

Kilbourn, Joanne
Burying Ariel - Gail Bowen   *m*   10

Lost, Emma
Thoroughly Kissed - Kristine Grayson   *r*   286

Mapstone, David
Concrete Desert - Jon Talton   *m*   182
Concrete Desert - Jon Talton   *w*   542

McGavock, Jill
Pascal's Wager - Nancy Rue   *i*   1080

Messenger, Ralph
Thinks. . . - David Lodge   *c*   1187

Monahan, Rory
The Temptation of Rory Monahan - Elizabeth Bevarly   *r*   221

Navarre, Jackson "Tres"
The Devil Went Down to Austin - Rick Riordan   *m*   156

Petrie
Mr. Mee - Andrew Crumey   *c*   1137

Phillips, Paul
Cradle of Dreams - Joseph Bentz   *i*   1013

Reed, Helen
Thinks. . . - David Lodge   *c*   1187

Robinette, Clay
If 6 Were 9 - Jake Lamar   *c*   1182

St. Vallier, Stella
Still of the Night - Meagan McKinney   *r*   375

Stanton, Gabriela "Gabby"
American Fuji - Sara Backer   *c*   1105

Unnamed Character
The Sputnik Sweetheart - Haruki Murakami   *c*   1208
To the Hermitage - Malcolm Bradbury   *c*   1118

PROSTITUTE

Dora
Bone House - Betsy Tobin   *c*   1236
Bone House - Betsy Tobin   *t*   989

Fusang
The Lost Daughter of Happiness - Geling Yan   *t*   1001
The Lost Daughter of Happiness - Geling Yan   *w*   551

Higgins, Doll
Slammerkin - Emma Donoghue   *t*   882

Paulinha, William Narcisco
Fixer Chao - Han Ong   *c*   1213

Pitman, Delia
The Seeds of Time - Carol Cail   *w*   466

Sabina
A Personal Devil - Roberta Gellis   *t*   901

Sandoval, Sandy
The Tin Collector - Stephen J. Cannell   *c*   1126

Saunders, Mary
Slammerkin - Emma Donoghue   *t*   882

Simpson, Deborah
Last Refuge of Scoundrels - Paul Lussier   *t*   934

Skye, Sunni
Natural Law - D.R. Schanker   *m*   165

Starr, Iris
Dr. Mortimer and the Barking Man Mystery - Gerard Williams   *t*   996

PSYCHIC

Flammarion, Dancy
Threshold - Caitlin R. Kiernan   *h*   693

Grant, Marbet
Probability Sun - Nancy Kress   *s*   799

Karan
A Shadow on the Glass - Ian Irvine   *f*   592

Mann, Summer
Special Effects - Kevin McCarthy   *s*   805

Matthews, Chance
Threshold - Caitlin R. Kiernan   *h*   693

Montella, Pat
Hang My Head and Cry - Elena Santangelo   *t*   978

Silvey, Deacon
Threshold - Caitlin R. Kiernan   *h*   693

Tibibnia, Ellen
The Doorkeepers - Graham Masterton   *h*   706

Waring, Eden
The Fury and the Terror - John Farris   *h*   676

Yann
The Merlin of the Oak Wood - Ann Chamberlin   *t*   863

PSYCHOLOGIST

Denison, Skye
Murder of a Sweet Old Lady - Denise Swanson   *m*   181

Frazer, Byron
Finding Ian - Stella Cameron   *r*   237

McCarron, Blue
The Last Blue Plate Special - Abigail Padgett   *m*   138

PUBLIC RELATIONS

Barr, Temple
Cat in a Leopard Spot - Carole Nelson Douglas   *m*   44

Giambelli, Sophia
The Villa - Nora Roberts   *r*   412

Hamilton, Tyler III
The Impossible Texan - Allie Shaw   *r*   424

Richardson, Rosie
Cause Celeb - Helen Fielding   *c*   1150

PUBLISHER

Chrysippus, Aurelius
Ode to a Banker - Lindsey Davis   *t*   877

Sloane, Todd
Looking for Laura - Judith Arnold   *r*   212

Smiricky, Sidonia
Two Murders in My Double Life - Josef Skvorecky   *c*   1228

RADIO PERSONALITY

Bridge, Nora
Summer Island - Kristin Hannah   *r*   293

Lewis, Jane
Plain Jane - Fern Michaels   *r*   380

Ryan, Kelly
Death Rides an Ill Wind - Kate Grilley   *m*   68

RAKE

Davenant, Maxwell "Max"
Miss Lacey's Last Fling - Candice Hern   *r*   301

Manning, Connor
A Scarlet Bride - Sylvia McDaniel   *r*   371

Sultan, Wesley Cross
A Few Corrections - Brad Leithauser   *c*   1184

RANCHER

Alvarez, Charlotte
Shannon: US Marshal - Charles E. Friend   *w*   484

Anthem, John
Texas Born - Kerry Newcomb   *w*   512

Benton, Reed
Summer Moon - Jill Marie Landis   *r*   342

Burbank, George
The Power of the Dog - Thomas Savage   *w*   538

Burbank, Phil
The Power of the Dog - Thomas Savage   *w*   538

Sunny Boy Blue
Juniper Tree Burning - Goldberry Long   *c*   1188

Tolbert, Eugene
Everyday People - Stewart O'Nan   *c*   1212

Trevisan, Paola
Mimi's Ghost - Tim Parks   *c*   1216
Mimi's Ghost - Tim Parks   *h*   717

Vera
The Biographer's Tale - A.S. Byatt   *c*   1124

Walker, Linda
The Songcatcher - Sharyn McCrumb   *c*   1197

Weatherspoon, Matt
Rides of the Midway - Lee Durkee   *c*   1146

Whitworth, Karlee
To Wed in Texas - Jodi Thomas   *r*   439

Young, Ruth
The Bonesetter's Daughter - Amy Tan   *c*   1233

Zielinsky, David
Crooked River Burning - Mark
   Winegardner   *c*   1245

RELIGIOUS

Anne
In the Company of Angels - N.M. Kelby   *t*   922

Bora, Katharina von
Storm - Reg Grant   *t*   904

Camfield, Daria
Beneath a Southern Sky - Deborah Raney   *i*   1077

Cley
The Beyond - Jeffrey Ford   *f*   581

Conor
Son of the Shadows - Juliet Marillier   *f*   608

Constable, Jasper
The Fields of Eden - Richard S. Wheeler   *t*   994

Cristo
Enemy Glory - Karen Michalson   *f*   610

Dane, Simon
Edge of the Wilderness - Stephanie Grace
   Whitson   *i*   1096

de St. Clair, Arnault
The Temple and the Crown - Katherine Kurtz   *f*   600

Dowling, Roger
Triple Pursuit - Ralph McInerny   *m*   116

Flatt, Alvin
Four of a Kind - Gilbert Morris   *i*   1063

Gardner, Sam
Just Shy of Harmony - Philip Gulley   *i*   1037

Garnet, Henry
A Fifth of November - Paul West   *t*   993

Hedrack
The Temple of Elemental Evil - Thomas M.
   Reid   *f*   623

Helewise of Hawkenlye
Ashes of the Elements - Alys Clare   *t*   865
Ashes of the Elements - Alys Clare   *m*   23

Joshua
The Parables of Joshua - Joseph F. Girzone   *i*   1036

Joy, Otis
The Reaper - Peter Lovesey   *m*   107

Kavanaugh, Timothy
A Common Life - Jan Karon   *c*   1179

Kirkwood, Griffin
Guardian of the Vision - Irene Radford   *f*   621

Leone, Orlando
The Champion - Carman   *i*   1026

Llewelyn
Enemy Glory - Karen Michalson   *f*   610

Lobsang
Thief of Time - Terry Pratchett   *f*   620

Lu-Tze
Thief of Time - Terry Pratchett   *f*   620

Luther, Martin
Storm - Reg Grant   *t*   904

Marie Francoise
The Burning Times - Jeanne Kalogridis   *t*   920

McLain, Daniel
To Wed in Texas - Jodi Thomas   *r*   439

Michel
The Burning Times - Jeanne Kalogridis   *t*   920

Mitchell, Joseph
Under the Color of Law - Michael
   McGarrity   *w*   505

Modeste, Damien
The Last Report on the Miracles at Little No Horse -
   Louise Erdrich   *t*   889

Mookerjee, Sri Billy Lee
The Song of the Earth - Hugh Nissenson   *s*   813

Moser, Thomas
The Faithful Narrative of a Pastor's Disappearance -
   Benjamin Anastas   *c*   1104

Newman, Leo
The Gospel of Judas - Simon Mawer   *c*   1195

Panic, Anton
Father Panic's Opera Macabre - Thomas
   Tessier   *h*   742

Pardoe, Christopher
Unholy Dying - Robert Barnard   *m*   4

Puyat, Pauline
The Last Report on the Miracles at Little No Horse -
   Louise Erdrich   *t*   889

Rob, Jahl
The Saints of the Sword - John Marco   *f*   607

Sahor
The Ring of Five Dragons - Eric Van
   Lustbader   *f*   645

Sherbrooke, Tysen
The Scottish Bride - Catherine Coulter   *r*   245

Simmons, Theophilius Henry
Church Folk - Michele Andrea Bowen   *i*   1021

Soldano, Bernard
Ship of Fools - Richard Paul Russo   *s*   825

Theodosius
The Veil of Years - L. Warren Douglas   *f*   572

Torquil
The Temple and the Crown - Katherine Kurtz   *f*   600

Welles, Regan
My Lord Pirate - Laura Renken   *r*   403

Williams, Roger
I, Roger Williams - Mary Lee Settle   *t*   979

Xavier
In the Company of Angels - N.M. Kelby   *t*   922

RESEARCHER

Ogelvie, Ian
Inspired Sleep - Robert Cohen   *c*   1133

RESISTANCE FIGHTER

Adams, Leslie
A Perfect Persecution - James R. Lucas   *i*   1059

RESTAURATEUR

D'Angelo, Nick
Walk on the Wild Side - Donna Kauffman   *r*   326

Dartigen, Framboise
Five Quarters of the Orange - Joanne Harris   *t*   910

Driver, Sally
Looking for Laura - Judith Arnold   *r*   212

Howe, Paul
This Flesh Unknown - Gary A. Braunbeck   *h*   659

Lawless, Jane
The Merchant of Venus - Ellen Hart   *m*   79

Roby, Miles
Empire Falls - Richard Russo   *c*   1224

Russo, Mary
The Trouble with Mary - Millie Criswell   *r*   248

Skinner, Dola Mae
Picture Rock - Stephen A. Bly   *i*   1020

Smith, Orpheus Beauregard "Bo"
In the Blood - Stephen Gresham   *h*   683

Taylor, Sydney
Reese's Wild Wager - Barbara McCauley   *r*   369

Whiting, Francine
Empire Falls - Richard Russo   *c*   1224

REVOLUTIONARY

Fawkes, Guy
A Fifth of November - Paul West   *t*   993

Marquez, Diamantino
Flight of the Swan - Rosario Ferre   *t*   893

RODEO RIDER

Cooper, Donna
Queen of the Rodeo - Michael Little   *w*   501

Griffin, Tyler
Queen of the Rodeo - Michael Little   *w*   501

McRay, Dillon
Dangerous Moves - Mary Morgan   *r*   387

ROGUE

MacGowan, Ramsay
The Fraser Bride - Lois Greiman   *r*   289

ROYALTY

Ahmose
The Horus Road - Pauline Gedge   *t*   900

Albert
Death at Epsom Downs - Robin Paige   *t*   955

Ali, Sher
The Long Love - Katharine Gordon   *r*   279

Beaufort, Charity
Royal Bride - Joan Wolf   *r*   450

B'Kah, Romlijhian
The Star King - Susan Grant   *r*   282

Bryan
Summers at Castle Auburn - Sharon Shinn   *f*   633

Chastain, Alexis
The Runaway Princess - Patricia Forsythe   *r*   270

Christina
Tempting - Susan Johnson   *r*   321

Conaire
The Destruction of the Inn - Randy Lee
   Eickhoff   *t*   888

Dekkeret
The King of Dreams - Robert Silverberg   *f*   635

Entipy
Sir Apropos of Nothing - Peter David   *f*   569

Gavril
The Chalice - Deborah Chester   *f*   565

George, Prince of Wales
The Tainted Snuff Box - Rosemary Stevens   *t*   983

Helena
Priestess of Avalon - Marion Zimmer
   Bradley   *t*   859

Kethrenan
The Inheritance - Nancy Varian Berberick   *f*   556

Lanson
The Devil's Mouth - Thomas Williams   *i*   1098

Louis XIV
Gardener to the King - Frederic Richaud   *t*   968

MacClintock, Roger
March Upcountry - David Weber   *s*   844

Maryn
The Fire Dragon - Katharine Kerr   *f*   594

Maxian
The Storm of Heaven - Thomas Harlan   *f*   587

Nefer Memnon
Warlock - Wilbur A. Smith   *t*   982

Ozma
The Emerald Burrito of Oz - John Skipp   *f*   636

Phenesa
The Chalice - Deborah Chester   *f*   565

Sameth
Lirael - Garth Nix   *f*   617

Theatana
The Mask and the Sorceress - Dennis Jones   *f*   593

RULER

Adamov, Augustus
Royal Bride - Joan Wolf   *r*   450

Alexander the Great
The House of Death - P.C. Doherty   *t*   881
The House of Death - P.C. Doherty   *m*   42

Ames
Metaplanetary - Tony Daniel   *s*   767

Apepa
The Horus Road - Pauline Gedge   *t*   900

Arutha
Krondor: Tear of the Gods - Raymond E.
   Feist   *f*   579

Auletes
Kleopatra - Karen Essex   *t*   890

Avall
Summerblood - Tom Deitz   *f*   570

Beryl
Dragons of a Lost Star - Margaret Weis   *f*   647

Carillon
Shapechanger's Song - Jennifer Roberson   *f*   625

Catherine the Great
To the Hermitage - Malcolm Bradbury   *t*   858
To the Hermitage - Malcolm Bradbury   *c*   1118

Constantine
Priestess of Avalon - Marion Zimmer
   Bradley   *t*   859

Constantius Chlorus, Flavius
Priestess of Avalon - Marion Zimmer
   Bradley   *t*   859

Darius
DoOon Mode - Piers Anthony   *f*   553

Edward I
The Demon Archer - P.C. Doherty   *t*   880

Elizabeth I
The Twylight Tower - Karen Harper   *m*   76
The Twylight Tower - Karen Harper   *t*   909
Virgin - Robin Maxwell   *t*   941

Florian
Knight or Knave - Andre Norton   *f*   618

Gayle, Tassis
The Saints of the Sword - John Marco   *f*   607

Hatusu
The Anubis Slayings - P.C. Doherty   *t*   879

Ila
Hammerfall - C.J. Cherryh   *s*   765

Johan
Johan - Clayton Emery   *f*   577

Kati
Empress of Light - James C. Glass   *s*   789

Kleopatra
Kleopatra - Karen Essex   *t*   890

Medea
God of the Golden Fleece - Fred Saberhagen   *f*   630

Merenptah
The Wise Woman - Christian Jacq   *t*   917

Naja
Warlock - Wilbur A. Smith   *t*   982

Pendragon, Uther
Uther - Jack Whyte   *f*   650
Uther - Jack Whyte   *t*   995

Prestimion
The King of Dreams - Robert Silverberg   *f*   635

Robero
The Shadow Sorceress - L.E. Modesitt Jr.   *f*   612

Swemmel
Through the Darkness - Harry Turtledove   *f*   644

Thebaw
The Glass Palace - Amitav Ghosh   *c*   1160

Ysa
Knight or Knave - Andre Norton   *f*   618

RUNAWAY

Bugg, Konstanze
The Mermaid of Penperro - Lisa Cach   *r*   234

Cathy
Chalktown - Melinda Haynes   *c*   1169

Cutler, Patrick
Dead North - Sue Henry   *m*   80
Dead North - Sue Henry   *w*   490

Lynch, Gabriel
Gabriel's Story - David Anthony Durham   *t*   886
Gabriel's Story - David Anthony Durham   *c*   1145

Sheehand, Hezekiah
Chalktown - Melinda Haynes   *c*   1169

Stansbury, Cordelia "Mary Westerman"
The Riddle of the Shipwrecked Spinster - Patricia
   Veryan   *r*   441

SAILOR

Guevara, John William
Tierra del Fuego - Sylvia Iparraguirre   *t*   915

Jardine, Tessa
A Great Catch - Michelle Jerott   *r*   319

Kite, William
The Privateersman - Richard Woodman   *t*   998

Tehidy, Thom
Corsair - Chris Bunch   *f*   560

SAINT

Mary, Mother of God
Our Lady of the Lost and Found - Diane
   Schoemperlen   *c*   1226

SALESMAN

Getz, Mike
Ordinary Horror - David Searcy   *h*   733

Gilmore, Truman
Duet for the Devil - T. Winter-Damon   *h*   750

SALESWOMAN

Delany, Carrington Rose "Carrie"
I Waxed My Legs for This? - Holly Jacobs   *r*   314

SALOON KEEPER/OWNER

Leuwen
The Philosophical Strangler - Eric Flint   *f*   580

Lou
The Pickup Artist - Terry Bisson   *s*   759

Murphy, John
Murphy's Lore: Fools' Day - Patrick Thomas   *f*   641

Sinclair, Reese
Reese's Wild Wager - Barbara McCauley   *r*   369

Toni
Dance of Knives - Donna McMahon   *s*   808

Wilder, Travis
The Dark Remains - Mark Anthony   *f*   552

SCHOLAR

Edel, Leon
Hotel Honolulu - Paul Theroux   *c*   1235

Merriem, Portia "Pip"
Lilies on the Lake - Katherine Kingsley   *r*   333

Mookherjee, Huree Chunder
Sherlock Holmes: The Missing Years - Jamyang
   Norbu   *t*   952

Moreston, Pearl
Rogue's Honor - Brenda Hiatt   *r*   303

Newman, Leo
The Gospel of Judas - Simon Mawer   *c*   1195

SCIENTIST

Archer, Grant
Jupiter - Ben Bova   *s*   760

Burke, Jessica
Someone to Watch over Her - Margaret
   Watson   *r*   446

Capelo, Thomas
Probability Sun - Nancy Kress   *s*   799

Carter, Samantha
The Morpheus Factor - Ashley McConnell   *s*   806

Catriona
Mr. Mee - Andrew Crumey   *c*   1137

Charnock, Jack
A River out of Eden - John Hockenberry   *w*   491

Chopra, Sulamith
The Chronoliths - Robert Charles Wilson   *s*   849

Copeland, Virgil
Limit of Vision - Linda Nagata   *s*   812

de Montchevreuil, Adrienne
The Shadows of God - J. Gregory Keyes f 595

Dempsey, Ariane
Voice of the Blood - Jemiah Jefferson h 689

Dove, Maurice
A Student of Weather - Elizabeth Hay c 1168

Duncan, Lisa
Area 51: The Grail - Robert Doherty s 773

Elle, Nan
Kingdom of Cages - Sarah Zettel s 851

Ford, Marion "Doc"
Shark River - Randy Wayne White m 193

Friemann, Lisa
The Cassandra Complex - Brian Stableford s 832

Fulla
The Biographer's Tale - A.S. Byatt c 1124

Grimnebulin, Isaac Dan Der
Perdido Street Station - China Mieville f 611

Hastings, Michael
Special Effects - Kevin McCarthy s 805

Hutchins, Priscilla
Deepsix - Jack McDevitt s 807

Jansen, Valkerie
Oxygen - John Olson i 1069

Karlstad, Egon
Jupiter - Ben Bova s 760

Lumet, Jack
Borrowed Tides - Paul Levinson s 800

Makarova, Xenia
Manifold: Space - Stephen Baxter s 756

Matthews, Chance
Threshold - Caitlin R. Kiernan h 693

Michelet, Ariana
Devil's Sea - Greg Donegan s 774

Miller, Morgan
The Cassandra Complex - Brian Stableford s 832

Moriarty, James
The Great Game - Michael Kurland m 99

Nash, Francis
Temple - Matt Reilly s 818

Nemoto
Manifold: Space - Stephen Baxter s 756

O'Hara, Elaine
Jupiter - Ben Bova s 760

O'Malley, Lisa
The Truth Seeker - Dee Henderson i 1045

Oppenheimer, J. Robert
America's Children - James Thackara c 1234

Panwar, Randall
Limit of Vision - Linda Nagata s 812

Queson, Randi
Melchior's Fire - Jack L. Chalker s 764

Schoenfeld, Aaron
Borrowed Tides - Paul Levinson s 800

Shepard, Lucas
The Living Blood - Tananarive Due h 672

Smohalla, Francine
A River out of Eden - John Hockenberry w 491

von Eichstatt, Karl Oelefse
Interlopers - Alan Dean Foster s 783

Washington, Melissa
Outer Perimeter - Ken Goddard s 790

Welland, Claire
Seeing Stars - Vanessa Grant r 284

Woodhull, Gob
Gob's Grief - Chris Adrian c 1102

SCOUT

Greenwood, Honore
Moon Medicine - Mike Blakely w 453

Kelly, Luther "Yellowstone"
Kelly and the Three-Toed Horse - Peter Bowen w 456
Kelly and the Three-Toed Horse - Peter Bowen t 857

SEA CAPTAIN

Ainsworth, Marcel
Summer's Bride - Catherine Archer r 211

Hall, Lucas
A Great Catch - Michelle Jerott r 319

Radnor, Gareth
Corsair - Chris Bunch f 560

SECRETARY

dy Cazaril, Lupe
The Curse of Chalion - Lois McMaster Bujold f 559

Hollingsworth, Nicholas "Nick"
Scandal in Venice - Amanda McCabe r 366

Trufant, Maci
Gob's Grief - Chris Adrian c 1102

Winslow, Don
License Invoked - Robert Asprin f 554

SECURITY OFFICER

Johnson, Alma
Tails You Lose - Lisa Smedman f 637

SERIAL KILLER

Duckworth, Morris
Mimi's Ghost - Tim Parks c 1216
Mimi's Ghost - Tim Parks h 717

Maldoror
Duet for the Devil - T. Winter-Damon h 750

McNab, Pat
Emerald Germs of Ireland - Patrick McCabe c 1196

SERVANT

Alice
A Fragment of Life - Arthur Machen h 704

Alpiew
Unnatural Fire - Fidelis Morgan m 125
Unnatural Fire - Fidelis Morgan t 949

Butler
Artemis Fowl - Eoin Colfer f 566

Cavan, Teresa
The Cavan Breed - Les Savage Jr. w 537

Celie
A Dish Taken Cold - Anne Perry t 959

Dolly
The Glass Palace - Amitav Ghosh t 902
The Glass Palace - Amitav Ghosh c 1160

Dovey
Get Along, Little Dogies - Lisa Waller Rogers w 533

Fiorinda
The King of Dreams - Robert Silverberg f 635

Graceful
Fire in Beulah - Rilla Askew t 853

Gupta
The Serpent's Shadow - Mercedes Lackey f 602

Joan
By Design - Madeline Hunter r 310

Johansson, Hilda
Green Grow the Victims - Jeanne M. Dams m 33
Green Grow the Victims - Jeanne M. Dams t 874

Kate
A Spell of Winter - Helen Dunmore c 1144

Kauffman, Dora
Lilac Blossom Time - Carrie Bender i 1010

Kean, Hester
The Birth of Blue Satan - Patricia Wynn m 200
The Birth of Blue Satan - Patricia Wynn t 1000

Lucine
Three Apples Fell from Heaven - Micheline Aharonian Marcom t 938

Phelan, Annie
Afterimage - Helen Humphreys t 913
Afterimage - Helen Humphreys c 1174

Tremayne, Lucinda-Ella "Rose"
Rose of Nancemillin - Malcolm MacDonald t 935

Unnamed Character
Bone House - Betsy Tobin c 1236
Bone House - Betsy Tobin t 989

Vishnu
The Death of Vishnu - Manil Suri c 1231

SETTLER

Gould, Henry Frye
The Far Field - Edie Meidav t 946
The Far Field - Edie Meidav c 1201

Haddad, Malik
Child of Venus - Pamela Sargent s 826

Kelsey, Andrew
An Ordinary Woman - Cecelia Holland w 493

Kelsey, Ben
An Ordinary Woman - Cecelia Holland w 493

Kelsey, Nancy
An Ordinary Woman - Cecelia Holland w 493

SHAMAN

Clah, Clifford
Shooting Chant - Aimee Thurlo w 543

Corn Flower
Raven Mocker - Don Coldsmith w 467
Raven Mocker - Don Coldsmith t 869

Ka
Song of the Axe - John R. Dann t 875

Red Shoes
The Shadows of God - J. Gregory Keyes f 595

Snakewater
Raven Mocker - Don Coldsmith w 467

SIDEKICK

BB
The Last Blue Plate Special - Abigail Padgett m 138

Daniels, Billy Bob
The Magic Wagon - Joe R. Lansdale w 499

Denny, Darla
K Falls - Skye Kathleen Moody w 509

Dulcie
Cat Spitting Mad - Shirley Rousseau Murphy m 129

Labala
Corsair - Chris Bunch *f* 560

Margal
The Evil Returns - Hugh B. Cave *h* 664

Mendark
A Shadow on the Glass - Ian Irvine *f* 592

Taita
Warlock - Wilbur A. Smith *t* 982

SORCERESS

Aurya
The Thirteenth Scroll - Rebecca Neason *f* 613

Brisane
Exiled from Camelot - Cherith Baldry *f* 555

Jewel
Sea of Sorrows - Michelle West *f* 649

Richina
The Shadow Sorceress - L.E. Modesitt Jr. *f* 612

Secca
The Shadow Sorceress - L.E. Modesitt Jr. *f* 612

SOUTHERN BELLE

Anderson, Elizabeth
The Outlaw Takes a Wife - Sylvia McDaniel *r* 370

Bonneaux, Julia
The Horse Soldier - Merline Lovelace *r* 355

Todd, Janet
When This Cruel War Is Over - Thomas
  Fleming *t* 894

SPACE EXPLORER

Boswell, Jasmine
The Star King - Susan Grant *r* 282

Lynx, Philip
Reunion - Alan Dean Foster *s* 784

Malenfant, Reid
Manifold: Space - Stephen Baxter *s* 756

SPACEMAN

Aguilera, Bartolomeo
Ship of Fools - Richard Paul Russo *s* 825

Casement, Danny
Spheres of Heaven - Charles Sheffield *s* 829

Dalton, Chan
Spheres of Heaven - Charles Sheffield *s* 829

Krislov, Alexei
Bouncing Off the Moon - David Gerrold *s* 787

Lumet, Jack
Borrowed Tides - Paul Levinson *s* 800

Nagel, Jerry
Melchior's Fire - Jack L. Chalker *s* 764

Pike, Gar
A Wizard in a Feud - Christopher Stasheff *f* 638

Schoenfeld, Aaron
Borrowed Tides - Paul Levinson *s* 800

Storm, Jack
The Sand Wars. Volume Two - Charles
  Ingrid *s* 796

SPACESHIP CAPTAIN

Clairveau, Marcel
Deepsix - Jack McDevitt *s* 807

Costa, Nikos
Ship of Fools - Richard Paul Russo *s* 825

Hutchins, Priscilla
Deepsix - Jack McDevitt *s* 807

Seafort, Nicholas
Children of Hope - David Feintuch *s* 779

SPACEWOMAN

Alea
A Wizard in a Feud - Christopher Stasheff *f* 638

Collier, Kellie
Deepsix - Jack McDevitt *s* 807

Li, An
Melchior's Fire - Jack L. Chalker *s* 764

Lotari, Kathy
Borrowed Tides - Paul Levinson *s* 800

SPINSTER

Hayes, Lizzie
Sister Noon - Karen Joy Fowler *t* 896
Sister Noon - Karen Joy Fowler *w* 483
Sister Noon - Karen Joy Fowler *c* 1154

Whitworth, Karlee
To Wed in Texas - Jodi Thomas *r* 439

SPIRIT

Edmonds, Daniel
Adams Fall - Sean Desmond *h* 671

MacIntyre, Malcolm
Night Visitor - Melanie Jackson *r* 313

Spivey, Septimus
7B - Stella Cameron *r* 236

Trevisan, Mimi
Mimi's Ghost - Tim Parks *c* 1216

SPORTS FIGURE

Buffalo, John
The Long Journey Home - Don Coldsmith *t* 868

Leone, Orlando
The Champion - Carman *i* 1026

Schwan, Brian
Spikes - Michael Griffith *c* 1164

Soulsby, Bird
Spikes - Michael Griffith *c* 1164

Sullivan, Jamie
Your Wish Is My Command - Donna
  Kauffman *r* 327

Thorpe, Jim
The Long Journey Home - Don Coldsmith *t* 868

Wilkins, Randy
The Hunting Wind - Steve Hamilton *m* 75

SPOUSE

Adams, Carrie
Longshadow's Woman - Bronwyn Williams *r* 448

Adams, Liz Hampton
The Hampton Passion - Julie Ellis *r* 264

Branscombe, Violet
Dr. Mortimer and the Barking Man Mystery - Gerard
  Williams *m* 195
Dr. Mortimer and the Barking Man Mystery - Gerard
  Williams *t* 996

Brewer, Madeleine
The Gospel of Judas - Simon Mawer *c* 1195

Buffalo Dreamer
Mystic Warriors - Rosanne Bittner *t* 855
Mystic Warriors - Rosanne Bittner *w* 452

Butler, Dick
Beloved Stranger - Clare Boylan *c* 1117

Butler, Lily
Beloved Stranger - Clare Boylan *c* 1117

Camfield, Nathan "Nate"
Beneath a Southern Sky - Deborah Raney *i* 1077

Carcera, Gina
Recent History - Anthony Giardina *c* 1161

Carcera, Luca
Recent History - Anthony Giardina *c* 1161

Christina
Tempting - Susan Johnson *r* 321

Coyle, Emma
A Trail to Wounded Knee - Tim Champlin *t* 864

Crosby, Julianna
Ribbon of Years - Robin Lee Hatcher *i* 1043

Dane, Genevieve LaCroix
Edge of the Wilderness - Stephanie Grace
  Whitson *i* 1096

Dashell, Eldon
Afterimage - Helen Humphreys *t* 913
Afterimage - Helen Humphreys *c* 1174

Dashell, Isabelle
Afterimage - Helen Humphreys *c* 1174
Afterimage - Helen Humphreys *t* 913

Davitch, Joe
Back When We Were Grownups - Anne
  Tyler *c* 1237

Dedham, Althea
Fire in Beulah - Rilla Askew *t* 853

Dengmei
Wintry Night - Qiao Li *t* 929

DeWitt, Agnes
The Last Report on the Miracles at Little No Horse -
  Louise Erdrich *c* 1149

Dias, Custodio
The Painter of Birds - Lidia Jorge *c* 1177

Dowling, Margaret
MacGregor's Lantern - Corinne Joy Brown *w* 463

Dunne, Livvy
The Magic of Ordinary Days - Ann Howard
  Creel *w* 471

Ferrer, Felix
I'm Gone - Jean Echenoz *c* 1147

Flaherty, Hanna
The Raptor Virus - Frank Simon *i* 1085

Flaherty, Russell
The Raptor Virus - Frank Simon *i* 1085

Fletcher, Alec
To Davy Jones Below - Carola Dunn *t* 885
To Davy Jones Below - Carola Dunn *m* 46

Ford, Jorie
Blue Diary - Alice Hoffman *c* 1171

Forth, Nefret
Lord of the Silent - Elizabeth Peters *m* 148
Lord of the Silent - Elizabeth Peters *t* 961

Fraser, Poppy
The Church Ladies - Lisa E. Samson *i* 1082

Gillian, Bucy
Grace - Jane Roberts Wood *w* 550

Goldman, Howard
A Perfect Arrangement - Suzanne Berne *c* 1114

Goodnight, Revelie
Code of the West - Aaron Latham *w* 500

TAXI DRIVER

Cavaco, Mike
Making over Mike - Lisa Plumley *r* 394

TEACHER

Banqueros, Felix
The View from Hell - John Shirley *h* 736

Briggs, Harry
Sleepeasy - T.M. Wright *h* 751

Bright, Anthea
The Bad Man's Bride - Susan Kay Law *r* 348

Brooks, Christine Bennett
The April Fool's Day Murder - Lee Harris *m* 77

Brooks, Melanie
Follow That Baby! - Isabel Sharpe *r* 423

Burke, O'Neil
Mary and O'Neil - Justin Cronin *c* 1136

Carpenter, Ernestine "Ernie"
Closer than the Bones - Dean James *m* 87

Cartier, Anne
Mute Witness - Charles O'Brien *m* 134
Mute Witness - Charles O'Brien *t* 953

Chastain, Alexis
The Runaway Princess - Patricia Forsythe *r* 270

Elinsky, Jakob
The 25th Hour - David Benioff *c* 1111

Flood, Elizabeth
Beulah Hill - William Heffernan *t* 911

Freemantle, Leonora
The Wedding Wager - Deborah Hale *r* 292

Garth, Isabel
The Gripping Beast - Margot Wadley *m* 187

Gillian, Grace
Grace - Jane Roberts Wood *t* 997
Grace - Jane Roberts Wood *w* 550

Griffith, Taylor
Suddenly Home - Loree Lough *i* 1058

Jackson, Mary
Private Vows - Sally Steward *r* 436

Kimball, Kate Stanislaski
Considering Kate - Nora Roberts *r* 411

Knight, Sam
Dead End - Helen R. Myers *r* 389

Li Quan
Safely Home - Randy C. Alcorn *i* 1005

Mary
Mary and O'Neil - Justin Cronin *c* 1136

McDolen, Kate
Wire Mesh Mothers - Elizabeth Massie *h* 705

Monahan, Tess
First Comes Love - Elizabeth Bevarly *r* 220

Mugabe, Karin
Child of Venus - Pamela Sargent *s* 826

Rossi, Carlotta "Charli"
I Do, but Here's the Catch - Pamela Burford *r* 232

Sailor, Jane
The Girl in the Face of the Clock - Charles
  Mathes *m* 110

Shaddler, Alterith
Ravenheart - David Gemmell *f* 584

Snowden, Brooke
Alyssa Again - Sylvie Kurtz *r* 341

Spenser, Leigh
Spring Rain - Gayle Roper *i* 1079

Sulaweyo, Irene
Sea of Silver Light - Tad Williams *f* 651

Thomas, Leah
A Husband to Hold - Cheryl Wolverton *i* 1101

Whittington, Katherine "Kate"
Summer Moon - Jill Marie Landis *r* 342

Wood, Molly
The Virginian - Owen Wister *w* 549

TEENAGER

Anton
On the Water - H.M. van den Brink *t* 991

Aten, Nick
Blood Crazy - Simon Clark *h* 666

Barksdale, Swayze
Taps - Willie Morris *c* 1205

Callahan, Nita
The Wizard's Dilemma - Diane Duane *f* 574

Cambian, Della Joan
Red Moon Rising - Billie Sue Mosiman *h* 712

Carclew, Fenella
Rose of Nancemillin - Malcolm MacDonald *t* 935

Carr, Randall
Children of Hope - David Feintuch *s* 779

Cathy
Chalktown - Melinda Haynes *c* 1169

Cleve, Lily
Eclipse - John Banville *c* 1107

Connor, John
T2: Infiltrator - S.M. Stirling *s* 834

Creighton, Melody
Gemini Rising - Brian McNaughton *h* 709

Cutler, Patrick
Dead North - Sue Henry *w* 490
Dead North - Sue Henry *m* 80

Cygnet
Primrose Past - Caroline Rose Hunt *t* 914

Daisy
We're So Famous - Jaime Clarke *c* 1132

David
On the Water - H.M. van den Brink *t* 991

Dingillian, Chigger
Bouncing Off the Moon - David Gerrold *s* 787

Dingillian, Douglas
Bouncing Off the Moon - David Gerrold *s* 787

Drake, Jim
Still Can't See Nothing Coming - Daniel
  Marshall *c* 1194

Drake, Mandy
Still Can't See Nothing Coming - Daniel
  Marshall *c* 1194

Dwyer, Jack
Prowlers - Christopher Golden *h* 679

Flaherty, Mark
Times and Seasons - Beverly LaHaye *i* 1053

Flammarion, Dancy
Threshold - Caitlin R. Kiernan *h* 693

Goldson, Ida
On Her Way Home - Harriet Rochlin *t* 973

Haldran, Andrew
Focus - Sallie Lowenstein *s* 801

Hardy, Lucinda
A Student of Weather - Elizabeth Hay *c* 1168

Hatcher, Molly
Prowlers - Christopher Golden *h* 679

Haufmann, Katherine
Fire on the Hillside - Melinda Rice *w* 530

Hayes, Sarah
Blood Crazy - Simon Clark *h* 666

James
Gabriel's Story - David Anthony Durham *c* 1145

Jenkins, Emily
Lick Creek - Brad Kessler *t* 923

Laughlin, Patrick
Downward to Darkness - Brian McNaughton *h* 708

Leth, Alazrian
The Saints of the Sword - John Marco *f* 607

Liangharad, Mahala
Child of Venus - Pamela Sargent *s* 826

Lirael
Lirael - Garth Nix *f* 617

Lynch, Gabriel
Gabriel's Story - David Anthony Durham *t* 886
Gabriel's Story - David Anthony Durham *c* 1145

Maika
The Funeral Party - Ludmila Ulitskaya *c* 1238

Maya
Motherland - Vineeta Vijayaraghavan *c* 1239

Mike
The Free Lunch - Spider Robinson *s* 824

Miniter, Jane
Downward to Darkness - Brian McNaughton *h* 708

Moore, Bobby
Grace - Jane Roberts Wood *w* 550

Newton, Paul
Darkness Demands - Simon Clark *h* 667

Paque
We're So Famous - Jaime Clarke *c* 1132

Pawli
The Curer - Adam Nichols *f* 614

Petinske, Angela "Tony"
Wire Mesh Mothers - Elizabeth Massie *h* 705

Ring, Kaelin
Ravenheart - David Gemmell *f* 584

Rodriguez, Kit
The Wizard's Dilemma - Diane Duane *f* 574

Sheehand, Hezekiah
Chalktown - Melinda Haynes *c* 1169

Slatter, Tug
Blood Crazy - Simon Clark *h* 666

Spring, Ian
Finding Ian - Stella Cameron *r* 237

Stella
We're So Famous - Jaime Clarke *c* 1132

Sulaweyo, Stephen
Sea of Silver Light - Tad Williams *f* 651

Tanzer, Owen
Prowlers - Christopher Golden *h* 679

Thurman, Donald
Destiny's Door - Judith Tracy *s* 838

Wallace, Kathy
The Lost - Jack Ketchum *h* 692

Wells, Hallie Lou
Get Along, Little Dogies - Lisa Waller
  Rogers *w* 533

TELEVISION PERSONALITY

McBride, Billy
Shock Talk - Bob Larson *i* 1054

McGowan, Alec
Morning - W.D. Wetherell   *c*   1242

Oliver
Cause Celeb - Helen Fielding   *c*   1150

TERRORIST

Charnock, Jack
A River out of Eden - John Hockenberry   *w*   491

Gerald
K Falls - Skye Kathleen Moody   *w*   509

THIEF

Apropos
Sir Apropos of Nothing - Peter David   *f*   569

Craer
The Vacant Throne - Ed Greenwood   *f*   586

de la Mouriere, Eve
The Wicked One - Danelle Harmon   *r*   294

Dortmunder, John
Bad News - Donald E. Westlake   *m*   192

Fowl, Artemis
Artemis Fowl - Eoin Colfer   *f*   566

Lamont, Bryce
Ghost Town - Ed Gorman   *w*   487

Malone, Cash
Gunning for Regret - Wolf MacKenna   *w*   502

Podarke, Emmlyn
Fool Me Twice - Matthew Hughes   *s*   795

Saint, Julianna
The Devil's Shadow - Hugh Holton   *m*   83

St. Clair, Luke
Rogue's Honor - Brenda Hiatt   *r*   303

Sally
The Buffalo Hunters - Gary McCarthy   *w*   504

Stodla, Frank
Ghost Town - Ed Gorman   *w*   487

Tacit
Sir Apropos of Nothing - Peter David   *f*   569

Wylie, Jed
Ghost Town - Ed Gorman   *w*   487

TIME TRAVELER

Ashe, Gordon
Time Traders II - Andre Norton   *s*   814

Brennan, Kelly
Time After Time - Constance O'Day-Flannery   *r*   391

Carson, Kit
The House That Jack Built - Robert Asprin   *s*   753

Ferguson, Jix
Highland Dream - Tess Mallory   *r*   361

Fox, Travis
Time Traders II - Andre Norton   *s*   814

Joseph
The Graveyard Game - Kage Baker   *s*   755

Lewis
The Graveyard Game - Kage Baker   *s*   755

Lytton, Tafaline "Taffy"
Night Visitor - Melanie Jackson   *r*   313

MacGregor, Jamie
Highland Dream - Tess Mallory   *r*   361

Matheson, Dylan
Son of the Sword - J. Ardian Lee   *f*   605

Murdock, Ross
Time Traders II - Andre Norton   *s*   814

St. Clare, Arden
To Tame a Rogue - Linda Kay   *r*   328

TOUR GUIDE

McPherson, Kate
Eternity - Tamara Thorne   *h*   743

Samuels, Rheada
Raven - Laura Baker   *r*   213

TOURIST

Norton, Kiru
Space Wasters - David Garnett   *s*   786

Norton, Wayne
Space Wasters - David Garnett   *s*   786

TRADER

Banouin
The Sword in the Storm - David Gemmell   *f*   585

Bent, Charles
Moon Medicine - Mike Blakely   *w*   453

Jeffords, Eames
Death Rides the Denver Stage - Lewis B. Patten   *w*   522

Menedemos
Over the Wine-Dark Sea - H.N. Turteltaub   *t*   990

Sostratos
Over the Wine-Dark Sea - H.N. Turteltaub   *t*   990

TRAPPER

Lovell, Pierre
Bodie Gone - Bill Hyde   *w*   495

TRAVELER

Horn
Return to the Whorl - Gene Wolfe   *s*   850

TWIN

Cranford, Peregrine
The Riddle of the Shipwrecked Spinster - Patricia Veryan   *r*   441

Cranford, Piers
The Riddle of the Shipwrecked Spinster - Patricia Veryan   *r*   441

Stanton, Cat
Lioness - Nell Brien   *r*   227

Woodhull, Gob
Gob's Grief - Chris Adrian   *c*   1102

Woodhull, Tomo
Gob's Grief - Chris Adrian   *c*   1102

UNDERTAKER

Eguchi
American Fuji - Sara Backer   *c*   1105

Slocombe, Drew
Dark Undertakings - Rebecca Tope   *m*   184

Youngren, Will
Life After Death - Carol Muske-Dukes   *c*   1209

UNEMPLOYED

Featherstone, Jake
American Empire: Blood and Iron - Harry Turtledove   *s*   839

Slocum
The Last Harbor - George Foy   *s*   785

VAMPIRE

Cambian, Della Joan
Red Moon Rising - Billie Sue Mosiman   *h*   712

Compton, Bill
Dead Until Dark - Charlaine Harris   *h*   685

Courbet, Jean Luc "Jack"
Bound in Blood - Thomas Lord   *h*   699

Courbet, Noel
Bound in Blood - Thomas Lord   *h*   699

Crepsley, Larten
Cirque Du Freak - Darren Shan   *h*   734

Daniel
Voice of the Blood - Jemiah Jefferson   *h*   689

Dashwood, Columbine
More than Mortal - Mick Farren   *h*   675

Fenrior
More than Mortal - Mick Farren   *h*   675

Malinari, Nephran
Avengers - Brian Lumley   *h*   702

Mentor
Red Moon Rising - Billie Sue Mosiman   *h*   712

Renquist, Victor
More than Mortal - Mick Farren   *h*   675

Ricari, Orfeo
Voice of the Blood - Jemiah Jefferson   *h*   689

VETERAN

Burnett, Tanner
The Outlaw Takes a Wife - Sylvia McDaniel   *r*   370

Corey, Steve
The Seduction of Ellen - Nan Ryan   *r*   417

Garrett, Andrew
The Horse Soldier - Merline Lovelace   *r*   355

Godwin
Murder on Good Friday - Sara Conway   *m*   26
Murder on Good Friday - Sara Conway   *t*   871

Haddam, Amos
One O'Clock Jump - Lise McClendon   *t*   942
One O'Clock Jump - Lise McClendon   *m*   112

Johnson, Evan
The Edge of Town - Dorothy Garlock   *t*   898

Jones, Fearless
Fearless Jones - Walter Mosley   *m*   126
Fearless Jones - Walter Mosley   *c*   1206

Mars, George Washington
The Killer Gun - Lauran Paine   *w*   519

Parrish, James
Shadows on the Land - James M. Vesely   *w*   547

Santo, Richard
613 West Jefferson - D.S. Lliteras   *i*   1057

Voxlauer, Oskar
The Right Hand of Sleep - John Wray   *t*   999

VETERINARIAN

Eberhard, Deirdre
Past the Size of Dreaming - Nina Kiriki Hoffman   *f*   588

Hunter, Colson
Beneath a Southern Sky - Deborah Raney   *i*   1077

LeBlanc, Sonsee
A Shelter in the Storm - Debra White Smith   *i*   1087

YOUNG MAN

YOUNG WOMAN

Author Index

This index is an alphabetical listing of the authors of books featured in entries and those listed within entries under the rubrics "Other books by the same author" and "Other books you might like." For each author, the titles of books described or listed in this edition and their entry numbers appear. Bold numbers indicate a featured main entry; light-face numbers refer to books recommended for further reading.

A

Aarsen, Carolyne
A Bride at Last 1002
The Cowboy's Bride 1002
A Family at Last 1002, 1041, 1050
A Family-Style Christmas 1002
A Hero for Kelsey **1002**, 1040, 1049, 1101
A Mother at Last 1002

ab Hugh, Daffyd
Far Beyond the Wave 555

Abbey, Edward
The Monkey Wrench Gang 124

Abbey, Lynn
Planeswalker 577
Simbul's Gift 556
Unicorn and Dragon 563

Abbott, Donald
How the Wizard Saved Oz 636

Abbott, Edwin A.
Flatland 833

Abbott, Jeff
The Jordan Poteet Series 119

Abe, Kobo
The Woman in the Dunes 581

Abe, Shana
Intimate Enemies **201**, 202, 246, 250, 253, 372, 431
A Kiss at Midnight 201, 202
The Promise of Rain 201, 202
A Rose in Winter 201, 202
The Secret Swan **202**
The Truelove Bride 201, 202, 331, 332, 368, 393, 437

Abel, Kenneth
Cold Steel Rain 1135

Abella, Alex
Final Acts 1131

Abnett, Dan
First and Only 643

Abrahams, Lionel
The Celibacy of Felix Greenspan 1125

Abrahams, Peter
Hard Rain 1148

Ackroyd, Peter
The Trial of Elizabeth Cree 960, 996

Adair, Cherry
Kiss and Tell 343

Adams, Alice
After the War 898, 922, 992, 997
Almost Perfect 1117, 1154, 1241
Last Lovely City 1211
Medicine Men 1209, 1237

Adams, Deborah
The Jesus Creek Series 113

Adams, Douglas
Dirk Gently's Holistic Detective Agency 786

Adams, Harold
A Way with Widows 889

Adams, Kylie
Fly Me to the Moon **203**, 271, 272, 349

Adamson, Isaac
Tokyo Suckerpunch 1219

Adcock, Thomas
The Neil Hockaday Series 38

Addison, Joseph
Tesseract 824, 849

Adkins, Patrick
Sons of the Titans 630

Adler, Paul
Saucer Hill 773

Adrian, Chris
Gob's Grief 894, 926, **1102**

Agee, James
A Death in the Family 1203

Agnon, S.Y.
Only Yesterday 1191, 1229

Aickman, Robert
The Unsettled Dust 731

Aiken, Ginny
The Bellamy's Blossoms Series 1082
A Bouquet of Love 1017
Camellia **1003**, 1028
Candy Kiss 1003
County Fair 1003
Crystal Memories 1003
Dream Vacation 1046
Lark 1003

Magnolia 1003
Victorian Christmas Keepsake **1071**

Aiken, Joan
Lady Catherine's Necklace 905

Aird, Catherine
After Affects 1
The Body Politic 1
A Going Concern 1
Injury Time 1
Little Knell **1**
Stiff News 1

Airth, Rennie
River of Darkness 930

Aitken, Judie
A Love Beyond Time 213

Aksyonov, Vassily
Generations of Winter 932, 981

Akutagawa, Ryunosuke
The Essential Akutagawa 700

Albert, Bill
Death at Epsom Downs **140**

Albert, Michele
A Great Catch **319**

Albert, Susan Wittig
Chile Death 53
The China Bayles Series 30, 34, 56, 139
Death at Epsom Downs 140, **955**

Albert, William
Death at Epsom Downs **955**

Alcorn, Angela
The Ishbane Conspiracy **1004**

Alcorn, Karina
The Ishbane Conspiracy **1004**

Alcorn, Randy C.
Deadline 1005
Dominion 1005
Edge of Eternity 1005
The Foulgrin's Letters Series 1033
The Ishbane Conspiracy **1004**
Lord Foulgrin's Letters 1004, 1005, 1034, 1098
Safely Home **1005**

Aldiss, Brian W.
Common Clay 752
Dracula Unbound 752
Frankenstein Unbound 652

Helliconia Spring 804
Helliconia Winter 752
An Island Called Moreau 768
Man in His Time 752
Supertoys Last All Summer Long **752**
A Tupolev Too Far 752
Vanguard from Alpha 821
The Year Before Yesterday 839, 841

Aldridge, Ray
The Emperor of Everything 851

Alef, Daniel
Pale Truth 1200

Alers, Rochelle
Going to the Chapel **204**
Harvest Moon 205
Heaven Sent 205
Hidden Agenda 205, 312
Just Before Dawn 205
My Love's Keeper 336
Private Passions **205**, 312
Reckless Surrender 204
Summer Magic 205

Alexander, Bruce
The Color of Death 949, 953
The Sir John Fielding Series 178, 200, 907, 958, 983, 1000

Alexander, Carrie
Black Velvet 221
The Madcap Heiress 244

Alexander, Karl
Time After Time 753

Alexander, Kathryn
The Forever Husband 1051
Heart of a Husband 1023, 1081
Twin Wishes 1041, 1075
A Wedding in the Family 1089

Alexander, Victoria
The Husband List 206, 215
The Marriage Lesson **206**, 362
Paradise Bay 206
Play It Again, Sam 206
The Wedding Bargain 206

Alfonsi, Alice
Some Enchanted Evening 286

Algren, Nelson
A Walk on the Wild Side 892

Alison, Jane
The Love-Artist **852**, 877, 987, **1103**

Manifold: Time 756, 849
Moonseed 756
The Raft 791
Raft 833
The Ring 799
Titan 756
Voyage 756

Bayley, Barrington J.
Eye of Terror 643

Bean, Frederic
Blood Trail 517
Border Justice 487
Lorena 501, 551
Murder at the Spirit Cave 456, 462, 465, 466, 475, 477, 486, 491, 505, 506, 507, 508, 509, 523, 526, 542, 543, 544
The Outlaw 461, 469, 522
The Pecos River 547
Renegade 453, 457
Santa Fe Showdown 455

Bear, David
Keeping Time 620, 772

Bear, Greg
Eternity 756
The Infinity Concerto 612
Moving Mars 826
Queen of Angels 812
Sisters 813

Beard, Julie
Romance of the Rose 235

Beaton, M.C.
Agatha Raisin and the Fairies of Fryfam 7
Agatha Raisin and the Witch of Wyckehadden 7
Death of a Dentist 6
Death of a Dustman 6, 7
Death of a Macho Man 6
Death of a Scriptwriter 6
Death of an Addict 6, 7
A Highland Christmas 6, 7
The Skeleton in the Closet 7, 110

Beattie, Ann
Another You 1176
Burning House 1110
Falling in Place 1185
Park City 1110
Perfect Recall **1110**, 1115, 1156
Picturing Will 1110, 1224
Secrets and Surprises 1110
What Was Mine 1110

Beaufort, Simon
The Sir Geoffrey Mappestone Series 59

Beaumont, Charles
The Howling Man 606
The Magic Man 646
Selected Stories 715

Beck, K.K.
Death in a Deck Chair 46
The Iris Cooper Series 93
The Jane da Silva Series 7
Young Mrs. Cavendish and the Kaiser's Men 45

Beck, Kathleen
My Darling Valentine 306

Becker, Stephen D.
The Blue-Eyed Shan 902

Becnel, Rexanne
The Bride of Rosecliffe 215
The Christmas Wish 237
Dangerous to Love 215

The Knight of Rosecliffe 215
The Maiden Bride 215
The Matchmaker **215**
The Mistress of Rosecliffe 210, 215, 250, 253

Begiebing, Robert J.
The Strange Death of Mistress Coffin 121

Belfer, Lauren
City of Light 33

Bell, Ann
Montana 1032

Bell, Clare
The Jaguar Princess 625

Bell, Donna
The Bluestocking's Beau 216

Bell, Hilari
A Matter of Profit **757**
Navohar 757, 813

Bell, James Scott
Angels Flight **1073**
Blind Justice 1009
Circumstantial Evidence 1009
The Darwin Conspiracy 1009
Final Witness 1009
The Nephilim Seed **1009**

Bell, Madison Smartt
Master of the Crossroads 1158
Years of Silence 1188

Bellow, Saul
The Actual 1184
The Dean's December 1122
Mr. Sammler's Planet 1125
Ravelstein 1137, 1187, 1228

Benard, Cheryl
Moghul Buffet 54
Turning on the Girls 1129

Benary-Isbert, Margot
The Wicked Enchantment 599

Benchley, Peter
Jaws 1128

Bendell, Don
Chief of Scouts 528

Bender, Carrie
Birch Hollow Schoolmarm 1010
Chestnut Ridge Acres 1010
Hemlock Hill Hideaway 1010
Lilac Blossom Time **1010**
A Treasured Friendship 1010
Woodland Dell's Secret 1010

Benedict, Helen
The Sailor's Wife 1230

Benford, Gregory
Artifact 825
Timescape 849

Benioff, David
The 25th Hour **1111**

Benjamin, Carole Lea
The Rachel Alexander and Dash Series 2, 8
The Rachel Alexander & Dash Series 20
The Rachel Alexander and Dash Series 47, 69

Benrey, Janet
Little White Lies **1011**

Benrey, Ron
Little White Lies **1011**, 1087

Benson, A.C.
The Hill of Trouble and Other Stories 719

Benson, Angela
Abiding Hope **1012**
Awakening Mercy 1012, 1021, 1066, 1092
A Family Wedding 1012
The Genesis House Series 1065
The Nicest Guy in America 1012
Second Chance Dad 1012
The Way Home 1012

Benson, Jessica
Lord Stanhope's Proposal 216, 247, 400
Much Obliged **216**

Benson, Margaret
Destiny **425**

Benson, Robert Hugh
Come Rack! Come Rope! 993
The Light Invisible 719

Bentz, Joseph
Cradle of Dreams **1013**, 1028, 1075
A Son Comes Home 1013, 1033, 1068, 1079, 1090
Song of Fire 1013

Berberick, Nancy Varian
A Child of Elvish 556
Dalamar the Dark 556
The Inheritance **556**
The Jewels of Elvish 556
The Panther's Hoard 556
Stormblade 616
Tears of the Night Sky 556

Berberova, Nina
The Book of Happiness 1238

Berenson, Laurien
The Melanie Travis Series 2, 8, 69

Berg, Elizabeth
Durable Goods 1112, 1198
Never Change **1112**, 1134
Open House 1106, 1112, 1133, 1140
The Pull of the Moon 1112
Range of Motion 1112
Talk Before Sleep 384
What We Keep 1112, 1120, 1178

Berg, Patti
Born to Be Wild **217**
Bride for a Night 217, 343, 376
If I Can't Have You 217
Looking for a Hero 217
Till the End of Time 217
Wife for a Day 217, 319, 407

Berger, Eileen
A Family for Andi 1014
The Highly Suspicious Halo 1014
The Missing Hydrangeas 1014
Reunions 1014, 1046
A Special Kind of Family **1014**, 1081
To Galilee with Love 1014

Berger, Thomas
The Return of Little Big Man 857, 954

Berglund, Edward P.
Disciples of Cthulhu 725
Shards of Darkness **656**, 728

Bergman, Andrew
Hollywood and LeVine 25, 91
The Jack LeVine Series 79
Tender Is LeVine 65

Bergren, Lisa Tawn
The Bridge 1015

The Captain's Bride 1015
Chosen 1093
Deep Harbor 1015, 1168
Firestorm 1015
Midnight Sun 1015, 1060, 1074
The Northern Lights Series 1020, 1042, 1096
Pathways **1015**
Porch Swings and Picket Fences 1017, 1046

Bernanos, Michel
The Other Side of the Mountain 937

Berne, Betsy
Bad Timing **1113**

Berne, Martine
A Perfect Rogue 218
The Prize **218**, 226

Berne, Suzanne
A Crime in the Neighborhood 1114
A Perfect Arrangement **1114**

Bernstein, Lisa
The Prize **218**

Berriault, Gina
The Lights of Earth 1154

Berry, Don
To Build a Ship 994

Berry, Wendell
Jayber Crow 911, 923

Bertin, Joanne
The Dragon and the Phoenix 607
The Last Dragonlord 594, 597

Betancourt, John Gregory
Johnny Zed 808
Rememory 798
Rogue Pirate 560

Betts, Heidi
Almost a Lady **219**, 240
Cinnamon and Roses 219, 371
A Promise of Roses 219

Bevarly, Elizabeth
A Doctor in Her Stocking 220
Dr. Irresistible 220, 221
Dr. Mommy 220, 232
First Comes Love **220**, 221, 423
He Could Be the One 221
How to Trap a Tycoon 221
Monahan's Gamble 221
Society Bride 220
The Temptation of Rory Monahan **221**
That Boss of Mine 220

Beverley, Jo
Deirdre and Don Juan 334
Devilish 222, 223, 294, 346, 347
The Devil's Heiress **222**, 223, 224
The Dragon's Bride 222, **223**, 224, 241
Forbidden Magic 241
In Praise of Younger Men **224**, 356
My Lady Notorious 228, 294, 317, 416
Secrets of the Night 222, 223
The Shattered Rose 210
Something Wicked 222, 223, 347, 364
Tempting Fortune 222, 223, 346

Beylen, Robert
The Way to the Sun 861

Biguenet, John
The Torturer's Apprentice 1109, **1115**, 1138, 1204, 1235

Billerbeck, Kristin
Forever Friends 1017, 1046

Author Index

Author Index

Author Index

Author Index

Author Index

Title Index

This index alphabetically lists all titles featured in entries and those listed within entries under "Other books by the same author" and "Other books you might like." Each title is followed by the author's name and the number of the entry where the book is described or listed. Bold numbers indicate featured main entries; light-face numbers refer to books recommended for further reading.

Title Index

Title Index

Title Index

Title Index

Title Index

Title Index

Title Index

Title Index

Title Index

Title Index

Title Index

Title Index

Title Index

Title Index

Title Index

Title Index

Title Index

Z

Title Index